GEORGIA OBITUARIES

1905-1910

Jeannette Holland Austin

HERITAGE BOOKS
2015

HERITAGE BOOKS
AN IMPRINT OF HERITAGE BOOKS, INC.

Books, CDs, and more—Worldwide

For our listing of thousands of titles see our website
at
www.HeritageBooks.com

Published 2015 by
HERITAGE BOOKS, INC.
Publishing Division
5810 Ruatan Street
Berwyn Heights, Md. 20740

International Standard Book Numbers
Paperbound: 978-1-58549-610-5
Clothbound: 978-0-7884-6095-1

PREFACE

Because the State of Georgia's Bureau of Vital Statistics did not begin keeping death records until 1919, a real problem exists in obtaining death information prior to that date.

The obituaries in this book were abstracted from *The Atlanta Georgian* and *The Atlanta Constitution* newspapers. *The Atlanta Georgian*, now extinct, published deaths of persons over the entire State, as did *The Atlanta Constitution*.

Thus, these newspaper abstracts helps to bridge the gap of the years, 1905 to 1910.

Abbreviations at the end of each entry are: AG (Atlanta Constitution) and AG (Atlanta Georgian) followed by the date of the newspaper. Please note that obituaries were not always published upon the actual date of death, but rather a day or two afterwards.

Often, the notice, or a similar notice, was reported two or three times, and usually contained different wording. One would suppose that the report of death was given by different relatives, and this might be the reason for such variables, even conflicting information. If the reader has a problem, the newspaper itself should be viewed (on microfilm) using a local library, which can obtain the microfilm from the University of Georgia. In some instances, additional information is contained in the obituary, or newspaper article, especially in the instance of accidents, murders, etc. However, all genealogical data was extracted for this book

Jeannette Holland Austin

ABBE, Frances Martha Neal, Mrs. d. 7/24, wife of Prof. Cleveland Abbe of Washington, D. C. She was dau. of Mr. and Mrs. David Neal, Atlanta. AG 8/4/1908

ABBOTT, Armistead T., age 68, d. Atlanta. AG 4/27/1910

ABBOTT, D. Q., Professor of Athens, Univ. of Ga. d., age 51. Leaves wife, two sons: Hunley, res. of Washington, D. C.; and Horace, age 12. Interred: Athens. AG 3/26/1907

ABBOTT, Josephine, Mrs., wife of Colonel B. F., d. Atlanta Wed. Interred: Family Vault, Oakland. AG 12/6/1910

ABEEL, J. Bartlett d. Sat. Chattanooga, Tenn. Interred: Forest Hill Cemetery. AG 12/17/1910

ABERCROMBIE, J. S., Mrs. of Douglasville d. 6/27. Husband, three children. AG 6/28/1909

ABERCROMBIE, Sarah T., Mrs., member of prominent Alabama family, d. Columbus, Ga. Daus: Mrs. William Chambers, Mrs. R. Howard, Mrs. R. G. Wright. Son: Henry Abercrombie. AG 1/30/1907

ABERNATHY, Nella, Mrs., age 21, wife of Roy, d. 290 Gordon St. Atlanta. Parents: Dr. and Mrs. E. H. Bacon, Eastman, Ga. ro: E. H. Bacon, Jr., Manchester, England. Sisters: Mrs. A. R. Colcord, Atlanta; Mrs. Badger Murrow, Tifton, Ga. AG 4/22/1908

ABIAS, Rosa, age 1 mo., d. 162 Gilmer St. Atlanta. AG 2/11/1909

ABIES, Sallie E., Mrs. d. Rison Ave. Huntsville, Ala. Two sons. AG 1/3/1910

ABLES, Snow, age 29, d. home of father in Dallas, Ga. Fri. He was connected with Sou. RR, conductor. Interred: Family burial grounds, Dallas, Ga. AG 12/23/1907

ABNEY, Emma, Mrs., wife of T. F., d. Howells Sta., Atlanta, Tues. Interred: Dallas, Ga. AG 10/30/1907

ABRAHAM, James Roy, age 1 yr., d. Jefferson, Ga. AG 2/8/1909

ACKER, Jim, colored, age 40, d. 19 Tyler St. Atlanta. AG 4/10/1907

ACREE, Katy Viola d. 9/8, age 10, dau. of Mr. and Mrs. W. H. Interred: Province Church yard. AC 9/11/1905

ACREE, T. P., age 55, d. 5 Mollie St., Atlanta. Wife, 4 children. AG 5/9/1910

ACREE, T. P., age 69, d. 201 Capitol Ave. Atlanta. AG 5/9/1910

ACTON, Lee, inf. son of Mr. and Mrs. L. L., d. 188 S. Boulevard, Atlanta, Tues. Interred: Westview. AG 7/23/1908

ADAIR, Guy, age 39, res. of Atlanta, d. Mon. Montgomery, Ala. Wife. Sis: Mrs. W. S. Griffin, Atlanta. Interred: Oakland. AG 7/6/1910

ADAIR, J. O., Mrs., age 64, d. 101 Butler St. Atlanta. AG 10/22/1909

ADAIR, Mary Jane, Mrs., age 78, d. 441 Peters St. Atlanta. AG 9/2/1910

ADAIR, Robert, unmd. d. Atlanta 5/16. AC 5/17/1905

ADAIR, W. P., Mrs. d. Hampton, Ga. 4/16. One sister. AC 4/18/1905

ADAMS, B. E., Mrs., age 65, d. Mon. 29 Joe Johnston Ave., Atlanta. Interred: Westview. AG 7/19/1910

ADAMS, Bessie, age 4, dau. of Mr. and Mrs. Charles, d. Fri. Interred: Carrollton, Ga., Family Grave Yard. AG 12/7/1907

ADAMS, Clara, Miss, age 25, d. Sun., 122 Means St., Atlanta. Interred: Hollywood. AG 8/7/1906

ADAMS, Earl, age 1 yr., d. 408 Central Railway Ave. Atlanta. AG 7/8/1907

1

ADAMS, Fannie Lou, colored, age mos., d. 63 Delbridge St. Atlanta. AG 9/26/1910

ADAMS, Fannie, Mrs. d. Rentz, Ga. Interred: Snow Hill Cemetery. She was formerly Miss Harris of Columbia Co. Sisters: Mrs. John T. Rogers, Rentz, Ga.; Mrs. Spears, Warren Co. AG 3/11/1909

ADAMS, Florence Reid, Miss d. 6/14 Eatonton, dau. of late Capt. I. H. Uncle: Sen.-elect George W. Adams. AC 6/16/1905

ADAMS, H. G. d. Elberton, Ga., buried 9/5. 5 sons, 3 daus. AG 9/6/1910

ADAMS, Harry, age 4, son of Mr. and Mrs. D. W., d. Atlanta Wed. Interred: Covington, Ga. AG 8/31/1910

ADAMS, Harry, colored, age 25, d. 101 N. Butler St. Atlanta. AG 2/7/1908

ADAMS, Harvey suicide Gainesville, Ga., age 42, in front of wife and children. AG 11/24/1910

ADAMS, Henry, age 17 mos., son of Mr. and Mrs. O. H., 103 Curran St., Atlanta, d. Sun. Interred: Hollywood. AG 3/22/1909

ADAMS, Henry, colored, age 1 yr., d. 103 Curran St. Atlanta. AG 3/22/1909

ADAMS, J. B. d. home Alabama City, Ala. Sat., age 40. Interred: Guntersville, Ala. AG 7/24/1906

ADAMS, J. K. d. Mon. Abbeville, Ga. Interred: Glenwood Cemetery, Thomaston, Ga. Age 72. Dau: Mrs. O. F. Paxson of Abbeville; Miss Bessie Adams, Atlanta. AG 8/18/1910

ADAMS, Jerry, age 84, d. home below Milton, Ga. Mon. Wife, 5 children. AG 3/15/1910

ADAMS, John, colored, age 49, d. Chattahoochee, Ga. AG 5/13/1907

ADAMS, Joseph A., Rev., Talbot Co. Baptist Min. of Box Springs, d. Jan. 30, age 72. Spent most of live in Talbot Co. AC 2/1/1905

ADAMS, Katie, Mrs., age 65, d. rear Westview Cemetery, Atlanta. AG 1/19/1910

ADAMS, L. C., Mrs., age 62, d. Fri. Atlanta. Interred: Westview. AG 9/10/1910

ADAMS, L. E., Mrs., age 79, d. Fri. 357 Marietta St. Atlanta. Interred: Oakland. AG 6/21/1907

ADAMS, Lizzie, Mrs., age 72, d. 158 Courtland St. Atlanta. AG 10/13/1906

ADAMS, Llewellyn, age 50, d. 72 Neal St. Atlanta. AG 11/8/1910

ADAMS, Llewelyn A., Mrs., age 50, wife of J. W., d. 72 Neal St., Atlanta, Sun. 8 children. Interred: Hartwell, Ga. AG 11/7/1910

ADAMS, Mary E., Mrs., d. 158 Courtland St. Atlanta, Sat. Interred: Oakland. AG 10/15/1906

ADAMS, Mary Helen, age 4 mos., dau. of Mr. and Mrs. N. G., d. 7/29 Athens, Ga. AG 7/30/1909

ADAMS, Odus V., colored, age 36, d. 327 Piedmont Ave. Atlanta. AG 7/9/1908

ADAMS, Preston killed himself after threatening wife, Cordele, Ga. 2/25. AG 2/25/1907

ADAMS, T. L., Col. d. bro's home, Washington. Interred: Bowman. Leaves widow. Daus: Miss Delrey, Mrs. Howard Arnold of Bowman, Mrs. Dr. B. C. Teasley, Hartwell. Son: Eldo H., Chester, S. C. AG 7/14/1906

ADAMS, W. W. d. Mon. Atlanta. Interred: Westview. AG 4/13/1909

ADAMS, Walton Lee, age 4, d. home of parents, Mr. and Mrs. Stanford Adams, Holt Ave., Vineville, Macon. Father, Mother, two little bros., little sister, survive. AG 7/17/1907

ADAMS, William C., age 22, d. 34 Morgan St. Atlanta. AG 10/25/1909

ADAMS, William H., age 53, d. Candler Bl. Atlanta. AG 4/13/1909

ADAMS, infant of Mr. and Mrs. J. C. d. 48 N. Lee St., Atlanta Sun. AG 11/19/1907

ADAMSON, Annie H., Mrs., age 42, d. 522 Central Ave. Atlanta. AG 1/16/1907

ADAMSON, Ruth, age 2 yrs., d. 31 Ridge Ave. Atlanta. AG 8/22/1910

ADAMS, Mary K., Mrs., age 72, d. 204 Courtland St., Atlanta, Mon. Son: Harry K., only surviving relative. AG 10/12/1909

ADAMS, Richard S., inf. son of Mr. and Mrs. R. A., 3 Tulip St., Atlanta, d. Mon. Interred: Roswell, Ga. AG 5/21/1906

ADAMS, Thomas, age 55, d. Sat. 8/23 Grady Hospital, Atlanta. Relatives in Mechanicsburg, Pa, where interred. Son: Thomas. AG 8/26/1907

ADDY, J. G., Mrs. d. res. of Dr. A. C. North near Newnan, Ga. Thurs. Three children. Interred: Family Burial Grounds. AG 8/7/1908

ADKINS, Adele, Miss, age 35, d. Tues. St. Josephs Infirmary, Atlanta. Res. of 236 Ivey St., Atlanta. Interred Augusta, AG 5/21/1907

ADKINS, Wallace, age 2, d. 278 Humphries St. Atlanta. AG 4/25/1910

ADLER, Jennie, Mrs., wife of L. C., merchant, d. Sun. Atlanta. AG 4/22/1907

ADLER, M., old merchant of Huntsville, Ala. d., age 70, native of Hungary. Res. of Huntsville since 1879. Ch: Mrs. E. Brown, Mrs. Sigmund Margon of Birmingham, and Sam Adler of New Orleans, AG 7/20/1908

AENCHBACHER, Ward A., age 24, d. Sat. 270 Sunset Ave., Atlanta. Interred: Oakland. AC 4/11/1910

AGEE, George L., age 42, d. Atlanta. AG 3/7/1910

AGNEW, Kate, Mrs., age 65, d. Covington. Interred: Columbia, S. C. AC 4/13/1905

AGRICOLA, Herman, inf. son of Mr. and Mrs. C. P., d. Sat. 100 E. Fair St., Atlanta. Interred: Westview. AG 5/20/1907

AIKEN, Frank M., Confederate Veteran, d. Sat. 36 Sontewall St., Atlanta. Interred: Westview. AG 2/24/1908

AIKEN, James F., age 18, d. Wed. father's res., J. W., 187 Humphries St., Atlanta. Interred: Hiram, Ga. AG 11/8/1910

AIKEN, Lucy, Mrs., age 83, d. Smyrna, Ga. Interred: Oakland. AG 3/1/1907

AIKIN, Ace A., age 29, d. Neal, Ga. AG 7/11/1907

AINSWORTH, James T., Rev. d. 12/6 Oglethorpe, Ga. Interred: Macon, Ga., Riverside Cemetery. AC 12/8/1905

AKEN, L. M., age 70, d. 36 Stonewall St. Atlanta. AG 2/24/1908

AKENS, G. W., Mrs., age 50, d. 333 N. Boulevard. Atlanta. AG 3/2/1907

AKERS, Ella Shepherd, Mrs., wife of G. W. Akers, d. Thurs. 33 N. Boulevard, Atlanta., dau. of Mrs. J. I. Shepherd. Sisters: Mrs. J. E. Maddox, wife of J. E.; Mrs. J. E. McKinley. Interred: Westview. AG 3/1/1907

3

AKERS, James, Mrs., age 45, d. McDonough Rd., Atlanta, Fri. Husband, several children. AG 4/15/1909
AKERS, W. T., Atlanta pioneer, d. Tues. 617 N. Boulevard, Atlanta. Interred: Sylvester Baptist Church. AG 1/10/1907
AKERS, Laura N., age 13, only child of Mrs. Bell H., and late John H., grdau. of Mrs. M. L. Haralson, d. Fri. Asheville, N. C. Funeral: Res. of aunt, Mrs. J. A. Carroll, Rice St. and Blvd., Atlanta. Interred: Oakland. AG 3/10/1910
AKIN, J. M., Mrs., old citizen of Barnesville, Ga., d. 6/15. AG 6/16/1906
AKIN, John Wesley, Hon., Pres. of Ga. Senate, d. Cartersville, Ga. 10/21. AG 10/19/1907
AKIN, Mary, Mrs., mother of Judge John W. Akin, d. yesterday Cartersville, Ga. Before marr. she was Mary Verdery of Augusta; was b. 7/6/1830, wife of Col. Warren Akin. AG 10/18/1907
AKINS, George Andrew, age 9 mos., son of Mr. and Mrs. Clark, d. Sun. 86 Wells St. Atlanta. Interred: Fairburn, Ga. AG 1/3/1910
AKINS, M. W. of Hampton, Ga. d. Jan. 15, age 57. Wife. Dau: Mrs. O. T. Hennessee. Interred: Berea Cemetery. AC 1/17/1905
ALARD, Ernest, age 22, d. 45 West End Ave. Atlanta. AG 11/30/1907
ALBERT, W. J., Col. d. Fri. 328 Houston St., Atlanta. Interred: Oakland. AG 5/12/1906
ALBRIGHT, Carrie J., Mrs. d. Sun. 21 Fortress Ave., Atlanta. Interred: Winder, Ga. AG 6/16/1908
ALBRIGHT, Josie Cornelia, Mrs., age 35, d. 21 Fortress St., Atlanta. Bur: Winder, Ga. Ch: Misses Ruby, Marie and Lucile and Hoyt Albright. Sis: Mrs. F. L Tuggle, Atlanta. Bros: G. V. Byrd, Commerge, C. and O. M. Byrd, Atlanta. AG 6/15/1908
ALCOTT, M. O., Mrs., mother of Mrs. Thompson, wife of Rev. C. J. Thompson, d. Sun. Interred: Clarksville, Va. AG 8/26/1909
ALDERHOLT, A. D., age 28, d. 505 Gordon St. Atlanta. AG 11/23/1910
ALDRED, Phoenie, Mrs., age 98, d. 181 W. Fair St., Atlanta, res. of Atlanta over 50 yrs. Ch: Mrs. Sallie Denham, Mrs. Martha Ward, Mrs. Bettie Aiken, Mrs. Fannie Latham, John W. Alexander of Atlanta. Interred: Oakland. AG 1/17/1908
ALEXANDER, C. H. who came to Union, S. C. 4 yrs. ago, d. Chester, S. C. He was b. Chester, age abt 50, m. Miss Lidie McLure, dau. of Maj. and Mrs. J. W. of Union. Dau: Frances. AG 1/21/1910
ALEXANDER, E. F., Mrs., age 50, d. Atlanta Wed. Ch: S. B., G. . and A. B Alexander, Misses Mary, Hoyt and Inez Alexander. Interred: Elberton, Ga. AG 3/11/1908
ALEXANDER, Eliza A., Mrs., age 78, d. 387 Luckie St. Atlanta. AG 1/28/1907
ALEXANDER, Emily, Mrs., age 50, d. Auburn Ave. and Courtland St. Interred: Elberton, Ga. AG 3/12/1908
ALEXANDER, I. W., Mrs., age 78, d. Mon. Baldwin, Ga. Interred: Harmony church. AG 6/10/1907
ALEXANDER, John, colored, age 59, d. 227 Neal St. Atlanta. AG 12/2/1910
ALEXANDER, John, son-in-law of G. A. Chastain of Atlanta, d. Mon. Eulaton, Ala. Interred: Eulaton, Ala. AG 9/22/1909
ALEXANDER, Kelly H., age 2 yrs., son of Mr. and Mrs. J. M., d. Sat. 153 Kelly St., Atlanta. Interred: Westview. AG 5/27/1907

4

ALEXANDER, Nellie Lou, age 2 mos., dau. of Mr. and Mrs. T. P., d. Riverside, Ga. Thurs. Interred: Hollywood. AG 4/30/1908

ALEXANDER, P. Eugene d. home of mother, Mrs. Mary E. Alexander, Pickens, S. C. 1/8/1908. He was former res. of Atlanta., age 34. Interred: Family Cem., 5 mi. N. of Pickens, S. C. AG 1/15/1908

ALEXANDER, S. W., Mrs., age 72, d. Mon. Baldwin, Ga. Interred: churchyard. AG 6/12/1907

ALEXANDER, Sarah, colored, age 47, d. 194 E. Ellis St. Atlanta. AG 1/8/1907

ALEXANDER, William, colored, age 31, d. 54 Crew St. Atlanta. AG 6/7/1907

ALEXANDER, William J., age 57, d. 62 Sylvan Ave., Atlanta, Tues. Leaves several children. Interred: South Bend Cemetery. AG 12/4/1907

ALEXANDER, Willie, colored, age 13, d. 349 Ira St. Atlanta. AG 1/22/1907

ALFORD, Berry, age 88, d. Old Soldiers' Home Wed., Atlanta. Enl. Confed. service 4/1/1861, Co., B., 12th Ga. Regt, served 4 yrs. AC 4/21/1910

ALFORD, C. A., age 36, of Hartwell, Ga., d. Mon. Parents, several bros., survive. Interred: Hartwell, Ga. AG 3/23/1908

ALFORD, E. B., while lying on death bed at Macon hospital, was indicted for double murder of his wife and mother-in-law. AG 1/19/1910

ALFORD, Lula, Mrs., age 44, wife of D. A., d. Bolton, Ga. Mon. Interred: Redan, Ga. Husband, 6 children, survive. AG 3/2/1909

ALFORD, Peter, colored, age 58, d. 74 Henry St. Atlanta. AG 10/7/1909

ALFORD, L. N. d. 8/21 W. Pt. Ga. where he had been res. 4 yrs., from Gabbettville, Ga. Wife. 3 ch. Sis: Mrs. J. N. Hogg; Mrs. A. J. Hogg. Bro: W. S. Alford, Ruston, La. Interred: Near Gabbettville, Ga. AC 8/22/1905

ALFRED, John F., aged man held in Cartersville jail for murder of wife, found guilty. AG 1/31/1907

ALGARY, Samuel shot and killed by Martha Wooten, acting in self defense, Clayton, Ga. AG 12/27/1910

ALGOOD, J. N. d. Mon. Atlanta. Interred: Villa Rica, Ga. AG 10/25/1910

ALLARD, Ernest L. d. Atlanta Wed. Interred: Buffalo, N. Y. AG 11/29/1907

ALLCOTT, M. O., Mrs. of Atlanta d. Pudacah, Ky. last Sun., dau. of Dr. and Mrs. C. J. Thompson of 20 East Ave. Atlanta. Interred: Clarksville, Va. AG 8/25/1909

ALLEN, Anna, colored, age 50, d. Grady Hospital. Atlanta. AG 4/10/1907

ALLEN, Charlotte G., inf. of Mr. and Mrs. C. F., d. 137 Venable St., Atlanta, Fri. Interred: Easley, Ala. AG 11/29/1907

ALLEN, D. C., Mrs., age 46, d. 143 Ashby St. Atlanta. 12 ch: Mrs. C. E. Allen, Mrs. Verlin Martin, Mrs. Buren Baker, Ethel, Velora, Helen, Daisy, Elizabeth & Rosalee Allen, Harold, Claude and Eugene Allen. Interred: Westview. AG 3/1/1908

ALLEN, E. C., age 60, d. Fri. Atlanta, 39 W. End Ave., Sun. Interred: Oakland. AG 7/27/1909

ALLEN, Elizabeth, Mrs., wife of late Joseph Allen, d. Thomaston Sat., age 83. Sis: Mrs. L. J. Battle. Sons: I. C. Thompson, Thomaston, Ga. AG 3/16/1909

ALLEN, Eva, age 1, dau. of Mr. and Mrs. L. W., d. Tues. Interred: LaGrange, Ga. AG 12/30/1908

ALLEN, F. B., colored, age 20, d. 101 N. Butler St. Atlanta. AG 10/3/1907

ALLEN, Flint of Oxford, Ala. d. Thurs. Interred: Oxford Cemetery. Wife survives. AG 12/17/1909

ALLEN, Fred J. d. Columbus, Ga. 11/11. AC 11/12/1905

ALLEN, G. W., age 52, d. 10/14 Broad St., Columbus, Ga. AC 10/16/1905

ALLEN, J. W., age 72, of Macon, Ga., d. 708 Ashby St. Atlanta. AG 9/21/1910

ALLEN, James, aged citizen, d. his home Woodlawn, in Talbot Co. Sun., age 80. Several children, all grown. AG 4/19/1910

ALLEN, James S., colored, age 47, d. 83 Elizabeth St. Atlanta. AG 12/22/1908

ALLEN, Jesse, age 103, of Columbus, Ga., gets Confederate Pension. AC 2/13/1905

ALLEN, John Rush, age 19, d. parents home, Mr. and Mrs. F. J., East Point, Ga Fri. One bro., one sister. He was grandson of Judge J. J. Martin. Interred: College Park Cemetery. AG 9/19/1908

ALLEN, Joseph Frank, inf. son of Mr. and Mrs. R. A., d. 35 Orange St. Atlanta, Sun. Interred: Westview. AG 5/31/1909

ALLEN, L. A., Mrs. d. Fri. Social Circle, Ga. Survived by three bros., 4 sisters. AG 5/18/1907

ALLEN, Lillian R., age 34, d. Davis and Fisher Sts., Atlanta. AG 3/29/1910

ALLEN, Lottie, colored, age 28, d. rear of 257 Decatur St., Atlanta. AG 12/14/1907

ALLEN, Lowry, infant son f Mr. and Mrs. Walker Allen, d. 550 Simpson St., Atlanta. Interred: Hollywood. AG 9/12/1907

ALLEN, Lucius, colored, age 39, d. rear 60 Gilmer St. Atlanta. AG 3/10/1908

ALLEN, Mary A., Mrs., age 61, d. Fri. 1 Bradley Ave., Atlanta, Sat. Interred: Highlands Cemetery. AG 12/26/1908

ALLEN, N. B., age 82, d. son's res., Pat Allen, Anniston, Ala. 3/29. Ch: Pat Allen, Anniston; L. T. and M. F. Allen, Atlanta; E. E. Allen, High P. F. Allen, N. C.; Mrs. G. L. Jameson, Anniston. Interred: Rome, Ga., former res. AC 3/30/1905

ALLEN, O. G., age 1, d. 137 Venable St. Atlanta. AG 11/30/1907

ALLEN, Patience, colored, age 50, d. 288 Auburn Ave. Atlanta. AG 8/21/1907

ALLEN, Robert d. Wytheville, Va., railroad man, age 72. Bro: R. B. Allen of Rome, Ga. AG 3/ 4/1907

ALLEN, S. A., Mrs., age 14, d. 110 Simpson St. Atlanta. AG 10/7/1907

ALLEN, S. L. O., Mrs., age 77, d. 639 Peachtree St. Atlanta. AG 1/3/1908

ALLEN, Sarah, colored, age 27, d. Atlanta. AG 1/17/1908

ALLEN, Sarah, Mrs. of Williamson, Ga., wife of Judge Robert H., d. Jan. 22, age 80. AC 1/23/1905

ALLEN, Thomas M., Judge, body reached Americus, Ga. from Atlanta 2/20. Age 71. AC 2/21/1905

ALLEN, Walter d. Waycross, Ga. 12/27. AG 12/27/1910
ALLEN, W. B., age 74, d. Mon. son´s res., W. H. Allen, 126
Elizabeth St., Atlanta. Interred: Huntsboro, Ala. AG 10/4/1910
ALLEN, Young J. d. Shanghai, China, m. Mary Houston of Ga. Ch:
Mrs. Mellie Loher, wife of Shanghai missionary; Mrs. Mary Turner,
NY; Alice and Ethel, Shanghai; Arthur H.; Judge Edgar; Arthur H.
(m. Jessie, dau. of O. S. Prior). AG 6/5/1907
ALLENSWORTH, Cora, Miss, age 23, dau. of James H., funeral from
res. of aunt, Mrs. C. P. Taylor, 86 Angier Ave., Atlanta. Father
resides College Park. AG 9/10/1910
ALLEY, A. R., Dr., age 65, d. Thurs. 83 W. Peachtree St.,
Confederate Veteran. AG 2/20/1907
ALLEY, Lizzie May, colored, age 1, d. 289 Fulton St. Atlanta. AG
8/11/1908
ALLEY, Mancil W., policeman, Atlanta force, from 1868, met tragic
end at Kimball Hotel, Atlanta. AG 5/4/1907
ALLGOOD, Drucilla, Mrs., age 59, d. Wed. 27 Bell St. Atlanta.
Interred: Villa Rica, Ga. AG 5/8/1907
ALLGOOD, J. N., shotmaker, Atlanta, d. from accident. Res. of 246
1/2 Decatur St. AG 10/24/1910
ALLISON, C. E., Mrs., age 52, d. Wed. 147 Davis St. Atlanta.
Interred: Cuthbert. AG 6/21/1907
ALLISON, Isabella, Mrs., age 63, d. 58 McDonough Rd., Atlanta,
Wed. Interred: Roswell, Ga. AG 5/12/1909
ALLISON, Kirby Lee, age 27, d. E. Hunter St. Atlanta. Interred:
Charlotte, N. C. AG 8/5/1910
ALLISON, Kitty, Miss, age 17, d. Tues. 27 Carlton St., Atlanta.
Interred: Roswell, Ga. AG 7/24/1907
ALLISON, Voniamen, age 10 mos., son of Mr. and Mrs. J. H., d.
Tues. Interred: Roswell, Ga. AG 6/3/1906
ALMAND, I. A., age 45, merchant, found dead Hillman, Ga. Tues.
Interred: Washington, Ga. AG 9/29/1909
ALMAND, Roy, age 3, d. Atlanta. AG 4/27/1910
ALMAND, W. B., 9 mos., d. 221 Berean Ave. Atlanta. AG 5/24/1907
ALMAND, William D., son of Mr. and Mrs. W. M., d. Fri. 66 Park
Ave., Atlanta. Interred: Westview. AG 5/24/1907
ALMON, G. H., age 27, d. Piedmont Hotel. Atlanta. AG 6/2/1910
ALMOND, Mary J., Mrs. d. Sat. 292 E. Cain St. Atlanta. Interred:
Washington, Ga. AG 8/11/1906
ALRED, Cora murdered by husband, John Franklin Alred, age 54, at
their home near Taylorsville, 11/1/1906, witnessed by their dau.,
Lula, age 16. AG 1/26/1907
ALSABROOK, J. C., age 39, d. Adamsville, Ga. Sun. Wife, three
children. Interred: Masons church yard. AG 6/27/1908
ALSABROOK, W. M., age 45, d. Luckie St. Atlanta. AG 11/25/1907
ALSTON, Nancy, colored, age 75, d. 86 Elm St. Atlanta. AG
10/19/1907
ALSTON, Susan Elizabeth, Miss of Atlanta, dau. of late Dr.
William Alston of Marietta, d. 2/6 res. of sis., Mrs. Charles
Willingham, 13 Cleburne Ave., Sun. Bro: F. Roland Alston,
Atlanta. Sis: Mrs. Sabina S. Nichols, Marietta. AG 2/7/1910
AMASON, John H. killed by lightning 7/13, age 25, unmd,
Washington, Ga. AG 7/14/1909
AMASSON, Renfroe, age 2, son of Mr. and Mrs. O. D., d. Tues.
Richmond Ave., Atlanta. Bur: Antioch Baptist Church. AG 5/7/1907

7

AMBLER, Robert Bruce, native of Accomack Co., Va., d. Atlanta, age 107. He was oldest Mason in USA. AG 5/31/1907

AMBROSE, Mary E., Mrs. funeral Mon. Nephew: G. Thomason. Interred: N.Y. AG 11/11/1907

AMES, F. H., Mrs. of Brunswick, d. F. Street, Ft. Son: Walter C. Ames. AG 10/20/1906

AMILON, E. H., age 48, d. 49-51 Houston St. Atlanta. AG 2/8/1907

AMOROUS, Martin, Mrs., wife of Hon. Martin, d. Fri. 251 Ivy St., Atlanta. Interred: Westview. AG 4/30/1906

ANDERSON, Addie M., Mrs, age 65, d. Fri. res. of bro-in-law: S. C. Morley, DeKalb Ave., Atlanta. Interred: Decatur, Ga. AG 1/15/1910

ANDERSON, Albert d. Tues. 28 Young Street, Atlanta. Interred: Indian Creek church yard. AG 6/6/1906

ANDERSON, Augustus, a section foreman d. Floster, Ga. AG 10/18/1907

ANDERSON, Axel H., age 16, d. 16 S. Jackson St. Atlanta. AG 7/22/1910

ANDERSON, Buie, Mrs. d. Emmitt (near Statesboro), Ga. Sun. Husband, 4 children. AG 9/3/1908

ANDERSON, Burle Bennett, age 21, d. res. of grandmother, Mrs. M. J. Spinks, Flat Shoals Rd., Atlanta, Thurs. Parents: Mr. and Mrs. R. B. Anderson. Interred: Oakland. AG 2/13/1908

ANDERSON, C. F., age 59, d. Mon. Grady Hospital, Atlanta, killed by train at Hiram. Interred: Floyd, Ga. AG 7/30/1907

ANDERSON, Charlie, negro, killed in Atlanta. AC 8/6/1905

ANDERSON, Clyde S. of Summit, Ga. d. Atlanta Mon. Interred: Garfield, Ga. AG 8/16/1910

ANDERSON, Dolly, Miss, teacher in Decatur, d. Sun. LaGrange, age 65. Bro: late Gen. Tige Anderson. Interred: Covington. AG 4/1/1907

ANDERSON, E., colored, 7 mos., d. 28 Fraser St. Atlanta. AG 2/4/1907

ANDERSON, Ellen, Mrs., age 57, d. 119 Jones Ave., Atlanta, Wed. Sons: H. C., A. F. Daus: Mrs. J. P. Howell, Mrs. P. H. Hutchinson. Interred: Hollywood. AG 5/19/1910

ANDERSON, Emma, Mrs., d. Sat. 234 Pulliam St. Atlanta Sun. Interred: Hollywood. AG 5/25/1908

ANDERSON, Emory F., Rev., 81, d. 10/3 res. Mrs. Jas T. Gresham (dau), College Pk. Bur: Westview. Bro: Dr. Lewis G. (d. Madison 1907, age 89). Ch: Mrs. C. H. Arnold; Misses Lucy, Furlow; John T.; Emory F., Jr.; Harry L., Andrew. AG 10/4/1909

ANDERSON, Esther, age 3, dau. of Mr. and Mrs. M. L., d. Thurs. 220 Berean Ave., Atlanta. Interred: Gainesville, AG 6/1/1907

ANDERSON, George A., colored, age 20, d. 321 E. Fair St. Atlanta. AG 3/1/1907

ANDERSON, Harold T. and wife, Louise, drowned when boat capsized in canal, Augusta, Ga. AG 5/21/1907

ANDERSON, Harry, colored, age 27, d. 97 Ivy St. Atlanta. AG 8/25/1908

ANDERSON, Harvey L., age 38, d. 294 Courtland St. Atlanta. AG 11/8/1909

ANDERSON, infant of Mr. and Mrs. G. M., d. Wed. at 78 Gaskill St., Atlanta. Interred: Sylvester cemetery. AG 5/23/1907

ANDERSON, J. J., Mrs. d. 94 Oak St., Atlanta. Interred: Westview. Husband. Sons: W. F., W. Lester (of Chicago). AG 9/1/1910

ANDERSON, J. L., Rev. found floating in River, Ellijay, Ga. AC 5/1/1905

ANDERSON, J. M., Mrs., age 30, d. Forest Park, Ga. Wed. Her death was second to occur in family within 2 weeks (Lucile, age 15 mos., dau., d. 10/17. Husband, 3 children, and her mother, survive. Interred: Elam Cemetery. AG 10/28/1909

ANDERSON, Jack, colored, age 26, d. 13 Green St. Atlanta. AG 3/28/1907

ANDERSON, James, colored, age 11, d. rear of 18 Benjamin St. Atlanta. AG 7/9/1908

ANDERSON, James, colored, age 26, d. 101 N. Butler St. Atlanta. AG 9/28/1909

ANDERSON, John T., Confederate Veteran, d. Wrightsville, Ga. Tues, age 74. Daus: Mrs. John Gunter, Miss Sarah Anderson. Sons: Will W. Anderson of South America; Lee and J. P. Anderson. AG 9/3/1908

ANDERSON, Judge, colored, age 82, d. Cloytville, Ga. AG 6/21/1909

ANDERSON, Lewis G., Dr., oldest graduate of Univ. of Ga. (1838), d. Madison, Ga. Bro: Rev. Emory Anderson. Nephews: Harvey L. and Andrew Anderson. Son: James C. Anderson, Morgan Co. He m. dau. of Barton Thrasher of Clarke Co. AG 7/11/1907

ANDERSON, Louise and husband, Harold T., drowned when boat capsized in canal. Augusta, Ga. AG 5/21/1907

ANDERSON, Louise, age 4, dau. of Rev. and Mrs. J. R., d. 121 Paynes Ave., Atlanta, Fri. Interred: Hollywood. AG 2/15/1908

ANDERSON, Lucile, age 15 mos., dau. of Mrs. J. M., d. 10/17, Forest Park, Ga. AG 10/28/1909

ANDERSON, Lucy, Mrs., age 55, wife of A. A., d. 89 Copenhill Ave. Atlanta, Sons: W. P., J. T., A. P., C. E. Dau: Mrs. C. E. Hardy. Parents: Mr. & Mrs. J. T. Alford, Redan. Sis: Mrs. J. A. Farmer; Mrs. Sandy Kelly, Lithonia; Mrs. Lizzie Floyd, Redan. Bros: J. A., S. W., L. H. & D. A. Alford, Atlanta. Interred: Lithonia, Ga. AG 5/25/1910

ANDERSON, Mack accidentally killed at a gin Douglas, Ga. AG 12/14/1907

ANDERSON, Marguerite Estelle, age 7, killed on Georgia Ave., Atlanta, by street car. AG 5/19/1910

ANDERSON, Martha J., Mrs., age 58, d. 89 Jett St. Atlanta. AG 6/3/1908

ANDERSON, Mary A., Mrs., age 54, d. 289 Central Ave., Atlanta, Mon. Interred: Cincinnati, Ohio, her old home. Husband: J. R. Son: G. . Daus: Mrs. Bert Sarvers, Mrs. Harry Wilson, Mrs. George Kent. AG 6/1/1909

ANDERSON, Matilda E., Mrs., age 79, d. Tues. Atlanta. Interred: Hollywood. One son, two daus., two bros., two sisters. AG 11/1/1910

ANDERSON, Overton, age 15, d. 64 Cameron St., Atlanta, Nov. 14. AG 11/16/1910

ANDERSON, Policeman shot by Clay Thomas 12 yrs. ago. Thomas killed by policeman. AG 8/6/1906

ANDERSON, R. O., Jr., inf. of Mr. and Mrs. R. O., d. near Wallace St., Atlanta, Mon. Interred: Peachtree Church yard. AG 12/9/1907

ANDERSON, Robert N., pioneer to Douglas Co., d. age 76, Confederate veteran. Wife, 4 daus., 2 sons, survive. AG 5/20/1907
ANDERSON, Susan V., Mrs., age 47, d. 315 Peachtree St., Atlanta. Interred: Hickory, N.C. AG 9/9/1907
ANDERSON, Victor suicide 12/25 Vienna, Ga., age abt 40. Wife, 2 children. AG 12/26/1910
ANDERSON, Virginia, inf. dau. of F. A., d. 428 Georgia Ave. Atlanta, Mon. Interred: Oakland. AG 11/22/1910
ANDERSON, W. T., age 64, d. Muscogee Co. 3/21. AC 3/22/1905
ANDREWS, Annie, Mrs., age 70, d. Thurs., 74 Cameron St., Atlanta. Interred: Camp Creek Church. AG 8/1/1907
ANDREWS, Carrie, Mrs., age 25, d. 44 Park Ave. Atlanta, Sat. Wife of J. G. Two children, her mother, Mrs. E. L. McCormack. 4 bros: G. W., R. F., C. R. and J. E. McComack. Sis: Miss Amelie McComack. Interred: LaGrange, Ga. AG 8/17/1908
ANDREWS, Catherine E., inf. dau. of Mr. and Mrs. Fred, d. 42 Jones Ave., Atlanta, Tues. Interred: Westview. AG 10/29/1907
ANDREWS, Charlie, negro, scalded to death, Atlanta Gas Light Co. accidentally. AG 11/22/1907
ANDREWS, Ezra, age 85, d. 239 S. Pryor St., Atlanta. Interred: Oakland. Wife, four children. AG 7/16/1908
ANDREWS, Ida, colored, age 43, d. 336 Fulton St. Atlanta. AG 9/10/1910
ANDREWS, Lula Marcella, inf. dau. of Mr. and Mrs. F. R., d. E. Pt., Ga., Tues. Parents, 2 sisters, 1 bro. Interred: Westview. AG 5/17/1910
ANDREWS, Margaret S., age 19 mos., dau. of Mr. and Mrs. J. S. Andrews, d. 20 Lucy St., Atlanta. Interred: Westview. AG 8/11/1906
ANDREWS, Margaret, Mrs., wife of John, d. Huntsville, Ala., Thurs, age 62. AG 10/8/1909
ANDREWS, Mattie W., Mrs., age 38, d. Sun. 50 Trinity Ave., Atlanta. Interred: Westview. 3 children. AG 11/22/1909
ANDREWS, Nancy, colored, age 2 yrs., d. 189 Maple St. Atlanta. AG 2/4/1907
ANDREWS, Perry, Mrs., age 59, d. Atlanta Fri., 367 North Jackson St. Interred: Westview. Husband, one dau., one son. AG 5/8/1909
ANDREWS, Rufus, colored, age 47, d. 45 Richmond St. Atlanta. AG 1/14/1907
ANDREWS, Sydney, Mrs., age 59, wife of Perry, d. Atlanta Fri., 367 North Jackson St. Son: George T. Love. Dau: Mrs. Thomas O. McBride. Sis: Mrs. T. J. Chadeayne, Conn.; Mrs. Mary Reed, Pa. Bro: James Heater, Ohio. AG 5/7/1909
ANGIER, Annie, Miss d. Thurs. res. of parents, Mr. and Mrs. Edgar A., Capitol Ave., Atlanta. Interred: Oakland. AG 2/20/1908
ANSLEY, Annie L., Mrs., age 58, d. 5/6 home of bro., Sam Hunt, Silver Creek, Ga. Sis: Mrs. R. M. Estes, Atlanta; Mrs. E. D. Estes, Cedartown; Miss Martha Hunt, Savannah. AG 5/7/1909
ANSLEY, Hattie Fuller, Mrs., wife of H. C., dau. of Rev. Fuller, d. Mon., Alexandria, Va. Bro: H. C. Ansley. News received by William S. Ansley, Atlanta. AG 1/1/1907
ANTHONY, Daniel Pittman, age 15 mos., son of Mr. and Mrs. E. Anthony, d. 119 Walton St. Atlanta, Wed. interred: Westview. AG 4/17/1907

ANTHONY, Garland, colored, age 83, d. 311 Park Ave. Atlanta. AG 5/4/1909

ANTHONY, George, age 36, d. Fri. 101 N. Butler St. Atlanta. Interred: Westview, Atlanta. AG 11/28/1908

ANTHONY, Mattie, colored, age 9, d. 229 Chestnut St. Atlanta. AG 12/12/1910

ANTHONY, Nathaniel, colored, age 2 mos., d. 275 E. Ave. Atlanta. AG 11/2/1907

ANTONINI, Sigmund, age 80, d. 122 Hill St., Atlanta, Sun. Interred; Westview. AG 12/12/1910

APPLETON, George, age 75, res. of Jacksonville, Fla., d. Atlanta Thurs. Son: George, Jr., Jacksonville. AG 5/21/1909

APPLING, Isadore Bradford, colored, age 7 mos., d. 112 Howell St. Atlanta. AG 6/21/1909

APPLING, Nellie, dau. of Mr. and Mrs. J. W. funeral Mt. Zion Church Sat. AG 2/20/1908

ARBERRY, J. W. d. several days ago. Funeral Sun. Interred: Westview. AC 4/16/1910

ARBERRY, Sallie, Mrs., age 60, wife of J. W., d. Thurs. 224 E. Linden St., Atlanta. Interred: Westview. AG 2/25/1910

ARCHER, Alonzo, age 11 mos., son of Mr. and Mrs. A. A., d. 645 E. Fair St., Atlanta, Mon. Interred: Westview. AG 11/19/1907

ARCHER, Carter, age 24, d. bro.'s res., Dr. M. S. Archer, Flat Shoals Rd., Atlanta, near Wesley Chapel. AG 5/26/1908

ARCHER, N. N. Mrs b.1831 Wilkes Co. d.Atlanta.Bro-J. W. Maddox.Daus-Mrs. W. H. Davis, Mrs. Horace Cranford. Sis-Mary Martin, Mittie Meynell. Gdaus-Cora & Maude Jones, Mrs. Jno McCarter, Miss A'Lama Steele. Ni-Mrs. W. S. Paris. AG 5/21/1907

ARCHER, Wilson B., Jr., age 6 mos., son of Mr. and Mrs. Wilson B., d. 41 Hayden St., Atlanta, Fri. Interred: Canton, Ga. AG 9/21/1907

ARCHER, William E. d. E. Point, Ga. Mon., oldest son f W. P. and Marietta. Bros: S. H., Orangeburg, S. C.; J. H., Sumter, S. C.; Pope C., Spartanburg, S. C. Interred: Pleasant Grove. AG 12/6/1909

ARCHIBALD, Walter H., age 52, d. Sun. Atlanta. Interred: Birmingham, Ala. Wife, 2 children, and one dau. AG 11/22/1909

ARD, Mattie, Mrs., age 32, d. Jackson St., Macon, wife of R. A. Ard. Leaves small child: Reuben. AG 6/4/1907

ARGO, Elizabeth, Mrs., age 35, d. Carmichael, Ga. AG 6/22/1910

ARGO, Fannie, Mrs., age 55, d. Thurs. Interred: Clifton Church yard. Atlanta. AG 9/24/1909

ARGO, Maggie L., Mrs., age 52, wid. of late W. R. Argo, d. 7/20, Macon. Ch: D. R., R. G., J. L., T. W. and Miss Annie Argo of Macon. Interred: Hazlehurst, Ga. AG 7/21/1908

ARMISTEAD, Vashie, Mrs., age 20, d. 30 Corley St., Atlanta, Sun. Interred: Hollywood. AG 9/23/1907

ARMISTEAD, W. S., age 60, d. Alms House. Atlanta. AG 11/23/1910

ARMOND, Adeline, colored, age 60, d. 60 Chamberlin St. Atlanta. AG 1/7/1907

ARMOUR, C. H., age 54, suicide, E. Point. AG 3/3/1910

ARMSTRONG, Adolphus, age 67, an inmate of Conf. Soldiers' Home, Atlanta, d. Wed. Enl. Co. B, 48th Ga. Vol. Inf. as Pvt. At Manassas, Petersburg, etc. Interred: Sandersville, Ga. AG 5/12/1909

11

ARMSTRONG, Elizabeth, Mrs., age 80, d. Cross Keys, Ga. AG 12/3/1908

ARMSTRONG, G. V., Mrs., age 74, d. Decatur, Ga. AG 5/12/1909

ARMSTRONG, J. Stinson, res. Atlanta 25 yrs., d. Montgomery, Ala., Sat. Conf. Vet., enl. Sullivans Island, 4th Ga. Cav. AG 4/20/1909

ARMSTRONG, James, Mrs. d. Scottsboro, Ala. Tues., wife of James Armstrong. Dau: Miss Marie. Sons: Phil, Andrew, Harry. She was sister to Mayor Harry M. Henderson and dau. of late Philip Henderson. AG 1/24/1907

ARMSTRONG, John H., age 8 mos., d. 11 Bluff St. Atlanta. AG 7/8/1907

ARMSTRONG, Samuel B., age 17 mos., son of Mr. and Mrs. Samuel Armstrong, d. 1056 Oglethorpe St., Atlanta. Interred: Mt. Pleasant cemetery. AG 4/9/1907

ARMSTRONG, Stewart I. of Atlanta killed in train wreck 54 mi. S. of Knoxville, Tenn. 3/21. AC 3/22/1905

ARMSTRONG, T. A., Mrs. of N. Dalton, Ga., d. 8/17. Interred: West Hill Cemetery. Ch: Miss Lula Armstrong and Walter Armstrong of Tilton; Oscar, Jesse and Sandy Armstrong, of Dalton. AG 8/13/1910

ARMSTRONG, Walter, 3 mos. son of Mr. and Mrs. T. S., d. Atlanta Mon. Interred: Westview. AG 6/30/1908

ARNES, Robert, age 5, son of Mr. and Mrs. J. B., d. near Clarkston, Ga. Sat. Interred: Greensboro, Ga. AG 12/21/1908

ARNETT, Walter R., age 28, d. 9 Highland Ave., Atlanta, Wed. Interred: Macon. AG 6/24/1909

ARNOLD, Ben H., age 27, res. of Atlanta, d. Jacksonville, Fla. Wife, two daus., parents, three bros, one sister. Interred: Atlanta. AG 12/16/1909

ARNOLD, Charles Steele, Capt. suicide 17 Baltimore black, Atlanta 2/23. Native of Augusta Co., Va., b. 6/18/1839. Interred: Virginia. AC 2/24/1905

ARNOLD, Chauncey N. funeral Jan. 23 Tallapoosa, Ga. Interred: Laurel Hill Cemetery. AC 1/24/1905

ARNOLD, D. S., age 77, d. 826 Marietta St. Atlanta. AG 2/20/1908

ARNOLD, Eliza, Mrs., age 43, d. Fri. near Skipperton, Ga. 5 bros., 2 bros., 9 children. AG 3/1/1908

ARNOLD, Ella M., Mrs., age 38, d. Atlanta Tues., wife of A. S. Three children. AG 7/23/1908

ARNOLD, Harriet, colored, age 46, d. 37 Wallace St. Atlanta. AG 9/2/1910

ARNOLD, Horace, colored, age 7, d. 133 Ira St. Atlanta. AG 3/31/1908

ARNOLD, infant of Mr. and Mrs. H. E. of Arnoldsville, Ga., d. res. of I. W. Prim, 38 Formwalt St., Atlanta, Sun. Interred: Arnoldsville, Ga. AG 3/23/1908

ARNOLD, John Barclay, son of Prof. L. W., d. at Norwood Thurs. Funeral at 111 S. Pryor St., Atlanta. Interred: Oakland. AG 6/29/1906

ARNOLD, John W. d. Jan. 14 Grantville. Ch: Mrs. John E. Dean; Mrs. Jannie Mootty; Misses Bessie and Ester Arnold, Grantville; Mrs. Dr. Simms, Talladega, Ala.; Mrs. Maude Perry, Bainbridge, Ga.; Park Arnold, Colorado Spgs, Colo. AC 1/15/1905

ARNOLD, M. A., Mrs., age 65, d. Jonesboro 5/31. Dau: Mrs. Charles H. Lyle, Jonesboro. AG 5/31/1910

ARNOLD, M. W., Mrs. d. Sun. 20 Stonewall St., Atlanta. Interred: Westview. AG 5/21/1907

ARNOLD, Margaret, Mrs., age 70, d. E. Atlanta. Interred: Macedonia Cemetery. AG 9/6/1909

ARNOLD, Rita, Miss, age 13, dau. of Mr. and Mrs. A. E., d. 53 Crew St., Atlanta, Sat. Interred: Westview. AG 2/10/1908

ARNOLD, S. D., Mrs., age 49, d. Atlanta. AG 5/11/1908

ARNOLD, Sallie, Mrs. of Washington, Ga. d. Atlanta Fri. Interred: Washington, Ga. Age 48. AG 5/9/1908

ARNOLD, T. E., wealthy farmer of Grantville (near Newnan), d. Sat. Sis: Mrs. W. A. Post, Grantville. AG 6/12/1908

ARNOLD, T. L. d. nephew's res., Talley Jenkins, 220 Calhoun St., Macon, age 72, unmd. Three bros. survive: Albert of Macon; Malcolm of Deveaux; Monroe of White Plains. Sis: Miss V. S. Arnold, Macon. Interred: Deveaureax, Ga. AG 4/19/1907

ARNOLD, Vista Eugene d. Sun., son of Mr. and Mrs. V. E., 139 Oglethorpe Ave., Atlanta. Interred: Westview. AG 5/28/1906

ARNOLD, W. T., age 61, d. res. of dau., Mrs. R. D. Fairman, 698 S. Pryor St. Atlanta. Ch: Mrs. M. M. Orr, Mrs. J. P. Burkholder, Mrs. R. D. Fairman, W. H. Arnold. Bro: Rev. J. W. Arnold, Perry, Ga. Interred: Westview. AG 2/24/1908

ARNOLD, William Edward (Teddy), age 24 d. 29 Luckie St. Atlanta. Thurs. Mother: Mrs. Frank M. Arnold of Kennebunkport, Me. Interred: Kennebunkport, Me. AG 9/25/1907

ARONSON, Archibald, age 7, son of Mr. and Mrs. S., d. Sun. Atlanta. AG 5/28/1906

ARRINGTON, G. A., age 56, d. 157 Chapel St., Atlanta, Fri. Wife, no. of children. Interred: Derring, Ga. AG 12/17/1910

ARRINGTON, Marie, age 9 mos., dau. of Mr. and Mrs. F. M., of 165 Magnolia St., Atlanta, d. Tues. Interred: Westview. AG 3/16/1909

ARRINGTON, Emily E., Mrs., age 62, wid. of James M., d. 197 Bass St. Atlanta. Son: Thomas D. Stepsons: A. B. & H. H. Arrington, Rome. Stepdau: Mrs. Thomas Evans, Rockmart, Ga. Several bros. and sisters. Interred: Rockmart, Ga. AG 6/2/1908

ARWOOD, Dora, Mrs., age 23, d. 85 Little St. Atlanta. AG 7/23/1909

ARWOOD, Walter B., age 30, d. 422 Woodward Ave., Atlanta, Mon. Wife, two children, father, three bros., three sisters. Interred: Austell, Ga. AG 12/30/1907

ASBERY, Victoria, colored, age 45, d. 190 Chappell St., Atlanta, Nov. 15. AG 11/16/1910

ASBURY, C. C., colored, age 33, d. rear 60 Orange St. Atlanta. AG 11/20/1907

ASBURY, E. N. d. Sat. 229 E. Hunter St. Atlanta. Interred: Woodville, Ga. AG 6/21/1907

ASBURY, Lena Pearl, Miss, age 27, d. 610 Washington St., Atlanta, Tues. Interred: Westview. AG 12/8/1909

ASBURY, J. W., age 77, of Greensboro, native Taliaferro Co., d. dau's home, Mrs. H. T. Evans. Ch: Dr. J. C. Asbury, Mrs. H. T. Evans of Greensboro. Bro: Richard Asbury, Thomson. Several grandchildren. Interred: Crawfordville. AG 11/2/1906

ASHFORD, J. K., age 62, d. 13 Ponce de Leon Ave. Atlanta. AG 6/9/1910

ASHFORD, John A., Dr. of Watkinsville d. 1/20, from blood poisoning caught from patient. AG 1/21/1910

ASHLEY, T. J., Mrs., age 19, d. 108 Loomis Ave. Atlanta, AG 12/16/1909

ASHLEY, W. E., age 26, d. Scottdale, Ga. AG 2/20/1909

ASHLEY, May, Miss, age 15, dau. of W. W., d. Chattahoochee, Ga., Fri. AG 12/10/1910

ASHWORTH, A. E., Mrs., age 61, d. Sat. 534 Woodward Ave., Atlanta. Sisters: Mrs. Susan Salter, Mrs. Jennie McKlendon, Miss Amanda Brannon. Two grandch. Interred: Oakland. AG 3/9/1908

ASKEW, Frank M., youngest son of J. L., of W. Point, Ga., d. 3/16. Bros: Dr. A. W., Alexander City; Dr. J. Lewis. Sts: Vollie. Interred: Pinewood Cemetery. AC 3/18/1905

ASKEW, James, age 59, d. Britian Hotel, Atlanta. AC 3/9/1910

ASKEW, John, age 60, d. St. Josephs Infirmary. Atlanta. AG 9/9/1907

ASKRAM, H. F., Mrs., wife of Dr. H. F., d. St. Clair Apts. Atlanta, 55 E. Harcis St. Mon., formerly Miss Lizzie Johnson. One dau. Sisters: Mrs. H. E. Williamson, Miss Ida Johnson, Atlanta, Miss Belle Johnson, NY. AG 6/9/1908

ASSELTINE, Hattie, Mrs., age 61, of Fruithurst, Ala., d. Atlanta Mon. Interred: Fruithurst, Ala. AG 3/1/1909

ATCHISON, Marguerite H., age 6, d. 73 Spring St. Atlanta. AG 11/21/1910

ATKINS, Nellie, colored, age 49, d. 131 Hilliard St. Atlanta. AG 7/6/1909

ATKINSON, A. J., age 78, d. 165 S. Humphries St. Atlanta. Interred: Mt. Zion. AG 12/12/1910

ATKINSON, Andrew J., age 75, d. 177 S. Humphries St. Atlanta. AG 12/12/1910

ATKINSON, D., age 33, d. 1 Middle St. Atlanta. AG 8/7/1908

ATKINSON, Harriet, inf. dau. of Mr. and Mrs. J. C., d. 347 Fraser St., Atlanta Sun. Interred: Marietta. AC 3/10/1910

ATKINSON, Ida L., Mrs., age 41, d. Atlanta Fri., wife of Rev. J. C. Formerly Miss Ida L. Williams (m. 1888). Interred: Jonesboro, Ga. AG 4/23/1910

ATKINSON, J. W., age 14 mos., son of Mr. and Mrs. Paul, d. Sun. 260 Greensferry Ave., Atlanta. Interred; DOrsey, Ga. AG 9/14/1907

ATKINSON, Lela Ruth, age 11 mos., d. 153 Middle St. Atlanta. AG 6/18/1907

ATKINSON, Ludie, Miss, age 15, dau. of Mr. and Mrs. D. V. Atkinson, d. Sun. 11 Lee St. Atlanta. Interred: Caseys. AG 3/16/1907

ATKINSON, Robert, engineer, d. accident Chattanooga, Tenn. Sun. Interred: Westview. AG 7/10/1906

ATKINSON, Ruth Lee, infant dau. of Mr. and Mrs. D., d. Sat. 153 Middle St., Atlanta. Interred: Mt. Zion church yard. AG 6/14/1907

ATKINSON, Walter of Montgomery, Ala. killed by train Oakland City. Body found Oct. 15th. Identified today. Mother: Mrs. Mollie Atkinson. AG 12/2/1906

ATTAMOS, Ezekiel, colored, age 30, d. 481 Glenn St. Atlanta. AG 6/7/1907

ATWELL, Sarah, Mrs., age 67, d. Tues. Macon. 3 daus., 2 sons of Macon survive. AG 4/29/1908

ATWOOD, Ethel L., Miss, age 82, d. 230 1/2 Peters St. Atlanta. AG 8/22/1910

ATWOOD, Mary Lee, age 3, dau. of Rev. and Mrs. J. W., d. Waycross, Ga., Sun. AG 10/14/1907

ATWOOD, Nancy E., Mrs., age 74, d. Roswell Rd., Atlanta, Mon. Interred: Crossroads church yard. AG 5/18/1909

AUDOUIN, Sarah, Mrs., age 84, d. 615 Second St., Atlanta. She was b. Jones Co. 1823, removed Macon before Civil war. She was wid. of late A. L. Audouin. Nephew: Chilly Audouin, Macon. AG 6/20/1907

AUERBACH, Joseph, age 58, b. N. Y., d. 296 Rawson St., Atlanta, Thurs. Wife. Sons: Clarence, Samuel. Daus: Misses Estelle, Henrietta. Bro-in-law: Harry Silverman. Interred: Oakland. AG 9/24/1909

AUGHTMAN, Mary, Mrs., wife of Willis, d. 82 Hightower St., Atlanta, Mon. Leaves husband, three sons, three daus. Interred: Family Burial Grounds, near College Park. AG 11/19/1907

AULT, C. W. of McRae, formerly from Buchanan, Ga., d. 8/19. Son: Eugene S., atty, Cedartown. Son-in-law: Hon. Price Edwards, atty, Buchanan. AC 8/22/1905

AULTMAN, Fannie, Mrs., age 85, d. Tues. Interred: Society Hill Church near Byron, Ga. Widow of late Solomon Aultman. 5 sons, 3 living in Macon. AG 9/23/1908

AUNY, Carrie, colored, age 47, d. 362 Greensferry Ave., Atlanta. AG 9/26/1907

AUSTELL, Ellen, colored, age 33, d. 148 Bedford Pl. Atlanta. AG 12/9/1910

AUSTIN, Alice, Mrs., age 53, d. Milledgeville, Ga. Atlanta. AG 11/20/1907

AUSTIN, Alice, Mrs., wife of J. N., d. Atlanta Sun., 15 Echo St., Atlanta, Mon. Interred: Oakland. AG 11/19/1907

AUSTIN, Elizabeth, Mrs. d. Copenhill Tues. Husband: J. C. Austin. Interred: Sandy Springs church yard. AG 10/6/1909

AUSTIN, G. F., Mrs., wife of Rev. of Hazlehurst, Ga., d. 2/15. Interred: Ocala, Fla. AG 2/16/1910

AUSTIN, George, inf. son of Mr. and Mrs. T. A., 14 Bellwood Ave., Atlanta, d. Tues. Interred: Wesleys Chapel. AG 3/18/1909

AUSTIN, J. D., Mrs., of 136 Jones Ave. Atlanta d. Sun. Interred: Villa Rica, Ga. Husband, 1 bro., 4 sisters, survive. AG 4/26/1908

AUSTIN, J. M. d. Ben Hill, Ga. Sun. Interred: Red Oak Church Yard. Age 80. Wife, 4 children, survive. AG 6/23/1908

AUSTIN, James L., age 54, d. 13 Porter St., Atlanta. Interred: Sandy Springs church yard. Wife, two bros., four sisters. AG 7/20/1909

AUSTIN, Lena, Mrs., age 31, wife of J. Lee, d. Atlanta Tues., 48 Kendall St. Interred: Sandy Springs. AG 5/13/1908

AUSTIN, Lucy, Mrs., age 39, d. Milledgeville, Ga. AG 4/28/1908

AUSTIN, M. E., Mrs., age 49, d. 3 E. North Ave. Atlanta. AG 10/8/1909

AUSTIN, Peyton Harrison, 11 mos. son of Mr. and Mrs. T. H. Austin, of 68 W. 5th St., Atlanta, died, a grandson of Mr. and Mrs. P. H. Snook. Interred: Westview. AG 6/13/1907

AUSTIN, J. C., 57, d. E. Pt. where buried. Dau: Mrs. W. C.
Carroll. Bros: J. M., Kenwood; Charles, Atlanta; W. H., Morrow;
J. L., Helen, AL. Sis: Mrs. Marrill, Heflin, AL.; Mrs. Graves;
Mrs. Carter; Mrs. Cook, The Rock, Ga. AG 2/28/1910
AUTEN, Hester Ann, Mrs. d. Thurs. 336 Hemphill Ave., Atlanta.
Dau: Mrs. R. H. Robb. Son: Dr. W. J. Auten. Nephews: Dr. J. T.
Gibson, W. F. Aiken, S. H. Ogletree. Interred: Westview. AC
3/31/1910
AVERA, Abner, son of W. G., d. Sparta, Ga. Sat. Interred: Berrien
Co., former home. AG 3/15/1910
AVERETT, E. T. buried Sandersville, Ga. Died Colorado Springs
Sun. where he went for his health. Leaves wife, one child. AG
9/11/1907
AVERETT, Mary R., Mrs., age 66, d. East Point, Ga. AG 2/27/1907
AVERITT, Phoebe, Mrs., age 68, d. res. of dau., Mrs. Rev. D. S.
Edenfield, 303 Grant St., Atlanta, Tues. Interred: Savannah. AG
12/30/1908
AVERY,, child of Mr. and Mrs. R. L. Avery, d. Dublin, Ga. 2/28.
AC 3/1/1905
AVERY, Fannie, colored, age 16, d. 101 N. Butler St. Atlanta. AG
11/6/1907
AWTREY, Louise, age 4, dau. of Mr. and Mrs. J. M., d. 74 Davis
St., Atlanta, Tues. Interred: Griffin. AG 7/23/1908
AWTRY, Louis, inf. son of Mr. and Mrs. J. T., d. Sat. 42 Summitt
Ave., Atlanta, Mon. Interred: Westview. AG 6/14/1909
AWTRY, Margaret, age 2, dau. of Mr. and Mrs. J. M., d. 6/21. 74
Davis St., Atlanta, Mon. Interred: Griffin, Ga. AG 6/22/1908
AYCOCK, Ella, Miss, age 17 yrs., d. Sat. Edgewood, Ga. Interred:
Tucker, Ga. AG 8/26/1907
AYERBACH, Isadore, age 11, d. 86 Gilmer St. Atlanta. AG 7/14/1909
AYERS, S. A., Conf. Vet., d. 620 DeKalb Ave., Atlanta, Tues.
Wife, 5 children. Interred: Toccoa, Ga. AG 2/22/1910
AYERS, Samuel , age 77, d. 620 DeKalb Ave. Atlanta. AG 2/24/1910
AYNARD, Gilbert, inf. son of Mr. and Mrs. L. E., d. 36 Bedford
Pl. Atlanta. Interred: Westview. AG 6/5/1908
BABB, J. N. of Battle Hill, Ga. d. Fri., age 70. Wife. Sons: E.
H., W. O. and James E. of Atlanta and T. J. Babb of Bonham.
Interred: McLand, near Powder Springs, Ga. AG 6/8/1906
BABB, Jennie A., age 3 mos., dau. of Mr. and Mrs. George, d. 68
Bradley Ave., Atlanta, Thurs. Interred: Westview. AG 3/31/1910
BABB, Louise, infant dau. of Mr. and Mrs. T. A., d. Tues. 286
Waldo St., Atlanta. Interred: Westview. AG 6/19/1907
BABER, Virginia, infant dau. of Mr. and Mrs. B. B., d. 235 E.
Pine St., Atlanta, Thurs. Interred: Madison, Ga. AG 3/20/1908
BACHELLER, W. M. funeral Sun. res. of William Lycett, 305 W.
Peachtree St., Atlanta. King: Judge and Mrs. C. B. Bacheller, R.
C. Bacheller, N. M. Bacheller, William Lycette. AG 10/5/1907
BACHELOR, Joseph, age 83, inmate of Confederate Soldiers´ Home,
Atlanta, d. Sun. Native of Eatonton. Enlisted 3rd Ga. Regt.,
transferred 66 Ga. AG 9/6/1909
BACHELOR, W. A., Capt. res. of Belaire 50 yrs., veteran of civil
war, shot and killed yesterday by W. T. Walton. AG 10/29/1906
BACHMAN, Sam, age 57, d. 24 Williams St., Atlanta. AG 10/18/1906
BACHMAN, W. S. d. Sat. 140 1/2 Houston St. Atlanta, Sun.
Interred: Bay City, Fla. AG 9/10/1910

16

BACON, Holcombe d. Aragon Hotel, Atlanta, Fri., age abt 32, unmd. Relative of Senator A. O. Bacon and son of late DeWitt C. Bacon of Albany. AG 3/10/1907

BADALESAS, John, age 23, d. Wesley Memorial Hospital, Atlanta. AG 4/27/1907

BADGER, Mary A., colored, age 71, d. Athens. ag 7/6/1909

BAER, A. Atlanta man, near to death in N. Y. AC 11/1/1905

BAGER, Georgia, age 3, d. 101 Butler St. Atlanta. AG 12/14/1909

BAGGARLY, Olin R., age 51, d. 237 Greensferry Ave. Atlanta, Mon. Wife survies. Interred: Westview. AG 6/2/1908

BAGGET, William, age 35, Marshall of Claxton, Ga., shot and killed 1/12 by William Bradley, son of Daniel Bradley, age 20. AG 1/12/1910

BAGGETT, Martha Jane,ge 11 mos., d. 69 Luckie St. Atlanta. Dau. of Mr. and Mrs. J. F. Baggett. Interred: South Bend Church. AG 5/11/1908

BAGWELL, Chester, son of Mr. and Mrs. C. A., d. Capitol View, Atlanta, Sun. Interred: Westview. AG 5/4/1908

BAGWELL, Eula, age 15, d. 29 Lucy Ave. Atlanta. AG 6/7/1910

BAGWELL, John D. of Gainesville of Gainesville d. 7/17, b. 9/18/1844 m. 2/7/1867 Miss Parrense Prater. Ch: Mrs. E. N. Gower, W. A., R. D., Bedford (of Indiana); Mrs. W. A. McLain, Clarkesville, Miss Addie and George. Confederate Veteran, Co. F, 43rd Ga. Bros, sis: William E., Forsyth Co.; James M. and Albert of Hall Co.; Dr. H. A. of INgleside; Mrs. C. M. Howington; Mrs. Noah Brogdon; Mrs. Ed Dericott of Pitts; Mrs. S. E. Gunter, Hall Co. AC 7/18/1905

BAGWELL, Martha E., Mrs., age 66, d. 3 Gartrell St. Atlanta. Interred: Gainesville. AG 9/2/1907

BAGWELL, Q. V., Mrs., age 36, d. 235 Capitol Ave. Atlanta. Wife of O. T. Bagwell of 30 Howell Mill Rd. Interred: Duluth, Ga. AG 2/7/1908

BAGWELL, M. V. res. of Bowman, Ga., d. Sun., age 66. Married twice. 2nd wife survives. 5 children by first marriage: Mrs. Alice Hulme, Emory, Van, John and Orrin Bagwell. Interred: Bowman cemetery. AG 11/15/1910

BAGWELL, Richard, Mrs. d. Tues. Norcross, Ga. Husband, 7 children, mother, father, Rev. and Mrs. Weldon Barnett, E. Point. Sisters, brothers. AG 12/23/1909

BAILEY, A. E., Mrs. of Toney, Ala., age 60, d. Husband, several children. AG 2/24/1910

BAILEY, B. E., age 67, d. West. 63 Sprinig St. Atlanta. Interred: Austell. AG 7/12/1907

BAILEY, Buford, age 11, d. Whitehall St. viaduct Atlanta. Ag 11/27/1907

BAILEY, Carl, Mrs., age 24, wife of William, d. Atlanta. AC 7/9/1909

BAILEY, Christine Isabella, age 1, dau. of Mr. and Mrs. Lee, d. 188 Jett St., Atlanta. Interred: Westview. AG 7/8/1910

BAILEY, Gleason, age 24, d. Tues. Clifton Forge, Va. Wife, one child. AG 8/11/1910

BAILEY, Grace Grosby, infant dau. of Mr. and Mrs. F. W., d. Wed. 94 Milledge Ave., Atlanta. Interred: Westview. AG 7/18/1907

BAILEY, Jemma, colored, age 22, d. 123 Wiley St. Atlanta. AG 9/21/1910

17

BAILEY, John, colored, age 40, d. Atlanta. AG 8/26/1907
BAILEY, L. M., age 2, d. 101 N. Butler St. Atlanta. AG 11/12/1907
BAILEY, Lizzie, colored, age 20, d. 175 E. Baker St. Atlanta. AG 12/19/1907
BAILEY, Mamie C., age 1, inf. dau. of Mr. and Mrs. J. M., d. 19 Larkin St., Atlanta, Sun. Interred: Sylvester. AG 11/11/1907
BAILEY, O. B., age 29, d. 43 Kennedy St. Atlanta. AG 6/16/1906
BAILEY, Paul, colored, age 27, d. 52 Leddell St. Atlanta. AG 12/5/1906
BAILEY, Robert Earle, age 3, son of Mr. and Mrs. S. W., d. 94 Milledge Ave. Atlanta. He is second child who has died in past two weeks (7/17). AG 7/30/1907
BAILEY, Samuel T., age 76, d. 12/30 at Woodbury, Ga. Interred: Macon, Ga., family burial grounds. AG 12/31/1909
BAILEY, W. B. d. 12/25, 173 E. Hunter St. Atlanta. Age 60. Ch: St. Elmo and Lariss. Interred: Sunnyside, Ga. AC 12/27/1905
BAILEY, W. H. d. his res. Sumter Co., Ga., age 72, 8/17. Wife. One dau: Dora. AC 8/17/1905
BAILEY, W. W., formerly of East Point, Ga., d. 3/3 Athens, Ga. Wife died year ago. 8 (one notice gives 7) small cchildren. Interred: College Park, Ga. AG 3/4/1908
BAILIFF, Marguerite, age 22 mos., dau. of G. T., d. 108 Center St. Atlanta, Fri. AG 6/17/1910
BAINBRIDGE, Arthur Edward, infant son of Mr. and Mrs. A. S., d. 12 Kent St. Atlanta, Wed. Interred: Augusta, Ga. AG 4/8/1909
BAKER, Annie, infant dau. of Mr. and Mrs. J. E., d. 213 Means St. Atlanta, Mon. Interred: Lawrenceville, Ga. AG 3/16/19109
BAKER, Bruno, colored, age 30, d. near Liddell's crossing. Atlanta. AG 8/3/1908
BAKER, B. L., Rev., age 67, of Monticello, Fla., d. sister's res., Mrs. J. H. Alexander, Atlanta. Confederate Veteran. Sisters: Mrs. Alexander, Mrs. Mary Spencer. Bro: Rev. Robert Baker, DeFuniak Springs, Fla. Son: Hansell, Brunswick. Interred: Monticello, Fla. AG 9/2/1910
BAKER, Cecil, age 3, d. 19 Rhinehardt St., Atlanta. AG 8/23/1909
BAKER, Comer, age 2 yrs., son of Mr. and Mrs. H. C., d. 188 Rawson St., Atlanta, Wed. Interred: Troy, Ala. AG 8/17/1910
BAKER, Courtney, negro, to die in gallows, Rome, Ga. AC 3/7/1905
BAKER, Daniel, colored, age 28, d. 15 Talisferro St.,A tlanta. AG 9/6/1910
BAKER, Ella d. Wed. Atlanta. Interred: Westview. AG 5/10/1906
BAKER, Erastus, age 6, d. 49 Kennedy St. Atlanta. AG 10/23/1907
BAKER, George, colored, age 42, d. 180 Bisbee Ave. Atlanta. AG 12/3/1908
BAKER, J. H. killed in Davis St. Plant, Atlanta Water and Electric Co., Sun., res. of 199 Plum St., Atlanta. Wife, 5 children. Interred: Sylvester Cemetery. AG 5/6/1907
BAKER, J. H., age 72, of Allapaha, Ga., d. 6/13 Atlanta. Interred: Town Cemetery, family lot. Son: P. O. of Allapaha. Dau: Mrs. B. F. Hill, Forsyth, Ga. Son-in-law: Judge J. B. Clements, Ocilla, Ga. Deceased owned 10,000 acres in Berrien Co. AG 6/16/1909
BAKER, Joe, age 28, colored, d. 37 Wallace St. Atlanta. AG 11/11/1909

18

BAKER, John, age 24, d. 60 E. Harris St. Atlanta, Wed. Interred: Evergreen, Ala. AG 11/6/1907

BAKER, John H., Col., age 81, Confederate Veteran, 13th Ga. Regt., d. Pike Co., near Zebulon, his home 4/7. AC 4/8/1905

BAKER, John Henry, colored, age 40, d. 379 Smith St. Atlanta. AG 1/13/1907

BAKER, John W., age 52, d. Sat. at Kimball House. Body sent to Greenville, S. C. Relatives reside in Batesville, S. C. AG 12/8/1906

BAKER, Katherine J., Mrs., age 36, suicide Wed., 36 W. 14th St., Atlanta. Interred: Family burying grounds. Daus: Minnie, Belle. Parents: Mr. and Mrs. S. J. Weaver. Her husband died abt yr. ago. AG 6/24/1909

BAKER, Lena, Mrs., age 40, d. Luckie St. Atlanta. AG 2/15/1909

BAKER, Louise, colored, age 1, d. 63 Rockwell St. Atlanta. AG 11/22/1909

BAKER, Lucile, infant dau. of Mr. and Mrs. C. F. Interred: Norcross, Ga. AG 3/26/1908

BAKER, Nola, Miss, age 19, d. Wed. res. of father, J. T. Baker, near College Park. Interred: Mt. Gilead Church. AG 5/31/1907

BAKER, Percy R., Mrs., formerly Miss Kate Lynn of Dalton, dau. of late Alex W. Lynn, d. San Diego, Calif. 6/13. Interred: Dalton, Ga. Son: Robert Lynn Baker. Sisters: Mrs. W. K. Moore, Mrs. E. P. Davis, Miss Victor Lynn. Bro: W. M. Lynn. AG 6/13/1910

BAKER, Rubie L., infant dau. of Mr. and Mrs. C. F., d. 8 Griffin St. Atlanta, Wed. Interred: Norcross. AG 3/25/ 908

BAKER, S. B., Colonel of Dublin d. Sun. at home of bro., Dr. T. M. Baker of Macon. Interred: Irwinton, family grounds. AG 10/3/1906

BAKER, Sallie E., age 47, wife of S. W., d. 271 Formwalt St. Atlanta, Fri. Leaves husband, 10 children. Interred: Westview. AG 10/30/1908

BAKER, Thomas, age 70, d. Phenix City, Ala. 5/10. AC 5/ /1905

BAKER, W. L. d. Washington St., Gainesville, age 66. Born Milledgeville. Res. of Habersham Co., Gainesville Ga., son of Rev. John W. Baker, Marietta. Ch: A. R., W. L., Jr., Mary Lou, Clifford, Bessie. Sis: Mrs. James Woodrow, Columbia, S. C. AG 4/27/ 908

BAKER, W. Paul, age 22, d. Atlanta Sun. Interred: Lithonia. AG 5/25/1908

BALCH, Annie, Mrs., age 23, d. 7/16 Huntsville, Ala. Husband survives. AC 7/18/1905

BALDER, Susan, colored, age 53, d. 307 Tumlin St. Atlanta. AG 9/26/1907

BALDWIN, Cornelia E., Mrs., age 72, d. son's home, J. C., Columbus, Ga. 6/28. Two sons, two sisters. Sons: J. C., Columbus, Ga.; Sam L., Hamilton, Ga. AG 6/ 9/ 909

BALDWIN, Evaline, Mrs. d. Fitzgerald, Ga. 2/ . Dau: Veina, Greenfield, Ind. Interred: Greenfield, Indiana. AC 2/23/1905

BALDWIN, L. D. killed 5/27 by train. Wife, 2 bros., 1 sister. AC 5/28/1905

BALDWIN, M. M., Mrs., mother of Rev. J. A., d. home of Ellerbee, Richmond Co., Thurs, age 90. AG 8/3/1906

BALDWIN, Moses, colored, age 31, d. 101 N. Butler St. Atlanta. AG 1/14/1908

BALDWIN, N. F., age 5, d. 17 Dainey St. Atlanta. AG 7/22/1910

BALKCOM, D. C., Mrs., age 22, d. 9/26 res. of parents, Mr. and Mrs. C. J. Roberts, Reid St., Macon. Interred: Cedar Ridge Cemetery. AG 9/27/1909

BALL, Annulet, infant dau. of Mr. and Mrs. Fred, d. Mell Ave., Atlanta, Wed. Interred: Decatur, Ga. AG 3/25/1908

BALL, James Nathan, age 4, son of Mr. and Mrs. T. E., d. Mon. 337 North Ave. Atlanta. AG 10/30/1906

BALL, John shot and killed by John A. Phillips, Sheriff, Bainbridge. AG 2/19/1907

BALL, Turner I., Capt. d. Cuthbert. Civil War Veteran. AC 4/13/1905

BALLARD, Anna Bang, age 7, dau. of N. H., d. Wed. Brunswick. AG 6/1/1907

BALLARD, H. A. killed Huntsville, Ala. 4/6 by Miss Oma Harding, age 21, dau. of Mrs. Mary Harding of Sparta, Tenn., his sweetheart. Then she killed herself. Uncle: Gov. Cox of Tenn. Father: A. C. Ballard, Briston, Tenn. AC 4/7/1905

BALLARD, Sarah, Mrs., wife of ex-Sen. Levi, d. Jan. 9 Palmetto. AC 1/10/1905

BALLENDER, Parks, colored, age 27, d. 101 N. Butler St. Atlanta. AG 7/9/1908

BAMBERG, W. M. d. Birmingham, Ala. AG 2/11/1910

BANCKER, Clara May, Mrs., age 60, d. 683 Piedmont Ave. Atlanta. AG 4/21/1908

BANDY, Minnie May, infant dau. of Mr. and Mrs. A. L., of 100 Emmett St. Atlanta, d. Sun. Interred: Norcross. AG 10/19/1908

BANIE, Thomas, colored, age 49, d. 117 Yonge St. Atlanta. AG 4/3/1908

BANKS, A. C., age 72, d. 15 N. Lee St. Atlanta. AG 4/ 0/1907

BANKS, Fannie, Mrs., age 75, widow of Dr. N. P., d. 7/20 res. of dau., Mrs. W. B. Watkins. AG 7/21/1906

BANKS, George T. d. Wynnton, Ga. 2/18, age 46. Wife, 4 children, 2 sisters. AG 2/19/1910

BANKS, John, colored, age 70, d. Fulton Co. Alms House, Atlanta. AG 12/30/1908

BANKS, John A., age 40, duputy sheriff of Richmond Co., d. 9/28. Leaves wife, 4 children. AG 9/29/1908

BANKS, Kate, Miss, age 21, d. Atlanta, Mon. Sis: Mrs. E. D. Tompkins, 136 W. Peachtree St., Atlanta. Parents: Mr. and Mrs. Thomas C. Banks. Interred: Barnesville, Ga. AG 6/29/1909

BANKS, Mamie, Mrs., age 4, d. res. of Mr. and Mrs. L. B. Banks, 70 Lowe St., Atlanta, Tues. Interred: Newnan, Ga. AG 12/18/1907

BANKS, Mary, colored, age 62, d. 115 Haynes St., Atlanta. AG 3/8/1909

BANKS, Mary M., Mrs., age 84, d. Atlanta. AG 8/1/1910

BANKS, Mattie, colored, age 55, d. rear of 55 Humphries St., Atlanta. AG 2/4/1908

BANKS, W. O., Mrs., age 18, d. 211 Angier Ave., Atlanta, Thurs. Interred: Cartersville, Ga. AG 5/10/1907

BANKS, Wilba, colored, age 16, d. East Point, Ga. AG 11/16/1910

BANKS, Will, colored, age 40, d. 101 Butler St., Atlanta. AG 10/30/1909

BANKSTON, Thelma, age 8 mos., dau. of Mr. and Mrs. L. J., d. 11 Hightower St., Atlanta, Wed. Interred: Roberta, Ga. AG 6/25/1908

BANNISTER, Kate, Mrs., wife of H. F., d. 39 Almo Ave., Atlanta, Mon. Interred: Rossville, Ga. AG 12/17/1907

BANNISTER, William S., age 73, d. Mon. 131 Jefferson St., Atlanta. Interred: Hollywood. AG 8/9/1910

BANNON, Michael, age 26, d. 58 Newport St., Atlanta. Relatives in Crawfordsville, Ind. AG 10/25/1907

BARBER, James M., colored, age 35, d. 419 Ira St., Atlanta. AG 7/17/1909

BARBER, T. H., age 73, d. Old Soldiers' Home, Atlanta. AG 1/17/1908

BARBER, Thomas F., Brig. Gen., 1st Military Governor of Hawaii, d. 3/17, N. Y. AC 3/18/1905

BAREFIELD, Cragie, colored, age 80, d. 5 Mercy St., Atlanta. AG 11/21/1910

BARFIELD, Charline, age 5, d. Mon. Parents: Mr. and Mrs. C. F., 422 Woodward Ave., Atlanta. Interred: Oakland. AG 10/30/1906

BARFIELD, George, colored, age 39, d. 240 Capitol Ave., Atlanta. AG 4/1/1907

BARFIELD, Joe, age 32, shot by Bud Touchstone, age 41, plantation of C. M. Patterson, near Sunnywide, Griffin. Wife, one child. Cannot survive. AG 7/12/1906

BARFIELD, Robert, age 65, colored, d. 156 E. Harris St., Atlanta. AG 4/7/1908

BARGE, Dennis, colored, age 78, d. 103 Greensferry Ave., Atlanta, 10/27. AG 10/ 8/1910

BARGE, Miles W., Mrs., age 26, wife of M. W., d. 119 Holderness St., Atlanta, Mon. Children survive. Parents: Mr. and Mrs. W. A. Collins, Campbell Co. Interred: Owl Rock Church yard. AG 9/20/1909

BARKER, A. M., Mrs., age 78, d. 14 N. Butler St., Atlanta. AG 10/3/1906

BARKER, C. T. d. 5/21 Commerce, Ga., age 55. Wife, 12 children. AC 5/23/1905

BARKER, Martha A., Mrs. d. Thurs. res. of son, W. A. Barker, Careys Station, age 75. Sons: James A., S. N., J. T., W. A. Interred: Bethel Church yard. AG 6/17/1910

BARKER, Minnie Ray, Miss d. Tues. 68 East Ave., Atlanta, dau. of late T. N. Barker. Mother, 3 sisters: Mary, Meta, Tommie. Bro: Russell L., of S. Dakota. Interred: Rockmart, Ga. AG 8/31/1910

BARKER, Walter W., Lt. Col., military funeral by 5th Regt. Wife, mother. AG 6/10/1910

BARKSDALE, Beverley E. of Longstreet, Pulaski Co., d. 12/16, res. of bro., A. B. AC 12/18/1905

BARKSDALE, Mary Elizabeth, age 73, d. Sat. son's res., R. O., Washington, Ga. Ch: Mrs. H. M. Sale, Tignall, Ga.; Mrs. Pauline Sledge of S. C.; Miss Mamie Barksdale; R. O., Wilkes Co.; T. J., Washington; N. G.; and Ben F. of Augusta. AG 3/1/1910

BARLOW, Leonard Jackson, colored, age 22, d. 415 Edgewood Ave., Atlanta. AG 12/29/1908

BARNARD, Miranda, colored, age 60, d. 177 Tanners alley, Atlanta. AG 4/13/1909

BARNARD, Sallie, Miss d. Atlanta. Kin: Misses Lucy and Kate Barnard. Interred: Columbus, Ga. AG 12/4/1907

21

BARNES, A. S. d. Sat. Atlanta. Interred: Jasper, Ala. AG 10/3/1908

BARNES, Abbie Lee, age 2 mos., dau. of Mr. and Mrs. H. T., d. 340 Mangum St., Atlanta. Interred: Hollywood. AG 5/7/1907

BARNES, Annie Laurie, infant dau. of Mr. and Mrs. J. E., d. Tues., 312 Woodward Ave., Atlanta. Interred: Hollywood. AG 3/3/1909

BARNES, C. E. W., age 1, d. 26 Cherry St., Atlanta. AG 11/9/1907

BARNES, C. W., age 21, d. Central Ave. railroad crossing, Atlanta. AG 8/19/1908

BARNES, Charles Elon Warner, age 2, son of Mr. and Mrs. Charles H., d. 26 Cherry St., Atlanta, Thurs. Interred: Hollywood. AG 11/8/1907

BARNES, Cornelius W., age 27, of Ingleside, Ga., fireman for Ga. railroad, d. accidentally. Interred: Decatur Cemetery. AG 8/18/ 908

BARNES, Eugenia, colored, age 42, d. 373 Chapel St. Atlanta. AG 11/25/1906

BARNES, Florence, age 11 mos., dau. of Mr. and Mrs. W. O., d. Mon. 689 Capitol Ave., Atlanta. Interred: Cartersville, Ga. AG 9/27/1910

BARNES, Florence, Mrs., age 33, d. 3 Ethel St.,tlanta. Interred: Emerson, Ga. AG 10/8/1909

BARNES, G. W. d. Bynum, Ga. 5/28. Interred: Coldwater. AC 5/31/1905

BARNES, Henry, age 33, d. 28 Milton St., Atlanta. AG 3/29/ 909

BARNES, Horace, age 11 mos., son of Mr. and Mrs. W. O., d. Mon. 686 Capitol Ave., Atlanta. Interred: Cartersville, Ga. AG 9/26/1910

BARNES, infant of C. W., d. 122 Glenwood Ave., Atlanta. AG 5/22/1910

BARNES, J. C. of Newton Co., age 66, Confederate Veteran, Co. L, 30th Ga. Regt., d. 7/7. Funeral at Macedonia Church. Daus: Mrs. W. W. Wilson of Jackson, Ga.; Mrs. W. W. Lott of South Georgia. Son: Hiram. AG 7/7/1910

BARNES, J. D. of Thomson, Ga. d. Jan. 8. AC 1/10/1905

BARNES, John E., age 72, of Old Soldiers' Home, Atlanta, d. Thurs. Funeral at dau.'s res., 1 Garnett St.,A tlanta. AG 12/29/1910

BARNES, Leola, colored, age 22, d. 1 Ladel St., Atlanta. AG 8/12/1908

BARNES, Maggie Mae, age 7 mos., dau. of Mr. and Mrs. H. T., d. 24 Strong St., Atlanta. Interred: Hollywood. AG 6/11/1909

BARNES, Mark M., age 39, d. 102 Jett St., Atlanta, Mon. Wife, 4 children. Interred: Hollywood. AG 1/31/1910

BARNES, W. C., colored, age 1, d. 53 Hilliard St., Atlanta. AG 2/15/1909

BARNETT, B. R., age 56, d. 63 Eugenia Ave., Atlanta, Sun. Interred: Montgomery, Ala. Wife, 11 children. AG 2/8/1910

BARNETT, G. M., age 38, d. Ormewood, Atlanta. Sun. Wife, 1 son, 2 dau, 4 bros, 3 sisters, father. Interred: Sylvester Cemetery. AG 8/23/1909

BARNETT, Isaac, age 8 mos., d. 170 Gilmer St.,A tlanta. AG 6/21/1907

BARNETT, Lavina, Mrs., age 52, d. Mon. 63 Eugenia St., Atlanta. Interred: Montgomery, Ala. AG 3/1/1910

BARNETT, Mary, Mrs., age 60, d. 12/1 Midland, Ga. AC 12/1/1905

BARNETT, Mattie, Mrs., age 42, d. Tues. 56 Berrien Ave., Atlanta. Interred: Westview. AG 9/22/1909

BARNETT, W. H. d. Augusta, Ga., Mon. Interred: Oakland Cemetery (Atlanta). AG 10/22/1907

BARNETT, Yetta, age 17 mos., dau. of Mr. and Mrs. Philip, d. 115 Connally St.,A tlanta, Fri. Interred: Oakland. AG 7/2/1909

BARNHART, S. L., age 28, d. Greenwood Ave., Atlanta. AG 7/30/1906

BARNHART, S. R., age 54, native of Greene Co., d. res. of mother at Penfield, Ga. Wife, 7 children. Bros: W. L., C. B., of Atlanta. AG 9/22/1909

BARNHART, Stephen L. d. Sat. Greenwood Ave., Atlanta. Interred: West Virginia. AG 7/30/1906

BARNWELL, John T. d. 14th St.,A tlanta. AG 4/23/1910

BARNWELL, Mattie Hackney, Mrs., age 57, widow of J. S., d. Wed. Washington, Ga. Interred: City Cemetery, Washington, Ga. Ch: Lyndon H. and Lila Barnwell of Washington. AG 11/12/1909

BARNWELL, Singie, Miss, dau. of Mr. and Mrs. J. T., d. Tues. Atlanta. Interred: Family Burial Grounds. AG 7/16/1907

BARR, G. Ray, age 41, d. Wed. Atlanta. One bro., one sister. Interred: Westview. AG 3/15/1910

BARR, Joseph H. d. 5/25 Phenix City, Ala. Wife, 6 children. AC 5/27/1905

BARRETT, Edmund, colored, age 49, d. 474 Smith St., Atlanta. AG 12/16/1908

BARRETT, Elizabeth, Mrs., age 70, d. Tues. Interred: Zebulon, Ga., family burial grounds. AG 5/14/1908

BARRETT, J. B., Mrs., age 45, d. Newnan, Ga., Tues. Interred: Covington. AG 10/30/1907

BARRETT, J. M., age 30, d. Atlanta. AG 4/7/1908

BARRETT, Lou, infant dau. of Mr. and Mrs. W. G., d. 520 Sunset Ave., Atlanta, Tues. Interred: Roswell, Ga. AG 6/2/1909

BARRETT, Mary, Mrs. d. 223-1/2 Peters St.,tlanta, Fri. Interred: Oakland. AG 6/20/1908

BARRETT, Oliver, age 2, son of Mr. and Mrs. T. W., d. 136 Main St., Atlanta, Body to be sent to Acworth, Ga. for interment. AG 12/18/1906

BARRETT, W. W., age 59, d. 398 E. Fair St., Atlanta, Tues. Interred: Westview. Wife: Mary. AG 6/30/1909

BARRON, Carrie, Mrs., age 28, d. 125 Windsor St., Atlanta. Mother, 4 sisters, 2 bros. Interred: LaGrange, Ga. AG 8/7/1908

BARRON, Ollie, Miss, age 20, d. 610 Chestnut St., Atlanta, Fri. Sis: Mrs. M. M. Shelverton, Mrs. John Dooley. Bro: Luther Barron. AG 10/12/1909

BARRON, R. A., age 30, d. Mon. 25 Stonewall St., Atlanta. Wife. Interred: Westview. AG 2/11/1908

BARROS, Dionies, native Greek, age 21, d. 85 Marietta St., Atlanta. Interred: Westview. AG 8/9/1910

BARROW, Annie, colored, age 3 mos., d. 131 Yonge St.,A tlanta. AG 9/3/1907

BARROW, D. C., Mrs., stepmother of Chancellor Barrow of Univ. of

Ga. and wife of Col. D. C. Barrow of Savannah, d. Sun. Savannah.
Interred: Athens, Ga. AG 12/27/1910
BARROWS,. Hildrey, Mrs., age 51, d. 95 Whitehall St., Atlanta. AG
3/8/1909
BARRY, Lizzie, colored, age 56, d. 423 Davis St., Atlanta. AG
3/10/1908
BARSKILIS, Demetry, age 86, native of Greeve, d. 111 Courtland
St., Atlanta. Interred: Greenwood. AG 8/5/1910
BARTH, Carl F., age 83, Atlanta pioneer 60 yrs. ago, d. Tivoli,
near Ormewood Park, Atlanta, Fri. Native of Germany 60 yrs. ago.
Wife: Pauline Huwald Barth. Sons: Carl, Paul, Raymond, Alfred.
Interred: Oakland. AG 12/3/1909
BARTLETT, Carl, age 8, d. Oakland City (Atlanta). AG 11/22/1909
BARTLETT, Elizabeth, Mrs., age 78, d. 73 Capitol Ave., Atlanta,
Tues. Dau: Mrs. J. G. Bloodworth. Sons: K. C. AG 6/23/1907
BARTLETT, Gena, Mrs., age 29, wife of J. C., d. Mon. 83 Paine
Ave., Atlanta. Interred: Newnan, Ga. Wife, 2 children. AG
7/30/1906
BARTLETT, Homer L., Dr. of Brooklyn, d. Thomasville, Ga. 2/3, age
74. Interred: Flat Bush, Long Island. AC 2/4/1905
BARTLETT, J. O. d. 9/2 Pebble St., S. Macon. Wife. Interred:
Family Burying Ground, 12 miles West of Macon. AC 9/3/1905
BARTLETT, William L., age 48, d. 1245 Marietta St., Atlanta, Sat.
Wife, 8 children. Interred: Hollywood. AG 7/28/1906
BARTON, Anne, Mrs., age 53, d. Woodward Ave., Atlanta, Sun.
Interred: Oakland. AG 9/28/1907
BNARTON, Frank, colored, age 23, d. 156 Auburn Ave.,A tlanta. AG
10/18/1907
BARTON, Martha J., Mrs., age 74, d. College Park, Thurs.
Interred: Canton, Ga. AG 5/21/1909
BARTON, Mollie, Miss, age 22, d. Mason and Turner Rds., Atlanta,
Thurs. Interred: Sharon Church. AG 9/21/1906
BARTOW, Annie, Mrs., age 45, d. 63 Walker St., Atlanta. AG
9/2/1909
BARTOW, John, colored, age 80, d. 122 Central Ave., Atlanta. AG
4/13/1909
BARWICK, J. W., Mrs., age 33, d. 203 Euclid Ave., Atlanta. AG
12/29/1910
BASKIN, N., Mrs., age 58, d. 47 Ponders Ave., Atlanta, Sun.
Interred: Hollywood. AG 9/14/1908
BASS, A. C., Dr. d. 5/12 Columbus, Ga. Sis: Mrs. James A. Lewis
of Columbus. AG 5/13/1907
BASS, H. C. d. 8/10 48 Tatnall St., Atlanta. AC 8/12/1905
BASS, Rosa, Mrs. d. Ardmore, Okla., Thurs. Funeral at res. of J.
L. Irwin, 335 Spring St.,A tlanta. Interred: Oakland. Son: J. A.
Dau: Miss Mamie. Bro: Rev. David Anderson. AG 9/11/1909
BASS, William, colored, age 26, d. 3 Bush St., Atlanta. AG
3/1/1907
BASSETT, W. B. of Bibb Co., d. Sun. Thomaston Rd. Wife, 2 sons,
dau. AG 10/11/1910
BATCHELLOR, George, son of J. S., suicide. Funeral 5/6,
Ellerslie, Ga. AG 5/6/1910
BATEMAN, Anna, Miss, age 32, d. home of bro., Col. J. N. Bateman,
503 N. Boulevard, Atlanta, Sun, age 42. Bro: Hon. O. C. Bateman
of Byron, Ga. Interred: Byron, Ga. AG 5/28/1907

BATEMAN, C. E., town marshal of Byron, shot Tues. by Attorney A. T. Harper at Byron depot, d. 12/10 from wounds, at Macon Hospital. AG 12/11/1909

BATES, Bessie, Mrs., age 20, d. 297 E. Fair St., Atlanta. AG 12/9/1910

BATES, Henrietta E., Mrs., age 65, teacher froM Boston, Mass., d. Sun. AG 10/14/1907

BATES, Ira C. d. 104 Davis St., Atlanta, Wed. Interred: Westview. AG 2/26/1908

BATES, Jennie, Mrs., age 55 (another notice sates age 41), d. Wed. 34 W. Fair St., Atlanta, wife of E. E. Bates. Several children. AG 6/22/1910

BATES, Martha A., age 68, d. Atlanta. AG 3/7/1910

BATES, Martha Quinn, Mrs., age 63, from Marietta, d. Atlanta Sat. AG 3/5/1910

BATES, Thomas, infant son of Mr. and Mrs. D. F., d. Fri. Ormond St., Atlanta. Interred: Westview. AG 6/5/1909

BATES, Wilson Allen of 162 Cypress St., Atlanta, funeral Sat. Interred: Oakland. Kin: M. L. Bates, C. J. Haden, Miss M. H. Allen, Mrs. Robert Winship, Charles R. Winship, George C. Walters, E. Woodruff. AG 5/3/1907

BATS, Peavy, colored, age 25, d. 101 N. Butler St., Atlanta. AG 2/26/1908

BATTLE, Anthony, colored, age 45, d. 217 Love St., Atlanta. AG 4/22/1909

BATTLE, C. E., Mrs., former music teacher, d. city hospital, Columbus, Ga. on 3/15, age 65. AG 3/16/1907

BATTLE, Ed, colored, age 25, d. 253 Frazer St., Atlanta. AG 9/8/1908

BATTLE, G. B., Mrs. d. 9/22 Omaha, Ga. Columbus relatives: Mr. and Mrs. Walter L. Meadows (dau.) and Hon. and Mrs. Charlton E. Battle. AC 9/25/1905

BATTLE, Lula, colored, age 34, d. 14 Electric Ave., Atlanta. AG 12/2/1910

BATTLE, M. C., Mrs., age 42, d. 748 Elliott St., Atlanta, Tues. Interred: Casey's Cemetery. AG 12/18/1907

BATTLE, Madison J., colored, age 46, d 506 Edgewood Ave., Atlanta. AG 10/1/1908

BATTLE, William A., Major, age 35, d. Thurs. res. of dau., Mrs. William L. Clay, Huntsville, Ala. First cousin: Mrs. Virginia Clay Clopton. AG 12/17/1909

BATTS, Peavie, negro, accidentally shot by Arthur Calhoun, negro, at 16 Berkle St., Atlanta, Sat. AG 2/2/1908

BAUGHAN, Benjamin F., d. 122 Hill St., Atlanta. Interred: Oakland. AG 6/27/1910

BAUKNIGHT, John funeral at bro.'s res., 460 Whitehall St., Atlanta, Sat. Interred: Westview. AG 2/20/1908

BAUKNIGHT, M. A., age 26, d. Home for Incurables, Atlanta. Mother: Mrs. M. S. Bauknight, 460 Whitehall St., Atlanta. Interred: Westview. AG 5/24/1907

BAUR, Foster, age 3, son of Mrs. Mary, d. Battle Hill, Atlanta, Wed. Interred: Westview. AG 10/7/1908

BAUSHELL, Pauline, Mrs., age 43, d. 885 Whitehall St., Atlanta., Thurs. Interred: Union City, Ga. AG 7/2/1909

BAXLEY, Joseph A., age 66, d. Old Soldiers' Home, Atlanta, Wed. Confederate Veteran, Co. 5, 5th Ga. Cavalry. Interred: Westview. AG 3/24/1910

BAXTER, M. E., Mrs., age 54, d. 395 Simpson St. Atlanta. AG 8/9/1910

BAXTER, Millard W., age 7, son of Mr. and Mrs. J. H., d. Mon., 214 Glenwood Ave., Atlanta. AG 8/19/1907

BAXTER, T. W., Mrs., age 46, d. 230 Ponce de Leon Ave., Atlanta. AG 8/9/1907

BAXTER, Walter, colored, age 28, d. Atlanta. AG 3/28/1907

BAXTER, Wreathie Mabelle, age 19 mos., dau. of Mr. and Mrs. W., d. 82 Glenwood Ave., Atlanta, Sun. Interred: Athens, Ga. AG 6/2/1908

BAYNE, H. V., age 67, d. 94 Oakland Ave., Atlanta. AG 12/9/1909

BAYNE, Pearl S., age 27, d. 94 Oakland Ave., Atlanta, Mon. Wife. Mother: Mrs. Ella Bayne. Bro: H. Z. Bayne. Sisters: Mrs. Addie Bosche, Mrs. Ida Johnson (wife of Dr. Allen D.), Miss Ella Lee Bayne. AG 6/28/1909

BAYNE, T. S., age 30, d. 94 Oakland Ave., Atlanta, Mon. Wife, mother, 5 sisters, 2 bros. AG 6/29/1909

BAZZAR, Philip, age 1, son of Mr. and Mrs. Charles, 54 Pratt St., Atlanta, d. Thurs. Interred: Westview. AG 4/30/1909

BEACHAM, Terry Taylor d. Mon. 58 W. Harris St. Atlanta. Interred: Westview. Wife, 5 sons, 4 daus., survive. AG 4/25/1906

BEAMONT, Joseph L., age 26, d. Pasadena, Cal. Sat., where interred. Former Atlanta resident. AG 11/21/1910

BEAVERS, Lizzie, Mrs., age 28, wife of G. E., d. 156 Courtland St., Atlanta. Sisters: Mrs. O. O. Adams, Mrs. C. O. Fagan, Misses Bessie and Iva May Covington. Ch: Emery, Clifton, William, John. Interred: Marietta, Ga. AG 11/16/1910

BECKMAN, William S. d. Sat. Res. of 240 1/2 Houston St., Atlanta. Wife, one dau. AG 9/10/1910

BELK, Edna, age 12, dau. of J. F., d. E. Pt., Sun. Interred: College Park Cemetery. AG 11/7/1910

BENNETT, Jack, colored, age 57, d. Oakland City, Ga. AG 11/17/1910

BERRY, Eva, Miss, dau. of Mr. and Mrs. E. J., d. Waycross, Ga. Funeral from Trinity Methodist Church. AG 10/18/1910

BERTSCHEIN, Lena, age 5, dau. of Ernest, d. near Mt. Airy, Ga., Mon. Child was at grandfather's house near Cornelia, Ga. when accident occurred. Interred: Eastview Cemetery, Mt. Airy, Ga. AG 11/15/1910

BETTS, W. P., Mrs. d. Wed. Athens, Ga. Husband: Dr. W. P. Ch: Mrs. O. A. Davis, Mrs. C. E. Underwood, Mrs. A. G. Hargrove, George A., Burke, B. M., L. N., W. F., P. T., J. L., and Bird Betts. AG 10/6/1910

BIBB, Josephine Martin, Mrs. d. in New York. Interred: Summerville cemetery, near Augusta, Ga. She was dau. of late Mrs. William H. Lucas who d. Bartow Co., Ga. several years ago, and wid. of late Capt. Peyton Bibb of US navy. AG 4/1/1907

BIBB, T. G., merchant of Waycross, d. 1/6. Wife, two stepchildren: Mrs. J. A. Farris, Savannah; Mrs. Ray, Jacksonville, Father: W. H. Bibb, Thomasville. Bros: J. K. Bibb, Waycross; W. H. Bibb, Jr., Thomasville, AG 1/7/1910

BICKART, Leo, father-in-law of A. Bluthenthal, d. 11/30 Atlanta, age 76. Wife: Louise. Son: Munroe. Daus: Carrie; Mrs. A. Bluthenthal. AC 12/1/1905

BIGGERS, William, colored, age 6 yrs, d. 13 Linden Way, Atlanta. AG 6/14/1907

BIGHAM, J. W., Mrs., age 55, found dead by husband Sat. Columbus, Ga. Interred: Cuseck. AG 9/20/1909

BIGHAM, James H., colored, age 1, d. 31 Blackgum St. Atlanta. AG 10/28/1908

BIGHAM, Willie, colored, age 1, d. 22 Blackgum St. Atlanta. AG 12/8/1910

BILBERT, Isaiah, colored, age 19, d. 291 Crumley St. Atlanta. AG 4/2/1909

BILLETER, Annie, age 35, d. Atlanta. AG 5/11/1910

BILLINGSLY, S. C., age 83, d. Co. Almshouse of old age. Atlanta. AG 6/23/1906

BILLUPS, E. S., Dr., age 79, of Watkinsville, formerly Atlanta, d. Jan. 6. Wife. Ch: A. C., Birmingham, Ala.; Mrs. Bell Johnson, Watkinsville. Interred: Oconee Cemetery. AC 2/7/1905

BILLUPS, Emily, Mrs. d. Wed. Atlanta. Interred: Athens, Ga. Age 73. AG 10/13/1910

BINDER, Lydia, young dau. of Mr. and Mrs. C. N., d. Mon. LaFrance St., Atlanta. Interred: Westview. AG 3/12/1907

BINGHAM, P. R., Dr., age 74, d. 10/15, 130 Julian St., Atlanta. Surgeon in Confederate Army. Wife, one son. Interred: Moreland, Ga. AC 10/16/1905

BINION, A. A., Mrs., age 77, d. 10/19 dau.´s res., Mrs. J. S. West, 1514 Second St., Macon. Interred: Cass Station. AG 10/20/1910

BINTON, Eddie shot down by negro cropper on plantation of Wilson Rives, Jeff Flegg, near Devereaux. AG 11/5/1906

BIRD, Bessie, colored, age 7 mos., d. 6 Victoria St. Atlanta. AG 3/3/1909

BIRD, George O., age 2, son of Mr. and Mrs. W. F., d. 71 Waddell St., Atlanta, Wed. Interred: Greenwood. AG 6/29/1910

BIRD, Gerald O., age 2 mos., son of Mr. and Mrs. W. F., d. 71 Waddell St., Atlanta, Tues. AG 6/28/1910

BIRDSONG, John T. killed Sat. S. of Macon on Sou. RR. AG 10/22/1907

BISHOP, Annie Murrell, inf. dau. of Mr. and Mrs. G. A., d. Freeman St., Atlanta, Mon. Interred: Rockmart, Ga. AG 6/21/1909

BISHOP, Henry R. d. Inboden, Va. Sat., well known in Atlanta. Mother: Mrs. Giles Bishop. Bro: J. M. Bishop, 270 E. Georgia Ave., Atlanta. AG 2/4/1908

BISHOP, Sarah Lou, age 5 mos., dau. of Mr. and Mrs. J. B., d. 955 Seaboard Ave., Atlanta. Interred: Roseland. AG 7/19/1910

BISHOP, T. C., Mrs., age 24, d. 149 W. Alexander St. Atlanta. AG 2/8/1909

BISHOP, Will killed by Joe Whitlington, Pike Co., Ga. Case postponed. AG 4/10/1907

BIVINS, Eunice, colored, age 42, d. 944 Peachtree St. Atlanta. AG 6/21/1907

BIXBY, Francis X., age 60, d. 381 Gordon St., Atlanta, Thurs. Interred: Westview. Sons: Carlos L., Samuel. AG 6/26/1908

BLACK, Bertha, Miss, dau. of M. M., merchant, d. 6/8 Mineral Bluff, Ga. Interred: Morganton Cemetery. AC 6/9/1905

BLACK, Charles Edward shot to death by father-in-law, Lon (Alonzo) Church, age 47, Howell Sta. Mon. AG 7/10/1906

BLACK, Clemintine, Mrs., former res. of Atlanta, d. Columbus, Ga. Thurs. Interred: Oakland. AG 12/30/1910

BLACK, Eugene P., age 64, d. Peachtree Rd. Atlanta. AG 3/11/1909

BLACK, J. R., age 48, d. 94 Garnett St. Atlanta Mon. Wife, 4 daus, 1 bro., 2 sisters. Interred: Monroe, Ga. AG 5/19/1908

BLACK, Josa R., age 48, d. 94 Garnett St. Atlanta. AG 5/20/1908

BLACKBURN, Anderson, colored, age 65, d. rear 79 Carnes St. Atlanta. AG 8/1/1907

BLACKBURN, Henry H., age 2, son of Mr. and Mrs. J. T., d. Sat. Interred: Chamblee, Ga. AG 5/2/1910

BLACKBURN, Tom J. d. Sun. train wreck, Ga. Railroad. Res. 32 Fitzgerald St., Atlanta. Wife: Lizzie Hardy Blackburn. AG 6/12/1906

BLACKMAN, Sarah, Mrs., age 79, d. 26 Hendrix Ave. Atlanta. AG 8/20/1907

BLACKMON, J. W. funeral Atlanta Thurs. AG 4/5/1910

BLACKMON, L. L., citizens of Wilkes Co., res. near Tignall, Ga., suicide, Washington, Ga., age 43. Survived by wife, 5 children. AG 4/22/1907

BLACKMON, Martha J., Mrs., age 65, d. 203 Glenn St. Atlanta. AG 9/3/1907

BLACKMON, T. J. funeral Tues. Atlanta. Interred: Oakland. AG 6/13/1906

BLACKSHEAR, Fannie L., age 36, d. Buffalo, N. Y. AG 7/20/1907

BLACKSTOCK, Jasper, age 71, d. Wed. Atlanta. Ch: R. H. Blackstock, Mrs. J. C. Bowden of Gainesville; Mrs. J. F. Clemmons of New Orleans; Mrs. E. W. Barksdale and C. A. Blackstock, Atlanta. Interred: Gainesville, Ga. AG 4/15/1909

BLACKSTOCK, Julia, Mrs., age 71, d. 62 Martin St. Atlanta Sun. Sons: R. H., C. A. Daus: Mrs. J. C.-----, Gainesville; Mrs. J. B.-----, New Orleans; Mrs.------Barksdale, Atlanta. AG 5/31/1909

BLACKWELL, Allen C., age 77, d. Oakland City, Atlanta, Wed. Wife. Sons: B. S., B., T. A. Daus: Mrs. R. R. Gibson; Mrs. Belle Crawley; Mrs. W. J. Knight; Mrs. G. W. Wise; Mrs. A. R. Grabb; Miss Marguerite Blackwell. AG 8/19/1909

BLACK, Ella, age 49, 226 Elliott Street, Atlanta. AG 11/9/1906

BLACK, Robert Covington, age 51, d. 365 Capitol Ave. Atlanta. Bur: Columbus, Ga. Sons: Sewell Black, Baltimore; George Black, Kansas City, Mo. Dau: Lula Black, Atlanta. Bro: R. P. Black. Father: Dr. R. C. Black, Americus, Ga. AG 7/23/1907

BLADES, Mary, Mrs., age 68, d. res. of Mrs. Sammons, 172 S. Forsyth St., Fri. Interred: Hollywood. AG 10/5/1907

BLAIR, Evie May, inf. dau. of Mr. and Mrs. John Blair of 32 Hills Ave., Atlanta, found dead in bed Tues. AG 10/30/1906

BLAIR, George Ernest, age 21, d. res. of father, Hon. D. W. Blair, Marietta, Ga., Sat. Father, mother, two bros., two sisters, survive. AG 5/21/1907

BLAIR, Katie, age 58, d. 22 Henry St. Atlanta. AG 7/18/1908

BLAIR, N. N., age 42, d. 24 Ellis St., Atlanta, Thurs. Wife, 5 children, 3 bros. Interred: Hollywood. AG 5/13/1910

BLAKE, David O., age 51, d. 30 Bedford Pl. Atlanta. AG 11/27/1910

BLAKE, Floyd, age 52, d. 72 Richmond St. Atlanta. AG 10/22/1906
BLAKE, Thomas, colored, age 44, d. 101 N. Butler St. Atlanta. AG
2/28/1908
BLAKELY, John, age 6, d. 107 Piedmont Ave. Atlanta. AG 11/4/1908
BLANCHARD, Noney, Mrs., age 24, d. Atlanta Sun. Husband: R. A.
Two bros, three sisters AG 8/2/1909
BLANCHARD, T. S., Hon. d. 6/14 Augusta, Ga. Interred: old home in
Alexander, Ga. AC 6/16/1905
BLANCHARD, Thomas A., age 65, d. 3/2 res. of son, Dr. C. A. 3
sons. Interred: Sharon Cemetery, Thomson, Ga. AC 3/3/1905
BLANCHARD, W. M. funeral Thurs. Atlanta. Interred: Westview. AG
5/10/1906
BLANKENSHIP, B. B., age 82, d. res. of dau., Mrs. M. T. Whaley,
14 Corput St. Atlanta. Interred: Rock Springs church, DeKalb Co.
AG 6/12/1907
BLANKENSHIP, Viola, age 4 mos., dau. of Mr. and Mrs. G. W., d.
117 Wells St., Atlanta. Interred: Westview. AG 8/6/1910
BLANTON, Clifford, colored, age 19, d. Grady Hospital. Atlanta.
AG 2/22/1907
BLANTON, Isaac A., age 67, d. 221 Crumley St. Atlanta. AG
7/8/1909
BLANTON, Selina W., Mrs., age 65, d. Tues. 350 E. Georgia Ave.
Atlanta, Wed. Interred: Williston, S. C. AG 6/15/1910
BLANTON, Lucius C., age 28, d. 178 Central. Interment: Farrar,
Ga. AG 11/17/1906
BLASINGAME, Howell, age one, son of Mr. and Mrs. I. M. of 62 Jett
St, Atlanta, d. Fri. AG 9/21/1906
BLASINGAME, Josie, Mrs., age 39, d. Atlanta. AG 1/25/1910
BLASTON, Sellma W., age 65, d. 350 Georgia Ave. Atlanta. AG
6/16/1910
BLAUVELT, W. C., age 50, d. 106 Forrest Ave., Atlanta, Tues.
Wife, one dau. AG 4/13/1909
BLECKLEY, Logan E., Judge, 80, d. Clarkesville. 1857 m. Caroline
Haralson (d.1887) Ch: Logan, Harrison, Mrs. Hugh Culberson. 1792
m. Clorie Herrin, had: Edwin, Barnell, Herrin, Sidney. Sil:
Hubert Culberson. Bur: Oakland. AG 3/6/1907
BLITCH, Leo W., Mrs. accidentally shot by Rena, his dau., while
playing with pistol Jan. 12. Husband, 7 ch. AC 1/13/1905
BLOCH, Joseph d. Sun. 827 Orange St. Macon, Ga. Interred: William
Wolff cemetery. AG 8/7/1907
BLOCK, Francis C., son of Frank E., d. 16 Kimball St. Atlanta,
age 40. Wife, father, mother. Bros: Dr. E. Bates and Hamilton
Block. Sisters: Miss Lucretia Block, Mrs. Hugh Bancker, Margaret
Block, age 4 yrs. Interred: Westview. AG 10/2/1907
BLOODWORTH, Cecil T., age 24, son of Mr. and Mrs. R. W., d. 122
Glenwood Ave., Atlanta, Mon. Interred: Macon, Browns Crossing. AG
9/23/1907
BLOODWORTH, Charles Douglas, age 17, son of J. G. C., of 142
Windsor St., Atlanta, drowned Sun. in Lakewood Lake. Nephew of
Hon. O. H. B. Bloodworth, Forsyth, Ga. AG 8/8/1910
BLOODWORTH, Douglas, age 17, drowned in Lakewood Sun., Atlanta.
Interred: Hollywood. AG 8/9/1910
BLOODWORTH, J. B., Mrs., age 27, d. Thurs. Gordon, Ga. Leaves
husband, 3 small sons. AG 11/8/1907

BLOODWORTH, R. M. d. Brunswick, Mon., widow. Sons: J. M., C. F. Dau: Mrs. C. F. Brown and 4 children who live in N. C. AG 2/28/1907

BLOOMFIELD, R. R., age 40, d. 108 S. Forsyth St. Atlanta. AG 2/8/1909

BLOOMFIELD, Elizabeth, age 21 mos., inf. dau. of Mr. and Mrs. P. J., d. St. Josephs Infirmary. Atlanta. Grandfather: late Peter Lynch. Father: P. J. Funeral res. of Mrs. Peter Lynch, 96 Trinity Ave. Interred: Oakland. AG 9/9/1907

BLOSSER, Rose Steinhagen, Mrs., age 32, d. 274 Spring St. Atlanta. AG 8/5/1907

BLOUNT, Carrie, colored, age 25, d. 409 Richardson St. Atlanta. AG 11/1/1909

BLOUNT, Horace, colored, age 8 mos., d. 20 Fort St. Atlanta. AG 10/8/1909

BLOUNT, J. F. of Orangeburg, S. C. in rr wreck in Macon 2/16. Died from injuries. Fiancee: Miss Clyde Buff. AG 2/17/1910

BLUE, William, colored, age 13, d. 103 Murry St. Atlanta. AG 7/9/1908

BOARTFIELD, Mary E., Mrs., age 71, d. 225 Woodward Ave., Sat. Ch: W. W. Boartfield, Atlanta, A. L. Boartfield, Rome, A. F. Boartfield, Sumter, S. C., Mrs. Susie Sewell, Mrs. Crutchshank, Atlanta. Interred: Westview. AG 2/2/1908

BOATWRIGHT, W. M. d. Thurs. 368 Auburn Ave. Atlanta. Interred: Lovett, Ga. AG 8/23/1907

BOAZ, George Russell, Capt., old Atlantan, d. Mon., first undertaker in Atlanta, succeeded by H. M. Patterson. Wife, son in Fla. survive. AG 1/22/1907

BOBO, George W. d. 183 Oakland Ave., Atlanta. Kin: George W. Bobo, W. G. Bobo, W. R. Griffin, J. A. Hall, Mrs. R. J. Hood. Interred: Oakland. AG 7/17/1908

BOBO, Hiram of Douglasville d. Sat. at home one-mi. E. of Douglasville. Age 67. Leaves wife, 3 sons, 4 daus. AG 2/5/1907

BOBO, Mary F., Mrs. d. Fri. 104 S. Pryor St., Atlanta. Interred: Roswell, Ga. AG 6/4/1910

BOBO, Mary Frances, Mrs., age 58, d. 104 S. Pryor St. Atlanta. AG 6/7/1910

BOBO, George W., age 52, d. 183 Oakland Ave., Atlanta, Thurs. ife. Son: Walton. Interred: Oakland. AG 7/17/1908

BODDIE, Grant, colored, age 30, d. 237 Meldon Ave. Atlanta. AG 7/11/1908

BODGEN, J. S., age 58, d. Mason and Turner Rd., Atlanta, Tues. Wife. Ch: Mrs. A. Gresham, C. B. and T. L. Bodgen. Interred: Mt. Harmony Church yard. AG 12/27/1910

BOE, Cornelius, negro, shot by Frank tappy, negro, Howell Mill Rd., Atlanta. AC 1/23/1905

BOGGAN, Patrick fell to death Mon, Birmingham Hotel, Birmingham, Ala. AG 4/6/1909

BOGGS, J. W., one yr., d. 508 Vine St. Atlanta. AG 5/8/1907

BOGGUS, William, Mrs., 32, wid. d. 571 Pryor St. Atlanta. Parents: Mr. & Mrs. H. A. Lankford. Son, dau. Bros: M. L. (S.C.), Arthur (Atlanta) & Matt Lankford. Sis: Emma Lankford; Mrs. Chas E. Von Kamp, Denver, CO. Bur: Westview. AG 4/1/1908

BOGMAN, A. M., Mrs., age 23, d. 140 Elizabeth St. Atlanta. AG 12/26/1907

BOHANAN, Chesterfield, age 20, d. 214 E. Georgia Ave. Atlanta. AG 7/29/1910

BOLAND, John L., Confed. Vet., d. St. Louis, Mo. He was b. Ballington, Va. 3 daus., 2 sons. AC 3/22/1905

BOLT, John of Heflin, Ala. d. Mon., interred beside his son, Charlie, who d. 2 yrs. ago. Wife, son, two small grandchildren. AG 9/21/1910

BOLT, John D., age 20, d. Atlanta. Interred: Anderson, S. C. Sister: Mrs. Lelia Tolbert, Sherman, Texas. AG 12/18/1909

BOLTON, D. E., age 54, d. Atlanta, Fri. Wife, 6 daus., 2 sons. Interred: Westview. AG 7/2/1910

BOLTON, Robert, age 48, d. 3 Foundry St. Atlanta. AG 11/21/1910

BOMAR, Junius O. d. 8/18 Atlanta. AG 8/25/1909

BOMAR, Louise Blasingame,, 22, dau. of Mrs. Wm A., grdau. of Benj. F. & Mrs. B. F., d. 11 Warren St. Atlanta. Sis: Mrs. J. F. Thomason, Columbia, S. C.; Mrs. John H. Evins; Sadie E. Bro: Junius O. (d. last Mon.). Bur: Oakland. AG 8/25/1909

BOND, C. T., Mrs., age 62, d. 6/31 Elberton, Ga. Interred: Concord Cemetery. Husband, 5 ch: Dr. Will Bond of Martin, Stephens Co.; Dr. Tom Bond; George Bond; Mrs. Addie Herndon; Miss Mamie Bond, of Elbert Co. AG 5/31/1910

BOND, Margaret, Mrs., age 84, d. Franklin, Tenn. AG 10/1/1909

BOND, Susie, age 25, died 342-1/2 Decatur Street, Atlanta. AG 12/8/1906

BOND, William D., Mrs., age 87, d. Franklin, Tenn. 9/29. Interred: College Park Cem., Atlanta. Former res. of Atlanta. Grson: A. H. Marchant, Atlanta. Daus: Mrs. Frank Hughs, Franklin Tenn.; Mrs. D. H. Marchant, Orangeburg, Tn. AG 9/30/1909

BONDURANT, Robert E., age 71, d. 150 Peeples St. Atlanta. AG 6/13/1910

BONE, Lonnie, age abt 15, shot, killed accidentally by Walter Hill, boy. AC 1/15/1905

BONES, Henry, a young man from Graniteville, S. C., d. Augusta, Ga. yesterday, run over by freight train. AG 6/26/1906

BONEY, Elizabeth, age 5, dau. of Mr. and Mrs. J. E., d. 377 Woodward Ave. Atlanta. Interred: Westview. AG 5/3/1906

BONEY, T. L., age 61, d. 69 Luckie St. Atlanta. AG 4/28/1908

BONNELL, W. A., age 63, d. 38 Cone St. Atlanta. AG 7/2/1908

BONNELL, William A., policeman, aged ct. officer run over by trolley in front of home, 253 Grant St., Atlanta, d. Wed. Confederate Veteran, known as "Uncle Billy." Interred: Oakland. AG 7/1/1908

BOOK, Nina, age 7 mos., d. 52 Walker St. Atlanta. AG 8/5/1908

BOOKER, C., colored, age 2 mos., d. 19 Ponders Ave. Atlanta. AG 11/1/1909

BOOKER, Willie May, colored, age 1, d. 272-A Bass St. Atlanta. AG 6/21/1909

BOON, Alfred of Valdosta shot by bro., Babe Boon in Echols Co., Wed., both under 21. Bro: Arthur. Sister. AG 10/30/1908

BOON, J. T., age 45, d. Wed. 304 East Ave., Atlanta. Wife, 4 children. AG 3/23/1910

BOON, William J. d. Wed. buried Perry, Ga. 9/9. Daus: Mrs. Kate Heard, Miss Addie Boon. Bros: W. O., Gus. Sis: Mrs. C. O. Kegg. AG 9/10/1909

BOONE, F. L., age 30, d. 92 Luckie St. Atlanta. AG 9/2/1909

BOONE, T. A., Mrs., age 35, d. Atlanta Tues, 31 Oak St. AG 2/22/1910

BOONE, T. O., Mrs., age 35, d. Atlanta. AG 2/25/1910

BOONE, W. R., Mrs., age 23, d. 606 Washington St. Atlanta. AG 10/19/1907

BOOTH, J. W., age 35, d. E. Lake. Atlanta. AG 10/7/1909

BOOTH, Jackson A. Logansville, Ga. 12/26/1906. Jackson died Sun, aged over 80 Leaves 6 children, two residents of Atlanta, one of Rome, and three in Walton Co., Ga. AG 12/26/1906

BOOTH, Jim killed by Lewis Gaddis Lumpkin Co. 3/26. AG 3/28/1910

BOOTH, O. D., Atlanta stable man, d. Wed. 446 Whitehall St. Interred: Westview. AG 7/28/1910

BOOTH, Oscar D., age 54, d. 406 Whitehall St. Atlanta. AG 7/28/1910

BOOTH, Sampson, age 70, d. Mon. Howell Sta., Atlanta. Wife. AG 8/30/1910

BORDEN, James L., colored, age 14 mos., d. 49 Wallace St. Atlanta. AG 7/23/1909

BORDERS, E. Darden, Mrs., age 20, d. res. of her father, J. T. Childress, Sun. Husband: E. Darden Borders, Conyers. Interred: Westview. AG 4/1/1907

BORDERS, Henrietta, Mrs., age 20, d. 311 Whitehall St. Atlanta. AG 4/1/1907

BORDERS, Thomas J., age 33, d. McDonough, Ga. Sun. Parents: Mr. and Mrs. Alexander Borders. Sis: Mrs. R. H. McCoy, Mrs. John O. Noel, Atlanta. Bro: Robert H. Borders, Macon. Interred: McDonough Cemetery. AG 6/10/1909

BORLAND, Thomas, age 40, res. of Waycross, d. Atlanta. Interred: Oakland. AG 12/31/1910

BORN, infant. of Mr. and Mrs. John T., of Hollywood, d. Sat. Interred: Masons Cemetery. AG 6/20/1910

BORN, J. M., Sr.,age 66, funeral Fri. res. 206 Woodward Ave. Atlanta. Interred: Oakland. Kin: J. M. Born, Jr., A. J. Haygood, Mrs. M. V. Tuggle. AG 12/26/1907

BORN, Sarah M., Mrs., age 77, wid. of late Judge James H., d. dau.´s res., Mrs. R. H. Randall, 658 Edgewood Ave., Atlanta. Interred: Lithonia, Ga. Daus: Mrs. Randall; Mrs. M. R. Ragsdale. 8 grandchildren. AG 7/12/1909

BOSEMAN, Chris killed by train 3/17 Mobile, Ala. AC 3/18/1905

BOSTICK, Arthur Clyde, age 49, d. 388 Grant St. Atlanta. AG 3/8/1909

BOSTWICK, Anna, colored, age 3 mos., d. 34 Mechanic Ave. Atlanta. AG 11/22/1909

BOSTWICK, Annie E., Mrs., age 67, d. 565 Central Ave. Atlanta. AG 11/15/1909

BOSTWICK, James G., age 42, d. Tues. 53 Park Ave. Atlanta. Interred: Oakland. AG 6/19/1907

BOSWELL, Elizabeth d. Ozark, Ala. AG 2/12/1907

BOSWELL, Emma, Mrs., age 29, d. Atlanta Fri., formerly res. 209 Peters St. Sister: Mrs. Sallie Boswell, Roswell, Ga. AG 2/15/1908

BOULDIN, Maud E., age 7, dau. of Mr. and Mrs. W. M., d. 142 E. Linden St., Atlanta, Mon. Interred: Westview. AG 2/4/1908

BOULIGNY, Alice H., Mrs., age 50, d. N. Kirkwood. AG 7/26/1907

BOULWARE, R. H., age 23, d. Atlanta. AG 2/8/1910

BOURMAN, N. R. d. 9/17 Lynchburg, Va. Confed. Soldier. Age 69. Wife, 7 children. AC 9/18/1905

BOURNE, Sydney, inf. son of Mr. and Mrs. P. Rufus, d. Mon. 277 Smith St. Atlanta. Interred: Sylvester. AG 6/6/1906

BOURN, W. C., age 25, d. 15 Bailey St., Atlanta, Sun. Mother: Mrs. M. A. Bourn. Wife, two children. Interred: Sylvester. AG 7/20/1908

BOURQUIN, Frank H. killed by live wire Savannah. (was to be married 12/22. AC 12/21/1905

BOVEY, Thomas L. d. Sat., b. Salem, Mass., age 61, settled Dallas, Tex. 10 yrs. in Atlanta. Ch: Mrs. Grace Boyd, Dallas, Tx; Mrs. May Forbes, Dallas, Tx; Warren H. Bovey, Houston, Tx. Interred: Dallas, Tx. AG 5/26/1908

BOWDEN, James L., inf. son of Mr. and Mrs. J. E., d. 578 Chestnut St., Atlanta, Fri. Interred: Westview. AG 2/15/1908

BOWDEN, John M., age 65, d. Grady Hospital, Atlanta, Sat. Interred: Conyers, Ga. AG 12/30/1907

BOWELL, Nannie Miss killed by lightning 4/9 Covington, Ga. res. of R. W. Boswell. AC 4/11/1905

BOWEN, C. E. d. Sun. 26 Morrison Ave., Atlanta. Interred: Westview. AG 9/23/1907

BOWEN, Caleb, Capt., age 80, d. Douglasville, Ga. 12/30. Confederate Vet., Co. C., 30th Ga. Regt. AG 12/30/1907

BOWEN, D. P., aged veteran, d. Thurs. Bowman, Ga. Several children survive, relatives in Ga. and S. C. AG 12/4/1909

BOWEN, E. L., age 39, d. 395 Woodward Ave., Atlanta, Wed. Wife. Son: Roy. Mother: Mrs. Emmie E. Bowen. Bro: F. A. Bowen. Sisters: Mrs. L. O. Dunwoody, Mrs. J. M. Payne, Mrs. K. A. Marston. Interred: Oakland. AG 2/17/1909

BOWEN, E. T., Mrs., age 50, d. near Decatur, Ga. Mon. Dau: Mary Bowen, age 6. Mother: Mrs. E. Plunket. Sisters: Mrs. mary Jackson, Mrs. Beckie Farmer, Miss Nannie Plunket. Interred: Smyrna, Ga. AG 7/27/1908

BOWEN, Hannah, colored, age 18, d. 101 N. Butler St. Atlanta. AG 3/29/1909

BOWEN, J. H. killed by Olin M. Thomason, Monroe, Ga. (committed to jail 7/13). AG 7/13/1908

BOWEN, Margaret E., Mrs., age 50, wife of E. T., d. Mead Rd., Decatur. Interred: Conyers. Dau: Mary E. Bowen, age 7. Mother: Mrs. E. Plunket. Sisters: Miss Nannie Plunket, Mrs. Mary Jackson, Mrs. Beckie Farmer. AG 7/28/1908

BOWEN, N. A. d. 9/15 Montgomery, Ala. AG 9/15/1910

BOWEN, Sarah, old negro and ex-slave, d. Douglasville, Ga. Aged abt 110. Children say aged 114. AG 5/28/1907

BOWEN, E. M., age 32, d. Atlanta Tues. Wife, two children. AG 10/7/1908

BOWERS, Billy, Uncle dead, pioneer citizen of Ga. AC 1/28/1905

BOWERS, Charles H., age 56, d. 310 Grant St. Atlanta. Interred: Hollywood. Wife, two sisters, and bro. in Virginia. AG 4/18/1910

BOWERS, J. W., pioneer of Cordele, Ga., d. Jan. 5. Wife, 2 children. Sis: Mrs. T. H. Westbrook. Interred: Cordele, Ga. AC 1/6/1905

BOWERS, May, Mrs. buried Comer, Ga. 5/20. She d. Westminster, S. C. Tues. dau. of D. P. Moon of Comer, Ga. AG 5/21/1908

BOWERS, S. G., tax collector of Hart Co., Ga., d. 6/5. AC 6/6/1905

BOWIE, Cornelia, Miss, age 69, d. Mon. bro.'s res., C. L. Bowie, 149 Little St. Atlanta. Interred: Dalton, Ga. AG 9/26/1910

BOWING, Lola, Miss, age 39, d. Atlanta Mon. Interred: Oakland. AG 7/11/1910

BOWLE, Cornelia, Miss, age 69, d. res. of bro., C. L. Bowle, 149 Little St. Atlanta. Interred: Dalton, Ga. AG 9/27/1910

BOWMAN, Otis B., inf. son of Mr. and Mrs. M. J. F., d. 310 Lee St., Atlanta. Interred: Westview. AG 11/23/1908

BOX, J. A., Confederate Veteran, d. 12/22 at Seddon, Ala. Interred: Family buring ground. Served under Gen. Joe Wheeler. Bro: L. F. Box, former judge. Wife, 8 children. AG 12/23/1909

BOYCOTT, Harry, age 42, (one notice says 66) d. Atlanta Mon. Interred: Westview. AG 3/1/1910

BOYD, Benjamin, res. of McCarmel, S. C., d. Atlanta Wed. Interred: McCarmel, S. C. AG 5/12/1909

BOYD, Cornelia, colored, age 32, d. 27 Greene St. Atlanta. AG 11/12/1910

BOYD, Ella, Mrs., age 49, killed by Central of Ga. train, Columbus, Ga. AG 2/25/1907

BOYD, Henrietta, colored, age 50, d. 9 Orme St. Atlanta. AG 10/18/1909

BOYD, John B. d. Perry, Fla., Thurs. Interred: Quitman, Ga. AG 11/14/1908 Children: Mrs. M. A. Tilley, Decatur; Marvin Boyd, Quitman; Miss Mary Boyd, Quitman. 3 bros., one sister. AG 11/14/1908

BOYD, J. T. of Snapping Shoals, Ga. d. 4/26, Confed. Vet. Wife, several children. AC 4/28/1905

BOYD, Minor, age 23, d. Jan. 5, native of Atlanta, son of James Boyd of Texas. Interred: Westview. AC 1/6/1905

BOYD, P. A., Mrs. of Calhoun Falls, S. C., d. Sun. Atlanta. AG 6/4/1910

BOYD, T. C., colored, age 63, d. 88 E. Cain St. Atlanta. AG 11/15/1907

BOYD, T. H., age 76, d. Atlanta, Sat. Interred: Thomson, Ga. AG 2/10/1908

BOYKIN, Josephine, colored, age 33, d. Newnan, Ga. AG 7/6/1909

BOYKIN, P. A., Mrs. d. 25 Cleveland St., E. Point, Ga. Mon. Mother: Mrs. M. J. Livesey. Three sons. Interred: Whitesbur, Ga. AG 10/19/1907

BOYKIN, P. A., Mrs. d. mother's res., Mrs. M. J. Livsey, E. Point, Ga. Interred: Whitesburg, Ga. AG 10/22/1907

BOYLE, W. A., age 37, d. Wed. 75 Foundry St., Atlanta. Interred: Oakhurst, Ga. AG 3/15/1910

BOYNTON, Hollis, Mrs., wife of H. A., d. Sun. 21 Windsor St., Atlanta. Interred: Oakland. Sister: Mrs. Joseph Singer. Bro: Isaac Mansfield, Chattanooga. Nieces: Mrs. George Tignor, Mrs. Tom Daniel. G 7/30/1907

BOYNTON, J. L., Mrs. of Edison, Ga. AG 8/27/1907

BOYNTON, Louise Mansfield, Mrs., age 59, d. 41 Windsor St. Atlanta. AG 7/3/1907

BOZEMAN, Nathan, Dr. d. NYC 12/17. Funera; Res. of Mrs. William Lee, College St. Macon. Interred: Rose Hill. AC 12/20/1905

BRACEWELL, Earl L. funeral 49 Howell St., Atlanta, Wed. Age 22.
Res. 49 Howell St. Interred: Westview. AG 3/25/1908
BRACEWELL, James S., age 48, d. Tues. 119 Auburn Ave. Atlanta.
Interred: Westview. AG 5/31/1910
BRACKETT, Charlie d. Sun. Funeral: Deep Spring (near Dalton,
Ga.). Age 32. Wife, one child. AG 2/22/1910
BRACKET, Mr. cut by Charlie Buchanan (in jail) at Marble Hill.
Wounds may be fatal. AC 7/18/1905
BRADBERRY, infant son of Mr. and Mrs. L. A., d. 178 Kirkwood
Ave., Atlanta, Tues. Interred: Buford, Ga. AG 2/4/1908
BRADBERRY, I. V., Mrs., 74, d. sis´s res., Mrs. Dobbins, Athens.
Bros: Dr. Hale, Athens; H. H. Hale, Atlanta. Ch: Ira, Mrs. Y. B.
& Miss Blanche Bradberry; Mrs. Chas. W. Heard, Mrs. Geo. Rice, J.
H. and Miss Bessie Bradberry. AG 10/27/1910
BRADBERRY, L. A. d. Atlanta. Interred: Buford, Ga. Wife: Mrs.
Josie. One child. Bros: F. C., M. L., T. E. Sis: Mrs. Hattie
Hudlow. AG 4/17/1908
BRADBURY, James R. d. Mon. Atlanta. Interred: Fairburn, Ga,
family burying grounds. AG 5/6/1908
BRADFORD, Cecil, age 2 mos., d. 667 E. Fair St. Atlanta. AG
2/22/1907
BRADFORD, J. A. of Gainesville d. 3/23, age 50. Wife, several
children. Interred: Scruggs Cemetery. AC 3/25/1905
BRADLEY, B. C., interred Tignall cemetery, Washington, Ga. Died
Mon. Age 68, Confederate Veteran. AG 8/1/1906
BRADLEY, D. L. d. Mobile, Ala. Thurs. Interred: Westview. Wife
lives 40-1/2 Alice St. Atlanta. AG 1/30/1908
BRADLEY, Edith, Mrs., b. England, age 50, wife of John, d.
Barksdale Drive, Ansley Park. Atlanta. AG 9/21/1909
BRADLEY, Ethel May, age 1 yr., d. 212 Clark St. Atlanta. AG
8/17/1907
BRADLEY, J. R., age abt 35. Waycross, Ga., 11/16. Bradley died at
home near A. B. & A. depot. Survivors: wife, 2 small children.
Remains carried to Tate, Ga. AG 11/17/1906
BRADLEY, Love A., Mrs., wife of J. P., d. Sat. Howell Sta.,
Atlanta. Interred: Casey´s Cemetery. AG 5/2/1910
BRADLEY, Luke, age 40, d. 736 Glenn St. Atlanta. AG 2/22/1907
BRADLEY, Mary J., Mrs. funeral 119 Estoria St. Atlanta. Interred:
Greenwood. AG 10/11/1910
BRADLEY, Mary Lou, colored, age 21, d. 7 Walker St. Atlanta. AG
9/2/1909
BRADLEY, N. B., age 77, d. Lizella, Ga., Mon. Wife. 4 cons. Ch:
Mrs. M. Birdsong, Macon; Mrs. M. L. Seale, Atlanta; John; Miss
Esther Bradley of Lizella. Interred: Lizella Cemetery. AG
5/12/1910
BRADLEY, Pearl Manning, age 21, d. 16 Bailey St., Atlanta, Sun.
Wife of E. E. Parents; Mr. and Mrs. C. A. Manning. AG 6/22/1908
BRADLEY, Virgil H., age 2 mos., son of Mr. and Mrs. J. P., d. 2
Carr St., Atlanta, Tues. Interred: Caseys. AG 9/1/1908
BRADLEY, Walter S.. Athens, 12/14, fireman on fgt train killed in
wreck by engine telescoping #2 local Seaboard at Carlton Thurs.
Engineer Pinkston jumped and saved his life. AG 12/14/1906
BRADLEY, William, son of Daniel of Hagan, age 20, shot and killed
William Baggett, age 35, Marshall of Claxton, Ga. 1/12. AG
1/12/1910

BRADLOVE, J. R., age 44, d. 88 McDonald St. Atlanta. AG 8/24/1908
BRADSHAW, Olivia, Mrs. d. 254 Clarke St., Atlanta. Interred:
Elberton, Ga. AG 2/10/1908
BRADWELL, Robert Walker, age 1, son of Mr. and Mrs. J. D., d.
College Park, Ga., Sat. Interred: College Park, Ga. Ag 6/22/1908
BRADY, J. S. of Dublin d. Sun. home of mother at Glenwood.
Interred: Dublin, Ga. AG 10/17/1906
BRAGG, Emory d. in fire Jackson St., Hawkinsville, Ga. H. T.
Bragg and family. AC 2/13/1905
BRAGGS, C. C. of Graves Springs, Ga. shot in stomach, dies from
wound. AG 2/23/1907
BRAKEFIELD, Clifford L., inf. son of Mr. and Mrs. Fred, d. Wed.
899 Marietta St., Atlanta. Interred: Hollywood. AG 8/8/1907
BRAMLETT, Alice, Mrs. d. res. near Lees Chapel (Dalton) Sun.
Interred: Poplar Springs Cemetery. AG 3/31/1910
BRAMLETT, H. P. d. Tues. Atlanta. Interred: Westview. AG
1/13/1910
BRAMLETT, Mabel, inf. dau. of Mr. and Mrs. G. W., d. 46 Powell
St., Atlanta, Mon. Interred: Sharon, Ga. AG 7/19/1909
BRAMLETT, Mattie Estelle, Mrs., age 24, wife of G. W. of 23
Berean Ave., Atlanta, d. Sat. Interred: Sharon, Ga. AG 8/12/1909
BRAMLETTE, L. J., Mrs., age 38, d. sister's res., Mrs. H. A.
Stephens, E. Point, Sun. Interred: Mt. Zion Cemetery. Parents, 5
sisters. AG 2/14/1910
BRANAN, J. J., Mrs. d. 3/30 New and Mulberry Sts., Macon.
Interred: Lumpkin, Ga., old home. Age 32. Husband, one son,
parents, survive. AG 3/31/1910
BRANAN, Myrtle Louise, age 18 mos., d. home of parents, Mr. and
Mrs. J. C. Branan of 380 Woodward Ave., Atlanta. Interred:
Oakland. AG 10/18/1906
BRANCH, Robert O., age 22, d. at King's Daughter's Hospital.
Atlanta. AG 2/22/1907
BRANCH, Susie P., wife of Prof. Thomas P. Branch of Ga. Tech, d.
Thurs. Children: Sarah, Thomas. Interred: Forsyth, Ga. AG
6/27/1907
BRAND, Annie Lou, age 3, dau. of Mr. and Mrs. C. T., d. Jonesboro
Rd. Mon. Interred: Sylvester Cemetery. AG 2/22/1910
BRAND, Bessie L., Mrs., (one notice states "Miss") age 21, d.
Thurs. 15 Kennedy St., Atlanta. Parents survive. Interred:
Sylvester. AG 5/7/1909
BRAND, G. A., age 52, d. Thurs. 68 Mason and Turner Rd., Atlanta.
Interred: Sylvester, Ga. AG 12/9/1910
BRANDON, DeWitt, age 4, d. Thurs., 693 E. Fair St. Atlanta.
Interred: Westview. AG 8/10/1906
BRANDON, J. C., age 16, d. College Park, Ga. AG 9/10/1910
BRANDON, John Clifton, age 18, son of Mr. and Mrs. G. H., d. Sun.
College Park. Bro., 3 sisters. AG 9/10/1910
BRANDON, Mamie, colored, age 27, d. 70 Markham St. Atlanta. AG
10/11/1909
BRANDT, Rosa A., Mrs., age 57, d. 249 Washington St. Atlanta. AG
9/26/1906
BRANNAN, Lee J. d. Grady Hospital Wed., of 85 Augusta Ave.,
Atlanta. Interred: Westview. Wife, five children. AG 4/10/1907
BRANNEN, Jack, colored, age 80, d. at Oakland City, Atlanta. AG

BRANNEN, Rudolph, age 8 mos., son of Mr. and Mrs. R., d. 24 1/2 Hunter St. Atlanta. Interred: Westview. AG 6/23/1910

BRANNON, Henry S., age 90, d. Tues. 352 Whitehall St., Atlanta. He was b. Newton Co. Res. of Atlanta 35 years. Sons: Henry S., Dr. J. S. Daus: Mrs. C. J. Beane, Shreveport, La., Mrs. Sallie Osborn, Alabama. Interred: Westview. AG 10/30/1906

BRANNON, J. C., age 40, d. 92 Luckie St. Atlanta. AG 11/15/1909

BRANTLEY, Benjamin d. Sun. Hazelhurst, Ga., where interred. Age 47. Wife, 4 small children. AG 4/19/1910

BRANTLEY, Georgia, Miss, age 18, eldest dau. of Major and Mrs. L. G., d. Tues. Main St., Lithonia. Interred: Conyers Cemetery. Relative of Joseph A. McCord and of Mr. and Mrs. J. D. Wester. AG 5/10/1906

BRANTLEY, Inez, inf. dau. of Mr. and Mrs. H. V., d. Sun. Atlanta. Interred: Oakland. AG 5/6/1907

BRANTLEY, J. A., Mrs., age 20, wife of J. A., d. Sun. Parents: Mr. and Mrs. H. R. Trowbridge. One bro. Interred: Westview.

BRANTLEY, Leonard L., inf. son of Mr. and Mrs. J. T., d. Mon. 127 Griffin St., Atlanta. Interred: Hollywood cemetery. AG 7/16/1907

BRANTLEY, Lucretia, Mrs. d. Sun. Atlanta. Interred: Westview. AG 4/2/1907

BRANTLEY, Quill F., Dr. age 24, d. 606 S. Pryor St. Atlanta. AG 4/15/1908

BRASELTON, Robert, Jr., age 14, son of Robert, d. Thurs., 93 S. Pryor St., Atlanta. Interred: Oakland. AG 8/23/1907

BRASWELL, B. D., Dr. d. Atlanta Wed. Interred: Ocilla, Ga. AG 6/25/1908

BRASWELL, Bartow B. burned to death. Uncle: A. Braswell, 772 Woodward Ave. Atlanta. Bur: Elberton. Par: Mr. & Mrs. B. B., Gainesville. Sis: Mrs. H. Powell, Atlanta; Mrs. I. J. Fen, Fla.; Ella, Gainesville. Bro: A. M., Atlanta. AG 1/12/1910

BRASWELL, J. C., inf. son of Mrs. W. T., d. Sun. 92 Orange St., Atlanta. Interred: Westview. AG 5/14/1906

BRATTON, Mary Laetitia, age 15 mos., dau. of Mr. and Mrs. Bratton, d. 16 Piedmont Place & 13th St., Atlanta, Wed. Interred: Oakland. AG 5/1/1907

BRAWNER, Sallie, Mrs., age 40, d. 659 Ashby St. Atlanta. AG 9/21/1909

BRAZELL, Annie M., Mrs. d. 17 Bedford Pl. Atlanta Fri. Parents: Mr. and Mrs. W. B. Hopson. Husband: James W. Brazell. 2 small children. Sis: Mrs. T. M. Sykes, Miss Birdie Hopson. Bro: W. S. Hopson. Interred: Hogansville, Ga. AG 4/2/1910

BRECKENRIDGE, Cabell, age 60, d. 17 W. Cain St. Atlanta. AG 11/15/1907

BREE, Alexander R., Mrs., b. Louisiana, Mo. dau. of late Gen. and Mrs. John L. Bernard. age 40, (one notice states age 68) d. Sun. 812 Piedmont Ave. Atlanta. Interred: Oakland. Daus: Misses Myrtle and Cora Bree. Interred: Westview. AG 9/28/1909

BREED, Richard, age 2, son of Mrs. Lillie Breed, d. 87 Carroll St., Atlanta, Sun. Interred: Hollywood. AG 9/23/1907

BRENNAN, Patrick J. d. 8/10 Washington, Ga. AG 8/10/1909

BRETT, Frank E. killed by Andrew A. Walline 8/1904. Pardon for Walline. AG 2/10/1908

BREUNING, Jasper, Mrs., age 54, widow of Sgt. Casper, d. 93 E.
Baker St. Atlanta 8/9. Ch: Mrs. Leo Maile; Mrs. C. C. Nichols;
Charles Breuning, N. Y. AC 8/10/1905
BREWER, Aurelle, Mrs., wife of L. S., d. Monroe, La. while
visiting dau., wife of Rev. J. V. Stanley, of Oklahoma; stopped
at her old home in Monroe, when she died. Telegram to Charles D.
McKinney, Atlanta. AG 11/8/1910
BREWER, F., colored, age 30, d. Brownsville, Texas. AG 5/4/1909
BREWER, Harry, colored, age 17, d. Fulton Co. Alms House. AG
8/7/1908
BREWER, L. H., Mrs., age 26, d. 101 N. Butler St. Atlanta. AG
10/13/1906
BREWER, William H., Hon. d. 1/17 Griffin, b. Walton Co.
10/22/1841, age 66. Wife, son, 5 daus. AG 1/18/1910
BREWSTER, Jane, colored, age 64, d. 2 Airline St. Atlanta. AG
8/25/1909
BREWSTER, P. H., Mrs. d. 2/26 College Park. Interred: College
Park Cemetery. 6 sons, 3 daus. AC 2/27/1905
BREWSTER, Preston, colored, age 60, d. 44 Whitehall Terr.
Atlanta. AG 12/24/1907
BREWSTER, Tomlinson C., age 75, d. Atlanta. AG 5/2/1910
BRICE, William, age 9 mos., d. 87 Jefferson St. Atlanta. AG
10/20/1909
BRIDGES, Annie, Mrs. interred Westview. Daus: Miss Bessie
Bridges; Mrs. Rubie Heflin, Atlanta. AG 1/13/1908
BRIDGES, J. W., Mrs. d. Sun. Atlanta. Interred: Westview. AG
1/14/1908
BRIDGES, James Weldon funeral Thurs. res. of Mrs. L. E. Gwynn,
409 Whitehall St., Atlanta. Interred: Oakland. AG 12/23/1909
BRIDGES, N. C., age 4 , d. Milledgeville, Ga. AG 1/11/1910
BRIDGES, Polly, age 7, dau. of Mr. and Mrs. N. C. Bridges, d. 22
1/2 W. Mitchell St., Atlanta, Mon. Bur: Westview. AG 3/8/1907
BRIDGES, Polly, dau. of Mr. and Mrs. N. C. Bridges, d. 22 1/2 W.
Mitchell St., Atlanta, Mon. Interred: Westview. AG 3/8/1907
BRIDGES, Robert H., age 74, d. Tues. Res. of 69 Travis St., Atlanta.
Bro. in Texas. AG 8/10/1910
BRIDWELL, Louise, age 8 mos., dau. of Mr. and Mrs. J. A., d.
Thurs. 18 Tifton St., Atlanta. Interred: Hollywood. AG 9/20/1907
BRIDWELL, William H., age 21, d. 86 Magnolia St., Atlanta, Thurs.
AG 10/9/1907
BRIGHTWELL, Fannie, colored, age 24, d. 171 Magnolia St. Atlanta.
AG 8/30/1910
BRIM, John Henry, son of Mr. and Mrs. A. L. of Pelham, d. at.
Interred: City cemetery. AG 1/22/1907
BRINKERHOFF, Marie E., Mrs., wife of W. H., d. Atlanta Wed. AG
4/8/1909
BRINKLEY, William, age 77, d. Blue Ridge, Ga. 2/15. 20 yrs. ago
came from Marietta. AG 2/16/1910
BRINSON, Elizabeth, 78, d. Swainsboro. Bros-T. J. (Savannah), A.
T. (Stillmore) & R. T. Durden (Summit). Sis-Mrs. Wm Stevens,
Midville; Mrs. A. L. Turner, Summit. Sons-S. E., Springfield; F.
R., Swainsboro; W. A., Cobbtown; D. E., Jacksonville; M. J.,
Springfield. Daus-Mrs. S. W. Sutton, Swainsboro; Mrs. A. S.
Turner & Mrs. J. W. Bowie, Summit; Mrs. J. K. Lanier, Stillmore.
AG 11/28/1908

BRISBINE, Paul, 1 yr., d. 5 E. North Ave. Atlanta. AG 2/8/1907
BRISCO, Egbert G., colored, age 34, d. 123 Ira St. Atlanta. AG 6/19/1909
BRISCOE, Katie, colored, age 48, d. 203 Martin St. Atlanta. AG 10/22/1909
BRISCOL, James, age 10, negro, killed by Riley Lowe, age 14, negro, with toy pistol, Atlanta. AG 1/4/1907
BRISENDINE, J. M., Mrs.,ge 54, d. Augusta, Ga. Tues. Dau: Mrs. G. S. Davis, 3 W. Delta Pl., Atlanta; Mrs. A. E. Stone, Darien, Ga.; Mrs. Mamie Thompson; Miss Hattie Brisendine, Augusta. Interred: Westview. AG 7/7/1909
BRITAIN, J. M., age 63, d. 315 E. Fair St. Atlanta. AG 2/27/1907
BRITT, Ed from Lanetta, Ala. drowned 7/3 in Chattahoochee River. AC 7/4/1905
BRITT, Luther W. d. Fri. First Ave., Columbus, Ga., age 60. Interred: Linwood. AG 3/10/1910
BRITT, M. M., Mrs., age 32, wife of Mark, d. 203 W. Kimball St., Atlanta Sun. Interred: Stone Mtn, Ga. AG 6/21/1909
BRITT, Mary Bell, Mrs. d. Randolph Ave., Macon, Ga., age 20, wife of W. T. Britt. Leaves husband, mother, 3 bros., sister, of Macon. AG 6/5/1907
BRITT, Mattie, Mrs., age 60, d. Atlanta Sun. Interred: Dawson, Ga. Leaves husband, A. I. Britt. AG 12/9/1907
BRITT, W. E. d. 160 Courtland St. Atlanta. AC 9/19/1905
BRITTAIN, E. G., age 26, d. Milledgeville, Ga. AG 10/18/1907
BRITTEN, J. M. d. 315 E. Fair St., Atlanta, Sat. Interred: Moreland, Ga. AG 2/26/1907
BRITTLE, Sam, age 22, d. Edgewood, Ga. AG 7/17/1907
BRITTON, Mary, Mrs. d. Sat. Atlanta. Interred: Westview. Husband, 5 children, three sisters. AG 9/20/1909
BROAD, L. P., Dr., age 68, d. 17 W. Cain St. Atlanta. AG 3/16/1908
BROAD, L. P., Dr. of Boston, Mass. d. Thurs. Atlanta. Interred: Natlick, Mass. He was b. 1840 Ashland, Mass. AG 3/13/1908
BROADBENT, Grace, Mrs., age 67, mother of W., d. 427 E. Georgia Ave. Atlanta, Sun. Interred: Westview. AG 9/23/1907
BROADNOX, Annie May, colored, age 22, d. 24 Grays alley. Atlanta. AG 8/15/1907
BROADSTREET, Lanth, age 2, son of Mr. and Mrs. T. W., d. E. Point, Ga. Tues. Interred: Hill Crest Cemetery. AG 12/30/1907
BROADWELL, Cecil, inf. son of Mr. and Mrs. R. C., d. 328 Windsor St., Atlanta, Sat. Interred: Buford, Ga. AG 2/8/1908
BROCK, Beatrice, colored, age 33, d. 127 Markham St. Atlanta. AG 9/14/1907
BROCKETT, Clinton T., Jr., Dr., age 24, d. Clarkston. funeral 4/7. Interred: Westview. Kin: Dr. Clinton T. Brockett, Sr., Mr. and Mrs. W. T. Comer. AG 4/6/1907
BROCKETT, Robert L., Prof., age 92, d. Corledge, Ga. AG 7/9/1908
BROCKMAN, R. A., Mrs., funeral was Mon. at Rock Springs Church. Interment: church yard. AG 11/12/1906
BROGDON, L. E., Mrs., age 23, d. Decatur, Ga. Mon. Interred: Decatur cemetery. AG 4/23/1907
BRONSTON, Charles J., Sr., widower several yrs, d. 4/15 Lexington, Ky. He eloped 2/1897 St. Louis w/Miss Belle Windom of Pudacah, Ky. His div. suit brought newspaper fame. AG 4/15/1909

Pudacah, Ky. His div. suit brought newspaper fame. AG 4/15/1909

BROOK, Clyde L., age 3, son of Mr. and Mrs. Andrew L., d. 83 Josephine St., Atlanta, Wed. AG 3/18/1909

BROOK, Maggie, colored, age 31, d. Hill St. on 10/2. AG 10/6/1910

BROOKS, A. T., colored, age 46, d. 233 Fox St. Atlanta. AG 8/26/1908

BROOKS, Belmont, age 24, d. 2/24 Columbus, Ga. Interred: Cusseta, Ga. AC 2/25/1905

BROOKS, Carrie, Mrs., age 25, d. Cordele, Ga. AG 12/2/1910

BROOKS, Clyde, age 39, d. 40 W. Peachtree St. Atlanta. AG 1/15/1907

BROOKS, Dora, colored, age 28, d. rear 245 Whitehall St. Atlanta. AG 2/11/1909

BROOKS, Eva E., Mrs., age 32, d. Jacksonville, Fla. Fri. Interred: Atlanta, Westview. Mother: Mrs. J. E. Beaton. Bro: J. W. Beaton. Sis: Mrs. D. B. Teabeaut, Atlanta. AG 12/11/1909

BROOKS, Fanida, dau. of Mr. and Mrs. George W., age 17, d. Lexington, Ga. Interred: Presbyterian Cemetery, Lexington. AG 7/26/1909

BROOKS, Fred, age 28, son of Mr. and Mrs. J. W., d. Atlanta Thurs. Bro: Alton, Birmingham, Ala. Sis: Mrs. Charles Sheldon. AG 5/5/1910

BROOKS, Frederick, age 28, d. Wed. 376 Ormond St., Atlanta. Interred: Westview. AG 5/6/1910

BROOKS, G. W., age 9, d. 111 Foundry St. Atlanta. AG 2/24/1908

BROOKS, George William, age 9, son of Mr. and Mrs. Edward, d. 111 Foundry St., Atlanta, Sat. Interred: Oakland. AG 2/20/1908

BROOKS, James H. of Atlanta killed Philadelphia 11/1, in car wreck. AC 11/2/1905

BROOKS, J. E., age 40, of Tupelo, Miss., d. Atlanta Thurs. AG 12/17/1909

BROOKS, J. L., age 46, d. 704 DeKalb Ave. Atlanta. AG 7/23/1907

BROOKS, J. P. d. Wed. Vineville, Ga. Interred: Ft. Hill Cemetery. AG 8/7/1908

BROOKS, John, colored, age 61, d. 108 Bramnes Ave., Atlanta, Oct. 19th. AG 10/20/1910

BROOKS, L., colored, age 35, d. 61 Whitehall Terrace, Atlanta. AG 1/1/1908

BROOKS, Laura J., Mrs., age 64, d. Sat. res. of dau., Mrs. F. M. Bridges, 250 Cooper St., Atlanta. Interred: Westview. She was wid. of A. A. Brooks. Ch: Mrs. F. T. Perkins, Mrs. F. M. Bridges, H. L. Brooks. AG 3/4/1907

BROOKS, Lula, colored, age 53, d. rear 103 E. Harris St. Atlanta. AG 7/23/1907

BROOKS, Mary, Mrs., age 61, d. 154 W. Mitchell St. Atlanta. AG 1/14/1910

BROOKS, R., colored, age 1 yr., d. rear of 376 Edgewood Ave., Atlanta. AG 10/9/1907

BROOKS, Roland W., Jr., inf. son of Mr. and Mrs. R. W., d. 172 S. Forsyth St., Atlanta Wed. Interred: Hollywood. AG 5/26/1908

BROOKS, William Cecil, age 13 mos., d. 16 Fowler St. Atlanta. AG 10/11/1909

BROOKS, W. M., Mrs., Rockmart, Ga. 11/7/1906. She was Miss Grace Tittle.   Survivors: Husband, a sister, 3 bros. She was a bride April last. Interment: Rockmart cem. AG 11/8/1906

BROOKSHIRE, W. B., age 72, d. Wed. dau.´s res., Mrs. J. E. Boston, 22 McAfee St. Atlanta. Son: J. L. AG 3/24/1910

BROOMFIELD, Currier, colored, age 60, d. 13 Chestnut St. Atlanta. AG 5/4/1909

BROTHERTON, William H., Capt., age 69, b. Polk Co., Tenn. 2/3/1839, d. Thurs. 235 S. Forsyth St. Atlanta. Bur: Oakland. Wife, 9 ch: Mrs. J. L. Small, William M., F. M., Charles H., Mrs. George I. Walker, R. L., Edgar, Mrs. John M. Berry (Rome), Harold P. AG 2/28/1908

BROTHWELL, Delia, Mrs., age 83, d. 74 Fraser St., Atlanta Thurs. Interred: Savannah, Ga. AG 2/6/1908

BROUGHTON, Frances Briscoe, age 4 mos., inf. dau. of Dr. and Mrs. Joseph, d. Tues. Gainesville, Ga. Res: 20 E. North Ave. Atlanta. Interred: Westview, Atlanta. Uncle: Rev. Len G. Broughton. AG 7/24/1907

BROUGHTON, L. M., colored, age 43, d. 96 Spencer St. Atlanta. AG 5/22/1910

BROVILLE, B. S., Dr. d. Hawkinsville, Ga. 2/12. AC 2/14/1905

BROWER, Eugenie, colored, age 44, d. 16 Grove St. Atlanta. AG 3/16/1908

BROWERS, H. L., Mrs. d. Fri. 258 Pulliam St., Atlanta. Interred: Cochran, Ga. AG 10/13/1906

BROWN, A. F., Mrs. d. Berkely, Ga. Husb. Ch: Otho, Atlanta; Luther, St. Louis, Mo.; Walter, Baltimore; Mrs. Lula Ash; Mrs. Quillia Thompson, Athens; Mrs. W. S. Stark, Commerce; Mrs. Rex Brown, Nashville, N. C. Bur: Carlton cem. AG 7/30/1907

BROWN, Ada, colored, age 31, d. 594 McDaniel St. Atlanta. AG 7/30/1908

BROWN, Albert, colored, age 60, d. 290 Rhodes St. Atlanta. AG 5/20/1909

BROWN, Allen, Dr. of Blackshear d. Mon., age 70. AG 8/8/1906

BROWN, Annie S., Mrs. d. Tues. New York City. Interred: Atlanta, Westview. AG 4/16/1910

BROWN, Arthur, ex-senator, Mrs. Anna Bradley indicted for shoting him., Washington. AG 2/15/1907

BROWN, B. B., age 20, brakeman for Sou. railroad, killed by freight train at Dames Ferry. Macon. Bros: J. B., W. L., C. S. and S. G. Brown. Sis: Mrs. Rosa May Parker. AG 2/15/1907

BROWN, Belle Oner, Mrs., wife of R. T., d. parents res. Paces Ferry Rd., Atlanta, Wed. (Mr. and Mrs. S. A. Wilson). Interred: Sardis. AG 10/23/1907

BROWN, Belle, colored, age unknown, d. rear of 18 Gilmore St. Atlanta. AG 5/28/1906

BROWN, Ben was run over by train, West Point, Ga. Saw-mill man. AG 10/8/1906

BROWN, C., colored, age 50, d. 101 N. Butler St. Atlanta. AG 3/19/1907

BROWN, C. B., age 78, d. Mon. 78 Jones Ave. Atlanta. AG 5/14/1906

BROWN, C. B., Mrs., age 29, d. 17 Willow St. Atlanta. AG 3/22/1907

BROWN, C. I., age 78, d. 325 S.Pryor St. Atlanta. AG 10/3/1906

BROWN, C. R., age 68, d. Mon. 341-1/2 E. Fair St. Interred: Westview. AG 2/5/1907

BROWN, Catherine M., Mrs., age 64, wife of Frederick M., d. New Orleans, La., Wed., formerly of Watertown, N.Y. Ch: Miss Kathleen Brown, Atlanta; Anthony, Atlanta; Miss Lydia M., Joseph M., Sheffield, Frederick W. Jr. AG 1/10/1908

BROWN, Cecil, age 3 mos., infant, found dead at home, 214 Echo St., Atlanta, Thurs. Interred: Elberton, Ga. AG 12/9/1909

BROWN, Celia, colored, age 52, d. 47 Haygood St. Atlanta. AG 4/28/1908

BROWN, Charles, inf. son of Mr. and Mrs. C. H., d. Mon. Interred: Westview. AG 6/1/1908

BROWN, Charlie, age 50, d. Fulton Co. barracks. AG 10/25/1906

BROWN, Clara, colored, age 3 mos., d. 19 Fairfax St. Atlanta. AG 12/9/1907

BROWN, Claude Key, colored, age 2 mos., d. 101 N. Butler St. Atlanta. AG 7/14/1909

BROWN, Dock, colored, age 50, d. Orme St. Atlanta. AG 3/1/1907

BROWN, E., colored, age 75, d. 99 E. Cain St. Atlanta. AG 7/8/1907

BROWN, E. G. of Nashville, Ga. d. Fri. AG 11/2/1908

BROWN, Edward, colored, age 55, d. Alms House. Atlanta. AG 12/12/1910

BROWN, Elisha M., age 65, d. 536 Walnut St. Atlanta. AG 4/ /1910

BROWN, Eliza, colored, age 50 d. Crumley St. Atlanta. AG 3/3/1909

BROWN, Eliza, Mrs. of Eufaula, Ala. d. Fri., age 82. Sons: Dr. Arthur, George, residents of Fla. AG 12/13/1909

BROWN, Evelyn, dau. of Mr. and Mrs. George, d. 11 Fitzgerald St. Atlanta Wed. Interred: Decatur, Ga. AG 5/6/1908

BROWN, Fannie Alma, dau. of Mr. and Mrs. W. L., age 1 yr., d. 14 Shelton St. Atlanta. Interred: Westview. AG 8/5/1910

BROWN, Fletcher, age 25, d. New York City. AG 1/21/1910

BROWN, G. W. suicide Columbus, Ga. AG 1/5/1910

BROWN, G. W., age 24, d. 69 Luckie St. Atlanta. AG 3/4/1907

BROWN, G. W., age 42, d. 280 N. Jackson St., Atlanta. AG 7/16/1907

BROWN, Garnett, colored, age 18, d. 27 Milton St. Atlanta. AG 7/16/1908

BROWN, George, age 42, d. Wed. 280 N. Jackson St. Atlanta. Wife, three children survive. Interred: Columbus, Ga. AG 7/11/1907

BROWN, George, colored, age 7 yrs., d. 77 Battle St. Atlanta. AG 6/18/1907

BROWN, Gladys, colored, age 28, d. 218 E. Ellis St. Atlanta. AG 12/17/1910

BROWN, Green, negro, d. Mon. 179 Butler St., Atlanta. AG 1/18/1908

BROWN, Gwendoline Bowen, age 2, dau. of Mr. and Mrs. J. J., d. Tues. 357 Lee St., Atlanta. Interred: Greenwood. AG 6/12/1907

BROWN, H. R. Mrs. d. Gadsden, Ala. Wed. AG 12/1/1910

BROWN, Harry P. of Griffin funeral Atlanta. Well known newspaper man. Interred: Oak Hill Cemetery. AG 4/27/1906

BROWN, Harry R. d. Ocean Park, Calif. Wife, child. Mother: Mrs. C. B. Rea. Sis: Mrs. M. R. Holland. Bur: Atlanta. AG 3/27/1908

BROWN, Henry, colored, age 26, d. 7 Trinity Ave. Atlanta. AG 12/26/1907

42

BROWN, Humphrey, colored, age 31, d. 336 W. Simpson St. Atlanta. AG 11/23/1910

BROWN, infant, 8 weeks old, son of Mr. and Mrs. E. G., d. Wed. Atlanta. Interred: Casey's Cemetery. AG 7/21/1910

BROWN, infant of Jessie, age two mos., d. 110 Walton St. Atlanta. AG 11/2/1907

BROWN, infant of Mr. and Mrs. Theodore, d. Howells Mill Rd., Atlanta, Wed. Interred: Sardis. AG 10/23/1907

BROWN, infant of Mr. and Mrs. J. W., age 13 mos., d. Mountain View Hospital yesterday. Interred: Perry, Ga. AG 7/12/1907

BROWN, I. N., Mrs., wife of mayor of Edgewood, Ga., d. Fri. Interred: Westview. AG 1/22/1907

BROWN, Isabelle C., Mrs., age 58, d. Tennille, Ga. AG 11/11/1909

BROWN, Isaiah, Mrs., age 88, d. 47 Crescent St. Atlanta. AG 2/4/1907

BROWN, J. A., age 76, d. 59 Richardson St. Atlanta. AG 4/7/1908

BROWN, J. Henry, Mrs., age 32, d. Wed. near Crumps Park, Macon, Ga., wife of Judge H. Henry. Dau: Gladys. Father, mother, 4 bros. Bro: W. J. Watson, Atlanta. Interred: Riverside, Macon, Ga. AG 9/10/1908

BROWN, J. J., one of Chattanooga's oldest citizens, d. Mon. He was b. Athens, Ga. in 1847, Conf. Soldier. AG 4/21/1909

BROWN, J. R., Dr. d. Calhoun St., Macon 9/23, druggist. Interred: Rose Hill. AG 9/24/1909

BROWN, J. T., age 58, d. 34 McLendon St., Atlanta. Wife, Daus: Mrs. E. M. Hardin, Mrs. L. T. Martin, Misses Ruth and Ethel. Son: Charles T. Interred: Westview. AG 3/29/1907

BROWN, James C., Jr., son of Mr. and Mrs. J. C., d. Fri. 71 Bearean Ave., Atlanta, Sat. Interred: Cool Springs Cemetery. AG 12/7/1907

BROWN, Jane, Mrs., widow of late Jesse Brown, d. yesterday 29 Hydrolia St., E. Macon. Dau: Mrs. Mat Garwood of Augusta. Sons: Jake, William and Jim Brown of Macon. Interred: Ft. Hill. AG 6/6/1907

BROWN, Jesse E., Hon. d. 8/15 Scottsboro, Ala., age 60. Born Jackson Co. Confederate Veteran. AC 8/17/1905

BROWN, Jesse O. O., Judge, judge of city court of Buford, d. Jan. 7, age less than 30. AC 1/121905

BROWN, Jessie, inf. dau. of Mr. and Mrs. J., interred Westview. AG 11/2/1907

BROWN, John, colored, age 88, d. 21 Hammock Pl. Atlanta. AG 12/17/1910

BROWN, John T., colored, age 56, d. 306 Hilliard St. Atlanta. AG 4/19/1907

BROWN, Joseph B., inf. son of Mr. and Mrs. B. W., 113 Main St., d. Tues. Interred: Griffin, Ga. AG 4/13/1909

BROWN, Joseph R., colored, age 6 mos., d. 293 1/2 Piedmont Ave. Atlanta. AG 3/28/1907

BROWN, Julius L., age 62, d. 187 Washington St. Atlanta. AG 9/5/1910

BROWN, Katie, colored, age 50, d. 301 Terry St. Atlanta. AG 12/17/1910

BROWN, Leonard T. killed Margaret Straud and then himself. Left wife. AG 2/12/1907

BROWN, Lewis, colored, age 54, d. 324 Walnut St. on 10/5. AG 1/6/1910

BROWN, Lillian M., Mrs., age 33, d. 15 Queen St., Atlanta, Wed. Bros: D. A. and J. E. Farrell. Sis: Mrs. F. F. Kennedy, Miss Margaret Farrell of Atlanta, Miss Annie B. Farrell of Worcester, Mass. Interred: Westview. AG 12/8/1910

BROWN, Lillie, age 10, negro, killed near Bogart, Ga. AG 4/21/1909

BROWN, Louise E., Mrs., age 57, d. 12/10 107 Logan St. Atlanta. Husband, 9 children. Interred: Clarkston, Ga. AC 12/11/1905

BROWN, Lula, Mrs., age 51, d. DeKalb Co. Thurs. Interred: Wesley Chapel church yard. AG 12/24/1909

BROWN, M. F., Mrs., age 45, d. Sun. E. Atlanta. Interred: Sylvester cemetery. AG 5/28/1907

BROWN, Mandy, age 5 mos., d. 11 Pickett St. Atlanta. AG 6/21/1906

BROWN, Martin L., colored, age 3, d. 533 Glynn St. Atlanta. AG 3/18/1909

BROWN, Mary E., age 71, d. 98 Pearl St. Atlanta. AG 5/11/1910

BROWN, Mary J., Mrs. d. Spring City, Tenn., widow. of late Polk Brown, age 59. Sis: Mrs. Harry Thomas. Daus: Mrs. Charles H. Mills, Spring City, Mrs. J. G. Crumbliss, Kingston. AG 12/17/1909

BROWN, Mary L., Mrs., age 29, d. Riverside, Ga. AG 9/14/1908

BROWN, Mary R., Miss, nurse, d. Thurs., shot by Martin L. Sterling, delirious patient, Washington, Ga. AG 1/8/1910

BROWN, Mary T., Mrs., wife of J. T., d. Calhoun St., Macon 3/22. Interred: Rose Hill. AC 3/22/1905

BROWN, Mary, Mrs. d. 4/1 Covington, Ga., age 80. Bro: Dr. James H. Weaver, Atlanta (decd). AC 4/3/1905

BROWN, Mary, Mrs., age 29, wife of W. I., d. near Riverside, Ga. Fri. Interred: Roswell, Ga. AG 9/12/1908

BROWN, Mattie, Miss, age 58, res. of Marietta, d. Atlanta Mon. Interred: Marietta, Ga. AG 7/6/1909

BROWN, Minner murdered Pike Co., Ga. 1906. Sheriff Harrison of Pike Co. arrested Wash Dinkins for murder. AG 3/25/1908

BROWN, Minnie Lou, Mrs. d. Mon. 57 Tye St., Atlanta. Interred; Hollywood. AG 10/30/1906

BROWN, Moses L., Capt., age 73, d. Decatur. Born Gwinnett Co., Ga. Confed Vet., 7th Ga. Regt. Married Miss Virgin Carter of Augusta (d. 1885). Ch: Mrs. Joseph E. Smith; Miss Nelle Brown; Moses L. Brown, Jr. Interred: Decatur. AG 9/26/1910

BROWN, P. C. of Merrlack, Ala. d. Wed., age 23. Wife, one child. AG 3/10/1910

BROWN, Ralph H., age 35, d. 261 Forrest Ave. Atlanta. AG 4/19/1907

BROWN, R. O. d. Ft. Gaines, Ga. 7/9, age 40. Wife, several small children. Father: Wiley Brown. AG 7/10/1909

BROWN, Nellie, colored, age 1, d. 124 E. Harris St. Atlanta. AG 2/22/1907

BROWN, Perino, age 85, d. Milledgeville, Ga. AG 3/10/1909

BROWN, R. Garvin, farmer of Jefferson Co., res. 6 mi. from Louisville, shot, fatally wounded by negro. Wife. AG 8/31/1908

BROWN, Rebecca, Mrs., wife of W. G., d. 113 W. Fair St., Atlanta. Interred: Westview. AG 8/7/1906

BROWN, Richard T., age 36, d. Atlanta. AG 4/13/1909

BROWN, Robert, colored, age 27, d. Atlanta. AG 7/29/1907

BROWN, Robert E., age 37, d. Mon. Atlanta. Interred: Oakland. AG 6/29/1910

BROWN, Ruby, age 14, dau. of Mr. and Mrs. J. D., d. McDonough Rd., Atlanta, Thurs. Interred: Clifton Church yard. AG 3/26/1909

BROWN, Ruth, Miss, age 16, dau. of J. F., d. Flat Shoals Rd., Atlanta, Thurs. Interred: Wesleys Chapel. AG 6/19/1908

BROWN, S. N., Mrs., age 38, d. 29 Luckie St. Atlanta. AG 1/22/1907

BROWN, S. T., motorman, killed. Charlie Walker to hang for his murder in Decatur, Fri. AG 7/28/1910

BROWN, Samuel T., age 31, d. Druid Hills. Atlanta. AG 4/25/1910

BROWN, Sanford V., Hon., d. 5/30 Hartwell, Ga. Wife, 6 children. AG 5/30/1910

BROWN, Sarah, colored, age 48, d. Mary St. Atlanta. AG 11/11/1907

BROWN, Sarah A. E., age 64, d. 46 Ella St. Atlanta. AG 3/7/1910

BROWN, Selwyn F., asst. supt. of Fulton Bag and Cotton Mills, d. Fri. Wife, two ch: Ruth and Annabelle Brown. From Augusta, Ga. Interred: Augusta. AG 8/1/1908

BROWN, Stephen M. d. yesterday at home, near Longstreet, Pulaski Co. Interred: Orange Hill, Hawkinsville, Ga. Wife, two small children. Bro: James Brown. AG 6/5/1907

BROWN, Stevenson, colored, age 17, d. Grady Hospital. Atlanta. AG 7/12/1907

BROWN, Terrell, inf. son of Mr. and Mrs. J. T. of 41 Crescent Ave., Atlanta, d. Sun. Interred: Sardis Church. AG 7/6/1908

BROWN, Thornton, age 2, d. res. of parents, Mr. and Mrs. G. N., 11 Fitzgerald St., Atlanta, Mon. Interred: Decatur, Ga. AG 10/28/1908

BROWN, Tom, age 43, d. Fulton Co. Jail. AG 11/7/1907

BROWN, Tommie, age 4, d. 1 Gallatin St. Atlanta. AG 1/7/1910

BROWN, Tommie, age 4, son of Mr. and Mrs. C. A., d. Thurs., 1 Gallatin St. Atlanta. Interred: Sardis church yard. AG 1/7/1910

BROWN, U. S., age 43, Hartwell, Ga. Merchant, d. DeKalb Ave., Atlanta Thurs. Wife survives. Interred: Hartwell, Ga. AG 2/27/1908

BROWN, Vesta, Miss d. at home near Stone Church (Dalton) Tues., dau. of William Brown, age 36. AG 6/15/1910

BROWN, W. J., Mrs., age 56, d. Sylvester St., Edgewood, Ga. Sun. Interred: Decatur, Ga. AG 5/25/1908

BROWN, W. R., Mrs. d. Anniston, Ala. 8/18. Interred: Oxford Cemetery. AG 8/19/1908

BROWN, W. S. committed suicide Marietta, Ga. Wife, 3 yr. old dau. AG 3/5/1908

BROWN, W. T. d. Grady Hospital 10/31, Atlanta. Interred: Westview. AG 11/11/1907

BROWN, W. T., age 80, d. 101 N. Butler St. Atlanta. AG 11/12/1907

BROWN, Warren, Mrs., mother of Hon. Edward T. Brown of Atlanta, d. Gainesville last night, age 77. Dau: Mrs. Luke Smith. Husband survives. AG 2/20/1907

BROWN, Wilder F., travelling man of Westmore, Mass., d. in room at Read House, Chattanooga, Tenn. 10/25. Interred: Westmore, Mass. AG 10/25/1909

BROWN, William instantly killed at Pelicanville near Brunswick with ax by Albert Thompson, both negroes. AG 4/17/1907

BROWN, William H., colored, age 43, d. 171 Martin St. Atlanta. AG 12/1/1908
BROWN, Willie, age 1 mo., d. 101 N. Butler St. Atlanta. AG 6/11/1909
BROWN, Willie, inf. son of Mr. and Mrs. W. D., d. Atlanta Thurs. Interred: Westview. AG 6/11/1909
BROWN, Wilson, colored, age 55, d. 32 Wilson St. Atlanta. AG 12/12/1910
BROWNE, George Y., inf. son of N. B., d. 14 Waddell St., Atlanta, Tues. AG 6/6/1906
BROWNELL, Lucia E., Miss d. 10/3 Atlanta. Interred: Alexander, La. Bros: Francis; Clarence. AC 11/1/1905
BROWNING, J. B., age 81, d. Old Soldiers' Home, Atlanta. AG 11/19/1909
BROWNING, R. E., age 76, d. Old Soldiers' Home. Atlanta. AG 11/8/1910
BROWNLEE, Bishop, colored, age 22, d. Fulton Co. Almshouse. AG 3/13/1908
BROYLES, C. E., Col., age 80, 36th Ga. in war, d. Antonito, Colo. Before his removal West in 1874, he was north Ga. lawyer. Ch: R. A. Broyles, Atlanta, C. E. Broyles, Jr., Ringgold, Mrs. Laura Boyd, Mrs. Sarah Boyd, Savannah. AG 10/22/1906
BRUCE, F. B.,ge 29, formerly of Atlanta, d. Cincinnati, Ohio, Sat. Wife, mother, Mrs. M. J. Bruce of 50 Woodward Ave., Atlanta. Bros: J. C. and Hugh G. Bruce. Interred: Newberry, S. C. AG 6/22/1908
BRUCE, Henry d. 8/11 Columbus, Ga., age 68. Native of Scotland. AG 8/12/1909
BRUCE, Robert, son of A. C., d. Sun. Norcross, Ga. Parents home: 327 N. Boulevard, Atlanta. Interred: Oakland. AG 8/5/1907
BRUCE, Stirling, son of, age 18, of Dawson Co., dragged to death Thus. AG 7/4/1908
BRUCE, Virginia, colored, age 3, d. 21 Wallace St. Atlanta. AG 8/31/1908
BRUNSON, Thomas Jefferson, age 5, son of Mr. and Mrs. R. C., d. 418 Whitehall St. Atlanta. Interred: Westview. AG 6/4/1910
BRUSES, Oscar, colored, age 26, d. 121 Hilliard St. Atlanta, Oct. 18. AG 10/20/1910
BRYAN, B. H., Miss, age 23, d. Birmingham, Ala. AB 2/12/1908
BRYAN, Beatrice H., Miss, age 23, d. Birmingham, Ala. Sun. Parents: Mr. and Mrs. E. J. Bryan, Birmingham. Interred: Atlanta, Westview Cemetery. AG 2/11/1908
BRYAN, Joe, negro, killed by W. J. Nixon, white man, Savannah, Ga. AG 12/26/1907
BRYAN, William, age 67, d. Confederate Soldiers' Home. Atlanta. AG 3/29/1909
BRYAN, Nellie May, age 18 mos., dau. of Mr. and Mrs. A. G., of Sparta, Ga. Interred: Atlanta, Greenwood Cemetery. AG 8/11/1910
BRYANT, Annie Celestia, age 1, d. 16 Wellington St. Atlanta. AG 10/7/1909
BRYANT, C. A., Mrs., age 27, d. 171 Majestic Ave., Atlanta, Fri. Interred: Masons church yard. AG 1/15/1910
BRYANT, George, negro, run over by switch engine 1/14. AG 1/15/1910

BRYANT, Gracie Bell, age 3 mos., d. 108 Foundry St. Atlanta. AG 5/8/1907

BRYANT, James, age 88, old citizen of Whitfield Co., d. Beaverdale, Ga., Fri. 12 children survive, all married. Wife survives. AG 9/10/1910

BRYANT, John H. d. 7/16, age 65, Huntsville, Ala. Confed. Vet. Wife, several children. AC 7/18/1905

BRYANT, John R., age 51, d. Atlanta Sun. Wife, 5 children. Interred: Covington, Ga. AG 5/22/1910

BRYANT, Lon, negro, shot Sat. by another negro may not survive. AG 3/25/1907

BRYANT, Mandy M., Mrs., age 52, d. 100 Estoria St., Atlanta, Wed. Husband, five children. Interred: Social Circle, Ga. AG 6/18/1908

BRYANT, Mary Aleen, age 7 mos., dau. of Mr. and Mrs. T. H., d. 16 Wellington St., Atlanta, Tues. Interred: Westview. AG 10/12/1910

BRYANT, Miss, age 10, killed by lightening 12/24, 12-mi. S. of Macon. Leaves father, mother two bros, four sisters. AG 12/24/1907

BRYANT, Nannie, Mrs., age 59, d. Sun. E. Point. Interred: Utoy Church yard. AG 2/22/1910

BRYANT, Ollie, colored, age 11, d. Reynoldstown, Ga. AG 11/15/1909

BRYANT, Robert Mays, age 23, d. 1 Pulliam St. Atlanta. AG 8/14/1908

BRYANT, W. H., Rev., well-known Baptist minister of Valdosta, Ga. d. Mon, age 61. Confederate veteran. Leaves widow, seven children. Funeral at Morven, Brooks Co. AG 6/20/1906

BRYANT, Weldon, age 17 mos., son of Mr. and Mrs. P. M., d. Sat. Interred: Masons church yard, Atlanta. AG 9/28/1907

BRYANT, William Q. robbed, killed by unknown parties Wed., Washington, Ga., aged nearly 60. AG 6/1/1906

BRYANT, William T., age 2, d. 82 Culver St. Atlanta. AG 7/29/1908

BRYANT, William Thomas, age 2, d. 82 Culver St. Atlanta. Son of Mr. and Mrs. W. M. Bryant. Interred: Oakland. AG 6/29/1908

BRYANT, James S. of Houston Co., Ga. d. Sun. Macon while visiting relatives. Funeral at Kathleen, Ga. Interred: Family Burial Ground. Sis-in-law: Mrs. J. S. Sclumeum, Macon. Wife, three sons, two daus., survive. AG 11/11/1907

BRYAN, William, of Confederate Soldiers' Home, Atlanta, d. Fri. He was b. Macon Co., Ga. 12/3/1841, enl. Conf. service 1/1/1862, Co. E, Phillips' Legion. Dau: Mrs. William H. Liggin, DeSoto, Ga. Bro: Fax Bryan, Vienna, Ga. AG 3/26/1909

BRYNE, William H., age 50, d. 27 Haynes St., Atlanta, Fri. Wife, 4 children. Daus: Helen, Lucile, Margaret. Son: John. AG 11/5/1910

BRYSON, Margie, Mrs., wife of Conductor Walter H., survivor of Druid Hills street car tragedy, funeral 316 E. Hunter St., Atlanta, Tues. Interred: Hollywood. AG 5/31/1910

BRYSON, Mary, Mrs. funeral Tues. Interred: Marietta, Ga. AG 4/5/1910

BUCHANAN, Andrew J., age 79, d. at Edgewood, Ga. AG 5/23/1907

BUCHANAN, Andrew Jackson (Uncle "Jack"), d. Tues., Candler Station, Atlanta, age 79. Interred: Oakland. AG 5/21/1907

BUCHANAN, Ellen, age 4, d. res. of parents, Mr. and Mrs. H. C. Holland, Lakewood Heights, Atlanta, Wed. Interred: Antioch Cemetery. AG 9/30/1909

BUCHANAN, Stacie, Mrs., age 77, d. 881 Marietta St. Atlanta. AG 3/22/1907

BUCHANAN, inf. of Mr. and Mrs. J. A., d. 120 S. Boulevard. Atlanta. AG 6/9/1906

BUCHER, Arthur S., Mrs., formerly known in Atlanta as Miss Ethel Butt, d. Wed. Winter Park, Fla. Husband, children, Conrad and Louise Bucher. Parents. Bro: Edward Butt, College Park. Interred: Winter Park, Fla. AG 10/20/1910

BUCK, Kate, Mrs., wife of Capt. B. B. of 17th Inf., d. Thurs. officers' qtrs, Ft. McPherson, age 36. Leaves 1 son, 2 married daus. She was native of Arizona. Interred: Washington, D. C. AG 6/14/1906

BUCKNER, Christina, 7-mo. dau. of Mr. and Mrs. C. E., d. 1 Weyman Ave., Atlanta, Thurs. Interred: Oakdale, Ga. AG 4/25/1907

BUCKNER, Julius, Jr., infant, d. Oakland City. Funeral Wed. at res. Oakland City. Interred: Westview. AG 6/6/1906

BUDD, James, Mrs. of Macon d. 7/27. Sis: Mrs. Willingham, Macon; Mrs. Frank Hawkins, Atlanta. Uncle: E. P. Knott, Atlanta. Dau. of Mrs. A. A. Coleman of Macon. Interred: Macon. AC 7/28/1905

BUFFINGTON, F. A., Mrs., age 50+, d. res. of dau., Mrs. Ora Wilson, Tilton, Ga., Sun. Interred: Rocky Face, Ga. Sons: James, John, Mark, Paul. AG 7/19/1910

BUGGS, Pauline, colored, age 1, d. 41 Bush St. Atlanta. AG 8/25/1910

BUICE, C. W. d. 9/12 Louisville, Ky. Interred: Atlanta, Oakland Cemetery. AC 9/14/1905

BUICE, Elisha, age 74, d. res. of dau., Mrs. Lizzie Edlemann, 67 W. Alexander St., Atlanta, Thurs. Confederate Veteran. Wife: Mrs. E. Ch: Mrs. Lizzie Edlemann, W. H. Buice. Interred: Oakland. AG 1/24/1908

BUICE, Madison, Major, age 77, d. Fitzgerald, Ga. Tues. Interred: Oakland. AG 10/9/1907

BUICE, R. M., Jr., infant son of R. M., d. Tues. 610 Marietta St., Atlanta. Interred: New Hope church yard. AG 5/31/1906

BUICE, Thomas J., infant son of Mr. and Mrs. A. S. interred Roswell, Ga. AG 9/14/1907

BUICKEM, Albertine, Mrs. d. Sat. Jackson St, age 73. Son: J. B. Daus: Frances, Mrs. W. F. Sanders. AG 1/13/1908

BULL, E. V., Mrs., age 67, d. Tues 137 Milledge Ave., Atlanta, wid. of late James A. Bull. Children: Mrs. J. H. Conkle of Lovejoy, Ga., Miss Ida Bull and Lon T. Bull. Res. 137 Milledge Ave. Atlanta. Interred: Jonesboro. AG 7/10/1907

BULL, William Tillinghast, Dr., New York surgeon, d. Savannah, Ga. Interred: New York. AG 2/22/1909

BULLARD, Edward, inf. son of Mr. and Mrs. J. H., d. Edgewood Wed. Interred: Bremen. AG 5/29/1906

BULLARD, H. N., Rev. d. Kansas City. Wife was Miss Mary Payne, sister of Miss Annie E. Payne, Atlanta teacher. AG 2/14/1908

BULLARD, Henry, Mrs., formerly Miss Mary Payne, d. Kansas City, Mo. Sis: Miss Annie Payne, Atlanta teacher. AG 2/13/1908

BULLARD, Ida, Mrs., age 34, wife of W. F., d. 214 W. Fair St. Atlanta. Interred: Mableton, Ga. AG 11/2/1907

BULLARD, John, Cobb Co. man who killed his dau. must hang 3/1. AG 2/19/1907

BULLARD, W. P., age 29, d. 101 N. Butler St. Atlanta Sat. Interred: Powder Springs, Ga. AG 11/19/1907

BULLARD, William A., age 77, d. Decatur, Ga. AG 5/21/1910

BULLOCK, Henry, age 89, Confederate veteran, d. Thurs. Rutland Dist., Macon. Leaves wife, w children. Mrs. August Meyers, James Bullock. AG 2/9/1907

BULLOCK, Virgil A., age 25, d. Mon. Interred: Logansville, Ga. AG 2/22/1910

BURAM, Vassie Haarm, mrs., age 30, d. at Fulton Tower (jail). AG 5/1/1907

BURCH, Harry, age 22, d. Central rr yards, Atlanta. AG 7/11/1907

BURCH, Harry, switchman, crushed to death Wed., age 23. Leaves wife, one child. Interred: Flippen, Ga. AG 7/11/1907

BURCKLE, William, Mrs. of Chattanooga, Tenn., funeral mother's res., Mrs. Wm. J. Garrett, 124 Washington St. Atlanta, Thurs. Interred: Westview. Sis: Mrs. Warren Boyd, Mrs. Estelle Garrett Baker of Atlanta. Husband, infant son. AG 6/9/1910

BURDEN, A. A., age 33, d. 542 Chestnut St. Atlanta. AG 12/17/1910

BURDEN, John, age 30, shot and killed by Will Smith, age 15, Sparta, Ga. AG 3/11/1907

BURDEN, John W., infant, d. 156 Wheeler St. Atlanta. AG 2/14/1910

BURDETT, infant of Mr. and Mrs. Jesse, age 4 mos., d. 10/29 Atlanta. AC 11/2/1905

BURDETT, Bessie, Mrs., age 20, d. 96 Powell St. Atlanta. AG 2/8/1907

BURDETT, C. E., age 30, d. 15 Fort Hood St. Atlanta. AG 10/1/1907

BURDETT, C. L. d. Sat. 13 Fort Hood Place, Atlanta. Interred: Hollywood. AG 9/28/1907

BURDETT, Cornelia, colored, age 39, d. Decatur, Ga. AG 12/11/1908

BURDETT, George Daniel, age 18 mos., son of Mr. and Mrs. John, d. Center Hill, Ga., Tues. Interred: Mt. Perrin Church yard. AG 6/21/1910

BURDETT, John, Mrs. d. Center Hill, Ga. AG 6/22/1910

BURDETT, Luther, age 13, son of W. B., d. 306 W. 4th St., Atlanta, Tues. Interred: Sandy Springs church yard. AG 12/15/1909

BURDETTE, Charles, inf. son of Mr. and Mrs. George, d. 58 Bellwood Ave., Atlanta, Sun. AG 2/24/1908

BURDETTE, Seaborn, colored, age 36, d. 302 Fort St. Atlanta. AG 12/29/1910

BURDETTE, W. C. funeral Mon. Atlanta. Interred: Godby's church yard. AG 6/4/1906

BURDGE, W. R., engineer, d. Jeff Davis St., Macon, yesterday, age 54. Leaves wife, son, 3 daus. Interred: Riverside. AG 1/20/1908

BURELL, W. A., age 54, d. 680 Ashby St. Atlanta. Interred: Dacula, Ga. AG 12/30/1910

BURFORD, Loyd, age 5, son of Mr. and Mrs. H. L., 120 Courtland St. d. Atlanta Mon. Interred: Jackson, Ga. AG 6/1/1909

BURGE, Charlotte, colored, age 90, d. 71 Valentine St. Atlanta. AG 7/9/1908

BURGE, George E., age 34, d. Fulton Co. Jail. AG 4/18/1910

BURGE, Lovey, Mrs. murdered 5/17. George Burge, husband, charged with murder, arrested at cousin's home, George McCravy. Son: Frank Britton. Dau: Lottie May Britton. AG 6/3/1909

BURGE, Rufus killed at Cordele, Ga. Bro: Will. AC 11/4/1905

BURGER, David, inmate of Confederate Soldiers' Home, Atlanta, d. Tues. Interred: Westview. Dau: Mrs. Phillips, Atlanta. Was Sgt. in Co. $, 4th Ga. Regt. AG 9/22/1909

BURGER, infant of Mr. and Mrs. B. H., d. 11 Hilliard St. Atlanta. AG 7/30/1906

BURGESS, Katherine Elizabeth, inf. dau. of Mr. and Mrs. B. F., d. Tues. Decatur, Ga. Interred: Wesley Chapel Cemetery. AG 8/25/1909

BURGESS, Lena, age 12 yrs., dau. of Jonathan of Decatur, Ga., d. Tues. Funeral at Wesley Chapel Church. AG 4/7/1910

BURGESS, Toronia, Mrs., age 38, d. 20 Howell St. Atlanta. AG 8/19/1909

BURGESS, W. A. , age 45, of Trion, Ga. killed Sat. by falling from cliffs. Raised in Morgan Co. Leaves wife, several children. AG 3/11/1907

BURK, Fannie, colored, age 48, d. 17 Liberty St. Atlanta. AG 5/8/1906

BURK, Harry, switchman, killed in yards of terminal station, Atlanta, Wed. AG 7/10/1907

BURKE, Eliza B., Mrs., age 70, d. 508 Peachtree St. Atlanta. AG 11/1/1909

BURKE, John, atty, d. 7/9 Huntsville, Ala. Leaves wife. AC 7/10/1905

BURKE, Martha, age 2 mos., d. 81 Doane St. Atlanta. AG 10/22/1906

BURKE, Ruby Lee, age 5 mos., d. Oakland City. AG 6/ 7/1907

BURKERT, Henrietta L., Mrs., age 79, b. Germany, 541 N. Jackson St. Atlanta. m. late John M. Burkert, New Orleans (dead 7 yrs.) Bro: Capt. Herman Outling, Milwaukee. Ch: Amelia, Henrietta, Paul. Grdau: Sara Henrietta Burkert. AG 6/15/1908

BURKETTE, Sarah, negro servant, killed by explosion of kerosene Oil at Skipperton, Ga. 12/7. AG 12/8/1910

BURKETT, William Philip, age 42, d. 6 Dixon P., Atlanta, Thurs. Wife, one child. Interred: Franklin, Ind. AG 7/31/1908

BURKS, J. B., age 70, d. Atlanta. AG 6/9/1910

BURKS, J. H. d. 366 Leggetts Ave., Atlanta. Wife, one dau., 5 sons. Interred: Westview. AG 6/8/1910

BURKS, J. H. funeral Thurs. E. Atlanta Baptist Church. Interred: Westview. Ag 6/9/1910

BURKS, John D., age 55, d. East Point, Ga. AG 4/13/1907

BURLINGAME, P., Mrs., age 88, d. 129 Hunnicutt St. Atlanta. AG 10/25/1906

BURLINGTON, S. P., Mrs., 88, of Moscow, NY d. dau's home, Mrs. Robt Ervin, 129 Hunnicutt St. Atlanta. Dau: Mrs. Alice McClair. Grch: Mrs. Preston P. Williams, Jonesboro, SC, Mrs. Robt A. Ervin, M. D. McClair. Bur: Walhalla, SC AG 10/20/1906

BURMEON, Mary, colored, age 67, d. 17 Howell St. Atlanta. AG 1/14/1908

BURNETT, A. A., Mrs. of Rome, Ga., d. Sat. home of sister, 210 W. Harris St. Atlanta. Interred: Romne. AG 7/10/1906

BURNETT, Callie Belle, Mrs. d. Mon. Norcross, Ga. Relative of Congressman T. M. Bell. Husband, 3 children, survive. Interred: White Co., Cleveland. AG 10/6/1909

BURNETT, E. P., Capt. d. Sun. Columbus, Ga., age 72, Vet. of Civil War. Wife, 3 children. Bro-in-law: G. Gunby Jordan. AG 1/4/1910

BURNETT, Henry of Jones Co. d. Jan. 24. Interred: Burial grounds near Haddock´s Station. AC 1/25/1905

BURNETT, Spencer, inf. son of Mr. and Mrs. R. A. of 92 Park Ave., Atlanta, d. Fri. AG 1/29/1910

BURNEY, Machen, negro, run over by yard engine, Adrain, Ga. AG 8/13/1906

BURNHAM, B. R., Admrs. Sale by Mrs. Josie C. Burnham, admx. AG 11/21/1907

BURNHAM, Norma, age 3, dau. of Mr. and Mrs. Richard, d. Fri. S. Macon. AG 4/25/1908

BURNHAM, T.Y., age 73, d. 48 Simpson St. Atlanta. AG 9/14/1908

BURNS, Christina, Mrs., age 83, d. grdau.´s res., Mrs. M. B. Seaborn, 60 W. Pine St., Atlanta, Mon. Interred: Westview. AG 2/4/1908

BURNS, Eliza, colored, age 29, d. 101 N. Butler St. Atlanta. AG 11/7/1907

BURNS, Frank, colored, age 62, d. 10 Mangum St. Atlanta. AG 5/18/1907

BURNS, Harry A., age 2 mos., d. 67 Jones Ave. Atlanta. AG 6/1/1907

BURNS, Harvie, son of Mrs. Samuel, d. Carrollton, Ga. first wk. Feb. AC 2/14/1905

BURNS, Hershel killed by Gordon McDonald. AG 3/1/1907

BURNS, Herchel. Macon, Ga. 12/25. As result of quarrel at Cochran, Ga., Sun., Gordon McDonald shot and killed Coley Cheney and Herchel. AG 12/25/1906

BURNS, Horace, colored, age 14, d. 101 N. Butler St. Atlanta. AG 4/21/1908

BURNS, Jimmie. Newnan, Ga., 12/14. Body of Jimmie Burns, old Irishman, who who resided alone in his hut near Sharpsburg, Ga. It is thought he was murdered. AG 12/14/1906

BURNS, Mary H., Mrs., wife of Michael H., d. 67 Jones Ave., Atlanta, Sat. AG 11/23/1907

BURNS, Samuel, Mrs., abt age 50, d. 2/12 Carrollton, Ga. Son: Harvie Burns (who d. Carrollton last wk.). AC 2/14/1905

BURNS, Sidney, Mrs. d. sister´s res., Mrs. Patrick Cassidy, Montgomery, Ala. Bros: C. T. Johnson, N. Y.; T. P. Johnson, Atlanta. Sis: Mrs. Cassidy; Mrs. John McGuire, Knoxville, Tenn.; Mrs. Patrick McGuire, Atlanta. AG 5/17/1910

BURNS, W. H., Mrs., age 36, d. Atlanta. Interred: Westview. AG 11/25/1907

BURNS, Walter, colored, age 35, d. rear of 41 Houston St. Atlanta. AG 10/13/1908

BURPITT, Grace Margaret, age 14 mos., dau. of Mr. and Mrs. W. P. Burpitt, d. Ellijay, Ga., Sat. Interred: Decatur. AG 7/30/1906

BURR, Mary Lucille, Mrs., wife of late Henry C., d. Fri. Griffin. She married Mr. Burr in 1870, mother of 4 children, one the late Capt. A. J. Burr who d. short while ago. AG 9/13/1909

BURROUGH, J. T., Mrs., age 56, d. 260 Simpson St., Atlanta, Thurs. Interred: Kingston, Ga. AG 12/9/1909

BURROUGHS, Louise, Mrs., age 72, d. 25 Doane St. Atlanta. AG 3/21/1910

BURSON, John, colored, age 62, d. 101 N. Butler St. Atlanta. AG 7/8/1909

BURT, Harry B., age 26, d. Wed. 73 Milledge Ave., Atlanta. Mother, four brothers, two sisters. Interred: Westview. AG 6/12/1907

BURT, Katherine, Sister d. 3/2 res. of sister, near Kennesaw. Born 7/8/1842, dau. of late Col. Ashmede Burt of Pendleton, S. C., early Gov. of Nebraska. AC 3/4/1905

BURT, W. Z., wealthy planter, of Buena Vista, found dead in Beaverun Creek 10/15. Wife, several children, survive. AG 10/16/1909

BURTEN, Bessie, Miss, age 25, d. Edgewood, Ga. AG 1/24/1907

BURTINI, Matt, Italian Marble worker, employed Carnegie Library, d. City Hospital, Columbus yesterday. Wife, children. Res. near Ponce de Leon Springs, Atlanta. Interred: Atlanta

BURTON, Alfred, Mrs., age 42, d. Tues. Chamblee, Ga. Husband. Daus: Addie, Maria, Pearl. Interred: Flat Rock Church yard. AG 8/16/1910

BURTON, Dora, Mrs., age 42, wife of Alfred, d. Tues. Chamblee, Ga. Interred: Flat Rock Church. AG 8/17/1910

BURTON, Edgar, inf. son of Mr. and Mrs. J. M., d. AG 2/14/ 9 0

BURTON, Ida J., Mrs., age 63, d. 574 New York Ave., Edgewood, Ga. Thurs. Interred: Social Circle, Ga. Two daus, one son, survive. AG 10/30/1908

BURTON, John C., minister, age 58, d. Stockade Rd. Wife of 381 E. Fair St. Atlanta. Interred: Social Circle. AG 8/4/1906

BURTON, Lizzie, age 27, d. 128 West Ga. Ave. Atlanta. AG 3/1/1907

BURTON, M. W., age 58, d. 245 Woodward Ave. Atlanta. AG 3/27/1909

BURTON, R. H., lifelong res. of Midville, Burke Co., Ga., d. 8/25. Interred: Bark Camp Cemetery. Wife. Son: Musgrove Burton, Midville. AG 8/30/1909

BURTON, Thomas L., ex-Confederate soldier, age 73, d. S. New Decatur, Ala. Tues. AG 7/2/1908

BURTZ, J. M., age 33, d. 83 Garden St. Atlanta. Interred: Marietta. AG 6/29/1908

BURTZ, Marguerite L., Mrs. lawsuit against co. for saw killing her husband. AC 4/6/1905

BUSH, Charles, age 60, d. 10/26 Atlanta. Interred: Westview. AG 10/27/1910

BUSH, Lennie W., age 31, d. Milledgeville, 10/13. AG 10/14/1910

BUSH, Ludy, colored, age 17, d. 183 Robbins St. Atlanta. AG 12/11/1908

BUSH, R. B., Rev. d. Covington, Ga. 10/6. Alabama minister, age 73. Large family. AC 10/7/ 905

BUSH, T. W., Professor of Madison, Ind. Bro: C. P. Bush, Gadsden, Ala. AG 8/14/1906

BUTCHER, Alfred Robert, age 51, d. Sun. 54 Connally St., Atlanta, Tues. Interred: Westview. AG 10/27/1908

BUTLER, A. G., Mrs., age 53, d. 743 Glenn St., Atlanta, Mon. Interred: Rock Springs Church. AG 1/11/1910

BUTLER, Annie, colored, age 29, d. 409 Richardson St., Atlanta. AG 10/1/1907

BUTLER, Anson Green, Mrs., age 53, d. Atlanta. AG 1/12/1910

BUTLER, Clarence, inf. son of Mr. and Mrs. A. J., 674 E. Fair St., Atlanta, d. Sat. Interred: Westview. AG 4/18/1910

BUTLER, Clarence J., age 11 mos., d. 670 E. Fair St. Atlanta. AG 4/18/1910

BUTLER, Elsie Pauline, infant of Mr. and Mrs. I. H., d. 68 N. Georgia Ave. Atlanta. Interred: Dallas, Ga. AG 3/22/1910

BUTLER, Francis E., age 4 mos., d. 138 Williams St. Atlanta. AG 5/9/1910

BUTLER, George, age 1, d. 275 Fraser St. Atlanta. AG 11/7/1907

BUTLER, George E., age 46, d. 69 McDaniel St., Atlanta. Wife, one dau: Jennie Butler. Sons: Roy, Carrie, Guy. One sister, three bros. Interred: Dallas, Tx. AG 11/7/1910

BUTLER, Henry, age 59, d. 424 Ira St. Atlanta. AG 5/8/1907

BUTLER, Henry, colored, age 8 mos., d. 226 W. Mitchell St. Atlanta. AG 7/9/1909

BUTLER, Holmes, age 3, d. Atlanta. AG 10/12/1909

BUTLER, J. E., Mrs. d. Tues. Eufaula, Ala. Funeral at sister's res., Mrs. J. E. Rabb, Gordon St., Atlanta. Interred: Westview. AG 12/29/1909

BUTLER, J. M. d. Tues. 525 Highland Ave., Atlanta. Interred: Rock Springs church yard. AG 5/1/1907

BUTLER, J. R., age 74, d. 84 Fortress Ave., Atlanta, Sun. Interred: Westview. Ch: J. E. Butler, Mrs. Roach, J. C. Butler, Atlanta, and C. R. Butler, Hull, Ga. AG 10/19/1908

BUTLER, J., Mrs., age 46, d. Tues. Grady Hospital, Atlanta. AG 10/2/1907

BUTLER, John G. d. Savannah 10/26. Son: George. AG 10/26/1907

BUTLER, John Henry, colored, age 7, d. 138 McDaniel St. Atlanta. AG 1/28/1907

BUTLER, Josephine, colored, age 45, d. Atlanta Heights. AG 10/2/1907

BUTLER, Kathleen, 5 mos. of Mr. and Mrs. G. J., d. 15 Fowler St. Atlanta. Interred: Westview. AG 10/18/1906

BUTLER, Lavonia, colored, age 33, d. 4 Berkele St. Atlanta. AG 9/28/1910

BUTLER, Mamie, Mrs., wife of Capt., William, of fire dept., funeral Mon. Atlanta. Interred: Westview. AG 8/8/1910

BUTLER, Mary, inf. dau. of Mr. and Mrs. W. A. of 25 Rhinehart St., Atlanta, Wed. Interred: Hollywood. AG 4/22/1908

BUTLER, Mary E., Mrs., age 66, d. Fri. 194 Kennedy St. Atlanta. Interred: Westview. AG 5/27/1907

BUTLER, Mattie, colored, age 36, d. St. Louis, Mo. AG 8/6/1907

BUTLER, Michael, age 10, son of Mr. and Mrs. R. E., d. Thurs. Hawkinsville, Ga. Interred: Orange Hill Cemetery. AG 8/17/1908

BUTLER, Robert Heiman, age 9, d. Atlanta. AG 9/1/1908

BUTLER, Sadie, colored, age 17, d. 424 Ira St. Atlanta. AG 8/5/1907

BUTLER, Sallie, colored, age 1 mo., died Piedmont Avenue, Atlanta. AG 1/29/1906

BUTLER, Susie, colored, age 38, d. 89 Reid St. Atlanta. AG 5/4/1909

BUTLER, Troupe interred: Washington, Ga. Body brought from Chattanooga, Tenn. He was age 81. Dau: Mrs. W. H. Toombs, Washington, Ga. He res. Chattanooga. AG 10/27/1909

BUTLER, Anderson C., age 45, Bibb Co. farmer, d. Houston Rd., Sat. Parents, 5 sisters, 3 bros. AG 12/17/1910

BUTLER, E. W., Mrs., wife of Hon. E. W., 3rd dau. of late Sen. Joshua Hill. Dau: Virginia. Sisters; Mrs. Hayes of Washington, D. C., Mrs. Belle Nash, Mrs. Richard Turnbull of Madison, Ga. Niece: Mrs. W. G. Obear, Atlanta. AG 10/16/1906

BUTT, John F., Rev., N. C. Minister, d. 11/2 Charlotte, N. C. AC 11/3/1905

BUTT, Kate, age 51, d. 294 Courtland St. Atlanta. Interred: Balirsville, Ga. AG 10/8/1909

BUTT, Lamar, age 21 days, d. 136 S. Moreland Ave. Atlanta. AG 5/21/1910

BUTT, M. C., Mrs., age 63, d. 525 Whitehall St. Atlanta. AG 5/8/1907

BUTT, William Thomas, Capt., ex-Confederate soldier, d. 6/24 Augusta. AG 6/25/1907

BUTTERWORTH, J. P., age 36, d. Atlanta Wed. Interred: Canton, Ga. AG 11/17/1910

BUTTRICE, T. H., Mrs., age 21, d. 17 W. Cain St. Atlanta. AG 9/3/1907

BUTTS, A. J., age 29, d. 169 Luckie St. Atlanta. AG 3/28/1907

BUTTS, Carrie, colored, age 28, d. 152 E. Harris St. Atlanta. AG 10/20/1908

BUTTS, Jere d. N. Orange St., Eufaula, Ala. Tues. Interred: Fairfiew Cemetery. He was b. Ga. 7/11/1855. Wife, two daus., one son. AG 9/10/1909

BUTT, Martha, Mrs., age 64, wid of Wm C., d. 525 Whitehall St., Atlanta. Bur: Norwood. Ch: R. I., W. C., Mrs. D. W. Wheeler, Mayfield, Ga.; Mrs. W. B. Cody, Atlanta. She was Miss Barksdale, dau. of Wm Barksdale of Warren Co. AG 5/7/1907

BUXTON, Bernard, age 4, d. Atlanta. AG 5/24/1906

BUZZETT, Mary Carmel, age 11 mos., dau. of Mr. and Mrs. W. D., d. grandmother's res., Mrs. J. J. Gannon, 42 Woodward Ave. Interred: Apalachicola, Fla. AG 6/22/1908

BYARS, Henry and Herbert, brothers, living 12 miles SW of Dawson, shot and robbed 9/11. AG 9/12/1908

BYARS, O. M. killed 12/1905 at dance in Spalding Co. Pardons granted: John Wesley, Landa and Newton Goodin of Spalding Co. for murder. AG 5/23/1907

BYARS, Robert, colored, age 28, d. Howell's Sta. Atlanta. AG 4/13/1907

BYERS, J. L., Mrs., age 77, d. 625 Washington St., Atlanta, Thurs. AG 11/11/1909

BYNES, Annie, colored, age 100, d. 239 Irwin St. Atlanta. AG 9/30/1910

BYNUM, John, ordinary of Columbia Co., ex-mbr Ga. legislature, d. Harlem last night, age 64. Interred: Harlem. AG 7/4/1907

BYNUM, O. H., Mrs. d. Courtland, Ala. Sun. Interred: City Cemetery, Decatur, Ala. Dau: Mrs. Luett P. Wallace, Decatur, Ala. Husband, three daus, son. AG 1/20/1910

BYRD, Ed, colored, age 29, d. Knotts Crossing. Atlanta. AG 8/21/1907

BYRD, George removed from jail in dying condition, to Macon city hospital. AG 12/26/1907

BYRD, Nettie, Mrs., age 60, d. 68 Atlanta Ave., Oct. 2. AG 10/3/1910

BYRD, W. D., age 64, d. Atlanta Sun. Wife, four daus. Mrs. T. B. Carroll, Miss Margaret Byrd, and W. C. Byrd. Interred: Canton, Ga. AG 8/10/1908

BYRNE, William M. age 50, d. Fri. 27 Haynes St. Atlanta. Interred: Westview. AG 11/5/1910

BYRNE, William M. d. Mon. res. of parents, Mr. and Mrs. W. M., Atlanta. Interred: Westview. AG 10/25/1910

BYRON, John, negro, taken from county jail Byron, Ga., shot, cremated. AG 10/26/1907

BYRON, G. S., Rev., age 74, d. Thurs. Atlanta, res. of Carrollton, Ga. Interred: Carrollton, Ga. AG 5/15/1908

CABANISS, J. W., Mrs. d. Sun. night Macon. Interred: Rose Hill. AG 1/30/1908

CABANISS, Juliet McKay, mrs., wid. of late George Augustus Cabaniss, d. 175 Augusta Ave., Atlanta, Fri. Interred: Oakland. AG 5/30/1908

CABBLE, Howard, age 2, son of Mr. and Mrs. John R., d. Fri., Atlanta. AG 6/10/1910

CABLE, J. J., Mrs., age 36, d. 25 Wylie St., Atlanta, Sat. Husband, several children. Interred: Concord, Ga. AG 12/10/1910

CAGLE, Billy, Uncle, age 105, d. near Powers Ferry, Atlanta, Wed. Ch: Billy, Jr., Burch, Marion, Daniel; Mrs. G. G. Cook; Mrs. Dick Beddington. He was b. S. C. 1803, came to Ga. age of 18. AG 2/19/1908

CAGLE, G. J. d. Sun. Haralson, Ga. AG 4/24/1907

CAGLE, Henry M., Gainesville, fatally shot by unknown person. AG 8/25/1906

CAGLE, Lily May, age 9, dau. of Mr. and Mrs. J., d. Flat Shoals Rd. Atlanta. Interred: Hollywood. AG 11/2/1907

CAIN, Eva, colored, age 20, d. 101 N. Butler St. Atlanta. AG 4/22/1909

CAIN, Harry M., age 11 mos., son of Mr. and Mrs. W. M., d. 392 Glenwood Ave. Atlanta. Interred: Antioch Church. AG 6/26/1908

CAIN, Lorena, age 9, dau. of Mr. and Mrs. M. A., d. Thurs. Vannoy St., Atlanta. Interred: Camp Creek church yard. AG 5/23/1907

CAIN, Mary E., age 29, d. Edgewood, Ga. AG 5/21/1907

CAIN, Richard, age 2, son of Mr. and Mrs. N. P. Cain, d. Fri. 14 High St. Atlanta. Interred: Roswell, Ga. AG 7/6/1907

CAIN, Sarah, colored, age 2, d. 270 Martin St. Atlanta. AG 8/14/1907

CAIN, Sarah C., Mrs., age 72, d. 34 N. Boulevard. Atlanta. AG 9/2/1909

CALDWELL, A. E., Mrs., age 63, d. Dr. Noble's Sanitarium. Atlanta. Interred: Newnan, Ga. AG 7/23/1907

CALDWELL, C. M., age 40, d. 651 Division St., Atlanta, Wed. Wife, two sons: C. H. and M. G. Caldwell of Macon. Interred: Americus, Ga. AG 1/3/1908

CALDWELL, J. W., Mrs., age 45, d. Marietta, Ga. AG 9/20/1906

CALDWELL, John Lawrence, age 65, d. 148 Richardson St. Atlanta. AG 3/3/1909

CALDWELL, Katie, Miss, age 23, d. 264-1/2 Decatur St., Atlanta, Sat. AG 2/8/1908

CALDWELL, Mary J., Miss, age 65, d. 92 Luckie St. Atlanta. AG 12/2/1909

CALDWELL, Mattie, colored, age 56, d. McDaniel St. Atlanta. AG 12/2/1910

CALDWELL, Jasper W., Mrs. d. Cherokee St. Husband; dau., Eleanor Caldwell. AG 9/20/1906

CALDWELL, E. B., Donalsonville, Ga., 11/12/ 906. Young son of John R. Caldwell fatally crushed by falling boiler. AG 11/12/1906

CALOWAY, William, colored, age 56, died 148 McDaniel St., Atlanta. AG 12/14/1906

CALHORNE, Henry, colored, age 30, d. 21 S. 20th St., Birmingham, Ala. AG 12/17/1910

CALHOUN, Carrie, colored, age 2, d. S. Pryor Rd. Atlanta. AG 7/16/1909

CALHOUN, Edward B., age 69, d. 94 Ponce de Leon Ave. Atlanta. AG 9/26/1910

CALHOUN, George E. d. 6/19 Macon, Ga. Wife was Miss Sallie Robertson. Dau: Elizabeth, age 7. Interred: Sardis Church. AG 6/21/1909

CALHOUN, Holt, age 5, son of A. D. Calhoun, fell into pile of cotton, smothered to death, Macon. AG 10/16/1906

CALHOUN, Ida, Miss, age 18, niece of Rev. C. M. Wilkinson, killed herself in Westview cemetery. AG 8/7/1906

CALHOUN, John, colored, age 16, d. 107 N. Butler St. Atlanta. AG 2/19/1907

CALHOUN, Julia, colored, age 26, d. 190 W. Peachtree St., rear, Atlanta. AG 7/12/1907

CALHOUN, Margaret M., Miss d. 2/15/1910. Honored by Joseph Habersham Chapter, D. A. R. AG 3/10/1910

CALHOUN, Margie, Miss, age 62, d. Tues. Atlanta. Interred: Oakland. AG 2/16/1910

CALHOUN, Mary Jane, Mrs., wife of Judge Lowndes, d. 10/21 Atlanta. Interred: Oakland. AC 10/23/1905

CALHOUN, Stella, age 10, dau. of Mr. and Mrs. W. B., d. 56 Wyman St., Atlanta, Wed. Interred: Sylvester. AG 1/16/1908

CALLAWAY, E. B., Mrs., age 50, d. 156 Gordon St. Atlanta. AG 4/20/1908

CALLAWAY, Eliza Phelan, Mrs. of Washington, Ga. d. Atlanta Wed. Husband: John I. Two daus. Cousin: E. C. Callaway. Interred: Washington, Ga. AG 7/7/1909

CALLAWAY, Emma Bernard, Mrs., age 50, d. 156 Gordon St. Atlanta Sun. Son: Roland. Wife of late William Callaway. Interred: Athens, Ga. AG 4/20/1908

CALLAWAY, J. M., Rev. d. LaGrange 5/11. Interred: West Point, Ga. Age 77. Wife. Ch: A. W. Callaway, LaGrange, Mrs. Oslin, Atlanta, Rev. Thomas Callaway, Pensavcola, Fla., Mrs. Charles D. Brady, Jersey City, N. J. AG 5/11/1908

CALLAWAY, Merrell P., Jr., son of Mr. and Mrs. M. P., d. 5/22, Macon. AG 5/23/1907

CALLAWAY, Roxie, age 39, veteran Atlanta newsboy, d. 357 Terry St. Atlanta. Interred: Westview. AG 7/21/1909

CALLAWAY, Tommie, colored, age 17, d. 8 Bishop St. Atlanta. AG 10/20/1908

CALLAWAY, W. W., Mrs., age 29, d. Washington St., E. Point, Ga. Thurs. Husband, four small children. Interred: Mt. Olive Church. AG 4/1/1910

CALLIS, John, age 34, d. Atlanta Mon. Interred: McDonough. AG 6/4/1906

CALLOWAY, Earl, age 6, son of Mr. and Mrs. . G., d. Mon. Ellenwood, Ga. Interred: Ellenwood church yard. AG 4/25/1906

CALLOWAY, Frank, colored, age 26, d. 150 E. Ellis St. Atlanta. AG 12/18/1907

CALLOWAY, Sam, colored, age 35, d. 200 Maple St. Atlanta. AG 10/1/1908

CALLOWAY, Willie, negro, killed at Hudson Camp #4, near Adamsville, Ga., Thurs. AG 8/1/1907

CALVIN, Sanders, colored, age 20, d. 68 Logans alley. Atlanta. AG 6/7/1907

CAMERON, Christina Katherine, infant dau. of Mr. and Mrs. J. S., d. Sat. 138 E. Pine St., Atlanta. Interred: vault at Oakland. AG 6/25/1907

CAMP,Benjamin A. d. 11/15 35 Bailey St., Atlanta. Interred: Oakland. AC 11/17/1905

CAMP, C. D. interred Douglasville Wed. AG 7/10/1906

CAMP, Evelyn L. d. 106 Windsor St. Atlanta. AG 3/28/1907

CAMP, Forrest E., eldest son of Mr. and Mrs. W. E., d. 14 St. Charles Ave., Atlanta, Sat., son of W. E. Camp. Interred: Westview. AG 11/2/1907

CAMP, Foster Hunter, age 4, son of Luther D. Camp of 38 Wheeler St., Atlanta, d. Fri. Interred: Woodstock, Ga. AG 8/4/1910

CAMP, H. W., Judge of Coweta Co., Ga. d. at home in Moreland yesterday., age abt 70. AG 1/1/1908

CAMP, Harry H., age 26, d. 62 S. Jackson St., Atlanta, Mon. Interred: Oakland. Parents: Mr. and Mrs. William M. Camp. Sisters: Mrs. C. W. Allen, Miss Ivy Camp, Miss Kate Camp. Bros: Charles, J. H., J. E. AG 12/20/1909

CAMP, Imogene, Mrs., age 28, d. Thurs. Marton Hotel, Atlanta, wife of W. H. Parents: Mr. and Mrs. R. E. Sims of Newnan, Ga. Interred: Newnan. AG 5/27/1910

CAMP, J. B., Miss, age 65, d. 129 Courtland St. Atlanta. AG 9/2/1909

CAMP, Margaret, Mrs., age 80, d. 9/22 63 S. Jackson St., Atlanta. Daus: Mrs. F. D. Mitchell, Mrs. W. G. Mitchell, Mrs. E. L. Church, Atlanta. Interred: Lithonia, Ga. AG 9/22/1909

CAMP, Pearl, colored, age 22, d. 101 N. Butler St. Atlanta. AG 7/9/1908

CAMP, William of Atlanta d. Boaz, Ala. Fri. Interred: Westview. AG 10/15/1906

CAMPBELL, Adrian F., age 7 mos., d. 101 N. Boulevard. Atlanta. AG 8/24/1908

CAMPBELL, Bessie May, Mrs., wife of O. F., d. 438 Pulliam St., Atlanta, Wed. Husband, one child, mother, father, two sisters, three brothers, survive. AG 5/22/1907

CAMPBELL, C. B. d. 10/1 Walnut St., Macon. AG 10/2/1909

CAMPBELL, C. H. formerly of Atlanta d. Tues. New York City. Interred: Macon, Ga. AG 3/27/1908

CAMPBELL, Catherine, Miss, age 79, d. 82 W. Harris St., Atlanta, Wed. Interred: Knoxville, Ga. AG 1/8/1908

CAMPBELL, E. F., Jr., inf. son of Mr. and Mrs. E. F. of 100 S. Boulevard, Atlanta, d. Sun. Interred: Westview. AG 9/6/1909

CAMPBELL, Emma, Mrs., age 65, d. son-in-law's res., Charles W. Bernhardt, 21 McAfee St., Atlanta, Wed. Daus: Mrs. Dora M. Smith, Mrs. Alice M. Jansen, Mrs. Bernhardt. AG 5/5/1909

CAMPBELL, Eudocia, Mrs. of Watkinsville, age 67, d. 1/24. Son: Thurmond Campbell, Watkinsville. Husband d. several yrs. ago. Interred: Watkinsville. AG 1/25/1910

CAMPBELL, George W., age 51, d. Atlanta. AG 3/15/1910

CAMPBELL, J. B., age 41, d. 110 W. Baker St. Atlanta. AG 2/24/1908

CAMPBELL, James, age 65, former res. of Atlanta, d. Augusta. Leave wife, 2 children. Interred: Oakland. AG 2/9/1907

CAMPBELL, Jane, Mrs., mother of Dr. J. L., d. Hapeville, Mon. Interred: Mt. Zion Church. AG 10/2/1907

CAMPBELL, Joe, age 24, d. 14 Fraser St. Atlanta. AG 1/14/1907

CAMPBELL, John Christopher, age 9 mos., d. 19 Park St. Atlanta. AG 9/8/1909

CAMPBELL, Lawrence, age 2, d. 226 E. Ellis St. Atlanta. AG 12/30/1910

CAMPBELL, Millard T., age 50, d. Nashville, Tenn. AC 4/13/1905

CAMPBELL, Nellie L., age 1 yr., d. 60 Neal St. Atlanta. AG 6/8/1907

CAMPBELL, Reau d. Chicago, formerly of Atlanta. Son: Franc. Dau: Miss Maie Campbell, 27 E. Alexander St. Atlanta. AG 6/1/1909

CAMPBELL, Theresa, Miss, dau. of Mrs. N., d. 123 Hill St., Atlanta, Mon. Mother, bros., Charles J. Campbell, sister, Miss Mary E. Campbell. Interred: Westview. AG 10/29/1907

CAMPE, Forrest E., age 21, d. 16 St. Charles Ave. Atlanta. AG 11/5/1907

CAN, Henry, age 9 mos., d. 153 Bedford Pl. Atlanta. AG 10/4/1910

CANADA, M. L., age 56, d. Tabernacle Infirmary. Atlanta. Interred: High Shoals, Ga. AG 11/12/1907

CANADY, Ingram hanged LaGrange, Ga. 3/20. AG 3/20/1908

CANDLER, Allen D., age 75, d. 657 Edgewood Ave., Atlanta, Oct. 26. AG 10/27/1910

CANDLER, Asa Griggs III, grandson of Asa G. of Atlanta, d. Hartwell, Ga. 2/8. Parents: Mr. and Mrs. Asa G. Candler, Jr. of Hartwell. Funeral 61 Elizabeth St., Atlanta. AC Interred: Westview. 2/11/1905

CANDLER, Walker, colored, age 8, d. 21 Dunlap St. Atlanta. AG 7/15/1909

CANNON, Bettie, colored, age 40, d. 194 Piedmont Ave., Atlanta. AG 5/23/1907

CANNON, Drucilla, colored, age 48, d. Union Depot. AG 3/29/1909

CANNON, Joe, negro, murdered by Jesse Cook, negro, who is condemned to hang 2/25. AG 4/21/1910

CANNON, Joe, negro, of Cartersville, shot and killed by Jesse Cook who is to hang 2/25. AG 1/15/1910

CANNON, John J. d. Sat. 44 Woodward Ave., Atlanta. Interred: Oakland. AG 8/12/1907

CANNON, Kyle, age 50, shot and killed at E. McRae by son-in-law, Julian Allagood. Cannon leaves family. Allagood m. his dau. a few mos. ago. AG 7/18/1906

CANNON, Mary, Mrs., age 59, d. her home near Clayton, Ga. Sat. She was niece of late Chief Justice Logan E. Bleckley. 3 bros., 3 sisters, 5 daus., 2 sons, survive. Interred: Bleckley Family Burial Grounds. AG 10/18/1909

CANNON, Roscoe P., age 18, killed at Gray's Saw Mill, Waycross, Ga. From Horry Co., S. C. abt yr. ago. Bro: Bert. Interred: Horry Co., S. C. AC 6/27/1905

CANNON, William R. funeral Sun. Interred: Westview, Atlanta. AG 5/14/1906

CANOFE, James, age 61, retired soldier, d. 91 W. Humphries St., Atlanta, Sun. Wife in Washington, D. C. Interred: Marietta, Ga. Natl Cemegery. AG 3/9/1908

CANTER, J. L., age 69, res. Ducktown, Tenn. d. Wed. Atlanta. Interred: Ducktown, Tenn. AG 1/29/1908

CANTRELL, Glenn Lewis, inf. son of Mr. and Mrs. J. C., d. 317 Ormond St. Atlanta. Interred: Hollywood. AG 6/4/1910

CANTRELL, Margaret Louise, age 1 yr., d. 198 Forrest Ave. Atlanta. AG 2/8/1909

CAPES, Leo S. dead from accidentally shooting himself a week ago with shotgun. Interred: New York, his home. AG 11/29/1909

CAPPERS, Frederick S., ae 72, citizen of Dalton, Ga., d. son's res., Frederick S. Cappers, Jr., 6 Venable St., Atlanta, Thurs. Interred: Dalton, Ga., Family Burial Ground. AG 1/9/1908

CAPPS, Chester L., age 3, son of Mr. and Mrs. W. L., d. 135 Lovejoy St., Atlanta, Mon. Interred: Chamblee, Ga. AG 10/13/1908

CAPPS, Hubert Otto, age 1, d. 50 Daniel St. Atlanta. AG 5/24/1907

CAPPS, Washington Tazewell, age 75, father of Rear Admiral W. L., d. 6/29, Norvolk, Va. AC 6/30/1905

CAPPS, William A., Mrs. d. Fri. Athens, Ga. Interred: Oconee Cemetery. Husband. Son, Dau. AG 7/11/1910

CARAKER, Leighter, inf. son of Mr. and Mrs. T. L. of Tennille, Ga., d. Sat. AG 5/9/1908

CARAWAY, Roger, age 19, son of Mr. and Mrs. R. J. of 188 Davis St. Atlanta d. Tues. AG 6/30/1908

CARD, Ella, colored, age 16, d. 259 Windsor St. Atlanta. AG 5/10/1906

CARDELL, Evelyn Louise, age 12, dau. of Mr. and Mrs. C. E. of Machen, Ga., d. Atlanta Thurs. AG 12/23/1909

CARDEN, David, 8 mos., son of Mr. and Mrs. Roscoe, d. Atlanta Thurs., 16 Whitehall St. AG 7/8/1910

CAREY, E. M., Mrs., age 69, d. 419 N. Jackson St. Atlanta. AG 7/30/1906

CAREY, Eva, Miss, age 22, d. res. of sister, Mrs. J. L. Oxford, Dalton. Parents: Mr. and Mrs. Dan Casey. Sis: Mrs. J. L. Oxford, Mrs. Will Manning, Miss Ella Casey. Bro: Cliff Casey. AG 6/17/1910

CAREY, John, Mrs. d. Sat., 419 N. Jackson St., Atlanta. Husband, two sons, Dan and Paul Carey of Utah. Four daus: Mrs. Peter F. Clark, Mrs. Charles N. Roberts, Agnes and Gertrude Carey. Interred: Westview. AG 7/30/1906

CAREY, W. A. d. Montgomery, Ala., 30 Sayre St., Wed. AG 4/28/1910

CARGILL, Frank, age 36, d. Fri. 188 Capitol Ave., Atlanta. Interred: Columbus, Ga. Ag 6/14/1907

CARGILL, John S., age 65, civil war vet. d. 188 Capitol Ave. Atlanta. Interred: Columbus, former home. Survivors: Wife and ch: E. K. Cargill, Columbus; James A. Cargill, Dallas, Texas. AG 9/4/1906

CARIAN, **Bessie**, age 10 mos., d. 43 Tye St. Atlanta. AG 10/20/1909

CARLISLE, **Carrie E.**, **Miss**, age 25, d. 655 N. Boulevard. Atlanta. AG 4/25/1910

CARLISLE, **Carrie**, **Miss**, age 23, d. 655 N. Boulevard, Atlanta, Sat., dau. of Mr. and Mrs. Felix W. Bro: Felix W., Jr. Sis: Kate. Interred: Opelika, Ala. AG 4/25/1910

CARLISLE, **Carrie**, **Miss**, age 23, d. 655 N. Boulevard, Atlanta., dau of Mr. and Mrs. Felix W. Bro: Felix W., Jr. Sis: Miss Kate. Interred: Opelika, Ala. AG 4/25/1910

CARLISLE, **Frank**, colored, age 27, d. 31 Liberty St. Atlanta. AG 6/15/1909

CARLISLE, **Hattie**, colored, age 50, d. 101 N. Butler St. Atlanta. AG 10/11/1907

CARLTON, **Charles E.**, age 8 mos., d. 506 S. Pryor St. Atlanta. AG 12/3 /1910

CARLTON, **Ernest**, age 30, d. Thurs. College Park. Parents, three bros, survive. Interred: College Park, Ga. AG 6/19/1908

CARLTON, **Junius**, age 14, son of John M., d. Bowersville, Ga. AG 8/6/1907

CARLTON, **M. A.**, **Mrs.**, age 6 , d. Tues. Woodlawn, Ga. AG 6/29/1910

CARLTON, **Paul V.**, age 40, d. Fri. 152 Holderness St., Atlanta. Interred: College Park, Ga. AG 4/22/1910

CARMAN, **Maydell**, age 4, dau. of Mr. and Mrs. W. M., d. Howells Mill, Atlanta, Thurs. Interred: Family Grounds. AG 10/25/1907

CARMICHAEL, **Georgia**, **Miss**, dau. of Mr. and Mrs. R. A., d. 663 Chestnut St., Atlanta, Fri., age 33. Interred: Smyrna, Ga. AG 11/9/1907

CARMICHAEL, **John B.**, age 34, d. 125 Terry St. Atlanta. AG 5/25/1906

CARN, **Lizzie**, colored, age 10 mos., d. 8 McGhee St. Atlanta. AG 1/31/1908

CARNES, **Ruth**, age 4, d. W. Hunter Rd. Atlanta. AG 7/24/1907

CARNES, **Ruby**, 3 yr. old dau. of Mr. and Mrs. G. W., d. Tues. Battle Hill. Interred: Westview. AG 7/24/1907

CARNES, **Z.**, **Dr.** d. Greenwood, Ind. (his home) 1/10, father of W. E. of Atlanta. AG 1/11/1910

CARNEY, **Lizzie**, age 22, d. Atlanta. AG 6/ /1910

CARPENTER, **Dora Thelma**, inf. dau. of Mr. and Mrs. C. A., d. Sun. 17 N. Boulevard, Atlanta. AG 5/13/1907

CARPENTER, **F.**, age 45, of Madison, Ga., d. Atlanta Tues. AG 3/22/1910

CARPENTER, **I. L.** funeral Wed. 145 S. Pryor St. Atlanta. Interred: Oakland. AG 9/21/1910

CARPENTER, **John W.**, age 57, d. home near Munnerlyn yesterday, farmer and Mason of Burke Co. Interred: Old Church. AG 2/27/1907

CARPENTER, **L. B.**, age 82, atty of Madison, Ga., d. Atlanta Tues. Interred: Madison, Ga. AG 3/23/1910

CARPENTER, **L. L.**, age 33, d. 44 Walton St. Atlanta. AG 9/22/1910

CARPENTER, Seaborn, colored, age 48, d. 20 Vine St. Atlanta. AG 5/22/1910

CARPENTER, R. A., age 58, of Columbus, Ga., d. 129 Courtland St. Atlanta. Interred: Tallapoosa, Ga. Wife, 4 children. AG 5/6/1909

CARR, H. M., age 21, d. 99 Cherokee Ave. Atlanta. AG 9/3/1907

CARR, Henry, age 9 mos., inf. son of Mr. and Mrs. J. H., d. Tues. 150 Bedford Pl. Atlanta. Interred: Casey's Cemetery. AG 10/4/1910

CARR, M. M., Mrs., age 62, d. Mon. 172 Western Ave., Atlanta. AG 7/16/1907

CARR, N., Mrs., age 62, d. 172 Western Ave. Atlanta. AG 7/17/1907

CARR, Robert H., age 29, d. 99 Cherokee Ave. Atlanta. AG 1/19/1907

CARR, Thomas H., Mayor, d. 10/1 Montgomery, Ala. AC 10/2/1905

CARR, Z. T., age 40, d. in room at 360 Decatur St., Atlanta Tues. Interred: Westview. AG 2/2/1907

CARRINGTON, W. S., aged citizen of Franklin, Ga., shot and killed by his 17-yr. old grandson, 11/22 (in jail). AG 11/23/1909

CARROLL, A. G., Dr., age 53, d. Sun. 128 Grant St. Atlanta. Interred: Villa Rica, Ga. AG 8/9/1910

CARROLL, Ethel J., age 8 mos., d. 5 Lindsey St. Atlanta. AG 8/20/1907

CARROLL, John S., age 79, d. Covington, Ga. Interred: Atlanta, Westview Cemetery. AC 8/22/1905

CARROLL, L. C., Mrs. interred South Bend Church. AG 9/14/1907

CARROLL, Lena, age 10 mos., d. Athens, Ga. AG 3/28/1907

CARROLL, N. W., Rev., Columbus, Ga., 11/13/1906. Minister of Christian Church died moments after performing marriage ceremony at Jordan City, suburb of Columbus of James Blakely and Dazzie Letford. AG 11/13/1906

CARROLL, Naomi Miriam, Mrs., widow, d.son's res., J. R. Carroll, East Point, Ga., Fri. 3 sons, one dau: J. R. adn B. F. Carroll of E. Point; J. T. Carroll, Roanoke, Ala.; Mrs. Charles Willis, E. Point. Interred: Utoy Cemetery. AG 3/13/1908

CARROLL, Thomas, age 81, of Sandersville, member of O'Hara traveling horse traders, brought to Atlanta, placed in vault beside other members of the band. Leaves several sons. Interred: Westview. AG 9/29/1910

CARROLL, William Stewart, inf. son of Mr. and Mrs. R. D., d. Rosalie St., Atlanta. Interred: Covington, Ga. AG 1/25/1910

CARROLL, William Wesley, age 63, of 38 Eads St.,A tlanta, d. Wed. Interred: Westview. AG 2/24/1910

CARRUTH, H. E., Mrs., wife of Probate Judge Carruth, d. Sat., date of late Judge Hunnicutt of Heflin, Ala. Leaves 5 children, all young. AG 4/30/1906

CARRUTHERS, H. A., Mrs., widow of H. A. of Walton Co., d. 10/0 res. of son, H. A. Carruthers, Winder, Ga., age 74. Sons: H. A., R. L., J. Y. Funeral at Bethebara Church, Walton Co. AG 10/11/1910

CARSON, Azlee, colored, age 6, d. 226 Lambert St. Atlanta. AG 9/8/1908

CARSON, Curtis, age 11 mos., d. 11 Oxford Ave. Atlanta. AG 4/19/1907

CARSON, D. I. d. recently. H. E. W. Palmer accompanied body to Connecticut for interment. AG 6/16/1909

CARSON, Elizabeth, Miss d. Sun. Atlanta. Interred: Westview. AG 11/22/1909

CARSON, George, colored, age 3, d. 226 Lambert St. Atlanta. AG 2/13/1908

CARSON, Mabelle, age 15, d. 91 Luckie St. Atlanta. AG 8/25/1908

CARSWALL, T. B., colored, age 4 mos., d. 13 Reed St. Atlanta. AG 1/17/1908

CARSWELL, Morris, Mrs. d. Blythe, Ga. 4/22. AG 4/22/1908

CARTER, Anthony, age 11, son of Mr. and Mrs. Frank M., d. Highland Ave., Atlanta, Mon. Interred: Clarkston, Ga. AG 8/11/1908

CARTER, Carwood, Marshal of Richland, Ga. killed by negro. AG 1/12/1907

CARTER, Edgar Ralph, age 7 mos., d. 400 Simpson St. Atlanta. AG 3/7/1909

CARTER, Gene, negro, shot and killed 7/26 by Dave Jones, negro, Spring Vale, Ga. AC 7/28/1905

CARTER, George W., age 69, d. 54 Piedmont Ave., Atlanta, Wed. Sons: C. E., W. M., of Atlanta. AG 2/24/1910

CARTER, Helen, Miss, age 16, dau. of Mrs. Ella S. Carter of 80 W. Peachtree St., Atlanta, d. Tues. Interred: Westview. AG 4/7/1909

CARTER, Iula, colored, age 32, d. 2 Fort St. Atlanta. AG 3/19/1907

CARTER, Jane, colored, age 53, d. 70 McDaniel St. Atlanta. AG 7/16/1907

CARTER, Jasper M., age 69, d. 28 Evans Drive, Ft. McPherson, Fri. Wife, several children. Interred: Antioch church yard. AG 7/18/1908

CARTER, John, colored, age 35, d. 101 N. Butler St. Atlanta. AG 8/17/1908

CARTER, Lawrence, age 13 days, d. 91 Central Ave. Atlanta. AG 6/22/1909

CARTER, M. C., colored, age 26, d. 204 W. Hunter St. Atlanta. AG 3/23/1908

CARTER, Margaret, Mrs. d. New Orleans, La. Tues. Dau: Mrs. Hugh L. Jackson, Atlanta. AG 12/19/1907

CARTER, Mary, Mrs., age 81, d. Mon. 624 DeKalb Ave., Atlanta. Son: W. T. Shelnutt. Dau: Mrs. Charles Haas. Interred: Oakland. AG 7/11/1910

CARTER, Mattie, colored, age 56, d. 5 Haygood alley. Atlanta. AG 8/13/1910

CARTER, P. W., age 64, d. 78 Grant St. Atlanta. AG 4/19/1907

CARTER, Rose, colored, age 27, d. 106 Tobent St. Atlanta. AG 12/16/1907

CARTER, S., colored, age 81, d. 514 W. Mitchell St. Atlanta. AG 12/6/1907

CARTER, Sanford, colored, age 30, d. rear of 139 E. Sumter St. Atlanta. AG 11/9/1907

CARTER, Susie A., colored, age 32, d. 71 Tattnall St. Atlanta. AG 2/11/1907

CARTER, Vivian Ellen, age 1, dau. of Mr. and Mrs. B. H., d. 488 St. Charles Ave., Atlanta, Mon. Interred: Villa Rica, Ga. AG 1/20/1908

CARTER, dau., age 12, of Tom Carter, d. Tucker, Ga. AG 10/11/1907

CARTER, Clio, colored, age 11 mos., d. 720 N. Jackson St. Atlanta. AG 9/28/1910

CARTER, W. L., father of ch. killed by J. G. Rawlins & Alf Moore (negro), Valdosta 1906. AG 12/3/1906

CASE, Henry d. E. Decatur, Ala. AG 9/7/1906

CASEY, R. H. H. d. Atlanta Sun. Interred: Sardis Church yard. AG 5/17/1910

CASEY, Thomas H. interred Cedartown, Ga. AG 12/9/1907

CASEY, W. E. d. Wed. 18 Dainey St., Atlanta. Funeral: Sardis Church. AG 8/8/1907

CASH, E. D., Mrs., age 63, funeral 12/23 Tunnel Hill, Ga. One sister, two bros. AG 12/18/1910

CASH, J. H. run over, killed by train. Remains brought to Atlanta. AG 1/15/1910

CASH, L. J., age 73, d. 8 Western Ave., Atlanta, Wed., Confed. Vet. 10 children. 6 bros., 4 grandchildren. Interred: Providence church yard. AG 12/29/1910

CASON, Anne S., Mrs., age 74, wid. of Adam F. Cason, dau. of Hampton Hudson. d. Sat. Funeral: Hepzibah Baptist Church, Burke Co. 1/24. Son: Adam Cason, Keysville. AG 1/28/1910

CASON, Frederick T., Jr., son of Mr. and Mrs. F. Q., age 5, d. 24 Highland Ave. Atlanta. AG 8/9/1910

CASON, R. E., Dr., dentist of Cartersville, d. Wed., age 72. Wife and 6 children survive. AG 1/24/1907

CASSELS, George W., Mrs., Atlanta pioneer, d. res. of son, L. J. Cassels, Kirkwood, Atlanta, Fri., age 56. Daus: Mrs. H. C. Davis, Columbia, S. C.; Miss Walter Cassels, Atlanta. Interred: Flemington, Ga. AG 6/8/1909

CASSELS, Luther Mallard of Atlanta, d. son's res., Thomas Mallard Cassels, Gadsden, Ala. 8/9. Dau: Mrs. Wm Burwell Pope. Sons: Raleigh Camp Cassels, Atlanta; Thos N. & Chas Green Cassels, Gadsden, Ala. Interred: Decatur, Ga. AG 8/10/1909

CASSIDY, Edward funeral 3/2 Macon, Ga., Oak St., age 64. Came to Macon from Ireland. Interred: Rose Hill Cemetery. AG 3/2/1910

CASSIDY, F. M. d. Atlanta Mon. Interred: Westview. AG 5/18/1910

CASSIRER, Margaret, age 10, d. 61 Hill St. Atlanta. AG 11/11/1909

CASTLEBERRY, Bennie, age 11, son of W. S. Castleberry of Phenix City, Ala. d. today. Columbus, Ga. AG 5/4/1907

CATE, Mary F., Mrs., age 40, d. res. Brown Mill Rd. Interred: Brooks Station. Husband: G. E. Cate. AG 9/19/1906

CATES, J. N., age 61, of 831 Marietta St., Atlanta, d. He was Confederate veteran. AG 3/4/1907

CATES, Jesse, Mrs., age 26, d. Sun. 68 Hendrix Ave. Atlanta. Interred: Rockmart, Ga. AG 5/20/1907

CATES, John N., age 61, d. 832 Marietta St. Atlanta. AG 3/5/1907

CATES, John R., age 50, d. Sandy Springs, Ga, where interred. AG 8/10/1910

CATES, S. M., age 50, d. Sun. Piedmont, Ala. Interred: Connally, Ga. AG 3/9/1910

CATHCART, George B., age 78, d. 131 W. Cain St. Atlanta. AG 2/25/1907

CATHERWOOD, T. B., well-known in Ga., d. his home at Lake Mary, Fla. Sun. Wife, 4 sons, survive: David K., Jacksonville; M. R., Waycross; John C., Dry Branch, Ga.; Frank F. of Lake Mary, Fla. AG 12/7/1908

CATLETT, Mary, Mrs., age 71, d. Sun. 354 Pulliam St., Atlanta. Interred: Nashville, Tenn. AG 1/31/1910

CATO, Archie W. funeral Tues. Atlanta. Interred: Hollywood. AG 4/5/1910

CATO, Moses, age 43, d. 122 Julian St. Atlanta. AG 11/3/1909

CAUBLE, J. L. d. Sat. Atlanta. Relatives in St. Louis, Mo. Interred: Westview. AG 8/25/1910

CAUDLE, Mollie E., inf. dau. of Mr. and Mrs. W. P. of 158 Jett St., Atlanta, d. Thurs. Interred: Westview. AG 4/2/1909

CAUSEY, M. J., age 73, d. 101 N. Butler St. Atlanta. AG 1/15/1908

CAUSEY, M. J., Mrs., age 73, d. Atlanta Mon., 480 Edgewood Ave. Interred: Westview. AG 1/14/1908

CAUTHORN, Percy C., only son of late Maj. B. F. Cauthorn, d. Nashville, Tenn. 4/21. Aunts: Mrs. Amos W. White, Thomaston; Mrs. Malcolm McPherson, Birmingham, AL; Mrs. Walter S. Tennant, Atlanta. Uncle: Thomas E. Cauthorn, N. Y. AG 5/3/1909

CAVALERI, E. E., Sr., age 83, d. res. of son, E. E. Calaleri, 60 Tyler St., Atlanta, Tues. Interred: Hollywood. AG 5/8/1906

CAY, Anais, Mrs., mother of John E., d. Charleston, S. C., Sun. Interred: Atlanta. Westview Cemetery. AG 4/12/1910

CAYLE, infant son of Mr. and Mrs. J. A., d. Wed. Atlanta. Interred: Hollywood. AG 9/15/1910

CAYLOR, C. K., Jr., age 16 mos., son of Mr. and Mrs. C. K., d. 25 Whitehall St., Atlanta, Sat. Interred: Westview. AG 7/24/1909

CEAUGUE, David H., age 68, Confed. Vet., d. Chattanooga, Tenn. 5/3. AG 5/4/1910

CERNIGLIA, Samuel Lawrence, age 16, d. Fri. res. of mother, Mrs. Josephine Cerniglia, 15 Clark St., Atlanta. Interment:estview. AG 10/6/1906

CHADWICK, Alonzo E. of Atlanta, d. Johns Hopkins Hospital, Baltimore, Md. AG 12/4/1907

CHAFFIN, James F., Mrs., age 65, d. 60 E. Alexander St. Atlanta. AG 2/19/1910

CHAFFIN, Jamie, Mrs., age 26, d. 206 Grant St. Atlanta. AG 7/29/1910

CHAFFIN, M. A., age 47, d. Sun. Atlanta. AG 2/19/1907

CHAFIN, Elizabeth, Mrs., age 31, d. Battle Hill Sun. Interred: Sylvester Cemetery. AG 3/9/1910

CHAFIN, Frank, son of Mr. and Mrs. F. L. of Washington, Ga., d. of burns. AG 1/26/1910

CHAFIN, J. N., age 21, d. Thurs. Roswell Rd. Atlanta. Interred: Sardis Church Yard. AG 11/26/1909

CHAFIN, John B., age 46, d. 71 Garden St. Atlanta Thurs. Bro: Edward B., Atlanta. Interred: Columbus, Ga. AG 5/9/1908

CHAFIN, S. E., Mrs., age 76, d. Mon. Atlanta. Son, one bro. Interred: Columbus, Ga. AG 10/4/1910

CHAIRMAN, George, age 23, a Greek, d. Atlanta Wed. AG 7/23/1908

CHALKER, Oscar, age 3, d. 176 Echo St., Atlanta, Fri. Interred: Kennesaw. AG 7/28/1906

CHAMBERLIN, Lizzie, Miss, age 30, d. 279 E. Hunter St. Atlanta. Interred: Westview. AG 8/22/1910

CHAMBERS, Allen A., inf. son of Mr. and Mrs. J. N., d. Bishop St., Atlanta, Sun. Interred: Moore's Mill, Ga. AG 3/9/1908

CHAMBERS, C. H., Mrs. d. Tues. Third St., Macon, age 43. Two children, husband, survive. Interred: Riverside, Macon. AG 12/23/1908

CHAMBERS, Carrie, Mrs., age 32, d. E. Point Tues. Interred: Macon. Husband. 5 small children. Mother: Mrs. Martha Howell, Macon. Bro: H. L. Howell, Ashburn, Ga. AG 5/5/1909

CHAMBERS, Edward Patterson, age 60, d. Atlanta 7/3, from Gainesville. Dau: Miss Marion. Wife, two daus. AC 7/4/1905

CHAMBERS, L. G., age 1, d. Hampton St. Atlanta. AG 10/25/1907

CHAMBERS, Lillian, age 1, dau. of Mr. and Mrs. Charley, d. 81 Hampton St., Atlanta Sat. AG 10/26/1907

CHAMBERS, Lucy May, age 7, dau. of Mrs. Blanche M., d. Tues. Interred: Hollywood. Res. 171 Plum St., Atlanta. AG 4/25/1906

CHAMBERS, Mary, age 52, d. 5 Gaskill St. Atlanta. AG 5/9/1910

CHAMBERS, Okey, age 19, son of Mr. and Mrs. B. F., d. Mon. 173 W. Pine St., Atlanta. Interred: Chamblee. AG 6/19/1907

CHAMBERS, R. P., unmd, formerly of Atlanta, suicide, Jacksonville. Parents: Mr. and Mrs. J. V., 88 Hendricks Ave., Atlanta. 5 sisters, 5 bros. Interred: Atlanta. AC 2/20/1905

CHAMBERS, Rachel, negro, shot, killed Tues. by George Tucker, negro, on Peters St. Atlanta. AG 7/24/1907

CHAMBERS, T. J., age 59, d. 134 Powell St., Atlanta, Mon. AG 7/11/1910

CHAMBERS, James. Valdosta, Ga. 12/10/1906. Old citizen of Valdosta found dead yesterday beside Atlantic Coast Line rr. AG 12/10/1906

CHAMBERS, Pearl, Mrs., age 19, d. Moreland Ave., Atlanta, Fri., wife of R. M. One small child. Funeral: Sardis Church. AG 5/8/1910

CHAMBLEE, M. J., Mrs. d. E. Point, Ga. Wed. Interred: Mt. Zion Church yard. AG 4/8/1908

CHAMBLISS, J. P., Mrs. d. Georgetown, Ga. 10/27. Husband, several grown children, survive. Interred: Family Cemetery, Georgetown. AG 10/28/1909

CHAMPION, Jacob, age 77, d. Soldier's Home, Atlanta. Interred: Westview. Was member of Co., G., 2nd Ga. Cavalry during Civil War, with Gen. Johnston at surrender. Niece: Mrs. E. E. Allen of 121 Crew St., Atlanta. AG 10/28/1908

CHAMPION, Loula A., Mrs., wife of J. P., d. Rose Hill Sun. (near Columbus). L   5 children. AG 10/1/1907

CHAMPION, Mary, Miss, age 65, d. 3/18 res. of Mrs. J. M. Gossett, sister, of Griffin. Bro: R. W. Chamption, A tlanta. Interred: Oak Hill Cemetery. AG 3/21/ 9 0

CHAMPION, R. I., an Illinois tourist, d. Fitzgerald, Ga. 3/15. Wife. 10 ch. Interred: Evergreen Cemetery. AC 3/17/1905

CHAMPION, Stewart assassinated 4/10 Tuscaloosa, Ala. AC 4/12/1905

CHANDLER, Carlton, son of Mr. and Mrs. G. C., d. 12/1907 Jonesboro Rd. Sun. Interred: Gillsville, Ga. AG 12/30/1907

CHANDLER, Harriett, age 33, d. 97 Dodd Ave., Atlanta. AG 12/1/1907

CHANDLER, Harry, age 14, son of A. M., killed yesterday by accidental shot from pistol of Robert Ulmer, age 16, Valdosta, Ga. AG 9/17/1907

CHANDLER, Lula, age 22, d. 203 Kennedy St. Atlanta. AG 3/10/1910

CHANDLER, Lula, colored, age 2, d. 233 Clark St. Atlanta. AG 8/14/1907

CHANDLER, Lula, Mrs., age 22, wife of H., d. 203 Kennedy St., Atlanta, Thurs. AG 3/17/1910

CHANDLER, Martha, Mrs., age 72, d. 20 Carlton St. Mon. Interred: Westview. AG 8/7/1900

CHANDLER, N. J., Mrs. of Bowden d. 2/19. AC 2/28/1905

CHANEY, Thelma, infant, d. 60 Robins St. Atlanta. AG 3/15/1910

CHAPEL, Alfred d. 8/30 Lyons, Ga. Resident of Fitzgerald, Ga. 10 yrs. Age 20. Wife, 2 small children. AC 9/3/1905

CHAPIN, J. B., age 46, d. 101 N. Butler St. Atlanta. AG 5/11/1908

CHAPMAN, Beulah V., dau. of Mr. and Mrs. H. K. d. 5/3. Interred: Gainesville, Ga. AG 56/4/1906

CHAPMAN, Martha, age 10, dau. of Mr. and Mrs. J. W., interred Kinsey, Ga. AG 9/28/1907

CHAPMAN, May, colored, age 11 mos., d. 58 Randolph St., Atlanta. AG 9/4/1907

CHAPMAN, Quinton C., age 6, grandson of Mr. and Mrs. E. C. Chapman, 457 Whitehall St., Atlanta, d. parent's res., Mr. and Mrs. John C. Chapman, Ft. Madison, Iowa. Interred: Westview. AG 8/3/1908

CHAPMAN, Robert Lee, age 5, son of Mr. and Mrs. J. W., d. Cedar St., Macon 8/3. Interred: Jones Chapel Cemetery. AC 8/14/1905

CHAPMAN, W. T., age 76, Confederate soldier, d. arnesville, Ga. Thurs. Ch: Mrs. E. W. Whitaker, Miss Sallie Chapman, C. H. Chapman, Atlanta. AG 5/5/1906

CHAPPEL, Frances, Mrs., age 82, killed in Griffin cyclone. AG 4/25/1908

CHAPPELL, Alfred, age 19, d. Fri. 1274 Marietta St. Atlanta. interred: Calhoun, Ga. AG 8/6/1910

CHAPPELL, Alfred C., age 19, d. 1274 Marietta St. Atlanta. AG 8/8/1910

CHAPPELL, Effie, age 2, d. 67 Alma Ave. Atlanta. AG 7/29/1910

CHAPPELLE, Patsy, colored, age 90, d. Newnan, Ga. AG 10/3/1907

CHAPPELL, Effie, age 8 mos., dau. of Mr. and Mrs. W. J., d. 61 Almo Ave., Atlanta. Interred: Mt. Zion Cemetery. AG 7/28/1910

CHASE, George W., Prof. d. Mon., age 76, Columbus, Ga. Born Brooklyn, N. Y. Confed. Vet., 6th and 19th Ga. Regts. 4 sons, 3 daus. AG 10/5/1910

CHASTAIN, Benjamin, age 80+, buried Rock Spring, Chickamauga Mon. Son: G. L. Chastain. AG 9/19/1906

CHASTAIN, E., age 7, d. 101 N. Butler St. Atlanta. AG 3/5/1907

CHASTAIN, Frances B., Mrs., age 52, d. dau.'s res., Mrs. W. G. Turner, 82 Park Ave., Atlanta. Interred: Oakland. Sis: Mrs. Moses Hollinsworth. AG 1/31/1910

CHASTAIN, Joseph, Mrs. of Valdosta, dau. of W. Z. Carter of DuPont, d. few days ago Thomas Co. 4 ch. Interred: Thomas Co., Ga. AC 2/15/1905

CHASTAIN, Josephine, age 5, dau. of Mr. and Mrs. J. A., d. 470 Decatur St., Atlanta, Fri. Interred: Anderson, S. C. AG 1/31/1908

CHASTAIN, W. L., age 63, d. 561 W. North Ave., Atlanta, Tues. Wife, two sons, T. P. and J. C., and two daus., Mrs. M. E. Mason, Mrs. N. C. Hawkins, survive. Interred: Hollywood. AG 11/24/1908

CHASTIN, Melvin, age 5, son of Mr. and Mrs. J. C., d. Sat. Atlanta. Interred: Family Burial Ground in the country. AG 11/2/1907

CHATHAM, E. H., Mrs., age 80, d. 101 Butler St., Atlanta. AG 12/16/1909

CHATHAM, Elizabeth, Mrs. d. several days ago Atlanta. Daus: Mrs. J. A. Whittemore; Mrs. George Rice, Atlanta; Mrs. G. C. White, Abbeville, Ala. Son: J. N. Chatham, Beaufort, Ga. AG 12/13/1909

CHEAT, Pearl, Mrs., age 26, wife of Paul, d. Atlanta Mon. AG 5/11/1908

CHEATHAM, L. P. d.Tilton, Ga. 4/11. Wife, 3 children. AG 4/12/1910

CHEMBER, Okey, age 19 yrs., d. 173 W. Pine St. Atlanta. AG 6/18/1907

CHENEY, Coley. Macon, Ga., 12/25. As result of quarrel at Cochran, Ga., Sun., Gordon McDonald shot and killed Coley Cheney and Herchel Burns. AG 12/25/1906

CHENEY, Robert Reeves, son of Mr. and Mrs. J. S., age 24, d. 119 E. Georgia Ave., Atlanta, Wed. Interred: Bairdstown, Ga. Bros: W. L., F. C. Sisters: Mrs. A. C. Hancock, Atlanta; Misses Eva, Florrie, Sarah Cheney, Atlanta. AG 7/8/1908

CHERRY, Claude C., age 20, d. 220 N. Jackson St. Atlanta, Mon. Bro: Pink Cherry. AG 5/30/1910

CHERRY, Elizabeth J., Mrs., age 72, d. Sat. 12 Atwood Ave. Atlanta. Interred: Griffin, Ga. AG 8/30/1910

CHERRY, J. M., age 61, vet. of Confederate army, Co. E, 5th Ga. Regt., d. Old Soldiers' home Mon. Interred: Westview. AG 1/4/1910

CHERRY, Nettie C., colored, age 28, d. 42 Bryan St. Atlanta. AG 8/14/1907

CHESHIRE, Eliza A., Mrs., wife of S. Jerome, d. Atlanta Thurs. Interred: Oakland. AG 1/15/1910

CHESTNUT, Earl, age 8 mos., infant son of Mr. and Mrs. J. C., d. Fri. 134 W. Alexander St., Atlanta. Interred: Westview. AG 9/21/1907

CHESTNUT, Mrs., aged lady, d. home of dau., Mrs. Jim Wilson of Attapulgus, Ga. Age 85. AG 3/4/1907

CHESTNUT, Ruby G., Mrs., wife of Thomas R., age 25, d. 99 Cherokee Ave. Atlanta. Two children, parents, four sister, one bro. Interred: Columbus, Ga. AG 7/9/1909

CHESTNUTT, Mary A., Mrs., wife of Judge O. L., d. Sat. res. of dau., Mrs. H. H. Britt, Tifton, Ga. Ch: Mrs. H. H. Britt, T. M., A. B., and Dr. O. Lee Chestnutt and Mrs. Mary Quick, of Tifton. AG 6/7/1910

CHESTNUTT, O. L., Judge d. Mon. Tifton, Ga. Interred: Oakgrove Cemetery. AG 5/25/1910

CHEWNING, Owen, age 7, son of Mr. and Mrs. M. J. of 53 Berne St., Atlanta, d. Fri. AG 7/17/1909

CHEWNING, Perry E., age 26, d. 34 W. 12th St. Atlanta. Wife, one child, mother, bro., one sister. Interred: Sardis Church. AG 9/2/1909

CHEWNING, Richard A., veteran of Lee's army, pioneer of Tucker, age 69, d. Tues. 9 ch, 22 tch, 2 gt-gch. Interred: Fellowship churchyard, Tucker, AG 1/23/1907

CHILDERS, Asbury, Mrs. d. Sun. 9 Plum St., Atlanta. Interred: Westview. AG 7/16/1907

CHILDERS, Dora, Mrs., age 23, d. 9 Plum St. Atlanta. AG 7/17/1907
CHILDERS, Clifford, age 3, son of Mr. and Mrs. J. W., d. Tues. Atlanta. Interred: Peachtree Church. AG 6/16/1908
CHILDRESS J. C., age 30, d. 211 Ivy St. Atlanta. AG 8/11/1908
CHILDRESS, H. K. W., age 67, d. 80 Belgrade Ave. Atlanta. AG 2/8/1907
CHILDRESS, Mary A., Mrs., age 61, d. Sun. 35 Inman Ave. Atlanta. Sons: W. W., D. R. Dau: Mrs. Hattie A. Bell. Interred: Rock Springs. AG 4/11/1910
CHILDRESS, W. A., Dr., Conf Vet., d. Ponders Ave. Atlanta. Bur: Goodwin's. Wife. Son: J. H. Daus: Mrs. Ada Northcutt, Mrs. A. J. Martin, Mrs. C. W. Bowman. Sis: Mrs. E. C. Mason, Flowery Branch. Bro: T. C. S., Fountain Inn, SC. AG 10/2/1909
CHILDS, B. B., Mrs. d. her home Rose Hill 2/16, age 26. Dau, age 2. Mother: Mrs. Dora B lakley. Two bros. Interred: Elmwood. AG 2/17/1910
CHILDS, Dennis E., age 23, d. Mon., son of Mr. and Mrs. W. S. Leaves father, mother, four sisters, four brothers. Res: 714 Oglethorpe St. Atlanta. AG 8/20/1907
CHILDS, Emily Blocker, inf. dau. of Mr. and Mrs. J. C., d. Sat. 189 Oglethorpe Ave., Atlanta. Interred: Westview. AG 3/21/1910
CHILDS, Erwin d. McCamy St., Dalton, Ga. Sat. Interred: Gordon Co., his old home. Age 22. Wife, and parents, Mr. and Mrs. W. B. Childs, survive. AG 11/7/1910
CHILDS, George W., colored, age 41, d. 23 Vine St. Atlanta. AG 7/29/1907
CHILDS, L. D., age 2, son of Mr. and Mrs. E. A., d. 133 Greenwich Ave., Atlanta, Mon. Interred: Westview. AG 1/14/1908
CHISOLM, Caroline H., Mrs., age 87, d. 15 Houston St., Atlanta, Mon. Interred: Oakland. AG 6/2/1908
CHISOLM, Harry A., age 44 d. 522 Central Ave., Atlanta, Thurs. Interred: Westview. AG 6/26/1908
CHOATE, Carrie, Mrs., age 35, d. Atlanta Fri. Interred: Westview. AG 8/1/1908
CHOLOVITIS, Henry, age 35, d. Grady Hospital. Atlanta. AG 6/8/1907
CHOVIN Eve, dau. of Charles, d. 8/24 Fitzgerald, Ga. AC 8/25/1905
CHREITZBERG, Hilliard F., Dr. d. Monroe, N. C., Mon. Interred: Oakwood Cemetery, Spartanburg, S. C. Father-in-law: Major A. H. Kirby. AG 10/12/1910
CHRISTIAN, Hugh, son of Mr. and Mrs. J. C., 686 Washington St. Atlanta. Interred: Westview. AG 6/4/1906
CHRISTIAN, Joseph, Judge of Superior Court of Virginia, d. 5/29, age 77, Richmond, Va. AC 5/30/1905
CHRISTIAN, L. W., Mrs., age 76, d. 365 Oak St. Atlanta. AG 11/21/1910
CHRISTIAN, Lois Cleveland, Mrs., dau. of Hon. and Mrs. Joe S. James, Douglasville, wife of J. H. Christian, d. Tues. Douglasville. Interred: Douglasville, Ga. AG 10/17/1906
CHRISTIAN, Paul Anderson, age 2, son of Mr. and Mrs. J. C., d. 534 Crew St., Atlanta, Wed. AG 11/26/1908
CHRISTIAN, T. C., age 28, d. 10 Ridge Ave., Atlanta, Fri. Interred: Hollywood cemetery. AG 11/23/1907
CHRISTIAN, Zera S., age 59, d. 56 Piedmont Ave., Atlanta. AG 7/15/1910

CHRISTIE, Monson, age 23, d. 127 S. Forsyth St., Atlanta, Mon., son of Mr. and Mrs. George. Bros: B. G., John. Sis: Mrs. Maud Whittaker, Mrs. J. L. Harris. Interred: Westview. AG 4/11/1910

CHRISTIE, J. R., age 57, d. Hancock Ave., Athens. Ch: Mrs. J. S. Holmes, Atlanta; Mrs. John Carithers, Newberry, S. C.; Mrs. John Duncan, Elberton; Carrie, Athens; Sam, Washington; Ruth, Balsam, N. C.; Carlisle, Athens. AG 12/15/1910

CHRISTOPHER, Louise, infnant, d. Jefferson St. Atlanta. AG 2/11/1910

CHUNG, Lee d. Sat. Atlanta. Interred: Westview. AG 6/27/1910

CHUNN, B. E., merchant of Woodbury, Ga. d. LaGrange sanitarium, apoplexy. Interred: Woodbury. AG 9/1/1906

CHUNN, Mattie Byrd, Mrs., age 28, wife of W. L., d. Atlanta. Interred: Woodbury, Ga. Mother: Mrs. M. A. Watson. Sis: Mrs. R. W. Cummins; Mrs. H. L. Dickson, Woodbury. AG 7/26/1909

CHURCH, Dalls, Mrs., wife of Dr. Charles A., d. Andersonville, Ga., Wed. Interred: Westview. AG 8/2/1906

CHURCH, E. J., age 43, d. Atlanta. AG 1/15/1910

CHURCH, E. J., age 52, d. 25 Carter St.,tlanta, Wed. Wife, three children. Interred: Casey's Cemetery. AG 1/13/1910

CHURCH, Richard of 133 Curran St., Atlanta, d. Fri. Interred: New Jersey. AG 6/15/1906

CHURCHILL, Samuel E., inf. son of Mr. and Mrs. S. R. of S. Moreland Ave., Atlanta, d. Fri. Interred: Sylvester. AG 3/21/1910

CHURCHILL, W. D., age 89, d. 228 Haynes St., Atlanta, Mon. Interred: Gainesville, Ga. AG 2/11/1908

CHYNOWETH, Major funeral Sat. Atlanta. Interred: Arlington Cemetery, Washington, D. C. AG 7/30/1909

CIDWELL, Guy, 17 yr. old son of Jake of Harlem, Ga., killed by freight train. AG 8/29/1907

CINCIOLO, Antonio, age 27, Gainesville merchant, d. Tues. Interred: Gainesville, Ga. AG 1/8/1908

CLANTON, Charles Murphy, age 1 yr., son of Mr. and Mrs. T. W., d. 182 Highland Ave. Atlanta. Interred: Westview. AG 5/19/1908

CLAPP, May, Miss of Columbus, Ga. d. Fri. AG 6/13/1908

CLARK, A. J., age 27, d. Grady Hospital. Atlanta. Interred: Flowery Branch, Ga. AG 8/26/1907

CLARK, Agnes, colored, age 43, d. 61 Leach St. Atlanta. AG 11/6/1907

CLARK, Alice, Mrs., age 40, d. 17 W. Cain St. Atlanta. AG 9/6/1906

CLARK, Amos shot by James Raley, Augusta, Ga. AG 3/16/1907

CLARK, C. N., Dr. d. Sheffield, Ala., Fri. Funeral, Atlanta. AG 11/27/1910

CLARK, Charles C., age 38, d. 27 Wiley St. Atlanta. AG 3/14/1910

CLARK, Charles C., age 38, d. Thurs. 41 Scott St. Atlanta, wife of J. S. 2 sons, 3 daus. AG 3/10/1910

CLARK, Edward Young Clark, Sr., age 70, d. 286 Washington St., Atlanta. AG 4/22/1910

CLARK, Emma E., Mrs., age 40, d. Troy, Ala. AG 8/22/1910

CLARK, George, age 35, d. 200 Murphy Ave. Atlanta. AG 9/2/1909

CLARK, John W., age 40, d. Sat. 58 Greenwood Ave., Atlanta. Interred: Oakland. AG 5/28/1906

CLARK, Leroy M., age 2 mos., son of Mr. and Mrs. L. P. of 6 Longley Ave., Atlanta, d. Thurs. Interred: Westview. AG 5/15/1908

CLARK, M. J., Mrs., age 54, d. 31 W. Peachtree Pl. Atlanta. AG 1/29/1907

CLARK, Mary L., infant dau. of Mr. and Mrs. W. A., d. Fri. 170 Fowler St., Atlanta. Interred: Westview. AG 5/27/1907

CLARK, Matilda, colored, age 41, d. 156 Ellis St. Atlanta. AG 11/30/1910

CLARK, Max, age 6, son of Mr. and Mrs. L. D., d. 170 Fowler St., Atlanta, Thurs. Interred: Westview. AG 10/18/1907

CLARK, Rufus of Franklin, Ga. d. home of sister, Mrs. Sallie Chivers 4/25. AG 4/29/1907

CLARK, Sadie, Mrs., age 30, d. 129 Courtland St. Atlanta. AG 7/6/1909

CLARK, W. J., age 80 yrs., d. Ellenwood, Ga. Wife, two children, Mrs. W. F. Matthews of Atlanta, W. H. Clark. AG 3/2/1907

CLARK, Willis, colored, age 48, d. 28 Proctor St. Atlanta. AG 4/20/1908

CLARKE, Edward Young, Sr., age 70, Atlanta pioneer, d. Thurs. 286 Washington St. Wife: Nora V. Sons: T. Y., Jr., Francis W. Confed. Vet. Interred: Oakland. AG 4/21/1910

CLARKE, Julia B., Miss d. 1/4 Clinton, S. C. where resided past 12 yrs., formerly from Virginia. AG 1/5/1910

CLARKE, L. H., wealthy farmer of Mitchell, Ga., d. Tues., leaving small son, two little daus. AG 9/10/1908

CLARKE, Lula, colored, age 40, d. Fulton Co. Alms House. Atlanta. AG 7/9/1908

CLARKE, M. E., Mrs., age 38, d. 190 Crew. St. Atlanta. AG 2/25/1910

CLARKE, Mary Lee, inf. dau. of Mr. and Mrs. W. A., d. Fri. 170 Fowler St. Atlanta. AG 5/24/1907

CLARKE, Max, age 6, d. 170 Fowler St. Atlanta. AG 10/19/1907

CLARKE, Robert, Jr., infant, d. 41 Leach St. Atlanta. AG 6/11/1910

CLARK, Bertie, colored, age 2 years, d. Moores alley, Atlanta. AG 12/20/1906

CLARK, M. E.,, wife of Geo. E., 38, d. Atlanta. Dau, sis: Mrs. J. J. Threlkeld, Mrs. R. W. Luck (Seal City, AL), Mrs. W. B. Jackson (Athens), Mrs. R. F. Winne (Watkinsville). Bro: A. M. Langford (Athens). Bur: Williamston, SC. AG 2/22/1910

CLAY, Cleveland, age 74, d. S. Kirkwood, Atlanta, Wed. Two sons, three daus. Interred: Clays Cemetery. AG 4/8/1909

CLAY, E. I., Mrs., age 67, d. 145 Walton St., Atlanta, Mon. Husband survives. Interred: Westview. AG 7/29/1908

CLAY, Henry, colored, age 32, d. 489 Glenn St. Atlanta. AG 4/19/1907

CLAY, Lizzie, negro, d. Macon. AC 7/12/1905

CLAY, M. D., age 35, d. 146 Ormond St. Atlanta. AG 4/13/1907

CLAY, Mary, colored, age 34, d. 21 Crew St. Atlanta. AG 4/7/1908

CLAY, Mary, inf. dau. of Mr. and Mrs. R. L., 78 Berean Ave. Atlanta, d. Thurs. Interred: Cool Springs. AG 7/2/1909

CLAYTON, C. D., age 34, d. Jackson, Miss. AG 9/28/1909

CLAYTON, Crit, colored, age 53, d. 68 Oliver St. Atlanta. AG 7/12/1909

CLAYTON, Donald W., inf. son of Mr. and Mrs. George A., d. 361 Cherokee Ave., Atlanta, Tues. Interred: Westview. AG 5/26/1908

CLAYTON, George A., Jr., age 7, son of Mr. and Mrs. George A., d. Thurs., 361 Cherokee Ave. Atlanta. AG 4/10/1907

CLAYTON, J. W., age 83, d. 104 E. Linden St. Atlanta. AG 4/22/1909

CLAYTON, M., colored, age 57, d. 418 Martin St. Atlanta. AG 12/24/1907

CLAYTON, Mary J., age 5 mos., d. 70 Cherry St. Atlanta. AG 6/26/1908

CLAYTON, Mary Lillie, age 6 mos., dau. of Mr. and Mrs. Joseph M., d. 70 Cherry St., Atlanta, Fri. Interred: Oakland. AG 6/26/1908

CLAYTON, Richard, Hon., age 68, school commissioner of Bartow Co., d. Sherman Hotel, Cartersville. Leaves wife, 3 sons: Julian, Ira, Harry of Atlanta. Interred: Cartersville. AG 5/13/1907

CLEMENS, Lizzie, colored, ate 45, d. 4 St. Charles Ave. Atlana. AG 12/26/1907

CLEMENT, W. L. of Big Creek, Duluth, d. 2/10. Wife. Ch: Dr. Dave, Norcross, Ga.; Dr. Ben, Cumming, Ga.; Ruby; Flonnie; Chandler; Steve. Interred: Sharon, AC 2/15/ 905

CLEMENTS, Capitola, Mrs., age 29, d. 116 Venable St. Atlanta. AG 5/18/1908

CLEMENTS, Claude, age 2, son of Mr. and Mrs. T. F., d. Mon. 18 Plum St. Interred: Westview. AG 5/28/1907

CLEMENTS, Eliza, Mrs. d. Cordele, Ga. 4/30.Daus: Mrs. J. S. Pate, Cordele, Mrs. Benefield, Moultrie. Sons: Jack, Nelson, Thomas (Moultrie). Interred: Zion Hope. AG 5/1/1906

CLEMENTS, Hattie Harvie, Mrs.; wife of Charles M., d. Buena Vista, Ga. 7/17. AC 7/18/1905

CLEMENT, Clyde H., age 33, of 39 Markham St. Atlanta d. train accident. Born Tunnel Hill, Ga. Parents: Dr. and Mrs. J. P. Clement. Bros: S. D. Clement, John G. Clement. Sisters: Misses Reo M. and Elma Clement. AG 9/12/1906

CLEMONS, P., colored, age 72, d. 176 W. Mitchell St. Atlanta. AG 1/8/1908

CLEN, Thomas, colored, age 57, d. 1 Lyons Ave. Atlanta. AG 10/13/1908

CLEVELAND, Alfred, son of Mr. and Mrs. A. L., d. Sun. Cherokee Ave., Atlanta. Interred: Family Burial Ground. AG 5/22/1910

CLEVELAND, B. J., age 70, d. 415 Ormond St. Atlanta. AG 9/4/1907

CLEVELAND, Henry E., age 1 day, d. 46 Howell Mill Rd. Atlanta. AG 11/4/1908

CLEVELAND, R. H., age 1 yr., d. 43 Moreland Ave. Atlanta. AG 11/11/1909

CLEVELAND, W. C., Greenville, S. C.'s wealthiest citizen, d., age 73. AG /1/1908

CLIETT, J. H. M., Mrs., age 55, d. Powersville, Ga. Husband and son, Furman Cliett, survives. Sister: Mrs. A. O. Cliet. Bro: Dr. J. D. Manard of Abbeville, GA. AG 5/22/1907

CLIFFORD, B. G., Dr., b. Haverhill, N. H. 12/1/1843, Vet. Conf. Army, Co. D, 23rd Regt., N. C., died Union, S. C. AG 2/8/1910

CLIFTON, James Hill, age 2, son of Mr. and Mrs. W. L., d. Sun. 278 Candler Ave., Atlanta. Interred: Westview. AG 5/22/1910

CLIFTON, Margaret, dau. of Mr. and Mrs. M. L., d. Sun. Interred: Westview, Atlanta. AG 5/14/1906

CLINE, J. T., age 10 mo., dau. of Mr. and Mrs. J. T., d. 52 Culver St., Atlanta, Thurs. Interred: Hollywood. AG 7/4/1908

CLINKSCALE, R. M., Confederate veteran, d. Sun. Interred: Westview. AG 3/16/1907

CLINKSCALES, Jennie, Mrs., age 68, d. 138 W. Pine St. Atlanta. AG 12/26/1907

CLISBY, Joseph, Mrs. d. Mon. Macon, Ga. Interred: Rose Hill. She was widow of late Joseph Clisby, owner of The Macon Telegraph. AG 4/7/1908

CLITON,J. S. d. 12/8 Thomasville, Ga., native of Lumpkin, Ga. AC 12/9/1905

CLOPTON, Dr. d. 5/19 Richmond, Va. Many yrs. pastor of Memorial Church, Anniston, Ala. AC 5/31/1905

CLOPTON, Lucile and Ruby buried Westview. Res. 652 S. Pryor St., Atlanta. Parents: Mr. and Mrs. Edwin. AG 5/1/1906

CLOTFELTER, J. G., native of Fulton Co., Ga., recently of Birmingham, Ala., d. 7/30. AG 7/30/1909

CLOYDE, Susan Todd, Mrs. d. Columbis S. C. 11/8. AG 11/10/1908

COACHMAN, Mariah, colored, age 59, d. 50 Rawson St., Atlanta. AG 12/5/1907

COBB, Essie Ruth, age 2, dau. of Mr. and Mrs. C. H., d. Anderson, S. c., Fri. Interred: Decatur cemetery. AG 12/14/1907

COBB, J. H. d. Tues. Atlanta. Interred: Live Oak, Fla. AG 5/31/1906

COBB, J. M., age 49, of Dawson, Ga., d. Atlanta Tues. Daus: Mrs. R. C. Ward, Miss Martha Cobb. Sons: J. M., Jr., T. A., Harry P. Interred: Shellman, Ga. AG 5/4/1910

COBB, James H. d. Temple, Ga., age 70. Bro: J. L., Atlanta. Ch: Dr. J. T. of Felton; William, postmaster at Temple; and Mrs. J. M. Wynn. Son: Felix N. Cobb, Atty. AG 9/28/1907

COBB, Jane, colored, age 54, d. Moreland Ave. Atlanta. AG 9/21/1910

COBB, L. O. of Temple, Ga. d. Sun. Leaves wife, 4 children. Interred: Pleasant Grove Cemetery. AG 5/7/1907

COBB, Lamar, Major d. Athens, Ga., Sat., son of Gen. Howell Cobb, bro. of Judge Cobb of Supreme Court; Judge Howell Cobb of Athens and Ordinary J. A. Cobb of Americus, Ga. Leaves wife, 3 sons, dau. AG 3/11/1907

COBB, Mary, colored, age 50, d. Colbert, Ga. AG 1/17/1908

COBB, Robert G., age 72, d. res. of son, R. H. Cobb, 173 Gordon St., Atlanta, Wed. Interred: Westview. AG 7/22/1909

COBB, W. H. killed. His wife, Mrs. Cobb, held. Royston, Ga. AC 8/12/1905

COBB, William shot by John F. Hillard, Milan, Ga. Recovery doubtful. AG 2/22/1910

COBBLE, Howard M., infant, age 2, son of Mr. and Mrs. John R., d. 169 Fowler St. Atlanta. Interred: Englewood, Tenn. AG 6/11/1910

COBBS, R. V., age 69, died at 31 E. Pavillon Street, Atlanta. AG 11/29/1906

COCHRAN, Emma, colored, age 44, d. Alms House. Atlanta. AG 8/24/1907

COCHRAN, G. A., age 15, son of Mr. and Mrs. E. A., d. 9/12. Interred: Mableton church yard. AC 9/14/1905

COCHRAN, George A., age 15, son of G. A., Sr., d. 9/13 26 White St., Atlanta. Interred: Mableton church yard. AC 9/15/1905

72

COCHRAN, Georgia, Mrs. d. Indianapolis, Ind. Interred:Atlanta. Leaves husband and one daughter, Mrs. Jessse Nichols. AG 5/29/1906

COCHRAN, infant of J. A., age 3 mos., d. E. Atlanta. AG 9/28/1907

COCHRAN, John B., age 74, d. 5 Vassar St., Atlanta. Wife. Dau: Mrs. J. B. Parry. Son: J. L. Interred: Westview. AC 4/2/1910

COCHRAN, Louise, age 2, dau. of Mr. and Mrs. James, d. Cherry Sta. Wed. Interred: Hollywood Cemetery. AG 12/15/1910

COCHRAN, Perlonia, Mrs., age 52, d. Greensferry Rd. Atlanta. Interred: Westview. AG 1/20/1910

COCHRAN, Z., Mrs., age 37, d. E. Atlanta. AG 9/3/1907

COCHRAN, Zenobia M., Mrs. d. 181 E. Georgia Ave., Atlanta, Sat. Interred: Stone Mountain, Ga. AG 6/27/1910

CODY, C. C., age abt 30, d. father's apt., L. L. Cody on Noble St. Interred: Oxford, Ala., his old home. Moved here few yrs. ago from Macon, Ga. AG 10/12/1909

CODY, C. P., Mrs., age 43, d. Atlanta. AG 1/11/1910

CODY, Lydia, Miss, age 22, d. 146 Wells St. Atlanta. Interred: Hollywood. AG 6/29/1908

COFER, Bettie May, age 15, dau. of Mr. and Mrs. P. A., interred Bogart, Ga. AG 9/11/1909

COFER, J. A., Dr., age 44, d. 11/17 Atlanta nephew's residence. AC 11/19/1905

COFER, Oscar A., age 20, son of Mr. and Mrs. C. L., d. Thurs., 214 Bass St. Atlanta. Interred: Westview. AG 9/13/1907

COFIELD, Annie, Mrs., age 36, d. 20 Gospero St., Atlanta, Tues. Interred: Lawrenceville. AG 9/30/1908

COGAN, James of Washington, Ga. suicide. AG 9/22/1908

COGGANS, Richard of Monroe Co., Ga., d. Colliers, Ga. Fri. Wife, several children. Interred: Cabiness Cemetery. AG 4/5/1910

COGGIN, John J. of 415 Bouleard, Atlanta, at death's door. AG 3/11/1907

COGGINS, Sarah, Mrs., age 72, d. 61 DeKalb Ave. Atlanta. AG 3/7/1907

COHEN, B., Mrs., age 71, d. 242 Central Ave., Atlanta, Wed. Interred: Hollywood. AG 9/15/1910

COHEN, Beher, age 83, d. 59 N. Butler St. Atlanta. AG 7/26/1907

COHEN, Dorothy Esther, age 10 mos., dau. of Mr. and Mrs. Dewald Cohen, d. 30 Orange St., Atlanta, Tues. Interred: Oakland. AG 7/28/1908

COHEN, Etta, Miss, age 51, d. Atlanta. Interred: Oakland. AG 9/6/1910

COHEN, Haskel, age 5, d. 166 Gilmore St. Atlanta. AG 12/17/1910

COHEN, M. M., age 60, d. 15 Warren Pl. Atlanta. Wife, 4 children. Interred: Oakland. AG 8/31/1910

COKER, Abraham, ge 2 mos., d. 42 Alice St. Atlanta. AG 6/12/1908

COKER, F. M. d. Washington St., Atlanta 9/12. Interred: Oakland. Confed. Vet. Moved to Coweta Co. when boy, then Pike Co. m. Miss Sallie A. Johnson, dau. of Dr. Green, Putnam Co. 5/17/1855. AC 9/14/1905

COKER, George Edward, age 13, son of Mr. and Mrs. E. A., d. Sun. Atlanta. Interred: Greenwood. AG 7/29/1908

COKER, Heyward S. killed Fri. at cotton mill, Roswell, age 34. Parents, several bros. and sisters. AG 9/26/1910

COKER, Isabella, Mrs., in 80´s, d. res. of Capt. W. C. Orr at Oxford 4/19. One of Calhoun Co.´s oldest citizens. AC 4/20/1905

COLBERT, Charley, negro, shot by Dozier Green, negro, d. Juliett, Ga. 9/20. AG 9/21/1909

COLBERT, Grace M., age 7, d. 295 Park Ave. Atlanta. AG 9/29/1909

COLE, A. A., age 56, d. Kirkwood Ave., E. Atlanta Mon. Interred: Lilburn, Ga. AG 11/23/1907

COLE, Charles C. d. Washington, D. C. 3/17. AC 3/18/1905

COLE, Clarke of Atlanta d. Montgomery, Ala. Leaves wife, one child. AG 11/23/1907

COLE, E. I., Mrs. funeral Tues. 6/30. Atlanta. AG 7/29/1908

COLE, E. I., Mrs., age 54, d. 145 Walton St., Atlanta. Interred: Westview. AG 6/30/1908

COLE, George Henry, b. 11/24/1838 Westport, d. 181 Ashby St., Atlanta. 1873 m. Julia E. Allen, Niagara Co., NY. To Atlanta, 1885. Dau: Mrs. H C. Roberts. Sis: Miss Minnie E. Cole, Atlanta. Bro: Austin H. Cole, Rochester, NY. AG 5/10/1907

COLE, Gordon, age 1, d. 117 Fraser St. Atlanta. AG 6/7/1907

COLE, Haygood, infant son of Mr. and Mrs. W. A., d. parents res., 4 Pelham St., Atlanta, Tues. Interred: Primrose Cemetery. AG 9/14/1909

COLE, J. D., age 64, d. Soldiers´ Home. Atlanta. AG 11/11/1907

COLE, James D. d. Soldiers´ Home Atlanta, Fri. Confederate Veteran. Dau: Miss Louise L. Cole, Augusta. Interred: Augusta, Ga. AG 11/9/1907

COLE, John killed by A. D. Strickland, Hazlehurst, Ga., who is jailed. AG 12/16/1907

COLE, Martha Burrell Overby, Mrs., age 78, wife of R. D. Cole of Newnan, (golden wedding anniversary was 1899) d. Tues. Nephew: E. M. Cole of Newnan. Her son d. no. yrs. ago. Mr. Cole´s bro., Matthew, d. few wks. ago. AG 3/12/1907

COLE, Martha, Mrs., age 80, d. Thurs. Interred: Decatur Cemetery. AG 7/10/1909

COLE, Ruth, age 2, of Mr. and Mrs. Howard Cole of Chicago., d. Thurs. at res. of Mrs. H. A. Dunwoody on Currier St., Atlanta, mother of Mrs. Cole. AG 2/22/1907

COLE, Sarah Stark, Miss, dau. of Mr. and Mrs. Thomas D., d. 9/21 Augusta, Ga. AC 9/23/1905

COLE, Thomas, age 18, d. Sun. Interred: Senoia, Ga. AG 7/23/1906

COLE, Thomas P. funeral 7/2. Interred: Oakland. Kin: V. E. Lambert, M. J. Cole, W. H. Cole. AG 7/1/1907

COLE, W. E., age 60, d. 34 Moreland Ave., Atlanta. Wife. Daus: Mrs. Geo. W. Price, Atlanta, Miss Edda Cole, Norfolk, Va. Sis: Mrs. L. A. Vickers, Shreveport, La. Bros: T. A., Americus, Ga., C. E., Columbus, Ga. Bur: Fairburn. AG 2/11/1909

COLE, William N., age 62, d. 12 Robinson St. Atlanta. AG 11/27/1910

COLEMAN, Francis, colored, age 34, d. 7 Ashley St. Atlanta. AG 7/9/1908

COLEMAN, Francis, infant, d. 485 W. Ashby St., Atlanta. AG 3/24/1910

COLEMAN, Hazel, age 3 yrs., dau. of Mr. and Mrs. W. T. Coleman, d. 63 Martin St. Atlanta. Interred: Oakland. AG 7/8/1907

COLEMAN, John, son of Mr. and Mrs. H. M., 301 W. 4th St., Atlanta, d. Sat. Interred: Hollywood. AG 2/20/1908

COLEMAN, Martha, inf. dau. of Mr. and Mrs. W. T., d. Wed. 93 Crew St., Atlanta, Thurs. Interred: Hollywood. AG 11/26/1908

COLEMAN, Mary, Mrs. d. Thurs. Funeral at res. of John Brooks, Center St., E. Macon. Interred: Ft. Hill. AG 10/11/1907

COLEMAN, Mary, Mrs., age 51, wid. 268 Central Ave., d. Tues. Buried: Oakland. AG 9/11/1906

COLEMAN, Sarah E., Mrs., age 82, d. 20 Park St. Atlanta. AG 12/27/1910

COLEMAN, Tommie, colored, age 3 mos., d. 101 N. Butler St. Atlanta. AG 11/3/1908

COLEMAN, W. T., age 39, d. 91 Crew St. Atlanta. Wife: Eva. Several children. Interred: Hollywood. AG 12/31/1910

COLES, Fred, colored, age 17, d. 60 Yonge St. Atlanta. AG 11/29/1907

COLES, Norman, colored, age 15, d. 10/27 60 Yonge St. Atlanta. AG 10/28/1910

COLLE, Carrie, colored, age 6, d. 101 N. Butler St. Atlanta. AG 11/25/1907

COLLIER, Emma, Mrs., age 38, d. 167 Rhodes St. Atlanta. Wife of H. E. Collier. Mother: Mrs. T. P. Gray. Interred: Fayetteville, Ga. AG 4/20/1908

COLLIER, George W., age 32, d. Piedmont Hotel. Atlanta. AG 1/25/1910

COLLIER, Harriet, colored, age 62, d. 233 Thurmond St. Atlanta. AG 7/15/1909

COLLIER, I. C., planter, d. Barnesville Sat., age 64. Son: J. C. Collier of Barnesville. Interred: Barnesville, Ga. AG 7/13/1908

COLLIER, J. W., age 63, d. 12 W. 11th St. Atlanta. AG 4/27/1910

COLLIER, L. W., Mrs. d. 3 miles from Comer, Ga., his home. AG 5/13/1907

COLLIER, Marion C., Mrs., age 40, d. 167 Davis St., Atlanta, Thurs. Husband, two bros., two sisters. Interred: Fayetteville, Ga. AG 4/2/1909

COLLIER, Minnie L., Mrs., age 24, d. 453 E. Georgia Ave. Atlanta. AG 6/12/1907

COLLIER, Wesley G., Mrs., wid. of late Wesley G., d. Peachtree Rd., Atlanta, Fri. Interred: Sardis Cemetery. Sons: John W., Charles F., Frank M., Sanford G. Dau: Mrs. Carrie L. Walker. AG 12/7/1908

COLLIER, William Henry, age 70, d. 50 Mills St. Atlanta. AG 8/6/1907

COLLINS, Clarence Earle, inf. son of Mr. and Mrs. J. E., d. 18 Ridge Ave., Atlanta, Sat. AG 6/5/1909

COLLINS, Dave, convict, negro, killed by Mr. Dickey (bro-in-law of Miss Hogg, the woman convict assaulted) Crystal Springs, Ga. AC 7/12/1905

COLLINS, Dina, colored, age 109, d. 292 Fulton St. Atlanta. AG 7/6/1909

COLLINS, J. T., age 55, of Hapeville, Ga., d. Mon. Wife, several children. Interred: Mt. Zion Church. AG 4/12/1910

COLLINS, J. T., age 57, d. Atlanta. AG 4/14/1910

COLLINS, Jonas E., age 63, d. Old Soldiers' Home, Atlanta. AG 8/19/1909

COLLINS, Lillian, colored, age 24, d. 101 N. Butler St. Atlanta. AG 1/31/1908

COLLINS, Martha, Mrs. d. 275 Whitehall St. Atlanta Thurs. Interred: Duluth, Ga. AG 6/2/1906

COLLINS, P. J., age 30, of Sycamore, Ga., d. AG 5/2/1910

COLLINS, R. S., formerly of Macon, d. Colorado. Interred: Rose Hill, Macon, Ga. AG 10/17/1908

COLLINS, Rozier, inf. dau. of Mr. and Mrs. R. T., d. 46 Lee St., Atlanta, Wed. Interred: Westview. AG 11/17/1910

COLLINS, T. A., Mrs. d. Jan. 11 Ellavilla, Ga. Husband. 4 ch. Interred: Ellaville, Ga. AC 1/12/1905

COLLINS, T. R., age 33, d. 17 W. Cain St. Atlanta. AG 8/20/1907

COLLIS, John d. Atlanta Mon. Interred: McDonough, Ga. AG 6/6/1906

COLQUITT, Lilla N., wife of W. W., d. 457 Piedmont Ave. Atlanta. She was Miss Lilla, dau. of Wm Neyle Habersham, Savannah. Ch: Lilla, Anna (Atlanta), Harriet (Savannah), Wm Neyle (Savannah), Joe Clay, Wellborn, Jr. (Atlanta). AG 7/3/1906

COLSON, M. J., Judge of Brunswick, d. Fri. Lived Brunswick for 40 years, age 60. Leaves wife, son: Col. J. T. Colson of Brunswick. AG 5/21/1907

COLVARD, John H., Col. d. Sat. Bowman, Ga. Interred: Holly Springs Cemetery. AG 4/30/1906

COMBEE, James P. d. 194 Bellwood Ave. Atlanta. AG 6/10/1907

COMBES, Daniel, colored, age 60, d. 20 Spinks alley. Atlanta. AG 8/5/1907

COMBS, Carl, age 2-1/2 yrs., inf. son of Mr. and Mrs. G. C., d. Mon. Atlanta. Interred: Locust Grove, Ga. AG 10/4/1910

COMBS, Daniel, negro, d. 20 Spinks alley, Atlanta, Fri. AG 8/3/1907

COMBS, I. E., Mrs., age 28, d. Atlanta Sun. Interred: Locust Grove, Ga. AG 9/13/1909

COMER, Annie, inf. dau. of Mr. and Mrs. R. S., d. Atlanta. Interred: Westview. AG 10/14/1907

COMER, L. J., Mrs., age 50, d. 834 Peachtree St. Atlanta. AG 10/18/1907

COMER, Sarah, Mrs., age 87, of Madison Co., d. 3/17. 5 sons (over age 50). 3 grandsons. Interred: Oconee Cemetery, Athens. Ch: Joseph T., Athens; A. F., Danielsville; W. J., Maysville; J. T. and H. T. of Comer. AC 3/20/1905

COMINGORE, David, musician, killed by freight train at Madison, Ga. 3/29. Bro. in Illinois. AG 3/30/1909

CONAWAY, T. J., age 69, d. 101 N. Butler St. Atlanta. AG 5/20/1909

CONDON-HENDRICK, L., Mrs., age 65, d. 388 Spring St. Atlanta. AG 3/11/1909

CONE, F. S. of Statesboro, d. Sat. Interred: East Side Cemetery. Bro: Major J. S. Cone, C. S. A. AG 9/7/1908

CONE, Hobart Douglas, age 2, son of Mr. and Mrs. E. H., d. 410 E. North Ave. Atlanta, Mon. AG 1/17/1910

CONE, Mary, Mrs., age 40, d. 92 Luckie St. Atlanta. AG 11/15/1909

CONE, Mary, Mrs. d. family home on Flanders St., S. Macon yesterday. Mother, two children. Interred: Ft. Hill cemetery. AG 4/1/1907

CONEY, Louise N., age 62, d. Atlanta. AG 2/11/1910

CONEY, Martha Catherine, age 2, son of Mr. and Mrs. J. F., Hawkinsville. Interred: Orange Hill. AG 10/29/1906

CONGDON, Elizabeth, Mrs.,ge 78, d. 28 E. Boulevard, S. Kirkwood, Atlanta. AG 12/14/1909

CONGER, A. killed by Jesse and Dempsey Taylor, Tifton, Ga., indicted 7/17. Sons: Abe and Barney Conger. AG 7/17/1908

CONGER, W. R., age 73, d. 63 Ponders Ave. Atlanta. AG 9/6/1910

CONKLIN, Curtis, age 2, d. 58 McDonough St. Atlanta. AG 10/5/1908

CONKLIN, D. H. of Titusville, Fla. d. Wed. Atlanta. AG 7/12/1906

CONLEY, Warren, negro, killed at camp meeting at Neal, Ga. yesterday. AG 9/2/1907

CONN, H. J., age 50, d. Tyner, Tenn. Wed. Wife. Interred: Atlanta. AG 4/30/1908

CONNALLY, J. M., age 76, d. 300 Ashby St. Atlanta. AG 2/8/1907

CONNALLY, Mary S., Mrs., age 66, d. 336 Pulliam St. Atlanta. AG 7/25/1910

CONNALLY, Rebecca F., age 45, d. 379 W. North Ave. Atlanta. Interred: Woodstock, Ga. AG 7/27/1907

CONNALLY, W. C., Dr., Paulding Co. physician, age 65, d. Dallas, Ga. AG 11/1/1907

CONNELL, Jesse Lee, age 18, son of Mr. and Mrs. R. L., d. 711 Marietta St., Atlanta, Mon. Interred: College Park, Ga. AG 7/14/1908

CONNELL, Mary Frances, Mrs., wife of late Dr. George T., d. dau.´s res., Mrs. Henry Strickland of Alpharetta, 3/22, age 69. Son: John, Atlanta. AG 3/24/1910

CONNELL, Nancy, Mrs., age 85, d. 12/1 Macon. Ch: J. J., J. T., of Macon. AC 12/1/1905

CONNER, Harriet J.,78, d. Kennesaw 12/10. Bur-New Bethel. Grs-Erastus Robertson, Ed Puckett, Virgil McConnell, John, Henry & Fred Boston. Ch-Mrs. F. A. Boston; P. L. Conner, Kennesaw, Ga.; Jno T. Conner, Tx, R. C. Conner, NY. AG 12/14/1907

CONNER, Lee J., Mrs., Knoxville, Tn. d. sis. res., Mrs. R. Lee Walker, 834 Peachtree St., Atlanta. Bro: Maj. George Rutzler, Charlotte, N. C. Husb: Lee J. (on isthmus of Panama). Parents: Mr. & Mrs. J. F. Rutzler. Bur: Oakland. AG 10/3/1907

CONNER, Wade d. 9/4 Monticello, Ga. Parents. One sis: Mrs. R. J. Warren, Monticello. Bros: H. E., Augusta; O. G., Cordele; Dr. Connor, Dallas, Texas. AC 9/6/1905

CONNOR, John H., retired merchant, d. Columbus 5/13, age 67. Interred: Church of the Holy Family. Never md. AG 5/14/1908

CONNOR, King, Mrs. d. 11/1, 427 E. Fair St. Atlanta. Interred: Westview. AC 11/2/1905

CONNORS, Lochrane, age 2, died 308 Peachtree Street, Atlanta. AG 12/12/1906

CONWAY, Leona, age 6, d. 16 Western Ave. Atlanta. AG 8/24/1908

CONWAY, W. O. d. 405 Central Ave., Atlanta, Wed. Wife, one bro., adopted mother and sister, Mrs. E. M. Blount and Mrs. W. O. Ballard. Interred: Westview. AG 9/22/1909

CONYERS, Gussie, colored, age 40, d. 101 N. Butler St. Atlanta. AG 4/2/1909

COOGLER, D. J., Mrs. d. Thurs. Conley, Ga. Interred: Forest Park, Ga. AG 8/15/1907

COOGLER, Roscoe P., age 20, d. Atlanta. Parents: Mr. and Mrs. J. Luther Coogler, 121 Estoria St. Interred: Jonesboro, Ga. Bro: A. E. Coogler. Decd was nephew of Probation Officer, S. J. Coogler. AG 11/14/1908

COOGLER, Sallie, Mrs., age 38, wife of T. W., d. Sun. Atlanta, 15 Hunnicutt St. Interred: Westview. AG 12/13/1909

COOK, Alberta, age 18, freshman class at Ga. Tech, d. Fri. Mother: Mrs. R. C. Cook, Covington. Bros: Joel R. Cook, student at Tech; H. Claude H. Cook, Atlanta. Sisters: Elizabeth and Janita Cook, Covington. Interred: Covington AG 6/14/1907

COOK, Benjamin, colored, age 51, d. 9 Lyons Ave. Atlanta. AG 3/29/1907

COOK, Charles, colored, age 7 mos., d. 123 Bell St. Atlanta. AG 5/14/1908

COOK, E. D., age 21, d. College Park Wed. Infant dau., 5 bros. Interred: Red Oak Church yard. AG 2/23/1910

COOK, Ellsdale, Miss, age 17, d. 16 Mayson Turner Rd. Atlanta, Oct. 1. AG 10/3/1910

COOK, Fannie, Mrs. d. Atlanta 9/4, age 73, wid. of Alex. Only dau: Miss Pearl Cook. Interred: Johnson Cemetery, 2 mi. E. of Covington. AC 9/6/1905

COOK, George, age 5, d. Flat Shoals Rd., Atlanta. Interred: Hardeman's church yard. AG 5/21/1908

COOK, George, colored, age 41, d. 32 Fortune St. Atlanta. AG 12/3/1907

COOK, H. P., age 73, Confederate veteran, d. Home for Incurables Thurs. Interred: Westview. Wife survives him. AG 9/28/1906

COOK, H. W. d. East Point, Ga., Wed., age 38. Wife, one dau. Interred: Union City, Ga. AG 11/8/1910

COOK, Hattie L., Mrs., age 84, d. 7 Longley Ave., Howell Station, Atlanta, Fri. Interred: Westview. AG 9/12/1908

COOK, Hiram, inf. son of Mr. and Mrs. J. T., grandson of Rev. and Mrs. W. A. Babb, d. 131 Meldrum St., Atlanta, Mon. Interred: Westview. AG 6/9/1908

COOK, I. J., age 73, d. 875 Whitehall St. Atlanta. AG 8/25/1909

COOK, Irene, Mrs. d. 12/25 Atlanta, age 31, dau. of Capt. Theophilus Cooper of USN. Interred: Baltimore, Md. AC 12/27/1905

COOK, J. H., age 65, d. Nickajack, Ga. AG 1/19/1910

COOK, Jesse, negro, condemned to die at Cartersville, Ga. for murdering 12/21 Joe Cannon, negro. To hang 2/25. AG 4/21/1910

COOK, Jesse, negro, shot Joe Cannon, negro, Cartersville 12/21. Cook to hang 2/25. AG 1/15/1910

COOK, Joseph d. Fri. 18 Formwalt St., Atlanta, Atlanta. Interred: Hollywood. AG 5/24/1907

COOK, Joseph L. d. 11/28 Atlanta. Interred: Westview. AC 11/31/1905

COOK, Lillian, Mrs., wife of T. A., d. Midway, Ga. 8/23. Husband, several small children. AC 8/24/1905

COOK, Oscar of 313 W. Fair St., Atlanta killed in railroad accident. Interred: Hollywood. AG 6/7/1906

COOK, Rena Estelle, Miss, age 24, d. Sat. Decatur. Mother, sister, 3 bros. AG 8/6/1910

COOK, Robert, colored, age 1, d. 46 Sunset Ave. Atlanta. AG 2/8/1907

COOK, Sallie, colored, age 34, d. 392 W. North Ave. Atlanta. AG 2/8/1908

COOK, W. W., Mrs., widow of W. W. Cook, d. Wrightsville Fri. 4th
death in family within a year. AG 8/7/1906

COOK, William Clarence, age 3, son of Mr. and Mrs. W. W., d. 302
East Ave. Atlanta. Interred: Oakland. AG 9/30/1909

COOKE, Catherine, dau. of Mr. and Mrs. L. A., d. Fri. 690 Ash
St., Macon. Interred: Ellaville, Ga. AG 9/7/1907

COOLEDGE, Norman F. , Mrs., age 80, d. Mon. res. of dau., Mrs. N.
G. Gable, Bolton, Ga. Funeral at Norcross, Ga. Son: F. J.
Cooledge, Atlanta. AG 5/13/1907

COOLEY, Ruth, Mrs.,a ge 22, d. Lakewood Ave. Atlanta. AG
12/14/1909

COOMBS, Frank B., inf. son of Mr. and Mrs. R. B. of Clarkston,
Ga., d. Tues. Interred: Clarkston. AG 4/13/1909

COON, Susan S., Mrs., age 86, d. 26 E. Kimball St. Atlanta. AG
11/22/1909

COOPER, A. B., age 26, d. 83 Windsor St. Atlanta. AG 12/14/1909

COOPER, Alice, age 10, d. 17 W. Cain St. Atlanta. AG 10/8/1909

COOPER, Archie B., age 26, d. 83 Windsor St., Atlanta, Sur.
Father and mother: Mr. and Mrs. G. W. Cooper. Wife, one dau.
Interred: Westview. AG 12/11/1909

COOPER, Charles, age 73, d. 101 Butler St. Atlanta. AG 10/11/1909

COOPER, Charles W. shot and killed by B. M. Pacquet, his son-in-
law, Charleston, S. C. 5/25. Cooper beat his wife who took refuge
with her father. Pacquet claims self-defense. AG 5/25/1910

COOPER, Estelle Camille, age 7 mos., dau. of Mr. and Mrs. John E.
S., 122 Cherokee Ave., Atlanta, Fri. Interred: Westview. AG
1/24/1908

COOPER, Eugene body found in rear of Cox home at Cass St.,
Cartersville, Ga., murdered, age 70. AG 12/12/1907

COOPER, Florine, colored, age 2 weeks, d. 149 Orme St. Atlanta.
AG 8/22/1910

COOPER, Floyd, colored, age 39, d. 90 Larkin St. Atlanta. AG
12/7/1910

COOPER, Frederick William, age 29, d. Fri. Atlanta, native of
Iowa. Mother: Mrs. M. J. Cooper. Sis: Miss Katherine. AG
8/15/1910

COOPER, Georgia, Mrs., age 54, died Butler Street, Atlanta. AG
12/10/1906

COOPER, Georgia, Mrs. of 228 Ira St., Atlanta, cut, beaten with
hatchet by her husband, John F. Cooper (who then shot and killed
himself), died at Grady Hospital, Atlanta, Sat. AG 12/8/1906

COOPER, H. E., age 31, d. 37 Irwin St., Atlanta, Wed. Sis: Miss
Hattie Cooper. Interred: Tallapoosa, Ga. AG 12/24/1908

COOPER, Hunter P., Dr., died 598 Peachtree St. Interment:
Westview. AG 8/27/1906

COOPER, Inez, Miss, age 43, d. Wed. Atlanta. Sis: Mrs. . L.
Wells, Mrs. A. A. Brearly, Miss Estelle Cooper. Bros: E. H., W.
M. Interred: St. Charles, S. C. AG 9/2/1910

COOPER, J. W., Mrs., age 72, d. 3/28 Huntsville, Ala. 8 Ch:
Carroll P. Cooper; Hon. Lawrence Cooper of Huntsville, Ala. AC
3/28/1905

COOPER, James E., colored, age 64, d. 14 Hancock Pl. Atlanta. AG
6/22/1908

COOPER, John F. shot wife, Georgia, then shot and killed himself.
AG 12/8/1906

COOPER, John T., age 29, d. 309 Pulliam St., Atlanta, Thurs. Mother: Mrs. Mary E. Sis: Misses Gertrude and Hattie Cooper; Mrs. Bertha Irby. Bro: Curtis Cooper. Bur: Marietta, Ga. AG 10/2/1908

COOPER, Mattie E., Mrs. d. Thurs. Iceville, Ga. Interred: Smyrna, Ga. AG 7/24/1909

COOPER, Pinkie, colored, age 33, d. 80 Yonge St. Atlanta. AG 3/1/1908

COOPER, Sarah F., Miss, age 27, d. Baltimore, Md. AG 8/20/1907

COPELAN, Corry d. Tues. Greensboro, Ga, age 50, buried 9/9. Wife, large family of children. AG 9/10/1909

COPELAN, W. D. of Greensboro, Ga. shot by negro Sat., age 23. Father: Corry Copelan. Interred: Greensboro, Ga. AG 8/17/1908

COPELAND, Alex, colored, age 45, d. Inman, Ga. AG 3/6/1908

COPELAND, Anthony, colored, age 55, d. 20 Westley Ave. Atlanta. AG 4/12/1909

COPELAND, J. L. d. Dasher, Ga., Mon., age 75. Interred: Union Cemetery. 6 children. AG 8/31/1910

COPELAND, Nettie, Mrs., age 60, d. Sun. 63 Atlantic Ave., Atlanta. Interred: Macon, Ga. AG 10/3/1910

COPPEDGE, Adeline J., Mrs., age 90, d. 167 W. Hunter St. Atlanta, Tues. Ch: Z. T. Coppedge, Emma Coppedge, Atlanta. Interred: Williamson, Ga. AG 3/10/1908

COPPS, J. M., Mrs., res. of Alexandria valley, Anniston, Ala., died. AG 8/22/1906

CORBET, Henry. His body send from Atlanta to be interred: Rutherfordton, N. C. AG 11/13/1907

COREY, Frances W., age 66, d. 17 W. Cain St. Atlanta. AG 9/3/1907

COREY, W. E., age 20 yrs., d. at 18 Dainey St. Atlanta. AG 8/9/1907

CORLEY, John, 8 mos., d. 165 McDaniel St. Atlanta. AG 6/3/1909

CORLEY, John W., age 28, d. 8 Highland Ave., Atlanta, Sun. Wife, one child, father, one bro., survive. Interred: Rock Springs. AG 7/6/1908

CORLEY, Lizzie, Mrs., age 35, d. 17 W. Cain St. Atlanta. AG 9/9/1908

CORLEY, S. P., Mrs., age 70, d. Thurs. Flat Shoals Rd. Atlanta. Husband, 5 children. Interred: Indian Creek Church Cemetery. AG 1/9/1908

CORN, A., age 25, d. Grady Hospital. Atlanta. AG 1/4/1910

CORN, N. A., age 25, d. Atlanta Sun. Mother resides Central, Ga. AG 1/3/1910

CORNELIUS, Bessie, colored, age 47, d. Milledgeville, Ga. AG 9/12/1908

CORNELIUS, Frank Rev., Prim. Bapt. minister of Clinch Co., shot and killed his home, 3-4 mi. from Dupont. Bro-in-law of W. H. Dame, assassinated two wks ago. AG 9/21/1906

CORNELL, G. P. d. Milledgeville Mon. Funeral at Indian Springs 8/30. Wife, one dau, Miss Lilly Cornell, and two sons. AG 8/31/1910

CORNELL, infant of Mr. and Mrs. A. J. d. Thurs. 3 Tumlin St., Atlanta. Interred: Hollywood. AG 8/1/1907

CORNELL, infant of A. F., d. Thurs., 3 Tumlin St., Atlanta. Interred: Hollywood. AG 8/1/1907

CORNETT, George, Confederate Veteran, d. 1894. Wife: Temperance. AG 8/10/1910

CORNETT, Rosa, Mrs., age 25, d. 2 Ethel St., Atlanta. AG 6/25/1910
CORNETT, Temperance, Mrs. d. Tues. res. of granddau., Mrs. A. M.
Lowe, 321 Peachtree St., Atlanta. Age 91, wid. of George Cornett,
Confed. Vet. who d. 16 yrs. ago. She was dau. of George Foster,
early settler of Charleston, S. C. who d. 100 ??? grdaus: Mrs.
V. C. Wilson, Mrs. L. V. Wilson, Mrs. A. M. Lowe. Grson: A. M.
Crenshaw of Logansville. AG 8/10/1910
CORRELL, Joseph Summerall, retired merchant of Raleigh, N. C., d.
Sat. Wife, 6 ch. Bro: W. B. Correll of Atlanta. Sisters: Mrs. H.
A. Deal, Greenville, S. C., Mrs. C. S. Roberts, Charlotte, N. C.
AG 7/22/1907
CORREY, W. J., Mrs. of Union Point, Ga., d. Fri. Interred: Union
Point, Ga. AG 3/29/1907
CORYELL, H. G., Mrs. of Marietta, age 40, d. 1/2. She was 1st
cousin of Chief W. P. Joyner of Atlanta and dau. of Col. James
W. Robertson. AC 1/3/1905
COSBY, Nellie Kate, age 6 mos., dau. of Mr. and Mrs. C. H., 60 S.
Delta Place Atlanta, d. Tues. Interred: Washington, Ga. AG
4/21/1909
COSKERY, Thomas W. funeral 3/11, Augusta, Ga. AG 3/11/1908
COSTAN, C. L., age 67, d. Confederate Soldiers' Home, Atlanta
Thurs, member of Co. K., No. 30, Miss, Orderly Sgt. AG 5/14/1908
COSTELO, C., age 45, d. 101 N. Butler St. Atlanta. AG 5/4/1909
COSTLEY, Mattie, Mrs., age 55, d. 258 Bellwood Ave. Atlanta.
Interred: Hollywood. AG 5/24/1910
COTES, S. M., age 50, d. Piedmont, Ala. AG 3/7/1910
COTTEN, Elizabeth J., Mrs., age 54, d. Decatur, Ga. AG 9/22/1908
COTTER, Edward P. of McRae, Ga., d. Sun. in Macon. Interred:
McRae Cemetery. AG 4/25/1910
COTTER, John of Augusta d. 8/23, blind, age 60. AC 8/24/1905
COTTON, Augustus S., age 40, d. Columbus, Ga. Sat. Interred:
Alexander City, Ala. Wife, one dau. AG 10/4/1910
COTTON, Joseph, colored, age 21, d. 26 Solomon St. Atlanta. AG
9/3/1909
COTTON, Willie, Miss, age 81, d. 52 Whitehall St., Atlanta, Tues.
Interred: Cartersville, Ga., Oak Hill Cemetery. She was buried
next to her father, William Cotton, who d. few years ago. AG
11/19/1909
COUCH, Altha May, Mrs., wife of Dr. A. B., d. Houston, Tx., Sun.
Husband, 6 sons: Dr. Albert T. Couch, Atlanta; Lonnie Couch,
Calif.; Emmett, Eddie, Earl and Lewis of Houston, Texas. Dau:
Altha May Couch. Interred: Houston, Tx. AG 8/3/1908
COUCH, Annie, colored, age 26, d. 428 McDaniel St. Atlanta. AG
11/20/1907
COUCH, Paul, Mrs. died Luthersville, Ga. Sat. of burns. AG
2/25/1907
COURIER, Francis, eldest son of Mr. and Mrs. John Courier, d.
res. on Norwich St., Brunswick, Ga., Wed. AG 2/15/1907
COURSEY, Daniel, Atlanta pioner, d. 165 W. Mitchell St., Atlanta,
Fri. Interred: Sharon Church. AG 3/9/1908
COURSEY, Roy, colored, age 15, d. Atlanta. AG 8/13/1910
COURT, Addie E., inf. dau. of Mr. and Mrs. Walter, d. 47
Jefferson St., Atlanta, Tues. Interred: Westview. AG 6/8/1910
COURT, Addie Elizabeth, infant, d. 47 Jefferson St. Atlanta. AG
6/8/1910

COURTNEY, George W., age 8 mos., d. 2 Todd St. Atlanta. AG 3/1/1907

COURTNEY, Lizzie Hamilton, Mrs. d. 7/14. Husband, bro., sister. Interred: Richmond AG 7/16/1909

COURTNEY, Mary E., Mrs., age 74, d. 24 E. Baker St. Atlanta. AG 7/14/1910

COURTNEY, T. L., Major of Richmond, Va. d. Thurs. Dau: Mrs. John R. Courtney, Atlanta. AG 1/10/1908

COVINGTON, Alex, colored, age 27, d. 101 N. Butler St. Atlanta. AG 12/16/1907

COVINGTON, E. M., colored, age 1, d. 98 Elliott St. Atlanta. AG 2/26/1908

COVINGTON, Ella T., Miss, age 21, d. 114 Glenwood Ave. Atlanta. AG 9/22/1908

COVINGTON, G. C., Mrs. d. 9/21/1909. Gov. Brown granted prisoner G. C. Covington permission to attend funeral. AG 9/22/1909

COVINGTON, G. C., Mrs., age 33, d. 69 Luckie St. Atlanta. Parents: Mr. and Mrs. F. A. Hargrove. Interred: Smyrna, Ga. AG 9/25/1909

COVINGTON, Isabelle, Mrs., wife of Melville L., d. DeKalb Ave., Atlanta. One son, dau. Interred: Carrollton, Ga. AG 6/16/1909

COVINGTON, W. E., planter of Upatoie, Muscogee Co., Ga., d. Wed., age 52. Wife, 4 children. Sister: Mrs. S. C. Jenkins of Columbus, Ga. AG 10/23/1907

COW, James Fur, colored, age 40, d. 325E Edgewood Ave. Atlanta. AG 2/19/1907

COWAN, J. E., age 28, of Doraville, d. Atlanta Wed. Interred: Doraville. AG 4/21/1910

COWAN, Lula, Miss, age 18, d. 116 Loomis St., Atlanta, Wed., dau. of Mrs. J. T. Bros: Zach, Charles, Grover, Edward. Sis: Mrs. W. O. Mann, Mrs. Thurza McDaniels, Miss Fannie May Cowan. Interred: Rockdale, Ga. AG 12/8/1910

COWAN, M. F., age 52, d. Sat. 200 Jett St. Atlanta Mon. Interred: Masons Cemetery. Wife, 7 children. AG 12/21/1908

COWDERY, L. L., age 54, of Columbus, Ga., d. res. of Troup P. Moreland, 337 S. Boulevard Atlanta Fri. Interred: Columbus, Ga. AG 4/8/1909

COWEN, Sarah, colored, age 38, d. 82 S. Humphries St. Atlanta. AG 11/30/1910

COWINGS, Harriet, colored, age 6, d. 339 W. Fair St. Atlanta. AG 12/31/1910

COWLES, Robert, negro, hanged Covington, Allegheny Co., Va. 3/17 for murder of J. A. Ruff. AC 3/18/1905

COWSEY, Janie, colored, age 40, d. 279 W. Mitchell St. Atlanta. AG 11/7/1907

COX, A. H., Mrs., of 414 Luckie St., Atlanta, d. Sat. AG 3/13/1909

COX, Albert T., Jr., inf. son of Mr. and Mrs. A. T., d. Sun. 247 W. Fair St., Atlanta. Interred: Westview. AG 2/22/1910

COX, C. M., age 24, d. 125 Windsor St., Atlanta, Thurs. Interred: LaGrange, Ga. Wife survivies. AG 4/10/1908

COX, Christie B., Mrs., wife of A. A. of 25 Hugh St. Atlanta d. Mon., age 41. Leaves husband, no ch. AG 7/10/1906

COX, Cornelia J., age 84, d. Cave Springs, Ga. AG 10/24/1906

COX, H. M., **Mrs.**, age 75, d. Howell Mill Rd., Atlanta, Tues.
Interred: Sardis church yard. 4 sons, 2 daus. AG 2/23/1910

COX, **Henry**, colored, age 19, d. 101 N. Butler St. Atlanta. AG
10/4/1907

COX, **Henry J.** killed. Res. of 38 Wheeler St. Atlanta. AC
5/16/1905

COX, **J.**, colored, age 60, d. rear of 116 Ellis St., Atlanta. AG
2/4/1908

COX, **J. P.**, age 41, d. Fri. 31 Cone St. Atlanta. Bros: W. B., H.
T. Interred: Oakland. Wife, two daus. AG 12/11/1909

COX, **Lowyel E.**, age 5 mos., son of Mr. and Mrs. Edward, d. Fri.
Howell Mill Rd., Atlanta. Interred: Stone Mountain, Ga. AG
6/27/1910

COX, **Mary**, age 2, dau. of Mr. and Mrs. R. E., of Abbeville, S.
C., d. Atlanta Wed. Interred: Abbeville, S. C. AG 5/4/1910

COX, **Orville Gustavus**, age 36, d. 317 Capitol Ave. Atlanta. AG
2/ 0/1909

COX, **T. S.**, age 2, inf. son of Mr. and Mrs. Joseph, d. Flat
Shoals Rd., Atlanta, Sun. Interred: Roswell, Ga. AG 3/9/1908

COX, **V. H.** d. Thurs. res. of father on Howell Mill Rd. Atlanta.
Interred: Sardis Cemetery. AG 10/12/1910

COX, **William** shot at New Holland, Ga. Robert Young charged with
murder. AC 12/1/1905

COX, **Silas**, colored, age 41, d. 113 Clarke St. Atlanta. AG
5/11/1908

COYNE, **Charles M.**, age 48, d. 123 Nelson St. Atlanta. AG
9/30/1910

COZAT, **W. A.**, age 70, d. 108 Pulliam St., Atlanta, Sat. Leaves
one son. AG 1/4/1908

COZENS, **Ellen, Mrs.**, age 56, died 69 Luckie St., Atlanta.
Interred: Westview. AG 8/29/1906

CRAFT, **Mary, Mrs.** funeral Tues. Interred: Oakland. AG 5/19/1908

CRAFT, **Regger**, 4 yr. old son of Mr. and Mrs. R., d. Thurs. 370
Formwalt St., Atlanta. Interred: Monroe, Ga. AG 5/31/1907

CRAIG, **Gracie**, colored, age 5, died of burns at Edgewood, Ga. AG
11/21/1906

CRAIG, **Julia A.**, **Mrs.**, age 76, d. 41 Gresham St., Atlanta, Wed.
at res. of dau., Mrs. Dr. Lyman H. Jones. Dau: Mrs. W. F. Barnes,
of Siluria, Ala. 3 bros., 4 sis: P. F. Stewart, Dawson, Ala.; S.
A. Stewart, Atlanta; T. S. Stewart, Ft. Payne, Ala.; Mrs. J. W.
Norman, Atlanta; Mrs. G. W. Ballentine, Houston, Ala.; Mrs. W. H.
Morgan and Mrs. G. M. Holdridge, Dawson, Ala. Interred: Snapping
Shoals, Ga. AG 8/1/1910

CRAIG, **Thada**, age 5 mos., d. 643 E. Fair St. Atlanta. AG
10/4/1907

CRAIG, **Tonie, Mrs.** d. Atlanta. Interred: Oakland. AG 11/23/1907

CRANDALL, **J. R.** of Macon d. Tues. Interred: Westview, Atlanta.
Wife, four ch: R. L. Crandall, George N. and John R. Crandall of
Macon, and Mrs. Robert G. Forsythe, Brooklyn, N. Y. AG 3/4/1908

CRANE, **Edward P.**, **Rev.**, former res. of Univ. of Pa., d. 3/21
Tallassee, Fla. He was b. NYC 1832. AC 3/22/1905

CRANE, **Mary, Mrs.**, age 33, d. Sun. E. Macon, Ga. Mother, two
children, sister, bro. AG 4/1/1907

CRANFORD, **L. F.**, age 63, Confed. Vet. of Macon, d. 3/18, New St.
Wife. Son, dau. Interred: Riverside Cemetery, Macon. AG 3/18/1909

CRANKSHAW, Hamilton, Jr., son of Mr. and Mrs. Hamilton, and bro. of Horatio L., Charles W. and Joseph Crankshaw, and Mrs. Margaret C. Thomas, d. 7 Peachtree Pl. Atlanta Sun. Interred: Oakland. AG 5/25/1908

CRANKSHAW, J. M., age 29, d. 110 Emmett St., Atlanta, Wed. Wife, one child. Mother: Mrs. Sarah Cranshaw. Interred: Sandy Springs, Ga. AG 7/6/1910

CRAVEN, Allen, age 45, d. 10 Rhinehart St. Atlanta. AG 10/5/1908

CRAWFORD, Bledsoe, 5-yr. old son of Mr. and Mrs. T. P., d. Sat. 297 East Ave., Atlanta. Interred: Westview. AG 5/27/1907

CRAWFORD, Elizabeth, inf. dau. of Mr. and Mrs. Hugh, d. 253 Crumley St., Atlanta, Thurs. Interred: Westview. AG 2/14/1908

CRAWFORD, Elizabeth Dismukes, Mrs., wife of Dr. J. M., age 55, d. Peachtree Rd., Atlanta Tues. Sons: Dr. J. H., Dr. E. D., Byron. Dau: Mrs. J. D. Rhodes. Interred: Westview. AG 12/6/1910

CRAWFORD, F. A., pioneer Atlantan, d. Mon. dau.'s res., Mrs. H. K. Taylor, 374 E. Georgia Ave., Atlanta. Interred: Oakland. AG 1/18/1910

CRAWFORD, F. O., age 70, d. 67 Augusta Ave. Atlanta. AG 1/19/1910

CRAWFORD, Franklin Alexander, Atlanta pioneer 60 yrs., age 70, d. 67 Augusta Ave. 1/17. Born in S. C. Wife. Dau: Mrs. H. K. Taylor, Atlanta. Son: C. W., N. Y. AG 1/17/1910

CRAWFORD, H. Clay, Mrs. d. Asheville, N. C. Tues, sister of Mrs. Walter E. Cason, Mrs. Carl Faries and Mrs. Ella Chisholm of Atlanta. Interred: Tallahassee, Fla. AG 9/18/1908

CRAWFORD, Hattie, colored, age 66, d. 119 Tattnall St. Atlanta. AG 8/26/1908

CRAWFORD, infant of C. . d. Fri. Atlanta. Interred: Antioch church yard. AG 5/10/1907

CRAWFORD, James H., Jr., age 2, d. Peachtree Circle. Atlanta. AG 11/23/1910

CRAWFORD, Joshua B., age 85, d. 674 W. Peachtree St. Atlanta. AG 3/3/1909

CRAWFORD, Kelsey killed Madison, Ga. by negroes, Ben Slaughter and John Russell. AC 4/30/1905

CRAWFORD, Lillian, Miss, age 23, d. 165 Kirkwood Ave. Atlanta. AG 7/28/1906

CRAWFORD, Lizzie Maud, wife of W. A., dau. of W. T. Akridge, d. Chapel Rd., Atlanta. Interred: Akridge buring grounds. AG 10/14/1907

CRAWFORD, M. C., Jr., colored, age 8 mos., d. 68 Delbridge St. Atlanta. AG 6/10/1907

CRAWFORD, Martha J., Mrs., age 45, d. 8 E. Tenth St. Atlanta, Sun. Husband: J. N. Dau. Bros: J. W. and Patrick Chandler. Interred: Peachtree church yard. AG 6/28/1909

CRAWFORD, Mary, inf. dau. of Mr. and Mrs. A. F., d. Marietta Rd., Atlanta. Interred: Palmetto, Ga. AG 8/16/1910

CRAWFORD, Mary L., colored, age 34, d. 257 Haynes St. Atlanta. AG 7/27/1907

CRAWFORD, N. E., Mrs., wife of J. B. age 66, d. 764 W. Peachtree St. Atlanta. Interred: Waco, Ga. AG 2/13/1908

CRAWFORD, Nannie, Mrs., wife of Dr. T. J., d. 270 Capitol Ave. Atlanta Sun. Dau: Mrs. T. A. Summers, Louisville, Ky. Interred: Cusseta, Ala. AG 5/30/1910

CRAWFORD, Oscar, colored, age 66, d. 156 Elliott St. Atlanta. AG 5/23/1907

CRAWFORD, Rebecca, Miss, age 84, d. 202 Waverly Way. Atlanta. AG 4/22/1909

CRAWFORD, W. J., Mrs., age 71, d. 28 Formwalt St. Atlanta. AG 5/6/1909

CRAWFORD, Della, colored, age 36, died 101 N. Butler St., Atlanta. AG 11/20/1906

CRAWLEY, James L. d. E. Fair Rd., Atlanta, Wed. Interred: New Hope church yard. AG 12/9/1909

CRAWLEY, William F., age 33, d. Sun. Atlanta. Atty of Waycross, Ga. Interred: Waycross, Ga. AG 7/11/1910

CREAMER, Rosetta, Mrs., age 87, d. 14 Circle St. Atlanta. AG 3/1/1907

CREEL, J. H. d. Wed. College Park, Ga. Interred: Family Cemetery, Clayton Co. AG 7/30/1909

CRENSHAW, A., Mrs., age 38, d. 262 W. Fourteenth St., Atlanta, Wed. Interred: Sandy Springs. Husband, 5 children, one bro. AG 9/24/1908

CRENSHAW, Annie Ruth, infant, d. 140 Emmett Ave. Atlanta. AG 5/24/1910

CRENSHAW, H. H. of S. Pryor St., Atlanta, d. Fri. Interred: Lynchburg, Va. AG 11/23/1907

CRENSHAW, James L., age 72, Confed. Vet., d. Old Soldiers' Home, Atlanta, Mon. Member of 9th Ga. Artillery. AG 3/9/1910

CRENSHAW, Lorena, Mrs., age 80, d. home of nephew, Prof. McLean of Agnes Scott Inst. Interred: Yorkville, S. C. AG 10/18/1906

CRENSHAW, Mark, age 3 mos., son of Mr. and Mrs. J. W., d. Sat. 10 McDonald St., Atlanta. Interred: Hollywood. AG 5/6/1907

CRENSHAW, W. H., age 55, d. 101 N. Butler St. Atlanta. AG 11/25/1907

CRESHAM, J. M. funeral Wed. Atlanta. Interred: Westview. AG 3/9/1910

CRESWELL, Frances, Mrs. of Macon burned to death to save grandchild. Interred: McIntyre Cemetery. AG 12/9/1907

CREW, Charles, age 17, d. Atlanta. AG 2/7/1908

CREWES, Martha E., Mrs., age 62, d. yesterday at home of son, J. S. Crewes of Albany. Interred: Greenwood, S. C. Funeral party: Dau., Mrs. Hill of Americus, Ga., Frank, John and Harry Crewes of Albany. AG 7/10/1907

CREWS, Charles D., age 42, d. 52 Williams St. Atlanta. AG 5/18/1907

CREWS, Daner d. Waycross, Ga. 12/27. AG 12/27/1910

CREWS, Harry, Mrs. d. Wed. Valdosta, Ga. Father: Chief of Police, C. Dampier. AG 11/27/1910

CREWS, J. W., Mrs. formerly of Atlanta, d. Richmond, Va. AG 1/3/1910

CRIDER, C. C., wealthy merchant, Hazlehurst, married two days, d. yesterday. Came from N. C. AG 9/10/1906

CRIM, Lucinda, Mrs., age 81, wife of late James Alexander Crim and mother of late Capt. Crim. d. 323 Pulliam St., Atlanta. Ch: Mrs. Bollings, Frankfort, Germany; Mrs. C. T. Shackelford; C. E. Crim, Atlanta. Interred: Oakland. AG 11/3/1908

CRITTLE, Crissie, colored, age 100, d. 245 Edgewood Ave. Atlanta. AG 10/31/1908

CROCKETT, James, age 47, d. Jonesboro Rd. Atlanta. AG 5/15/1907

CROCKETT, Louise F., Miss, age 34, d. Atlanta, Sat. Interred: Marietta, Ga. AG 7/24/1909

CROCKETTE, Jonnie, Miss, d. yesterday, Jonesboro, Ga. Three sisters, one, Mrs. E. O. Waldrop. AG 10/10/1906

CROFT, Tom, age 19, res. of W. Point, Ga., d. Wed. Interred: West Point, Ga. AG 3/11/1908

CROLEY, William, colored, age 40, d. 80 Grady Ave. Atlanta. AG 3/25/1908

CROME, Addie, age 41, d. 562 1/2 Decatur St. Atlanta. AG 8/14/1907

CRONHEIM, Augusta, age 81, d. Atlanta. AG 1/12/1910

CROOK, Ben, colored, age 28, d. 187 Fort St. Atlanta. AG 6/12/1907

CROOMS, Mary H., Mrs., age 67, d. Kennesaw, Ga. Interred: Oakland. AG 5/24/1906

CROSBY, Ed, age 21, d. 101 N. Butler St. Atlanta. AG 10/25/1906

CROSBY, Minnie, age 20, colored, d. 64 Fort St. Atlanta. AG 12/17/1910

CROSSLEY, B. D., age 41, d. 61 Bedford Place, Atlanta, Sat. Interred: Conyers, Ga. AG 12/30/1907

CROSSLEY, J. E., Confederate Veteran, d. Soldiers' Home, Atlanta several days ago. Interred: Emerson, Ga. AG 12/18/1907

CROSS, R. J., pioneer citizen of Rome, Confederate veteran, d. 11/8/1906, at res., E. First St., Atlanta. Remains shipped to Chattanooga. Survivors: Two daughters, Mrs. D. Turner of Lendale and Elizabeth Harris. 91 descendants. Interred: Bethany. AC 12/20/1905

CROSS, Sarah, Mrs., aged abt 70, d. yesterday while visiting her son, A. P. Cross, Tallapoosa, Ga. AG 1/28/1908

CROUGH, Margaret J., Mrs. d. res. of bro., Thomas Crouch, on Rose Hill, Columbus, Ga., Wed. 4 bros., one sister. AG 7/8/1910

CROW, Addie, Mrs., age 24, wife of B. H., d. res. of mother, Mrs. Sarah Lamb, 23 E. 13th St., Atlanta Wed. Interred: Sardis graveyard. AG 9/24/1907

CROW, Charles, age 17, of Marietta, Ga. d. Thurs. Parents: Rev. and Mrs. J. J. Crow, two brothers, survive. Interred: Marietta, Ga. AG 2/7/1908

CROW, Martha M., Mrs., age 71, d. 19 S. Moore St. Atlanta. Dau: Mrs. Elizabeth Murray. Interred: Utoy Church. AG 4/10/1908

CROW, Mary Ann, Mrs., aged 50, run over by L. & train near Kennesaw Sat. and instantly killed. Mrs. Crow left Marietta to visit relatives at Holly Springs. AG 12/17/1906

CROW, Myron, inf. dau. of Mr. and Mrs. C. E., d. First Ave. Atlanta, Mon. Interred: Lawrenceville, Ga. AG 5/12/1908

CROW, Susie, colored, age 18, d. 503 Glenn St. Atlanta. AG 2/8/1909

CROWBARD, Ethel, colored, age 22, d. 44 Orange St. Atlanta. AG 3/16/1908

CROWDER, Nancy, Mrs. d. 10/14, age 80, wid. of Col. Terrell Crowder, Forsyth, Ga. Interred: Family burying grounds. AC 10/16/1905

CROWLEY, J. L., Mrs., Jr., age 31, d. Old Soldiers' Home, Atlanta. Interred: Southbend Cemetery. AG 6/8/1903

CROWLEY, John, of Augusta fire dept., killed 8/27 by falling chimney. AG 10/27/1910

CROZIER, G. C., colored, age 53, d. 103 Cain St. Atlanta. AG 10/9/1907

CRUM, J. d. 101 N. Butler St. Atlanta. AG 12/16/1907

CRUM, John F., Confederate veteran, d. Soldiers' Home, Atlanta, Mon. Interred: Westview. AG 2/26/1908

CRUMBLEY, George Lovette, age 22 mos., son of Mr. and Mrs. William D. Crumbley of Marietta, d. res. of grandparents, Mr. and Mrs. G. W. Key, 42 Hood St., Atlanta. Interred: Westview. AG 7/14/1906

CRUMLEY, Mary, colored, age 71, d. 99 Randean St. Atlanta. AG 2/8/1907

CRUMLEY, R., colored, age 56, d. 257 Orme St. Atlanta. AG 1/14/1908

CRUMLEY, Susan J., Mrs., age 51, d. 206 Chapel St., Atlanta, Tues. AG 7/7/1908

CRUMLEY, Emma, colored, age 19, died 57 Orange St., Atlanta, AG 12/20/1906

CRUMPLER, Mary, age 20, d. 17 W. Cain St. Atlanta. AG 10/18/1907

CRUMPTON, Amanda, age 10, accidently killed by brother, Archie Crumpton, playing with shotgun. AG 6/20/1907

CRUNCH, Henry, age 11, son of Mrs. Lillie Crunch, head crushed in fall in elevator shaft. AG 8/4/1906

CRUSSELLE, James A., Mrs. funeral 6/23 from res. 117 E. North Ave. Atlanta. Kin: James A. Crusselle, J. W. Souther, Dunwoody, Ga., J. N. Crussell, W. H. Crussell, H. G. Crusselle, Mrs. Lula Spruill. AG 6/22/1908

CRUSSELLE, Willie Lewis, Miss, age 20, dau. of Mr. and Mrs. W. F., d. 536 Spring St., Atlanta, Wed. AG 10/1/1908

CRYMES, Janie Lou, age 16 mos., dau. of Mr. and Mrs. W. H., d. 198 Wylie St., Atlanta, Mon. Interred: Sylvester. AG 3/9/1908

CRYMES, M. E., Mrs., age 57, d. 157 Randolph St. Atlanta. AG 4/22/1909

CRYMES, Sarah, Mrs., age 60, d. 69 Doane St. Atlanta. AG 1/11/1910

CRYNES, B. L., age 67, died Fri. at his res., 37 Berrien Ave., Atlanta. Survived by 4 daus., one son, one sister. Interment: Sylvester cemetery. AG 12/8/1906

CUBA, Joe, age 42, d. Atlanta Tues. Wife, 6 children. Interred: Hollywood Cemetery. AG 9/1/1909

CUBA, Josie, age 42, d. 101 Butler St. Atlanta. AG 9/2/1909

CULBERSON, Margaret, Mrs., age 80, widow of late Col. A. B., funeral Thurs. Atlanta. Interred: Oakland. Son: Hon. Hubert L. Culberson. AG 6/30/1910

CULBREATH, Susan, Miss, age 67, d. Atlanta Tues. Sis: Mrs. Margaret McMichael, Alice Culbreath. Bur: Westview. AG 4/1/1908

CULPEPER, N. W., Confederate Veteran d. Thurs. Interred: Westview. AG 4/2/1909

CULPEPPER, Mary Anne, Mrs. d. Muscogee Co. res. of dau., Mrs. J. O. Boggs 6/16, age 78. Funeral at Pine Grove Church. AG 6/17/1910

CUMMINGS, Arthur Campbell, Gen. d. Abington, Va., age 83. Commanded 33rd Regt. AC 3/20/1905

CUMMINGS, Francis, Mrs., age 79, d. 339 Whitehall St. Atlanta. AG 7/1/1910

CUMMINGS, Imus Willingham, Dr., age 28, d. res. of W. F. Bird, 75 Waddell St., Atlanta, Sun. Parents, one bro. Interred: Arnoldsonville, Ga. AG 11/7/1910

CUMMINGS, Leah,, mother of Mrs. B. H. Rawls of Dublin, d. 2/24 her home in Wilkinson Co. She was dau. of late Rowell Stanley of Laurens Co. Bro: Marshall Stanley. Sis: Mrs. Gussie W. Robinson. Interred: Stanley Burial Ground. AG 2/25/1909

CUMMINGS, Thelma, colored, age 7, d. 159-B Howell St. Atlanta. AG 8/23/1909

CUNNINGHAM, Ben, colored, age 20, d. 11 Riggin St. Atlanta. AG 11/21/1910

CUNNINGHAM, Elizabeth, age 8 mos., dau. of Mr. and Mrs. M. D., d. Anthony, Fla. Tues. Interred: Atlanta, Oakland. AG 10/28/1908

CUNNINGHAM, Elizabeth, Mrs., age 74, d. home of dau., Mrs. F. P. Duncan, 250 S. 4th St. Gadsden, Ala. Survivors: Mrs F. P. Duncan, George Cunningham, Shreveport, La. AG 8/31/1906

CUNNINGHAM, Emily, Mrs., age 49, d. 119 Neal St. Atlanta. Interred: Oakland. AG 6/27/1910

CUNNINGHAM, J. F., age 51, d. Athens, Sun. Funeral at Winterville, Ga. AG 5/4/1910

CUNNINGHAM, John, colored, age 23, d. 2-1/2 Central Ave. Atlanta. AG 11/9/1907

CUNNINGHAM, John R., son of Mr. and Mrs. T. G., age 3 mos., d. 8 High St. Atlanta. Interred: Utoy Cemetery. AG 4/29/1909

CURBOW, J. H., age 2, d. 110 Logan St., res. of parents, Mr. and Mrs. E. E., of Atlanta. AG 8/18/1909

CURRIE Louis, Confed. Vet., d. 10/27 Atlanta. Interred: Westview. AG 11/1/1905

CURRIE, W. C., age 58, d. Atlanta. Interred: Aberdeen, N. C. AG 10/8/1907

CURRY, Annie, negro woman, jumped from bridge 2/10, Broad St., Albany, Ga. when mother refused to give her $1. AG 2/12/1907

CURRY, J. H., Mrs., age 58, d. Sun. Cleveland Ave., Vineville (Macon). Interred: Cedar Ridge Cemetery. She was wife of J. H. Curry, Merchant. AG 10/6/1908

CURRY, Manly B., Major, formerly of Macon, d. Atlanta. Buried with military honors. Bur: Arlington, Va. Natl Cemetery. Father-in-law: Sen. A. O. Bacon. Three ch., wife, survive. AG 12/20/1907

CURRY, Richard, old citizen of Monroe Co., d. Juliette, Ga. Sat., aged abt 75. Wife, 5 ch. Bur: Forsyth, Ga. AG 9/26/1910

CURRY, W. L., Rev., old Baptist minister of Pelham, Ga. d. 10/19/1907. AG 10/19/1907

CURTIN, Thomas, Judge, native of Richmond, Va., d. Bristol, Tenn. 8/16, age 53. Cousin of Justin McCarthy. AC 8/17/1905

CURTIS, Farris Hendrix, age 2, inf. son of Mr. and Mrs. H. C., d. Tues. 15 (or 68) Newport St. Atlanta. Bur: Ellijay. AG 7/24/1907

CURTIS, Melville, age 9, son of Dr. and Mrs. C. F. of East Lake, d. from fatal burns. Interred: Greenwood. Bro: Glen. Sisters: Addie, Helen. AG 1/29/1907

CUTRIGHT, Sally, colored, age 35, d. 144 E. Harris St. Atlanta. AG 3/23/1908

DABNER, Alice, colored, age 24, d. 100 W. Pine St., rear. Atlanta. AG 9/6/1910

DABNEY, Harold, infant son of Mr. and Mrs. W. J., Decatur, Ga. d. Tues. AG 8/27/1907

DAGGERT, Jule condemned to gallows for murdering Zack Kendrick last Dec. To be hanged at Appling, Ga. 4/19. AG 4/18/1910

DAILEY, George W., age 65, d. Atlanta Tues. Interred: Mt. Zion church yard. Sons: Herbert, Avery. AG 9/15/1909

DAILEY, Martha (Mattie), d. Grady Hospital Mon. from train accident. Age 16, dau. of Mrs. M. M. Dailey of Oakland Ave., Oakland City. Interred: Fairburn. AG 10/23/1906

DALE, Lillie Jacobs, age 26, d. 102 1/2 Decatur St. Atlanta. AG 5/24/1907

DALEY, Ellen, Mrs. d. Sun. 250 Courtland St., Atlanta. Interred: Oakland. AG 4/20/1909

DALLAS, Alfred B., colored, age 33, d. 455 Auburn Ave. Atlanta. AG 2/11/1909

DALLAS, G. J., age 76, d. 220 Gordon St. Atlanta. AG 12/27/1910

DALLIS, George T., age 58, d. Atlanta. AG 3/29/1909

DALTON, Ernest L., inf. of Mr. and Mrs. T. P., d. Sun. Atlanta. Interred: Westview. AG 5/6/1907

DALY, Josephine Esputa, Mme. d. Washington, D. C., well known singer, music teacher, former Atlanta res. AG 4/15/1909

DALY, Margaret, inf. dau. of Mr. and Mrs. J. L., d. Sun. Atlanta. Interred: Hollywood. AG 5/25/1908

DALY, Matthew d. 3/31 Macon, age 75. Came to Macon from Ireland, res. of Macon more than 40 yrs. Interred: Riverside. Daus: Mrs. Redmond, Mrs. J. W. O'Hara, Mrs. E. D. Huthnance. AG 4/1/1910

DALYRUPLE, Essie May, inf. dau. of Mr. and Mrs. J. H., d. 122 Marietta St., Atlanta, Wed. Interred: Hollywood. AG 5/21/1908

DAMERON, Robert P., age 60, d. Thurs. 22 Pierce St. Atlanta. Interred: Sharon Church yard. AG 7/1/1910

DAMS, Mary E., Mrs., age 72, funeral Sat. dau.'s res., Mrs. T. Brooks, 96 Cherokee Ave., Atlanta. Interred: Acworth, Ga. Sons: J. R., J. A. AG 2/14/1910

DANCE, Wayne, age 8, son of Mr. and Mrs. J. N. Dance, d. 307 Oakland Ave. Atlanta. AG 5/17/1907

DANFORD, F. M., colored, age 9 mos., d. 527 (B) Lilliard St. Atlanta. AG 9/26/1907

DANFORTH, Elizabeth Drakeford, age 20 mos., d. Wed. College Park. Interred: College Park Cemetery. AG 5/31/1906

DANIEL, Alice May, age 11, of 62 Ponders Ave., Atlanta, d. Wed. Interred: Casey's Cem. AG 8/12/1909

DANIEL, Annie Katherine, age 52, d. 17 Trinity Ave. Atlanta. AG 4/21/1910

DANIEL, Benjamin F., Dr., Decatur physician, age 58, d. Decatur Mon. Former res. of Union Point. Sons: Robert, John. Sis: Mrs. F. G. C. Peek, Atlanta; Mrs. E. D. Bryan, Woodstock. Bro: J. C., McDonough. Interred: Decatur Cemetery. AG 6/28/1910
DANIEL, Carrie, colored, age 4 mos., died 30 Adams St., Atlanta. AG 12/26/1906
DANIEL, Carrie, Mrs. d. Sun. Atlanta. Interred: Prattville, Ala. AG 12/30/1907
DANIEL, Clem Archer, age 41, d. Atlanta. AG 5/24/1910
DANIEL, Clyde, age 15, son of Mr. and Mrs. G. P., d. S. Atlanta Fri. AG 4/10/1908
DANIEL, E. S., Mrs., age 55, d. 294 Courtland St. Atlanta. AG 2/8/1909
DANIEL, F. A., Mrs.,ge 28, d. 101 N. Butler St. Atlanta. AG 12/30/1907
DANIEL, Felix A., Mrs. d. Grady Hospital, Atlanta, Sun. AG 1/1/1908
DANIEL, Ida, colored, age 2, d. 87 Means St. Atlanta. AG 8/28/1907
DANIEL, J. H., age 62, d. Thurs. Edgehill Ave., Atlanta. Member of Comanche Tribe of Red Men. AG 8/11/1910
DANIEL, Jennie, age 57, d. 17 Postell St. Atlanta. AG 3/15/1910
DANIEL, John H., age 62, d. Thurs. 10 Edgehill Ave., Atlanta. Interred: Sardis Church. AG 8/12/1910
DANIEL, Joseph, age 9, son of Mr. and Mrs. W. T., d. Sat. Peachtree Rd., Atlanta. Interred: Rossville, Ga. AG 10/8/1907
DANIEL, Julia, age 11, dau. of Mr. and Mrs. C. L., d. Sun. 22 Cherry St. Atlanta. Interred: Rome, Ga. AG 5/6/1907
DANIEL, L. P., age 76, d. Thurs. Atlanta. Relatives in Canada. AG 10/13/1910
DANIEL, Mary, age 2, dau. of Mr. and Mrs. E. G., d. 93 Capitol square, Atlanta, Tues. Interred: Millen, Ga. AG 10/6/1908
DANIEL, Miller J., Dr. d. Griffin, Ga. 6/5. Born Zebulon (Pike Co.) 10/12/1829 m. Miss Virginia Towns of Griffin (d. several yrs. ago). Sons: Judge Robert T., Capt. Milton J., Jr. of Griffin. Sis: Mrs. J. G. Rucker, Atlanta. AC 6/6/1905
DANIEL, Otis, negro, killed by West Cochran while returning home with his 2 children, Griffin, Ga. AG 7/6/1910
DANIEL, Rosa, colored, age 57, d. 193 Murry Ave. Atlanta. AG 5/10/1907
DANIEL, Sarah, colored, age 75, d. 10 Piedmont Way. Atlanta. AG 9/29/1909
DANIEL, T. A., Mrs., whose home is near Hoschton, Athens, Ga., suicide. She leaves husband and several children. AG 12/15/1906
DANIEL, Thomas, farmer, Flowery Branch, formerly of Gainesville, will probably die from overdose of an opiate. AG 4/6/1907
DANIEL, Will, colored, age 85, d. 230 Martin St. Atlanta. AG 5/21/1907
DANIELS, Adolphus, negro youth, charged with killing his mother and stepfather, Macon, Ga. AG 12/3/1909
DANIELS, J. Kelso, age 7 mos., son f Mr. and Mrs. George, d. Hapeville, Ga. Wed. Interred: College Park, Ga. AG 10/23/1907
DANIELS, Jack, age 3 mos., d. 826 Marietta St. Atlanta. AG 11/12/1910

DANIELS, Mattie, colored, age 22, d. 187 Little St. Atlanta. AG 5/24/1907

DANNENBERG, Joseph d. NY City. Funeral Sun. Interred: Family lot, Macon, Ga. AG 10/18/1910

DARDAMER, Kate, Mrs., age 51, d. Decatur. AG 7/25/1910

DARDEN, E. E., age 54, d. Tues. 101 Capitol Ave., Atlanta. Wife. Ch: G. B., R., and Miss Mollie Darden. Interred: Sharon, Ga. AG 10/18/1910

DARDEN, G. N., colored, age 41, d. 240 W. Hunter St. Atlanta. AG 3/1/1908

DARDEN, Maude Estell, Miss, age 22, only dau. of Mr. and Mrs. W. A., d. E. Fair Rd., Atlanta, Fri. Interred: Washington, Ga. AG 6/20/1908

DARDEN, C. B., age 46, d. Fri. Washington, Ga. Sis: Mrs. John R. Asbury, Crawfordville, Ga. Husband, 5 children: Birdie and Mary Darden of Washington; Wallace Darden, W. E. Darden, Gainesville; Gordon Darden, Nashville, Tenn. AG 2/4/1907

DARDEN, K. K., age 54, d. 101 Capitol Ave. Atlanta, Oct. 18. AG 10/20/1910

DARNELL, Charles F., age 64, d. 125 Grant St., Atlanta, Wed. Wife. Dau: Mrs. H. F. Schroeder, of Manila. Son: M. H. Schroeder, Atlanta. Interred: Westview. AG 5/31/1910

DARNELL, S. A., Col., b. Pickens Co. 12/28/1845 d. 191 Angier Av. Educ. Cleveland, Tn. Un. Army, 5th Tn Regt. 2/22/1871 m. Susie Hotchkiss (survives). Ch: Mrs. W. A. Jones, Jasper; S. A., Jr., Atlanta. Bur: Natl cem. Marietta AG 9/10/1906

DAUTREY, C. E., Mrs. of Lakewood Heights, Atlanta, d. Thurs. AG 12/24/1909

DAVENPORT, J., age 35, d. Grady Hospital. Atlanta. AG 3/29/1907

DAVENPORT, J. B., Major of New Orleans, d. Atlanta Sat. Interred Tues. Austell. Sister from Texas. AG 8/7/1906

DAVENPORT, Max, son of late J. C. of Waycross, d. Fri. Wife, a bride of only a few months. Mother. 3 bros: James C. of Atlanta, Jim of Atlanta, Eugene of Norcross. AG 5/30/1910

DAVENPORT, Thomas W., pioneer to Bostwick, Ga., d. Sat. Interred: Bostwick, Ga. AG 2/24/1903

DAVES, Joel T., Mrs. d. Bur: Westview. Kin: Mrs. Joel T. Daves, Sr., C. W. Smith, Geo. A. Mell, Armintius W. Wright, W. B. Bonnell, Homer Wright, Dr. E. L. Bardwell, Albert Wright Collier, R. N. R. Bardwell, Jno W. Collier. AG 4/17/1908

DAVID, E. C., Atlanta photographer, d. hotel room, Albany, Ga. Interred: Sylvester Cemetery. AG 3/10/1909

DAVID, Maude, Miss d. Tues. res. of parents, Mr. and Mrs. E. C. David, Ormewood, Atlanta. Interred: Family burial ground. AG 7/18/1907

DAVIDSON, A. T., Mrs. d. 33 Gresham St. Atlanta, Tues. Interred: Westview. Husband, several children. AG 4/17/1907

DAVIDSON, David L., Dr., age 66, d. Tues. res. of Mr. Arnold, 232 Angier Ave., Atlanta. Son: T. W. Davidson, LaLoma, Mexico. Dau: Mrs. Y. B. Early, Waxahachie, Texas. AG 12/29/1909

DAVIDSON, Julia, Miss of Cornelia, Ga. d. Wilmington, N. C. Interred: Cornelia, Ga. AG 5/18/1906

DAVIDSON, Kate, colored, age 3, d. corner Orme and Mills St., Atlanta. AG 3/3/1908

DAVIDSON, Lucile colored, age 5, d. 97 Mills St. Atlanta. AG 9/11/1908

DAVIDSON, Mary L., Mrs., age 50, d. 33 Gresham St. Atlanta. AG 4/19/1907

DAVIDSON, Ola, colored, age 25, d. 101 N. Butler St. Atlanta. AG 9/12/1908

DAVIDSON, S. W., age 47, of Gainesville, Ga., d. Sun. Atlanta. Wife, 8 children. Bros: Lawton, Edward, both of Atlanta. Interred: Gainesville, Ga. AG 8/22/1910

DAVIES, E. A., Mrs., age 68, d. 419 Woodward Ave., Atlanta, Thurs. Husband, 4 sons, dau. Interred: Westview. AG 11/3/1906

DAVIES, John R., age 70, d. Wed. 103 Oglethorpe St. Atlanta. Interred: Westview. Wife. Son: Thomas B. AG 4/30/1909

DAVIES, M. E., Mrs., wid. of Rev. Bartow, d. 8/22, 422 Whitehall St., Atlanta. Son: M. M., Atlanta. Daus: Sallie, Daisy. AC 8/22/1905

DAVIS, A. J., Mrs. d. Tues. 30 White St. Atlanta. Interred: Hollywood. AG 5/15/1907

DAVIS, A., Mrs. d. Sat., wife of prominent farmer. Several children survive. AG 10/18/1909

DAVIS, Amanda, colored, age 39, d. 101 Butler St. Atlanta. AG 10/20/1909

DAVIS, Andrew, age 17, dying of Bright's disease, pardoned by prison commission on conviction of larceny. To go to mother's home in Atlanta. AG 11/14/1906

DAVIS, Annie, colored, age 57, d. 50 Clifton St. Atlanta. AG 9/8/1908

DAVIS, Biddie, Miss, age 20, dau. of Mrs. Mattie, d. Mansfield, Ga. from fire. AC 12/8/1905

DAVIS, Buck, colored, accidentally shot, killed yesterday by Mattie Griffin, colored. AG 7/12/1907

DAVIS, C. A., Mrs. d. 900 Marietta St. Atlanta Mon. Sons: rnest, Dudley. Daus: Misses Katie, Lorena. AG 6/21/1909

DAVIS, Charles, age 24, d. Atlanta. Interred: Westview. AG 8/7/1908

DAVIS, Charles, age 13, d. 291 Central Ave. Atlanta. AG 12/28/1910

DAVIS, DeWitt, son of Mr. and Mrs. Fred Davis, d. 70 Jefferson St. Atlanta, Wed. AG 4/10/1907

DAVIS, E. Burney, Mrs., age 60, d. 16 Richardson St. Atlanta. AG 4/24/1908

DAVIS, E. D., age 54, d. 376 N. Boulevard. Atlanta. AG 1/7/1907

DAVIS, Eddie, age 18 mos., son of Mr. and Mrs. S. D., d. 710 Chestnut St. Atlanta. Interred: Casey's Cemetery. AG 8/12/1910

DAVIS, Eliza, colored, age 53, d. 106 Robbins St. Atlanta. AG 3/30/1909

DAVIS, Elizabeth, inf. dau. of Mr. and Mrs. E. R., d. Sun. DeGress Ave. in Inman Park. Interred: Westview. AG 8/12/1907

DAVIS, Elizabeth A., Mrs., age 67 (one notice says age 56), d. Sat. 567 Marietta St. Atlanta. Husband: R. B. Interred: Westview. AG 4/23/1910

DAVIS, Elizabeth, Mrs., age 35, d. Ocala.,Fla. AG 3/29/1907

DAVIS, Eugenia, Mrs., age 63, d. 214 Grant St. Atlanta. AG 2/8/1910

DAVIS, F. T., age 32, d. 135 Spring St. Atlanta. AG 11/25/1907

DAVIS, Fannie, colored, age 55, d. 84 Oliver St. Atlanta. AG 9/6/1910

DAVIS, Florence, colored, age 1 mo., d. 28 Morris alley. Atlanta. AG 10/21/1908

DAVIS, Frank J., age 28, d. Hampton, Va. Interred: Hollywood Cemetery, Atlanta. AG 10/5/1908

DAVIS, Fred drowned Rome, Ga. Res: 237 E. Hunter St., Atlanta. Interred: Oakland. AG 8/12/1907

DAVIS, Fred, age 26, d. Rome, Ga. AG 8/14/1907

DAVIS, George W., res. of Brunswick, age abt 20 yrs., d. He was native of N. C. AG 4/10/1907

DAVIS, Giles, colored, age 60, d. 25 Mangum St. Atlanta. AG 12/8/1910

DAVIS, H. H., age 28, d. Federal prison, Atlanta, Nov. 3. AG 11/5/1910

DAVIS, Harry, young man, killed in railroad yards, Atlanta. He was from Lumber City, Ga. AC 9/11/1905

DAVIS, Hattie interred Westview Cemetery. AG 11/23/1907

DAVIS, Hester, Mrs., age 30, d. Tues. 30 White St., West End, Atlanta. Interred: Hollywood. AG 5/13/1907

DAVIS, Homer, age 17, nephew of Sheriff Davis, shot and killed himself 7/3, Dahlonega, Ga., accident. AG 7/4/1908

DAVIS, Homer J. d. Copper Hill, Tenn. Parents, 4 sisters, 4 bros. Interred: Chamblee, Ga. AG 7/8/1910

DAVIS, Horace, age 12, son of Mr. and Mrs. John W., d. Thurs. 21 Glenn St. Atlanta. Interred: Fayetteville, Ga. AG 9/10/1910

DAVIS, I. T. d. Atlanta Sun. Interred: Dublin, Ga. AG 11/23/1907

DAVIS, I. T. d. Irwinton, Ga. Mon. AG 4/1/1908

DAVIS, infant of Octavia, negro, d. 283 Magnolia St. Atlanta. AG 5/22/1910

DAVIS, infant of Jennie, colored, d. Mangum St. Atlanta. AG 5/25/1906

DAVIS, J. B., Jr., age 47, d. E. Point, Ga. AG 2/26/1908

DAVIS, J. E. killed by Harry Hale in Johnson City, Tenn. last May. Hale was soldier at Ft. McPherson, Co. M., 17th Inf., arrested Oakland City. AG 7/12/1907

DAVIS, Jacob d. Midville, Ga. 5/10. Age 40. Interred: Macon, Ga. AC 5/11/1905

DAVIS, James, age 91, d. res. of son, William, at Harmony, Ga., Wed. Interred: Mt. Zion Cemetery. He moved here from Ky. 10 yrs. ago. AG 12/30/1910

DAVIS, John A., Capt. of Albany d. 4/9/ Ch: Joseph S., Mayor of Albany; Mrs. S. D. Jones; Mrs. A. D. Jones; Mrs. D. W. Shaffer; Mrs. R. L. Jones of Albany; Mrs. Lott Warren, Atlanta. AC 4/9/1905

DAVIS, John H. d. Wilmington, N. C. 8/16, age 47. He was merchant at Marietta, Ga. AC 8/17/1905

DAVIS, Joseph, age 85, of Atlanta, Mexican and Civil War veteran, d. Dallas, Texas 3/13. He was b. Cass Co., Ga., father of 18 children. 50 grandchildren, etc. AG 3/13/1909

DAVIS, Julia, Mrs., age 77, mother of John L. Davis, d. Davisville, Ala. yesterday. Interred: Davisville. Leaves 3 sons, 4 daus. AG 9/11/1907

DAVIS, Kearney, age 22, d. Atlanta Tues. Interred: Red Oak Church. AG 10/28/1908

DAVIS, L. B., Mrs., age 70, d. 394 Spring St. Atlanta. AG 11/30/1907

DAVIS, Lawrence Betrand of Georgia, suicide, at Lima, Peru. AG 9/9/1908

DAVIS, Lucy, colored, age 60, d. 267 Haynes St. Atlanta. AG 4/29/1909

DAVIS, Lula, colored, age 23, d. 41 Howell St. Atlanta. AG 11/21/1910

DAVIS, M. D., age 73, d. 27 Echo St., Atlanta, Sat. Interred: Masons Church yard. AG 9/11/1909

DAVIS, Marshie, Mrs., age 19, d. Thurs. Macon Hospital. Interred: Riverside. AG 9/20/1907

DAVIS, Mary A., Mrs., age 83, d. 215 Hilliard St. Atlanta. Bur: Westview. Formerly of Toccoa. Son: Lewis Davis, Lawton, OK. Daus: Mrs. M. E. Lawson, Mrs. C. T. Blackmer, Emma Davis, Atlanta, Mrs. Virginia Lewis, Zolfo, Fla., Mrs. I. C. --------------

DAVIS, Mary E., Mrs., age 47, d. Thurs. 41 Scott St., Atlanta, wife of J. S. 2 sons, 3 daus. AG 3/10/1910

DAVIS, Mary J., Mrs. d. Fri. Macon. Interred: Cedar Ridge. She was widow of late J. F. Davis. Ch: E. B. Davis, Mrs. E. S. Braswell. Bros: all live Macon. AG 6/20/1908

DAVIS, Melford, Confed. Vet., d. 9/4 Columbus, Ga. AC 9/6/1905

DAVIS, Melviss, Mrs., age 62, d. 830 W. Peachtree St., Atlanta, 10/4. AG 10/5/1910

DAVIS, N. A., Mrs., age 50, d. 76 Carroll St. Atlanta. AG 2/11/1909

DAVIS, Nathan, colored, age 65, d. near South Bend Dist. Atlanta. AG 2/7/1908

DAVIS, O., colored, age 70, d. E. Hunter St. Atlanta. AG 11/25/1907

DAVIS, Otheia, Mrs., age 40, d. Columbia, S. C. AG 1/21/1910

DAVIS, Pearl, colored, age 19 yrs., d. 31 Newton St. Atlanta. AG 8/9/1907

DAVIS, R. A., colored, age 60, d. 131 Yonge St. Atlanta. AG 1/17/1908

DAVIS, R. B., Mrs., age 54, of 45 Plum St. d. Grady Hospital. Atlanta. Bro: J. T. Williamson. AG 8/26/1907

DAVIS, R. M., age 42, d. Atlanta Sat. Interred: Sylva, N. C. AG 11/16/1908

DAVIS, R. M., Mrs., age 38, d. Sun. 65 W. Baker St., Atlanta. Interred: Sylva, N. C. AG 9/2/1907

DAVIS, Robert, age 32, former Atlantan, d. Cincinnato, Ohio. Interred: Atlanta, Westview. AG 7/24/1909

DAVIS, Rufus A., inf. son of Mr. and Mrs. W. T. of 11 Pope St., Atlanta, d. Thurs. Interred: South Bend. AG 3/18/1909

DAVIS, S. M., postmaster, d. 2/4 Calhoun, Ga. AC 2/5/1905

DAVIS, Sarah, age 9 mos., infant dau. of Mr. and Mrs. Charles B., d. Sun. 145 Alexander St., Atlanta. Interred: Norcross, Ga. AG 7/8/1907

DAVIS, Thomas, age 21, died at 357 North Avenue, Atlanta. AG 12/10/1906

DAVIS, Virgil, colored, age 3 mos., d. 272 Auburn Ave. Atlanta. AG 4/22/1909

DAVIS, W. A., Capt. d. 369 Orange St., Atlanta., Sat., b. on farm 8 mi. E of Atlanta 4/4/1847. Confed. Soldier, age 16, Co. B, 2nd Ga. Battn of Cavalry. Md. 1868 Mary R., dau. of J. W. and Susan (Barlow) Summers. Ch: Hattie B., Edwin, Mabel C., Gussie M. Mr. Davis' father was Elisha Davis, native of Burke Co., Ga. AG 1/21/1907

DAVIS, W. A., Dr., age 57, d. 29 Houston St., Atlanta. AG 12/18/1910

DAVIS, W. A., Mrs., Monarch, Palmyra, NY. AG 7/9/1908

DAVIS, Walter, age 1 mo., d. 17 Corley Place. Atlanta. AG 9/3/1907

DAVIS, Will, colored, age 4 yrs., d. 53 Logan alley, Atlanta. AG 9/9/1907

DAVIS, William buried Arlington, Ga. yesterday, Masonic hnors. AG 10/22/1906

DAVIS, William, colored, age 50, d. 101 N. Butler St. Atlanta. AG 5/4/1908

DAVIS, William, age 82, former res. of Fla., d. Mon. corner Whiteford and DeKalb Aves., Atlanta. Bro-in-law of M. T. LaHatte. Sons: Sidney, Frank, Willie of Atlanta. Daus: Mrs. Robert Carnes, Eastman, Ga. and Miss Minnie Davis. AG 6/6/1906

DAVIS, William Dwight, age 14 days, d. 49 Kirkwood Ave. Atlanta. AG 1/3/1907

DAVIS, William Popham of Atlanta d. 534 S. Pryor St. Sun. Born Leighland, Somerset, Entland 3/29/1831. To America 1875. Wife: Diana K. Dau: Mrs. J. B. Wilhelm. AG 12/27/1910

DAVIS, William, Mrs. d. Elbert Co., Sun. Interred: Stinchcomb Church. Husband survives. AG 11/1/1910

DAWSON, Elaine, infant, d. 231 Tumlin St. Atlanta. AG 6/9/1910

DAWSON, Flora, age 7, d. Emmett St. Atlanta. AG 10/18/1906

DAWSON, Lizzie, colored, age 42, d. 94 Richmond St. Atlanta. AG 3/10/1908

DAWSON, Oscar, colored, age 35, d. Valdosta, Ga. AG 7/9/ 909

DAWSON, Vivian, age 1 yr., inf. dau. of Mr. and Mrs. E. W., d. Sun., corner Piedmont Ave. and Tumlin Sts. Atlanta. AG 8/26/1907

DAWSON, W. C., age 60, d. Atlanta Tues. Interred: Greensboro, Ga. Bro: J. H. AG 6/30/1909

DAY, Howard, age 24, d. 80 1/2 Capitol Ave. Atlanta. AG 11/22/1909

DAY, Lillian Louise, age 5 mos., dau. of Mr. and Mrs. C. P. Day, d. Mon. 206 W. Alexander St. Atlanta. Interred: Hollywood. AG 7/24/1906

DAY, S. W., Mrs. d. Mon. 132 Oakland Ave., Atlanta, age 64. Lived Atlanta since Civil War. Husband: Hon. S. W. Sons: Thomas J., Albert L. AG 8/3/1908

DAY, Sarah A., Mrs., age 64, d. 132 Oakland Ave. Atlanta. AG 8/5/1908

DEAL, Mary A., Mrs., age 79, d. dau.'s res., Mrs. W. M. Richardson, 215 Howell St., Atlanta, Tues. One dau, one son: T. J. Deal, Atlanta. Interred: Lithonia, Ga., Union Cemetery. AG 3/18/1908

DEAN, Clarence, age 30, d. 175 Magnolia St., Atlanta, 2/27, in saloon. AC 2/28/1905

DEAN, E. O. d. Comer, Ga. 5/25. Wife. One son. AC 5/27/1905

DEAN, Gary, negro fireman for Sou. Railroad, killed in accident, Augusta, Ga. AG 2/11/1907

DEAN, Mattie Lee, age 7 mos., d. 162 Nelson St. Atlanta. AG 6/14/1907

DEAN, Maude, murdered by Arthur Glover on 10/20/1906. AG 11/16/1906

DEAN, W. L., Dr., age 50, d. 34 1/2 North Forsyth St. Atlanta. AG 10/25/1906

DEAN, Warren, colored, age 51, d. 18 Gunby St. Atlanta. AG 9/2/1909

DEAN, Willie, colored, age 35, d. 219 Walnut St. Atlanta. AG 11/15/1909

DEAS, Marshal fatally wounded Sat. afternoon Cairo, Ga. by W. A. and Nim Maxwell, while making arrest. AG 8/5/1907

DEAVERONS, Mattie, Mrs., age 23, d. corner Auburn Ave. and Courtland St. Atlanta. AG 7/1/1907

DEBOIS, Elizabeth, Mrs., age 102, d. Mobile, Ala. 7/24. Born Ireland 7/15. AC 7/25/1905

DEBRAY, B., Mrs. d. 11/14, 326 Lee St., Atlanta. Interred: Mt. Zion. Son: Late Patrolman DeBray (murdered). Several Children. AC 11/16/1905

DECIA, F., Mrs., age 35, d. Atlanta 6/28. Husband, two children AG 6/28/1909

DECK, Fannie, Mrs. d. Greenbush, Ga., age abt 80. Ch: Mrs. T. B. Mitchell, Attalia, Ala.; Mrs. G. C. Wallace, Atlanta; Mrs. C. B. Wood, Greenbush; Mrs. Beulah Trevitt; Miss Joe Deck; Mrs. Howard, of Dalton, Ga. AG 6/16/1910

DECKNER, Robert H., inf. son of Mr. and Mrs. Carl H., d. Wed. Stewart Ave. Atlanta. Interred: Mt. Zion Church. AG 8/27/1907

DECOSTIE, Charles d. 342 S. Boulevard, Atlanta, Fri. Leaves wife, two daus., Misses Martha and Minette. AG 10/22/1909

DEE, William Van, suicide, Walton St., Atlanta, Wed. Interred: Westview. AG 1/11/1908

DEEN, W. H., vet. and Mason, d. 1/26 near Waverly Hall, Ga. AG 1/27/1910

DEESE, Lacy Lee, age 2 yrs., d. at Pasteur Institute. Atlanta. AG 7/25/1906

DEFORE, Robert d Macon 4/25 from accident. AG 4/26/1909

DEFRANCASCHI, infant of Mr. and Mrs. A., d. 7/29 Athens, Ga. AG 7/30/1909

DEGIVE, Catherine, 11 mos., dau. of Mr. & Mrs. Henry L., d. 176 Juniper St. Interred: Oakland. AG 12/28/1906

DEGIVE, Laurent, age 82, d. Rock Lodge, Fla. AG 3/21/1910

DEIGNAN, Richard, age 74, wealthy merchant, d. Columbus, Ga., Confederate soldier. Unmd. Funeral: Catholic Church. AG 9/1/1906

DEJOURNETTE, William, age 70, d. Old Soldiers; Home, Atlanta, Sat. Interred: Rome, Ga. AG 4/5/1910

DEKLE, Jessie L., Mrs. died Mon. at res., 172 S. Pryor St., Atlanta. Funeral: Central Baptist Church. AG 12/26/1906

DEKLE, Jessie S., Mrs., age 19, died 172 S. Forsyth St., Atlanta. AG 12/26/1906

DEKLE, Oscar, negro, shot, killed by Offr Guy Presley, Valdosta. AG 12/26/1906

DEKLE, W. W. d. at home at Excelsior, Ga. (near Statesboro). Wife, two sons, John R. of Savannah and Edgar of Statesboro. 2 daus. Funeral at Lower Lotts Creek Church. AG 9/14/1908

DELANEY, Nancy, Mrs., age 61, d. 95 N. Humphries St., Atlanta. Interred: Westview. Husband: Patrick Delaney. AG 5/21/1908

DELAY, Fannie, Mrs., age 55, wife of R. J., d. 2/17, 100 Fortress Ave., Atlanta. 10 Ch. Interred: Oconee Co. AC 3/19/1905

DELAY, Frank T., age 62, d. Wed. res. of niece, Mrs. J. T. Haden, 81 Bryan St., Atlanta. Interred: Oakland. Sisters: Mrs. Sarah Johnson, Mrs. Mary Wofford. Bro: Russell DeLay, Texas. AG 1/13/1910

DELAY, J. T., age 62, d. 81 Bryan St. Atlanta. AG 1/14/1910

DELERIDGE, Rebecca, colored, age 60, d. 101 N. Butler St. tlanta. AG 3/26/1908

DELOACH, J. D. d. S. Kirkwood, Atlanta, Wed. Interred: Sylvester. AG 2/6/1908

DELONG, Carrie May, age 25, d. Milledgeville, Ga. AG 4/2/1909

DELONG, Carrie May, Miss, age 26, of 38 Julian St., Atlanta, d. Wed. AG 3/3/1909

DELONG, Marion drowned Chattahoochee River, near Roswell bridge. Interred: Ebenezer, Ga. 7/28. AG 7/30/1909

DELORME, Hazel L., inf. dau. of Mr. and Mrs. J. W., interred Greensboro, N. C. AG 5/25/1908

DELPHEY, Mary, age 2, dau. of J. C. Delphy, d. 32 Reinhardt St. Atlanta. Interment: Westview. AG 8/22/1906

DEMPSEY, James T., age 2, son of Mr. and Mrs. B. C., Lambert St., Atlanta, d. Mon. Interred: Hollywood cemetery. AG 11/23/1907

DEMPSEY, M. W., Mrs. of Smyrna, Ga. d. Thurs., res. of Smyrna 48 yrs. Son: W. A. Dempsey of 198 Foundry St., Atlanta. AG 9/20/1907

DEMPSEY, Sallie, Mrs.,ge 71, d. sister's home, Mrs. R. E. McWaters, 61 Bass St.,A tlanta, Thurs. Bros: C. C., G. W. and S. C. Stovall, Atlanta. AG 12/17/1909

DEMPSEY, William A., age 27, of 198 Foundry St., Atlanta. d. Inman yards. Atlanta. AG 10/3/1907

DENCON, Ernest, colored, age 8, d. 31 Tattnall St. Atlanta. AG 11/17/1907

DENEEN, John, 75, Atlanta pioneer 40 yrs., d. dau's res., Mrs. W. L. Bridwell, 215 Ashby St., Atlanta. Wife: Catherine. Daus: Mrs. W. L. Bridwell, Mrs. Emma Trotti, Mrs. Mary Stevens of Los Angeles, Calif. Interred: Westview. AG 12/4/1907

DENEEN, Katherine, Mrs., age 75, wife of late John, d. 215 Ashby St., Atlanta, Sun. Daus: Mrs. Walter Bridwell, Mrs. J. T. Trotti, Mrs. Mary Stevens, Los Angeles, Calif. Interred: Westview. AG 7/6/1908

DENHAM, Lula, Mrs., age 60, d. 14 Viola St. Atlanta. AG 5/30/1908

DENICO, Geneva, colored, age 21 days., d. 16 Mechanic Ave. Atlanta. AG 8/17/1908

DENKIN, May Belle, 4-yr. old dau. of Mr. and Mrs. Donald of 340 Cottage St., Augusta, d. yesterday. AG 5/21/1907

DENMAN (or DENNARD), Lula, Mrs., age 36, d. 292 Cameron St.
Atlanta on 10/4. Interred: Hollywood. AG 10/6/1910
DENNARD, Erwin L. d. 1/6 Perry, Ga, age 53. Sis: Mrs. Dudley M.
Hughes. He was twice married. AG 1/7/1910
DENNARD, Leonora A., Mrs., age 43, d. Mulberry St., Macon. Ch: C.
B., F. E., Mrs. J. S. Smithson, Mrs. O. C. Attaway. Interred:
Jeffersonville, Ga., decd's old home. AG 5/7/1907
DENNARD, Lula A., Mrs., age 65, d. 91 English Ave. Atlanta.
Interred: Westview. Husband, several children. AG 4/17/1907
DENNARD, Mary Aline, age 9 mos., dau. of Mr. and Mrs. W. F.
Dennard, Jr., d. 54 Beecher St. Atlanta. Interred: Hollywood. AG
3/16/1907
DENNARD, Valeria, wife of late Erwin L., d. 6/13 Perry, Ga. 4
sisters, 1 bro: Mrs. Ansley, Americus; Mrs. Irwin, Atlanta; Mrs.
Willingham, Macon; Miss Mattie Tharpe and A. H. Tharpe of Perry.
AG 6/13/1910
DENNARD, W. F., Mrs., age 38, wife of W. F., d. Sun. 7 Lovejoy
St. Atlanta. Interred: Hollywood. AG 6/14/1909
DENNEY, W. M. d. 12/5 Bowman, Ga., age 55. Wife, two bros.,
survive. AG 12/6/1909
DENNIS, Caroline, Mrs., age 81, d. 3 Moreland Ave. Atlanta. AG
1/16/1907
DENNIS, David L. d. Mon, age 65, d. Atlanta Mon. Dau: Mrs. H. E.
Garrett, Atlanta. Sons: J. A., Atlanta; W. P., Oklahoma.
Interred: Westview. AG 7/6/1909
DENNIS, Etta, Mrs., age 44, d. 140 Oliver St. Atlanta, Fri.
Interred: Hollywood. AG 10/20/1906
DENNIS, Francis A., age 1, son of Mr. and Mrs. J. A. of 17
Fortress Ave., Atlanta, d. Tues. Interred: Red Oak, Ga. AG
5/10/1909
DENNIS, Frank, inf. son of Mr. and Mrs. G. W., d. 125 Main St.,
Atlanta, Wed. Interred: Hollywood. AG 2/19/1908
DENNIS, John, age 45, d. 101 N. Butler St. Atlanta. AG 4/13/1909
DENNIS, John T., Mrs., age 38, d. Eatonton 7/9, dau. of Mr. and
Mrs. John R. Gatewood of Americus. Several bros. and sisters. AC
7/12/1905
DENNIS, Mary J., age 11 mos., d. 95 Clara St. Atlanta. AG
5/10/1907
DENNIS, Mattie, Miss, age 59, d. S. Boulevard and Bryan Sts.
Atlanta. AG 3/27/1909
DENNIS, Mertie G., inf. dau. of Mr. and Mrs. J. H., d. Sat. 17
Fortress St.,Atlanta. Interred: Red Oak. AG 2/28/1910
DENNY, Willis F. of Atlanta d. 8/17 Denver, Colo. Wife, mother. 2
ch. Mrs. Denny was formerly Miss Gertrude Moreland, dau. of Maj.
A. F., and sis. of Dr. A. C. Moreland of Forsyth and Mrs. C. D.
Maddox, Atlanta. AC 8/18/1905
DENNY, Susie, Mrs., age 40, of 18 Reinhardt St. d. while facing
lunacy chg. AG 8/23/1906
DENSON, Frank funeral 1 Fox St., Atlanta Wed. Interred: Highland
Cemetery. AG 3/25/1908
DENSON, James A., age 3 mos., son of Mr. and Mrs. W. F., d. 8
Ella St., Atlanta. Interred: Hollywood. AG 8/30/1910
DENSON, W. J. killed by electric shock Tues. Funeral at res. 390
Whitehall St. Atlanta. Interred: Locust Grove. AG 7/18/1906
DENT, Susan, Mrs., age 32, d. 69 Luckie St. Atlanta. AG 6/9/1906

DENTON, Elizabeth, Mrs. d. son's res., J. M. Denton, Atlanta, Sun. Interred: Calhoun, Tenn. AG 11/23/1907

DENTON, Hixley, inf. son of Mr. and Mrs. J. I., d. Tues. 270 State St. Atlanta. AG 3/15/1910

DENTON, Mattie Kate, Mrs., age 21, d. 28 Orange St. Atlanta. AG 2/8/1909

DENTON, Susie, age 7, dau. of Mr. and Mrs. W. M., interred: Westview. AG 9/14/1907

DENZER, Albert, Mrs., formerly Miss Emma Mayer of Atlanta, d. Berne Switzerland, 8/7. Interred: Cypress Hill Cemetery, New York. AG 8/30/1910

DERDEN, John Henry, age 53, d. 72 Willow St. Atlanta. AG Interred: Westview. 5/8/1909

DERNELL, Charles T., age 64, d. 125 Grant St. Atlanta. AG 6/2/1910

DERRETTE, Margaret, inf. dau. of Mr. and Mrs. J. H., funeral 102 Connally St., Atlanta. Interred: Oakland. AG 6/4/1906

DERRICK, E. T., Mrs. d. 148 Trinity Ave., Atlanta, Mon. Grsons: J. D., W. B., G. W., F. B. and Ralph Hudson. Bros: A. D. and G. B. Adair. Sisters: Mrs. A. J. Moore, Mrs. Warren H. Campbell. Interred: Gainesville, Ga. AG 1/21/1908

DERRICK, Frances, infant, d. 200 Lee St. Atlanta. AG 3/10/1910

DERRICK, Jesse, Mrs. was perhaps fatally burned Wed. Father-in-law: Wallace D. Derrick. AG 4/28/1906

DESAUSSURE, Alexander Dr., Mrs. d. 5/2 98 E. Pine St., Atlanta, age 60, b. Camden, S. C. Ch: John, S. D. (Cheneyville, Ala.) and Mrs. O. F. Randall, Misses Ida and Louise, Atlanta. AG 5/3/1906

DESAUSURE, Ida C., Mrs. funeral 5/4 at res. 98 E. Pine St. Atlanta. AG 5/4/1906

DESPONEY, Gordon, age 23, d. Atlanta. AG 2/14/1910

DEVARIS, Jennie, age 6, dau. of Mr. and Mrs. P., funeral Brunswick 4/19. AC 4/21/1905

DEVENEY, Mary G., Mrs., age 84, d. home of son-in-law, J. D. Ruffin at Gentian, 5-mi. N. of Columbus, Ga. Interred: Ingram Burying Ground. AG 5/14/1908

DEVEREAUX, Annie, Mrs., wid. of late D., d. res. of D. A. Green near Adamsville, Ga. Sun. Interred: Oakland. 2 sisters, 2 bro. AG 4/26/1908

DEVERERUX, Mima, Milledgeville, 11/16 condemned negro, hanged. AG 11/16/1906

DEVINE, A. J., colored, age 68, d. 53 Randolph St. Atlanta. AG 11/24/1910

DEVINE, Horace McDavis, colored, age 10 mos., d. 16 Lyons St. Atlanta. AG 1/10/1907

DEWBERRY, Ben F., age 49, d. Buford, Ga. Gwinnett Co. AG 8/25/1908

DEWBERRY, Gilas, age 75, d. Battle Hill Sun. Interred: Hollywood. Dau: Mrs. G. A. Fletcher. AG 1/17/1910

DEWBERRY, Minnie Belle, colored, age 4, d. 101 N. Butler St. Atlanta. AG 10/8/1909

DEWELL, Margaret May, Miss d. Sun. E. Point. Bros: A., G.P. 4 sisters. Interred: Mt. Gilead Cemetery. AG 12/12/1910

DEWOLF, Walter S. d. Sat. Columbus, Ga. Interred: Linwood. AG 10/5/1909

DEWOLF, Walter S., Mrs., formerly of Columbus, Ga., d. Chatham, Va. 6/4. She was Miss Carrie Porter, dau. of Mr. and Mrs. J. C. Porter. Mother, 3 bros: John Porter, Atlanta; Robert Porter, Birmingham; William Porter, Columbus. Daus: Mrs. Claud Miller, Columbus; Miss Kate DeWolf, Chatham, Va. Funeral: First Baptist Church, Columbus, Ga. AC 6/6/1905

DEWS, R. C., missing manager of Macon Phonograph Co., found in field near house of Senator A. O. Bacon, Macon. Wife, one child of Decatur, Ga., survive. Bro: H. W. Dews., Jr. AG 7/6/1906

DEWSON, George B., Mrs., age 48, d. 85 Washington St. Atlanta. AG 3/10/1909

DEXTER, Sarah, Mrs., wife of P. B., d. 3/4 Columbus, Ga., age 27. Husband survives. AG 3/4/1910

DIAL, child, age 2 of Mr. and Mrs. Troy, formerly of Atlanta, d. Logansville, Ga. at home of grandparents, Mr. and Mrs. Marion Hodges. AG 1/15/1908

DIAL, Hubert killed 6/5 93 Fortress Ave. Atlanta. Trial of Andrew J. Taylor for murder. AG 6/10/1909

DIAL, P. D. d. 89 Fortress St., Atlanta Mon. Interred: Westview. AG 5/12/1909

DIAL, T. B., age 26, killed in auto accident in Hapeville, Ga. AG 8/1/1910

DICK, Samuel K., age 69, d. 1/24 Marietta where lived 30 yrs. Wife. Sons: Jackson, Sam, Jr. Sis: Mrs. Ellen Hines, Atlanta; Mrs. C. R. Harris, Atlanta; Mrs. J. A. Smith, Bainbridge; Mrs. Sam Grace, Maryville, Tenn. AG 1/25/1910

DICKENSON, Willie O., age 15, d. Bolton, Ga. AG 11/19/1909

DICKERSON, Annie May, colored, age 16, d. 17 1/2 Chestnut St. Atlanta. AG 11/15/1909

DICKERSON, J. S., Mrs., wife of merchant of Ocilla, Ga., d. yesterday,. Interred: Mud Creek, her former home. AG 6/8/1906

DICKERSON, Lena, colored, age 32, d. 258 Williams St. Atlanta. AG 8/19/1908

DICKERSON, Martha, age 68, d. E. Point, Ga. AG 2/21/1907

DICKERSON, Martha Ann, 79, wid of Jno T., d. E. Pt. Ch-T. T., Birmingham; Mrs. A. O. Fowler, E. Point; Mrs. A. J. Mangum, Belton, Mo.; Rev. J. R., Prescott, Ark.; Mrs. M. W. Gober, E. Point; J. P., Woodstock. Bur-Little River. AG 12/19/1907

DICKERSON, O. A., Mrs., age 60, d. Atlanta Sun. Husband, W. R., d. abt week ago. Interred: Union Point, Ga. AG 1/27/1908

DICKERSON, W. R., age 69, d. 113 Sampson St., Atlanta 1/20/1908. Wife: O. A. AG 1/27/1908

DICKEY, G. W., age 40, d. 118 Curran St., Atlanta, Wed. Wife survives. Interred: Riverview. AG 3/26/1908

DICKEY, James L., age 63, d. 381 Peachtree St. Atlanta. AG 11/1/1910

DICKEY, Mary I., Mrs., age 89, d. Wed. Sis: Mrs. Dora Calloway, 21 McDaniel St., Atlanta. Interred: Greenwood Cemetery, AG 3/11/1909

DICKEY, T. B., infant, 2 weeks old, d. Edgewood, Ga. AG 8/4/1906

DICKINSON, Christine, colored, age 9 mos., d. 111 E. Cain St. Atlanta. AG 8/7/1908

DICKSON, Anna, Miss of Oxford, age 65, d. 5/4. Bro: Judge Capters Dickson. AC 5/6/1905

DICKSON, C. A., Mrs., wife of Judge C. A., of Newton Co., d. Oxford, Ga. 7/7. AG 7/8/1910

DICKSON, Georgia S., Mrs., age 21, wife of H. C., d. 112 Trinity Ave., Atlanta, Wed. Parents: Mr. and Mrs. J. H. Whatley. Husband survives. AG 8/19/1908

DICKSON, Marion, colored, age 7 mos., d. 34 1/2 Greensferry Ave. Atlanta. AG 2/15/1909

DICKSON, Tom, colored, age 13, d. Sparta, Ga. AG 2/8/1909

DICKSON, W. I. d. Mon. Vineville, Ga. Interred: Riverside Cemetery, Macon. AG 9/11/1907

DICKSON, Lizzie, Mrs., age 37, d. Wiley St. Atlanta. AG 12/12/1910

DILBECK, Gertrude, age 4, dau. of Mr. and Mrs. John, d. Roswell Rd. Atlanta Mon. Interred: Sardis Church. AG 9/21/1909

DILLARD, William Henry, son of Mrs. R. S., interred Westview. AG 3/10/1908

DILLARD, William Henry, age 7 mos., son of Mrs. M., d. 18 Rhinehart St., Atlanta, Mon. Interred: Westview. AG 3/9/1908

DILLARD, Will drowned 3/10, body recovered 20 mi. from Montgomery, Ala. 4/5. Father: Capt. W. T. Dillard, 111 Whitman St. Atlanta. Interred: Oakland. AG 4/6/1909

DILLIARD, Mamie, colored, age 22, d. 58 Fain St. Atlanta. AG 4/2/1909

DIMMOCK, William R., Atlanta citizen, d. 114 N. Jackson St. Survivors: Wife, son, Avery Miller Dimmock, age 14; bros., Thomas W. Dimmock, Carrollton, A. E. Dimmock, Valdosta; sister, Mrs. L.

DIMON, Maggie C., Mrs., age 55, d. 12/7 Columbus, Ga. Interred: Rose Hill Cemetery. AC 12/9/1905

DISMER, George, age 13. Funeral Wes., res., 70 Connally St. Atlanta. Interred: Oakland. AG 10/24/1906

DISON, John T., painter, d. 144 Marietta St. Atlanta 9/30. Wife in Birmingham, Ala. AC 11/1/1905

DITMORE, Amanda, Mrs., age 83, d. 376 Glenn St. Atlanta. AG 2/19/1907

DIX, A. S., Rev. funeral at Vineville Baptist Church, Macon. Interred: Riverside. AG 12/29/1910

DIXON, infant of Mr. and Mrs. W. D., d. Sat., Atlanta. Interred: DeKalb Co., Ga. AG 4/25/1910

DIXON, E. H., Mrs., age 85, grandmother of Claud and Clarence Henry, of Dalton, Ga., d. her res. near Spring Place. AG 6/27/1910

DIXON, Fannie, Mrs., Pres. of Free Kindergarten Assn, age 60, d. today. Sons: Thomas, Marshall. AG 10/23/1907

DIXON, George, colored, fell from the mizzenmast of the schooner "Josephine", 90 ft., killed yesterday, Savannah, Ga. AG 9/12/1907

DIXON, George W., Capt. of Augusta d. Sat. Lived Augusta 30 yrs. Age 53. AG 2/24/1908

DIXON, John of Dublin accidentally killed at saw-mill of S. T. Hall. AG 7/16/1906

DIXON, Lucy, colored, age 43, d. 302-A W. Fair St. Atlanta. AG 9/24/1907

DIXON, R. Emmett d. New Orleans, La. Wed. Interred: Woodbury, Ga. AG 10/3/1908

DIXON, Warren, age 62, d. Jonesboro, Ga., Fri. 3 sons, 4 daus. AG 9/10/1910

DOANE, Alonzo B., age 37, formerly of Hapeville, d. Mon. Tampa, Fla. Wife, 5 yr. old son, E. A. Parents: Mr. & Mrs. E. A. Doane, 21 W. Peachtree Pl. Atlanta. Sis: Mrs. J. P. Riley, Atlanta. Bur: Mt. Zion Cem., Hapeville, Ga. AG 5/25/1910

DOBBINS, Estell, age 31, d. Ashby St. Atlanta. AG 9/8/1909

DOBBS, A. A., age 74, d. Sun. 349 Little St., Atlanta. Interred: Cartersville. Dau: Mrs. R. R. Ray, Cartersville. AG 7/29/1907

DOBBS, Adelia, colored, d. Spellman Hospital. Atlanta. AG 5/31/1907

DOBBS, Dora, colored, age 15, d. Pittsburg, Pa. AG 1/18/1907

DOBBS, J. M. killed 12/8 railroad accident. Mrs. Todd of Rockmart, Ga. notified. AC 12/10/1905

DOBBS, Susan, Mrs., age 73, d. dau.'s res., Mrs. A. J. Luther, Cascade Ave., Atlanta, Tues. Daus: Mrs. A. J. Luther, Mrs. Fanny Rogers, Mrs. Molly Wheeler. Son: Willard Dobbs. Interred: Villa Rica, Ga. AG 1/21/1908

DOBBS, W. G., age 19, d. Atlanta. AG 11/19/1909

DOBBS, Charles O., age 30, d. Rockmart Fri. Funeral res. of John Dobbs, cousin. Wife survives. AG 8/23/1909

DODD, Green Taliaferro, age 71, Atlanta pioneer, b. St. Clair, Ala. 7/7/1834, d. 372 W. Peachtree St. Atlanta. m. 1st Miss Calloway, had ch: John (decd); Thomas; Augustus; Charles (decd); Mrs. W. C. Warren; Nellie Dodd. m. 2nd Miss Henrietta Chapman of Atlanta, had ch: Philip, age 16; Mary, age 14. Interred: Oakland. Son of John Dodd of Hall Co., Ga. who d. age 79 Calhoun Co., Ala.; grson of Jesse Dodd, Rev. War Soldier under Washington. Interred: Oakland. AC 7/9/1905

DODD, J. T., Dr., age 78, Clayton Co. pioneer, d. Tues., Riverdale. Surgeon in Civil War. Wife, 14 ch. 1st wife: Mattie Shadrick, 8 ch. By 2nd wife: 10 ch. Surviving ch: J. M., A. M., Dr. W. T., Norwood, W. H., Walter, P. S., Claude and Osceola. Daus: Mrs. Alberta Allen, Mrs. Maggie Bishop, Mrs. R. J. Brown, Mrs. Joe Walker, Miss Pearl Dodd. Interred: Hollywood. AG 9/25/1907

DODD, Mary L., Mrs. d. 188 Bellwood Ave., Atlanta, Sun. Interred: Family burial grounds, Collins Springs. AG 10/8/1907

DODD, Thomas, Capt., Georgia man, V. P. of RR, d. Laredo, Texas. He was b. 5/1840 Bartow Co., Ga. AG 1/14/1907

DODGE, Maybelle, Miss, age 35, d. sister's res., Mrs. W. T. Callahan, E. Point, Ga., Sun., dau. of late Rev. W. A. Dodge. Bro: W. A. Dodge, Jr. Interred: E. Pt. Methodist Church cemetery. AG 4/18/1910

DODGEN, Homer C., age 15, son of Mr. and Mrs. N. W. B., d. Mason and Turners Ferry Rd., Atlanta, Tues. Interred: Harmony church. AG 10/22/1907

DODGEN, W. A., age 53, d. 66 Hood St. Atlanta. AG 5/24/1907

DODGON, Jessie, Mrs., age 29, d. Wed. 23 Dalney St. Atlanta. Interred: Hollywood. AG 5/26/1910

DODSON, Francis A., infant son of Mr. and Mrs. Joseph N., d. Fri., 59 Marcus St. Interred: Clarkston. AG 6/29/1907

DODSON, John H., infant son of Mr. and Mrs. Joseph N., d. Mon. 59 Marcus St., Atlanta. Interred: family burying ground in the country. AG 6/5/1907

DODSON, Joseph H., age 5 mos., d. 59 Marcus St. Atlanta. AG 6/6/1907

DODSON, Nancy, Mrs., age 72, d. Columbus, Ga. AG 10/17/1908
DODSON, Virgil, son of N., age 21, d. Jacksonville, Fla. Bros: W.
N., Jacksonville; W. E. M., Atlanta. AG 2/15/1910
DOERFLINGER, W. F., citizen of Brunswick, Ga. d. Baltimore, Johns
Hopkins Hospital. Interred: Brunswick. AG 6/1/1907
DOHN, Henry, son of Mr. and Mrs. Adolph, d. Fri. Macon. AG
5/9/1908
DOKE, Thomas A., age 59, d. Atlanta. AG 5/21/1910
DOLAN, Evelyn, age 16 mos., dau. of Mr. and Mrs. W. K., d.
Atlanta Fri. Interred: Westview. AG 3/29/1907
DOLAN, Grace G., Mrs. funeral 22 Woodston St., Atlanta. Interred:
Westview. Husband: James Dolan. Dau: Mrs. G. D. Kirkland. Son: W.
K. Dolan. AG 8/7/1906
DOLLAR, Alfred A., inf. son of W. E., d. 3 Ellis St., Atlanta.
Interred: Westview. AG 6/13/1906
DOLLAR, Anna May, inf. dau. of Mr. and Mrs. James W., d. 3
Ponders Ave., Atlanta, Wed. Interred: Collins Spring Church. AG
2/26/1907
DOLLAR, H. C., Dr., age 60, d. Atlanta. AG 4/21/1908
DOMINI, John funeral 5/12, German Luthern Church. Atlanta. AG
5/11/1907
DOMMATT, L. D., age 40, d. 101 N. Butler St. Atlanta. AG
11/20/1907
DOMMOTH, Lena, Mrs., age 40, d. Atlanta, Mon., 49 Armstrong St.
Interred: Westview. AG 11/19/1907
DONALD, Guy, inf. son of Mr. and Mrs. John M. of 44 Harold St.,
Atlanta, d. Mon. Interred: Hollywood. AG 5/21/1908
DONALD, Mary, colored, age 33, d. 568 Glenn St. Atlanta. AG
12/22/1908
DONALDSON, John, age 30, d. Grady Hospital. Atlanta. AG 8/24/1906
DONALDSON, Thelma, age 2, dau. of Mr. and Mrs. S. P., d. 7
Richards St., Atlanta, Wed. Interred: Nancys Creek church yard.
AG 6/30/1910
DONAVAN, John A. LWT contested. He d. 2 wks ago. Mrs. Charles R.
White of LaGrange (sister) and Mrs. Annie Terry, Columbia, S. C.,
admrs. Sis-in-law: Mrs. John Ware named as heir. AC 5/9/1905
DONAVAN, John A. of Atlanta d. LaGrange 4/27 at res. of bro-in-
law: Charles R. White. Bro-in-law: Capt. John R. Ware. Wife was
formerly Miss Brady of LaGrange. AG 4/28/1905
DONCHOO, Mary Leak, infant, d. 167 Rhodes St. Atlanta. AG
5/24/1906
DONEHOO, Lula Eloise, inf. dau. of Mr. and Mrs. J. W., d.
Bellwood Rd., Atlanta, Sat. Interred: Fayetteville, Ga. AG
6/13/1908
DONEHOO, N. M., Mrs., age 72, d. 107 Jefferson St., Atlanta, Wed.
Two children. Interred: Oneonto, Ala. AG 3/18/1908
DONEHOO, Nannie Lou, age 1, dau. of Mr. and Mrs. J. A., d. 95
Ella St., Atlanta, Thurs. Interred: Adamsville, Ga. AG 9/27/1907
DOOLEY, Martin J., age 52, d. 59 Luckie St. Atlanta. Interred:
Westview. AG 7/9/1906
DOOLEY, O. W., age 20, d. Atlanta Tues. Interred: Westview.
Mother, one sister. AG 7/14/1909
DOOLITTLE, Charles V. d. Atlanta Sat. Interred: Westview. Wife,
and father survive. AG 5/25/1908

DOONAN, DeSales d. Boston, Mass. Sat., res. 244 Washington St., Atlanta. Interred: Oakland. AG 9/29/1908

DOONAN, J. J. of Atlanta d. Tues. Interred: Oakland. AG 1/13/1910

DOONAN, James F. DeSales, age 31, d. Boston, Mass. AG 10/1/1908

DORMAN, Felix, age 14, d. 122 Central Ave. Atlanta. AG 8/10/1906

DORMAN, Blarney, son of Police J. W., Richland, Ga., shot, killed Tues. by negroes. Arrested: George Green, Bob Simmons, Lee Robinson, Stewart Co. jail. Blarney had just retd from Loyd, Fla. where engated in sawmill business. AG 12/26/1907

DORR, J. W., Mrs. d. Sat. Interred: Oakland. AG 12/28/1909

DORR, Walter Richmond, inf. son of Mr. and Mrs. George C., d. 113 Woodward Ave., Atlanta, Thurs. Interred: Westview. AG 11/23/1907

DORRNAN, Harry, age 25, d. Atlanta Thurs. Interred: Oakland. AG 4/8/1910

DORSETT, J. E., age 68, d. 22 Walker St. Atlanta. AG 8/31/1908

DORSEY, Anna, old negro woman, scared to death by storm at Americus, Ga. 6/14/1906.

DORSEY, B. H.. Jonesboro. Leon T. Milner charged with murder. AG 8/30/1906

DORSEY, C. Percy of East Point killed by Emmett Nelson near Shady Dale, Jasper Co., Ga. Bros: James R. Dorsey; John Dorsey. Percy m. 2 yrs. ago to Miss Cloe West of Butler, Ga. AG 2/16/1907

DORSEY, Dan, Mrs. d. Mon. Barnesville. Survived by husband, two small children. Interred: Family Burial Lot. AG 12/23/1908

DORSEY, Ed, colored, age 17, d. 101 N. Butler St. Atlanta. AG 9/17/1907

DORSEY, G. E., colored, age 1, d. rear of 73 Fort St. Atlanta. AG 3/5/1908

DORSEY, Lucile, colored, age 3, d. Grady Hospital. Atlanta. AG 3/25/1907

DORSEY, Mahaley, colored, age 40, d. 257 Thurmond St., Atlanta. AG 10/14/1907

DORSEY, Margaret, colored, age 60, d. rear 125 Central Ave. Atlanta. AG 1/18/1907

DORSEY, Robert, age 25, d. Memphis, Tenn. Thurs. Mother: Mary Dorsey, 308 Oakland Ave. Atlanta. Bur: Westview. AG 11/16/1908

DORTCH, A. F., Mrs. d. Broad St., Hawkinsville, Thurs. Husband, 9 children. Interred: Orange Hill. AG 7/23/1908

DOSTER, Cassie, Mrs. interred Manfield, Ga. Mon. AG 5/21/1906

DOSTER, G. H. shot yesterday by M. S. Ezell. Both are unmd. Leaves mother, father, four bros., four sisters. AG 5/15/1907

DOSTER, H. V., age 62, d. 321 Peachtree St. Atlanta. AG 2/16/1910

DOSTER, J. H., age 63, Confederate veteran, d. Thurs. at Soldiers' Home, Atlanta. Member of Co. H., No. 43, Ga. Volunteers. AG 5/10/1907

DOSTER, John, planter of White Plains, Ga. d. 10/27. Interred: Family burial ground. AC 10/29/1905

DOUBS, P. F., age 64, veteran of civil war, d. Soldiers' Home, Atlanta, Thurs. Interred: Westview. AG 6/15/1906

DOUGHERTY, Amanda, colored, age 50, d. 16 Madison Ave. Atlanta. AG 8/24/1908

DOUGHERTY, Edwin F., Jr., inf. son of Mr. and Mrs. Edwin F., and grandson of Mr. and Mrs. D. B. Carson and Mr. and Mrs. D. O. Dougherty, d. 800 Peachtree St., Atlanta, Mon. Interred: Westview. AG 3/10/1908

DOUGHERTY, Frank, negro, killed by William Frederick, negro. Augusta, Ga. AG 4/5/1909

DOUGHERTY, Mary Floyd, Mrs., age 62, d. W. Peachtree St. Atlanta. AG 10/20/1909

DOUGHERTY, Will, age 27, d. Clarkston, Ga. AG 3/10/1910

DOUGHTY, William Henry, Dr. d. 3/27. Interred: City Cemetery, Augusta. AC 3/28/1905

DOUGLAS, Eugenius L., Colonel, once noted lawyer of Cuthbert, d. yesterday, age 80, Confederate veteran. AG 2/1/1907

DOUGLAS, Georgia, Mrs., age 39, d. 125 N. Jackson St., Atlanta, Fri., wife of O. S. Father: Capt. J. C. Hendrix. Sis: Mrs. Andrew Anderson; Mrs. J. W. Davidson. 4 children. AG 3/21/1910

DOUGLAS, R. O., Capt. d. Atlanta Thurs. Interred: Westview. He was b. LaGrange 8/25/1842, Conf. Vet., Co. E, 41 Ga. Son of late John Douglas of LaGrange. Ch: Peyton Douglas, Mrs. R. T. Crosser. Sisters: Mrs. Rebecca Lowe Gunston, Hot Springs, Va., Mrs. James M. Coulter, Baltimore, Md. AG 7/31/1908

DOUGLAS, Robert Allen, age 65, d. 294 Courtland St. Atlanta. AG 8/1/1908

DOUGLAS, Virginia, Mrs., age 61, d. S. Kirkwood, Ga. Wed., wife of Capt. R. O. Son: Peyton. Interred: Westview. AG 4/22/1908

DOWDY, A. N., age 53, d. 146 E. Linden St., Atlanta, Fri. Wife: Mrs. A. N., 4 children. Interred: Westview. AG 1/11/1908

DOWDY, Lula, age 14, dau. of Mr. and Mrs. A. H., d. 15 Bluff St. Atlanta, Sat. Interred: Redan, Ga. AG 5/11/1908

DOWLING, Raymond suicide Waycross, Ga. Wife, 4 children. Ag 11/7/1910

DOWMAN, George, d. 1905. From obituary of Mrs. A. W. Dowman. AG 11/19/1906

DOWMAN, A. W., Mrs., age 81, b. London, Engl., dau's home, Mrs. George Adahold. Res. Edgewood, Ga., then Campbell Co. 7 ch: Dr. George Dowman, N. C.; J. H. Dowman, Charleston, W. Va.; Charles E. Dowman, Atlanta; J. W. Dowman, Selina Dowman, Atlanta; Albert Dowman, Mrs. J. Suber and Mrs. George Adahold of Campbell Co. AG 11/19/1906

DOWNING, James W., age 6, son of Mr. and Mrs. James, d. 135 Cooper St. Atlanta. Interred: Westview. AG 10/13/1908

DOX, Frank H. d. 10/15 118 S. Forsyth St. Atlanta. AC 10/16/1905

DOXEY, Laura H., Mrs., age 38, d. 25 W. Georgia Ave. Atlanta. AG 7/14/1910

DOYLE, Alfred, age 55, d. 4/15 Atlanta. Relatives in Griffin,a. AC 4/17/1905

DOYLE, George, age 6 mos., d. 23 Corput St. Atlanta. AG 3/10/1909

DOYLE, Nancy Whippey, Mrs., age 64, wife of Dr. John Doyle, d. 392 S. Boulevard, Atlanta, Thurs. Interred: Ohio. AG 7/23/1908

DOZIER, Anna, inf. dau. of Mr. and Mrs. C. A. of 24 Oak St., Atlanta, d. Mon. AG 7/20/1909

DOZIER, James, colored, age 55, d. 22 Spinks alley. Atlanta. AG 3/12/1908

DOZIER, Orin, age 26, d. 12/29 Flovilla, Ga., son of W. B. AG 12/30/1910

DRAKE, Addie C., Mrs. d. Sun. Atlanta, age 72. Sisters: Mrs. J. W. Christian, Mrs. C. Boyles, Mrs. Annie Bennett, Mrs. George Hawley, Mrs. Annie Taylor, Mrs. Eugenia Marchman. Interred: Westview. AG 5/28/1906

DRAKE, Charlie shot and killed by Jim Simms, colored, Athens, Ga. AG 3/1/1907

DRAKE, Decai, colored, age 27, d. 329 Magnolia St. Atlanta. AG 9/25/1909

DRAKE, Ed, colored, age 19 yrs., d. corner Hunnicutt and Orme Sts. Atlanta. AG 8/20/1907

DRAKE, Elvira, Mrs. of Union City, Ga. d. Fri., wife of J. C. Bro: D. T. Summers, Opelika, Ala. Interred: Senoia, Ga. AG 6/10/1910

DRAKE, F. L., formerly of Atlanta, d. Thurs. Shreveport, Ala. Interred: Thomaston, Ga. Father: Dr. John C. Thomaston. Bro: Edward A., Atlanta. AG 7/17/1909

DRAKE, Forrest, age 6 mos., died 144 Wells St. Atlanta. AG 12/26/1906

DRAKE, G. W., age 54, d. Roswell Rd. Atlanta Thurs. Son: W. L. AG 2/17/1910

DRAKE, Mary D., colored, age 49, d. 105 Richmond St. Atlanta. AG 9/21/1909

DRAKEFORD, A., colored, age 52, d. 26 Bradberry alley. Atlanta. AG 4/20/1908

DRAPER, Emma M., age 59, d. 34 Cone St. Atlanta. AG 12/31/1910

DRAPER, Franklin, died at 24 Luckie Street, Atlanta. AG 11/26/1906

DRASBACH, H. C. stabbed 10/3/1903. He was policeman. Memorial erected at English Lutheran Church. Atlanta. AC 5/6/1905

DREAUX, Norman Melo, infant of Mr. and Mrs. Melo, d. Wed. 380 Grant St. Atlanta. Interred: Hollywood. AG 6/27/1907

DREGER, Ruth Elizabeth, inf. dau. of Mr. and Mrs. W. T., d. 139 N. Jackson St., Fri. Interred: Westview. AG 11/2/1907

DRENNAN, J. W., age 34, d. 39 Curran St. Atlanta, Fri. Interred: Westview. AG 4/27/1907

DREW, Polly Williams, Mrs. d. 4/7 Montpelier Ave., Macon. Interred: Riverside. Husband. Ch: Thomas, Virginia. Father, 2 sisters, 4 bros. AG 4/8/1910

DREWRY, Farrell, 4 mos., d. 189 Cherokee Ave. Atlanta. AG 1/28/1907

DREYFUS, Charlotte, Mrs. d. 12/8 dau.´s res., Mrs. H. C. Sommer, 451 Washington St., Atlanta. Interred: Memphis, Tenn. AC 12/10/1905

DRIVER, Floyd, age 20, d. Haynes St. Atlanta. AG 6/14/1907

DRIVER, H. A., age 23, d. Atlanta Wed. Interred: West Point, Ga. Parents, several bros., sisters. AG 7/16/1908

DRIVER, Kate, Miss, age 65, res. of Americus, Ga., d. Atlanta. Interred: Westview. AG 3/22/1910

DROHAN, Ethel, Miss d. Atlanta, injuries from auto accident. Interred: Baltimore, Maryland. AG 10/13/1910

DROMGOOLE, C. C. of Richmond, Va. d. Knoxville, Tenn., Cumberland Hotel. AC 7/8/1905

DROSKIN, Sam, age 10 mos., d. 110 Gilmer St., Atlanta. AG 7/11/1910

DRUB, L., age 50, d. Sat. 277 Decatur St. Atlanta. Interred: Hollywood. AG 4/13/1908

DRYMON, Frank, age 19, d. 101 N. Butler St. Atlanta. Interred: Spartanburg, S. C. AG 11/20/1907

DUBIGNON, Fleming Grantland, age 57, d. 33 Peachtree Pl. Atlanta.
AG 11/22/1909
DUBOIS, Ben, Mrs. d. Thurs. E. Pt. Husband. Son: Wallace.
Interred: Ligonier, Ind. AG 4/28/1910
DUBOIS, Dan, Mrs., age 39, d. E. Point, Ga. AG 4/28/1910
DUBOSE, Jessie, Mrs., age 54, d. 124 S. Pryor St. Atlanta, Mon.
Husband survives. Interred: Clarkston, Ga., Family Cemetery. AG
4/21/1908
DUBOSE, Otis, negro,, age 13, d. lockjaw, Atlanta. AG 1/7/1910
DUBOSE, Mary H., Mrs., age 70, wife of Rev. J. E., d. Decatur.
Ch: John A., William T., Samuel W., Elias; Mrs. W. S.
Featherstone; Carrie, Fannie and Sallie. Bur: Decatur, Ga. AG
4/16/1908
DUDLEY, Sarah E., Mrs., age 76, d. 365 Haynes St. Atlanta, Mon.
Sons: A. M., W. W. Dau: Mrs. W. R. Jones, Columbus, Ga. Sis: Mrs.
Mary Morison, Mrs. Minnie Morrison. Bros-in-law: F. B. and J. C.
Morrison. AG 12/17/1910
DUDLEY, W. F., age 70, Russell Co., Ala. farmer, d. 6 mi. W. of
Columbus, Ga. yesterday. Confederate Veteran and father of 10
living children. Son, R. L. Dudley, Columbus, Ga. AG 12/23/1908
DUFFEY, George, colored, age 3 yrs., d. Solomon St. Atlanta. AG
3/1/1907
DUGER, R. E., age 1, d. 129 N. Jackson St. Atlanta. AG 11/2/1907
DUGGAN, Mack, Mrs. d. Wed. Sandersville, Ga., dau. of Judge and
Mrs. P. R. Taliaferro. Ch: Annie Nora, Lizzie Belle, Roy, Mack,
Charles. AG 4/17/1908
DUGGAN, Jas H., Mrs., 42, d. 10/3 Wilkinson Co. Dau. of Dr. Benj.
F. Stanley, grdau. of Ira E. Stanley, ggrdau. of Gov. Thos
McCall. GrUnc: Col. Hugh McCall. Bro: Rollin Maury Stanley. Sis:
Mrs. Lucy McArthur. Bur: Stanley Cem. AG 10/4/1909
DUHME, John W., age 33, former Atlantan, d. Savannah, Ga.
Interred: Westview (Atlanta). 2 bros: Charles, Phil. AG
11/16/1910
DUHME, M. A., Mrs.,a ge 64, d. 45 W. Alexander St. Atlanta. AG
2/24/1908
DUHME, Mary Anne, Mrs., age 65, d. dau.´s res., Mrs. William
Butler, 45 W. Alexander St., Atlanta, Fri. Ch: John W., Charles
H., P. J.; Mrs. William Butler. Interred: Westview. AG 2/20/1908
DUKE, Birdie, Mrs., wife of J. L., d. 920 Fifth Ave., Columbus,
Ga. 7/7. Interred: Rose Hill, Ala. AC 7/9/1905
DUKE, Elizabeth, Miss, age 78, d. Atlanta Thurs. Bro: T. E. Duke,
E. Point. AG 2/17/1910
DUKE, J. R., Mrs., age 27, d. 63 Bartow St. Atlanta. Interred:
Cedartown, Ga. AG 8/5/1910
DUKE, M. E., Mrs., age 73, d. res. of son, late Richard Duke, 120
Western Ave., Atlanta, Sun. Interred: Fairburn, Ga. AG 9/23/1907
DUKE, Mary F., Mrs. funeral Sun. 50 Westland Ave. Interred:
Fairburn, Ga. AG 2/8/1910
DUKE, Mary Frances, age 51, d. 50 Western Ave. Atlanta. AG
2/7/1910
DUKE, Samuel M., Confederate veteran, d. Griffin, age 79. Wife,
two children: Robert L. Duke of Griffin and Walter Duke of
Atlanta. AG 4/2/1907
DUKE, T. M., age 62, d. Thurs. 407 Fraser St. Atlanta. AG
8/25/1910

DUKES, Mahulda, Mrs., age 75, d. 2/13, 16th St., Columbus, Ga. AC 2/15/1905

DUKES, R. F. d. 12/28. Interred: Fairburn, Ga. AC 11/30/1905

DUKES, Ruth, colored, age 5, d. 101 N. Butler St. Atlanta. AG 12/6/1907

DUKES, William, colored, age 7 mos., d. 956-B Fort St. Atlanta. AG 5/12/1909

DUMPHREY, Weston M., Mrs., widow of R. S., d. 7/20, age 76, res. of Columbus, Ga. 60 yrs. AC 7/21/1905

DUMPHREY, William d. Louisville, Ky. from swallowing false teeth. Former Georgian. AG 4/20/1907

DUNAWAY, W. E., Mrs., age 50, d. Atlanta Fri. Sis: Mrs. Woods, White, Atlanta. Interred: Jackson, Tenn. AG 8/6/1910

DUNAWAY, W. H., age 56, d. 315 Edgewood Ave. Atlanta. AG 4/10/1907

DUNBAR, Harry, age 38, d. Sun. Atlanta. Interred: Chamblee, Ga. AG 12/8/1909

DUNBAR, Rebecca Hopkins, Mrs., wife of Mayor William Dunbar of Augusta, Ga., d. home on lower Green St. last night. Sons: Hon. C. E. Dunbar, Dr. Stiles Dunbar, Wadley, Ga., Frank Dunbar, Augusta. AG 4/15/1907

DUNCAN, Ben, colored, age 47, d. 10 George St. Atlanta. AG 2/13/1908

DUNCAN, Charles, age 5 mos., inf. son of Mr. and Mrs. James, 19 Bluff St., Atlanta, d. Fri. Interred: Caseys Cemetery. AG 7/17/1909

DUNCAN, Flo, age 5, d. 101 N. Butler St. Atlanta. AG 6/21/1907

DUNCAN, Griff, negro engineer at light plant, shot and killed last night by Jesse Willis, colored. AG 2/14/1907

DUNCAN, Harriet, colored, age 80, died 245 Mangum Street, Atlanta. AG 11/20/1906

DUNCAN, J. D., Mrs., age 50, d. McDonough Rd., Atlanta, Wed. Husband, one child, survive. Interred: Family Burial Ground. AG 12/15/1909

DUNCAN, J. L., Mrs. d. Milner, Ga. 4/16. Interred: Milner Cemetery. AC 4/20/1905

DUNCAN, K. S. of Valdosta, saloonist, suicide. Leaves wife. AG 7/30/1906

DUNCAN, Malcolm, youngest son of late Judge C., d. Wed. Perry, Ga. Interred: Evergreen Cemetery. Age 28. Bros: J. P., C. C. Sis: Mrs. Stella Carter of Perry; Mrs. Sila Pate, Hawkinsville. AG 9/10/1910

DUNCAN, M. M., age 71, d. corner Pine and 14th Sts. Atlanta. Interred: Sandy Springs Cemetery. 2 sons, 2 daus. AG 1/27/1910

DUNCAN, Neal, colored, age 40, d. 67 Chapel St. Atlanta. AG 7/11/1908

DUNCAN, P. Mellican, age 19, son of Mr. and Mrs. P. W., d. 91 Carroll St. Atlanta. Interred: Caseys. AG 7/20/1907

DUNCAN, Robert C., age 4 mos., son of Mr. and Mrs. H. C. of Hapeville, d. Sat. Interred: Hapeville. AG 8/23/1909

DUNCAN, Robert Emmett d. Wed. Vineville, Ga. Interred: Toomsboro, Ga. AG 3/20/1908

DUNCAN, Roy, Jr., age 7 mos., d. 65 Johnson Ave. Atlanta. AG 7/25/1910

DUNCAN, Samuel, inf. son of Mr. and Mrs. J. D., d. Sun. 424 Marietta Sat., Atlanta. Interred: Westview. AG 7/22/1907

DUNCAN, W. R., Mrs. suicide 4/5 Lilburn, Ga. AG 4/6/1909

DUNCAN, William, colored, age 57, d. 390 Houston St. Atlanta. AG 7/16/1909

DUNFORD, Annie, Mrs., wife of Capt. J. W., d. Atlanta 11/23. Bur: Westview. Relatives: Mrs. Maggie Brazile; Miss Josie Prater; Mrs. Bell Prater; Mr. and Mrs. E. L. Prater; Mrs. T. B. McNaron, Albertville, Ala.; J. B. Prater. AC 11/24/1905

DUNIGAN, Nannie, Mrs., age 24, d. Buford, Ga. AG 7/6/1909

DUNLAP, David J., age 89, d. Soldiers´ Home, Atlanta. AG 5/28/1906

DUNLAP, John G., age 59, d. 22 Rankin St. Atlanta. Wife. Bros: Samuel C. Dunlap, Carnesville; Edgar Dunlap, Atlanta. Sisters: Mrs. C. H. Strickland, Mrs. W. H. Strickland, Mrs. F. R. Bell, Mrs. W. D. Harwell, Interred: Oakland. AG 11/3/1908

DUNLAP, Philip S., Mrs. d. Tues. res. of husband in Kirkwood. Interred: Westview. AG 7/18/1906

DUNN, Budd, colored, age 59, d. at rear of 39 McDaniel St. Atlanta. AG 2/8/1907

DUNN, E. N., Mrs. buried Pinewood Cemetery 4/24. Son: Albert, Pine Bluff, Ark. Dau: Miss Euphra Dunn of W. Point, Ga. Sis: Miss Jula Jeter, Atlanta. AC 4/25/1905

DUNN, James P. S., age 82, d. 303 Cherokee Ave. Atlanta. AG 5/15/1907

DUNN, R. I. E., Mrs., age 20, d. Dallas, Texas. Husband: R. I. E. of Atlanta. She was md. 5 mos. ago. AG 2/23/1910

DUNNAWAY, Clyde H., age 2, d. 6 Berean Ave. Atlanta. AG 2/22/1907

DUNN, Ella, Mrs., age 26, d. McDonough Rd., Atlanta Tues. Husband: H. G. Several children. Interred: Morrow Station, Ga. AG 7/7/1909

DUNSTER, Henry, Mrs., age 76, d. 17 W. Cain St. Atlanta. AG 8/20/1907

DUNTON, Gertrude, age 39, d. Atlanta. AG 2/11/1910

DUNWOODY, Mary Parker, Mrs., wife of Felix, suicide Macon. Age 18, bride of 18 mos. AG 6/12/1906

DUPRE, John Samuel, Col. d. bros. res., Col. P. P., Canton, Ga. 8/24. Interred: Town Cemetery. AC 8/25/1905

DUPRE, Mary B., age 20, d. 98 Boulevard Pl. Atlanta. AG 11/30/1910

DUPREE, Conductor, of Kathleen, Ga., d. Macon train wreck. AG 2/15/1911

DUPREE, Watt, colored, age 34, d. Rome, Ga. AG 10/30/1908

DURDEN, Nellie O., age 18 mos., dau. of Mr. and Mrs. J. M., d. 175 Fern St. Atlanta, Fri. Interred: Green Mountain, Ga. AG 6/25/1910

DURE, George A. d. Wed. Macon. Son: Leon Dure. Interred: Rose Hill Cemetery, Macon. AG 3/20/1908

DUREN, J. F., age 21, d. Tues. res. of parents, Mr. and Mrs. G. W., 299 Bellwood Ave. Atlanta. Interred: Fairburn, Ga. AG 9/28/1910

DURHAM, Charles Wesley, son of Mr. and Mrs. E. F., age 1, d. 9 Todd St. Atlanta. Interred: Westview. AG 8/19/1909

DURHAM, James, colored, age 19, d. 101 N. Butler St. Atlanta. AG 5/20/1909

DURHAM, Lamar, colored, age 30, d. 113 Violet St. Atlanta. AG 11/1/1910

DURHAM, Lula, Mrs. d. res. of son, J. C. Durham, 14 Viola St., Atlanta, Sat. Interred: Westview. 3 daus, 2 sons. AG 6/1/1908

DURHAM, Willis E., infant son of Mr. and Mrs. E. F., d. Sat. 22 1/2 Marietta St., Atlanta. Interred: Westview. AG 6/25/1907

DURRENCE, Lilla, Miss, dau. of Mr. and Mrs. J. W., d. Sat. Glennville, Ga. AG 6/15/1908

DUVAL, Antoinette, inf. dau. of Mr. and Mrs. W. N., d. 51 Currier St. Atlanta, Tues. Interred: Westview. AG 11/16/1910

DWYER, J. F. d. Thurs. Macon. Interred: old home, Tullahoma, Tenn. Wife. Dau. in Jacksonville. AG 2/27/1910

DYAR, Allen S., Dr., age 48, of New Orleans, d. Atlanta. AG 12/27/1910

DYCHE, Arthur murdered Fri. night, Macon. Father: R. B. Dyche of Monroe Co. Interred: Macon, Ga. AG 6/26/1907

DYE, Martha Helen, age 7 mos., dau. of Mr. and Mrs. J. T., d. 975 S. Pryor St., Atlanta, Mon. Interred: Antioch Church. AG 4/21/1908

DYE, Wade, colored, age 55, d. 41 Taylor St. Atlanta. AG 7/19/1909

DYER, B. V., age 27, d. Atlanta Tues. AG 11/16/1910

DYER, Hugh A., age 4 mos., inf. son of Mr. and Mrs. W. W. of 10 Augusta Ave., Atlanta, d. Mon. Interred: Smarrs, Ga. AG 7/6/1909

DYER, Lula, Miss, age 18, d. 10/1, 169 Bellwood Ave. Atlanta. Interred: Auburn. AC 10/3/1905

DYER, Millie, Mrs., age 76, d. 301 N. Ave. Atlanta. AG 12/28/1910

DYER, W. L., age 30, d. Fri. res. of uncle, Rev. W. W. Brinsfield, 48 English Ave. Atlanta. Interred: Pinson, Ga. AG 5/3/1907

DYSON, George, Mrs. funeral Thurs., Washington, Ga., age 80. Children: Mrs. C. H. Smith, Mrs. J. R. Turner, Joseph R. Dyson. Interred: City cemetery. AG 5/24/1907

EADS, Daniel, age 65, killed by train Chattahoochee, Ga. AG 4/18/1910

EADS, Henry, colored, age 62, d. Fulton Co. barracks. AG 2/27/1907

EAKES, E. E. E., age 29, d. Atlanta Sat., son of Rev. and Mrs. M. H. Eakes. Wife, three small children, three bros., one sister. Interred: Lithonia, Ga. AG 12/21/1907

EAKES, Roy, age 8, son of E. E., d. 5/3 19 Hardin St., Atlanta. Nephew of Rev. Dr. Eakes, Lithonia, Ga. AG 5/3/1906

EARL, M. J., Mrs., age 55, d. 129 Lake Ave. Atlanta. AG 12/8/1910

EARLE, William G., inf. son of Mr. and Mrs. J. D., d. Bellwood Ave., Atlanta, Wed. Interred: Hollywood. AG 9/1/1908

EARLEY, Charles T., colored, age 2, d. 188 Chestnut St. Atlanta. AG 11/15/1909

EARLY, Willie May, colored, age 8 mos., d. 64 Moody Pl. Atlanta. AG 7/19/1909

EARP, O. H., Jr., age 3 mos., d. 1 Chamberlin St. Atlanta. AG 6/22/1908

EARP, Ottis Ratcliffe, age 3 mos., d. 1 Chamberlin St. Atlanta. AG 6/22/1908

EART, O. H., Jr., age 3 mos., son of Mr. and Mrs. O. H., d. Chamberlin St., Atlanta, Fri. Bur: Lynchburg, Va. AG 6/19/1908

EASON, Joel, age 11 mos., d. 232 Luckie St. Atlanta. AG 6/6/1907
EASON, Susan, Mrs., age 83, d. 217 Truman St., Atlanta, Mon.
Interred: Manassas, Ga. AG 1/21/1908
EAST, Ellen, Mrs. d. London, England. Sis: Mrs. Thomas McWhinney.
AG 8/14/1907
EASTIN, Laura G., Miss, age 17, d. res. of mother, Mrs. H. C.
Bailey, 296 Forrest Ave. Atlanta Thurs. Interred: Paris, Tx., old
family home. AG 6/5/1908
EATON, Margaret O., age 1, dau. of Mr. and Mrs. J. R. of 39
Egleston St., Atlanta, d. Fri. Interred: West Pointa, Ga. AG
4/8/1909
EATON, Thomas J., age 6, son of Mr. and Mrs. T. B., d. 272 W.
Fifth St., Atlanta, Sat. Interred: Hollywood. AG 6/27/1910
EBARDT, Charles, age 34, d. 278 S. Boulevard. Atlanta. AG
3/24/1910
EBERHARDT, Emma, Mrs., age 62, d. 260 Lee St. Atlanta. Three
daus., 3 sons, all of Atlanta. Interment: Westview. AG 4/4/1907
EBERHARDT, J. B., Capt. d. 1/24 Carlton, Ga., age 69, Conf. Vet.
40 yrs. res. Madison Co. Wife. Ch: Misses Mattie and Lizzie;
Harry, Hamilton of Carlton; Dr. Pope, Elberton; Robert,
Taylorsville. AG 1/25/1910
EBERHARDT, Robert, Col., age 72, vet. 2 wars d. 260 Lee St,
Atlanta. Lt-Col., 38th Ga., Army of N. Va. Came Atlanta from
Oglethorpe Co. Wife, 4 sons: John L., Thomas L., R. W., Harry.
Daus: Mrs. D. E. Moncrief, Jennie, Gussie. AG 1/18/1907
EBERHARDT, Willie, Mrs., age 25, d. East End Tues. Interred:
Forest Park, Ga. AG 5/1/1907
ECHOLS, Aley Figures, age 18, son of Mr. and Mrs. Ewing Echolds,
d. 7/8 Huntsville, Ala. AC 7/10/1905
ECHOLS, B. V., colored, age 46, d. 179 Auburn Ave. Atlanta. AG
1/8/1908
ECHOLS, Elmo, age 10, d. Atlanta. AG 8/14/1908
ECHOLS, Helen, age 1 yr., dau. of Mr. and Mrs. Fred, d.
grandparents res., Mr. and Mrs. J. J. Miller, 194 Edgewood Ave.,
Atlanta, Thurs. Interred: Rock Springs Cemetery. AG 7/4/1908
ECHOLS, John R., age 27, d. Sat. Atlanta. Interred: Westview. AG
5/14/1906
ECHOLS, K., colored, age 54, d. 19 Fair St. Atlanta. AG 4/29/1909
ECHOLS, R. L., colored, age 22, d. 32 Morris St. Atlanta. AG
12/11/1908
ECHOLS, Stephens, colored, age 49, d. 510 N. Boulevard. Atlanta.
AG 7/12/1907
ECHOLS, W. S., colored, age 39, d. 51 Morris St. Atlanta. AG
2/8/1909
ECKERLE, Edna, age 11, dau. of Mr. and Mrs. O. A., d. Fri.
Edgewood Ave., Atlanta. AG 4/16/1910
ECKLES, Alma, Mrs., age 16, wife of J. Z., of 131 Kirkwood Ave.,
Atlanta, d. Thurs. Interred: Lutherville, Ga. AG 10/7/1910
EDDISON, Willie, infant, d. Atlanta. AG 5/24/1906
EDDY, Annie Mrs., age 67, d. dau.´s res., Mrs. G. W. Himebaugh,
22 Rosalie St., Atlanta, Thurs. Interred: Columbia, Tenn. 3
children survive. AG 4/30/1908
EDENFIELD, John d. Stillmore, Ga., age 68. Leaves large family.
AC 11/12/1905

EDENS, Addie Sue, Miss, age 42, dau. of Rev. J. F. Edens, Sr., d. Atlanta Thurs. Bros: B. M., V. H., J. F. Sis: Mrs. J. C. Brannan, Mrs. A. H. Martin. AG 12/1/1910

EDGAR, A. R., Mrs., age 24, wife of A. R., d. 46 Harold Ave., Atlanta, Mon. Husband, two sons, John and Marcel Edgar. Daus: Misses Ruby and Annie. Bros: Sgt. R. J. Brown, Atlanta. AG 6/23/1908

EDGAR, Maude, Mrs., age 26, d. Wed. 38 W. 12th St., Atlanta. Interred: Caseys. AG 7/26/1907

EDGE, Mattie, Mrs., wife of late P. W., d. Mon. Austell, many yrs. res. of Macon. Son: John. AG 3/6/1907

EDGE, Sallie, Mrs., age 55, wife of G. H., d. 668 E. Fair St. Atlanta. Interred: College Park. AG 10/21/1908

EDGEMON, J. F. Chattanooga, Tenn., 11/13/1906. Collision between Cincinnati Southern and Belt railway trains 11/13 killed J. F. Edgemon of Athens, Ga., switchman on Belt train. AG 11/13/1906

EDMONDS, Henry interred Sardis Church, Atlanta. AG 2/14/1908

EDMONDS, Henry, age 60, Atlanta pioneer, d. Cox Cross Rds., Thurs. Son: Walter Edmonds of 361 W. Third St. Interred: Family Burial Grounds. AG 2/13/1908

EDMONDS, Mary, Miss, age 63, d. Fri. res. of sister in E. Pt. One bro., two sisters. Interred: Palmetto, Ga. AG 9/9/1910

EDMONDSON, G. W., age 63, d. 9/29 son-in-laws res., W. N. Seymore, Columbus, Ga. Interred: Brooks Station, Ga. AC 10/1/1905

EDMONDSON, Joseph H., age 86, d. 468 S. Pryor St. Atlanta. AG 11/27/1910

EDMONDSON, Nettie and William murdered by Ben Clements, Decatur. Edward Edmondson, John F. Helms, J. P., told how their bodies were found in house fire. Aged father: Bob Clements, wife, 7 small children. AG 2/25/1909

EDMUNDS, J. P., Mrs., sister of Congressman C. B. Slemp of Virginia, d. Roosevelt Hospital, New York. Interred: Bristol, Tenn. Funeral: Big Stone Gap. AG 1/17/1910

EDWARDS, A. M., Mrs., age 23, wife of A. M., d. Atlanta Thurs, dau. of Mr. and Mrs. W. P. West of Cedartown, Ga. She lived near Milledgeville, Ga. 4 bros., 4 sisters. Interred: Cedartown, Ga. AG 1/9/1908

EDWARDS, C. C., Mrs. d. Campbellton Rd. Atlanta, Mon. Interred: akland. AG 5/6/1908

EDWARDS, C. E., age 75, d. Soldiers' Home, Atlanta. AG 4/3/1908

EDWARDS, E. R., colored, age 27, d. 20 Newman St. Atlanta. AG 3/28/1907

EDWARDS, Ed, colored, age 38, d. Atlanta. AG 12/17/1910

EDWARDS, Eli, young son of Dr. and Mrs. J. H., d. 161 Bedford Place, Atlanta, Wed. Interred: Caseys. AG 3/28/1907

EDWARDS, Eliza, Mrs., age 84, d. 211 South Ave., Atlanta, Thurs. Son: C. L., Dallas, Texas. Dau: Mrs. J. W. Hooten, Atlanta. Interred: Forsyth, Ga. AG 7/29/1909

EDWARDS, Elizabeth, Mrs., age 83, d. 11 Augusta Ave., Atlanta, Sat. INterred: Canton, Ga. AG 5/25/1908

EDWARDS, Ernest, age 31, of Adairsville, Ga., d. Wed. Interred: Nelson, Ga. AG 6/4/1909

EDWARDS, Fannie, Mrs. of Logansville, Ala. d. Atlanta. AG 5/17/1909

EDWARDS, Helen, age 18 mos., dau. of Mr. and Mrs. W. B., of Simmsville, Ga. d. Thurs. Interred: Hollywood. AG 6/17/1910

EDWARDS, James E., age 79, b. Rutherford Co., N. C., inmate of Confederate Soldiers' Home, Atlanta, d. Jan. 8. Fought side-by-side with J. W. Nelson, interred same way. After war, settled Lowndes Co. Interred: Westview. AC 1/9/1905

EDWARDS, James M., age 4, son of Mr. and Mrs. B. E., d. Mon. parents home, 117 Nelson St., Atlanta. Interred: Forest Park. AG 3/2/1909

EDWARDS, John M., Capt., age 67, d. 267 Capitol Ave., Atlanta. Confederate army. Ch: Hines M., William, Bessie. Sis: Mrs. Ann Kidd, Milledgeville. Bro: Capt. Jack Edwards, Decatur. Bur: Milledgeville. AG 11/20/1906

EDWARDS, Joseph A., Mrs., wife of Dr. J. A., d. 163 Bellwood Ave., Atlanta, Sun. Interred: Marietta, Ga. AG 9/28/1907

EDWARDS, Julia, negro, age 42, d. Columbus, Ga. 7/ . AG 7/22/1907

EDWARDS, L. G., Mrs., age 40, d. Atlanta. AG 9/2/1910

EDWARDS, Maude, Miss, age 26, dau. of Mr. and Mrs. John, of Copenhill, Tenn., d. 131 S. Pryor St., Atlanta Thurs. Interred: Knoxville, Tenn. One bro. AG 5/7/1909

EDWARDS, Pearl Atlee, age 2, dau. of Mr. and Mrs. W. C., d. 148 Dill Ave. Atlanta, Fri. Interred: Flovilla, Ga. AG 5/28/1909

EDWARDS, Savannah, Mrs., age 48, d. res. near Peyton's Station, on River car line, Fri. Bro: J. W. Dudley. Interred: Casey's Cemetery. AG 2/27/1909

EDWARDS, W. E., Mrs. funeral Tues. from res. 88 Kirkwood Ave., Atlanta. Interred: Jonesboro. Kin: Mrs. S. J. Coogler, W. B. Maddox, J. L. Coogler, A. B. Coogler, J. B. Edwards, J. W. Fields, J. A. Fullerton, Matt Barnett. AG 9/28/1907

EDWARDS, W. E., Mrs., age 19, d. 69 Luckie St. Atlanta. AG 10/1/1907

EDWARDS, W. E., Mrs., dau. of Policeman S. G. Coogler of Atlanta, d. Atlanta Mon. Res: Kirkwood. AG 9/23/1907

EDWARDY, Alberta, Mrs., age 80, d. dau.'s res., Mrs. Pilgrim, 102 Ormond St., Atlanta, Sun. Husband, child, father. Interred: Westview. AG 5/31/1909

EGAN, Joe, age 1, son of Mr. and Mrs. M. J., d. Sun. 7 Tumlin St., Atlanta. Interred: Stephens church yard. AG 11/29/1909

EGART, Anne Josephine, age 2 mos., d. 281 S. Pryor St. Atlanta. Dau. of Mr. and Mrs. J. T. Egart. Interred: Oakland. AG 7/12/1909

EGGART, Fannie L., Mrs. d. 121 Capitol Ave. Atlanta. Interred: Westview. Two children, one sister, two brothers, Dr. Allen Hargrove, John Hargrove. AG 11/5/1906

EICHBAUM, Bertha, Miss, dau. of Mrs. James, of Demorest, Ga., d. Wed. Interred: Macon, Ga. Bros: Sol, Emanuel. Sis: Miss Effie. AG 3/18/1909

EIDSON, Elmer, age 28, d. res. of parents, Mr. and Mrs. N. C. Eidson, near Dunwoody, Ga. Interred: Prospect cemetery. AG 12/23/1907

EIDSON, George G., age 61, d. 27 Plum St. Atlanta. Son: Hugh. Bro: Isaac. Sisters: Mrs. Will Brown, Austell, Ga., Mrs. Trumer Hamby, Smyrna, Ga. Interred: Collins Springs. AG 9/4/1908

EIDSON, Mattie, Mrs., age 42, d. Wed. 377 Whitehall St., Atlanta. Interred: Collings Springs Cemetery. AG 7/21/1910

EINSTEIN, Samuel A., b. Savannah, Ga. 1851, d. Amsterdam, Ga. Interred: Savannah. Wife, two daus., mother, two sisters, all of N. Y. AG 3/21/1910

EINSTEIN, Sol, age 50, of Cincinnati, bro. of Sims Einstein of Atlanta, d. Mon. in Cincinnati. AG 9/10/1910

ELAM, G. A. d. Scottdale, Ga., Thurs. Interred: Indian Creek Cemetery. AG 4/1/1910

ELCHELBERGER, Adam L., age 81, d. Oakland City. AG 7/9/1909

ELDER, G. B. d. Flovilla, Ga. 9/5. AC 9/11/1905

ELDER, H. B., old citizen of Stewart Co. d. 6/19, res. of dau., Mrs. J. Thad Williams, Richland, Ga. Dau: Mrs. R. T. Humber, Lumpkin, Ga. Wife, several children, grandchildren. Interred: Cemetery, Lumpkin, Ga. AG 6/20/1908

ELDER, J. T., Jr., age 3 yrs., d. 220 1/2 Decatur St., Atlanta, Sat. Interred: Norcross, Ga. AG 7/6/1908

ELDER, Marie, colored, age 2 mos., d. 78 Jones alley. Atlanta. AG 1/16/1907

ELDER, Robert David, age 3 mos., d. 84 S. Jackson St. Atlanta. AG 3/8/1909

ELDER, Thomas G., age 34, d. 45 Pulliam St. Atlanta. Wife, Mrs. Lelia Rogers Elder. Daus: Mary, Mildred. Father: E. F. Bros: J. W., J. D., E. E. Sis: Mrs. E. P. Leahey, all of Anniston, Ala. Bro: J. T., resides Atlanta. Interred: Westview. AG 3/25/1907

ELIZABETH, Mrs., age 71, d. 709 Marietta St. Atlanta. AG 1/22/1907

ELKAN, Edward, age 45, d. 370 Washington St. Atlanta. Bro-in-law: Moses Blum. Interred: Oakland. AG 3/25/1907

ELKIN, Embree, age 2, dau. of Mr. and Mrs. J. O., d. 48 Clay St., Atlanta. Interred: Lawrenceville, Ga. AG 8/10/1910

ELKIN, Embru, age 2, dau. of Mr. and Mrs. J. O., d. Tues. 48 Clay St., Atlanta. Interred: Lawrenceville, Ga. AG 8/9/1910

ELKIN, Nona, inf. dau. of Mr. and Mrs. J. O., d. Willow St., Atlanta, Mon. Interred: Family Cemetery. AG 8/3/1908

ELKINS, Elijah d. 76 Spring St., Atlanta Sun. Native of England. Wife, son. AG 9/18/1906

ELKINS, John D. accidentally shot and killed himself 12 mi. from Hazlehurst Sat. He was from Locust Grove, Ga. AG 2/8/1910

ELLA, Mary B., age 49, wife of E. A., d. 181 Griffin St., Atlanta, Tues. Interred: Hollywood. AG 4/8/1908

ELLER, Amos E., age 52, d. 152 Majestic Ave. Atlanta. AG 8/22/1910

ELLINGTON, Asbury F., Rev., age 54, d. 50 Orme St., Atlanta, Tues. Sons: W. B., Olin F., Frank G., Rouse S. Interred: Westview. AG 5/4/1910

ELLINGTON, J. C., age 51, d. Sun. Columbus, Ga. Wife, 2 children. AG 1/27/1908

ELLIOTT, Charles C., age 30, d. Atlanta. AG 3/14/1910

ELLIOTT, D. M., age 62, d. Atlanta. AG 1/27/1910

ELLIOTT, Delia, Mrs.,ge 25, d. E. Point, Ga. Sun. Interred: Hollywood. Husband, three small children. AG 10/6/1908

ELLIOTT, E. J. , age 50, d. Grady Hospital. Atlanta. AG 2/4/1907

ELLIOTT, J. M., Dr. of Troup Co., Ga. to hang for murder of G. L. Rivers. AG 6/19/1909

ELLIOTT, Julia Mary, age one, dau. of Mr. and Mrs. R. H., d. 110 Neal St. Interment: Hollywood. AG 9/21/1906

ELLIOTT, Louie, inf. son of Mr. and Mrs. R. H., d. Sun. 110 Neal St. Atlanta. Interred: Hollywood. AG 6/27/1910

ELLIOTT, Mintie K., age 15 mos., dau. of Mr. and Mrs. John, d. 188 E. Linden St. Atlanta, Fri. AG 8/15/1910

ELLIOTT, J. C. d. cell, 3rd floor, Tower. Wife of 2 mos. AG 8/31/1906

ELLIOTT, Louie, infant son of Mr. and Mrs. R. H., d. 110 Neal St. Atlanta. Interred: Hollywood. AG 6/28/1910

ELLIS, Carl Gilbert, age 3 mos., d. Atlanta. AG 4/15/1910

ELLIS, Charles A., age 64, Confed. Vet., d. Sun. Old Soldiers' Home, Atlanta. AG 3/21/1910

ELLIS, Charles H.ral Tues. Atlanta. Interred: Macon, Ga. AG 3/22/1910

ELLIS, E. C., Mrs. d. Thurs. E. Pt. Interred: Utoy Church yard. AG 10/28/1910

ELLIS, E. P., Mrsd. of DeKalb Co. d. Thurs., age 72. Leaves husband, two married children. Interred: Masters' grave yard. AG 6/14/1906

ELLIS, F. N., Mrs. d. Wed. Atlanta. Interred: Cleveland, Tenn. AG 9/1/1910

ELLIS, H. M., colored, age 2 mos., d. 386 McDaniel St. Atlanta. AG 4/28/1908

ELLIS, John J., Confed. Vet., age 65, d. 4/30. AC 5/1/1905

ELLIS, Lucile, age 23, dau. of Rev. and Mrs. H. J. Ellis, d. Mon. Washington, Ga. Oldest of three daus. Interred: city cemetery. AG 2/6/1907

ELLIS, M. A., Mrs., age 64, d. 16 Harold St. Atlanta. Interred: Norcross, Ga. AG 7/27/1907

ELLIS, M., Mrs., age 78, d. 5 Chamberlin St. Atlanta. AG 12/28/1907

ELLIS, Margaret Earle, inf. dau. of Mr. and Mrs. Frank, d. Mon. 102 Angier Ave. Atlanta Wed. Interred: Westview. AG 5/21/1906

ELLIS, Mary E., Mrs., age 76, d. Milledgeville, Ga. AG 1/11/1910

ELLIS, Mary F., Mrs., age 53, d. Mon. S. Macon, Ga., wife of Rev. C. H. Son lives in Macon. AG 3/24/1908

ELLIS, Mary, Mrs., age 52, d. Atlanta. AG 8/21/1907

ELLIS, Nathan, colored, age 42, d. 101 Butler St. Atlanta. AG 10/8/1909

ELLIS, Roswell, Capt., 86, vet. Mexican, Civil wars, d. neph's res., R. J. Atkinson, 3/30 Greenville, Ga. Uncle of late Gov. W. Y., late Judge Thos D., T. E. & R. J. Atkinson. 2nd wife: Miss Lizzie Rutherford, Columbus. AG 3/3/1909

ELLIS, S., colored, age 27, d. 23 Leach St. Atlanta. AG 12/30/1907

ELLIS, S. E., Mrs., over 50 yrs, enroute Millen, Ga. from Furman, S. C., suicide. AG 2/27/1908

ELLIS, W. G., Mrs. d. Atlanta Tues. Bros: C. F. and Will Collier. Daus: Lillie and Carrie Collier of Macon. Funeral from Collier home on Highland Ave. Atlanta. AG 8/21/1907

ELLIS, William, age 87, d. dau's res., Mrs. Emma E. Bailey, 4443 Courtland St., Atlanta, Mon. Interred: Westview. AG 6/25/1906

ELLISON, E., colored, age 16, died 218 Edgewood Avenue, Atlanta. AG 12/11/1906

ELLISON, Rena, negro woman, found dead Mon. 124 Gilmer St., Atlanta. AG 7/22/1901

ELLISON, Sallie L., Mrs., wife of Toombs, d. at Gentian Sun, age 36. Parents: Mr. and Mrs. G. W. Hamer; three sisters, 4 bros. AG 11/10/1908

ELROD, Joseph F. d. N. 9th St., Griffin, Ga., Fri., age 36. AG 2/29/1908

ELSAS, Clara, Mrs., wife of Jacob, Pres. of Fulton Bag and Cotton Mills, funeral 215 Washington St., Atlanta, Jan. 8. 6 sons (from NY), 2 daus. (Atlanta). AC 1/8/1906

ELSNER, Martha, Miss, age 17, dau. of Mr. and Mrs. J., d. Tues. Interred: Hollywood. AG 8/21/1906

EMERSON, Andrew Waldo d. yesterday Savannah, Ga., age 27. Came to Savannah 1904 from Augusta. Wife, three little girls. AG 12/27/1907

EMERSON, Lizzie, colored, age 33, d. 95 Luckie St. Atlanta. AG 2/16/1908

EMERY, Paul Jones, age 22, d. 116 Logan St. Atlanta. Interred: Glenn, Ga. AG 3/21/1910

EMMA BROWN, Mrs., age 20, wife of C. B., d. 72 Venable St., Atlanta, Wed. Mother: Mrs. S. R. Smith. Bros: H. H. and A. D. Robinson. Sis: Mrs. W. T. Robinson, Mrs. J. A. Albert. Interred: Hollywood. AG 6/16/1909

EMORY, Annie Lucile Randall, age 3 yrs., d. 116 Logan St. Atlanta. AG 5/1/1907

EMORY, George S., age 90, d. Sun. at res. of dau., Mrs. M. B. Hand, 102 W. Cain St., Atlanta. He was b. Harris Co., res. of Atlanta over 40 yrs. Funeral at State Line, Ga. AG 3/12/1907

EMORY, Lucile, 8 yrs., dau. of Mrs. Sarah L. Emory, d. two weeks ago. AG 5/10/1907

EMORY, Nathaniel, colored, age 68, d. rear of 54 Butts St. Atlanta. AG 11/27/1909

EMORY, Sarah L., Mrs., age 44, wife of G. W., d. Thurs. 116 Logan St., Atlanta. Mother, husband, 5 children, survive. AG 5/10/1907

EMORY, Sarah, Mrs., age 44, d. 116 Logan St. Atlanta. AG 5/13/1907

ENELL, William, colored, age 27, d. 16 Hammock St. Atlanta. AG 10/23/1907

ENGLAND, Pauline, Miss, age 22, d. Sun. W. Baker St. Atlanta. Interred: Westview. AG 8/16/1910

ENGLAND, Allison, single. Blue Ridge, Ga. 12/22. John and Arthur Harper met England in public road near Mineral Bluff, Ga. and shot and killed him. AG 12/22/1906

ENGLISH, Emily, Mrs., age 65, d. 40 Cone St. Atlanta. AG 8/14/1907

ENGLISH, John H., age 75, d. Nashville, Tenn. AG 2/25/1907

ENGLISH, Lizzie, colored, age 31, d. College Park, Ga. AG 9/26/1910

ENGLISH, Lottie, Mrs., age 29, d. 96 Jones Ave. Atlanta. AG 10/3/1906

ENGLISH, Richard, Jr., colored, age 24, d. 12 Phoenix alley. Atlanta. AG 3/18/1908

ENGLISH, T. H., Mrs., age 28, d. Fri. 96 Jones Ave. Leaves husband, one child. Interred: Collins Springs. AG 9/29/1906

ENLOE, Anna E., Miss, age 23, d. Thurs. 40 Park St. Atlanta. Interred: Dillard, Ga. AG 8/23/1906

ENLOE, Mary E., Miss, age 23, d. 40 Park Ave. AG 8/24/1906

ENTRICAN, Susie Frances, inf. dau. of Mr. and Mrs. H. G., d. 47 Longley Ave., Atlanta, Tues. Interred: Caseys. AG 11/26/1908

EPLAN, Bessie P., Mrs., age 74, d. 306 Central Ave. Atlanta. AG 11/24/1910

EPPERSON, Joseph funeral at Varnelia, Ga. 3/29. Age 40. Wife, 5 children. AG 3/29/1910

EPPS, Columbus, young farmer of Hancock Co. d. a few miles S. of Sparta, age 33. Leaves wife, 4 small children. AG 3/25/1907

EPPS, Daisy, Mrs., age 28, d. Atlanta, Fri. Sis: Mrs. S. K. Rossignol, 106 Cherokee Ave. Bro: H. D. Spink, Atlanta. Interred: Oakland. AG 2/8/1908

EPPS, Georgia, colored, age 67, d. 366 Richardson St. Atlanta. AG 12/22/1908

EPPS, John, colored, age 18, died Fulton Co. Jail. Atlanta. AG 12/26/1906

ERHARDT, Charles d. 278 S. Boulevard, Atlanta, Tues. Wife. AG 3/23/1910

ERIE, Samuel, citizen of Marietta, d. Whitlock Ave. yesterday, age 65, unmd. AG 4/10/1907

ERSKINE, Wallace, actor, suicide, Columbus, Ga. AG 12/20/1907

ERVIN, Elizabeth, Mrs., age 80, d. Sun. 206 Echo St., Atlanta. Interred: Casey's Cemetery. AG 4/25/1910

ERWIN, J. R., Mrs., age 80, d. Atlanta Sun. Son: W. R. Smith, Chapel, S. C. Husband survives. Interred: Chapel, S. C. AG 7/13/1908

ERWIN, Willie S., young son of Gen. Manger of Tallulah Falls RR, W. S. Erwin), d. Cornelia, Ga. AG 8/31/1907

ERWIN, James D., Dr., d. Erwinton, S. C. Bro: Marion Erwin, US Dist. Atty, Macon. Sis: Late Mrs. Evan P. Howell, Atlanta; Mrs. Ida L. Woodward, Augusta. Ch: P. A., J. L., T. C., Dr. C. W. (Allendale, S. C.), A. M., Macon. AG 3/18/1909

ESKEW, Floyd D., inf. son of Mr. and Mrs. J. L., d. 115 Neal St., Atlanta, Sun. Interred: Riverdale, Ga. AG 7/27/1908

ESSELBORN, C. A., age 27, d. 554 North Blvd. Atlanta. AG 9/2/1910

ESSELBORN, Carl A. d. Atlanta Tues. age 26, from NY City where parents reside. Father: Adolph Esselborn. AG 8/30/1910

ESTES, Clifford G., age 20, d. Atlanta. AG 5/21/1910

ESTES, Emma, age 42, wife of James H., d. Fri. 372 E. Georgia Ave. Atlanta. Interred: Westview. AG 6/1/1907

ESTES, Frances E., age 60, d. 77 Nutting St. Atlanta. AG 12/4/1908

ESTES, M. V., age 65, d. Fri., old res. of Atlanta, Confed. veteran. Children: J. M., G. T., T. R.; Mrs. Mary F. Wash of Pa. Interred: Westview. AG 5/24/1907

ESTES, Ralph, age 5 mos., infant son of Mr. and Mrs. J. H., d. Wed. Atlanta. Interred: Westview. AG 6/12/1907

ESTES, Richard H. (Dick), age 61, formerly of Columbus, Ga., d. Dallas, Tx where buried. Bro: Charles E., Columbus. AC 9/3/1905

ESTES, W. E., formerly of Hapeville, Ga., was accidentally killed by wife, Savannah, Ga., age 48. 3 yrs. ago he md. Mrs. Swift, Columbus, Ga. Parents: Mr. and Mrs. J. H. Estes, Atlanta. AG 1/13/1908

ESTES, William d. Farley, Ala. Sun., age 50. Wife survives. AG 3/1/1910

EUBANKS, G. W., colored, age 50, d. 224 W. Mitchell St. Atlanta. AG 5/13/1907

EUBANKS, Mary Lou, 2 yrs. dau. of Mrs. S. A., 171 Kelly St. Interment: Tate. AG 9/20/1906

EUBANKS, Smith, colored, age 2 mos., d. 276 Auburn Ave. Atlanta. AG 4/10/1907

EUBANKS, Thomas F., age 61, d. 127 Plum St. Atlanta. AG 3/28/1907

EVANS, A. M., age 61, d. yesterday, res. of H. K. Perry, pioneer citizen to Atlanta. AG 9/9/1907

EVANS, A. W., Jr., age 3 mos., son of A. W. Evans of Sandersville, d. Mon. at res. of Supreme Ct Justice Beverly D. Evans, 330 W. Peachtree St., Atlanta. Interred: Sandersville. AG 7/17/1906

EVANS, A., Mrs. d. 5/29 4-mile, Ala. where buried. Husband, 8 children, one a week old. AC 5/31/1905

EVANS, Alice Bell, colored, age 2, d. 14 Maple alley. Atlanta. AG 7/29/1907

EVANS, Annie Curtiss, Mrs., age 48, d. Sun. 237 E. Fair St. Atlanta. Husband: David Evans. 3 sisters, 2 bros., 4 children. Interred: Westview. AG 7/11/1910

EVANS, Archie, Confed. Vet., age 88, d. Huntsville, Ala. 7/15. AC 7/15/1905

EVANS, Cary, colored, age 12, d. 201 N. Ashby St. Atlanta. AG 9/11/1908

EVANS, Effie, inf. dau. of Mr. and Mrs. R. L., d. Edgewood Ave., Atlanta. Interred: Redan, Ga. AG 12/1/1907

EVANS, Elizabeth, Mrs., age 62, d. E. Point Fri., wife of J. G. Sons: J. A., E. J. of E. Point, E. M. of Munain, Minn., C. C. of Cincinnati. Dau: Mrs. L. A. Whitsit, Mansena, N. Y. Interred: College Park Cem. AG 2/11/1910

EVANS, Frank, son of W. H. (Bibb Co. legislator), killed 7/22 by train. AG 7/23/1909

EVANS, George, age 40, d. 101 N. Butler St. Atlanta. AG 12/3/1907

EVANS, J. Floyd of Gillsville, Ga. d. Thurs. Wife, 3 ch: E. P. Evans, Gillsville, Ga.; James Evans, Atlanta; Sandy Evans, Clarkesville, Ga. 2 grandchildren, 2 gr-grandchildren. Interred: Family Cemetery. AG 4/16/1908

EVANS, J. W., age 55, of Douglasville, Ga., d. 17 W. Cain St. Atlanta. AG 9/2/1909

EVANS, Mehalia, colored, age 62, d. 176 Elizabeth St. Atlanta. AG 10/20/1909

EVANS, N. H., age 70, inmate of Conf. Soldiers' Home, Atlanta, d. Sat. Enlisted 3/18/1862, Pvt. in Echols' Artillery, in many battles around coastal Ga. and coastal S. C. AG 4/10/1909

EVANS, O., colored, age 2, d. 101 N. Butler St. Atlanta. AG 10/20/1908

EVANS, T. A. d. 2/14 Greensboro, Ga., age 50. Wife, 5 children. AG 2/14/1910

EVANS, T. A., merchant of Jonesboro, d. Mon., age 50. Wife, 5 children. AG 2/16/1910

EVANS, Toccora E., Mrs., age 52, d. Atlanta Thurs, 94 Nelson St. Interred: Westview. Son: C. E. Sisters: Mrs. Izora Smith, Mrs. Ida Robinson, Mrs. Stella McArthur, Ft. Valley, Ga. AG 1/7/1910

EVANS, W. D., Mrs., wife of Wadley's citizen, d. 7/22. Two small children. AG 7/23/1909

EVATT, Charles W., age 66, d. Tues. 389 Whitehall St., Atlanta Wed. Interred: Oakland. Daus: Mrs. J. A. Riviere, Mrs. D. B. Grant of Atlanta; Mrs. H. K. Hicks, Augusta, Ga. AG 5/5/1909

EVE, Lucile, colored, age 3 mos., d. 16 E. Ellis St. Atlanta. AG 8/11/1908

EVERATT, John S., Jr., inf. son of Mr. and Mrs. John S., Sr., d. Thurs., 739 Glenn St., Atlanta. Interred: Hollywood. AG 5/13/1910

EVERETT, E. Quincy funeral Mon. 362 Peachtree St. Atlanta. Relatives: Mrs. E. Quincy Everett, Mrs. Frances G. Everett, Mr. and Mrs. Clarence Everett, Mr. and Mrs. W. O. Jones, Mr. and Mrs. Thomas B. Lumpkin. Interred: Oakland. AG 5/28/1906

EVERETT, George W. d. Lumpkin, Ga., age 75. Bro: M. L. Everett, Stewart Co. AG 10/8/1907

EVERETT, James A. d. 618 N. Boulevard, Atlanta, Sun. Wife, two sons: A. E., J. B. Daus: Mrs. W. B. Lovett, Mrs. A. S. Grey. AG 6/2/1908

EVERETT, T. H., age 58, d. dau.'s res., Mrs. G. W. Latham, Cascade Ave., Atlanta, Mon. 8 children, two sisters. Interred: Greenwood. AG 10/27/1908

EVERIDGE, Peyton, age 19, d. Broad St., E. Macon, Ga. 9/27. Interred: Roberts, Ga. Mother, father, four brothers, sister. AG 9/28/1908

EVERITT, R. M. d. Covington 10/31, age 87. Son: R. E. 4 sons, 3 daus. Interred: Westview. AG 11/1/1910

EVES, Mary Augusta, Miss of Beech Island, S. C. d. Augusta, Ga. Relative: Judge William F. Eve. AC 8/25/1905

EWING, F. M., age 72, d. Clarkston, Ga., Confed. Vet. Ch: E. A.; Mrs. Mary Dempsey; Misses Uta and Bertie Ewing. Interred: Conyers, Ga. AG 12/26/1910

EWING, James Edward, age 2, son of Mr. and Mrs. H. C., d. Oxford, Ga. 5/26. Interred: Oxford Cemetery. AC 5/27/1905

EYSTER, J. C., Mrs., Moultrie, 11/7/1906. L. L. Daughtrey recd telegram of death of his sister of New Decatur, Ala., dau. of Mr. and Mrs. G. W. Daugherty of Moultrie. AG 11/9/1906

EZELL, C. T., Mrs. d. Monticello, Ga. 4/1. Ch: Dr. Howard of Oliver; Roy of Atlanta; Ruby of Monticello; Bessie of Monticello; C. B. Interred: Monticello Baptist Church Cemetery. AG 4/2/1910

EZZARD, Clara P., Mrs., Tues. Funeral at res. of Thomas A. Day, 132 S. Pryor St. Atlanta. General Clement A. Evans will officiate. Interment: Oakland. AG 11/13/1906

FABER, Savannah Georgia, Mrs., age 23, d. 9/13 Columbus, Ga., wid. of Edward A. Born Savannah, Ga. Ch: E. S. and Elmer, Columbus; Mrs. Oliver McIlhenny, Washington, D. C. AC 9/14/1905

FADER, George H., aged port pilot, d. Cumberland Island, Ga. AG 12/5/1907

FAGAN, Christopher A., age 61, Atlanta pioneer, d. 42 Capitol Ave. Atlanta Mon. Wife, 4 children. Interred: Oakland. AG 5/14/1908

FAGAN, Mary,, age 88, wid. of H. B., d. dau.'s res., Mrs. W. N. Sheridan. Ch: Mrs. W. C. Horton, Mrs. M. C. O'Shields, Mrs. Sheridan, Mrs. S. A. Owings, Mrs. Charles Benner (Macon), Mrs. J. L. Loftis and J. D. Fagan (Austell). AG 6/8/1910

FAGAN, Virginia May, age 6, d. 205 Oak St. Atlanta. AG 12/27/1910
FAIN, Charles F., age 34, d. Wed. Interred: Fairburn, Ga. AG 4/24/1907
FAIN, Herschel d. Fri. Atlanta. Interred: Marietta. AG 5/14/1906
FAIN, Joel C., Jr., son of Mr. and Mrs. Joel C., of Birmingham, Ala., funeral Tues. res. of child's aunt, Mrs. C. J. Sullivan, Atlanta. Interred: Oakland. AG 9/6/1910
FAIR, Annie May, age 5, d. 235 Capitol Ave. Atlanta. AG 11/4/1908
FAIR, Howard d. Tues. Marietta, aged abt 48, for 25 yrs. a porter in Ga. Hse of Representatives. AG 4/19/1910
FAIR, Margaret Elizabeth, d. Newnan, Ga. 6/10 res. of J. T. Fair. Dau. of Col. James M. Toole of Maryville, Tenn. and relict of Stuart A. Fair, Dandridge, Tenn. Uncle: Late Major Campbell Wallace of Marietta. 2 sons, 2 daus. AC 6/11/1905
FAIR, Mary A., Mrs., age 69, d. Oakland City, Ga. Wed. Interred: Indiana, Pa. AG 8/14/1908
FAIRBANKS, H. W., Mrs., age 80, d. Sat. Interred: Westview. AG 9/21/1909
FAIRBANKS, Henrietta F., Mrs., age 79, wid. of Franklin T., of 249 Spring St. Atlanta, d. home of Mrs. S. A. Medlin, 55 Alexander St. Interred: Westview. Daus: Mrs. L. C. Melee, Mrs. J. F. Morris. Nephew: Fred Renteen. AG 9/21/1909
FAIRBROTHER, Howard, age 50, d. Wed. Piedmont Hotel, Atlanta. Interred: Augusta, Ga. Unmd. Bro: Nathaniel of Augusta. Sis: Mrs. Sarah M. F. Batteyh, Boston. AG 4/22/1908
FAIRFAX, Willie, colored, age 2 mos., d. 507 W. Mitchell St. Atlanta. AG 12/17/1910
FALCOVITZ, Mike, age 50, d. Sun. 158 E. Ellis St., Atlanta. Funeral Tues. Interred: Oakland. Wife survives. AG 4/5/1910
FALKS, James H., Dr. d. 90 E. Pine St., Atlanta Thurs. Interred: Westview. AG 12/2/1909
FALL, A., colored, age 37, d. 10 Solomon St. Atlanta. AG 1/14/1908
FALL, Rosa I., colored, age 0, d. 68 Fitzgerald St. Atlanta. AG 9/3/1909
FALVEY, John J., Jr., d. home of father, J. J., 217 Gordon St., age 26, unmd. AG 9/11/1906
FAMBRO, Catherine, colored, age 60, d. Hamlet, N. C. AG 5/12/1909
FAMBROUGH, Harriett L., age 2, dau. of Mr. and Mrs. W. M., d. 293 Highland Ave., Atlanta, Thurs. Interred: Bolton, Ga. AG 9/15/1910
FANNIN, James H., Mrs. d. LaGrange, wife of Colonel James H. Ch: Julia Fannin of LaGrange; Mrs. T. S. Whitfield; Mrs. Wilbur Coney of Savannah; Mrs. Will Holt of Montgomery; Jim Fannin of San Francisco. Interred: Hill View. AG 2/19/1907
FANNIN, Ruth, age 14 mos., dau. of Mrs. Elsie, d. Atlanta Wed. Interred: Westview. Ag 7/16/1908
FANNING, Bird P., age 23, d. 401 Ormond Ave., Atlanta, Sat. Interred: Hollywood. AG 10/14/1907
FANNING, Bryan, age 67, dl 401 Ormond St., Atlanta, Wed. Wife: Emma. Sons: W. R., W. W., E. L. Daus: Misses Louise and Emmie. AG 5/25/1910
FARABE infant, of Mr. and Mrs. Luther, d. 12/8 Commerce, Ga. Interred: Gray Hill Cemetery. AC 12/9/1905

FARGO, Isabella, Mrs. d. Augusta, Ga. 7/30. Ch: George F., C. T., Mrs. George Lamback. AC 8/1/1905

FARGURSON, Cora, Mrs., age 25, d. 38 Ormond St. Atlanta. AG 7/15/1910

FARLEY, two negro daus., age 16 and 14, daus. of John Farley, Eatonton, Ga. quarrelled. Older girl killed her sister. AG 4/30/1906

FARLEY, Cornelia, colored, age 61, d. Atlanta School of Medicine. AG 2/16/1908

FARLEY, Mary Jane, Mrs., age 75, d. 283 Lawson St. Atlanta. AG 5/3/1906

FARLEY, Mary, Mrs., age 78, d. 5/2. AG 5/3/1906

FARLEY, W. A., Rev. d. 9/1 Hamilton, Ga. Once School commissioner of Harris Co., and res. of Seale, Ala. AC 9/2/1905

FARLEY, Bessie L., Mrs., age 19, d. Atlanta. AG 12/28/1910

FARLOW, Leila, Mrs., age 22, dau. of Mr. and Mrs. M. Y. Davenport, d. 76 Alma St., Atlanta, Thurs. Survived by her husband and one child. AG 9/27/1907

FARMER, Annie Mrs., age 39, d. Atlanta. Interred: Campbells Crossing. Husband: E. Farmer. two sons, one dau. AG 2/14/1910

FARMER, Charity, Mrs. d. Sun. 329 Chestnut St. Atlanta. Interred: Westview. AG 7/29/1907

FARMER, Ernest, age 2, son of Mrs. Mamie, d. E. End, Ga. Mon. Interred: Lawrenceville, Ga. AG 3/23/1908

FARMER, J. A., age 56, d. Atlanta Wed. Wife, 4 children, Mrs. Ross Hunter, Miss Mary Farmer, Will Farmer, J. A. Farmer, Jr. Interred: Covington, Ga. AG 3/18/1908

FARMER, J. W. d. Sat. Crawfordville, Ga. where buried. Wife. Dau: Mrs. R. E. L. Harris. AG 11/9/1907

FARMER, M. C., Mrs., age 52, d. Sun. Atlanta. Interred: Prospect Church, Lawrenceville, Ga. She md. 3/4/1883 C. L. Farmer. Survived by husband, 4 children. AG 1/30/1908

FARMER, Mary, infant dau. of Mrs. Lillie Farmer, d. Fri. Interred: Westview. AG 7/6/1907

FARMER, Mary Elizabeth, age 1 mo., d. 17 Corley St. Atlanta. AG 7/6/1907

FARMER, N. C., Mrs., age 49, d. Northern and Third Sts., near East Lake, Ga. Sun., wife of C. L. Interred: Lawrenceville, Ga., family grounds. AG 1/27/1908

FARMER, Rendy R., Mrs., age 56, d. Chapel Rd., Atlanta. Husband, 6 sons: S. D., W. T. Howard, Joseph E. J., T. J. Daus: Mrs. H. M. Hendrix, Mrs. John Meister, Mrs. James Dunn. Interred: Westview. AG 6/20/1908

FARNEY, Corley, colored, age 21, d. 388 W. North Ave. Atlanta. AG 3/18/1908

FARNSWORTH, R. L., age 30, d. Sapulpa, Okla. several days ago. Interred: Westview. Sisters: Mrs. Lee Hardeman, Miss Clio Farnsworth. Bro: John Farnsworth. AG 12/24/1908

FARR, Luther, age 22, son of Superintendent J. D. Farr of Walton Cotton Mill, d. Monroe Co. Interred: Roswell. AG 1/18/1907

FARR, T. J., Mrs. died her res., 48 Terry St., Atlanta. Survivors: Husband. Interment: Hollywood cemetery. AG 1/29/1906

FARR, W. R. B. C., Professor. Funeral: his late res. Peachtree Rd, Atlanta, Wed. Interment: Oakland. AG 12/18/1906

121

FARRAR, M. K., age 28, d. Sun. 87 Hampton St., Atlanta. Wife, 3 small children. Interred: Chamblee, Ga. AG 3/23/1908

FARRIES, M. L., age 75, inmate of Confederate Soldiers' Home, Atlanta, d. Wed. Bro: Thomas A. Ferries, Valdosta, Ga. AG 4/7/1909

FARRIS, Camelia, Mrs., age 70, d. res. of dau., Mrs. W. W. Harris, 83 W. Harris St., Atlanta. Son: F. B. Farris. Interment: Westview. AG 10/27/1906

FARROW, Gus, colored, age 80, d. Fulton Co. Alms House. AG 4/8/1908

FARROW, H. P., Colonel, age 73, d. 123 S. Pryor St. Atlanta. AG 2/12/1907

FASSETT, W. R., Mrs. d. Mon. from wounds from boiler explosion 10/3, Toomsboro, Ga. Husband. Interred: Family burial grounds. AG 10/12/1910

FAST, Pauline, Mrs., age 28, d. 58 Connally St., Atlanta, Tues. Husband: R. W. Fast, three small children. Interred: Westview. AG 12/30/1908

FAUSTMAN, Katharine Eleanor, inf. dau. of Mr. and Mrs. J., d. 178 Ivy St. Atlanta Sat. Interred: Lawrenceville, Ga. AG 6/1/1908

FAUS, Daniel, colored, age 90, d. 108 Richmond St. Atlanta. AG 9/8/1908

FAVER, Dinah, colored, d. 10/4, age 89, 39 Lowes alley, Atlanta. AG 10/5/1910

FAVER, Kate R., Mrs., age 67, d. Mon. 47 W. Cain St., Atlanta. Bur: Stevens, Ga. AG 11/13/1906

FAVORS, Frank, colored, age 35, d. Arlington, Ga. AG 11/17/1907

FAVORS, Mattie, Mrs. d. Wilkes Co., Ga. Sister: Mrs. Mollie Reynolds, Lexington, Ga. Son: Dr. W. H. Reynolds, Lexington, Ga. AG 6/20/1908

FEAGIN, Fred, age 25, of Tifton, Ga. fell from rr train at Jacksonville, Fla. AG 6/1/1907

FEAGIN, W. P., age 44, d. 239 Howell St., Atlanta, Wed. Husband. 8 sons: Elmore, George, Howard, Willie, Leon, Claude, James, Olin. Dau: Nonie. Bro: H. E. W. Palmer. AG 6/16/1909

FEARS, H. Clay, Rev. d. home of Thomas Shackleford near Rutledge, Ga. AG 1/28/1908

FEARS, Lena, Mrs., wife of Parks, d. 11/24 Athens, Ga. 5 sons. AC 11/27/1905

FEARS, Louis Beane, young son of Mr. and Mrs. J. T., d. 320 Grant St. Atlanta Fri. Interred: Westview. AG 6/26/1908

FEARS, Sarah J., Mrs. funeral 7/14 Oakland Cemetery. Relatives: Mary Grant Prochoska, Daniel Grant, Peter G. Grant, Capt. James W. Morrow. AG 7/13/1909

FEARS, Sarah J., Mrs., age 64, d. Memphis, Tenn. AG 7/16/1909

FEATHERS, Roxana, Mrs., age 60, d. res. of dau., Mrs. J. L. A. Fair, 15 Harwell St., Atlanta, Mon. Interred: Hollywood. AG 5/16/1910

FEATHER, Joanna, inf. dau. of Mr. and Mrs. C. W., d. 78 Hardin St. Atlanta Mon. Interred: Panthersville, Ga. AG 1/3/1910

FEDDER, Ellen, Mrs., age 40, d. 101 N. Butler St. Atlanta. AG 4/13/1909

FELDER, Calvin W., Capt., age 85, Vet. of Seminole War, d. 5/30 Americus, Ga. Son: former Mayor John B. Daus: Mrs. Lavender Ray; Mrs. Jane R. Shaw, Atlanta; and 3 others. AC 5/31/1905

FELTON, W. H., Dr., b. Oglethorpe Co. 6/19/1823, son of John (d. 1870, age 80, Cass Co.) & Mary D. (d. 1859), d. 9/24 Cartersville. Son: Dr. Howard. m. (1) 1844 Ann Carlton, d. 1851, dau. of J. R., Athens. 1 dau., Mrs. Ann (Jno F.) Gibbons, Ark.; (2) Rebecca Latimer, dau. of Maj. Chas, DeKalb Co. AG 9/25/1909

FELTON, William H., Dr., d. 10/1909. Monument erected Cartersville. AG 2/1/1910

FENELON, Lena, dau. of L. L., d. Mon. Covington. Interred: Westview Cemetery, Covington, beside her mother, who d. few mos. ago. AG 5/25/1910

FENN, Eula L., Mrs., wife of L. H., d. 512 Central Ave. Atlanta., age 45. Daus: Mrs. John H. Abbott, Miss Myrtis L. Fenn. Sis: Miss Ella Caudle; Mrs. C. H. Moore, Greenville, Ga. Bros: John Caudle, William Caudle, Norfolk, Va. Interred: Greenwood. AG 10/20/1910

FENN, Hannah, Mrs., age 72, d. 82 Gilmore St. Atlanta. AG 4/15/1910

FENN, Laura F., Mrs., age 75, d. Sun. at son's res., L. F. Fenn, 106 Martin St., Atlanta. Sons: F. C., L. J., L. H., Jefferson. Interred: Oakland. AG 9/2/1907

FENNELL, Mary, Mrs., age 49, d. Atlanta Mon. Interred: Westview. AG 9/9/1908

FERGUSON, B. P. of Barnesville, Ga. d. Milner, Ga. 4/15. AG 4/16/1910

FERGUSON, D. W., age 70, citizen of Waleska, Ga., Confederate Veteran, d. Mon. Interred: Canton, Ga. Wife. Sons: W. D., Washington, D. C.; C. P, Waleska; Dr. V. W., Atlanta. Dau: Mrs. P. M. Tate, Fairmount, Ga. AG 12/15/1908

FERGUSON, George H., Dr. d. Thurs. Indian Springs, Ga. Interred: Burghard's Chapel. Relatives in NYC. AG 7/27/1907

FERGUSON, John killed by Miss Flossie Edwards last Sun. Accident Rome, Ga. AG 6/15/1907

FERGUSON, Ruby Louise, inf. dau. of Mr. and Mrs. R. H., d. 12 Lynch St., Atlanta, Wed. Interred: East End Baptist Church. AG 10/1/1908

FERGUSON, Taylor B. d. Brunswick, Ga. News reached Atlanta. Rev. A. C. Ward of Atlanta attended funeral. AG 8/11/1910

FERGUSON, Virginia, age 2, dau. of Mr. and Mrs. H. B., d. 414 S. Pryor St., Atlanta, Sat. Interred: Westview. AG 8/10/1908

FERGUSON, William J., age 35, d. 541 Whitehall St., Atlanta, Mon. Mother. Bros: B. F., Barnesville; E. L., Atlanta. Sis: Misses Hattie and Sallie Ferguson and Mrs. J. H. Turner, Atlanta. Interred: Milner, Ga. AG 5/10/1909

FERRALL, Elizabeth T., Mrs., wife of Capt. G. A., d. Tues. She was b. 1832, m. in 1850. Leaves 5 children, husband. AG 5/8/1907

FERREL, R. L., age 28, d. 101 N. Butler St. Atlanta. AG 7/8/1909

FERRELL, E. D., Mrs. d. Valdosta Mon. E. D. Ferrell and family attended funeral Montgomery. AG 8/12/1909

FERRELL, E. G., age 28, d. of knife wound, Grady Hospital, Atlanta. AG 9/5/1906

FERRELL, E. J. stabbed to death 9/3 by Tommie Lucas in saloon on Decatur St. AG 9/10/1906

FERRELL, Sarah, colored, age 59, d. 176 Hilliard St. Atlanta. AG 7/6/1909

FERRIS, Pierre Soule., age 60, b. Pontiac, Mich. 1849, d. 7/8 311
E. N. Ave., Atlanta, son of Dr. Wm. F. (French). Lvd Mexico, Tx,
Atlanta 18 yrs. Wife was Miss Jennis Whiteside, Cincinnati. Ch:
Mrs. D. Frank Looper, Edna, Donald, Ralph. AG 7/8/1909
FETTER, Elyde E., age 21 mos., d. 54 South Ave. Atlanta. AG
8/31/1908
FEW, L. J. of Madison, Ga. d. Sat. Interred: in new cemetery.
Leaves wife, one child. AG 2/24/1908
FIELD, Emma, Miss, age 55, d. Sun. Atlanta. AG 11/29/1909
FIELD, Lida A. d. Dalton. Sis-Mrs. S. A. Wylly, Chicago; Mrs. C.
E. Rembert, San Francisco; Minnie, Atlanta. Bros-D. M., Porto
Rico; Frank, New Orleans; Jno & Chas. H., Dalton; James P., 16
Baltimore Pl. Atlanta. Bur-Westview. AG 11/30/1908
FIELD, W. G., Judge, d. Thurs., age 76, Confed. Vet. Res. of
Elberton, Ga. 20 yrs, from S. C. AG 9/2/1910
FIELDMAN, C. L., age 27 d. Atlanta Wed. Interred: Edwardsville.
AG 7/23/1908
FIELDS, Claude, age 39, d. 222 Central Ave. Atlanta. Interred:
Indianapolis, Ind. AG 7/27/1907
FIELDS, Mary C., Mrs., age 45, d. 12 Bunker St. Atlanta. AG
8/1/1910
FIELDS, Oscar Ballard, age 16, d. Wed. Flora Ave., in Edgewood,
Atlanta, Interred: Hollywood. AG 5/23/1908
FIELDS, Sarah, Mrs., age 79, d. 147 Curran St. Atlanta. AG
3/15/1910
FIELDS, W. M., age 42, d. Edgewood, Ga., Sat. Interred: Oakland.
AG 7/7/1908
FIFE, George C., Jr., age 6, d. 124 Milledge Ave., Atlanta.
Interred: Westview. AG 10/25/1907
FILMORE, W. A. d. Thurs. Atlanta, age 65. Interred: Natl
Cemetery, Marietta, Ga. AG 11/8/1907
FINCH, Dorothy May, age 1, dau. of Mr. and Mrs. C. O., d. Mon.
160 Peeples St. Atlanta. Interred: Westview. AG 6/8/1909
FINCH, J. F., res. of Athens, d. 10/ 8 38 E. Georgia Ave.,
Atlanta, age 65. Interred: Athens, Ga. AC 10/19/1905
FINCHER, Phieta, age 1 yr., dau. of Mr. and Mrs. T. C., d. Howell
Sta., Wed. Interred: Cross Roads Church. AG 4/17/1907
FINCHER, Rebecca, Mrs. interred Westview. AG 1/20/1908
FINCHER, S. D., age 1, d. East Atlanta. AG 4/10/1907
FINCHER, Virginia Inez, dau. of Mr. and Mrs. B. L., d. 11/18 425
Woodward Ave., Atlanta. Interred: Rock Springs Church. AC
11/19/1905
FINCHER, W. T., Dr., age 60, d. at Spring Place, Ga., his farm,
Murray Co. Survivors: Wife, Mrs. E. G. Quares, May and Willie
Fincher. Cousin: W. A. Fincher. AG 8/20/1906
FINCHER, F. M., age 31, d. Atlanta, Sun. Wife, father, one
sister, 3 brothers, all of Atlanta. Interred: Covington, Ga. AG
11/7/1910
FINCHER, J. A. funeral Wed. Atlanta. Interred: Westview. AG
5/25/1910
FINCHER, J. L. b. Forsyth Co.-d. Dalton, age 59. Daus: Mrs. E.
Moore, Mrs. W. A. Young, Roanoke, Ala. Bro: J. D. Fincher,
Atlanta. Sis: Mrs. Sallie Wallace, Mrs. Roselle Thomas, Whitfield
Co., Mrs. Mattie Townsend, Atlanta. AG 9/10/1908

124

FINDLEY, William F., Col., lawyer, ex-mayor of Gainesville, d. 5/26, age 58. AC 5/27/1905

FINICAL, B. F., age 74, old Federal soldier, d. Tues. res. of dau., Mrs. J. D. Adams, 380 Simpson St., Atlanta. Ch: Mrs. C. Clare, Mrs. J. A. Wilder, Mrs. J. D. Adams. Served in 1st Minn. Vols. Interred: Fitzgerald, Ga. AG 10/18/1910

FINK, Alice A., Mrs. d. 12/12, 233 Oak St. Atlanta. Husband and child. Interred: Westview. AC 12/14/1905

FINKELL, Ella, Mrs., wife of A. E., died. Son: George D. Finkell of Philadelphia. Funeral at res: 361 Washington St., Atlanta. AG 8/4/1906

FINKENSTADT, Minnie, Miss, age 35, d. 307 Mangum St. Atlanta. AG 1/25/1910

FINLEY, George L., colored, age 31, d. 144 Markham St. Atlanta. AG 6/10/1907

FINLEY, J. A. funeral Tues. Interred: Opelika, Ala. AG 2/14/1907

FINLEY, James, age 60, former Atlantan, Kimball Hse, 27 yrs, d. Baltimore, Md. 8/27. AG 8/29/1906

FINLEY, W. H. d. LaGrange, Ga., Elmrose Hotel, owner of LaGrange ice plant, native of Kentucky, citizen of LaGrange several mos. Interred: Kentucky. AG 2/15/1908

FINN, S., age 79, funeral Atlanta. Interred: Oakland. AG 6/4/1906

FISCHER, Rosa Marie, age 6 mos., dau. of Mr. and Mrs. O. J., d. 9/10 Ft. McPherson, Ga. Interred: Westview. AC 9/11/1905

FISH, Robertine, Mrs., age 80, 111 Nelson St., Atlanta, d. Her husband d. 20 yrs. ago. Family from Covington. AG 11/3/1906

FISHER, John, colored, age 49, d. 26 Bushby St. Atlanta. AG 3/1/1908

FISHER, R. M., fireman, killed in fire Atlanta. Interred: Westview. AG 7/23/1908

FISHER, Raymond M. funeral 7/22. Kin: J. E. Leffew, H. M. Fisher. AG 7/21/1908

FISHER, W. G., age 27, d. King's Daughter's Hospital. Atlanta. AG 4/10/1907

FISHER, W. M., abt 70, d. Howell Mill Rd., Atlanta, Wed. Daus: Mrs. J. A. Geddie, Mrs. Lillian Sherman, Atlanta. AG 12/29/1909

FISHER, Walter G., age 27, d. Home for Incurables, Sat. Funeral at 258 Decatur St., Sun. Interred: Oakland. AG 4/6/1907

FISHER, Benjamin, age 68, d. son's res., Atlanta. Wife. AG 5/2/1910

FISHMAN, M., colored, age 50, d. 88 Cain St. Atlanta. AG 2/22/1907

FISK, Sarah, wife of T. F., of E. Point, d. Thurs, age 70. 9 children. Interred: East Point Cemetery. AG 1/27/1910

FITE, E. E., Mrs., age 49, d. Sat. W. Huntsville, Ala. AG 1/31/1910

FITE, Flossie, inf. dau. of Mr. and Mrs. O. A. of Hartwell, Ga., d. Sun. Interred: Westview. AG 4/13/1908

FITE, Rebah Blanch, Miss, age 21, d. res. of parents, Mr. and Mrs. W. W. Fite, 505 Piedmont Ave., Atlanta, Sun. Sis: Misses Mansol and Ethel. Bro: W. Interred: Westview. AG 5/9/1910

FITHIAN, M. L. OF 140 Spring St., Atlanta d. Wed. Interred: Jacksonville, Fla. AG 9/23/1908

FITTS, E. B. d. 160 Richardson St., Atlanta, Fri. Interred: Westview. AG 11/8/1907

FITZGERALD, Thelma, age 6, d. 67 Gaskill St. Atlanta. AG 8/25/1908

FITZGIBBONS, Mary, Mrs., age 65, d. 250 Spring St. Atlanta. AG 12/22/1908

FITZPATRICK, Robert funeral Thurs. Age 77, of 283 Marietta St., Atlanta. Interred: Natl Cemetery, Marietta, Ga. AG 3/26/1908

FITZPATRICK, E. J., Mrs., wid., d. 4/19 Lithonia, age 79. Sis: Mrs. Bell Mabry, Jonesboro. Ch: Mrs. G. A. Bass, Lake City, Fla.; Mrs. C. M. White, Clarkston; Mrs. W. T. Milner, Covington; Mrs. Idka Anthony, W. Pt.; Jennie. AC 4/20/1905

FITZWATER, Mr., Special Agent of Seaboard rr., drowned Sun., Savannah. Interred: Munroe, N. C. AG 7/24/1906

FLADMM, M., age 40, d. Atlanta. AG 12/10/1910

FLAHERTY, John B., age 35, d. Buckhead, Ga. AG 11/19/1909

FLANAGAN, Annie, Miss, former teacher in State St. School, d. sister;s res., Mrs. W. W. Wilson, 14 Johnson Ave., Atlanta, Wed. Sis: Mrs. Wilson, Mrs. Dana Gibbs, Miss Nonie Flanagan. Interred: Westview. AG 3/26/1908

FLANAGAN, Mildred, inf. dau. of Mr. and Mrs. R. A., d. 33 Larkin St., Atlanta, Mon. Interred: Antioch Church. AG 5/17/1910

FLEISCHER, P., Mrs., age 71, d. Tues. Macon, res. of dau., Mrs. S. Blouenstein, Mulberry St. Son: Dave. Interred: William Wolff Cemetery. AG 1/13/1910

FLEMING, George M. d. Mon. Smyrna, Ga., age 52. Wife. Dau: Mrs. Ruby Kemp. Parents: Mr. and Mrs. John N. Fleming. Bros: C. A., Richard, Monroe, Robert, H. L., J. E. and Dr. Albert Fleming. Sis: Mrs. C. A. Green, Misses Mary and Luda Fleming. Interred: Fair Oaks, Smyrna, Ga. AG 8/23/1910

FLEMING, Gilbert N., age 50, d. Mon. 133 Greensferry Ave., Atlanta. Interred: Oakland. AG 8/7/1906

FLEMING, Job, son of S. T., d. 2/4 Bowersville, Ga., age 23. AC 2/5/1905

FLEMING, Julia, Mrs. d. Atlanta Thurs. Interred: Westview. AG 5/18/1909

FLEMING, M. C., Mrs., age 66, d. 58 Mills St. Atlanta. 4 children. Interred: Westview. AG 5/13/1908

FLEMING, Mary Lee, age 9 mos., d. 19 Highland Ave. Atlanta. AG 6/7/1907

FLEMING, Susan C., Mrs., age 68, wife of R. H., of Atlanta, d. 180 Cameron St., Sat. Sons: J. D., C. A., E. M., E. H. Daus: Mrs. Mary Rodgers, Mrs. Seabelle White. Interred: Camp Creek Church, Lilburn, Ga. AG 11/27/1910

FLETCHER, B., age 48, d. Wed. res. of sister, Mrs. C. W. Eddings, 30 Bedford Place, Atlanta. Wife. Daus: Mrs. Frank Roman, Mrs. Al Owens, Atlanta. Interred: Westview. AG 9/22/1909

FLETCHER, Julia, Mrs., age 76, d. McDonough Rd., Atlanta, Wed. Interred: Bowden, Ga. AG 7/14/1909

FLETCHER, Louis B., age 48, d. 30 Bedford Place. Atlanta. AG 9/25/1909

FLETCHER, Nellie May, age two, dau. of Mr. and Mrs. Ayer, d. 630 S. Pryor St., Atlanta, Mon. Interred: Westview. AG 5/12/1908

FLETCHER, Ouida, colored, age 25, d. Grady Hospital. Atlanta. AG 8/20/1907

FLETCHER, Richard M., Dr. d. 6/17 Madison, Ala., age 74. Confed. Vet. Wife, 8 children. AC 6/19/1905

FLETCHER, Ziba d. 9/4 1546 First Ave., Columbus, Ga., age 49. Interred: Bullochville, Ga. AC 9/6/1905

FLEURNEY, Mrs., d. union sta., Macon yesterday while on her way to Atlanta. AG 9/11/1906

FLEXNER, Frank, age 65, d. Chattanooga, Tenn. AG 4/13/1909

FLINT, Alma C., Miss, age 22, d. Fri. 224 E. Hunter St., Atlanta. Interred: Harlem, Ga. AG 7/20/1907

FLOOD, Leila, Mrs., wife of Samuel F., age 40, d. 160 Spring St., Atlanta Mon. Interred: Oakland. Husband, 3 sons, C. P. Goldsmith, John and Samuel F. Flood, Jr., and one dau., Miss May Flood, survive. AG 10/28/1908

FLORENCE, Bertha, age 26, wife of H. E., d. East Point and Dorsey Aves., Atlanta, Thurs. AG 12/15/1910

FLORENCE, George, infant son of Mr. and Mrs. R. A. of Marietta, d. Wed. AG 12/24/1908

FLORENCE, John H. of Hampton, Ga. d. 7/23, buried Berea cemetery. Age 73. Dau: Miss Sallie Florence. AC 7/25/1905

FLOURNOY, Annie, Mrs., age 65, d. Thurs. 50 Bellwood Ave., Atlanta. Interred: Marietta, Ga. AG 4/30/1909

FLOWERS, A., Mrs., old res. of S. Macon, d. Fri. 1724 Third St. Sons: James T., J. F., Macon. Daus: Mrs. James E. Reed, Mrs. T. C. Hickey, Mrs. Terrissa McDonald, Mrs. W. M. Newberry, Jr. AG 9/7/1907

FLOWERS, Annie, Mrs., age 25, dau. of Mr. and Mrs. B. S. Eltson of Athens, Ga., d. 129 Courtland St. Atlanta. AG 10/20/1908

FLOWERS, Ed, age 35, of S. Macon d. 5/21 at Roff home. Leaves several bros. AC 5/22/1905

FLOWERS, Eula Taylor, Mrs. d. Conyers St., Covington 11/21. 5 children, the youngest being few wks old, survive. AG 11/22/1909

FLOYD, B. F., age 62, d. 102 Butler St. Atlanta. AG 3/19/1907

FLOYD, Clara, Mrs., age 26, d. 208 Cooper St. Atlanta. AG 3/16/1907

FLOYD, Cora L., Mrs. d. Thurs. 208 Cooper St. Atlanta. 8-yr. old dau. survives. AG 3/15/1907

FLOYD, James S., Jr., son of Mr. and Mrs. James S., funeral 85 E. 15th St., Atlanta Fri. AG 10/28/1909

FLOYD, Lee d. Lindale, Ga. InterredL Pleasant Hope. AG 4/20/1908

FLOYD, Mary, colored, age 40, d. 272 Williams St. Atlanta. AG 3/16/1908

FLOYD, Mary, Mrs., age 91, wid. of late John J., Judge of Flint Circuit, d. dau's res., Mrs. George H. Hammond, Decatur, Ga., Mon., only surviving child. Mrs. Floyd was b. 2/21/1817 Madison, Ga. Interred: Covington, Ga. AG 2/4/1908

FLOYD, Minnie, Miss, age 26, dau. of Mrs. L. J., Leggetts Ave. Atlanta, d. Wed. Bur: Bethel Church, near Stone Mtn. Bros: D. J. and J. M. Floyd, Rock Hill, S. C. Sis: Mrs. Maggie Henderson; Mrs. Sallie Allen; Mrs. Gillie Wells. AG 3/31/1910

FLUKER, J. M., Sr., age 61, d. 451 Whitehall St., Atlanta Thurs. Wife. Sons: E. R., J. M., Jr. Daus: Mrs. George Carey, San Francisco, Cal.; Mrs. W. R. Branham; Mrs. W. H. Adams, Atlanta. Bur: Oakland. AG 3/25/1909

FLUKER, Lucy, Miss, age 28, d. Atlanta Sun. Parents: Mr. and Mrs. W. H. Fluker, Washington, Ga. Several bros. and sisters. AG 6/8/1908

FLYNN, Robert interred Oakland. AG 10/22/1907

FLYNN, Thomas F., age 17, d. 41 York St. Atlanta. AG 8/21/1907

FLYNN, W. M., Capt., age 75, d. 66 Stonewall St., Atlanta, Tues. Interred: Oakland. Confederate veteran. AG 4/17/1907

FLYNT, Gertrude A., dau. of Mr. and Mrs. T. J., age 24, d 99 Hill St. Atlanta. Sis: Misses Regina and May Flynt. Bros: Joseph M., J. Edward and George T. Flynt. AG 3/28/1910

FLYNT, G. G., Mrs., wife of Col. G. G., mother of Dr. Harry, Atlanta and Atlanta postmaster, J. W., died at home, Rest Haven. AG 12/29/1906

FLYNT, Wash, Mrs., age 79, d. res. of son-in-law, T. W. Duncan, Jackson, Ga. Tues. AG 2/11/1910

FOLDS, Thomas E., age 62, funeral Sat. Interred: Pinehurst, Ga. AG 4/22/1910

FOLDS, James DePass, infant, d. Grady Hospital. Atlanta. AG 7/30/1906

FOLDS, Thomas E. funeral Atlanta Sat. Interred: Pinehurst, Ga. AG 4/23/1910

FOLKS, George, colored, age 35, d. Atlanta from gunshot wound. AG 5/29/1906

FOLKS, William B., age 38, d. 17 W. Cain St. Atlanta. AG 2/20/1909

FOLL, E. F., Mrs., age 70, d. 72 Fairlie St. Atlanta. AG 3/22/1907

FOLSOM, Owen, son of P. G., Red Land Dist., Valdosta, Ga., d. AG 7/31/1908

FONTAINE, Robert A., age 73, d. 128 Whitehall Terr. Atlanta. AG 5/24/1910

FONTS, J. C., age 10 mos., d. 172 Griffin St. Atlanta. AG 12/17/1909

FONVILLE, G. A., Mrs., age 75, d. 385-C Luckie St., Atlanta, Wed. Interred: Anniston, Ala. AG 2/16/1910

FORBES, Sam, age 27, d. 25 Savannah St. Atlanta. AG 7/22/1907

FORD, Allora, Miss, age 28, d. Fri. 60 Eada St. Atlanta. Three aunts survive. Interred: Rex, Ga. AG 7/16/1909

FORD, DeSaussure Rucker, Mrs. of Augusta d. Sister: T. W. Rucker, Atlanta. Grson: T. W. Rucker, Jr. Interred: Augusta, Ga. AG 2/14/1908

FORD, Hilliard, colored, age 49, d. 229 Little St. Atlanta. AG 8/25/1910

FORD, Marie, age 8 yrs, died Presbyterian Hospital, Atlanta. AG 12/26/1906

FOREORS, Otis, colored, age 5, d. Strong St. Atlanta. AG 1/28/1908

FORRESTER, John W., age 66 d. 11/7 Albany, Ga. Double funeral with bro., R. A., who d. few minutes later. Buried beside their other bro., J. R., who d. 1909 Albany. AG 11/8/1910

FORRESTER, R. A. d. Leesburg, Ga. 11/10. Wife, 8 children. His bro., upon hearing, d. few minutes later, John W. Forrester. Double funeral in Albany. Bur. beside another bro., J. R., who d. Albany 1909. AG 11/8/1910

FORSYTH, W. G., age 84, Atlanta (Marthasville) pioneer, d 85 Dohne St., Atlanta. Has invalid wife, 2 grandch. AC 1/5/1905

FORT, Tomlinson, Col., age 72, son of late Dr. Tomlinson Ft., native of Milledgeville, Ga., d. Wed. Chattanooga, Tenn. Interred: Milledgeville, Ga. AG 12/15/1910

FORTNER, J. R. d. 11/8 from broken neck Atlanta. AG 11/8/1910

FORTNER, Warren, age 10, d. 276 Hemphill Ave. Atlanta. AG 7/8/1907

FOSTER, infant son of Mr. and Mrs. W. H., d. East Point, Mon. Interred: College Park Cemetery. AG 8/23/1910

FOSTER, C. D., age 18, suicide, 105 Luckie St. Atlanta. AG 3/7/1910

FOSTER, C. J., Mrs., 32, d. 433 Luckie St. Atlanta. Husb., parents. Sis: Mrs. Jason Cannon, Mrs. R. F. Cox, Mrs. C. W. Young, Central, S. C. Bros: W. G. Stephens, Abbeville, S. C., S. C. Stephens, Central, S. C. Bur: Westview. AG 8/3/1908

FOSTER, Charles, age 35, married, was run over by freight car last night. Wife was visiting relatives in Goodwater, Ala. No children. AG 5/3/1907

FOSTER, George W. d. Cincinnati Tues, formerly of Atlanta, aged abt 75 yrs. Interred: Cincinnati. AG 11/10/1909

FOSTER, Gladys, age 2, dau. of Mr. and Mrs. . H., d. Washington St., E. Point, Ga., Tues. Interred: College Park, Ga. AG 1/29/1908

FOSTER, Henry, colored, age 46, d. Nashville, Tenn. AG 11/28/1908

FOSTER, John, age 1, son of Mr. and Mrs. C. P., d. S. Kirkwood, Atlanta, Mon. Interred: Marietta. AG 7/28/1908

FOSTER, John, colored, age 4 mos., d. 7 Campbell St. Atlanta. AG 7/29/1908

FOSTER, Joshua Hill, Mrs. d. 7/4, age 78, formerly Miss Frances Cornelia Bacon, b. Liberty Co., Ga. 5/17/1828 m. 2/24/1853. Bro: Major R. J. Bacon, Baconton, Ga. Nephew: Hon. A. O. Bacon, US Senator from Georgia. Ch; T. J.; Mrs. J. M. Dill, Bessemer, Ala.; Prof. S. B., Orange, Tx.; Rev. James H., Anniston; Ellen, Tuscalooa; Prof. C. C., Waco, Tx.; Judge Henry Bacon Foster, Tuscaloosa; Prof. Edwin H., Tuscaloosa. 12 grchildren. AC 7/5/1905

FOSTER, Lucy, colored, age 47, d. 112 Chaffee St. Atlanta. AG 10/3/1907

FOSTER, Mary B., Mrs., age 49, d. 30 E. 11th St. Atlanta. AG 2/15/1910

FOSTER, Mary Elizabeth, Mrs., age 44, d. 62 Queen St. Atlanta. AG 2/8/1909

FOSTER, Mattie E., Miss, age 39, d. 111 Whitehall Terrace, Atlanta, Thurs. Mother: Mrs. V. A. Foster. Sis: Mrs. J. A. Barnes, Mrs. Iola McMillan, Misses Hattie E. and Inez Foster. Bros: W. J., J. C. Interred: Westview. AG 6/11/1909

FOSTER, Maurice, colored, age 20, d. Grady Hospital. Atlanta. AG 10/25/1900

FOSTER, Sarah, Mrs., age 65, d. Mon. 15 Clifford St.,tlanta. Ch: Mrs. Laura Chamberlin; Misses Mamie and Clifford Foster and W. J. Foster. Interred: Westview. AG 4/12/1910

FOSTER, Thomas M., age 66, d. Atlanta Sat. Interred: Monroe, Ga. AG 2/19/1910

FOSTER, T. M., Rev. of Winder d. Sat. in Atlanta, age 70. Wife, 9 children, three sons. AG 2/21/1910

FOSTER, V. A., Mrs. d. Savannah Sun. Remains brought to Atlanta. AG 1/31/1910

FOSTER, Willie, colored, age 28, d. 265 Fraser St. Atlanta. AG 8/19/1909

FOSTER, W. B., Judge, d. Lindale, Ga. 7/17. He was ordinary of Walker Co. 22 yrs. Leaves wife, two sons, two daus. AG 7/18/1908

FOUTE, William Edward, Judge d. res. of dau., Mrs. Albert S. Heywood, Worcester, Mass, Thurs. Judge Foute was b. E. Tenn. 65 yrs. ago. Wife, 3 daus. survive. AG 8/4/1908

FOWLER, Annie L., age 9, dau. of Mr. and Mrs. J. L. of 188 Magnolia St., Atlanta, Fri. Interred: Indian Creek, Ga. AG 8/12/1909

FOWLER, Bayard, M., age 40, d. 894 Peachtree St. Atlanta. AG 8/12/1908

FOWLER, B. M. funeral 8/12, res. of B. B. Crew, 33 W. Harris St., Atlanta. Interred: Oakland. Kin: C. M. Goodman, B. B. Crew, ALex C. King, Jefferson Fenn, C. R. Merritt, Miss H. P. Fowler, Miss Grace Fowler, B. M. Fowler. AG 8/11/1908

FOWLER, C. M., age 30, d. Tues. Funeral res. of M. W. Gober Chattahoochee Ave., E. Point, Ga. Interred: Hillcrest. Mother, two brothers, J. W. and A. M. Fowler, and one sister, Mrs. Flora Brown. AG 12/23/1908

FOWLER, James S., age 71, d. 38 Hilliard St. Atlanta. Wife, 4 sons: J. A., W. A., J. G., T. L. Daus: Mrs. L. A. Hamilton, Mrs. Mamie Davis, Mrs. Esther Bradley. Bros: L. C., H. S. Interred: Dacula, Ga. AG 9/9/1910

FOWLER, J. C., age 71, d. Fri. 88 Hilliard St. Atlanta. Interred: Dacula, Ga. AG 9/10/1910

FOWLER, Oma Kathleen, inf. dau. of Mr. and Mrs. R. L., d. 69 Kirkwood Ave. Atlanta. Interred: Fayetteville, Ga. AG 6/30/1909

FOWLER, R. C., Mrs., age 75, d. son's res., W. C. Fowler, 281 Rawson St. Atlanta. Sons: R. E., Montgomery, Ala.; Walker F., Aberdeen, Miss.; W. C., Atlanta. Sis: Miss Lizzie Taylor, Montgomery, Ala. Interred: Montgomery, Ala. AG 7/17/1908

FOWLER, Sarena, Mrs., Interment: Wesley Chapel church yard. AG 12/28/1906

FOWLER, Vernon, age 15, son of T. A. of Ingleside, Ga., d. Thurs. Interred: Indian Creek Church yard. AG 10/13/1910

FOY, Thomas pushed from 3rd store window of Stuart House, Atlanta. Thomas Mitchell acquitted. AG 11/9/1907

FRAGAN, Mary, Mrs., age 88, d. 765 Marietta St. Atlanta. AG 6/9/1910

FRAMBES, H. S. d. Sat. N. Highland Heights, Macon. Leaves wife, 2 sons, 3 daus. Interred: Riverside. AG 10/6/1907

FRANCIS, Henry L., Mrs. d. 282 Ponce De Leon Ave. Atlanta. AG 9/8/1908

FRANCIS, Julia E., Mrs. d. 135 Juniper St. Atlanta. Interred: Westview. AG 7/25/1910

FRANCIS, Maude Talmadge, Mrs., formerly Maude Talmadge of Athens, age 40, d. sister's res., Mrs. Rutherford Lipscomb, 282 Ponce de Leon Ave. Atlanta. Husb: Henry L. Francis. Sons: John and Thomas Henry Francis. Bur: Westview. AG 9/5/1908

FRANE, L. P., Mrs. d. 3/29 Ft. Valley. Fun: Nashville, Tn. Ch: Mr. Hawthorne, Nashville; Mrs. Jas Palmer, Nashville; Mrs. McCarty, Oxford, Miss.; Mrs. Chisholm, Atlanta; Mrs. J. P. Heath, Ft. Valley; Mrs. W. F. George, Decatur. AC 3/30/1905

FRANKLIN, A. E., age 75, died Thurs. at res., Ezzard St., Atlanta. AG 11/22/1906

FRANKLIN, Bessie, age 2, d. 211 Echo St. Atlanta. AG 9/1/1908

FRANKLIN, Jonas, negro, killed Albany, Ga. Body brought to
Thomasville. Killed by train. AG 11/12/1907

FRANKLIN, Louise, age 1 mo., d. Mon. Atlanta. Interred: Westview.
AG 10/25/1910

FRANKLIN, L. W., Mrs., age 22, d. 66 Almo Ave. Atlanta. Interred:
Indian Creek Cemetery. AG 11/11/1907

FRANKLIN, Moses J., age 39, funeral Fri. Interred: Oakland.
Suicide. AG 4/1/1910

FRANKLIN, M. J., age 40, d. 373 S. Pryor St. Atlanta. AG 4/2/1910

FRANKLIN, William Joseph, age 61, d. Atlanta. AG 1/20/1910

FRANKLIN, Willie, inf. of Mr. and Mrs. John interred Oakland
Cemetery. A 10/19/1907

FRANSON, Viola, age 6 mos., dau. of Mr. and Mrs. M., d. Atlanta
Mon. Interred: Westview. AG 12/28/1908

FRASER, James D., age 60, d. Atlanta. Sat. Wife, several
children. Interred: Edgefield, S. C. AG 2/20/1908

FRASER, Thomas, inf. son of Mr. and Mrs. T. P., d. Atlanta Sun.
Interred: Westview. AG 4/25/1910

FRASIER, Ann Mary, Mrs. d. Mon., Florence hotel, Marietta St.,
Atlanta. Interred: Frankfort, Ky. AG 1/8/1907

FRASIER, Scott J., age 26, d. Tues. Grady Hospital, Atlanta. AG
5/13/1907

FRAZER, Haywood, age 29, son of Mrs. Carrie, d. Columbus, Ga.
5/29. AC 5/30/1905

FRAZER, John L., Mrs. d. 6/29 McRae, Ga. AC 6/30/1905

FRAZER, J. D., age 60, d. 235 Capitol Ave. Atlanta. AG 2/24/1908

FRAZIER, Ulysses, colored, age 21, d. 224 W. Mitchell St.
Atlanta. AG 2/7/1908

FREDERICK, Charles J., age 63, d. sis. res., Mrs. W. E. Wardlaw,
Columbus, Ga. Bro: F. M. Frederick, Columbus. AG 11/21/1910

FREEDMAN, Jake, age 5 mos., d. 260 E. Hunter St. Atlanta. AG
1/18/1907

FREEMAN, Ada, colored, age 41, d. 45 Merritts Ave., rear.
Atlanta. AG 4/19/1907

FREEMAN, A. C., Jr., age 7, of Arcadia, Fla., killed in train
crash, Monticello, Ga. crossing. AG 6/28/1910

FREEMAN, A. C., Mrs. of Arcadia, Fla. killed in train crash,
Monticello, Ga., crossing. AG 6/28/1910

FREEMAN, Bertha, age 2 mos., inf. dau. of Mr. and Mrs. R. F., d.
53 Almo St. Atlanta. Wed. Interred: Decatur, Ga. AG 4/30/1908

FREEMAN, Bertha, Mrs., wife of Roy, d. 53 Almo Ave., Atlanta.
Interred: Decula, Ga. AG 3/1/1908

FREEMAN, C. O. of 37 Carnegie Place, Atlanta, d. from rat powder.
AG 6/25/1907

FREEMAN, Ella, colored, age 19, d. 277 W. Fair St. Atlanta. AG
9/25/1909

FREEMAN, G. W., age 48, d. Atlanta Wed. Farmer of Cabaniss, Ga.
Wife, two sons, one dau., survive. AG 12/10/1908

FREEMAN, Homer, Mrs. d. Atlanta Wed. She was dau. of J. O. Perry;
had been married 1 yr. AG 6/15/1906

FREEMAN, Lula, colored, age 11, d. 164 Irwin St. Atlanta. AG
9/11/1908

FREEMAN, Marvin F., of West Point, Ga., Fri., Presbyterian
Hospital. Interment: West Point. Survivors: 3 bros., W. R. and H.
C. Freeman of Atlanta, and G. P. Freeman of West Point.

FREEMAN, Mary, colored, age 10 mos., d. 39 Norris St. Atlanta. AG 11/15/1907

FREEMAN, Mary I., Mrs., age 80, d. Douglasville Sat. Ch: William of Oklahoma, Dock of Tenn., Charlie of Polk Co., Ga., Jay of Vienna, James, Mrs. Mollie Hutson, Misses Savannah and Lula. AG 2/28/1910

FREEMAN, Oce, colored, age 10, d. Gray and Strong Sts. Atlanta. AG 10/11/1909

FREEMAN, Oscar, colored, age 7, d. 395 Hilliard St. Atlanta. AG 10/3/1908

FREEMAN, William J., age 40, suicide at 130 Ivy Street, Atlanta. AG 11/20/1906

FREEMAN, W. J., night clerk, Marion Hotel, Atlanta, suicide at sister's home, Mrs. Will Meador, 130 Ivy St., Atlanta. Wife, formerly Miss Cora Lou Harris of Knoxville, was visiting father, Dr. Harris, dentist, Knoxville. AG 11/19/1906

FREENEY, A. E., age 39, d. Atlanta Tues, son of J. G. Bro: G. W. AG 5/3/1910

FREETCH, E. A., age 52, d. 217 Fox St., Atlanta. AG 3/26/1910

FREIDMAN, Celia, Mrs.,ge 64, d. 14 N. Boulevard, Atlanta, Tues. Interred: Oakland. AG 6/16/1908

FREISLEBEN, Abe, Mrs., res. of Atlanta many yrs., d. Mon. Kansas City, while visiting dau., Mrs. Louis Ehrlich. Husband survives. AG 6/27/1910

FREISLEBEN, H., of West Point, Ga. d. in train wreck. AG 3/2/1907

FRENCH, E. A. funeral 317 Fox St., Atlanta, Sat. Interred: Hollywood. AG 3/26/1910

FRENCH, Henry S. of College Park, Ga., age 46, d. Fri. Wife. Son: Clayton. Daus: Mrs. John McDonald, Misses Susie and Caroline French. Interred: Westview. AG 5/6/1910

FRESHER, Harry J., age 24, d. 610 N. Boulevard. Atlanta. AG 3/7/1907

FRETWELL, John, age abt 30, jumped from incoming Seaboard train at Simpson St. Tues.; probably won't recover. AG 10/16/1906

FRETWELL, Robert Henry, inf. son of Mr. and Mrs. R. F. of Chattahoochee, Ga., d. Thurs. Bur: Mason's Church. AG 6/5/1908

FREY, Maude H., Mrs. d. Tues Milledgeville. Interred: Riverside Cemetery, Macon. Ga. She was b. York Shoal, S. C. AG 9/10/1908

FREY, Vivian Harriet, age 5, dau. of Mr. and Mrs. F. P., d. 166 Nelson St., Atlanta. Interred: Westview. AG 8/30/1910

FRIDDELL, Annie, age 1 yr. d. 18 Alaska Ave. Atlanta. AG 12/27/1907

FRIDDELL, Edward, age 3, son of Mr. and Mrs. Henry, d. 13 Alaska Ave., Atlanta, Fri. Interred: Casey's Cemetery. AG 1/24/1908

FRIDELL, Annie, inf. dau. of Mr. and Mrs. Samuel L., d. 13 Alaska Ave., Atlanta, Wed. Interred: Caseys. AG 12/26/1907

FRIEDMAN, Abraham, age 2 mos., d. 260 Hunter St. Atlanta. AG 2/14/1908

FRIESE, Charles J. d. Fri., age 60. Sparta, Ga. AG 5/27/1907

FRINLEY, Willie, colored, age 6 yrs., d. 301 Chappell St. Atlanta. AG 3/2/1907

FROBEL, Annie, Miss, age 97, formerly lived in Atlanta with her nephew, W. K. Mower, d. Montgomery, Ala. Mon. at home of Mr. Mower's sister, Mrs. M. S. Raoul. Interred: Christ cemetery, Alexandria, Va. AG 4/16/1907

FROST, George W., age 79, d. 442 W. Peachtree St. Atlanta. AG 10/7/1909

FROST, Jessie, colored, age 57, d. 124 Crescent St. Atlanta. AG 12/9/1907

FROTHER, Jeanna, infant, d. 78 Hardee St. Atlanta. AG 1/4/1910

FRYER, Annie, Miss d. parents home, Mr. and Mrs. R. C. Fryer, Atlanta. Sis: Mrs. C. L. Stockton, Atlanta. AG 7/22/1909

FRY, Herbert, Capt., river pilot, drowned in lower river 4/19. Columbus, Ga. AG 4/20/1908

FRY, Robert, colored, age 67, d. 11 Bradley Ave. Atlanta. AG 10/25/1907

FUGAZZI, A., Mrs., age 57, d. 279 Whitehall St. Atlanta. AG 3/29/1907

FUGAZZI, Mary, Mrs., wife of A., d. 279 Whitehall St., Atlanta, Fri. AG 3/30/1907

FULAYSON, L., colored, age 47, d. 89 Howell St. Atlanta. AG 1/31/1907

FULCHER, J. A., Mrs. of Athens, d. 3/2. Ch: Mrs. Cicero Blassengale of Monroe, Ga.; Dorothy, little dau. Sisters: Mrs. W. H. Kethum, Savannah; Mrs. George H. Christian, Atlanta; Mrs. W. K. Harley, Chicago, Ill.; Mrs. C. A. Lanier, Athens. AG 3/3/1910

FULENWIDER, H. E., Mrs., age 40, d. 17 W. Cain St. Atlanta. Interred: Westview. AG 7/13/1908

FULLBRIGHT, Marian, Miss, age 35, *d. res. of sister, Mrs. Edward Baker, 109 State St., Atlanta, Fri. Interred: Boneville, Ga. Mother, two sisters, three bros., survive. AG 11/14/1908

FULLER, A. L., age 47, d. 67 Elmo St., Atlanta, Wed. Wife, two children, three bros. AG 7/22/1909

FULLER, Carrie, Mrs., wife of John W., d. 520 Washington St., Atlanta, Tues. Ch: John H. Fuller, Mrs. J. S. Dickert, Miss Robbie Fuller. Interred: Westview. AG 4/14/1908

FULLER, Eugene, age 4 mos., d. Grady Hospital. Atlanta. AG 6/18/1907

FULLER, Ezekiel, Capt. d. Clarkesville, Ga. 5/28. Veteran citizen of Habersham Co. Age 73. Only wife survives. AG 5/30/1905

FULLER, Fannie, Mrs., age 34, d. 105 Venable St. Atlanta. AG 1/25/1910

FULLER, Frederick D., colored, age 5 mos., d. 368 Smith St. Atlanta. AG 7/12/1909

FULLER, George M., age 69, inmate of Old Soldier's Home, Atlanta, d. Thurs. Pvt. in Co. A., 10th Confed. Cavalry. AG 5/21/1909

FULLER, Mary H., age 60, d. 60 Ponders Ave. Atlanta. AG 11/15/1909

FULLER, Nancy A., Mrs., age 74, d. 180 Murphy Ave. Atlanta. AG 8/22/1910

FULLER, R. C., Mrs. of Chicago, former res. of Atlanta, d. Wed. Bur: Oakland Cemetery. Sons: O. C., Watson, Atlanta. AG 3/26/1909

FULLER, Rosamond C., Mrs., age 77, widow of E. Q., mother of Olin C. Fuller and Watson Fuller, d. 3/24 Chicago. Funeral: Central Congregational Church, Atlanta. AG 3/26/1909

FULLER, Susan, Mrs., wid. of Rev. R. W., formerly of Atlanta, d. Alexandria, Va. Interred: Oakland. Ch: Mrs. H. C. Ansley, Alexandria, Va.; Mrs. D. L. C. Genake, Dawson, Ga.; Robert, Washington, D. C.; Phoebe, Atlanta; Mrs. W. B. Rodman, Charleston, S. C. Sis: Mrs. Robt P. King, Atlanta. AC 11/21/1905

FULLER, Virginia, age 18 mos., dau. of Mr. and Mrs. R. C., d. 307 Mangum St. Atlanta, Tues. Interred: Westview. AG 7/6/1910

FULLER, W. A., Capt., Conf. Vet, d. Atlanta 12/28. 1860 m. Miss Lula Asher (d.1872) Murray Co.:4 ch: Baxter C., etc. 1874 m. Miss Susan Alford, Griffin. Ch: Wm A., Nina K., Lela Bell, Annie Laurie, Nellie Louise. Bur: Oakland. AC 12/29/1905

FULLER, W. H., Mrs., age 45, d. 190 S. Pryor St., Atlanta Thurs. Bur: Westview. Husband, 2 ch: Frances and Bruce. AG 9/24/1908

FULTON, George R., wife of Samuel, d. 32 Rosalie St. Atlanta. Interred: Oakland. AG 6/28/1910

FULTON, Lessie, colored, age 17, d. 347 Meldon Ave. Atlanta. AG 3/7/1907

FULTON, William M., age 45, d. 172 Capitol Ave. Atlanta. AG 4/22/1909

FULTON, Samuel, Mrs., age 69, d. 22 Rosalie St. Atlanta, Mon. Husband, 2 ch: W. H., Mrs. J. G. Norvill AG 6/27/1910

FURKS, W. M., Dr. funeral 8/22. WIfe 9 ch. Interred: Near Siloam, Ga. AC 8/24/1905

FURLOW, Charles T., Mrs. of Clarkesville, Ga. d. Sun. Ch: Floyd, Carl, Meriwether, Hal, Eugene. Interred: Americus, Ga. AG 12/12/1910

FURMAN, H. S., age 67, d. several days ago at 44 Hayden St., Atlanta. Interred: Westview. AG 2/23/1910

FURSE, John H., Lt., U. S. N. killed by wave while at post on battleship Illinois, bur. yesterday, Savannah. Fiancee: Miss Bertha Batchelor. AG 10/5/1907

FUSS, Allen J., age 50, d. rr yards 2/18. Bro: Leroy. Wife, 8 children. AG 2/18/1910

FUTCH, James E., Mrs. d. Harville, Ga. 8/25. Husband, and father and mother, Mr. and Mrs. Lamb Lanier, survive. Interred: Family Burial Ground. AG 8/26/1908

GAAR, W. S. d. Las Vegas, N. M. Funeral Atlanta Thurs. Interred: Westview. AG 12/23/1909

GAAR, Alameda, Mrs., age 85, d. grdau's home, Mrs. Lucie B. Huey, 201 S. Forsyth, Atlanta. Bur: Westview. Ch: Mrs. Lucie Bentley, Mrs. S. S. Scudder, W. J. C. Gaar. Grch: Mrs. W. W. Whittington, Mrs. W. M. Perryman. AG 1/1/1907

GABOURY, Philip S., age 9, son of Mr. and Mrs. J. A. of Jacksonville, Ala., killed in railway collission at Woodward, Ala. Parents, sister, 4 bros. AG 10/4/1910

GADD, J. E., age 69, Confederate Veteran, d. Old Soldiers' Home, Atlanta, Tues. Member of Co. K, N. C. Vols., wounded battle of Gettysburg. AG 12/8/1909

GADDIS, Georgia, Miss d. Thurs., res., corner E. Fair and Pine Sts., Atlanta. Interred: Sylvester cemetery. AG 5/31/1907

GADDY, Emily, Mrs., age 84, d. res. of son, W. P., 35 Simpson St, Atlanta, Sun. Interred: Chamblee, Ga. AG 6/28/1909

GADLE, J. J., Mrs., age 35, d. 25 Wiley St. Atlanta. AG 12/12/1910

GAFFNEY, J. M. funeral 2/10 Dalton, Ga. He d. home near Rocky Face, was native of Ireland, d. age 74. AG 2/11/1910

GAILEY, S. C., Mrs., age 55, d. Fri. 94 Berean Ave. Atlanta. Sons: S. F., Theo. Daus: Beulah, Lallie; Mrs. W. H. Botet. Interred: Alto, Ga. AG 9/10/1910

GAILLARD, S. G., Mrs. d. Griffin Tues, age 82. 5 children, one sister, one bro. Son-in-law: T. M. Berry. Interred: Oak Hill Cemetery. AG 9/1/1908

GAINER, Ruba, negro, playing with gun accidentally killed on Dr. J. W. Brinson, Sr. place, Wrightsville, Ga. AG 11/19/1907

GAINES, M., colored, age 78, d. 60 Orange St. Atlanta. AG 5/11/1908

GAINES, Philip B., age 18, res. of Brunswick for past 8 yrs., d. Tues., 1608 Gloucester St. Atlanta. AG 3/1/1907

GAINES, S. E., Mrs., age 74, d. 206 Means St. Atlanta. AG 2/4/1908

GAINES, Sarah A. Mrs., age 83, d. Fri. son's res., R. B. Gaines, Jonesboro Rd., Atlanta. Interred: Cass Station. AG 9/10/1910

GAINES, Sarah E., Mrs., age 73, widow, d. res. of sil, D. A. McNabb, 206 Means St., Atlanta, Sun. Ch: Mrs. D. A. McNabb, Mrs. Viola Finch, Mrs. Mary Murphy, J. Y. and G. W. Gaines. Interred: Canton, Ga. AG 2/2/1908

GAITHER, I., age 65, d. Mon. 116 Garden St., Macon. Son: J. F. Daus: Annie, Lizzie. AG 11/16/1910

GALBRAITH, E. d. Helena, Ga. Sun. Interred: Glenwood, Ga. AG 2/23/1910

GALE, Charles W., Englishman, age 35, d. 9/4 Columbus, Ga. where he moved to two yrs. ago from Atlanta. AC 9/6/1905

GALESRAITH, E. d. 2/20 Helena, Ga. AG 2/21/1910

GALHOUSE, Henry J., age 70, d. McDonough Rd. Invalid wife and three ch: John H., Alice, and Mrs. Oscar M. Bilsendine. Interred: Oakland. AG 10/26/1907

GALLAGHER, Edward Francis, age 25, of Atlanta d. 280 Formwalt St. 1/21. Wife. Father: Frank. Foster Mother: Mrs. Kate Brennan (reared him; mother d. soon after his birth). Several adopted bros., sisters. Bur: Hartsville, Ga. AG 1/21/1910

GALLAWAY, C. B., age 70, d. Memphis, Tenn. AC 12/1/1905

GALLAWAY, Thomas Jackson, age 18 mos., son of Mr. and Mrs. E. L., d. 11/12 Mell Ave., Atlanta. Interred: Hollywood. AC 11/13/1905

GALLOWAY, Ida M., Mrs., age 40, wife of T. S., d. 53 Lindsay St. Atlanta, Mon. Interred: Decatur cemetery. AG 2/16/1909

GALLOWAY, William Oliver, age 2, son of Mr. and Mrs. E. O., d. 21 Jett St., Atlanta, Mon. AG 11/2/1907

GALMOND, Mary, age 6 mos., died McDonald St. Atlanta. AG 8/22/1906

GAMBLE, J. A., Mrs., age 39, d. Tallapoosa, Ga, Thurs. Husband survives. Interred: Waco, Ga. AG 5/20/1910

GAME, M. T., Dr., age 48, d. 29 Luckie St. Atlanta. AG 3/26/1908

GAMMON, Joshua, age 46, d. Bibb Co. 4/24. AC 4/15/1905

GANGER, Edward, formerly of Atlanta, d. Philadelphia, Pa. AG 7/6/1907

GANN, David, Mrs. d. Athens, Ga. 12/23, age 79, grmother of D. D. & Fred Beussee of Athens. Ch: W. H. Gann, Mrs. E. S. Edge, Mrs. N. Hauser of Hartwell. Fun: Oconee St. Church. AG 12/24/1909

GANNON, John J., age 52, d. Sat., 42 Woodward Ave., Atlanta. AG 8/10/1907

GANTT, Dora, colored, age 17, d. 188 Currier St. Atlanta. AG 10/28/1908

GANTT, F. R., colored, age 1, d. 63 Tattnall St., Atlanta. AG 12/21/1907

GARCIA, Felix d. Aucon, Panama Canal Zone 10/7. Wife and family res. Jacksonville, Fla. Mother, sis., bro., in Atlanta. AC 11/1/1905

GARIBOLD, W. J. d. Athns Fri., age 50. Aged parents, one bro., Horace Garibold, three sisters. AG 2/8/1910

GARLAND, R. H. J., age 73, d. 294 Courtland St. Atlanta. AG 11/19/1909

GARNER, Augustus, age 14, d. Atlanta. Interred: Hampton, Ga. AC 11/23/1905

GARNER, Beatrice, inf. dau. of Mr. and Mrs. Dock od 367 W. North Ave., Atlanta, d. Fri. Interred: Caseys. AG 10/12/1908

GARNER, E. G. d. 5/3 1116 Marietta St.,tlanta. Interred: Kennsaw. AG 5/4/1906

GARNER, Elmer, colored, age 50, d. 19 Lowe alley. Atlanta. AG 3/27/1909

GARNER, Freddie, age 4, son of Mr. and Mrs. T. S., 57 Almo St., Atlanta, d. Mon. Interred: Westview. AG 6/8/1909

GARNER, Mary J., Mrs., age 68, d. Sun. 78 Tennille St., At,anta. Interred: Auburn, Ga. 9 children. AG 2/8/1910

GARNER, Thomas, inf. son of Mr. and Mrs. E. G., d. Thurs. Interred: Kennesaw, Ga. AG 10/25/1907

GARNER, Thomas, age 1 mo., d. 1116 Marietta St. Atlanta. AG 10/25/1907

GARNER, William Wallace, age 21, d. Atlanta. AG 1/12/1910

GARNER, infant of Mr. and Mrs. C. W. of 18 Paynes Ave., Atlanta d. Thurs. Interred: Riverdale Church, Clayton Co. AG 1/31/1908

GARNIE, Mary W., Mrs. d. 10/22 res. of son-in-law: Justice John S. Candler (Ga. Sup. Ct.) at Edgewood (Atlanta). Widow of Col. Isidore V. Garnie, Jacksonville, Fla. (He d. 1873). One dau: Mrs. Robert M. Freeman, Atlanta. AC 10/23/1905

GARRETT, C. C., Mrs., age 50, wife of C. C. of Lithia Springs, d. 5/22. Husband, 3 sons, 3 daus. Interred: Douglasville, Ga. AC 5/23/1905

GARRETT, C. W., Mrs., age 77, d. Sun., 126 Fraser St. Atlanta. Interred: Oakland. AG 10/15/1906

GARRETT, J. M., Mrs. d. 9/21 Montgomery, Ala. Interred: Greenwood Cemetery. AG 9/22/1910

GARRISON, Clarence, colored, age 2, d. 2 Maple St. Atlanta. AG 12/31/1910

GARRISON, Isabella, Mrs., age 57, d. Thurs. Willow St., E. Atlanta. Son: Homer Garrison. Dau: Mrs. Annie Murray. AG 6/2/1906

GARRISON, Mary Leak, Mrs., age 65, d. 30 E. Cain St. Atlanta. AG 10/3/1910

GARRISON, W. M., age 25, d. 11 Stonewall St., Atlanta, Wed. Wife. Interred: Haralson, Ga. AG 3/18/1909

GARROW, Mary, Mrs., age 53, wife of George, d. Wed. 255 Hill St., Atlanta. Dau: Mrs. J. L. Trammell. Sons: Fred, Ralph. Sis: Mrs. J. R. Maxwell. Interred: Greenwood. AG 9/15/1910

GARTNER, Marie, age 6 mos., d. 20 St. Charles Ave. Atlanta. AG 6/6/1907

GARTRELL, Annie, Miss, dau. of late Col. John O., d. Tues. 92 S. Pryor St. Atlanta. Sisters: Lizzie, Lucy, Ina. Bro: J. B. She was niece of late Gen. Gartrell. Interred: Marietta. AG 5/10/1906

GARVIN, Mary, inf. dau. of Mr. and Mrs. W. T., d. Fri. 24 Doane St., Atlanta. Interred: Lula, Ga. AG 2/14/1910

GARWOOD, W. A., Jr., age 18 yrs., son of Mr. and Mrs. W. A., d. 529 Central Ave., Atlanta, Tues. Bur: Jasper, Ga. AG 10/23/1907

GASTON, D. I., Mrs., age 36, d. 259 Glenwood Ave., Atlanta, Wed. Husband, two sons, Bob Willie and Joe Sam Gaston, survive. Interred: Cartersville, Ga. AG 11/3/1908

GASTON, Georgia, age 5, dau. of Mr. and Mrs. W. B., d. College Park, Ga. Mon. Interred: Crest Hill Cemetery. AG 3/22/1910

GASTON, Jennie, Miss, age 22, d. Atlanta Sat., res. of Carrollton, Ga. AG 12/18/1909

GASTON, Martha, Mrs., age 64, 61 Hayden St. Atlanta. Interred: Oakland. AG 10/17/1906

GASTON, Verdery Imogene, age 6 mos., d. 267 Glennwood Ave. Atlanta. AG 3/27/1909

GASTON, W. D., Mrs., age 44, d. Egan Park, Atlanta, Mon. Interred: Newnan, Ga. AG 1/4/1910

GATES, Jack, colored, age 44, d. 32 Fort St. Atlanta. AG 3/3/1909

GATES, Lamar, colored, age 31, d. 18 Jennings St. Atlanta. AG 12/9/1910

GATES, Morney, colored, age 36, d. 70 N. McDaniel St. Atlanta. AG 8/14/1907

GATEWOOD, Roberta, colored, age 20, d. Birmingham, Ala. AG 11/27/1907

GATINS, Annie Mrs., wife of John, d. 291 Central Ave., Atlanta, Sat. Res. Atlanta 45 yrs. Son: Joseph A., Washington, D. C.; Will, Atlanta. Daus: Mrs. J. D. Clark, Washington, D. C.; Miss Cele Gatins and Miss Nell Gatins. AG 10/24/1908

GATINS, Annie, Mrs. d. 9/14 Washington, D. C. Sis: Mrs. J. H. Clarke. Mother, 3 sisters, 2 bros. Sis: Miss Nettie Gatins, Asst. Principal of Walker St. School. Interred: Atlanta. AC 9/15/1905

GATTIS, Elizabeth, colored, age 3, d. 227 Lambert St. Atlanta. AG 5/7/1907

GAUDLACK, Gracie, colored, age 26, d. 18 Lowndes St. Atlanta. AG 10/31/1908

GAUEDY, Musette, Miss, age 26, d. Atlanta. Interred: Hollywood. 8/25/1906

GAULT, Lawrence L., age 2, son of Mr. and Mrs. W. H., d. 1278 Marietta St., Atlanta, Fri. AG 2/14/1908

GAVAN, John H., age 75, d. 294 Courtland St. Atlanta. AG 12/9/1909

GAWDET, Evelyn, inf. dau. of Mrs. E. G., d. Wed. Interred: Westview. AG 8/21/1907

GAY, Edward H., age 39, d. 324 Spring St. Atlanta, 10/2. Interred: Westview. AG 10/3/1910

GAY, J. J., age 30, d. near Chamblee, Ga. Tues. Leaves wife, father, mother. Interred: Corinth Church. AG 7/25/1906

GAY, Robert, colored, age 54, d. Edgewood, Ga. AG 12/3/1908

GAY, Willie, colored, age 1, d. 269 Irwin St. Atlanta. AG 12/30/1910

GAY, William, colored, age 44, d. 119 Haynes St. Atlanta. AG 12/9/1907

GAY, William E., Col., d. home of Mrs. E. B. Griffin (dau) Sat., Cuthbert. Sons: Col. R. D., J. M. Daus: Mrs. L. E. Gay, Mrs. J. M. Raives; Mrs. E. B. Griffin; Mrs. J. L. Saunders. AG 2/10/1908

GAZAWAY, Libbie, age 7, dau. of W. R., of Flat Shoals Rd., Atlanta, d. Sat. Interred: Wesley Cemetery. AG 12/10/1910

GEASLEY, Mary, colored, age 32, d. 193 McDaniel St. Atlanta. AG 2/8/1909

GEBHARD, infant of J. C., d. Sat. Atlanta. AG 10/19/1907

GEDDING, Edward, Dr., age 74, d. Augusta, Ga. He was first American to graduate from Univ. of Berlin, Germany, age of 21. AG 6/25/1906

GEENS, M. B. d. Sun. Atlanta. Interred: Moscow, Ky. AG 12/17/1907

GEER, Stella, Mrs., wife of M. E., d. Thurs. Husband, 4 children. Interred: Easley, S. C. AG 10/21/1910

GELLESPIE, Minnie, Miss d. Sun. S. Pryor St. Interred: Westview. Bros: Frank, James, Edward, Atlanta. AG 2/22/1910

GENGRECH, Elsie, Miss, age 19, d. Atlanta Fri. Parents, several sisters. Interred: Riggsville, Mich. AG 4/2/1910

GENNTISON, Ralph, inf. son of Mr. and Mrs. Nicholas, 334 Central Ave., Atlanta, d. Wed. Interred: Oakland. AG 4/13/1909

GENTLES, Caroline, Mrs. of Tilton, d. res. of son, John. Funeral: Tilton, Ga. AG 6/9/1910

GENTRY, A. O., age 25, killed in railroad wreck near Chattanooga, Tenn. AG 7/9/1906

GENTRY, Mattie, Mrs., age 44, d. 125 Paines Ave. Atlanta, Thurs, wife of J. M. 7 children. Interred: Douglasville, Ga. AG 7/8/1910

GENTRY, Ralph C. d. 153 Bedford St. Atlanta. AG 8/22/1910

GENTRY, Ruby, age 5, d. 125 Paine Ave. Atlanta. Interred: Douglasville, Ga. AG 8/1/1907

GEORGE, A. T., Jr., infant son of Mr. and Mrs. A. T., d. Mon., 79 Whitehall St., Atlanta. Interred: Lithonia, Ga. AG 9/10/1907

GEORGE, Frank, age 21, d. Atlanta. AG 1/12/1910

GEORGE, Harold E., age 19, d. Atlanta. AG 1/12/1910

GEORGE, Jesse C., age 22, d. 101 N. Butler St. Atlanta. Member of Conesauga Tribe, No. 23, Red Men. He lived Battle Hill, Ga. Interred: Westview. AG 10/25/1907

GEORGE, M. F., age 4, d. 117 Nelson St. Atlanta. AG 11/6/1907

GEORGE, Mary Frances, age 4, dau. of Mr. and Mrs. J. M., d. Nelson St., Atlanta, Sat. Interred: Forest Park, Ga. AG 11/2/1907

GEORGE, Nahall, Mrs., age 25, d. 58 North Butler St.,A tlanta, Fri. Husband: Charles. Two small children. Interred: Westview. AG 4/2/1910

GEORGE, Victor, colored, age 25, d. 101 N. Butler St. Atlanta. AG 5/20/1908

GEORGE, William A., age 15, young Greek d. Atlanta. Interred: Westview. AG 12/9/1907

GEORGE, Louis, age 21, d. 17 W. Cain St. Atlanta. AG 9/28/1909

GERAKETES, Victor, infant, d. 20 Gilmer St. Atlanta. AG 6/13/1910

GERASANOS, Nicholas, age 28, a Greek, d. Atlanta Thurs. Interred: Westview. AG 7/23/1908

GERMANY, Caroline, colored, age 66, d. 332 N. Butler St. Atlanta. AG 2/16/1907

GERRELL, Annie, colored, age 35, d. 49 Rawson St. Atlanta. AG 4/20/1908

GERSHON, A., Mrs. of 46 Brotherton St., Atlanta, d. Thurs. Husband, 4 children. Interred: Westview. AG 7/12/1906

GERSHON, Aaron, age 76, d. 46 Brotherton St. Atlanta. AG 2/15/1909

GETLER, Elise, Mrs., age 43, d. 294 Courtland St. Atlanta. Interred: Westview. AG 1/8/1907

GETTIS, Joseph, Mrs. of Tilton, Ga. d. 5/3, age 31. AG 5/4/1910
GIANONE, Marcia, Mrs., age 22, ife of F. P., d. Thurs. Cleburne
Ave., Atlanta. Interred: Oakland. AG 3/10/1910
GIBBS, Annie S., age 22, d. 113 Rawson St. Atlanta. Bur:
Oakland. Mother: Mrs. W. W. Gibbs. Sis: Misses Ella and Emma
Gibbs; Mrs. C. M. Quillian of Blue Ridge; Mrs. T. M. Walker and
Mrs. Jack Head. Bros: William H., Samuel H. AG 3/15/1910
GIBBS, Elsie, colored, age 32, d. rear 19 Forrest Ave. Atlanta.
AG 3/30/1908
GIBBS, Florence Angus, Mrs., age 31, wife of Dana, d. 1 Augusta
Ave., Atlanta, Wed. AG 3/17/1910
GIBBS, W. H., age 45, d. Western Heights. Atlanta. AG 9/17/1907
GIBSON, Adeal, colored, age 34, d. 379 Hilliard St. Atlanta. AG
9/21/1908
GIBSON, Berry, colored, age 1 mo., d. 106 Gilmer St. Atlanta. AG
9/14/1908
GIBSON, Charlie, age 14, d. Thurs., 364 Frazier St. Atlanta. AG
9/28/1906
GIBSON, Cornelia, colored, age 27, d. 48 Old Wheat St. Atlanta.
AG 11/7/1907
GIBSON, E. Park, Judge d. today Milledgeville, Ga. Leaves wife, 5
children. AG 10/19/1907
GIBSON, J. B., Mrs., age 74, d. 26 Peeples St., Atlanta, Oct. 16.
AG 10/18/1910
GIBSON, J. W., Jr., age 15 mos., d. 204 Echo St. Atlanta, Oct. 2.
AG 10/3/1910
GIBSON, Lady, Miss, age 24, d. Atlanta Tues. Interred: Griffin,
Ga. Mother: Mrs. Mary Gibson, Griffin. AG 3/18/1909
GIBSON, Laura, colored, age 60, d. 131 E. Harris St. Atlanta. AG
9/4/1908
GIBSON, Nother, colored, age 55, d. 187 W. Mitchell St. Atlanta.
AG 2/20/1907
GIBSON, S. E., Mrs., age 49, d. 97 Martin St., Atlanta. Interred:
Cedar Grove, Ga. AG 9/14/1907
GIBSON, Albert J. d. Sat. Newberry, S. C., age 50. Ch: Mrs. I. H.
Hunt, Mrs. O. B. Cannon, Mrs. J. N. McCaughrin, Miss Nina Gibson
of Newberry; & Mrs. C. L. Reed of Petersburg, Va. Wife died
several yrs. ago. Interred: Rosemont. AG 2/2/1910
GIBSON, Earnest, Mrs., murdered at home (Lindale) 11/8/1906. His
nurse, Matilda Brewer, from Lexington, Ky, in custody. Ag
11/9/1906
GIDDENS, Fitz, age 21, d. Wilson Hotel, Willacoochee, Ga. 12/29.
He was son of Ed Giddens. AG 12/31/1909
GIES, Walter C., age 28, former Atlantan, d. Nashville, Tenn.
Aunt: Mrs. W. H. Sutton o f 252 Capitol Ave. Atlanta. Interred:
Atlanta. AG 3/2/1910
GIGNILLIAT, Flora Kate, inf. dau. of Mr. and Mrs. E. S., d. Sat.
Girard Ave. Atlanta. Interred: Marietta, Ga. AG 7/22/1907
GILBERT, Catherine, mrs., age 69, d. Thurs. res. of dau., Mrs. J.
R. Harris, 10 Bailey St., Atlanta. Interred: Hollywood. AG
5/3/1907
GILBERT, H. B., Mrs., age 43, d. Peachtree Inn Apts., Atlanta,
Sat. Dau: Miss Frances Gilbert. Parents: Capt. and Mrs. R.
Parker. Leaves bro. Interred: Jacksonville, Fla. AG 12/1/1907

GILBERT, J. O., Dr., age 36, d. 347 Ponce de Leon Ave. Atlanta. AG 4/18/1910

GILBERT, Julia, Mrs., age 75, d. Thurs. Georgetown, Ga., wife of R. T. Gilbert. Daus: Mrs. J. B. Shelley of Eufaula, Ala. and Mrs. W. F. Adams of Cincinnati. AG 11/27/1910

GILBERT, L. P., age 55, d. Edgewood, Ga., Thurs. Interred: Madison, S. C. AG 10/9/1908

GILBERT, Lillian, infant, d. 18 Reinhardt St., Atlanta. AG 3/10/1910

GILBERT, Mary, Miss, age 50, d. Atlanta. 1/2 bros: Hugh, Charles and William Smith of Lindale, Ga. Cousin: Mrs. H. Strickland, Duluth, Ga. Interred: Westview. AG 3/22/1910

GILBERT, J. B., Jr., son of Mr. & Mrs. J. B. Interred: Westview. AG 12/31/1906

GILDEWELL, M. S., Mrs., age 50, died Culver Street, Atlanta. AG 11/19/1906

GILES, Columbus Richard, Dr., age 58, d. 591 Whitehall St. Survivors: wife, 5 ch: Mrs. W. T. Spratt, Jr., Oakland City; Rolf Giles, Phila., Pa.; Carl, Norman, Elo and Miss Ruth Giles, Atlanta. AG 12/27/1906

GILES, Harriett Elizabeth, Miss, res. of Spellman Univ., Atlanta, death mourned. AG 11/15/1909

GILES, Vera May, Miss, age 44, d. 140 Jett St. Atlanta. AG 2/27/1907

GILFILLAN, David, Mrs., age 42, of Decatur, d. Fri., wife of David, sone of best known cotton mill man in South. Sons: Malcolm, John. Dau: Mrs. Charles Binger, Birmingham. Interred: Westesby, N. Y. AG 5/8/1909

GILL, G. N., age 63, d. 125 Windsor St. Atlanta. AG 11/27/1907

GILL, H. D., Dr., age 40, d. 11 Arthur St. Atlanta. AG 11/11/1909

GILLAM, Addie Mary, colored, age 5, d. 159 N. Butler St. Atlanta. AG 5/23/1907

GILLEBEAU, J. L., Rev. of Cadle, Ga. d. 3/24, age 44. Wife. 4 ch. Interred: Scruggs Cemetery. AG 3/25/1905

GILLELAND, S. O., age 48, d. 168 Sidney St. Atlanta. AG 2/22/1907

GILLELAND, Susie E., Mrs., wife of J. H., d. Jeff Davis St., Macon, Ga. yesterday. Leaves husaband, 6 children. AG 2/4/1907

GILLESPIE, Angelena, Miss, age 28, dau. of Mr. and Mrs. G. C., d. 121 E. North Ave. Atlanta. Sis: Mrs. W. S. Joplin, S. Pittsburg, Tenn.; Miss May Gillespie, Atlanta. Bros: Joseph, Frank, Jacob. Interred: S. Pittsburg, Tenn. AG 11/24/1910

GILLESPIE, Early of Atlanta, age 46, from Barnesville, d. 441 Capitol Ave. Wife. Dau: Ruth, age 6. Mother: Mrs. Sarah Gillespie. Kin: H. N. Smith, E. N. Smith. He md. Cornelia, sis. of Rev. Dr. I. J. Van Ness, Nashville, Tenn. AG 2/12/1908

GILLESPIE, James, age 80, d. 224 Park Ave. Atlanta. AG 11/1/1909

GILLIAM, Thomas M., colored, age 1, d. 76 Inman Ave. Atlanta. AG 4/28/1908

GILLIELAND, W. L., age 39, d. Tues. Atlanta. Interred: Roswell, Ga. AG 7/6/1910

GILLMAN, Jessie, inf. dau. of Mrs. Mary of 86 Glenn St. Atlanta d. Sat. Interred: Westview. AG 6/1/1908

GILLMAN, M. M., Mrs., age 50, d. Tampa, Fla. AG 2/25/1907

GILLON, C. M., colored, age 45, d. 224 Elliott St. Atlanta. AG 10/30/1909

GILMER, W. M. of 138 W. Pine St., Atlanta, killed Sun. by engine of Central of Ga. rr. of which he was a switchman. AG 7/30/1906

GILMORE, A. A., age 22, d. mother's res., Oak St., Macon, Wed. AG 12/9/1910

GILMORE, Frank, colored, age 38, d. 319 Bell St. Atlanta. AG 4/13/1909

GILMORE, James H. d. 9/22 Talbotton, Ga. where buried. AC 9/23/1905

GILREATH, America Allen, Mrs., age 79, d. 321 E. Hunter St. Atlanta. AG 10/13/1908

GILREATH, Carrie A., Miss, age 54, d. Wed. 321 E. Hunter t. Atlanta. Sisters: Mrs. H. T. Martin, Mrs. J. P. Burgess, Mrs. Will England, Mrs. A. B. Collier. Bros: J. W. F. and J. E. Gilreath. Interred: Cass Station, Ga. AG 10/28/1909

GILREATH, Hoyt, infant, age 15 mo., son of Mr. and Mrs. Frank C., d. 65 Queen St., Atlanta, Fri. AG 5/20/1910

GILREATH, Miller H. of Cartersville now E Pine St. Atlanta. Bros-Paul, Mayor, Cartersville; James H.; L. R. Sis-Mrs. G. N. Tumlin, Sulphur Spgs, Tx. Ch-Frank C., Miller H., Jr., Joel Benjamin, Mattie, Mrs. Ella M. Satterfield. AG 11/2/1906

GILSTRAP, Luella, (or Leila age 2 mos., dau. of Mr. and Mrs. T. F., d. 30 Saxon St., Atlanta, Thurs. Interred: Marietta. AG 4/1/1910

GINN, Gertrude, Mrs., age 19, d. 7 Bennett St. Atlanta. Funeral at Harmony Church. AG 9/14/1906

GINN, Gladys, inf. dau. of Mr. and Mrs. L., d. 141 Venable St., Atlanta, Mon. Interred: Hollywood. AG 5/16/1910

GINN, Louise, Mrs., age 26, d. Thurs. 141 Venable St., Atlanta. 3 wks. old dau. Husband: L. H. Ginn. Besides infant, two girls, one boy, survive. AG 1/27/1910

GINN, Mary J., Mrs., age 59, wife of J. N., d. 586 Chestnut St., Atlanta, Fri. Five ch., 4 sons: J. R., L. H., R. T., Atlanta, and W. J. of Athens. Dau: Mrs. E. M. Jones, Atlanta. Interred: Athens, Ga. AG 11/20/1903

GIPPERICH, Hilda, Miss, age 21, d. sister's res., Mrs. J. J. Foote, Edgewood, Ga. Sister: Mrs. William Carder, Atlanta. Bro: Carl Gipperich, New York. Interred: Westview. AG 2/24/1908

GITT, Lee, suicide Tues. Atlanta. Interred: Westview. AG 5/25/1908

GIVENS, Joseph, age 51, res. 29 Luckie St., killed in accident in Atlanta. Body taken to Louisville, Ky. to aged parents. Interred: Birmingham, Ala. AG 8/12/1908

GIVINS, Adam, negro, run over by yard engine, Adrain, Ga. AG 8/13/1906

GLASE, William, wealthy bachelor, d. mysteriously Dawson, Ga. Mrs. L. J. Atkinson (wife of his 1/2 bro.) jailed. Glase's mother d. recently. AG 9/30/1909

GLASS, Carrie, colored, age 23, d. 62 Fair St. Atlanta. AG 7/16/1909

GLASS, Columbus H., age 28, killed Marietta, Ga., brakeman for Atlantic RR. Unmd. Father in New Hope, Ala. AG 6/2/1909

GLASS, Fannie, Mrs. suit filed for death of husband. AC 11/2/1905

GLASS, L. C., age 40, d. 168 Tyler St. Atlanta. Interred: Covington, Ga. AG 11/11/1907

GLASS, Rosa Mary, Mrs., age 35 d. Tues. 158 W. Fair St. Atlanta. Husband: Philip. Interred: Oakland. AG 9/29/1909

GLASS, S. C., age 77, former res. of Covington, d. res. of dau., Waynesboro, Ga. 5/16. Wife, several children, two in Covington. Sons: Steve, L. C.,A tlanta. AC 5/18/1905

GLASS, Virginia J., b.1832 Atlanta, d. 2/23 Arlington Hotel, Waynesboro where res. w/dau., Mrs. H. S. Kaylor. Res. Oxford 20 yrs. Ch: Steve, Atlanta; James, Covington; Mrs. Lee; Mrs. Mumford, Atlanta. Bur: Covington. AG 2/23/1909

GLATZ, J., age 83, d. 79 Augusta Ave., Atlanta, Sat. Interred: Oakland. AG 6/22/1908

GLEASON, E. A., Mrs., d. home of dau., Mrs. Isham meadows of Motts, Ala. yesterday. AG 7/21/1906

GLEASON, Harriett, Mrs. d. Sun. Cleveland, Ohio, former res. of Atlanta, age 75. Ch: Henry, Lucy. AG 9/24/1910

GLENN, Aaron, colored, age 51, d. 23 Howell St. Atlanta. AG 12/31/1910

GLENN, Grady, age 4, d. 101 N. Butler St. Atlanta. AG 11/27/1907

GLENN, M. W., son of Willie, of 262 Pulliam St., Atlanta, killed accidentally in Monroe, La. Interred: Atlanta. AG 2/13/1908

GLENN, Mattie, colored, age 35, d. 97 W. Peachtree St. Atlanta. AG 9/26/1907

GLENN, Vinie, colored, age 40, d. 115 Rockwell St. Atlanta. AG 3/22/1907

GLENN, Willie, age 61, d. 389 Whitehall St., Atlanta, Thurs. Interred: Hollywood. AG 4/8/1910

GLISSOM, W. C. killed by son, George, age 25, at Hillis (Waynesboro), Ga. AC 12/14/1905

GLOER, I. D., age 82, d. Bowman, Ga. Sat., father of late J. A. Gloer. Son: I. G., oldest son, survives. AG 10/18/1909

GLOER, Joseph A. d. 2/28 Bowman, Ga. Wife, 3 children. AC 3/1/1905

GLORE, Lenox A., age 1, d. 2 Bibb St. Atlanta. AG 7/1/1907

GLORE, Senie, infant dau. of Mr. and Mrs. Thomas A., d. Fri., 2 Bibb St. Atlanta. Interred: Comer, Ga. AG 6/29/1907

GLOSSUP, J. A., age 49, d. Atlanta Fri. Bro: W. B. AG 3/19/1904

GLOVER, Arthur, to hang for murder of Maude Dean in Sibley Mill 10/20. Augusta, 11/16/1906. AG 11/16/1906

GLOVER, Gordon, 2 mos. old son of Mr. and Mrs. W. W. Glover of 31 Longley Ave., Atlanta, suffocated by bed clothing. Interred: Duluth. AG 8/3/1906

GLOVER, Henry Christian, inf. son of H. H., d. Ft. McPherson, Ga. Interred: Savannah, Ga. AG 12/17/1910

GLOVER, Minnie, colored, age 23, d. 11 Talbot alley. Atlanta. AG 12/ 8/1910

GLOZIER, Willie May died from burns, 13 Corley St., Atlanta. Mother: Mrs. Ida Glozier, wid. Interred: Hollywood cemetery. AG 12/14/1907

GOBER, Eliza A., Mrs., age 67, d. 145 Luckie St., Atlanta, Mon. Interred: Lawrenceville, Ga. AG 11/19/1907

GODARD, Daniel d. 6/9 res. of dau., Mrs. M. J. Evans, Griffin, Ga. Age 64. 5 sons, 4 daus. AG 6/10/1910

GODFREY, B. F., age 77, d. 148 W. Peachtree St. Atlanta. AG 1/22/1907

GODWIN, Mary Lee, 1 yr., d. 77 McDonald St. Atlanta. AG 1/16/1907

GODWIN. W. T. d. Sat. LaGrange. Ch: Dr. William, Mrs. J. R. Roberts of Columbus, Mrs. Mattie Stratford of Ala., Mrs. William Cotton and Mrs. Pink Whitman of LaGrange. AG 12/17/1907

GOETZ, Eva, Mrs., age 78, old Atlanta res., d. res. of dau., Mrs. O. Wrege, 454 Houston St., Fri. 2 sons, 2 daus. Interred: Westview. AG 12/9/1910

GOETZ, Margaret, Mrs. d. Fri. Griffin, Ga. Interred: Oakland Cemetery, Atlanta. AG 5/26/1906

GOFF, Sarah D., Mrs., age 44, d. 55 Garnett St. Atlanta. AG 7/8/1907

GOINS, Ernest shot and mortally wounded by his bro-in-law, James Ford, Rutland, 10 mi. from Macon. AG 5/10/1906

GOLATT, Bob, negro, sentenced to be hanged 4/17 for murder of Eady Moore, negro woman, Appling, Ga. AG 3/26/1908

GOLDBERG, Sadie, Miss, sis. of B. B. of N. Y., burned to death 12/27 Thomasville, Ga. Age 20. Interred: N. Y. AC 12/28/1905

GOLDEN, Hillis M., age 11 mos., son of Dr. and Mrs. J. B., d. parents res. Wed. Interred: Temple, Ga. AG 6/18/1908

GOLDEN, Jack, age 5, son of Dr. and Mrs. J. B., d. 540 Chestnut St., Atlanta, Fri. Interred: Temple, Ga. AG 9/19/1908

GOLDEN, Leslie L., colored, age 18, d. 240 Decatur St. Atlanta. AG 8/31/1908

GOLDEN, Ruby Pearl, age 7 mos. d. Howell Mill Rd. Atlanta. AG 9/28/1909

GOLDSMITH, Emma, colored, age 63, d. Grady Hospital. Atlanta. AG 4/10/1907

GOLDSMITH, J. Meador d. Tues. Marion Hotel. Funeral at res. 856 Peachtree St., Atlanta. Interred: Oakland. AG 10/28/1909

GOLDSMITH, John H., Mrs., wife of City Comptroller, J. H., d. Farlington Flats Apts, Atlanta, Mon. Bur: Oakland. Stepdau: Mrs. Turner Goldsmith. Nephews: P. B. Simms, R. B. Simms. AG 5/12/1908

GOLDSMITH, Margaret H., Mrs., wife of J. H., Jr., grandson of City Comptroller, J. H. Goldsmith, d. 271 E. North Ave. Atlanta. Leaves husband, two children. Interred: Cedartown. AG 7/31/1906

GOLDSTEIN, Isadore, age 26, d. 23 Piedmont Ave. Atlanta. AG 9/10/1910

GOLDSTIN, John Thomas, colored, age 8, d. 173 E. Cain St. Atlanta. AG 12/10/1908

GOLDWIRE, Jim, negro politician, suicide, Valdosta, Ga. AG 3/1/1908

GOLIGHTLY, A. R. of Cedartown d. Sun. Philpot St., citizen of about 20 yrs. AG 12/9/1907

GOLPHIN, Jacob, negro boy, d. yesterday. Killed by train. AG 1/22/1908

GOLUCKE, J. W., age 5, d. Newton, Ga. AG 10/29/1907

GOMEZ, Mattie L., Mrs., wife of N. M., d. Sun. Winder, Ga. Bro: John A. Webb, Tunnell Hill, Ga. Sis: Abbie Webb, Atlanta. Dau: Mrs. N. K. Smith. Interred: Myrtle Hill, Rome, Ga. AG 5/17/1910

GOODE, Charles, age 4, son of Eli W. Goode, d. Thurs. from dog bite, Hawkinsville. AG 1/7/1907

GOODE, S. W., age 45, d. Milledgeville, Ga. AG 11/17/1907

GOODHEART, E. H., Sr. d. Sun. Washington, D. C. Wife. Sons: E. H., Jr.; Clarence, New Mexico; Richard. AG 2/28/1910

GOODMAN, George, colored, age 41, d. 45 Delbridge St. Atlanta. AG 7/10/1907

GOODMAN, John, age 68, Confederate veteran, committed suicide Moultrie, Ga. yesterday. Wife, 12 children. AG 9/5/1906

GOODMAN, Laura, Mrs., age 28, d. 307 Whitehall St., Atlanta, Wed. Mother: Mrs. M. G. Marshall. One sis. Interred: Decatur, Ga. AG 12/7/1910

GOODMAN, Morris, age 51, res. of Wellborn, Ala., d. Atlanta Sun. Interred: Westview. AG 7/19/1909

GOODMAN, Mathyars, 19, son of C. A., Atlanta, fiancee, step-sis, Sarah Frances Ellis, killed train wreck. Bur: Fayetteville, fam. cem. Sis: Mary, Norwood; Lillie May, Birmingham. Bros: Luther, Stockbridge; Lewis, Fayetteville.

GOODNER, J. P. d. N. Rome, Ga. this morning, age 52. Wife, large family of children. AG 8/6/1907

GOODSON, J. H., age 48, d. 757 Seaboard Ave. Atlanta. AG 8/31/1910

GOODSON, A. J., age 50, d. Union City, Ga., Fri. Interred: Smithville, Tenn. AG 7/17/1908

GOODSON, H. A., age 62, d. 112 Cherokee Ave. Atlanta. Interred: Westview. AG 1/22/1907

GOODWIN, Martha, Mrs., age 46, d. Mon. S. Kirkwood, Ga., dau. of Judge Aaron Collins of Cartersville, Ga. Dau: Mrs. C. T. Walthour. Interred: Rome cemetery, Cartersville. AG 8/12/1907

GOODWIN, Will, age 19, d. Sat. 226 Grant St., Atlanta. Interred: Kinston, Ga. AG 7/19/1909

GOODWIN, Willie, age 19, d. 33 Cone St. Atlanta. AG 7/19/1909

GOODWYN, Thomas H., Jr., infant, d. 504 Highland Ave. Atlanta. AG 1/25/1910

GOODYEAR, Beaman murdered Mon. Douglas, Ga. AG 2/26/1909

GOOGER, William, colored, age 35, d. Maple St. Atlanta. AG 9/10/1910

GOOLSBY, William T. killed by train Tues. Interred: Lawrenceville, Ga. AG 9/21/1910

GOOSBY, Fannie, colored, age 23, d. 101 N. Butler St. Atlanta. AG 4/2/1909

GORDON, Albert, age two, son of Mr. and Mrs. L. Z., d. 163 Marietta St., Atlanta, Thurs. Bur: Munroe, S. C. AG 1/17/1908

GORDON, Frank A. suicide Macon 5/17. Interred: Forsyth, Ga. AC 5/11/1905

GORDON, Frank B., Major d. Tues. Washington, D. C. Mrs. John B. Gordon left Atlanta to attend funeral, his mother. Interred: Atlanta. AG 1/24/1907

GORDON, John B., Gen. d. 1/11/1904 Boyton, Fla. AG 5/24/1907

GORDON, Louis, age 44, d. Terminal Hotel. Atlanta. AG 10/19/1907

GORDON, M. B., Mrs., age 50, of 57 Fraser St., Atlanta, d. Sun. Ch: Charles, Daisy, Will, Hugh Long. AG 11/23/1908

GORDON, M., Mrs., age 32, d. 125 Pulliam St. Atlanta. AG 10/22/1909

GORDON, Motor, age 6, colored, killed by Henry West and John Hardgrave, negroes. AG 12/7/1907

GORDON, Mariah, age 82, died 123 Thurman St., Atlanta. AG 12/26/1906

GORE, M. S. A., age 69, d. 578 S. Pryor St. Atlanta. AG 10/14/1907

GORE, S. A., Mrs. d. 570 S. Pryor St., Atlanta. Interred: Rome, Ga. AG 10/14/1907

GOREE, Mary Alice, Mrs. d. 455 Courtland St., Atlanta, Tues. Interred: Chattanooga, Tenn. Husband: C. P. Ch: Roy, Wisdom and Miss Aline. AG 10/23/1908

GORMAN, Arthur Poe, Senator, democrat, d. AG 6/4/1906

GORMAN, D. E. d. Chamblee, Ga. 4/6. Interred: Prospect Church cemetery. Wife, 4 children. AG 4/10/1909

GORMAN, J. A., Mrs. d. Waycross, Ga. Wed. Interred: Kettle Creek Cemetery. Husband, several children. AG 8/7/1909

GORMAN, Noah, age 40, d. Thurs. Scottdale, Ga. Leaves wife, 7 children. AG 6/14/1906

GORMAN, Samuel, colored, age 6 mos, died 111 Markham St., Atlanta. AG 12/11/1906

GOSS, Sarah, Mrs., age 44, d. Sun. 53 Garnett St. Atlanta. Interred: Tampa, Fla. AG 7/8/1907

GOSSMAN, Joseph, age 9 mos., d. 704 Woodward Ave. Atlanta. AG 5/10/1907

GOSWICK, Herbert L., age 8, son of Mr. and Mrs. W. E., d. Memphis, Tenn., Sat. Interred: Roswell, Ga. AG 10/19/1908

GOTHOUSE, Agnes R., Mrs., age 63, d. McDonough Rd. Atlanta. AG 8/23/1909

GOUGE, A. B., Mrs., age 65, d. Mon. res. son-in-law, Rock Springs, Ga. Interred: Rock Springs Church yard. AG 1/4/1910

GOULD, David B., age 51, d. Oconomowac, Wisconsin. AG 11/8/1909

GOVER, Mercy, age 10, colored, d. 4 N. Forsyth St. Atlanta. AG 1/14/1907

GOWDER, Marian, colored, age 23, d. 101 N. Butler St. Atlanta. AG 8/7/1908

GOWER, Henry, age 1, d. Ft. McPherson, Ga. AG 12/17/1910

GRACE, John B., age 19, d. 592 Edgewood Ave. Atlanta. AG 12/14/1908

GRADEN, infant of Z. E., age 7 mos., interred Turners church yard. AG 9/28/1907

GRAHAM, Mary E., age 25, died at Home for Incurables. AG 12/11/1906

GRAHAM, Ella, colored, age 39, d. Atlanta. AG 8/11/1910

GRAHAM, Hugh H. West Point, Ga., 11/12/1906. While duck hunting 11/11 on Chattahoochee river, near Riverside, Ala., accidentally shot, killed by A. K. Anthony. AG 11/13/1906

GRAHAM, J. S., age 55, d. Ellenwood Mon. Wife, 5 children. Interred: Ellenwood, Ga. AG 6/29/1909

GRAHAM, John Isham, age 8, d. 11 Crew St. Atlanta. AG 9/28/1909

GRAHAM, P., age 21, d. parents res. 335 Rawson St., Atlanta, Wed. Interred: Westview. AG 6/13/1908

GRAHAM, Mary Cecil died Mon. Interment: Westview. AG 12/12/1906

GRAHAME, A. M., Mrs., age 20, d. 119 E. Fair St. Atlanta. AG 5/20/1908

GRAMLING, J. A. funeral from res. in Bolton, Ga. 12/1. Kin: J. A. Gramling, C. B. Gramling, E. C. Gramling, W. A. Gramling, W. R. Gramling, Miss Nina Gramling, Fitzhugh Knox, Mollie Baber, C. C. Witt. AG 11/30/1907

GRAMLING, Charles K., age 28, d. Sat. Marietta, (where born). Interred: Marietta Cemetery. Wife. One child. Parents. 3 sisters, Mrs. J. D. Reynolds and Misses Emmalela and Pauline Gramling. Bros: John K; and T. A. Gramling, Jr. AG 8/29/1910

GRANT, **Charles**, colored, age 21, d. 101 N. Butler St. Atlanta. AG 4/8/1908

GRANT, **Christine S., Miss**, age 14, dau. of Ed Grant, d. 195 Euclid Ave., Atlanta. Interred: Decatur. AG 8/4/1910

GRANT, **Daniel**, colored, age 23, d. 57 Emmett St. Atlanta. AG 2/8/1909

GRANT, **Daniel**, colored, age 23, d. 57 Emmett St. Atlanta. AG 2/8/1909

GRANT, **Edgar**, age 13, d. 18 Cornelia St. Atlanta. AG 3/5/1908

GRANT, **Emma, Miss**, age 23, youngest dau. of late Policeman Grant of Atlanta who was slain in Pittsburg riot, d. Stockbridge Thurs. AG 3/10/1910

GRANT, **George W., Sr.**, age 80, d. Sun. son's res., George W. Grant, Jr. 177 Rawson St., Atlanta. Interred: Griffin. AG 5/14/1906

GRANT, **J. C., Mrs.**, age 23, d. Atlanta. AG 3/7/1910

GRANT, **James T.**, age 2 mos., d. 181 South Ave. Atlanta. AG 8/22/1910

GRANT, **John A., Capt.** funeral 6/8, Atlanta. Dau: Mrs. William G. Haynes of Columbia, S. C. AG 6/29/1907

GRANT, **John A., Capt.**, age 70, d. 159 E. North Ave. Atlanta. AG 6/10/1907

GRANT, **Laurence**, age 18, son of Ed L. Grant, d. 195 Euclid Ave. Atlanta. Second child to die of typhoid fever, the other being his 13-yr old dau. a mo. ago. AG 9/13/1906

GRANT, **Mary, Mrs.**, age 75, d. Milledgeville, Ga. AG 10/13/1906

GRANT, **Sarah Jefferson**, age 2 yrs., dau. of Mr. and Mrs. W. A., d. 67 Grant St. Tues. Interred: Hollywood. AG 6/16/1908

GRANT, **infant** son of Mr. and Mrs. Wallace, d. 61 York Ave., Atlanta, Sun. AG 7/5/1909

GRANTHAUS, **Nannie, Mrs.** d. Harris Co., Ga. AC 12/1/1905

GRANT, **Hugh Inman**, age 10, eldest son of John W., d. Peachtree St. Grandparents: Hugh T. Inman (maternal); Mrs. William D. Grant (paternal). Nephew of Edward Inman, Mrs. John M. Slaton, Mrs. Hugh Richardson. Bur: Oakland. AG 6/6/1906

GRANT, **Mary J.,,** wid of C.F., Saratoga, NY, dau of Jos Wood, Knoxville, Tn, d. Atlanta. Bro: Thos J. Wood, Brooklyn. Ch: Mrs. R.G. Thompson, Atlanta; Mrs. E.W. Krutch, Knoxville, Mrs. E.L. Sprague, Lexington, Ky. Bur: Knoxville. AG 7/2/1909

GRAUL, **Alice**, age 3, dau. of Mr. and Mrs. Charles, d. Atlanta Thurs. Interred: Westview. AG 7/30/1908

GRAUPE, **Henry**, inf. son of Mr. and Mrs. Oscar, funeral near Buckhead, Thurs. Interred: Sardis Church yard. AG 3/17/1910

GRAVE, **Alice**, age 3, d. Atlanta. AG 7/31/1908

GRAVER, **Carrie Bragg, Mrs.**, dau. of Gen. Braxton Bragg, buried W. Chester Village, N. Y. Born on Bragg Plantation, Newbern, N. C. Wife of Arthur Sherman Graver from New Haven, Conn. AC 6/25/1905

GRAVES, **John Verner**, age 17, son of Mr. and Mrs. W. R., d. College Park, Ga. Fri. 5 sisters, 5 bros. AG 3/26/1910

GRAVES, **Sterling P.**, age 52, d. 199 Courtland St., Atlanta, Fri. Interred: Lexington, Ky. Wife survives. AG 6/26/1908

GRAY, **Alfred**, colored, age 35, d. 85 Park St. Atlanta. AG 9/29/1909

GRAY, **C. M.** d. 7 Dainey St., Atlanta, Sat. Wife, three children. Interred: Dallas, Ga. AG 8/28/1909

GRAY, C. M., age 36, d. 129 Courtland St. Atlanta. AG 9/2/1909

GRAY, David, colored, age 50, d. 159 Auburn Ave. Atlanta. AG 5/6/1908

GRAY, E. T. funeral 11/30 Macon. AG 12/1/1910

GRAY, Ella, colored, age 22, d. 223 Irwin St. Atlanta. AG 7/17/1907

GRAY, H. L., Mrs. d. Jackson, Ga. Sun. Husband survives. AG 8/31/1910

GRAY, Howard L., age 5 mos., son of Mr. and Mrs. C. M., d. 310 State St. Atlanta Wed. Interred: Dallas, Ga. AG 2/17/1909

GRAY, Josephine, colored, age 28, d. 68 Holland St. Atlanta. AG 8/20/1908

GRAY, Louise, dau. of Mr. and Mrs. W. T., Athens, Ga., d. 7/29. Interred: Farmington, Ga. AG 7/30/1909

GRAY, Lucy, colored, age 54, d. 167 Old Wheat St. Atlanta. AG 4/19/1907

GRAY, Nancy C., Mrs., age 77, d. Atlanta Mon. Ch: J. W. Gray, Fayetteville, Ga.; T. W. Gray, Memphis, Tenn; Mrs. W. H. Timmons and Mrs. Mary McElroy. Interred: Fayetteville, Ga. AG 10/6/1908

GRAY, Sarah, wife of Col. John W., d. 11/10 Adairsville, Ga., age 74, formerly Miss Venable m. 56 yrs. ago. Ch: Josephine M.; Hon. J. R., Atlanta; Mrs. W. W. Trimble. AC 11/11/1905

GRAY, William, colored, age 27, d. 101 N. Butler St. Atlanta. AG 3/27/1908

GREAVES, Henry Shorter d. Clinton, Ga., age 77. He m. Martha, dau. of Thomas W. and Pallie Stewart of Jones Co. Dau: Annie, wife of James A. Stewart. Bur: Clinton cemetery. AG 1/21/1908

GREEN, Alice, colored, age 42, d. rear 229 Rawson St. Atlanta. AG 3/10/1908

GREEN, Benjamin E., Colonel, son of General Duff Green, of Dalton, d. last night., age 86. He was b. Elkton, Ky. 2/5/1822. AG 5/13/1907

GREEN, Cal of Brunswick, Ga., engineer, killed in wreck yesterday on railroad. Survived by father, mother, three children. AG 4/17/1907

GREEN, Claudine, Miss d. Sat. Interred: College Park. AG 3/1/1909

GREEN, Eliza J., Mrs., age 67, d. 327 E. Hunter St. Atlanta. AG 10/3/1906

GREEN, Elizabeth, inf. dau. of Mr. and Mrs. J. Howell Green of Decatur, Ga., funeral Mon. Interred: Decatur. AG 10/24/1910

GREEN, Emily, Mrs., age 26, wife of Dr. Thomas E., d. Wed. 655 S. Pryor St., Atlanta. AG 8/22/1906

GREEN, Enisell, colored, age 30, d. 254 Williams Ave. Atlanta. AG 7/17/1909

GREEN, Estelia, colored, age 1, d. 61 Kennesaw alley. Atlanta. AG 11/9/1910

GREEN, George, young blacksmith of Grays, Ga., d. 1/26 Macon from gunshot wounds inflicted by Clifford Chambliss (in jail), druggist at Grays. 3 small children, mother. AG 1/27/1910

GREEN, George R., age 2, son of Mr. and Mrs. G. J., d. 22 Simpson St., Atlanta, Thurs. Interred: Augusta, Ga. AG 4/30/1908

GREEN, H. D., Washington, D. C. d. Rallston, Va. 8/28. Wf: Mary, dau. of Judge B. Y. Martin, Ga. Supr. Ct. Uncle: Judge J. J. Martin, E. Point, Ga. Daus: Margaret, Carro; Mrs. W. C. Harrison, N. Y. Sons: Chas. B., H. D., W. L. AG 9/7/1907

147

GREEN, H. W., age 24, d. Atlanta Tues., son of Y. J. of Linesville, Ala., where interred. AG 11/16/1910

GREEN, J. E., Mrs., age 50, d. 104 DeKalb Ave. Atlanta. AG 4/ 7/1907

GREEN, J. W. of Villa Rica, Ga. d. last night. Wife, 7 children. AG 7/31/1906

GREEN, Jack, colored, age 35, d. Anniston, Ala. AG 10/29/1907

GREEN, James W. died his res., 1293 Marietta St., Atlanta. Survived by mother, 2 sons, one dau. Interment: Casey's cemetery. AG 12/8/1906

GREEN, Jessie L., Miss, age 30, d. 11/17 Kirkwood (Atlanta. Relatives: Mr. and Mrs. J. W. Green, Dr. and Mrs. S. T. Sinclair, Mr. and Mrs. J. S. Nance, Mr. and Mrs. W. L. Brown, Judge and Mrs. J. F. Green. Interred: Oakland. AC 11/19/1905

GREEN, John, colored, age 32, d. 106 Thurmond St. Atlanta. AG 2/16/1908

GREEN, John, colored, age 55, d. 22 Air Line St. Atlanta. AG 6/3/1909

GREEN, Julius killed at Mullis (near Dublin), Ga. 12/27. W. Bowden charged with murder. AC 12/29/1905

GREEN, L. F., Mrs., age 64, d. 327 E. Hunter St., Sat. Survived by husband, 5 children. Two ch: Roy, Richard of Birmingham and Jacksonville. Interred: Hollywood. AG 9/29/1906

GREEN, Martin, son of James, Thomasville. Chas Hughes murdered. AG 12/27/1906

GREEN, Minnie, Miss, age 45, d. Tues. Bishopville, S. C. Interred: Loackapoka, Ala. Several bros, one is Dr. Z. Green, Newnan, Ga. AG 12/29/1909

GREEN, Morris H., age 26, d. Mon. bro.'s res., C. C. Green, 398 Spring St., Atlanta. Interred: Ft. Gaines, Ga. AG 4/20/1910

GREEN, Morris H., age 26, d. res. of bro.., C. C. Green, 398 Spring St., d. Atlanta. Mother: Mrs. Carrie W. Green. Bros: C. C., Capt. E. A. Sis: Mrs. Chester Garvin of Ala. Interred: Ft. Gaines, Ga. AG 4/21/1910

GREEN, N., colored, age 84, d. 21-1/2 Clifford St. Atlanta. AG 11/21/1907

GREEN, Philip, Jr., age 2, son of Mr. and Mrs. Philip B., d. Tues. 40 Lucile Ave., Atlanta. Interred: Westview. AG 3/11/1908

GREEN, Richard M., infant, d. Maxwellton, Ga. AG 2/16/1910

GREEN, Tempy A., Mrs., age 60, d. 11/1, 88 St. Pryor St., Atlanta. Daus: Annie; Mrs. Mattie Morgan. AC 11/2/1905

GREEN, Thomas, age 31, d. Mon. res. of mother, Mrs. Mary Harris, 253 E. Fair St., Atlanta. Interred: Hollywood. AG 7/10/1906

GREEN, W. E., age 39, died his res. 330 Ponce de Leon Ave., Atlanta, Tues. Funeral: Ponce de Leon Baptist Church. Survived by wife and 3 children. AG 12/18/1906

GREEN, W. L., Merchant of Valdosta, d. Jan. 30, formerly of Howell, Ga. Interred: Thomasville. AC 2/1/1905

GREEN, W. Lee, age 30, res. Garnett St. Atlanta. young man from Marietta, run over by train. Interred: Marietta. AG 7/31/1908

GREEN, W. P., age 46, d. 604 S. Pryor St., Atlanta. Wife, one child. Interred: Jonesboro. AG 7/21/1906

GREEN, Will, age 30, d. Grady Hospital. Atlanta. AG 4/10/1907

GREEN, William, colored, age 75, died 45 Matthews St., Atlanta. AG 12/14/1906

GREENE, Alma, colored, age 11 mos., d. 222 Brown Ave. Atlanta. AG 4/13/1909

GREENE, C. C., Dr., age 49, d. 352 Whitehall St. Atlanta. AG 9/5/1906

GREENE, Thomas E., Mrs., died Wed. Interred: Spring Place, Ga. AG 8/23/1906

GREENHALSH, Mrs. of Knoxville, age 70, d. Tues. at res. of son-in-law, F. G. Painter, Roberta, Ga. Interred: Family lot near Knoxville, Ga. AG 4/21/1910

GREENLEA, M. A., colored, age 2, d. 336 Richardson St. Atlanta. AG 3/16/1908

GREENTREE, Nellie May, age 4 mos., d. 17 Early St. Atlanta. AG 5/8/1907

GREENWAY, E. W., liveryman of Bowman, Ga. d. Thurs. Wife, three small ch. AG 8/4/1906

GREENWAY, L. C., Mrs., age 60, d. 11 E. Alexander St. Atlanta. Interred: Westview. AG 6/ 3/1910

GREENWOOD, Fort, colored, age 45, d. 6 Newman St. Atlanta. AG 2/25/1907

GREENWOOD, J. E., colored, age 55, d. 40 Turner's alley. Atlanta. AG 2/13/1908

GREER, Claude, colored, age 19, d. 200 Mason and Turner Aves. Atlanta. AG 3/7/1907

GREER, Helen Thomas, age 6, only dau. of Mr. and Mrs. M. Greer, d. Sun. 225 Ivy St., Atlanta. Interred: Westview. AG 4/22/1907

GREER, Martha, Mrs., age 53, d. Wed. College Park, Ga. Interred: College Park Cemetery. AG 6/2/1906

GREER, Mary, Mrs., age 40, killed in Griffin cyclone. AG 4/25/1908

GREER, R. S., age 69, d. Fri. 97 Hardee St., Atlanta. Wife. Ch: S. W., S. A., L. G.; Mrs. M. E. Schaffield; Mrs. S. L. Reeves; Mrs. M. E. Wofford; Mrs. W. B. Payne; Miss Carrie Greer. Interred: Rock Springs. AG 6/4/1910

GREER, Robert, age 31, d. Cartersville, Ga. AG 6/11/1910

GREER, W. A., age 66, d. 482 Whitehall St., Atlanta. Wife, two daus: Miss Lizzie, Mrs. H. G. Greer. Interment: Westview. AG 10/6/1906

GREER, Will, negro, d. 8/16 while resisting arrest in Columbus, Ga. AG 8/17/1910

GREGG, Charlie, colored, age 30, d. Grady Hospital. Atlanta. AG 5/1/1907

GREGGS, Martha, Mrs., age 56, d. E. Point, Ga. Mon. Interred: Westview. AG 5/22/1910

GREGORY, Frank, age 24, d. 286 E. Georgia Ave., Atlanta, Wed. Interred: Crandel, Ga. AG 3/9/1910

GREGORY, Isla, Mrs., age 73, d. res. of son-in-law, C. A. Morgan, Columbus, Ga. Daus: Mrs. C. A. Morgan, Mrs. W. H. Smith, Mrs. S. J. Johnson. AG 6/21/1910

GREGORY, Sallie, Miss, age 60, d. Monroe Co. Tues. Interred: Sandy Creek, Butts Co. AG 2/11/1910

GREGORY, Willie, Miss, age 21, dau. of W. M. Gregory of Rockville, d. Tues. She was to have been married Sun. AG 7/26/1906

GRENADE, J. E. of Howard St., Atlanta, d. Tues. Presby. Hosp. from injuries recd Fulton Foundry near Kirkwood. AG 1/2/1907

GRENADE, James E., age 38, d. Presbyterian Hospital. Atlanta. AG 1/3/1907
GRESHAM, A. M., Mrs. of Birmingham, Ala., formerly Miss Aurelia Anderson of Atlanta, d. Mon. res. of uncle, Thomas A. Clayton, 119 E. Fair St. Atlanta. Interred: Westview. AG 5/19/1908
GRESHAM, Adeline, colored, age 60, d. 188 Orme St., Atlanta, 10/24. AG 10/25/1910
GRESHAM, Annie Lou, colored, age 2, d. 180 Hilliard St. Atlanta. AG 11/3/1909
GRESHAM, J. G., colored, d. 20 Liberty St. Atlanta. AG 3/27/1909
GRESHAM, Julia, age 23, d. 32 Fortune St. Atlanta. AG 10/22/1906
GRESHAM, Lee, colored, age 1 mo., d. 12 Love St. Atlanta. AG 8/11/1908
GRESHAM, Lola E., age 2, dau. of Mrs. J. H. Gresham, 302 East Ave., d. Mon. Interred: Stone Mountain. AG 9/26/1906
GRESHAM, Mollie, colored, age 39, d. rear 173 Fort St. Atlanta. AG 9/2/1909
GRESHAM, Myrtle, Mrs., age 24, d. 60 George St. Atlanta. AG 1/7/1907
GRESHAM, T. C., age 76, d. Oak St., Macon, Ga. 1/27. Dau: Mrs. J. R. Robinson, Macon. Son: W. R., Putnam Co. AG 1/28/1910
GRESHAM, W. C., age 43, of E. Point, d. Savannah 1/30. Interred: College Park. Wife. Three children. Bros: James T. Gresham, Atlanta; Charles A. Gresham, NYC. AG 1/29/1910
GRESHAM, William A., Jr., age 1, son o f Mr. and Mrs. W. A., d. 474 S. Pryor St., Atlanta, Mon. Interred: Pickens, S. C. AG 10/13/1908
GRESHAM, W. C., age 19, d. E. Pt., Ga. Mon. Wife, one child. Interred: Jonesboro, Ga. AG 11/22/1910
GRIBBIN, Lois, age 14, d. Fitzgerald, Ga. AG 5/18/1908
GRIER, Bob, colored, age 24, d. Chattahoochee, Ga. AG 2/14/1908
GRIER, Samuel, colored, age 16, d. 8 Golden Ave. Atlanta. AG 11/4/1908
GRIFFETH, Ethel, Miss d. 216 S. Pryor St. Atlanta. Wed. Bro: Dr. J. O. Griffeth, Atlanta physician. Interred: Danielsville. AG 3/13/1907
GRIFFETH, Milton B. of Bogart, Ga. d. 8/27. Funeral: Betheraba Church, Oconee Co. AG 8/28/1909
GRIFFIN, Frank, colored, age 54, d. 55 Trenholm St. Atlanta. AG 11/9/1907
GRIFFIN, Jesse R., Confederate Veteran, d. Carrollton, Ga., age 58, Jan. 13. Wife. Son: Hugh Lee Griffin of Dental College, Atlanta. AC 1/15/1905
GRIFFIN, Julia, colored, age 18, d. 138 Fort St. Atlanta. AG 5/6/1909
GRIFFIN, Lula Brown, Mrs., wife of C. M., d. Covington 2/22, dau. of late Dr. Griffin. AG 2/23/1910
GRIFFIN, Mamie, Miss d. Covington, Ga. AG 6/26/1908
GRIFFIN, Robert L., age 50, d. 17 West Cain St. Atlanta. AG 8/22/1906
GRIFFIN, Sallie, Miss, age 52, d. 265 W. Ashby St. Atlanta. AG 3/17/1910
GRIFFIN, Sallie, Mrs., age 35, d. 265 Ashby St., Atlanta, Wed. Interred: Carrollton, Ga. AG 3/17/1910
GRIFFIN, W. L., age 51, d. Fitzgerald, Ga. AG 7/8/1907

GRIFFIN, Walter, age 3, son of Mr. and Mrs. J. R., d. E. Point, Ga., Mon. Interred: Holly Springs. Ag 5/31/1910
GRIFFIN, Laura E., 57, dau of Mrs. M.V. Keller, d. 92 E Av. Atlanta. Ch: Mrs. N.K. Tyer, Lake Pk, FL; Irene, Rannie; Mrs. A.T. Averett; Dane, San Antonio; F.M. Bro: C.W. Keller. Sis: Mrs. C.B. Peeples, Mrs. G.W. Terry, Valdosta. AG 4/8/1909
GRIFFIN, Mary, Mrs., 57, wid. of E. A. Griffin, b., reared Atlanta, d. 41 Houston St. Bur: Oakland. Daus: Mrs. A. L. Pitman, Mrs. J. F. Wood, Miss Lizzie Griffin, Atlanta, Mrs. G. G. Maner, Birmingham. Sons: Charles, David L. AG 3/29/1909
GRIFFITH, Jack of 169 Central Ave. Atlanta d. Atlanta Sat. Interred: Statham, Ga. AG 7/27/1908
GRIGGS, Eliza, colored, age 22, d. 28 Dover St. Atlanta. AG 9/6/1910
GRIGGS, James M., Judge d. Father-in-law: Hon. D. R. Stewart, Cuthbert, Ga. AG 1/19/1910
GRIGGS, W. B., colored, age 30, d. Hill Park. Atlanta. AG 12/28/1907
GRIGGS, Alfred F., Dr., son of Dr. Asa W., W. Pt., d. Reno, Nev. 11/9. Wife, son, 2 bros, 2 sis: Prof. Asa W., Mabank, Tx; Dr. R. S.; Carrie Lou; Mrs. Oscie Smith, W. Pt.; Dr. Willie, Slaughter, La. Aunt: Mrs. 4. L. Winter. AG 11/10/1908
GRIHLE, Alma, Mrs., age 40, wife of C. C., d. 10/17 Columbus, Ga. AC 10/19/1905
GRIMES, Emaline, colored, age 57, d. 5 1/2 Alabaster alley. Atlanta. AG 11/15/1909
GRIMES, Harriet G., Mrs., age 60, d. 239 W. Fair St., Atlanta, Mon. Interred: Westview. AG 5/19/1909
GRIMES, P. M., age 52, d. Wesley Memorial Hospital. Atlanta. AG 8/6/1907
GRIMES, Thomas, ex-Congressman, 4th Dist., funeral Columbus, Ga. Confed. Vet. Interred: Linwood Cemetery. AC 11/1/1905
GRISWELL, Nancy E., Mrs., wife of C. A., d. 307 Means St., Atlanta Fri. Interred: Dallas, Ga. AG 12/7/1907
GRISWOLD, Harry G., Rev. d. Cordele, Ga. Jan. 22. AC 1/25/1905
GRISWOLD, Annie G., Mrs., age 59, died Luckie Street, Atlanta. AG 12/10/1906
GRIZZARD, Joseph, age 78, d. Tues. Interred: Smyrna, Ga. AG 5/1/1907
GROGAN, Ella, Mrs., age 36, d. 64 Magnolia St., Atlanta, Tues. Husband: T. B. Two children. Interred: Chamblee. AG 7/6/1909
GROGAN, Jacob W., age 86, d. 442 E. Georgia Ave. Atlanta. AG 8/31/1910
GROGAN, J. W., age 35, d. Tues. 442 E. Georgia Ave., Atlanta. Interred: Acworth, Ga. Wife survives. AG 8/31/1910
GROMLEY, Marjorie, infant, d. 215 Oakland Ave. Atlanta. AG 2/7/1910
GROODZENSKY, Louis, age 10 mos., died 95 Piedmont Ave., Atlanta. AG 12/17/1906
GROOM, Ella, age 47, d. Atlanta. AG 1/25/1910
GROOVER, D. R., lawyer of Statesboro d. 4/15, age 54. AC 4/17/1905
GROOVER, W. E., Mrs. buried Mon. Hollywood cemetery. Res: 133 Jett St. Atlanta. AG 9/14/1907

GROSS, Margaret, colored, age 52, d. 101 N. Butler St. Atlanta. AG 12/28/1907

GROUT, O. D., Dr., age 66, Auburn, Ala. pioneer, d. Sat. Dau: Mrs. C. S. Yarbrough, Auburn. 2 bros, 2 sis: Clifford Grout, C. C. of Auburn; Mrs. Peake, Pensacola, Fla.; Mrs. McCloud, Louisville, Ky. Interred: Auburn, Ala. AG 5/26/1910

GROVELAND, Jim, colored, age 24, d. Chattahoochee, Ga. AG 1/16/1907

GRUBBS, D. G. Funeral at res. Whiteford St. in Edgewood, Ga. AG 12/26/1906

GRUBBS, E. G., age 23, killed by switch engine North Ave, Atlanta. AG 12/26/1906

GRUBBS, Ed of Gladesville, Ga. d. Wed. in Macon Hospital from accident. Wife, several children. AG 9/10/1908

GRUBBS, Edna, age 1, dau. of Mr. and Mrs. J. E., d. 267 Waldo St. Atlanta. AG 8/11/1908

GRUBBS, G. E., age 23, of Whiteford Avenue, Edgewood, driver for Guthman's Steam Laundry, killed by Southern switch engine on tracks at North Ave. AG 12/24/1906

GRUBBS, Marvin, age 4, inf. son of Mr. and Mrs. George W., d. Wed., 149 Alexander St., Atlanta. Interred: Westview. AG 8/8/1907

GRUBBS, T. J., age 86, d. 109 Garden St. Atlanta, Ga. AG 3/2/1907

GRUBBS, Wilson L., age 77, d. 457 E. Fair St. Atlanta. Interred: Oakland. AG 7/2/1908

GRUFER, John C., age 62, d. 482 Houston St. Atlanta. AG 2/8/1910

GUERRADDIE, Julia, Mrs., age 73, d. Thurs., Macon, 2110 Second St. Sons: Virgil, Walter, Cunningham G. of Macon. Dau: Mrs. Walter Williams, Moultrie, Ga. AG 12/13/1907

GUERRY, C. E., Mrs., age 76, d. dau.'s res., Mrs. F. W. Carlisle, 655 N. Boulevard, Atlanta, Sun. Interred: Opelika, Ala. AG 3/29/1909

GUERRY, Hattie, Mrs. d. Rome, Ga. Thurs. Funeral res. of A. T. Hall, Vineville. Interred: Rose Hill. AG 8/10/1907

GUEST, G. W., Mrs. d. Thurs. Campbellton Rd. Atlanta. Interred: Union Church yard. AG 7/1/1910

GUFFIN, J. M., age 45 yrs., of Conyers, assaulted Atlanta by unknown man, d. Grady Hospital 8/21. AG 9/14/1906

GUINN, W. A., Colonel, Blue Ridge, Ga., assassinated McCaysville, Tenn. 3 weeks ago by John Ellis of Fannin Co. (confessed). Mrs. Guinn, wife, held for complicity. AG 1/11/1907

GUINN, W. A., Colonel. Blue Ridge, Ga., 12/7/1906. Col. Guinn died of of gunshot wounds. (assassinated). AG 12/7/1906

GULLATT, William C. d. Washington, Ga. Tues. Interred: Augusta, Ga. Wife, 6 small children. AG 3/11/1909

GULLFOYLE, Nellie, Miss, age 40, d. aunt's res., Mrs. Thomas Hastings, 238 Richardson St., Atlanta, Mon. Bro: Owen Guilfoyle, S. C. Interred: Oakland. AG 6/14/1909

GUNBY, William J. of Rome, Ga. d. Thurs. at Home of Incurables, age 38. He md. Miss Sharp of Rome. Survived by wife, one child. Interred: Oakland. AG 3/14/1907

GUNN, Frank of Houston Co., planter, funeral son's res., Alderman Will Gunn, Orange St., Macon. He d. fam. res., 6 mil. from Perry. Sons: Will and Frank of Macon, and a younger son of Houston Co. Dau: Mrs. Albert Taylor, Macon. AG 2/8/1910

GUNN, Frank, colored, age 52, died 54 Wells Street, Atlanta. AG 11/19/1906

GUNN, Harrel, age two, son of J. R., d. 4/30 Macon. Interred: Riverside Cemetery. AC 5/2/1905

GUNN, William R. d. Sat. 45 Luckie St., Atlanta. AG 1/25/1910

GUNNELL, Ida, age 2, d. 209 East Ave., Atlanta, Ga. AG 3/18/1909

GUNNELS, C. W., age 47, of Dawson, Ga., d. Fri. Interred: Dawson, Ga. AG 11/14/1908

GUNTER, Nannie, Miss, age 85, d. Atlanta Sat. Interred: Oakland. AG 7/4/1908

GUNTER, Ola Paul, infant, d. Lakewood Heights, Atlanta. Interred: Lawrenceville. AG 5/24/1906

GUNTHARPE, Annie L., Mrs., age 27, wife of O. W., 463 Georgia Ave., Atlanta, d. Sun. Interred: Macon. Husband, two wks. old baby. AG 2/28/1910

GURR, T. E. d. Dawson, Ga. Sat. Wife. Age 35. Two children. AG 11/8/1910

GUSS, John, colored, age 32, d. Fulton co. barracks. AG 3/1/1907

GUTHMAN, Caroline, Mrs., age 74, d. 305 S. Pryor St. Atlanta Mon. Interred: Oakland. Sons: Manuel, A. H. AG 5/14/1908

GUTHMAN, Emanuel C., age 43, d. 33 Cone St. Atlanta. Funeral from residence of Isaac Hans, 383 S. Pryor St. Interred: Oakland. Guthman's mother d. abt 2 mos. ago. Bro: Albert L. Sisters: Mrs. Edward Guthman, Chicago, Ill.; Mrs. Isaac Haas, Atlanta. AG 7/13/1908

GUTHRIE, G. W., age 66, Vet. of Civil War, Tige Anderson's Brigade, moved Atlanta from Carrollton abt 10 yrs ago., lived 107 Kirkwood Ave. Sons: J. E., G. H., J. C. Dau: Miss Echsan, Atlanta. AC 2/18/1905

GUTTUN, Mose, colored, age 28, d. rear 125 Magnolia St. Atlanta. AG 3/8/1909

GUYTON, Thomas E., age 49, d. 147 Peeples St., Atlanta, Fri. Interred: Anderson, S. C. Sister: Mrs. F. A. McCorkle. AG 4/13/1907

GWALTNEY, L. R., Dr. funeral 7/20, Rome, Ga. Born Virginia 80 yrs. ago. AG 7/21/1910

HAAS, Bertha, Mrs., 57 d. 384 Whitehall St. Sons: Leopold, Jr., Morris, Gustave, Henry. 2 daus. To America 4 yrs. ago w/her 2 sisters to join sons; she's sis-in-law of Mrs. Jacob Haas and sis. of Henry Rosenbaum. Bur: Oakland. AG 12/12/1906

HABERSHAM, William Waring, age 83, bro. of Mrs. Charles King of Rome, d. yesterday N. Augusta. He was born Savannah 1/12/1824. Nieces: Mr. R. G. Clark, Rome; Mrs. J. W. Jackson, Augusta. AG 12/1/1906

HABGOOD, Manch P., age 33, d. 274 Chestnut St. Atlanta. AG 1/21/1910

HACKETT, Emma, colored, age 6, 217 East Fair St. rear, Atlanta. AG 11/9/1906

HADIN, Elbin, dau. of T. J., age 10, killed by assassin's bullet intended for T. J. Hadin. M. V. Culpepper of Girard, Ala. arrested. AG 9/18/1908

HAFER, Maddie, Miss, age 17, dau. of W. H. of 356 Formwalt St., Atlanta, d. Sun. Father, 2 sisters, Mrs. T. W. Buflin, Miss Susiee Hafer. Bros: Harry, Austell, Fred. Interred: Austell, Ga. AG 4/13/1908

HAGAN, Essie, Mrs., wife of G. W., d. Tues. Donalsonville, Ga. Interred: Rocky Ford, Ga. AG 7/23/1908

HAGAN, John W., Mrs. of Valdosta, Ga. d. Sat., age 73, dau. of late Owen Smith who d. a few years ago, aged more than 90 yrs. AG 10/3/1907

HAGER, Mary, Mrs., age 72, d. res. of dau., Mrs. H. L. Jordan, 87 Richardson St., Atlanta, Sat. Interred: Birmingham, Ala. Dau: Mrs. Jordan and Mrs. G. H. Stephenson of Bessemer, Ala. Son: C. G. Hager, Barnwell, Ala. AG 12/7/1908

HAGERMAN, Willie F., Mrs., age 62, d. 154 Simpson St. Atlanta. Interred: Hollywood. Daus: Mrs. T. A. Small, Mrs. E. E. Alred, Mrs. Sallie Schefler, Mrs. W. E. Neilson. Son: T. D. AG 12/30/1910

HAGGARD, E. L., age 70, d. Tues. 17 Marcus St. Atlanta. Three sons, three daus. survive. Interred: Montreal, Ga. AG 7/31/1907

HAINES, A. H., who recently moved to Cordele, d. yesterday. Son lives in Columbus, Ga. AG 4/6/1907

HAINES, Fannie E., Mrs., age 47, d. 44 Eugenia St. Atlanta. AG 7/1/1907

HAINES, Marie, Mrs., wife of George, d. Augusta, 3/12, age 50. AG 3/13/1908

HAIRSON, C. C., age 65, d. Atlanta. AG 7/30/1908

HAIRSTON, Charles A., age 65, d. Atlanta Tues. Interred: Hollywood. AG 7/30/1908

HAIRSTON, Joel, inf. son of Mr. and Mrs. J. B., d. Kirkwood Tues. Interred: Peachtree Road Church, church yard. AG 10/30/1907

HAIRSTON, Katie, Mrs., age 36, wife of A. M., d. 38 McDonough St., Atlanta. Leaves husband, 8 children. Interred: Antioch church yard. AG 11/21/1907

HAKINS, A. J., Mrs., age 82, d. 4th St., Macon, Ga. AC 5/24/1905

HALE, Dayton, Mrs., age 50, d. Mon. 324 Myrtle St., Atlanta. Sons: R. F., Marion, Dayton, Jr. Bur: Westview. AG 6/16/1908

HALE, James E., age 45, d. E. Atlanta. AG 8/14/1908

HALE, Sarah Augusta, Miss, age 62, d. Hancock Ave., Athens. Bro: Dr. Hale of Athens; Hope H. Hale of Atlanta. AG 5/4/1910

HALEY, Hugh, son of Mr. and Mrs. Thomas H., of Ocala, Fla., d. Savannah, Ga. Interred: Elder Cemetery, Indian Springs, Ga. 4 bros., 1 sister (Fla.). Relatives in Atlanta and Macon. Grson of late W. A. Elder, Sr. of Indian Springs, Ga. AG 11/17/1910

HALEY, Mary Elizabeth, Mrs., mother of Sheriff S. N. Haley, d. Elberton, Ga. Sun., age 82. Son: George. Had 10 children, 8 survive. AG 5/17/1910

HALL, Andrew, age 57, d. 291 S. Boulevard. Atlanta. AG 9/3/1909

HALL, B. C., age 52, d. Thurs. 40 Girard Ave., Atlanta. Interred: Westview. AG 8/8/1907

HALL, Bob, negro, of 356 Butler St., Atlanta, killed Wed. by falling earth. AG 6/5/1907

HALL, C. H., Dr., 70, College St, Macon. Survivors: Wife, Dr. Thos & C. H. Hall, Jr., Macon, Mrs. S. R. Jacques, Mrs. Kate Taylor, Macon, Mrs. Ellis Talbott, Richmond, Va. Bur: Rose Hill. AG 9/10/1906

HALL, Charles W. of Bowman d. yesterday. Wife. Ch: Mrs. W. A. Carrington, Mrs. J. L. Smith, Bowman; Howell Cobb Hall, Athens; Charles S. Hall, Birmingham, Ala.; George A. Hall, Elberton; R. E. L. Hall, Norfolk, Va. AG 9/24/1907

HALL, Charles, Mrs. d. Atlanta Thurs. One dau. AG 1/20/1910
HALL, Emmala, Mrs., age 64, of 215 Ivy St., Atlanta, d. Thurs. Interred: Westview. AG 1/21/1910
HALL, George C. d. Mon. 88 Ellis St., Atlanta. Interred: Westview. AG 10/18/1910
HALL, Harry Alton, age 1, son of Mr. and Mrs. G. S., d. 680 E. Fair St. Atlanta. Interred: Columbus, Ga. AG 7/27/1907
HALL, Hulda, Mrs., age 78, d. Sat. 620 Chestnut St., Atlanta. Interred: Acworth, Ga. AG 9/10/1910
HALL, J. T., age 51, d. 4 Confederate Ave. Atlanta. AG 3/21/1910
HALL, J. T., Mrs. d. 1/14 Elm St., Macon. Husband, 2 sons, 2 daus. Interred: Riverside Cemetery. AG 1/15/1910
HALL, Jennie Theresa, Mrs., age 51, d. 4 Confederate Ave., Atlanta, Thurs. Interred: New Haven, Con. AG 3/17/1910
HALL, Joe Sim, age 1, son of Mr. and Mrs. W. H., d. near Lakewood Heights, Atlanta. Interred: Elberton. AG 8/3/1908
HALL, John, colored, age 41, d. 88 Haynes St. Atlanta. AG 4/15/1908
HALL, John P., age 45, b. Harris Co. 3/24/1828, to Atlanta 1860, d. dau.'s res., Mrs. J. J. Barnes, 282 Whitehall St. Atlanta. Wife. Ch: Mrs. J. J. Barnes, Mrs. J. M. Daniel, Mrs. W. R. Shropshire, T. O. Hall. Bur: Oakland. AG 4/8/1909
HALL, John S., age 75, Confederate veteran, d. Wed. at Soldiers' Home, Atlanta. Interred: Westview. AG 5/10/1907
HALL, Julia M., Mrs., age 71, d. nephew's res., Hon. Joseph Hill Hall, 243 Hardeman Ave., Macon, Sun. Interred: Rose Hill Cemetery. AG 10/18/1910
HALL, Louise, colored, age 1 yr., d. 404 Crumley St. Atlanta. AG 10/4/1907
HALL, Louise, colored, age 4, d. 21 Palson St. Atlanta. AG 9/2/1910
HALL, Lyman, Capt., Pres. of Ga. Tech., expected to die Danville, N. Y. AC 8/12/1905
HALL, M. A., Mrs., age 66, died her res., Kirkwood. Interment: Adel, Ga. AG 12/16/1906
HALL, Margaret S., inf. dau. of Mr. and Mrs. George D., d. Tues. Bonnie Brae. Interred: Westview. AG 5/31/1906
HALL, Mary D., Mrs., age 60, d. 188 W. Peachtree St. Atlanta. AG 10/22/1909
HALL, Mary J., Mrs., age 73, d. Fri. 163 Mill St., Atlanta, Sat. Interred: Westview. AG 10/2/1909
HALL, Mary, Mrs., age 82, d. Tues. Mason and Turner Rds., Atlanta. Interred: Masons church yard. Dau: Mrs. T. C. Sparks. Grch: C. A. Jones, of USS Salem; Roscoe Jones, Hapeville; Dewey Jones, Levinia Jones; Nat Jones, Atlanta. AG 12/29/1909
HALL, Oscar, colored, age 27, d. 31 Elm St. Atlanta. AG 3/4/1908
HALL, Robert, age 34, d. W. Hunter St. Atlanta. AG 6/6/1907
HALL, T. N., age 60, d. 5/7, 181 W. Peachtree St. Atlanta. AC 5/9/1905
HALL, W. N., Capt., age 106, d. 3/1, Statesboro, Ga. Served in 5th Ga. Cav., Civil War. Wife, 6 children. Interred: Statesboro, Ga. AC 3/4/1905
HALL, Will, negro, shot, killed by Berry Cannon, negro, Wrightsville, Ga. AG 2/4/1907

HALL, William D., colored, age 59, d. 205 McDaniel St. Atlanta. AG 5/24/1910

HALLEY, G. T., age 43, d. 27 Prospect Place. Atlanta. AG 3/8/1909

HALLEY, Weston, colored, age 25, d. 189 Howell St. Atlanta. AG 11/1/1909

HALLIDAY, Agnes, Mrs. of Eufaula, Ala. d. Sat., age 95. Numerous grandchildren and gr-grandchildren who res. in various pats of Ga. AG 12/13/1909

HALLMAN, Judson d. Tues. Unadilla, Ga. Wife and father survive. Well-known in Macon. Interred: Shiloh Church. AG 9/3/1907

HAM, P. H., of Elberton, Ga., received news that his son was killed in Philippine Islands, soldier in army. AG 2/4/1907

HAMBRICK, A. R., Mrs., age 28, d. 42 S. Jackson St., Atlanta, Fri. Ch: Fred, Otis, Claud. Husband. AG 12/9/1910

HAMBRICK, Fred, 6 mos. old, d. 200 Haynes St. Atlanta. AG 10/3/1906

HAMBRICK, Lucy J., Mrs., age 78, d. res. of nephew, John W. Cochran, New Market, Ala. AG 7/11/1910

HAMBRICK, Mac, age 7 mos., son of Mr. and Mrs. James H., d. Thurs. 22 Oglethorpe Ave. Atlanta. Interred: Duluth, Ga. AG 7/21/1910

HAMBRIGHT, Annie Morris, age 3 mos., d. 300 E. Pine St. Atlanta. AG 10/11/1909

HAMBRY, Gordon killed by Western & Atlantic train. Funeral: family res., corner Neal and Lindsay Sts. Interment: Casey´s. AG 12/18/1906

HAMBURGER, Louis, Major of Columbus, Ga. buried Linwood cemetery. AG 5/28/1907

HAMBY, Gordon of Western Heights. Death under investigation. Legs were crushed by train in Western & Atlantic yards last Sat. He died later at Grady Hospital. AG 12/22/1906

HAMBY, Wilmer, age 2, son of Mr. and Mrs. B. B. of 105 Park Ave., d. Mon. Interred: Smyrna, Ga. AG 5/25/1908

HAMES, Jay O., age 15, son of Mr. and Mrs. W. J. M., d. 152 Richardson St., Atlanta, Tues. Bro: F. W. H. Hames. Sisters: Misses Carolyn and Louise H. hames. Interred: Conyers, Ga. AG 7/14/1908

HAMEY, Magnolia, colored, age 20, d. 102-1/2 Decatur St. Atlanta. AG 7/9/1908

HAMILTON, Berta L., age 3, dau. of Mr. and Mrs. M. C., d. 52 Savannah St., Atlanta, Mon. Interred: Bogart, Ga. AG 10/2/1907

HAMILTON, Dock, colored, age 40, d. 59 Hilliard St. Atlanta. AG 12/17/1910

HAMILTON, Fannie d. 12 Shelton St. Atlanta. AG 10/22/1906

HAMILTON, J. T., Capt. d. 12/1, Confederate Veteran, res. of Athens, Ga. Wife survives. AG 12/2/1909

HAMILTON, John C., age 53, d. 37 Warren St., Kirkwood, Ga., Sat. Wife, 3 children, 3 bros., George W., W. R. and Clarence Hamilton, of Atlanta police force, one sister, Mrs. L. L. Hendrix. Interred: Conyers, Ga. AG 6/26/1908

HAMILTON, Joseph, age 7 mos., d. 101 N. Butler St. Atlanta. AG 7/17/1909

HAMILTON, Leah, colored, age 98, d. 155 Bell St. Atlanta. AG 3/30/1909

HAMILTON, Louise funeral Wed. Marietta, Ga., inf. dau. of Mr. and Mrs. J. M. Hamilton. AG 5/23/1906
HAMILTON, Susie, colored, age 28, d. 431 Richardson St. Atlanta. AG 12/24/1907
HAMILTON, T. M., Mrs., age 60, d. Hapeville, Ga., Tues. Husband, 4 ch: D. F., T. M., Jr. of Hapeville; Mrs. J. T. Medlock, Jonesboro; Mrs. C. J. Stanford, Lovejoy, Ga. Interred: Co. Line Church, Jonesboro, Ga. AG 5/25/1910
HAMILTON, Sallie, Mrs., wife of Dr. C. J. for past 8 yrs., Anniston, Ala., d. W. 15th St. AG 9/11/1906
HAMIL, J. L. d. 4/20 Barnesville, Ga., age 60. Veteran of Civil War. Wife. Dau. AC 4/22/1905
HAMMOCK, Addie M., age 17, d. Conyers, Ga. AG 11/8/1910
HAMMOCK, Addie May, age 19, d. res. of mother in Kirkwood (Atlanta) Fri. Interred: Conyers, Ga. AG 11/5/1910
HAMMOCK, Andrew, age 17, son of Mr. and Mrs. W. J., d. Sun. 215 Peters St., Atlanta. Interred: Westview. AG 5/30/1910
HAMMOND, Annie Mrs., age 78, d. dau.'s res., Mrs. John W. Clay, S. Kirkwood, Ga., Mon. Interred: Westview. Sons: D. L., J. F. and A. W. Hammond. Daus: Mrs. Clay, Mrs. Maggie Dunn. AG 5/19/1908
HAMMOND, Clifford, son of Mr. and Mrs. P. L., d. 33 Cooper St., Atlanta, Tues. Interred: Statham, Ga. AG 7/6/1910
HAMMOND, E. W., Judge of Griffin, age 62, d. 8/17. Res. Culloden, Atlanta, Griffin (1866). 1869 md. Sallie Andrews, Griffin. Daus: Miss Jane, Mrs. J. E. Drake, Mrs. E. W. Beck, Griffin. Sis: Mrs. M. O. Bowdoin. Bro: George H. AG 8/18/1908
HAMMOND, Howard, age 20, son of Dr. L. P. of Rome, Ga., d. Arizona. AG 8/25/1906
HAMMOND, J. W. hanged Winston-Salem, N. C. for murdering wife, Henrietta, 4/19. AC 9/3/1905
HAMMOND, Laura F., Mrs., wife of late Nathaniel J., d. dau's res., Mrs. James Gilbert, 724 Piedmont Ave., Atlanta. Interred: Oakland. AG 12/30/1908
HAMMOND, O. C., age 37, d. 132 Venable St., Atlanta Fri. Interred: Hollywood. AG 9/19/1908
HAMPTON, E. R., age 57, of 134 Powers St., d. Wed. Interred: Westview. AG 11/26/1908
HAMPTON, Frank L. d. Utica, N. Y. Thurs. Sister: Mrs. Julia L. McKie, Atlanta. Bro: John Hampton, Cornelia, Ga. Interred: Westview. Leaves wife, and mother, Mrs. C. D. McKie. AG 12/21/1908
HAMPTON, L. L., colored, age 5 mos., d. 35 Matthew St. Atlanta. AG 12/24/1907
HAMPTON, M., Miss, age 71, d. Pouland, Ga. AG 6/1/1907
HAMPTON, R. E., age 57, d. 134 Powers St., Atlanta, Wed. Sister: Miss Annie Hampton. Interred: Westview. AG 11/26/1908
HAMPTON, Wade, age 30, d. several days ago at Grady Hospital, Atlanta. Interred: Westview. He was from Johnson City, Tenn. AG 7/12/1907
HANCK, Nellie Rice, age 14, dau. of Mrs. Francis, d. Scottdalle, Ga. Mon. Interred: Stonewall, Ga. AG 3/10/1910
HANCOCK, Alice, Miss, dau. of W. J. of Wilcox Co., d. 6/17 while caring for her baby sister. AG 6/18/1909

HANCOCK, **Charner P., Mrs.** d. Riverdale, Ga. Her husband d. several days ago. Son: B. F. Daus: Mrs. Henrietta Creel of College Park, and Mrs. E. E. Wallace. Interred: Popular Springs church yard. AG 5/9/1910

HANCOCK, **Charner T.,** age 86, d. Riverdale, Ga., Thurs., pioneer citizen of Clayton Co. Wife. Son: B. F. Daus: Mrs. Henrietta Creel, College Park; Mrs. E. E. Wallace. AG 5/5/1910

HANCOCK, **F. T., Mrs.** d. Varnells, Ga. Wed. Interred: Phelps, Ga. Age 80. Dau: Mrs. Bob Saylors of Varnella, Ga. AG 10/28/1910

HANCOCK, **Fred,** infant, d. 177 Echo St. Atlanta. AG 1/25/1910

HANCOCK, **George, Mrs.,** died her res. near Ponce de Leon Ave., Atlanta, last night, 11/12th. Tues. Interment: Westview. AG 11/13/1906

HANCOCK, **Grace,** age 8 mos., d. 95 McAfee St. Atlanta. AG 4/15/1910

HANCOCK, **J. Fred** funeral 2/4/1908. AG 2/3/1908

HANCOCK, **Lillie,** age 32, d. 37 Estoria St. Atlanta. Interred: Roswell, Ga. AG 12/30/1910

HANCOCK, **M. J., Mrs.,** age 78, d. Sun. 115 Washington t., Atlanta. Interred: Conyers, Ga. AG 3/1/1908

HANCOCK, **Mary, Mrs.** d. 9/11, 114 Luckie St., Atlanta. Interred: Oakland. AC 9/14/1905

HANCOCK, **Perry H.,** age 64, d. 84 Powell St., Atlanta, Mon. Interred: Roswell, Ga. AG 6/28/1910

HANCOCK, **Sarah Rebecca, Mrs.,** wid. of C. J., d. 11/16 son's res., W. E., Moreland, Ga. Sons: W. E., W. L. Interred: Oakland. AC 11/19/1905

HAND, **Fannie, Miss,** age 55, d. Atlanta, Wed. Interred: Leary, Ga. AG 12/16/1909

HANDLY, **George T.,** age 79, d. at Confederate Soldiers Home, Atlanta. AG 9/5/1906

HANEY, **Hannah J., Mrs.,** age 87, d. 48 Center St., Atlanta, Thurs. Sons: Henry P., T. W. Interred: Jacksonville, Fla. AG 4/22/1909

HANEY, **J. R.,** age 65, d. 901 Marietta St. Atlanta, Thurs. Interred: Hollywood. AG 1/7/1910

HANEY, **Levi,** age 71, d. 414 Central Railroad St. Atlanta. AG 8/1/1907

HANEY, **Lucy Elizabeth,** age 10 mos., dau. of Mr. and Mrs. C. F., and grdau. of Henry P. Haney, d. Wed. 111 Simpson St. Atlanta. Interred: Casey's Cemetery. AG 8/25/1910

HANGER, **J. Edward, Sr., Mrs.** d. Washington, D. C. 1132 Lamont St. Sons: J. E., Jr., Hebert B., Albert, former res. of Atlanta. AG 4/5/1909

HANIELTER, **Ida M., Miss,** age 65, d. Hapeville Thurs. Interred: Westview. AG 6/17/1910

HANNA, **George D.** of 99 Ormond St., Atlanta, d. Fri. Hagerstown, Md. while visiting relatives. Wife, several children. Funeral in Atlanta. AG 4/22/1910

HANNA, **R. M., Rev.** d. Chosea, Ala., Wed, age 786. Sons: W. H. of Chosea Springs, Ala. and R. L. of Louisiana. Bro: A. T. Hanna, Anniston, Ala. AG 11/8/1910

HANNAH, **J. B., Mrs.,** wife of J. B., Professor at Emory College, d. this morning, dau. of Pres. Elder C. E. Bowman. Son: James, age 4. Infant dau., father, mother, one bro. in London. AG 6/17/1907

HANNAH, J. P., Judge, d. Herod, Ga. Interred: Cedar Hill Cemetery 7/18. AG 7/19/1910

HANNERS, J. M., age 63, d. Columbus, Ga. 12/5. Interred: Smiths Station, Ala. AC 12/7/1905

HANSELL, Lelia, age 1, d. 430 Highland Ave. Atlanta. AG 6/22/1908

HANSELL, Mary, Mrs., mother of Capt. Hansell, asst secy of senate, d. Thomasville Mon. AG 8/14/1906

HANSELL, William A., Capt., of 23 Washington St., Atlanta, d. Fri. AG 1/3/1907

HANSELL, Wm A., Capt. bur-Oakland. Kin-Mr. & Mrs. Andrew J. Hansell, Mr. & Mrs. Lewellyn P. Hillyer, Mr. & Mrs. Wm A. Hansell, Jr., Mr. & Mrs. Francis M. Whittle, Capt. & Mrs. Robt M. Clayton, Mrs. J. H. Keiner, Dr. Wm Crenshaw. AG 1/7/1907

HANSFORD, Lena, Miss, res. of Atlanta, d. res. of sister, Mrs. W. B. Coleman, Talladega, Ala., Thurs. Interred: Talladega, Ala. AG 10/3/1908

HANSON, Eugene J., age 23, son of Col. and Mrs. J. T., d. Mon. 141 Lawton St., Atlanta. Interred: Westview. AG 6/4/1907

HANSON, Henry M., age 16, son of Mr. and Mrs. Peter, d. 31 Hale St. Atlanta, Sat. Interred: Westview. AG 3/21/1910

HANSON, Samuel d. 12/28 Charlotte, N. C. Cousin: Mrs. Philip Brown, Portland, Maine. Interred: Portland, Maine. AC 12/29/1905

HANUS, J. L. d. Tues. West Point, Ga., age 60. AG 12/17/1910

HANYE, infant of Mr. and Mrs. Robert, of Battle Hill, d. Interred: Hapeville, Ga. AG 8/4/1910

HARBIN, Easle Louise, age 1, d. 158 S. Boulevard. Atlanta. AG 12/8/1910

HARBIN, O. W., age 75, d. 9 Lattimer St. Atlanta. AG 11/30/1910

HARBUCK, Carl Franklin, age 7 mos., d. 390 E. Hunter St., Atlanta. AG 6/21/1906

HARBUCK, G. E., vet. fireman d. 100 Walker St., Atlanta, Sun. Interred: Utoy church yard. Ch: W. E. Harbuck, Waco, Tx.; Mrs. Minnie Bourn, Atlanta. Bros: Pink, John. AG 7/21/1908

HARBUCK, Minnie Lee funeral Mon. in Harley, Ga. Parents res. 75 Ponders Ave. AG 5/14/1906

HARBUCK, Willie, Mrs., age 33, d. 120 Courtland St. Atlanta. AG 7/24/1909

HARDAGE, Lou, Miss d. Marietta, Fri. Bros: Thomas, Kennesaw; Jessie, Rockmart; William, Marietta; James, Largo, Fla.; Robert, Tucker. Sisters: Mrs. Harriet James, Douglas Co., Miss Lucinda Hardage, Miss Mary Ware, Cobb Co. AG 5/21/1908

HARDAGE, Lucy F., age 70, d. Powder Spgs. Ch: Mrs. Z.B. Moon, Atlanta; Mrs. A.H. Culpepper, Homerville; Ethel, Powder Spgs; Robt, Charlotte, NC.; Otis M.; Garrett M., Powder Spgs; Wm T., Atlanta. Sis: Mrs. Martha Varner, Mrs. S. E. Boyd. AG 5/16/1910

HARDAWAY, E. Atkinson, age 29, d. Ft. McPherson, Ga. AG 2/1/1907

HARDEE, Elizabeth, Miss killed Boston, Mass. Interred: Savannah, Ga. AG 3/13/1908

HARDEMAN, Morgan Callaway, age 14, son of Mr. and Mrs. U. G. of Decatur, Ga., d. Sat. Mother, father, two sisters, four bros., survive. Interred: Oxford, Ga. AG 12/4/1909

HARDEMAN, Vernon, age 17, d. Eufaula, Ala. Mon. Two bros., four sisters. AG 9/22/1909

HARDEMAN, W. G., of Wadley, Ga. d. Thurs. Atlanta., age 40. Bro. is Repr. Hardeman of Louisville, Ga. AG 7/4/1908

HARDEN, Alex, colored, age 20, d. 267 Piedmont Ave. Atlanta. AG 12/24/1907

HARDER, K. F., infant, d. 23 Josephine Ave. Atlanta. AG 1/19/1910

HARDIN, Augustus D., Jr., age 11, son of Mr. and Mrs. Augustus D., 64 Bass St., Atlanta, accidentally killed by parlor *rifle. Interred: Central, S. C. AC 1/7/1905

HARDIN, Catherine, Mrs., age 80, d. Thurs. Greenville, Ga. Interred: Westview. AG 9/23/1910

HARDIN, F. C., Mrs. d. Atlanta Sun. Husband, 4 children survive. Interred: Harmony Grove, Ga. AG 5/14/1906

HARDIN, J. M., Mrs., age 59, d. 15 Bradley St., Atlanta, Fri. Interred: Red Oak, Ga. Husband, 5 children, survive. AG 12/7/1908

HARDIN, James, age 60, d. 57 Fulton St., Atlanta, Mon. Leaves dau. as only relative. AG 1/22/1909

HARDIN, Maggie, colored, age 44, d. 82 W. Merritts Ave. Atlanta. AG 12/8/1910

HARDIN, Marvin, age 27, bro. of Dr. L. Sage Hardin, d. 267 Capitol Ave. Atlanta. Interred: Blacksburg, S. C. AG 10/8/1907

HARDIN, Matilda, Mrs., age 60, d. 618 Chestnut St. Atlanta. AG 11/1/1910

HARDIN, Vannesse, Mrs., wife of R. S., age 48, d. 112 Richardson St., Atlanta. Interred: Hawkinsville, Ga. Husband, and one bro., L. D. Coley. AG 9/14/1908

HARDING, Oma, Miss, age 21, dau. of Mrs. Mary Harding of Sparta, Tenn. killed herself and H. A. Ballard, her sweetheart, Huntsville, Ala. 4/6. AC 4/7/1905

HARDSFIELD, T. M., Mrs. died Thurs., Riverside, Ga. Survived by husband and one child. AG 12/20/1906

HARDWICKE, L. W., age 79, of Atlanta d. Tues. 454 Bass St. Wife: Anna. Daus: Mrs. R. S. Pendle, Birmingham, Ala.; Mrs. L. Davenport; Misses Anna May and Mabel Hardwicke, Atlanta. Sons: W. L., L. O., E. A., G. A., Atlanta. AG 3/2/1910

HARDY, Annie, age 45, d. 130 Orme St. Atlanta. AG 10/25/1906

HARDY, Grady, age 6, son of Mr. and Mrs. J. B., funeral Fri. Interred: Indian Creek Church burying grounds. AG 6/17/1910

HARDY, J. R., Mrs., age 23, d. Wed. Atlanta. Husband, one child. Parents: Mr. and Mrs. W. H. Hardin. AG 6/30/1910

HARDY, McNease, farmer, age 78, farmer in south Atlanta, d. Sun. Interred: Maysville, Ga. AG 10/22/1906

HARE, Susan Bullard, Mrs. of Auburn, Ala. d., wid. of Joseph S., Lee Co. tax collector. Sons: Prof. Cliff, Auburn College; Fred, New Mexico; Crossland, Montgomery; Francis, Monroeville. Sisters, bros: Mrs. R. M. Greene, Mrs. W. S. Harris, Mrs. Elizabeth Wms, Opelika; Mrs. Sallie Richards, Weatherford, Tx.; Mrs. J.S.N. Davis, Woodbine, Ga.; Dr. C. C. Bullard, Opelika, Ala, Col. R. L. Bullard, Monterey, CA; Dan Bullard, Oakbowery. Bur: Auburn. AG 8/9/1910

HARE, W. F., Mrs., age 55, d. Grady Hospital, Atlanta. AG 9/3/1907

HARGETT, Milus, negro, of Harris Co., d. after placed in jail, Columbus, Ga. AG 9/1/1909

HARGIS, W. H., age 69, inmate of Confederate Soldiers' Home, Atlanta, d. Tues., C. B, Phillips Legion of Cavalry. Former res. of Bartow Co. AG 6/24/1909

HARGRAVES, Benjamin W., age 44, d. Thurs. 221 Whitehall St. Atlanta. Wife was Miss Frances Daniel of Wilson, N. C. Ch: Elizabeth, Frances, Helen, John Daniel, Benjamin W., Jr., William, James. Interred: Westview. AG 7/11/1907

HARGROVE, Harry, John Groover Burch killed him, Eastman, Ga. AG 12/27/1906

HARGROVE, James T. d. Habersham Co. 7/28, only son of Rev. J. W. Hargrove of Gaskill St., Atlanta. AG 7/29/1909

HARGROVE, M. F., Mrs. d. 1/16 res. of dau., Mrs. John A. Dunwody, Vineville Ave., Macon, Ga., age 76. Sons: S. J., H. M. Interred: Marshallville, Ga. AG 1/17/1910

HARION, Thomas, age 64, d. 6/4 E. Highlands, Columbus, Ga. AC 6/26/1905

HARKINS, J. C., Mrs. interred Calhoun, Ga. Three children survive. AG 5/21/1906

HARLAN, J. T., Mrs., age 32, d. 222 Sydney St., Atlanta, Sat. Interred: Clarksville, Tenn. AG 3/21/1910

HARLING, M. A., Mrs., age 49, d. 52 S. Jackson St., Atlanta, Mon. Interred: Johnston, S. C. Husband, two sons, one dau., survive. AG 12/6/1909

HARMEN, M., age 22, died at N. Butler Street, Atlanta. AG 12/10/1906

HARMON, Samuel S., age 6 mos., d. 306 Wylie St. Atlanta. AG 7/15/1909

HARMON, babe, age 8 mos., of Mr. and Mrs. J. R. found dead, Taylor Ave., Atlanta, Fri. Interred: Hillcrest. AG 1/9/1908

HARMOND, Richard E. d. Ft. Worth, Tex. Fri. Uncle: C. H. Langston, Atlanta. AG 11/2/1907

HARP, Alex, negro murdered by John Royal, negro, who was sentenced to life. Columbus, Ga. AG 11/29/1907

HARP, Henrietta J., Mrs., age 46, d. 11/14, 27 McDaniel St., Atlanta, Wed. Interred: Westview. AG 11/16/1910

HARP, LaFayette, Sheriff, age 75, at home near Cusseta, Chattahoochee Co. 11/8/1906. AG 11/9/1906

HARPER, Alice H., Miss, age 64, d. sister's res., Mrs. A. H. Walles, 26 Capitol Pl. Atlanta. Interred: Marlborough, Md. AG 4/30/1908

HARPER, Charles T., Jr., colored, age 14, d. 413 Auburn Ave. Atlanta. AG 11/23/1910

HARPER, D. C., Mrs., age 60, d. Brown Mill Rd. Atlanta. AG 10/6/1906

HARPER, Gussie P., Mrs., age 25, d. Atlanta Thurs. Husband: R. H., 455 Grant St., Atlanta. 2 children. Interred: South Bend Church yard. AG 12/1/1910

HARPER, Hattie J., Mrs., 56, d. 699 S. Pryor St. Atlanta. Mother: Mrs. J. W. Watson, Kissimee, Fla. Sons: N. C., J. M., of Atlanta. Bros: J. M. Watson, Kissimmee; Wm Watson, Tx. Sis: Mrs. W. Sears, Miss Sue Watson, Kissimmee. AG 12/8/1910

HARPER, J. A., Mrs., wife of Dr. J. A., d. 22 Windsor St., Atlanta, Mon. Interred: Oakland. AG 12/30/1907

HARPER, James G., age 28, d. Kimball House. Atlanta. AG 6/9/1910

HARPER, Joe, colored, age 5 mos., d. 15-A Horton St. Atlanta. AG 6/1/1907

HARPER, John convicted of killing Sheriff Keith of Chatsworth, Ga. to hang 5/29. AG 5/7/1908

HARPER, John, age 25, d. 10 Reed St. Atlanta. AG 3/8/1907

HARPER, Kate, colored, age 26, d. 313 N. Piedmont Ave. Atlanta. AG 12/10/1908

HARPER, M., colored, age 64, d. 142 Baker St. Atlanta. AG 2/22/1907

HARPER, M. A., Mrs., age 42, d. 22 Windsor St. Atlanta. AG 1/1/1908

HARPER, Mary J., Mrs., age 63, d. 5 Stonewall St. Atlanta. AG 8/24/1906

HARPER, Minnie, Mrs., wife of William A. of 84 Hendrix Ave., Atlanta, d. Wed., age 35. Husband, 4 children. Interred: Oakland. AG 7/12/1906

HARPER, Thomas J., age 68, Atlanta pioneer, d. 48 Formwalt St., Atlanta. Interred: Oakland. Wife was Miss Dora A. Morrell of Michigan. Sisters: Mrs. M. Moss, Covington, Ga.; Mrs. L. Cornwell, Griffin, Ga. AG 12/9/1907

HARPER, Tom of Atlanta found drowned by Sam Williams, negro, and cousin, Will Dillard, and two negroes, Dick Johnson and Bob Goodwin, 7 mi. below Montgomery, Ala. AG 3/27/1909

HARREL, Pauline Virginia, age 14 mos., dau. of Mr. and Mrs. C. M., d. 28 Mason Ave., Atlanta, Thurs. AG 12/17/1909

HARRELL, J. W., former legislature and state senator, d. near Cat Creek (Valdosta) Jan. 10. Wife, 8 ch. Aged abt 70. AC 1/12/1905

HARRELL, Mary, Mrs. of Cumming, Ga. d. Atlanta Sat. Interred: Westview. AG 5/2/1910

HARRELL, Porter, age 24, d. Atlanta Fri. Father: T. A., Louisville, Ga. AG 1/28/1910

HARRELL, W. P. Mrs. Sallie Freeney, Eastman, Ga. found guilty of his murder. AG 5/24/1907

HARRELL, W. P. of Eastman, Ga. killed some mos. ago by Mrs. Sallie Freeney. AG 7/17/1907

HARRELL, W. P., citizen of Dodge Co. shot and killed Sat. by Mrs. Sallie Freeney. Leaves wife, several children. AG 3/11/1907

HARRINGTON, J. W., Mrs., age 60, Fri., d. E. Pt. Ch: Mrs. R. P. Thompson, W. J. Malone, Rome, Ga. Interment: College Park cemetery. AG 11/9/1906

HARRINGTON, James E., age 28, d. North Tower, Sou. RR. Atlanta. AG 7/8/1907

HARRINGTON, Josie F., Mrs., age 46, d. 375 Capitol Ave. Atlanta. AG 11/1/1909

HARRINGTON, N. T., age 38, d. Atlanta Mon. Interred: Duluth, Ga. AG 3/9/1910

HARRIS, A. G., Mrs., age 48 d. AG 4/12/1910

HARRIS, Abe, colored, age 48, d. 150 E. Cain St. Atlanta. AG 2/14/1908

HARRIS, Albert, colored, age 8 mos., d. 1 Cooks alley. Atlanta. AG 9/2/1909

HARRIS, Andrew, colored, age 45, d. 125 Howell St. Atlanta. AG 3/28/1907

HARRIS, Annie B., age 11, dau. of Mr. and Mrs. J. M., d. Sat. 14 English Ave. Atlanta. Interred: Caseys. AG 8/5/1907

HARRIS, Belle Holmes, Miss of Winterville, Ga. (near Athens) d. sister's home, Mrs. J. H. Stone, Lumpkin St. Leaves two bros., four sisters. AG 8/11/1908

HARRIS, Burdell, colored, age 28, d. Jacksonville, Fla. AG 10/1/1908

HARRIS, Carter B., Capt., age 65, bro. of late Pres., Benjamin, d. Murfreesboro, Tenn. Confed. Vet. Wife. 1 dau. 1 son. AC 12/9/1905

HARRIS, Charles, colored, age 52, d. 201 E. Harris St. Atlanta. AG 3/25/1907

HARRIS, Charles, colored, age 7 mos., d. 366 Sims St. Atlanta. AG 4/27/1907

HARRIS, Charles A. of Cuthbert, Ga. d. 3/2. Ch: Mesdames L. C. Toombs and A. C. Moye, C. S., T. R. and J. W. Harris, all of Cuthbert. Was 73 in Jan. AC 3/4/1905

HARRIS, Charlie, negro lynched at Pearson, Ga. by mob after murdering Harden Pearson. AG 5/7/1907

HARRIS, Clara J., Miss d. Sat. Atlanta. Interred: Stone Mtn, Ga. AG 10/24/1910

HARRIS, E. A., Mrs. of Talbotton, Ga. d. 311 Whitehall St., Atlanta, Fri., wife of E. A. Interred: Talbotton, Ga. AG 1/10/1908

HARRIS, Edward, cotton mill man, formerly of Columbia, S. C. murdered by Frank Rossi and wife, Grace Rossi, 8/14. AG 1/20/1910

HARRIS, Elizabeth, Mrs., age 63, wid. of Fleming
Harris, Confed. Soldier d. Tues. home of dau., Mrs. Harrison, Ft. McPherson. AG 9/11/1906

HARRIS, Elizabeth, age 1, d. 16 DeGress Ave. Atlanta. AG 8/14/1907

HARRIS, Elizabeth, Mrs. funeral Sun. Interred: Hollywood. AG 1/19/1907

HARRIS, Elliot, age 38, d. Sun. Macon Hospital. Bros: E. B., C. H., T. B. and Howell Harris of Macon. Leaves wife, 2 children. Interred: Rose Hill. AG 9/2/1907

HARRIS, Estelle, age 1 mo., d. 132 Bellwood Ave. Atlanta. AG 6/18/1907

HARRIS, Eugene, age 12, d. 279 Chapel St. Atlanta. AG 9/22/1910

HARRIS, Francis, colored, age 4 mos., d. 278 Rhodes St. Atlanta. AG 8/19/1908

HARRIS, Frank, negro porter for J. E. Simms Grocery, hit on head by wty from 4th story of Muscogee Mills, Columbus. AG 9/29/1906

HARRIS, G. A., age 3, d. 52 Formwalt St. Atlanta. AG 2/24/1908

HARRIS, Hannah L., Mrs., wife of L., d. 2/13, 1025 First Ave., Columbus, Ga. AC 2/15/1905

HARRIS, Harriet, colored, age 72, d. 3 Wilson St. Atlanta. AG 10/18/1909

HARRIS, Harriett, colored, age 54, d. 17 Auburn Ave. Atlanta. AG 9/17/1907

HARRIS, Henry, colored, age 19, d. rear of 176 E. Harris St. Atlanta. AG 6/8/1907

HARRIS, Henry, colored, age 8 days, d. 105 S. Bell St. Atlanta. AG 9/1/1908

HARRIS, Homer, Mrs., wife of Superintendent Harris of co. farm, d. Jackson, Ga., Sat. 4 children, father, several bros, sisters, husband, survive. AG 10/11/1910

HARRIS, Horace, colored, age 2, d. 10 Solomon St. Atlanta. AG 3/3/1909

HARRIS, I. M., Mrs. d. Tues. Atlanta. Interred: Westview. AG 5/1/1907

HARRIS, J., colored, age 20, d. 389 E. Hunter St. Atlanta. AG 2/8/1907

HARRIS, J. J., age 74, d. Alms House, Atlanta. AG 5/11/1910

HARRIS, James, colored, age 82, d. 32 Tyler St. Atlanta, 10/27. AG 10/28/1910

HARRIS, J. L., Dr., former Atlanta physician, d. Rome, Ga. Fri., where interred. AG 10/21/1910

HARRIS, Jane E., Mrs., age 83, d. 102 Forrest Ave. Atlanta. AG 4/22/1909

HARRIS, Joel Chandler left no LWT. Estate turned over to Mrs. Harris, admx. Leaves valuable property in West End. He was known as "Uncle Remus". Sons: Julian, Lucien, Joel, Jr. Dau: Evelyn. AG 7/7/1908

HARRIS, Joseph D., age 3 mos., young son of Mr. and Mrs. G. S. Harris, d. Thurs. 131 Griffin St., Atlanta. Interred: Hollywood. AG 4/10/1907

HARRIS, Josephine, age 76, died at Home for Incurables. AG 11/22/1906

HARRIS, Kate, Mrs., age 25, d. Atlanta. AG 3/27/1909

HARRIS, Lizzie, colored, age 34, d. 70-A Fort St. Atlanta. AG 4/13/1909

HARRIS, Lizzie, colored, age 60, d. 150 E. Cain St. Atlanta. AG 3/8/1909

HARRIS, Lundy, Dr. suicide Sun., Cartersville, Ga. Interred: Oxford, Ga. Dau: Faith. Wife survives. AG 9/20/1910

HARRIS, M. J., Mrs., age 69, d. Presbyterian Hospital. Atlanta. AG 5/23/1907

HARRIS, Mary, colored, age 33, d. Grady Hospital. Atlanta. AG 8/29/1907

HARRIS, Mary E., Mrs., age 56, d. East Point Mon. Husband, several children. Interred: Mt. Zion. AG 8/14/1906

HARRIS, Matt, Mrs., age 72, d. Monroe, Ga. AG 10/13/1908

HARRIS, Nora, colored, age 30, d. 12 Croney's alley. Atlanta. AG 9/22/1908

HARRIS, Norval T., age 21, found dead from bullet in temple, Washington, Ga. Woman, Diasy, suspected. AG 8/29/1910

HARRIS, Rachel, colored, age 57, d. 454 Smith St. Atlanta. AG 12/29/1908

HARRIS, Rena, Miss, age 32, d. New York City. AG 11/17/1907

HARRIS, Ruby, inf. dau. of Mr. and Mrs. J. L., d. 107 Jefferson St. Atlanta Sat. Interred: Casey's Cemetery. AG 5/9/1908

HARRIS, S. A., Mrs., age 72, d. McDonough Rd. Sun. Son: J. F. Harris of E. Atlanta. Dau: Mrs. Mamie Granade of Conyers. AG 1/27/1908

HARRIS, Samuel, colored, age 3 weeks, d. rear of 94 Nelson St. Atlanta. AG 1/31/1908

HARRIS, Sarah, Mrs., age 76, d. res. of dau., Mrs. H. C. King, 102 N. Butler St., Atlanta, Tues. Dau: Mrs. M. L. Queen. 3 granddaus: Mrs. J. B. Webb, Mrs. Charles Chisholm, Miss Clara Miller. Interred: Oakland. AG 6/22/1910

HARRIS, Sheppard, negro butler, shot and killed by Robert Wilkes. Wilkes given 10 yrs. (He was negro butler of C. T. Ladson). AG 9/21/1910

HARRIS, Solomon, age 16, found dead in pine thicket from gunshot wounds. Missing since Wed. Atlanta. AG 12/23/1907

HARRIS, Stoneman, colored, age 39, d. Howell Station. Atlanta. AG 12/4/1908

HARRIS, T. L., Mrs. d. Wrightsville, Ga. Mon. Husband, 7 children. AG 5/31/1910

HARRIS, Thomas, age 53, d. 564 Decatur St. Atlanta. AG 4/2/1910

HARRIS, Tillie, Mrs. of Waycross d. 6/13. Son: Willie Joe, age 14. Her father resides Homerville. Interred: Homerville, Ga. AG 6/15/1909

HARRIS, Tom, negro, d. from gunshot wounds in Columbus, Ga. AG 10/2/1907

HARRIS, W. H., age 72, d. Atlanta, res. of dau., Mrs. George H. Fauss, 640 N. Boulevard, Wed. Son: W. H., Jr. Daus: Mrs. Wynie Graves, Atlanta; Mrs. James H. Taylor, Hawkinsville; Miss Myrtle Harris, Munsey, Ind. AG 3/9/1910

HARRIS, Waverly H., age 26, d. Jonesboro, Ga. Interred: Sewanee, Ga. AG 10/14/1907

HARRIS, Will, colored, age 42, d. 24 Brooks alley. Atlanta. AG 10/23/1907

HARRIS, Will killed by train Sat. Wife, 5 children. Interred: Canton. AG 7/23/1906

HARRIS, Willie, colored, age 22, d. Haynes St. Atlanta. AG 1/28/1908

HARRIS, infant of Mr. and Mrs. J. L., d. 107 Jefferson St., Atlanta, Fri. Interred: Caseys. AG 2/7/1908

HARRISON, Glenn F., age 25, d. 33 Stonewall St. Atlanta. AG 3/18/1909

HARRISON, Hazel, age 15 mos. dau. of Mr. and Mrs. N. C., d. 769 Ash St., Atlanta, Mon. AG 8/20/1907

HARRISON, J. P., inf. of Mr. and Mrs. George W., d. Mon. E. Point, Ga. AG 5/21/1910

HARRISON, John A., age 44, d. 326 Woodward Ave. Atlanta, Tues. Interment: Lawrenceville. AG 8/22/1906

HARRISON, John D. d. Winder, Ga. Sat. AG 5/8/1906

HARRISON, John W. of Atlanta d. Tampa, Fla. He was b. Va. and md. Miss Dulsy Ruffin of Hillsboro, N. C., a sister of Mrs. C. L. Pettigrew, 522 N. Boulevard, Atlanta. AG 3/28/1907

HARRISON, Josh, age 60, d. Thurs. 26 Mechanic St., Atlanta. Interred: Smyrna. AG 1/11/1907

HARRISON, Mildred, dau. of Z. D., Jr., d. Tues. E. Point, Ga. Interred: Oakland. AG 5/30/1906

HARRISON, Pearl, Mrs., age 39, d. 11 Loomis Ave. Atlanta. AG 12/2/1909

HARRISON, Randolph, Mrs. killed in Griffin cyclone. AG 4/25/1908

HARRISON, Ruby C., age 2, d. 151 Emmett St. Atlanta. AG 11/25/1906

HARRISON, Ruth, Miss, age 19, d. Grady Hospital. Atlanta. AG 8/4/1906

HARRISON, S. P., Mrs., age 35, d. Hapeville, Ga. Fri. Husband, 3 small children. Interred: Mt. Zion Church yard. AG 4/21/1910

HARRISON, Sarah, Mrs., age 43, d. 87 Martin St. Atlanta. AG 4/10/1907

HARRISON, William Edgar, age 5, d. Thurs. Interred: Casey's Cemetery. AG 5/10/1906

HARRISON, Ladosia V., wife of James B., d. 7/5. run down, killed by S. Decatur rr car. Lawsuit mentioned. Two sons, five daus. AG 7/12/1907

HARRISON, W. B., Mrs., 55, d. Lavonia 1/25 dau. of Saml J. Trible. Bros: Col. Saml J., Athens; G. W., Calhoun & J. A. Trible. Sis: Mrs. A. W. Martin; Mrs. W. T. Adams. Ch: Mrs. W. H. Addington; Mrs. J. P. Sims, James; Walter N., Lucy. AG 1/25/1910

HART, Charles W., age 28, d. 193 Glennwood Ave. Atlanta Tues. Wife, one child. Parents: Mr. and Mrs. S. Hart. One bro., three sisters. Interred: Oakland. AG 6/30/1909

HART, E. P., Mrs.,a ge 34, d. Atlanta Sat., wife of W. S., of 1292 Marietta St., Atlanta. Interred: Chattanooga. AG 11/7/1910

HART, Edna P., Mrs., age 34, d. Marietta St. Atlanta. AG 11/8/1910

HART, Eula, Miss, age 22, d. Mon. father's res., Rev. J. M. Hart, College Park. Interred: Antioch Church yard. AG 6/27/1910

HART, Glenn, age 4 mos., d. 192 Stewart Ave. Atlanta. AG 4/19/1907

HART, Irma Lee, age two, dau. of Mr. and Mrs. Tyre Hart, d. Mon. 192 Sgewart Ave. Atlanta. Interred: Dallas. AG 5/7/1907

HART, Jesse D., age 12, d. Atlanta. AG 3/10/1909

HART, young son of Alderman and Mrs. Jesse B. Hart died today, Macon. AG 7/17/1906

HARTFORD, E., age 56, of 62 Rinehardt St., Atlanta, d. Fri. Grady Hospital, age 62. Wife. Interred: Westview. AG 8/18/1906

HARTFORD, Lee, age 4 mos., one of twins, of Mr. and Mrs. R. L., d. 124 W. Harris St., Atlanta, Thurs. Interred: Hollywood. AG 5/12/1910

HARTLEY, Henry killed by Southern train Wed., Macon. Interred: Macon. Relatives not found. AG 10/5/1907

HARTLINE, M. E., Mrs. d. age 73 Chattnooga, Tenn. Sons: M. J. Hartline of Kensington, Ga., M. M. Hartline, of Atlanta; three others living in Atlanta and Oklahoma. AG 1/28/1908

HARTMAYER, Robert, age 50, d. 5/16 Atlanta. AC 5/17/1905

HARVELL, Audrey, age 4 yrs., dau. of Mr. and Mrs. W., d. 24 Williams St., Atlanta, Sat. Interred: Greenwood. AG 5/9/1910

HARVELL, William, colored, age 71, d. 36 Battle St. Atlanta. AG 3/27/1909

HARVEY, Josephine, Mrs., age 62, wife of George S., d. 214 E. Fair St. Atlanta. 6 children. Interred: Sylvester, Ga. AG 11/7/1910

HARVEY, Cal, colored, d. 80 Reed St. Atlanta. AG 8/11/1908

HARVIL, Claude, inf. dau. of Mr. and Mrs. J. J., d. Sun. res. of parents, 67 Woodward Ave. Atlanta. AG 4/30/1906

HARWELL, E. M., Rev., age 85, d. dau.'s res., Mrs. R. F. Youngblood, 177 Mills St., Atlanta, Fri. Interred: Comer, Ga. Ag 6/22/1908

HARWELL, J. E., Mrs., age 33, d. res. of Mrs. W. A. Coppedge, 365 Grant St., Atlanta. She was dau. of late W. A. Wilson. Husband survives. Interred: Wilson church, Adamsville, Ga. AG 4/24/1907

HARWELL, John M., Capt., Confed. Veteran d. Atlanta 4/30. Interred: Oakland. AC 5/1/1905

HARWELL, Lizzie, Mrs., age 32, d. 365 Grant Ave. Atlanta. AG 4/26/1907

HARWELL, Manning McCord, infant son of Mr. and Mrs. W. A., d. Sun. 168 E. Hunter St., Atlanta. Interred: Westview. AG 5/28/1907

HARWELL, Mathis, negro, dropped dead Wed. Atlanta. AG 5/12/1909

HARWELL, Mattie, Mrs., wife of W. E., of Hayston, Ga., d. 4/19. Ch: John R., Atlanta; Thomas, Washington; Mrs. C. O. Osborn, Mansfield; Grady; Ellen. AC 4/20/1905

HARWELL, Myddleton P. shot and killed. Wife lives Summerville, Ga. AC 3/27/1905

HARWOOD, Mary, Mrs., age 62 of 71 Curran St., Atlanta, d. Fri. AG 4/2/1909

HASLETT, Merta, age 17 mos., only child of W. R., d. 39 W. Linden St., Atlanta, Tues. Interred: Westview. AG 6/9/1908

HASLEY, Joe, age 17, d. Tues., 6 Savannah St., Atlanta. Interred: Sylvester cemetery. AG 9/11/1907

HASSON, Henry Clay d. Atlanta. Interred: Oakland. AG 10/3/1910

HASTEY, Emily, Mrs., wife of A. J., age 68, d. 5th Ave., Columbus, Ga., Jan. 21. AC 1/23/1905

HASTINGS, C. E., Jrs., infant son of Mr. and Mrs. C. E. Hastings, d. Mon. 144 Wylie St. Atlanta. Interred: Sylvester cemetery. AG 6/25/1907

HASTINGS, Carrie Louise, inf. dau. of Mr. and Mrs. L. M., of E. Pt., Ga., d. Thurs. Interred: LaGrange, Ga.

HASTY, Callie, Mrs., age 19, d. 975 E. Fair St., Atlanta, Wed. Interred: Westview. Husband, C. A. Hasty. Parents: Mr. and Mrs. C. H. Carter. AG 3/11/1909

HASTY, Mary Ethel, age 8 mos., d. 64 Fulton Terrace, Atlanta. AG 10/18/1909

HASTY, A., colored, age 35, died at Formwalt Street, Atlanta. AG 11/19/1906

HATCELL, Lula, colored, age 26, d. Middlebrooks Rd. Atlanta. AG 11/30/1910

HATCHER, J. F. d. Harlem, Ga. 11/11. AC 11/13/1905

HATCHER, Margaret P., age 3, d. 29 Luckie St. Atlanta. AG 12/29/1908

HATCHER, Mary E., Mrs., wife of Harvey, age 61, d. 92 Luckie St. Atlanta. Interred: Westview. AG 8/17/1908

HATCHER, Reuben d. 2/12 Hawkinsville, Ga. AC 2/14/1905

HATCHER, W. A., farmer, d. 8 mi. s. of Adrain, Ga., killed accidentally by wife. AG 10/11/1907

HATCHER, Harvey b. 1837 Bedford Co. Va. s. of Henry & Mary Ann d. 1/15 Beaufort, SC. m. Franklin Co. Va. 11/30/1869 Pattie L.(d. 11/21/1881) m. 12/30/1885 Murfreesboro, Mrs. Mary Myers. Ch: Harvey, Jr.; Frances Hall, Mobile. AC 1/16/1905

HATHCOCK, Edward, age 59, d. Sat. Howell Mill Rd., Atlanta. Interred: Family burial ground. AG 8/12/1907

HATHCOCK, William N., age 76, d. 160 Whitehall Terrace, Atlanta, Mon. Bros: I. S., M. L., J. L., L. E. and W. C. AG 5/9/1910

HAUNSON, Eugene J., age 22, d. Mon. res. of parents, Mr. and Mrs. J. T. Haunson, 241 Lawson St., Atlanta. Interred: Westview. AG 6/5/1907

HAUSE, E. V. P., Confederate veteran, d. Mon. at Soldiers' Home, Atlanta. Interred: Westview. AG 7/10/1907

HAUSER, George, age 69, Confederate Veteran, d. Athens. Wife, two children, Emil Hauser of Wadley and Mrs. Hinton Booth of Statesboro. AG -/28/1908

HAUSMAN, Paul, Mrs., age 31, d. 457 Washington St. Atlanta, Mon. Husband, 6 yr. old son. Her bro. in N.Y. AG 8/7/1906

HAVE, J. V., colored, age 7 mos., d. 178 E. Ellis St. Atlanta. AG 10/7/1907

HAVERTY, James J., nephew of James J. of Rhodes-Haverty Co., Atlanta, and son of late Michael Haverty, d. N.Y. last Wed., age 33. Mother: Mrs. Michael Haverty of 191 S. Forsyth St., Atlanta. Body retd to Atlanta. AG 1/25/1908

HAVERTY, Michael d. Spring of 1907. AG 1/25/1908

HAWES, Ila, Mrs. of 681 Marietta St., Atlanta, committed suicide Thurs. Husband: B. H. Hawes. Child: Lillie Belle. Her mother: Mrs. G. W. Wood. AG 9/6/1906

HAWES, Samuel, Mrs. d. Bainbridge, Ga. 6/28. Husband, several children. AG 6/29/1909

HAWK, Mary, negro, shot and killed by Clarence Singleton, negro, Thurs. who then committed suicide. AG 5/25/1906

HAWKES, Ben J., age 65, d. Austin, Tx. AG 11/5/1910

HAWKES, William M. funeral Sun. Americus, Ga. AG 11/21/1910

HAWKINS, A. S. of Dalton, Ga. d. Fri. He came from Murray Co. 4 yrs. ago. 9 children. Wife died 9/1910. AG 11/7/1910

HAWKINS, B. B. d. 286 Crumley St., Atlanta. Interred: Westview. AG 6/14/1906

HAWKINS, F. P., Mrs., age 32, d. 11/5 Milledgeville, Ga. Husband, several children. AG 11/5/1910

HAWKINS, Fred, son of Jere, Gainesville murdered by Henry E. Cagle. AG 8/27/1906

HAWKINS, Henry, colored, age 72, d. 18 Lyons Ave. Atlanta. AG 12/24/1907

HAWKINS, J. E B., age 11, d. 29 Luckie St. Atlanta. AG 8/24/1908

HAWKINS, J. G., age 57, d. Covington Rd. Atlanta. AG 4/29/1909

HAWKINS, Lois Lee, age 1 mo., dau. of Mr. and Mrs. J. W., d. 199 Carter St., Atlanta. Interred Westview. AG 10/14/1907

HAWKINS, Maggie, colored, age 45, d. 256 Currier St. Atlanta. AG 7/20/1907

HAWKINS, Martha, colored, age 29, d. 18 Lyons St. Atlanta. AG 10/26/1907

HAWKINS, Mary, Mrs., age 65, d. 236 S. Pryor St. Atlanta. AG 2/24/1910

HAWKINS, Nathan, ex-Gov., d. 4/27 Nashville, Tenn., age 83. He was a native of Ky. AC 4/28/1905

HAWKINS, Samuel Hugh d. 5/26 Americus, Ga. Wife, 4 daus., 2 sons: William E., Atlanta. Interred: Oak Grove Cemetery. AC 5/28/1905

HAWKINS, T. H., Mrs., 44, of Athens, d. Atlanta. Son: T. H., Jr. Old res., "Cherokee Hall", Oglethorpe Co. 3 sis., 1 bro: Mrs. T. B. Sutton, Wilkes Co.; Mrs. J. R. Crane, Athens; Mrs. James H. Hall, Arnoldsville; R. W. Davis, Winterville. AG 8/5/1910

HAWKINS, Vina, Mrs., wife of Allen, bur. yesterday St. Lukes cemetery, Prosperity, S. C. AG 9/19/1906

HAWKINS, W. H., Mrs., age 65, d. S. Pryor St., Atlanta, Tues. Husband. 5 ch: Mrs. R. A. Clark, Mrs. D. B. Sheldon, Judge K. J. Hawkins, W. H. and B. H. Hawkins. AG 2/23/1910

HAWKLAND, Annie, Mrs. of Social Circle Funeral 2/18. From Norway 20 yrs. ago to Mass., then Jonesboro, then E. Pt., then Social Circle, Ga. Interred: Westview. Husband: Sam. Son-in-law: James Irwin, 665 E. Fair St. Atlanta. AC 2/19/1905

HAWLEY, Joseph, age 78, b. Stewartsville, N. C., former Connecticut Senator, d. 3/18. Leaves 3 daus. AC 3/18/1905

HAWTHORN, A. E. d. Nashville, Tenn. Wife, 2 children, 5 sisters, Mrs. E. A. McCarthy, Miss.; Mrs. James Palmer, Nashville; Mrs. M. H. Chisolm; Mrs. J. P. Heath, Atlanta; Mrs. Homer F. George, Decatur, Ga. AG 3/11/1908

HAYDEN, Early suicide Jasper Co., Ga. 2/23. Interred: Monticello, Ga. Res. of Oxford many yrs. AC 2/25/1905

HAYDIN, Nelson, colored, age 28, d. Blondtown, Ga. AG 3/4/1908

HAYES, Emma, colored, age 45, d. 8 Bradley Ave. Atlanta. AG 7/8/1907

HAYES, Lillie, Mrs., age 32, d. Woodward Ave. and Boulevard. Atlanta. Two small children. Interred: Chamblee, Ga. AG 2/26/1908

HAYES, Luther B., age 28, d. 204 Courtland St. Atlanta. AG 9/2/1909

HAYES, Richard, age abt 50, suicide, on W. W. Timmons' plantation, 2 miles N. of Tifton, Ga. Leaves wife, 5 children. AG 9/25/1907

HAYES, T. E., age 49, d. near Lakewood Heights, Ga. Mon. AG 1/20/1908

HAYES, Thomas G., former Atlantan, d. New Orleans, newspaper man with Daily News. AG 1/5/1907

HAYES, Thomas, age 35, d. Tues. Dalton, Ga. Interred: Deep Springs Cemetery. AG 6/30/1910

HAYES, Vernie, Mrs., age 22, d. 92 Davis St., Atlanta, Sat. Interred: Jonesboro, Ga. AG 5/9/1910

HAYES, Shuly, colored, age 20, died 417 Foundry St. Atlanta. AG 12/26/1906

HAYGOOD, Josephine, colored, age 6 mos., d. 11 Chestnut St. Atlanta. AG 2/8/1909

HAYGOOD, Oscar, colored, age 25, d. 237 Lee St. Atlanta. AG 8/14/1907

HAYNES, Claude, age 13, d. E. Point, Ga., Sun. Parents, two bros., one sister. Interred: Buford, Ga. AG 7/13/1908

HAYNES, George W., age 69, d. 13 Willow St. Atlanta. Sons: J. J., G. W., Jr., W. E., and J. H. Daus: Mrs. C. J. Johnson, Mrs. W. H. McDaniel, Miss Lillie Haynes. Interred: Decatur, Ga. AG 4/20/1910

HAYNES, Joseph, colored, age 17, d. 50 Oakland Ave. Atlanta. AG 3/25/1907

HAYNES, S. F., former Atlanta, d. Huntsville, Ala. 2/14. AG 2/15/1910

HAYNES, Julian L., 8 mos. son of Mr. & Mrs. Wm G., d. home of A. D. Adair, 94 Washington St. Atlanta. Haynes came Atlanta from Columbia, S. C. 6/8 to attend funeral of Capt. John A. Grant, father of Mrs. Haynes. Bur: Westview. AG 6/29/1907

HAYNIE, T. F., colored, age 10 mos., d. 186 Irwin St. Atlanta. AG 10/9/1907

HAYS, Anna Hill, Mrs., age 70, formerly of Washington, D. C., d. Wed. res. of dau., Mrs. William Gray Obear, 196-A Capitol Ave., Atlanta. Interred: Madison, Ga. AG 5/31/1910

HAYS, Annie, colored, age 28, d. 32 Garibaldi St. Atlanta. AG 12/28/1910

HAYS, Henry, colored, age 38, d. 15 Piedmont Ave. Atlanta. AG 8/7/1908

HAYS, J. L., Hon. d. 5/22 Newton Co., age 65, Confed. Vet. Wife, one son. Interred: Family Cemetery near Hayston, Ga. AC 5/23/1905

HAYSFIELD, M., Mrs., age 62, d. Griffin, Ga. AG 12/14/1909

HAZARD, Manly drowned Tallulah Falls, funeral 27 Baltimore block, Atlanta, Thurs. Interred: Westview. AG 8/12/1909

HAZELRIGS, Dolly, Miss d. 69 Plum St., Atlanta, Sun. Interred: Tucker, Ga. Father, 2 bros, 2 sisters. AG 8/2/1909

HAZLIP, T. J. of Putnam Co. d. near Jacksonville, Fla., fell from moving train. Leaves father. AG 11/9/1907

HAZZARD, Frank, age 71, of Bibb Co., Ga., d. Sun. at Soldiers' Home, Atlanta. Interred: Westview. Served in Co. K, 12th, Ga. Regt. AG 7/29/1907

HEAD, Emily, dau. of Mr. and Mrs. Hugh, d. Columbia, S. C. Wed. Funeral: Mr. and Mrs. E. H. LeVert, 26 Dixie Ave., Inman Park, Atlanta. Interred: Oakland. AG 11/3/1908

HEAD, J. F., Mrs. of E. Point d. Wed. Interred: Utoy Cemetery. Two sons, two daus, husband. AG 1/13/1910

HEAD, J. W., age 43, d. 61 Wymen St. Atlanta. AG 2/15/1909

HEAD, Martha, Mrs., age 87, d. Hapeville, Ga. Tues. Interred: Mt. Zion Church. AG 6/8/1910

HEAD, Sallie C., Mrs., age 71, d. 177 Cherokee Ave. Atlanta. Interred: Tunnel Hill, Ga. AG 3/3/1908

HEAD, W. K. Polk d. 3/19, age 59, Dahlonega, Ga. AC 3/22/1905

HEARD Cencia, colored, age 50, d. 77-B Bell St. Atlanta. AG 12/30/1908

HEARD, E. J., Mrs., age 64, d. res. of son, A. A. Webb, Lakewood Heights, Atlanta, Thurs. One son, four bros., two sisters, survive. AG 12/24/1909

HEARD, Henry, colored, age 60, d. 4 Raines row. Atlanta. AG 7/24/1909

HEARD, J. E., age 34, d. Wed. 317 W. Third St. Atlanta. Interred: Family burying ground. AG 1/12/1910

HEARD, J. G., age 34, d. Atlanta Wed., 317 W. Third St. Interred: Family burying ground. AG 1/13/1910

HEARD, Mamie, colored, age 25, d. rear of 313 Spring St. Atlanta. AG 3/5/1908

HEARD, S., Miss, age 39, d.. her res. in East Point (Atlanta) Wed. Interred: Mt. Olive. AG 1/3/1907

HEARD, J. L., Policeman, killed 9/24/1906 by Wiley Brooks, negro, arrested Brownsville. AG 12/4/1906

HEARTSILL, A. L., Mrs., age 67, d. res. of dau., Mrs. John Warmack, Ridgedale, Tenn. She was wife of A. L. Heartsill of Cleveland and mother of B. L. Heartsill, Mrs. George W. Brown, nashville, Mrs. John Warmack, Ridgedale. AG 12/17/1909

HEATH, John, colored, age 20, d. 76 Old Wheat St. Atlanta. AG 4/10/1908

HEATH, Mattie, age 29, d. 323 Fulton St. Atlanta. AG 4/28/1908

HEATH, Natalie, age 20 mos., son of Mr. and Mrs. A. T., d. 22 Howell P., Atlanta, Wed. Funeral res. of grandparents: Col. and Mrs. Albert Howell, 283 Gordon St., Atlanta. Interred: Westview. AG 7/9/1908

HEATH, W. T., age 62, d. Tues. Clarkston, Ga. Interred: Norwood, Ga. Two sons, one dau. AG 4/17/1907

HEATH, Will, colored, age 28, d. N. Butler St. Atlanta. AG 3/3/1909

HEATH, William Austell, age 56, former res. of Atlanta, d. Fri. his home Columbia, S. C. Nephew of Gen. Albert Austell of Atlanta. AG 12/10/1910

HEDRICK, T. L., age 65, d. Atlanta. Interred: Tanners church yard. AG 12/23/1907

HEERY, W. H., age 32, d. Fri. 16 1/2 Edgewood Ave. Atlanta. Interred: Oakland. AG 10/20/1906

HEERY, Neal, son of Mr. and Mrs. C. W. d. 143 Spring St. Atlanta. Interred: Westview. AG 6/1/1908

HEFNER, Floyd, age 19, d. 239 Capitol Ave. Atlanta. AG 12/4/1909

HEGMAN, J. M. d. Atlanta 7/21. Interred: Westview Cemetery. AG 7/30/1909

HEINBERG, Frieda, Mrs., age 73, d. Sun. Atlanta. Interred: Oakland. AG 12/13/1909

HEINSOHN, T. K.. Sylvester, Ga., 12/17/. Committed suicide yesterday. Survived by wife, one child,
a boy 12 yrs old. AG 12/17/1906

HEIRNDEN, Lucile, age 16 mos., dau. of Mr. and Mrs. Virgil, d. 1083 Marietta St., Atlanta, Thurs. Interred: Highland Cemetery. AG 7/28/1910

HELD, Mary H., Mrs., age 47, d. Wed. Atlanta. Son: Benjamin. Interred: Anniston, Ala. AG 10/27/1909

HELLER, Clara,a ge 41, d. 520 Washington St. Atlanta. AG 3/28/1910

HELLIG, John d. Grady Hospital Atlanta Wed. Interred: Brooklyn N. Y. Ammunition man for wild west show. AG 10/15/1908

HELM, Louis, colored, age 44, d. 276 Meldrum St. Atlanta. AG 7/1/1907

HELMS, Dock of Rockdale Co., d. 3/12, former res. of Atlanta. Wife, 5 children. Relatives: Hon. Tobe Helms, Conyers, Ga. and Robert Helms of Henry Co. Interred: Union Methodist Church, Rockdale Co. AG 3/10/1910

HELMS, L. A., age 79, d. Macon, Ga. AG 2/14/1910

HEMBREE, Lois, Mrs., age 19, wife of R. L., and dau. of Mr. and Mrs. H. H. Walker, d. parents res., 178 McDaniel St., Atlanta, Wed. Interred: Westview. AG 10/9/1907

HEMPHILL, C. H., age 25, d. 101 N. Butler St. Atlanta. AG 11/17/1907

HEMPHILL, H. W., age 64, of Toccoa, Ga., d. res. of N. W. Williams, 256 Luckie St., Atlanta, Thurs. Interred: Toccoa. AG 8/27/1908

HEMPHILL, L. A., Mrs., age 47, d. 49 Pickett St. Atlanta. Four children. AG 9/2/1909

HEMPHILL, Mabel Hillyer, Mrs., age 49, d. 514 Peachtree St. Atlanta. AG 11/11/1909

HENAGAN, Kate, Mrs., age 60, d. College Park, Ga. AG 12/28/1910

HENDERSON, infant of Josie Henderson, age 9 mos., d. 320 Mangum St. Atlanta. AG 10/25/1900

HENDERSON John J., age 44, d. 44, d. 24 Chapel St. Atlanta. Wife: Mrs. Floy Henderson, two children, survive. Interred: Memphis, Tenn. AG 7/26/1907

HENDERSON, A. S. d. Sat. res. of son, Clifford, Decatur, Ala. Bro: W. B., Decatur. Native of Knoxville, Tenn. AG 10/18/1910

HENDERSON, Andy, age 40, d. Coca-Cola alley. Atlanta. AG 2/16/1908

HENDERSON, C. B. d. Baltimore, Md. Thurs. Interred: Westview. He was res. of Hapeville, Ga. Wife survives. AG 6/5/1908

HENDERSON, C. B. of Hapeville, Ga. d. Baltimore, Md. Thurs. Wife survives. Interred: Westview, Atlanta. AG 6/5/1908

HENDERSON, Carrie, colored, age 36, d. 39 Elm St. Atlanta. AG 5/30/1906

HENDERSON, Celia, colored, age 78, d. rear 429 E. Fair St. Atlanta. AG 11/9/1907

HENDERSON, Dorothy, inf. dau. of Mr. and Mrs. R. T., Funeral: 9 Loomis Ave. Atlanta. Interred: Oakland. AG 6/6/1906

HENDERSON, Emma, colored, age 35, d. 101 N. Butler St. Atlanta. AG 4/26/1907

HENDERSON, George R. of Mansfield, d. while plowing yesterday, of Covington, aged about 50. AG 2/15/1907

HENDERSON, Hester, colored, age 34, d. rear 17 Peters St. Atlanta. AG 3/18/1909

HENDERSON, John B., Mrs., age 64, d. Rossville, Ga. 2/23. Sis: Mrs. Laura Trimmer, Rossville. Dau: Mrs. J. H. Wann of Chattanooga, Tenn. Sons: Charles B., L. G. and Harold. Interred: Rossville, Ga. AG 2/23/1910

HENDERSON, J. W., colored, age 18, d. Lula, Ga. AG 5/8/1909

HENDERSON, Julia, colored, age 38, of Athens, Ga., d. Atlanta. AG 12/27/1910

HENDERSON, Leslie, colored, age 20, d. 215 Hubbard St. Atlanta. AG 2/26/1908

HENDERSON, Mary, colored, age 21, d. 363 Chapel St. Atlanta. AG 5/4/1909

HENDERSON, Mary T., Mrs., age 36, d. Mon. 247 Juniper St., Atlanta. Wife of J. A. 3 children. Father: S. R. Turner. AG 8/9/1910

HENDERSON, Mike, colored, age 57, d. 308 Martin St. Atlanta. AG 2/1/1908

HENDERSON, Nettie C., Mrs., age 41, d. Sat. 14 Alaska Ave., Atlanta. Interred: Social Circle, Ga. AG 6/15/1907

HENDERSON, Oliver H., 9 yrs., d. 107 Ridge Ave. Atlanta. AG 2/16/1907

HENDERSON, Pauline R., Mrs., widow of late Judge John T. of Atlanta, d. dau.'s res., Mrs. Paul R. Sledge, Augusta, Ga. Ch: Mrs. Paul R. Sledge, Augusta; Hon. W. B. Henderson, Atlanta. Interred: Westview. AG 4/2/1909

HENDERSON, R. H. of Brooks, Fayette Co., Ga., age 45, suicide 6/22. Bro-in-law: Dr. N. W. Gable. Wife, six daus. AG 6/23/1908

HENDERSON, R. L. T. of St. Louis, Mo. d. News recd in Atlanta by mother and sister, Mrs. L. T. Henderson and Miss Nina Mae Henderson. Decd removed out west no. of yrs. ago. AG 4/5/1910

HENDERSON, R. Still d. Mon. Stockbridge, Ga. Wife, 4 sons, 2 daus. Interred: Old Concord Cemetery. AG 11/15/1910

HENDERSON, Rosa, colored, age 37, d. 101 N. Butler St. Atlanta. AG 10/13/1908

HENDERSON, Roy Tye, formerly of Atlanta, d. St. Louis 4/4. Mother: Mrs. L. T. Henderson. Sis: Miss Mae Henderson. One bro. in Calif. Relative: John L. Tye, Atlanta. Grmother: Mrs. M. A. Tye, McDonough. AG 4/8/1910

HENDERSON, Sallie, Mrs., age 81, d. 14 Brown St., Atlanta, Sun. Interred: Clarkston. Sons: J. W., R. A. Daus: Mrs. G. W. Brooks,

172

Mrs. L. E. Morris. AG 4/5/1909

HENDERSON, Sam, colored, age 65, d. 706 Robins St. Atlanta. AG 3/10/1908

HENDERSON, T. J. d. Waugh St., Dalton, Ga., Sat., age 71, Confed. Vet. Wife: Mrs. H. C. Dau: Miss Cora Lee. Sons: L. J. and Lowry of Chattanooga, Tenn. Interred: West Hill. AG 9/26/1910

HENDERSON, Una, Miss, age 14, dau. of Mr. and Mrs. Daniel, d. Wed. Fitzgerald, Ga. Interred: Ocilla, Ga. AG 12/17/1909

HENDERSON, V. E., age 27, d. Montreal, Ga. AG 12/4/1908

HENDERSON, W. C., Mrs. d. Henderson's Crossing, S. Atlanta. Interred: Westview. AG 5/3/1906

HENDERSON, Wesley D., age 52, d. Fri. Atlanta. Interred: Hampton, Ga. AG 6/25/1910

HENDRICKS, C. N., age 64, d. 11/22 Old Soldiers' Home. Atlanta. Interred: Westview. AC 11/23/1905

HENDRICKS, H. M., age 46, d. 30 Leggett Ave., Atlanta, Thurs. Wife. Daus: Mrs. M. G. Winters, Mrs. T. N. Parris. AG 3/24/1910

HENDRICKS, Willie, colored, age 17, d. 53 Humphries St. Atlanta. AG 3/1/1907

HENDRIX, Lawyer shot and killed by Lucius Narpin, his bro-in-law, a negro. AG 5/22/1906

HENLEY, Carrie Irene, age two, dau. of Mr. and Mrs. O. K., d. 225 E. Fair St., Atlanta, Fri. AG 5/22/1909

HENLEY, J. B. of Baconton, Ga. d. res. of Sanders Barnett, a negro tenant, 12/28. Wife, 3 children. AG 12/29/1910

HENLEY, Richard McD., age 4, d. 225 E. Hunter St. Atlanta. Son of Mr. and Mrs. O. Henley. Interred: Westview. AG 9/25/1909

HENNY, Viola, colored, age 7, d. 179 Connally St. Atlanta. AG 12/17/1910

HENRY, Dora A., Mrs., wife of J. S., d. 44 Clay St. Atlanta, Tues. Interred: Westview. AG 4/1/1908

HENRY, Edward d. Ft. Missoula, Mont. recently, remains to Atlanta Fri. AG 9/10/1909

HENRY, Mattie, Mrs., age 34, wife of W. J., d. 280 Chestnut St. Atlanta Thurs. Interred: Dalton, Ga. AG 3/12/1908

HENSON, James, infant son of Mr. and Mrs. J. B. of 168 Echo St., Atlanta, d. Sat. Interred: Hollywood. AG 12/21/1908

HENSON, Lloyd, veteran of Civil war, d. Ellijay Sun., age 80 yrs. AG 6/25/1907

HENSON, M. M., Mrs., formerly of Atlanta, d. Newnan, 8/8. Interred: Oak Hill. AG 8/9/1906

HENSON, Mabelle, age 11 mos. d. Atlanta. AG 9/1/1908

HENSON, William H. d. Mon. his res., Marietta Rd. Atlanta, age 60. Confederate Veteran, Co. D, 48th Ga. Interred: Westview. 1/1/1907

HERBERT, Preston, colored, age 56, d. Birmingham, Ala. AG 3/1/1908

HERCHOVITCH, Edward, age 46, a tailor,, d. 29 Piedmont Ave. Atlanta. Wife, three children survive at 55 102 St. NYC. Interred: Oakland. AG 12/24/1908

HERDER, K. F., Jr., inf. son of Mr. and Mrs. K. F., d. 31 Josephine Ave. Atlanta Sun. Interred: Westview. AG 1/17/1910

HERMAN, H. H., age 74, d. Girard, Ala. 5/28. Leaves wife, 11 children. AC 5/30/1905

HERNDON, C. J., age 69, d. 338 W. North Ave., Atlanta, Thurs.

Wife, several children. Interred: Westview. AG 5/13/1910

HERNDON, Ernest, a*ge 1 mo., son of Mr. and Mrs. I. E., d. Sun. 95 Chappell St., Atlanta. Interred: Westview. AG 5/6/1907

HERNDON, Sarah M., Mrs., age 66, d. Tues. 61 E. Ellis St. Atlanta. Dau: Mrs. Bessie Avery. Interred: Macon. AG 5/22/1907

HERNDON, William G., age 79, d. Sat. 17 Chamberlain St. Atlanta. Bro: Dr. H. C. Herndon. Sis: Mrs. Elizabeth Hunt, Oxford, N. C. AG 11/27/1910

HERNDON, William M. d. 70 Bradley Ave., Atlanta, Sun. Interred: Westview. AG 10/19/1907

HERNDON, Z. T. of Columbus, Ga., d. Macon, age 59. One son, four daus. AG 6/10/1909

HERREN, Elizabeth, Mrs., age 79, d. 335 Peters St. Atlanta. Interred: Westview. AG 5/1/1906

HERREN, Neals Edward, age 18 mos., son of Mr. and Mrs. Ol Herren, d. Fri. at 215 Glenwood Ave. Atlanta. Interment: Westview. AG 10/27/1906

HERRINGTON, Lettie, colored, age 45, d. 481 Fort St. Atlanta. AG 8/14/1907

HESKA, Essa, finfant, d. Scottdale, Ga. AG 6/9/1910

HESLEY, Gaynell, age 1 yr., d. 165 Hunnicutt St., Atlanta. AG 8/26/1907

HESS, Daniel, age 78, d. while leaving from Westview cemetery. Wife: Kate Green Hess. Bro: Philomon, Columbus, Ohio. Interred: Oakland. AC 12/4/1905

HESTER, C. J., age 48, d. 55 Piedmont Pl. Atlanta, Sun. Interred: Hominy Grove Baptist Church yard. Wife, two sons, one sister, one bro. AG 8/3/1909

HESTER, C. Y. d. Waycross, Ga. 7/24. Interred: Quitman, Ga. AG 7/24/1909

HESTER, Frank, negro, shot and killed in basement, Walton and Bartow Sts., Atlanta. Toombs Hightower, arrested. AG 7/7/1906

HESTER, Simeon, age 70, d. res. of son, W. S., Union Pt., Ga., Wed. Son: C. S. Near relative of Hon. John Temple Graves. AG 12/18/1910

HETZER, Ada, Mrs., age 32, d. 92 Luckie St. Atlanta. AG 10/25/1909

HETZER, Ada, Mrs., age 32, d. Sun. Husband: Fred. Interred: Savannah, Ga. AG 10/25/1909

HEWATT, William A., age 10, d. Copenhill. AG 9/6/1910

HEWEY, Mary, colored, age 22, d. 84 Elizabeth St. Atlanta. AG 7/19/1909

HEYMAN, Mamie, Mrs., age 42, suicide 322 Whitehall St., Atlanta. Interred: Oakland. Husband: Emil Heyman. Sons: Harry L., Oscar. AG 11/26/1908

HEYS, Samuel of Americus, Conf. Vet., d. 3/3. AC 3/4/1905

HEYSER, E., Mrs., former resident of Madison, Ga., d. Macon Mon. Interred: Madison, Ga. AG 4/8/1908

HIBBETT, Andrew, negro, hanged 4/6 Nashville, Tenn for murdering his mother-in-law, Mary Norvelt. AC 4/6/1905

HICKEY, Marion Elizabeth d. Wed. 104 E. Fair St. Atlanta. Interred: Augusta, Ga. 6/7/1906

HICKLIN, Charles, colored, age 28, d. 59 W. Hunter St. Atlanta. AG 11/7/1907

HICKMAN, J. S., railroad machinist of S. Macon d. Mon. Wife, several children. AG 2/16/1908

HICKMAN, **Merrell**, age 9 mos., son of Mr. and Mrs. G. U., d. 6 Rhinehart St., Atlanta Mon. Interred: Greenwood. AG 6/22/1908

HICKOK, R. D., age 65, d. 205 Oglethorpe Ave. Atlanta. AG 3/7/1907

HICKOK, **Robert D.**, age 65, d. Tues. res. of son, Robert D. Hickok, Jr., Atlanta. He was b. Ohio, coming to Atlanta 7 yrs. ago. Vet. of civil war. Son: Robert D., Jr. AG 3/5/1907

HICKS, negro, shot by Fred Wilson, Russellville, Ga. AG 7/30/1907

HICKS, **Annie**, colored, age 25, d. Fulton Co. Alms House. AG 3/30/1908

HICKS, **Charley** d. Oxford 11/10. Bro-in-law: J. Z. Johnson. AC 11/13/1905

HICKS, **Clara**, colored, age 55, d. 14 Graves St. Atlanta. AG 12/4/1908

HICKS, **Clark**, **Mrs.** of Bibb Co., Houston Rd., d. 5/23. Interred: Shiloh Cemetery. AC 5/24/1905

HICKS, F. M., age 84, d. 92 Kelly St. Atlanta. AG 5/24/1910

HICKS, **Oscar L.** d. res. of M. V. Murray on First St., Macon 2/.10. Interred: Oxford, N. C. AG 2/11/1910

HICKS, R. B., age 73, d.58 Hampton St. Atlanta. AG 8/20/1906

HICKS, **William P.** d. Wed. res. of son, E. E. Hicks, 4 mi. north f Dublin, age 80. Interred: Wrightsville, Ga. AG 9/9/1910

HICKS, I. H., Mrs., aged 20, died at Howell Station, Atlanta. AG 12/5/1906

HICKS, **Minnie**, age 24, died 24 Chestnut Street, Atlanta. AG 12/8/1906

HIGGINBOTHAM, **Wilford** d. West Point, Ga., Tues. Wife, 2 children. AG 12/17/1910

HIGGINS, P., colored, age 50, d. 20 Garibaldi St. Atlanta. AG 10/13/1909

HIGH, J. M., LWT of J. M. High, filed Wilkinson Co. Sis: Miss Emma C. High. Daus: Hattie, Elizabeth, Dorothy. Bros: Forrest, Mark, St. Louis. Sis: Mrs. Birney, Macon, Emma High, Atlanta. Wife: Mrs. Hattie Wilson High. AG 11/9/1906

HIGH, M. M., late merchant of 528 Peachtree St. 250 employees of J. M. High Co. attended. Wife, 3 daus: Hattie, Elizabeth and Dorothy. Bros: Forrest, Mark of St. Louis. Sisters: Mrs. Birney, Macon, Emma High, Atlanta. AG 11/5/1906

HIGH, W. B., **Mrs.** d. Jan. 30 Valdosta. 6 sons, 1 dau. Husband. Interred: Corinth Church. AC 2/1/1905

HIGHBEE, **Sebina**, **Miss**, age 50 of 21 Lawn St., Atlanta, d. Mon. Bros: C. A. Highbee of Philadelphia, Pa., and Dr. C. L. Highbee of Clinton, Ky. Sis: Miss Nellie Highbee. AG 10/18/1909

HIGHTOWER, C. B., age 19, d. Grady Hospital. Atlanta. AG 8/4/1906

HIGHTOWER, **Cliff**, colored, age 19, d. Fulton Co. Barracks. AG 11/6/1907

HIGHTOWER, **Daniel C.**, age 28, d. Tues. 517 Courtland St., Atlanta. Interred: Barnesville, Ga. AG 9/21/1910

HIGHTOWER, **David**, father of late Dr. G. H. of Dalton, and grfather of Walter Hightower of Atlanta, d. Gordon Co. Sat. Age 87. AG 2/22/1910

HIGHTOWER, **Harry H.**, **Mrs.**, age 50, d. 167 W. Peachtree St. Atlanta. AG 12/3/1908

HIGHTOWER, John W., age 60, died at 204 Courtland Street, Atlanta. AG 11/20/1906

HIGHTOWER, S. C., age 19, street car conductor d. Fri. Grady Hospital, injured in wreck. Wife. Parents live Dahlonega. Wife's Father: W. S. Keown, 268 E. Hunter St. Intered: Dahlonega. AG 8/4/1906

HIGHTOWER, L. L., infant, age 5 mos., d. 62 Mangum St. Atlanta. AG 8/23/1906

HIGHTOWER, S. J., age 74, d. Mon. Old Soldiers' Home, Atlanta. Interred: Westview. Confed. Vet., enl. 5/1862, Pvt., Co. H., 5th Ga. Regt. Lost arm in fighting around Atlanta when Sherman was advancing. AG 8/31/1910

HIGHTOWER, W. J., age 57, d. 357 Capitol Ave. Atlanta. Interred: Dublin, Ga. Wife, 7 children: Mrs. W. S. Prescott, Atlanta; Misses Willie, Louise, Maudie and Ruth; Darte Hightower. Mother: Mrs. Elizabeth Hightower, Dublin. AG 3/22/1909

HIGHTOWER, Walter, funeral home of mother. Interment: Riverside. AG 12/27/1906

HIGHTOWER, Walter, of 144 Gaskell St., Atlanta, was discovered in a room with a young woman in his own house by his 7-year old son, Henry. He killed Bessie Jones, then himself. AG 12/24/1906

HIGHTOWER, Wayne, age 9, killed by explosion of old shell, Atlanta. Interred: Westview. AG 4/10/1909

HILBURN, F. F., Mrs. d. E. Point, Tues. Interred: College Park, Ga. AG 10/23/1907

HILBURN, Indiana, Mrs., age 45, wife of R. R., d. Mon., 47 S. Boulevard, Atlanta. Leaves husband, three children. Interred: Aragon, Ga. AG 10/3/1906

HILBURN, Maggie, Mrs., wife of F. F., age 24, d. 63 Garden St. Atlanta. Interred: College Park, Ga. AG 10/23/1907

HILBURN, R. E., Mrs., age 65, d. 365 Luckie St. Atlanta. AG 2/20/1908

HILDERBRAND, Ethel, age 8 mos., inf. dau. of Mr. and Mrs. L. L., d. 547 Chestnut St.,tlanta, Tues. Interred: Mt. Paron Church yard. AG 7/14/1909

HILDERBRAND, Vivian, age 2, dau. of Mr. and Mrs. L. L., d. 1265 Mildren St., Atlanta, Mon. Interred: Sardis Church. AG 1/20/1908

HILL, Albert, a Union Veteran, d. Chattanooga, Tenn. Mon., age 79. He was b. Erie, Pa. in 1830, member of 130th Ohio Vols. Wife, one dau., Mrs. Ruth Howie, of Michigan. AG 12/23/1909

HILL, Alford, colored, age 23, d. Grady Hospital. Atlanta. AG 8/14/1907

HILL, C., colored, age 30, d. Memphis, Tenn. AG 12/26/1907

HILL, Caroline H., Mrs., wife of Charles D., Sol. Gen, Fulton Superior Ct., d. 644 Piedmont Ave., Mon. Interred: Oakland. She was dau. of late Col. D. G. Hughes. Son: Harvey Hill. Bro: Hon. Dudley M. Hughes of Danville, Ga. AG 4/23/1907

HILL, Charles D., Jr., age 4, d. 267 Capitol Ave. Atlanta. AG 8/31/1908

HILL, Duncan C., Hon., age 74, d. W. Palm Beach, Fla. Interred: Family Cemetery near Ophelia, Ga. Ch: C. P. Hill, Ophelia, Ga.; Mrs. A. P. Anthony, W. Palm Beach, Fla. Bros: L. J. Hill, Atlanta; W. W. Hill, Sr., Washington, Ga. AG 3/5/1908

HILL, Cora, colored, age 28, d. 11 Rawson St. Atlanta. AG 4/3/1908
HILL, Ella May, age 2, d. 17 Venable St. Atlanta. AG 11/12/1910
HILL, Ellen, colored, age 9 mos., d. 33 Elm St. Atlanta. AG 2/16/1908
HILL, Elmira, colored, age 21, d. 18 Randolph St., Atlanta. AG 10/23/1907
HILL, Erskine, colored, age 85, d. 68 W. Cain St. Atlanta. AG 8/24/1908
HILL, G. C., Mrs., age 22, d. Sun. 234 Formwalt St. Atlanta. Interred: Westview. Parents: Mr. and Mrs. Walter Watts. 4 sisters, 4 bros. AG 3/21/1910
HILL, George, age 23, d. Grady Hospital. Atlanta. AG 3/22/1907
HILL, Gordon, age 19, d. corner Decatur and Moore Sts. Atlanta. AG 10/13/1908
HILL, Ida E., Mrs., age 53, d. 47 Ponders Ave. Atlanta, Thurs. AG 1/10/1908
HILL, Jim, negro, d. Atlanta. AC 6/25/1905
HILL, John, colored, age 55, d. 93 Greensferry Ave. Atlanta. AG 6/9/1908
HILL, John J., Dr., Washington, Ga., 11/13/1906, age 54, physician of NE Ga. Survivors: wife and one dau. Interment: city cemetery. AG 11/13/1906
HILL, Julia, Mrs., age 39, wife of late Dr. C. M. Hill, d. 17 W. Cain St. Atlanta. Bro: W. P. Hill of Atlanta. Sis: Mrs. Minnie L. Reed, LaGrange. Son: Charles M. Hill, Pensacola, Fla. Interred: Westview. AG 3/25/1907
HILL, Kate, colored, age 21, d. Grady Hospital. Atlanta. AG 6/7/1907
HILL, L. D., Jr., age 12, son of Mr. and Mrs. L. D. Hill of Gough, Ga. d. yesterday. AG 2/26/1907
HILL, Lilla, Miss, age 30, d. 69 Luckie St. Atlanta. AG 3/4/1907
HILL, Lula, colored, age 38, d. 270 Williams St. Atlanta. AG 12/30/1907
HILL, M. E., Miss, age 65, d. 523 Highland Ave., Atlanta, Fri. Three bros. Interred: Marietta. AG 7/23/1908
HILL, Mary, colored, age 24, died 142 Fraser St., Atlanta. AG 12/17/1906
HILL, Mary, Mrs., age 58, d. 92 Woodson St. Atlanta. AG 5/12/1909
HILL, Monih, colored, age 47, d. 46 Moon St., Atlanta. AG 10/14/1907
HILL, Morris, age 2, dau. of Mr. and Mrs. J. L., d. 79 Martin St., Atlanta, Tues. Interred: Indian Creek Cemetery. AG 9/9/1908
HILL, Nathan S., age 52, d. Sun. 698 E. Fair St. Atlanta. Interred: Sylvester cemetery. AG 4/23/1907
HILL, Pope, Macon atty, found dead McRae, Ga. (shot). AG 4/5/1909
HILL, R. A. of Homer, Ga., age 32, d. Atlanta Sat. at Grady Hospital. AG 12/22/1908
HILL, Richard d. 10/25 Abbeville, S. C. Wife. Bros: James A., W. E. AG 10/25/1910
HILL, Roxie, colored, age 31, d. 124 Gilmore St. Atlanta. AG 11/1/1909
HILL, S. M., Mrs. funeral 10/6 Macon, Ga. Interred: Riverside. AG 10/7/1910

HILL, Susie, Miss, age 24, dau. of Mr. and Mrs. W. F., d. 124 Garden St., Atlanta, Sun. Interred: Westview. AG 11/23/1907

HILL, T. J., age 10, d. Fri. Atlanta. AG 2/27/1910

HILL, T. J., age 40, d. Sat. Interred: Westview. AG 2/28/1910

HILL, Thomas, colored, age 33, d. 571 Chestnut St. Atlanta. AG 11/14/1908

HILL, Thomas H., colored, age 33, d. 313 Fraser St., Atlanta, Oct. 16. AG 10/18/1910

HILL, V. D., age 21, d. Grady Hospital. Atlanta. AG 3/29/1907

HILL, Velma D., age 27, d. Grady Hospital, Atlanta, Thurs. Mother lives 1503 Third St., Columbus, Ga. Sister, Brother. AG 3/28/1907

HILL, W. T. shot and killed 5 miles from Birmingham, Ala. 4/8. AC 4/9/1905

HILL, Walter Bernard d. 12/28 Athens. Born 9/9/1851 Talbotton, son of Judge Barnard Hill and Miss Mary Clay Birch (cousin of Henry Clay). AC 12/29/1905

HILL, Wellborn, age 58, d. 17 W. Cain St. Atlanta. AG 8/27/1907

HILL, William P., city atty, age 47, citizen since 1885, died. Wife. Sis: Mrs. Todd Reed, LaGrange. Cousins: Charles D. and Ben H. Hill, Atlanta. Interred: Westview. AG 8/11/1909

HILLBURN, Frank, age 36, d. Grady Hospital. Atlanta. AG 3/2/1907

HILLEY, Lucy, Mrs. d. Sun. 106 Center St. Atlanta. Funeral res. of son, 188 State St. Interred: Westview. Sons: R. S., R. I. and C. O. Daus: Mrs. Susan E. Tinsley, Mrs. W. T. Whiting, Mrs. W. T. Chambers, Mrs. Sarona E. Heard. AG 5/14/1906

HILLHOUSE, Hamp, colored, age 19, d. Terminal St. Atlanta. AG 2/13/1908

HILLHOUSE, Henry, negro porter for Sou. RR, killed Wed. by train. Atlanta, res. of 48 John St. AG 2/12/1908

HILLS, Mathew L., infant, d. 41 Mills St. Atlanta. AG 6/11/1910

HILLSON, J., Rev., colored, d. Sat. Atlanta. Interred: Cartersville. AG 12/14/1907

HILSMAN, A. P., scalded by vat of water at Fulton Bag and Cotton Mills several days ago, d. Thurs. Grady Hospital, Atlanta. Wife, three children, survive. AG 12/27/1907

HILSON, J. H., colored, age 72, d. 40 Newton St. Atlanta. AG 12/16/1907

HILTON, Jessie, Mrs., age 30, d. Atlanta Fri. Mother, sister, one child, of E. Atlanta. AG 1/15/1910

HILTON, John, age 12, d. 36 Park Ave., Atlanta. AG 10/20/1908

HILTON, Richard W., age 71, d. 400 N. Boulevard. Atlanta. AG 6/22/1909

HIND, Thomas, 72, d. Atlanta. Ch: Mrs. W. H. Webb, Atlanta; Mrs. Everett Libby, Winona, MS; Mrs. Miles Gallager, Oakland, CA; J. C., Dawson; Rev. A. T., Waleska: W. G., San Francisco; H. F., Brit. Columbia. Bur: Tallapoosa. AG 5/30/1910

HINES, Elizabeth, colored, age 25, d. 101 Maple St. Atlanta. AG 7/20/1907

HINES, Matthew, age 21, d. Atlanta. Interred: Utoy Church. AG 5/8/1906

HINES, Rachel, colored, age 57, d. rear 21 W. Alexander St. Atlanta. AG 7/2/1908

HINMAN, George, age 79, d. 584 Washington St. Atlanta. AG 6/18/1907

HINMAN, George, Mrs. d. Augusta, Ga. Mon., funeral at son's res., Dr. Thomas P. Hinman, 359 W. Peachtree St., Atlanta. Interred: Oakland. Kin: George B. Hinman, Dr. R. M. Hinman, F. W. R. Hinman, R. M. Stiles, Dr. Thomas P. Hinman. AG 12/9/1907

HINTON, Asbury, colored, age 34, d. 39 Hills St. Atlanta. AG 10/20/1908

HINTON, Lizzie, colored, age 28, d. 222 Chestnut St. Atlanta. AG 11/12/1907

HINTON, Susan W., Mrs., age 78, d. 68 Garibaldi St. Atlanta. AG 6/2/1910

HIPP, R. L., Senator, killed by John R. Williams 4/11 Cullman, Ala. AC 4/12/1905

HIROSOWITZ, Jacob, age 41, d. 110 Decatur St. Atlanta. AG 3/1/1908

HIRSCH, Lillian Florine, dau. of Mr. and Mrs. Idadore, d. Macon Hospital, Macon, Ga. AG 8/30/1908

HIRSCH, Lillian, Mrs., age 32, d. Battle Creek, Mich. AG 12/14/1909

HIRSH, Bertha, Mrs., age 37, d. 352 Whitehall St. Atlanta. AG 10/8/1907

HITCHELL, H. E., age 38, d. 224-1/2 Peters St., Atlanta, Sun. AG 9/18/1906

HITCHINS, Maggie, Mrs., age 70, d. Atlanta Sun. Interred: Westview. AG 1/13/1908

HITT, Frank B., age 22, d. 56 E. Ellis St. Atlanta. AG 2/22/1907

HITT, Joseph Woolfolk, age 31, d. 376 Spring St., Atlanta, d. Fri. Interred: Augusta. Mother: Mrs. Lucy W. Hitt, 386 Spring St., Atlanta. AG 1/5/1907

HITT, Martin, charged with murdering his wife, Nancy, near Folsom, Ga. last May, d. 7/8 Cartersville, Ga. in his cell. AG 7/9/1910

HITT, Nancy, Mrs. killed by husband, Martin Hitt, 5/1910, Folsom, Ga. AG 7/9/1910

HITT, Ottillie, age 63, d. Thurs. 335 Formwalt St. Atlanta. Son: A. H. Hitt. Interred: Westview. AG 1/31/1907

HITT, V. G., Dr. d. Jan. 17. Interred: Augusta, Ga. Age 64, res. of Atlanta since 1896 from Augusta. Wife. Sons: Joseph W., W. Moultrie, Jr., E. G.. Dau: Lucile. Bros: R. G., W. M. and J. E. Hitt. AC 1/18/1905

HIX, Josephine, colored, age 51, d. 104 Fort St. Atlanta. AG 3/13/1908

HOBBS, Nancy, Mrs., age 86, d. Hemphill, Ga. Mon. Son: R. H. Interred: Hemphill, Ga. AG 5/3/1910

HOBBS, Rachel Cox, age 79, d. 610 Piedmont Ave. Atlanta. Daus: Mrs. C. G. Lippold, Mrs. T. F. Smith. Son: A. B. Hobbs. Interred: Owensboro, Ky. AG 3/15/1907

HOBBS, Sarah H., Mrs., age 88, of Stewart Co., d. son-in-law's, George Overby. Eldest son: Richard Hobbs, Lumpkin, Ga. AG 8/5/1907

HOBBS, Sue, Mrs., age 55, d. 169 Central Ave., Atlanta. Daus: Miss Beatrice Hobbs, Mrs. J. J. Arline. Interred: Oglethorpe, Ga. AG 1/24/1908

HOBGOOD, Monch, age 33, d. 274 Chestnut St. Atlanta. AG 1/21/1910

HOCH, Kate, Mrs., wife of Hans, d. Mon. Atlanta. Interred: Westivew. AG 10/3/1910

HODGE, Susie, Mrs.,a ge 48, d. 101 N. Butler St. Atlanta. AG 9/8/1908

HODGES, A., colored, age 17, died at Kirkwood, Ga. AG 12/10/1906

HODGES, F. B., Mrs. buried last Monday. Hartwell, Ga. AG 6/13/1910

HODGES, John H., age 47, d. 6/13 Hartwell, Ga., son of Hon. and Mrs. F. B. He md. Miss Annie Gossett of Easley, S. C. Sons: Walter, Jack. Bro: Judge Waller I. Hodges of Hartwell. Sis: Mrs. J. E. Linder. AG 6/13/1910

HODGES, Margaret, colored, age 45, d. 33 Old Wheat St. Atlanta. AG 8/14/1908

HODGES, Mary, Mrs., age 90, d. Oakland City, Ga. AG 2/14/1908

HODGES, Ollie E., Mrs., age 56, d. 534 E. St. Charles Ave. Atlanta. AG 9/8/1908

HODNETT, Mary A., Mrs., age 79, d. Haralson, Ga. AG 1/18/1908

HOFFINE, Samuel, age 66, d. Tues. res. of son, Amiel Hoffine, of Douglasville, Ga. Interred: Greensboro, N. C. AG 6/8/1910

HOFFMAN, Abraham W., age 72, d. 742 Glenn St. Atlanta. Wife, 5 ch: Mrs. Gay Nell McManmon, Mrs. Lula Wofford, Mrs. T. F. Clements, Miss Kate Hoffman, Rex Hoffman. AG 4/27/1907

HOFFMAN, Agnes, inf. dau. of Mr. and Mrs. A. C. of Augusta, Ga., d. Mon. Atlanta. Interred: Westview. AG 12/23/1909

HOFFMAN, George Joseph, age 5 mos., d. 228 Spring St. Atlanta. AG 7/12/1907

HOFFMAN, Jacob d. age 72, Atlanta resident, 374 Washington St. Leaves wife, two children: Mrs. M. Hirsch and Gus Hoffman. Interred: Oakland. AG 7/1/1907

HOFFMAN, James F., age 42, d. Tues. 228 Spring St. Atlanta. Wife. Interred: Hollywood. AG 3/22/1910

HOFFMAN, Joseph, 9 mos. old son of Mr. and Mrs. James Hoffman, d. 185 Plum St. Atlanta. Interred: Hollywood. AG 7/12/1906

HOFFMANN, Hubert and Adolph, age 9 and 7, d. 228 Spring St. Atlanta. AG 9/6/1910

HOFMAN, R. A., colored, age 45, d. 41 Leonard St. Atlanta. AG 5/12/1909

HOFMAYER, Dora, Mrs., wife of L. J., d. Thurs. Atlanta. Leaves husband, her mother, Mrs. Morris Barwald of 321 Washington St.,A tlanta. Bros: Fred, Mont, Edwin and Morris Barwald. Interred: Albany, Ga. AG 11/12/1909

HOGAN, C. V., Mrs. of Atlanta d. city hospital, Columbus. Interred: Chipley, Ga., her old home. Survived by husband, two childen. AG 1/8/1907

HOGAN, New, age 23, d. London City, Canada. AG 8/6/1907

HOGE, Annie, Miss, d. High St., Macon. Survivors: Three bros., Solomon, John S. and George F.; two sisters, Misses Addie and Julia. AG 9/12/1906

HOGG, D. M. d. 8/10 Atlanta. Interred: Sharon Church yard. AC 8/12/1905

HOLBROOK, Elijah G., age 19, d. res. of parents, Mr. and Mrs. T. M., 11 Oliver St.,A tlanta, Sun. One bro., two sisters. Interred: Westview. AG 12/5/1910

HOLBROOK, F. M. and wife murdered Watkinsville 5/9. Old couple. AC 5/11/1905

HOLBROOK, J. C., age 76, d. 171 Griffin St. Atlanta. AG 2/27/1907
HOLBROOK, Julia E., Mrs. d. 9/12 383 Auburn Ave. Atlanta.
Interred: Oakland. AC 9/14/1905
HOLBROOK, William C., Rev., age 76, d. 22 Alaska Ave., Atlanta,
Mon. Son: H. P. Bro: A. L. Sis: Mrs. F. C. Weems, Texas.
Interred: Oakland. AG 7/13/1909
HOLBROOK, William H., age 36, d. 124 Peeples St. Atlanta. AG
9/12/1906
HOLBROOK, William T. d. Fri. Norcross, Ga. Interred: Oakland.
Sis: Miss Lula Holbrook, of Norcross. AG 9/2/1910
HOLCOMB, Angie, Mrs., age 68, d. 120 S. Boulevard. Atlanta. AG
9/6/1910
HOLCOMB, J. R., age 57, d. 231 Central Ave. Atlanta. AG 9/10/1910
HOLCOMB, infant of Sarah Holcomb, age 2 mos., d. 169 Fort St.
Atlanta. AG 10/25/1900
HOLCOMBE, John R., age 57, d. Sun. Atlanta. Wife, mother, 3 sons,
one dau. Interred: Westview. AG 9/10/1910
HOLCOMBE, Onie, Mrs., age 28, d. Atlanta. AG 9/8/1909
HOLCOMBE, W. H., age 69, d. 284 N. Jackson St. Atlanta. AG
8/1/1910
HOLDEN, Blanch, Mrs., age 38, d. Atlanta. AG 1/11/1910
HOLDEN, Lula May, age 2, d. 170 Randolph St. Atlanta. AG 9/2/1909
HOLDEN, W. O., Mrs. of Crawfordville d. Atlanta Sat. She was
formerly Miss Cornelia Rhodes of Crawfordville. Ch: Mrs. Anthony,
of Fla.; Mrs. A. H. Beazley and Misses Nellie and Marcia Holden
of Crawfordville. Husband: W. O. AG 5/31/1910
HOLDER, J. J. funeral Sun. Atlanta. Interred: Lula, Ga. AG
9/10/1910
HOLDER, James J., age 65, d. Fri. 69 Ponders Ave. Atlanta. Wife.
Sons: W. R., J. D., J. B. Daus: Mrs. W. R. Greer, Mrs. M. M.
Coly, Katherine, Harriet H. Interred: Lula, Ga. AG 9/10/1910
HOLDER, N. E. d. Macon 6/7. AC 6/8/1905
HOLDER, Roscoe, colored, age 4, d. 101 N. Butler St. Atlanta. AG
11/20/1907
HOLDER, T. J. d. Mon. Hawkinsville. Daus: Miss Rosa Holder; Mrs.
Lizzie Markert, of Cordele. Son: W. J. Holder of Savannah.
Interred: Hawkinsville, Ga. AG 9/6/1910
HOLDT, Margaret A., wife of Arthur E., d. Kirkwood, Fri. Ch:
Ernest, Herbert, Robert, Helen, Edna. Father: James H. Blake,
Locust Grove, Ohio. Bro: Henry C. Blake, Atlanta. Sis: Mrs. E. W.
Bixby, Ironton, Ohio. Bur: Oakland. AG 12/30/1907
HOLINGSWORTH, Jennie Rose, age 2, dau. of Mr. and Mrs. C. J., d.
338 Highland Ave., Atlanta, Tues. Interred: Oakland. AG 2/19/1908
HOLLAND, Benjamin of Maysville, Ga. d. 7/22, age 95 yrs., 6 mos.
Oldest citizen. AC 7/25/1905
HOLLAND, Edmund d. 904 DeKalb Ave., Atlanta, Sun. Interred:
Oakland. Wife, 7 children. AG 8/3/1909
HOLLAND, Emma V., Mrs., age 54, d. 58 W. Peachtree St, Atlanta,
Mon. Husband: J. H. Holland. Interred: Lexington, Ky. AG
6/30/1908
HOLLAND, George, age 48, manufacturer of Huntsville and Decatur,
Ala., d. 8/17 res. of Ernest Holland, Church St. Interred:
Decatur, Ala. AG 8/18/1909
HOLLAND, Harry L., age 26, d. Sat. Interred: Lexington, Ky.
Father: J. H. Holland, Lexington, Ky. AG 10/29/1906

HOLLAND, Leona May, age 4, inf. of Mr. and Mrs. E. E., d. 187 Smith St. Atlanta. Interred: Stone Mountain, Ga. AG 10/18/1907

HOLLAND, Mary E., Mrs., age 85 d. Thurs. 86 Park Ave. Atlanta. Sons: Dr. Frank Holland of Atlanta; S. J. Holland of Chicago. Niece: Miss Mary Strother, Atlanta. Interred: Westview. AG 4/6/1907

HOLLAND, Mary Rosabell, Mrs., age 38, d. 269 Glenn St. Atlanta. Parents: Mr. and Mrs. J. D. arbrough. Bros: B. C., J. H., J. F. and J. E. Yarbrough. Sis: Mrs. A. D. Reeves, Miss Lily Yarbrough. Interred: Westview. Parents, 4 bros., 3 sisters, survive. A

HOLLAND, Mattie, colored, age 18, d. 341 Piedmont Ave. Atlanta, Nov. 3. AG 11/5/1910

HOLLAND, Minnie E., Mrs., d. 11 Clifford St. her funeral Mon. St. Luke's Church. Atlanta. Interred: Westview. Two sons, dau. AG 2/5/1907

HOLLAND, William, colored, age 53, d 486 McDaniel St. Atlanta. AG 9/30/1909

HOLLAND, William, night watchman, murdered, Atlanta. Wife: Lucinda. AG 5/12/1910

HOLLAWAY, Arthur, colored, age 16, d. 328 Fulton St. Atlanta. AG 9/2/1909

HOLLEMAN, C. A., age 45, d. Milledgeville. AG 1/14/1907

HOLLEN, C. S. accidentally killed by train near Chattahoochee Sta. Wed. Interred: Canton, Ga. AG 4/28/1910

HOLLEY, Frank R., Mrs. d. Wed. She was b. uniondale, Pa., member 2nd Baptist Church, res. of Atlanta 10 yrs. Husband, several bros, sisters. AG 9/28/1906

HOLLEY, Smithie Jane, age 47, d. 41 Kirkwood Ave. Atlanta. AG 8/1/1908

HOLLEYMAN, W. F., age 65, d. Fri. Decatur, Ga. Wife, two daus: Mrs. Olin F. Pattillo, Mrs. T. R. Weams. Confederate Veteran, druggist. Interred: Decatur, Ga. AG 11/26/1909

HOLLIDAY, James, colored, age 23, d. 163 Rockwell St. Atlanta. AG 8/25/1910

HOLLIDAY, Robert A., Dr., funeral was Sun. at his res., 411 Spring St., Atlanta, Interment: Westview. Survivors: Wife, three children, two brothers. AG 11/12/1906

HOLLIFIELD, James L., age 61, d. 555 Spring St. Atlanta. AG 5/13/1907

HOLLINGSWORTH, Allin, inf. dau. of Mr. and Mrs. L. D., d. Wed. 352 W. North Ave., Atlanta. Interred: Rex, Ga.

HOLLINGSWORTH, Frances, Miss, age 16, d. 12 Dillon St. Atlanta. AG 11/1/1909

HOLLINGSWORTH, Gladys M., infant, d. 13 Josephine St. Atlanta. AG 3/21/1910

HOLLINGSWORTH, Ira B. d. and buried Pelham, Ga. 7/26. AC 7/28/1905

HOLLINGSWORTH, Jane, Mrs., wife of Dr. Joseph, d. Sat. Highland Ave. and Greenwood Sts. Interred: Westview. AG 9/14/1907

HOLLINGSWORTH, Mattie, colored, age 28, d. 49 Gartrell St. Atlanta. AG 11/1/1910

HOLLINGSWORTH, R. H., age 78, d. Leggett St., Atlanta. Wife. Sons: William of Lithonia; Judge Wyman of Fayetteville; Edgar of Atlanta. Dau: Mrs. Ellis of Hazlehurst. Interred: Lithonia Cemetery. AG 12/27/1910

HOLLIS, J. J., Mrs. d. Thurs., age 71, Douglasville, Ga. One of first settlers, b. Campbell Co., Ga. Husband. Ch: J. A. Hollis, Atlanta; R. L. Hollis, Atlanta; T. E. Hollis, Atlanta; Mrs. R. F. Ellis, Montgomery, Ala. AG 9/9/1910
HOLLIS, M. C., Mrs., age 65, d. 44 Eugenia St., Atlanta, Wed. Interred: Westview. Ag 11/7/1910
HOLLIS, Mattie Lee, age 2, dau. of Mr. and Mrs. W. H., d. 67 Larkin St., Atlanta, Sun. AG 8/3/1908
HOLLIS, Prince, old negro man, shot and killed Sun. by Bud Thomas, negro. AG 2/4/1907
HOLLOMAN, D. L., age 50, d. Atlanta Mon. Five ch. Interred: Westview. AG 12/17/1907
HOLLOWAY, E. S., colored, age 35, d. 215 Clarke St. Atlanta. AG 5/6/1908
HOLLOWAY, F. L., Mrs., age 65 d. Wed. Howell Mill Rd., Atlanta. Interred: Caseys. AG 7/25/1907
HOLLOWAY, Grover interred Decatur, Ga. AG 12/30/1907
HOLLOWAY, Howard, age 22, son of Mrs. W. T., d. 1 mi. e. of Douglasville, Ga., 2/14/ AG 2/20/1908
HOLLOWAY, Lindsay of Dawson Co., prisoner in Tower (Atlanta) released to attend his wife's funerl. AG 11/13/1907
HOLLOWAY, Mary Clair, age 17, dau. of Mr. and Mrs. E. F., 115 Crew St., Atlanta, d. Sat. AG 3/5/1910
HOLLOWAY, Munch, negro, d. Americus, Ga. Was conficted of forgery, in co. gang. AG 6/12/1906
HOLLOWAY, Oma Jane, age 16 mos., d. Mon. parents res., Mr. and Mrs. P. A. Holloway. Leaves wife. Interred: Gainesville, Ga. AG 9/14/1909
HOLLOWAY, Sue, Miss d. few wks. ago. Atlanta. Fund raised for memorial. AC 1/9/1905
HOLLOWAY, W. T., Mrs. d. 1 mi. e. of Douglasville, Ga. yesterday. AG 2/20/1908
HOLLY, O. A., age 19, d. Flat Shoals Rd. Atlanta. AG 11/8/1909
HOLLY, Will, Mrs. of Jackson, Ga., dau. of Butt's Co. Judge, J. H. Ham, d. Jan. 15. Husband, son. AC 1/7/1905
HOLMES, Ardaway, age 8 mos., son of Mr. and Mrs. C., d. 12/10 Decatur, Ga., DeKalb C. Interred: Caldwell, Ga. AC 12/11/1905
HOLMES, Clifford W., age 20, d. 132 Ashby St. Atlanta. AG 12/18/1910
HOLMES, Eliza, colored, age 55, d. 33 Richmond St. Atlanta. AG 7/19/1909
HOLMES, Fannie, Mrs., age 16, d. several days ago. Interred: Westview. AG 7/21/1906
HOLMES, J. O., Mrs. d. Sat. Culloden, Ga. AG 4/1/1907
HOLMES, J. W., Rev., age 24, formerly of Roswell, d. Atlanta Tues. Interred: Roswell, Ga. Wife, two children. AG 6/1/1909
HOLMES, John D., age over 90 yrs., d. Sun. Interred: Methodist cemetery. Survived by wife who was Miss Hardin of Lagrange; three sons, W. P., W. H. and I. F. Holmes. Two daus: Mrs. Belle Reynolds, Miss Virgie Holmes. AG 6/10/1907
HOLMES, M. J., Mrs., wife of Richard, d. 62 Rankin St., Atlanta, Sat. AG 2/8/1908
HOLMES, Perry, trunkmarker, 48 Culver St., Atlanta, d. Wed. Wife, 5 children. Interment: Westview. AG 9/13/1906

HOLMES, Ruby, Miss, age 19, d. 14 Formwalt St. Atlanta. AG 9/29/1910

HOLMS, Cora, infant dau. of Mr. and Mrs. F. O., d. Mon. 215 Berean Ave. Atlanta. Interred: Westview. AG 6/18/1907

HOLSENBACH, Lonie, colored, 4 mos., died 3 Baltimore, Atlanta. AG 12/26/1906

HOLSENBECK, Willie Marguerite, age 8, d. Thomson St. Atlanta. AG 9/9/1908

HOLSHOUSER, T. W., Mrs., age 36, d. Fri. 96 Jones Ave., Atlanta. Husband, one son. Interred: Hollywood. AG 9/9/1910

HOLT, Abner T. funeral held Vineville 2/26. AG 2/27/1909

HOLT, P. R., Dr. d. 6/4, age 81, Newnan, Ga. Born Talbot Co., surgeon in Confed. Army. Ch: Mrs. H. P. Bloun, Atlanta; Mrs. A. D. Skelly, Ft. Valley; Frank, Montezuma; Mrs. H. D. Wakefield, N. Y.; J. R., Newnan; P. E., Albany. AC 6/6/1905

HOLT, R. W., negro, d. Macon train wreck. AG 2/15/1911

HOLTON, Eva J., Mrs. d. Fri., funeral 8/22 Folks St., Waycross. Husband, 3 children (2 sons, 1 dau.). AG 8/23/1909

HOLTON, Evans of Hawkinsville killed 5/9/1906. Reward offered. AG 1/15/1907

HOLTZCLAW, Henry, age 77, d. at Confederate Soldiers Home. Atlanta. AG 10/3/1906

HOLTZCLAW, Nancy J., Mrs., age 59, d. 311 Courtland St. Atlanta. AG 10/25/1906

HOMER, Louise Lovelace, Mrs., wife of Henry of W. Point, d. 3/3, age 82. Last member of family of eight, each having lived to age 80. Husband is age 92. AC 3/4/1905

HONEA, Edgar C., age 19, d. E. Point, Ga. AG 8/5/1907

HONEY, Edgar of 12 Circle Street, East Point, Ga., age 18, drowned Sun. Interred: Smyrna, Ga. AG 8/5/1907

HOOD, John V. R. d. Sat. Oakland City, Ga. Sun. Interred: Hollywood. AG 5/25/1908

HOOD, R. E., Mrs., mother-in-law of A. G. Sherman, d. 7/27. AG 8/28/1909

HOOD, W. M., age 70, Confed. Vet., d. 125 Spring St. Atlanta. Wife. several children. Interred: Westview. AC 5/1/1905

HOODY, Seeson, colored, age 41, d. 3 Thompson alley. Atlanta. AG 10/25/1907

HOOK, Josephine H., Miss, age 70, of Lookout, Tenn., d. Atlanta Wed. Interred: Chattanooga, Tenn. AG 8/19/1908

HOOKER, DeWitt H., Jr., age 1 yr., d. 39 Oak St. Atlanta. AG 10/11/1909

HOOKS, Mrs. d. Mon., wife of J. T., Carrollton, Ga. Children: Clyde Hooks, Cleveland, Ohio; Oma Hooks, Thomasville, Ga.; Stella Hooks, Thomasville, Ga. AG 12/21/1907

HOOPER, John Quincy, Jr., age 2, d. Fri. Riverside, Ga. Interred: Westview. AG 9/24/1910

HOOPER, infant dau. of Mr. and Mrs. Z. N. Hooper, d. near Bolton, Ga. Fri. Interred: Hollywood. AG 5/4/1907

HOOTEN, J. W., age 64, d. 211 South Ave., Atlanta, Sun. Wife, 7 ch: A. M., of Griffin; C. M. of Manchester; J. W. of Atlanta; Misses Mittie, Lillie, Virginia and Annie Lou Hooten of Atlanta. AG 5/9/1910

HOOVER, John S., age 36, d. Wesley Memorial Hospital. Atlanta. AG 3/28/1907

HOOVER, John Smith, formerly of Canton, Ohio, d. Tues. Interred: Canton, Ohio. Wife in Atlanta survives. AG 3/26/1907

HOOVER, L. C., Mrs., age 60, d. near Morrow Sta. Sat. Son: A. T., Atlanta. Dau: Mrs. W. B. Thompson, Atlanta. Interred: Hollywood. AG 6/5/1909

HOPGOOD, Ora Lee, Mrs., age 22, d. 267 1/2 Peters St. Atlanta. AG 9/30/1910

HOPKINS, Francis, printer, found dead in cell at station house yesterday, Washington, Ga. AG 5/23/1907

HOPKINS, Lucile, age 2, dau. of Mr. and Mrs. L. A. interred: Greenwood cemetery. AG 10/14/1907

HOPKINS, Mary, age 13, d. 23 Waldo St. Atlanta. AG 10/18/1909

HOPKINS, Roy Eugene, age 2, d. 51 Daniel St. Atlanta. AG 9/9/1908

HOPKINS, Mary, age 1, dau. of Mr. and Mrs. L. S. of 22 Waldo St., Atlanta, d. Sun. AG 10/18/1909

HOPPER, Guy, age 4 mos., son of Mrs. Nora, 61 Tennille St., Atlanta, d. Mon. Interred: New Hope. AG 5/3/1909

HOPPER, Sarah C., Mrs., age 42, d. Birmingham, Ala. AG 3/14/1910

HORN, Nancy, Mrs., age 94, d. Harget, Harris Co., Ga. 8/13. From N. C. AC 8/15/1905

HORNE, Samuel, colored, age 3 mos., d. 297 Terry St. Atlanta. AG 9/2/1909

HORNER, J. Fred, age 50, d. Atlanta Sun. Wife, one ch. Interred: Westview. AG 2/2/1908

HORNER, W. Frank d. Atlanta. Interred: Greenwood. AG 7/19/1910

HORNSBY, Fred W. d. Tues. Lakewood Hgts., Atlanta. Interred: South Bend. AG 10/17/1907

HORNSBY, Johnnie Pet funeral at res. Lakewood Heights, Atlanta, Sun. Interred: S. Bend Cemetery. AG 9/28/1907

HORTON, Andrew W., Dr. of Alabama, age 35, d. Atlanta Fri. Interred: Pelham, Ala. AG 2/27/1910

HORTON, Richard, colored, age 51, d. 36 Oliver St. Atlanta. AG 8/19/1908

HORTON, Virgil A. S., age 72, d. Old Soldiers' Home, Atlanta. Confederate Veteran. Interred: Westview. AG 7/11/1908

HORTON, W. J., Mrs. d. Sat. 444 Peachtree St. Atlanta. Interred: Augusta. AG 5/20/1907

HOUCHIN, J. W., age 75, d. 163 Peeples St. Atlanta. He was b. London 1832, came to America 1869; to Atlanta 1886. Wife: Laura. Ch: J. R., Atlanta; Mrs. Octavia Smith (Arp) of Cartersville; Mrs. Catherine Higgins, N. Y. AG 5/18/1907

HOUGE, F. W., Mrs., d. Mon., Lakewood Heights, Atlanta. Interred: New Hope. AG 2/27/1907

HOUGH, M., Mrs., age 68, d. 362 N. Jackson St. Atlanta. AG 5/8/1907

HOULT, Nellie E., Mrs., age 58, d. 40 W. Linden St. Atlanta. AG 8/24/1908

HOUSE, E. V. P., age 82, d. Soldiers Home, Atlanta. AG 7/10/1907

HOUSE, John Hayden, age 1, son of Mr. and Mrs. John M., d. Atlanta Mon. Interred: Wesleys Chapel church yard. AG 6/23/1908

HOUSE, M. J., Mrs., age 66, d. N. Peachtree Rd., Atlanta, Wed. Son: C. C. House. Interred: Mt. Perrin church yard. AG 2/27/1908

HOUSE, Margaret Del, little dau. of Mr. and Mrs. John House, d. Fri. Jefferson, Ga. Buried: Bethany. AG 7/23/1906

HOUSE, Mary Ruth, age 2, dau. of Mr. and Mrs. C. D. of 343

Formwalt St., Atlanta, d. Wed. Interred: Hollywood. AG 5/26/1908

HOUSE, S., colored, age 764, d. Atlanta. AG 11/25/1907

HOUSER, John A., Capt. of Ft. Valley, Ga., d. 3/.15, age 83. Wife was Miss Jones of Charleston, S. C. Ch: F. C., Macon; Mrs. W. M. Reese, Thomasville; Mrs. Alva B. Greene, Ft. Valley. Confed. Vet. AG 3/15/1910

HOUSTON, Edwin, Sheriff of Troup Co., d. 8/13 res. of mother-in-law, Mrs. T. S. Baker, W. Pt., Ga. Sis: Mattie Lou Houston, Dawson, Ga. Son: W. R., W. Pt. Wife. Interred: Pinewood Cemetery. AC 8/15/1905

HOUSTON, William, colored, age 22, d. 36 Gray St. Atlanta. AG 11/8/1910

HOUTEN, J., age 30, d. 111 Capitol Ave. Atlanta. AG 11/25/1907

HOWARD, A. G., Mrs. d. 9/12 Wadley, Ga. AC 9/14/1905

HOWARD, Annie, colored, age 1 yr., d. 11 Victoria St. Atlanta. AG 6/18/1907

HOWARD, Claud, colored, age 3, d. 11 Victoria St. Atlanta. AG 4/10/1908

HOWARD, Cura, colored, age 31, d. 725 N. Jackson St. Atlanta. AG 3/27/1909

HOWARD, E. G., Mrs., age 82, widow of late Dr. H. A., d. Oakland City Wed. Daus: Mrs. R. C. Howard, Mrs. A. D. Jay, Mrs. A. B. Graves. Sons: Rev. J. A. of Texas, A. J. of N. C., and T. A. of Atlanta. Interred: Montgomery, Ala. AG 12/15/1909

HOWARD, Ella, colored, age 50, d. 246 Vine St. Atlanta. AG 10/8/1909

HOWARD, Florence, colored, age 30, d. 130 Bell St. Atlanta. AG 2/13/1908

HOWARD, George, young man of Donalsonville, Ga. killed yesterday by train. AG 1/21/1908

HOWARD, Georgia O., Mrs., d. yesterday at home of Col. B. S. Walker, Monroe, Ga. AG 7/28/1906

HOWARD, John F., Hon., tax assessor of Thomas Co., d. 2/22. 6 ch. Wife died 2 yrs. ago. AG 2/23/1905

HOWARD, John F., Mrs. d. 1903 Thomas Co., Ga. AC 2/23/1905

HOWARD, Joseph, age 14, son of Mr. and Mrs. M. E., d. Tues. 17 Ashby St., Atlanta. Bro: Hugh. Sis: Mrs. N. B. Wright, Savannah, Georgia; Maude and Mozelle. Interred: Westview. AG 8/6/1907

HOWARD, Louis, negro, shot and killed at negro church, Monroe Co. AG 10/3/1906

HOWARD, Pollie, colored, age 58, d. 216 E. Cain St. Atlanta. AG 9/12/1908

HOWARD, Robert, age 28, d. Eden Park, E. Point, Ga. Thurs. Interred: Hill Crest Cemetery. Wife, two children, parents. AG 7/30/1909

HOWARD, Will, colored, age 19, d. 101 N. Butler St. Atlanta. AG 12/16/1907

HOWARD, William, colored, age 56, d. 243 Vine St. Atlanta. AG 1/10/1907

HOWARD, son, age 14 mos. of Frank Howard, planter, hung himself on swing while playing at home, Crawford, Ala. Columbus, Ga. AG 4/29/1907

HOWARD, Verner Allen, Jr., 10 weeks old son of Mr. and Mrs. V. A. Howard, died res., 425 Luckie St., Atlanta, Thurs. Interment: Easley, S. C. AG 12/26/1906

HOWE, **Martha V., Mrs.**, age 73, d. 154 Whitehall St., Atlanta Tues. 6 ch: John, Emmett; Mrs. Robert Braselton; Mrs. W. H. Allen; Mrs. Ernest Layham; Miss Ollie Howe. AG 3/15/1910

HOWE, **S. R., Mrs.**, age 77, d. Thurs. res. of dau., Mrs. P. E. Carlisle, 348 E. Georgia Ave., Atlanta. Interred: Hollywood. AG 7/23/1908

HOWELL, A. H. G., age 75, d. Hemphill, Ga. Wed. Wife, 6 children, 2 boys, 4 girls. Interred: Mt. Gilead Cemetery. AG 5/14/1908

HOWELL, B. J., age 45, d. Tilton, Ga., Sat. Interred: Westview. Two Children, mother, two sisters. AG 6/29/1908

HOWELL, B. J., Mrs., age 46, d. Tifton, Ga. Sat. Interred: Westview. Two children, mother, two sisters, survive. AG 7/29/1908

HOWELL, **Dee,** colored, age 85, d. 80 Greensferry Ave. Atlanta. AG 3/18/1909

HOWELL, E. B., Mrs. of Newberry, Fla., d. Valdosta, formerly Miss Kate Martin of Valdosta m. Dr. E. B. Howell 12/1908, niece of Mrs. W. S. West and T. G. and J. G. Cranford of Valdosta. AG 8/28/1909

HOWELL, **Gene** shot, killed by Will Askea yesterday, 4 miles from Hartwell, Ga. AG 12/26/1907

HOWELL, **John Wiley,** age 3, son of Mr. and Mrs. W. S., d. 23 Fulton St. Atlanta, Mon. Interred: Casey's Cemetery. AG 6/29/1909

HOWELL, **Katie,** colored, age 29, d. 142 N. Boulevard. Atlanta. AG 11/24/1910

HOWELL, **Katie, Mrs.**, age 58, d. 22 Henry St., Atlanta, Fri. Dau: Mrs. N. N. Blair. Interred: Hollywood. AG 7/18/1908

HOWELL, M. S., age 80, d. 4/28, Confed. Vet. Ch: Mrs. M. J. Palmer, J. F. Howell, >Mrs. O. M. McCarthy, Mrs. A. M. Clay, Mrs. Annie Nelly, George and Paul Howell. Interred: Sylvester cemetery. AG 4/29/1906

HOWELL, **Millard F.** d. Wed. Philadephia, Pa. Interred: Rome, Ga., Myrtle Hill cemetery. AG 4/10/1907

HOWELL, **Vallie May,** age 6 mos., d. 641 Woodward Ave. Atlanta. AG 5/21/1910

HOWELL, **William Francis,** age 8 mos., son of Mr. and Mrs. W. E., funeral Wed. Jonesboro Rd., Atlanta. Interred: Greenwood. AG 9/28/1910

HOWELL, **William P.**, age 8 mos., d. Jonesboro Rd. Atlanta. AG 9/29/1910

HOWE, **H. H., Mrs.**, age 64, d. 10 Gillett St., Atlanta, Oct. 18. AG 10/20/1910

HOWLAND, **Emma, Mrs.**, native of Kansas, age 74, wife of Alonzo, d. Tues. res. of dau., Mrs. W. H. Moore, 332 Gordon St. AG 7/10/1906

HOYLE, D. W. F., age 68, d. Columbus, Ga. yesterday. Born and raised in Tenn. Leaves wife, several children. AG 11/30/1907

HOYLE, **George S.**, age 58, killed by railway train at College Park. AG 10/6/1906

HOYLE, W. S., Mrs., age 57, d. E. Pt., Atlanta, Mon. One son, two daus., two bros. Interred: Pomona, Ga. AG 12/17/1910

HOYLE, **George F., Major,** age 65 of College Park, recruiting officer of US Army, hit by Atlanta train Tues. AG 10/1/1906

HOYT, **Lizzie M., Mrs.**, age 74, d. 584 Peachtree St. Atlanta. AG 7/28/1910

HUBARD, **Lelia, Mrs.**, age 82, wife of R. T., d. Atlanta Sun. Res. 19 Orange St. Interred: Westview. Dau: Martha. Father: Prof. J. B. T. Moss. Sis: Miss Kathleen Moss. Bros: B. M. and Howard K. Moss. AG 7/29/1908

HUBBARD, **Ervie, Mrs.**, age 31, d. 190 Echo St., Atlanta, Fri. Interred: Casey's Cemetery. AG 6/10/1910

HUBBARD, **Ethel**, age 11 mos., dau. of Mr. and Mrs. Henry G., d. Fri. Atlanta. Interred: Family burying ground. AG 7/6/1906

HUBBARD, **Jim**, colored, age 19, d. 101 N. Butler St. Atlanta. AG 5/4/1907

HUBBARD, **John W.**, d. Capitol Ave., Atlanta, formerly from Wilkes Co., age 74. Interred: City Cemetery, Washington, Ga. AG 6/31/1909

HUBBARD, **Julia**, colored, age 23, d. Berkele St. Atlanta. AG 5/12/1909

HUBBARD, **Randall**, colored, age 58, d. 101 Rawson St. Atlanta. AG 3/22/1909

HUBEN, **Joseph**, infant, d. 66 Connally St. Atlanta. AG 5/25/1906

HUBERT, **Moses**, colored, age 29, d. 101 N. Butler St. Atlanta. AG 2/26/1908

HUCKABEE, **Dozier**, shot and killed by Gene Bryant, negro, Sun. Columbus, Ga. AG 2/19/1907

HUCKABY, **Charles**, infant son of Mr. and Mrs. W. C., d. 95 Means St., Atlanta, Sat. Interred: Concord, Ga. AG 6/10/1910

HUCKABY, **Lilla**, colored, age 24, d. 58 Moody Place. Atlanta. AG 1/19/1907

HUCKABY, **Tantie, Mrs.**, age 70, d. Wed. Atlanta. Sis: Mrs. John LeRoy, Lowndesville, S. C. Nephew: W. C. Tennett, 365 Capitol Ave., Atlanta. Cousins: Mrs. A. M. Perkerson, Tom Moore, Atlanta. Interred: Lowndesville, S. C. AG 9/16/1909

HUDDLESTON, **G. W., Mrs.**, sister of Mrs. Rolfe Hunt of Atlanta, d. Jackson, Miss. Her bro. d. Colorado Springs, Col. few wks ago. Several children, husband, father, mother, one bro. in Tenn., sister in Chicago. AG 5/8/1906

HUDDLESTON, **John W., Mrs.** d. Eufaula, Ala. 7/15. Dau: Mrs. Clayton D. Tullis, Montgomery. AG 7/16/1909

HUDGENS, **M. L., Mrs.** d. Tampa, Fla., former res. of Atlanta, and formerly Miss Pallie M. Whittle. Mother: Mrs. Lottie Whittle. 2 sisters, 4 stepchildren, one child.

HUDGENS, **M. L., Mrs.**, former res. of Atlanta, formerly Miss Pallie M. Whittle. Mother: Mrs. Lottie Whittle. 2 sisters, 4 stepchildren, one child. AG 2/28/1910

HUDGENS, **Mildred Lee**, age 1 mo., d. 14 Dodd Ave. Atlanta. AG 4/19/1907

HUDGINS, **Bradley**, inf. son of Mr. and Mrs. B. B., d. Wed. Gainesville, Ga. at 166 N. Jackson St. Atlanta. Interred: Westview.

HUDGINS, **Jack** of East Point, age 55, d. Atlanta. He lived with sister, Mrs. Bowden in East Point. AG 1/12/1907

HUDGINS, **Charles Augustus**, rr engineer, killed wreck, Powder Springs Fri. Bur: Cedartown. Wife, two children, survive, Sarah, age 5, Miller Wright, age 2. Sister: Miss Mamie Hudgins. Mother, brother, Cartersville. Brother, Texas. AG 3/2/1907

HUDSON, **Bessie Lee**, age 4 mos., dau. of Mrs. W. D. Hudson, d. Sat., Atlanta. AG 2/11/1907

HUDSON, Clara May d. Sun. W. Hunter St. Atlanta. Interred: Westview. AG 5/14/1906

HUDSON, Cora Lee, Mrs. d. 243 S. Boulevard, Atlanta, Fri. Husband: E. M. Interred: Newnan, Ga. AG 7/11/1908

HUDSON, Desty, Mrs., age 68, d. 753 Whitehall St. Atlanta. Interred: Buford, Ga. AG 5/11/1908

HUDSON, Eddie P., age 19, son of Mrs. Sarah, d. several days ago. AG 12/14/1907

HUDSON, Ethel May, Miss interred Oakland. AG 7/20/1906

HUDSON, Everett Frank, age 2 yrs., son of Mr. and Mrs. Roscoe, d. 11/12, 34 Savannah St. Atlanta. Interred: Cool Springs, Ga. AC 11/13/1905

HUDSON, Forrest P., Mrs. d. Montreal, Ga. Tues. Husband: F. P. Interred: Tucker, Ga. AG 12/30/1907

HUDSON, George G., from Atlanta, suicide, Birmingham, Ala. AG 3/29/1910

HUDSON, George, Hon., citizen of Jefferson Co., Ga., d. age 83. Wife, several children. Interred: Old Providence Church. AG 9/27/1907

HUDSON, Hazel, age 2, dau. of Mr. and Mrs. T. R., d. 23 Powell St., Atlanta, Wed. Interred: Hollywood. AG 3/18/1908

HUDSON, J. L., Jr. funeral Sun. 320 Hemphill Ave., Atlanta. Interred: Westview. AG 5/2/1910

HUDSON, J. T. d. Atlanta Sat. Interred: Sardis cemetery. AG 1/20/1908

HUDSON, John, Mrs. murdered by John Hudson and Henry Campbell, all negroes. AG 1/9/1908

HUDSON, L. D., Mrs., age 38, wife of Sheriff, of Spalding Co., d. 6/6. Interred: Midway Church, 4 mi. E. of Griffin. Several children. AG 6/7/1910

HUDSON, M. A., Mrs., age 46, d. 414 Luckie St. Atlanta. AG 10/29/1907

HUDSON, M. M. (Phil) d. 6/24 Columbus, Ga. Funeral: Prospect Church near Waverly Hall, Ga. AC 6/26/1905

HUDSON, Marie, colored, age 11 mos., d. 43 Martin St. Atlanta. AG 3/22/1909

HUDSON, Martha Ann, Mrs., age 46, d. 414 Luckie St., Atlanta. Ch: Mrs. Ozmer, W. G. Hudson, Earl Hudson. Interred: Oakland. AG 10/26/1907

HUDSON, N. E., Mrs. funeral Tues at home in Jones Co., Ga. Interred: Family Burial Grounds. AG 6/23/1908

HUDSON, R. N., age 57, d. Atlanta Sun. Interred: Cartersville. AG 1/18/1910

HUDSON, Stella E., Mrs. d. 706 Sells Ave., Atlanta. Interred: Westview. AG 7/30/1906

HUDSON, W. L. d. Thurs. Interred: Cummings, Ga. AG 6/29/1906

HUES, E. C., convict, d. from cruelty and neglect. AG 5/5/1909

HUEY, Annie, Mrs., age 10, dau. of Mr. and Mrs. G. H., d. 27 Echo St., Atlanta, Mon. Interred: Mason's cemetery. AG 11/23/1907

HUEY, Buchanan, age 53, d. 93 Garibaldi St., Atlanta. Interred: Stamps Chapel church yard. AG 4/25/1910

HUEY, E. B., age 53, d. 93 Garibaldi St. Atlanta. AG 4/25/1910

HUEY, Hannah, Mrs., age 83, d. Flat Shoals Road, near E. Lake, Atlanta, Fri. Leaves husband, two sons, three daus. Interred: Family Grave Yard, near E. Lake. AG 11/23/1907

HUEY, T. M., age 45, d. Chattahoochee River. Atlanta. AG 5/18/1908

HUFF, Elizabeth, age 80, died at Howell Station. AG 11/26/1906

HUFF, Emily, Mrs., age 26, d. 72 Gillett St., Atlanta, Tues., wife of O. C. Sis: Mrs. J. P. Sewall, Miss Jennie Allen. Interred: College Park Cemetery. AG 11/8/1910

HUFF, James, age 23, d. Decatur and N. Boulevard. Atlanta. AG 5/6/1908

HUFF, James E., age 29, d. Atlanta Mon. Interred: Madison, Ga. AG 7/27/1909

HUFF, Jeremiah C., Mrs., b. Clarke Co. 7/4/1821. Maiden name: Elizabeth Norton m. 8/1848 Thos Wells (d. 1847) Son: Montgomery Wells. m. 11/1853 Mr. Huff. Ch: Jeremiah C., M. S. Clayton Huff. 9 grch, 5 grgrch. Bur: Oakland. Husband, daus, Misses Sarah and Cordella Huff. AG 11/26/1906

HUFF, Louise, age 6 mos., d. 101 N. Butler St. Atlanta. AG 3/29/1909

HUFF, Louise, inf. dau. of Mr. and Mrs. H. L. of 224 Smith St., d. Atlanta. Interred: Mansfield, Ga. AG 3/29/1909

HUFF, Mollie, age 2, dau. of Mr. and Mrs. M., 203 Cooper St., Atlanta, d. Wed. Interred: Mansfield, Ga. AG 7/15/1909

HUFF, Rand, colored, age 58, d. 162 Williams St. Atlanta. AG 8/20/1908

HUFF, Willie Beck, age 2, d. 203 Cooper St. Atlanta. AG 7/16/1909

HUGGINS, Bluford funeral 1/2 Carrollton, Ga. Died. 12/31/1904, age abt 75. Sexton of Carrollton Cemetery. AC 1/3/1905

HUGHES, Abbie, Mrs., wife of J. I., age 35, d. 69 Luckie St. Atlanta. Bro-in-law: G. W. Watkins. Husband, one child, her father, survive, James W. Johnson. AG 8/19/1908

HUGHES, Charles Edward, age 11 mos., d. 17 Stonewall St. Atlanta. AG 6/9/1908

HUGHES, Charles Edward, inf. son of Mr. and Mrs. H. H. of 17 Stonewall St., Atlanta. Interred: Greenwood. AG 6/8/1908

HUGHES, E. W., age 70, Confed. Vet., d. Soldiers' Home, Atlanta. Interred: Westview. He enlisted in 40th Ga. Regt., Co. G. AG 9/27/1910

HUGHES, E. W., age 76, d. Old Soldiers' Home. Atlanta. AG 9/28/1910

HUGHES, J. I., Mrs., age 85, d. Atlanta. Interred: Fairburn, Ga. AG 8/19/1908

HUGHES, J. M., aged citizen of Catoosa Co., d. Sun., age 88. Wife, 7 children. AG 8/9/1910

HUGHES, J. M., Rev., citizen of Cumming, Ga., d. Wed. Interred: Ebenezer cemetery. AG 6/1/1907

HUGHES, J. W., Mrs. d. Columbus, Ga. Fri. Res. 118 Estoria St. Atlanta. Interred: Westview. AG 5/8/1906

HUGHES, John S., age 65, d. Atlanta Sun. Interred: South Bend church yard. Sons: John, Willard. 3 sisters, 2 bros. AG 6/28/1909

HUGHES, Lacey d. Efland, Orange Co., N. C. trying to save friend, Earl S. Faucett who also browned. Both unmd. AC 5/22/1905

HUGHES, Malcolm, age 8 mos., inf. son of Mr. and Mrs. H. H., d. 36 Jones Ave., Atlanta, Tues. Father resides San Antonio, Tx. AG 5/11/1910

HUGHES, Marguerite, age 19, died 10 Daniel St., Atlanta. AG 12/28/1906

HUGHES, Nettie Lee, inf. dau. of J. W., Jr., d. Wed. home of grandmother, 75 Berean Ave., Atlanta. Interred: Westview. AG 6/7/1906

HUGHES, Nina, Miss, age 24, d. Thurs. 17 W. Cain St. Atlanta. Interred Oakland. AG 9/14/1907

HUGHES, R. F. d. Piedmont, Ala. 4/11. AC 4/13/1905

HUGHES, R. M., age 41, d. 413 Pulliam St. Atlanta. AG 9/17/1907

HUGHES, Robert M., age 41, Atlanta letter carrier for 10 years, buried Cummings, Ga. AG 9/14/1907

HUGHES, Sena, Mrs., age 81, d. Ft. McPherson, Ga., Fri. Interred: Mt. Zion Church yard. AG 4/10/1909

HUGHES, Susie, Mrs., age 61, d. Sat. 668 Woodward Ave., Atlanta. Interred: Marvin church yard. AG 2/4/1910

HUGHES, Margaret, Miss, dau. of Mrs. A. L. Hughes, d. 10 Daniel St. Bur: Good Templars. Pallbearers: R. R. Hudson, Raymond Sherrill, Chas Hughes, Carl Hughes, Wm Smith, L. M. Porter, AG 12/26/1906

HUGHEY, John, age 56, d. Atlanta. AG 2/8/1910

HUGHLEY, Lucinda, Mrs., age 82 d. res. of dau., Mrs. Flora Rapp, Howell Mill Rod., Atlanta, Sun. Daus: Mrs. Flora Rapp, Mrs. H. C. Ramsey, Mrs. H. H. Fudge, Mrs. C. W. Smith, all of Atlanta. Interred: Oakland. AG 4/22/1907

HUGULEY, Sam, colored, age 23, d. Grady Hospital. Atlanta. AG 8/5/1907

HUIETT, J. M., age 69, from N. Y. two years ago, d. Tues. St. George, Ga. Interred: Oakview. AG 12/9/1909

HUIE, Hilda, Miss, dau. of Capt. and Mrs. Joseph H., funeral Sun. Interred: Philadelphia Cemetery, Forest Park, Ga. 6 bros., 2 bros: Mrs. Luther Murphy, Roger Huie (Anniston, Ala.); Edgar Huie, Mrs. Robert Chapman, Lucile Huie (Forest Park); Mrs. Lorna Shelnutt, E. Pt., Ga.; Mrs. George M. Murphy, Atlanta; Mrs. Edgar Murphy, Atlanta. AG 9/23/1910

HULL, C. D., age 52, d. 10 Grand Ave. Atlanta. AG 8/9/1907

HULL, Julia M., Mrs., age 82, d. 160 Pine St. Atlanta. AG 6/21/1906

HULL, Mark T., age 64, d. 84 Lowe St. Atlanta. AG 5/15/1907

HULME, Robert d. near Elberton yesterday. He was son of Dillard Hulme of Elbert Co. Leaves wife. AG 2/15/1907

HULME, Rubie R., Miss, age 19, dau. of Mr. and Mrs. W. H. of Elberton, Ga., d. Tues. Atlanta. Interred: Elberton, Ga. AG 9/28/1910

HULSEY, Adda, Miss, sis. of late Mrs. H. C. Sawtell, d. Thurs. 311 Formwalt St., Atlanta, age 67, dau. of late William Hulsey of DeKalb Co. Bro: J. J. Hulsey, Decatur. Interred: Oakland. AG 8/1/1907

HULSEY, B. Jeff d. Sun. near Gainesville. Wife. Sons: John M., Julius M., and Roe. Daus: Mrs. Manas, Mrs. Neese. AG 3/1/1910

HULSEY, Marion J., Mrs., age 65, wife of Judge W. H., former mayor and ordinary of Fulton Co., d. 74 Forrest Ave., Wed., Atlanta. Interred: Oakland. AG 1/9/1907

HULSEY, Sarah, Mrs., wife of J. J., d. several days ago. Interred: Panthersville Presbyterian church yard. AG 12/14/1907

HUMBER, Charles, Mrs. d. home of mother, Mrs. E. H. Garrard, near Dennis Sta., Putnam Co. Interred: Arat. Leaves husband, 6 children. AG 11/9/1907

HUMBERT, **Minerva Mary, Mrs.** of Newberry, S. C., d. E. Main St., Mon., age 79. Husband: Rev. J. W. Bro: H. H. Kinard, Newberry. Sis: Mrs. A. Coke Smith, wid. of Bishop A. Coke Smith of Norfolk, Va. Niece: Mrs. E. H. Aull, Newberry. Nephews: Dr. James P. Kinard of Winthrope College, John M. Kinard of Newberry. Interred: Rosemont Cemetery. AG 11/8/1910

HUMPHREY, **Alma, Miss**, age 24, d. Tues. Atlanta. Bro: Amos Humphrey. Sis: Mrs. G. Little, Miss Lizzie Humphrey. Interred: Bainbridge, Ga. AG 7/19/1910

HUMPHREY, **Henry**, age 37, d. 9/21 Tuscaloosa, Ala. Interred: Madison Co. AG 9/22/1910

HUMPHREY, **James I.**, age 11, of Atlanta shot dead by his uncle in hunt near Aiken, S. C., age 11, son of Charles A. of 372 Courtland St., Atlanta. Uncle: B. F. Tyler. AG 12/28/1907

HUMPHREY, **Pearl**, colored, age 21, d. 475 Smith St. Atlanta. AG 4/28/1908

HUMPHREY, **W. M.**, age 45, died of accident, Ga. RR. Atlanta. AG 8/18/1906

HUMPHRIES, **A. D.**, age 52, d. Tues. Hapeville, Ga. Wife, 5 children. AG 6/22/1910

HUMPHRIES, **Albert Sammes**, infant, d. 56 Woodward Ave. Atlanta. AG 6/13/1910

HUMPHRIES, **Alma, Miss**, age 22, d. 65 Houston St. Atlanta. Interred: Bainbridge, Ga. AG 7/22/1910

HUMPHRIES, **Bertie**, inf. dau. of Mr. and Mrs. J. D., d. Mon. 73 Butler St. Atlanta. Interred: Westview. AG 2/21/1910

HUMPHRIES, **Bettie, Mrs.**, age 47, wife of J. M., d. 65 Greenwood Ave., Atlanta, Wed. 4 children. AG 3/3/1910

HUMPHRIES, **Susie, Mrs.**, age 50, d. 163 Love St. Atlanta. Sat. Interment: Caseys. AG 9/1/1906

HUNKLER, **Mary J.**, age 4 mos., d. 65 W. Georgia Ave. Atlanta. AG 4/1/1907

HUNLEY, **Lon**, old negro, found dead in a house in the Bottom, Columbus, Ga. AG 11/3/1906

HUNNICUTT, **G. H.**, carpenter, dropped dead, res. of E. Point. Interred: East Point. AG 1/21/1910

HUNNICUTT, **George W.** d. Wed. 15 Estoria St., Atlanta. Interred: Westview. Wife, three daus., one son, survive. AG 5/23/1907

HUNNICUT, **infant** of C. H., colored, d. 51 Humphries St. Atlanta. AG 5/25/1906

HUNNICUTT, **Nellie Mae, Miss**, age 16, d. Sun. 17 Estoria St., Atlanta, dau. of G. W. Hunnicutt. Interred: Westview. AG 5/27/1907

HUNNICUTT, **R. H.**, age 38, d. Ponce de Leon Ave. Atlanta. AG 1/25/1910

HUNNICUTT, **W. O., Mrs.**, age 24, d. Macon 4/11. Husband, parents. Md. abt 3 yrs. Interred: Mt. Pleasant Cemetery. AC 4/12/1905

HUNT, **A. F.**, age 35, d. 321 Whitehall St. Atlanta. AG 11/12/1907

HUNT, **A. F.**, merchant of Hartwell, Ga. d. Sun. Interred: Hartwell, Ga. AG 11/11/1907

HUNT, **Abigail, Mrs.**, mother of Misses Anna E. and Ethel Hunt, d. Fri. 39 E. Third St. Atlanta, age 66. Former res. of Wooster, Ohio, where interred. AG 10/21/1910

HUNT, Annie Mongin, Mrs., age 73, d. 111 Logan St. Atlanta Mon. Interred: Westview. Son: W. B. Sis: Mrs. E. J. Martin, Mrs. B. M. Hunter. Bro: Major J. M. Barnard, LaGrange. AG 1/4/1910

HUNT, Cicero funeral Tues. Interred: Douglasville, Ga. AG 7/6/1910

HUNT, F. W. of Atlanta, body found drowned in Altamaha River. Interred: Savannah. AG 12/19/1907

HUNT, Frank P., age 55, d. Wed. Decatur, Ga. Wife. Bro: F. A. Hunt, Bullochville, Ga. Ch: Gordon Hunt, Mrs. E. H. Carson. Interred: Decatur, Ga. AG 3/3/1909

HUNT, Gertrude, Miss, age 65, d. 39 Carnegie Way. Atlanta. Interred: Sandersville, Ga. AG 6/23/1910

HUNT, Hoke murdered by Jim Reed at Chattahoochee Church near Flowery Branch last year. His trail this morning Hall Superior Court, Gainesville. AG 1/28/1907

HUNT, I. S., Mrs. d. Thomson 6/14. Husband, son, dau. AC 6/16/1905

HUNT, Olin C. d. Laurel, Ms. b. 1867 Monroe Co., Ga. Bros: Rev. Wolfe, Atlanta; Homer L., Atlanta; J. S., Milner; Dr. D. Roy, Myrick, Ms.; Col. F. M., Purvis, Ms. Mother: Mrs. F. C. Sis: Louise; Mrs. D. Macune, Rose Hill, Ms. AG 1/21/1907

HUNTER, Annie, colored, age 29, d. 181 E. Harris St. Atlanta. AG 10/7/1909

HUNTER, Bertie J., Mrs., age 22, d. 153 Emmett St. Atlanta. AG 6/7/1907

HUNTER, Carson, colored, age 24, died at Terminal Sta. Atlanta. AG 12/28/1906

HUNTER, Ellen, colored, age 30, d. 45 Wells St. Atlanta. AG 9/22/1910

HUNTER, Hattie, colored, age 3, d. Atlanta. AG 12/9/1910

HUNTER, J. W., Jr., colored, age 25, d. 27 Rosbery St. Atlanta. AG 7/12/1907

HUNTER, Joseph A. killed in railroad wreck Somerset, Ky. Res: Clara St., Atlanta. Interred: Hollywood. AG 8/2/1906

HUNTER, Julia E., Mrs., age 35, d. 51 Garden St., Atlanta, Thurs. Interred: Hollywood. AG 8/7/1908

HUNTER, Melinda, colored, age 68, d. 74 Inman Ave. Atlanta. AG 3/1/1908

HUNTON, John W., Mrs. d. 3/11, Griffin, formerly Miss Briscoe of Walton Co. Husband, mother, one child, Mary Briscoe Hunton. AG 8/11/1908

HURD, L. J., age 76, d. 306 E. Hunter St. Atlanta, Sun. Confed. Vet., Co. E, 5th Ala. Sons: W. F., Washington, D. C.; Howard L., Atlanta. Bro: Albert H., Lee, Mass. AG 7/12/1909

HURD, S. J. d. Sun. 306 E. Hunter St. Atlanta. Interred: Newnan, Ga. A 7/13/1909

HURDIE, Louise, age 13 mos., dau. of Mr. and Mrs. J. W. Hurdie, d. Sun. Montezuma, Ga. AG 2/5/1907

HURLEY, Annie Mary, age 2 mos., dau. of Mr. and Mrs. J. T., d. 88 W. Fair St., Atlanta, Fri. Interred: Oakland. AG 12/14/1907

HURLEY, Savillah Henrietta, inf. dau. of Rec. and Mrs. H. C., d. 265 S. Boulevard, Atlanta, Wed. Interred: Westview. AG 7/31/1908

HURST, J. M., Sr., age 89, d. 308 E. Linden Ave., Atlanta, Sat. Wife, two sons. Interred: Social Circle, Ga. AG 4/16/1910

HURST, J. N., age 80, d. 10/31. Wife, large family. Interred: City Cemetery, Opelika, Ala. AC 11/3/1905

HURSTON, Rosa, age 6 yrs., dau. of Mr. and Mrs. Hurston of 102 Chapel St., Atlanta. Interred: Hollywood. AG 7/12/1906

HURT, Martin, colored, age 31, d. 101 N. Butler St. Atlanta. AG 7/19/1909

HURT, Martin, young negro of 226 E. Ellis St., Atlanta, d. Fri. from bullet hole recd in fight with wife, Alice. AG 7/16/1909

HUSH, Abe suicide Cottonton, Ga., on Chattahoochee river, Fri. last. AG 5/6/1910

HUSON, G. J. of Thomasville d. Mon. res. of cousin, Mrs. T. M. Armistead, 315 Whitehall St., Atlanta. Huson b. Conyers, age 56. Wife. Bro: R. W. Huson, Conyers. Four daus., one son. Interment: Conyers. AG 10/3/1906

HUSTACE, Augustus d. N. Y. Survived by wife and mother. AG 4/29/1907

HUTBROAD, DR. d. Leipsic 4/17. AC 4/18/1905

HUTCHENS, George O., infant son of Mr. and Mrs. G. D. Hutchens, d. 302 E. Fair St., Atlanta, Sun. Interred: Bainbridge, Ga. AG 7/23/1906

HUTCHENSON, R. B., Dr. of Draketown, Ga. d. 7/27, age 80. Son: Dr. E. B. Nephews: Hon. Thomas A. Hutcheson, Ordinary of Haralson; W. R. Hutcheson, atty; Hon. E. R. Griffith, representative. AC 7/28/1905

HUTCHESON, J. E., middle-aged man of Bremen, Ga. d. in Gentry's Livery Stable Wed. Leaves wife, 3 children. AG 2/8/1908

HUTCHINS, Alexander, age 80, d. Milledgeville. Interred: Pleasant Hill Cemetery. Ch: Josh, Odden, Tyler, Earl; Mrs. Dan Rey, Macon. Bros: J. H., Jack, Auburn, Ga. AG 9/6/1909

HUTCHINS, Earl E., age 14, son of J. P., d. Wed. 161 Randolph St., Atlanta. Interred: Augusta, Ga., home of parents. AG 5/23/1907

HUTCHINS, Elsie, Miss, dau. of C. C., d. Hawkinsville 5/9. AC 5/10/1905

HUTCHINS, Frank d. Sat. Atlanta. Interred: Antioch Baptist Church. Sis: Mrs. T. A. Bowen of East Point, Ga. AG 1/14/1907

HUTCHINS, Jack, age 58, d. Atlanta. AG 1/15/1907

HUTCHINS, Mary, inf. dau. of Mr. and Mrs. G. D., d. Sat. 302 E. Fair St. Atlanta. Interred: Hollywood. AG 3/5/1910

HUTCHINS, Nathan Louis, Judge b. Lawrenceville, Ga. 10/4/1835, son of Nathan L. and Mary Dixon (Holt) Hutchins (she was dau. of Hines Holt, Sr.), d. 6/8 Lawrenceville. Ch: N. L., Jr., Lawrenceville; Mrs. Charles H. Brand, Athens; Mrs. R. Iverson Randolph of Atlanta and Mrs. Hooper Alexander of Decatur. Confed. Vet., Lt. 3rd Ga. Battn of Sharpshooters. He m. 1866 Miss Carrie Orr of Lawrenceville. One bro survives: Clarence L. of Suwanee. Sis: Lee Winn, Greensboro; Mrs. W. H. Powell, Lawrenceville; W. H.; Victor; Eve; Blanch. Nephew: Dr. Miller B. Hutchins, Atlanta, which decd reared as his gdn, also: Mrs. Julia Iverson Patton and Mrs. Minnie

HUTCHINSON, Alice, Mrs. funeral at bro-in-law, L. B. Hutchinson, 140 Rawson St., Atlanta. Interred: Oakland. AG 4/9/1908

HUTCHINSON, Eileen (or Ellen) Jeannette, age 10 mos., dau. of Mr. and Mrs. Paul H., d. Tues. 113 Jones Ave., Atlanta. Interred: Westview. AG 6/7/1910

HUTCHINSON, Thomas S., Conf. Vet., d. Wed., interred 3/3 in City Cemetery, Greensboro, Ga. Wife, 4 children: Mrs. W. G. Armor, Greensboro; Tol S. Hutchinson, Greene Co.; T. M. Hutchinson, Monticello. AG 3/4/1910

HYATT, Eddie, age 7 mos., d. 101 Butler St. Atlanta. Son of M. and Mrs. R. H. Hyatt. Interred: Westview. AG 7/10/1909

HYATT, W. W., d. Thurs., 306 E. Pine St., Atlanta. Leaves wife, children, mother, two sisters, four brothers. AG 3/9/1907

HYMAN, J. J., Rev. dying ar Arabi, Ga., age 72. AC 8/24/1905

HYNDMAN, James W., Jr., age 20 mos., son of Mr. and Mrs. J. W., of 54 Terry St., Atlanta, d. grandmother's home, Mrs. O. H. Snider, 337 E. Hunter St. Atlanta Mon. Interred: Decatur, Ga. AG 5/12/1908

HYNDS, Ruth Carr, Mrs., age 34, d. Howell Park Sanitarium. Atlanta. AG 9/5/1906

ICKES, Fannie M., Mrs. d. Thurs. 101 Courtland St. Atlanta, age 80. Son: Charles Spangler, only son, d. 6 mos. ago. Sis. lives Abbottstown, Pa. Interred: Pennsylvania, old home. AG 9/23/1910

INGLE, S. L., age 36, d. 101 Butler St. Atlanta. AG 9/2/1909

INGRAHAM, John, colored, age 49, d. 268 Auburn Av.e, Atlanta, Nov. 2. AG 11/5/1910

INGRAHAM, John M., age 68, d. Home for Incurables. Atlanta. Interred: Westview. Wife, son, 3 daus. AG 4/20/1908

INGRAM, Bat, age 46, d. Sun. Geneva, Ga. Bro: Arthur G. of Marvin. Sis: Mrs. B. W. Williams of Opelika, Ala. and Mrs. Frank Tignor of Columbus, Ga. Interred: City Cemetery, Opelika, Ala. AG 5/25/1910

INGRAM, George, age 57, funeral Sat Atlanta. Survived by: Dr. R. F. Ingram and Mrs. E. A. Battle, of Atlanta; Julian and William Ingram of Union Pt., and James J. Ingram, of Greensboro. Interred: Hollywood. AG 6/10/1910

INGRAM, Lavina, Mrs., age 79, d. Thurs. Oakland City, Atlanta. Husband: J. W. Ch: C. L. and Frances Ingram. Interred: Brooks Station, Ga. AG 7/22/1909

INGRAM, Nora E., Mrs., wife of W. R., d. Wed. res. 114 Niles St., Howell's Sta., Atlanta. Interred: Hollywood. AG 8/23/1907

INGRAM, Paul J., age 17, son o f Mrs. Mary, d. Fri. 123 Powers St., Atlanta. AG 4/16/1910

INGRAM, Robert, age 73, d. Jackson. Bur: Atlanta, Hollywood Cem. Sons: W. D., of Jackson, and Robert, Jr., Atlanta. Daus: Mrs. Lizzie Kirk, Mrs. Lula Breadwater, Mrs. Ida Britt, Mrs. Fannie Waters, Miss Hattie Ingram, Atlanta. AG 8/25/1910

INGRAM, Sarah, Mrs., age 41, wife of R. L., d. 11/13, 904 Marietta St., Atlanta. Interred: Hollywood. AC 11/14/1905

INMAN, Hugh T., age 63, d. 420 W. Peachtree St. Atlanta. AG 11/17/1910

INMAN, Walker P. d. Sat. 478 Peachtree St. Atlanta. Interred: Oakland. AG 11/25/1907

INZER, Reuben A., age 1, son of Mr. and Mrs. G. W. of 19 Echo St., Atlanta, d. Mon. Interred: Maloney Springs, Ga. AG 8/3/1909

IRBY, Ed, colored, age 65, d. 3 McMillan St. Atlanta. AG 8/22/1910

IRBY, Virginia, Mrs., age 65, from Eufaula, Ala., d. Columbus, Ga. 5/28 res. of Mrs. M. C. Barlow. Bro: Virgil Crawford of Eufaula, Sheriff of Barbour Co. AC 5/30/1905

IRBY, Virginia, Mrs., age 65, from Eufaula, Ala., d. Columbus, Ga. 5/28 res. of Mrs. M. C. Barlow. Bro: Virgil Crawford of Eufaula, Sheriff of Barbour Co. AC 5/30/1905
IRVINE, Ruth A., Mrs. funeral Sat. res. of son, William S., Macon. Interred: Riverside. AG 12/7/1910
IRVINE, Ruth H., Mrs., age 80, d. 1106 Walnut St., Macon, Thurs. Interred: Rose Hill. AG 12/17/1910
IRVIN, John F.. Lumpkin, Ga., 11/16/1906. Irvin died yesterday. Survivors: wife, four children. AG 11/16/1906
IRWIN, A. Walter, aged plumber, found dead near res. at Center Hill Sun., abt 60 yrs. old. AG 12/14/1908
ISENBURG, Edward, inf. son of Mr. and Mrs. J. H. of E. Atlanta, d. Mon. Interred: Sylvester. AG 7/13/1909
IVEY, P. A., funeral Tues. at res. 208 Richardson St., Atlanta. Interred: Hollywood. AG 8/21/1906
IVIE, B. F., age 68, d. 14 Fulton Terr. Atlanta Wed. Interred: Stone Mtn, Ga. AG 7/2/1908
IVIE, Mary L., Mrs. d. Sun. Atlanta, mother of late Theodore Ivie. Sisters: Mrs. J. W. Christian, Mrs. C. Boyles, Mrs. Annie Bennett, Mrs. George Hawley, Mrs. Annie Taylor, Mrs. Eugenia Marchman. Interred: Westview. AG 5/28/1906
JABOLEY, James, age 1, d. 52 Pratt St. Atlanta. AG 12/27/1910
JACK, Etta, Mrs., age 26, d. Atlanta Sun. Husband: J. R. Parents: Mr. and Mrs. Bagwell of Carbon Hill, Ala. Sis: Mrs. J. J. Hill, Mrs. Ella Candiess, Mrs. Essie West, of Ala. Interred: Oakland. AG 7/5/1909
JACK, Lou, Mrs., age 66, d. Wed. at res. of adopted dau., Mrs. Charlie Austin, 98 Alexander St., Atlanta. Interred: Oakland. Bro: Ed Holland. Half-sis: Mrs. A. M. Little. AG 9/27/1906
JACKSON, A. J. of Atlanta d. Anniston, Ala. 9/27. Came to Ala. to escape race riots. AG 9/27/1906
JACKSON, A. M., colored, age 23, d. rear of 174 Butler St. Atlanta. AG 11/2/1907
JACKSON, Ada, colored, age 25, d. 231 W. Hunter St. Atlanta. AG 8/7/1908
JACKSON, Allene, Miss, age 25, d. 399 Frasier St. Atlanta. AG 2/11/1907
JACKSON, Alton, two yr. old son of Jesse Jackson died hours after father, 1086 Marietta St. Atlanta. AG 3/1/1907
JACKSON, Anderson A., inf. of Mr. and Mrs. T. A., d. 689 Woodward Ave., Atlanta, Tues. Interred: Westview. AG 7/20/1909
JACKSON, Andrew d. Comfort, Texas 7/16, son of Mrs. A. M., of Gainesville, Ga. Wife, one child. Interred: Gainesville, Ga. AC 7/18/1905
JACKSON, Arthur, age 48, native of Scotland, stone-cutter, d. 58 Walton St., Atlanta, Fri., age 48. Interred: Westview. AG 8/4/1906
JACKSON, Artie May, colored, age 19, d. Atlanta. AG 9/21/1909
JACKSON, Bradford, eldest son of Mr. and Mrs. A. C., d. Watkinsville, Ga. Sat, student Ga. Mil. Inst. 3 sisters, one bro., nephew, Mr. A. J. Haygood, Atlanta. AG 6/25/1908
JACKSON, Elizabeth, age 78, d. 214 Lawton St. Atlanta. AG 1/19/1910
JACKSON, Emily, colored, age 50, d. 197 Lambert St. Atlanta. AG 12/18/1907

JACKSON, Emma, colored, age 25, died, 21 Kennesaw, Atlanta. AG 11/20/1906

JACKSON, Essie, colored, age 17, d. 144 Bedford Pl. Atlanta. AG 5/6/1909

JACKSON, Gilbert, Jr. d. McDonough Rd. Fri. Interred: Family burial ground. AG 1/14/1907

JACKSON, Guy P., colored, age 3, d. 103 Mooney St. Atlanta. AG 10/13/1908

JACKSON, Hazra, colored, age 2 mos., d. 134 W. Pine St. Atlanta. AG 12/14/1907

JACKSON, Henry, colored, age 3, d. Spencer St. Atlanta. AG 12/17/1910

JACKSON, J. F., Jr., inf. son of Mr. and Mrs. J. J., d. 110 Plum St., Atlanta, Wed. AG 6/8/1910

JACKSON, J. W. d. Sun. 7 Louisa Ave., Atlanta, Tues. Interred: Sylvester cemetery. AG 12/9/1907

JACKSON, Jesse d. hours before his two-yr. old son, Alton, 1086 Marietta St. Atlanta. AG 3/1/1907

JACKSON, John, colored, age 17, d. 34 Groove St. Atlanta. AG 7/8/1907

JACKSON, John, colored, age 18, d. St. Louis, Mo. AG 3/15/1907

JACKSON, John, colored, age 50, d. 33 High St. Atlanta. AG 7/13/1908

JACKSON, John B., age 3 mos., d. 145 Capitol Ave. Atlanta. Interred: Westview. AG 11/17/1907

JACKSON, John Breckenridge, Jr., son of Mr. and Jrs. J. B., d. 545 Capitol Ave., Atlanta, Sun. Interred: Westview. AG 11/19/1907

JACKSON, Katie, colored, age 30, d. rear of 49 Pulliam St. Atlanta. AG 12/5/1907

JACKSON, Leo Kate, colored, infant, d. 284 Piedmont Ave. Atlanta. AG 5/24/1910

JACKSON, Lizzie, colored, age 26, d. rear 91 Garnett St. Atlanta. AG 5/26/1908

JACKSON, Louise, 8 mos., d. 17 Corley St., Atlanta. Interred: Westview. AG 9/22/1906

JACKSON, M. L., colored, age 56, d. 32 Diamond St. Atlanta. AG 10/23/1907

JACKSON, Manda, colored, age 50, d. Fulton CO. alms house. AG 4/13/1909

JACKSON, Margaret, colored, age 68, died 13 Webster St., Atlanta. AG 12/26/1906

JACKSON, Martha, colored, age 50, d. 1 Beckwith St. Atlanta. AG 10/18/1909

JACKSON, Mary, colored, age 26, d. 93 Haynes St. Atlanta. AG 3/10/1908

JACKSON, Mary, Mrs., age 62, wife of Andrew, d. 1 Wayman Ave., Atlanta, Wed. Husband, 3 sons: R. E., F. M. and W. E. Daus: Mrs. W. P. Archer, Mrs. E. Morris, Mrs. D. F. McManus, Mrs. J. F. Wilson. Interred: Antioch Church. AG 5/6/1908

JACKSON, Mattie, colored, age 13 days., d. 18 Magnolia St. Atlanta. AG 1/15/1907

JACKSON, Miles, colored, age 50, d. Macon, Ga. AG 3/5/1908

JACKSON, **Minnie Turner**, 41, 24 Rosalie. Atlanta. Sis: Mrs. A. C.
McCalla, Conyers; Mrs. J. R. George; Mrs. T. J. Shepard; Mrs. L.
C. Stovall. Bros: Dr. C. H., Conyers); L. H., E. H., Elberton, C.
G. & J. H. Turner. Interred: Conyers. AG 4/1/1908
JACKSON, **Moses**, colored, age 45, d. 140 Houston St. Atlanta. AG
3/1/1908
JACKSON, **N. P., Jr.**, age 22, d. Atlanta. AG 5/11/1910
JACKSON, **Paul**, colored, age 17, d. 49 Williams St., rear.
Atlanta. AG 1/22/1907
JACKSON, **Peter**, colored, age 45, d. in country. AG 7/10/1907
JACKSON, **R. A.**, age 26, d. Sat., 26 Capitol Ave. Aglanta.
Interred: Westview. AG 8/26/1907
JACKSON, **R. L.**, age 16, d. 26 Capitol Ave. Atlanta. AG 8/26/1907
JACKSON, **Ruby Lee**, age 6 mos., d. res. of parents, 6 sisters, one
bro. AG 8/19/1909
JACKSON, **S.**, colored, age 1 yr., d. 31 N. Boulevard Atlanta. AG
1/12/1907
JACKSON, **Sarah**, 4 mos. dau. of Mr. and Mrs. I. M. Jackson, d.
Sun. 1968 Marietta St. Atlanta. Interred: Westview. AG 9/25/1906
JACKSON, **Sarah**, age 12, dau. of Mr. and Mrs. W. J., d. 12 Esteen
St., Atlanta, Tues. Interred: Decatur Cemetery. AG 2/16/1910
JACKSON, **Sarah**, colored, age 26, d. Atlanta. AG 7/9/1908
JACKSON, **Tom**, colored, age 82, d. 197 Lambert St. Atlanta. AG
11/7/1907
JACKSON, **W. A.**, age 76, d. res. of son, Dr. W. A., 180 W. North
Ave., Atlanta, Wed. Confed. Vet., 1st Md. Regt. Interred:
Baltimore, Md. AG 11/8/1910
JACKSON, **W. L.**, d. Lizella, Ga. Jan. 18. Interred: Family grounds
near decd's home. AC 1/20/1905
JACKSON, **Walter, Dr.**, civil war phys. d. 9/22 home of 51 yrs.,
Montgomery, Ala. Dau: Mrs. S. W. Foster, Atlanta. Native, Elmore
Co., Ala., b. Ellersley, nr Millbank, home of gr-father, Bolling
Hall. 5 bros. were Confederates. AG 9/28/1906
JACKSON, **William**, colored, age 50, d. 116 Rockwell St. Atlanta.
AG 3/3/1908
JACKSON, **Willie** fatally stabbed Marietta, Ga. by Johnson
Flannagan. Flannagan says it was accident. Both negroes. AG
3/25/1909
JACKSON, **Wilton**, colored, age 29, d. 88 Haygood Ave. Atlanta. AG
12/17/1910
JACOBS, **Lillian, Miss**, age 26, d. Tues. Atlanta. Relatives res.
Greenville, S. C. AG 5/22/1907
JACOBS, **Ollie T., Mrs.**, age 42, d. 486 Houston St. Atlanta. AG
9/2/1909
JACOBS, **Robert W.**, age 42, d. 101 N. Butler St. Atlanta. AG
8/14/1908
JACOBS, **William A.**, inf. son of Mr. and Mrs. J. W., d. Fri. 945
Marietta St., Atlanta. Bur: Parker's churchyard. AG 8/24/1907
JACOBSON, **S. D.**, age 78, d. 93 Gilmer St., Atlanta. Wife. AG
9/30/1909
JAILETTE, **Annie, Mrs.**, wife of W. M., d. E. Point, Ga., Fri.
Interred: Sharon Church yard. AG 11/2/1907
JAILLETTE, **Bessie, age 14**, d. Sat., typhoid fever, 27 Markham
St., Atlanta. Interred: Fairburn. AG 7/30/1906

JAMES, **Albert**, youngest son of Capt. T. J. James, 11/11/1906.
Remains will be carried to Atlanta. Student, Adrian High School.
AG 11/12/1906

JAMES, **Carrie**, colored, age 27, d. Armour Sta. Atlanta. AG
12/18/1910

JAMES, **Hattie**, colored, age 41, d. 125 Currier Ave. Atlanta. AG
8/22/1910

JAMES, **Jack**, Cartledge, Augusta. James, a bro-in-law of Cartledge.
Shot, killed by Fred Cartledge, bro. of Councilman, James L.
Cartledge. AG 8/20/1906

JAMES, James F., Capt. d. 11/12 Anniston, Ala. AC 11/13/1905

JAMES, **Kate**, **Miss**, age 69 d. sister;s res., Mrs. J. M. Kerdr,
Walker St., Atlanta. AG 1/31/1910

JAMES, **Lelia**, **Mrs.** d. Sat. 28 Carnegie Way, Atlanta, wife of W.
B. James. Interred: Ellijay, Ga. AG 6/1/1907

JAMES, **Leo**, age 3 mos., d. 101 N. Butler St. Atlanta. AG 7/8/1909

JAMES, **Lizzie**, colored, age 50, d. 185 W. Mitchell St. Atlanta.
AG 5/4/1908

JAMES, **Mary L.**, colored, age 32, d. 321 Chapel St. Atlanta. AG
2/27/1907

JAMES, **Morris**, colored, age 1 yrs., d. 110 Mildred Ave. Atlanta.
AG 5/7/1907

JAMES, **S.**, colored, age 67, d. 174 W. Hunter St. Atlanta. AG
12/18/1907

JAMES, **W. B.**, **Mrs.** d. 3/30 Ashburn, Ga. Husband, 3 sons. AC
3/30/1905

JAMESON, **Ida**, **Mrs.**, wife of D. B. R., d. 11/1 Columbus, Ga. (Rose
Hill). Interred: Waverly Hall, Ga. AC 11/2/1905

JAMIESON, O. M. d. Newberry Hotel, Newberry, S. C., age 50.
Interred: Chalybeate, Miss. AG 2/2/1910

JANES, **Mary E.**, **Mrs.** d. Ft. Valley Tues, dau. of late Dr. S. G.
Hillyer. Her husband, Dr. John W. Janes, d. abt 18 mos. ago in
Atlanta. Bro: Rev. J. L. D. Hillyer, Atlanta. Interred: Forsyth.
AG 7/18/1906

JANKS, **Sam**, colored, age 7 mos., d. 91 Pear St. Atlanta. AG
11/25/1907

JAQUES, **Joe**, negro, shot and killed Columbus, Ga. AG 3/25/1907

JARILETTE, **Bessie**, age 14, d. 27 Markham St. Atlanta. AG
7/30/1906

JARMAN, P. B., age 27, m. four yrs. ago, d. Leaves mother, two
sisters, two brothers. AC 8/22/1905

JARNAGIN, O. L., policeman, killed by Ernest Wells, Knoxville,
Ga. AG 3/18/1906

JARNIGAN, infant of Walter Jarnigan, age 6 mos., d. 118 Cherokee
Ave. Atlanta. AG 11/2/1907

JARRARD, **Estelle**, age 2, dau. of Mr. and Mrs. L. M., d. Wed. 154
Park Ave., Atlanta. Interred: Albany, Ga. AG 9/2/1910

JARRELL, **James**, age 28, d. Mon., near James Ferry, north of
Macon, Ga. He was nephew of Richard Burden of Macon. AG 8/11/1908

JARRELL, James G., Dr., Savannah physician, d. Tues. AG 9/21/1910

JARRELL, **Stephen** of Macon funeral 8/12. Family res. near Dames
Ferry. Died Mon. Interred: Family Burial Ground. AG 8/12/1908

JARRETT, **Frances A.**, **Mrs.**, age 58, d. Thurs., 49 Gartrell St.,
Atlanta. Interred: Oakland. Two sons, one dau. AG 3/26/1909

JARRETT, J. A., age 66, d. Sun. 49 Gartrell St., Atlanta, Mon. Bur: Westview. Confed. Vet., 1st N. C. Cavalry. Wife, two sons, J. O. and R. C. Jarrett. Dau: Miss Mary E. Jarrett. AG 11/16/1908
JARRETT, M. Z., age 32, d. 235 Capitol Ave. Atlanta. AG 11/23/1910
JARRETT, R., age 50, d. 704 DeKalb Ave. Atlanta. AG 7/12/1907
JARVIS, Harry L., Mrs., wife of Dr. H. L. of Gainesville, Fla. d. AG 8/31/1906
JARVIS, Mamie E., Miss, age 33, d. res. of bro., Dr. J. L. Jarvis, 398 Whitehall St., Atlanta. Interred: Rome. AG 6/1/1907
JARVIS, Mary, Mrs., wife of John S., d. 39 Carnegie Way, Atlanta, Thurs. Interred: Oakland. AG 1/10/1908
JARVIS, W. L. d. 39 Carnegie Way, Atlanta Mon. Interred: Oakland. AG 9/20/1907
JARVIS, W. S., age 83, d. 39 Carnegie Place, Atlanta, Thurs. Interred: Westview. AG 9/19/1907
JAY, D. B., ex-judge of city court, Fitzgerald, Ga., d. 8/16. Wife, 3 children. AG 8/17/1910
JEFFERS, Norma C., Mrs., age 25, d. 387 E. North Ave. Atlanta. AG 8/8/1910
JEFFERS, Thomas, Mrs., age 25, d. Sat. 387 E. North Ave. Atlanta. Interred: Westview. AG 8/8/1910
JEFFERSON, John, colored, age 27, d. 136 Hilliard St. Atlanta. AG 10/7/1909
JEFFERSON, Will, colored, age 16, d. railroad accident at MCDaniel St. Crossing. Atlanta. AG 1/7/1907
JEFFORDS, Anna E., Mrs., age 35, d. 267 Capitol Ave. Atlanta. AG 10/11/1909
JEKYLL, George, age 80, d. 674 Washington St. Atlanta. AG 2/15/1909
JENKINS, Allen W., colored, age 61, d. 26 Richmond St. Atlanta. AG 11/22/1909
JENKINS, Annie, Mrs., age 24, d. Knoxville, Tenn. Tues. Interred: Westview. AG 2/2/1907
JENKINS, Avina, age 4 mos., d. 39 Tennille St. Atlanta. AG 4/10/1907
JENKINS, C. J., age 50, d. Grady Hospital, Atlanta, Thurs. Interred: Westview. AG 1/31/1908
JENKINS, Charles, colored, age 60, d. 82 S. Dillon St. Atlanta. AG 1/14/1908
JENKINS, Douglas, inf. son of Mr. and Mrs. John B. of 8 Loomnis Ave., d. Thurs. Interred: Oakland. AG 6/7/1906
JENKINS, Edward, colored, age 1, d. 155 East Ave. Atlanta. AG 12/23/1908
JENKINS, Floyd, age 26, d. 294 Courtland St. Atlanta. AG 8/25/1909
JENKINS, Horace, colored, age 5, d. rear 18-A Williams St. Atlanta. AG 10/19/1907
JENKINS, J. F., age 54, d. Atlanta Tues. Ch: W. H. Jenkins, Miss Annie Jenkins of Atlanta. AG 1/14/1908
JENKINS, J. W. d. 5/29 Lithonia, Ga. Wife, 7 children. Interred: Lithonia Cemetery. AC 5/30/1905
JENKINS, James B., age 56, d. 11 Tumlin St., Atlanta, Wed. Interred: Casey's Cemetery. AG 5/31/1910

JENKINS, Jane, colored, age 85, d. 5 Trenholm St. Atlanta. AG 4/7/1908

JENKINS, Laura, colored, age 55, d. 537 Walton St. Atlanta. AG 7/6/1907

JENKINS, May, Miss, age 20, d. 230 S. Boulevard. Atlanta. Interred: Westview. AG 3/28/1907

JENKINS, Paul, inf. son of Mr. and Mrs. A. S., d. 99 Lambert St., Atlanta, Tues. Interred: Peachtree Creek. AG 7/23/1908

JENKINS, Peter, colored, age 56, d. 54 Hill St. Atlanta. AG 3/30/1908

JENKINS, Ruth Marian, age 12, da. of Mr. and Mrs. D. L., d. 277 Central Ave., Atlanta, Sun. Interred: Westview. AG 7/27/1908

JENKINS, Thomas, age 65, d. Sun. 830 Marietta St., Atlanta. 3 sons, 4 daus. Interred: Westview. AG 8/30/1910

JENKINS, W. Eugene, age 82, d. McDonough, Ga. AG 11/15/1909

JENNINGS, C. A. B., Rev. drowned near Spartanburg, S. C. Mon, well-known in Atlanta. Sis-in-law: Mrs. Ed Clinkscales, Atlanta. J. A. Wingo of Atlanta is cou. of Dr. Jenning's wife. AG 5/26/1908

JENNINGS, Henry, Mrs., wife of Police Chief Henry, d. Wed. 209 Kimball St., Atlanta. Son: Julian H. Dau: Lillian. AG 12/18/1907

JENNINGS, J. J., Mrs. of Oconee Co. d. 3/19, age 65. Several children. AC 3/20/1905

JENNINGS, Tindia, Mrs., age 42, d. 599 Marietta St., Atlanta, Sat. AG 2/8/1908

JENNINGS, W. H., Mrs., age 77, d. Thurs. 524 Washington St. Atlanta Fri. Daus: Mrs. Isaac Martin, Mrs. G. P. Yelverton. Interred: Palatka, Fla. AG 11/20/1908

JENNINGS, W. M., Mrs. interred Westview Cemetery. AG 2/10/1908

JENSEN, Fred, age 34, d. King's Daughters Hospital. Atlanta. AG 1/31/1907

JERGAN, Harold, age 14, d. Atlanta. AG 6/9/1910

JERNIGAN, L. M., Mrs. d. White Plains, Ga. Wed. Sister: Mrs. Willie Tappan, Atlanta. AG 2/28/1908

JERNIGAN, Willie, inf. son of Mr. and Mrs. W. A., d. 118 Cherokee Ave., Atlanta, Fri. Interred: Oakland. AG 11/2/1907

JERSEY, Ida, colored, age 30, d. 101 N. Butler St. Atlanta. AG 4/28/1908

JERVEY, E. T., age 63, d. Marietta, Ga. AG 12/27/1910

JESTER, John Robert, Jr., age 18 mos., son of Rev. and Mrs. J. R., d. 236 Peeples St., Atlanta, Wed. Interred: Westview. AG 7/16/1908

JETT, J. B. d. 10/18, age 80, 32 Doane St. Atlanta. Confed. Vet. AC 10/19/1905

JETT, Viney, Mrs., age 45, d. 27 Bush St., Atlanta, Sun. AG 23/1/1907

JETTY, Thomas A., age 29, of 6 Delta Pl. Atlanta, d. Atlanta Wed. Wife. Parents: Mr. and Mrs. M. T. Jetty, Dallas, Texas. AG 3/3/1909

JEWELL, Henry, Dr. d. Wed. on Decatur trolley car. Interred: Decatur, Ga. AG 11/12/1909

JEWETT, H. R., age 51, d. 20 Edgewood Ave. Atlanta. AG 11/11/1909

JINKS, Will, age 34, d. Southern railroad depot. Atlanta. AG 3/28/1907

JIMERSON, Earl, age 17, d. 8/23 res. of mother, Mrs. Mary, Phenix City, Ala. AC 8/25/1905

JOBIONSKI, Katie, wife of C. R., d. Mon. Bellwood Ave., Atlanta. Interred: Hollywood. AG 8/14/1907

JOHNS, W. B., age 67, d. 24 Beecher St. Atlanta. AG 9/21/1908

JOHNSON, A. C. V., Mrs., age 74, d. Mon. Atlanta. Interred: Westview. 5 sons, 1 dau. AG 8/10/1909

JOHNSON, A. W., age 50, d. Thurs. Wylie St. Atlanta. Interred: Westview. AG 5/24/1906

JOHNSON, Addie, age 43, d. 297 Pulliam St. Atlanta. AG 8/5/1908

JOHNSON, Adeline, colored, age 65, d. 169 Houston St. Atlanta. AG 6/14/1907

JOHNSON, Albert, age 2, son of Mr. and Mrs. J. A., d. 12 Bender St. Atlanta, Mon. AG 3/23/1908

JOHNSON, Alce killed by husband, Eli, negroes 9/17, Adairsville, Ga. AC 9/18/1905

JOHNSON, Amanda, Mrs., age 64, d. Columbus, Thurs. Interred: Riverdale cemetery. AG 2/1/1907

JOHNSON, Annie, colored, age 26, d. 186 E. Ellis St. Atlanta. AG 12/3/1907

JOHNSON, Annie P., Mrs., age 66, d. 408 Luckie St. Atlanta. AG 7/18/1908

JOHNSON, Annie, Miss, age 51, d. 294 Courtland St. Atlanta. AG 3/18/1909

JOHNSON, Arthur, Mrs., age 25, d. parents home at Monrovia, Ala. 6/28. She was dau. of D. K. Wall. AC 6/30/1905

JOHNSON, B., colored, age 33, d. 12 Orme St. Atlanta. AG 12/18/1907

JOHNSON, Bonham, Mrs. d. res. parents near Oak Hill, Ga., aged 20. Leaves husband. AC 7/28/1905

JOHNSON, Brooks, age 10, d. 104 N. Butler St. Atlanta. AG 10/25/1907

JOHNSON, Brooks, age 11, d. 29 White St., Atlanta, Sun. Interred: Westview. AG 10/26/1907

JOHNSON, C. S., Judge of Griffin d. 2/12. Married twice. Several children. AC 2/14/1905

JOHNSON, Charles D., age 35, shot himself res. of sister, Mrs. Edward Early, 145 E. Fair St. Atlanta, Tues. Interred: Westview. AG 12/15/1910

JOHNSON, Clarence funeral Sun. Interred: Greenwood Cemetery. AG 9/26/1910

JOHNSON, D., colored, age 65, d. Fulton Co. barracks. Atlanta. AG 1/19/1907

JOHNSON, Dan, colored, age 50, d. 1 Mitchell Pl. Atlanta. AG 12/10/1908

JOHNSON, dau of Mr. and Mrs. T. B., d. 9/18 Wadley, Ga. 3 yrs. ago they lost another baby girl, age 13 mos. AG 9/19/1908

JOHNSON, Dennis, age 80, former Atlantan, d. Dalton, Ga. 3/10. He was b. Lewis Co., N. Y. in 1830, ageing age 78. Interred: West Hill Cemetery. AG 3/12/1908

JOHNSON, Dock, colored, age 45, d. 11 Phoenix alley. Atlanta. AG 3/3/1908

JOHNSON, E. J. d. Atlanta Mon. Interred: Tallahassee, Fla. AG 10/22/1907

JOHNSON, **Ed**, colored, age 25, d. 101 N. Butler St. Atlanta. AG 2/6/1907

JOHNSON, **Ed**, colored, age 20, d. Grady Hospital. Atlanta. AG 7/19/1907

JOHNSON, **Edwina**, age 2 yrs., dau. of Mr. and Mrs. W. Dan Johnson, d. Wed. 56 Highland Ave., Atlanta. Interred: Oakland. AG 6/27/1907

JOHNSON, **Effie**, colored, age 28, d. 23 Travis St. Atlanta. AG 12/24/1907

JOHNSON, **Eliza**, colored, age 45, d. 15 Rhodes St. Atlanta. AG 9/6/1910

JOHNSON, **Eliza**, age 40, d. Thurs., Confederate Ave. Interred: Westview. AG 8/9/1906

JOHNSON, **Ella**, colored, age 38, d. 238 Vine St. Atlanta. AG 5/26/1908

JOHNSON, **Ella**, mother of the wife of Frank Strong, murdered by him (negro). Also, his wife is dying of wounds. AC 2/24/1905

JOHNSON, **Evelyn**, age 9 mos., dau. of J. B., d. College Park Thurs. Interred: Griffin, Ga. AG 6/29/1906

JOHNSON, **F. C.**, Rev. d. 2/23 Villa Rica, Ga., buried Old Chambers grave yard. AC 2/25/1905

JOHNSON, **Fannie Tripp**, Mrs. of Cartersville, wid. of Col. Abda, d. age 74. Leaves 3 daus: Mrs. J. W. Aiken, Cartersville; Mrs. M. L. Johnson and Mrs. Lillie Bradley. Son: Col. Albert Sidney Johnson of Texas. AG 1/23/1907

JOHNSON, **Flem**, age 15, negro, killed his brother. Athens, Ga. AG 12/30/1907

JOHNSON, **Frank** d. 12/20 Atlanta. Accident. AC 12/20/1905

JOHNSON, **Frank**, colored, age 33, d. 101 N. Butler St. Atlanta. AG 12/16/1908

JOHNSON, **Franklin**, age two mos., son of Mr. and Mrs. R. A., d. 25 Johnson Ave., Atlanta, Mon. AG 9/14/1909

JOHNSON, **G. L.**, Dr., age 74, d. Palmetto, Ga. Unmarried. AG 4/27/1907

JOHNSON, **George A.**, age 25, d. Thurs. night 30 N. Boulevard, Atlanta. Interred: Gloster, Ga. AG 6/29/1907

JOHNSON, **Henry,**c olored, age 21, d. Macon, Ga. AG 3/1/1908

JOHNSON, **Hopie Nevill**, Mrs., wid. of M. W. of Lexington, Ga., d. Tues. 62 Johnson Ave. Interred: Lexington, Ga. Ch: H. B., W. D., M. S., J. M. and N. L. Johnson; Mrs. Frank Mills, Miss Lucy C. Johnson, all of Atlanta. AG 2/26/1908

JOHNSON, **infant** of Mr. and Mrs. W. Z., age 2 yrs., d. 29 Curran St., Atlanta, Thurs. Interred: Caseys. AG 2/7/1908

JOHNSON, **Isaac W.**, 68, d. 192 E. Baker St. Atlanta. Dau: Mrs. J. W. Sharp. Sis: Mrs. Pink Arnold, Mrs. Lucy Merriweather, both of Senatobia, Miss. Bros: Edward L. and Macon C. Johnson, of Crawford Co., Ga. Interred: Crawford. AG 5/25/1910

JOHNSON, **J. A.** ("Taylor") d. 5/29 res. of son, Ernest, in Girard, Ala., age 79. Confed. Vet. AC 5/30/1905

JOHNSON, **J. E.**, age 37, d. 340 Edgewood Ave., Atlanta. AG 9/9/1907

JOHNSON, **J. H.**, Sr., age 70, d. 840 Piedmont Ave., Atlanta. AG 4/2/1910

JOHNSON, **J. S.**, age 66, d. 49 Pickett St. Sat. Leaves wife, 7 children. Interred: Oakland. AG 7/7/1906

JOHNSON, **J. Sidney**, age 35, of Terrell Co., planter, d. 4/11.

Son: E. Johnson of Dawson. Wife, 2 children. Interred: Bethel Church graveyard. AC 4/13/1905

JOHNSON, J. W., Mayor, father of Mary Johnson, age 66, d. 5/21 Richmond, Va. Confed. Vet. AC 5/23/1905

JOHNSON, Jack, colored, age 50, d. 200 Gilmore St. Atlanta. AG 9/5/1906

JOHNSON, James A., Mrs. d. Sat. Columbus, Ga. Formerly Miss Nettie Mizell, sister of Alderman C. W. Mizell. Husband, 2 little boys. AG 8/30/1910

JOHNSON, Janie, Mrs., age 74, d. 707 Woodward Ave., Atlanta. AG 10/19/1907

JOHNSON, Jennie Howell, Mrs., age 24, of 274 Oak St., Atlanta, d. Fri. Husband, two daus, parents, survive. AG 8/28/1909

JOHNSON, Jessie, infant, d. 65 Lindsay St. Atlanta. AG 6/11/1910

JOHNSON, John A., Judge, age 80, d. Cullman, Ala. 8/24. Confed. Vet. AC 8/25/1905

JOHNSON, John of 25-1/2 S. Pryor St., Atlanta. d. Grady Hospital last Fri. Interment: Westview. AG 9/26/1906

JOHNSON, John A., age 48, farmer, Moultrie, assassinated last night. AG 9/6/1906

JOHNSON, Joseph, age 30, d. Charlotte, Ga. AG 8/14/1907

JOHNSON, Joseph A., Mrs. d. 302 Luckie St., Atlanta, Tues, age 80, pioneer to Atlanta. Celebrated 57th wedding anniversary last Aug. Sons: George E., J. V., W. L., O. B. Interred: Oakland. AG 9/25/1907

JOHNSON, Joseph E., son of Mrs. M. J., d. Charlotte, N. C. Age 31. Interred: Oakland, Atlanta. Sisters: Mrs. Leon I. McRae, Mrs. John C. Maddox, Kate Johnson. AG 8/14/1907

JOHNSON, Joseph H., 70, son of Rev. Marcus D.C., d. Atlanta. Conf. Vet. Bro: Mark W. Daus: Mrs. J. A. Droege, Providence, RI.; Mrs. Lt. Ralph Hayden, Ft. Clark, Tx.; Mrs. A.S. Hook, Atlanta; Mrs. A.L. Sloan. Son: Jos. H., Jr., NY. AG 4/1/1910

JOHNSON, L. C., age 39, d. 4 Rosehill Ave. Atlanta Sun. Wife, 6 children. AG 3/29/1909

JOHNSON, L. P., Mrs., age 55, d. 87 E. North Ave. Atlanta. Interred: Decatur, Ga. AG 5/14/1910

JOHNSON, Lamar, son f Mr. and Mrs. R. C., 455 Grant St., Atlanta, d. Sun. Interred: Harlem, Ga. AG 6/14/1909

JOHNSON, Laura, Mrs. d. 45 Glenn St., Atlanta, Thurs. Husband: W. D. AG 4/8/1909

JOHNSON, Laura B., Mrs., wife of late Hardtin T., d. Macon, age 65. Daus: Mrs. Julian Rogers, Atlanta; Miss Emmie and E. M. and Herbert. AC 8/18/1905

JOHNSON, Len, colored, age 3 mos., d. 124 Glenn St. Atlanta. AG 2/6/1907

JOHNSON, Letitia P., Mrs., age 55, d. 87 E. North Ave., Atlanta, Thurs, wife of J. L. Son: Paul C. Daus: Mrs. L. H. Magill; Ruth, Lois. Bros: W. G. and J. O. Wells, Atlanta, and W. M. Wells, Macon. Sis: Mrs. J. L. Phillips, Lithonia; Mrs. G. R. Wells, Monroe, Ga.; Miss Sallie Wells, Atlanta. Interred: Decatur, Ga. AG 5/12/1910

JOHNSON, Lucy, colored, age 8, d. 14 Fifth St. Atlanta, AG 11/19/1909

JOHNSON, Ludia, colored, age 21, d. 36 Majestic Ave. Atlanta. AG 9/30/1910

JOHNSON, Luther, colored, age 28, d. 309 Walnut St. Atlanta. AG 11/23/1910

JOHNSON, Mabel, age 11, d. 101 Butler St. Atlanta. AG 10/22/1909

JOHNSON, Marie, colored, age 113, d. 35 Granger St. Atlanta. AG 2/1/1908

JOHNSON, Mark, colored, age 8, d. Chattanooga, Tenn. AG 3/4/1907

JOHNSON, Martha, colored, age 47, d. 36 Germunda St. Atlanta. AG 10/14/1907

JOHNSON, Mary, colored, age 105, d. 84 Roy St. Atlanta. AG 2/24/1908

JOHNSON, Mary, colored, age 3, d. 4 McGee alley. Atlanta. AG 4/22/1907

JOHNSON, Mary A., Mrs., mother of Benjamin T., d. 130 Grant St., Atlanta, Wed. Sons: B. T. of Atlanta, John D. of Conyers, Middleton of Tampa, Fla. and Whitson. AG 1/29/1908

JOHNSON, Mary E., Mrs., age 53, d. Sun. Atlanta. Interred: Conyers, Ga. AG 5/2/1910

JOHNSON, Mary, Miss, age 38, d. 37 Tye St. Atlanta. AG 8/17/1907

JOHNSON, Matilda, colored, age 48, d. 201 Butler St. Atlanta. AG 8/19/1909

JOHNSON, Melo, negro from Macon, brakeman of Central Railroad, d. rail accident. AG 7/23/1906

JOHNSON, Melvin L., colored, age 7, d. 26 Tyler St. Atlanta. AG 9/4/1908

JOHNSON, Miller, negro, found dead on 14th St., Cordele, Ga. 6/14. AG 6/15/1906

JOHNSON, Mose, colored, age 53, d. 37 Selma St. Atlanta. AG 11/27/1910

JOHNSON, Mr., Jim Johnson found guilty of murdering his father. Moultrie, Ga. AG 10/11/1906

JOHNSON, O. T., colored, age 13 days, d. 60 Spruce St. Atlanta. AG 10/5/1908

JOHNSON, Ollie L., age 10, dau. of Mr. and Mrs. B. ., d. Sun. parents res., 250 Glennwood Ave., Atlanta. Interred: Oakland. AG 10/3/1910

JOHNSON, Oliver, age 36, d. 27 Townes St. Atlanta. AG 3/3/1909

JOHNSON, Oscar, colored, age 33, d. 16 Central St. Atlanta. AG 12/12/1910

JOHNSON, P., colored, age 93, d. 37 Poplar St. Atlanta. AG 2/19/1907

JOHNSON, P. N., Dr., age 51, d. 294 Courtland St. Atlanta. AG 1/22/1907

JOHNSON, Pearl, Miss, age 18, dau. of Mr. and Mrs. W. S., d. Thurs. Clarkston, Ga. Interred: Clarkston. AG 5/28/1909

JOHNSON, Polly, colored, age 56, d. 92 Old Wheat St. Atlanta. AG 12/12/1910

JOHNSON, R. of Americus, d. train wreck Macon. AG 2/15/1911

JOHNSON, R. Clyde of Chattanooga, Tenn. d. Atlanta, Mon. Bro: Arthur W. Interred: Chattanooga, Tenn. AG 2/7/1910

JOHNSON, Richard, colored, age 3 yrs., died 9 Spinks Ave. Atlanta. AG 12/28/1906

JOHNSON, Robert funeral. Interred: Elizabeth, N. J., former home. Kin: J. H. Johnson, Thomas Weaver. AG 10/16/1907

JOHNSON, Robert, age 60, d. 22-B Carnegie Way, Atlanta. AG 10/18/1907

JOHNSON, Rosaline, inf. dau. of J. B., d. Mon. College Park. Interred: Griffin. AG 5/28/1906
JOHNSON, Rebecca, Miss, age 80, d. Sun. Atlanta. Niece: Miss Pearl Cook, 60 Baker St., Atlanta. Interred: Covington, Ga. AG 8/30/1910
JOHNSON, Sallie, colored, age 39, d. 890 Walnut St. Atlanta, on 10/27. AG 10/28/1910
JOHNSON, Sallie, Mrs., age 44, d. 100 Connally St. Atlanta. AG 1/18/1907
JOHNSON, Sam, colored, age 40, d. 178 Orme St. Atlanta. AG 5/1/1907
JOHNSON, Sam, colored, age 54, d. 113 Bell St. Atlanta. AG 5/21/1907
JOHNSON, Sarah E., Mrs. d. dau.´s home, Mrs. I. A. Abbott, First Ave., Columbus, Ga., Sun., age 79. Formerly of Heard Co. Son: E. W. Johnson. AG 10/5/1909
JOHNSON, Stephen, colored, age 55, d. 13 Clifton St. Atlanta. AG 9/9/1908
JOHNSON, Susan H., age 59, d. 251 Courtland Ave. Atlanta. AG 1/4/1910
JOHNSON, T. J., age 65, d. 465 Grant St., Atlanta, Nov. 12. AG 11/16/1910
JOHNSON, T. W., turpentine man of Blakely, Ga. d. Fri. Children: Mrs. J. W. Calahan, Bainbridge; wife of J. A. McLaurin of Blakely; Will A. Johnson of Blakely. AG 3/16/1907
JOHNSON, Tom, colored, age 35, d. 149 1/2 Auburn Ave. Atlanta. AG 5/10/1906
JOHNSON, W. A. L., Mrs., age 24, d. Fri. Lakewood Heights, Atlanta. Husband survives. Interred: Marvin Church. AG 7/21/1906
JOHNSON, W. H., Macon, Ga. 12/1/1906, Deputy, US Dist. Court, died in train crash. AG 12/1/1906
JOHNSON, W. P., Mrs. d. dau.´s res., Mrs. George H. Sims., 408 Luckie St., Atlanta, Thurs. Daus: Mrs. N. Q. Pope, Mrs. L. N. Hollingsworth, Mrs. W. T. Eason, Mrs. George H. Sims. Interred: Sardis Cemetery. AG 7/16/1908
JOHNSON, Walter, colored, age 39, died 43 Carter Street, Atlanta. AG 12/8/1906
JOHNSON, Will, age 26, for criminally assaulting Mrs. Richard Hembree near her home at Battle Hill 8/15th, given death sentence. AG 12/1/1906
JOHNSON, Will, colored, age 32, d. 10 Grady Ave. Atlanta. AG 2/15/1909
JOHNSON, William A., age 22, d. res. of parents, Mr. and Mrs. W. M. Atlanta, Interred: Gloster, Ga. AG 11/19/1907
JOHNSON, William G., Rev. d. Eatonton, Ga. Leaves wife. Several ch: M. Johnson; Mrs. L. DeLoach, Atlanta. Sis: Mrs. Frank C. Coker, Sr. Bro: B. F. Johnson, Atlanta. Interred: E. Putnam. AC 4/21/1905
JOHNSON, William M., age 50, d. Tues., 475 Whitehall St., Atlanta. Interred: Oakland. AG 1/23/1907
JOHNSON, Willie May, colored, age 4, d. 169 McDonough Rd. Atlanta. AG 12/22/1908
JOHNSTON, C. E., colored, age 57, d. 292 Fulton St. Atlanta. AG 7/17/1909
JOHNSTON, Henrietta, Mrs. d. Lumpkin, Ga., age 64. AG 12/24/1907
JOHNSTON, J. A., Mrs. of Jacksonville, Fla. d. at home of W. J. Gay, Ft. Gaines, Ga. 4 small ch and husband, survive. Husband is son of Hon. John B. Johnston of Dade City, Fla. AG 7/25/1907

JOHNSTON, John William, aged 69, Bibb Co., Civil War Vet., d. yesterday. Served with Macon Vols. throughout war. Ch: O. H., Savannah; J. W., Jr.; Mrs. Arthur Jobson; Mrs. Frank Taylor; Misses Carrie and Sallie Johnston, Macon. AG 7/17/1907

JOHNSTON, Lawrence L., age 33, d. Moreland Ave., Atlanta, Fri. Wife, four children. Father: G. P. Johnston. Interred: Gloster, Ga. AG 10/2/1909

JOINER, George, colored, age 33, d. 388 Chestnut St. Atlanta. AG 4/15/1908

JOINER, Emma, Mrs.. Abbeville. Dau. of Thomas Mitchell d. Vienna. AG 8/25/1906

JOLLEY, Salley, Mrs., age 56, d. 60 S. Delta Place, Atlanta. AG 7/30/1906

JOLLY, D. W., Mrs. d. Sat. 42 Mills St., Atlanta. Interred: Jackson, Ga. AG 5/6/1907

JONES, A. B., age 54, d. 4/19 Columbus, Ga., Front St. Interred: Union, Ga. AC 4/21/1905

JONES, Addie M., colored, age 13 mos., d. 29 Collier St., Atlanta, 10/3. AG 10/5/1910

JONES, Alfred E. d. Tues. 274 Jones Ave. Atlanta. Wife, 4 children. Interred: Chamblee, Ga. AG 6/15/1910

JONES, Amaretur, inf. dau. of Mr. and Mrs. Arthur, d. Thurs. 5 Bryan St., Atlanta. Interred: Westview. AG 5/31/1907

JONES, Andrew, colored, age 29, d. 172 Clarke St. Atlanta. AG 3/27/1908

JONES, Annie Ione, Mrs., age 26, wife of W. R., D. 70 Crew St., Atlanta, Fri. Dau: Mrs. C. R. Powell, Sparta, Ga. Interred: Westview. AG 12/10/1910

JONES, Bertha M., Miss, age 22, dau. of Mr. and Mrs. W. A., d. E. Atlanta Fri. Interred: Marvin church yard. AG 7/16/1909

JONES, Bessie, Miss died 144 Gaskill St. Interment: Rock Springs. AG 12/26/1906

JONES, Bessie. Walter Hightower shot and killed her. See Hightower, Walter. AG 12/27/1906

JONES, C. W., Mrs. who res. short distance from city limits of Rome, on Black's bluff road, d. Fri. Interred: Cartersville. Age 45. One sister, four bros. AG 3/25/1907

JONES, Charlotte, Mrs. funeral St. Lukes Episcopal Church, Atlanta, Sun. Interred: Westview. AG 4/25/1910

JONES, Clifford, colored, age 26, d. 315 Hilliard St. Atlanta. AG 8/22/1910

JONES, Clifford, Mrs. d. Sat. Interred: Forest Park, Ga. AG 8/2/1909

JONES, Cornilice, colored, age 39, d. 261 Williams St. Atlanta. AG 10/3/1907

JONES, Daisy, age 9, dau. of Mr. and Mrs. W. D. of Carbondale, Ga., d. Thurs. Interred: Cox Grave yard, near Phelps. AG 3/21/1910

JONES, Dan, negro, shot in back with army rifle. Res. of 47 Rawson St., Atlanta. Jim Grant, negro, did shooting, still ar large. AG 6/20/1910

JONES, Dennard, age 6 mos., d. 462 Crew St. Atlanta. Interred: Westview. AG 11/2/1907

JONES, Doc, colored, age 28, died 101 N. Butler Street, Atlanta. AG 12/8/1906

JONES, E. J., age 29, d. 101 Butler St. Atlanta. AG 12/14/1909
JONES, Earnest killed auto accident Sat. Atlanta. Interred:
Westview. Wife, two children. AG 12/13/1909
JONES, Edna M., age 1, d. Atlanta. AG 5/14/1910
JONES, Eliza A., colored, age 28, d. 210 Fraser St. Atlanta. AG
8/14/1907
JONES, Ella, colored, age 28, d. 37-B Battle St. Atlanta. AG
7/19/1909
JONES, Elmira, Mrs. d. Elberton, Ga. Interred: Falling Creek
Cemetery. Several children. AG 4/15/1909
JONES, Enoch, Hon. d. 12/19 Fairburn. April 14th would have been
age 75. m. Miss Elizabeth Travis of Clayton Co. 19 ch, 11
survive: Lovic, Bartow, Walter, Ed, Felton, Luther, Mrs. Ida
Posey, Mrs. Sallie Martin, Mrs. Mattie Boyd, Mrs. Minnie
JONES, Evelyn D., age 1 yr., d. 245 North Jackson St. Atlanta. AG
6/18/1907
JONES, Everhart, age 43, d. Tues. Atlanta. Interred: Westview. AG
7/6/1910
JONES, Frank M. d. Thomasville, Ga. Wed. Uncle of Hon. W. I.
McIntyre, W. J. Hammond and Thomas Jones of Thomasville, Ga. and
Charlton Jones of Birmingham, Ala. AG 10/27/1910
JONES, Frederick R., age 57, d. Mon. 14 Bluff St.,A tlanta.
Interred: Waco, Ga. AG 6/28/1910
JONES, Hamilton, colored, age 40, d. 178 E. Cain St. Atlanta. AG
6/8/1908
JONES, Harry A., infant of Mr. and Mrs. M. H., d. Sat. 167 Jones
Ave. Atlanta. AG 6/15/1907
JONES, Hattie, colored, age 34, d. 107-A Randolph St. Atlanta. AG
9/10/1910
JONES, Henrietta, colored, age 52, d. 127 Glenn St. Atlanta. AG
10/7/1909
JONES, Henry Edward, age 17, son of Mr. and Mrs. John S., d.
12/25 Dunwoody by accidental gun discharged by Wyman Jones, his
cousin. Interred: Casey's Cemetery. AC 12/28/1905
JONES, Herbert, inf. son of Mr. and Mrs. J. Tom, d. Mon. 348
Mangum St., Atlanta. Interred: Westview. AG 5/14/1906
JONES, Hilliard, colored, age 34, d. 332-B Terry St. Atlanta. AG
11/28/1908
JONES, infant of Mr. and Mrs. R. H., d. Atlanta. Interred:
College Park, Ga. AG 9/23/1907
JONES, J. A., colored, age 2, d. 175 Beckwith St. Atlanta. AG
10/12/1907
JONES, J. H. of Lumpkin d. Fri. AG 6/25/1907
JONES, J. H., Mrs., age 83 of Elberton, Ga., widow of late Major
J. H. Jones, d. Sun. Heirs: T. A. and W. O. Jones, Mrs. R. M.
Heard, Mrs. J. J. Burch, Mrs. Lavonia Gardiner, Mrs. Mamie
Blackwell, Miss Nora Jones. AG 12/29/1909
JONES, J. Herbert died Thurs. at Grady Hospital, Atlanta.
Survivors: bros., M. J. and C. A. Jones; 3 sisters, Mrs. M. D.
Bagwell, Mrs. J. M. DeFoor and Mrs. R. E. Boyle. Interment:
Westview. AG 12/21/1906
JONES, J. Horace, age 56 (or 61), of Lorraine, N. Y., d. Atlanta
Wed. Wife. Sis: Mrs. W. K. Booth of Atlanta. AG 4/7/1909
JONES, J. M., age 20, d. 108 Merritts Ave. Atlanta. AG 8/5/1908

JONES, J. William, Dr., confed. historian, b. 9/25/1836 Louisa
Ct. Hse, Va., d. Columbus 3/17. Bur: Hollywood. Sons: Carter
Helm, Oklahoma City; E. Pendleton, Hampton, Va.; Frank Wm, NY.;
M. Ashby, Columbus; Howard Lee, Charleston. AG 3/18/1909
JONES, James H., age 78, d. 41 Stewart Ave., Atlanta, Fri.
Interred: Sylvester Cemetery. Son: William H. Dau: Mrs. L. A.
Neely. Three bros., three sisters. AG 10/8/1909
JONES, James H., age 78, d. Fri. 71 Stewart Ave., Atlanta.
Interred: Sylvester Cemetery. AG 10/8/1909
JONES, Jethro of Carrollton, Ga. murdered by Charlie and West
Sumerlin, negroes. AG 1/15/1908
JONES, Jim, a Jenkins Co. murderer, must hang on 5/26. AG
5/12/1909
JONES, John, colored, age 46 d. 42 Vernont. Atlanta. AG
12/11/1908
JONES, John A., Capt. of Chattooga Co., 9th Ga. Regt., d. Tues.
Formerly of Decatur. Father: John, Sheriff of DeKalb Co. Ch: Dr.
E. G. Jones, Mrs J. L. Campbell, Atlanta. Bro-in-law: Dr. W. S.
Kendrick. Interred: Chattooga Co. AG 2/25/1909
JONES, John B. d. in fight at house of Mabel Turner, Macon. Tom
Jones, cousin, charged with manslaugher. AG 3/9/1910
JONES, John G., age 36, d. Chattanooga, Tenn. AG 11/4/1908
JONES, John H. suicide, Atlanta, age abt 28. From Canton, Ga. AG
1/29/1907
JONES, John N., Hon. d. Sun., Main St., Fairburn, Ga. Interred:
Fairburn Cemetery. He was age 70, removed to Fairburn from
Jackson Co. Wife, one adopted dau., Mrs Sam Foster of Texas. Bro:
Hon. B. F. Jones, Fairburn. AG 3/9/1909
JONES, Jonas A. d. Sat. Chattahoochee, Ga. Interred: Hollywood.
AG 5/2/1910
JONES, Katie, Mrs., age 51, d. Fri. 452 E. Fair St. Atlanta.
Leaves husband, 5 children. Interred: Westview. AG 4/27/1907
JONES, L., colored, age 63, d. 287 Piedmont Ave. Atlanta. AG
4/23/1908
JONES, L. J., Mrs., age 55, d. Mon. res. of dau., Mrs. C. L.
Childs, 330 Washington St., Atlanta. Interred: Covington, Ga. AG
7/16/1907
JONES, Lalle, Miss, age 26, funeral at parents, 26 Dunn t.,
Atlanta. Interred: Master's graveyard. AG 3/28/1907
JONES, Laura, Mrs., age 40, d. Chattahoochee, Ga. Sat. Interment:
Chattahoochee burying ground. AG 8/18/1906
JONES, Lawrence, infant, d. Atlanta. AG 6/11/1910
JONES, Leonard, colored, age 27, d. 259 Park Ave. Atlanta. AG
2/8/1909
JONES, Lillie Mary, age 4, dau. of Mr. and Mrs. J. C., d. 83 Echo
St., Atlanta Thurs. Interred: Norcross, Ga. AG 10/18/1907
JONES, Lorina, colored, age 64, d. 28 Grady Lane, Atlanta, Nov.
10. AG 11/16/1910
JONES, Lula, colored, age 32, d. 7 Old Wheat St. Atlanta. AG
4/13/1907
JONES, Lula, Miss,, age 12, niece of Mrs. W. E. Shepperd, d.
Madison, Ga. 4/7. Interred: Waynesboro, Ga. AG 4/8/1908
JONES, Luther, age 2, son of Mr. and Mrs. T. L., d. Lakewood
Heights, Atlanta, Wed. Interred: Masons Church. AG 10/2/1908

JONES, M., colored, age 9 days, d. 176 S. Forsyth St. Atlanta. AG 1/1/1908

JONES, M. W., colored, age 23, d. Tarrytown, N. Y. AG 5/14/1908

JONES, Martha A. d. Sun. E. Macon, Ga. AG 8/4/1908

JONES, Mary, colored, age 19, d. rear 274 Washington St. Atlanta. AG 7/23/1909

JONES, Mary, colored, age 34, d. Bradberry Ave. Atlanta. AG 2/15/1909

JONES, Mary E., age 2, d. 58 Harold Ave. Atlanta. AG 11/24/1910

JONES, Mary E., Mrs., age 80, d. Wed. 58 Harold Ave. Atlanta. Son: B. C. Jones. Interred: Charleston, S. C. AG 9/28/1910

JONES, Mary Eliza, Mrs., widow of Confederate officer, d. Columbus, Ga., age 60. Sis: Mrs. Lizzie Rutherford Ellis. AG 8/30/1910

JONES, Mary Elizabeth, age 3 mos., dau. of Mr. and Mrs. S. D., d. 121 S. Pryor St., Atlanta, Tues. Interred: Oak,and. AG 10/22/1907

JONES, Mary, Miss, age 80, d. Sat. 156 Wheeler St., Atlanta. Interred: Westview. AG 9/24/1910

JONES, Maud, Mrs., age 42, d. Grady Hospital. Atlanta. AG 9/3/1907

JONES, Melissa, age 6 mos., dau. of Mr. and Mrs. C. E. of 227 Jones Ave., Atlanta, d. Wed. Interred: Chamblee, Ga. AG 4/21/1909

JONES, Melmina, negro, killed by train Cordele, Ga. 1/30. AG 2/1/1910

JONES, Melva Clarence, age 2, son of Mr. and Mrs. M. C., d. 291 East Ave. Atlanta Tues. Interred: Dillard, Ga. AG 5/13/1908

JONES, Melvin, colored, age 32, d. 101 N. Butler St. Atlanta. AG 3/15/1907

JONES, Milton, age 14, d. 1 Cloverlane, Atlanta. AG 9/3/1907

JONES, Minnie A., colored, age 36, d. 206 Williams St. Atlanta. AG 11/3/1908

JONES, Nannie, Miss, age 36, dau. of Mrs. Mattie Jones, first grade teacher, Fraser St. School, d. uncle's res., Dr. Amos Fox, 533 Washington St., Atlanta, Mon. Interred: Oakland. Kin: Mrs. Mattie Jones, Misses Azale and Lela Jones, Mrs., D. E. Jones. Interred: Oakland. AG 10/2/1907

JONES, Nellie B., Miss d. Mon. Macon, Ga. AG 11/8/1910

JONES, Ophelia, granddau. of Mr. and Mrs. H. C. Jones, 83 Jefferson St., Atlanta. Interred: Westview. AG 4/25/1910

JONES, P. C. suicide Fitzgerald, Ga. 12/17. AG 12/18/1909

JONES, Paul, age 10, son of Rev. E. W. Jones of Atlanta Heights. Interred: Fairburn. AG 8/7/1906

JONES, R. A., agent of Central RR, d. Thurs. Eatonton, Ga. Leaves wife, small child. AG 3/9/1907

JONES, R. A., Mrs., age 70, d. Hampton St., Atlanta. Interred: Rock Springs church yard. AG 6/2/1908

JONES, R. B., d. Mon. near Lumpkin, Ga. Interred: Weston, Ga. AG 12/8/1909

JONES, R. E. L., age 40, son of Mrs. Mary E., d. 127 S. Forsyth St., Atlanta. Interred: Westview. AG 2/27/1910

JONES, Robert, colored, age 37, d. 12 Brown St. Atlanta, on 10/24. AG 10/28/1910

JONES, Robert Porter, age 30, second son of late evangelist, Samuel P. Jones, d. Cartersville this morning. Leaves wife, son, mother, bro., 4 sisters. AG 1/26/1907

JONES, Robert W., age 30, d. Cartersville, Ga. AG 1/29/1907

JONES, Robert Williams d. N. Moreland Ave. Atlanta. AG 12/14/1908

JONES, Roy, negro, indicted by grand jury for assault with intent to murder, etc., was killed this morning by Deputy George Shiflett, resisting arrest, Hartwell, Ga. AG 10/4/1907

JONES, Ruby, age 7 yrs., d. Atlanta Thurs. Res. with parents at Manassas, Ga. AG 8/12/1909

JONES, Ruth, colored, age 1 year, Fort Street, Atlanta. AG 11/9/1906

JONES, S. K., Mrs., age 57, d. 195 Whitehall St. Atlanta. AG 3/3/1908

JONES, Sallie, Miss, age 26, d. 101 N. Butler St. Atlanta. AG 3/29/1907

JONES, Sam, age 55, negro, killed near Orchard Hill, Ga. 7/7. Ralph Miller, nephew of Jones' wife, arrested. AC 7/9/1905

JONES, Sam P. d. Reynolds, Ga. 11/5. Wife. several children. AC 11/7/1905

JONES, Samuel Porter, Rev., Ga. evangelist d. near Perry, Ark. His body to rest in rotunda at capitol on Hunter St. side Fri. AG 8/15/1906

JONES, Sarah Kingsbery, Mrs., age 57, d. 195 Whitehall St., Atlanta, Sun. Sons: Hugh K., Stanley, and Will R. Jones. Interred: Rockmart, Ga. AG 3/1/1908

JONES, Savannah, colored, age 19, d. 270 Mangum St. Atlanta. AG 10/1/1908

JONES, Seaborn A. shot and killed 5/29 by Gus Ragan. AG 5/30/1908

JONES, Steve, colored, age 26, d. Grady Hospital. Atlanta. AG 6/23/1907

JONES, Sudie, colored, age 25, d. 101 N. Butler St. Atlanta. AG 1/8/1908

JONES, T. W., age 71, d. 32 Larkin St. Atlanta. AG 4/22/1909

JONES, Temple, Miss d. 12/17, age 70, Waynesboro. One son: Harvey. Interred: old Cemetery. AC 12/18/1905

JONES, Thelma, age 2 mos., dau. of Mr. and Mrs. B. S., d. 227 Bellwood Ave., Atlanta, Mon. Interred: Hollywood. AG 4/19/1910

JONES, Thomas Olin, formerly of Covington, age 56, d. 316 Hemphill. Atlanta Fri. Musician. Interred: Covington. Wife, two sons: C. J., G. H. Daus: Mrs. J. W. Sneed, Misses Lula, Cassie, Avis. AG 10/20/1906

JONES, Thomas W., age 71, d. 32 Larkin St., Atlanta, Fri. Wife, 8 children. Interred: Adamsville. AG 4/17/1909

JONES, W. B., age 68, d. home of son, A. B. Jones, Dublin, Ga. Sat. Interred: Northview Cemetery. AG 8/1/1906

JONES, W. F., colored, age 35, d. 85 W. Linden St. Atlanta. AG 3/10/1908

JONES, W. L., age 65, d. 984 DeKalb Ave. Atlanta. AG 12/27/1910

JONES, Wallace, colored, age 4 mos., died 52 Sunset Ave., Atlanta. AG 11/21/1906

JONES, Walter shot by Will Walden, Waverly Hall, Ga. Sat., negroes. Walden escaped. AG 11/16/1909

JONES, Will, colored, age 29, d. 121 E. Cain St. Atlanta. AG 8/30/1910

JONES, William, age 37, d. 101 N. Butler St. Atlanta. AG
8/25/1909
JONES, William, colored, age 55, d. 131 Magnolia St. Atlanta. AG
12/9/1907
JONES, William R., age 64, d. 10 Atwood St., Atlanta, Wed. Wife.
Interred: Westview. AG 5/2/1909
JONES, Willie, colored, age 33, d. 250 Williams St. Atlanta. AG
7/19/1909
JONES, Willis Benham, 28, son of Rev. Jos. J., nep. of Rev. Sam,
d. Clinton, Il. Bur: Cartersville. Sis: Mrs. A. B. Cunyus,
Cartersville, Mrs. John G. Simpson, Charlotte, N. C., Mrs. B. L.
Sims, Murfreesboro, Tn, Hattie, Helen. AG 7/26/1907
JORDAN, Birkett Fry d. Atlanta, age 50. Wife, two small children.
Three sisters. AG 10/20/1906
JORDON, Effie, Miss d. Gulfport, Miss. some days ago. AC
7/10/1905
JORDAN, Eliza, Mrs., 61, wife of C. D. d. 22 Homer St, bur.
Caseys. AG 8/19/1906
JORDAN, Emma, colored, age 35, d. 38 Drummond St. Atlanta. AG
7/23/1907
JORDAN, Flora L., age 40, d. 55 S. Jackson St., Atlanta, Nov. 3.
AG 11/5/1910
JORDAN, Grace, colored, age 6 mos., d. 165 Butler St. Atlanta. AG
2/12/1908
JORDON, H. C. of Blue Ridge, Ga. killed in train wreck 54 miles
s. of Knoxville 3/21. AC 3/22/1905
JORDAN, Henry E., age 64, died Sun. at res., Jonesboro Rd. Res.
of Fulton Co. all his life. Survivors: Wife, 8 children.
Interment: South Bend Church yard. AG 11/26/1906
JORDAN, Henry R., age 59, Confederate vet., d. Soldiers Home,
Atlanta Tues. (inmate for 5 years). AG 11/5/1906
JORDAN, J. T., age 72, formerly of Atlanta, d. res. of Mrs.
Joseph Mabbett, Quitman, Ga., Wed. Wife survives. Interred: Oak
Hill Cemetery. AG 12/17/1910
JORDAN, John J. d. Mon. Nephews: T. E. Harper, W. R. Buchanan, H.
T. Grogan, W. T. Jordan, G. S. Jordan, J. H. P. Jordan. Interred:
Lakewood Hts churchyard. Wife, 3 children, 2 bros., survive. AG
6/4/1906
JORDAN, John M. d. Sat. Howell Sta. Atlanta. Wife, 4 children
survive. AG 4/27/1907
JORDAN, Luther, colored, age 21, d. Moore St. Crossing. Atlanta.
AG 4/10/1907
JORDAN, Martha M., Miss, age 83, d. Tues. Flat Shoals Rd.
Atlanta. Interred: Clarkston, Ga. AG 5/10/1907
JORDAN, Nancy E., Mrs., age 78, d. 37 Columbia Ave. Atlanta. AG
9/30/1910
JORDAN, R. A., age 27, d. 101 N. Butler St. Atlanta. AG 7/14/1908
JORDAN, R. A., age 30, of 205 Kennedy St., Atlanta, d. Mon.
Parents: Mr. and Mrs. W. N. Jordan of Dacula, Ga. AG 7/13/1908
JORDON, R. B. d. 6/7 Roanoke, Ala. AC 6/9/1905
JORDAN, Raymon Adelene, inf. of Mr. and Mrs. J. A., d. Mon.
Atlanta. AG 1/3/1910
JORDAN, Robert, colored, age 2, d. 101 N. Butler St. Atlanta. AG
6/21/1909

JORDAN, Savilla, age 82, d. Sun. Flat Shoals Rd., Atlanta. Interred: Clarkston. AG 6/25/1907
JORDAN, Thomas N., age 17, d. Tabernacle Infirmary. Atlanta. AG 4/4/1907
JORDAN, Ulis, age 20, d. Chattahochee Ave., Atlanta. Parents, two bros., one sister. Interred: Cornelia, Ga. AG 5/6/1909
JORDAN, W. E., Jr., age 4, son of Mr. and Mrs. W. E., d. 53 Shelton St., Atlanta, Mon. Interred: Westview. AG 1/21/1908
JORDAN, Warren, age 68, d. Wed. Atlanta. Interred: Westview. AG 7/7/1910
JORDAN, Winston, age 15, son of Mr. and Mrs. Charles, d. Wed. E. Macon. Bros: Thomas, Bridges. AG 10/3/1907
JOWERS, B. T., age 21, d. 49 Neal St., Atlanta. AG 5/4/1909
JOYNER, H. B. d. Sun. Macon, Ga. Interred: Riverside Cemetery. Wife, several children. AG 9/20/1909
JOYNER, Howlett, Mrs. formerly Miss Goodman, Cobb Co. d. 114 Erwin. Husb's bro-W. R. Ch-Jas W., Alex, Robt, W. H., Mrs. J. D. Dameron, Mrs. S. G. Jordan, Miss Margaret. Bur: Marietta. AG 9/11/1906
JOYNER, Joseph, inf. son of Mr. and Mrs. J. C., d. 132 McDonald Rd., Atlanta, Wed. Interred: Antioch church cemetery. AG 5/19/1910
JOYNER, Susan M., Mrs., age 55, d. 114 Irwin St. Atlanta. AG 9/12/1906
JUBALEY, Charles, Mrs., age 23, d. 101 N. Butler St. Atlanta. AG 7/9/1909
JUDSON, John M., age 44, d. 66 Robbins St. Atlanta. AG 10/18/1909
JUHAN, Louis, Macon Merchant, d. 9/10, res. of bro., W. J. Juhan, Oglethorpe St., age 34, unmd. Bros: W. J., Macon; C. J., Texas. A married sister in Texas. AG 9/11/1909
JUHON, Bessie, age 5 years, died Savannah Street, Atlanta. AG 11/29/1906
JUSTICE, J. G. of Marcus, Ga. d. 9/23, age 75. Unmd. AG 9/24/1910
KADEL, Adam, age 50, d. Fri. 145 Ira St., Atlanta. Wife, son. Interment: Westview. AG 10/27/1906
KADEL, Richard, age 68, d. 693 S. Pryor St., Atlanta, Mon. Wife. Ch: Mrs. C. T. Waddill, Mrs. G. L. Grabbs, Mrs. W. M. Rainey, P. F. Kadel. Interred: Westview. AG 7/14/1908
KAGLEMACHER, Gus, d. Mon. E. Atlanta, near Sylvester Church. Wife, 4 children survive. AG 6/13/1906
KAHNWELLER, J., Mrs., age 65, d. 240 Courtland St. Atlanta. AG 1/1/1908
KAHN, Rebecca, Mrs., age 45, d. Atlanta. Funeral: res. of sister, Mrs. Susie Leibman, 245 Whitehall St., Atlanta. Survivors: Dau., Miss Myrtle Kahn; sister, KAHNRebecca, Mrs., contd....Mrs. Susie Leibman. AG 12/16/1906
KAHN, Valentine, age 80, Macon pioneer, d. NYC visiting son. 8 ch: Mrs. Edgar Mayer, Mrs. Henry Framer, Norten and Edgar Kahn of NYC; Mrs. Jake Heniger, Lee, Mayer, and Felix H. Kahn of Texas. Interred: William Wolff cem. AG 7/6/1907
KALBISCH, Zesal, colored, age 1 yr., dau. of Mr. and Mrs. S. E. of 78 Gilmer St. Atlanta. Interred: Hollywood. AG 3/3/1909
KALMON, Henry C., age 26, d. Atlanta Fri. Interred: Albany. Parents, several bros. and sisters. AG 8/1/1908

KAMPKIN, infant of Mr. and Mrs. A. K. d. 7/6 Ft. Gaines, Ga. Mrs. Kampkin had just arrived from China where res. for past several yrs. AG 7/7/1909

KAPLAN, Louis H., age 52, of Anniston, Ala. d. Atlanta Tues. Son: Robert, Anniston, Ala. AG 3/9/1910

KAPTUCH, Mike killed Sat. by Foder Kaminski, a Russian, Statesboro, Ga. AG 8/6/1907

KARLSRUHER, Regina, Mrs., age 80, d. 357 Pulliam St., Atlanta, Thurs. Daus: Miss Adline Karlsruher; Mrs. G. Strauss. AG 11/3/1908

KARR, Mary Elizabeth d. Tues., age 70. 3 sons, 3 daus. Interred: Sardis Church yard. AG 2/12/1907

KARWISCH, Annie R., Miss, age 33, d. Atlanta Wed. Interred: Oakland. Father. Bros: J. M., B. H Uncles: Ben Karwisch and John Hackman. AG 3/2/1910

KARWISCH, Annie, Miss, age 33, d. 175 Kirkwood Ave. Atlanta. AG 3/3/1910

KATCOFF, Dora, Miss, age 13, d. Atlanta Tues. 53 Armstrong St. AG 5/13/1908

KAUFMAN, Julius, age 49, d. St. Josephs Infirmary. Atlanta. AG 5/24/1907

KAUFMAN, Lester F., inf. son of Mr. and Mrs. L. F., d. 29 Uncle Remus Ave., Atlanta, Thurs. Interred: Westview. AG 5/13/1910

KAUFMANN, Florence, age 10, d. res. of grandparents, Mr. and Mrs. Henry Wolfe, 161 S. Forsyth St., Atlnata, Tues. Interred: Oakland. AG 5/26/1908

KAY, J. M., Mrs. d. 43 Stewart Ave., Atlanta, Wed. Interred: McDaniel, Ga. AG 6/25/1908

KEAN, William H., Major, age 65, d. Mon. Forrest Ave., Atlanta. Native of Geneva, N. Y., res. of Atlanta several years. Interred: Geneva, N. Y. AG 10/11/1910

KEAN, Mary E., Mrs., 70, d. 529 Highland Ave. Atlanta res. since Civil War. Daus: Mrs. C. B. Boatenreiter, Miss Minnie Kean. Sons: John, Charles E. Sis, bro: Mrs. Geo. Kimball, Joseph Boutell. Bur: Oakland. AG 9/2/1910

KEAN, William H., b. 1870 Corinth, Miss, of Atlanta Journal, d. 7 Cain St. Leaves Mother. Sis: Minnie Kean, Mrs. Charles E. Boatenreiter. Bros: John, Charlie. Wife: Martha. Daus: Mary, age 5, Martha, age 6 wks. Bur: Oakland. AG 7/14/1906

KEE, J. W. d. 12/7, 664 Highland Ave. Atlanta. Interred: Westview. AC 12/10/1905

KEE, Serita, inf. dau. of Mr. and Mrs. F. W., d. Mon., 82 McClendon St., Atlanta. Interred: Westview. AG 10/18/1910

KEEL, Lavinia, Mrs., age 57, d. 167 Magnolia St. Atlanta. Interred: Covington, Ga. AG 5/4/1907

KEELING, Frank E., age 29, d. Hawkinsville, Ga. AG 11/1/1909

KEESE, Addie, Mrs., age 77, d. 145 Ira St. Atlanta. Interred: Westview. AG 6/8/1908

KEESE, M. A., Mrs. d. Anderso, S. C. Children: Mrs. Henry Dunwody, Mrs. Arminius Wright, and Rodgers Keese, of Atlanta. AG 6/14/1907

KEE, Joe, alias Kwang Sing, chinaman, dead. Son in Athens. AG 8/20/1906

KEHELEY, W. A., age 55, d. 8 Homer St. Atlanta Tues. Wife survives. Interred: Fair Oak, Ga. AG 5/26/1908

KEITH, Ben d. Chattanooga, Tenn. buried Rising Fawn, Ga. Vet. of Spanish-American War. Wife, father, several brothers. AG 5/13/1910

KEITH, Emily Katherine, age 3 yrs., dau. of Mr. and Mrs. S. J., d. 79 Lovejoy St., Atlanta, Wed. AG 12/15/1909

KEITH, Sheriff killed by John Harper. Chatsworth, Ga. AG 5/7/1908

KEITH, W. Harvey, Mrs., 76, d. Clermont, Ga. Dau: Mrs. J. J. Boggs, White Co. Sons: M. Q., J. W., O. V. Bros: J. C. (Atlanta) & R. B. Hardie (Gainesville). Sis: Mrs. J. W. Blackwell, Mrs. R. S. Blackwell. Bur: Concord church. AG 12/4/1909

KELL, Ann, Mrs., age 65, d. 101 N. Butler St. Atlanta. AG 10/9/1907

KELLAM, C. H., age 20, res. of Talbotton, Ga., d. Mon. Parents: Mr. and Mrs. W. T. Kellum. Interred: Talbotton, Ga. AG 11/8/1910

KELLCHER, Margaret, Miss, age 24, d. New Kimball Hotel. Atlanta. AG 2/20/1907

KELLER, C. D. B., age 1, d. 3 Findley St. Atlanta. AG 9/21/1909

KELLEY, Blanche, age 6 mos., dau. of Mr. and Mrs. Gordon, d. Thurs. Panthersville, Ga. Interred: Mt. Carmen Church. AG 4/8/1910

KELLEY, Henry of Henry Co., d. Kelleytown, 3/10, age 76. Wife, 4 children. AG 3/10/1910

KELLEY, J. M., Dr. d. 6/29 Griffin, age 56, b. Wilkes Co., Ga. Wife. Dau: Mrs. A. J. Dunham. Sons: Marion F., M. Hewlette. Bros: B. A., Washington, Ga.; G. W., Louisville, Ga. AG 6/30/1909

KELLEY, John, colored, age 15, d. 101 Butler St. Atlanta. AG 7/12/1909

KELLEY, J. T. d. Panthersville Sat. Ch: Frank, W. B., Dr. O. G., Mrs. T. O. Poole, Mrs. C. C. Cobb, Mrs. C. E. Brantly, Misses Pearl and Estelle. Interred: Chapel near Decatur. AG 2/19/1910

KELLEY, Poney, negro, murdered by William Musgrove and Bill Kelley and Mack Forbes, negroes, Newton Co., Ga. AG 2/25/1908

KELLOGG, Milo P. d. 807 Piedmont Ave., Atlanta, Wed. Interred: Newnan, Ga. Wife, son: William Kellogg. Sister: Mrs. R. M. Gann. AG 5/7/1908

KELLUM, Mary F., Mrs., age 71, d. 193 W. North Ave. Atlanta. AG 6/18/1909

KELLY, Alonzo S., age 52, d. 352 Haynes St. Atlanta, Wed. Wife, 2 children. Father: G. W. Kelly. Bros: W. P., A. G. Interred: Columbus, Ga. AG 12/15/1910

KELLY, Annie, Mrs., age 17, wife of Joseph, d. 757 Ashby St., Atlanta, Thurs. AG 3/5/1908

KELLY, Bert of Westminster, S. C. killed by train at Toccoa, Ga. while walking tracks. AG 7/8/1908

KELLY, Bessie, Mrs., age 21, wife of J. S., d. 72 Neal St., Atlanta Mon. Interred: Anderson, S. C. AG 1/27/1908

KELLY, D., Rev., colored, age 59, d. 20 Chestnut St., Atlanta. AG 1/29/1908

KELLY, Edgar, age 27, d. Decatur Orphans' Home. AG 6/15/1909

KELLY, H. Solon, age 70, Confederate Veteran, d. Madison Co., Huntsville, Ala., Wed. AG 6/19/1908

KELLY, J. C., Mrs. d. Fri., age 50. Sons: C. C., O. L. Dau: Mrs. Gifford, of Gifford, S. C. AG 11/5/1910

KELLY, J. H., age 78, d. Panthersville Wed. Leaves wife, 3 sons, one dau. Interred: Clifton church yard. AG 12/30/1908

KELLY, J. K., Mrs., wife of J. A., d. Cliateville, Ga. 4/18. Sis: Mrs. W. S. West. Bros: T. G. and J. Crawford of Valdosta. AC

KELLY, J. W., age 26, d. 125 McMillan St. Atlanta. AG 10/3/1906

KELLY, Jack, 4 mos. son of Mr. & Mrs. C. H., 119 Garnett St. buried Westview. AG 9/20/1906

KELLY, N. E., Mrs., age 76, d. Atlanta, 362 Gordon St. Son: R. L. Interred: Sylvester Cemetery. AG 10/31/1908

KELLY, Nancy, Mrs. d. Sat. Atlanta. Interred: Westview. AG 12/5/1910

KELLY, P. H., Mrs., age 48, of Fitzgerald, Ga., d. Sat. Husband, 3 daus. survive. AG 4/22/1910

KELLY, Pearl, Miss d. Atlanta Sat. Interred: Clarkesville, Ga. AG 10/14/1907

KELLY, Reid H., colored, age 39, d. 237 Jonesboro Rd. Atlanta. AG 9/22/1908

KELLY, Richard, colored, age 21, d. 59 Biggers Ave. Atlanta. AG 1/9/1907

KELLY, Richard, son of Henry and Mary Usher, negroes, of 19 Moseley St. d. Sun. mysteriously. Parents held. AG 1/7/1907

KELLY, Rosa, Mrs. of 364 Decatur St., Atlanta d. Tues. AG 8/14/1906

KELLY, Samuel, Capt., ex-Confederate, d. Thurs. Charlotte, N. C., age 69. Was military prisoner at Ft. Delaware a year. AG 8/3/1906

KELLY, T. B., colored, age 49, d. 232 Fort St. Atlanta. AG 10/30/1909

KELSEY, Fannie, age 59, d. Savannah, Ga. AG 1/1/1908

KELSEY, Maggie F., colored, age 16, d. 16 Dunlap St. Atlanta. AG 5/6/1909

KEMBERLY, Cleo, age two, dau. of Mr. and Mrs. S. E., d. 112 Middle St., Atlanta, Mon. Interred: Flat Rock Church. AG 5/25/1908

KEMP, Eliza, colored, age 65, d. 335 Fort St. Atlanta. AG 1/28/1908

KEMP, Josie, son of Josha, killed by lumber cart, Mt Vernon, Ga. AG 11/1/1906

KEMP, J. W., Mrs., age 71, d. 282 E. Georgia Ave. Atlanta. Dau-in-law: Mrs. F. E. Kemp. Interred: Sandy Springs, Ga. AG 9/2/1910

KEMP, W. B., Mrs. d. Byron, Ga. 8/22. Husband, one child. Interred: Sardis Church Cemetery. AC 8/24/1905

KEMP, Walter Lee, age 16 mos., d. 164 McAfee St. Atlanta. Parents: Mr. and Mrs. J. A. Kemp. Interred: Hollywood. AG 10/8/1909

KEMPNER, Amelia, Mrs. funeral Wed. Interred: Oakland. AG 6/14/1906

KENAN, Thos Holmes, Dr, Conf. Vet, son of Col. Augustus Holmes Kenan, grson of Dr. Thomas Holmes Kenan, d. 174 Forrest Ave., Atlanta, age 74. Sons: Louis H., I. Kirtland. Daus: Lucy, Henrietta. Bur: Family plot, Milledgeville. AG 4/11/1910

KENDALL, Homer, age 21, d. res. of parents, Mr. and Mrs. Ben Kendall, in Cottondale, Mon. Interred: Cornelia, Ga. AG 1/21/1908

KENDALL, R. J., Mrs.,ge 48, d. 67 E. Harris St., Atlanta, Wed. Interred: Norcross, Ga. Sis: Mrs. Laura McNabb. Husband survives. AG 7/16/1908

KENDER, Daniel, colored, age 56, d. 56 South Ave. Atlanta. AG 7/8/1907

KENDRICK, John R., Mrs. d. 2-mi. W. of Sharon Wed, age 60, wife of Hon. John R. of Taliaferro Co. in State Legislature. Ch: Mrs. W. S. Wright, F. C. Manoe, Atlanta, Mrs. O. C. Stote?, W. M. and I. Ruff Kendrick of Sharon. AG 1/21/1910

KENDRICK, Zach murdered 12/1909 by Jule Daggert who is to be hanged at Appling. 4/19. AG 4/18/1910

KENDRICKS, L., Mrs., age 26, d. Longhorn St. Atlanta. AG 11/7/1907

KENNABREW, Miss, of Elberton, Ga., d. in house with bro-in-law, D. S. Kerlin. AG 2/11/1907

KENNEDY, Annie, Mrs., wife of Michael, d. Atlanta Wed. 4 children. Interred: Decatur, Ga. AG 4/17/1908

KENNEDY, Charles, colored, age 17, d. rear of 166 Whitehall St. Atlanta. AG 3/1/1908

KENNEDY, James W., age 76, of Winterville, Ga. d. Sun. Son: Walter Kennedy, Atlanta. Dau: Mrs. Cora L. Avary, Atlanta. Interred: Oakland. AG 12/7/1908

KENNEDY, John C. suicide Sat. Sandtown Road. Bro: Albert Kennedy. Interred: Family Burial Grounds. AG 12/30/1907

KENNEDY, M. J., age 45, d. 131 Garden St. Atlanta. Interred: Westview. Wife, 2 children, survive. AG 5/24/1906

KENNEDY, Mike Calvert, Jr., inf. son of M. C. of 120 Niles Ave. Atlanta, d. Mon. Interred: Decatur, Ga. AG 6/16/1908

KENNEDY, Mollie E., Mrs., wife of T. C., d. 9/14 Campbellton Rd., Atlanta. 7 boys, 4 girls (11 children). Interred: Wilson Burying ground. AC 9/15/1905

KENNEDY, Myrtle, Miss, age 19, d. sister's res., Mrs. M. L. Hatchett, 119 Columbia Ave., Atlanta, Thurs. Interred: Westview. AG 8/26/1909

KENNEDY, T. N. d. 119 Columbia Ave. Atlanta Sun. Interred: Westview. AG 5/12/1908

KENNEDY, Toombs, age 3, son of Mr. and Mrs. I. G., buried yesterday Cuthbert, Ga. Mrs. Kennedy is grandniece of General Robert Toombs. AG 5/1/1906

KENNEDY, Walter d. Statesboro, Ga. 1/20, son of Mr. and Mrs. Stephen of Emmit. AG 1/21/1910

KENNEDY, Wilson killed by Elmer Mahan, age 13, Rome, Ga. (indicted). AG 1/25/1907

KENNEY, Dan G., age 52, d. 92 Venable St. Atlanta. AG 7/19/1907

KENNON, Mary E., Miss interred Salem, Ala. Parents: Mr. and Mrs. R. L. Kennon. Bros: R. L., Jr. of Birmingham, Ala.; W. P. of Augusta, Ga.; Herbert of Atlanta. Sisters: Pauline, Lillie, Louise, Elsie, Helen. AG 2/27/1908

KENNY, Henry Gratton, age 13, son of Mr. and Mrs. E. P., grandson of late James Lynch, d. 3/4 Atlanta, S. Pryor St. Interred: Oakland. AC 3/5/1905

KENT, A., colored, age 19, d. 354 Piedmont Ave. Atlanta. AG 12/18/1907

KENT, Charles Austin, inf. son of Mr. and Mrs. C. O., d. Sun. 181 Emmett St., Atlanta. Interred: Roswell, Ga. AG 3/1/1908

KENT, Dora, Mrs., age 48, d. Sun. 23 Narrows Ave., Atlanta. Interred: Loganville, Ga. AG 5/30/1910

KENT, E. A., Dr., d. Fri. 519 Ponce de Leon Ave., Atlanta, Sun. Interred: Westview. AG 9/13/1909

KENT, Edward, Dr b. 4/1/1866 Hamilton, Ont. d. Atlanta m. Decatur, MI 1897 Lena Lyle.Ch: Edwd A, Jr; Marion. Bros: Harry, Altoona, PA; Jas, Blooming Pr, MN. Sis: Mrs. Frank Stockton, Margaret Kent,Ont; Mrs. Boyd, Brandon, MN. AG 9/11/1909

KENT, Gertrude, age 3, dau. of Mr. and Mrs. Charles, d. Edgewood, Ga., Sun. Interred: Luxompi, Ga. AG 2/24/1908

KENT, Irvin of Ala. was killed and Jailer A. A. Phelts wounded Sun. when mob stormed Muscogee Co. jail to get Henry Taylor, negro charged with attacking young woman. Kent was res. of Phenix City, Ala., age 22, unmd. AG 12/12/1910

KENT, Julius, colored, age 21, d. 101 Butler St. Atlanta. AG 11/3/1909

KENYON, F. J. d. River St., Athens, Sat. Interred: Oconee Cemetery. Age 45. Wife, little dau. AG 2/5/1910

KEOWN, W. S., age 54, d. 268 E. Hunter St. Atlanta. Wife, 3 children. Interred: Goster, Ga. AG 4/20/1908

KERBY, Bessie C., Miss, age 45, of 55 Wayman St., Atlanta, d. Atlanta Sat. Interred: Greenwood. AG 8/17/1908

KERER, George B., son of Mr. and Mrs. Frank E. of Montgomery, Ala. d. Thurs. Grainesville, Ga. Funeral res. of Patrick Calhoun, 156 Crew St., Atlanta. Interred: Norcross, Ga. AG 5/10/1907

KERLIN, D. S. of Elberton, Ga., d. in house with his sister-in-law, Miss Kennabrew within few hours of her death. AG 2/11/1907

KERR, Mittie, Mrs., age 58, d. Atlanta Fri. Interred: Decatur, Ga. AG 11/27/1910

KERR, O., age 53, d. Grady Hospital, Atlanta. AG 2/8/1907

KERRISON, Louis, age 11 mos., d. 216 E. Pine St. Atlanta. AG 3/29/1907

KERY, Winnie Miss, age 17, d. 25 Walnut St. Atlanta. AG 12/26/1907

KETTERER, August, age 73, native of Germany, to Atlanta 40 yrs. ago, d. 66 Conally St. Wife: Katharine. Ch: Henry, Oscar; Mrs. A. C. Huber, Mrs. J. B. Hewett, Mrs. William Kling, Mrs. O. K. H. Alcorn, Atlanta. Bur: Westview. AG 2/2/1908

KETTLE, Sam, age 44, d. 167-1/2 Decatur St., Atlanta. AG 4/4/1907

KEY, A. J., Mrs., d. Fri. 26 Rock St., Atlanta. Interred: Rock Springs Church. AG 1/19/1907

KEY, Fannie, Mrs., age 48, d. 26 Rock St. Atlanta. AG 1/22/1907

KEY, George Pierce, age 9, d. Wed. res. of grandfather, G. W. Key, 42 Hood St. Atlanta. Interred: Westview. AG 5/26/1910

KEY, Mamie Lou, age 14, dau. of G. M., d. Mon. N. Boulevard, Atlanta. AG 8/1/1910

KEY, Mary, Mrs., age 75, d. Atlanta Mon. Interred: Westview. AG 3/10/1909

KEY, William Bibb, age 72, d. Peachtree Road, Atlanta. AG 11/4/1908

KEYS, I. H., Union Soldier during Civil War, d. Mon. Dalton, Ga., age 60. Wife, 5 children. AG 1/5/1910

KICKLIGHTER, Gussie, Miss of Glennville, Ga., d. Sat. Interred: Beard Creek Cemetery. AG 7/20/1908

KIDD, Henry, colored, age 16, d. 101 N. Butler St. Atlanta. AG 3/4/1907

KIEBOLD, Therese, Mrs., age 40, d. Atlanta Wed. 72 W. Peachtree St. Interred: Westivew. Husband: J. P. Son: Robert. AG 11/26/1908

KIEL, Mamie, Mrs., age 35, d. 10 Oliver St. Atlanta. AG 7/29/1908

KILBY, Frank W. of Anniston, Ala. killed by railroad wreck near Greensboro, Ga. Interred: Atlanta. AG 12/16/1909

KILE, Catherine Keith, inf. dau. of Mr. and Mrs. J. W., d. 28 Elm St., Atlanta, Sun. Interred: Westview. AG 7/27/1908

KILGER, V., Mrs., age 54, d. 143 Piedmont Ave. Atlanta. AG 1/24/1907

KILGO, Thomas, colored, age 20, d. rear of 266 Pulliam St. Atlanta. AG 11/15/1907

KILGORE, Bettie, Mrs., age 50, wife of Jack, d. Howells Mill Road, Atlanta, Sun. Interred: Casey's. AG 1/27/1908

KILGORE, Claudie, Miss, age 20, dau. of Mr. and Mrs. Jackson Kilgore of Villa Rica d. yesterday. AG 8/9/1906

KILGORE, J. H., age 52, of Winder. Merchant. Died 9/22. Wife, 7 children. Interred: Winder Cemetery. AG 9/22/1909

KILGORE, John E., age 48, d. 101 N. Butler St. Atlanta. AG 2/8/1909

KILGORE, Missouri, Mrs., age 35, d. 14 Chestnut St., Atlanta, Fri. Interred: Newnan, Ga. AG 12/14/1907

KILGORE, Rufus, age 22, d. Atlanta. AG 9/2/1909

KILGORE, S. M., Mrs., age 44, d. 17 W. Cain St. Atlanta. AG 9/18/1908

KILGORE, Sarah, Mrs., age 63, d. dau's res., Mrs. J. E. Gifford, College Park. Daus: Mrs. C. H. Branan, College Park; Mrs. Inie Riddle, Oxford, Ala.; Mrs. Addie Durham, Heflin, Ala. Son: James J., Anniston, Ala. Bur: Heflin. AG 7/31/1908

KILLEN, Elizabeth, Mrs., age 75, d. Riverside Thurs. Nephew: John Dudley. Interred: Casey's Cemetery. AG 5/6/1910

KILLIAN, Horace M., age 39, d. 16 W. Ellis St. Atlanta. Interred: Louisville, Ky. AG 7/23/1907

KILLINGSWORTH, T. M. d. 4/20 Fitzgerald, Ga. Widow, 12 children. Interred: Ft. Gaines, Ga. AC 4/21/1905

KILPATRICK, I. J., Mrs., d. 267 Peachtree St., Atlanta, Wed. Interred: Eden, Ga. AG 1/16/1908

KILPATRICK, Sarah Frances, Miss, second dau. of Mr. and Mrs. Edward, d. Tues. Eatonton, Ga. Interred: Family Burial Grounds at Harmonyh. AG 10/30/1908

KILPATRICK, T. G., age 30, d. Macon, Ga. Survived by mother, Mrs. T. J. Kilpatric, 4 bros. AG 4/28/1908

KILPATRICK, W. H., Mrs., wife of Prof., principal of Columbus High School, d. yesterday. Interred: Marianna, Fla., her former home. AG 5/30/1907

KIMBALL, J. B. d. Pasadena, Calif. 3/23, formerly of Columbus, Ga. AG 4/2/1907

KIMBERLY, Walter, inf. son of Mr. and Mrs. J. T. of 130 Logan St., Atlanta, Thurs. Interred: Ben Hill, Ga. AG 10/23/1908

KIMBRELL, Mrs. J. H., age 59, d. 111 Kirkwood Ave. Atlanta. AG 7/11/1907

KIMBRO, Samuel B., Mrs., age 82, d. Peachtree Inn, Atlanta. AG 4/18/1910

KIMBRO, V. A., Mrs., age 83, d. Peachtree Inn, Atlanta, Sat. Dau: Mrs. F. M. Farley. Interred: Westview. AG 4/16/1910

KINDELL, Pearl, colored, age 18, d. 101 N. Butler St. Atlanta. AG 5/20/1909

KING, Albert, colored, age 40, d. 2 Allens alley. Atlanta. AG 6/6/1907

KING, Ben, aged printed, d. Atlanta Tues. Father: Cary A. King of Forsyth, Ga., survives. AG 8/19/1908

KING, Ben T., age 59, d. 101 N. Butler St. Atlanta. AG 8/20/1908

KING, Bessie Augusta, age 14 mos., dau. of Mr. and Mrs. W. C., d. Lexington, Ga. 5/17. Interred: Atlanta. AC 5/18/1905

KING, C. E., age 37, d. corner Kirkwood Ave. and Willow St. Thurs. Member of Cherokee Tribe, No. 1, Improved Order of Red Men. AG 5/24/1907

KING, Charles E. d. 9/14 Halcyon. Interred: Westview. AC 9/15/1905

KING, Charles Rufus, Dr., b. Carroll Co., Ms. 2/28/1841, res. Atlanta d. 356 N. Jackson St. Sons: R. DeWitt, Chas. Surgeon & Clyde Randolph. Daus: Misses Irma Lee & Mabel. Bro: Dr. H. R., 110 Ivy St. Bur: Westview. AG 11/27/1909

KING, Della, Miss, age 50, d. Peachtree Rd. Atlanta. AG 8/14/1907

KING, E. J., Mrs., age 21, d. Presbyterian Hospital. Atlanta. AG 1/7/1907

KING, Elba d. Columbia, S. C., Sun. Interred: Bowman, Ga. Leaves young bride. He was son of J. W. King of Bowman, Ga. AG 11/15/1910

KING, Florence M., age 57, d. 129 Courtland St. Atlanta. AG 6/20/1907

KING, Frank, age 18, d. 199 Forrest Ave. Atlanta. AG 12/30/1908

KING, Frank, age 19, d. 299 Forrest Ave., Atlanta, Tues. AGX 12/29/1908

KING, Green, negro, killed Macon 12/7/1905. Hal Schofield charged. AC 12/14/1905

KING, H. H., former res. of Savannah, d. Eustus, Fla. AC 4/22/1905

KING, J. Gadsden, Major, Atlanta, d. dau's res., Mrs. Harry W. Young, 254 Peeples St., res. Atlanta 30 yrs; born Charleston, S. C. 1831. Survivors: Sons, Alex C., suicide 142 S. Pryor St. Atlanta. Interred: Westview. AG 8/29/1906

KING, J. M., age 62, d. 66 W. Georgia Ave. Atlanta. AG 7/8/1909

KING, J. R. of Marietta d. Fri., age 50. One dau. Interred: Oakland. AG 1/15/1910

KING, J. R., age 57, d. Atlanta. AG 1/20/1910

KING, J. R., Mrs. d. Marietta. Funeral: Atlanta. Interred: Oakland. AC 2/19/1905

KING, J. W., age 69, Confed. Vet., d. Mon. 80 Powell St., Atlanta. Interred: Sylvester Cemetery. AG 10/18/1910

KING, John T. who was shot in pistol duel yesterday with I. S. McConnell, E. Macon merchant, d. city hospital. AG 2/20/1907

KING, Lizzie, Mrs., age 40, d. Egan, Ga. Tues. Interred: Hill Crest Cemetery, East Point, Ga. AG 5/31/1910

KING, Miles P., age 57, d. 293 Forrest Ave. Atlanta. AG 3/29/1907

KING, Mitchell, age 23, d. at Flat Rock, N. C. AG 8/20/1906

KING, Morris C., nephew of late Willis King, d. Wed. Atlanta. Interred: Hollywood. AG 6/6/1906

KING, Nellie, colored, age 48, d. 49 Biggers St. Atlanta. AG 7/31/1907

KING, R. L., Mrs., age 37, of Dillsboro, N. C., d. Atlanta Sun. Interred: Dillsboro, N. C. AG 7/25/1910

KING, Robert, Mrs. suicide, near Fellowship, Hart Co., Ga. She lost child several mos. ago. Interred: Fellowship Cemetery. AG 7/15/1910

KING, Susan, colored, d. 58 Brown's alley. Atlanta. AG 5/18/1908

KING, Tessie B., Mrs., age 31, d. Germania Ave., Decatur, Ga., Sun., wife of J. B. Interred: Duluth, Ga. AG 5/2/1910

KING, Thomas killed by lightening at Howell's Sta. Atlanta. Interred: Caseys. AG 6/25/1907

KING, Thomas, age 78, d. Tues. Dalton, Ga. Wife. Ch: Mrs. Sallie Thacker, Mrs. Headrick, Mrs. Mattie Higest, of Oklahoma; John and Tom King, of Texas; Will King of Calif.; and Dr. Jim King and Alex King of Tilton. AG 6/22/1910

KING, Violet, colored, age 80, d. 213 N. Piedmond Ave. Atlanta. AG 12/14/1908

KING, W. A., age 255, d. 45 Johnson Ave. Atlanta. Bro., sister, survive. Interred: Antioch church yard. AG 2/26/1908

KING, W. B., age 50, d. E. Point Sun. Interred: Cress Hill Cemetery. AG 1/17/1910

KING, West, colored, age 27, d. 101 N. Butler St. Atlanta. AG 12/16/1908

KING, Will, colored, age 19, d. Grady Hospital. Atlanta. AG 1/7/1907

KING. W. J., Rev. d. 3/4 Adairsville, Ga., Conf. Vet. Wife, one child. Interred: Enon. AC 3/5/1905

KINGSBERY, Charles S., Judge d. 380 Peachtree St. Atlanta Tues. Interred: Oakland. AG 8/27/1908

KINGSLEY, Mrs., wife of James, citizen of Pavo, Ga., d. AG 6/8/1906

KINNEBREW, E. C., Mrs. d. 11/23 Wray St. Athens. AC 11/27/1905

KINNEY, Willie May, inf. dau. of Mr. and Mrs. William, d. Sat., Lakewood Dr. Atlanta. Bur: Greenwood Cemetery. AG 6/4/1910

KINNON, A. J. of Bellaire, Mich. d. 12/6 Fitzgerald, Ga. AG 12/6/1909

KINNON, Ann, colored, age 85, d. 26 Bellman St. Atlanta. AG 7/8/1909

KINSEL, Charles M. d. Columbus, Ga. Tues. Born Dresden, Germany, came to Columbus in 1859. AG 10/13/1910

KINZLE, Ernestine, Mrs., age 55, of Ft. Myers, Fla. d. 239 Forrest Ave. Atlanta Wed. Sons: Capt. A. L. Kinzie, etc. Interred: Ft. Myers, Fla. AG 6/2/1909

KIRBY, Clarence, age 36, d. Sun. 315 E. Fair St., Atlanta. Interred: Westview. AG 8/19/1907

KIRBY, George, colored, age 27, d. 101 N. Butler St. Atlanta. AG 3/1/1908

KIRBY, Hannah, colored, age 18, d. 428 Foundry St. Atlanta. AG 5/31/1907

KIRCHER, Ferdinand, age 76, d. Home for Incurables. Atlanta. AG 10/25/1906

KIRCUS, M. J., Mrs., age 62, d. 664 Ashby St.. Atlanta Mon. 3 daus, two sons. AG 4/22/1907

KIRKLAND, R. R. d. Atlanta Thurs. Wife, 5 sons, dau. survive. Interred; Conyers, Ga. AG 9/24/1908

KIRKLEY, C. P., age 78, d. Sat. Funeral at res. of dau., Mrs. Reynolds, 225 Glenwood Ave., Atlanta. Interred: Hollywood. AG 7/30/1906

KIRKMAN, Everett Lee, age 2, son of Mr. and Mrs. E. E. Kirkman, 29 Ashland Ave., Atlanta. Interred: Hollywood. AG 7/23/1906

KIRKPATRICK, John C., Mrs., age 64, d. Kirkwood, Ga. AG 12/16/1909

KIRKPATRICK, M. E., Mrs., age 72, d. 56 W. Peachtree Pl. Atlanta. AG 11/30/1910

KIRKPATRICK, W. L., Mrs. d. Anniston, Ala. Tues. res. of bro., R. P. Milan, 289 Forrest Ave. Ch: R. L. (Atlanta), W. A., Charles (Birmingham), Mrs. L. G. Jones (Anniston). Interred: Cartersville, Ga. AG 7/6/1910

KIRKSEY, William d. Milledgeville, Ga. Wed. Interred: Atlanta, Oakland Cem. Father: George, Augusta. AG 9/23/1909

KISER, A. T., age 64, d. DeKalb Ave. Atlanta. AG 8/1/1908

KISER, P. H., Mrs. d. Fairburn, Ga., age 44. Husband. Dau: Miss Cloudie Kiser. Interred: Fairburn Cemetery. AG 10/4/1910

KISER, W. C. of Fairbrn, Ga., d. S. Main St. 8/31, age 55. Leaves son and brother. Relative of M. C. Kiser of Atlanta. Interred: Fairburn Cem. AG 8/31/1909

KISSELL, Howard F., inf. son of Mr. and Mrs. N. C., d. 176 Venable St., Atlanta, Wed. Interred: South Bend. AG 1/9/1908

KISSLER, J. A., Professor, musician, d. res. of dau., Mrs. E. Harrison, 240 Central Ave. Atlanta Tues. Interred: Oakland. AG 4/2/1907

KISTER, Mary C., age 48, d. 150 Glenwood Ave. Atlanta. AG 10/25/1906

KITCHENS, Aaron, Mrs., age 56, d. Sun. E. Point, Ga. Funeral: Forest Park Church. AG 8/5/1907

KITCHENS, Arthur, colored, age 50, d. 55 Newton St. Atlanta. AG 7/14/1909

KITCHENS, C. B., Mrs. d. 115 Washington St. Atlanta Mon. Interred: Canton, Ga. AG 5/14/1908

KITCHENS, Lorene, dau. of Mr. and Mrs. W. Terrell Kitchens (Postmaster), d. Sat., abt 4 yrs. old. AG 3/19/1907

KITCHENS, W. A., Mrs., age 29, d. 137 Simpson St., Atlanta, Mon. AG 2/10/1908

KITCHENS, Willie, age 10, son of Rev. William Kitchens of Mitchell, Ga., d. yesterday Sandersville, Ga. where taken for treatment. AG 12/24/1908

KITE, Bertha, Mrs., age 23, d. Sun. 19 Church St. Atlanta. Interred: Columbus, Ga. AG 12/30/1907

KITE, Beulah, Mrs., age 33, d. 138 Grant St. Atlanta. AG 7/23/1909

KITTREDGE, H. T. d. Sat. Atlanta. AG 6/8/1909

KLASSET, John Andrew, age 30, d. 56 Walnut St. Atlanta. Father: Charles. Interred: Oakland. AG 5/9/1908

KLASSET, Mary, Mrs., wife of F. W., d. Mon. 114 Park Ave. Atlanta. Interred: Oakland. AG 1/25/1910

KLATT, E. W. d. Macon Tues. Interred: Riverside Cemetery. Wife survives. AG 11/8/1910

KLEIN, Charles A., age 56, native German, sometime res. of Atlanta, d. 76 N. Boulevard, Atlanta. Interred: Oakland. AG 8/1/1910

KLENLE, Herman, age 55, d. Norfolk, Va., age 55. AC 12/7/1905

KLINE, inf. dau. of Mr. and Mrs. R. J., d. 179 Wiley St. Atlanta. AG 6/29/1910

KLINE, S. F., age 24, formerly of Savannah, suicide, 140 S. Pryor St. Atlanta. Sis: Elizabeth Kline, 1253 W. Broad, Savannah. Div. AG 8/28/1906

KLING, D. V. Jay, age 80, d. 133 Cooper St. Atlanta. AG 2/26/1908

KLOECKLER, Theresa, Mrs. d. Sun. Birmingham. Funeral at St. Anthonys Chapel, Atlanta. AG 10/18/1910]

KNIGHT, Annie May, age 1, dau. of Mr. and Mrs. Frank, d. 64 Glenn St., Atlanta, Thurs. Interred: Hollywood. AG 6/24/1909

KNIGHT, J. R., Mrs., age 50, d. 4/20. Dau: Clarice Knight. 1/2 sister: Mrs. E. W. Whilden, Waycross, and Mrs. E. A. Ashe, Jacksonville. Bros: Peter and Owen Griffin of Ware Co. and Leander Griffin of Sparks. AG 4/21/1908

KNIGHT, John, inf. son of Mr. and Mrs. W. R., funeral, res. Mason and Turner Rds. Atlanta, Sun. Interred: Masons Church yard. AG 7/25/1910

KNIGHT, M. M., Mrs., died Valdosta. Interred: city cemetery. AG 8/25/1906

KNIGHT, Oscar killed by Arthur Hogan, negroes, Macon. AC 7/16/1905

KNIGHT, Ray, Capt. d. 64 Ivy St. Atlanta. In Regt. w/Sherman. 4 sons. Daus: Nellie m. English army officer, res. Scotland; Grace m. Prof. John Daniel, Nashville, Tn. Wife's bro: Will N. Harbin, Ga. novelist. Bur: Decatur, Ala. AG 4/30/1908

KNIGHT, Sarah A., Mrs. d. Tues. 200 Jett St. Atlanta, wife of John F. Interred: Masons Church yard. AG 3/24/1910

KNIGHT, Thelma Inez, age 3 mos., dau. of Mr. and Mrs. N. C., d. Wed. Douglasville, Ga. Interred: Greenville, S. C. AG 9/23/1910

KNIGHT, W. C., Hon., age 83, d. Cedartown 11/17. Confed. Vet. Interred: Greenwood Cemetery. AC 11/18/1905

KNIGHT, W. S., suicide at New Holland. Interred: Dacula. AG 8/7/1906

KNOBLOCH, Katie, Miss, age 22, formerly of Macon, dau. of late W. C., drowned in mill pond, Florence, S. C. Bur: Rose Hill Cemetery, Macon, Ga. Sisters: Mrs. C. C. Arnett, Meridian, Miss., Miss Lillian Knobloch, Anderson, S. C. Bro: W. C. Knobloch, US Navy. AG 6/9/1908

KNOLL, Mat, age 65, d. East Point. AG 3/27/1909

KNOTT, Dorothy May, infant, d. Washington St. Atlanta. AG 2/11/1910

KNOWLES, Richard, colored, age 49, d. 101 N. Butler St. Atlanta. AG 5/11/1908

KNOX, Daniel C. killed Fri. by railway train Atlanta. Interred: Hollywood. AG 10/15/1906

KNOX, Georgia, Mrs., wid. of Peter, Atlanta pioneer 20 yrs. ago from Newton Co., d. 443 E. Fair St. Bur: Social Circle. Daus: Mrs. Ella K. Cumminham, Mrs. Robt V. Haslett, Mrs. Edw. P. Wood. Sons: Walter I., Robt F., Charles H. AG 1/3/1907

KNOX, John, negro, killed by Irvin Bailey, Washington, Ga., negroes. Acquitted. AG 11/12/1907

KODEFF, Bonsie, colored, age 10 mos., d. Chattanooga, Tenn. AG 6/10/1907

KOEWN, W. S., Mrs., age 50, d. 268 E. Hunter St. Atlanta. AG 5/4/1908

KOHN, Joseph, age 48, d. Asheville, N. C. AG 10/7/1909

KONG, **Loo Hing**, Chinaman, age 51, d. W. Mitchell and Mangum Sts. Atlanta. AG 5/11/1908

KONTZ, **Anton L.** of Atlanta d. Sat. 145 W. Peachtree St. at res. of A. J. Smith. Bro: Judge Ernest C. Kontz. Parents came to Atlanta from Germany in 1849. AG 11/23/1907

KONTZ, **Lena, Mrs.**, age 82, d. 110 Davis St. Atlanta. AG 1/18/1907

KONTZ, **W. L.**, age 56, d. 145 W. Peachtree St. Atlanta. AG 11/25/1907

KOONSE, **Henry**, colored, age 40, d. Dothan, Ala. AG 12/12/1910

KOSCHE, **Charles Walker**, age 10 mos., son of Mr. and Mrs. Walter, d. 178 Franklin St., Atlanta, Tues. Interred: Hollywood. AG 7/21/1908

KRAMER, **E. G., Mrs.**, wife of Hon. E. G. Kramer and sis. of L. C. and L. P. Mandeville, d. Carrollton, Ga. yesterday. AG 1/10/1908

KREIS, **Robert Charles**, age 8, d. 163 Jett St. Atlanta. AG 11/15/1909

KRIES, **V. C., Mrs.**, age 64, d. 18 Trinity Ave. Atlanta. AG 2/23/1907

KROUSE, **Henry E.** d. Fri. Denver, Colo., railroad man of Atlanta. Interred: Oakland Cemetery. AG 7/19/1909

KRÜGER, **Edward**, Prof. interred Westview Sun. AG 5/14/1906

KRUMHOLZ, **Mary Rosalie, Mrs.** accidentally killed by husband, H. B., Mon., 139 S. Forsyth St., Atlanta. Interred: Hollywood. AG 8/8/1907

KRUMHOLZ, **Rosalie, Mrs.** murdered by husband, H. B. 8/6, 139 S. Forsyth St., Atlanta. Mother: Mrs. J. J. Jenkins. AG 10/2/1907

KUHN, **Sophie, Mrs.**, age 80, d. Edgewood, Ga. AG 2/20/1908

KULE, **Lime**, Chinaman, age 73, d. 101 Butler St. Atlanta. AG 10/18/1909

KURFEES, **H. G., Mrs.**, age 29, d. Park St. Atlanta. AG 12/30/1907

KYLE, **Napoleon B.**, age 68, d. 24 Leonard St. Atlanta. AG 9/28/1909

KYLE, **Thomas**, age 65, d. 24 Leonard St. Atlanta. AG 4/6/1907

A. Kysor, 14 St. Clair Ave. Atlanta. Wife. Sons: S. A., William. Dau: Mrs. Jessie Hopkins of Hemlock, N. Y. Interred: Cattaraugus, N. Y. AG 3/17/1910

L'ENGLE, Charles S., Atlantan, d. Mon. 164 Ponce de Leon Ave. Wife, 6 children survive. Interred: Westview. AG 6/18/1907

LABORS, Jim, negro, run over, cut in two by electric car near Lindale, Ga. AG 9/16/1907

LACE, Ben, negro, body found in river, Bay Street, Augusta, Ga. by John Hurt, negro, while fishing, 3/11. AG 3/11/1907

LACKEY, J. M., age 65, d. Tues. 14 McAfee St. Atlanta. Interred: Cartersville. Wife, Mary. Ag 4/17/1907

LACKEY, Thomas d. 2/9 Rose Hill. AC 2/12/1905

LACOSTE, James C., Confed. Vet., who took part in first guns at Ft. Sumter, d. age 68, Birmingham, Ala. AC 12/27/1905

LACY, George Edward, 709 Highland Ave., Atlanta. AG 11/9/1906

LADD, Roland d. Tues. Interred: Hollywood. AG 9/17/1907

LADE, Barbara Alice, age 11 mos., d. 856 Davis St. Atlanta. AG 10/20/1908

LAFITT, Eva, Miss, age 25, d. 92 Luckie St. Atlanta. AG 8/25/1909

LAFITTE, James A., age 61, d. 96 Cooper St. Atlanta. AG 3/16/1907

LAFLIN, T. C., former Atlantan, d. Thurs. home of wife's bro., Charles R. Harvey, Plainfield, Ind. Res. of N. Jackson St., Atlanta. Wife survives him. AG 6/1/1907

LAHATTE, Charles Burge, Dr., age 70, d. 124 S. Pryor St., Atlanta Thurs. Dau: Mrs. Emmett Brogdon, 330 Grant St., Atlanta. Interred: Gainesville, Ga., his old home. AG 5/1/1908

LA HATTE, Elizabeth, Mrs., 82, b. Edgefield, S. C., moved Augusta, Ga. w/parents, Mr. & Mrs. Isham Windham, later Muscogee Co., d. son's res., M. T., 32 Garnett. Bur: Oakland. Hus: Charles Henry La Hatte of NY, Ga Meth. Preacher. 12 of her ch' lived to maturity. 5 survive. Four sons served Confederate army. Husband died Atlanta. Children: Rev. Dr. C. B. LaHatte of Atlanta; M. T. LaHatte, Atlanta; Mrs. Alda Carraway, Philadelphia; Miss Fannie LaHatte, Atlanta; Mrs. Charles P. Bedingfield, Atlanta. AG 12/11/1906

LA HATTE, John Holton, infant son of Mr. and Mrs. C. O., d. Mon. 425 Washington St. Atlanta. Interred: Gainesville, Ga. AG 8/8/1910

LAHRMAN, Henry, age 63, d. Knoxville, Tenn. 6/18. AC 6/19/1905

LAIR, Mary A., Mrs., age 69, d. Oakland City, Ga. AG 8/14/1908

LAIRD, D. T., a saloon passenger on steamship City of Atlanta which arrived today from Savannah (N. Y.) found dead. Aged abt 60. AG 3/25/1907

LAIRD, Esmeralda Marie, age 18 mos., dau. of Mr. and Mrs. E. G., d. grandmother's res., Mrs. A. J. Foster, 20 Elliott St., Atlanta, Fri. Interred: Westview. AG 6/20/1908

LAIRD, W. A. d. Atlanta. Interred: Westview. AG 2/2/1908

LAIRD, W. D., age 78, d. Clarkston, Ga. Thurs. AG 4/22/1909

LAMAR, C. A., Mrs., age 46, d. 101 N. Butler St. Atlanta. AG 2/12/1907

LAMAR, Dunbar, planter at Beech Island, S. C. d. yesterday N. Augusta, Ga. Leaves wife, 8 children. Bros: Casey, Colonel, and Dr. A. W. Lamar in Nashville, Tenn. AG 5/21/1907

LAMAR, Katie, Miss, age 46, d. Sun. Grady Hospital, Atlanta. Wife of Charles A. Lamar of 497 Whitehall St., Atlanta. AG 2/11/1907

LAMAR, Richard N., age 62, co. school commissioner of Baldwin Co., d. 7/31 Milledgeville. Wife, 3 children, dau., and son in NY, one son in Calif. Bro: L. J. Lamar. AG 7/31/1909

LAMAR, Sarah, Mrs., age 75, d. 27 Corley Ave. Atlanta. AG 9/10/1908

LAMB, Emma, Mrs., age 30, d. 41 W. 12th St. Atlanta. AG 2/7/1910

LAMB, Harold C., ifant, d. 183 Randolph St. Atlanta. AG 1/25/1910

LAMB, Rhoda Adele, dau. of Mr. and Mrs. C. A., d. 19 Bluff St., Atlanta, Sun. Interred: Howells Mill Rd. Cemetery. AG 2/24/1908

LAMB, Sarah H., Mrs., age 56, d. Fri. Buckhead. 5 children, 1 bro., 4 sisters. AG 2/25/1910

LAMBERT, Bessie, age 10, killed Houston, Tex. Fri. by explosion. Interred: Bethesda church yard, Atlanta. AG 11/11/1907

LAMBERT, William J., age 31, d. Tues. 107 Ivy St. Atlanta. Interred: Oakland. Bros: V. E., Peter and John Lambert. Sis: Mrs. H. G. Kenney, Mrs. G. W. Brown. AG 9/29/1909

LAMBERT, William J., age 31, d. Tues. 107 Ivy St. Atlanta. Interred: Oakland. Bros: V. E., Peter and John Lambert. Sis: Mrs. H. G. Kenney, Mrs. G. W. Brown. AG 9/29/1909

LAMBRETH, Aletha, Mrs., age 64, d. 9 Corley Ave., Atlanta, Thurs. Interred: Rome, Ga. AG 12/24/1909

LAMDIN, A. M. d. Waco, Texas while visiting dau., Mrs J. D. Williamson. Funeral: Barnesville, Ga. AG 7/7/1909

LAMON, Margaret, Miss, age 40, d. W. Mitchell St. Atlanta. AG 7/11/1910

LAMPKIN, Susie, colored, age 20, d. 370 N. Butler St. Atlanta. AG 4/28/1908

LANCASTER, Neal, age 28 shot and killed by bro., John T. Lancaster, age 34, Mon. Bessie, age 12, and Charlie, age 7, children of Neal Lancaster, watched. Parents: Mr. and Mrs. L. M. Lancaster, 521 Marietta St., Atlanta. 7 other siblings: Henry, Carlton, Otis, Paul and Willie Lancaster; Mrs. W. M. Carman; Mrs. J. W. Stalvey. AG 7/27/1908

LANCASTER, Percy Lee, age 2 mos., d. 352 1/2 Decatur St. Atlanta. AG 10/18/1909

LAND, J. M., age 71, d. 135 Luckie St. Atlanta. AG 3/23/1908

LAND, Katie, Mrs., age 50, d. 172 Rawlins St. Atlanta. AG 12/9/1909

LAND, Laura A., Mrs., age 61, d. Thurs. Atlanta. Interred: Woodstock, Ga. AG 9/10/1910

LAND, William S., Ordinary, Washington, Ga., d., age 60. Dau: Emmie Lane, Washington. Son: H. Lane, Atlanta. Bro. Sis: Miss Annie Lane, Washington. Interred: Washington, Ga. AG 5/7/1910

LANDERS, Emmett, age 3, son of Mr. and Mrs. J. C. of 86 Echo St., Atlanta, d. Wed. AG 9/1/1909

LANDERS, Esther, Miss, age 14, dau. of Mr. and Mrs. E. T., of Temple, Ga., d. Interred: Mt. Zion Church, Hapeville, Ga. AG 7/8/1910

LANDERS, Louis D. d. Mon. Atlanta. Interred: Westview. AG 10/27/1909

LANDRETH, Elizabeth, Mrs., age 75, d. res. of dau., Mrs. J. C. Nobles, Blue Springs. Interred: Bluff Creek Church cemetery. AG 2/24/1910

LANDRUM, John, colored, age 52, d. 14 Mangum St. Atlanta. AG 10/18/1907

LANDRUM, M. V., Mrs., age 70, d. Atlanta. AG 3/8/1909

LANE, Joe W., Dr., son of Charles, d. Helena, Ga., Thurs. AG 11/27/1910

LANE. K., Mrs., age 74, d. 808 Marietta St. Atlanta. AG 7/21/1908

LANE, Loring, age 60, d. 33 Cone St. Atlanta. Interred: Brooklyn, N. Y. AG 3/22/1909

LANE, Lucile, Mrs., age 43, d. 335 E. Georgia Ave. Atlanta. AG 11/2/1907

LANE, Ludie, Mrs. d. several days ago. Interred: Conyers, Ga. AG 11/2/1907

LANE, W. J., superintendent of Valdosta St. RR Co. d. Valdosta mysteriously. The unmd son of A. H. Lane and nephew of Sen. W. S. West. AG 7/13/1906

LANE, W. S., Major, age 63, d. Liberty St., Washington, Ga. Fri. Interred: City Cemetery. Dau: Miss Emmie Lane of Washington, Ga. Bro: Dr. M. H. Lane of Atlanta. Sis: Miss Annie Lane of Washington, Ga. AG 5/9/1910

LANEY, E. W., age 26, d. Wed. 155 Whitehall Terrace, Atlanta. Interred: Morrow Station. AG 9/11/1907

LANEY, G. L., Mrs., age 53, d. 101 N. Butler St. Atlanta. AG 7/20/1907

LANEY, J. L., Mrs., age 54, funeral at family res., 127 Berne St., Atlanta, Fri. Interred: Westview. AG 9/20/1907

LANEY, Waddell, infant, d. Atlanta. AG 5/26/1906

LANFORD, Alfred, colored, age 20, d. corner Edgewood Ave. and Randolph St. Atlanta. AG 8/20/1908

LANFORD, Simeon of Anniston, Ala., formerly from S. C., d. 10/25. Dau: Miss Sue Lanford. Sons: M. D. and E. H. of Anniston, Ala.; S. L., Tyler, Tx.; E. R., Oklahoma City; C. W., Weaver, Ala. AG 10/5/1910

LANG, Goldin, negro, shot to death by negro, Fitzgerald, Ga. AG 8/7/1906

LANG, James, colored, age 40, d. 317 Fort St. Atlanta. AG 11/30/1910

LANGFORD, John H., age 47, d. 101 N. Butler St. Atlanta. AG 6/18/1909

LANGFORD, Roy, age 18, d. Sun. Tucker, Ga. Interred: Zion Hill church yard. Parents: Mr. and Mrs. W. P. AG 2/14/1910

LANGLEY, C. D., Mrs., age 32, d. 69 Luckie St. Atlanta. AG 6/27/1907

LANGLEY, Ernest, age 15, d. Washington, Ga. from stab wound. Rafael Altman being hunted. AG 5/18/1907

LANGLEY, Fred W., age 9 mos., d. 15 Tumlin St. Atlanta. AG 7/9/1906

LANGLEY, Leroy, young son of Mr. and Mrs. H. H., d. 896 Marietta S., Atlanta. Interred: Marietta, Ga. AG 3/12/1907

LANGLEY, Georgia,, formerly of Atlanta, wife of Thomas J., d. Anniston, Ala. Ch: Mrs. C. B. Palmer, Mrs. J. A. Rasbury (Atlanta), Irene Langley (Anniston), Laura Langley (W. Point), Fred F. Langley (New Orleans). Bur: Atlanta. AG 1/20/1908

LANGSTON, Annie Lee McFaul, Mrs., wife of Arthur C. Langston, d. Mon. res. of her father, Dr. J. W. McFaul, 371 Marietta St., Atlanta. Interred: Oakland. Survived by husband, father, mother, one bro. AG 1/22/1907

LANGSTON, Annie M., Mrs., age 64, d. 270 Peachtree St., Atlanta, Sat. Husband: Thomas L. Sons: Porter, Wade. Dau: Mrs. G. W. Morrow. Sis: Mrs. William Goddard. Interred: Westview. AG 5/8/1910

LANGSTON, Arthur C., Mrs., dau. of Dr. and Mrs. J. W. McFaul, d. 371 Marietta St. Atlanta. AG 1/22/1907

LANGSTON, B. B., Mrs., d. Tues. Lived Bolton, Ga. Interred: Austell, Ga. AG 6/25/1907

LANGSTON, Louis L. d. 12/12. Funeral res. of father, J. W. Langston, 42 12th St., Atlanta. Interred: Oakland. AC 12/14/1905

LANGSTON, Milton, colored, age 30, d. Inman yards. Atlanta. AG 2/26/1908

LANGSTON, T. C., age 30, d. 29 Luckie St. Atlanta. Interred: Maysville, Ga. AG 9/12/1908

LANGSTON, T. L., Mrs. funeral from res. 790 Peachtree St., Atlanta. Interred: Westview. Relatives: Capt. T. L. Langston, Mrs. William Goddard, Porter Langston, Mr. and Mrs. Gilham Morrow, Mr. and Mrs. Wade Langston. AG 5/8/1910

LANGSTON, Will, colored, age 27, d. 16-1/2 Madison Ave. Atlanta. AG 12/30/1907

LANHAM, Laura B., Mrs., age 45, d. Jakin, Ga. AG 9/18/1908

LANIER, David E., age 67, Confederte Veteran, d. Third Ave., Decatur, Tues. Wife, three sons: J. D., C. P., C. Z. Daus: Mrs. J. W. Lindsay, Mrs. J. E. Camp, Miss Peal Lanier. AG 12/22/1908

LANIER, David S., age 67, d. Decatur, Ga. AG 12/23/1908

LANIER, David S. S., age 32, d. East End, Ga. AG 1/28/1907

LANIER, Florence, Miss, age 36, d. Fri. 135 Pearl St. Interred: Decatur. AG 8/3/1906

LANIER, Golden, age 7, son of Mr. and Mrs. J. L., d. Sun. Hawkinsville, Ga. Interred: Orange Hill Cemetery. AG 5/18/1910

LANIER, J. C., age 23, d. Mon. at East End near Decatur. He was a member of the Cherokee Tribe, No. 1, of Red Men. Ag 1/14/1907

LANIER, Lillian, age 6 mos., d. 122 Simpson St., Atlanta. AG 2/19/1908

LANIER, Lillian, inf. dau. of Mr. and Mrs. Roland, d. 122 Simpson St., Atlanta, Mon. Interred: Norcross, Ga. AG 2/19/1908

LANIER, R. W., formerly of Valdosta, near George, Ga., murdered, robbed by negro. AG 2/19/1907

LANIUS, T. P., age 75, old citizen of Oxford, Ga., d. Rehoboth, Ga. 2/11. Wife. AC 2/14/1905

LANSHAN, W. d. Los Angeles, CA, Mon. 4 yrs. ago was res. of Atlanta. Interred: Texas. AG 8/1/1910

LARD, J. M., age 81, d. Hiram, Ga., res. of M. Chancer. Confederate Soldier. AC 2/14/1905

LARISEY, Randolph, inf. son of Mr. and Mrs. J. A., d. 96 Cooper St., Atlanta, Thurs. AG 1/30/1908

LARKIN, Benton G., age 70, Confed. Vet., d. Old Soldiers' Home, Atlanta. Dau: Mrs. Warlick, Americus, Ga. Interred: Americus. AG 10/3/1910

LARKIN, Benton G., age 70, d. Confederate Soldiers' Home, Atlanta. AG 10/4/1910

LARKIN, Fabius, age 35, d. North Ave. rr. crossing. AG 2/8/1909

LARSON, Marie, Miss, age 55, d. at King's Daughters' Hospital. Atlanta. AG 7/21/1906

LARUED James W., age 11, d. East Point, Ga. AG 8/31/1908

LASENBY, Alford, colored, age 52, d. 40 N. Jackson St. Atlanta. AG 9/8/1908

LASENBY, John Robert, colored, 2 yrs., d. 252-Irwin St. Atlanta. AG 5/21/1907

LASHLEY, James Pinkney d. Jonesboro, Ga. 6/26, age 27. AG 6/27/1908

LASSETER, Dora, Mrs., age 30, d. Atlanta, Fri. AG 3/20/1908

LASSETER, Chester d. Fri. Colquitt, Ga., age 21. He m. Miss Alice Powell of Decatur Co. 3 weeks ago. AG 1/31/1910

LASSITER, Edward, age 10, son of Mr. and Mrs. E. V., d. in Bonie Brae Mon. Interred: Riverdale, Ga. 6/10/1907

LASSITER, Georgia Ann, Mrs., age 77, d. 62 Formwalt St. Atlanta. AG 3/8/1909

LASSITER, William, age 50 killed by son, Harry Lassiter, age 18. Leaves wife, 4 children. AG 10/25/1907

LATA, Harriet N., Mrs., formerly of Macon, d. 10/11 res. of husband, E. D. Latta, Charlotte, N. C. Born Macon, Ga. 1853, being age 57. Ch: Nisbet Latta, San Francisco; E. D. Latta, Jr., Charlotte; Miss Acton Latta, Charlotte. AG 10/12/1910

LATHEM, Mary B., Mrs., age 71, died Sun. at res., Crumley St., Atlanta. Body to be sent to Gainesville, Ga. AG 11/12/1906

LATHROP, J. A., Confederate Veteran, d. 709 Marietta St., Atlanta, Sat. Interred: Westview. AG 2/10/1908

LATIMER, Casper F., inf. son of Mr. and Mrs. W. R., d. 2 Delta Pl. Atlanta Mon. AG 4/12/1910

LATIMER, George T., age 63, d. 315 N. Jackson St. Atlanta. AG 3/27/1909

LATIMER, Moses, colored, age 45, d. rear 70 Woodward Ave. Atlanta. AG 10/9/1907

LATIMER, Robert P. d. Centerville, Ga. 10/1, where buried. Age 45. AC 10/3/1905

LATIMER, W. R., Mrs., age 22, d. 315 N. Jackson St., Atlanta, Thurs. Interred: Westview. AG 4/2/1909

LATIMER, Wash, colored, age 50, d. Fulton Co. barracks. Atlanta. AG 2/22/1907

LATIMORE, Aty, colored, age 3 mos., d. 31 Griffin St. Atlanta. AG 2/7/1908

LAUBENSTEIN, Philip, Mrs. d. 24 Langley Ave., Howell St., Atlanta, Sun. Interred: Westview. AG 3/1/1908

LAW, Will, colored, age 61, d. 55 Delbridge St. Atlanta. AG 8/14/1907

LAWELL, J. R., age 57, d. Columbus, Ga. 5/26. AC 5/27/1905

LAWHORN, Annie, Miss, age 25, d. Atlanta, Fri. Interred: Augusta. AG 8/3/1908

LAWLER, John, old citizen of Madison Co., Ala. d. Tues. at home at Brownsboro., age 74. Ch: W. B., W. J., N. W.; Miss Tommie Lawler; J. J. Lawler; Mrs. Sam Cobb. AG 1/24/1907

LAWLER, R. C., Mrs., age 70, d. 281 Rawson St. Atlanta. AG 7/18/1908

LAWLESS, Charles d. Wed. Wife, two children survive. Interred: Mason's church yard. AG 2/8/1907

LAWLESS, Emma, Mrs., wid. of George, d. 315 Luckie St., Atlanta, Thurs. Sons: A. G., George W. Daus: Mrs. Dora Bush, Miss Frankie Lawless. AG 6/11/1909

LAWLESS, George W., Sr. of 315 Luckie St., Atlanta funeral Tues. Wife, 4 ch: Miss Dora and Frank Lawless, A. G., G. W., Jr. Interred: Westview. AG 5/21/1906

LAWLESS, Henry J., age 19 mos., d. Sat. Atlanta. Interred: Mason's churchyard. AG 6/4/1910

LAWRENCE, B. R., Mrs., age 40, d. 131 S. Pryor St. Atlanta. AG 8/14/1908

LAWRENCE, Bertie, age 21, d. 267 Ashby St. Atlanta. AG 4/25/1910

LAWRENCE, Bertie, age 21, dau. of Robert S. Roberts, d. 267 Ashby St. Atlanta. One child survives. Interred: Westview. AG 4/25/1910

LAWRENCE, Blanche, Mrs. d. Mon. on Jonesboro Rd., S. Atlanta. Leaves husband, W. J. Lawrence, and two small children. Interred: Harlem, Ga. AG 6/19/1906

LAWRENCE, Drew A. d. Long St., Girard, Ga., Thurs. Wife, 6 children. Bro: Alderman C. A. Lawrence. Interred: Girard Cemetery. AG 9/10/1910

LAWRENCE, E. A., Mrs., age 50, d. 26 McMillian St. Atlanta. AG 2/24/1908

LAWRENCE, George Elkin, age 4 yrs., son of Mr. and Mrs. W. C., d. Atlanta Sun. Interred: Oakland. AG 7/26/1909

LAWRENCE, H. A., age 47, d. Grady Hospital. Atlanta. Interred: Sparta, Ga. AG 7/23/1907

LAWRENCE, Lacy, age 14, son of Mr. and Mrs. C. H., d. 11/17, 341 Jackson St. Atlanta. Interred: Brunswick. AC 11/19/1905

LAWRENCE, Mary, Mrs., age 26, wife of W. J., d. 59 Fortress Ave. Atlanta. Interred: Dallas, Ga. AG 8/23/1909

LAWRENCE, Mrs., widow of ex-Sen. of Springfield, Ill. to Atlanta, d. Dau: Mrs. Susan Dana. AC 3/14/1905

LAWRENCE, Pad, negro, Buncombe District, Rockmart, Ga., burned to death Sat. night. AG 3/21/1907

LAWRENCE, Susie Louise, 8 mos., inf. dau. of Mr. and Mrs. W. H., d. Atlanta Tues. Interred: Antioch church yard. AG 5/11/1910

LAWS, Annie W., Miss, age 27, dau. of Mr. and Mrs. S. M., d. 1 Bibb St. Atlanta. Interred: Hollywood. AG 9/3/1908

LAWSHE, Annie E., Mrs. d. 345 Edgewood Ave. Atlanta. AG 8/27/1907

LAWSHE, P. B., Col., 75, b. NJ, d. Hartwell, Ga. Bur-Oakland. Minn, Gainesville, Atlanta. Ch-Chas, Frank, Edward, Clarence, Mable (Atlanta), Paul (Portland, Ore.), Mrs. Jno Thornton, Mrs. Celia Van Dusen, Mrs. Estelle Van Vlick. AG 5/3/1906

LAWSON, Claudia T., Mrs. d. Cordele, Ga., Sat. dau.'s res., Mrs. Claudia Pate. Interred: Perry, Ga. Son: Hugh of Perry. Daus: Mrs. Claudia Pate, Cordele; Mrs. Mattie Cheeves, Montezjma. One bro., 5 sisters. AG 6/4/1910

LAWSON, Dorothy, age 3, dau. of Mr. and Mrs. Lawson, d. Atlanta. AG 9/14/1908

LAWSON, Jake, colored, age 25, d. Fulton Co. barracks. AG 3/5/1907

LAWSON, Mattie, Miss, age 55, d. Thurs. Home for Incurables. Atlanta. AG 7/20/1906

LAWSON, Olivia, Mrs., age 23, d. 276 Woodward Ave. Atlanta. AG 9/2/1910

LAWSON, Susie, Mrs., age 32, d. Atlanta Thurs. Interred: Riverview Cemetery. AG 10/9/1908

LAWSON, T. B., Mrs., widow, d. Lumpkin, Ga. Sun., age 71. AG 12/24/1907

LAWTON, William J., age 48, d. 148 Forrest Ave. Atlanta. Wife two daus. Interred: Westview. AG 10/8/1909

LAYFIELD, G. M., Mrs., widow, d. 102 W. Peachtree St., Atlanta, Tues. Ch: Mrs. W. R. Lyons, Miss Clifford Layfield, Jesse Layfield. AG 12/14/1910

LAYFIELD, J. R., age 84, d. Fri. 36 Chapel St., Atlanta. Interred: Enterprise, Ala. AG 9/23/1910

LAYFIELD, Joseph, age 20, d. res. of bro-in-law, Alderman T. L. Bowden, Columbus, Ga., Mon. Res. of Chattahoochee Co. Parents, 4 bros., 4 sisters, all of Chattahoochee Co. AG 10/27/1910

LAYTON, Barney T. d. 8/7/ AG 8/7/1909

LAZARUS, Nathan, age 37, d. Grady Hospital. Atlanta. AG 7/12/1907

LEACH, A. F., age 53, d. Scottdale, Ga. Leaves wife, 8 children. Two bros: H. C. and E. N. Leach. Interred: Indian Creek Church. Member of Chippewa Tribe No. 3, Red Men, of Ingleside, Ga. AG 7/3/1907

LEACH, C. H., infant of, 126 Confederate Ave. Atlanta d. Mon. Interred: Sylvester, Ga. AG 6/8/1908

LEACH, J. W., Mrs., wife of J. W., d. near Scottdale, Ga. Fri., age 23. Interred: Indian Creek Church Yard. AG 1/4/1908

LEACH, Liza, Miss, age 74, d. res. of Mr. and Mrs. J. L. Stevens, 11 Bradley St., Atlanta, Thurs. Interred: Ackworth, Ga. AG 5/15/1908

LEACH, Mary Elizabeth, age 3, d. 41 W. 7th St. Atlanta. AG 9/1/1908

LEAGUE, T. B., age 36, d. Atlanta Mon., 303 Wiley St. Sis: Mrs. Lula Pug. AG 6/8/1909

LEAH, E. M., age 37, d. 92 Luckie St. Atlanta. AG 3/29/1909

LEAK, Billie, age 1 mo., inf. son of Mr. and Mrs. J. T., d. 181 Nelson St. Atlanta. Interred: Oakland. AG 8/15/1907

LEAK, Thomas d. Colorado Springs Wed. Funeral, Atlanta. Interred: Hollywood. AG 12/17/1910

LEAK, Thomas F., age 55, d. Colorado Springs, Colo. AG 12/17/1910

LEAKE, Bunion killed by trestle train Atlanta according to his bro., Mark. A. Leake of Cartersville. AG 6/27/1907

LEAKE, Edgar N., son of Mr. and Mrs. J. S. of Madison, Ga., nephew of Lee Douglas. Father, mother, two sisters of Madison. AG 3/29/1909

LEAMON, William Webster, age 77, d. 104 W. Alexander St., Atlanta, Wed. Interred: Westview. Res. of Atlanta 14 yrs. Came from Nova Scotia. Bro: J. R. Leamon. Several nieces, nephews. AG 12/9/1909

LEARMONT, John, age 80, native of Scotland, d. Fri., 65 W. Peachtree St., Atlanta. Wife, three children, Misses Marion and Jesse Learmont, and J. B. Learmont. Interred: Hollywood. AG 5/11/1907

LEATHERWOOD, Ernest Clifford, age 8 mos., son of Mr. and Mrs. C., d. 510 Sunset Ave. Atlanta. AG 3/3/1908

LEAVENS, Addison, age 62, d. College Park, Ga. AG 1/11/1910

LECHLEITNER, Katharine, Mrs., age 88, d. 266 Rawson St. Atlanta. Interred: Oakland. AG 12/18/1910

LEDBETTER, Alma May, age 14 mos., d. 72 Culver St. Interred: Westview. 8/25/1906

LEDFORD, Irvin A., age 2, son of Mr. and Mrs. A. A., d. 85 Lindsay St., Atlanta, Sun. AG 7/12/1909

LEDFORD, John Adam, age 24, d. 19 Wellborn St. Atlanta, Thurs. Interred: Westview. AG 8/1/1908

LEDOYAN, Victor E., age 1, son of Mr. and Mrs. Emmile Le Doyen, Fri., res., 69 Fairlie St., Atlanta. Funeral: Patterson's. AG 11/9/1906

LEE, Alonzo F., age 59, d. 91 Luckie St. Atlanta. AG 12/16/1908

LEE, Amanda, Mrs., age 60, d. Thurs. Grady Hospital. Atlanta. Interred: Westview. AG 9/7/1906

LEE, Chester, third son of Moses, farmer res. 2 miles from Milltown, Ga., d. 12/16. AG 12/17/1908

LEE, Ed, colored, age 50, d. 42 Olwin St. Atlanta. AG 8/29/1907

LEE, Fitzhugh, Gen. funeral Richmond, Va. AC 5/3/1905

LEE, Grace Louise, inf. dau. of Mr. and Mrs. T. J., d. Flat Shoals Rd., Atlanta, Sat. Interred: Wesley Chapel. AG 6/13/1908

LEE, Grace Louise, inf. dau. of Mr. and Mrs. T. J., d. Flat Shoals Rd., Atlanta, Sat. Interred: Westview. AG 6/13/1908

LEE, Henry colored, age 30, d. 265 Martin St. Atlanta. AG 6/12/1907

LEE, Henry, age 48, d. 167 Davis St., Atlanta, Thurs. Wife, 7 children, survive. Interred: Irwinton, Ga. AG 4/9/1903

LEE, infant of Mr. and Mrs. J. Z., d. Atlanta Thurs. Interred: Lithonia, Ga. AG 10/16/1907

LEE, J. W. d. 12/12. Funeral dau.'s res., Mrs. Mattie Farris, 269 Simpson St., Atlanta. Interred: Casey's Cemetery. AC 12/14/1905

LEE, J., Mrs., age 70, d. Fri. Lakewood Heights, Atlanta. Funeral at her old home in Jackson, Ga., Sun. Several children survive. AG 9/28/1907

LEE, Jefferson, old citizen of Concord, Ga., age 83, d. 12/22. Son: J. H. Lee. AG 12/23/1909

LEE, Jenny, colored, age 6 days, died 66 Chamberlin, Atlanta. AG 12/26/1906

LEE, John A., age 75, res., Sandtown Rd, Sat. Survivors: Wife, 3 sons: J. R., J. M. and T. F. Lee; 2 daus., Mrs. Katie Livsey, Mrs. Fannie Sewell. Funeral: Utoy Church. Interment: churchyard. AG 11/17/1906

LEE, John D., Veteran, d. Macon 5/5. AC 5/6/1905

LEE, John Parker, Rev., formerly of Atlanta, d. 11/22, res. of dau. in Los Angeles, Cal., age 90. AG 12/1/1910

LEE, Leo, colored, age 24, d. 101 N. Butler St., Atlanta. AG 7/21/1908

LEE, Lola Mosley, age 30, d. 69 Simpson St. Atlanta. Interred: Westview. AG 8/26/1907

LEE, Martha, age 4 mos., d. 65 Johnson Ave. Atlanta. AG 9/30/1910

LEE, Mary, colored, age 88, d. Grady Hospital. Atlanta. AG 6/23/1907

LEE, Mary C., age 88, negro, d. Thurs. During slavery days Aunt Mary belonged to Major Augustus Lee of Covington. She lived Atlanta since 1863. AG 6/21/1907

LEE, Mattie, Mrs., age 50, d. yesterday, Main St., E. Macon. Interred: Hampton, Ga. AG 5/11/1907

LEE, Mildred, Miss d. New Orleans, La. 3/27, youngest dau. of Gen. Robert E. Lee. AC 3/27/1905

LEE, Myrtle R., Miss, age 47, d. Wesley Memorial Hospital. Atlanta. AG 7/26/1907

LEE, Nellie, age 6 mos., d. McDonough Rd., Atlanta, Sun. Interred: Westview. AG 5/9/1910

LEE, Paul, colored, age 27, d. 101 N. Butler St. Atlanta. AG 7/9/1908

LEE, Rosa, age 4 mos., d. Cornell, Ga. Interment: Fayetteville. AG 0/6/1906

LEE, Roy, colored, age 3, d. 433 Ira St. Atlanta. AG 3/30/1908

LEE, W. H. of Haralson, Ga. d. res. of bro-in-law, J. D. Cole, yesterday. AG 1/3/1908

LEE, W. L., age 35, killed train wreck near Rome, Ga. AG 3/28/1910

LEE, Walter, formerly of Atlanta, d. Los Angeles, Calif. Sun. 10/4. Sister: Miss Theo Lee, Atlanta. AG 10/ /1908

LEE, Young, age 35, d. 48 E. Hunter St. Atlanta. AG 2/16/1908

LEFKOWITZ, Louis d. Fulton Co. Jail Fri. Relatives are in Russia. AG 7/3/1910

LEGARDE, Augustine, colored, age 30, died Spelman seminary. AG 12/21/1906

LEGG, J. A., age 58, d. Atlanta Tues. Bros: J. B. and T. E. Legg, Atlanta. AG 6/ 6/1908

LEGGINS, Eliza, colored, age 26, d. 40 Dover St. Atlanta. AG 3/ 3/1908

LEHMAN, Elmer, age 32, Oakland City, Ga. AG 11/9/ 906

LEHMAN, Elmer, Miss. Funeral: Baptist Tabernacle. Survivors: Parents, Mr. and Mrs. Charles Lehman, 3 sisters, 3 bros. AG 11/9/1906

LEIGH, Mary Brewster, Mrs., wife of Capt. Thomas, d. 2/13 Newnan, Ga. Bro: Col. P. H. Brewster, Atlanta. Husband, 4 children. AC 2/14/ 905

LEIGH, S. M., Mrs., wife of Anselin, formerly Mrs. S. M. Carlton, d. 3/10 Palmetto, Ch: Mrs. Judge H. M. Reid, Atlanta; Mrs. Hal L. Johnson; Dr. J. A. Carlton, Palmetto. Sis: Mrs. J. M. McCool; Mrs. T. C. McLendon; Mrs. O. ----

LELAND, Agnes J., Mrs., age 55, d. College Park. AG 12/30/1908

LEMANDO, Thelma, colored, age 1, d. 23 Reid St. Atlanta. AG 6/ 6/1908

LEMING, Arie, age 6, son of Mr. and Mrs. George, d. 28 Girard Ave., Atlanta, Wed. Interred: Sandy Springs Church yard. AG 8/19/1908

LEMMON, N. F. H., Mrs., age 64, d. 117 Cherokee Ave. Atlanta. Son: C. F. Daus: Mrs. D. Z. Armour, Mrs. R. V. Downs. AG 7/31/1907

LEMMON, N. S. H., Mrs. of 29 Bell St., Atlanta funeral 8/1. Kin: C. T. Lemmon, J. E. Downs, W. T. Arthur, Mrs. Minnie Myers, Mrs. Mamie Jones, W. D. Laird. AG 7/31/1907

LEMON, Helen Mae, colored, d. 435 Auburn Ave. Atlanta. AG 8/26/1909

LEMON, Jane, colored, age 61, d. 37 King St. Atlanta. AG 5/24/1910

LEMONS, Minnie, colored, age 40, d. 167 McDonough St. Atlanta. AG 6/12/1908

LENARD, Tinsey, colored, age 80, d. 12 Winship alley. Atlanta. AG 3/26/1908

LENOX, Luther, colored, age 43, d. 110 Foundry St. Atlanta. AG 11/3/1908

LEONARD, Sophie, colored, age 55, d. 6 Davis St. Atlanta. AG 8/24/1908

LEPPERT, Carrie, Miss, age 31, d. Atlanta. Res. with sister, Mrs. Charles Schoen, 148 Trinity Ave. Mother: Mrs. Carrie Leppert. Interred: Cincinnati, Ohio. AG 10/7/1909

LESLIE, B. D., colored, age 18, d. 463 Lee St. Atlanta. AG 12/26/1907

LESTER, late representative from Ga. Washington, D. C., memorial services to his memory in House Sun. 2/10. AG 1/18/1907

LESTER, A. N. of Athens, Ga. d. 7/27. Wife, several children. AC 7/28/1905

LESTER, David, colored, age 13, d. 57 McDaniel St. Atlanta. AG 7/22/1907

LESTER, James G., Mrs. of Atlanta, formerly of Covington, d. Sat. Interred: Covington. Husband: J. G. Lester. AG 9/4/1906

LESTER, Lucinda, colored, age 25, d. 67 Greensferry Ave. Atlanta. AG 5/4/1909

LESTER, Mary Frances, age 8, dau. of Dr. and Mrs. J. A., d. 11/10 Fayetteville, Ga. AG 11/10/1908

LESTER, R. E., age 62, d. Terry St. Atlanta. AG 3/1/1907

LESTER, R. F., Dr., age 65, d. 53 Terry St., Atlanta, Mon. AG 2/25/1907

LESTER, Sol M., son of Abe of Macon, found on banks of Ocmulgee River 11/26, age 22. AC 11/27/1905

LESTER, T. N., Mrs. of Winder, Ga. d. 8/10 Atlanta. Husband, several children. interred: Winder, Ga. AC 8/12/1905

LESTER, Walter H., age 25, d. Fri. Interred: Thomasville, Ga. Parents; Mr. and Mrs. Robert E. Lester. Sister: Miss Lucy Lester, all of Thomasville. AG 7/6/1907

LESTER, William, colored, age 74, d. 161 Connally St. Atlanta. AG 1/3/1908

LEVEATT, Emily, colored, age 30, d. Fraser St. Atlanta. AG 12/17/1910

LEVERT, C. E., Mrs., age 49, d. 91 W. Harris St. Atlanta Tues. Interred: Oakland. AG 9/9/1908

LEVITT, Julius, age 50, d. Atlanta Wed. AG 12/8/1909

LEWELLYN, Mary, Mrs., age 20, d. 101 N. Butler St. Atlanta. AG 12/26/1907

LEWIS, Alfred, negro, shot by Willie Snyder, white man of Liberty Co., Savannah, Ga. 3/19. AC 3/20/1905

LEWIS, Alice, colored, age 30, d. 318 Decatur St. Atlanta. AG 12/29/1910

LEWIS, Anna, colored, age 44, d. Benjamin St. Atlanta. AG 1/28/1908

LEWIS, Bill, colored, age 38, d. Fulton Co., Ga. AG 10/19/1907

LEWIS, C. B. d. Sat. Ozark, Ala. Wife was Miss Maud White of Atlanta. AG 9/10/1910

LEWIS, Crawford J., age 13, son of Mr. and Mrs. T. L., d. Mon. 11 Queen St. Atlanta. Interred: Westview. AG 5/7/1907

LEWIS, E. S. d. Savannah Thurs. from accident. Res: 406 Oakland Ave., Atlanta. Interred: Westview. AG 11/5/1910

LEWIS, Ellen, Mrs., age 62, d. 176 Ivy St. Atlanta. Tues. AG 12/18/1907

LEWIS, Eugene, colored, age 38, d. 283 Piedmont Ave. Atlanta. AG 8/20/1907

LEWIS, George, age 28, eldest son of Editor Sidney Lewis of The Sparta Ishmaelite, d. 5/29. Bro: Robert, Atlanta. Sis: Miss Bessie. AC 5/30/1905

LEWIS, George A., age 39, merchant of Monroe, Ga., d. Mon. Wife survives. Interred: Monroe, Ga. Ag 7/7/1908

LEWIS, Henry J., age 32, d. Sun. Red Oak, Ga., son of Mr. and Mrs. James Lewis. Interred: Family burial ground, Red Oak, Ga. AG 7/22/1907

LEWIS, Laura, colored, age 39, d. 124 Glenn St., Atlanta, 10/11. AG 10/14/1910

LEWIS, Lucinda, colored, age 60, d. 101 Butler St. Atlanta. AG 10/18/1909

LEWIS, Milton, colored, age 21, d. 27 Howell Place, Atlanta. AG 9/10/1908

LEWIS, Ophelia S., age 4 mos., d. 406 Oakland Ave. Atlanta. AG 8/1/1908

LEWIS, T. S. near death at his home, 647 Peachtree St., Atlanta. AG 12/29/1908

LEWIS, Tom, Confederate veteran of Hancock Co., d. yesterday at home in Powelton, 7 miles N of Sparta. AG 2/20/1907

LEWIS, William, age 80, Fulton Co. alms house. AG 11/9/1906

LEYDEN, Claude L. d. apt. in Peachtree Inn, 291 Peachtree St., Atlanta, Sat. Mother, one sister, Mrs. Haynes, Jacksonville, Fla., survive. AG 9/26/1908

LEYDEN, Rhoda C., Mrs., wid. of Major A., d. Tues. Peachtree Inn, age 82. Husband was Confed. Vet. Interred: Oakland. AG 9/21/1910

LICHTENSTEIN, Sylvia, inf. dau. of Mr. and Mrs. Max, of 72 Connally St., Atlanta, d. Sun. Interred: Oakland. AG 11/22/1909

LIDDELL, Mary, colored, age 43, d. 131 Tanner's alley. Atlanta. AG 11/20/1907

LIDDELL, Maude Friday, Mrs., age 24, d. 53 Oglethorpe St. Atlanta. AG 12/4/1908

LIGGETT, M. C. d. 12/13 Broxton, Ga., son of B. R. AG 12/17/1910

LIGHT, L. W., age 39, d. 599 Chestnut St. Atlanta. Interred: Westview. AG 5/6/1908

LIGONS, John, colored, age 23, d. 5 Louis alley. Atlanta. AG 12/19/1907

LILES, N. B. of E. Macon d. Tues. home of son, J. E. Liles, Willingham St., Macon. Sons: J. E., J. D., J. A. of Macon. Dau: Mrs. Fannie Pearce, Tenn. AG 5/26/1908

LILLY, Thomas, age 56, d. 1042 E. Fair St. Atlanta, Oct. 19. AG 10/20/1910

LILY, John, aged Confederate veteran, 243 Oakland Ave., Atlanta, Wed. Mr. Lily and Police Chief Jennings fought side by side through the civil war. Survived by wife, one dau., 5 sons. AG 11/14/1906

LINAM, Adrina A., Mrs., age 61, d. res., 154 Ira St., Atlanta. She was wife of Patrolman Tony Linam. Interment: College Park. AG 11/20/1906

LINCH, Helen Ruth, inf. dau. of Mr. and Mrs. R. W., d. 5 Mayes St., Atlanta, Mon. Interred: Oakland. AG 10/8/1907

LINCH, W. C., Capt., died 11/24/1906, Senoia, Ga. Capt. He was born 1839 Coweta Co. Enlisted 1861, 7th Ga., Co. A; wounded several times. After war, was in mercantile business at Newnan. Survivors: Wife, 4 grown children. AG 11/24/1906

LINCHAN, Kate, Miss, age 41, d. 45 Gray St. Atlanta. AG 3/16/1907

LIND, Edmund G., Atlanta architect, d. res. of son-in-law, Rev. William H. Laird, Wilmington, Del. 7/14, age 91. Res. Atlanta since 1882. AG 7/22/1909

LINDSAY, John, colored, age 34, d. 26 Dews St. Atlanta. AG 7/12/1907

LINDSEY, Jane, colored, age 50, d. Oakland City, near Atlanta. AG 9/26/1907

LINDSEY, M. A., age 55, d. 112 Forrest Ave. Atlanta, Wed. Wife. Son: E. S., Rome, Ga. Daus: Jennileu, M. A., Theresa. Interred: Flovilla, Ga. AG 12/15/1910

LINDSEY, Martha A., Mrs., age 86, d. 84 Cooper St., Atlanta, Tues. Mother-in-law of S. C. Kicklighter. 5 grchildren. Interred: Oakland. AG 7/31/1906

LINDSEY, W. A., age 26, d. 17 W. Cain St. Atlanta. AG 10/3/1907

LINGERFELT, Carter killed at Mt. Pisgah Church, Gilmer Co. Sat. by Jim and Bunyan Kimmons, two Baptist preachers, in self-defense. AG 12/26/1910

LINGO, Martha, Mrs., age 66, d. Tues. E. Macon, Ga. Interred: Ft. Hill Cemetery. AG 12/4/1907

LINK, William L., age 51, d. 204 Plum St., Atlanta, Wed. Wife. Sons: Calhoun, Robert, Harold, Joe. Bros: S. J. and R. S. Link, of Abbeville, S. C. Sis: Mrs. K. H. Porter, Wilmington, N. C. Interred: Westview. AG 5/5/1910

LIPPETT, James Chesnut, age 12, Mon. res. of father, F. B. Lippett, 252 East Pine Street, Atlanta, AG 11/13/1906

LIPPMAN, B., Mrs. d. Tues. Interred: Oakland. AG 11/13/1907

LIPSCOMB, John Daniel, age 8, d. Atlanta. AG 3/18/1909

LIPSCOMB, Priscilla, colored, age 55, d. 312 Piedmont Ave. Atlanta. AG 3/7/1907

LIPSCOMB, Thomas Coleman, age 4, d. 232 W. Peachtree St. Atlanta. AG 1/7/1907

LIPSCOMB, Thomas, Mrs., wife of former co. commissioner of Durham, N. C., suicide 11/25. AG 11/26/1909

LIPSEY, John, negro, hanged near courthouse, Carrollton, Ga. for attacking Mrs. Ed Windham (in critical condition). AG 8/29/1907

LISLE, Mamie d. Sat. 227 Ross St. Macon. Interred: Riverside. Parents: Mr. and Mrs. J. M. Lisle. Two bros, one sister. AG 12/1/1907

LITCHWORTH, M. L., Mrs., age 54, widow, d. 175 Hampton St., Atlanta, Sat. AG 9/5/1908

LITCHWORTH, Margaret C., age 55, d. 176 Hampton St. Atlanta. AG 9/8/1908

LITES, Moses, Mrs., age 63, d. 615 Edgewood Ave., Atlanta, Fri. Daus: Misses Mabelle and Levine. Sons: Guinn, Hoyt, Ben. Interred: Oakland. AG 9/24/1909

LITTLE, Anna Dickinson, 14 mos., dau. of Mr. and Mrs. S. D. of 180 Angier Ave., Atlanta, d. Sun. Interred: Alberta, Ga. AG 5/2/1910

LITTLE, Annie, colored, age 28, d. 200 Markham St. Atlanta. AG 6/12/1907

LITTLE, Ben, colored, age 65, d. 194 Martin St. Atlanta. AG 4/13/1909

LITTLE, Dave, colored, age 48, d. 7 Davis St. Atlanta. AG 9/2/1909

LITTLE, Dock, negro, died in fire on plantation of T. Marshall. His wife, Clara, arrested. AG 6/4/1910

LITTLE, E. D., Dr., formerly of Atlanta, d. Smyrna, Ga. Thurs. Wife, 4 daus., 1 son. Interred: Suwanee, Ga. AG 5/27/1910

LITTLE, Fannie M., colored, age 24 yrs., d. 160 Hilliard St. Atlanta. AG 4/22/1907

LITTLE, George, Dr., age 45, d. Atlanta. AG 2/19/1910

LITTLE, J. D., Merchant of Forsyth, Ga., d. Wed. Wife survives. Interred: Forsyth, Ga. AG 4/22/1908

LITTLE, J. D., age 47, d. Atlanta. AG 4/23/1908

LITTLE, Joseph F., age 36, d. St. Louis, Mo. AG 6/3/1910

LITTLE, W. F., age 33, d. N. Y. City. AG 5/24/1910

LITTLEFIELD, Kay, son of N. N. of Cordele, d. Sat., age 20. AG 1/31/1910

LITTLEJOHN, Mary, age 27, d. Alexander, Ga. AG 8/14/1907

LITTLEJOHN, T., colored, age 32, d. Oakland City. AG 4/28/1908

LITTLE, Kinchew D., age 81, d. Tues. Elberton where buried. Wife. Sons: Charles E., Nashville, Tenn.; Beman, Dayton, Ohio; Lewis, Ala., Forrester. Daus: Mrs. Maggie Little Lee, Louisville, Ky.; Mrs. Ada Little Mixon, Atlanta. AG 12/9/1910

LIVELY, Ernest (or Alice), age 4, d. 131 English Ave., Atlanta. Interred: Highland Cemetery. AG 8/1/1910

LIVELY, Henry M., Mrs. d. yesterday. Wife of Mayor Henry M. Lively, two-yr. old dau. Formerly Miss Mary Carmichael of Turin, Ga. AG 7/28/1906

LIVELY, Mary Escott, Miss, age 26, d. Fri. 365 Glenn St. Atlanta. Dau. of Mr. and Mrs. W. E. Lively. Bros: Earle R., Elbert W., Owen. Sisters: Miss Ruth H. Lively; Mrs. S. P. Hollingsworth. Interred: Westview. AG 9/11/1909

LIVINGSTON, Georgia, dau. of Mr. and Mrs. E. E., d. Mon., 1 Boundary St. Macon. Interred: Riverside. AG 7/31/1907

LIVINGSTON, Mary E., age 25, d. 628 Chestnut St. Atlanta. AG 7/23/1907

LIVINGSTON, S. H. d. Thurs. Atlanta. Wife, one dau, Miss Annie Livingston, and stepson, C. W. Allen, survive. Interred: Westview. Member of Mohawk Tribe No. 5, Improved Order of Red Men. AG 6/2/1906

LIVINGSTON, William J., age 77, d. 100 Pine St. Atlanta. AG 8/23/1909

LIVSEY, E. R., age 26, suicide in Chattanooga, Tenn. Ten. Mother: Mrs. Alice Livsey, 115 Auburn Ave., Atlanta. Interred: Loganville, Ga. AG 5/26/1908

LIVSEY, W. C., age 26, d. Atlanta Tues. Mother: Mrs. Alice Livsey. Two sisters, three bros. Interred: Logansville, Ga. AG 10/30/1907

LIVSEY, W. L. d. Presbyterian Hospital, Atlanta, Mon. Intered: Logansville. AG 10/30/1906

LLEWELLYN, Mary, Mrs. d. Thurs. Atlanta. Interred: Hollywood. AG 12/26/1907

LLORENS, Bernard, age 52, d. 230 E. Cain St., Atlanta, Sat. Interred: Hollywood Cemetery. AG 3/29/1909

LLOYD, C. H., Mrs. of 92 Fowler St., Atlanta, d. Thurs. AG 12/31/1909

LLOYD, Esther Louise, age 3, dau. of Mr. and Jrs. J. A., d. Wed. Decatur. AG 8/8/1907

LLUPO, Ruth, Mrs., age 19, d. 280 Simpson St., Atlanta, Tues. Interred: Oakland. AG 4/13/1909

LOCKE, Arthur Hall, age 60, formerly of Charleston, S. C., then Linden Ave. Atlanta, now NYC, d. Greenville, S. C. 2/19. Sis: Mrs. O'Hear (& her son-in-law, Chessly Howard). Dau: Belle Locke, now Mrs. Capt. Wm. J. Snow. Bro: Edwin H., d. Charleston sev. yrs. ago). Mother d. Boston yrs. ago. Niece: Mrs. Chessly B. Howard, 99 Merritts Ave. AC 2/20/1905

LOCKETT, Julia K., Mrs. d. Tues. res. of J. A. McCrary, Barnesville, Ga. Sis: Mrs. Loula K. Rogers, Barnesville. Bro: Dr. T. R. Kendall. AG 6/22/1910

LOCKETT, Uriah S. d. Americus, Ga. 4/19, Confed. Vet. AC 4/20/1905

LOCKHART, Fred T., Hon., lawyer, d. res. Greene St., Augusta. He was b. Lincoln Co. 1850. Leaves wife, 4 children in Augusta. AG 1/26/1907

LOCKHART, Minnie, age 10 mos., d. 101 N. Butler St. Atlanta. AG 6/21/1909

LOCKHART, Minnie, inf. dau. of Mr. and Mrs. T. J., d. Atlanta Sun. Interred: Westview. AG 6/21/1909

LOCKHART, Sarah, nee Turner, age 80, d. Atlanta Mon. Born Co. Cork, Ireland, Atlanta pioneer woman in 1851. AG 1/11/1910

LOCKHART, Thomas, age 50, d. 27 Bellwood Ave., Atlanta, Thurs. Wife. Interred: Westview. AG 4/8/1910

LOCKHART, Ware, colored, age 26, d. 20 Beerman St. Atlanta. AG 9/2/1910

LOCKRIDGE, Samuel, age 52, of 409 Ormond St., Atlanta, d. Tues. Interred: Gloucester, Ga. Wife, 5 children. AG 12/29/1909

LOFTIN, James H., age 75, d. 94 Woodward Ave., Atlanta, Wed. Interred: Elberton, Ga. AG 9/23/1908

LOFTIS, Artemisia, Mrs., age 89, d. 546 Woodward Ave. Atlanta. AG 12/9/1909

LOGAN, C., colored, age 50, d. 272 Williams St. Atlanta. AG 4/23/1908

LOGAN, Crimson, colored, age 40, d. 254 Williams St. Atlanta. AG 11/4/1908

LOGAN, J. P., age 37, d. 17 W. Cain St. Atlanta. AG 10/3/1906

LOGAN, John P., age 26, son of Mr. and Mrs. Frank Logan of Greenwood, S. C., d. Fri. at Presbyterian Hospital, Atlanta. Interred: Oakland. AG 9/29/1906

LOGAN, Paul, colored, age 6 mos., d. 10 Martin St. Atlanta. AG 3/8/1907

LOLLAR, Joseph, youngest son of Mr. and Mrs. John B., d. Jasper, Ala., aged abt 26. AG 8/2/1906

LOMAX, Mose, colored, age 32, d. 17 Gumby St. Atlanta. AG 5/7/1907

LONCRAWFORD, Addie, age 18 mos., dau. of Mr. and Mrs. T. J., 77 Emmett St., Atlanta, d. Mon. Interred: Sardis. AG 5/31/1909

LONDON, Frank O., age 49, d. 24 N. Broad St. Atlanta. AG 2/22/1907

LONG, Andrew, age 45, d. Fulton Co. Alms House. Atlanta. Interred: Westview. AG 11/9/1907

LONG, Edward, age 81, d. Mon. Macon. Was b. Co. Cork, Ireland, Came to Macon, Ga. 60 yrs. ago. Ch: J. D. Long, Mrs. Patricia Murphy, both of Macon. Interred: Rosehill. AG 1/28/1908

LONG, Hall, age 18 mos., son of Mr. and Mrs. T. A., d. 704 Woodward Ave., Atlanta, Sat. Interred: Westview. AG 9/14/1907

LONG, Harvey C., age 3, d. Atlanta, son of C. F. AG 7/25/1910

LONG, infant son of Mr. and Mrs. Cleve, d. N. Dalton, Ga., Sat. Interred: West Hill Cemetery. AG 11/7/1910

LONG, Lois, age 8, d. 41 Almo Ave. Atlanta. AG 9/10/1910

LONG, Rose, colored, age 7 mos., d. 26 Smith St. Atlanta. AG 7/6/1909

LONG, W. D., age 18, d. 89 Walton St. Atlanta. Interred: Ala. AG 8/20/1906

LONG, W. H., Mrs., age 81, d. Sun. res. of dau., Mrs. Sarah Taylor, 451 N. Jackson St. Atlanta. Widow of Col. W. H. Long. Sons: W. H. Long, Judge H. L. Long, Leesburg, Ga. AG 10/15/1906

LONG, Zed, negro, removed from East Point jail and lynched by mob. AG 9/24/1906

LOOMIS, Charles E., Confederate veteran committed suicide last night, Atlanta, Soldier's Home. he was b. 10/23/1834 Lexington Co., S. C. Bro: Aiken, S. C. AG 1/1/1907

LOOMIS, Luther, colored, age 22, d. 227 Fort St. Atlanta. AG 7/17/1909

LOOMIS, C. E., Conf vet, suicide. Interred: Columbia, SC. Survivors: bro. J. H. LOOMIS, C. E., Loomis, Aiken, SC.; sis-Mrs. L. B. Brewer, NY. AG 12/31/1906

LOONEY, M. H., Mrs., age 50, wife of D. F., many yrs. detectie in Atlanta, d. Birmingham, Ala. Three ch. One is Ernest O. Looney. AG 2/16/1907

LOONEY, Sallie E., Miss d. Cornelia, Ga. Wed, age 64. Bros: B. A., Cornelia; D. S., Birmingham. Sis: Mrs. R. T. Harrison, Atlanta; Mrs. A. Chatham, Maysville, Ga. Interred: Cornelia, Ga. AG 4/8/1909

LOOPEY, Henry, age 42, d. 113 Magnolia St. Atlanta. AG 10/22/1906

LOOR, M., colored, age 9 mos., d. Fulton Co. almshouse. AG 9/14/1908

LOPEZ, Moses E. d. Mon. 190 W. Peachtree St., Atlanta. Children: Mrs. Dr. J. H. Hines and P. H. Lopez of Atlanta. Interred: Washington, D. C. AG 6/5/1907

LORCHEN, Lizzie, colored, age 1 mo., d. 235 Piedmont Ave. Atlanta. AG 9/24/1907

LORD, Elizabeth, Mrs., age 35, d. 74 Neal St. Atlanta. AG Interred: Hollywood. 5/24/1910

LORD, J. T., planter of Commerce, Ga., d. 2/10/ AC 2/12/1905

LORIE, Gussie, colored, age 27, d. Chicago, Ill. AG 7/21/1908

LORING, J. M., age 60, d. Lowe Village (Huntsville, Ala.) 10/27. Several children. AC 10/31/1905

LORING, Leona, Mrs., age 23, wife of Marvin, d. 3/21 Huntsville, Ala. Two small children. AC 3/22/1905

LORME, Estelle, 8 mos. old, d. 129 Kelly St. Atlanta. AG 9/5/1906

LOTT, Elizabeth A., Mrs. funeral 8/1 Columbus, Ga. AC 8/1/1905

LOUBENSTEIN, P., Mrs., age 20, d. 24 Langley Ave. Atlanta. AG 3/3/1908

LOUD, Charles D., Col., Mt. Vernon atty, shot in Honduras 10/17. AG 10/20/1906

LOUDENBER, F. W., age 57, d. 3/18 Chattanooga, Tenn. Wife. 5 children. AC 3/20/1905

LOUDETTE, Fred J., father of Mrs. J. H. Crutchfield, Atlanta, at home of son, Eugene Loudette, Columbia, S. C. AG 11/12/1906

LOVE, Ed H., Colonel d. Atlanta. AG 10/29/1907

LOVE, James W., Capt., Confed. Vet., d. 3/17 Ft. Valley, Ga. He md. 1865 Mrs. A. E. Moore. AC 3/18/1905

LOVE, L. L., Mrs., age 87, former res. Columbus, Ga. d. 3/21 res. of niece, Mrs. C. P. Miller, Talbot Co. Grch: Mrs. John Strother, Charleston, W. Va.; Robert Foot Love, Marietta; Miss Mittie Love Porter, Dallas, Ga. AC 3/25/1905

LOVEJOY, Frank, colored, age 57, d. 39 Inman St. Atlanta. AG 8/17/1907

LOVEJOY, John H., age 77, d. 73 W. Alexander St., Atlanta, Wed. Interred: Oakland. AG 10/7/1908

LOVELACE, E. H. d. Greenville, S. C. Interred: Atlanta. AG 11/17/1907

LOVETT, Harry, age 15, drowned Tybee (Savannah). Body found today 7/23. AG 7/23/1908

LOVETT, Lester, age 11, son of Mr. and Mrs. E. A. Lovett of Wrightsvill killed by train. AG 10/23/1906

LOVICK, James H. believed to be murdered. Father: J. H. Lovick, Columbus, Ga. AG 1/11/1908

LOVING, Harriet, Mrs., age 91, d. res. of dau. Huntsville, Ala. Came to Huntsville 75 yrs. ago. Ch: Mrs. J. W. Martin, Huntsville, Ala.; Mrs. D. S. Turner, Birmingham; Abe Loving, Ga. AG 12/9/1909

LOWE, Annie, Miss, age 18, member of Girls High School, d. Fri. 135 Nelson St., Atlanta. Mother: Mrs. M. A. Lowe. Sis: Mrs. R. E. Lowe. Bros: William H., Frank B. Interred: Westview. AG 9/21/1907

LOWE, Asa, age 77, d. 75 Glennwood Ave. Atlanta. Wife, one dau. Interred: Westview. AG 3/17/1910

LOWE, P., colored, age 1 mo., d. rear of 40 Orange St. Atlanta. AG 11/22/1909

LOWE, Pauline, colored, age 22, d. 44 Berkle St. Atlanta. AG 11/22/1909

LOWE, Robert J. d. Tues. Eufaula, Ala. AG 11/1/1910

LOWE, W. B. estate. Litigation over est. ended Fri. Mrs. H. P. Woodruff, Savannah; Mrs. Lula Spencer, Newnan; A. J. Lowe, nieces, nephew vs. exrs. AG 12/20/1907

LOWE, W. S., farmer, Bibb Co., d. today, Clinton Rd., Macon. Age 55, leaves family. AG 11/1/1906

LOWELL, Jennie B., Mrs., age 36, d. 96 W. North Ave. Atlanta. Husband: W. G. 3 sons, two sisters, two bros. AG 4/29/1909

LOWENTHAL, Sarah, Mrs., age 63, d. Thurs. Interred: Oakland. Widow of late Louis Lowenthal. AG 9/24/1909

LOWER, W. F., age 39, d. Tues. 218 Central Ave. Atlanta. Interred: Westview. AG 6/27/1907

LOWER, William F., age 38, d. Tues. 218 Central Ave. Atlanta. AG 6/25/1907

LOWNDES, Theodosia, Mrs., age 54, d. E. Point. AG 1/19/1910

LOWRANCE, Ordie S., Mrs., age 61, d. 17 W. Cain St. Atlanta. AG 9/3/1907

LOWRY, H. A., age 51, d. Auburn Ave. and Courtland Sts. Atlanta.
AG 9/21/1908

LOWRY, H. C., age 51, d. Atlanta Fri., res. of Sumter, S. C.,
visiting relatives. Interred: Sumter, S. C. Wife survives. AG
9/19/1908

LOWRY, J. W., age 39, d. Milledgeville, Ga. Thurs. Res. of 51
Simpson St., Atlanta. Interred: Atlanta. AG 3/24/1910

LOWRY, John A. d. Sun. Dalton, age 66, Confed. Vet. Wife, 3 ch:
Mrs. L. E. Hollinger of T. Worth, Tx.; Mrs. Joe Russell, Atlanta;
Miss Effie Lowry of Dalton, Ga. AG 4/5/1910

LOWRY, Robert, Col., ex-Gov. of Miss., Conf. Vet., age 78, d.
Jackson, Miss. Native of Chesterfield, S. C. 7 children. AG
1/20/1810

LOWRY, Selina, Mrs., age 83, d. 367 Edgewood Ave. Atlanta. AG
1/10/1907

LOWRY, Wheeler d. Atlanta Wed., former res. of Dalton, Ga., son of
W. T. Wife, 2 children. Interred: Dalton, Ga. AG 3/26/1910

LOYD, Pope, age 68, of Paces Ferry Rd. d. Wed., Atlanta. Wife
survives. Interred: Mt. Perrin. AG 12/10/1908

LOYD, W. S. of Fayette Co., Ga. accidentally killed himself. AC
11/4/1905

LUCAS, Ellen, colored, age 49, d. 116 Pratt St. Atlanta. AG
5/4/1908

LUCAS, J. T., age 38, d. Sun. Atlanta. Interred: Athens, Ga. AG
4/11/1910

LUCAS, J. V., Hon. d. Ivy Joy, Union Co., Ga. 9/1, Confed. Vet.
One child, Mrs. Collie Lanes King. AC 9/3/1905

LUCILE, Cornelia, colored, age 44, d. 5 Halley alley. Atlanta. AG
9/29/1910

LUCK, George W., age 56, d. 67 Greenwood Ave. Atlanta. Wife, 7
children. Interred: Gainesville, Ga. AG 3/17/1910

LUCK, James P., age 88, d. Oakland City. AG 12/17/1910

LUCKIE, Jackson accidentally shot and killed by John Austin of
Sargent, Ga. (near Newnan). AG 11/29/1909

LUCKIE, Howard, colored, age 45, died Palmer brick yard. Atlanta.
AG 12/26/1906

LUCK, James P., 88, Campbell Co., d. dau.´s res: Mrs. Irene C.
Grizzard, Oakland Cty. Sons: J.J., Cherokee Co.; Capt. A.M., Sgt.
A.D., police. Daus: Mrs. Mary Godwin, Tx.; Mrs. Georgia A. Stone.
Bur: Sharon Church, Union City. AG 12/17/1910

LUDD, Betty, mrs., age 54, d. 12/19 Courtland St., Atlanta. One
son. Interred: Westview. AC 12/19/1905

LUDWIG, Alex S. funeral Tues. Interred: Westview. AG 5/19/1908

LUDWIG, Henry E., age 58, d. Milledgeville, Ga. AG 8/14/1907

LUIDLEY, Anna, colored, age 62, d. 291 Auburn Ave. Atlanta. AG
9/14/1908

LUKE, Joe, colored, age 34, d. rear 38 Fraser St., Atlanta. AG
3/6/1908

LUKENBILL, E. A., Mrs., age 71, d. 548 Washington St., Atlanta,
Mon. Ch: E. D., E. H., J. S., H. C.; Mrs. N. W. Johnson, Mrs. C.
A. Hopper, Miss Lillie Lukenbill; Mrs. H. D. Ellis. Interred:
Westview. AG 11/10/1908

LUKENHILL, R. H., age 50, d. Fernandina, Fla. AG 3/17/1910

LUMMUS, Louis E. d. Mon. Columbus, Ga., age 49. Wife, 3 children.
Bro: F. E. Lummus. Aged mother. AG 12/15/1910

241

LUMPKIN, Alice, colored, age 38, d. 42 Genenden St. Atlanta. AG 7/21/1908

LUMPKIN, Amanda, age 40, d. 73 Fort St. Atlanta. AG 10/25/1906

LUMPKIN, Dodd, Mrs., age 74, d. res. of dau., Mrs. Lucy Johnson, Elberton, Ga. Interred: Oglethorpe, Ga., near home of John S. Bacon, beside husband. Sons: Dan, Thomas B. Daus: Mrs. Lucy Johnson, Mrs. Ada Oglesby. AG 3/3/1909

LUMPKIN, Frank, dying of incurable disease, convicted in Muscogee Co., Ga. in 1903 for burglary, sentence commuted. AG 11/14/1906

LUMPKIN, George B., age 65, d. 8/30 Lexington, Ga. AC 10/3/1905

LUMPKIN, Joe, colored, age 14, d. Grady Hospital. Atlanta. AG 1/14/1907

LUMPKIN, Joe, negro, shot and killed by Lowe Little, negro, age 15, Atlanta, Thurs. AG 1/10/1907

LUMPKIN, Ollie, age 10, d. 250 Glennwood Ave., Atlanta, Oct. 2. AG 10/3/1910

LUMSFORD, Hulsey d. 3 Lindsay St., Atlanta, Fri. Interred: Montreal, Ga. AG 5/24/1907

LUNSFORD, Alton, son of Mr. and Mrs. Evans, d. Wed. Covington, Ga. He was youngest child of Mr. and Mrs. Lunsford. AG 5/6/1910

LUQUIRE, Mary Ann, Mrs., age 62, d. Tues. 296 McDaniel St., Atlanta. Interred: Augusta, Ga. Sons: E. C. and Hugh of Augusta. Dau: Mrs. F. R. Miller, Atlanta. AG 12/28/1909

LUTHER, H. T., age 5 mos., d. 240 Edgewood Ave. Atlanta. AG 8/19/1908

LUTHER, Upton H., age 67, died, Rochester, N. Y. several days ago. Body to be brought to Atlanta. Funeral, Sun., Barclay & Brandon chapel. AG 11/17/1906

LYCETT, Edward, Sr., age 73, d. Fri. res. of Mr. and Mrs. Abraham at LaGrange. Funeral res. of grson, Edward Lycett, Jr., 305 W. Peachtree St., Atlanta, Sat. Interred: Westview. AG 5/8/1910

LYKES, M. J., Mrs., age 18, d. 534 Pulliam St. Atlanta. AG 11/29/1907

LYLE, Clara, Mrs. d. Springvale, Ga. 2/18. AG 2/19/1910

LYLE, Estelle, age 23 mos., dau. of Mr. and Mrs. S. T., 110 Lowe St., Atlanta, d. Sun. Interred: Westview. AG 6/14/1909

LYLE, Fannie, Mrs., age 78, wife of James, d. Cornell, Ga. Sun. Interred: Forest Park church yard. AG 3/9/1908

LYLE, Harry E. confessed to killing his wife and child 1/1/1907, saying it was accident. AG 5/15/1907

LYLE, Isabel Rose, age 20 yrs., d. 294 Courtland St. Atlanta. AG 7/1/1907

LYLE, Isabella, Miss, sister of E. C. Lyle who res. 85 Washington St., Atlanta, d. Fri. Interred: Oakland. AG 6/29/1907

LYLES, Mattie murdered. R. V. L. Day charged with murder. Douglas, Ga. AG 2/26/1909

LYNAM, J. G., Major, officer of Conf. Army, d. Jan. 16 371 Peachtree St., Atlanta. Born in Ireland 75 yrs. ago. Settled Miss. Major in 9th Miss Regt. Wife, 4 daus. AC 1/17/1905

LYNAN, Maria, age 66, wid. of James, d. 1/8, 227 S. Pryor St. Atlanta, b. Galway Co., Ire., America age 13. Lvd & Md. Dalton, Ga. Ch: Mrs. John Corrigan, Miss Joe Lynan, Mrs. Mary Berry, Miss Kate Lynan, Mrs. William Otis, Columbia, S. C.; Sister Carmel of Sisters of Mercy, Savannah. Sons: John and Arthur Connelly. 5 grch. AC 1/9/1905

LYNCH, Eugene, Mrs., age 70, d. Tues, Oglethorpe St., Macon. 4 daus., 2 sons of Macon survive. Interred: Willard, Ga. AG 4/29/1908

LYNCH, Hugh d. Wed. 98 Irwin St., Atlanta. Interred: Oakland. AG 6/14/1907

LYNCH, Hugh funeral Fri., 6/14. Kin: Mrs. John T. Connally, James Lynch, Mrs. Annie Hamilton, Mrs. Kate Wooten. AG 6/13/1907

LYNCH, infant son of Mr. and Mrs. John H., d. Sun. Interred: Westview. AG 5/14/1906

LYNCH, Wallace, colored, aged 59, died 230 W. Mitchell St. AG 12/5/1906

LYNCH, Wylie, colored, age 50, d. Fulton Co. Almshouse. AG 7/13/1908

LYNN, Lydia, Mrs., age 52, d. Lakewood Heights, Atlanta, Sun. Interred: South Bend Church yard. 3 sons, 5 daus, 2 bros., survive. AG 11/29/1909

LYNN, Ozier, age 3, son of Mr. and Mrs. J. C., d. res. of grandfather, W. P. Rutledge, Cheshire Rd., Atlanta, Mon. AG 8/4/1908

LYNN, S. A., Confederate Veteran, d. Soldiers' Home, Atlanta, Sat. AG 3/9/1908

LYNN, W. Z., age 79, Confed. Vet., d. Dublin. Wife, 3 sons, 2 daus. AG 5/25/1910

LYON, W. M., age 66, d. 17 W. Cain St. Atlanta. AG 12/22/1908

LYONS, Amanda, colored, age 50, d. 66 Eliza Ave. Atlanta. AG 2/8/1908

LYONS, John T., age 49, d. 273 Formwalt St. Atlanta, railroad accident. Wife. 7 children. Oldest son is 21. AG 9/25/1909

LYON, N. A., Mrs. d. Western Av. & Davis St., Atlanta, wife of Prof. G. W. Ch: Mrs. J. T. Casey, A. A. Lyon, Mrs. A. D. McDonald, Mrs. J. P. Casey, G. W. Lyon, Jr., W. M. Lyon, Miss Bessie Lyon, Mrs. H. C. Sigman. Sisters: Mrs. Laura Malcom, Mrs. Bessie Garrett, Social Circle, Mrs. Emma Lyon, Atlanta. Bro: Augustus Williams. Interred: Hollywood. AG 2/9/1907

LYON, W. M., age 65, Confederate Veteran, 42nd Ga., d. Atlanta. Interred: Oakland. Dau: Mrs. W. H. Barker. Stepdaus: Mrs. Dora Hurst, Mrs. J. R. Slider. Bros: J. A. Lyon; James A. Lyon, Crescent, Oklahoma. Sisters: Mrs. Thomas Mize, Mrs. J. F. Ozee, Crescent, Oklahoma. AG 12/21/1908

MABRE, M. J., age 79, Atlanta pioneer, Conf. Vet., d. 76 Park Ave., Atlanta. From Newton Co. to Atlanta in 1850. Daus: Mrs. Fannie Chastain, Mrs. W. M. Hollingsworth, Mrs. R. A. Wilder, of Atlanta. AC 1/31/1905

MABRY, S. S., Mrs., age 68, d. 70 Wells St., Atlanta, Sun. Interred: Westview. AG 12/20/1909

MACHANAN, J. H., Confed. Vet., res. of Old Soldiers' Home, Atlanta. Interred: Westview. AG 7/6/1910

MACK, Albert, colored, age 17, d. 261 Orme St. Atlanta. AG 4/7/1908

MACK, Mike, Jr., age 5, d. Tues., Madisonville, Tenn. Remains arrived Atlanta. Interred: Oakland. AG 5/19/1910

MACK, Nellie W., age 67, d. East End, Atlanta. AG 6/16/1906

MACKAY, Mary, Mrs., age 73, d. 122 Bellwood Ave., Atlanta, Fri. Sons: S. J., J. M. Daus: Mrs. Rebecca Stells, Mrs. Parish Hamilton, Mrs. J. Ivy, Mrs. Kate McLucas. Interred: Marietta, Ga. AG 4/2/1910

MACKEY, Howard, colored, age 36, d. Decatur and Butler Sts. Atlanta. AG 7/6/1909

MACON, George B., age 2 mos., d. 221 Cooper St. Atlanta. AG 6/12/1908

MADDOX, infant son of Mr. and Mrs. J T., d. 23 Tifton St. Atlanta, Mon. Interred: Westview. AG 5/31/1910

MADDOX, Apha Roe, age 3, son of Mr. and Mrs. J. E., 38 Lake Ave., Atlanta, d. Sat. Interred: Westview. AG 7/26/1909

MADDOX, C. J., age 38, d. 129 Courtland St. Atlanta. AG 6/26/1908

MADDOX, Delia, colored, age 49, d. Atlanta. AG 7/16/1908

MADDOX, Dora, colored, age 31, d. 413 Richardson St. Atlanta. AG 5/4/1908

MADDOX, E. C., Mrs., age 33, d. 386 Central Ave. Atlanta. AG 3/21/1910

MADDOX, Ella, Mrs., age 55, wife of W. C., d. Howell Mill Rd., Atlanta, Tues. 7 children. Interred: Sardis Church. AG 4/29/1908

MADDOX, George, colored, age 37, d. 14 Battle St. Atlanta. AG 9/21/1909

MADDOX, H. T. d. Tues. Interred: Prospect Church, near Chamblee, Ga. AG 11/13/1907

MADDOX, J. A. of Harris Co., Ga. d. 7/4 Whitesville, Ga., age 65. Bro: W. N. Wife, 5 children. Interred: Family burial grounds near Whitesville, Ga. AC 7/4/1905

MADDOX, J. B., age 23, d. Atlanta Thurs, wife of J. B. Interred: Jackson, Ga. AG 4/17/1908

MADDOX, Martha, colored, age 46, d. 141 Gardner St. Atlanta. AG 2/28/1908

MADDOX, Silvia, colored, age 54, d. 164 Elliott St. Atlanta. AG 4/13/1909

MAFFETT, Loyd, age 7, d. 47 Oakhill Ave. Atlanta. AG 12/22/1908

MAGRITIS, Vesalois, age 70, d. 101 N. Butler St. Atlanta. AG 4/15/1908

MAHER, John T., age 51, d. Tues. Atlanta. Interred: Augusta, Ga. 3 sisters, Misses Mary and Ellen Maher and Mrs. George A. Delhi. AG 10/27/1909

MAHER, William R., age 42, d. 59 Broyles St. Atlanta, res. of sister, Mrs. Frank Giles. Interred: Oakland. AG 9/3/1908

MAHONEY, Mattie, colored, age 27, d. 20 Spink alley. Atlanta. AG 12/24/1907

MAIER, J. Roy, age 23, son of Mr. and Mrs. A. D. of 68 Queen St., Atlanta, d. Tues. Interred: Oakland. Uncle: H. A. Maier. AG 5/19/1909

MAILE, Leo, age 46, suicide Fri. 93 E. Baker St. Atlanta. Interred: Westview. AG 7/5/1909

MAIN, H. K, Dr. of Dalton, Ga., d. 21 Humphries St., Atlanta, Mon. Interred: Hill City. AG 12/28/1909

MAJOR, Henry P., colored, age 29, d. 376 Jackson Pl, Atlanta, 10/4. AG 10/5/1910

MAJORS, Cicero H. d. Atlanta Sat. Interred: Oakland. AG 8/12/1909

MALCOM, Edgar Franklin, infant, d. Atlanta. Interred: White Plains, Ga. AG 1/27/1910

MALIA, John d. Decatur, Ala., res. of cousin, Mrs. Holland. Interred: Louisville, Ky. AG 10/13/1910

MALINE, Sarah H., Mrs. d. W. Peachtree St., Atlanta, Thurs. Ch: H. W., Robert, Sallie. AG 10/20/1910

MALLEN, Jack E., age 5 mos., son of Mr. and Mrs. K. E., d. 57 E. Fair St., Atlanta, Thurs. Interred: Westview. AG 12/30/1908

MALONE, Charles W., age 35, d. Chapel St. Atlanta., Thurs. Interred: Oakland. AG 3/27/1908

MALONE, Nancy, age 3, dau. of Mr. and Mrs. A. W., d. Savannah, Ga. Wed. where interD. of Augusta; Mrs. Lewis Schley. AG 9/23/1907

MALTBIE, William N., Col. d. Fri. Crawfordville, Ga. where buried. AG 5/27/1910

MAN, Sarah, Mrs., age 80, d. 95 Venable St. Atlanta. AG 12/11/1908

MANASSAH, Samuel, age 50, d. 101 N. Butler St. Atlanta. AG 12/22/1908

MANDERS, Frank, age 2, d. 128 Estoria St. Atlanta. AG 10/20/1909

MANDRAM, Lizzie, Miss, age 60, d. 20 Bradley St. Atlanta. AG 3/26/1908

MANER, Claude d. mother's res., Mrs. W. E. Maner, near Gilmer, Ga. Thurs. Wife, 2 small children, mother, three brothers (Lama, Dora and E. Gus Maner), survive. Interred: Collins Spring. AG 11/3/1908

MANIER, Emma, inf. dau. of Mr. and Mrs. S., d. 27 Kennedy St., Atlanta. Interred: Hollywood. AG 10/6/1908

MANIER, John, Marshal of Pretoria, Ga. shot, killed by Pete Thomas, negro. AC 4/17/1905

MANLER, Officer killed by Andrew Johnson, negro, several weeks ago. AG 1/3/1908

MANLEY, Boyd, age 20, d. mother's res., Heard St., Elberton, Ga. Bro: Julian. Mother: Mrs. Mary Manley. AG 3/9/1910

MANLEY, J. A., Mrs. d. 12/5 Carnesville. Bros: R. H. and T. O. Brugess, Carnesville. Husband. Several grown children: Hubert T.; Miss Lillian; Mrs. Maud Manley Whitesides, Chester, S. C. AC 12/7/1905

MANLEY, John T., age 54, d. 151 Lee St. Atlanta, Tues. Wife, one dau, Miss Thelma Manley. One son: Carl C. Manley. Interred: Hampton, Ga. AG 5/25/1910

MANLEY, M. J., Mrs. d. Atlanta. Funeral res. of W. S. Rea, 320 E. Hunter St., her nephew. AG 4/27/1906

MANLY, John C., age 57, d. 325 Pulliam St., Atlanta, Sun. Interred: Oakland. Member of Comance Tribe of Red Men. Wife. Ch: Mrs. J. H. Savage, Miss Lillie Manly, and John T. Manly of Atlanta. AG 10/3/1910

MANN, Bertha, age 1, dau. of Mr. and Mrs. S. C., 23 Clay St., Atlanta, d. Sun. Interred: Tucker, Ga. AG 7/26/1909

MANN, Florida McArthur, Miss, age 22, d. Baxley, Ga., foster dau. of Mrs. G. T. Melton, dau. of Hon. Henry Mann of Tattnall and late Mrs. Florida McArthur Mann. AC 4/23/1905

MANN, James H., age 66, ex-Confederate soldier, formerly of Ga., body found floating in Tenn. River. He disappeared 4/15. AG 4/26/1906

MANN, Mary B., Miss, dau. of Mr. and Mrs. James of 71 Venable St., Atlanta, d. Mon. Interred: Westview. Survived by parents, three bros., two sisters. AG 12/15/1908

MANN, Mary, Mrs., age 53, d. 73 Tennille St., Atlanta. AG 4/2/1910

MANNING, Bernard, age 4 mos., son of Mr. and Mrs. Ernest, d. 58 Ridge Ave. Atlanta. Interred: Westview. AG 8/17/1908

MANNING, C. A., age 53, d. 101 N. Butler St. Atlanta. AG 9/9/1908

MANNING, E. A., age 52, d. Tues. 16 Bailey St. Atlanta. Interred: Westview. AG 9/9/1908

MANNING, Frank J., age 29, d. Atlanta Sat. 14 W. North Ave. Interred: Boston, Mass. AG 6/2/1908

MANNING, L. C. shot to death at Phileman, Ga. Tues. by John B. Wilkinson. AG 4/21/1910

MANNING, Margaret E., Mrs., age 37, wife of C. C. of 48 Lindsey St., Atlanta, d. Fri. Interred: Westview. AG 6/5/1908

MANNING, Pearl Bradley, Mrs. d. 16 Bailey St., Atlanta Sun. Interred: Westview. AG 6/23/1908

MANOS, Calloxi, inf. dau. of Mr. and Mrs., d. 57 Pulliam St. Atlanta., Mon. Interred: Westview. Ag 11/22/1910

MANSFIELD, Fred L., former state senator, d. Sat. Athens, Ga. Prominent in E. Tenn. politics. Funeral in Chattanooga, Tenn. AG 6/4/1910

MANSON, Mabel H., Mrs., age 29, d. E. Ellis St. Atlanta. AG 7/29/1908

MANSON, Mable H., Mrs., age 80, d. 101 E. Ellis St., Atlanta Sat. Interred: Westview. AG 7/29/1908

MAPP, Lillian, colored, age 10 mos., d. 41 Brandon St. Atlanta. AG 6/22/1908

MAPP, Margaret, colored, age 3, d. rear of 330 Decatur St., Atlanta. AG 5/10/1906

MAPP, Raymond, age 2, d. Decatur, Ga. AG 1/11/1910

MAR, Charles P., age 38, d. mother's res., Mrs. Sarah Mar, 41 Jefferson St., Atlanta, Fri. Interred: Acworth, Ga. AG 8/14/1908

MARBUT, Mary, Mrs. d. E. Atlanta Wed. Interred: Sylvester. AG 3/26/1909

MARBUT, Nancy, Mrs., age 35, d. E. Atlanta. AG 3/27/1909

MARBUT, Samuel P., age 65, d. 24 Kelly St. Atlanta. AG 2/16/1910

MARCUS, Rosa, colored, age 15 mos., d. 209 E. Baker St. Atlanta. AG 11/22/1909

MARKIES, Julius, Mrs. of 264 Auburn Ave., Atlanta, wife of a merchant, d. 6/9, age 24. Leaves husband, 3 children. AC 6/10/1905

MARKS, Caesar d. Hot Springs, Ark. Funeral res. of sister, Mrs. Eugene Raney, New Decatur, Ala., Wed. Mother, 4 sisters, 2 bros. survive. AG 10/6/1910

MARKWALTER, Frank H., Jr., son of Mr. and Mrs. Frank, d. Thurs. Macon. Interred: Rose Hill. AG 8/7/1908

MARLAND, William, Major, former postmaster of Andover, Mass., d. Griffin, Ga. 4/17. Born 1839 Andover, Mass. Wife, 3 children. AC 4/18/1905

MARR, Sarah, Mrs., age 80, d. 95 Venable St., Atlanta, Thurs. Three children survive. AG 12/10/1908

MARS, Charles d. Wed. Atlanta. Interred: Westview. AG 6/1/1908

MARS, J. A. d. Wed. 322 Capitol Ave., Atlanta. Interred: Westview. AG 5/30/1908

MARSENGILL, E. O. d. yesterday, age 24, son of Hon. J. M. Marsengill of Atlanta. AG 10/12/1909

MARSH, E. W. est. insolvent. J. G. St. Almond, exr. See details. AC 5/6/1905

MARSH, M. W. d. Mon. Atlanta. Interred: Westview. AG 6/25/1908

MARSHALL, Nina, infant dau. of Mr. and Mrs. W. H., d. Tues. 69 Bedford Place, Atlanta, Wed. AG 2/17/1909

MARSHALL, Oliver, colored, age 22, d. 101 N. Butler St. Atlanta. AG 3/10/1908

MARSHALL, Thomas J. of Reynolds, Ga. d. Jan. 8, Conf. Vet., age abt 70. 4 sons, 2 daus. AC 1/10/1905

MARSHALL, William, colored, age 31, d. 115 Butler St. Atlanta. AG 8/5/1908

MARTIN, Alice, age 17, dau. of Mr. and Mrs. Amos, d. 350 Windsor St. Atlanta, Thurs. Interred: Sylvester cemetery. AG 6/10/1910

MARTIN, Aline, age 3, dau. of Mr. and Mrs. W. H., d. Wed. Sheffield, Ala. Interred: Westview, Atlanta. AG 10/22/1909

MARTIN, Annie H., Mrs., wife of T. J., d. Sat. at Peachtree Inn. Husband survives. Interred: Inona, Minn. AG 4/25/1910

MARTIN, Annie, age 18 mos., d. 101 Butler St. Atlanta. AG 11/22/1909

MARTIN, Annie H., Mrs., wife of T. J., age 38, d. Peachtree Inn. Atlanta. Interred: Winona, Minn. AG 4/25/1910

MARTIN, Benjamin Walker funeral res. College Park Wed. Interred: College Park Cemetery. AG 5/23/1906

MARTIN Dan, colored, age 84, d. 88 Humphries St. Atlanta. AG 3/22/1909

MARTIN, Felix B. drowned Ocean View, near Norfolk, Va. Sat. Interred: Family Cemetery, Madison, Ga. Parents: Mr. and Mrs. W. F. Martin. Bro: Wilfred Martin. AG 7/28/1908

MARTIN, George, age 40, d. 36 English Ave. Atlanta. AG 8/27/1909

MARTIN, Harriet, colored, age 82, d. 50 Scott St. Atlanta. AG 12/2/1910

MARTIN, Henry, infant, d. 30 Luckie St. Atlanta. AG 3/28/1910

MARTIN, Herschel B. d. Sat. 74 S. Jackson St., Atlanta. Interred: Westview. AG 4/25/1910

MARTIN, Herschel Porter, age 30, d. 74 S. Jackson St., Atlanta, Sat. Wife. Bro: W. D. Martin. Interred: Westview. AG 4/23/1910

MARTIN, J. . d. 8/30 Jeffersonville, Ga. Bro: A. F. ac 9/3/1905

MARTIN, J. P. of Marion, N. C. d. Savannah, Ga. 6/26. AC 6/27/1905

MARTIN, James E. killed in auto accident 12/24 in NY. Bro-in-law: William Gould Brokaw of Atlanta. Mr. and Mrs. Frank S. Ellis received telegram in Atlanta. AC 12/26/1905

MARTIN, Jerre T., age 58, formerly of Harris Co., farmer, Columbus, Ga., d. Jan. 3. AC 1/5/1905

MARTIN, Katherine, age 4 mos., d. 101 N. Butler St. Atlanta. AG 2/8/1909

MARTIN, Mark, Mrs. d. 2 Oak St., Dalton, Ga., Fri. Husband, 2 sons, 3 daus. AG 12/17/1910

MARTIN, Mary Frances, age 71, d. Inman yards. Atlanta. AG 2/2/1910

MARTIN, Nellie May, age 18, d. 130 English Ave. Atlanta. AG 4/27/1910

MARTIN, Omer O., Miss, age 22, d. parents res., Mr. and Mrs. A. J. Martin, 95 Powell St. Atlanta, Tues. Interred: Oakwood, Ga. AG 9/28/1909

MARTIN, Otis, age 3, son of Mr. and Mrs. E. H. of E. Point, Ga. d. Thurs. Interred: East Point Cemetery. AG 12/31/1909

MARTIN, R. F., res. of Crawford, Ga., d. Mon. Wife, two nephews, George H. Jones and J. E. Martin of Atlanta. Nieces: Mrs. C. G. Childs, Mrs. B. H. Hartsfield of 236 Park St. Atlanta. AG 11/22/1909

MARTIN, Ruth, age 3, dau. of Mr. and Mrs. Walter, d. Hemphill Ave. and Bishop Streets, Atlanta, Thurs. Interred: Lula, Ga. AG 12/17/1908

MARTIN, Sarah, Mrs. d. Sun. Columbus Rd., Macon, age 22. Husband, two small children survive. AG 7/7/1908

MARTIN, Theodore, age 2 mos., d. 56 Poplar St., Atlanta. AG 10/28/1908

MARTIN, Thomas M., Jr., age 2, son of Mr. and Mrs. Thomas M., d. Tues. 29 1/2 Walker St. Atlanta. Interred: Newnan, Ga. AG 12/2/1909

MARTIN, U. R., Jr., age 10 mos., son of Mr. and Mrs. U R., d. 54 Oglethorpe Ave., Atlanta. Interred: Hollywood. AG 7/20/1908

MARTIN, W. C., age 27, d. 46 Elizabeth St. Atlanta. AG 11/8/1910

MARTIN, Wiley d. Sun. Decatur, Ala. AG 10/1/1909

MARYS, Morton, Col., age 27, d. Richmond, Va. 12/22. Father of P. Thornton Marys, Morton Marys, Jr. and Mrs. J. S. B. Thompson, all of Atlanta. AG 12/17/1910

MASHBURN, Bertha, Mrs., age 21, d. Sun. 690 E. Fair St., Atlanta. Interred: Conyers, Ga. AG 9/10/1910

MASHBURN, Carrie, Mrs. d. Wed. Atlanta. Interred: Williamston, S. C. AG 5/23/1909

MASHBURN, Violet, age 6 mos., dau. of C. R., d. 690 E. Fair St., Atlanta. AG 10/27/1910

MASON, Charles B., age 67, d. Mon. Inman yards, Atlanta. Interred: Greensboro, Ga. AG 2/22/1910

MASON, Cliff, Mrs. d. Fri. at father's home, Dr. J. W. Quillian, Augusta Ave., Atlanta. Husband, one infant. AG 5/23/1909

MASON, Emma Frances, age 7 mos., dau. of Mr. and Mrs. E. W., 345 S. Boulevard Atlanta, d. Thurs. Interred: Macon. AG 8/14/1908

MASON, George William, age 12 days, d. 103 Chapel St. Atlanta. AG 3/27/1909

MASON, Lizzie, Mrs., age 38, wife of Matthew, d. 218 N. Jackson St., Atlanta, Thurs. Dau: Evelyn. Several other children. Interred: Montgomery, Ala. AG 8/12/1909

MASON, Marvin Q., age 2, inf. son of Mr. and Mrs. J. H., d. 19 Krogg St., Atlanta, Fri. Interred: Culberson, Ga. AG 5/8/1910

MASSEE, Sanford D., pioneer res. of E. Macon, d. 3/3 family home on Ft. Hill, age 68. Wife, 4 sons, 2 daus. Interred: Riverside. AG 3/4/1910

MASSEY, Dora, Mrs., age 34, wife of T. R., d. Mon. 564 Moreland Ave. Atlanta. AG 2/22/1910

MASSEY, Leila, Mrs., age 39, d. Atlanta. AG 5/12/1910

MASSEY, Lela, Mrs., age 22, d. Hollis Springs, Ga. Wed., wife of W. N. Two children. AG 5/11/1910

MASSEY, M., Mrs., age 38, d. Hood St. 10/20, Atlanta. AG 10/25/1910

MASTRAVES, Maggie, Mrs., age 44, d. Mon. Atlanta. Interred: Westview. Husband. AG 6/1/1909

MATHES, Rachel Elizabeth, age 23 mos., dau. of Rev. and Mrs. N. B., d. Riverdale, Ga. Sun. Interred: Westview. AG 9/15/1909

MATHEWS, J. J., Mrs. d. Cuthbert, Ga. Sat., age 80. Mother of large family. AG 12/21/1908

MATHEWS, Matty, colored, age 23, d. 27 Adams Alley. Atlanta. AG 12/29/1908

MATHEWS, Ramon and Ed Britt from Lanett, Ala. drowned in Chattahoochee River 7/3. AC 7/4/1905

MATHIS, inf. son of Mr. and Mrs. C. P., d. 68 S. McDaniel St., Atlanta, Wed. Interred: Ellijay, Ga. AG 6/16/1910

MATHIS, Amanda, Mrs., age 78, d. 695 E. Fair St., Atlanta, Wed. Interred: Duluth, Ga. Four daus. survive. AG 5/6/1908

MATHIS, Herman, colored, d. 80 Elizabeth St. Atlanta. AG 5/3/1906

MATHIS, Paul, age 4, d. 172 S. Forsyth St. Atlanta. AG 9/26/1910

MATSON, John Sharp, age 68, d. 311 Myrtle St. Atlanta. AG 4/14/1910

MATTHEWS, Charles P. d. Sat. parents home, Mr. and Mrs. Homer Matthews, in Edgewood. Interred: Sylvester Cemetery. AG 10/18/1909

MATTHEWS, Charles Pressly, age 9 mos., d. Edgewood, Ga. AG 10/18/1909

MATTHEWS, F. C., Mrs., age 73, d. Decatur, Ga., Thurs. Son: Charles. Two sisters. Interred: Decatur Cemetery. AG 5/13/1910

MATTHEWS, George F., alias George Morris, killed himself with pistol, Collins St., Atlanta. 2/27. Interred: Louisville, Ga. AC 3/1/1905

MATTHEWS, George P., inf. son of Mr. and Mrs. T. R., d. 10/27, 35 Haralson St., Atlanta. Interred: Westview. AG 10/28/1910

MATTHEWS, Gertrude, Miss, age 18, d. 291 Capitol Ave., Atlanta, Sun. Parents: Mr. and Mrs. Ed Matthews. Sisters: Misses Grace, Beatrice, Edith. AG 9/21/1909

MATTHEWS, Helen Margaret, dau. of Mr. and Mrs. M. E., d. Wed. 291 Capitol Ave. Atlanta, Thurs. Interred: Oakland. AG 6/10/1909

MATTHEWS, Jessie E. d. Atlanta Sun. Interred: Talbotton, Ga. AG 7/25/1910

MATTHEWS, Lessie D., Mrs., age 33, d. Sun. NY City, formerly res. of Atlanta. Interred: Westview. AG 7/2/1910

MATTHEWS, M. E. funeral from res., 291 Capitol Ave., Atlanta, Tues. Interred: Oakland. AG 4/5/1910

MATTHEWS, Mark J., age 21, d. 133 Peeples St. Atlanta. AG 5/18/1908

MATTHEWS, Mary, colored, age 36, d. 84 W. Harris St. Atlanta. AG 9/2/1909

MATTHEWS, Mary, Mrs., wife of John V., d. Sat. Huntsville, Ala. Grdau. of late Gov. Reuben Chapman, of Alabama. Married abt a yr. AG 10/3/1910

MATTHEWS, Robert A., Mrs. d. 10/18, 58 Ponders Ave., Atlanta. AC 10/19/1905

MATTHEWS, Sarah, colored, age 6, d. 80 Elizabeth St. Atlanta. AG 9/26/1910

MATTHEWS, W. T., merchant, d. 4/18 Columbus, Ga., age 38. Wife, several children. AG 4/19/1910

MATTHEWS, infant of C. F., colored, d. rear of 166 Capitol Ave. Atlanta. AG 6/6/1906

MATTINGLY, Herbert H. d. Wed. 97 E. Pine St. Atlanta, age 35. Wife. Father: Judge Robert Mattingly of Lima, Ohio. AG 8/1/1910

MATTISON, Ella A., Mrs., wife of Alexandria, age 64, d. 724 Highland Ave. Atlanta. Husband. Sons: M. W., of New Orleans; A. W. Daus: Mrs. Charles A. Smith, Mrs. G. W. Akers, Mrs. H. D. Smith, Jr., Misses Daisy and Jennie Mattison. Interred: Westview. AG 6/29/1910

MATTISON, Mary, Miss, dau. of G. A., d. 4/28 Talladega, Ala., age 17. AG 4/28/1910

MATTOX, Fannie T., Mrs., age 62, d. Washington, D. C. Tues. Interred: Westview, Atlanta. Son: Harry L. Good. Sister: Mrs. T. J. Harwell, LaGrange, Ga. AG 9/12/1908

MATTOX, John, Judge d. 3/13 Summerville, Ga., Ordinary of Chattooga Co. 28 yrs. Wife, 3 grown children. AC 3/14/1905

MAULDIN, Ernest, age 1, d. 208 Echo St. Atlanta. AG 11/1/1909

MAUND, Mrs. suicide Atlanta. Interred: Riverdale Cemetery, Macon. AG 2/20/1909

MAURY, Ethel, Miss d. Atlanta Sat. Interred: Marlboro, Mass. AG 6/6/1906

MAXEY, Willie May, colored, age 1, d. 429 Richardson St. Atlanta. AG 12/24/1908

MAXWELL, A. E., Mrs., bride of 3 mos., d. Atlanta Thurs., formerly Miss Ramsey of Asheville, N. C., age 20. Interred: Asheville, N. C. AG 9/3/1908

MAXWELL, Corrie, age 14, son of J. A. O. of Amsterdam, Ga., d. Interred: Calvary Cemetery. AG 2/24/1910

MAXWELL, Henry, colored, age 49, d. 92 E. Cain St. Atlanta. AG 8/23/1909

MAXWELL, J. T., Mrs. d. 9/20. Interred: Family Burial Ground at Max. AG 9/20/1909

MAXWELL, John B. d. Bowden, Ga. 11/5. Former res. of Hartwell, Ga. Wife, 7 sons and daus. 11/30th he would have been age 94. AC 11/7/1905

MAXWELL, Julia, negro, age 4, d. from burns E. Rome, Ga. AG 2/3/1908

MAXWELL, Rena, age 31, d. 178 Luckie St. Atlanta, Tues. Sister and mother survive. Interred: Kingston, Ga. AG 11/22/1910

MAXWELL, Young shot Jan. 2 by John Turner at Hartwell, Ga. Hart Co. negroes. AC 1/4/1905

MAY, Douglas, young res. of Montgomery, Ala. d. 9/10. AG 9/11/1909

MAY, William A., age 52, d. 4/25 res. of son-in-law, Frank Williamson, 536 Washington St., Atlanta. Wife, dau. survive. Interred: Westview. AG 4/25/1906

MAYERS, S. F. D. d. Soldiers' Home, Atlanta, Sun. Interred: Oakland. AG 5/1/1906

MAYES, Sam suicide 3/17 at Commercial Hotel, Gadsden, Ala., grieving over dau.'s death. AC 3/18/1905

MAYFIELD , Charles R. d. Mon. San Antonio, Texas. Funeral: Atlanta. Interred: Oakland. AG 12/2/1909

MAYFIELD, Charlie, colored, age 47, d. Atlanta. AG 5/22/1910

MAYFIELD, J. R., age 53, d. 21 Welborn St., Atlanta. 6 children. Interred: Jackson, Ga. AG 5/3/2920

MAYFIELD, Nancy, Mrs., age 70, d. 683 Woodward Ave. Atlanta. Daus: Mrs. R. C. Humphries, Atlanta; Mrs. Katie Mansee, San Antonio, Tx. Sons: G. A., S. L., J. P., J. . and C. M. Interred: Fairburn, Ga. AG 1/27/1910

MAYHUGH, Joseph T., son of W. T., of 177 Griffin St., Atlanta, d. Sat. Interred: Westview. AG 6/25/1906

MAYNARD, Katie O., Mrs., age 21, d. Atlanta Wed., wife of E. Herbert Maynard. Parents: Mr. and Mrs. E. F. Marston of 102 Ivy St. AG 12/2/1909

MAYO, Alice Rosa, inf. dau. of Mr. and Mrs. Joseph, d. 12 Hoke St., Atlanta, Thurs. Interred: Casey's Cemetery. AG 3/18/1908

MAYO, David M. d. Americus, Ga., age 43, son of late David A. Wife, 2 children, 4 bros., sister. AG 10/6/1910

MAYO, infant, son of Mrs. W. R., d. 99 Davis St., Atlanta, Sun. Interred: Hollywood. AG 3/23/1908

MAYO, Lorena, Mrs., age 41, d. Atlanta Fri. Riverdale, Ga. Husband, parents, two children. AG 9/24/1910

MAYO, W. R., Mrs. d. 99 Davis St., Atlanta, Tues. Interred: Hollywood. AG 3/25/1908

MAYSON, Carrie B., Mrs., age 44, d. 20 W. 15th St. Atlanta. AG 2/24/1910

MAYSON, J. Wiley, age 6 mos., son of Cliff, d. 127 Cleburne Ave., Atlanta, Tues. Interred: Gainesville, Ga. AG 12/15/1909

MAYSON, Mary E., age 5, dau. of City Atty James L. Mayson, d. Jan. 11. Abt 6 mos. ago, Mrs. T. C. Mayson, his mother, expired. AC 1/12/1905

MAYSON, T. C., Mrs., mother of City Atty, James L. Mayson, d. abt. June 1904. AC 1/12/1905

MCADAMS, Elnora, age 2, dau. of W. A., d. 223 D'Alvigny St., Atlanta, Fri. Interred: Hollywood. AG 12/18/1910

MCADAMS, R. O., Mrs. d. Atlanta Thurs. Interred: Abbeville, S. C. AG 11/23/1907

MCAFEE, W. W., age 79, Atlanta pioneer, d. res. son-in-law: Mrs. M. O. Thompson, 503 Washington St., Atlanta. Wife: Ella. Dau: Mrs. John B. Goodwin. Interred: Oakland. AC 11/4/1905

MCALPINE, M. C., Mrs. d. Talladega, Ala. 6/17. Known as "Grandmother McAlpine." AG 6/17/1910

MCBEAN, Alexander, Dr., former Georgian, suicide in prison cell, Houston, Texas. He was b. Logansville, Ga., age 44. Father, physician, d. several yrs. ago. AC 3/25/1905

MCBURNEY, J. C., former Atlantan, d. Jersey City 4/3. Ch: E. P., Atlanta; Mrs. Kendrick Morton, Marietta. Three ch res. Jersey City. Interred: Westview. AC 4/4/1905

MCCALL, B. F. of Jennings, Fla., d. Valdosta, Ga. AG 2/16/1910

MCCALLA, Charles R., age 64, d. Sat. 137 Richardson St., Atlanta. Wife, several children. AG 4/17/1909

MCCALLA, Harry E., age 85, d. 39 McDaniel St. Atlanta. AG 2/7/1910

MCCALLA, Walter of Shiloh d. Sun. AG 1/18/1910

MCCARLEY, Paul d. 44 Colquitt Ave., Atlanta, Wed. Interred: Westview. AG 4/7/1910

MCCARTHY, Helen, age 3 mos., dau. of W. R., d. 1163 E. Fair St., Atlanta. Interred: Sylvester Cemetery. AG 12/15/1910

MCCARTY, Molly, Mrs., age 49, d. 11/9 Macon, Ga. Interred: St. Josephs Cemetery. Husband, 2 daus: Misses Blanche and Ruth. Sons: H. J., E. J., Willie, Leo. AG 11/8/1910

MCCASH, Marie, dau. of Mr. and Mrs. Barton Stone McCash, d. 2/26, 170 N. Jackson St., Atlanta. Interred: Westview. AC 2/27/1905

MCCASLIN, Charles, age 59, funeral Sun. Atlanta. Interred: Nashville, Tenn. AG 9/26/1910

MCCASSERTY, W. N., Mrs. d. Columbus, Ga. Thurs., age 26. Husband, one dau. Interred: Dadeville, Ala. AG 2/27/1910

MCCAW, Mary, Mrs., widow of James of Tenn., d. dau.´s res., Mrs. E. L. Peek, Macon, Ga. 4/8. Interred: Rose Hill. AC 4/8/1905

MCCAY, Andy, colored, age 44, d. 59 Biggers St. Atlanta. AG 4/8/1908

MCCLAIN, Amanda B., Miss, age 50, d. 15 Highland Ave., Atlanta. Interred: Charleston. Mother: Mrs. James Clarkston. 3 bros. 2 sisters. AC 11/23/1905

MCCLELLAND, W. R. d. Thurs. Atlanta, age 43, son of late John F., Presbyterian minister. Wife: Bessie. AG 9/1/1910

MCCLELLAND, W. R., age 43, d. Stewart Ave. Atlanta. AG 9/2/1910

MCCLENDON, Emily, colored, age 66, d. 432 Crumley St. Atlanta. AG 3/18/1908

MCCLENDON, Mary A., Mrs. d. 429 Woodward Ave., Atlanta, Thurs. Interred: Oakland. AG 5/13/1910

MCCLESKEY, J. R., Rev. d. Washington, Ga. 11/13, age 65. Leaves wife, 5 children. AG 11/13/1908

MCCLINK, Janie, colored, age 42, d. 101 N. Butler St. Atlanta. AG 12/6/1908

MCCOLGAN, Charles L., age 47, d. Atlanta Thurs. Interred: Oakland. AG 2/14/1910

MCCOLLOUGH, M. A., Mrs. d. Tues. Round Oak in Jones Co., Ga., age 76. Six children, several grandchildren of Macon survive. AG 12/23/1908

MCCOMBS, Calvin, colored, age 49, d. 145 Clarke St. Atlanta. AG 11/28/1908

MCCONNELL, Anna, Mrs. d. Mon. Pleasant Grove, Ga. AG 10/20/1910

MCCONNELL, Anna, Mrs., age 53, of Clayton Co., d. Salina, Mon. 2 sons, 2 daus. One son in Chicago, one son in N. Y. AG 10/18/1910

MCCONNELL, J. R., age 33, d. 72 Hendrix Ave., Atlanta, Tues. Interred: Augusta, Ga. Mother: Mrs. J. P. McConnell. Bro: J. D. McConnell, both of Atlanta. AG 3/11/1908

MCCOOK, G. W., Mrs. d. 3/4 Lizella, Ga. Husband, several small children. Parents: Mr. and Mrs. M. G. Newsom. Bros: Henry, Frank, Clifford, Edward and Bradford Newsom. Sis: Mrs. Robinson, Mrs. C. E. Hurt. AG 3/5/1910

MCCOOL, E. J. dropped dead in postoffice Fri., Atlanta. Interred: Brockton, Mass. AG 6/20/1908

MCCOOL, Edward J., age 35, d. Atlanta. AG 6/22/1908

MCCORD, Courtney G. B. funeral Sat. Atlanta. Interred: Westview. AG 4/16/1910

MCCORD, J. C., age 63, d. 482 Ashby St., Atlanta, Wed. Wife. Daus: Mrs. E. D. Hasty, Mrs. Robert Leach, Miss Gertrude McCord. Sons: Homer and D. Interred: Sylvester, Ga. AG 5/19/1910

MCCORD, Mary, Miss, age 18, only dau. of Mr. and Mrs. H. Y., 272 Juniper St. d. Wesley Memorial Hospital, Atlanta. Interred: Westview. 4 bros: Burton, Harry, Jeff Davis and Ashby McCord. AG 10/30/1908

MCCORMACK, W. H., age 65, d. 154 Greenwich Ave., Atlanta, Tues. Interred: Westview. AG 9/9/1908

MCCORMICK, William, younger son of M., of Sparta, Ga., d. 10/29. AC 10/31/1905

MCCOWAN, Louise, age 2, dau. of Mr. and Mrs. James, d. 47 Venable St. Atlanta, Tues. Interred: Westview. AG 6/15/1910

MCCOWN, Robert d. 12/17. Wife. several children. Interred: Atlanta, Oakland Cemetery. AC 12/19/1905

MCCOY, Annie Mrs., age 40, d. Decatur, Ga. AG 2/7/1910

MCCOY, Mollie, age 64, d. 276 W. Fifth St. Atlanta. AG 11/14/1908

MCCOY, T. T., age 53, of Lee Co., Ala., farmer, d. 10 mi. W. of Columbus, Ga. AC 10/16/1905

MCCOY, Winslow T., age 44, d. Thurs. Kirkwood (Atlanta). Interred: Greenwood. AG 6/17/1910

MCCRARY, negro, to hang for attacking Perry Lee Coukle, 10-yr. old white girl, Jonesboro, Ga. AC 3/31/1905

MCCRARY, Dolly B., Mrs., wife of J. A., of LaGrange, d. Atlanta. Interred: LaGrange, Ga. AG 7/11/1910

MCCRARY, James S., age 41, d. 155 Holderness St. Atlanta. AG 11/30/1910

MCCRARY, Rebecca, colored, age 40, d. 101 N. Butler St. Atlanta. AG 3/3/1909

MCCRARY, Walter E. suicide 9/12 Columbus, Ga. AG 9/18/1909

MCCRAVEN, Charles, age 19, d. parents res., Mr. and Mrs. Samuel McCraven, near E. Point, Ga., Sat. Interred: Family Cemetery. AG 8/3/1908

MCCRAW, James, colored, age 21, d. 101 N. Butler St. Atlanta. AG 3/4/1908

MCCREARY, Mamie, dau. of Mr. and Mrs. I. N., d. Mon. 450 Walnut St., Atlanta. Father, mother, 5 sisters, little bro., survive. AG 7/7/1908

MCCREE, Charlotte J., inf. dau. of Mr. and Mrs. Thomas H., d. Mon. 21 Peachtree Circle, Atlanta. Interred: Westview. AG 5/31/1910

MCCULLEY, Edward T., age 28, d. Wed. 116 Center St., Atlanta. Interred: Westview. AG 9/22/1910

MCCULLEY, Lavinia, Miss, age 20, d. res. of parents, Mr. and Mrs. W. G. McCulley, Church St., Huntsville, Ala. AG 10/1/1909

MCCULLOCH, W. W., Mrs. d. Sun. Marietta, Ga., where interred. Dau. of late Pat Lynch, Jr., grdau. of Pat Lynch, Atlanta pioneer. Husband, 3 children, 4 sisters, Mrs. G. Biggers of Atlanta; Mrs. M. Haynes of Los Angeles, CA; Mrs. K. Posse of Nashville; Mrs. Mel T. Johnson of Lawrenceville. Bros: John H. and E. J. Lynch. AG 8/30/1910

MCCULLOM, Jewett Dashwood, age 2, son of Dr. and Mrs. W. W., d. Lakewood Heights, Atlanta, Sun. Interred: Holly SPrings, Ga. AG 10/25/1909

MCCULLOUGH, Emma, Mrs., former res. of Covington, d. Norman Park, Ga. 8/10 (sister's res.). AG 8/17/1910

MCCULLOUGH, George, colored, age 62, d. 38 McDaniel St. Atlanta. AG 3/3/1909

MCCULLOUGH, Matilda, colored, age 57, d. 38 N. McDaniel St. Atlanta. AG 4/22/1909

MCCULLOUGH, Mattie, colored, age 26, d. 9 Trayholms alley. Atlanta. AG 9/6/1910

MCCULLY, G. W., age 56, d. 333 Woodward Ave. Atlanta. AG 4/17/1908

MCCUTCHEN, W. P. of Dalton, Ga., d. Sun., age 83. Interred: Donegan Cemetery. AG 11/1/1910

MCDANDISH, C. S. d. 11/30, 871 N. Boulevard, Atlanta, age 58. Wife, 3 small children. interred: Westview. AC 12/1/1905

MCDANIEL, Carl, age 7, d. 52 College St. Atlanta. AG 9/2/1909

MCDANIEL, Emma, Miss d. Mon. Atlanta. Interred: Westview. Mother: Mrs. Frances E. McDaniel. Bros: J. E., H. L. and W. J. McDaniel Sis: Misses Mary and Annie McDaniel. AG 8/10/1909

MCDANIEL, Grace A., age 5, dau. of Mr. and Mrs. V. S., funeral 680 DeKalb Ave. Interred: Oakland. AG 6/13/1906

MCDANIEL, Helen, age 2, one of twin daus. of Mr. and Mrs. C. A., d. Norcross, Ga., Tues. Gr.dau. of Dr. Thomas Terrell Key and niece of James Lee Key of Atlanta. She was Miss Maude Key of Atlanta before marriage. Funeral at Norcross. AG 5/3/1910

MCDANIEL, J. Stewart, age 22, son of Mr. and Mrs. J. E., d. College Park Fri. AG 4/15/1909

MCDANIEL, James, age 34, d. 86 Fairbiew Ave., Atlanta, Thurs., son of Mr. and Mrs. Ben. Wife, one child. Interred: Westview. AG 1/28/1910

MCDANIEL, James M., 80, b. 9/29/1829 S. C., Atlanta pioneer, d. dau's res., Mrs. A. P. Johnson, 345 Ponce de Leon Ave., Atlanta. Sons: G. W., W. M., J. B. Daus: Mrs. J. E. Christopher, Mrs. J. J. Murphy. 7 grch, 1 gr-grchild. AG 2/11/1909

MCDANIEL, Josephine E., Mrs., age 41, d. Atlanta Wed. Dau: Miss Viola McDaniel, 19 Bush St. Atlanta. AG 3/18/1909

MCDANIEL, Julia, Mrs., age 69, d. Tues. Clarkston, Ga. Interred: Liberty Church yard. AG 8/17/1910

MCDANIEL, Louis Sylvester, age 21 mos., son of Mr. and Mrs. Sylvester, d. 2 Virgil St. Atlanta. Bur: Oakland. AG 1/17/1910

MCDANIEL, Paul, age 26, colored, d. 12 Lowndes St. Atlanta. AG 11/27/1910

MCDANIEL, Paul Taft, colored, age 12 days, d. 460 Piedmont Ave., Atlanta. AG 9/29/1909

MCDANIEL, Samuel, Mrs., d. Duluth, Ga., Wed, formerly Miss Lizzie Hargrove of Smyrna, dau. of Mr. and Mrs. F. A. Hargrove. Bro: W. A. Hargrove, Atlanta. Sis: Mrs. Roy Walters, Atlanta; Miss Estelle Hargrove, Smyrna. AG 5/6/1910

MCDAVID, John A., age 53, d. 78 Hightower St., Atlanta, Thurs. Interred: Westview. AG 12/9/1910

MCDIARMID, Essie, Mrs., age 84, d. Atlanta 12/12/1907. Interred: Lochmaddy, Scotland. Son: Dr. John McDiarmid of Deland, Fla. AG 6/25/1908

MCDONALD, child, age 6 yrs., son of Mr. and Mrs. J. A., d. 10/17 Waycross, Ga. Interred: Waresboro, Ga. AG 10/18/1910

MCDONALD, Carrie, Mrs., age 24, d. 407 Simpson St. Atlanta. AG 6/8/1908

MCDONALD, G. F., Capt., d. 12/28 Montgomery, Ala. AC 12/29/1905

MCDONALD, Howard L., inf. son of Dr. and Mrs. Paul, d. Bolton, Ga. Wed. Interred: Family Burial Ground. AG 3/11/1908

MCDONALD, J. O of Carrollton, Ga., d. 2/26, son of Hon. H. A. of Bowdon, age 30. Wife. No children. AC 2/28/1905

MCDONALD, Julius W., age 24, d. Richardson and Pulliam Sts. Atlanta. AG 5/6/1908

MCDONALD, Kate, Miss, age 17, dau. of J. R., funeral 10/2. Interred: Kettle Creek Cemetery. AG 10/3/1910

MCDONALD, Marvin d. from wounds Montgomery, Ala. Shot by C. B. Gardner at Ozark, Ala. Tues. AG 1/27/1910

MCDONALD, Mary E., Mrs., age 48, d. 571 Woodward Ave., Atlanta, Wed. Husband: J. H. Daus: Mrs. Dora Smith, New Albany, Miss.; Miss Alice McDonald, Atlanta. Son: Frank A. McDonald, Atlanta. AG 7/29/1909

MCDONALD, Myrtice V., Mrs., age 73, formerly of Atlanta and Augusta, d. res. of son, T. H. McDonald, Brooklyn, N. Y. Fri. Bro: Prof. William Teck, Atlanta. Interred: Augusta, Ga. AG 8/11/1908

MCDONALD, Paul A., former Atlantan, committed suicide 11/27, Hot Springs, Ark. hotel. AG 11/28/1908

MCDONALD, Ruth, age 14 mos., dau. of Mr. and Mrs. John T. of 112 Plum St., Atlanta, d. Fri. Interred: Westview. AG 5/30/1908

MCDONALD, Sarah, Mrs., age 83, d. res. of dau., Mrs. M. A. Harrison, E. Point, Ga. Daus: Mrs. Harrison, Mrs. Maggie Thompson, Atlanta, and Mrs. Mary Brotherton, Texas. Interred: Fairburn, Ga. AG 11/22/1909

MCDONALD, Will of Covington d. 6/3, age 30. Wife, one little girl. AG 6/4/1909

MCDONALD, Wilson, age 11 mos., son of Mr. and Mrs. J. G., d. College Park, Ga. Interred: Carters Springs, Ga. AG 9/2/1909

MCDONALD, J. C., Mrs., dau. of S. G. Hillyer, d. Ft. Valley. Bros: Rev. J. L. D., J. F., Rome & L. P. Hillyer, Macon. Sis: Mrs. W. A. Turner, Miss L. C. Hillyer, Decatur, Mrs. T. L. Robinson, Anniston, Mrs. R. G. Owen, Cuthbert. AG 6/2/1908

MCDOWELL, J. N., age 51, d. 294 Courtland St. Atlanta. AG 9/9/1908

MCEACHERN, Marian committed suicide Thurs. AG 1/3/1908

MCELHANEY, Mary, Mrs., age 32, d. 59 Lake St. Atlanta. Husband: J. T. One son, one dau, three bros., two sisters. Interred: Rome, Ga. AG 8/23/1909

MCELROY, C. T., **Mrs.** d. Hapeville Wed. Husband, 4 children.
Father: T. M. McHugh, Atlanta. Interred: College Park Cemetery.
AG 5/25/1910

MCELROY, **Maggie, Mrs.**, age 57 (or 87), d. 38 Tye St., Atlanta,
Tues. Interred: Lithonia, Ga. AG 11/16/1910

MCFALL, D. H., Judge, d. Austin, Texas. Md. 1900 Miss Rosa
Russell of Columbus, Ga. Son: Charles R. AC 3/22/1905

MCFERRIN, R. A., Dr., former coal merchant of Atlanta and
stepfather of Gerald Hannah of Atlanta and General Harvey H.
Hannah of Tenn., d. Oliver Springs, near Knoxville, Tenn. 7/4. AG
7/4/1908

MCGARRITY, T., **Mrs.**, age 69, d. College Park Wed. Dau: Mrs. H. J.
Wyatt of E. Point. Sons: R. W., W. T. of Fairburn, Ga. Interred:
Fairburn, Ga. AG 2/23/1910

MCGAUGHEY, J. D., Dr. of Wallingford, Conn. d. Mon. Wife, one
son, two daus. Bros: W. G., F. S., and C. B. McGaughey, and one
sister, Mrs. L. E. Bradford, all of Atlanta. Interred:
Wallingford, Conn. AG 11/1/1910

MCGEE, E. K., **Mrs.** d. Tues. res. of son, Dr. H. H. McGee, 113
Liberty St., Savannah. Native of Screven Co. where lived until
recently. Ch: Dr. McGee, Savannah; Mrs. J. L. Sheppard,
Haleondale. Interred: Union Baptist Church. AG 6/30/1909

MCGEE, **Jim**, colored, age 29, d. 9 Alexander St. Atlanta. AG
12/17/1910

MCGEE, **Sarah, Mrs.**, age 67, d. 213 Greensferry Ave., Atlanta,
Thurs. Sis: Mrs. Mary G. Wilson, Mrs. J. J. Barfield; Miss Andrew
McGee. Bros: M. S., J. M., Dr. L. M. and Prof. J. T. McGee.
Interred: Mt. Gilead Church yard. AG 4/8/1910

MCGEHEE, W. B. d. Sat. Waverly Hall, Ga. AG 1/17/1910

MCGHEE, **M. V., Mrs.**, age 30, d. Atlanta Thurs. Husband: W. V.
McGhee, Chipley, Ga. Interred: Chipley, Ga. AG 1/3/1908

MCGHEE, **Zach, Mrs.**, wife of correspondent of Savannah Morning
News, d. Providence Hospital, Washington. Formerly Miss Helen
Irwin of Spartanburg, S. C. AG 10/13/1908

MCGILL, J. H., **Mrs.** d. 8/10 Atlanta. Husband. Interred: Hollywood
Cemetery. AC 8/12/1905

MCGINNIS, **Sidney**, age 11, d. 109 Main St. Atlanta. AG 10/11/1909

MCGINTY, C. E., **Mrs.**, age 57, d. 69 Luckie St. Atlanta. Ten
children. AG 7/10/1908

MCGINTY, **Marjorie**, age 2, d. 53 Park Ave. Atlanta. AG 7/30/1908

MCGINTY, V. A., age 66, formerly of Atlanta, d. Dodge Co. Sat.
Survived by son, R. E.; dau., Mrs. J. B. Stribling of McRae, Ga.
Interred: Norcross, Ga. AG 12/26/1908

MCGOUGH, **Graham**, age 23 killed by lightning at home of B. L.
McGouch, Railroad St., Fayetteville, Ga. AG 6/6/1906

MCGOUGH, **Russell**, age 14, grandson of B. L. McGough, struck by
lightning, Railroad St., Fayetteville, Ga. AG 6/6/1906

MCGRIBB, Henry C., age 60, d. Kirkwood, Ga. AG 8/11/1908

MCGUIRE, **Lillian M.**, colored, age 1, d. Edgewood, Ga. AG
12/16/1908

MCGUIRK, **Hugh**, age 54, d. 24 King St. Atlanta. Interred:
Westview. AG 12/30/1910

MCGUKIN, Mary, **Mrs.** d. Atlanta Sun., age 74. Ch: John McGukin and
Mrs. H. T. Yergan. AG 6/20/1910

MCGUKIN, **William**, age 76, d. Atlanta. AG 3/21/1910

MCHAN, Augustus, age 4, son of Mr. and Mrs. T. W., d. 211 N. Jackson St., Atlanta, Fri. Parents, one sister, two brothers. Interred: Westview. AG 10/7/1910

MCHUGH, Eleanor, age 17 mos., dau. of Mr. and Mrs. Charles A., d. Atlanta Thurs. Interred: Westview. AG 7/2/1909

MCHUGH, Mary Louise, Mrs. d. Fri. 37 Moreland Ave., Atlanta. Interred: Westview. AG 4/11/1910

MCHUGH, T. P., age 65, inmate of Confederate Soldiers' Home, Atlanta, d. Fri. Enl. 3/1861 Pvt., Co. F, 24th Ga. Vols. Two bros. AG 4/30/1909

MCINTIRE, James W., age 28, d. Southern Hotel. Atlanta. AG 11/22/1909

MCINTOSH, George A., colored, age 1, d. 32 Hammond St. Atlanta. AG 10/18/1909

MCINTYRE, Joe, Mrs. d. Elberton, Ga., Sun. Born and reared near Winterville, Oconee Co., where interred. Husband survives. AG 11/1/1910

MCINTYRE, Virginia, Mrs., age 43, d. Sun. sister's res., Mrs. P. H. Kirt, E. Pt. Sis: Mrs. D. C. Harris, Mrs. A. P. Baldwin, Mrs. P. H. Kirt, Miss Clara Coggins. Bros: B. W. and S. M. Coggins. Interred: Flat Rock. AG 5/22/1910

MCKAMY, D. K. of Dalton, Ga. d. Jan. 6 Thornton Ave. AC 1/7/1905

MCKEE, Carl Wesley, age 13, d. Atlanta. AG 1/17/1910

MCKEE, Georgia Mariah, Mrs., age 65, d. 12/6 Columbus, Ga. Born Savannah, lived Columbus 50 yrs. Sons: Wylly, Savannah; Bourke, Troy, Ala. AC 12/8/1905

MCKELVEY, James H., age 49, d. East End, Ga. Sun. Wife, 4 children. AG 6/15/1908

MCKELVEY, Mary Elizabeth, Miss d. 10/1. Interred: Greenville, S. C. AC 10/3/1905

MCKELVY, James, Mrs. d. Roanoke, Ala. Wed. Interred: West End (Atlanta). AG 7/2/1909

MCKENAN, William, age 68, d. 84 Hurt St. Atlanta, 10/2. AG 10/3/1910

MCKENNA, Leonora, 11 mos. old dau. of Mr. and Mrs. W. A., d. Macon 8/30. Interred: Rose Hill. AG 9/1/1909

MCKENNY, David M. d. 4/7 Athens, Ga. AC 4/8/1905

MCKENZIE, L., Mrs., age 49, d. 280 Ormond St. Atlanta. AG 5/16/1910

MCKINLEY, Junia, Miss of Atlanta d. 1908. Bro: Nathaniel. AG 5/12/1909

MCKINLEY, Nathaniel, d. Selma, Ala., formerly of Atlanta, removed to Selma in Jan. Sis: Mrs. Frances Scales. Bro: Joseph E. Nie*ce: Miss Estelle Whelan. His sis, Miss Junia McKinley of Atlanta d. last yr. AG 5/12/1909

MCKINNEY, J. D. d. Ridgeland, S. C., former res. of Waycross, Ga., age abt 60. AG 10/18/1910

MCKOWN, Maggie,, age 23, wf of R. C. Parents: Mr. & Mrs. Andrew Burnham. Sis: Mrs. H. P. Brown, Cornell; Mrs. J. W. McKinley; Mrs. T. A. Scoggin, Dalton; Lula, Nellie. Bros: Paul E., W., Berkley, CA.; Jack, Conley. Bur: F. Cem. AG 8/3/1908

MCLANE, Burrell, white, killed in race riot Turner, S. C. AC 6/6/1905

MCLAUGHLIN, Leonard Frank, Dr. of Americus, Ga., native of Meriwether Co., former res. of Rome and Greenville, d. Wife, 8 ch. AC 1/10/1905

MCLEAN, Kate E., age 71, d. Fri. Atlanta, 28 Brown St. Interred: Oakland. AG 7/27/1908

MCLENDON, E. P., age 52, d. Box Springs, Ga. AC 3/18/1905

MCLENDON, Edgar H., age 46, d. Springfield, Mo. Tues. Mother and father: Mr. and Mrs. N. A. McLendon, 139 Washington St., Atlanta. Bro: Charles. Sis: Mrs. Ella Henderson. AG 2/23/1910

MCLENDON, Herschell L., age 24, d. 31 Cone St. Atlanta. AG 2/8/1909

MCLENDON, Mack d. Jernigan, Russell Co., Ala. AC 2/15/1905

MCLENDON, Mary A., Mrs., age 71, d. 429 Woodward Ave., Atlanta, Thurs. Sons: Thomas A., Alonzo L. Daus: Mrs. Lee Hagan, Mrs. Joseph H. Duncan. Nephew: W. M. Zirkle. Interred: Oakland. AG 5/12/1910

MCLENDON, Melton, colored, age 13, d. 101 N. Butler St. Atlanta. AG 3/10/1909

MCLENDON, Nathan, colored, age 60, d. Nov. 13, Atlanta. AG 11/16/1910

MCLEOD, Rochelle, Miss, age 16 d. N. Highlands, Columbus, Ga. AG 1/30/1908

MCLINDON, J. W., Mrs. of Lakewood Heights, Atlanta, d. Thurs. Husband, two children. AG 11/11/1909

MCLUCAS, J. H. T., Mrs. of Dallas, Ga. d. Atlanta Fri. Interred: Hampton, Ga. AG 10/2/1909

MCMAHON, Lucinda, Mrs. d. 12/27, age 72, Hampton, Ga. Ch: Mrs. J. W. Stephens; Mrs. E. H. Hair; Mrs. J. T. Manley of Pomona; Mrs. G. W. Avary, Newton Co.; Mrs. Fannie Whittle; A. F. McMahon, Atlanta. Interred: Family grounds. AC 12/29/1905

MCMAKIN, I. K., age 84, d. 6/23 Hatchechubbee, Russell Co., Ala. AC 6/25/1905

MCMASTERS, H. B., Dr. of Waynesboro funeral held Sun. Interred: Waynesboro, Ga. AG 8/24/1908

MCMASTERS, M. B., age 50, d. 602 Chestnut St. Atlanta. AG 11/15/1909

MCMICHAEL, David d. Jackson, Ga. Sat. Mother: Mrs. McCune McMichael. Wife was Miss Doe of Griffin. Sis: Miss Marie McMichael, Mrs. Kate Valentine of Jackson, Mrs. E. M. Boyd of Kissimmee, Fla. Bro: William. AG 2/8/1910

MCMILLAN, A. D., age 50, d. Atlanta Sun., prominent merchant of Wrightsville, Ga. Interred: Fayetteville, Ga. Interred: Fayetteville, Ga. AG 7/29/1908

MCMILLAN, George M., Jr., age 16, d. 8 Boulevard Terr., Atlanta, Sun., son of Dr. and Mrs. G. M. Bro: Virgil. Interred: Ochlochnee, Ga. AG 7/25/1910

MCMILLAN, J. O. d. 2/26 Washington Ave., Macon, age 53 Wife, one brother. AG 2/27/1909

MCMILLAN, M. A., Mrs., age 55, d. 16 Young St., Atlanta, Mon. Husband: J. F. One son. AG 11/10/1908

MCMULLEN, J. J., age 36, d. 38 Formwalt St. Atlanta, Mon. Interred: Orchard Hill, Ga. Wife, 3 small children. Bros: W. W., O., Jr. AG 10/13/1908

MCNABB, Mary A., inf. dau. of Mr. and Mrs. F. E., d. 203 Means St., Atlanta, Thurs. Interred: Hollywood. AG 7/8/1910

MCNAIR, Sim, colored, age 49, d. 368 S. McDaniel St. Atlanta. AG 12/27/1910

MCNEAL, William H., age 39, d. Chattanooga, Tenn. Interred: Luxomni, Ga. AG 8/16/1910

MCNEALY, Florence, Mrs. d. 2nd Ave. Atlanta Sat, age 46. Husband, 5 children. Interred: Riverdale Cemetery. AG 12/17/1910

MCNEW, Doris, inf. dau. of Mr. and Mrs. J. H., d. 171 Jones Ave., Atlanta, Mon. Interred: Westview. AG 6/21/1910

MCNEW, Doris, inf. dau. of Mr. and Mrs. J. H., of 171 Jones Ave., Atlanta, d. Mon. Interred: Westview. AG 6/21/1910

MCNINCH, Maggie, Miss, age 50, d. 120 Wells St. Atlanta. AG 5/12/1910

MCNINCH, Maggie, Mrs. d. Tues. 120 Wells St., Atlanta. Interred: Williamston, S. C. AG 5/11/1910

MCPHERSON, A. S., age 31, d. Atlanta Thurs. Interred: Newton, Miss. AG 5/12/1910

MCPHERSON, Orrin S., age 31, d. Atlanta Thurs. Interred: Newton, Miss. AG 5/13/1910

MCRAE, Joe, colored, age 32, d. 22 Garibaldi St. Atlanta. AG 9/2/1909

MCREE, E. J., Hon., of Lowndes Co., Ga. legislature, d. home at Kinderton, 6 mi. from Valdosta. AG 3/25/1908

MCSWEENEY, M. B., former Gov. of S. C., d. 9/29 Baltimore, Md., age 55. Widow, 6 children. AG 9/29/1909

MCWATTY, T. F. d. near Spread, Ga. 3/1, age 57. AG 3/2/1910

MCWHORTER, J. H., Mrs., age 32, d. Atlanta Sun. 389 E. Georgia Ave. Interred: Westview. AG 11/7/1910

MCWILLIAMS, W. A., age 49, d. bro.'s res. George W., Roswell Rd., Atlanta, Tues. Interred: Oakland. AG 9/24/1908

MEACHAM, Arthur V., age 4 mos., son of Mr. and Mrs. G. N., d. Tues. 40 York St. Atlanta. Interred: Decatur, Ga. AG 8/17/1910

MEADOR, James J., age 70, d. 101 N. Butler St. Atlanta. AG 10/13/1908

MEADOR, Lillie Ray, Mrs., age 42, d. Atlanta. AG 11/8/1909

MEADORS, Jason L., Mrs. d. 6/4 Lanett, Ala. Husband, 3 children. Father: S. J. Costley. Sis: Mrs. J. W. Barrow; Mrs. Halston Darden. Interred: Pinewood Cemetery. AC 6/6/1905

MEADOWS, H. H. suicide Atlanta. Interred: Terre Haute, Ind. Wife, one child. AG 11/24/1910

MEADOWS, Mose, colored, age 70, d. 29 Tyler St. Atlanta. AG 3/22/1909

MEDLEY, Myrtice, Mrs., age 44, d. 767 Ashby St. Atlanta, Fri. Interred: Casey's Cemetery. AG 6/5/1909

MEDLIN, P. M. T., age 68, pioneer res. Atlanta, d. 107 Simpson St. Mon. Wife, one dau: Mrs. E. E. Butler, Chattanooga, Tenn. Sons: C. R. and J. T. Medlin, Atlanta. Interred: Smyrna, Ga. G 6/8/1909

MEDLIN, W. H., age 64, d. Atlanta Thurs. Interred: Smyrna, Ga. AG 10/22/1909

MEDLOCK, Riley O., age 48, d. Empire Bld. Atlanta. AG 6/26/1908

MEEKINS, Vinie, colored, age 58, d. 29 Lee Ave. Atlanta. AG 7/23/1909

MEERS, Annie A., inf. dau. of Mr. and Mrs. L. D., d. McDonough Rd. Atlanta, Mon. Interred: Clinton Church yard. AG 4/14/1908

MEGRITIS, Pasalois, age 60, d. 142 Auburn Ave., Atlanta. AG 4/14/1908

MELCHER, Lillie B., Mrs., age 52, d. Marlborough Apts. Atlanta. Husband: R. B. Dau: Miss Reina Melcher. Interred: Louisville, Ky. AG 8/17/1908

MELDAU, John, son of Mr. and Mrs. F. F., d. 12/25, 62 W. McDonald St., Atlanta. Interred: Westview. AC 12/27/1905

MELL, John L., Jr., age 21, d. Atlanta Sat. 456 Capitol Ave. Interred: Oakland. AG 6/15/1908

MELSON, Ella, Mrs., age 60, wife of B. F., d. 33 Crew St., Atlanta, Thurs. Interred: Newnan, Ga. Husband, one dau, Miss Ida Melson, survive. AG 9/19/1908

MELVIN, L. J., Mrs., age 64, d. Egan Park, E. Point, Ga. Wed. Interred: Crest Hill. One dau: Mrs. Georgia Reid, survives. AG 11/3/1908

MENASSEH, Samuel d. Grady Hospital, Atlanta, Fri. Res. 84 Kelly St. Interred: Oakland. AG 12/21/1908

MENGER, Mattie E., Mrs., wife of John M., d. Chattanooga, Tenn. Mon. Sons: J. C., Montgomery, Ala.; William R., Lenir City; Dan C., Chattanooga. Daus: Mrs. L. D. Perry, Misses Anna, Jennie and Lida. AG 12/23/1909

MERCER, Homer, colored, age 2 mos., d. 53 Ezzard St. Atlanta. AG 2/15/1909

MERCHANT, Fannie, Mrs., age 28, former res. of Atlanta, d. Oklahoma City last Wed. Interred: Atlanta, Oakland Cemetery. AG 12/7/1910

MERIWETHER, Sarah C., Mrs., age 68, d. Sun. home of son-in-law, S. C. Pelot, 18 Dunlap St. Atlanta. Interred: Monticello, Ga. AG 4/30/1906

MERRILL, S. M., Dr., ex-chaplain of US Army, d. Jasper, Ga. 6/26. Interred; Marietta, Ga. AG 6/26/1908

MERRITT, Alwyne, age 15, d. 88 Wells St. Atlanta. AG 1/25/1910

MERRITT, Lula, age 38, d. 235 Capitol Ave. Atlanta. AG 2/14/1910

MERRITT, N. A., Mrs., age 67, d. 12/21 Macon, Ga. res. of dau., Mrs. T. W. Johnson. Son: George A., New York. AG 12/17/1910

MERRITT, Ralph T., age 2, son of Mr. and Mrs. W. P., 30 S. Delta St., Atlanta, d. Sat. Interred: Chestnut Mtn, Ga. AG 4/2/1910

MERRITT, Roger, negro, charged with attacking young girl, to be hanged 6/3, Fulton Co. AG 4/19/1910

MERTIN, Alice, infant, d. 380 Windsor St. Atlanta. AG 6/11/1910

METHELE, Annie, colored, age 35, d. 26 Capitol Ave. Atlanta. AG 5/4/1909

METHVIN, Lillian, Mrs., age 31, d. Atlanta Sun. Interred: Lindale, Ga. AG 12/5/1910

METZGER, Eugene, age 36, d. Chattanooga, Tenn. AG 9/21/1910

MEW, Larence, Jr., age 1 mo., d. Sat. Atlanta. Res. of 165 Bellwood Ave. Atlanta. Interred: Westview. AG 9/24/1910

MEWBORN, W. E., Mrs., age 61, d. Atlanta. AG 2/8/1909

MEWBOURNE, S. M. d. Bowman, Ga. 10/26. Large family survives. AG 10/27/1908

MEYERS, Mary Ella, age 26, d. 22 12th St. Atlanta. AG 5/11/1910

MICHAEL, J. C., age 38, d. 135 Curran St., Atlanta, Thurs. Wife: Mattie. Sis., res. Conyers, Ga. AG 4/22/1909

MICHALL, Ben of Macon d. Fri. 367 Walnut St. AG 5/9/1908

MIDDLEBROOKS, Perry, Mrs. of Madison, Ga. d. Thurs., dau. of late Albert Foster and niece of Judge Fred Foster. Mother: Mrs. Louise Tunnell. Bro: J. H. Foster, Madison, Ga. Interred: Madison, Ga. AG 9/22/1910

MIDDLETON, Caroline, Miss, age 16, d. E. Lake, Atlanta, Fri. Interred: Charleston, S. C., beside her mother. AG 8/12/1909

MIDDLETON, D. S., Mrs. d. 6/27 Rising Fawn, Ga. Leaves dau., age 12. AG 6/28/1910

MILAM, I. V., age 48, d. Atlanta. AG 6/11/1910

MILAM, J. F., age 23, d. 23 Haywood Ave. Atlanta Sun. Wife, one child. Sis: Mrs. T. V. Adamson. Bros: W. J. and C. D. Milam. Interred: Morrow, Ga. AG 4/18/1910

MILAM, Wiley, Sr., old citizen of Henry Co., age 86,, d. res. of son. Wife died yrs. ago. Sons: William W., Stockbridge; Wesley; James of Henry Co. Dau: Mrs. Jack Harwell, Atlanta. Interred: Concord Cemetery. AG 10/18/190

MILES, J. G. d. 12/27, 27 Oliver St. Atlanta. Interred: Casey´s Cemetery. AC 12/28/1905

MILES, L. O., age 75, d. Atlanta. AG 2/15/1910

MILL, Eugene Van, age 10 mos., son (another reference says this is a dau., Eugenia) of Mr. and Mrs. P. C., d. Fri. 46 Kelly St. Atlanta. Interred: Westview. AG 9/23/1910

MILLER, Belle, colored, age 18, d. 183 Clarke St. Atlanta. AG 5/11/1908

MILLER, Charles . d. in Paris 12/8, a cousin of Mrs. Logan Williamson and Mrs. Hugh M. Willet of Atlanta. Wife was before marriage, Miss Alice Porter of Ga. AG 12/10/1908

MILLER, George, age 21, d. 310 State St. Atlanta, Wed. Wife, mother, several bros. Interred: Holly Springs, Ga. AG 9/3/1908

MILLER, Hayward, colored, age 18, d. Atlanta. AG 11/1/1910

MILLER, Henry, inf. son of Mr. and Mrs. P. W., d. 114 Capitol Ave., Atlanta, Wed. AG 6/16/1910

MILLER, Henry L., infant, d. 196 Capitol Ave. Atlanta. AG 6/16/1910

MILLER, J. W., age 40, d. 187 Chapel St., Atlanta. Interred: Douglasville, Ga. AG 5/10/1906

MILLER, Jack, Mrs. d. Hawkinsville, Ga. 2/11. AC 2/14/1905

MILLER, James d. Tues., buried 1/19 Charleston, S. C., oldest member of police force. AG 1/20/1910

MILLER, James A., keeper of Columbus stockade, d. Columbus 7/2. AG 7/4/1908

MILLER, Joseph F., formerly of Columbus, Ga., but past 20 yrs. inmate of state sanitarium, d. 9/15. Interred: Columbus, Ga. AG 9/16/1909

MILLER, Lizzie, Mrs., age 26, d. Atlanta Wed., wife of W. T. Two children. Interred: Westview. AG 4/7/1910

MILLER, Luther, inf. son of Mr. and Mrs. L. E. N., d. Chattahoochee, Ga. Tues. Interred: Masons Cemetery, Atlanta. AG 7/7/1909

MILLER, Marjorie, Miss, the New Orleans young woman who was drowned 8/29 in river at Tallulah Falls, Ga., funeral Tues. Father: Rev. Walter Miller. Sis: Edith Miller. AG 9/28/1910

MILLER, Mark Olive, age 23, d. Grady Hospital Atlanta Wed. AG 6/17/1908

MILLER, Mary Edna, Mrs., age 69, d. dau.'s res., Mrs. R. D. Beattie, 150 Courtland St., Atlanta, Fri. Bros: John N., W. J. and Dr. James N. Flowers. Sis: Mrs. S. B. Braswell. Nephew: Dr. A. P. Flowers. Interred: Chamblee, Ga. AG 3/26/1909

MILLER, Mattie J., Mrs., age 20, d. 48 W. Alexander St., Atlanta, Sat. Interred: Hollywood. Husband: G. W. Parents: Mr. and Mrs. Joseph Brown, Rome, Ga. AG 10/3/1908

MILLER, Mattie S., Mrs., wife of Frank, d. Mon. Huntsville, Ala., age 28. Three small children. AG 2/2/1910

MILLER, Ollie May, Miss, dau. of Mrs. Mary S., d. Atlanta. Sis: Mrs. Lamar Griggs. AG 8/15/1910

MILLER, Peter, age 66, ex-Confederate soldier, d. 5/17. AG 5/18/1906

MILLER, Preston, Mrs. funeral Sun. Interred: Oakland. AG 5/21/1906

MILLER, Ranzy, age 25, d. Atlanta Sun. 15 Rankin St. Wife, 3 children, 2 bros, mother, survive. AG 10/25/1909

MILLER, Rosa, colored, age 26, d. 4 Belabridge St. Atlanta, 10/3. AG 10/5/1910

MILLER, Saluda, Miss, age 38, d. Denver, Colo. AG 3/22/1909

MILLER, W. H., Mrs. of Terrell Co., Ga. d. Dawson, Ga. Interred: New Bethel Cemetery. AG 3/27/1909

MILLER, Wallace d. Columbia, S. C. Sis: Mrs. J. Brown, Hawkinsville. Bro: Norman P. Miller, Hawkinsville. Interred: Augusta, Ga. AG 1/31/1910

MILLIGAN, Harricott W., age 6, d. 1 High St. Atlanta. AG 7/14/1908

MILLIGAN, Mary L., Mrs., wife of J. C., d. 147 South Ave., Atlanta, Fri. Interred: Westview. AG 4/10/1909

MILLING, Edward, age 45, d. 101 Butler St. Atlanta. AG 10/7/1909

MILLING, Nellie d. Fri. Atlanta. Interred: Fairburn, Ga. AG 4/18/1910

MILLING, Nellie, age 10, d. Atlanta. AG 4/19/1910

MILLS, Gladys, age 9 mos., son of Mr. and Mrs. W. H., d. Mon. Atlanta. Interred: Westview. AG 5/3/1910

MILLS, Oma, inf. son of Mr. and Mrs. W. S., d. 68 Jefferson St. Atlanta. Interred: Casey's Cemetery. AG 9/27/1909

MILLWOOD, Harry, inf. son of Mrs. Mattie, d. Howell St., Atlanta, Sun. Interred: Caseys Cemetery. AG 6/21/1909

MILLWOOD, Janie P., Mrs., age 28, d. 12 Josephine St. Atlanta. AG 1/20/1910

MILNER, Amanda J., Mrs., age 63, d. 644 Washington St. Atlanta. AG 3/18/1909

MILNER, Robert F., age 59, postmaster at Newnan, d. 12/20. Wife. 5 ch. Son of late Jonathan Milner. AC 12/21/1905

MILNER, W. R., formerly of Atlanta, d. Shannon, Ga., near Rome, Thurs. Wife, 2 ch. Sis: Mrs. W. B. Cone, Mrs. Emma Moseley of Atlanta. Bros: J. S. Milner of Stillmore, and T. P. Milner of Texas. Interred: Westview. AG 4/23/1910

MILTON, Annie, Mrs., age 62, d. dau's res., Mrs. R. J. Holt, Masons Ave., Edgewood, Ga., Wed. Dau, and one son, Charles A. Milton. Interred: Oakland. AG 10/1/1908

MILTON, Charles, age 27, d. 129 Courtland St. Atlanta. AG 5/18/1908

MILTON, R. M., age 29, d. Atlanta. AG 7/29/1908

MIMS, Chlorinda, Mrs., age 90, d. res. of son, M. A. Mims, near E. Point, Ga., Mon. Sons: M. A., J. S., W. H. H., H. J. and J. P. Daus: Mrs. S. R. Oliver, Mrs. M. C. Godby. Interred: Red Oak Church yard. AG 7/14/1908

MIMS, Willie, colored, age 2, d. 3 Johnson's Row. Atlanta. AG 7/6/1909

MINER, J. M., age 60, d. 166 Juniper St. Atlanta. Daus: Mrs. W. L. Curry, Hawkinsville; Mrs. E. Smith, Dublin. Bros: C. O. and W. R. Thigpen, Sandersville, J. L. Thigpen, Bainbridge, T. J. Thigpen, Davisboro. Interred: Oakland. AG 9/5/1908

MINOR, D. C., Jr., inf. son of Mr. and Mrs. D. C., of Edgewood, Atlanta, d. Wed. Interred: Stone Mountain, Ga. AG 7/29/1909

MINOR, M. L., Sr., age 76, d. E. Atlanta. AG 12/16/1909

MINOR, Sarah, Mrs. d. Fri. E. Atlanta. AG 5/2/1910

MINTOR, Mary, colored, age 51, d. 101 N. Butler St. Atlanta. AG 9/29/1909

MINTZ, Thomas B., age 7 mos., d. 491 S. Pryor St. Atlanta. AG 9/6/1910

MITCHAM, W. D., age 42, d. Atlanta Mon. Interred: Westview. Bros: J. S., C. B., G. A. Sisters: Mrs. Anna Hardin, Mrs. O. N. Rauschenberg, Mrs. C. L. Peacock. Interred: Westview. AG 10/7/1908

MITCHEL, Deborah Sue, Miss, age 29, d. 343 N. Boulevard. Atlanta. AG 9/12/1908

MITCHELL, Albert V., age 25, d. 182 Hunnicutt St. Atlanta. AG 4/21/1910

MITCHELL, Albert V., age 25, d. 182 Hunnicutt St., Atlanta, Tues. Wife. Mother: Mrs. J. T. Mitchell. Interred: Auburn, Ga. AG 4/20/1910

MITCHELL, Anna L., colored, age 2, d. 7 Dora St. Atlanta. AG 10/8/1909

MITCHELL, Charles, colored, age 35, d. 101 N. Butler St. Atlanta. AG 4/22/1909

MITCHELL, Frank, colored, a ge 25, d. 121 Reid St. Atlanta. AG 5/8/1908

MITCHELL, Horace, son of Mr. and Mrs. W. T., d. 12/24, 318 Whitehall St. Atlanta. Interred: Oakland. AC 12/27/1905

MITCHELL, Ida, Mrs., wife of F. G., d. Tues. 1055 Walnut St., Macon. Interred: Newbern, N. C., former residence. AG 11/17/1910

MITCHELL, J. J., age 25, d. Fri. Interred: Cross Roads church yard, Atlanta. AG 6/29/1908

MITCHELL, J. W., inf. son of Mr. and Mrs. J. J., 25 Pope St., Atlanta, d. Sat. Interred: Stockbridge, Ga. AG 5/9/1910

MITCHELL, James A. d. Cincinnati, Ohio, prominent lawyer of Bowling Green, Ky, where buried. Wife and son, Samuel, survive. AG 5/29/1906

MITCHELL, John, colored, age 1 day, d. 262 Fraser St. Atlanta. AG 11/19/1909

MITCHELL, L. A., age 78, d. Sun. dau.'s res., Mrs. J. B. Stanley, 109 Bryan St. Atlanta. Daus: Mrs. Stanley; Mrs. E. L. Sisk. Interred: Conyers, Ga. AG 3/21/1910

MITCHELL, Lizzie, age 25, colored, d. 260 Fraser St. Atlanta. AG 11/27/1910

MITCHELL, Lizzie, colored, age 29, d. 101 N. Butler St. Atlanta. AG 5/1/1908

MITCHELL, Lu R., Miss, age 53, of Eastman, Ga., d. Atlanta, Wed. Interred: Eastman, Ga. AG 3/24/1910

MITCHELL, Mamie, Mrs., age 49, d. Atlanta. AG 4/18/1910

MITCHELL, Nannie, Mrs., age 49, d. Atlanta Sun., wife of T. W. Nieces: Misses Lillie and Margarete Norman. Interred: Marietta, Ga. AG 4/18/1910

MITCHELL, Robert, colored, age 25, d. 11 Lowe St., Atlanta. AG 5/8/1906

MITCHELL, Ruby, Miss, age 18, d. Atlanta Wed. Relatives in Huntsville, Ala. AG 6/101/1909

MITCHELL, Hiram Carl, age 3, son of Mr. and Mrs. J. T., d. 9 Guyton St., Atlanta, Fri. Interred: Collins Springs Church. AG 5/9/1908

MITCHELL, Irene Caroline, Miss d. 343 N. Boulevard, Atlanta, Wed. Interred: Oakland. Mother: Mrs. Russell C. Mitchell. Bros: Eugene M., Gordon F., Robert M., Russell C., Jr. Sis: Mrs. W. M. Timmons; Jessie, Clara, Lillian. AG 10/23/1908

MITCHELL, Lizzie, age 25, colored, d. 260 Fraser St. Atlanta. AG 11/27/1910

MITCHELL, Ora Sue, fun. 9/13 343 N. Blvd. Atlanta. Bur: Oakland. Kin: Mrs. Russell C. and Eugene M. Mitchell, Willis M. Timmons, Robert M., Jessie, Irene, Clara, Gordon F. & Russell C. Mitchell, Jr., Arthur Neal Robinson. AG 9/11/1908

MITCHELL, Russell C., 67, b. Madison Co. Conf Vet d. 1/19 Atlanta, 343 Blvd. Ch-Eugene, Gordon, Robert, Russell, Jr., Miss Jessie, Ona Sue, Aline, Irene, Clara, Killian. Bro-L. B. Sis-Mrs. Frank Rice. Sson-Arthur Neal Robinson. AC 1/17/1905

MIXON, Ida, colored, age 40, d. 101 N. Butler St. Atlanta. Ag 3/18/1909

MIXON, Lizzie, dau. of Mr. and Mrs. B. F., d. Sun. Eatonton, Ga. Interred: Ft. Hill Cemetery. AG 9/29/1908

MOBBS, Milton, inf. son of Mr. and Mrs. C. E., d. 83 Stewart Ave. Atlanta. Sun. AG 1/3/1910

MOBLES, Milton, age 11 mos., d. 83 Stewart Ave. Atlanta. AG 1/3/1910

MOBLEY, Clinton of Burke Co. near Waynesboro, Ga. murdered. Mose Reed charged. AC 5/16/1905

MOBLEY, Dorothy Elizabeth, age 1 yr., dau. of Mr. and Mrs. Stuart Mobley, d. 5/3, 46 Culberson St., Atlanta. AG 5/4/1906

MOBLEY, Emma, Mrs., age 37, wife of L. D., d. 772 E. Fair St., Atlanta, Mon. Interred: Newnan. AG 9/22/1908

MOBLEY, Ethel, Mrs., dau. of James Davis of Atlanta, d. Jan. 6 Muscogee Co., her home. AC 1/8/1905

MOBLEY, Stacy, Mrs., age 25, d. E. Point, Ga. AG 3/8/1909

MOCK, J. L. came to Atlanta 4 mos. ago from Newark, N. J., suicide, 345 Myrtle St. AG 12/22/1909

MOCK, John R., age 40, d. 28 E. Alexander St. Atlanta. AG 5/20/1909

MOFFET, infant son of Mr. and Mrs. F. E., d. 223 Capitol Ave., Atlanta, Sun. Interred: Marietta, Ga. AG 6/27/1910

MOFFETT, Sadie J., Mrs., age 27, d. Ingleside, Ga. Sat. Interred: Marietta, Ga. AG 6/20/1910

MOFFITT, Amanda, colored, age 34, d. 87 Fort St. Atlanta. AG 11/22/1909

MOLAND, Emma, colored, age 33, d. 101 N. Butler St. Atlanta. AG 9/1/1908

MONAGHAM, John B. tribute Atlanta Wed., who d. Tues. Interred: Westview. AG 8/17/1910

MONNISH, Rosa F., Mrs. Dr. suicide Tues. Atlanta. Interred: Westview. AG 4/22/1909

MONROE, Laura L., Mrs., of 73 Foundry St.,tlanta, d. Tues. Interred: Marietta, Ga. Husband, two small children, parents, several bros. and sisters. AG 10/27/1909

MONROE, Nellie, colored, age 21, d. 143 Currier St. Alanta. AG 12/16/1908

MONTAG, Robert, age 8, son of Mr. and Mrs. Sigmund, d. Tues. 430 S. Pryor St., Atlanta. Interred: Oakland. AG 5/ /1910

MONTAGUE, Charles W., age 50, d. 220 S. Boulevard. Atlanta. AG 9/2/1909

MONTGOMERY, L. D., Jr., inf. son of Mr. and Mrs. L. D., of 67 Love St., Atlanta. Funeral Sun. Interred: Westview. AG 6/4/1906

MONTGOMERY, Mattie B., Mrs., age 42, of Greensboro, Ga., d. Atlanta Mon. Mother, three bros. Interred: Greensboro, Ga. AG 6/22/1908

MONTGOMERY, R. O., Dr., res. of St. Joice, S. C., d. Wed, age 55. A 4/7/1909

MONTGOMERY, T. F., colored, age 34, d. 192 Summit Ave. Atlanta. AG 10/1/1909

MONTIETH, Susie, Miss d. Tues. Sis: Mrs. George T. Latimer, 315 N. Jackson St., Atlanta. Interred: Oakland. AG 4/9/1908

MONTIETH, Emma N., age 51, d. 5/7 571 S. Pryor St. Atlanta, wife of R. A. Sons: Eugene, Robert S., Wharton H., Paul L. Daus: Mrs. G. F. Prince, Mrs. Louie Cabell. Bros: Ed. B. Douglas, Miami; Raford Douglas, Washington Terr. AG 5/8/1906

MOODIE, R. B., father of Mrs. David W. Yarborough of Atlanta, d. Dayton, Ohio. AG 9/28/1909

MOODY, Della, colored, age 27, d. 3 Box St., Atlanta. AG 5/24/1906

MOODY, George W. found dead Wellborn St., Atlanta, Fri. Interred: Red Oak, Ga. AG 11/27/1910

MOODY, James d. Tunnel Hill, Ga. Tues, age 25, son of J. A. Moody. AG 12/9/1910

MOODY, John T., infant of Mr. and Mrs. Edward M., d. Sat. Atlanta. Interred: Mason's churchyard. AG 6/4/1910

MOODY, W. R., Major, age 67, d. 138 East Ave. Atlanta. AG 5/12/1909

MOON, Lee, colored, age 26, d. 38-A Mozeley St. Atlanta. AG 7/14/1908

MOON, Roberta, colored, age 27, d. 7 Cravens alley. Atlanta. AG 8/5/1908

MOON, Walter Z., son of former Capt. Z. B. of Atlanta, d. 242 Formwalt St., Atlanta, Fri. Interred: Tifton, Ga. Wife, two children survive. AG 12/26/1908

MOORE, Amos C., age 76, d. Old Soldiers' Home. Atlanta. AG 8/20/1908

MOORE, Annie, age 5 mos., dau. of Mrs. Emma, d. Wed. Atlanta. Interred: Westview. AG 12/9/1909

MOORE, Annye, Miss d. Sat. Atlanta. Interred: Antioch church yard. AG 5/26/1906

MOORE, Charles, colored, age 23, d. 178 1/2 Decatur St. Atlanta. AG 11/22/1909

MOORE, Clara, Mrs., age 67, d. Milledgeville, Ga. AG 12/3/1908

MOORE, dau., age 8 mos. of Mr. and Mrs. J. M., d. Angier Ave., Atlanta, Fri. Grandparents: Mr. and Mrs. Mims. AG 7/4/1908

MOORE, Dock, colored, age 85, d. 61 Leonard St. Atlanta. AG 11/27/1909

MOORE, E., Mrs. d. Mon. 548 Washington St., Atlanta. Interred: Oakland. Husband: E. S. Sis: Mrs. Nettie Smith of Punta Gorda, Fla. AG 12/13/1910

MOORE, Edy, negro, killed by Bob Golatt. He is to hang 4/17. Appling, Ga. AG 3/26/1908

MOORE, Estel, age 14, d. 188 Haynes St. Atlanta. AG 5/4/1909

MOORE, Evelyn, age 3, dau. of Mr. and Mrs. E. A., d. Atlanta Thurs. Interred: Westview. AG 11/3/1908

MOORE, George, colored, age 49, d. 44 Lyons Ave. Atlanta. AG 3/29/1909

MOORE, George, age 68, Conf. Vet., 1st S. C. Regt., father of Atlanta attys, Charles J. and Jesse L., d. Olive Springs, Ga. (Marietta) Tues. Interred: Olive Springs, family grounds. Wife: Mrs. Nancy. Dau: Miss Fannie Moore. AG 7/22/1909

MOORE, Gertrude Marcia, age 8 mos., dau. of Mr. and Mrs. J. M., d. 159 Whitehall St., Atlanta, Sat. Interred: Oakland. AG 7/6/1908

MOORE, Harriet, inf. dau. of Mr. and Mrs. Berrien Moore, interred Westview. AG 10/21/1910

MOORE, Herschel, age 17 mos., son of Mr. and Mrs. H. B., d. Wed. 13 Berean St. Atlanta. Interred: Hollywood. AG 8/25/1910

MOORE, Hulda, colored, age 50, d. 71 Inman Ave. Atlanta. AG 9/21/1910

MOORE, Isaac D., Dr. d. White Plains, Ga. Thurs, age 82, Civil War Surgeon. Daus: Mrs. R. J. Reid, Toccoa; Mrs. George W. Tappan, White Plains; Mrs. Paul Brown, Sandersville; Mrs. Charles Hardy, Washington; Mrs. Ophelia and Miss Mattie Moore, White Plains. Sons: John Sidney, Thomas C., Robert. AG 6/22/1910

MOORE, J. Comer d. Athens. AG 9/13/1908

MOORE, John, colored, age 23, d. 328 Simpson St. Atlanta. AG 8/19/1908

MOORE, John B., age 63, d. 1/4 Macon, res. of dau., Mrs. C. L. Rogers, Morgan Ave. 5 daus. survive. AG 1/5/1910

MOORE, John S. shot by wife in self-defense, killed. AG 12/27/1907

MOORE, John W., formerly of Atlanta, d. Plant City, Fla. Tues. Interred: Oakland, Atlanta. AG 5/21/1908

MOORE, Lena, Miss, age 21, d. 21 Evans Dr., Ft. McPherson, Ga., d. Sun., dau. of R. D. AG 7/11/1910

MOORE, Marie Arline, Miss, pupil at Calhoun St. School, age 14, d. Atlanta. AC 2/12/1905

MOORE, Mattie, Mrs. d. Summerville, Ala. 2 bros., 4 sisters. AC 3/25/1905

MOORE, Maude, Mrs., age 19, of 116 Courtland St., Atlanta, d. Mon. Husband, parents, two sisters, two brothers. Interred: Loganville, Ga. AG 7/20/1909

MOORE, Patience, colored, age 54, d. Wiley St. Atlanta. AG 12/11/1908

MOORE, Raymoth Holcombe, age 6 mos., dau. of Mr. and Mrs. R. B. of Asheville, N. C., d. res. of grandparents, Dr. and Mrs. T. R. Whitley, Douglasville, 6/4. AG 6/5/1909

MOORE, William d. Athens Fri. Interred: Bowman, Ga. Wife, 3 children, father, mother, bro., 2 sisters, Mrs. Iduma Bray of Arnoldsville and Mrs. Willis Vaughan of Elberton. AG 1/31/1910

MOORE, William R., millionaire merchant, buried Memphis, Tenn. AG 6/14/1909

MOORE, Willie Lee killed by train, res. of 22 Whitehall Terrace, Atlanta. Interred: Antioch. AC 11/30/1905

MOREL, Reid, age 10, son of Hon. J. J., Mayor of Sylvania, drowned in creek 7/19. AC 7/21/1905

MORELAND, A. F., Major, age 80, d. 28 Moreland St. Atlanta. Interred: Westview. AG 9/2/1909

MORELAND, Ross A., Mrs. funeral, age 69 of Osceoda Co., Fla. Fri. Interred: Orlando Cemetery. Dau: Mrs. W. B. Summerall, Atlanta. Sis: Mrs. Mary Davis, Orlando, Fla. AG 3/1/1910

MORGAN, Brooks, Mrs. d. 8/30 res. of parents, Mr. and Mrs. Frank E. Block, 550 Peachtree St. Atlanta. AC 9/3/1905

MORGAN, Docia Belle, Mrs., age 21, d. Brown Hill Rd., Atlanta, Wed. Interred: Antioch Church. Husband, two small children, parents, 5 bros, 3 sisters. AG 10/15/1908

MORGAN, G. J., Mrs., age 69, d. Sat. Sandy Springs, Ga. Interred: Cross Roads Church yard. AG 3/21/1910

MORGAN, George Elbert, age 4, son of Cleo, d. 108 West Ave. Atlanta. Interred: Hollywood. AG 12/12/1910

MORGAN, J. B., Mrs., mother-in-law of Charles T. Hopkins, d. 403 N. Boulevard, Atlanta. Interred: Decatur Cemetery. AG 5/31/1910

MORGAN, John, colored, age 40, d. 367 Chapel St. Atlanta. AG 4/28/1908

MORGAN, M. J., Mrs., age 80, of LaGrange, d. 3/29. Son: Dave, Atlanta. Grch: E. E. Dallas, Atlanta. AC 3/30/1905

MORGAN, Minnie, Miss, age 22, d. Atlanta Wed. Parents: Mr. and Mrs. John T. Morgan of 491 Piedmont Ave., Atlanta. Two bros., three sisters. AG 7/29/1908

MORGAN, Nancy Hill, age 70, d. 402 N. Boulevard. Atlanta. AG 6/2/1910

MORGAN, Orphy, colored, age 29, d. Garnett St. Crossing. Atlanta. AG 9/4/1908

MORGAN, S. C., Mrs. d. 9/18 53 Beecher St. Atlanta. Husband, 3 children. Interred: Westview. AC 9/19/1905

MORGAN, infant of Burt and Sinthy, colored, d. 149 Howell St. Atlanta. AG 5/3/1906

MORGANSTERN, G., age 61, d. 98 E. Georgia Ave. Bur: Westview. Wife. Ch: Mrs. J. S. Morris, A. A. Morris, Mrs. Max Morris, Mrs. M. L. Shatzen, Mrs. J. C. Morris, Misses Sophie, Theresa and Tillie Morganstern, Edward Morganstern. AG 2/2/1910

MORING, A. E., Mrs., age 66, d. dau.'s res., Mrs. Walter E. Cason, 27 E. Harris, Atlanta. Daus: Mrs. C. F. Faires, Mrs. Ella Chisolm, Mrs. Walter E. Cason, Atlanta; Mrs. H. Clay Crawford, Tallahasse, Fla. Interred: Westview. AG 7/3/1908

MORLEY, George W., age 58, d. 9 Wellborn St. Atlanta. AG 11/27/1910

MORMAN, Ina, colored, age 52, d. 101 Butler St. Atlanta. AG 7/16/1909

MORRELL, J. A., age 57, d. Atlanta. Interred: Weford, Mich. AG
4/2/1910

MORRIS, A. S., fireman, of Macon, killed railroad accident. AG
6/12/1906

MORRIS, Amina funeral Atlanta Sun. Interred: Westview. AG
5/30/1910

MORRIS, C. W. (of C. S.), age 69, funeral 172 Old Wheat St.
Atlanta Fri. Interred: Oakland. Wife. Son: Dave. Daus: Mrs. Clara
Williams, Miss Addie Belle Morris. AG 3/4/1910

MORRIS, Charles A., Jr., inf. son of Mr. and Mrs. C. A., interred
Hollywood Cemetery, Atlanta. AG 3/26/1908

MORRIS, Clifford, age 4, son of Mr. and Mrs. C. W., d. Mason and
Turner Rd., Atlanta, Wed. Interred: Harmony Church yard. AG
11/3/1908

MORRIS, Corinne colored, age 2, d. 27 Johnson St. Atlanta. AG
12/14/1908

MORRIS, Dillie, Miss, age 68, d. 28 Berrien Ave. Atlanta. AG
8/19/1908

MORRIS, E. H. d. 9/29 Phenix City, Ala. AC 10/1/1905

MORRIS, E. J. d. San Bernardino, Calif. interred Atlanta. AG
12/26/1908

MORRIS, Eugene, colored, age 26, d. 198 E. Cain St. Atlanta. AG
4/7/1908

MORRIS, J. Emory, age 58, d. 418 Luckie St. Atlanta Sun. Wife, 4
children. Interred: Emerson, Ga. AG 5/30/1910

MORRIS, J. H., Mrs., age 29, d. 165 Stewart Ave., Atlanta, Sat.
Interred: Decatur, Ga. AG 7/6/1908

MORRIS, J. M., Mrs., age 60, d. Tues. Atlanta. Daus: Mrs. H. C.
Nowell, Atlanta; Mrs. J. E. Haws, Griffin. Interred: Griffin, Ga.
AG 5/4/1910

MORRIS, James Allen, Mrs., wife of J. A., d. Mon. 17 Kimball St.
Atlanta. Interred: Oakland. Husband, 3 children. AG 5/6/1908

MORRIS, Janie, Mrs., age 31, d. Thurs., 8 Cab Ave., Atlanta.
Interred: Casey's Cemetery. AG 6/10/1910

MORRIS, John, colored, age 16, d. Alms House, Atlanta. AG
8/30/1910

MORRIS, John A., age 65, d. 205 S. Forsyth St. Atlanta. AG
11/1/1909

MORRIS, L. G., age 84, d. 48 Woodward Ave., Atlanta, Sun.
Interred: Oakland. Ch: Miss Mary Morris, Mrs. A. M. Allen, Mrs.
J. R. Holcombe, J. F. and C. H. Morris. AG 10/3/1908

MORRIS, Lelia P., Mrs., age 60, d. 131 S. Pryor St. Atlanta. AG
5/6/1908

MORRIS, Leroy G., age 84, d. 48 Woodward Ave. Atlanta. AG
10/5/1908

MORRIS, Lizzie, Miss, age 59, d. 15 Currier St. Atlanta, Wed.
Interred: Marietta, Ga. AG 5/6/1908

MORRIS, Mattie, Mrs. d. Fri. Chattahoochee Ave., E. Point, Ga. 4
sons, 2 daus. Interred: Bowden, Ga. AG 6/17/1908

MORRIS, Milton, age 1, son of Mr. and Mrs. J. O., d. Buckhead,
Ga., Sat. Interred: Sardis church yard. AG 11/28/1908

MORRIS, O. T., Hon. d. 10/5 Dallas, Ga. Wife, 7 ch. Bros:
William, Texas; Melton, Okla. AC 10/7/1905

MORRIS, R. W. d. 11/20 Macon. He was from Mesina, where buried.
AC 11/20/1905

MORRIS, Victoria, Mrs., age 60, d. 544 Pulliam St., Atlanta, Fri. Interred: Cedar Grove church yard. Two sons, two daus., three sisters, survive. AG 12/11/1909

MORRIS, W. O., age 58, d. 28 Center St., Atlanta, Fri. Interred: Sardis. AG 7/27/1908

MORRIS, William Absalom d. res. of sister, Mrs. Kate Livingston, Fri., Rex, Ga. Sis: Mrs. Livingston, Mrs. Brannan, Mrs. Hinton. Bro: Richard Morris, of Norcross. Interred: Burke Cemetery, Stockbridge, Ga. AG 5/30/1910

MORRIS, William J., age 65, d. Marietta and Bartow Sts. Atlanta. AG 7/16/1908

MORRISON, Tom, age 53, d. 34 West Fair St. Atlanta. AG 1/11/1910

MORROW, Hampton, colored, age 57, d. 153 E. Harris St. Atlanta. AG 5/14/1908

MORROW, Jennie, Mrs. d. Fri. Bellevue, Ga. (near Macon), age 55, wife of W. C. AG 3/21/1908

MORSE, J. M. d. 9/12 Valdosta, Ga. Wife, several children. AC 9/14/1905

MORSE, Mildred, age 1, d. 64 E. Georgia Ave. Atlanta. AG 11/12/1910

MORSE, W. H., age 38, d. Tues. Atlanta. Wife survives. Interred: Abbeville, S. C. AG 4/21/1908

MORTON, Edward T. of Jones Co. d. his res. College St., Macon 6/18, age 76. Interred: Grays, Ga. AC 6/19/1905

MORTON, Harry, age 30, d. Atlanta Thurs., res. of Boston, Mass. AG 4/22/1909

MORTON, John, son of G. S., d. Young Harris, Ga. 7/16. Interred: Hebron, Banks Co. AC 7/18/1905

MORTON, Sammie, Miss d. Sun. Atlanta, native of Colquitt, Ga. Interred: Colquitt. AG 6/4/1906

MOSELEY, Ella, Mrs., age 38, d. Atlanta. AG 3/3/1910

MOSELEY, Emma, Mrs., age 44, d. 604 Woodward Ave., Atlanta 9/13. Interred: Hollywood Cemetery. AC 9/14/1905

MOSELEY, R. C., Mrs. of Comer, Ga., age 38, d. Atlanta Tues. Husband: Dr. R. C. Interred: Comer, Ga. AG 3/2/1910

MOSELY, Emma J., Mrs., age 67, d. Sun. 150 Love St., Atlanta. Son: J. R. Bros: John, Ernest and Theodore Minter. Sis: Mrs. W. B. Cone. Interred: Laurens, S. C. AG 8/22/1910

MOSELY, H. H. d. 8/23 Mansville, Ga., former res. of McDonough, Ga. Wife, several children. AC 8/25/1905

MOSLEY, Bertha Mae, colored, age 4, d. 278 Martin St. Atlanta. AG 6/21/1909

MOSS, Amanda J., Mrs., age 73, Marthaville (Atlanta) pioneer, d. Wed. Dau: Mrs. Lizzie Price. Grson: J. W. Price. Grdau: Mrs. Edna Price Billingsly. 5 sisters, 3 bros. AG 7/21/1910

MOSS, Jesse d. Flovilla, Ga. Sun., age 45, native of Butts Co. 3 daus., 2 sons. AG 2/16/1910

MOSS, Mary, colored, age 1 mo., d. 180 Randolph St., rear, Atlanta. AG 12/11/1908

MOSS, Mary, Mrs., age 62, d. nephew's res., Chester Cornwell, 111 Holderness St. Atlanta, Mon. Sis: Mrs. Lizzie Cornwell, Griffin, Ga. Bro: Late Thomas J. Harper. Interred: Covington, Ga. AG 5/31/1910

MOSS, Ralph, age 21, son of Dr. and Mrs. T. J. of Riverdale, Ga. d. Sun. Interred: Hollywood. AG 5/25/1908

MOSS, Vestle, age 11, d. Atlanta. AG 2/7/1910

MOTE, Mary C., age 76, d. Walnut St. 4/26. Interred: Hollywood. AG 4/27/1906

MOTEN, M. L., colored, age 3, d. 211 W. Mitchell St. Atlanta. AG 12/22/1908

MOTT, H. B., age 46, d. 310 Luckie St. Atlanta. AG 11/17/1910

MOTT, H. O., age 47, d. 310 Luckie St., Atlanta, Wed. Wife, 9 children, 4 sisters. Interred: Harrison, Ohio. AG 11/16/1910

MOYERS, Julia, Mrs., age 18, d. 92 Luckie St. Atlanta. AG 8/31/1908

MOZLEY, Ada, Mrs., age 57, widow. of Dr. Hiram, d. Sat. Atlanta. Dau: Mrs. Sanford W. Gay. Before marriage she was Miss Ada Berry of Greenville, S. C. Interred: Westview. AG 3/23/1908

MOZO, Dorsey, age 12 mos., son of Mr. and Mrs. W. B., d. Thomas St., St. George George 4/18. First person who died in St. George Colony. Interred: Colony Cemetery. They came from St. Marys, Ga. 3 weeks ago. AC 4/20/1905

MUELLER, Mary, Mrs., age 47, d. 87 Hubbard St., Atlanta, Sept. 30. Interred: Westview. AG 10/3/1910

MUELLER, Samuel F., age 79, d. 11/12, 105 Herbert St., Atlanta. Interred: Westview. AC 11/13/1905

MULCAHY, James, Mrs., age 35, d. Jackson, Ga., Thurs. Funeral: Atlanta. AG 4/28/1910

MULKEY, Jimmie, age 6, d. 98 Brighton St. Atlanta. AG 10/21/1908

MULKEY, Sarah A., Mrs., wife of J. A., age 59, d. 75 Almo Ave. Atlanta. 3 sons, 2 daus. Interred: Ellijay, Ga. AG 9/21/1908

MULLIGAN, Alice, Mrs., age 51, d. 107 Piedmont Ave., Atlanta. Sat. Daus: Mamie Mulligan, Mrs. Ceila Schwartz. Interred: New Haven, Conn. AG 2/19/1910

MULLIGAN, Harricott W., age 6 mos., dau. of Mr. and Mrs. William J., d. 1 High St., Atlanta, Sun. Interred: Westview. AG 7/13/1908

MULLIN, Madeline, age 1, d. 180 Kennedy St. Atlanta. AG 9/6/1910

MULLINS, James M., aged citizen, d. bro.'s res., L. F. Mullins, 10/26, Smiths Station, Ala. Age 74. AG 10/27/1909

MULLINS, M. T., Mrs., age 70, d. Griffin Thurs. 9 children. AG 12/18/1910

MUNSON, F. B., the Atlanta, Birmingham and Atlantic RR inspector, d. railroad accident. Wife. Interred: Rogersville, Tenn. AG 6/30/1909

MURCHANSON, D. H., deputy sheriff, Blakely, Ga., fatally shot Mon. by negro, John Fowler. Wife, 7 children. AG 3/3/1909

MURDAUGH, Mattie, colored, age 26, d. 92 W. Cain St. Atlanta. AG 5/12/1909

MURDEN, Maggie, colored age 10 days, d. 32 Fortune St., Atlanta. AG 12/10/1908

MURDOCK, Earle, age 12, son of Mr. and Mrs. J. A., d. 55 Howell St. Atlanta. AG 9/28/1910

MURDOCK, S. C., Miss, age 72, d. Thurs. White Mill Rd., Atlanta. Interred: Panthersville Presbyterian church yard. Sis: Mrs. C. Doby. AG 12/31/1909

MURNANE, Sarah Agnes, infant dau. of Mr. and Mrs. W. C. of 81 Emmett St., Atlanta, d. Wed. Interred: Westview. AG 10/28/1909

MURPH, J. J., Mrs., wife of J. J. of Marshallville, Ga. d. Fri. AG 6/20/1908

MURPHEY, John A., age 48, formerly of Atlanta, d. Jacksonville, Fla. Fri. Interred: Oakland. Wife. Son: Gregory. Bro: J. W. Murphy. AG 5/17/1909

MURPHEY, Richard J. d. Denver, Colo. 5/26. Funeral: Augusta, Ga. Wife, formerly Miss Maude McDaniel of Atlanta. AG 6/4/1908

MURPHY, Anna M., Mrs., age 48, d. 811 Lawston St. Atlanta, Oct. 2. AG 10/3/1910

MURPHY, Anna, Mrs., wife of J. L., d. 311 Lawton St. Atlanta, d. Sun. Ch: James, Richard, Clarence, Wiley, Lillian. Interred: Westview. AG 10/3/1910

MURPHY, Anthony, age 34, son of late Anthony Murphy, Sr., d. Mon. Atlanta. Mother, 3 sisters: Mrs. Charles E. Sciple, Mrs. Annie Tanner, Mrs. Boykin Robinson. Bros: R. E., John K., Charles C. Interred: Oakland. AG 2/28/1910

MURPHY, Florence Leona, inf. dau. of Mr. and Mrs. C. F., d. 30 Lynch St., Atlanta, Tues. Interred: Casey's Cemetery. AG 3/10/1908

MURPHY, Fred C., age 29, d. Sun. res. of parents in East Point, Ga. Interred: Mt. Zion. AG 6/20/1910

MURPHY, John burned to death in jail at Wadley, Ga. 12/26. AG 12/27/1909

MURPHY, Lizzie, colored, age 44, d. 101 N. Butler. Atlanta. AG 5/11/1908

MURPHY, Louise, Miss d. Fri. Atlanta. Mother in Oklahoma. AG 10/2/1909

MURPHY, Oliver drowned Yazoo Lake, Vicksburg, Miss. Wed. Ch: Miss Cleo Murphy, Mrs. Flowers, Mrs. Drenard (Fla.), Mrs. Carter. AG 5/31/1909

MURPHY, William Ulrick, inf. son of Mr. and Mrs. A. J., d. Atlanta, Sat. Interred: Augusta, Ga. AG 5/30/1910

MURPHY, Anthony, 80, Atlanta pioneer b. Ire. d. 12/28, Conf Vet. In 1862 chase of "Texas" after "General". Wife. Ch: Emmett, Jno K., Tony, Chas C., Mrs. G. H. Tanner, Mrs. Chas E. Sciple, Atlanta; Mrs. Boykin Robinson, NY. AG 12/29/1909

MURRAH, T. T. was shot and instantly killed yesterday. J. A. Hastey is charged. Chipley, Ga. AG 6/11/1906

MURRAY, C. T. d. Tues. Interred: Oakland. AG 10/12/1909

MURRAY, E. H., Mrs. d. 9/30 Ft. Valley, Ga. Husband, 3-yr. old dau. AC 10/2/1905

MURRAY, J. B. d. 10/17 Atlanta. Interred: Clayton, Ga. AC 10/19/1905

MURRAY, John, colored, age 22, d. Atlanta. AG 12/17/1910

MURRAY, Mamie, colored, age 10, d. 77 Leonard St. Atlanta. AG 4/12/1909

MURRAY, T. A., Mrs., age 72, d. E. Point, Ga. Sun. Husband, 3 sons, one dau. Interred: Oakland. AG 9/6/1909

MURROW, Mary, Mrs., age 73, d. 1320 Marietta St. Atlanta. Wed. 4 grandchildren. Interred: Oakland. AG 9/16/1909

MURRY, Charles Norman, inf. son of Mr. and Mrs. Robert, d. Capitol heights, Atlanta, Thurs. Interred: Stone Mtn, Ga. AG 5/19/1910

MURRY, Evelyn, Mrs., age 79, d. 3/24 707 8th St., Columbus, Ga. AC 3/26/1905

MURTREY, E. L., age 40, d. Roswell Rd., Atlanta, Mon. Wife, 7 children. Interred: Sandy Springs Church yard. AG 10/11/1910

MYERS, Herman, his LWT mentioned, former mayor of Savannah. Wife: Mrs. Virginia Myers. AG 4/3/1909

MYERS, Lewis, colored, age 60, d. 1 Hollins St., Atlanta, Nov. 15. AG 11/16/1910

MYERS, Luther A. d. Fri. Macon, Ga. Interred: Winston-Salem, N. C. Father, mother, two bros, all of N. C. AG 5/9/1908

MYERS, Thomas P., age 52, d. Atlanta Sun. Interred: Conyers, Ga. AG 1/31/1910

MYERS, W. W., pioneer to Bartow Co., d. 11/24 Cassville. Ch: Mrs. W. Pittard, Cassville; H. B. Myers, Gadsden, Ala. AC 11/25/1905

MYERS, Ella, wife of Wm, 35, d. 32 D'Alvigny St. Atlanta. Dau: Mrs. Delia House. 5 small ch. Sis: Mrs. S. Edgar, Mrs. Dora Edgar, Mrs. S. A. Robertson, Mrs. Nancy Mander, Callie Allen. Bros: Steve & Grover Allen. Interred: Mt. Harmony. AG 5/8/1910

NABORS, Lamar, age 24, d. 101 N. Butler St. Atlanta. Interred: Cornelia, Ga. AG 10/14/1907

NAILS, W. M., inf. dau. of., aged 3 weeks, d. 353 W. North Ave., Atlanta, Mon. Interred: Forest Park, Ga. AG 7/14/1908

NAILS, Walter Clyde, age 4 mos., infant son of Mr. and Mrs. W. M., d. Tues. 355 W. North Ave., Atlanta. Interred: Forest Park, Ga. AG 6/26/1907

NAIL, Mary Anna, Mrs., age 36, d. 15 Willow St. Atlanta. AG 1/11/1910

NANCE, James H., age 26, d. Thurs. at res. of mother, Mrs. M. J. Nance, in Oakland City, Atlanta. For 5-6 yrs. resided New York. Dau lives in N. Y. AG 2/14/1907

NANCE, William Chester, age 3, d. 160 Grant St. Atlanta. AG 10/7/1909

NANTZ, Selina, Mrs., wife of J. A., d. 209 N. Liberty St., Spartanburg, S. C., age 53. Several children. Interred: Oakwood. AG 9/28/1910

NASH, Alfonso, colored, age 84, d. 86 Jeptha St. Atlanta. AG 3/22/1909

NASH, Eugene, 2 days old, d. 53 Shelton St. Atlanta. AG 10/24/1906

NASH, Jennie G., Mrs., age 23, d. 718 Woodward Ave. Atlanta. AG 1/25/1910

NASH, Josie, Mrs., age 49, d. Main St. Atlanta. Several children. Interred: Peachtree Church. AG 6/3/1909

NASH, Lucie, Mrs., age 22, d. 139 Williams St. Atlanta, Thurs. Interred: Lilburn, Ga. AG 8/27/1908

NASH, M. L., Mrs., age 55, d. 955 Marietta St., Atlanta. AG 5/15/1907

NASH, Miles Ashton, infant son of Mr. and Mrs. J. M., Jr., d. Wed. 445 Luckie St. Atlanta. AG 6/14/1906

NASH, Wellborn, age 2 mos., d. Fri., son of Mr. and Mrs. W. A., res. near Connally, Ga. Interred: Noah's Ark. Cemetery, Clayton Co. AG 10/11/1907

NASH, William Allen, 18 mos. inf. of Mr. and Mrs. N. R., d. 11/18 47 E. 12th St., Atlanta. Mother also died. Interred: Dunwoody, Ga. AC 11/19/1905

NATHAN, Edward, age 16 mos., son of Morris Nathan, d. 142 Peachtree St., Atlanta, Wed. AG 5/19/1909

NATIONS, William LeRoy, age 3 mos., son of Mr. and Mrs. J. M., d. Campbellton Rd., Atlanta, Thurs. Bur: New Hope Cem. AG 5/6/1909

NAZARRNUS, George B., age 60, d. Wesley Memorial hospital. Atlanta. AG 1/31/1907

NEAL, C. O., age 73, d. 12 Clark St. Atlanta. AG 3/14/1910

NEAL, Clinton, age 4 mos., d. 65 Johnson Ave. Atlanta. AG 7/6/1909

NEAL, Georgia, Mrs. of Mitchell, Ga., wife of William, co. surveyor of Warren Co., age 60, d. yesterday. AG 10/11/1907

NEAL, John A., Jr., colored, age 5, d. 263 Greensferry Ave. Atlanta. AG 8/30/1910

NEAL, Stephen, Dr. d. 9/8 Cordele, Ga. Wife, 5 children. Interred: Cordele. AG 9/9/1909

NEALON, Martin N., father of Thomas W. and Joseph N., d. 9/2, age 91. Interred: Dalton, Ga. AC 9/3/1905

NEALY, Ernest A., age 39, d. Fri. 376 E. Georgia Ave. Atlanta. Interred: Westview. AG 9/24/1910

NEEL, Tom, age 34, d. Norfolk, Va. Interred: Atlanta, Westview Cem. Bros: W. S., Jr., Robert, Atlanta; Raymond, San Francisco. Sis: Mrs. L. A. Patrick, Social Circle, Ga. Parents: Mr. and Mrs. W. S., residents of Atlanta. AG 9/9/1909

NEELEY, Henry, negro, railroad employee, stabbed and killed Sat. by unknown assailtant. AG 12/1/1907

NEELY, Mary, age 7, d. Maiden Lane, College Park. AG 12/18/1910

NEELY, E. A., age 29, d. 376 E. Georgia Ave. Atlanta. AG 9/26/1910

NEESE, Eliza, age 76, d. 81 Bradley Ave. Atlanta. AG 2/28/1908

NEESE, Eliza, Mrs., age 76, d. 81 Bradley Ave., Atlanta, Wed. Interred: Cherokee, Ga. AG 2/27/1908

NEESE, Susan, Mrs., age 67, d. Thurs. 65 Kennedy St., Atlanta. Interred: Roswell. Husband, three children survive. AG 7/6/1907

NEISLER, Samuel, age 34, d. 101 N. Butler St. Atlanta. Interred: Richmond, Va. Leaves bride of 4 mos., father, sister, one bro. AG 4/28/1908

NELMS, E. C., Mrs., age 40, d. Atlanta Fri. Interred: Dawson, Ga. AG 7/17/1908

NELMS, Eugene R., age 19, d. mother's res., Mrs. Emma Nelms, corner Hampton and Emmett Sts., Atlanta, Tues. Interred: Smyrna. AG 9/30/1908

NELMS, Hattie, Miss d. 3/15 Griffin, Ga. Sis: Mrs. F. D. Peaby, Columbusp Mrs. Henry C. Burr, Griffin; Mrs. H. I. Watt; Mrs. Mattie Smith. Ch: Albert Nelms, Houston, Tx; John L. Nelms, Tx. AC 3/17/1905

NELMS, Joe, age 5, son of Mr. and Mrs. W. L., grandson of Ordinary Nelms of Franklin Co., d. yesterday. AG 5/7/1907

NELON, Leo C., age 26, d. 309 Peachtree St., Atlanta, Fri. Interred: Akron, Ohio. Mother: Mrs. Daniel Nelon of Akron, Ohio. AG 4/17/1909

NELSON, Andrew, colored, age 73, d. 2 State St. Atlanta. AG 3/10/1908

NELSON, Annie C., Mrs., wife of M. C., d. Wed. Atlanta. Interred: Decatur Cemetery. AG 6/9/1910

NELSON, B. S., planter of Twiggs Co., Ga., d. Wed. Interred: Family Burying Ground. AG 12/1/1910

NELSON, E., colored, age 90, d. 44-B Trenholm St. Atlanta. AG 11/29/1907

NELSON, J. M. d. 3/24 Cordele, Ga. Wife, dau. Interred: Perry, Ga. AC 3/25/1905

NELSON, J. W., age 53, b. Twiggs Co., Ga., inmate of Confederate Soldiers' Home, Atlanta, d. Jan. 8. Fought side-by-side with James E. Edwards, buried same way. After war, settled Lowndes Co. Interred: Westview. AC 1/9/1905

NELSON, William, colored, age 79, d. 163 E. Cain St. Atlanta. AG 5/18/1907

NERENBAUM, Morris, age 49, d. Denver, Colo. AG 1/25/1910

NESBETT, Jane, colored, age 20, d. 170 E. Ellis St. Atlanta. AG 9/26/1910

NESBIT, infant of J. L., d. 295 Oak St. Atlanta. 10/5. AG 10/6/1910

NESBIT, Amandy colored, age 52, d. 364 McDaniel St. Atlanta. AG 6/22/1909

NESBIT, Ida, colored, age 38, d. 361 Fulton St. Atlanta. AG 1/31/1908

NESBIT, James, colored, age 51, d. 230 Ira St. Atlanta. AG 1/19/1907

NESBITT, Robert, colored, age 23, d. 1 Ponders Ave. Atlanta. AG 7/9/1908

NESSMITH, C. D. of Atlanta d. Wed. College Park. Interred: College Park Cemetery. AG 8/8/1907

NETHERLAND, Lula, age 10 mos., d. Flat Shoals Rd. Atlanta. AG 10/22/1909

NEUBERGER, Max, drowned Tybee Island last night. Wife: Miss Levy of Augusta and infant survive. AG 7/21/1906

NEVITT, John, Mrs. d. Philadelphia, funeral 12/28 Athens, Ga. Interred: Oconee Cemetery. AG 12/29/1910

NEW, Olivia, Mrs., age 67, d. Wed. 399 Rawson St. Atlanta. Interred: Carrollton, Ga. AG 7/10/1907

NEW, Percy, colored, age 22, d. Grady Hospital. Atlanta. AG 6/1/1907

NEWBORN, J. T. interred Westview Cemetery, Atlanta. Member of Conesauga Tribe of Red Men, No. 6. AG 2/19/1908

NEWBORN, J. T., age 36, d. 17 W. Cain St. Atlanta. AG 2/19/1908

NEWBORN, Thomas funeral 3/18 Bowman, Ga. Several children survive. One is Harvey G. AG 3/21/1910

NEWBY, E. F., Merchant of Skipperton, Ga., d. 2/2. Interred: Gordon, Ga. AC 2/4/1905

NEWCOMB, Edith, Mrs., age 69, d. Sun. 49 Ocmulgee St., Atlanta. Son: William, Jr. AG 8/8/1910

NEWCOMB, Robert, colored, age 2, d. Jefferson St. Atlanta. AG 7/24/1909

NEWMAN, Agnes E., age 71, d. Rome, Ga. AG 6/1/1907

NEWMAN, Agnes, Mrs., age 71, d. Rome, Ga., at home of Miss Fannie Berrien. AG 5/31/1907

NEWMAN, Fannie, Mrs., age 40, d. corner Loomis and Cherokee Ave. Atlanta. Interred: LaGrange, Ga. AG 5/21/907

NEWMAN, Grace, Miss, age 19, d. 319 Crew St. Atlanta. AG 1/18/1907

NEWMAN, H. G., Mrs., age 31, d. 101 N. Butler St. Atlanta. AG 6/22/1908

NEWMAN, Jesse, negro, known as "Uncle Jesse", age 109, d. in fire Thomasville, Ga. AG 2/14/1910

NEWMAN, Rachel, Mrs., age 30, d. Atlanta Wed., 315 Edgewood Ave. Interred: Hollywood. AG 6/19/1908

NEWRITER, Kate, Mrs., age 65, d. Chapel Ave. Atlanta. AG 12/22/1908

NEWSOM, G. H., Mrs., age 52, of Davisboro, Ga. d. Atlanta. Son: Dr. N. J. Dau: Miss Fannie M. Newsom, Davisboro, Ga. Interred: Davisboro. AG 5/10/1909

NEWSOM, Ginnie H., Mrs., age 52, d. 394 Courtland St. Atlanta. AG 5/12/1909

NEWSOM, Moses H., age 67, d. 111 Kirkwood Ave. Atlanta. AG 2/4/1907

NEWSOME, J. A., Jr., age 37, d. Atlanta. AG 1/19/1910

NEWSOME, James C., age 62, d. Washington, Ga. 8/12. Interred: City Cemetery. 7 children survive. AC 8/14/1905

NEWSOME, Robert, age two, son of Mr. and Mrs. J. H., d. Thurs. Interred: Fairburn, Ga. AG 7/24/1909

NEWTON, Agnes, colored, age 60, d. 49-B Bumsted St. Atlanta. AG 3/4/1908

NEWTON, Clarence W., age 2, son of Mr. and Mrs. J. D., 79 Bellwood Ave., Atlanta. Interred: Marietta, Ga. AG 11/11/1907

NEWTON, Connie, Miss, age 25, d. 69 Luckie St. Atlanta. AG 7/11/1907

NEWTON, Corinne, Miss, age 25, d. Wed. Interred: Pickens, S. C. AG 7/11/1907

NEWTON, D. J. d. 8/24 Savannah, Ga. AC 8/25/1905

NEWTON, James, colored, age 55, d. 34-1/2 Greensferry Ave. Atlanta. AG 1/28/1908

NEWTON, Leila, Miss, age 24, d. res. of parents, Rev. and Mrs. H. M. Newton, 73 W. Ga. Ave. Atlanta, Mon. Interred: Westview. AG 8/14/1906

NEWTON, Mary L., colored, age 1, d. 302 Foundry St. Atlanta. AG 12/17/1910

NEWTON, Rosa, colored, age 25, d. 5 Hollins St. Atlanta. AG 9/9/1908

NEWTON, Susie, Miss d. 11/5 Athens, Ga. AC 11/7/1905

NEW, Ethel C., Miss, age 15, d. res. of parents, Mr. and Mrs. G. W. New, 127 Rhodes St., Atlanta. Interred: Westview. AG 6/23/1908

NICHOLS, Allen J., ged 51, d. 60 Greens Ferry Ave. AG 11/3/1906

NICHOLS, Barbara, Mrs., age 60, d. 39 Queen St., Atlanta, res. of son, D. L. Nichols, Fri. Husband: B. C. Nichols. Sons: John T., D. L. of Atlanta. Dau: Mrs. J. C. King, Baldwin, Ga. Interred: Commerce, Ga. AG 10/27/1906

NICHOLS, Eliza, colored, age 64, d. 82 Sampson St. Atlanta. AG 1/15/1907

NICHOLS, John M. d. Albany, Ga. Interred: Marietta, Ga. AG 7/7/1910

NICHOLS, Miriam Lumpkin, Mrs. d. Tues. Funeral: Mrs. Porter King, 79 Merritts Ave., Atlanta. She was dau. of Rev. Jack Lumpkin of Oglethorpe Co., Ga and niece of Chief Justice Joseph Henry Lumpkin and Gov. Wilson Lumpkin. AG 1/1/1908

NICKERSON, Reuben, Capt., pioneer of Athens, d. Hill St. 1/19, age 81. Son: Thomas H., Athens. AG 1/20/1910

NILES, Samuel D. funeral Inman Park Presbyterian Church, Atlanta. Interred: Westview. AG 11/14/1907

NILES, Samuel D., his LWT filed for probate by atty George L. Bell and Mrs. May B. Niles, extrx. AG 11/20/1907

NILSON, Anders d. Sat. Atlanta, Recently removed from Avika, Sweden to this country. AG 5/22/1909

NIPPER, J. D., age 61, d. 131 Ashby St. Atlanta. Interred: Westview. AG 7/11/1907

NIVINS, W. M., colored, age 48, d. 1632 Cain St. Atlanta. AG 9/8/1909

NIX, Carlton, young son of Mr. and Mrs. E. C. Nix, d. 539 Pulliam St., Wed. Interred: Columbus, Ga. AG 3/28/1907

NIX, Eliza, Mrs., age 64, d. Sat. res. of Dr. R. B. Cuthbert, Dean St., E. Rome, Ga. She was grandmother of Mrs. Cuthbert. Interred: Anniston, Ala. AG 5/21/1906

NIX, Ella, Mrs., age 35, d. 101 N. Butler St. Atlanta. AG 5/18/1907

NIX, Ella, Mrs., d. Tues., 101 S. Ave. Atlanta. Interred: Oakland. AG 5/17/1907

NIX, George S., age 36, d. 118 S. Pryor St. Atlanta. AG 5/1/1907

NIX, infant of Mr. and Mrs. Claud, d. yesterday 67 Woodward Ave. Atlanta. Interred: Westview. AG 4/30/1906

NIX, Ivie, mrs. funeral Wed. Howell Mill Rd. at Brown memorial Church, Atlanta. Interred: White Co., Ga. AG 9/28/1910

NIX, J. C., Mrs., age 53, d. Grady Hospital. Atlanta. AG 10/25/1900

NIX, Juliette Carr, Mrs. d. 21 Ashby St., Atlanta, Sun. Son: Edwin M. Nix, Miss Nellie Nix. AG 10/22/1906

NIX, Thomas, inf. son of Mr. and Mrs. V. H., d. Tues. Atlanta. Interred: Westview. AG 5/13/1907

NOBLE, Stephen N., age 60, d. res. near Longs Sta., Rome, Ga., Wed. Interred: Bolingbroke, Ga. AG 6/13/1908

NOEL, J. O., Jr., age 1 day. d. 17 W. Cain St. Atlanta. AG 7/9/1908

NOGGLE, J. H., Mrs., age 56, d. 44 Carroll St. Atlanta. AG 6/10/1907

NOGGLES, W. C. d. Wed. near Mallorysville, age 83. Wife, 9 children. Interred: Mallorsville, Ga. AG 7/16/1909

NOLAN, Lola, age 5, d. 266 Ashby St. Atlanta. AG 3/19/1907

NOLLEY, Ben, colored, age 43, d. 4 Middlebrooks row. Atlanta. AG 4/9/1908

NORMAN, Callie Speer, Miss, age 30, d. Wed. 34 Forrest Ave. Atlanta. Interred: Dawson, Ga. AG 7/28/1910

NORRIS, George C. funeral from ces. 426 Capitol Ave., Atlanta, Sun. Interred: Westview. AG 12/30/1907

NORRIS, J. C., age 76, Confed. Vet., d. Sun. 261 E. Georgia Ave., Atlanta. Interred: Westview. Wife, three children. Only son: A. L. Norris. AG 8/1/1910

NORRIS, John F., age 41, d. 52 Carroll St. Atlanta. AG 8/20/1906

NORRIS, Mary, age two, dau. of Mr. and Mrs. E. B., 254 Oak St., Atlanta, Wed. Interred: Westview. AG 7/7/1909

NORRIS, Mary, Mrs., age 74, d. dau.'s res., Mrs. M. E. Adams, 64 Nelson St., Atlanta, Fri. Daus: Mrs. Adams, Mrs. Georgia Blackstock, Mrs. Joe Reynolds. Sons: John, Bill, Enoch, Joe. AG 5/28/1909

NORRIS, R. J., **Mrs.**, age 75, d. res. of dau., Mrs. J. S. Allrid, 9 mi. W. of Phenix City, Ala. 6/30. Interred: Philadelphia Church. One son, one dau. AG 7/1/1909

NORRIS, **Sarah**, d. 32 Dixie Ave. Atlanta, Thurs. Husband: Walter R. AG 7/8/1910

NORRIS, **Thomas C.**, age 46, d. Sat. 48 Gartrell St., Atlanta. Interred: Oakland. AG 6/15/1908

NORRMAN, G. L., age 65, suicide Majestic Hotel, Atlanta, Tues. Interred: Oakland. AG 11/13/1909

NORSE, **Clara**, colored, age 23, d. 24 Graves St. Atlanta. AG 11/9/1910

NORTH, A. C., Dr. d. Greenville St., Newnan, Ga. 1/28, age 72. Sons: H. H., N. L. Dau: Mrs. Frank B. Cole, Newnan. Wife. AG 1/28/1810

NORTH, **Elizabeth**, age 66, d. Oakland City, Ga. AG 6/18/1907

NORTH, **Henry**, age 85, d. 15 Pope St. Atlanta. AG 7/25/1910

NORTHCUTT, A., **Mrs.**, age 79, d. dau's home, Mrs. Campbell Wallace, Kennesaw Av. Atlanta, wid. of J. J. of Marietta. Sons: C. S., Ellijay, R. H.. John D. Daus: Mrs. J. H. Barnes, Mrs. Campbell Wallace, Mrs. F. B. Wellons. AG 7/28/1906

NORTON, **Frank**, age 25, d. 75 Crew St. Atlanta. AG 7/11/1907

NORTON, **Marjorie Pauline**, inf. dau. of Mr. and Mrs. Sam, d. 168 Curran St., Atlanta, Tues. Interred: Flat Rock Cemetery. AG 9/15/1909

NORTON, **Smith**, age 15 mos., son of Samuel, d. Mon. East Point. Interred: Flat Shoals church yard. AG 9/26/1906

NORTON, **Susie**, **Mrs.**, age 84, d. Thurs. dau.'s res. Eagan, Ga. Interred: East Point Cemetery. Three daus. AG 12/24/1909

NORTON, **Wylie J.**, age 61, d. 30 Crew St. Atlanta. Interred: Roswell, Ga. AG 8/9/1910

NORTON, W. R., engineer for Sou. Railroad, killed in accident, Augusta, Ga. AG 2/11/1907

NORVELL, **Samuel Morgan**, inf. son of Mr. and Mrs. John G., d. Thurs. 32 Rosalie St., Atlanta. Interred: Oakland. AG 11/20/1908

NORWACK, **Rosa N.**, **Mrs.** d. Sun. 38 Hill St. Atlanta. Interred: Ohio. Husband, two children. AG 3/8/1907

NORWOOD, **Charles**, age 21, former Atlantan, d. New Orleans Fri. Mother: Mrs. H. A. Norwood of 426 E. Fair St., Atlanta. Sisters: Mrs. C. H. Thomas, Mrs. McMillan. Bro. Interred: Atlanta. AG 1/31/1908

NORWOOD, **James F.**, age 55, d. 167 1/2 Decatur St. Atlanta. AG 3/19/1907

NORWOOD, **James F.**, age 55, d. 58 George St. Atlanta. Wife, two daus., two sons. AG 3/16/1907

NORWOOD, **James Oscar**, age 61, d. Hogansville, Ga. Mon. Wife. Daus: Mrs. W. M. Hill, Miss Mamie Norwood. Son: Pickens Norwood. Sis: Mrs. P. F. Williams, Mrs. H. E. Jackson, Mrs. W. F. Crimple. Interred: Hogansville, Ga. AG 4/19/1910

NORWOOD, **Jo**, age 61, d. 27 Luckie St. Atlanta. AG 4/19/1910

NORWOOD, **Laura**, colored, age 50, d. 21 Solomons St. Atlanta. AG 10/8/1907

NOWELL, Frank, son of Mr. and Mrs. J. W., d. Wed. Macon, Columbus Rd. AG 12/17/1908

NUDGEN, Charles, age 34, d. rr accident, Powder Springs, Ga. AG 3/4/1907

NUNN, C. H. d. 11/11 Decatur Rd., age 50. Interred: Decatur. AC 11/12/1905

NUNN, F. G., Mrs. of 228 S. Pryor St., Atlanta, d. New Kimball House Sun. Interred: Rutledge, Ga. AG 7/6/1909

NUNN, J. B., Mrs. d. Augusta, Ga. Mon. Interred: Atlanta, Oakland Cemetery. Husband, 3 children, survive. AG 4/22/1908

NUNN, J. B., age 70, d. Sun. 704 DeKalb Ave., Atlanta. Family in Waynesboro, Ga. Interred: Swainesboro, Ga. AG 10/30/1906

NUNN, R. J., Dr., age 79, d. 7/29 Savannah, Ga. He was b. Wexford, Ireland 1831, came to Savannah in 1850. AG 6/29/1910

NUNNALLY, A. O., Mrs., age 69, d. 29 Luckie St. Atlanta. AG 12/3/1908

NUNN, C. W., age 66, d. Wed. 278 Woodward Ave. Atlanta. AG 12/23/1909

NUSSBAUM, Gus, former Macon merchant, d. NY. last week. He md. Clara Dreyfous, sis. of Ed, now of Atlanta. AG 12/24/1907

O'CONNOR, John H., suicide, of Macon, Ga., 19 Bradley St., d. Atlanta Fri., son of E. D. O'Connor. Wife was going to live with her father, R. A. Starnes. Wife, 2 daus., Mildred, age 3, and Louise, age 19 mos., survive. AG 11/19/1909

O'CONNOR, M. A., Mrs., 71, d. Pulliam St., Atlanta. Ch: Mrs. P. O'Connor, Commerce; Sister M. Clare, Augusta,; Lillie & Bernie, Atlanta. Bro: Frank Fesler, San Francisco. Sis: Mrs. N. Rakestraw, Mrs. K. F. Sale. Bur: Westview. AG 2/26/1908

O'DONNELLY, Margaret, Miss, age 50, d. 294 Gordon St. Atlanta. AG 4/15/1910

O'HANLON, C. J., Mrs. d. Augusta Sat. Interred: Rose Hill Cemetery, Macon. AG 10/6/1908

O'HARA, Maggie, girl wife of Tom, leader of the great O'Hara Clan, buried Westview Cemetery, Atlanta, 4/1. AC 4/2/1905

O'HARA, R. T., age 76, d. dau.'s res., Mrs. Arthur Golden, Macon, Holt St. 4/25. Interred: Milledgeville, Ga. AC 4/28/1905

O'KEEFE, Lawrence E., Capt., , age 72, d. 213 Ponce de Leon Ave. Atlanta. Confederate veteran, Co. C, 17th Ga. Leaves wife, 5 sons, dau., 2 sisters. AG 1/18/1907

O'NEAL, Letitia, colored, age 22, d. 179 Connally St. Atlanta. AG 8/29/1907

O'NEAL, O. O., age 66, d. 10/19 Macon, Ga. Wife, 2 sons, 3 daus. Interred: O'Neal burial ground. AG 10/20/1910

O'NEAL, W. B., age 32, d. 45 Woodward Ave., Atlanta, Sun. Interred: College Park. Wife, 3 ch, bro., two sisters. AG 3/29/1909

O'NEIL, Annie, Miss, age 23, d. Thurs. Atlanta. AG 8/1/1907

O'PRY, Corrinne, Mrs., age 58, d. 720 Spring St., Macon 11/16. Husband: J. J. Son: Groves. Interred: Her old home in Alabama. AG 11/17/1910

O'REAR, Rebecca, Mrs., age 84, d. res. of dau., Mrs. T. L. Moore, Whitesburg, Ga., Fri. 2 daus. AG 11/21/1910

O'ROURKE, Edmund Arthur, age 50, d. Wed. 508 Capitol Ave. Atlanta. Wife. Bros: Vincent, Atlanta; Gerald, Tx. Sis: Mrs. Wilfred Tempest, Pontefract, Engl. Bur: Westview. AG 8/17/1910

O'SHIELDS, Benjamin, age 1 year, inf. son of Mr. and Mrs. J. M., d. Wed. 26 Lindsay St., Atlanta. Interred: Suwanee, Ga. AG 7/31/1907

O'SHIELDS, Elizabeth, Mrs., age 80, d. Sun., 492 Chestnut St., Atlanta. Interred: Hollywood. AG 6/20/1910

O'SHIELDS, Harry, age 76, old res. of Atlanta, d. 751 Marietta S. Sat. Interred: Hollywood cemetery. AG 2/3/1908

O'SHIELDS, Maggie, age 11, dau. of Mr. and Mrs. B. F., d. 55 Tennelle St. Atlanta. Interred: Hollywood. AG 11/2/1907

O'SHIELDS, R. F., age 47, d. 117 Holderness St. Atlanta Mon. Interred: Westview. AG 2/17/1909

O'SULLIVAN, Eddie John, son of E. J., of 12 E. Fair St., Atlanta, d. from fall. Age 25. AG 3/9/1910

O'TYSON, Morris, age 56, d. 58 Hood St. Atlanta. Interred: Westview. Wife, two sons. AG 9/21/1909

OAFIELD, William, age 27, d. Atlanta. AG 9/9/1908

OAKES, Larseny, age 76, d. 14 Bellwood Ave. Atlanta. AG 11/8/1910

OAKES, Larseny, age 76, d. Mon. Atlanta. Daus: Mrs. George Humphries, Mrs. Wylie Fowler, Mrs. Mary Daly, Mrs. Henrietta Mullins. Interred: Hollywood. AG 11/7/1910

OAKFORD, Frank, age 53, d. Victoria Apts, 87 W. Peachtree St.,tlanta. Wife, and parents, Mr. and Mrs. Samuel Oakford, survive. Interred: Philadelphia, Pa. AG 11/20/1908

OAKFORD, Frank C. d. Victoria Apts., W. Peachtree St., Atlanta, Sun. Interred: Westview. AG 12/7/1908

OAKSHETTE, Mary Hill, Mrs., age 51, d. 371 Peachtree St., Atlanta, Mon. Husb. in Providence, R. I., two daus. of Atlanta. AG 1/13/1908

OATES, William C., Gen., former Gov. of Alabama, funeral Sun. Montgomery, Ala. AG 9/10/1910

ODELL, W. J. d. Tues. Atlanta. AG 2/19/1907

ODOM, William, colored, age 36, d. 44 Parsons St. Atlanta. AG 11/17/1910

OESCHGER, I.. Funeral at German Lutheran Church. Atlanta. AG 7/17/1906

OESCHGER, Ignatz, age 61, d. 17 W. Cain St. Atlanta. AG 7/18/1906

OETJEN, Henry, age 52, d. Atlanta. Interred: Augusta, Ga. AG 4/25/1910

OGDEN, Emily, Mrs. d. 4/20 Tifton, Ga., widow of A., age 54. Sons: John W., Adolphus, Archibald. Interred: Tifton Cemetery. AC 4/23/1905

OGLE, Bertha, Mrs., age 26, d. 384 Cooper St. Atlanta. AG 11/24/1910

OGLE, Mary S., Mrs., age 30, d. mother's res., Mrs. M. V. Ogle, 869 Marietta St., Atlanta, Sun. Interred: Citizens Cemetery, Marietta, Ga. AG 7/12/1909

OGLETREE, Alice May, colored, age 11 mos., d. 8 Phoenix alley. Atlanta. AG 6/26/1908

OGLETREE, M. F., Mrs., age 70, d. 65 Larkin St. Atlanta. AG 11/17/1907

OGLETREE, S. R., pioneer citizen of Quitman Co., Ga., d. 10/22 Georgetown, Ga., near his home, age 78. Vet. of Civil War. 7 grown sons and daus. Interred: Georgetown, Ga. AG 10/23/1909

OLDFIELD, A. N., age 62, d. Cornelia, Ga. AG 3/4/1907

OLDHAM, Frank d. Birmingham, Ala. Tues. Mother, wife, two children survive. Interred: Atlanta, Oakland Cem., Fam. Vault. AG 6/7/1906
OLIFF, John W. d. Fri. Statesboro, Ga. Leaves wife, three children. AG 11/11/1907
OLIVE, Sarah, Mrs., age 63, d. 3/24 Girard, Ga. Husband, 7 children. AC 3/25/1905
OLIVER, Augustus, son of John L., murdered. Grady Tarver, teenager, charged, Americus, Ga. AC 3/18/1905
OLIVER, Dorothy, Miss, age 19, dau. of Mr. and Mrs. S. A., d. 138 Hunnicutt St., Atlanta, Mon. Interred: Oakland. AG 1/21/1908
OLIVER, Henry Carson, son of Mr. and Mrs. E. L., d. Mon., S. Macon. AG 6/9/1908
OLIVER, James, age 2 mos., d. 224 Smith St. Atlanta. AG 2/8/1909
OLIVER, Jettie, age 21, d. Grady Hospital. Atlanta. AG 8/20/1907
OLIVER, M., age 50, d. Fulton Co. jail, Atlanta. Interred: Westview. AG 5/10/1907
OLIVER, S. C., age 73, d. Red Oak, Ga., Fri. Wife, 3 sons, G. W., J. A. and W. D. Daus: Mrs. P. C. Flynn, Mrs. M. J. Cook. Interred: Red Oak Christian Church. AG 4/30/1908
OLIVER, Thurmond d. Elberton Tues. Interred: Elmhurst Cemetery. AG 4/28/1909
OLIVER, M., age 50, d. Fulton Co. jail. Atlanta. AG 5/10/1907
OLLINGER, Joseph, age 65, d. Mobile, Ala. AG 11/30/1907
OLSEN, Elleff, age 63, steward on steamer "Charles H. Evans" drowned at Mallory Docks, Brunswick, Sun. AG 8/27/1907
OLSON, Andrew, age 44, d. Atlanta Sun. Interred: Westview. Wife, 4 children. His father lives in Sweden. AG 5/17/1909
ONTER, J. L., age 69, d. 69 Luckie St. Atlanta. AG 1/29/1908
ORCHARD, James, Mrs. Received news in Atlanta that she d. Dallas, Texas. Before marriage was Mary Keen, dau. of Robert Keen of Augusta, and mother, Phinizy Bowdre. Interred: Dallas, Tx. AG 1/1/1908
ORGAIN, J. C., Mrs., age 40, d. Delta Ave. Atlanta. AG 2/15/1909
ORGAIN, Martha, age 1 yr., d. 290 Atlanta Ave. Atlanta. AG 7/1/1907
ORME, Julia, Miss d. Mon. 428 Peachtree St., Atlanta. Age 35. Bros: Joseph T., Wilson (Alpine, Ky.). She was dau. of late Dr. William P. Orme, Atlanta pioneer, and niece of Dr. F. H. Orme. AG 1/13/1908
ORMON, Henry, colored, age 20, d. Birmingham, Ala. AG 2/7/1908
ORMSLEY, Alice of Savannah died. Inquest held. Arrested: George H. Tholken, Miss Lizzie Spinner. AG 9/27/1906
ORR, A., colored, age 27, d. 7 Smiths alley. Atlanta. AG 12/9/1908
ORR, Bessie, age 14 mos., dau. of S. C., d. Center St. Atlanta. Interred: Canton, Ga. AG 6/29/1906
ORR, J. A., age 60, d. 17 W. Cain St. Atlanta. Interred: Oxford, Ga. AG 5/1/1907
ORR, Mattie, colored, age 6 mos., d. 27 Kingsley St. Atlanta. AG 10/2/1907
ORR, W. H., age 37, d. Atlanta Fri. Interred: Spellman, Ga. AG 3/27/1908
ORR, W. V. d. Piedmont Ave. and Center St.,tlanta, Tues. Interred: Canton, Ga. Age 76, left two sons. AG 1/8/1908

ORR, William, colored, age 52, d. 10 Whitney St. Atlanta. AG 1/28/1908

ORTON, George N., age 77, d. 92 Luckie St. Atlanta. AG 7/12/1909

OSBORN, E. O., age 28, of Watkinsville, Ga., d. Atlanta Sun. AG 6/14/1909

OSBORN, G. C., age 62, d. E. Point Tues. Interred: Palmetto. AG 4/25/1906

OSBORNE, Etta, infant dau. of Mr. and Mrs. T. J., d. 177 Griffin St., Atlanta, Tues. Interred: Caseys. AG 9/17/1907

OSBORNE, Jacquelyn, age 18 mos., dau. of Mr. and Mrs. J. J., d. Fri. 43 Augusta Ave. Atlanta. Interred: Westview. AG 8/15/1910

OSBORN, M. E., Mrs., age 73 d. viewing body of Sam Jones capitol rotunda. Niece: Miss Willie Ellett, Brooklyn. Grdau: Katherine Storey, 36 Zachery St. Daus: Mrs. W. R. Storey, 36 Zachery St., Mrs. J. T. Goodrum, 15 Garnett St. AG 10/19/1906

OSBOURN, Robert B., age 23, d. Atlanta Fri. AG 11/23/1907

OSBURN, Mary Lizzie died. Relatives: Mrs. A. M. Bergstrom, Mr. and Mrs. W. R. Stoy, Mr. and Mrs. J. T. Goodrum, Mr. and Mrs. Wheeler Mangum, J. L. Patrick, Mrs. Julia Osburn, Mrs. Mary Jones. AG 10/20/1906

OSBURN, Mary Lizzie, Mrs., dau. of Nat Mangum, sister of Wheeler Mangum. Daus: Mrs. W. R. Storey, Mrs. J. T. Goodrum. d. Fri. Interment: Oakland. AG 10/20/1906

OSLIN, Lewis,ge 3, d. 456 South Boulevard. Atlanta. AG 11/2/1907

OSLIN, Louis, age 3, son of Mr. and Mrs. Alfred, d. 456 S. Boulevard, Atlanta, Fri. Interred: Smyrna, Ga. AG 11/2/1907

OSTLUND, Sadie, Miss, age 21, of Red Wing, Minn., d. Atlanta Wed. Sis: Miss Lillie Ostlund, Minn. AG 8/26/1909

OTMAN, Sarah, Mrs., age 62, wife of William, d. 61 Hightower St., tlanta, Mon. AG 11/17/1907

OTTLEY, Charles W., age 36, d. Baltimore, Md. AG 5/13/1907

OTTLEY, Charles W., Dr., bro. of John K., Atlanta, d. Jno Hopkins Hospital. Aged 36, b. Columbus, Miss., son of Col. John K. Mother: Mrs. E. G. McCabe, Atlanta. Bros: John K., Atlanta; Ernest, Cedartown. Bur: Columbus, Ga. AG 5/8/1907

OUTHOUSE, Willard M., age 2, of Rockmart, Ga., d. Atlanta. AG 9/21/1910

OUTLER, Robert A. of Phenix City, Ala. d. 3/28. Members of Red Man Creek Tribe attended funeral. AC 3/30/1905

OVERBY, B. H., Mrs., wife of B. H., d. Thurs., 83 Lowe St., Atlanta. Son: B. H., Jr. Sisters: Mrs. J. E. Byrnes, Birmingham, Ala.; Mrs. Walker, Tarrytown, Ga. Bro: R. L. Odum, Rockdale, Ga. Interred: Hollywood. AG 8/15/1907

OVERBY, Bartow H., age 61, d. Soldiers' Home, Atlanta. AG 7/20/1907

OVERBY, Lula, Mrs., age 42, d. 101 N. Butler St. Atlanta. AG 8/17/1907

OVERBY, W. H., Mrs., age 44, d. 267 Capitol Ave., Atlanta. AG 5/31/1907

OVERTON, J. H., Mrs., 70, past Atlanta res. b. DeKalb Co. d. 1/17 son's res., J. M. Ch: Mrs. G.M. Anderson, Mrs. W.M. Almand, Atlanta; Mrs. Jno Reagan, Lithonia; Mrs. G.R. Cheshire; W.B., Chattanooga. Bur: Grove Level, Dalton. AG 1/18/1910

OWEN, Annie, Mrs. d. 8/30 Rose Hill (Columbus), Ga., wid. of G. R. 5 ch. Bro: J. A. Allen, Opelika, Ala. She was dau. of late J. A. Allen of Oak Bowery, Ala., where she was buried. AC 9/2/1905

OWEN, J. E., Mrs. d. 55 Mills St. Atlanta. Interred: Westview. AG 5/19/1908

OWEN, J. Frank, age 29, d. 11 Capitol Ave., Atlanta, Sat. Connected with Davison-Paxon-Stokes Co. Parents: Mr. and Mrs. G. G. Owen. Sisters: Nettie, Mamie, Sanger and Mildred. Interred: Westview. AG 11/23/1907

OWEN, Janie, Mrs. d. 181 E. North Ave., Atlanta. Husband: John, 5 children. AG 3/1/1908

OWEN, Mary E., Miss, age 50, d. 187 Smith St. Atlanta, AG 5/24/1907

OWEN, Pauline, inf. dau. of Mr. and Mrs. B. A., 105 Meldrum St., Atlanta, d. Sun. Interred: Dallas, Ga. AG 7/26/1909

OWEN, Ruth C., Mrs., age 45, wife of late Judge Patrick H., d. res. of dau., Mrs. J. W. Cason, 161 W. Pine St., Atlanta, Thurs. Interred: Westview. AG 8/7/1908

OWENS, C. J.,ge 62, d. Old Soldiers' Home. Atlanta. AG 12/2/1910

OWENS, Charley, colored, age 3, d. 56 Douthy St. Atlanta. AG 11/14/1908

OWENS, Henry, colored, age 27, d. 101 N. Butler St. Atlanta. AG 2/15/1909

OWENS, John, age 10, son of Mrs. Owens of Spring Place, Ga., shot to death 6/16. Has 12-yr. old bro. AG 6/17/1908

OWENS, K., colored, age 21, d. Sugar Hill, Ga. AG 9/3/1907

OWENS, Mary, Mrs., age 28, d. Marietta Road. Atlanta. AG 10/20/1909

OWENS, Phillip, colored, age 22, d. 101 Butler St. Atlanta. AG 9/2/1909

OWENS, Robert O., age 23, son of Mr. and Mrs. W. T. of Edgewood, Ga. d. Sat. Interred: Lithonia, Ga. AG 12/7/1908

OWENS, S. L., Mrs., age 31, (or age 35) d. 129 Courtland St. Atlanta. Interred: Kestler, Ga. AG 9/28/1909

OWENS, Will, colored, age 22, d. 31 Dora St. Atlanta. AG 3/16/1908

OWENSBY, S. E., Mrs., age 44, d. Oklahoma. AG 11/19/1909

OWINGS, Elizabeth Reeves, Mrs., age 90, d. res. of dau., Mrs. Walker G. Brown, 147 Cooper St., Mon, Atlanta. Interred: Westview. AG 1/22/1907

OWINGS, F. D., Gen. accidentally shot in Rockwood, Tenn., killed, 11/7. AC 11/7/1905

OXFORD, J. L., Confederate Veteran, d. n. of Dalton, Ga. Thurs., aged abt 60. Wife, 2 daus., 3 sons. AG 10/30/1909

OXFORD, Katie, Mrs., wife of Rev. J. J., d. Thurs. 453 Gordon St., Atlanta. Ch: W. E., G. T., J. T., Clifford, Paul, Anna and Katherine. AG 6/22/1910

OXFORD, Mary C., Mrs., age 63, d. 28 Lowndes St., Atlanta. Daus: Mrs. John Matton, Millen, Ga.; Mrs. Mattie R. Craig, Texas. Sons: G. T., Atlanta; R. W., Jackson, Ga. Bur: Barnesville. AG 6/7/1910

OZMER, Gladys G., Miss d. 9/12 133 Hunnicutt St., Atlanta. Interred: Oakland. AC 9/14/1905

OZMER, J. W., Mrs. d. Tues. Atlanta. Interred: Redan, Ga. Husband, 9 children. AG 6/2/1909

PACE, son of James P., age 18, killed while hunting, Dallas, Ga. by 14-yr. old son of Will Cohran. AG 12/28/1910

PACE, Celie, Mrs., age 83, d. 12/10 at sister's res., Mrs. McDonald, 24 Howell St., Atlanta. Interred: Ellenwood, Ga. AC 12/11/1905

PACE, E., Mrs., age 57, d. 92 Luckie St. Atlanta. AG 8/26/1908

PACE, Robert Lee, age 38, d. 76 Metroplitan Ave., Atlanta, Nov. 4. Interred: Rex, Ga. AG 11/5/1910

PADEN, J. T., age 54, d. Sat. Cheshire Bridge Rd., Atlanta. Wife. Interred: Rock Springs Church yard. AG 1/31/1910

PADEN, John, colored, age 2 yrs., d. 12 Air Line. Atlanta. AG 5/10/1907

PADGET, Charles, young man res. several miles Sou. of Valdosta, d. blood poison. Age 23. AG 7/9/1908

PADGETT, Berry, colored, age 54, d. W. Third St. Atlanta. AG 2/16/1908

PADGETT, E. R. funeral today. Interred: Hollywood Cemetery. AC 11/30/1905

PADGETT, J. W., flagman for Sou. RR., accidently run over in Jesup, Ga. yard. Leaves wife, 2 small children. AG 2/9/1907

PADGETT, M. A., age 79, d. Confederate Soldiers' Home, Atlanta, Thurs. Relatives: Augusta, Ga. Enl. 6/8/1861 Confed. Servive, was Sgt. in Co. B, Hampton's Legion. AG 12/23/1909

PADGETT, Marion Henry, inf. son of Mr. and Mrs. Hardy, d. Barksdale Drive, Atlanta Tues. Interred: Westview. AG 5/19/1909

PAGE, infant of Mr. and Mrs. H., d. 65 Tumlin St., Atlanta, Wed. Interred: Griffin, Ga. AG 1/8/1908

PAGE, J. C., Mrs., wife of J. C., d. Greenwood St., Atlanta Sat. Husband, two children, survive. Interred: Hurtsboro, Ala., her old home. AG 10/18/1909

PAGE, Mattie, Mrs., age 47, d. 220 S. Boulevard. Atlanta. AG 12/14/1909

PAGE, Sarah, colored, age 64, d. 51 N. McDaniel St. Atlanta. AG 3/29/1909

PAGE, Thomas Gene, age 21, d. Atlanta Mon. Interred: Turrin, Ga. Bro: H. Page. AG 3/16/1909

PAIGE, John, Dr. d. Salt Lake City, Utah, formerly res. of Savannah, age 45. AC 3/28/1905

PAINE, Edward T., Capt., age 85, d. East Lake, Ga. Son: Thomas B. AG 8/21/1908

PAINE, J. W., Mrs., age 73, d. 176 Edgewood Ave., Atlanta, Sun. Husband, 13 ch. Interred: Bishop, Ga. AG 3/29/1909

PAINTER, Emily May, age 36, d. 4 Baltimore Pl. Atlanta. AG 6/21/1906

PALM, Anna, colored, age 109, d. 10 Travis St. Atlanta. AG 1/18/1907

PALMER, Curtis, colored, age 18, d. 36 1/2 Greensferry Ave. Atlanta. AG 4/1/1907

PALMER, Nellie W., age 1 yrs., d. 60 Sylvan St. Atlanta. AG 6/8/1907

PALMER, William, age 47, d. Fri. Atlanta, from Clinton, S. C. AG 3/1/1907

PALMER, William, age 36, d. 267 Capitol Ave. Atlanta. AG 3/4/1907

PALMER, William Wallace, age 39, d. 115 1/2 N. Pryor St. Atlanta.
AG 2/25/1907
PAPE, Nina Anderson, Mrs. funeral 9.23 Savannah, Ga. She d. 9/20
Biltimore, N. C. Dau. of late Col. Edward C. Anderson. Dau: Nina.
Bro: E. M. Anderson. Sis: Miss Sallie W. Anderson. AC 9/23/1905
PAPPS, Annie, Miss, age 19, dau. of Mr. and Mrs. John, d. 610 N.
Boulevard Mon. Interred: Westview. AG 10/17/1906
PARHAM, George, colored, age 61, d. 40 Greenunden St. Atlanta. AG
11/22/1909
PARIS, Mary A, Miss, age 17, d. Wed. Hill St., Atlanta. Interred:
Casey´s Cemetery. AG 7/22/1910
PARISH, Joseph, age 64, d. dau´s res., Mrs. J. H. ?assenger, 83
Perry St., Atlanta, Sun. Interred: Tallapoosa, Ga. AG 3/1/1909
PARK, D. S., age 54, d. Wed. Confederate Soldiers´ Home, Atlanta.
He enl. 8/8/1862, served throughout war, including battle of
Peachtree Creek. Interred: Westview. AG 3/10/1909
PARK, E. F. Miss, age 19, d. 101 N. Butler St. Atlanta. AG
11/25/1907
PARK, Effie May, Miss interred Rossville, Ga. AG 11/23/1907
PARK, Henry Edgar d. 74 Richardson St. Atlanta Fri. Age 40. Wife,
4 children. Interred: Decatur, Ga. AG 9/2/1910
PARK, Nelson, age 10, son of Hon. C. J. of Riverside, Ga. d.
8/23. Interred: Ridge Grove Cemetery. AC 8/24/1905
PARK, Pearl, Mrs., age 22, wife of J. A., dau. of Mr. and Mrs. W.
A. Jack, d. 459 Washington St. Atlanta. Sis: Misses Myrtle, Anna
and Maud Jack; Mrs. L. O. Montgomery; Mrs. C. L. Nicholson; Mrs.
O. O. Hull. Bro: W. H. Jack. Interred: Westview. Husband,
PARKER, Annie, Miss, dau. of Mrs. Frank, d. 9/1, Lizella, Ga. AG
9/2/1910
PARKER, C. W., Dr., age 80, d. 305 Peters St. Atlanta. AG
5/20/1909
PARKER, Cecil, Mrs., age 18, d. 110 Powell St. Atlanta. AG
8/31/1908
PARKER, Charles, age 10, killed by train, Columbus, Ga. AG
1/10/1907
PARKER, Eliza, colored, age 105, d. 118 Amy St. Atlanta. AG
10/8/1909
PARKER, G. A., age 22, of 701 S. Pryor St., Atlanta, d. Mon.
Interred: Littleton, Mass. Father and mother: Mr. and Mrs. E. B.
Parker. AG 12/28/1909
PARKER, Glenn E., age 4 mos., d. Ellijay, Ga. AG 7/6/1907
PARKER, Herbert, age 4 mos., d. 628 DeKalb Ave. Atlanta. AG
7/13/1908
PARKER, Herman, Georgian, drowned off Fla. coast, while guest of
Stuart Bennett of N. Y. who also drowned, yacht wreck, Key West,
Fla. AG 12/27/1910
PARKER, J. C., Rev. funeral Cairo, Ga. 3/9. Interred:
Sandersville, Ga. AG 3/9/1907
PARKER, J. W., Mrs., age 80, d. 119 Athens. Interred: Oconee
Cemetery. AC 11/11/1905
PARKER, Jim, colored, age 39, d. Howell Station, Ga. AG 1/1/1908
PARKER, Jim, colored, age 52, d. 24 Roseberry St. Atlanta. AG
8/11/1908
PARKER, Jim, negro fireman for Seaboard Air Line RR, shot,
killed. AG 3/27/1908

PARKER, John, age 25, d. Fulton Co. barracks. AG 10/25/1906

PARKER, Johnny Lee, age 1, inf. son of Mr. and Mrs. J. L., d. Tues. 52 Fortress Ave., Atlanta. Interred: Hollywood. AG 8/28/1907

PARKER, Joseph killed Jan. 2 at Wollen Mills, intersection of Wells St. and Sou. R. R., Atlanta. Married only 5 weeks. Res. 371 1/2 Decatur St. AC 1/4/1905

PARKER, Joseph R., age 61, d. Atlanta 8/17. Sons: V. C., Calvin W., Atlanta; Lee. AG 8/18/1909

PARKER, Leona, age 10 mos., d. 19 Daniel St. Atlanta. AG 9/6/1907

PARKER, Lucy, Mrs., age 59, d. dau.'s res., Mrs. W. D. Rhodes, 19 Josephine St., Inman Park, Atlanta, Wed. Interred: Sylvester Cemetery. AG 3/10/1909

PARKER, Minnie J., Mrs., age 26, d. 115 Grant St.,tlanta, Fri., wife of W. O. Parents: Mr. and Mrs. J. P. Henderson. Sis: Mrs. Claud Parker, Misses Ola, Jessie, Essie, Marie and Bessie Henderson. Interred: Greenwood. AG 5/8/1910

PARKER, Nellie, Mrs., age 26, d. 115 Grant St., Atlanta. AG 5/8/1910

PARKER, Paul, age 5, son of Mr. and Mrs. P. H., d. Wed. E. Pt. Interred: Dallas, Ga. AG 4/21/1910

PARKER, Peggie, colored, age 52, d. 40 Kuhrt St. Atlanta. AG 3/18/1908

PARKER, R. J., age 78, d. near E. Lake, Ga. Sat. Interred: Family Cemetery. AG 8/3/1908

PARKER, Sarah M., Mrs., age 82, d. Sat. Atlanta, 701 S. Pryor St. Son-in-law: Harry Greenwood. Interred: Littleton, Mass. AG 5/4/1908

PARKER, W. L., age 76, d. Tues. Funeral dau.'s res., Mrs. M. H. Mahan, 526 Pulliam St., Atlanta. Interred: Westview. AG 2/11/1909

PARKER, W. O., Mrs. funeral 115 Grant St., Atlanta, Sun. Interred: Greenwood. AG 5/9/1910

PARKS, Albert murdered by Homer Pace Mon., Bibb Co. AG 10/23/1907

PARKS, Alvin, age one, son of Mr. and Mrs. A. T., 520 Capitol Ave., Atlanta, d. Tues. AG 9/19/1906

PARKS, George, colored, age 11, d. 200 Love St. Atlanta. AG 12/17/1910

PARKS, James, colored, age 9 mos., d. 27 Grover St. Atlanta. AG 7/23/1909

PARKS, Lizzie, Miss, age 65, d. Atlanta Sun., from Odessadale, Ga. Cousin: G. H. Hardy, Odessadale. AG 3/22/1909

PARKS, Phillis, colored, age 21, d. 399 Martin St. Atlanta AG 7/6/1909

PARKS, Rosa Lee, colored, age 11 yrs., d. 3 Mitchell Place. Atlanta. AG 2/19/1907

PARKS, S., colored, age 48, d. rear 227 Haynes St. Atlanta. AG 1/29/1908

PARKS, Welcome, age 59, d. Newnan, Ga. AG 7/28/1910

PARR, Beatrice, infant of Mr. and Mrs. N. I., d. S. Macon 5/29. Interred: Riverside Cemetery. AC 5/31/1905

PARR, Calvin of Athens d. 12/29, age 66. Wife, 5 grandchildren. Several bros. and sisters. AG 12/30/1910

PARR, J. S., age 68, d. Grady Hospital Atlanta. Wife, several children. Interred: Antioch Church. AG 7/18/1908

PARR, Jack, age 1, d. 77 McDonald St. Atlanta. AG 6/22/1909

PARR, William, age 70, d. 1094 Marietta St., Atlanta Thurs. Interred: Tallassee, Ala. AG 10/23/1908

PARRIS, L. W., age 46, Atlanta pioneer cigar-maker, d. 223 Peters St. Sun, native of Berlin. Wife: Mrs. Lucy Parris, one dau. Interred: Meansville, Ga. AG 10/8/1907

PARRISH, I. P., merchant of Bremen, Ga., d. 10/26. Interred: Bremen. AG 10/27/1910

PARROT, J. B., Mrs. d. 1/20 Clinton, S. C., wife of late Rev. J. B. AG 1/21/1910

PARROTT, Charles C., Mrs. d. Greenville St., Newnan, Ga. 7/12, wife of Charles C., dau. of late Judge John S. Bigby. Son: Bigby Parrott. Dau: Miss Mary Parrott. AG 7/13/1909

PARROTT, W. L., former res. of Atlanta, d. Hot Springs, Ark. several days ago. AG 5/28/1909

PARROTT, Walter W., Mrs. d. 5/24. Funeral 5/26. Interred: Westview. AG 5/24/1906

PARSON, Lee, inf. son of Mr. and Mrs. Lee, d. Thurs. Atlanta. Interred: Westview. AG 1/3/1908

PARSONS, B. F., aged Hawkinsville, Ga. man, d. Sat. Interred: Orange Hill Cemetery. AG 11/17/1907

PARSONS, Charles, age 29, d. Home for Incurables. Atlanta. Interred: Hollywood. AG 4/20/1908

PARSONS, Martha, Mrs., wife of Wm Henry, age 52, d. 131 Capitol Ave., Atlanta, dau. of Dr. & Mrs. Jas F. Bozeman. Martha b. Columbus, Ga. 12/16/1855. Dau: Mrs. Marion McHenry, Jackson. Aunt: Mrs. J. B. O'Brien, Nashville, Tn. AG 6/26/1907

PARSONS, Mary Allgood, Mrs., wife of late F. C. Parsons, d. Pickens, S. C., Fri., age 64. Bros: W. B. Allgood, D. A. Allgood, Pickens, S. C.; E. F. Allgood, Anderson Co. Sis: Mrs. W. T. Bowen, Mrs. William Craig, Pickens Co. AG 3/22/1909

PARSONS, W. P., age 66, d. Strouds, Ga. Thurs. Interred: Family Burial Grounds. Wife, several sons and daus. AG 5/8/1910

PARTEE, Levi, colored, age 60, d. 29 Howell St., Atlanta, 10/23. AG 10/25/1910

PARTELL, Emma, colored, age 51, d. 157 Fraser St. Atlanta. AG 1/14/1908

PARTRIDGE, Orbrey, age 9 mos., d. 89 Pearl St. Atlanta. AG 4/22/1909

PARTRIDGE, Sarah A., Mrs., age 48, d. Atlanta. AG 1/11/1910

PARTRIDGE, William C., age 1, d. 126 East Love St. Atlanta. AG 4/10/1907

PASCHAL, J. L., Mrs. d. McDonough Rd. Fri. Husband, two children survive. Interred: Marvin churchyard. AG 4/6/1907

PASCHALL, W. G., age 65, d. 640 Highland Ave., Atlanta. AG 2/14/1908

PASS, C. C., age 64, d. 175 Cameron St. Atlanta. AG 11/6/1907

PATCH, Walker N., age 6 mos., son of Mr. and Mrs. Walter, 27 Dewey St., Atlanta, Sun. Interred: Westview. AG 11/11/1907

PATCH, William H., age 2, son of Mr. and Mrs. W. B., res. of 87 Windsor St., Atlanta, Tues, in Augusta. Interred: Westview. AG 7/7/1910

PATE, Cordia, age 28, d. Atlanta. AG 1/11/1910

PATE, David F., age 54, d. Inman yards. Atlanta. Interred: Oakland. Wife, 4 sons, 4 daus. AG 2/15/1910

PATE, Elijah of Albany, Ga. d. rr accident, rr engineer. AC 2/23/1905

PATE, Isabella J.,55, 524 Whitehall, Atlanta. Hus-J. L. Ch-H. L., Jesse, Atlanta; J. T., Lithonia; C. Q. Pate, Mrs. W. A. Bradford, Cartersville; Mrs. Joseph Freeman, Centersville; Mrs. D. F. Jackson, Baxley. Bur: Lawrenceville. AG 5/7/1907

PATILLO, James, b. Greene Co. 7/13/1821, d. 3/21 West Pt. m. 7/18/1843 Sara W. Oslin. Ch: W. F., Atlanta; Mrs. S. P. Callaway, LaGrange; Mrs. W. A. Callaway, Atlanta; Mrs. T. B. Stubbs, Montgomery, AL; R. S., Whitesville. Bur: Pinewood. AC 3/22/1905

PATON, Florence, colored, age 7, d. 91 Weldon's alley. Atlanta. AG 6/12/1907

PATRICK, C. L. of Morgan Co., d. Mon. near Madison, Ga. Several sons and daus. AG 11/15/1910

PATTEE, Finney, Mrs. of Athens d. Atlanta Sat. Husband: James H. Interred: Boston, Mass. Nephew: L. T. Smith. AG 4/10/1909

PATTEN, Silas, age 52, d. Atlanta Sun. Interred: Auburn, Ala. AG 6/14/1909

PATTERSON, A. C., Mrs., age 44, d. Tues. 53 E. Ellis St., Atlanta. Interred: Paducah, Ky. Husband: A. C. AG 10/27/1909

PATTERSON, Albert N., age 58, d. Sun. 40 Plum St., Atlanta. Interred: Oakland. Wife, mother, Mrs. M. R. Patterson, and two bros., W. J. and S. S. Patterson. AG 5/20/1907

PATTERSON, Alice A., Mrs., age 27, wife of George T. of E. Pt., d. Mon. Interred: Brooks, Ga. AG 5/3/1910

PATTERSON, Boyd, Jr., colored, 7 mos., d. 140 McDaniel St. Atlanta. AG 1/7/1907

PATTERSON, Charles N. of Cartersville, Ga. d. Atlanta Sun. Interred: Cartersville. AG 6/28/1909

PATTERSON, George, age 70, d. 11/16 Old Soldiers' Home, Atlanta. Came from Augusta yr. ago, where buried. AC 11/17/1905

PATTERSON, Griffith William D., Dr., age 72, d. 415 Greenwood Ave. Atlanta. AG 10/25/1909

PATTERSON, Hattie, Mrs., age 29, d. 615 Chestnut St.,A tlanta, Wed., wife of Charles M. Three small children, her parents, survive. AG 5/6/1909

PATTERSON, J. E., Mrs., age 71, d. Kirkwood (Atlanta). Daus: Mrs. T. F. Baird, Mrs. J. E. Watson of Atlanta, and Mrs. L. D. Wade, of Brunswick. Sons: J. H., of Shreveport, La., and J. C., of Kansas City, Mo. Interred: Newnan, Ga. AG 6/23/1910

PATTERSON, J. M. d. Tues. Hapeville, Ga., age 75. Wife, 6 children. Interred: McDonough, Ga. AG 9/21/1910

PATTERSON, Lamar E., age 2 mos., son of Mr. and Mrs. Z. B., d. 8 Bibb St., Atlanta, Fri. Interred: Casey's cemetery. AG 1/24/1908

PATTERSON, Lucy, colored, age 45, d. 198 Fraser St. Atlanta. AG 11/21/1910

PATTERSON, Margaret, Mrs., age 77, d. 67 Stonewall St.,tlanta, Thurs. Sons: S. S., J. W., Atlanta. Dau: Mrs. R. W. Allen, New York. Interred: Oakland. AG 5/21/1909

PATTERSON, N. A., Judge, age 83, d. Johnson City, Tenn. Wife, son, daus. AG 4/28/1910

PATTERSON, John K. of Stewart Co. d. Lumpkin, res. of John, John T. Patterson, age 87. Sons: Dr. Fred, Cuthbert; Dr. J. C., Lumpkin; Dr. J. W., Dawson; Dr. E. C., New Orleans; J. E., Miss. Interred: Family Cem., Wesley Chapel. AG 1/18/1910

PATTERSON, J. E., Mrs., age 71, d. Kirkwood (Atlanta). Daus: Mrs. T. F. Bat of Bremen, Ga., d. 10/26. Interred: Bremen. AG 10/27/1910

PATTERSON, N. A., Judge, age 83, d. Johnson City, Tenn. Wife, son, daus. AG 4/28/1910

PATTILLO, J. W., Mrs., age 37, d. Magazine Rd. Atlanta Sat. Interred: Macedonia Church. AG 6/1/1908

PATTILLO, Lake, colored, age 16, d. 101 N. Butler St. Atlanta. AG 2/4/1908

PATTILLO, W. P., age 72, d. 171 E. Fair St. Atlanta 4/12. Interred: Oakland. AG 4/13/1909

PATTMAN, J. W., age 89, d. 173 Alexander St. Atlanta. AG 2/25/1907

PATTON, Emma E., Miss, age 57, d. 326 Washington St. Atlanta. AG 3/3/1908

PATTON, Francis C., age 2 yrs., d. 96 N. Lawn St. Atlanta. AG 5/12/1910

PATTON, J. B., Sr., one of Rome's oldest citizens, d. today. Survivors: Wife, 4 children, Harry, Joe and Charlie Patton; Mrs. F. N. Shropshire, Atlanta. AG 9/1/1906

PATTON, Oliver B. d. Huntsville, Ala. Wife. Ch: Mrs. Richard Miller, Mrs. James L. Darwin, Miss Shelby Patton, Dr. Irvine Patton, Dr. O. B. Patton, Huntsville, Humes Patton, Minnesota, Mrs. R. W. Walker, Ft. Oglethorpe, Ga. AG 12/13/1909

PATTON, R. M., age 30, d. 69 Luckie St. Atlanta. Interred: Albany, Ga. AG 8/29/1907

PATTY, Ezekiel, age 14 mos., son of Mr. and Mrs. C. ., d. Atlanta Fri., 126 Curran St. Interred: Rock Springs Church. AG 1/4/1908

PAUL, Alex, age 45, committed suicide Lexington, Ga. Wife, 7 children. AG 9/15/1906

PAUL, G. S., age 83, d. Soldiers' Home. Atlanta. AG 9/21/1908

PAUL, J. S., age 83, Confederate Veteran d. Soldiers' Home, Atlanta Fri. Interred: Marietta, Ga. One son, two daus. AG 9/19/1908

PAULSON, Edith, Miss, age 20, in Portland, Oreg. recd Mon. by her bro., Joe Paulson of Atlanta. AG 3/12/1907

PAUSE, Clarence, age 14, d. 101 N. Butler St. Atlanta. AG 3/11/1909

PAYNE, C. M., Mrs., age 67, wife of late Columbus M., d. 160 Spring St., Atlanta, Mon. Dau: Mrs. F. F. Flood, Atlanta. Sis: Mrs. P. A. Creed, Conyers. AG 10/19/1908

PAYNE, Elizabeth, Mrs., wid. of Rev. N. H. Cou: Mrs. Lucian L. Knight, Atlanta, d. while she and dau., Annie, were visiting dau., Mrs. H. N. Bullard, Mound City, Mo. Sons: Portner, Philadelphia; Howard. Bur: Natl Cem. Marietta. AG 8/10/1906

PAYNE, Emily H., Mrs. d. Memphis, Tenn. Mon. res. of dau. Funeral: Macon. Interred: Rose Hill. Dau: Mrs. W. W. Carnes, Memphis, Tenn. Sons: Dr. George F. Payne, Atlanta; W. S. Payne, Montgomery. AG 8/3/1910

PAYNE, Emma, Miss d. Sat. Atlanta. Interred: Bridgeport, Ala. AG 11/23/1908

PAYNE, Emma, Miss, age 37, d. 101 N. Butler St. Atlanta. AG 11/25/1906

PAYNE, Mattie, Mrs., age 67, d. 160 Spring St. Atlanta. AG 10/20/1908

288

PAYNE, Ruth, Mrs., age 18, d. Sat. 104 Jones Ave., Atlanta. Husband survives. Interred: Duluth. AG 1/4/1907

PAYNE, Sarah Ann, Mrs. d. age 69, son's res., W. L. Payne, 213 Central Ave., Atlanta, Wed. Interred: Decatur Cemetery. Dau: Mrs. M. E. Smith of Albany. Sons: W. L., S. M., J. M., Atlanta. AG 6/9/1910

PAYTON, Mattie, age 51, colored, d. 172 Bradley alley, Atlanta. AG 11/11/1909

PAYTON, Winnie, colored, age 47, d. 109 Houston St. Atlanta. AG 10/3/1907

PEABODY, E. P. funeral 9/22 Waycross, Ga. Father-in-law: Col. S. W. Hitch. AG 9/23/1910

PEACE, Fannie, Miss d. Sat. 603 Sells Ave. Atlanta. Interred: Westview. AG 5/20/1907

PEACOCK, Billie Jones, age 2, son of Rev. and Mrs. E. H., d. corner Simpson and Orme Sts., Atlanta, Thurs. Interred: Hollywood Cemetery. AG 12/14/1907

PEACOCK, C. E., Mrs., age 66, d. 201 Chapel St., Atlanta, Wed. Ch: J. S. Peacock, Mrs. Ella Cooper, Mrs. Cora Wagner, Mrs. Lula Robins, Mrs. Minnie Smith, Atlanta. Interred: Mt. Gilead Church. AT 1/30/1908

PEACOCK, Josephine Banks, Mrs., wife of G. J., d. Wynnton, Ga., age 62. Leaves husband, 4 children. AG 7/25/1906

PEACOCK, L. M. of Eastman d. 6/28, age 62. Wife, 6 children. AG 6/29/1909

PEACOCK, P. L. d. Thurs. Cochran. His wife was buried one week ago Wed. AG 2/22/1907

PEACOCK, Ray, age 23, d. 312 Bellwood Ave. Atlanta. AG 4/23/1908

PEACOCK, Samantha, Mrs., widow of D. W., of Clayton Co., d. Sat. Morrow, Ga. AG 9/26/1910

PEARCE, J. R. d. 9/15. Interred: Fitzgerald, Ga., family burying ground. Parents: Mr. and Mrs. W. R. Pearce. 4 bros, one sister. AG 9/16/1909

PEARCE, Mary M., Miss, dau. of Prof. H. J., Pres. of Brenau College, d. res. of grandparents, Mr. and Mrs. John S. Matthews, Mon., Columbus, Ga. AG 12/17/1910

PEARCE, Arthur, colored, age 30, d. Memphis, Tenn. AG 11/8/1910

PEARL, Fannie L., age 28, d. 603 Sells Ave. Atlanta. AG 5/21/1907

PEARSON, Albert E., age 74, d. Columbus, Ga. 1/15. Wife, 8 children. AG 1/15/1910

PEARSON, Geraldine C., Mrs., age 39, d. Atlanta. AG 10/5/1908

PEARSON, H. M., Mrs. d. 149 Summitt Ave., Atlanta, Mon. Interred: Knoxville, Tenn. AG 4/29/1908

PEARSON, Harden shot and killed by negro farm hand, Charlie Harris near Dearing, Ga., 25 miles W of Augusta. Negro was then lynched. AG 5/7/1907

PEARSON, Joe, colored, age 20, d. Grady Hospital. Atlanta. AG 9/5/1906

PEARSON, Orie, inf. dau. of Mr. and Mrs. D. C., 195 Echols St., Atlanta, d. Fri. Interred: Caseys Cemetery. AG 7/17/1909

PEARSON, Sarah P., Mrs., age 88, d. Wed. Funeral dau.'s res., Mrs. Mary A. Goodhardt, 23 McDaniel St. Interred: Westview. Leaves two daus. AG 4/8/1909

PEARSON, Vienna V., Mrs., age 73, d. 223 Capitol Ave., Atlanta, Thurs. Son: C. D. Pearson, Macon. Interred: Eatonton, Ga. AG 3/13/1908

PEARY, Walter, colored, age 17, d. 84 Gray St., Atlanta, Oct. 27. AG 10/29/1910

PEASE, Charles R., age 31, killed in train wreck near Rome, Ga., Tues. Interred: Morrison, Ill. AG 10/30/1908

PEAVEY, Alva E., young son of Mrs. M. O. Peavey, 333 E. Luckie St., Atlanta, d. Mon. AG 7/10/1906

PEAVY, Arthur R., carpenter, killed by falling from top of Forsyth Bldg., tlanta, Sat. Res. of 17 Holderness St. Interred: Peachtree Church yard. AG 8/1/1910

PEAVY, Cora, Miss accidentally killed Thurs. Atlanta. Interred: Peachtree Church yard. AG 9/10/1910

PEBWORTH, Annie, Mrs., age 48, d. Atlanta Tues. Interred: Montgomery, Ala. One dau: Mrs. Agnes Schenck, E. Point. AG 2/22/1910

PECK, Harry L., age 50, d. 10 Boulevard Terr. Oct. 27, Atlanta. Wife, Jessie. Dau: Frances E. Sis: Mrs. D. B. Curtis of Oshkosh, Wis. and Mrs. Arthur Snell of Fargo, W. Dak. Interred: Westview. AG 11/1/1910

PECK, Mrs. of Senoia, Ga. d. Sun. AG 4/24/1907

PEEDE, Harlette, Mrs., wife of J. A. of Sibley, Ga., d. Sat. Interred: Rose Hill Cemetery, Macon, Ga. AG 12/13/1909

PEEDE, Meryl, age 2, son of Mr. and Mrs. F. A. of Butler, Ga. d. Thurs. res. of C. P. Spillers on Western Heights. Interred: Butler, Ga. AG 12/28/1907

PEEK, Eva L., Miss, N. Blvd. school teacher, Atlanta, d. by falling from window. Sis: Miss Belle Peek. Mother res. 76 Waddell St. AG 11/27/1910

PEEK, Green, colored, age 87, d. 92 Younge St. Atlanta. AG 10/3/1907

PEEK, Henry, Judge d. 11/9 Athens, Ga. Born 1805. Son: Hon. W. L. AC 11/12/1905

PEEK, James M., 73, d. 92 Luckie St. Atlanta. Sons: T. D., E. G. Daus: Mrs. Sydney West, Chattanooga; Mrs. G. M. Littleton, Norris, SC.; Thoenia Peek, Central, SC. Sis: Susie Peek; Mrs. Tobe Clay, Marietta. Bur: Central, SC. AG 8/19/1909

PEEK, John C., age 78, d. 97 Ivy St. Atlanta. AG 3/10/1908

PEEPLES, Annie Wright, in Memoriam, d. 7/22. She md. 4/4/1900 Thomas Jackson Peeples. AG 7/30/1907

PEEPLES, Thos J., Mrs., husb son of Judge Cincinnatus, d. 481 Piedmont. Atlanta. Bur: Westview. Formerly Annie, dau. of Wm C. Wright. Sis: Mrs. Jno W. Wing, Mrs. Chas Phinizy, Athens. Bros: Philip (Augusta) & Ronson Wright (NY) AG 7/24/1907

PEGRAM, Sarah Frances Leigh, Mrs., widow of Capt. Robert. of Confed. Nacy, d. 8/14, age 80, Norfolk, Va. AC 8/15/1905

PELFRY, Clio, inf. dau. of Mr. and Mrs. Alonzo, d. Atlanta Mon. Interred: in the country. AG 10/29/1907

PELFRY, Willie, age 3 mos., son of Mr. and Mrs. J. A., 139 Jefferson St., Atlanta, d. Fri. Interred: Caseys Cemetery. AG 3/26/1909

PELHAM, Ambrose, Rev., age 84, preacher 60 yrs. d. Enterprise, Ga. Leaves wife, four children. AG 5/10/1907

PENCE, T. B., age 61, d. 69 Luckie St. Atlanta. AG 4/28/1908

PENDER, W. D., aged citizen of Brunswick, d. Thurs. home of dau.,
Mrs. C. C. Crofton, 1007 G Street. AG 10/27/1906

PENDERGAST, J. J., **Mrs.** d. Mon., 26 Orange St. Former res. of
Macon. One son, two sisters, of Goggins, Ga. AG 7/27/1909

PENDLETON, George W. d. Tues. E. Point, Ga. Interred: Westview.
AG 5/10/1906

PENDLETON, S. B., **Mrs.**, age 36, d. Atlanta. AG 12/6/1908

PENDLEY, John L. d. Marble Hill, Ga. Interred: Tate, Ga. AC
11/16/1905

PENDLEY, P. d. 214 Bryan St. Atlanta. Interred: Westview. AG
6/13/1906

PENN, C. A. killed by railroad car Valdosta, Ga. 2/1906. Suit
filed by wife. AG 4/30/1906

PENNY, H. H. d. Thurs. 96 Terry St., Atlanta, Sat. Interred:
Westview. AG 12/14/1907

PENT, **Lawrence J.**, age 12, son of Mr. and Mrs. L. F., 43 Tifton
St., Atlanta, d. Fri. Interred: Hollywood. AG 2/27/1910

PENT, **Lawrence J.**, son of Mr. and Mrs. L. F. funeral Sun.
Interred: Rose Hill. AG 2/28/1910

PENTICOST, J. C., former Winder, Ga. citizen, recently of Albany,
d. Thurs., age 28. Leaves wife, formerly Miss Blanche Hazlett of
Lawrenceville. Interred: Family Burial Ground near Winder. AG
9/26/1908

PENWICK, **Henry A.**, **Mrs.** d. Sat. Brunswick, Ga. Leaves husband,
two small children. AG 8/27/1907

PEPPERS, J. M., age 23, of Suwanee, killed at Suluth by train. AG
7/16/1906

PERCELL, **Hubert**, age 10 mos., d. 17 Tennessee Ave. Atlanta. AG
4/26/1907

PERINGTON, **Frank**, colored, age 57, d. 151 Connally St. Atlanta.
AG 4/8/1908

PERKERSON, **Ellen Eulalia, Miss**, dau. of Mrs. A. M., b. 6/1/1879,
d. 205 Spring St., Atlanta, Mon. Interred: Fam. Cem., Mt. Zion.,
by her 4 bros., W. T, H. M., E. J. and A. M. AG 3/22/1909

PERKINS, **Caroline**, colored, age 60, d. 88 Bell St. Atlanta. AG
4/13/1909

PERKINS, **Cora E.**, **Mrs.**, age 29, d. Atlanta Thurs., wife of
Charles E. of 506 S. Pryor St., Atlanta. Kin: C. E. Perkins,
James Whitmire, S. P. Marbut, Ab Marbut, Arthur Marbut, T. L.
Morgan. AG 8/7/1908

PERKINS, **infant** of Mr. and Mrs. P. P., d. 27 Kirkwood Ave.
Atlanta. AG 11/5/1906

PERKINS, J. H., Judge, Confed. Vet., d. Greensboro, Ga., interred
old family burying ground near Greshamville. He was native of
Greene Co. Ch: Earl Perkins, Mrs. Mamie Oswaltz, Fairbolt, Ala.,
Mrs. Susie Smith, Greshamville. AG 12/3/1909

PERKINS, J. R. d. Broxton, Ga. 4/12. Friends in South Ga. and
Cheraw, S. C. AC 5/14/1905

PERKINS, J. S., **Mrs.** of Jennings, Fla. d. 5/12. Dau. of A. S.
Johns of n. Fla. Leaves husband, young child. AG 5/12/1906

PERKINS, **Joe**, colored, age 27, d. Birmingham, Ala. AG 8/28/1907

PERKINS, **Sarah** killed 192 Butler St., Atlanta several mos. ago.
Albert White, negro, charged. AG 11/17/1910

PERKINS, W. E., age 50, d. McLendon St., Atlanta, Tues. Wife, 2 daus: Misses Helen and India Perkins. One son. Interred: Westview. AG 7/7/1909

PERRANT, W. W., age 72, d. 11/11 Stockbridge, Ga. Interred: Oakland. AC 11/12/1905

PERRINE, Carry, Mrs., age 65, d. Mon. 264 Boulevard, Atlanta. Husband, two sisters. AG 5/8/1906

PERRY, infant of Mr. and Mrs. John Archibald, d. Winder, Ga., Fri. AG 10/3/1910

PERRY, Allen S., age 44, planter of Americus, d. 2/12. 5 ch. Bro: James R. Perry, Americus, Ga. AC 2/14/1905

PERRY, L. C., age 38, d. 439 Davis St. Atlanta, Tues. AG 11/16/1910

PERRY, Lecty, Mrs., wife of C. E., age 48, d. 109 N. Pryor St. Atlanta. Son and dau. survives. Interred: Westview. AG 7/8/1907

PERRY, Mrs. killed by her husband, Herbert, negroes, Salem, Ala. 12/29. AG 12/30/1910

PERRY, Sadie, Miss, age 22, d. College St., Decatur, Sun. Interred: Decatur Cemetery. AG 5/22/1910

PERRY, Sallie, colored, age 70, d. 217 W. Hunter St. Atlanta. AG 3/22/1907

PERRY, Violer, colored, age 29, d. 48 Bynum St. Atlanta. AG 1/8/1908

PERRYMAN, Allie, Mrs., age 36, d. 147 Chapel St. Atlanta. AG 2/1/1907

PERRYMAN, B. A., age 80, d. Heflin, Ala. Ch: Mrs. J. R. Little, Miss Hattie, Frank M., Jep of Atlanta; Mrs. Morgan, Eula, Dave and Gus of Heflin, Ala. AG 6/8/1906

PERRYMAN, Virgil H., age 76, d. 147 Chapel St. Atlanta, Thurs. Wife, two sons, V. E. and W. M., survive. Dau: Miss Dora. Interred: Westview. AG 12/4/1908

PERRY, Leroy Griffin, age 1 mo., inf. son of Mr. and Mrs. N. V., d. home of W. C. Gill, Ormewood Park, Atlanta, Tues. AG 10/9/1907

PERRY, Rachel, Mrs., age 74, nat. of England, d. 26 Formwalt St., Atlanta. Son: Oliver H. of Hecla, S. D. Son-in-law: E. T. Davis, Chicago. Daus: Mrs. Dean, Madison, Wis.; Mrs. Hardesty, Birmingham, Ala. Bur: Providence, R. I. AG 10/30/1908

PERSON, Annie Maud, colored, age 13, d. 152 1/2 Butler St. Atlanta. AG 9/9/1910

PERSON, Edward, colored, age 40, d. 8 Grace St. Atlanta. AG 12/17/1910

PERSONS, Ogden G., Mrs. d. Forsyth, Ga. 10/13, wife of Col., dau. of A. W. Bramblett of Forsyth. Interred: Oakland. AC 10/16/1905

PERSONS, Sarah, Mrs. d. home of her dau. at Juliette, Ga., Fri. Leaves several children. Interred: Culloden. AG 1/14/1907

PETERS, J. D., Sr. of Lowndes Co. d. 7/12, age 85. Born in S. C., moved to Lowndes Co., Ga. 1820. Interred: Old Union Church, near Milltown, Ga. AC 7/12/1905

PETERS, Rebecca, Miss, age 22, d. Sun. res. of parents, Mr. and Mrs. J. R. Peters, Kirkwood Ave. Atlanta. Interred: Gloster, Ga. AG 4/30/1907

PETERSON, Martha, Mrs. d. Douglas, Ga., age 70. AC 2/12/1905

PETTIJOHN, John F., age 39, d. Grady Hospital. Atlanta. Interred: Athens, Ga. AG 5/1/1907

PETTIS, Rosser Hamilton, Charlotte, N. C. drummer found in Savannah River last Sat., abt 3 miles below Augusta. AG 6/3/1908

PETTUS, Edmund W., Mrs., age 82, wife of Sen., d. Sun. Interred: Live Oak cem. beside son, late Francis L. Pettus. AG 7/16/1906

PETTUS, E. W., Mrs., age 35, d. 24 Bradley St. Atlanta. Husband exonerated of blame by coroner's jury. AG 2/28/1907 AG 3/1/1907

PETTUS, Mattie, Mrs., age abt 45, d. Jan. 14, fell off back porch of Roscoe Clark, 21 Fortress Ave., Atlanta. Husband: S. J. Pettus, Buckhead, Ga. AC 1/15/1905

PETTY, Evelyn, age 2, d. 71 Oakland Ave. Atlanta. AG 9/1/1908

PETTY, Kate, Mrs., mother of Mrs. Jere Blanton, d. 6/28 Huntsville, Ala. Interred: Belfast, Tenn. AC 6/30/1905

PETTY, Lula, colored, age 37, d. 118 E. Fair St., rear, Atlanta. AG 6/10/1907

PETTY, M. L., Mrs., d. Thurs. 49 Milledge St., Atlanta. AG 10/6/1906

PETTY, Marguerite J., age 19 mos., dau. of Mr. and Mrs. W. O., of 219-B E. Fair St., Atlanta, d. Mon. Interred: Powder Springs, Ga. AG 7/21/1908

PEYTON, Katie, age 1, d. 73 Bellwood Ave. Atlanta. AG 7/9/1908

PHANES, Louisa, Mrs., age 68 d. Fairburn, Ga. Wed. Interred: College Park Cemetery. Husband, 6 sons, 4 daus. AG 9/10/1908

PHARR, Mary E., Mrs. d. 3/18, age 76. Bro: Henry W. Miller. Sisters: Mrs. A. E. Edge, Misses Carrie and Lou Miller. AG 3/18/1908

PHELPS, C. W., Mrs. d. 430 Pulliam St., Atlanta. Interred: Westview. AG 12/1/1907

PHELPS, Charles W. d. 430 Pulliam St., Atlanta, Fri. Interred: Westview. AG 2/24/1908

PHELPS, Elizabeth, Mrs. d. Columbus, Ga. yesterday, age 65. Dau: Mrs. W. D. Affeck of Columbus, Ga. Interred: Notasulga, Ala. AG 11/20/1907

PHELPS, Henry M. d. Birmingham, Ala. Fri., age 16, son of Mr. and Mrs. W. C. Phelps of Edgewood, Ga. AG 11/9/1907

PHELPS, Lilla, colored, age 48, d. Henry St. Atlanta. AG 8/26/1909

PHELPS, Lorena, Mrs., age 39, d. 6 Lynch St. Atlanta. Ag 6/25/1910

PHEW, Willie, colored, age 22, d. 101 N. Butler St. Atlanta. AG 3/7/1907

PHILEN, E. M., fireman, fell from truck to death 7/13 Birmingham, Ala. AG 7/14/1909

PHILIP, Peter C., age 50, d. Wed. 336 Simpson St. Atlanta. Wife, one child. Interred: Augusta, Ga. AG 6/30/1910

PHILIPS, Mary, colored, age 46, d. 263 Chapel St. Atlanta. AG 7/1/1907

PHILIPS, Nellie, inf. dau. of Mr. and Mrs. Andrew, 122 Main St., Atlanta, d. Wed. AG 7/7/1909

PHILIPS, Newton M., Jr., age 12, d. Mon., 202 Courtland St.,tlanta. Interred: Kansas City. AG 6/7/1910

PHILIPS, R. L., Mrs., formerly Miss Minnie Kirby of Dalton, Ga., d. Mon. Tuscon, Ariz, age 34. Husband, one small child. AG 5/4/1910

PHILIPS, Rachel, colored, age 2, d. 40 Kurht St. Atlanta. AG 5/4/1909

293

PHILIPS, William, age 53, d. 9/1 Phenix, Ala. Wife. 2 sons. Interred: Bethany Church, near Alexander City, Ala. AC 9/3/1905

PHILLIPS, Mr. killed by desperado, William Fowler, Cartersville, Ga. AG 9/2/1910

PHILLIPS, A. F., Mrs., age 60, d. 544 Washington St. Atlanta. Interred: Lafayette, R. I. AG 4/10/1907

PHILLIPS, A., Mrs. d. Fri. 279 Glenn St. Atlanta. Interred: Westview. AG 6/21/1907

PHILLIPS, Ben, negro, killed 12/2 by live wire. AC 12/4/1905

PHILLIPS, Ben H. d. Sat. Atlanta. Interred: Westview. AG 10/24/1910

PHILLIPS, Bleckley, age 26, d. Sun. at Roanoke, Ala., son of Mr. and Mrs. G. D. of 51 Clark St., Atlanta. Interred: Roanoke, Ala. AG 5/21/1907

PHILLIPS, Buena, Mrs., wife of Joseph, d. East Point Mon. Husband, 4 children. Interred: Antioch, 4 mi. from Fairburn. AG 4/23/1907

PHILLIPS, C. E., age 62, of 218 Kirkwood Ave., Atlanta, d. Fri. Wife, one son, 3 daus, two bros. AG 11/26/1909

PHILLIPS, C. E., age 64, d. 101 Butler St. Atlanta. AG 11/27/1909

PHILLIPS, C. L., age 27, son of Virgil, d. near Oakland City, Ga. Sun. Interred: Fairburn, Ga. AG 10/13/1908

PHILLIPS, Clyde, colored, age 25, d. city stockade. Atlanta. AG 8/24/1908

PHILLIPS, J. A., age 42, d. 2/21, 285 E. Georgia Ave. Atlanta. Mother: Mrs. N. E. Phillips of Atlanta. 4 sisters, 2 bros. Interred: Westview. AG 2/22/1910

PHILLIPS, J. C., age 78, d. 25 Terrell St., Atlanta. Interred: Norcross, Ga. AG 12/8/1909

PHILLIPS, Julia E., age 2 mos., dau. of Mr. and Mrs. L. S., d. Atlanta. Interred: Westview. AG 3/31/1910

PHILLIPS, Julius, Mrs. A. Tosewitz, San Francisco. Bros: Hugh Phillips, Eagle Pass, Tx.; Felix Phillips, Athens, Ga. Interred: Oakland. AG 7/18/1908

PHILLIPS, Katie B., Miss, age 18, d. 441 Pulliam St. Atlanta. AG 3/23/1908

PHILLIPS, Lester, age 19, d. E. Point, Ga. Sun. Interred: Cress Hill Cemetery. Mother, four bros., two sisters. AG 6/14/1909

PHILLIPS, Lizzie, Mrs. d. mother;s home, Mrs. Wilkinson, LaGrange, Sun. She was wid. of late D. E. Phillips. Interred Hill View. Sisters: Mrs. Frank Tatum, Lula and Kate Wilkinson, LaGrange. Little dau. AG 1/1/1907

PHILLIPS, Lottie Regina, inf. dau. of Mr. and Mrs. J. E., d. Sat. 18 Formwalt St., Atlanta. Interred: Hollywood. AG 5/27/1907

PHILLIPS, R. E., Mrs., age 59, d. 50 Daniels St., Atlanta Wed. Interred: Westview. AG 12/26/1907

PHILLIPS, R. L., age 42, d. Kirkwood, Ga. AG 7/12/1909

PHILLIPS, R. L. of East Point d. Thurs. Wife survives. Interred: East Point Cemetery. AG 10/2/1908

PHILLIPS, Rebecca, Mrs. d. Thurs. S. Kirkwood (Atlanta). Interred: Sylvester cemetery. AG 6/25/1910

PHILLIPS, Rosalie, inf. dau. of Mr. and Mrs. Milton, d. Sun. Grady Hospital, Atlanta. Res: 29 Hilliard St. Interred: Westview. AG 7/24/1907

PHILLIPS, Susan, Mrs., age 87, res. of Home for Old Women, d. last Sat. Interred: Augusta, Ga., her old old home. AG 3/10/1908
PHILLIPS, T. J. d. Atlanta Sat. Interred: Oak Hill, Griffin, Ga. He was son of W. R. Phillips, merchant for 20 yrs. in Texas. AG 1/2/1907
PHILLIPS, Thomas R. of E. Point, Ga. d. Sat, age 56. Interred: E. Point Cemetery. Wife, 7 children, and bro. survive. AG 5/9/1908
PHILLIPS, W. C. funeral 11/20 Bolling Springs Missionary Baptist Church. Swainsboro, Ga. AC 11/22/1905
PHILLIPS, W. C., Capt. d. Covena 9/1. Confed. Vet., age 74. Interred: Boil Spring Church. AC 9/6/1905
PHILLIPS, H. W., 52, d. Lowell, Ms. Mother: Mrs. N. E., Atlanta. Bros: L. W., 115 Garden St., Eugene, John. Sis: Mrs. E. R. Watson, Mrs. Lee Wingate, Atlanta; Mrs. Hitty Davis, Blacksburg, SC.; Mrs. Chas Edwards, Tyler, Tx. AG 5/14/1909
PHILLIPS, J. A., Capt., age 70, d. 5/28 Fitzgerald, Ga. Born Emanuel Co. m. Margaret McArthur. Daus: Sadie L. (decd); Ida E. (Mrs. J. H. Harris). Interred: Tifton, Ga., beside Sadie AC 5/30/1905
PHILLIPS, M. W., Mrs., age 77, wid. of Gen. Wm Phillips of Marietta, d. son´s res., George D., 51 Clarke St., Atlanta. Interred: Marietta Cemetery. Sons: W. W., Cartersville; George D., Atlanta; M. T., Newnan; H. M., Marietta. AG 12/13/1909
PHILLIPS, Julius, age 51, d. 52 Fulton St., Atlanta, Fri. Wife was Miss Irene Franklin, dau. of A. Franklin. Two children. Sisters: Mrs. Simon Michael, Athens; Mrs. Jake Phillips, San Antonio, Tx.; Mrs. M. Manassee, Atlanta;
PHILPOTT, Lucy, age two, dau. of Mr. and Mrs. Walter W., d. 22 Lynch Ave., Atlanta, Sun. Interred: Caseys Cemetery. AG 7/12/1909
PHINIZY, Shepherd, age 30, d. at county jail. Atlanta. AG 4/6/1907
PHRIMES, Cistoria, colored, age 38, d. Milledgeville, Ga. AG 7/29/1908
PICKARD, David B., age 75, d. Old Soldiers´ Home. Atlanta. AG 5/21/1910
PICKENS, Bertha, age 2, dau. of Mr. and Mrs. C. H. of 176 Poplar St., Atlanta. Interred: Caseys. AG 9/1/1908
PICKETT, Agnes Iola, age 3 yrs, d. res. of parents, Mr. and Mrs. J. L. Pickett, 223 W. Fair St. Atlanta. Interred: Westview. AG 7/20/1906
PICKETT, Cornelia, Mrs., age 32, wife of George M., d. 32 Grady Pl., Atlanta, Fri. AG 1/25/1908
PICKETT, E. S., Mrs., age 75, d. 21 Hood St. Atlanta. AG 3/4/1907
PICKETT, G. M., Mrs. d. Fri. Interred: her old home, Columbus, Ga. Leaves husband, one bro., Grafton Kimbrough of Columbus. She was formerly Miss Cornelia Kimbrough, b. Columbus, Ga. AG 1/31/1908
PICKETT, Lawrence D., 22, d. 90 Woodward Av. Atlanta. Wife, 1 ch. Par: Mr. & Mrs. E. L. Bros: J. B., W. E., J. M., Dahlonega; Louis G., F. B. Sis: Mrs. W. M. Carroll, Mrs. W. P. Edmondson, Miss M. L. Pickett. Bur: Westview. AG 10/11/1909
PICKETT, Margaret E., inf. dau. of Mr. and Mrs. F. S., funeral Wed., res. Glendale Ave. Interred: Wesley Church yard. AG 5/25/1910

PICKETT, S. F. M., age 77, d. Atlanta Tues, 37 Glendale St. Interred: Covington, Ga. 4 daus., 7 sons, 3 bros., 3 sisters. AG 1/11/1910

PICKETT, Thaddeus, age 64, of Ball Ground, Ga., d. Atlanta Sat. Son: R., Ball Ground. AG 8/7/1909

PICKRELL, Mattie Bell, age 3, dau. of Mr. and Mrs. L. A., d. Fri., 31 Tennelle St., Atlanta. Interred: Monroe, Ga. AG 5/11/1907

PIERCE, C. H., age 33, of Battle Hill, Ga., d. Atlanta Mon. Parents: Mr. and Mrs. R. E. Pierce. Sis: Misses E. G. and L. M. Pierce. Bro: J. R. AG 6/1/1909

PIERCE, Ed, negro, taken from sheriff Tues. and lynched by mob. AG 7/12/1906

PIERCE, Elsie, age 1, dau. of Mr. and Mrs. B. F., d. 31 Berean Ave., Atlanta. Interred: Sylvester Cemetery. AG 8/1/1910

PIERCE, George W., age 42, d. 52 Hendrix Ave., Atlanta, Thurs. Wife, four children. AG 8/7/1908

PIERCE, Gladys, age 1 mo., d. 309 Auburn Ave., Atlanta. Interred: Stone Mountain, Ga. AG 10/19/1907

PIERCE, J. W. d. Wed. Interred: Palmetto, Ga. Veteran of civil War. Wife, two daus, Mrs. M. L. Camp, Mrs. H. C. Baggett; two sons, E. J. and F. J. Pierce, survive. AG 5/8/1907

PIERCE, Ophelia, age 21, d. 73 King St. Atlanta. AG 2/1/1907

PIERCE, Quitman d. 11/4 604 Edgewood Ave. Atlanta. Interred: Hollywood Cemetery. AC 11/16/1905

PIERCE, S. B. found with throat cut, Valdosta, Ga., probable suicide. AG 5/7/1907

PIERCE, Sam Maddox, nephew of Hon. S. P. Maddox of Dalton, Ga., killed under train at Ramhurst, Murray Co., age 16. AG 2/19/1910

PIERCE, William, age 30, d. 101 N. Butler St. Atlanta. AG 12/6/1908

PIERSON, Charles, age 23, d. 18 Grady Pl. Atlanta. Interred: Westview. AG 8/17/1908

PIERSON, F. R., Mrs., age 35, d. Atlanta Thurs. Sister resides Milledgeville, Ga. AG 10/2/1908

PIERSON, S., Mrs., age 28, d. 101 N. Butler St. Atlanta. AG 12/3/1908

PIKE, Helen Olivia, age 4, d. 28 W. Peachtree St. Atlanta. AG 11/11/1909

PILKINTON, J. W., Judge d. Thomaston, Ga. Tues., age 65. AG 9/28/1910

PILLER, J. W. d. 706 N. Boulevard, Atlanta, Fri. He was b. Oglethorpe Co. 1850. Res. of Atlanta 4 yrs. Wife, 5 sons, Eugene Latimer, Arthur S. Word and George Piller, Atlanta, and Theodore H. Piller. 4 daus. AG 10/22/1909

PINCKARD, Fannie G., Mrs. d. 67 E. Merritts Ave., Atlanta Thurs. Interred: Westview. Husband. Daus: Mrs. A. S. Magbee, Mrs. P. S. Holt, Mrs. W. C. Ewing, Miss Lillian Pinkard. Son: L. R. AG 4/8/1909

PINCKARD, Lucian d. Sat. Allegheny, Pa. Interred: Atlanta, Westview. AG 9/13/1909

PINE, Theodore of Asheville, N. C. d. 6/10. Res. of NY and Chicago. Interred: Ossing. AC 6/11/1905

PINION, Charles William, inf. son of Mr. and Mrs. C. E., 757 Seaboard Ave. Atlanta, d. Mon. Interred: Oakland. AG 6/29/1909

PINION, Mary, Mrs., age 41, d. 70 Whitehall Terrace. Atlanta. AG 3/18/1909

PINION, Maud M., Miss, age 35, d. Mon. res. of parents, Mr. and Mrs. S. B. Pinion, 710 Marietta St., Atlanta. Bros: Luther, Charles B., L. H. and J. V. Interred: Oakland. AG 5/3/1910

PINKSTON, John Ray of Albany, Ga. d. Sat. Asheville, N. C. Ag 2/4/1908

PINKSTON, W. R., Rev., age 63, d. dau's res., Mrs. J. G. Dodd, 70 Fraser St., Atlanta, Wed. Interred: Cordele, Ga. AG 6/16/1910

PINNELL, James R., age 64, d. Martin St., Atlanta Thurs. Son: N. J. Dau: Mrs. L. E. Chastain,A tlanta. Wife. Interred: Peachtree Church yard. AG 9/11/1909

PINNELL, Robert, 38, of Atlanta, d. St. Joseph, Mo. Sis: Mrs. W. D. Armistead, Willie Pinnell, Mrs. W. C. Stovall, Mrs. W. M. Watkins, Mrs. Ed Joyner, Atlanta; Mrs. McDonald, Conyers; Mrs. Nash, Columbus. Bros: George, John. AG 10/12/1909

PINSEN, Annie, colored, age 16, d. 71 Robin St. Atlanta. AG 1/18/1907

PIPKIN, C. J., age 50, d. 893 Seaboard Ave. Atlanta. Interred: Westview. AG 10/14/1907

PITCHFORD, Minnie R., age 9 mos., d. 250 Ashby St. Atlanta. AG 4/10/1907

PITMAN, Shetrich, colored, age 20, d. 21 Berkle St. Atlanta. AG 9/24/1907

PITT, L. J., Mrs., age 56, d. corner Boulevard and Woodward Ave. Atlanta. AG 11/2/1907

PITT, Laura, Mrs., wife of T. W., funeral from res. of dau., Mrs. Will McAfee, 48 Hill St., Atlanta, Sun. Interred: Westview. AG 11/2/1907

PITTMAN, C. M., Mrs., age 70, d. 1 Garnett St. Atlanta. AG 12/22/1908

PITTMAN, Charles, young negro, switchman, killed by Central of Ga. train. Macon. AG 8/14/1907

PITTMAN, H. B., Mrs. d. 4/28 Waycross, Ga. Husband, several children survive. Interred: Lott Cemetery. AG 4/29/1908

PITTMAN, infant son of Mr. and Mrs. William, d. Wed. 196 Woodward Ave., Atlanta. AG 8/17/1910

PITTMAN, John, colored, age 47, d. 28 Whites alley. Atlanta. AG 1/28/1908

PITTMAN, Julia A., young dau. of Mr. and Mrs. A. C., d. 79 Whitehall Terr. Atlanta, Tues. Interred: Sylvester cemetery. AG 4/24/1907

PITTMAN, Rosa, colored, age 40, d. 133 Fowler St. Atlanta. AG 8/11/1908

PITTMAN, T. Jasper of Phenix City, Ala. d. res. of dau., Mrs. J. J. Smith, Columbus, Ga., Sun. Confed Vet. Wife, 3 daus. AG 5/17/1910

PITTMAN, Tommie, colored, age 47, d. 15 Holland St. Atlanta. AG 8/6/1907

PITTMAN, W. C., age 49, d. Manchester, Ga. AG 11/15/1909

PITTMAN, W. X. of E. Pt., d. Thurs. Husband, 5 daus., 3 sons. Interred: Mt. Zion. AG 4/21/1910

PITTMAN, W. Z., Mrs., of E. Point, d. Thurs. Husband, daus., 3 sons. Interred: Mt. Zion Church. AG 4/21/1910

PITTS, Annie, colored, age 27, d. 292 Fort St. Atlanta. AG 3/18/1909

PITTS, Bertha shot and killed by Albert Hopkins, few weeks ago in Waycross, Ga. Self-defense. AG 5/30/1910

PITTS, Emmet, negro, killed at saw mill of A. G. Lane near Ellerslie, Ga. AG 1/29/1907

PITTS, G., colored, age 5 mos., d. 220 Fort St. Atlanta. AG 11/21/1907

PITTS, Luke, colored, age 5, d. 836 Peachtree St., Atlanta, 10/22. AG 10/25/1910

PITTS, N. P., Mrs. d. Newborn, Ga. Interred: Newborn 8/10. Husband, 3 children. AG 8/11/1910

PITTS, W. M., Mrs., age 66, d. son's res., W. J. Pitts, 92 Greensferry Ave. Atlanta. Son: N. J. Interred: Cornelia, Ga. AG 8/12/1910

PLASKETT, Charles G., Qtr Master Sgt., of Ga. 12th U. S. Cavalry, Ft. Oglethorpe, Ga., killed by switching engine tonight, which was to take him back to Ga. AG 10/1/1907

PLASTER, D. L., age 73, d. Atlanta Mon. Interred: Rock Spring Church. AG 5/12/1908

PLASTER, Joshua A., age 64, d. Fri. Atlanta. Interred: Sardis Church. AG 2/14/1910

PLATT, Mary Lou, age 26, d. Asheville, N. C. Interred: Oakland. AG 6/8/1908

PLEASANT, Tenwa, colored, age 3 mos., d. 130 Bell St. Atlanta. AG 2/19/1907

PLUMMER, infant of Mr. and Mrs. C. A., d. 368 W. North Ave., Atlanta, Fri. Interred: Tucker, Ga. AG 1/10/1908

PLUNKETT, Charles, Mrs., age 38, wife of J. A., d. 143 English Ave., Atlanta, Fri. Interred: Hollywood. Husband, 4 sons, 2 daus, mother, 1 bro., 2 sisters, survive. AG 7/24/1909

PLUNKETT, infant, son of Mr. and Mrs. J. A. d. Careys Sta., Ga. Thurs. Interred: Hollywood. AG 5/21/1908

PLUNKETT, John W., age 29, d. Sat. 457 Hazel St., Macon, Ga. Parents: Mr. and Mrs. H. A. Plunkett. 2 bros., 5 sisters. Interred: Evergreen Cemetery. AG 11/7/1910

POGUE, S. H. d. Thurs. Bro: J. J. Pogue, Lima, Ohio. AG 7/6/1906

POGUE, S. H., blind pencil seller, d. in jail Thurs. Interred: Harriman, Tenn. Bro: J. J. Pogue of Lima, Ohio. Left wife, 4 children. AG 7/7/1906

POHLMAN, H. F., Mrs., age 35, d. Atlanta, Mon. Dau: Mrs. W. H. Bennett. Grdau: Mrs. Ben Lee Crew. Interred: Bainbridge, Ga. AG 11/1/1910

POINDEXTER, Miriam, Miss, age 50, d. 50 1/2 Jones Ave. Atlanta. AG 7/19/1909

POLHILL, J. H., Mrs., wife of druggist of Fitzgerald, Ga., d. 7/16. AG 7/16/1908

POLK, Lawrence, Mrs., age 25, d. Decatur Mon. Had been married only one yr. Interred: Westview. AG 12/15/1908

POLLARD, G. W., age 77, d. Soldiers' Home, Atlanta, Fri. Dau: Mrs. F. C. Exley f 1 Gordon St., Savannah, Ga. AG 1/11/1908

POLLS, Fannie, colored, age 43, d. 345 Woodward Ave. Atlanta, rear. AG 1/19/1907

POLTAN, William D., colored, age 44, d. 156 Bell St. Atlanta. AG 6/10/1907

PONDER, Amos of Monroe Co. d. Tues., age 68. Wife, several children. Interred: Family Burial Ground. AG 10/8/1909

PONDER, George, colored, age 30, d. alms house. Atlanta. AG 11/21/1910

PONDER, L. H., age 36, d. Macon. AG 10/8/1906

PONDER, S. K., age 1, d. 350 Mangum St. Atlanta. AG 10/29/1907

PONDER, Susie Katherine, inf. dau. of Mr. and Mrs. H. P., d. 350 Mangum St., Atlanta. Mon. Interred: Hollywood. AG 10/26/1907

PONDERS, Willie, colored, age 80, d. 294 W. Mitchell St., Atlanta, on 10/4. AG 1/6/1910

POOL, Violet, colored, age 66, d. 72 Eliza St. Atlanta. AG 1/1/1908

POOLE, Daisy E., Miss d. Thurs. res. of bro., Norman T. Poole, 200 Folk St., Atlanta. Parents: Mr. and Mrs. D. B. C. Poole. 4 bros., 3 sisters. AG 10/6/1910

POOLE, Elizabeth H., Mrs., age 62, d. 457 Gordon St. Atlanta 9/24. Husband: W. F. Sons: William, C. F., T. O., Harry G. Dau: Bessie. Bro: J. S. Gilbert, Atlanta. Sis: Mrs. S. A. Taliaferro, Atlanta. Interred: Westview. AG 9/24/1909

POOLE, Joseph, age 15, d. Presbyterian Hospital. Atlanta. AG 5/1/1907

POOLE, Lawrence D. P., Jr., age 17, d. Wed., son of Mr. and Mrs. L. D. P., 16 Warren St., Atlanta. Interred: Nashville, Tenn. AG 6/8/1910

POOLE, Thomas H. d. Early Co., Ga. Funeral 3/7 at Douglasville, Ga. Interred: Family Cemetery. Wife, 3 children. AG 3/9/1910

POOR, infant of J. W. d. 146 Rockwell St., Atlanta, Tues. Interred: Woodstock, Ga. AG 10/9/1907

POORE, William L. of Canon, Ga. suicide last night. Wife, thee children, mother, three brothers, two sisters. AG 1/18/1907

POPE, Burwell, former res. of Atlanta, d. Gadsden, Ala. Wife was Miss Clifford Cassels of Atlanta. Several bros. Interred: Gadsden, Ala. AG 5/14/1909

POPE, Cliff G., age 42, former Atlantan who m. Miss Maie Walker of Atlanta (d. several yrs. ago), d. Jackson, Miss. Interred: Atlanta, Oakland Cem. AG 7/8/1909

POPE, Fannie, Mrs., age 24, d. 200 Jones Ave. Atlanta. AG 6/12/1908

POPE, Helen, Mrs., widow of late Dr. Sampson Pope, d. Newberry S. C. yesterday. AG 8/14/1906

POPE, Josiah P., citizen of Jasper Co., d. Monticello, Ga. Tues., age 84. AG 6/30/1910

POPE, Mit, age 31, formerly of Atlanta, d. NY. Parents: Mr. & Mrs. R. S. Pope, Atlanta. Bros: R. S., Jr., Atlanta; W. W., Brownsville, Tx. Sis: Mrs. J. A. Inzer, Gadsden, Ala.; Mrs. C. H. Shelton, Atlanta. Bur: Westview. AG 9/2/1910

PORCH, George, colored, age 80, d. Fulton Co. barracks. Atlanta. AG 11/12/1910

PORCHER, Esther G., Mrs., age 77, d. 10 Piedmont Pl. Atlanta. AG 7/25/1910

PORTER, Anathy B., age 70, former Georgian, kills himself in New York. AG 6/3/1908

PORTER, B. H., age 63, d. 20 W. Peachtree Place. Atlanta. AG 6/18/1907

PORTER, G. A., Jr., inf. son of Mr. and Mrs. G. A., d. Atlanta Wed. Interred: Hollywood. AG 4/21/1909

PORTER, G. A., age 7 mos., d. 37 Almo Ave. Atlanta. AG 4/22/1909

PORTER, Helen, Miss, only dau. of F. R., d. 11/25 Newborn, Ga., age 22. AC 11/26/1905

PORTER, Katie P., Miss d. res. of Mr. and Mrs. Andrew M. Soule Sat., Athens, Ga. (sister) Interred: Baltimore, Md. AG 9/27/1909

PORTER, Mary Kate, Mrs., age 20, wife of G. T., d. Cooper St., Atlanta, Mon. Interred: Concord, Ga. AG 4/20/1909

PORTER, Massie, Mrs., age 56, d. 12 1/2 N. Pryor St. Atlanta. AG 6/21/1906

PORTER, Son, colored, age 25, d. Fulton C. Alms House. AG 2/26/1908

PORTER, Walter funeral Thurs, 12/1, Sacred Heart. Relatives: Mr. and Mrs. W. B. Porter, Mrs. Anna E. Gramling, Dr. Robert E. Gramling, Mrs. Kate Hardin, Mrs. Barbara K. Porter, Mrs. Anne Spalding. AG 11/30/1910

PORTER, Walter B., age 55, d. 624 Peachtree St. Atlanta. AG 11/30/1910

POSEY, Hubert, shot and killed by Mrs. Mollie Bowie and her son, Henry, because he did not marry "sis" Bowie, who was 2nd cousin to Posey. AG 1/21/1907

POSS, C. C., age 61, d. Sun. AG 11/2/1907

POSS, Clements, inf. son of Mr. and Mrs. J. P., d. Wed. 304 Wiley St., Atlanta, Thurs. Interred: Sylvester. AG 7/8/1909

POSS, J. T., age 36, d. 25 Clark St. Atlanta. AG 9/2/1909

POSS, M. J. Kenney, Mrs., age 60, d. 15 Verner St., Atlanta, Mon. Interred: McCollum, Ga. AG 2/24/1908

POSS, Maggie, age 4, dau. of Mr. and Mrs. C. C., d. 175 Powell St. Atlanta, Tues. Interred: Smyrna, Ga. AG 12/18/1907

POST, Nancy Ellen, Mrs., age 39, d. Mon. 175 Curran St. Atlanta. Leaves mother, several sisters. AG 5/21/1906

POSTON, R. A., age 30, d. police station, Atlanta. AG 5/21/1907

POTTER, Ella, Miss, dau. of Mr. and Mrs. George A., d. Thurs. 340 Lee St., Atlanta. Interred: Westview. AG 8/8/1907

POTTER, Ella, Miss, dau. of Mrs. Julia S. Potter, d. 8/8/1907. AG 8/26/1907

POTTER, G. G., Mrs., age 87, d. 340 Lee St. Atlanta. AG 2/14/1907

POTTER, Lester, age 2, d. Nelson, Ga. AG 11/21/1907

POTTER, Julia S., Mrs., age 58, d. dau.'s res., Mrs. S. M. Willingham, Masons & Turners Ferry Rd. Res: 340 Lee St. Daus: Ella (d. 8/8), Mrs. J. G. Worley, Marietta, Hennie, Eula and Hattie, George A., Jr. Interred: Oakland. AG 8/27/1907

POTTS, Elizabeth LeRoy, Mrs., age 20, d. Peachtree Rd. Atlanta. AG 4/13/1909

POTTS, Ethel May, age 3, d. 101 N. Boulevard. Atlanta. AG 8/25/1908

POTTS, Frank M., age 74, d. 21 E. Fifth St. Atlanta. AG 1/11/1910

POTTS, Margaret, 4 mos. infant of Mr. and Mrs. W. T., d. Edgewood, Thurs. Interred: Conyers. AG 8//1906

POUND, Abel F., Col, d. 112 Crew St., Atlanta, Sun. Interred: Oakland. Wife, 3 daus., Mrs. F. E. Winburn, Mrs. G. R. Edmundson, Miss Grace Pound. Sons: Theodore F., Linton. Bros: T. S. Pound, Birmingham; Long Pound, Columbus, AG 3/13/1909

POUND, E. E., Mrs. d. Jackson 10/24, age 69. Ch: O. A. Pound, Atlanta; Robert Pound, Nashville; Mrs. J. M. Currie, Jackson; Mrs. E. K. Williams, Ft. Leavenworth, Kans.; Mrs. J. T. Harris and Miss Eloise Pound, Jackson, Ga. AG 10/24/1910

POUND, Jere, age 15, son of Jere M. Pound, accidentally killed 5/7 at Dr. Allen's plantation, near Milledgeville, by playmate. AG 5/7/1910

POWELL, B. F., age 46, d. Sun. 631 Washington St. Interred: Mt. Zion Church yard. AG 3/25/1907

POWELL, B. J., age 46, d. 631 Capitol Ave. Atlanta. AG 3/25/1907

POWELL, G. A., age 55, d. 419 Pulliam St. Atlanta. AG 12/14/1909

POWELL, George H. d. Tues., Macon. Interred: Aiken, S. C. AG 10/6/1906

POWELL, Green B.,Mrs., age 67,d . 11/24 Waycross, dau. of Edmund Gresham. Ch: Walter & Jesse Greer (w/husb, Jesse Greer); Dr. Louis Powell. Sis: Adeline Gresham; Mrs. R.H. Burkon, Midville. Bros: Job A. & Jones Gresham. Bur: New Cem. AC 11/26/1905

POWELL, John Edward, age 8 mos., d. 203 E. North Ave. Atlanta. AG 6/21/1906

POWELL, L. E., Dr. d. Waynesboro 9/26. Wife, one child. AG 9/27/1909

POWELL, Lizzie, Mrs., age 44, d. Tues. Wallace Mill Rd., Atlanta, dau. of Mrs. M. E. Jones. Sis: Mrs. Frank Williams. Bros: J. M., G. M., W. C. and D. C. Jones. Dau: Mary Powell. Interred: Westview. AG 8/17/1910

POWELL, Mary J., Mrs., age 68, d. Thurs. 70 Crew St., Atlanta. Interred: Rutledge, Ga. AG 8/8/1907

POWELL, Mary, Miss, age 19, d. Wallace Mill Rd. Atlanta. AG 12/2/1910

POWELL, Mary, Mrs., age 59, d. 191 E. Pine St., Atlanta, Mon. AG 1/27/1908

POWELL, Oscar W., age 39, of 50 Robins St., Atlanta, killed by live wire. Wife survives. Interred: Caseys Cemetery. AG 3/9/1910

POWELL, Thomas, colored, age 33, d. 101 N. Butler St. Atlanta. AG 3/11/1909

POWELL, Thomas murdered in Americus, Ga. His bro., Meig, charged. AC 12/15/1905

POWELL, W., colored, age 60, d. 8 Millens Ave., Atlanta. AG 11/17/1907

POWELL, Warren Connally, Jr. d. Sat. Parents: Mr. and Mrs. W. C. Powell, 737 W. Peachtree St., Atlanta. Interred: Westview. AG 6/20/1910

POWER, Herman, age 22 mos., son of Mr. and Mrs. William A., d. 3/17, 815 Piedmont Ave., Atlanta. Interred: Sandy Springs, Ga. AC 3/19/1905

POWERS, James R., age 37, d. Alexandria, Ga. AG 6/20/1910

PRATHERS, Maggie, colored, age 42, d. 202 Edgewood Ave. Atlanta.
AG 2/27/1907
PRATT, N. A., Dr., eminent scientist, chg of largest gun powder
manufactory of Confederacy. AG 11/1/1906
PRATT, N. A., Mrs., age 73, wid., d. Tues. dau's home, Mrs. J. S.
Kennedy, Decatur. Husband d. few mos. ago. Sons: N. P., Atlanta,
George L. Daus: Mrs. J. S. Kennedy, Decatur, Miss Fannie L.
Pratt, Baltimore. Interred: Decatur. AG 4/17/1907
PRESLY, P. A., Mrs., age 63, d. son's res., Emmett C. Pressly, 36
Hayden St., Atlanta, Mon. Sons: Robert H., Emmett C. AG 6/8/1908
PRESSNELL, Charles, age 43, d. Montgomery, Ala. Tues, son of Mr.
and Mrs. G. W. Sis: Mrs. W. A. Norwood, of Michigan; Mrs. R. F.
Murphy, Atlanta. Interred: Oakland. AG 5/18/1910
PRESTON, Abbie, Mrs., age 57, d. Sun. 636 Ashby St., Atlanta.
Interred: Westview. AG 4/8/1907
PRESTON, Ben Smith, age 22, d. 17 West Cain St. Atlanta. Desc. of
Edmund Randolph. Grandfather: Col. J. L. T. Preston, Lexington,
Va. Grandmother: Mrs. Margaret Preston, poetess. Father: Rev.
John Alexander Preston. Mother was Miss Courtland Smith of
Hampden-Sidney, Va. Bro: Edmund Randolph Preston, Charlotte, N.
C. Aunt: Mrs. A. J. McKelway, Decatur. Interred: Lexington, Va.
AG 9/1/1908
PRESTON, C. M., age 22, d. 58 Berean Ave. Atlanta. AG 8/23/1909
PRESTON, J. R. d. Macon 10/28, age 43. Ch: J. A., W. F., Ella,
Nina. Funeral: Ft. Valley. AC 10/29/1905
PRESTON, J. R. d. Macon 10/28, age 43. Children: J. A., W. F.,
Ella, Nina. Funeral: Ft. Valley. AC 10/29/1905
PRESTON, James M., age 84, d. Howell Mill Rd. Atlanta. AG
12/3/1908
PRESTON, Vera, age 7 mos., d. res. of parents, Flat Shoals Rd.,
Sun. Interred: Sylvester cemetery. AG 10/22/1906
PRESTON, William Harwell, inf. son of Mr. and Mrs. C. M., d. 80
Gaskill St., Atlanta, Thurs. Interred: Sylvester cemetery. AG
6/18/1908
PREYER, Grant, colored, age 60, d. 101 N. Butler St. Atlanta. AG
11/19/1909
PRICE, Doyal, age 6 mos., son of Mr. and Mrs. W. H. Price, d.
Tues. Atlanta. Interred: Indian Creek. AG 1/9/1907
PRICE, Ide killed by Orville Cargile across Ocmulgee River on
Jasper Co. side 9/5. Cargile arrested. AG 9/6/1909
PRICE, J. B. of Columbus, Ga. fell from window 6/6 Greensville,
Ga. Interred: Columbus, Ga. AC 6/8/1905
PRICE, J. M., age 87, d. Sun. East Atlanta. Interred: Peachtree
church yard. Wife survives. AG 5/13/1907
PRICE, J. W., age 65, d. 314 Winsor St. Atlanta. AG 5/8/1907
PRICE, James H., Dr., d. 668 N. Boulevard. Atlanta. Interred:
Westview. AG 7/23/1907
PRICE, John R., Mrs. d. 11/2 Flippen, Ga. AC 11/3/1905
PRICE, John W., Judge, age 81, Confed. Vet., native of
Louisville, Ky., d. Phoebus, Va. where buried. AC 7/21/1905
PRICE, M. P., Mrs., age 72, d. 110 Irwin St. Atlanta. AG
10/4/1907
PRICE, Mary E., Mrs., age 68, d. Chattahoochee, Ga., Mon.
Interred: Masons church yard. AG 5/18/1909
PRICE, Mimmock, Mrs. killed in a storm, Victory, Ga. AG 5/3/1909

PRICE, Otis, age 18, d. 81 S. Pryor St. Atlanta. AG 9/24/1907

PRICE, Scott, colored, age 50, d. Fulton Co. Barracks. Atlanta. AG 1/15/1907

PRICE, W. T., colored, age 34, d. 299 Auburn Ave. Atlanta. AG 3/22/1907

PRICHARD, A. C., age 77, d. Grady Hospital. Atlanta. AG 1/22/1907

PRICHARD, Homer C., age 1, d. 16 Meldrum St. Atlanta. AG 6/10/1907

PRICHARD, W. H., Mrs. d. Elm St., Barnesville, Ga., Mon., age 70. Husband d. several yrs. ago. Bro: E. T. Crowder. Sis: Mrs. Williamson. AG 11/22/1910

PRICKETT, E. M, age 13, d. Fri. res. of mother, Mrs. Hattie Prickett, E. Point, Ga. Interred: Chattanooga, Tenn. AG 11/26/1909

PRIDE, Mary, colored, age 19, d. 287 Rhodes St. Atlanta. AG 3/18/1908

PRINCE, M. L., negro, aged 125 yrs. AG 4/15/1908

PRINTLE, Peter, colored, age 50, d. 305 Tumlin St. Atlanta. AG 12/14/1908

PRIOR, Robert, age abt 40, struck 10/23 by train Dublin, Ga. He lived on East side of river. AG 10/24/1910

PRISCOCK, Jennie, Mrs., age 62, d. Sun. res. of niece, Mrs. J. J. Akridge, 265 Cherokee Ave., Atlanta, wife of M. J. Sisters: Mrs. Harriett Bridewell, Mrs. Ella Moore, Mrs. Georgia Calvo. AG 11/9/1907

PRITCHETT, Dorothy Helen, dau. of Mr. and Mrs. R. J., d. 45 Park Ave., Atlanta, Thurs. Interred: Westview. AG 4/19/1907

PRITCHETT, Gideon, pioneer citizen of Edison, Ga., age 87, funeral Sat. AG 7/12/1909

PRITCHETT, Porter Lee, age 16, d. 12 Milton St. Atlanta. AG 7/2/1908

PRITCHETT, Sallie, Mrs., age 47, d. 207 Echo St., Atlanta. Interred: Casey´s Cemetery. AG 6/15/1908

PRITCHETT, William E., age 57, d. Wed. 191 Foundry St. Atlanta. Interred: Stone Mountain, Ga. AG 7/11/1907

PROCTOR, Orena, age 1 mo., d. 147 Bellwood Ave. Atlanta. AG 12/2/1910

PROFFIT, J. S., age 45, d. railroad accident. AG 12/18/1909

PRUDEN, Alonzo, colored, age 69, d. 25 Randolph St. Atlanta. AG 2/24/1908

PRUETT, James H., age 7 mos., d. 14 S. Moore St. Atlanta. AG 9/3/1907

PRUITT, Eunice, Mrs., wid. of Maj. W. B. of Athens, d. Dougherty St. 2/6, age 66. Son: John, California. Sis: Mrs. Charles McAllister, Athens. AG 2/8/1910

PUCKET, infant dau., age 2 mos. of Mrs. S C. Puckett, 6 Henry St., Atlanta, d. Sat. Interment: Westview. AG 9/18/1906

PUCKETT, E. M., age 13, d. E. Point, Ga. AG 11/27/1909

PUCKETT, J. R., age 71, d. 124 Main St. Atlanta. AG 1/20/1910

PUCKETT, Mary Brown,, infant dau. of Mr. and Mrs. Sallie Puckett, d. Thurs., 6 Henry St. Interred: Westview. AG 10/13/1906

PUGESLEY, Mary J., colored, age 67, d. 215 Auburn Ave. Atlanta. AG 4/28/1908

PUGH, LaRue Herring, age 2 mos., d. Gainesville, Ga. AG 9/28/1909

PUGIN, Byron A., age 67, d. 56 Carnegie Way. Atlanta. AG 7/10/1909

PULHAM, Dennis, colored, age 29, d. 24 Doray St. Atlanta. AG 9/3/1909

PULLEN, Sarah E., Mrs., age 34, d. Atlanta. AG 11/8/1910

PULLEN, William, colored, age 35, d. Lexington, Ky. AG 6/6/1906

PULLEN, Sarah E., Mrs., 84, d. grdau.'s res., Mrs. R. M. Crumley, Atlanta. Dau: Mrs. Fannie Amis, Washington, D. C. Grch: Mrs. J. Clifford Carroll, Baltimore; James A. Morris, NY.; Mrs. B. M. Crumley. BurPULLEN, Sarah E., Mrs.

PULLIAM, Richard, colored, age 8 days, d. 736 N. Butler St. Atlanta. AG 12/16/1908

PURCELL, Henry, age 24, d. 54 Brotherton St. Atlanta Tues. Mother: Mrs. H. J. Purcell. Bros: Frank, J. Interred: Hollywood. AG 4/22/1908

PURCELL, R. B., age 35, d. Howells Mill Rd., Atlanta, Tues. Wife, 4 ch. Member of Powhattan Tribe, No. 8, Red Men. Interred: Norcross, Ga. AG 2/12/1908

PURCELL, Thomas F., age 40, d. 336 E. Georgia Ave. Atlanta. Interred: Oakland. AG 11/17/1907

PURIFOY, J. L., Mrs., age 41, d. Adamsville Rd., Thurs. Husband: J. L., 7 children, survive. Interred: Westview. AG 2/6/1908

PURSE, J. M., for yrs. a res. of Brunswick, Ga., d. Waycross, Ga. 9/28. Wife, 4 children: Mrs. Hoyt Gale, Cleveland, Ohio; Mrs. Oscar Lott; Mrs. W. W. Sharpe, Jr.; and a son, of Waycross. AG 9/28/1910

PURSELEY, Hezekiah, age 80, d. 124 Curran St. Atlanta. AG 9/4/1906

PURTELL, Alton B., age 19, d. Washington, D. C. AG 9/1/1908

PURVINE, Martha, Mrs. of N. Dalton, d. Sun., age 60. Several children. AG 5/3/1910

PURVIS, Lona, age 3, d. 68 West Tenth St. Atlanta. AG 3/10/1909

PURVIS, Lona, age 3, d. 68 West Tenth St. Atlanta. AG 3/10/1909

PURVIS, W. R., of Len, Ga. (near Glennville), d. Sat. Interred: Beards Creek Church. AG 8/17/1908

PURYEAR, Sallie, Miss d. Sun., age 22. Interred: Dalton, Ga. AG 5/3/1910

PUSATERI, Joseph, age 15, son of Mr. and Mrs. L.., d. Sat. Atlanta. Interred: Westview. AG 9/14/1907

PUTE, Mattie C., Mrs. d. 6/3, age 47, Macon. Wife of George T. Pute. AC 6/5/1905

PYE, George, colored, age 78, d. 206 Smith St. Atlanta, Oct. 25. AG 10/27/1910

PYE, Lucinda, colored, age 64, d. 67 Rockwell St. Atlanta. AG 1/3/1908

PYE, Ruby, colored, age 1, d. 360 Smith St. Atlanta. AG 9/25/1909

PYRON, Thomas J. d. Kennesaw Thurs. Leaves wife, two sons, two daus. His late res. at 110 W. Harris St. Atlanta. AG 6/29/1906

QUARLES, dau. of Mr. and Mrs. J. S. Quarles d. Wed., North Rome, Ga. AG 8/10/1906

QUARTERMAN, Richard, colored, age 22, d. 219-1/2 Butler St. Atlanta. AG 3/1/1908

QUEEN, D. M. buried 6/24 Atlanta, Oakland Cemetery. Res. of 318 Simpson St. Confed. Vet. AC 6/26/1905

QUIGG, Henry, Dr. d. Conyers yesterday. Wife, one son, Henry Quigg. Grdaus: Mrs. Agnes Quigg Tucker, Miss Marie Davis. Grsons: Bayard Quigg. Came to American from Ireland when a boy, locating in Ga. AG 12/3/1907

QUILLIAN, Mary Roberta, Mrs., age 45, d. 266 Crew St. Atlanta. AG 7/9/1908

QUILLIAN, Pearce, son of J. P. of Belton, Ga., age 32, d. Orient, Okla. Uncle: Rev. M. J. Cofer. AG 5/22/1907

QUILLIAN, W. F., Dr., age 62, d. 11/1 Cartersville dau.'s res., Mrs. John Willie Jones. Wife, 5 ch: Mrs. John Willie Jones, Cartersville; Dr. W. E., Atlanta; O. L., Nashville; Prof. W. T., Jr. and Garnett of Wrightsville, Ga. AC 11/1/1905

QUINN, E. C., age 56, d. Mon. 313 Windsor St. Atlanta. Interred: Gloster, Ga. Wife, several children. AG 7/19/1910

QUINN, Hattie B., Mrs., age 34, d. res. of father, J. T. Ream, 349 Oak St., Atlanta, Tues. Son: Charles. Two small children. Bro: C. E. Ream. AG 4/13/1909

QUINTOULES, Alex, age 33, a Greek, d. Tues. Atlanta, 120 W. Mitchell St. AG 7/27/1909

RACE, W. W., age 24, d. Inman yards. Atlanta. AG 12/24/1907

RAGAN, Louis killed by Joe Wallace Hawkinsville, Ga. Jan. 21. AC 1/24/1905

RAGAN, William, age 66, d. 417 Glenwood Ave. Atlanta. AG 6/12/1908

RAGLAND, Jessie, Mrs. d. 230 Ponce de Leon Ave., Atlanta, Sun. Interred: Talbotton, Ga. Two children. AG 6/14/1909

RAGLAND, Mildred, dau. of Mr. and Mrs. J. M., 107 Center St., d. Wed. Interred: Palmetto, Ga. AG 6/10/1909

RAGLAND, Henry Ellis, age 1, son of Mr. and Mrs. Eugene, d. Thurs. 401 Euclid Ave. Atlanta. Interred: Marietta, Ga. AG 12/31/1909

RAGSDALE, Ida, Mrs. d. near E. Point, Ga. Wed. Husband: J. W. Parents: Mr. and Mrs. T. D. Chappeller. Sisters: Mira and Eula Chappelier. 5 bros. Interred: Hill Crest. AG 10/23/1908

RAGSDALE, John 12/8. Interred: Hogansville, Ga. AC 12/10/1905

RAGSDALE, John William, inf. son of Mr. and Mrs. C. F., d. 57 Bonnie Brae Ave., Atlanta, Sun. Interred: Draketown, Ga. AG 8/3/1908

RAGSDALE, Lovey, lover, Will Gresham. AG 8/25/1906

RAGSDALE, Walter, age 3 mos., son of Mr. and Mrs. J. P., d. Sat. 51 Hendrix Ave., Atlanta. Interred: Westview. AG 5/2/1910

RAGSDALE, Elijah, Mexican, Civil Wars Vet., b. 1812 d. 8/21/1909 dau.'s res., Mrs. C. R. McCalla, 137 Richards St. Atlanta. Bur: Powder Spgs. Sons: M. R., James P. Daus: Mrs. G. P. Lowry, Mrs. I. N. Scott, Mrs. Carrie Bennett. AG 8/23/1909

RAHRER, Lillie, Miss, age 24, d. Fri. 283 Marietta St., Atlanta. Interred: Westview. AG 8/30/1910

RAINES, I. R., age 57, d. 707 Chestnut St., Atlanta, Mon. Wife, four children. Interred: Hollywood. Powhatan Tribe of Red Men officiated at funeral. AG 7/14/1908

RAINES, Robert, farmer in sou. Upson Co., killed by nephew, Charley Bailey. (in jail). AG 10/11/1909

RAINEY, Peter, negro, age 25, half-witted, shot and killed by 14-yr old negro boy, Harvey. AG 10/3/1906

RAINS, Sarah B., Miss, age 22, dau. of Mr. and Mrs. D. W., d. 707 Chestnut St. Atlanta, Thurs. Interred: Hollywood. AG 4/25/1907

RAINWATER, Leila M., Mrs., age 28, d. 15 Atwood St. Atlanta. AG 12/22/1908

RAKESTRAW, R. M. d. at his home near Starrsville Sun., age 87. Leaves wife, several children. Interred: Rakestraw burying ground. Son: R. A. Rakestraw of Atlanta Police Force. AG 5/1/1906

RALEY, Ella, Miss, age 24, dau of Mr. & Mrs. C. P., d. 40 Tattnall St. Atlanta. Bur: Westview. Sis: Mrs. M. A. Erlich, Mrs. Guy Mitchell, San Francisco, Mrs. R. Brown, Chattanooga, Tenn.; Mrs. E. Danne, Atlanta. Bro: Charles. AG 10/7/1908

RALPHS, W. C., age 78, d. at Soldiers Home. Atlanta. AG 2/22/1907

RAMEY, J. M., Mrs., age 60, of Griffin d. res. of son, Milton Ramey. Interred: Covington, Ga. Sons: Will of Atlanta, Milton of Griffin. AG 2/27/1910

RAMEY, Ralph, age 33, d. East Point, Ga. AG 5/24/1907

RAMEY, Warren A., age 15, d. 17 W. Cain St. Atelanta. AG 8/7/1908

RAMOS, Frank, age 24, d. 220 S. Boulevard. Atlanta Sun. Bro., one sister. Interred: Mt. Zion church yard. AG 6/14/1909

RAMOS, Stella, Miss, age 19, d. Hapeville Orphans' Home. AG 9/29/1910

RAMPLEY, M. C. d. 9/30 Carnesville, Ga. where interred. AC 10/1/1905

RAMPSPECK, Theodore, age 58, d. Decatur, Ga. AG 11/15/1909

RAMSEY, A. K., Hon., Capt., member of Legislature from Murray Co., shot and killed Sun., 18 miles from Dalton, Ga., his home at Ramsey. Shot by Jim Franklin. Left 10 children. AG 4/26/1906

RAMSEY, Clara May, age 2, d. 100 Powers St. Atlanta. AG 8/13/1910

RAMSEY, C. A., Mrs., 67, d. 1/17 Valdosta. Ch: Mrs. J. G. Stevens & F. H. Ramsey, Valdosta; Mrs. Jefferson Davis, Quitman; Mrs. W. D. Collier, Marco, FL; Thomas Ramsey, Tampa, Fl; Mrs. H. B. Harrison, Albany, NY. Bur: Valdosta. AC 1/18/1905

RAMSPECK, G. A. of Decatur d. 2/17. Wife: Mrs. Margaret M. Daus: Mrs. C. M. C. Gilmore, Decatur, Ga.' Mrs. E. P. Thomas, N. Y.; Mrs. W. R. Harper, Philadelphia. Son: J. L., of Decatur. AC 2/19/1905

RANDALL, Elizabeth, age 2, dau. of Mr. and Mrs. H. I., d. Wed. AG 4/26/1907

RANDALL, Frances, age 2, dau. of Mr. and Mrs. O. R., d. 459 Cherokee Ave., Atlanta, Sun. Interred: Martin, Ga. AG 11/29/1909

RANDALL, James Ryder d. Augusta, Ga. Tues. AG 1/15/1908

RANDALL, R. A., age 68, d. 108 Julian St. Atlanta. Wife, five children. Interred: Vining, Ga. AG 6/29/1908

RANDALL, W. C., age 73, d. Mon. S. Macon, Ga., Confederate Veteran. AG 6/23/1908

RANDER, Beulah, colored, age 16, d. 153 E. Linden St., Atlanta, Oct. 23. AG 10/27/1910

RANGER, C. H, age 72, d. 220 S. Boulevard. Atlanta. AG 1/3/1908

RANGER, Charles H. d. several days ago. Interred: Westview. AG 1/3/1908

RANKIN, J. G., Mrs., age 72, d. res. of son, John S. Rankin near Stone Mountain, Ga. Sons: John S.; C. A., of Lithonia. Dau: Miss Jennie Rankin, Stone Mountain. Interred: Family Burial Ground, Stone Mountain. AG 1/25/1908

RANKIN, Sam, age 23, d. Somerset, Ky. AG 5/13/1907

RANKINS, Charlie, colored, age 30, d. 150 Larkin St. Atlanta. AG 1/24/1907

RANSOM, A. McB., age 35, d. 294 Courtland St. Atlanta. AG 7/26/1909

RANSOM, C. A., Jr., infant son of Mr. and Mrs. C. A., d. 18 Oliver St. Atlanta. Interred: Hollywood. AG 3/17/1910

RANSOM, L. A., Capt. of Atlanta d. before reaching Greenwood, S. C. Age 58. Born S. C. Wife. Son: Ronald (who m. Miss Mary Brent Smith, dau. of Gov. and Mrs. Hoke Smith). Interred: Westview. AG 9/20/1910

RANSOM, Vertra, age 7, dau. of Mr. and Mrs. V. S., 94 McDonald St., Atlanta, d. Sun. Interred: Hollywood. AG 7/26/1909

RANSOME, Annie B., Mrs., age 24, d. Sat. 35 Lawshe St., Atlanta. AG 8/26/1907

RANSOME, B. Frank funeral Wed. Atlanta. Interred: Westview. AG 11/13/1907

RANSOME, J. T., age 1 mo., d. 146 Griffin St. Atlanta. AG 1/29/1908

RANSOME, James, age 30, d. Grady Hospital Atlanta Sun. Interred: Hollywood. AG 6/30/1908

RANSOM, A. McBr. d. bro-in-law's res., Judge J. S. Powell, Newnan. Bur: Newnan. Mother: Mrs. G. A. Ransom, Newnan. Bros: M. S., Atlanta; T. J., Tx. Sis: Mrs. J. S. Powell; Mrs. L. N. Rogers, Newnan; Mrs. Willie Blackiston, Tx. AG 7/26/1909

RANSOM, James, age 30, 106 Luckie St., Atlanta, d. Sun. Mother: Mrs. M. J. Ransom. Sister, 6 yr. old son. AG 7/29/1908

RAPPOLEL, Annie, colored, age 2, d. 145 Sims St. Atlanta. AG 11/17/1907

RASBURY, Officer, Atlanta police force, met tragic end at Kimball Hotel. Atlanta. AG 5/4/1907

RATCLIFF, W. D. killed accidentally Jan. 24 Tifton, Ga. Wife, no ch. From Fayetteville, N. C. AC 1/26/1905

RATTEREE, Elizabeth J., Mrs., age 47, d. 38 Granger St., Atlanta, Fri. Husband. Ch: Mrs. E. R. Slyder, W. L. Ratteree. AG 4/15/1909

RATTAREE, James M. age 35, d. 59 Ellis St. Atlanta. AG 11/12/1910

RATTAREE, U. L., age 2, son of Mr. and Mrs. A. L., d. Sun. 165 Rhodes St., Atlanta. Interred: Hollywood. AG 8/5/1907

RATTAREE, U. S., age 1, d. 160 Rhodes St. Atlanta. AG 8/6/1907

RAUSFMANN, Walter W. buried Lawrenceville, Ga. Tues. AG 5/21/1906

RAUZIN, Michael, age 53, d. 203 E. Hunter St. Atlanta. AG 8/28/1907

RAWLINGS, B. T., Mrs. funeral Mon., family res., "Belleview:, Sandersville, Ga. AG 10/18/1910

RAWLINGS, Ernest B., inf. son of Mr. and Mrs. J. H., d. 83 Travis St., Atlanta, Mon. Interred: Dallas, Ga. AG 3/1/1910

RAWLINGS, R. H., Mrs., age 23, d. Thurs. Atlanta. Husband: R. H. Rawlings, Sandersville, Ga., son of Judge Rawlings. One child. Interred: Sandersville, AG 12/31/1909

RAWLINS, Charles, colored, age 77, d. 487 Sims St., Atlanta, Nov. 15. AG 11/ 6/1910

RAWLINS, Hazel, Miss d. Mon. sister's res., Mrs. W. C. Warfield, 374 Capitol Ave. Atlanta. Interred: Sidell, Ill. AG 5/31/1910

RAWLINS, Hilliard L., age 38, d. Atlanta Sun. Interred: Gloster, Ga. AG 9/14/1909

RAWLINS, J. G., Valdosta, Ga. 12/4/1906. Rawlins hanged for murder of Carter children. Buried McRae, Ga. AG 12/4/1906

RAWLINSON, Sarah F., Mrs., age 71, d. Mon. 55 Garnett St. Atlanta. Ch: B. H., J. W.; Mrs. C. R. Golden, Mrs. H. G. Meyer, Mrs. E. J. Jenkins, of Atlanta, and Mrs. J. T. Welsh, Dillon, S. C. Interred: Newberry, S. C. AG 10/24/1910

RAWLS, David d. home of dau., Mrs. Jane Seals. He was oldest citizen of Johnson Co. AG 10/25/1907

RAY, Arabella, age 78, d. 10 Chestnut St. Atlanta. AG 6/10/1907

RAY, C. B., brakeman, Sante Fe RR, killed in wreck 9/21. Body to arrive Atlanta Fri. Parents: Mr. and Mrs. John A. Ray, 366 Luckie St., Atlanta. Killed San Bernardino, CA. AG 10/16/1907

RAY, Clarence C., age 2 mos., d. 386 Fraser St. Atlanta. AG 8/8/1906

RAY, David R., age 77, d. Mon. Confederate Soldiers' Home, Atlanta. Native of Walton Co. Served Co. C, 9th Ga. Vols. Interred: Westview. AG 7/19/ 9 0

RAY, Eugenia, son of Mr. and Mrs. E. R., d. Mon. Interred: Westview. AG 8/19/1907

RAY, John, colored, age 85?, d. 182 Markham St. Atlanta. AG 11/21/1910

RAY, John Thomas, age 2, son of Mr. and Mrs. C. P., d. 43 Pickett St., Atlanta, Tues. Interred: Oakland. AG 5/3/1910

RAY, Martha, infant dau. of Mr. and Mrs. J. A. Ray d. 366 Luckie St. Interred: Hollywood. AG 10/15/1906

RAY, Mrs., widow, d. Atlanta, age 68. Daus: Mrs. J. E. Alexander and Mrs. J. N. T. Cawhern. Interred: Casey's Cemetery. AC 7/14/1905

RAY, Nancy L., Mrs., wife of J. W., age 73, d. 404 Houston St. Atlanta. Interred: Rock Springs Cemetery. AG 8/17/1908

RAY, Sarah A., Mrs., age 73, d. home of dau., Mrs. E. J. Wylie Montgomery, Ala. She was wid. of late Harris Ray, Macon. Interred: Rose Hill, Macon, Ga. AG 7/25/1907

RAY, W. F. funeral Thurs. Interred: Westview. AG 6/2/1906

RAY, William R., age 46, d. Mon. Atlanta. 6 children. Interred: Tucker, Ga. AC 3/29/1910

RAY, William R., infant, d. Atlanta. AG 3/29/1910

RAYDEN, Ella, age 12, negro girl of Foundry and Haynes St., Atlanta, d. Atlanta from too much booze. AG 5/21/1906

RAYMER, G. O., age 40, d. Atlanta Mon. Interred: Westview. AG 6/1/1909

RAYMER, George O., age 44, d. 129 Courtland St. Atlanta. AG 6/3/1909

RAYSOR, John M., age 67, d. sis. res. Mrs. Mary Jordan, 186 Crow St. Atlanta. Dau: Mrs. Robt T. Clayton, Birmingham, Ala. Bro: Geo. D. Raysor, Quitman, Ga. Sisters: Mrs. Joseph Mabbett, Quitman, Ga.; Mrs. Mary Jordan, Atlanta. AG 4/10/1908

REA, J. B., age 49, d. 24 South Boulevard. Atlanta. AG 11/4/1908
READ, A. A., age 77, Anniston, Ala. pioneer d. 2/15. Interred:
Cedartown, Ga. Wife. AG 2/16/1910
READ, Harrison, age 9 mos., son of Mr. and Mrs. M. R., d. Fri. 89
Hampton St. Atlanta. Interred: Casey's Cemetery. AG 9/10/1910
REAGAN, E. J., Judge, Zebulon, Pike Superior Court, announced
death of his little granddau. AG 4/10/1907
REAGAN, Emma, Mrs., age 50, d. 107 W. Peachtree St. Atlanta Tues.
Interred: Adairsville, Ga. old home. AG 1/8/1908
REAGIN, Chloreun, age 2, d. Edgewood Ave., Atlanta. AG 9/9/1907
REAGIN, E. O., Mrs., age of former sheriff of Dekalb Co., d.
Decatur Tues. Husband, large family survives. Interred: Lithonia
Cemetery. AG 6/2/1908
REALER, F. E., Mrs., wife of F. E. d. Mon. 99 E. Linden Ave.,
Atlanta. Interred: Jeffersonville, Ga. AG 7/30/1907
REAVERS, John, colored, age 21, d. 22 Tyler St., Atlanta, Oct.
27. AG 10/29/1910
REDD, Eugenia W., Mrs., wid. of C. A., d. yesterday, Columbus,
Ga. age 75, member of Weems family. Son: W. A. Redd. Dau: Mrs.
Fielder, Columbus, Ga. 2 bros. AG 2/4/1908
REDDING, Augustus H. of Ellerslie, Ga., d. Wed., age 30. Wife.
One dau. Parents: Mr. and Mrs. G. A. Redding. AG 5/5/1910
REDDING, Elizabeth, Mrs., age 85, d. Wed. dau.'s res., Mrs. R. W.
Ellis, 267 Central Ave. Atlanta. Dau., two bros, John and Samuel
Bishop of Manchester, Iowa, one sister, Mrs. L. V. Deye.
Interred: Westview. AG 10/6/1910
REDDING, J. B., Mrs. d. 10/1 Macon, age 87, Spring St. Interred:
Rose Hill. AG 10/2/1909
REDDING, Jack, negro killed by negro, Ike Sloppy, Findley, Ga. AG
6/7/1906
REDDING, John, Capt. d. Cuthbert, Ga. Sat. AG 8/5/1907
REDDING, Mary, Miss d. father's home, Ellerslie, Ga. Bro: Prof.
A. H. Redding. AG 6/9/1908
REDWINE, Ruth, Mrs., age 35, d. 112 McDaniel St. Atlanta.
Interred: Fayetteville, Ga. AG 3/29/1910
REED, D. W., Dr. d. age 83 Adel, Ga. AG 2/11/1910
REED, Eddie, colored, age 31, d. 133 Formwalt St. Atlanta. AG
3/28/1907
REED, Emma, Mrs., age 42, d. 180 E. Baker St. Atlanta. AG
10/14/1907
REED, George M., age 26, d. 398 Auburn Ave. Atlanta. AG
10/29/1909
REED, Georgia, Mrs., age 22, d. 527 W. North Ave. Atlanta. AG
7/30/1906
REED, Ina B., Mrs., teacher at Center St. Grammar School,
Atlanta, found dead over desk. AG 5/3/1907
REED, John C., Col. d. Montgomery Wed. Interred: Atlanta,
Oakland. AG 1/13/1910
REED, Leonard of New Hope, Ga., d., age 31. Wife, two small
children. AG 2/23/1910
REED, Lucy, colored, age 53, d. 250 Fraser St. Atlanta. AG
3/3/1909
REED, Maggie, colored, age 35, d. Magnolia St. Atlanta. AG
4/7/1908

REED, Mamie E., age 29, d. 25 Wyley St. Atlanta, Sat. Interred: Gainesville, Ga. AG 6/10/1910

REED, Minnie E., Mrs., age 29, d. 25 Wylie St. Atlanta. AG 6/11/1910

REED, Sarah B., Mrs. d. 29 Edwards St., Atlanta, Thurs. Interred: Oakland. AG 10/16/1907

REED, Will, painter of Bellwood Ave., Atlanta, overdosed on morphine for love of a woman. AG 7/20/1908

REEDER, Sarah E., Mrs., age 76, d. 373 S. Moreland St. Atlanta. AG 5/14/1910

REEDER, Wesley E., age 3, son of Mr. and Mrs. J. E. Reeder of 412 Simpson St., Atlanta, d. Sun. Interred: Oakland. AG 10/15/1906

REEDER, Sarah E., 76, d.Atlanta.Ch-M.O., W.L., C.H., Atlanta; J.E., Ft. Worth, Tx.; Mrs. M.E. Davis; Mrs. V.G. Griffin, Atlanta; Mrs. W.K. York, Rocky Mtn. Sis: Mrs. E.F. Kerr, LeDill, Tn. Bro: Hardy Mattax, Okla. Bur: Oakland. AG 5/13/1910

REED, Jessie, colored, age 20, died from gunshot wound, Atlanta. AG 11/19/1906

REESE, B. P., age 1, d. 17 Tennille St. Atlanta. AG 5/21/1907

REESE, D. A., age 51, d. Atlanta Wed 148 Ira St. 5 children. AG 2/11/1909

REESE, Fannie, Mrs., age 59, d. 403 Pulliam St. Atlanta. AG 12/22/1908

REESE, Susan, colored, age 64, d. 37 Beard St. Atlanta. AG 2/7/1908

REESE, Wallace, young son of Mr. and Mrs. J. T., d. Mon. 17 Tennelle St., Atlanta. Interred: Greenwood. AG 5/13/1907

REESE, William J., colored, age 32 yrs., d. 14 Granger St. Atlanta. AG 8/9/1907

REEVES, Annie, colored, age 38, d. 95 Terry St. Atlanta. AG 5/31/1907

REEVES, Charlotte Thelma, dau. of Mr. and Mrs. W. O., age 13, d. 12/7, 862 Third St., Macon. Interred: Riverside. AC 12/8/1905

REEVES, Ella J., colored, age 30, d. 79 Hilliard St. Atlanta. AG 7/12/1907

REEVES, Elsie, colored, age 6 mos., d. 21 Randolph St. Atlanta. AG 1/16/1907

REEVES, Fannie, colored, age 42, d. 143 E. Cain St. Atlanta. AG 12/30/1907

REEVES, James, colored, age 43, d. 95 Terry St. Atlanta. AG 12/29/1908

REEVES, James, colored, age 75, d. 21 Smith St. Atlanta. AG 3/3/1909

REEVES, Luther P., age 32, d. 400 Magnolia St. Atlanta. AG 7/20/1907

REEVES, Luther P., son of Mr. and Mrs. F. M., d. Thurs. Senoia, Ga. Interred: Senoia, Ga. AG 9/20/1907

REEVES, Marion, age 12, d. Fri. Sat. Interred: Westview. AG 8/24/1907

REEVES, Mary T., Mrs., age 41, d. 44 Robins St., Atlanta, Sat. Husband: W. R. Interred: LaVergue, Tenn. AG 4/10/1909

REEVES, Nancy, Mrs., age 70, d. Wed. 10 Circle St., Atlanta. Interred: Casey's Cemetery. Husband, 5 children. AG 9/22/1910

REEVES, W. F., age 54, d. 388 E. Fair St. Atlanta. AG 10/6/1906

REEVES, **Walter**, age 18, d. Thurs. mother's home, Mrs. T. W.
Reeves, College Park. Interred: Jones' Chapel church yard. AG
5/24/1906

REEVES, **Willie May**, **Miss**, age 15, d. res. of parents, Mr. and
Mrs. J. T., corner Bishop St. and Hemphill Ave., Atlanta, Fri.
Interred: Westview. AG 10/8/1909

REEVES, **W. W.**, age 38, d. 153 Walton St., unmd. 3 bros., 5
sisters. Interred: Co Line Church, Gwinnett Co. AG 9/11/1906

REID, **Alexander Sidney**, **Capt.**, Putnam Co.'s repr. to state
legislature, d. 12/2. Confederate Veteran. Wife. Dau: Mrs. Rogers
Davis, Atlanta. He was cousin of Mrs. W. D. Grant and John M.
Slaton of Atlanta. AG 12/3/1909

REID, **C. W.**, age 58, d. Bolton (Atlanta). AG 9/21/1910

REID, **Charles Sidney**, age 1 yr., d. 414 Edgewood Ave. Atlanta. AG
6/21/1906

REID, **Florence M.**, **Mrs.**, age 28, d. 129 Courtland St. Atlanta.
Interred: Logansville, Ga. Husband, two children, survive. AG
9/2/1909

REID, **Irene Frances** d. Wed. 52 Mills St. Atlanta. Interred:
Westview. AG 5/10/1906

REID, **Louis H.**, **Dr.**, age 64, d. 257 Crumley St., Atlanta, Thurs.
Interred: Washington, D. C. AG 6/26/1908

REID, **Mary K.**, age 60 days, d. 288 Courtland St. Atlanta. AG
8/29/1907

REID, **R. R.** d. Sat. Forsyth, Ga. Interred: Oakland. AG 5/7/1907

REID, **Roxie**, colored, age 24, d. 101 N. Butler St. Atlanta. AG
5/11/1908

REID, **Scott**, colored, age 31, d. 89-A Alexander St. Atlanta. AG
6/19/1909

REID, **W. R.**, **Mrs.**, wife of former Senator of Crawfordville, d.
Thurs. Survivors: Mother, sister, Mrs. T. E. Bristow of
Crawfordville, and Mrs. Arthur Dickerson of Va., husband, and 6
children. Interred: Crawfordville. AG 9/22/1906

REID, **Will** d. Grady Hospital, Atlanta Mon. overdose of morphine.
Interred: Marietta, Ga. AG 7/22/1908

REIGER, **Louis**, age 45, d. Fri. nephew's home, Theodore Fichter,
Peachtree Rd., Atlanta. Wife, 3 children, and sister: Mrs. Kate
Fichter, survive. AG 11/26/1909

REIGER, **William**, age 26, d. at Piedmont Sanitarium, Atlanta.
Interred: New York. AG 5/18/1907

REINAU, **Francis D.**, age 65, d. 127 N. Pryor St. Atlanta. AG
12/30/1908

REINHARDT, **Sam**, colored, age 16 yrs., d. 101 N. Butler St.
Atlanta. AG 2/8/1807

REINHARDT, **Victor** of Charlotte, N. C. d. in Philadelphia. AG
1/13/1910

RELIFORT, **Calvin**, colored, age 88, d. 258 Love St. Atlanta. AG
4/13/1909

RENARD, **Joseph F.**, **Capt.** ("Uncle Joe"), age 68, d. 51 E. Georgia
Ave. Atlanta. Born Charleston, S. C., moved Atlanta. In war as RR
engineer. Wife was Miss Alice Weaver. Dau: Mrs. Henry M. Wood.
Interred: Oakland. AC 5/21/1905

RENDER, **Leary**, colored, age 53, d. 11 Lemon St. Atlanta. AG
2/7/1908

RENFROE, J. W., Mrs., age 76, d. sister's home, Mrs. John King, Cleburne, Tx. Body to Atlanta. Survivors: sis, Mrs. King; granddau., Mrs. Sidney P. Cooper, Hendersonville, N. C.; grandson, Renfroe Jackson, Atlanta. AG 12/5/1906

RENFROE, Olive McNeil, inf. son of Mr. and Mrs. Ernest, d. Wed. 85 Garibaldi St. Atlanta. Interred: Westview. AG 7/16/1907

RENT, H. B., Mrs. of Adrian, Ga., d. 7/10 res. of father, W. T. Kendrick, Columbus. Interred: Riverdale Cemetery. AC 7/12/1905

RENTFROW, James K., age 62, d. Lee Co., Phenix City, Ala., 5/19. Wife, 4 children. AG 5/20/1910

RENTZ, T. H., Mrs. d. Grovania, Ga. Sis: Mrs. R. F. Napier, Hawkinsville. AG 1/31/1910

RESPESS, Judge, colored, age 45, d. 41 Traynham St. Atlanta. AG 4/2/1909

REVIS, Charles, colored, age 42, d. 20 Terry St. Atlanta. AG 7/19/1909

REYNOLDS, A. B., age 60, d. Fri. 27 Abbott St. Atlanta. Interred: Westview. AG 5/3/1907

REYNOLDS, A. N., Mrs. d. Mon. Atlanta. Interred: Kentucky. AG 1/8/1907

REYNOLDS, Alma E., age 8 mos., inf. dau. of Mr. and Mrs. L., d. 4 W. East Ave., Atlanta, Mon. Interred: Macon, Ga. AG 2/10/1908

REYNOLDS, Carl,a ge 15, d. rr accident at 29 Luckie St. Atlanta. AG 3/7/1907

REYNOLDS, J. P., age 45, d. Griffin, Ga. AG 9/28/1909

REYNOLDS, J. T. of Tifton d. Fri. AG 7/7/1906

REYNOLDS, Jack, Capt., formerly of Columbus, d. Hurtsboro, Ala. Sun. age 65. Veteran of civil war under Pat Cleburne. Wife survives. AG 11/1/1907

REYNOLDS, John B., age 34, d. Atlanta. AG 1/12/1910

REYNOLDS, L. O., Mrs., age 42, of 243 Peachtree St., Atlanta, d. Atlanta Fri. Dau: Mrs. Cora Baker. Son: Charles. Bro: R. L. Kirkley. AG 3/26/1910

REYNOLDS, Leila O., age 42, d. Atlanta. AG 3/28/1910

REYNOLDS, Lizzie, colored, age 25, d. 101 N. Butler St. Atlanta. AG 4/10/1907

REYNOLDS, Lizzie, Mrs., wife of W. H., d. 176 Crumley St., Atlanta, Thurs. Parents: Mr. and Mrs. John Gavin. 4 sisters. AG 1/9/1908

REYNOLDS, Mary Jane, Mrs. funeral at res., East Point, Ga. AG 1/19/1907

REYNOLDS, R. F., age 70, Confed. Vet., d. dau.'s res., Mrs. Joseph Peavy, S. Macon, Ga. 11/21. Interred: Cedar Ridge Cemetery. AC 11/22/1905

REYNOLDS, C. W., age 60, died 218 E. Georgia Avenue, Atlanta. AG 12/8/1906

REYNOLDS, Thomas L., age 56, died Fri., Grady Hospital. Printer, lived Atlanta for last 20 years. Interment: Conyers, Ga. AG 11/17/1906

REYNOLDS, Thomas S., 50, died at Grady Hospital, Atlanta. AG 11/19/1906

RHEA, Katherine Leonard, age 4 mos., dau. of Mrs. J. C., granddau. of Mrs. Fitzhigh Lee, d. Catoosa Springs 7/13. Mrs. J. C. Rhea's husband in Phillippines. Present: Mrs. Fitzbugh Lee, Miss Virginia Lee, Capt. Fitzhugh Lee. AC 7/14/1905

RHEBERG, Richard, age 6 mos., son of Mr. and Mrs. S. C., d. Sun Covington, Ga. Interred: Westview. AG 8/21/1906

RHODES, Abra drowned Silver Lake Fri. Interred: Blue Ridge, Ga. AG 7/24/1909

RHODES, Abvaniah, aged 11 mos, died 187 Smith Street, Atlanta. AG 12/5/1906

RHODES, Annie May, inf. dau. of Mr. and Mrs. J. A., d. Mon. Atlanta. Interred: Springfield, Mo. AG 5/13/1908

RHODES, Carl, 5 mos. son of Mrs. Grace Rhodes, d. Tues. Interred: Hollywood. AG 7/10/1907

RHODES, Emma, age 18, d. 164 Orme St. Atlanta. AG 10/22/1906

RHODES, Frank P., age 74, merchant of Lexington, Va., father of Ernest L. Rhodes of Atlanta, d. Thurs. Lexington where interred. AG 12/18/1910

RHODES, J. M. of Commerce, Ga. d. 2/11, age 84. Served War of 1837 and Civil War. Son: Major Rhodes, Athens. AC 2/12/1905

RHODES, J. S. d. Great Bend, Kansas. Interred: Cartersville, Ga. Bro: R. V. Rhodes, 60 Venable St.,A tlanta; A. L. Rhodes, 28 McAfee St., Atlanta. Sister resides Smyrna. AG 7/26/1909

RHODES, Sarah, Mrs., age 77, d. 172 W. North Ave. Atlanta. AG 9/3/1907

RHYNE, W. L., age 17, d. 2/21 Augusta, bro.'s res., W. H. Harden, 1632 Broad St. Interred: Okahumpka, Fla. Son of G. R. Rhyne of Okahumpka, Fla. AC 2/23/1905

RICE, Gladys Corinne, age 3, dau. of Mr. and Mrs. J. H., d. 18 Waddell St. Atlanta, Thurs. Interred: Conyers, Ga. AG 4/10/1908

RICE, James A., Sr. funeral Thurs. from res. W. Hunter St., Atlanta. Interred: Westview. AG 10/4/1907

RICE, Jane E., Mrs., age 22, d. 28 Rosalie St. Atlanta. AG 11/1/1910

RICE, Loy Frank, age 4, son of Dr. and Mrs. William H., d. 210 Grant St., Atlanta, Wed. Interred: Westview. AG 1/17/1908

RTCE, Mamie, Mrs., age 27, d. 76 Poplar St., Atlanta, Wed. Interred: Casey's Cemetery. AG 1/13/1910

 Albany, Ga., 12/2/1906. An aged negro working on city street force was run down and killed by Albany & Northern switch engine this morning. AG 12/3/1906

RICE, Millie, age 14, d. Scottdale, Ga. AG 3/15/1910

RICE, Nancy E., Mrs., age 42, d. Thurs. 142 Confederate Ave. Atlanta. Interred: Bethel Church yard. AG 7/1/1910

RICE, Rudolph G., age 62, d. Fri. 26 Broyles St. Atlanta. Wife, 5 sons: H. Ivey, Alt. Ivey, Gordon Ivey, Joseph Ivey, James Ivey. Daus: Mrs. Mary Carter, Mrs. Hattie Harp, Miss Bessie Ivey. Interred: Oakland. AG 7/14/1906

RICE, Lessie, Miss, Madison, Ga. 11/13/1906. Dau. of Mr. and Mrs. Ed Rice, died died Sun., buried yesterday. Mr. Rice, publisher of The Madison Advertiser before going to Gate City

RICE, S. E., infant of, died at res., Atlanta. Interment: Westview. AG 11/26/1906

RICH, Julia, Mrs., age 25, d. 269 Courtland St. Atlanta. AG 3/25/1907

RICHARDS, Alvin l., age 7 mos., d. 119 W. Alexander St. Atlanta. AG 7/21/1908

RICHARDS, D. H., age 4 mos., d. 592 Edgewood Ave. Atlanta. AG 11/1/1909

RICHARDS, E. T., age 1, d. Ft. McPherson, Ga. AG 11/20/1907

RICHARDS, Emma, dau. of Mrs. Minnie, d. Tues. Interred: Westview. AG 11/19/1907

RICHARDS, Emma Phelma, dau. of Mr. and Mrs. R. M., d. Sun. Interred: Westview. AG 11/19/1907

RICHARDS, HenryB., age 64, d. 607 Chestnut St. Atlanta. AG 10/7/1909

RICHARDS, Lizzie, Mrs. d. Tues. 197 1/2 Decatur St., Atlanta, age 59. AG 8/14/1906

RICHARDS, M. E., Mrs. d. Sun. St. Augustine, Fla. Interred: Rose Hill Cemetery, Macon, Ga. AG 7/7/1908

RICHARDS, S. P., pioneer Atlantan, funeral 4/20 Atlanta. AG 4/19/1910

RICHARDS, Samuel P., age 86, d. 112 Washington St. Atlanta. Interred: Oakland. AG 4/20/1910

RICHARDSON, Alva, colored, age 40, d. Ft. McPherson. AG 11/20/1909

RICHARDSON, Annie, colored, age 29, d. 36 Dowmans Ave., Atlanta. AG 2/20/1908

RICHARDSON, Annie, Mrs., age 44, d. 124 Garnett St. Atlanta, Sun. Ch: Nita, Grace, Harold, Charles. Interred: Westview. AG 11/21/1910

RICHARDSON, B. V., Mrs., age 58, d. 6 Longly Ave. Atlanta. Interred: Oakland. Children: Mrs. Charles Millwood, Mrs. Alonzo Moody, W. R. Richardson. AG 6/ /1907

RICHARDSON, Falby, colored, age 63, d. Hooper St. Atlanta. AG 8/22/1910

RICHARDSON, J. A., Mrs. funeral Thurs. res. of Dr. Noble, 980 Peachtree St., Atlanta. Relatives: Dr. and Mrs. George H. Noble; J. A. Richardson. AG 11/23/1910

RICHARDSON, James, negro, who killed his wife several days ago at 9 Liddell St., Atlanta. wants to hang. AG 4/22/1908

RICHARDSON, James B., age 37, d. Atlanta Fr. Leaves wife. No issue. Interred: Gaffney, S. C. AG 6/15/1906

RICHARDSON, James H., age 43, d. Atlanta Thurs. Sis: Mrs. J. W. Dill, Epps, Ala. Interred: Epps, Ala. AG 8/7/1909

RICHARDSON, John R. of Atlanta d. 2/26, age 70. Interred: Westview. AC 2/27/1905

RICHARDSON, Laura L., Mrs., age 40, d. 62 Tumlin St. Atlanta. AG 8/22/1910

RICHARDSON, Lucy J., Mrs., age 68, d. 300 Spring St. Atlanta. AG 11/24/1910

RICHARDSON, Mattie, Miss, age 19, dau. of Mr. and Mrs. D. T., d. 198 Fora Ave., Atlanta, Sun. Interred: Sylvester Cemetery. AG 6/29/1908

RICHARDSON, Moses, Dr., Norcross pioneer, d. 3/17. He was b. Newton Co. 1830. In 1862 organized Co. 1, 16th Ga. Regt., Confed. Vet. AC 3/18/1905

RICHARDSON, Mrs., sister of Mrs. Palmer, widow, d. when a runaway horse overturned their buggy, Monroe, Ga. AG 5/11/1907

314

RICHARDS, Alvin, Jr., age 7 mos., son of Mr. and Mrs. A. L., d. 119 W. Alexander St., Atlanta, Fri. Interred: Jonesboro, Ga. AG 7/17/1908

RICHIE, Lela, colored, age 27, d. 36 Elm St. Atlanta. AG 11/15/1909

RICH, Mary M., Mrs., 80, d. Swainsboro. Bur: Pine Grove Cem. Twice marr., 1st, William N. Moore (d. yrs. ago); 2nd, William Rich (d. 22 yrs. ago). Ch: S. S. & Jas M. Moore, Summertown, Ga., Mrs. Nancy Sumner, all by 1st husb. AG 12/17/1909

RICKETTS, Lawrence D., age 22, d. 690 Woodward Ave.,tlanta. AG 10/12/1909

RICKETTS, Lula, Mrs. d. 33 Fitzgerald St. Atlanta. AG 1/25/1910

RICKET, M., colored, age 31, died 239 Courtland St., Atlanta. AG 12/10/1906

RIDDER, Mary, colored, age 60, d. Fulton Co. Alms House. AG 2/1/1908

RIDDLE, A. J., Mrs., age 41, former Atlanta res., d. Chattanooga Wed. Interred: Westview. AG 12/17/1910

RIDGE, James Franklin, age 82, d. 153 Courtland St., Atlanta Tues. Son: J. Frank. Sister: Mrs. J. T. Dennis of Louisville, Ky. Interred: Kentucky. AG 11/26/1908

RIDLEY, Lee Little, Miss, age 24, d. Oakland City. AG 12/3/1908

RIDLING, Nancy, Mrs., age 78, d. 363 Simpson St. Atlanta. AG 7/29/1910

RIDLING, Eva Estelle, infant, d. 10 Simpson St. Atlanta. Interred: Westview. AG 1/21/1910

RIE, Edward C., suicide, age 33, Mobile, Ala. Interred: Ninety Six, S. C. AC 12/29/1905

RIGDON, W. C., formerly of Culloden, Ga., now of Pelham, d. Macon 9/10, age 28. Wife, two infant children. Bros: H. T. Fitzpatrick, Culloden, Ga.; Rev. R. M. Rigdon, Macon. Sis: Mrs. F. W. Hammock, Culloden, Ga. AG 9/11/1909

RIGELL, Helen, Miss, dau. of Thomas, d. 2 mi. from Milltown, Sat. Interred: Milltown, Ga. AG 7/5/1909

RIGGINS, Carrie, colored, age 50, d. 108 Bradley alley. Atlanta. AG 10/13/1908

RIGGINS, Josephine, colored, age 44, d. 198 Orme St. Atlanta. AG 9/6/1910

RIGGINS, Lorenzo, colored, age 1, d. 574 Glenn St. Atlanta. AG 2/4/1908

RILEY, D. Frank, Rev., age 57, d. 696 Forsyth St. Atlanta. AG 4/13/1907

RILEY, Harriet, colored, age 87, d. 252 Marietta St. Atlanta. AG 5/21/1907

RILEY, Jennie, colored, age 15, d. 199 Fort St. Atlanta. AG 11/25/1906

RILEY, Julia, inf. of Mr. and Mrs. P. J., 85 Ella St. Atlanta, d. Mon. Interred: Westview. AG 6/8/1909

RILEY, Mary, colored, age 50, d. 3 Melvin St. Atlanta. AG 3/25/1907

RILEY, Minnie, Mrs., age 36, d. 82 Culver St. Atlanta. AG 5/18/1908

RIPLEY, Dwight, Major, age 80, of Brooklhn, N. Y., father of Dr. Henry McHatton of Macon, d. Wed. Confederate Veteran. Leaves wife. Dau: Mrs. Joseph Norris. AG 12/19/1907

RIPLEY, T. Alexander, age 41, d. Chattanooga, Tenn. AG 11/7/1907
RISS, Dora, colored, age 1 mo., d. rear of 403 Whitehall St. Atlanta. AG 2/8/1909
RITCH, J. S., age 60, blacksmith, d. near Decatur Sat. Interment: Covington. AG 9/18/1906
RITCH, John Harvey, age 8, d. 267 Capitol Ave. Atlanta. AG 11/3/1908
RITCH, Missouri, Mrs., age 56, d. Upatoie (near Columbus), Ga. AC 2/15/1905
RITCH, Sarah F., Mrs. d. Sat. Boss Ave., Atlanta. Interred: Hollywood. AG 5/2/1910
RITTENBERRY, Mrs., age 70, funeral at res. on Clinton St., E. Macon. Son: George. Two married daus. AG 11/ /1907
RITZELL, J. W., age 35, d. Atlanta Tues. Wife. Interred: Westview. AG 3/26/1908
RIVERS, G. L. shot and killed by Dr. J. M. Elliott in Troup Co. 9/1908. AG 6/19/1909
RIVERS, George fatally shot by Dr. Elliott, veterinary surgeon, LaGrange, Ga., Bull St. Elliott has wife and 6 weeks old baby. Wife has 7-yr. old dau. AG 9/1/1908
RIVERS, John, colored, age 41, d. 149 Washington St. Atlanta. AG 3/10/1908
RIVERS, Willie T., colored, age 2 yrs., d. 21 Bush St. Atlanta. AG 4/19/1907
RIVIERE, G. P., Mrs. of Pelham, Ga. buried 5/4 Methodist Cemetery. Sis: Mrs. A. M. Lambdin of Barnesville. AC 5/6/1905
ROACH, Edward, age 14, son of Dr. Roach, former Atlantan, accidently killed himself with pistol at mother´s home, Charlotte, N. C. where he removed abt 12 yrs. ago. AG 9/27/1906
ROACH, Jack, age 45, d. Atlanta. Interred>: Westview. AG 3/15/1910
ROACH, John interred Westview. AG 3/15/1910
ROACH, T. C., age 1, d. 99 Curran St. Atlanta. AG 12/10/1910
ROACH, Thomas C., inf. son of Mr. and Mrs. R. L., d. 99 Curran St., Atlanta, Thurs. Interred: Hollywood. AG 12/9/1910
ROACH,Ellen Mitchell, 75, wid of Dr.E.J., dau. of Alex W. Mitchell, d. 153 Whitehall St. Atlanta. Daus: Mrs. W. R. Colburn, Colburn, Ga.; Mrs. R. E. Hinman; Miss Aurelia Roach; Mrs. John M. Speer. Son: E. J. Bro: C. B. Mitchell. AG 9/1/1910
ROAN, Lucy J., Mrs. d. Wed. Fairburn, Ga. AG 3/17/1910
ROAN, Steven H., Dr., age 23, d. 185 Cherokee Ave. Atlanta. Father: B. H. H. Roan. Uncle: Judge Roan. Interred: Fairburn, Ga. AG 7/24/1907
ROBERDS, Paul T., age 8, d. Lakewood Heights. Atlanta. AG 2/11/1909
ROBERSON, Bessie, age 3, d. 165 Venable St. Atlanta. AG 3/14/1910
ROBERSON, C. W., age 26, d. 371 E. Hunter St. Atlanta. AG 2/8/1909
ROBERSON, Ethel, colored, age 25, d. 176 W. Hunter St. Atlanta. AG 9/17/1907
ROBERSON, John Douglas, age 10 mos., d. 165 Venable St. Atlanta. AG 1/3/1907
ROBERSON, Mollie, age 10, oldest dau. of W. M. Roberson of Wayne Co.,d. last Fri. Interred: Jesup cemetery. AG 2/6/1907

316

ROBERSON, Roy, colored, age 1, d. 50 W. Clifton St. Atlanta, Nov. 5. AT 11/5/1910

ROBERSON, W. E., age 1, d. 34 Ezzard St. Atlanta. AG 2/22/1907

ROBERT, B. F., age 73, d. 168 Crew St. Atlanta. AG 2/25/1907

ROBERT, Charles d. Wed., Atlanta, native of London, England. AG 5/22/1907

ROBERT, George Benjamin, age 11 mos., son of Mr. and Mrs. H. C., d. 244 Peeples St., West End, Atlanta. Interred: Westview. AG 6/2/1906

ROBERTS, Charles d. at Presbyterian Hospital. Atlanta. AG 5/24/1907

ROBERTS, David M., Judge, of Eastman, Ga., age 73, d. Atlanta, Thurs. Wife. Sons: Hon. J. H., Dodge Co. representative; Paul A. of Eastman; S. A., Jacksonville, Fla. Interred: Eastman, Ga. AG 7/29/1910

ROBERTS, E. E. G. d. Atlanta Fri. Wife: Kate. Dau: Miss Lizzie Roberts. Sons: E. E. G., Jr., Samuel. Interred: Anniston, Ala. AG 4/17/1909

ROBERTS, E. M., age 67, d. 249 Spring St. Atlanta. AG 9/3/1907

ROBERTS, E. W., Mrs. d. Sun. Elberton, Ga., age 60, proprietor of the Hotel Roberts. Interred: Elmhurst Cemetery. Daus: Mrs. L. P. Eberhardt of Elberton and Mrs. Charles Parks of Cornelia. AG 7/25/1910

ROBERTS, Edward, colored, age 40, d. 353 McDaniel St. Atlanta. AG 5/1/1908

ROBERTS, G. W., Mrs. of N. Dalton, d. 9/12. Husband, 5 children. Interred: West Hill Cemetery. AG 9/10/1910

ROBERTS, Irma, infant dau. of Mr. and Mrs. J. W., d. Thurs. Beecher St, Atlanta. Interred: Fairburn. AG 5/31/1907

ROBERTS, J. P., age 20, of Louisville, Ga., drowned 7/30 in Willacoochee River, near Olympia. AG 7/31/1908

ROBERTS, J. W., age 79, d. 29 Luckie St. Atlanta. AG 7/30/1906

ROBERTS, James A., age 63, d. at Confederate Soldier's Home. AG 8/18/1906

ROBERTS, James H., age 25, d. res. of parents, Mr. and Mrs. B. F. Roberts, near Ben Hill, Ga. Interred: Wesley Chapel church yard. AG 1/4/1908

ROBERTS, James, Mrs. killed. Her husband charged with murder, Lafayette, Ga. 3/3. AC 3/4/1905

ROBERTS, Joe, age 35, colored, d. Macon, Ga. AG 3/6/1908

ROBERTS, Lula, Mrs., age 25, d. 4 Bradley Ave. Atlanta. Interred: Gainesville, Ga. AG 11/8/1907

ROBERTS, M. S., Mrs., age 78, d. 602 W. Peachtree St. Atlanta. AG 3/6/1908

ROBERTS, Martha, Mrs. d. yesterday, one of oldest residents of Hancock Co. Interred: Culverton cemetery. AG 1/24/1907

ROBERTS, Nancy, Mrs. d. Fri. 54 Ella St., Atlanta, Sat. Interred: Westview. AG 12/21/1907

ROBERTS, P. A. d. Sun. Monticello, Ga. AG 10/18/1910

ROBERTS, Phoebe, colored, age 50, d. 52 Railroad St. Atlanta. AG 12/3/1907

ROBERTS, Rose, colored, age 29, d. 21 Old Wheat St. Atlanta. AG 10/12/1907

ROBERTS, Sarah, colored, age 37, d. 25 Dover St. Atlanta. AG 12/29/1908

317

ROBERTS, Susie, age 6 mos., d. 21 Old Wheat St. Atlanta. AG
10/25/1900

ROBERTS, Sylva J., Mrs., age 38, d. Atlanta Sun. Interred:
Buford, Ga. Husband: F. J. Two children, four bros., four
sisters, and father, survive. AG 9/13/1909

ROBERTS, T. F. d. Lakewood, Ga. AG 5/21/1907

ROBERTS, T. J. killed Sat. night on Lakewood car line, Atlanta.
Interred: Caseys. AG 5/21/1907

ROBERTS, Vonie, Miss, age 25, dau. of Mr. and Mrs. J. W., d.
Berean Ave. Atlanta Mon. AG 1/29/1907

ROBERTS, W. E., age 68, d. Grady Hospital. Atlanta. AG 7/16/1907

ROBERTS, W. G., Dr., age 72, Confederate Veteran, enl. Co. E,
35th Ga. Regt. 1861, d. Old Soldiers' Home, Atlanta, Tues. AG
1/4/1910

ROBERTSON, Amelia B., age 48, d. 53 Viola St. Atlanta. AG
11/19/1909

ROBERTSON, Anthony R. of Troup Co. d. few mi. from LaGrange Jan.
11. Interred: Hill View. Wife, 3 sons, 1 dau., all grown. AC
1/13/1905

ROBERTSON, B. P., Mrs. d. Brevard, N. C., wife of Rev. B. P. News
reached Atlanta. Interred: Gaffney, S. C. AG 6/21/1910

ROBERTSON, D. C., Mrs., mother of Prof. T. H., d. res. of son,
Thweatt Robertson 6/29, age 77, Gainesville, Ga. 12 ch. Interred:
Late family home near Bolding's Bridge. AC 6/30/1905

ROBERTSON, E. G., formerly of Oxford, Ala. d. 9/14 Corinth, Miss.
AC 9/15/1905

ROBERTSON, Ethel, Mrs., age 25, d. 176 W. Hunter St. Atlanta. AG
9/17/1907

ROBERTSON, Frank G., age 61, d. Mon. 221 E. Fair St. Atlanta.
Interred: Westview. Wife, one son, one dau. AG 6/8/1909

ROBERTSON, Grace, age 8, dau. of Mr. and Mrs. G. W. of 62 Hood
St., Atlanta, d. Wed. AG 10/28/1909

ROBERTSON, H. M., Mrs., age 56, d. 81 McDaniel St., Atlanta, Sun.
Interred: Mableton, Ga. AG 7/21/1908

ROBERTSON, Inard, age 1, son of Mr. and Mrs. E. C., of 94 Ira
St., Atlanta, d. Fri. AG 8/7/1909

ROBERTSON, J. O., age 72, d. Thurs. Atlanta, formerly of Canton,
Ga. AG 9/23/1910

ROBERTSON, J. T., age 35, d. 60 Gartrell St. Atlanta. AG
12/30/1910

ROBERTSON, John, Mrs. d. Mon. at Jewells, near Sparta, Ga. Leave
husband, John, 5 small children. AG 9/19/1906

ROBERTSON, Mamie Clare, Mrs., age 21, wife of W. H., d. 76 Dodd
Ave., Atlanta, Tues. Parents: Mr. and Mrs. W. P. Smithson.
Interred: Kennesaw, Ga. AG 2/16/1908

ROBERTSON, Mary, colored, age 16, d. Grady Hospital. Atlanta. AG
8/20/1907

ROBERTSON, N. H., Mrs., age 21, d. 76 Dodd Ave. Atlanta. AG
2/19/1908

ROBERTSON, Ulaf O., age 62, d. Roxboro, Ga. AG 8/5/1908

ROBERTSON, W. B., age 28, d. Sun. Interred: Anniston, Ala. AG
11/5/1906

ROBERTSON, W. P., Mrs. of Rutledge, Ga. d. 5/7 at home of dau-in-
law, Mrs. M. H. Higginbotham. AG 5/8/1906

ROBINS, W. M., Hon. d. Salisbury, N. C., res. of son. Age 77. In Civil War. AC 5/6/1905

ROBINSON, Adam M. d. 11/16, 358 Pulliam St., Atlanta, age 78. Interred: Lawrenceville. AC 11/17/1905

ROBINSON, Ambrose, colored, age 18, d. 5 Phenix alley. Atlanta. AG 12/23/1908

ROBINSON, Charles, colored, age 51, d. rear of 102 Martin St. Atlanta. AG 10/12/1908

ROBINSON David, infant. son of Mr. and Mrs. David, d. 11/15 Atlanta. Interred: Hollywood. AC 11/17/1905

ROBINSON, E. A., age 27, d. 22 Lansing St., Atlanta, 10/12. AG 10/14/1910

ROBINSON, Fred, colored, age 14 days, d. 9 Kennett St. Atlanta. AG 9/9/1910

ROBINSON, George, colored, age 55, d. 256 Love St. Atlanta. AG 7/8/1907

ROBINSON, Gilbert, colored, age 45, d. 54 John St. Atlanta. AG 8/11/1908

ROBINSON, J. A., age 35, d. Wed. Philadelphia, Pa., his home for past 8 yrs., formerly atty of Atlanta. Leaves wife, formerly Miss Jennie Campbell of Stone Mtn. No issue. Interred: Oakland. AG 6/14/1906

ROBINSON, J. L., Mrs., age 49, d. Atlanta Tues. Interred: Waukesha, Wisconsin. AG 1/13/1910

ROBINSON, J. T., age 2, son of Mr. and Mrs. J. L. of 434 Woodward Ave. Atlanta, d. Wed. AG 7/8/1909

ROBINSON, J. W., Mrs., age 35, d. Fri. Atlanta. Interred: Englewood, Tenn. AG 6/10/1910

ROBINSON, James E., age 43, d. Philadelphia, Pa. AG 6/16/1906

ROBINSON, Joe, Judge, d. Garrard Co., Ky. Mrs. Kate Daniel of Columbus, Ga. received telegram. AC 3/22/1905

ROBINSON, Julia, colored, age 36, d. 60 Hilliard St. Atlanta. AG 2/7/1908

ROBINSON, Lula I., inf. dau. of Mr. and Mrs. H. D., d. Thurs. Lakewood Heights, Atlanta. Interred: Lawrenceville, Ga. AG 12/24/1909

ROBINSON, M. A., Mrs., wife of M. A., d. Sun. Dau: Mrs. W. C. Blankenship. Interred: Oakland. AG 3/19/1907

ROBINSON, M. M., Mrs., age 21, d. 127 Powell St. Atlanta. AG 2/23/1907

ROBINSON, Mamie, colored, age 30, d. Spring St. Atlanta. AG 11/17/1910

ROBINSON, Mason, colored, age 60, d. 514 Bedford Place. Atlanta. AG 2/16/1908

ROBINSON, May, colored, age 55, d. rear of 150 Whitehall St. Atlanta. AG 10/31/1908

ROBINSON, Minnie, Miss d. 3/18 Glennville, Ga. Interred: Watermelon Creek Cemetery. AG 3/18/1908

ROBINSON, Myrtis, Mrs., age 23, d. Atlanta Sat. Interred: Westview. AG 7/25/1910

ROBINSON, Nathaniel, colored, age 1, d. 296 Chapel St. Atlanta. AG 9/9/1909

ROBINSON, Rachael, colored, age 60 yrs., d. 26 Johnson Ave. Atlanta. AG 8/28/1907

ROBINSON, W. F., Rev. funeral 9/20. Bro-in-law: Prof. Harry H. Stone. AC 9/21/1905

ROBISON, A. N., Mrs., age 85, d. 51 Daniel St. Atlanta. AG 1/29/1907

ROBISON, Mattie, colored, age 19, d. 191 N. Butler St. Atlanta. AG 1/12/1907

ROCKWELL, Sarah of Lumpkin, Ga., age 73, d., widow of late John R. Rockwell, merchant, who was bro of Mrs. W. H. and R. B. Harrison of Atlanta. Several children survive. AG 6/4/1908

RODEN, Lottie Myrtle d. Sun. parents home, Mr. and Mrs. Charles J., corner of Pine and 14th Sts., Atlanta, Mon. Interred: Hollywood. AG 10/18/1909

RODOLPH, William of Lee Co., Ala. 8/30, dau.´s res., Mrs. T. H. Reese, Hannah, Ala. Interred: Concord Church. AC 9/3/1905

ROE, Levi G. of Monticello, Ark., d. Sun. Interred: Dalton, Ga. Age 26. AG 5/3/1910

ROGAN, William, age 66, d. 417 Glenwood Ave., Atlanta, Thurs. Interred: Oakland. Wife survives. AG 6/12/1908

ROGERS, Everett, colored, age 16, d. Atlanta. AG 10/11/1909

ROGERS, F. R. d. 8/11 College St., Macon, age 63. Ch: Annie, Lelia, J. Frank. AG 8/12/1910

ROGERS, Gary, age 31, d. Atlanta. AG 1/27/1910

ROGERS, George, age 3 mos., d. 129 Courtland St. Atlanta. AG 9/21/1909

ROGERS, George, inf. son of Mr. and Mrs. Milton, of Union City, Ga., d. Thurs. Interred: Vega, Ga. AG 9/16/1909

ROGERS, J. W., age 74, d. 53 Jones Ave. Atlanta. AG 11/1/1909

ROGERS, Jessie, age 18, d. East Lake, 10/28. AG 10/28/1910

ROGERS, Jessie, Miss, former Atlanta res., d. Graysville, Tenn. recently. Funeral res. of sister, Mrs. M. R. Courter of East Lake, Thurs. (Atlanta) Interred: Greenwood. AG 10/27/1910

ROGERS, John Christian funeral 449 S. Pryor St. Atlanta Wed. Interred: Oakland. AG 3/23/1910

ROGERS, John Christian, age 73, Atlanta pioneer, d. 449 S. Pryor St., Atlanta, Mon., Confed. Vet. Wife. Daus: Mrs. M. W. Chambers of S. C.; Mrs. J. R. Ransom and Miss Josephine Rogers of Atlanta. AG 3/21/1910

ROGERS, Lula Z., Mrs. d. San Antonio, Texas Tues., wife of Z. B., Elberton, Ga. citizen. Leaves husband, one child, several bros. AG 12/17/1907

ROGERS, Martha, Mrs., age 105, widow, b. Chesterfield, S. C. 3/16/1805, old Griffin res. since 1861, buried 1/7. Dau: Mrs. W. H. Bishop, age 80+. Grandson: J. W. Bishop, Griffin. Grdau: Mrs. Thomas Capps, Henry Co. AG 1/8/1910

ROGERS, Thomas E., Reidsville. Fatally crushed. Interred: Shiloh. AG 8/17/1906

ROGERS, W. B., age 20, d. 23 Egleston St. Atlanta. AG 9/18/1908

ROGERS, Wess, negro, shot and killed by Jim Stinson, negro, Columbus, Ga. (captured). AG 3/28/1907

ROGERS, William J. d. Atlanta. Interred: Augusta, Ga. AG 11/11/1907

ROLAND, Effie, colored, age 25, d. 26 Inis alley. Atlanta. AG 7/16/1908

ROLING, Roy, colored, 3 mos., d. Rhodes Street, rear. AG 2/8/1907

ROLLESTONE, Harry, age 56, b. Ballinamallard, co. Fermanagh, Ireland, d. Tues. Grady Hospital, accident. Came Atlanta over 30 yrs. ago. Survivors: 2nd wife, ch: James, Moreton, Maude. Interred: Westview. AG 10/30/1906

ROOD, E. H. d. Wed. Ramhurst, Ga. Res. of Ringgold, age 64. Wife, 2 daus, one son. AG 12/9/1910

ROOF, Joe, colored, age 30, d. Grady Hospital. Atlanta. AG 3/29/1907

ROOKS, Helen, age 3 yrs., d. Grady Hospital. Atlanta. AG 9/6/1907

ROOKS, Maggie, Mrs. of 95 Central Ave., Atlanta, d. Tues. Interred: Quitman, Ga. AG 10/27/1909

ROOKS, R. C., age 1, d. 148 Madison Ave. Atlanta. AG 7/19/1907

ROONEY, Ernest M., age 31, d. 57 N. Forsyth St., Atlanta. funeral Sun. Shriner and Elk. Survived by mother and brother. AG 6/9/1906

ROOT, Sam, colored, age 20, d. 33 Cone St. Atlanta. AG 2/24/1908

ROPER, J. D., age 21, d. Grady Hospital. Atlanta. AG 7/7/1906

ROPER, J. L., age 60, of Paulding Co. d. 3/6 Hiram, Ga. Funeral at Powder Springs, his birthplace. 5 children. Son: J. O. AG 3/9/1910

ROPER, son, age one, son of Mr. and Mrs. W. B. Roper, d. 188 Haynes St. Tues. Interred: Powder Springs. AG 9/19/1906

ROSE, George H., age 39, d. Sun. 161 Pearl St. Atlanta. Interred: Decatur, Ga., Miller Burial Grounds. AG 12/13/1909

ROSE, H. P., Hon. of St. Marys, Ga. d. 7/7. Judge of City Court. Interred: Savannah. Wife, 7 children. AG 7/7/1909

ROSE, J. T., Mrs., age 31, wife of J. T., d. Tues. 27 E. 14th St., Atlanta. Interred: Delta, Ohio, her former home. They were marr. over yr. ago. AG 4/20/1910

ROSE, Kathleen, inf. dau. of Mr. and Mrs. W. H. C., d. Fri. 309 Spring St., Atlanta. Interred: Westview. AG 5/24/1907

ROSE, Lilly, colored, age 3, d. Mayson St., Edgewood, Ga. AG 4/3/1908

ROSE, O. A. V., Capt., age 70, former Atlantan, bro. of R. M., d. New London, Conn. where interred. Sons: Jay G. and Russell W. of New London, Conn. Daus: Mrs. Ernest Levy, Demopolis, Ala., Mrs. Samuel Cranford, Matley, Va. AG 8/26/1908

ROSE, Paul, age 11, son of Mr. and Mrs. A. A., d. 109 E. Georgia Ave., Atlanta, Tues. Interred: Barnesville, Ga. Grson of Mr. and Mrs. E. W. Rose, and nephew of Mr. and Mrs. J. W. Shinholser. AG 2/19/1908

ROSENBURY, Charlotte S., Mrs. LWT probated. Charles Ward Rosenbury qualified as exr. Fulton Co. AG 9/26/1908

ROSENBURY, Charlotte, Mrs., age 72, d. 470 N. Jackson St. Atlanta. AG 10/13/1906

ROSENFELD, Julia, age 4 mos., dau. of Mr. and Mrs. L., d. Atlanta Thurs. Interred: Oakland. AG 7/16/1908

ROSENFELD, Morris, Mrs., age 34, d. Milledgeville Tues. Interred: Oakland Cemetery, Atlanta. AG 4/21/1909

ROSENFELD, Rosa, Mrs., age 45, wife of M., of Atlanta, d. Milledgeville, Ga. Tues. Husband, three children. AG 4/20/1909

ROSS, George, Jr. d. Wichita, Kansas. Sister: Mrs. Warren H. Fogg, Atlanta. AG 3/1/1907

ROSS, Hester, colored, age 80, d. Pine and Emmett Sts. Atlanta. AG 11/1/1910

ROSS, Martha, Miss, age 57, d. 272 Forrest Ave. Atlanta. AG 8/11/1908

ROSS, S. L., Mrs., age 70, mother of R. L., d. Columbus, Ga., former res. of Opelika, Ala, where buried. AG 8/14/1907

ROSS, Savannah, Mrs., age 72, d. Atlanta Wed. Son: Edward M. Ross, Los Angeles, Calif. Bro: S. A. Carter. Sis: Mrs. Little, Macon. AG 3/11/1909

ROSSELLE, Robert L., age 4 mos., son of H. L., d. 80 Ivy St. Atlanta. AG 7/1/1910

ROSSER, Beula, Mrs., wife of L. N., d. Wed. Atlanta. Interred: Conyers, Ga. AG 9/9/1910

ROSSER, Frank Q., Dr. d. Yuma, Calif., father of Quincy Rosser of Atlanta. Interred: McDonough, Ga. AG 6/9/1906

ROSSER, James P., Dr., age 71, Atlanta physician 13 yrs. from Conyers, d. Mon. 351 Cherokee Ave., Atlanta, age 71. Bros. and sister: Judge E. B. Rosser, Atlanta; W. K. Rosser, Birmingham; Mrs. A. D. Moseley, Atlanta; Mrs. Bettie Swann, Conyers; Mrs. F. S. Treadwell, Atlanta; Mrs. Mollie Gaither, Mansfield; Mrs. Z. B. Cook, Ft. Smith, Ark. Rosser md. Georgia Middlebrooks, Walton Co. AG 2/11/1908

ROSSER, Louis Albert, inf. son of Mr. and Mrs. L. N., d. 61 Bonnie Brae Ave., Atlanta, Wed. Interred: Conyers, Ga. AG 9/1/1909

ROSSER, M. J., age 60, d. Howell Mill Rd., Atlanta. Three ch. Bro: Judge E. B. Rosser, Atlanta. Interred: Sandy Springs AG 1/29/1908

ROSSER, Mattie, colored, age 40, d. corner Peters and Fair Sts. Atlanta. AG 12/21/1907

ROSSER, R. T., age 66, d. Soldiers' Home. Atlanta. AG 1/17/1908

ROSWELL, Lou Underwood, Mrs., wid of Christopher, dau. of Judge John W. H. Underwood, d. 1st Ave, Rome. Sis-Mrs. D. D. Plumb; Mrs. Charles R. Clark, Augusta; Mrs. Jno R. Pitts, St. Augustine, FL. Son-W. S. Daus-Minnie, Bessie. AG 6/17/1907

ROTHSCHILD, Charles, age 65, d. corner Washington and Clarke Sts. Atlanta. AG 11/2/1907

ROTHSCHILD, Jennie, Mrs. d. Wed. 301 S. Pryor St. Atlanta. Interred: Savannah, Ga. Husband, Charles, and dau., Mrs. Sol Samuels, survive. AG 5/8/1907

ROUAN, Mr. of Smyrna, Ga. d. Sat. Burned to death. AG 2/3/1908

ROUECHE, George W. suicide 10/30 Covington, Ga. Circus man. Mother resides Meadeville, Pa. AC 10/31/1905

ROUGHTON, Martha, Mrs., age 74, interred Hollywood Cemetery. Ch: J. F. and M. P. Roughton, Mrs. A. D. WOod. AG 5/15/1908

ROUGHTON, Willis C., old Atlanta res., d. Thurs., 111 Estoria St. Interred: Hollywood. Wife, three ch: Dr. J. F. Roughton, M. P. Roughton, Mrs. A. D. Wood, Rome, Ga. AG 7/26/1907

ROUNTREE, Ephraim, age 66, d. Riverdale, Ga., Sun. 5 sons, 1 dau. Interred: Riverdale Baptist Church yard. AG 5/16/1910

ROUNTREE, William D., former Madison Co., Ala. commissioner, d. W. Huntsville, Ala., age 60. Bachelor. Sis: Mrs. C. P. Nunnally, Birmingham. Bros: H. S., of Denver; C. F., Glendars, Miss.; Charles A. and J. G. of Huntsville. AG 11/8/1910

ROWAN, S. M., Mrs. d. Thurs. 247 Oak St., Atlanta, res. of son, Dr. W. J. Rowan. Interred: Flippen, Ga. AG 7/24/1909

ROWDEN, Mary J., Miss of Ellenwood d. Mon. age abt 73. Nephew: Rev. J. T. Rowden, Stockbridge Baptist Church. Funeral at Tanners Church. AG 10/4/1910

ROWE, Dan, negro, was shot and killed by Snowden Swygert, 2 miles from Haralson, Ga. 9/3. AG 9/3/1909

ROWE, George W., age 56, d. 308 W. Fourth St. Atlanta. AG 10/8/1909

ROWE, Gerald S., age 2, son of Mr. and Mrs. J. W., d. 308 W. Fourth St., Atlanta, Sat. Interred: Conyers, Ga. AG 11/16/1907

ROWELL, G. S. killed in duel by Ephraim Murphy, Gough, Ga. AG 7/18/1906

ROWLAND, Ann, Dr., age 74, d. 90 Park Ave., Atlanta Tues. Wife, one son. Came to Atlanta from Brunswick, formerly of St. Louis. Interred: St. Louis, Mo. AG 3/11/1908

ROWLAND, Elizabeth, Mrs., age 31, d. 314 Williams St. Atlanta. AG 5/12/1909

ROWLAND, Harllee, age 19 (or 79), d. Sat. Atlanta. Interred: Decatur cemetery. AG 9/2/1907

ROWLAND, Julius N. funeral Fri. Wife survives. Interred: Oakland. AG 6/8/1906

ROWLAND, S., Mrs., age 18, d. 17 W. Cain St. Atlanta. AG 8/31/1908

ROWLAND, T. H., colored, age 6, d. 383 Richardson St. Atlanta. AG 11/27/1907

ROWLEY, Bernice Mae, age 3 yrs., d. 271 E. North Ave. Atlanta. AG 3/29/1907

ROWLEY, Verner May, age 3, d. res. of aunt, Mrs. A. L. Sweet, 271 E. North Ave., Atlanta, Fri. Interred: Rochester, Minn. AG 3/29/1907

ROYSTON, Lucy, Mrs. of Jonesboro, Ga., age 65, d. 8/11. Son: Julian B. Sisters: Mrs. Emma C. Bonds, Cross Plains, Tx.; Mrs. W. H. Thompson, Tifton, Ga. Interred: Royston, Ga. AG 8/11/1908

RUBLER, John T., age 52, d. 88 Garden St. Atlanta. AG 2/11/1907

RUCKER, Edward, colored, age 81, d. 152 Piedmont Ave. Atlanta. AG 11/29/1907

RUCKER, Eva J., age 1, d. 396 Houston St. Atlanta. AG 7/27/1907

RUCKER, Jessie G., Mrs. d. 413 Washington St., Atlanta. AG 6/28/1910

RUCKER, Julian, Miss d. Gainesville, Ga. Interred: Oakland. AG 10/3/1910

RUCKER, Sarah Elizabeth, age 3, dau. of W. A., d. Sat. Elberton, Ga. Interred: Elmhurst Cemetery. AG 8/23/1910

RUCKER, Walter, colored, age 35, d. 84 Fort St. Atlanta. AG 10/3/1907

RUCKER, Walter, colored, age 5, d. 101 N. Butler St. Atlanta. AG 1/8/1908

RUCKER, Victoria, colored, age 27, died 284 N. Piedmont Ave. AG 12/11/1906

RUDERMAN, Rosa, age 4, d. Grady Hospital. Atlanta. AG 11/5/1906

RUDOLPH, Louise, age 5 mos., dau. of Mr. and Mrs. E. C., 40 Morrison Ave., Atlanta, d. Tues. Interred: Forsyth, Ga. AG 5/12/1909

RUFF, Guy, age 4, son of Mr. and Mrs. G. W., d. Atlanta Sun. Interred: Marietta, Ga. AG 6/22/1908

RUFF, Lenton, colored, age 39, d. 101 N. Butler St. Atlanta. AG 1/14/1907

RUFF, Lizzie, Mrs., age 50, wife of J. M., farmer of Vesta, Oglethorpe Co., d. Tues. Interred: Vesta, Ga. AG 7/1/1909

RUFF, Margaret, 7 mos. old dau. of Mr. and Mrs. B. Z. Ruff, who died Tues. at family res.,interred Westview cemetery. AG 12/26/1906

RUKER, Mary Jane Elizabeth, Mrs. d. Wed. Funeral res. of Mrs. William Powell, 81 Walton St., Atlanta, Fri. Interred: Oakland. AG 3/13/1908

RUMSEY, Ruby, age 2, d. 56 Poplar St. Atlanta. AG 9/30/1908

RUMSEY, Velma, age two, dau. of Mrs. Rose Rumsey, d. Mon. Atlanta. 31 N. Moore St. Interred: Oakland. AG 6/13/1906

RUSH, George W., Dr. d. 3/4, lineal descendant of Benjamin Rush, signer of Declar. of Indep., age 42, native of Opelika, Ala. Lived Savannah 15 yrs. Wife, 2 children. AC 3/5/1905

RUSH, James Asbury, age 52, died 562 1-2 Decatur St. Atlanta. AG 12/26/1906

RUSHING, Sarah, Mrs., wife of John L. of Byron, d. Perry, Ga. 3/30, only dau. of Mr. and Mrs. L. S. Townsley. Bro: S. S. Townsley, Atlanta; L. S. Townsley, Jr., Perry. AC 4/2/1905

RUSHTON, Ella, Mrs., dau. of late Maj. Samuel B. Wight, Conf. Soldier. Graduate of Wesleyan Female College in 1873. Sisters: Mrs. A. P. Coles, Mrs. W. S. Wilson, Atlanta, Mrs. C. W. Tift, Albany. Bros: Ed L. Wight, Samuel B. Wight, Atlanta, Charles H. Wight, Jacksonville, Fla. Mother: Mrs. Samuel B. Wight. Grandchildren: Irene Tift, Clyde, Jr. and Clara Belle, Jr., ch of Mr. and Mrs. Clyde King. AG 6/29/1908

RUSHTON, Robert E., Mrs., d. 255 Capitol Ave., Atlanta, Tues. Kin: Robert R. Rushton, Clyde L. King, William W. Rushton, Robert Rushton, Jr., Charles E. Rushton, Misses Alice May, Ella B. and Margaret Rushton, Mrs. Samuel B. Wight, Charles W. Tift, W. S. Wilson, A. P. Coles, Sam Wight, Ed L. Wight. AG 7/29/1908

RUSK, T. R. d. Cotton Row (Augusta) 3/17. AG 3/17/1910

RUSKING, William, colored, age 80, d. 20 Doray St. Atlanta. AG 1/28/1908

RUSSELL, Anna W., Mrs., mother of Hon. Charles R., d. Columbus, Ga., Tues. Widow of Charles R. Russell. Age 70. 4 children. Relatives in Texas. AG 12/15/1910

RUSSELL, Annie, Mrs. d. 55 Whiteford Ave., Atlanta, Sun. Interred: Oakland. AG 4/20/1908

RUSSELL, F. E., Mrs., age 38, d. 197 Lawton St. Atlanta, Mon. Husband survives. AG 8/23/1909

RUSSELL, George, colored, shot, killed Macon, Ga. AC 6/5/1905

RUSSELL, James E., son of J. M. Russell, atty, d. 5/22 Birmingham, Ala. Age 21. AG 5/21/1908

RUSSELL, Jennings, age 2, son of Mr. and Mrs. Fred J., d. Atlanta Tues. Interred: Newberry, S. C. AG 3/18/1908

RUSSELL, Lee, 6 mos. old son of ex-Judge R. B., recent candidate for Gov., native of Lee Co., d. Fri., Winder. Lee is 3rd child of judge to die, only 8 now living; oldest is 13. AG 9/8/1906

RUSSELL, Leila, colored, age 26, d. 101 N. Butler St. Atlanta. AG 7/10/1908

RUSSELL, Lucile, age 7, dau. of Mr. and Mrs. Robert, d. 25 Longley Ave. Atlanta, Wed. Interred: Hollywood. AG 5/7/1908

RUSSELL, Myron L., age 33, d. 146 Gordon St. Atlanta. AG 11/8/1909

RUSSELL, Sadie, Mrs., age 83, d. Atlanta. AG 6/19/1909

RUSSELL, Sarah L., Mrs., age 75, wife of late James G., d. Kimball House, Atlanta, Fri. Ch: Mrs. J. C. Courtney, Mrs. A. H. Benning, J. B. Russell. AG 4/17/1908

RUSSELL, Stephen B. d. Augusta, Ga. 11/11, age 35, native of S. C. Also lived Anniston, Ala. for sometime. AG 11/11/1909

RUSSELL, Tempie, colored, age 44, d. 242 Luckie St. Atlanta. AG 7/6/1907

RUSSER, M., Mrs. d. 5/13 res. of son, 4th St., Macon. Interred: St. Josephs cemetery. AG 5/13/1907

RUSSLE, Castus, colored, age 10 mos., d. 284 Connally St. Atlanta. AG 6/3/1909

RUSSON, Rolland W., ex-Mayor, d. 9/13 Dallas, Ga. AC 9/14/1905

RUST, Margaret, Miss, age 12, d. 10/15 Battle Hill. Interred: Westview. AC 10/16/1905

RUST, Nora P., Mrs. suicide Mon. home in Battle Hill, Atlanta. Interred: Westview. AG 6/10/1909

RUST, Sarah S., Mrs., age 80, d. Albany, Ga. 11/25 at dau.'s res., Mrs. P. L. Hilsman. She lived Albany since 1844. Son: R. S., Atlanta. AC 12/27/1905

RUTHERFORD, Mamie, Mrs., wife of R. T., d. Sun. 46 Plum St., Atlanta. Interred: Hollywood. AG 5/9/1910

RUTHERFORD, Margaret, Mrs., age 43, d. Inman, Ga. AG 10/18/1909

RUTHERFORD, Newton T. d. Sun. Marietta, Ga. Leaves wife, several children. Interred: City cemetery. AG 9/10/1907

RUTHERFORD, O. W., Mrs., age 25, d. Tues. Mayson and Turner Rds. Atlanta. Interred: Masons Church cemetery. AG 8/10/1910

RUTLEDGE, D. F., Mrs., age 44, d. 17 W. Cone St. Atlanta Wed. Interred: Loganville, Ga. AG 4/9/1908

RUTLEDGE, Drucilla, Mrs., age 49, d. Atlanta. AG 9/21/1909

RUTLEDGE, Edward B., colored infant, d. rear 123 N. Butler St. Atlanta. AG 5/26/1906

RUTLEDGE, Oscar, age 9, d. Wed., son of Mr. and Mrs. J. O. of E. Lake, Ga. AG 10/12/1909

RUTLEDGE, Priscilla, Mrs., age 49, of Jackson, Ga., d. Atlanta Thurs. Interred: Jackson, Ga. Daus: Misses Estell and Myrtis. Son: Emery, Jackson, Ga. AG 9/16/1909

RUTLEDGE, Virgil H., age 23, d. 68 Formwat St. Atlanta. AG 3/10/1910

RUTZLER, J. F., age 79, d. son-in-law's home, B. Lee Walker, 834 Peachtree St. Atlanta. Son: George F. Rutzler. Interred: Savannah, Ga. AG 10/29/1907

RYAN, J. A. of Boston, Mass. killed by passenger train Tifton, Ga. Interred: Tifton Cemetery. AC 6/25/1905

RYAN, Frank T., Capt., d. Sun. Funeral: Presbyterian Church, Atlanta. AG 6/25/1907

RYAN, Mattie, Mrs., age 86, died Grady Hospital. Atlanta. Interred: Oakland. AG 8/27/1906

RYAN, Paul, age 28, d. 177 Woodward Ave., Atlanta, Sun. Interred: Oakland. Bro: F. P. Ryan. Sis: Miss Annie Louise Ryan. AG 11/29/1909

RYAN, Stephen A. d. 727 Peachtree St., Atlanta, Thurs. Interred: Westview. He was b. Atlanta 50 yrs. ago. Funeral: 6/13. Wife, Mrs. Daisy E. Ryan, dau. of Dr. H. F. Askram. Dau: Edith. Mother: Mrs. John Ryan. Bros: John F. Ryan, Kansas City, Charles I., A. J. Ryan, R. A. Ryan. Sisters: Miss Ida Ryan, Mrs. H. L. Kuhrt. AG 6/12/1908

RYAN, William d. Sat. Atlanta. Interred: Westview. AG 8/30/1909

RYDER, Ed Morrison, Mrs., wife of A. D., d. father's home, Col. W. M. Morrison, Decatur. Interred: Oakland. AG 2/22/1910

RYLES, Liles, colored, age 32, d. 44 Ripley St. Atlanta. AG 3/16/1908

RYMAN, E. W., Col. of Fitzgerald, Ga. d. today. AG 2/20/1908

SAGE, Ira Y., Capt., age 60, d. 614 Peachtree St., Atlanta Sat. Interred: Oakland. AG 11/16/1908

SALBIDE, Manuel d. Newnan, Ga. 6/18. He was b. 1849 Biscay Province, Spain. AC 6/19/1905

SALE, Cornelius R. of Washington, Ga., pioneer of Wilkes Co., d. Jan. 26 Washington, Ga., age 75. Wife, 3 children. AC 1/26/1905

SALISBURY, Samuel d. 3/29 Columbus, Ga., age 53, oldest son of late Major W. L., banker. Wife, 7 children. AG 3/29/1910

SALLES, Julia, colored, age 18 days, d. 10 Phoenix alley. Atlanta. AG 10/1/1909

SALM, Grover, age 13, d. 72 Walton St. Atlanta. AG 11/12/1910

SALOSHIN, Gustav d. 67 Garnett St., Atlanta, age 82, Hebrew citizen from Cincinnati 1868 where res. after coming to America from birthplace, Breslau, Germany. Survived by wife, 5 ch, 15 gr-children, one gr-grandchild. Children: Louis Saloshin, Mrs. M. Lang, Mrs. I. A. Saloshin of N. Y.; Mrs. M. Waldman of Houston, Texas, Fred Saloshin of Atlanta. AG 12/12/1906

SALTER, Ada, Mrs., wife of W. C. of Newton Co., age 48, died. AG 6/17/1907

SALTER, F. F., Mrs., age 77, d. 23 Bailey St. Atlanta. AG 1/19/1910

SALTER, Susan O., Mrs., age 83, d. 359 Ormond St. Atlanta. Interred: Social Circle, Ga. AG 7/25/1910

SALYOR, Walter, colored, age 30, d. 158 E. Baker St. Atlanta. AG 11/9/1910

SAMMON, S. Q., Mrs. of Lawrenceville, Ga. d. Interred: Lawrenceville Cemetery. AG 12/12/1910

SAMONS, M. J., Mrs., age 83, d. bro.'s res., J. S. Montgomery, 56 Summitt Ave.,tlanta, Wed. Interred: Hogansville, Ga. AG 10/17/1907

SAMS, Oliver, colored, age 55, d. 297 Garibaldi St. Atlanta. AG 9/2/1909

SAMS, Robert W. of Americus, Ga., age 41, d. Sat. Interred: Oakland. Mother: Mrs. C. P. Sams of Americus. Sis: Mrs. W. B. Worthy, Americus. Bro: R. W. Sams, Atlanta. AG 5/2/1910

SAMUELS, Bettie, colored, age 54, d. 56 Delbridge St. Atlanta. AG 4/28/1908

SANDERS Sallie, Mrs., age 60, d. 6/14 Phenix City, Ala. AC 6/16/1905

SANDERS, C., colored, age 3 yrs., d. 159 Houston St. Atlanta. AG 2/1/1907

SANDERS, E., colored, age 53, d. Cutler, Ga. AG 5/11/1908

SANDERS, G. A., age 50, d. Fri. 69 Luckie St. Atlanta. Interred: Westview. AG 7/6/1907

SANDERS, J. I. d. Tues. 171 Chapel St., Atlanta. Wife, three ch: Mrs. L. L. Price, LaGrange, L. Sanders, T. Sanders. Interred: Columbus, Ga. AG 10/30/1906

SANDERS, J. M. d. Winder 1/14, age 73. Bro: Dr. W. H. Bush, Winder, Ga. Mother of large family. AG 1/15/1910

SANDERS, J. W., Mrs. d. home pf parents, Mr. and Mrs. Jim Brown, near Stilson, Ga., Thurs. She was bride only fe mos. Interred: Black Creek Church. AG 9/29/1908

SANDERS, Jessie Marie, colored, age 3, d. 145 Houston St. Atlanta. AG 7/8/1907

SANDERS, John, age 9, d. 132 W. Mitchell St., rear. AG 2/27/1907

SANDERS, Lucius, colored, age 32, d. 101 N. Butler St. Atlanta. AG 8/20/1908

SANDERS, Maner P., age 46, d. Wed. Atlanta. Interred: White Plains, Ga. Bro: L. B. Sanders, Atlanta. AG 5/1/1907

SANDERS, Maude, age 9 mos., d. 157 Courtland St. Atlanta. AG 7/12/1907

SANDERS, Minnie, colored, age 35, d. Memphis, Tenn. AG 3/30/1908

SANDERS, Myrtle Lee, age 9 yrs., d. 133 Whitehall St., Atlanta. AG 6/14/1907

SANDERS, Princeola, age 2, dau. of Mr. and Mrs. R. S., d. Sun. Atlanta. Interred: Roswell, Ga. AG 7/20/1908

SANDERS, R. G., Jr. d. Tues. Lizella, Ga. Funeral at Mt. Parson Church. AG 9/2/1910

SANDERS, Sarah J., age 55, d. 34 Carlton Ave. Atlanta. AG 5/18/1907

SANDERS, William, age 48, d. Macon Mon. Res. Anderson St., S. Macon. Wife, 6 children. AG 6/9/1908

SANDERS, Wilson, olored, age 30, d. Montreal, Ga. AG 4/28/1908

SANDS, Mattie, Mrs., age 39, d. Chipley, Ga. AG 11/24/1910

SANFORD, George, colored, age 46, d. 87-A Bell St. Atlanta. AG 7/22/1907

SAPPINGTON, John d. Sun., bur. family grounds near Barnesville. Age 83. AG 5/4/1910

SARGENT, Josephine Frances, age two, dau. of Mr. and Mrs. irving E. Sargent, d. 344 E. Linden St., Atlanta, Mon. Interred: Westview. AG 4/2/1907

SASSINE, Sidney, colored, age 51, d. 125 Bell St. Atlanta. AG 7/12/1907

SATTERFIELD, Julia H., Mrs., age 38, wife of V. E., 66 Houston St., Atlanta d. Thurs. AG 10/23/1908

SATTERFIELD, Regina, 11 mos. old infant of Mr. and Mrs. T. C. Satterfield, d. 33 Doane St. Atlanta. Interred: Dahlonega. AG 3/19/1907

SATTERFIELD, Vashti, age 49, d. 429 E. Fair St. Atlanta. AG 5/13/1907

SATTERWHITE, Floria, Miss, dau. of Mrs. G. A., d. yesterday, Cuthbert. AG 2/9/1907

SATTERWHITE, G. A., Mrs. d. Cuthbert, Ga. 5/23. Dau: Mrs. Elmore Jolly, Dawson, Ga., survives. AG 5/24/1907

SATTERWHITE, Milledge, colored, age 18, d. 147 Houston St. Atlanta. AG 3/10/1908

SAUNDERS, Elizabeth Louise, Mrs. d. Thurs., dau. of Mr. and Mrs. H. R. Smith, Macon, Ga. Interred: Riverside Cemetery, Macon. AG 11/11/1908
SAUNDERS, J. H., colored, age 36, d. 55 Yonge St. Atlanta AG 10/8/1907
SAUNDERS, William E., Sr., age 75, d. S. Kirkwood (Atlanta) 4/1 of old age. Wife. Ch: Mrs. R. B. Neal, Starkville, Miss.; C. E., Greenwood, Miss.; Miss Genevieve and William E. J. of Atlanta. Interred: Starkville, Miss. AC 4/2/1905
SAVAGE, Charles, colored, age 49, d. 142 E. Ellis St. Atlanta. AG 12/9/1907
SAVER, T. W., Mrs., age 76, d. E. Macon yesterday. Two daus and two bros. J. A. Smith of Knoxville, Tenn., Dr. R. C. Smith of Elberton, Ga. AG 2/20/1907
SAVIDGE, Charles L., age 35, d. 294 Courtland St. Atlanta. AG 8/11/1908
SAWTELL, Ella Hulsey, Mrs., age 57, wid. of late H. C., d. Sun. 311 Formwalt St., Atlanta. Interred: Oakland. AG 7/16/1907
SAWTELL, H. C., age 66, d. 311 Formwalt St. Atlanta. AG 6/27/1907
SAWTELL, Henry, pioneer to Atlanta, d. Tues. 311 Formwalt St. Atlanta. ex-Confed. soldier. Wife, 6 children, Misses Oma, Sue and Augusta Sawtell; Mrs. Myrtys Sawell Lokey; Henry D. and Albert Sawtell. AG 6/26/1907
SAWTELL, Henry C. estate left to 6 ch: Misses Oma, Susie and Katie, Albert and Henry D. Sawtell; Mrs. Lokey. AG 8/21/1907
SAWTELL, I. Y. d. 143 Richardson. Res. Atlanta 50 yrs; Born Athens, Tenn. 1859 md. Eliza, dau. of Dr. G. H. Roberts, Villa Rica. Sons: T. R., E. M. & L. P. Sawtell. Daus: Misses Mary, Annie, Estelle, Dorn. Bur: Westview. AG 12/26/1906
SAWYER, A. A., Mrs., age 72, d. Lumpkin, Ga. Dau: Mrs. J. C. Huff, 243 Capitol Ave., Atlanta. Interred: Oakland. Funeral 6/5. AG 6/8/1908
SAWYER, Daniel Linsey, age 57, d. 35 Auburn Ave., Atlanta, Wed. Wife survives. Interred: Rutledge, Ga. AG 9/24/1908
SAWYER, Green, colored, age 55, d. 106 Decatur St. Atlanta. AG 12/19/1907
SAWYER, Irene, age 1, d. 101 N. Butler St. Atlanta. AG 11/11/1907
SAWYER, Tom, City Marshal, d. Abbeville, Ga. jail yesterday. Wife, two children. Had been delirious. AG 8/9/1906
SAXE, Mary Estelle, Miss d. Thurs. res. of bro., George H. Saxe, 320 S. Boulevard, Atlanta. Interred: Oakland. AG 8/2/1906
SAXON, Mildred, Mrs., age 65, d. res. of son, J. C., 5/17. Widow of Joshua Saxon. 14 ch, 7 survive. Interred: Bethlehem Church. AG 5/18/1910
SAXTON, Joseph, age 1 yr, d. 325 Peachtree St. Atlanta. AG 3/16/1907
SAYE, Mary Frances, age 6, d. Tues. res. of parents, Mr. and Mrs. Edward D., 328 Luckie St. Atlanta. Interred: Oakland. She was niece of Mrs. Kate Jolly. AG 9/29/1909
SAYE, R. A., Atlanta pioneer, d. Thurs. Interred: Oakland. AG 2/25/1910

SCALES, Ethel May, age 1, d. 228 Cooper St. Atlanta. AG 8/31/1908

SCARRATT, Dorothy, age 11 mos., d. Grady Hospital. Atlanta. AG 6/18/1907

SCHAEFFER, Annie, age 4 mos., d. Todd Rd. Atlanta. AG 9/3/1909

SCHALL, George Frederick, age 23, son of Mr. and Mrs. George, d. Mon. Plona Ave. Atlanta. One bro. Interred: Riverside. AG 8/20/1907

SCHELL, Claude C., age 3, son of Mr. and Mrs. W. A., d. Sat. S. Atlanta. Interred: South Bend Church yard. AG 6/15/1908

SCHELL, Martha, Mrs. d. several days ago. Interred: Westview. AG 12/14/1907

SCHESINGER, Nettie Weis, Mrs., age 76, dau. of Jacob Weis, mayor of Neuera, Hungary, wid. of 5 yrs., d. 258 S. Pryor St. Atlanta. Ch: Col. Harry L.; M. B.; Mrs. Ralph Victor; Mrs. H. Utitz, NY. In America 40 yrs. Bur: Oakland. AG 3/19/1907

SCHEUER, E. Miss, age 17, d. Cartersville, Ga. AG 2/22/1907

SCHICK, Katy, Mrs., age 24, wife of Michael, d. Tues. Melton St., S. Atlanta. Interred: Westview. AG 7/31/1907

SCHIKAN, Catherine, Mrs., age 81, Atlanta pioneer (to Marthasville), b. 1826 Germany, d. 115 Oglethorpe Ave., Atlanta. Daus: Miss Minnie Schikan, Mrs. John Jentzen, Atlanta; Mrs. C. B. Pope of Waycross. Interred: Oakland. AG 7/16/1907

SCHMELTZER, Pauline, age 72, d. 101 N., Butler St. Atlanta. AG 11/29/1907

SCHMIDT, W. F. d. Atlanta Mon. Interred: Marietta, Ga. AG 9/23/1907

SCHMIDT, W. H. d. Old Soldiers' Home Atlanta, Mon. Interred: Westview. AG 3/3/1909

SCHNEIDER, Julius, Professor, funeral Tues. Interred: Westview. Res. 452 S. Boulevard, Atlanta. AG 5/31/1906

SCHNUB, G., age 63, d. Battle Hill, Ga. AG 8/11/1908

SCHOEN, Moses, age 26, of Atlanta, d. Sun. bros. res., Isaac Schoen, 306 Washington St. Interred: Oakland. Born 5/22/1882 Louisville, Ky., to Atlanta age 12. AG 3/7/1910

SCHOFIELD, Edward, Mrs.,a ge 49, d. Mon. Vineville, Ga. Husband, two children. AG 8/4/1908

SCHOMBERG, Carl, Jr., age 2, son of Mr. and Mrs. Carl, d. 280 N. Jackson St., Atlanta, Thurs. Interred: Columbus, Ga. AG 2/28/1908

SCHROEDER, A. B., age 30, d. Wed. res. at Faith's Crossing. Leaves wife. Interred: Abbeville, S. C. AG 8/21/1907

SCHULER, Perry, colored, age 24, d. 225 Smith St. Atlanta. AG 12/24/1908

SCHULZ, Louise C., age 3, dau. of Mr. and Mrs. W. F., d. 371 Peachtree St., Atlanta, Fri. Interred: Westview. AG 10/5/1907

SCHUTZE, Daniel C., age 78, d. Stone Mountain, Ga. Tues. Interred: Family Cemetery. AG 7/2/1908

SCHWALB, Fritz, age 19, dornwd 6/7, Tybee (Savannah). AG 6/8/1908

SCMITZ, George. Macon, Ga., 12/12. Death (appendicitis) of city fireman at city hospital, generally deplored. AG 12/12/1906

SCOFIELD, Gerrit Smith funeral 66 Forrest Ave., Atlanta, res. He d. Gardiner, Mont., age 58. Wife was formerly Miss Katherine Evans, Brooklyn, N. Y. Bro: F. M. Schofield. 2 sisters, bro. in N. Y. Interred: Westview. AG 6/7/1906

SCOGGINS, Jane A., Mrs., age 77, d. 5/20 res. of dau., Mrs. George W. White, Columbus, Ga. AC 5/22/1905

SCOGIN, W. E., administrator's sale, Fulton Co., 1st Tues. Oct. 1906. W. C. Baggett, admr. AG 9/29/1906

SCOTT, Alice Chandler, age 2, d. 36 E. North Ave. Atlanta. AG 9/3/1909

SCOTT, Cheney, colored, age 82, d. 281 Terry St. Atlanta. AG 9/8/1908

SCOTT, Cooper B., age 65, buried 4/8 Gainesville. Res. 22 yrs. of Gainesville. From Charleston, S. C. Alleged to be man who fired first canon at Ft. Sumter. AC 4/9/1905

SCOTT, Cynthia A., Mrs., age 5, d. Sun. 178 Jones Ave., Atlanta, wife of J. E. Ch: George E.; Mrs. J. C. Reese. Sis: Mrs. W. H. Rice. AG 4/11/1910

SCOTT, D. T., age 32, d. Atlanta Wed., 180 Woodward Ave. Interred: Greenwood Cemetery. Wife, one child. AG 3/18/1909

SCOTT, E. G., age 41, d. Fulton co. Tower. AG 2/20/1908

SCOTT, Ed, colored, age 19, d. rear of 326 Fort St. Atlanta. AG 11/15/1909

SCOTT, Fletcher, colored, age 35, d. rear 131 W. Fair St. Atlanta. AG 2/20/1908

SCOTT, G., colored, age 4 yrs., d. 162 Irwin St. Atlanta. AG 1/3/1907

SCOTT, George W., Capt., Confed. Vet., d. Fri. Oliver, Ga. Bur: Ogeechee Cemetery. Age 84. One son, one dau. AG 5/30/1910

SCOTT, Hannah, colored, age 65, d. 23 Elm St. Atlanta. AG 12/10/1910

SCOTT, Harold, age 2, son of Mr. and Mrs. C. E., d. E. Point, Ga. Tues. Interred: Webbs cemetery. AG 9/1/1908

SCOTT, J. E., Hartwell, Ga., 11/13/1906, oldest citizen, died Sun. night. Buried yesterday by Masonic fraternity. AG 11/13/1906

SCOTT, Jane E., Mrs., age 68, d. 98 East Linden St. Atlanta. AG 3/7/1907

SCOTT, John, colored, age 50, d. 335 W. Fair St., Atlanta, Oct. 15. AG 10/18/1910

SCOTT, Joseph A. d. Thurs. 19 Longley Ave., Atlanta. Interment: Westview. Wife, one child. AG 9/7/1906

SCOTT, K., colored, age 2 yrs., d. 77 Dawson St., rear. Atlanta. AG 2/19/1907

SCOTT, Lily May, age 13, d. 631 Highland Ave. Atlanta. AG 3/3/1909

SCOTT, Lot, age 80, d. 9 Inman Ave. Atlanta. Interred: Rock Springs Church AG 4/26/1907

SCOTT, M. E., Mrs., age 55, d. 522 W. Hunter St. Atlanta Thurs. Daus: Misses Jessie and Gertrude. Son: Luther Scott. AG 6/19/1908

SCOTT, Marie, inf. dau. of J. A., d. Wed. Interred: Greenwood. AG 6/21/1907

SCOTT, Marshall, colored, age 22, d. 9 Graves St. Atlanta. AG 8/14/1908

SCOTT, Mary Belle, age 11 dau. of Mr. and Mrs. Arthur S. of Macon, d. Sat. Atlanta. Interred: Oakland. AG 12/28/1908

SCOTT, Mattie, Mrs., age 31, d. 55 E. Harris St., Atlanta, Oct. 28. AG 10/29/1910

SCOTT, Rosanna, d. sil's res: H. A. DuPre, Powder Spgs. Ch: Mrs. E. J. Maddux, Doraville; S. Scott, Chickamauga: Mrs. H. A. DuPre, Powder Springs; Mary and Sara Scott; W. W. Scott; Mrs. E. A. White, Atlanta. Bur: Powder Spgs. AG 12/1/1907

SCOTT, Sarah, colored, age 80, d. rear of 138 Fraser St. Atlanta. AG 6/1/1907

SCOTT, Thomas Jefferson, Jr., age 14, son of Mr. and Mrs. J. C. of Comer, Ga., d. Fri. Interred: Comer. AG 3/13/1909

SCOTT, Virginia E., age 1, dau. of Mr. and Mrs. W. L., d. 631 Highland Ave. Atlanta. Interred: Westview. AG 10/30/1908

SCOTT, W. E., age 66, Grady Hospital, Atlanta. AG 11/9/1906

SCOTT, W. J., Mrs., widow (husband d. 5 yrs. ago) of Atlanta, d. Jan. 31 415 Piedmont Ave. AC 2/1/1905

SCOTT, William B., Confederate Veteran, age 67, d. 12 Carlton St. Atlanta. Interred: Griffin, Ga. Daus: Mrs. Lizzie Taylor, Mrs. Lennie Murphy. Son: W. B. Scott, Jr. AG 5/21/1908

SCREVEN, Thomas E., Mrs. d. 8/12 69 Crew St. Atlanta. AC 8/12/1905

SCREVENS, W. J. d. Inman yards, Atlanta 12/9/1908. Sis: Mrs. R. P. Burton of 464 Benton Blvd., Los Angeles, Calif. Interred: Waycross, Ga. AG 12/23/1908

SCROGGINS, Alex, age 53, d. 167 E. Harris St. Atlanta. AG 10/25/1900

SCROGGINS, Rhoda C., Mrs., age 80, d. 21 Cornelia St., Atlanta, Sun. Interred: Hollywood. AG 2/28/1910

SCROGGINS, T. A., age 34, d. 523 W. Hunter St. Atlanta. AG 9/6/1910

SCRUGGS, Conway, age 11, son of Mr. and Mrs. William E., d. Fri. 47 Culberson St. Atlanta, grandson of Col. W. L. Scruggs, former minister to Venzeuela. Interred: West Point, Ga. AG 9/2/1910

SCRUGGS, L. Houston, Col. d. Nashville, Tenn. 7/30. Confed. Vet., 4th Ala. Inf. Sis: Ella; Mrs. Otey Robinson. Bro: J. W., Huntsville, Ala. AC 8/1/1905

SCRUGGS, Lillian P., Mrs. d. Mon. Crew St.,A tlanta. Interred: Jackson, Ga. AG 4/5/1910

SCRUGGS, W. J., Prof., d. Ft. Valley 11/12. Wife. Ch: Mrs. R. E. Brown and Mattie Scruggs, Ft. Valley, William Scruggs (atty at Harvard), Philip Scruggs, Auburn, Ala. AC 11/13/1905

SCUDDER, James, negro, hanged 4/6 Nashville, Tenn. for murdering his 3-yr. old child, James Alfred Scudder. AC 4/6/1905

SCUDDER, Samuel S., age 69, Confed. Veteran, 12th Ga., Regt., d. 350 Formwalt St. Atlanta. Wife, two sons: W. Russell, Frank S. 3 bros, one sister. AG 11/14/1908

SEABLOOM, Annie, Miss, age 22, d. 148 Davis St. Atlanta. Interred: Ormond, Fla. AG 4/10/1908

SEAGO, A. K. d. Wed. New Orleans. Interred: Atlanta, Oakland Cemetery. AG 6/30/1910

SEALE, Sarah Alice, age 6 mos., inf. dau. of Mr. and Mrs. M. J., d. Atlanta Tues. Interred: Greensboro, Ga. AG 7/13/1909

SEALS, John H., age 76, d. Milledgeville, Ga. AG 2/11/1909

SEALS, Lou H., Mrs., age 77, wid. of late Prof. W. B. Seals, died 220 S Boulevard, Atlanta. She was born Eatonton. Survived by one son: N. T. Seals. Interment: Westview. AG 12/20/1906

SEALS, William, colored, age 31, d. 249 Fraser St. Atlanta. AG 10/29/1907

SEAMORE, L. E., Mrs., age 49, d. Sun. Griffin. Interred: Oakland. AG 8/27/1907

SEARCEY, Willie, colored, age 1, d. 81 Greensferry Ave. Atlanta. AG 2/4/1908

SEARCY, James K., age 45, d. Atlanta. AG 5/20/1910
SEBELL, Sallie, infant, d. 214 E. Hunter St. Atlanta. AG 8/4/1906
SEDBERRY, John H., age 39, d. 114 Luckie St. Atlanta. AG 11/1/1909
SEDDON, Leonara E., 20 mos. dau. of Mr. & Mrs. W. M. Seddon, d. Thurs. Cascade Ave. Atlanta. Bur: Oakland. AG 3/30/1907
SEELY, U., Sr., Mrs. d. Thurs. Newark, N. J. 7 children, one is F. L. Seely, of Atlanta. Interred: Newark, N. J. AG 9/15/1910
SEIDELL, Emma A., Mrs., age 60, d. Washington, D. C. AG 12/11/1908
SEITINZER, Thomas F., age 54, d. Tues. 310 N. Boulevard, Atlanta. Interred: Westview. Wife, 5 children, survive. AG 6/12/1907
SELBY, small child of W. H. Selby, Sylvania, Ga., 11/12/1906, fatally burned by fire, AG 11/13/1906
SELF, Lott, age 34, d. 69 Luckie St. Atlanta. Res. of Tallapoosa, Fla., where interred. AG 4/25/1908
SELF, W. I. of Conyers, Ga. d. Thurs. Wife survives. Interred: Conyers, Ga. AG 2/14/1908
SELIG, Jacob d. Mon., 2/4, Chicago, Illinois. Interred: Oakland cemetery, Atlanta. AG 2/11/1907
SELLARS, Ellen, age 3, d. 101 N. Butler St. Atlanta. AG 2/27/1907
SELLARS, Otis, age 6 mos., d. 92 Connally St. Atlanta. Interred: Hollywood. AG 6/21/1907
SELLARS, Paul M., age 2, son of Angel, d. Wed. 68 McDonald St. Atlanta. Interred: Hollywood. AG 7/21/1910
SELLERS, Ruth, age 17 mos., dau. of Mr. and Mrs. A. D., d. Wed. 781 Marietta St. Atlanta. Interred: Westview. AG 8/4/1910
SELLS, C. H. d. 61 E. Tenth St., Atlanta, Fri. Interred: Stone Mtn. Wife, one son, H. G. Dau: Miss Carrie Wells. AG 9/12/1908
SELLS, Thomas R., Mrs. d. 3/22, NW of Columbus. AC 3/23/1905
SELMAN, J. H., Mrs., age 53, d. 17 W. Cain St. Atlanta. AG 11/7/1907
SENGELLTON, Carolina Livingston, age 55, d. 221-A Luckie St. Atlanta. AG 12/14/1908
SENTELL, Emma, Mrs., wife of John H.,, age 50, d. Fri., 748 N. Boulevard, Atlanta. Bur: Sandy Springs churchyard. AG 6/29/1907
SERCEY, Jasper, age 22, killed Wed. by engine in construction camp. Interred: Hollywood. AG 9/19/1907
SESSAMON, Lucy, age 12, died at 131 S. Pryor Street, Atlanta. AG 12/10/1906
SESSOMS, A., orig. from N. C., age 74, is dying at Waycross. Son: Alex, Jr. Dau: Mrs. Pauline Swain of Mexico. AG 3/21/1910
SETTLES, Eva Pearl, inf. dau. of Mr. and Mrs. E. S., d. Sun. Interred: Sewanee. AG 6/4/1906
SETZ, John Hallman, inf. son of Mr. and Mrs. J. W., d. 376 Spring St. Atlanta, Tues. Interred: Marietta. AG 7/20/1909
SEWELL, Edna Maude, Miss, age 15, dau. of Mr. and Mrs. O. T. of 16 Spencer St. Atlanta, d. Wed. Bur: Smyrna, Ga. AG 5/21/1908
SEWELL, Elma, Mrs., age 30, d. 74 Mangum St., Atlanta, Mon. Husband, 2 children. Interred: Highland Cemetery. AG 11/15/1910
SEWELL, Milt, Mrs. of Roscoe, Ga., Coweta Co., d. Sun. 6 mi. from Whitesburg. Dau: Dolly, age 14. AG 11/6/1907
SEXTON, Susan, Mrs., age 62, d. Exposition Grounds. Atlanta. AG 1/16/1907
SEZEAR, Peter, age 48, d. 127 Richardson St. Atlanta. AG 2/1/1907

SHACKELFORD, J. F., Dr. d. Columbus, Ga., Sun., age 70, prominent
druggist. He was an asst. surgeon in the famous Pickett division
during civil war; was at Gettysburg. AG 6/19/1906
SHACKELFORD, M. A., Mrs., age 34, d. Tues. 64 N. Forsyth St.,
Atlanta. Interred: Westview. Husband, two children, M. T. and
Rubye Shackleford. Two bros: H. H. and J. W. Lane. AG 12/28/1909
SHACKELFORD, Georgia, 61, d. dau.'s res., Mrs. R. P. Recht, 494
Spring St. Atlanta. Son: M. A. Sis: Mrs. A. C. Wilkinson,
Hogansville, Ga.; Mrs. Lizzie Phillips, Winnsboro, Tx. Bro: R. M.
Stinson, Hogansville. Bur: Westview. AG 4/19/1910
SHACKLEFORD, J. B. d. res. of mother Sun., Columbus, Ga., age 45.
2 sisters, 2 bros. AG 8/23/1910
SHACKLEFORD, Sarah, Miss, age 80, d. Griffin, Tues., dau. of
Capt. A. B. Shackleford. AG 12/17/1910
SHACKLEFORD, Susan, Miss d. Sat., age 73, Belmont, Ga. Interred:
Hopewell Church, Hall Co., Ga. AG 1/28/1908
SHACKLEFORD, Nell Wheeler, Miss, age 18, d. Fri. aunt's home,
Mrs. Minnie McLeod, 43 Greenwood Ave., Atlanta. Interred:
Montgomery. Sis: Misses Genevieve and Estell Shackleford. Bro:
Elmwood Shackelford. AG 2/11/1910
SHADDEN, J. H., age 71, d. 17 W. Cain St. Atlanta. AG 5/6/1908
SHAEFER, Fred, Jr., infant of Mr. and Mrs. Fred, d. Mon. College
Park, Ga. Interred: Westview. AG 6/19/1907
SHAFER, Francis Aubrey, age 4, son of Mr. and Mrs. F. B., d. 98
Whitehall Terrace, Atlanta. Interred: LaGrange, Ga. AG 6/18/1908
SHAFFER, J. M., Mrs., age 82, d. home of dau., Mrs. E. J. Henry,
Hawkinsville, Ga. Fri. Ch: Mrs. E. J. Henry; P. W. Russell,
Macon; A. W. and M. A. Russell, Atlanta. AG 4/26/1908
SHAFFER, Mary, Miss, age 18, dau. of Mr. and Mrs. L. F., d. 12
Fortune St. Atlanta, Thurs. Interred: Sharon Church. AG 3/20/1908
SHAMSTULSKY, John, age 52, d. 1/11, Chattanooga, Tenn. AG
1/11/1910
SHANDS, Joseph F. d. Sun. 50 Houston St. Atlanta. Interred: Ft.
Meyer, Fla. AG 5/25/1907
SHANKS, J. H., age 73, d. 3/30 Girard, Ga., age 73, Confed. Vet.
AC 3/31/1905
SHANNON, George, negro, found dead McDonough Rd., Jackson Co. AG
1/25/1910
SHANNON, James M. b. Cabaniss, Monroe Co., Ga. 9/11/1839, d. age
69. In 1820 bros., James, oseph and John, left river Shannon, N.
Ireland, to America. AG 10/18/1907
SHANNON, Samuel, age 82, d. Soldiers' Home. Atlanta. AG
10/19/1907
SHARKEY, Martha Elizabeth, age 6 mos., d. 29 Luckie St. Atlanta.
Dau. of Mr. and Mrs. E. E. Sharkey. Interred: Palmetto, Ga. AG
7/10/1909
SHARMAN, C. B., Mrs., age 73, old Atlanta res., d. Willow St.,
Mon. Interred: Oakland. AG 11/19/1907
SHARP, Clyde, Mrs., wife of Z. D., d. Mon. res. of sister, 146 W.
Pine St., Atlanta. Interred: Westview. AG 10/4/1907
SHARP, James B., father of Dr. James of Atlanta, d. Forsyth, Ga.
Wed. Wife. Sons: Dr. James, Atlanta; Norman, Newnan, Ga.; Cyrus,
Forsyth. AG 4/15/1909
SHARP, M. E., Mrs., age 68, d. Wed. 100 E. Georgia Ave. Atlanta.
Son: B. Sharp. AG 8/29/1907

SHARPE, Alex, colored, age 42, d. 157 Fraser St. Atlanta. AG 5/11/1908

SHARPE, William H., age 57, d. 263 Rawson St., Atlanta Wed. Wife. Son: Henry. Dau: Annie. AG 6/16/1909

SHARPSTEEN, Hannah, Mrs., age 74, d. 6 McLinden St., Edgewood, Ga., Fri. Interred: Westview. AG 10/12/1907

SHARUS, Aaron, colored, age 75, d. 95 Thurmond St. Atlanta. AG 7/30/1908

SHAVER, Jack H. d. Wed. Atlanta. Interred: Mt. Zion. AG 9/19/1907

SHAW, Augustus of Atlanta d. 41 Houston St. 11/5. Wife. Daus: Flora, Bessie. Son: Augustus, Jr. He was b. Jackson Co., Ga. 8/21/1834. Interred: Westview. AC 11/6/1905

SHAW, Calvin, Rev., age 93, d. Raleigh, N. C. Chaplain in Civil War. AC 7/14/1905

SHAW, James C., Macon businessman, age 60, d. yesterday. Wife, one dau., Miss Annie Laurie Shaw. Bros-in-law: Jud S. Hill and A. B. Subers of Macon. AG 5/24/1907

SHAW, John R., age 61, d. Collage Park, Ga. Tues. Interred: Americus. Wife, three sisters. AG 2/27/1907

SHAW, Lula, colored, age 37, d. 476 W. Mitchell St. Atlanta. AG 9/11/1907

SHAW, Osmer L., son of Mrs. L. F., d. Valdosta, Ga., age 19. AG 8/28/1909

SHAW, S. E., Miss, age 53, d. Mon. 209 Spring St. Atlanta. Interment: Hollywood. AG 9/4/1906

SHAW, Nell McWhirter, Mrs., age 27, wife of P. P., dau. of Jas McWhirter, d. 186 Rawson St. Bur: Westview. Bros: Robert & James McWhirter, St. Louis, Mo. Sis: Mrs. Edward Belliveau, Charleston, S. C.; Annie & Agnes McWhirter, Atlanta. AG 6/10/1907

SHAW, R. E., Miss, age 53, d. 209 Spring St. Atlanta. AG 9/4/1906

SHEAT, William H., age 82, d. 211 E. North Ave. Thurs. Wife, 8 children. Interred: Westview. AG 11/3/1906

SHEATS, A. Y., Capt. of Kingston d. 7/26. He was b. Clarke Co., Ga. 12/1830, Capt. Co. I, 40th Ga. Regt. Md. twice, last to dau. of Dr. William Irby of Laurens, S. C. Two ch, one: S. I., Kingston, Ga. AG 7/27/1909

SHEATS, John E. of Atlanta d. 64 Bass St. Tues, age 32. Wife, 3 children, Edith,Agnes, Harold. Interred: Westview. AG 5/25/1910

SHEATS, Nannie J., Mrs., age 52, d. 78 Richardson St., Atlanta, Sun., wife of W. H. 4 children. Interred: Westview. AG 12/5/1910

SHEATS, S. F., Mrs., age 70, d. 211 E. North Ave. Atlanta. AG 11/7/1907

SHEATS, Susan F., Mrs., age 76, d. 211 E. North Ave., Atlanta. Interred: Westview. Mother of 8 children. AG 11/6/1907

SHEEHAN, Elizabeth, Mrs., of Atlanta, age 67, d. Ellenwood, NY. Daus: Mrs. Jos. N. Moody; Mrs. Claude N. Kress, NY. Descended from McCarthy-Mores of Ire. She was Elizabeth McCarty before marrying late Cornelius Sheehan. AG 8/24/1906

SHEELY, Laura V., Mrs., age 58, d. 692 1/2 S. Pryor St., Atlanta, Sat. Dau: Mrs. Allie Raiford. Son: Andrew. Interred: Sparks, Ga. AG 11/21/1910

SHEETS, Georgia, Miss, dau. of Mr. and Mrs. Wood Sheets, d. Atlanta Fri. Interred: Winder. AG 2/2/1907

SHEFFIELD, Duncan killed by son, Luther, on Christmas eve., 12/24/1907. Luther, age 25, married, has one child, abt 5 weeks old, held. AG 1/1/1908

SHELBY, Mamie, dau. of Mr. and Mrs. L. S., D. 27 Simpson St., Atlanta, Sun. Interred: Westview. AG 12/9/1907

SHELDON, F. E., formerly of Chicago, d. 12/25 Atlanta. AC 12/27/1905

SHELL, William S., age 2 mos., d. 214 E. Hunter St., Atlanta, home of parents, Mr. and Mrs. G. Interred: Hollywood cemetery. AG 12/1/1907

SHELLMAN, Tom, epileptic, drowned in river Wed., Columbus, Ga., had been shot in head. AG 7/25/1907

SHELLS, Sallie, colored, age 17, d. 43 Rawson St. Atlanta. AG 8/14/1907

SHELNUTT, Sallie, Mrs., wife of J. H., d. 194 S. Pryor St.,A tlanta Tues. Ch: Mrs. F. C. Martin, Waterloo, N. Y.; Mrs. J. H. Triplett, Atlanta; E. L. Shelnutt, Atlanta. Interred: Newnan, Ga. AG 12/22/1908

SHELTON, A. M., Mrs., age 51, d. Atlanta. AG 5/20/1910

SHELTON, Annie M., Mrs., d. 29 Ellis St., Atlanta, Wed. Interred: Westview. AG 5/19/1910

SHELTON, A. C., age 55, d. Atlanta Wed. Interred: Utoy church yard. AG 8/30/1903

SHELVERTON, Norman, Colonel interred Oakland. Wife, one son, survive. AG 1/24/1908

SHELVERTON, W. Edwin, age 83, d. Austell, Ga. Mon. Interred: Westview. Wife, two sons. AG 4/20/1909

SHENUTT, Sallie, Mrs., age 62, d. 194 S. Pryor St. Atlanta. AG 12/24/1908

SHEPARD, Annie Laurie, colored 379 W. Third St. killed in Atlanta race riot. AG 9/24/1906

SHEPARD, James T., age 50, d. 24 Rosalie St. Atlanta. AG 11/12/1910

SHEPARD, Laura, colored, age 80, d. 6 Martin alley, Atlanta, Nov. 11. AG 11/16/1910

SHEPARD, Martha, Mrs. funeral Sun. Interred: Marietta, Ga. AG 9/14/1907

SHEPARD, Will, negro, killed by John Holiday, Donalsonville, Ga. AG 12/30/1907

SHEPHERD, Amanda, colored, age 63, d. 92 W. Cain St. Atlanta. AG 4/9/1908

SHEPHERD, Charles T., Mrs. d. Thurs. 42 Luckie St., Atlanta. Interred: Marietta, Ga. AG 9/13/1907

SHEPHERD, Martha, Mrs., age 68, d. 42 Luckie St. Atlanta. AG 9/14/1907

SHEPPARD, Charles met tragic end at Kimball Hotel, Atlanta. AG 5/4/1907

SHEPPARD, S. H. d. Sat. at res. of Miss Orrie Colbert, Spring St., Macon where he had res. 4 yrs. Leaves wife, 3 children: William S., Augusta; Samuel H., Pt. Loma, CA; Mrs. W. C. Wardlow, Augusta. Interred: Augusta. AG 3/4/1907

SHERARD, Ward mortally wounded by Foster Pressley Sat. night on boat in Savannah River. AG 11/13/1907

SHERIDAN, Robert B., age 69, d. Columbus, Ga. 6/5. Formerly of Macon. AG 6/6/1906

SHERIDAN, W. W., Jr., inf. of Mr. and Mrs. W. W., d. 604 Whitehall St. Atlanta. Interred: Hollywood. AG 7/7/1909

SHERLIN, Samuel C., Jr., age 19, d. 101 N. Butler St., Atlanta., d. Wed. Interred: Niota, Tenn. AG 1/3/1907

SHERMAN, Bessie, Miss, age 21, d. 17 W. Cain St. Atlanta. AG 9/9/1908

SHERMAN, David B. of Donalson, Ga. d. 8/4, formerly of Blakely, Ga. Proprietor of several saw mills. Young wife, one child. Interred: Blakely, Ga. AG 8/4/1908

SHERMAN, Henry T. of Donalsonville, Ga., formerly of Blakely, Ga., d. Dothan, Ala., Sat. Bro: David . Sherman d. month ago. Interred: Lumpkin. AG 9/7/1908

SHERMAN, Lula Hood, Mrs., age 35, d. 135 Jett St., Atlanta, Tues. Husband: F. T. 3 children, parents, Mr. and Mrs. J. F. Franklin. Interred: Flowery Branch, Ga. AG 3/2/1909

SHERMAN, Sim, colored, age 50, d. 372 N. Butler St. Atlanta. AG 10/9/1907

SHERRAN, Thomas E., age 6 mos., son of Mr. and Mrs. E. J., d. 55 Almo Ave., Atlanta, Sat. Interred: Oakland. AG 9/28/1908

SHERRELL, Laura, colored, age 52, d. Atlanta. AG 10/30/1908

SHERRON, E. J., age 20, d. Atlanta. AG 3/7/1910

SHERWOOD, George C., age 64, d. E. Ellis St. Atlanta. AG 4/2/1910

SHERWOOD, John M., age 22, d. 25 Ellis St. Atlanta, son of Mr. and Mrs. E. C., sent to Columbus, Ga. Thurs. for interment. AG 9/26/1907

SHETZEN, Florence, age 11, d. 284 W. Fair St., Atlanta. Interred: Oakland. AG 8/10/1906

SHEWMAKE, John T., of Augusta drowned at Tybee, was cousin of Claude Shewmake, wholesale grocer of Atlanta. Wife was Miss Mamie Harris of Augusta, niece of Mrs. George R. Sibley. AG 8/8/1906

SHEWORD, Aamer, colored, age 9 mos., d. 382 Crumley St. Atlanta. AG 10/25/1906

SHIELDS, Annie, colored, age 38, d. 10 Golden Ave. Atlanta. AG 12/17/1910

SHIELDS, Annie, Miss d. Tues. res. of sister, Mrs. R. H. Shaw, 174 W. Alexander St., Atlanta, Thurs. Interred: Oakland. AG 9/26/1907

SHIELDS, Columbus, Mrs. of Stockbridge, Ga., d. Sat. Husband, two children. AG 10/18/1910

SHIELDS, E. S., age 69, d. 10/27 Atlanta. Interred: Stockbridge, Ga. AG 10/28/1910

SHIELDS, Emma, Miss, age 23, d. 69 Luckie St. Atlanta. AG 9/26/1907

SHIELDS, Hannon, inf. son of Mr. and Mrs. J. A., d. 21 Center St., Atlanta, Thurs. Interred: Westview. AG 5/27/1910

SHIELDS, J. W., age 67, d. Sun. 187 Echo St. Atlanta. Interred: Austell, Ga. AG 3/23/1910

SHIELDS, John W., Sr., age 49, d. 274 Central Ave., Atlanta Fri. Another notice says age 94. AG 3/26/1910

SHIELDS, Julia M., Miss, age 33, d. 779 Piedmont Ave. Atlanta. AG 4/22/1908

SHIELDS, Emmie L., Miss, age 24, d. Atlanta, Wed. Father, W. S. Shields. Sisters: Mrs. R. H. Shaw, Miss Willie Shields, Atlanta, Mrs. Elmer E. Morris, Cameron, W. Va. Bros: E. A., A. S. of Atlanta. Interred: Oakland. AG 9/24/1907

SHIELDS, Florence, colored, age 59, died Larkin St., Atlanta. AG 11/26/1906

SHIELDS, Lizzie, Miss d. 267 Woodward Ave., Atlanta, Sun. Interred: Westview. AG 6/25/1906

SHINE, E. E. d. 7/3 S. Macon, age 55. Wife, 5 children. Interred: Liberty Chapel Cemetery. AC 7/5/1905

SHINN, G. H., Dr. d. in Boston, 9/6. (Memorial). Founder of Universalist Church in Atlanta. AG 9/28/1907

SHIPLEY, E. E., Rev., age 70, d. Baltimore, Md., Sun. Dau: Mrs. B. Mifflin Hood, 93 Elizabeth St., Atlanta. Wife: Laura D. AG 3/29/1910

SHIPP, Forrest J., age 17 mos., died 8 Ella St. Atlanta. AG 8/22/1906

SHIPP, Mary Lee, age 13, dau. of Mr. and Mrs. W. M., d. 135 Fraser St., Atlanta, Mon. AG 12/7/1908

SHIPPEY, C. B. of Atlanta, age 31, d. Tucson, Ariz. Bro: J. K. Shippey, 63 Milledge Ave., Atlanta. Interred: Westview. AG 2/6/1908

SHIRLEY, J. F., age 47, former Atlantan, d. Thurs., Bolives, Tenn. Interred: Hollywood. AG 6/10/1910

SHISSLER, T. B., native of Iowa, came Atlanta 20 yrs., ago, d. 222 Lee St., West End, Atlanta, Mon. Interred: Oakland. Leaves widow, one dau., Mrs. Kate Shissler, age 10. AG 12/9/1907

SHIVER, S. M., Mrs. d. hospital, Nashville, Tenn., wife of S. M. Shiver, engineer on Seaboard road, Abbeville, S. C. AG 8/1/1906

SHIVERS, Anna P., age 2, d. Hayden St. Atlanta 10/22. AG 10/25/1910

SHOCKLEY, Lillian, age 34, d. 42 Dunn St. Atlanta. AG 9/8/1908

SHOCKLEY, Ruth, Miss, age 47, d. 296 S. Pryor St., Atlanta, Fri. Sis: Misses Leo and Iva Shockley of Atlanta; Mrs. F. A. Lewis of Nacoma, Tx. Bro: R. W. Shockley of Atlanta. Interred: Cartersville, Ga. AG 5/8/1910

SHOEMAKE, Ella, colored, age 31, d. 18 Rawson St. Atlanta. AG 3/10/1909

SHOEN, Clara, Mrs., wid. of Louis, d. Thurs. 252 S. Pryor St., Atlanta. She was b. Bavaria, Germany; lived Atlanta since 1884. Sons: Isaac, Sam, Moses. Interred: Oakland. AG 8/9/1906

SHONAKE, Marie, colored, age 55, d. 284 Connally St. Atlanta. AG 10/15/1909

SHOPE, L. E., Mrs., age 54 d. Atlanta several days ago. Interred: Baxter, Union Co., Ga. AG 6/17/1907

SHORDER, Robert, age 1 mo., d. 71 Johnson Ave. Atlanta. AG 9/12/1908

SHORE, Fannie B., Mrs., wife of Charles E., d. 452 Piedmont Ave., Atlanta, Thurs. Interred: Oakland. AG 2/20/1908

SHORT, C. S., Mrs. d. Dalton, Ga. AG 12/12/1910

SHORT, Frank killed accident near Blue Ridge 12/19. Interred: Washington, Ga. Bros: Tas, Roy, of Atlanta. Parents: Mr. and Mrs. D. M., Washington, Ga. Bros, sis: Rube, of Blue Ridge; James, John and Marion, Washington; Mrs. C. R. Cooper, Washington; Mrs. R. A. Lawton, Macon; Mrs. Thomas Humphries, Atlanta; Mrs. J. E. Dickerson, Atlanta; Effie, Washington. AC 12/21/1905

SHORT, W. A., age 55, died at Edgewood, Ga. AG 12/17/1906

SHOT, Willie, colored, age 24, d. 59 S. Boulevard. Atlanta. AG 10/11/1907

SHOWERS, A. J., colored, age 21, d. Detroit, Mich. AG 1/28/1908
SHRIMPTON, James, Mrs., age 66, d. 167 Oglethorpe Ave. Atlanta.
AG 3/3/1910
SHROPSHIRE, Charles M., age 30, d. 133 Windsor St. Atlanta. AG
7/19/1909
SHROPSHIRE, I. S., Mrs., age 60, d. Wed. 133 Windsor St.,
Atlanta. Husband. Sons: R. R., Marlebridge. Daus: Mrs. W. B.
Bently, Misses Frankie and Inis Shropshire. Interred: Westview.
AG 9/15/1910
SHROPSHIRE, W. F., age 63, d. at 13 Windsor St. Atlanta at bro.´s
res., I. S. Shropshire. Confederate Veteran, Co. K, 1st Ga.
Cavalry. Bros: W. R., I. S., of Atlanta. Sis: Mrs. W. L. Cole,
Senoia, Ga. AG 1/3/1907
SHROPSHIRE, W. R., Jr. d. Spokane, Wash., res. of 604 Washington
St., Atlanta. Interred: Oakland. AG 1/15/1910
SHUBERT, Benjamin, age 22, killed as he swung off moving street
car. Bro: William. AG 2/21/1910
SHULER, Lillian, Mrs., wife of A. C., d. 616 S. Pryor St.,
Atlanta, Tues. Interred: Felton, Ga. AG 12/18/1907
SHUMATE, M. C., Mrs., age 82, d. 25 Fortress Ave. Atlanta. AG
10/9/1907
SHUMATE, Perry, Mrs., age 82, d. 25 Richardson St., Atlanta,
Tues. Ch: Edward, J. B., Mrs. Fannie Zurline. Other ch live
Texas, and dau. in Pope Co., Ga. Interred: Pope Co., Ga. AG
10/9/1907
SHUMATE, F. F., age 88, Conf. Vet., d. Ingleside. Sis: Mrs. J. C.
Thompson, Macon. Sons: W. L., Dallas, Tx.; J. B., Atlanta; C. T.,
Birmingham; D. A., Decatur; R. T., Dalton. Dau: Mrs. George D.
Ferguson, Dalton. Bur: Decatur. AG 8/19/1908
SHUTTLESWORTH, Alice, Mrs., age 42, d. Sat, formerly Mrs. William
Travis of Fayetteville, Ga. Ch: Willie Kate Travis, Rembert P.
Travis. 4 sisters, 2 bros. Interred: Fayetteville, Ga. AG
6/25/1907
SIDDONS, Bertha, Mrs., age 28, d. 177 Woodward Ave. Atlanta. AG
5/18/1908
SIGMAN, Emmett R., age 59, d. 25 Postell St. Atlanta. AG
1/19/1907
SIGMAN, Jane, colored, age 52, d. 219 Martin St. Atlanta. AG
6/23/1907
SIKES, dau., age two, of Charley Sikes, burned to death
Cobbtown, Ga. 10/4. Bur: Cedar Creek Church Cem. AG 10/4/1909
SIKES, Effie, age 14, d. Charlotte, N. C. AC 3/30/1905
SIKES, Lester James, age 1, son of Mr. and Mrs. P. M., d. 29
Edwards St., Atlanta, Fri. Interred: Oakland. AG 8/15/1910
SIKES, Matt, age 40, killed in drunken pistol duel by Watt
Chance, age 28, friends, both of Alexander, Ga. Sat. Interred:
Alexander. AG 7/23/1906
SIKES, Thomas H. d. Thurs, age 75, Glennville, Ga. AG 8/10/1909
SILAS, Robert, formerly of Columbus, Ga., d. 9/4 Cedartown. Wife,
mother, bros., sisters. Interred: Columbus, Ga. AC 9/6/1905
SILVA, E. F., age 72, Confederate veteran, d. Soldiers´ home,
Atlanta. Interred: Westview. AG 3/25/1907
SILVERMAN, Max, age 42, d. Elberton, Ga. Sun. Funeral, 39 E.
Ellis St. Atlanta. Interred: Oakland Cemetery, Atlanta. AG
11/16/1908

SILVERMAN, Millie, age 9, dau. of Isaac, d. 147 Piedmont Ave. Atlanta, in fire. AC 8/7/1905

SIMMONDS, Harry B., age 65, d. Presbyterian Hospital. Atlanta. AG 7/20/1907

SIMMONS, Annie, colored, age 17, d. Clifton Ave. Atlanta. AG 9/6/1910

SIMMONS, Carrie Alberta, age 9 mos., dau. of Mr. and Mrs. John D., d. 22 Augusta Ave., Inman Park, Atlanta, Tues. AG 3/16/1909

SIMMONS, Fred, colored, age 61, d. Fulton Co. barracks. Atlanta. AG 7/12/1907

SIMMONS, H. B. d. Wed. Atlanta. Interred: Westview. AG 7/22/1907

SIMMONS, Helena, colored, age 13, d. 13 Linden alley. Atlanta. AG 10/3/1908

SIMMONS, Marion, colored, age 20, d. 15 Lowes alley. Atlanta. AG 3/22/1907

SIMMONS, Oscar, colored, age 17, d. 186 Orme St. Atlanta. AG 6/21/1909

SIMMONS, William J., age 67, d. Soldiers' Home, Atlanta. AG 1/ /1910

SIMMONS, William S., age 75, d. Tues. 22 Hansell St., Atlanta, Wed. Wife, three sons: W. B., C. C., and H. T. Simmons. AG 5/19/1909

SIMMONS, I. E., Mrs., age 65, died at 54 Hampton Street, Atlanta. AG 11/29/1906

SIMMS, Becky, old negro drowned in creek July 4, Covington, Ga. AG 7/7/1906

SIMMS, G. W., colored, age 80, d. 27 Parsons St. Atlanta. AG 10/9/1907

SIMMS, Fannie d. 1/19 bur: Pinewood Cem. WPt. Daus: Mrs. C. C. Pugh, Auburn; Mrs. Willie Johnson, St. Mtn. Sis: Mrs. McDonald, Mrs. W. A. Camp. Bros: W. T. Sheppard, Baltimore; J. S. Sheppard, Atlanta; Levi Sheppard, Selma, AL. AC 1/21/1905

SIMON, Charles Henry, age 54, d. 267 Capitol Ave. Atlanta. Merchant. Interred: Westview. AG 7/2/1908

SIMON, Ezemine, colored, age 10, d. 140 Glenn St. Atlanta. AG 8/12/1908

SIMPKINS, William, Mrs., age 23, d. 101 N. Butler St. Atlanta. AG 12/3/1908

SIMPSON, Anne Elizabeth, age two, dau. of Mr. and Mrs. Ben L., 43 W. 5th St., d. Fri., Macon, Ga. Interred: Westview. AG 1/7/1910

SIMPSON, Arthur B., age 27, d. 109 S. Moreland Ave. Atlanta. Interred: Gainesville, Ga. AG 11/2/1907

SIMPSON, C. A. accidentally killed Macon last Fri. night. AG 1/1/1907

SIMPSON, Claude d. 11/16 Atlanta, age 24. Interred: Clarkston, Gaz. AC 11/17/1905

SIMPSON, David, colored, age 4, d. 69 James St. Atlanta. AG 12/12/1910

SIMPSON, F. C., Mrs., 22, bur. Washington, Ga. 3 sisters, 3 bros: Mrs. Katherine Hill & Mrs. Joseph A. Terry, Washington, Ga.; Mrs. Barrett, Milledgeville; Robert & William Harper, Wilkes Co.; Prof. George Harper, Warrenton. AG 6/22/1910

SIMPSON, F. M., age 63, d. 32 White St. Atlanta. AG 11/3/1909

SIMPSON, Grace M., Mrs., age 58, wife of F. M. (24 yrs.), d. 32
White St. Atlanta Mon. Daus: Mrs. E. L. Ficken, Mrs. G. W.
Ficken, Mrs. S. L. Cochran, Atlanta. Interred: Westview. AG
6/1/1909
SIMPSON, Ida M., Mrs. d. 157 Flat Shoals Rd., Atlanta, Thurs.
Interred: Gainesville, Ga. AG 3/13/1908
SIMPSON, Leacher H, Mrs., wife of R. M., d. Sat. Atlanta.
Interred: Martin, Ga. AG 10/26/1907
SIMPSON, Lena, 11 mos. dau. of Mr. and Mrs. J. C., d. Perry, Ga.,
Wed., a twin. AG 9/20/1907
SIMPSON, Leonard, age 20, d. E. Point, Ga. Interred: Waverly
Hill, Ga., his old home. AG 11/11/1909
SIMPSON, R. C., age 37, d. 109 S. Moreland Ave., Atlanta, Sun.
Interred: Gainesville, Ga. AG 11/2/1907
SIMPSON, Ray, son of Mr. and Mrs. George, d. Forest Park, Ga.
Mon. Interred: Forrest Grove church. AG 10/26/1907
SIMPSON, Stella, Miss, dau. of Mr. and Mrs. C. N. of Cuthbert,
Ga., d. Sun. in Augusta. AG 4/11/1910
SIMPSON, Victory, dau. of Mrs. Jessie of 114 Powell St., Atlanta,
d. Wed. Atlanta. AG 6/24/1908
SIMS, Alice, Mrs., wife of John, dau. of Dr. Dismuke of Irwin
Co., Ga. Husband, Merchant of Loflin, Russell Co., Ala. Suicide
4/9. 7 children. AC 4/11/1905
SIMS, B. H., age 48, suicide. Wife. Son in Hancock Co. Dau. AG
2/9/1910
SIMS, Debbie, colored, shot and killed by Richard Jackson,
Donalsonville, Ga. AG 3/22/1907
SIMS, Elizabeth, Mrs., age 80, d. Sat. res. in Hapeville. Leaves
81 direct descendants. She was mother of Mrs. Mary Southard,
Cartersville, Ga.; J. F. Sims, Irondale, Ala.; Hon. J. L. Sims,
mayor of Hapeville; Mrs. Jannie Ball, Hapeville; Mrs. Mattie Orr,
Virginia; Mrs. Alice Nolan and Mrs. Sallie Thrailkill of
Hapeville. Sis: Mrs. W. A. Dodge, East Point, Mrs. J. M. Johnson,
Atlanta. Bro: J. J. Jones, Atlanta. AG 2/4/1907
SIMS, George W., Conf. Vet., d. 2/10 Macon. Dau: Mrs. T. J.
Weaver 1st St., Macon. Interred: Rose Hill. AG 2/11/1910
SIMS, George W., son of late R. H. of Griffin, age 47, d. res. of
sister, Mrs. F. A. Robinson, 274 E. Cain St. Atlanta, Mon. Wife,
one sister, Mrs. F. A. Robinson, and bro., C. R. Sims of
Houstson, Tx. Interred: Griffin, Ga. AG 5/26/1908
SIMS, L. D., age 42, d. E. Point, Ga. Tues. Wife, 6 children.
Funeral: Jonesboro, Ga. Interred: Family Cemetery. AG 3/11/1908
SIMS, Lizzie, colored, age 14, died 103-A Randolph St., Atlanta.
AG 11/20/1906
SIMS, M. H., Mrs., age 66, d. 67 DeKalb Ave. Atlanta. AG 8/1/1910
SIMS, Susan, Mrs. buried Perry, Ga. yesterday. She d. home of her
son, Howard Sims, Macon, Sun. Leaves 5 daus., three sons. Age 77.
AG 4/9/1907
SIMS, T. H., age 64, d. Tues. Forest Park, Ga. Interred: Forest
Park Cemetery. AG 8/31/1910
SIMS, W. A., age 67, Confederate veteran, d. 14 Formwalt St.,
Atlanta, Sat. Interred: Bogart, Ga. AG 2/15/1908
SIMS, Wayne, Mrs. d. Peachtree Rd., Atlanta, Tues. Interred:
Sardis Church. Dau: Mrs. D. N. Williams, Atlanta. Sons: Glenn and
Will Holmes of El Paso, Tx. AG 4/20/1910

SIMS, Willie H., age 19, d. Sun. Atlanta. Interred: Sharon, Ga. AG 8/1/1910

SINCLAIR, Marguerite, inf. dau. of Mr. and Mrs. William, d. 6 Brotherton St., Atlanta, Sun. Interred: Westview. AG 2/19/1910

SINEATH, Ulmer, telegraph operator at Sparks, Ga., killed 4/2 by freight train Valdosta, Ga. AG 4/3/1909

SINGER, J. R. d. Cleveland, Ohio, former res. of Atlanta. Interred: Americus, Ga. Wife survives. AG 10/16/1907

SINGER, Joseph E., age 61, d. Thurs. 174 Washington St., Atlanta. Wife, Mrs. Julia Singer. Ch: H. Leon Singer, Mrs. George S. Tigner, Joseph L. Singer, Mrs. Thomas S. Daniel. Mother: Mrs. Louisa Singer, over 90 yrs. Bros: John G., F. S. of Lumpkin. Several sisters. Joseph b. Lumpkin, Ga. 1840. After war lived Eufaula, Ala., to Atlanta 1883. Md. Josephine Mansfield 1869, and after her death, her sister, Miss Louise Mansfield. Interred: Oakland. Kin: Louisa Singer, Lumpkin, Ga., H. Leon Singer, Dr. and Mrs. George S. Tigner, Joseph L. Singer, Thomas H. Daniel, Atlanta. AG 8/1/1907

SINGER, Mary W., Mrs., age 57, d. dau.'s res., Mrs. W. A. Woodson, 238 Crew St., Atlanta, Fri. Ch: Mrs. W. A. Woodson, Mrs. Julian Watson, George W. Singer, St. Augustine, Fla. AG 2/15/1908

SINGLETERY, T. A., Mrs., wid. of Joseph, Thomas Co. pioneer, d. 6/29, age 75. Ch: M. A. Lindsey, Atlanta; J. Fred, Mrs. Olivia Lindsey, Ochlochnee; Mrs. I. J. Clancy, Augusta; Mrs. C. E. Stringer, Pine Park. Bur: Bowen Cem. AG 6/30/1910

SINGLETON, Clarence, age 24, of 316 Spring St., Atlanta, negro, committed suicide after killing Mary Hawk, negro. AG 5/25/1906

SINGLETON, Ida, Miss, age 35, d. 201 Capitol Ave. Atlanta. Interred: Gainesville, Ga. AG 8/5/1910

SINGLETON, Noah, old negro janitor at Wesleyan Female College, d. Sat. AG 12/1/1907

SINGLETREE, A. S., colored, age 15, d. 136 Chestnut St. Atlanta. AG 10/3/1907

SINKFIELD, Carlos, colored, age 21, d. 333 Smith St. Atlanta. AG 8/13/1910

SINKLER, Cynthia, age 46, d. 104 Fort St. Atlanta. AG 10/22/1906

SINOR, Paul, infant son of Mr. and Mrs. W. H., d. Mon. 105 Main St., Atlanta. Interred: Caseys. AG 8/27/1907

SINQUEFIELD, Mollie P., Mrs., wid. of Lt. F. A., d. 8/2 Louisville, Ga. Stepch: W. R. Sinquefield; Mrs. W. A. Stone of Louisville. AG 8/2/1909

SISEMORE, E. A., age 68, d. Carey, Ga. AG 2/24/1910

SISK, Laura, age 33, d. 624 DeKalb Ave. Atlanta. AG 9/9/1908

SISSON, Mell shot by Arthur Thomas, Blue Ridge, Ga. Died 3/19. AC 3/20/1905

SIVLEY, R. E., Mrs., age 66, d. res. of dau., Mrs. Bun Wylie, 75 Peachtree St., Atlanta, Wed. Husband: Major R. E. Sivley, Richmond, Va. Interred: Hollywood Cemetery, Richmond, Va. AG 12/30/1908

SIXSMITH, Ethel May, age 18 mos., dau. of Mr. and Mrs. Albert Sixsmith, d. Wed. 79 Johnson Ave. Atlanta. Interred: Oakland. AG 1/9/1907

SIXSMITH, Joseph, age 75, d. Tues. Hemphill, Ga. Ch: J. G., E. W., W. W.; Mrs. M. E. Whitfield. Interred: Sharon Church yard. AG 7/6/1910

SKATES, Elizabeth, Mrs., wid. of Wm, d. Fri. dau´s res., Mrs. W. S. Taylor, 370 Pulliam St. Atlanta. Bur: Sylvester. AG 5/10/1907

SKATES, W. M., d. Flat Shoals Rd., Atlanta, Mon. Wife, three daus: Mrs. W. S. Taylor, Mrs. C. A. Williams, Mrs. J. M. Davis, Macon. Interred: Sylvester Church. AG 8/7/1906

SKATES, W. M., Mrs., age 59, d. Fri. 374 Pulliam St., Atlanta. Interred: Sylvester cemetery. AG 5/11/1907

SKIFF, Margaret A., Mrs., age 79, d. 175 S. Pryor St., Atlanta, Fri. No relatives. Interred: Williamsburg, Mass. AG 12/21/1907

SKINNER, Ernest, age 19, d. 79 Trinity Ave., Atlanta, crushed to death oper. candy factory elevator. Bur: Blythe, Ga. AG 7/2/1910

SKINNER, Lester, age 15, an orphan, drowned in river 5/6, Columbus, Ga. AG 5/7/1906

SKINNER, Marlin d. 10/15 Covington, Ga., age 25. Wife was formerly Miss Bessie Jenkins, Atlanta (m. 8 mos. ago). Interred: Starrsville, Ga. AG 10/16/1905

SKINNER, Marlin, age 4, son of Mr. and Mrs. M. T., d. 830 Marietta St., Atlanta, Tues. AG 8/3/1909

SKIPPER, Lillian, inf. dau. of Mr. and Mrs. E. S., d. Mon. 37 Savannah St., Atlanta. Interred: Hollywood. AG 5/13/1907

SKOTZY, Abe d. 17th St. Columbus, Ga. Wed., age 49. Wife, 5 sons, 3 daus. Interred: Linwood Cemetery. AG 2/11/1910

SLACK, Adam, colored, age 60, d. 137 Glenn St. Atlanta. AG 3/19/1907

SLACK, Henry Lee, age 69, of Newnan, Ga., d. Atlanta Thurs. Confed. Vet. Wife, one sister. Interred: Madison, Ga. AG 4/1/1910

SLACK, John H., bro. of Charles H. of The Nashville American, d. Bristol, Tenn. Sun., age 45. Wife, one little dau. AG 5/30/1910

SLACK, Hester, colored, age 3, died 137 Glenn St., Atlanta. AG 12/17/1906

SLATER, Jennie S., Mrs., age 47, wife of A. J., d. 136 Rawson St. Atlanta, Thurs. Son: W. F. Wiggins. Daus: Mrs. J. E. Oxford, Mrs. Charles E. Marshall, Jr.; Misses Pansy and Lillie Slater, Atlanta. Interred: Hollywood. AG 7/30/1909

SLATON, infant son of Mr. and Mrs. J. T., d. 18 Narrow St., Atlanta, Tues. Interred: Westview. AG 5/31/1910

SLATON, J. T., inf. son of Mr. and Mrs. J. T., d. 11 McDaniel St. Atlanta. Interred: Sylvester cemetery. AG 11/14/1907

SLAUGHTER, John, age 40, d. Atlanta Sun. He was res. of Resaca, Ga. AG 12/13/1909

SLAUGHTER, John, age 63, d. 101 Butler St. Atlanta. AG 12/14/1909

SLEDGE, Madison, colored, age 3 mos., d. 101 N. Butler St. Atlanta. AG 5/12/1909

SLOAN, Ben P., 75, b. 1832 Seneca, SC, d. son´s res, 442 Fraser St. Ch: A. L., Atlanta, T. M., Avondale, AL.; B. C., Cassville; Dave F. & Mrs. M. B. Jarmon, Charlottesville, Va.; Hattie Sloan, Atlanta; Mrs. W. S. Kilby, Anniston, AL. AG 3/5/1907

SLOCUM, Nathan, age 39, unmd, Jones Co., Ga. planter, found murdered. His brother found him. AC 3/17/1905

SLOCUM, Odessa, Mrs., wife of T. H., age 28, d. Macon. Interred: Roberta, Ga. AC 10/7/1905

SLOCUMB, D. H. d. city hospital last Fri., Macon. Res., 613 Adams St. Interred: Riversale. AG 1/8/1907

SLOMBERG, Herman, 20, d. Jonesboro. Bur: Roseland. AG 1/31/1910

SLORENS, Bernard, 52, d. 230 E. Cain St. Atlanta. AG 3/29/1909

SMALL, A. B. d. Wed. Lorane, Ga. Family res. College St., Macon. Interred: Riverside, Macon. AG 7/31/1908

SMALLWOOD, George, colored, age 23, d. 101 N. Butler St. Atlanta. AG 8/7/1908

SMART, A. G., age 67, d. 263 Peachtree St. Atlanta. AG 2/25/1907

SMART, Arthur G. d. Fri. Atlanta. AG 2/25/1907

SMEDLEY, George, age 1, son of Mr. and Mrs. G. O., funeral Fri. Interred: Westview. AG 8/28/1909

SMITH, A. E., Mrs. died Sun. Relatives from New York. AG 12/17/1906

SMITH, Adelphia Ann, Mrs., mother of late C. B. Chapman, George A. Smith of Macon, and wid. of late Col. George A. Smith of Confederate Army, d. Sun. Interred: Rose Hill Cemetery, Macon. AG 5/17/1909

SMITH, Adline, colored, age 60, d. county jail. Atlanta. AG 12/29/1908

SMITH, Alice, Mrs., age 5, d. Forest Park, Ga., Sun., where interred. AG 8/9/1910

SMITH, Allen, age 9 mos., son of R. W., d. 21 Paine Ave., Atlanta, Sun. Interred: Hollywood. AG 12/5/1910

SMITH, Alpha Robert, age 54, d. Woodward Ave. Atlanta. AG 8/26/1909

SMITH, Amanda, negro, her body found by police yesterday. AG 9/16/1907

SMITH, Andy, age 45, d. 101 N. Butler St. Atlanta. AG 4/13/1909

SMITH, Anna H., Mrs., age 59, b. Columbia, S. C. d. 160 Park Ave. Atlanta 8/31. Principal, Fair St. School; m. Whiteford S. Smith, Charleston (d. sev. yrs. ago). Dau: Mrs. Frank Hill. Grdaus: Mrs. Annie Whitefoord; Emma Hill. AG 9/2/1909

SMITH, Annie, Mrs., age 78, d. E. Point, Ga. Sat. AG 2/29/1908

SMITH, Arthur, Mrs., age 37, d. 102 Middle St., Atlanta, Wed. Interred: Utoy Church. Husband, two children. AG 10/1/1908

SMITH, B. S. of Macon d. 8/24, Third St. AC 8/25/1905

SMITH, Bobbie, Mrs., age 37, d. 102 Middle St. Atlanta. AG 10/5/1908

SMITH, Byron K., age 2, son of Mr. and Mrs. W. R., d. 35 Tudor St. Atlanta, Fri. Interred: Westview. AG 4/17/1908

SMITH, C. S., age 69, (or 79), Confederate Veteran, d. 1 Garnett St. Atlanta. Interred: Westview. AG 8/8/1910

SMITH, C. W. d. Tues. College Park, Ga. Wife, 6 children. Interred: Westview. AG 6/15/1910

SMITH, Chan, Mrs., widow, d. 10/21 Atlanta. One child: Maynard Smith. Interred: Oakland. AC 10/23/1905

SMITH, Charles, age 22, d. 445 Glenn St. Atlanta. AG 9/2/1910

SMITH, Charles, age 30, d. Atlanta Fri. AG 10/2/1909

SMITH, Charles, res. of Atlanta, age 25, electrocuted Thurs. in Decatur, repairing telegraph wires. Unmd. Interred: Calhoun, Ga. AG 9/2/1910

SMITH, Charles H, Mrs, wid of Bill Arp d. Cartersville 6/22. Ch: Mrs G.H. Aubrey, Mrs W.W. Young, Mrs S.O. Brumby, Marian Smith; Ralph, Jacksonville; Royal R, Athens; Hines, Rome; Carl, Mex; Frank, Tx. Bro: C.L. Hutchins, Sewanee. AG 6/22/1909

SMITH, Charley, colored, age 18, d. 211 Irwin St. Atlanta. AG 12/3/1907

SMITH, Claude, colored, age 21, d. 12 Overholm St. Atlanta. AG 10/19/1907

SMITH, Clifford A., age 31, d. Sat. 555 Whitehall St., Atlanta. Wife, one child. Bro: M. J. Sisters: Mrs. W. D. Bagwell, Mrs. R. E. Boyle, Mrs. J. M. DeFoor. Interred: Westview. AG 9/9/1907

SMITH, Clinton, colored, age 33, d. 169 Auburn Ave. Atlanta. AG 12/23/1908

SMITH, Columbus, age 17, d. corner Boulevard and Woodward Ave., Atlanta. AG 10/18/1907

SMITH, Crawford K., Mrs., age 45, d. Atlanta. AG 4/18/1910

SMITH, Davis, Mrs., d. Tues. home of dau-in-law, Mrs. Martha Smith, 53 King St., Atlanta, bur: Mt. Airy. Survivors: Dau: Mrs. H. B. Deas, New York. Sons: Edwin Smith, Chattanooga; Sidney Smith of Cornelia, Ga. AG 11/14/1906

SMITH, Dofty, Mrs., wife of L. A., d. Wed. Funeral at res. of Capt. T. J. Donaldson, 910 Peachtree St. Atlanta. Interred: Oakland. AG 4/25/1907

SMITH, E. C., colored, age 7 mos., d. 231 Fraser St. Atlanta. AG 3/3/1909

SMITH, E. J., age 67, d. Confederate Soldiers' Home, Atlanta. Member of Co. I, 70th Ga. Vol. Inf. Leaves 2 bros, one in Marietta, one in Ala. AG 6/16/1906

SMITH, E. T., age 34, d. 385 E. Georgia Ave., Atlanta. Interred: Westview. AG 6/19/1903

SMITH, Earl P., age 35, son of Mr. and Mrs. Jesse, d. 385 E. Georgia Ave., Atlanta, Fri. Interred: Westview. Parents, one sister, Mrs. S. N. Quinn, survive. AG 6/20/1908

SMITH, Edward, Jr., age 14 mos., son of Mr. and Mrs. Edward E. Smith of Atlanta, d. Tues. Interred: Brunswick. AG 2/5/1907

SMITH, Elbert, age 10, d. 43 Hightower St. Atlanta. Interred: Westview. AG 6/11/1910

SMITH, Eliza, Mrs., age 77, d. Adairsville, Ga. Thurs. Interred: Atlanta, New Hope. AG 4/15/1909

SMITH, Elizabeth, Mrs. d. 153 Davis St., Atlanta, Fri. Interred: Martin, Ga. Sons: J. T., W. R., J. S. Daus: Mrs. R. W. Jones, Mrs. Ellen Creek, Mrs. Lou Hardy. AG 12/26/1908

SMITH, Elizabeth, Mrs., age 64 d. 678 S. Pryor St. Atlanta. Sons: R. L., I. B. Daus: Mrs. R. L. Nabors, Miss Dorothy and Irene Smith, husband, survive. Interred: Hollywood. AG 12/24/1908

SMITH, Elmer Harold, age 6 mos., son of Mr. and Mrs. William, of 305 E. Hunter St., Atlanta, d. Thurs. Interred: Conyers, Ga. AG 3/18/1909

SMITH, Emily, Mrs., age 79, burned to death from exploding lamp 12/30, Columbus, Ga. Two daus. AG 12/30/1910

SMITH, Emma, colored, age 44, d. 371 N. Butler St. Atlanta. AG 9/18/1908

SMITH, Erwin L., infant of Mr. and Mrs. F. B., d. 11/14, 67 Irwin St., Atlanta. Interred: Hollywood. AC 11/16/1905

SMITH, Esther Kathleen, dau. of Mr. and Mrs. M. J., 106 Ponce de Leon Ave., Atlanta, d. Thurs. Interred: Oakland. AG 4/9/1908

SMITH, Evelyn, inf. dau. of Mr. and Mrs. J. W., d. 127 Richardson St., Atlanta. Interred: Hollywood. AG 1/27/1910

SMITH, F. H. d. yesterday Tallapoosa, Ga. Veteran of civil war. Native of New England. AG 2/5/1907

SMITH, Fannie W., Mrs., age 58, d. Atlanta Tues. Sons: H. A., W. W. Res. 74 S. Boulevard. Interred: Oakland. AG 6/9/1908

SMITH, Fannie, Miss interred Powder Springs, Ga., Mon. AG 9/14/1907

SMITH, Fannie, Mrs., age 66, d. 70 Glass St. Atlanta. AG 12/27/1910

SMITH, Fleming murdered 12/12/1908. W. B. Lyens and his son, Archie Lyens, charged. Cordele, Ga. AG 7/30/1910

SMITH, Flora, Mrs., age 40, d. Hemphill Rd., Atlanta, Atlanta, Tues. Interred: Lithia Springs, Ga. AG 6/22/1910

SMITH, Frances, colored, age 20, d. Fulton Co. Alms House. AG 9/2/1909

SMITH, Francis Xavier, age 8, son of Mr. and Mrs. J. B., d. Jonesboro Rd., Atlanta, Wed. AG 6/4/1908

SMITH, Frank, colored, 212 Clark St., killed race riot Atlanta. AG 9/24/1906

SMITH, Frank d. res. of his father, James Smith, near Veazey, Ga. AG 3/4/1910

SMITH, Frank, age 29, d. Roseland Camp. AG 11/24/1910

SMITH, Fred, Jr. d. Fri. Whitesville, N. C., inf.son of Mr. and Mrs. F. B. Interred: Atlanta, Hollywood Cemetery. AG 2/27/1910

SMITH, G. B., age 70, d. 101 N. Butler St. Atlanta. AG 12/3/1907

SMITH, G. W., colored, age 41, d. 33 Davis St. Atlanta. AG 11/12/1907

SMITH, George of Oliver, elderly, killed by train Adrian, Ga. AG 9/25/1906

SMITH, George, farmer, Sparta, killed yesterday, thrown from wagon. Age about 40. AG 8/1/1906

SMITH, George B., 70. Ch: Rev. James A. Smith, Bainbridge; Mrs. C. A. Carpenter, Atlanta; Mrs. Bertha Shaw, Atlanta; Mrs. Claude Gardner, Macon; G. C. Smith, Louisville, Ky.; Mrs. George Miller, Powder Springs. Bur: Oakland. AG 12/1/1907

SMITH, George M., age 34, from Chattanooga, Tenn., d. 12/26 res. of father, G. W. Smith, Columbus, Ga. AC 12/27/1905

SMITH, Grafty, Mrs., age 32, d. 123 E. 12th St. Atlanta. AG 4/26/1907

SMITH, H. H., Mrs. d. Mon. AG 7/4/1906

SMITH, H. L., Mrs., age 38, d. Peachtree Rd., Atlanta, Thurs. Interred: Family Burial Ground. AG 2/6/1908

SMITH, Hannah, colored, age 42, d. 144 Houston St. Atlanta. AG 4/7/1908

SMITH, Harry M., Mrs. d. 60 Morrison Ave., Atlanta, Wed, age 26. Interred: LaGrange. AG 6/3/1909

SMITH, Helen, infant dau. of Mr. and Mrs. William Smith, d. Sun. Atlanta. Interred: Westview. AG 6/25/1907

SMITH, Henry killed in Macon, Printer, by L. D. Strong who was granted pardon. AG 10/17/1907

SMITH, Henry D. killed by L. D. Strong last Mon., Macon. AG 5/8/1907

SMITH, Hildredth H., Dr., age 88, father of Gov. Hoke Smith, d. 582 W. Peachtree St., Atlanta, Mon. He m. Miss Hoke, dau. of Michael Hoke and sister of Gen. R. F. Hoke of N. C. AG 9/14/1908

SMITH, Holmes funeral Thurs. Interred: Westview. AG 1/16/1908

SMITH, Hoyd, age 2, son of Mr. and Mrs. W D., d. 39 Tennille St., Atlanta, Wed. Interred: Norris, Ga. AG 7/20/1910

345

SMITH, Hoyt, age 2, son of Mr. and Mrs. W. T., d. 38 Tennille St., Atlanta, Wed. Interred: Morris. AG 7/21/1910

SMITH, Ida, colored, age 47, d. 25 Fain St. Atlanta. AG 12/22/1908

SMITH, Ike C. d. 12/27 Murphy, Ga., age 40. Wife. 5 sons, dau. AC 12/29/1905

SMITH, Izara I., Mrs., age 55, d. Ringgold, Ga. AG 12/17/1910

SMITH, J. A., age 81, d. 250 Bass St. Atlanta. Interred: Oakland. AG 8/14/1907

SMITH, J. E., age 63, d. 189 McDaniel St. Atlanta. Wife, two sons, C. D. and Sam Smith. Daus: Misses Ruth, Maggie and Julia Smith and Mrs. Charles Cates and Mrs. Edward South. Interred: Cherokee Co. AG 6/22/1908

SMITH, J. F., Mrs. d. Toccoa, Ga. 4/23. Bros: W. G. Edwards; D. W. Edwards, Toccoa; L. A. Edwards, Westminster, S. C.; S. T. Edwards, Orange, Texas. AC 4/25/1905

SMITH, J. H., age 36, died at 101 N. Butler Street, Atlanta. AG 12/21/1906

SMITH, J. Henley, age 78, d. 50 Norcross Ave. Atlanta. AG 2/27/1907

SMITH, J. I., age 40, d. Jacksonville, Fla. AG 8/24/1908

SMITH, J. T. Z. of Griffin d. Fri., age 52. Wife survives. Res. Griffin 27 yrs. Interred: Oak Hill Cemetery. AG 6/25/1906

SMITH, J. W., age 60, d. Grady Hospital. Atlanta. AG 10/25/1900

SMITH, Jacob L., Hon. d. 9/12 Swainsboro, Ga., age 80. Native of S. C. Interred: New City Cemetery "Westview". AC 9/14/1905

SMITH, Jane, Mrs., age 79, wife of John W., before marriage, Miss Henderson, b. Goshen Hill Township, d. res. of dau., Mrs. J. C. Lake, South Union, S. C. Dau: Mrs. John G. Smith, Greenville; Mrs. M. C. Lake. AG 1/5/1910

SMITH, Janie, colored, age 25, died Grady Hospital, Atlanta. AG 12/26/1906

SMITH, Jessie T., age 75, d. Tues. res. 76 DeKalb Co. Interred: Oakland. AG 2/27/1907

SMITH, Jim, colored, age 30, d. 31 Cone St. Atlanta. AG 7/24/1909

SMITH, Joel, age 65, d. Forest Park Thurs. Wife, one dau, two sons. Interred: Forest Park church yard. AG 4/8/1910

SMITH, John, colored, age 28, d. 276 Henry St. Atlanta. AG 8/19/1908

SMITH, John, colored, age 65, d. Fulton Co. Almshouse. AG 2/7/1908

SMITH, John M., age 67, d. Wed. 383 Central Ave., Atlanta. Wife, 3 sons, 2 daus., 2 bros., 2 sisters. Interred: McDonough. AG 2/19/1907

SMITH, John S., pioneer to Winder, Ga. buried yesterday at Chapel Church. AG 7/19/1907

SMITH, John Wesley, colored, age 2 mos., d. 61 Logan alley, Atlanta. AG 9/4/1907

SMITH, Johnnie, member of O'Hara Clan, bur. Tues. at Westview, age 17. AG 7/31/1906

SMITH, Joseph W., age 14, son of Mrs. L. E., d. 4/21 Macon, 653 Elm St. Interred: Rose Hill. AC 4/22/1905

SMITH, Juanita, Mrs., wife of Dr. W. P., d. 5/18 Swainsboro, Ga. Parents: Mr. and Mrs. J. A. Coleman. Sis: Mrs. Frank Mitchell. AG 5/19/1910

SMITH, Kate, Mrs., age 23, d. Atlanta. AG 3/14/1910

SMITH, Katie Bell, age 24, d. Atlanta Fri. Res. of 38 Dillon St. Interred: Roswell, Ga. AG 3/10/1910

SMITH, L. A., Mrs., wife of L. A., d. Wed. Thurs. Atlanta. Interred: Oakland cemetery. AG 4/24/1907

SMITH, L. C., age 58, d. Wed. College Park, Ga. Interred: Mt. Zion Church. Two daus. AG 8/27/1907

SMITH, Laura, Miss, age 38, d. E. Point, Ga. Tues. Interred: Fairburn, Ga. AG 5/19/1909

SMITH, Lee, colored, age 34, d. 44 Sunset Ave. Atlanta. AG 2/25/1909

SMITH, Lee, colored, age 42, d. Alms House. Atlanta. AG 8/5/1907

SMITH, Lester d. Thurs. 3 Plyant St., Atlanta, res. of parents. Interred: Oakwood, Ga. AG 10/21/1910

SMITH, Lester, inf. son of J. P., d. 3 Pyiant St., Atlanta, Thurs. Interred: Oakwood, Ga. AG 10/20/1910

SMITH, Lillian, colored, age 1, d. 259 Fort St. Atlanta. AG 3/18/1909

SMITH, Lizzie, Mrs., age 28, d. of typhoid fever, 17 McMillan St. A   8/31/1906

SMITH, Lodge, age 63, d. 101 N. Butler St. Atlanta. AG 2/15/1909

SMITH, Louis, colored, age 46, d. 196 Butler St. Atlanta. AG 4/22/1908

SMITH, Louis A., age 78, d. Old Soldiers´ Home, Atlanta. AG 11/19/1909

SMITH, Louise M., Mrs., age 48, d. Fri. 20 Walnut St., Atlanta. Ch: Edward, Emma, Bertha; Mrs. A. Steele. Interred: Tyron, Ga. AG 10/28/1910

SMITH, Love, Miss, Thomson, Ga., 11/12/1906, age 30, dau. of Hon. John E. Smith, Pres. of Bank at Thomson, member of Legislature of McDuffie.Co., etc., burned to death, home of father, 3 miles from town. AG 11/12/1906

SMITH, Lowry, age 1 yr., d. 550 Walnut St. Atlanta. AG 4/19/1907

SMITH, Loy, inf. son of Mr. and Mrs. D. W., d. 147 Bedford St., Atlanta, Sun. Interred: Commerce, Ga. AG 2/10/1908

SMITH, Lula M., Mrs., age 49, d. 20 Walnut St., Atlanta, Fri. 4 children. Son: E. J.Smith. Daus: Mrs. T. Steele, Misses Bertha and Irma Smith. AG 10/28/1910

SMITH, Luther, age 7 mos., son of Mr. and Mrs. R. W., d. Thurs. 29 Bellwood Ave., Atlanta. Interred: Casey´s Cemetery. AG 9/9/1910

SMITH, Luther W., Mrs. d. Jonesboro Rd., near Lakewood Heights, Atlanta, Mon., age 21. Bro: Carlton Chandler d. mo. ago of same disease. Husband, one child, parents, Mr. and Mr. G. C. Chandler. Interred: South Bend Cemetery. AG 1/14/1908

SMITH, M. J., Miss, age 38, d. Washington St. Atlanta. AG 11/25/1907

SMITH, M. L., Mrs. d. 1/28 Jackson, 62, formerly Lutie Hall. Bro., Sis: Jno I. Hall, Macon; Mrs. Jubal A. Watts, Harpersville, MS. Nephs: Cols. J. E. & M. P. Hall, Macon, Bob Hall. Nie: Mrs. W. C. Murray, Griffin. Bur: Jackson. AG 1/29/1910

SMITH, Malissa, Mrs., age 48, d. 2 Pulliam St. Atlanta. AG 3/3/1909

SMITH, Mamie, colored, age 6, d. 101 N. Butler St. Atlanta. AG 4/20/1908

SMITH, Marshal B., Mrs. d. Atlanta Sat. Interred: Opelika, Ala., City Cemetery. She was Miss Crawford Kimball of Cedartown, Ga. before marriage. AG 4/19/1910

SMITH, Marshall, colored, age 30, d. 43 Richmond St. Atlanta. AG 3/29/1909

SMITH, Martha E., Mrs., Atlanta pionner, d. Thurs. 269 Lee St. Atlanta, age 79. Daus: Mrs. Etta Irvin, Mrs. L. D. Lowe, Miss Hattie Smith. Interred: Oakland. AG 9/2/1910

SMITH, Martha H., Mrs., age 46, d. 116 Bellwood Ave. Atlanta. Interred: Auburn, Ga. AG 10/4/1907

SMITH, Martin, colored, age 33, d. 101 N. Butler St. Atlanta. AG 12/3/1908

SMITH, Mary A., Mrs., age 75, wife of Dr. C. D., d. Maysons Ave., Edgewood Thurs. Interred: Newnan, Ga. AG 8/7/1908

SMITH, Mary C., Mrs., age 31, d. Phoenix, Arizona. AG 4/6/1907

SMITH, Mary E., Miss, age 61, d. Wed., 135 W. Hunter St. Atlanta. Interred: Westview. AG 8/2/1906

SMITH, Mary E., Mrs., age 35, d. 104 Echo St. Atlanta. AG 4/27/1910

SMITH, Mattie, colored, age 31, d. 289 Chapel St. Atlanta. AG 8/11/1908

SMITH, Mattie Lee, age 2-1/2 yrs., dau. of Mrs. Daisy Smith, d. Wed. 49 Ocmulgee St. Atlanta. Interred: Hollywood. AG 6/27/1907

SMITH, Maude, Mrs., age 25, wife of W. A., d. Sandy Springs Sun. Dau: Elizabeth. Father: Henry Gadis. Interred: Sandy Springs. AG 9/27/1909

SMITH, McNeal, Judge of Probate Court, Autauga Co., Ala., d. Prattville, Ala. 12/30. Wife, 4 children. AG 12/30/1910

SMITH, Minnie, dau. of Mr. and Mrs. M. Smith, d. Tues. Interred: Westview. AG 4/2/1907

SMITH, Minnie Miss, young dau. of Mr. and Mrs. M. Smith, d. Tues. Atlanta. Interred: Westview. AG 4/4/1907

SMITH, Minor, 7th in family of 9 to d. of consumption, d. Thurs. Savannah. He was b. Perry, Ga., age 21. Sisters; Fannie, Bessie. AG 5/20/1907

SMITH, Myrtis, Miss, principal of Fraser St. School, d. Atlanta Sat. Parents: Dr. and Mrs. R. T. Smith, 565 Washington St., Atlanta. Interred: Oakland. AG 11/23/1907

SMITH, Myrtle, Miss, age 19, d. Sun. Atlanta. AG 6/14/1909

SMITH, Nancy, Mrs., age 63, d. Tues. Hemphill, Ga., wife of J. H. Ch: J. G., E. W., W. W.; Mrs. M. E. Whitfield. Interred: Sharon Church yard. AG 7/6/1910

SMITH, Nannie J., Mrs., age 23, d. 92 Center St. Atlanta. Husband: Perry B. Smith. Son, dau. Mother: Mrs. M. A. Dobbins. 4 sisters, 2 bros. Interred: Oakland. AG 8/31/1910

SMITH, Naomi, Miss, age 16, dau. of Mr. and Mrs. J. M. of 76 Julian St., Atlanta, d. Mon. Interred: Hollywood. AG 10/7/1908

SMITH, Nathan, colored, age 21, d. 149 N. Butler St. Atlanta. AG 12/30/1910

SMITH, Nellie, age 2, d. 41 Jefferson St. Atlanta. AG 10/22/1909

SMITH, Nellie Lois, age 8 mos., dau. of Mr. and Mrs. J. B., d. Mon. 126 E. 12th St. Atlanta. Interred: Hollywood. AG 8/30/1910

SMITH, Nettie, colored, age 36, d. 131 Houston St. Atlanta. AG 2/8/1907

SMITH, Nora Belle, Miss, age 16, dau. of Mrs. Fannie, d. 43 Hightower St., Atlanta, Wed. Interred: Westview. AG 4/8/1908

SMITH, Orson Mann, Mrs., wife of Pres. R. W. Smith, d. Wed. LaGrange, Ga., old age. Came to LaGrange from Dalton, Ga. in 1885. AG 8/29/1907

SMITH, Owen, aged more than 90, of Valdosta, Ga., d. ca 1900 Valdosta, Ga. AG 10/3/1907

SMITH, Pauline, dau. of Mr. and Mrs. W. A., d. 13 Middle St., Atlanta, Mon. Interred: Rex, Ga. AG 3/12/1907

SMITH, Pearl, Miss, Fri., res. of father, W. E. Smith, 27 York Ave., Atlanta. Interment: Westview Cemetery. AG 11/9/1906

SMITH, Perry N., inf. son of Mr. and Mrs. P. B., d. 92 Center St., Atlanta, Mon. Interred: Oakland. AG 11/19/1907

SMITH, R. M., age 25, d. Thurs. Atlanta. Interred: Marietta. AG 8/15/1907

SMITH, R. M., age 70, d. res. of son, A. C. Smith, at Deep Springs, Ga., Sun. 4 sons. AG 8/9/1910

SMITH, R. S., Mrs. d. Gordon, Ga. 10/27, age 67. Husband. 9 children. AC 10/29/1905

SMITH, Rebecca, Mrs., age 65, d. 129 Courtland St. Atlanta. AG 12/4/1908

SMITH, Reuben, colored, age 32, d. Kirkwood. AG 11/22/1909

SMITH, Richard, colored, age 5 days, d. 145 Houston St. Atlanta. AG 12/3/1908

SMITH, Richard Ranson, age 77, funeral 11/22 at Girard, Ala. Confed. Vet. AC 11/2/1905

SMITH, Robert Lee, inf. of Mrs. Rosa Smith, d. Fri. Interred: Mason's churchyard, Atlanta. AG 5/18/1907

SMITH, Robert M., son of Mr. and Mrs. W. P., age 1, d. 12 Guyton St. Atlanta. Interred: Hollywood. AG 8/9/1910

SMITH, Robert Windsor, age 68, d. Atlanta Mon. AG 2/8/1910

SMITH, Ruby, dau. of Mr. and Mrs. W. W., d. Columbus 11/10. Grandfather: James Hughes, 75 Berean Ave., Atlanta. Interred: Cool Springs, Ga. AC 11/12/1905

SMITH, Russell, age 20, d. Atlanta Thurs. Res. 491 Simpson St. AG 9/3/1908

SMITH, Ruth Allen, dau. of Mr. and Mrs. H. C., d. 68 Stonewall St., Atlanta, Wed. Interred: Westview. AG 3/26/1908

SMITH, S. H., infant, d. Atlanta. AG 1/12/1910

SMITH, S. J., Mrs., age 54, d. Atlanta. AG 1/14/1910

SMITH, S. R., Mrs., age 60, d. 114 W. Alexander St. Atlanta. AG 11/23/1910

SMITH, Sallie, Mrs., age 55, d. 206 S. Forsyth St., Atlanta, Sun., wife of R. D. 4 sons, 1 dau. AG 11/21/1910

SMITH, Sam, age 52, d. 101 N. Butler St. Atlanta. AG 3/5/1907

SMITH, Samuel, inf. son of Mr. and Mrs. S. H., d. 1/10. Interred: Westview. AG 1/11/1910

SMITH, Samuel W., Dr. d. 1/10 Columbia, S. C. Bros: Dr. Henry Louis Smith, Alphonso Smith, Prof., Univ. of Va. AG 1/11/1910

SMITH, Sarah A., Mrs., age 80, d. res. of dau., Mrs. W. C. Mount, Wynnton, Ga. 2/25. AC 2/25/1905 SMITH, Mary, Mrs. murdered her home near Pearson, Ga. 2/8. 10-yr. old grand dau. survives. AC 2/10/1905

SMITH, Sarah, Mrs., age 77, d. res. of son, F. M. Smith at Selfville, Blount Co., Ala. Sat. while visiting. Funeral at Rocky Creek Church. Sister, two sons. AG 4/5/1910

SMITH, Spencer, age 5 mos., son of Mr. and Mrs. C. D., d. Armour Sta., Tues., Atlanta. Interred: Lula, Ga. AG 7/20/1910

SMITH, Sydney S., age 16 mos., son of Mr. and Mrs. W. W., d. Mon. Columbus, Ga. Grparents: Mr. and Mrs. M. E. Hughes, 54 Berean Ave., Atlanta. Interred: Cool Springs Cemetery. AG 1/5/1910

SMITH, Syvilla, Mrs. d. Mon. E. Point. Father, mother, husband, and three small children. Interred: Roswell, Ga. AG 7/20/1908

SMITH, T. D., Mrs., nee Stokes, d. Dublin. Sons: Robt, Sylvania; Thos, Vidalia; Mark, Columbus. Sis: Mrs. Stanley Melton, Opelika, Ala.; Mrs. L. I. Beall; Mamie Smith; Mrs. Fannie Robinson, Dublin; Mrs. Nannie Duncan, Jackson. AG 3/11/1909

SMITH, T. L. d. Atlanta Sun., age 38, res. of 228 Crew St. Wife, 9 children. Interred: Milledgeville, Ga. AG 3/21/1910

SMITH, T. M., Mrs., age 33, d. Atlanta. Interred: Emerson, Ga. Husband: T. L., 4 children. AG 10/27/1908

SMITH, T. M., Mrs., age 83, d. 101 N. Butler St. Atlanta. AG 10/30/1908

SMITH, T. T., age 82, clerk in charge of post office at Ft. McPherson, d. Thurs. he was first white child born in city of Forsyth, Ga; lived Atlanta no. of years. Interred: Forsyth. AG 8/3/1906

SMITH, Terrell Bayne, age 11, son of Mr. and Mrs. A. E., d. 511 Woodward Ave. Atlanta. Interred: Oakland. AG 4/20/1910

SMITH, Thomas E., age 3, son of Mr. and Mrs. Thomas, d. 167 Currier St. Atlanta. Interred: Westview. AG 6/23/1910

SMITH, Thomas L., age 47, d. Constitution, Ga. AG 7/23/1909

SMITH, Tom, colored, age 23, d. Chattahoochee, Ga. AG 5/28/1906

SMITH, Tony, age 2, son of Mr. and Mrs. W. W., d. Main St., Sun. Interred: Riverside. AG 8/17/1908

SMITH, Victor, 3rd son of Charles H. Smith (Bill Arp) of Cartersville, d. New York. Mother, 3 sisters, two bros-Miss Marian Smith, Mrs. Stella Brumby, Mrs. W. W. Young, Cartersville; Hines Smith, Rome; Royal Smith, Birmingham. AG 3/16/1909

SMITH, W. H., Mrs. formerly of Moultrie, d. Sun. at Pelham, Ga. Interred: Camilla. She was Miss Anna McWlvey. leaves husband, 3 wks. old boy. AG 3/14/1907

SMITH, W. I., age 28, d. Grady Hospital, Atlanta. AG 2/1/1907

SMITH, W. J., 78, Conf. Vet., b. Gwinnett Co., d. Eagan, Ga. Sons: W. H., John L, J. R. Daus: Mrs. W. H. Bell; Mrs. W. Z. Smith; Mrs. J. H. Abbott; Mrs. H. H. Butler. Wife: Delilah. 19 grch. Res. DeKalb Co.; Henry Co. teacher. AG 12/17/1910

SMITH, W. Joel, age 74, d. 172 Capitol Ave. Atlanta. AG 10/21/1908

SMITH, W. T. d. Sat. Elberton, Ga. Wife, several children, two grown sons in Texas. AG 2/2/1910

SMITH, Will, colored, age 30, d. 10 N. Butler St. Atlanta. AG 12/19/1907

SMITH, Will, postmaster at Boliver, Tenn., killed 12/27 by Ran Marsh. AC 12/28/1905

SMITH, Will, colored. Columbus, Ga., 12/11. Body found near home of George Alexander on Pore Place, 6 mi. E of city. AG 12/11/1906

SMITH, William, age 5 yrs., son of Mr. and Mrs. W. G., d. 21 Venable St., Atlanta, Sun. Interred: Clarkston, Ga. AG 12/13/1909

SMITH, William D., age 28, d. Grant Park. Atlanta. AG 8/14/1907

SMITH, William G., inf. son of Mr. and Mrs. L. M., d. Sat. 92 S. Pryor St. Atlanta. Interred: Oakland. AG 7/6/1908

SMITH, William, Hon. of N. Warren, Ga. d. 5/29. AC 5/30/1905

SMITH, Willis B., colored, age 39, d. 31 Doray St. Atlanta. AG 2/12/1907

SMITH, Zachariah H., age 73, pioneer citizen to Atlanta, d. Wed. 195 E. Hunter St., Atlanta. Interred: Oakland. AG 9/27/1906

SMITH, Zola, inf. dau. of Mr. and Mrs. H. P., d. 90 Center St. Atlanta Thurs. Interred: Norcross, Ga. AG 3/12/1908

SMITHWICK, Minnie C., Mrs., age 42, wife of A. A., d. 644 S. Pryor St., Atlanta, Thurs. Husband. Parents: Mr. and Mrs. Carmichael, Monroe, Ga. Interred: Jackson, Ga. Her infant son died less than week ago. AG 4/22/1909

SMOOT, Kate, Mrs. d. 63 White St., Atlanta, Wed. Interred: Westview. AG 12/17/1910

SMULLYAN, Alexander, age 21, died at Home for Incurables. Atlanta. AG 12/28/1906

SMULLYAN, David R., age 3, d. 343 Edgewood Ave. Atlanta. AG 9/7/1906

SMULLYAN, Isadore, age 60, d. 163 Trinity Ave. Atlanta, d. Thurs. Wife, several children. Interred: Oakland. AG 8/8/1910

SNAVEL, John, Mrs., died Sun. Interment: Trinity. AG 9/20/1906

SNEAD, E. C. age 24, d. Atlanta Mon., son of Mr. and Mrs. M. P. of 34 S. Jackson St., Atlanta. Interred: Westview. AG 12/22/1908

SNEAD, E. C., age 24, son of Mr. and Mrs. W. F., d. Atlanta Mon. Interred: Westview. AG 12/23/1908

SNEED, E. C., age 23, d. Milledgeville, Ga. AG 12/23/1908

SNELLING, James M., Confed. Vet., age 76, d. 153 E. Fair St., Atlanta. Wife. Sons: J. F., H. A., M. P. Daus: Misses Bessie, Sarah and Odia. Grdau: Mrs. Annie DeLisle. Interred: Westview. AG 4/1/1910

SNELLINGS, George, Mrs. d. Flatwoods, 8 mi. from Elberton, Ga. Mon. Interred: Family burying ground, Eliam District. 6 children, one son and married dau. in Yazoo, Miss. AG 4/7/1909

SNELLINGS, W. H., Sr. d. Sun. Elberton, Ga., Confed. Vet. Wife, 2 daus., 3 sons. AG 11/15/1910

SNELSON, Mattie, colored, age 10, d. rear of 84 Thurmond St. Atlanta. AG 2/19/1908

SNELSON, W. E., age 50, d. Atlanta Fri. Interred: Stone Mountain, his home. AG 11/14/1908

SNIDER, Albert d. 3/17 Griffin, Ga., age 70, b. and reared in Columbus, Ga. Bro: W. F., Columbus, Ga. AG 3/18/1909

SNIDER, M. E., Mrs., age 68, d. Thurs., 46 Garden St. Atlanta. Interred: Oakland. AG 9/28/1906

SNOW, J. W., Mrs. of Savannah, Ga. killed herself in N. Y. AG 5/6/1910

SNOW, John, age 80, d. 4/   Survivors: Mrs. J. C. Linder, Mrs. W. I. Hailey, Guy Snow, and Lace and Bernice Snow of Texas. AC 4/2/1905

SNOW, Lucy, Mrs., age 30, wife of William J., d. 87 Courtland St. Atlanta, Thurs. AG 3/12/1908

SNOWDEN, Eliza Lee, Mrs., age 66, d. Mon. Atlanta. Sons: R. H., Birmingham; W. E., Elberton, Ga. Interred: Charleston, S. C. AG 5/3/1910

SNYDER, J. C., age 35, d. Atlanta. AG 11/27/1910

SOCKWELL, J. C., Jr., age 3 mos., d. 9 Dainey St. Atlanta. Interred: Hollywood. AG 5/11/1908

SOCKWELL, John L. d. 11/13. Interred: Hollywood. AC 11/16/1905

SOLOMON, Avarilla, Mrs., wid. of W. L., d. Sat. Macon. Interred: Twiggs Co. Son: W. W., Mulberry St. Macon, Rev. J. C., W. W., J. F. AG 1/3/1910

SOLOMON, Carey E., Capt. d. Montezuma 4/10, one of oldest and wealthiest citizens. Ch: J. W., Mrs. C. E. Reid, Mrs. W. W. Hooks. Interred: Perry, Ga. AG 4/13/1909

SOLOMON, Marks, age 65, son-in-law of late Marcus Peyser of Macon, d. 8/31 Montgomery, Ala. Interred: Wm Wolff Cemetery, macon, Ga. Wife, 5 sons. AG 9/1/1910

SOMMERS, A. H., age 73, d. Clarkston, Ga. Mon. Wife. Sons: B. C., C. E., G. F., J. B. AG 5/16/1910

SORROUGH, Howell, colored, age 1, d. 418 Auburn Ave. Atlanta. AG 10/9/1907

SORROW, Nancy, Mrs., age 65, wife of W. J., d. Fri. 24 Bradley St., Atlanta. Interred: Redan, Ga. AG 8/10/1907

SORROW, Pluma, Mrs., age 38, d. Sat. Merrimack, Ala. Husband, 2 children. AG 10/3/1910

SOUTH, Effie May, age 7, d. Mon. 375 W. North Ave. Interment: Hollywood. AG 8/14/1906

SOUTH, Horace P., age 22, d. 1 Dillon St., Sun. Interred: Roswell, Ga. Ag 7/17/1906

SOUTH, Mary A., Mrs., age 56, d. Fri. 530 Walnut St., Atlanta. AG 12/24/1909

SOUTHER, Mary Lou, dau. of Mr. and Mrs. J. N., former residents of Macon, but now res. of Griswoldville, funeral 8/14. AG 8/14/1908

SOUTHER, Nora L., Mrs., age 35, d. yesterday on Main St., E. Macon. Interred: James, Ga. AG 7/25/1907

SOWELL, Daniel, Rev., age 40, d. Atlanta Thurs., 135 Luckie St. AG 1/3/1908

SOWELL, W. J. run over by trolley car in N. Augusta Thurs. died. AG 11/3/1906

SPAIR, Jack, (from Nova Scotia) superintendent of M. Hanna's plantation, 6 mi. from Thomasville, d. 9/28. AG 9/29/1908

SPAIR, James Russell, colored, age 20, d. 219 Irwin St. Atlanta. AG 9/30/1908

SPALDING, R. D., Dr. admn of estate closed Tues. Estate valued at $630,000. Exrs: Mrs. Anne Spalding, Jack J. Spalding. AG 5/5/1909

SPALDING, R. D., Dr. funeral Sun. in Atlanta. AG 12/1/1907

SPALDING, Robert D., age 74, d. Peachtree Rd. Atlanta. Kin: Jack J. Spalding, R. D. Spalding, Jr., W. D. Spalding. AG 11/30/1907

SPANGLER, Charles H., age 52, d. res. of mother, 101 Courtland St., Atlanta, Tues. Interred: Abbotstown, Pa. AG 12/15/1909

SPANGLER, Charlie, age 52, d. 101 Courtland St. Atlanta. AG 12/17/1909

SPANGLER, Malcolm, age 2, son of Mr, and Mrs. S. E. of 35 Stonewall St., Atlanta, d. Wed. AG 12/29/1909

SPANNON, George W. d. 3/17 Colorado Springs, Colo. AC 3/18/1905

SPANSELL, Mary B., Mrs., age 68, d. 99 LaFrance St. Atlanta. Sons: Wallace of Washington, D. C.; Roland, Philadelphia. Sis: Mrs. Kate Morgan, Montezuma, Ga. Interred: Cartersville, Ga. AG 4/25/1910

SPARKS, L. E., Mrs.,ge 50, d. Atlanta 483 Woodward Ave. Tues. Interred: Morrow, Ga. AG 5/12/1908

SPARKS, Nancy D., Mrs., age 82, d. Wed. at home of son, William C. Sparks, 96 Pulliam St. Atlanta. Interred: Oakland. AG 7/18/1906

SPATES, Lee, age 1, son of Mr. and Mrs. O. O., d. 43 Stewart Ave., Atlanta, Tues. Interred: Bremen, Ga. AG 2/11/1908

SPATOLA, Fannie, Mrs. d. Sat. home of sister, Mrs. Katie Andress, Jacksonville, Fla. Interred: Hollywood cemetery, Atlanta. AG 4/23/1907

SPEAR, James, Mrs., formerly of Atlanta, d. Fri. Douglasville, Ga. AG 12/17/1910

SPEAR, S. S., Rev., age 75, d. 183 E. Pine St. Atlanta. AG 12/2/1909

SPEED, A. L., colored, age 21, d. 223 Clarke St. Atlanta. AG 2/26/1908

SPEIGHTS, Hillie May, Mrs., age 18, wife of C. W., d. parents res., Mr. and Mrs. J. Howell Vaughn, 16 Pope St., Atlanta, Sun. Interred: Hill Crest. AG 9/14/1908

SPEIGHTS, William T., age 75, d. 72 Arnold St., Atlanta, Fri. Daus: Mrs. F. J. Liley, Mrs. R. R. Nash. Sons: G. E., R. B. Interred: Westview. AG 11/5/1910

SPEIR, J. P., Prof., age 64, d. 61 Houston St. Atlanta. AG 4/7/1908

SPELL, Andrew Calhoun, died E. Harris St., Atlanta. Came from Abbeville, Ga. Interment: Abbeville, Ga. AG 11/26/1906

SPENCE, Maude, Mrs., wife of William Nesbit Spence of 1245 Marietta St., age 26, d. Atlanta. Interred: Thomaston, Ga. Sis: Mrs. A. A. Andrews of 350 Pulliam St., Atlanta. AG 7/11/1908

SPENCE, William Nesbit, Mrs. d. Atlanta Fri. Interred: Thomaston, Ga., her former home. AG 7/11/1908

SPENCER, B. A., Mrs., age 80, d. 145 W. Mitchell St. Atlanta. Interred: Covington, Ga. Son. Dau: Mrs. W. E. Woodson. AG 7/12/1909

SPENCER, Carey, colored, age 10 mos., d. 226 Foundry St. Atlanta. AG 7/14/1908

SPENCER, Ford, age 40, d. 92 Luckie St. Atlanta. AG 9/12/1908

SPENCER, Nancy, Mrs., age 91, d. 26 Georgia Ave. Atlanta. AG 6/21/1906

SPENCER, Samuel, 1847-1906, a Georgian, Confederate Soldier, first Pres. of Sou. Railway Co., monument erected by employees of co. AG 5/7/1910

SPENCER, Samuel, Macon, Ga., 11/29/1906. Pres. of Sou. rr. killed in rail accident near Richmond, Va. Half-Sisters: Mrs. Frank E. Calloway, Atlanta; Mrs. Stanford E. Moses, wife of Lt. Moses of US Navy. AG 11/29/1906

SPICER, Nellie M., age 10 mos., d. 26 McMillan St. Atlanta. AG 6/20/1910

SPIER, Alfred funeral at Locust Grove. He d. Frees Homes, Cherokee Co., Ga. AG 6/29/1907

SPIER, Jackson P., Prof., age 69, d. 61 Houston St., Atlanta, Fri. Res. Atlanta 30 yrs. Wife: Helen. Son: William K. Dau: Miss Alma Speir. Interred: Fairburn, Ga. AG 4/3/1908

SPINK, Elizabeth S., Mrs. funeral Fri. Atlanta. Interred: Hollywood. AG 7/22/1910

SPINK, Paul W., age 32, d. 17 W. Cain St. Atlanta. Interred: Westview. Three bros. AG 11/25/1907

SPINKER, Clarence, age 1, son of Mr. and Mrs. J. A. of 47 Almo Ave., Atlanta, Fri. Interred: Caseys. AG 11/14/1908

SPINKS, Elizabeth S., Mrs. LWT filed for probate Wed. Atlanta. Exrs: F. R. Spink, B. C. Spink, R. C. Spink, sons. Legacy to son, William C. Spink. AG 8/4/1910

SPINKS, Jack, son of F. B., drowned in Sweetwater Creek near Austell 7/1. Bro: Roy. AG 7/1/1908

SPINKS, Melissa, Mrs., age 61, d. 57 Tattnall St. Atlanta. AG 1/11/1910

SPINKS, Obediah, age 38, interred Hollywood cemetery. Funeral, res. of parents, Mr. and Mrs. J. W. Spinks, at Riverside. AG 10/15/1906

SPINKS, R. J. d. Jan. 26 Atlanta, Conf. Vet., Co. L., Wofford's Brigage, Phillips' Legion. AC 1/26/1905

SPINKS, R. L., age 46, d. 121 Garnett St., Atlanta, Oct. 16. AG 10/18/1910

SPINKS, Susan, Mrs., age 88, d. 750 Elliott St. Atlanta. Dau: Miss S. A. Spinks. Interred: Tilton, Ga. AG 9/10/1908

SPIVEY, George Washington, age 36, d. Wed. Atlanta. Came from Moultrie to Atlanta for treatment. Wife, one child. Interred: Moultrie. AG 1/10/1907

SPIVEY, James shot accidentally at shooting gallery, killed 3/29, Douglas, Ga. AC 3/30/1905

SPIVEY, Marion, age 4, d. Grady Hospital. Atlanta. AG 11/5/1906

SPIVEY, Maud, Mrs., age 19, d. Wed. Husband, one child. Parents: Mr. and Mrs. O. H. Juhan. Interred: Stone Mountain, Ga. AG 9/16/1909

SPIVEY, Randall, age 20, d. Bellwood Ave. Crossing. Atlanta. AG 12/22/1908

SPRADLIN, L. B., age 35, d. 53 Cameron St., Atlanta, Mon. Wife, 3 children. Mother: Mrs. Julia Spradlin. Bros: G. H., T. W., Augustus, Rufus and Henry Spradlin. AG 11/22/1910

SPRATLIN, Nannie, Mrs., age 28, d. Wed. 7 Tumlin St., Atlanta. Interred: Casey's cemetery. AG 5/23/1907

SPRAYBERRY, Hubert, age 3, son of Mr. and Mrs. Newton, d. 14th and Spring Sts., Atlanta, Fri. Interred: Harmony church yard. AG 1/10/1908

SPRAYBERRY, T. F. killed at East Point by Central Ga. freight train Thurs. Survived by wife, 2 children, mother, father. AG 12/21/1906

SPRAYBERRY, William and age wife d. last Sun. Panthersville, DeKalb Co. Investigation, body exhumed. AG 11/17/1910

SPRINGER, J. M., Mrs., age 29, d. 548 Washington St. Atlanta. AG 4/28/1908

SPRINGER, Jennie, Mrs. of 548 Washington St., Atlanta d. Sat. Interred: Oakland. AG 4/26/1908

SPROULL, J. C., Mrs., age 84, of Rome d. Wed. at res. of Mrs. R. T. Fouche, 106 Second Ave. Two daus., one son: Mrs. W. H. Mitchell, Nashville, Tenn., Mrs. R. T. Fouche, Rome, Ga., J. C. Sproull, Richmond, Ky. AG 10/5/1906

SPRUELL, Mary A., Mrs., age 86, d. Tues. res. of son, T. E. Spruell, Roswell Rd., Atlanta. Daus: Mrs. Minda Henson, Mrs. Mary Garmon, Mrs. Georgia Thompson (of Angley, Ala.) Interred: Sardis Church. AG 3/9/1910

SPURLIN, J. B. , age 38, died Atlanta. AG 12/10/1906

STACKS, Carrie, colored, age 24, d. Gordon, Cascade Ave. Atlanta. AG 12/8/1910

STACY, J. H., son of Mr. and Mrs. Frank of Temperance Hill settlement (Dalton, Ga.), age 16, funeral 3/5. AG 3/5/1910

STAFFORD, J. W., Jr., 17 mos. son of Mr. and Mrs. J. W. Stafford, d. yesterday 518 Monroe St., Atlanta. AG 4/10/1907

STAFFORD, Lizzie, Mrs., age 66, d. dau.´s res., Mrs. Walter Boyd, 76 E. Fair St., Atlanta, Sat. Interred: Grantville, Ga. AG 9/28/1908

STAFFORD, Mary E., Mrs., age 75, d. dau.´s res., Mrs. H. E. Glass, 697 N. Boulevard. Atlanta. Interred: Barnesville, Ga. AG 3/3/1908

STAHLI, G. G., age 58, d. 482 Decatur St. Atlanta. AG 11/4/1908

STALL, Kate, Mrs., age 55, d. Thurs. 161 Richardson St., Atlanta. Interred: Westview. AG 2/25/1910

STALLINGS, D. W., age 57, d. 129 Grant St., Atlanta, Fri. Wife, two children: R. H. Stallings, Mrs. Lucy Roberts. Bro: J. W. Stallings. Interred: Oakland. AG 7/4/1908

STALLINGS, Jack, colored, age 1 yr., d. 209 Love St. Atlanta. AG 4/19/1907

STALLINGS, James E., age 43, d. corner Venire and Rawlins Sts., Atlanta, Thurs. Interred: Westview. Wife. AG 4/17/1909

STALLINGS, Mary, age 3 yrs., d. E. Point, Ga. AG 4/15/1910

STALLINGS, R. G., Mrs., wife of Dr. R. G., d. 78 King St., Atlanta several days ago. Interred: Westview. AG 1/8/1908

STALLINGS, W. H., Mrs. of Augusta d. Buffalo, N. Y. 7/26 res. of son, George. Son: William. Interred: Family burial ground, Richmond Co., Ga. AC 7/27/1905

STALLINGS, Wilmer Gertrude, age 3, dau. of Mr. and Mrs. J. E., d. Grant St. Atlanta, Wed. Interred: Westview. AG 4/17/1907

STALLON, Bettie, colored, age 80, d. Alms House. Atlanta. AG 9/4/1907

STAMPS, C. N., age 24, son of J. B., d. Wed. Thomaston, Ga. He had been living in Lumber City. AG 8/12/1910

STAMPS, J. B., age 82, d. Center St., Atlanta, Sept. 30. AG 10/3/1910

STAMPS, Melvin, inf. son of Mr. and Mrs. S. L., d. near East Lake, Ga. Wed. Interred: Parker´s Cemetery, E. Lake, Ga. AG 9/10/1908

STANCELL, Nora U., Miss, dau. of Mr. and Mrs. M. D., d. 91 Walton St., Atlanta, Sat. Interred: Loganville. AG 8/3/1908

STANDRIDGE, Lula May, infant, d. Sun. 22 Tifton St., Atlanta. Interred: Austell, Ga. AG 5/14/1906

STANFILL, Lawrence of Hahira, Ga., d. 2/12, eldest som of L. M., Merchant of Valdosta. AC 2/15/1905

STANFORD, J. E., age 63, inmate of Soldier's Home, Atlanta, d. Tues. Interred: Westview. AG 7/18/1906

STANFORD, Josephine, Miss, res. of Sparta, d. Broad St., age 87. Sister: Miss Anne Stanford. Interred: Sparta cemetery. AG 2/27/1907

STANFORD, M. H., age 19, d. 341 E. Hunter St. Atlanta. AG 11/20/1907

STANFORD, Martha, Miss d. 6/4 Sparta, Ga. Leaves two aged and afflicted sisters: Miss Josephine and Miss Ann Stanford. Near Relatives: Oscar and Gunby Jordan of Columbus and George Young of Atlanta. AC 6/6/1905

STANFORD, Virginia, age 2 days, d. 111 W. Cain St. Atlanta. AG 5/11/1908

STANLEY, Emma, age 40, d. 228 1/2 Marietta St. Atlanta. AG 12/27/1907

STANLEY, Emma, Mrs. d. res. of sister, Mrs. Ella Gibson, 228 1/2 Marietta St., Atlanta. funeral Thurs. Interred: Hollywood. AG 12/26/1907

STANLEY, Gilbert, colored, age 80, d. 310 Highland Ave., Atlanta, 10/13. AG 10/14/1910

STANLEY, H. S., age 70, d. Soldiers' Home, Atlanta, Sat. Was Pvt. in Co. 1, 16th Ga. Vols. during Civil War. Interred: Westview. AG 10/14/1907

STANLEY, J. T., age 21, d. 92 Lovejoy St., Atlanta, Sun. Parents: Mr. and Mrs. J. M. Stanley. Interred: Tucker, Ga. AG 2/11/1908

STANLEY, John R., inf. son of Mr. and Mrs. J. H., d. 18 Larkin St., Atlanta, Mon. Interred: Prospect Cemetery. AG 2/22/1910

STANLEY, Nancy Annie, Mrs. d. dau's home, Mrs. M. E. Simpkins, Lithonia, Ga. Fri. Dau: Mrs. N. F. Dodson, Cullman, Ala. Sons: C. L., E. T. and J. B. Stanley of Atlanta. Interred: Family Burial Ground, Henry Co. AG 2/20/1908

STANLEY, Paul, age 65, d. 640 Capitol Ave. Atlanta. AG 5/24/1907

STANSELL, Mary F., Mrs., age 68, d. 99 LaFrance St. Atlanta. AG 4/25/1910

STANSELL, Richard A. of Dover, Ga., age 67, d. Oxford 5/27. Wife. Interred: Dover Cemetery. AC 5/28/1905

STANTON, George, colored, age 1, d. 237-A Rhodes St. Atlanta. AG 9/2/1909

STANTON, George, colored, age 1, d. 237-A Rhodes St. Atlanta. AG 9/2/1909

STANTON, John P. of Chicago, Ill. found dead in his room at Terminal Hotel, Atlanta, Mon. AG 3/29/1910

STANTON, John P., age 50, d. Terminal Hotel. Atlanta. AG 3/3/1910

STANTON, W. L., former Atlanta res., d. California recently. Funeral: Atlanta. Interred: Westview. Wife. Daus: Mrs. W. T. Forbes, Athens, Ga.; Misses Lucy and Catherine Stanton; Frank, Hawthorne. AG 5/8/1909

STANTON, W. L., former Atlanta, d. California. Interred: Westview. AG 5/7/1909

STAPLE, Elizabeth, colored, age 2, d. 48 Gartrell St. Atlanta. AG 12/2/1910

STAPLES, Annie Mary, infant dau. of Mr. and Mrs. J. M. Staples at Atoka, Ind. Terr. Mrs. A. M. Burke, mother of Mrs. Staples, Atlanta. AG 2/2/1907

STARK, J. H., age 64, d. 224 Greensferry Ave. Atlanta. AG 7/6/1909

STARKE, Mary, Mrs., age 35, d. 17 W. Cain St. Atlanta. AG 8/20/1906

STARNES, Frances, inf. dau. of Mr. and Mrs. Herbert, d. 16 W. End Ave., Atlanta. Interred: Lawrenceburg, Tenn. AG 2/22/1910

STARNES, Hattie, Mrs., age 15, wife of J. J., d. 15 Latimer St., Atlanta, Thurs. AG 10/2/1908

STARNES, N. C., Mrs., age 65, d. Fri. 190 Mason and Turner Rd., Atlanta. Interred: Elliotts Cemetery. AG 10/8/1909

STARNES, W. D., Mrs., age 36, d. Tues. Atlanta. Interred: Bakers burying ground. AG 6/15/1910

STARNES, W. L., Dr. of Mableton d. Sun. Wife, two children. Children: J. N. Starnes, O. H. Starnes, Mrs. J. M. Gloer, Mrs. Emma Smith, P. P. Starnes of Atlanta, and T. J. Starnes of Austell. AG 6/25/1907

STARR, Elmer C. d. 10/5 Stockbridge, Ga., age 37. Wife, 6 small children. Interred: Flippen, Ga. AG 10/6/1910

STARR, Eugene, colored, age 3, d. 101 N. Butler St. Atlanta. AG 3/25/1907

STARR, Isaac, colored, age 27, d. Masons Ave. Atlanta. AG 12/6/1908

STARR, Lucile, age 10 mos., dau. of J. W., d. 98 Davis St., Atlanta, Thurs. Interred: Sunnyside, Ga. AG 6/29/1906

STARR, Nell, inf. dau. of Mr. and Mrs. J. S., d. near Center Hill Sun. Interred: Westview. AG 7/5/1909

STARR, Ruby, age 13, d. E. Point Tues. Interred: Crest Hill. AG 10/8/1907

STATEN, Samuel, old citizen of Echols Co., Ga., d. yesterday. He was an uncle of J. L., W. T., J. B. and Charles Staten of Valdosta. Aged abt 75, never married. Interred: Bunt church. AG 5/12/1906

STEED, infant of Mr. and Mrs. E. E., d. Glendale Ave., Edgewood, Ga. Mon. Interred: Hollywood cemetery. AG 11/19/1907

STEED, J. E., age 1 mo., d. Edgewood, Ga. AG 11/20/1907

STEED, Jim shot and instantly killed by Rob Anderson, negro. AG 6/25/1907

STEEL, George M., age 6, d. 69 Luckie St. Atlanta. AG 3/31/1908

STEELE, Elizabeth, inf. dau. of Mr. and Mrs. J. O., 93 Edgewood Ave., Atlanta, d. Tues. AG 6/30/1910

STEELE, Elizabeth D., Mrs., age 66, d. 481 Spring St. Atlanta. Interred: Philadelphia, Pa. AG 3/3/1909

STEELE, H. H., Mrs., age 45, d. Wed. Atlanta. Interred: Albany, Ga. AG 5/23/1908

STEELE, John W., age 27, suicide 22 Gospero St. Atlanta. AG 6/21/1907

STEELE, L. A., Mrs. d. 11/8 Albany, Ga. To Albany abt 50 yrs. ago from Virginia. Ch: Mrs. Samuel Weldon, Mrs. Sallie McIntosh. AG 11/8/1910

STEELE, Sarah H., Mrs., age 41, d. 701 E. Fair St., Atlanta, Thurs. Husband: B. S. AG 10/23/1908

STEELE, W. O., Mrs., age 38, dau. of late Wesley Collier, d. 25 Baltimore Pl., Atlanta. Mother: Mrs. W. G. Collier. Bros: John W., Frank M., Charles F. and Sanford Collier. Sis: Mrs. Carrie Walker. Interred: Sardis Church. AG 2/27/1907

STEGALL, M. C., Sheriff, funeral 10/30 Bainbridge, Ga. Wife, 6
children. Murdered by negro (lynched 10/27). AC 10/31/1905
STEGALL, Raymond, age 18, d. Fri. 69 Simpson St., Atlanta.
Interred: Austell. AG 8/31/1906
STEINER, J. E., age 34, d. 33 Cone St. Atlanta. Interred:
Westview. AG 3/22/1909
STEINHAGEN, R. T., Mrs. d. 274 Spring St. Sun. Interred:
Westview. Dau: Mrs. Clarence Blosser, Miss Florence Steinhagen.
AG 3/4/1907
STELLERS, S. C., Mrs., age 65, d. Mon., Atlanta. Interred:
Waynesboro, Va. AG 1/13/1908
STELLE, M. A., of DeKalb Co. since 1823, b. Pendleton Dist., SC
3/17/1821; 1849 m. Martha (d. 1883), dau. of Robt H. Smith. Bur-
Rock Spring Ch. Daus-Mrs. J. S. A. Tilly; Mrs. M. C. Medlock.
Sons: W. O.; L. J.; R. S. AG 5/23/1907
STENGISS, R. C., age 20, d. College Park, Ga. AG 9/17/1907
STEPHANS, A. M. funeral held Macon, Ga. 2/27. AG 2/27/1909
STEPHENS, Alexander H., age 58, d. Mon. Macon. AG 12/16/1909
STEPHENS, Annie, Miss d. Tues. Lake Geneva, Ill. Funeral Fri.
Atlanta. Interred: Oakland. Mother: Mrs. John Stephens, 147 N.
Jackson St. Atlanta. AG 6/9/1910
STEPHENS, Annie, Miss funeral Fri. Atlanta. Interred: Oakland. AG
6/10/1910
STEPHENS, C. W., age 58, d. in Bonnie Brae. Interment: Oakland.
Wife, several children. AG 10/25/1906
STEPHENS, Camilla A., Mrs., age 79, d. 1/10 Macon, Ga. Interred:
Buchanan. Grson: D. L. Doster, 2nd St., Macon. Sons: J. M.,
Macon, W. H., Bremen, Mrs. W. P. Stevens, Macon. AG 1/11/1910
STEPHENS, Clarence G., inf. son of Mr. and Mrs. M. C., d. Mon.
Hapeville, Ga. Interred: Tanner's Church yard. AG 10/18/1910
STEPHENS, D. V., Mrs. d. 18 Alden St. Ch: Mrs. C. E. Budding,
Mrs. S. A. Brown, Mrs. W. T. Stephens, Mrs. C. P. Gibson, Mrs. C.
A. Whidby, Mrs. W. H. Gooddy, Mrs. W. F. Dennard, Mrs. J. W.
Robts, J. A. Stephens. Bur: Fairburn. AG 2/20/1906
STEPHENS, Della, colored, age 24, d. 101 N. Butler St. Atlanta.
AG 9/21/1908
STEPHENS, E. A., Mrs., wife of Col. E. A. of McDonough, d. Sun.
She was dau. of Mr. and Mrs. B. B. Carmichael of McDonough, Ga.,
and dau-in-law of Mr. and Mrs. E. W. Rose, Atlanta. Interred:
McDonough, Ga. AG 3/9/1908
STEPHENS, Essie, colored, age 22, d. 40 Brown St. Atlanta. AG
11/20/1909
STEPHENS, Fannie , colored, age 64, d. 101 Butler St. Atlanta. AG
7/19/1909
STEPHENS, Georgia, Mrs., age 51, d. 62 Bonnie Brae Ave. Atlanta.
Sis: Mrs. Emma Walker. Ch: Marion C., John T., C. G.; Mrs. W. T.
Evans, Mrs. W. B. Winburn, Mrs. W. C. Hitchcock, Atlanta; Mrs. A.
J. Corley, Chattanooga, Tn. AG 4/15/1909
STEPHENS, J. C., Mrs., age 46, d. 152 Ormond St. Atlanta. AG
9/30/1908
STEPHENS, J. M., Mrs. d. 56 Park St., Atlanta West End, Atlanta,
Mon. Husband survives. Sons: James, Robert, Charles, Graves,
Frank. Dau: Nannie. Interred: Westview. AG 12/24/1907
STEPHENS, John T., age 1, d. Magazine Rd. Atlanta. AG 8/11/1908

STEPHENS, Lena, colored, age 51, d. 94 W. Linden Ave. Atlanta. AG 9/26/1907

STEPHENS, Lillie, colored, age 9 days, d. 354 Smith St. Atlanta. AG 5/8/1909

STEPHENS, Louis, inf. son of Mr. and Mrs. W. G., d. 15 Alice St., Atlanta, Wed. Interred: Westview. AG 7/9/1908

STEPHENS, Lucy, Mrs., age 40, d. 56 Carroll St. Atlanta. AG 9/12/1908

STEPHENS, Mattie, Mrs., age 30, d. Atlanta. AG 3/29/1910

STEPHENS, Minnie, Mrs., age 38, d. Tues. 36 Walnut St. Atlanta. Husband: W. T. 4 sons, 1 dau, 2 bros., 6 sisters, father. Interred: Jonesboro, Ga. AG 1/5/1910

STEPHENS, Minnie, Miss, age 22, d. parents' res., Mr. & Mrs. W. M. Bearden, College Pk. Bros: A. E. Stephens, E. Pt; Thomas & Arthur, Atlanta. Sis: Mrs. Ella Keith, E. Pt.; Mrs. Lela Ivey, Carrollton. Bur: Crest Hill Cem. AG 8/12/1910

STEPHENS, Peter, negro, d. Macon train wreck. AG 2/15/1911

STEPHENS, Robert, age 45, d. Thurs. Tifton, Ga. Wife, 3 children. Vet. of Spanish-American War. AG 12/17/1910

STEPHENS, S. M., Mrs., age 48, d. 56 Park St. Atlanta. AG 12/26/1907

STEPHENS, Sandy, colored, age 37. d. rear 106 W. Baker St. Atlanta. AG 9/26/1910

STEPHENS, Thelma, age 2 mos., d. 101 N. Butler St. Atlanta. AG 9/22/1908

STEPHENS, Will, colored, age 24, d. 327 Hilliard St. Atlanta. AG 12/28/1910

STEPHENSON, Charles Barclay, age 5, d. 63 Martin St. Atlanta. AG 3/22/1907

STEPHENSON, Jennie, Mrs., wife of Hon. L. F., of Rocky Plains, Ga., d. 2/22. Ch: John, James (Covington); Mrs. W. B. Harvey (Snapping Shoals); Miss Mary Stephenson (Rocky Plains). Interred: Hopewell Church. AC 2/24/1905

STEPHENSON, Mrs., age abt 20, wife of John, killed accidentally in Cedartown, Sat. Leaves 2 mos. baby. AG 3/4/1907

STERCHI, J. H., age 81, d. 99 Ira St. Atlanta. Two daus., one son. AG 8/19/1909

STEVENS, D. V., age 68, d. 18 Allen St. Atlanta. AG 2/22/1907

STEVENS, J. L., age 51, d. Mon. Atlanta. Wife, 5 children. Interred: Newnan, Ga. AG 2/28/1910

STEVENS, Joseph, colored, age 8 days, d. 25 Hollins St. Atlanta. AG 9/8/1908

STEVENS, M., Mrs., age 80, d. Greensferry Rd., near Bolton, Ga. Husband: Cash Stevens, two children. Interred: Mason's churchyard. AG 1/17/1908

STEVENS, Mary Lou, Mrs., wife of J. R., d. Mon. Gordon, Ga. AG 1/27/1910

STEVENS, Ralph, colored, age 65, d. 331 Fort St. Atlanta. AG 4/7/1908

STEVENS, Tilman, colored, age 44 d. 105 Chapel St. Atlanta. AG 11/25/1907

STEVENS, W. M., age 60, d. Mulberry St., Macon, 8/9. Wife, several relatives. AG 8/10/1909

STEVENSON, Lillie, colored age 15, d. 46 Daniel St., Atlanta. AG 9/11/1907

STEVENSON, Robert, colored, age 59, d. 56 Daniel St. Atlanta. AG 7/23/1909

STEVENS, Sandy, age 70, died at 68 Markham Street, Atlanta. AG 11/19/1906

STEWART, A. J., Mrs., age 39, d. 44 Norcross St., Atlanta, Mon. AG 9/21/1909

STEWART, Allen J., inf. son of Mr. and Mrs. E. R., d. Conley, Ga. Wed. AG 2/13/1908

STEWART, Arthur, age 18, drowned in Chattahoochee River, Columbus, Ga. AC 8/1/1905

STEWART, B. J., Mrs., age 73, d. 59 McDaniel St. Atlanta. AG 9/6/1907

STEWART, Callie, colored, age 1, d. 53 Old Wheat St. Atlanta. AG 12/11/1908

STEWART, Elizabeth, age 18 mos., dau. of Mr. and Mrs. R., of 38 LarkinSt., Atlanta, d. Sun. Interred: Westview. AG 6/27/1910

STEWART, Emma, Mrs., age 69, former res. of Wrightsville, Ga., wife of W. H. H., d. son´s res., P. A., 402 N. Jackson St., Atlanta, Thurs. Husband. Dau: Mrs. Leila Daley, 152 Forrest Ave. Atlanta. Interred: Westview. AG 6/11/1909

STEWART, Helen, age 44, d. 480 E. Fair St. Atlanta. AG 6/29/1910

STEWART, Helen, Mrs., wife of J. R., d. 480 E. Fair St., Atlanta, Mon. Interred: Wesley Chapel churchyard. AG 6/28/1910

STEWART, Hillie, colored, age 39, d. rear of 327 Fort St. Atlanta. AG 7/10/1909

STEWART, J. M., age 61, d. 447 Central Ave. Atlanta. Interred: Oakland. AG 3/17/1910

STEWART, J. W., Mrs. d. Mon. E. Huntsville, Ala. Husband, one small child. Age 30. Before marriage was Miss Mayme Moore. AG 4/5/1910

STEWART, Jesse, colored infant, d. 124 E. Ellis St., Atlanta. AG 5/26/1906

STEWART, John O. d. 7/27, age 75, b. Newton Co., Confed. Vet. m. Miss Kittie Dixin in 1858. Sons: P., Rome; J. B., Atlanta; Dr. Joseph, Griffin. AC 7/28/1905

STEWART, Lizzie, age 27, colored, d. 408 Mangum St. Atlanta. AG 11/27/1910

STEWART, Lizzie, Miss funeral res. of R. J. Rice, 800 Mangum St. Atlanta. AG 6/17/1910

STEWART, Margaret, Mrs. d. Ben Hill, Ga. Tues., mother of J. C. and P. G. Stewart. Interred: Family Burial Grounds. AG 12/18/1907

STEWART, Marion E., age 6, d. 111 S. Pryor St., Atlanta. AG 5/1/1907

STEWART, Mary, colored, d. age 80, 201 Walnut St., Atlanta. AG 1/24/1907

STEWART, Mira A., Mrs., age 4 , wife of Robert S., d. Sun. AG 8/3/1908

STEWART, R. S., age 32, d. suicide, corner Gilmer and Fort Sts. Atlanta. AG 4/4/1907

STEWART, S. C., age 56, d. Atlanta, Sat. Wife: Mrs. Mollie. Sons: A. M., D. C. Interred: McDonough, Ga. AG 9/23/1907

STEWART, Susan C., Mrs. d. 19 North Lee St., Atlanta, Sat. Interred: Oakland. AG 7/6/1908

STEWART, Thomas O. d. Sparta 12/28, age 75. Wife. 4 sons. 4 daus. AC 12/29/1905

STILLWELL, W. R., Rev., aged 60, Methodist minister, d. Thurs. Wesley Memorial Hospital. Interred: McDonough. AG 2/8/1907

STINSON, J. A., age 46, d. 205 Decatur St., Atlanta. Funeral: Thurs. Atlata. Wife. Sons: John, William. Bro: W. M. Stephenson. Sis: Mrs. R. Peeples, Vicksburg, Miss. AG 6/17/1910

STINSON, Oscar killed himself and sweetheart, Edna Wamble, negroes, Woodbury, Ga. AC 5/3/1905

STOCKS, G. W., Mrs., age 57, d. 63 Loomis St. Atlanta. Husband: Rev. George W. Ch: Dr. C. L. Stocks, Miss Rosebed Stocks, Atlanta, C. E. Stocks, Barnesville, C. W. Stocks, Milledgeville, G. T. Stocks, Newnan, Mrs. W. R. Waldrop, Jacksonville, Fla. Interred: Barnesville, Family Cemetery. AG 7/2/1908

STOCKS, J. W. d. 447 E. Fair St. Atlanta. Interred: Oakland. 3 nieces, 3 nephews. AC 11/19/1905

STOCKTON, Joseph Penn, inf. son of Mr. and Mrs. R. E., 252 Formwalt St., Atlanta, age 2 mos., d. 252 Formwalt St. Atlanta. Wed. Interred: Hollywood Cemetery. AG 8/25/1909

STOCKTON, Otis, infant son of Mr. and Mrs. Walter, d. Sun. 430 Windsor St. Atlanta. Interred: Westview. AG 6/25/1907

STOCK, Henry E., age 68, d. Decatur, Ga. AG 4/2/1910

STOKELY, M. C., Mrs., age 72, d. Wed. at home of dau., Mrs. L. M. Johnson, 79 Park Ave., Atlanta. Interred: Crawford, Ga. AG 6/14/1906

STOKES, Isaac, colored, age 34, d. 101 N. Butler St. Atlanta. AG 8/25/1909

STOKES, Jim, colored, age 27, d. 31 Fort St. Atlanta. AG 9/4/1908

STOKES, Nellie, Miss, age 13, d. Fri., home of parents, Mr. and Mrs. W. J. Stokes, Houston Rd., Atlanta. Three sisters, two bros. Interred: Mt. Pleasant Church. AG 7/11/1908

STOKES, Zeb, colored, age 42, d. 91 Hilliard St. Atlanta. AG 10/3/1908

STONE, Bessie, Miss d. Mon. Interred: Villa Rica, Ga. AG 6/10/1907

STONE, Ellison, age 70, d. Athens 5/5. Wife. Sons: J. H., G. E., E. P., C. D. AC 5/6/1905

STONE, Emma A., Mrs., age 62, d. 98 Washington St. Atlanta. AG 9/21/1909

STONE, I. T. d. Bibb Co. Sun., age 50. Interred: Howard, Ga. AG 8/14/1906

STONE, Willie Myrtle, age 1, dau. of Mr. and Mrs. W. G., d. 12 Dillon St., Atlanta, Thurs. Interred: Cross Hill, S. C. AG 11/11/1909

STONEY, C. Louis, Jr., inf. son of Mr. and Mrs. C. L., d. 675 Peachtree St., Atlanta, Sat. Interred: Westview. AG 6/8/1908

STORY, L. M., age 24, son of J. A. of Phenix City, d. 2/23. Interred: Hopewell Church, Alabama. AC 2/25/1905

STORY, Martha funeral at res. 36 Zachry St., Atlanta, Wed. Interred: Oakland. AG 5/11/1910

STORY, Martha, age 6, d. 36 Zachry St. Atlanta. AG 5/11/1910

STORY, Tom, colored, age 32, d. 101 N. Butler St. Atlanta. AG 3/15/1907

STORY, Zorah, Mrs. d. Thompson, Ga. Bur: Briar Creek. Husband: W. D. Two small children. Bros, sis: H. F. Norris, W. A. Norris, C. D. Norris, J. F. Norris, J. P. Norris, Dr. C. E. Norris, Mrs. T. B. Johnson, Mrs. D. B. Printup. AG 6/10/1909

STOVALL, Abda C., 94, d. Oglesby, 12/7. Ch: Mrs. Brock, Banks Co.; Mrs. Nancy Mize, Elbert Co. (by 1st wife); Hon. A. S. J., Elberton; James T., Commerce; Mrs. Minnie McCurry; J. Ben, Elbert Co. (by 2d wife). Bur: Elmhurst Cem. AG 12/8/1909

STOVALL, Bessie, Mrs. d. Sat. Atlanta. Interred: Oakland. AG 5/24/1907

STOVALL, Walter B., age 34, d. Atlanta Thurs, son of Mr. and Mrs. C. C. Bros: W. O., G. W., L. L., Atlanta, and E. C. of Baltimore, Md. AG 2/11/1909

STOW, Kate, Miss d. Tues. Atlanta at res. of M. R. Berry, 47 Walton St. Interred: Oakland. AG 7/14/1908

STOW, Maud, Mrs., age 27, d. 78 Ponders Ave., Atlanta. Husband: M. H. Five children. Father: Sam Spradling. Two bros. AG 9/30/1909

STOWE, Elizabeth Dowdell, age 3, dau. of Dr. and Mrs. I. N., d. 55 St. Charles Ave., Atlanta, Wed. Interred: Opelika, Ala. AG 6/16/1909

STOWE, H. W., age 26, d. Wed. 112 Pearl St. Atlanta. Interred: Conyers. AG 6/2/1907

STOWELL, Frank, age 35, d. Boulevard and Woodward Ave. Atlanta. AG 2/20/1908

STOWELL, Rosie Lee, age 2 mos., d. 59 Elmo Ave. Atlanta. AG 9/12/1908

STOWERS, George, age 77, d. Soldiers' Home. Atlanta. AG 9/8/1908

STRADLEY, C., Mrs., age 71, d. dau.'s res., Mrs. W. M. Fulks, 172 W. Alexander St., Atlanta. Bur: Dalton, Ga. Sons: W. G., H. C. Daus: Mrs. Fulks, Mrs. F. B. Quillian, Atlanta, Mrs. A. P. Rutherford, Galveston, Tx. AG 7/22/1909

STRAIN, Elizabeth J., Mrs., age 73, d. 188 Capitol Ave., Atlanta, Sun. Interred: Cleveland, Tenn. Dau: Miss Alice G. Strain. AG 2/10/1908

STRAND, Lottie, colored, age 32, d. 460 Piedmont Ave. Atlanta. AG 11/21/1910

STRANGE, Ibbie Louise, Mrs., age 84, d. 414 S. Pryor St. Atlanta. Ag 7/15/1910

STRAUD, Margaret of 1731 T. Street, Washington, Ga. found dead in buggy shop. Leonard T. Brown killed her, then himself. AG 2/12/1907

STRAUTER, Will, colored, age 36, d. 110 Bradley St. Atlanta. AG 11/22/1909

STRAWN, Elizabeth, Mrs., widow of late F. F., of Social Circle, Ga., d. Fri. AG 3/13/1909

STREET, Ben, colored, age 56, d. 34 Tyler St. Atlanta. AG 10/1/1909

STREET, Bertha, Miss, age 35, d. 235 Capitol Ave. Atlanta Tues. Interred: Oakland. Bro: C. E. Street. AG 8/19/1908

STREET, G. H., Mrs., age 51, d. 169 Milton St. Interred: Caseys. AG 8/25/1906

STREET, George T. d. Wed. 148 Windsor St. Interred: Westview. Wife: Ida M. Daus: Marian, Louise. AG 3/26/1908

STREET, John, Mrs. d. Wed. 701 E. Fair St., Atlanta. AG 8/28/1907

STREET, Nora, Mrs., age 26, d. E. Point, Ga. AG 1/25/1910

STREET, Susie M., Mrs., wife of John, d. Wed. 701 E. Fair St. Atlanta. Interred: Redan, Ga. AG 8/27/1907

STREET, Vernon, age 1, d. 701 E. Fair St. Atlanta. AG 8/14/1907

STREETER, Annie, colored, age 29, d. 89 Newton St. Atlanta. AG 12/3/1908

STREETER, James, colored, age 4 mos., d. rear of 484 Woodward Ave. Atlanta, AG 6/13/1909

STREETMAN, J. N., Mrs., Sr. d. 8/31 Lumpkin, Ga. Husband, 6 children. She was sister of late Judge Wimberly. AG 8/31/1910

STRIBLINE, Harry L., age 45, killed in wreck of Southern RR. Interred: Decatur Cemetery. AG 12/17/1909

STRICKLAND, C. H., Mrs. d. Jan. 7 Waycross. AC 1/8/1905

STRICKLAND, C. T., Jr., age 6, son of Mr. and Mrs. C. T., d. 10/24 Waycross, Ga. AG 10/25/1910

STRICKLAND, E. M., Mrs. interred Indian Creek grave yard. AG 9/14/1907

STRICKLAND, Eliza, mrs., age 47, d. Jan. 12 Atlanta. AC 1/14/1905

STRICKLAND, Henry killed by wagon Sat. Interred: Fairburn, Ga. AG 10/8/1907

STRICKLAND, Henry, age 15, d. Peters and Walker Streets. Atlanta. AG 0/7/1907

STRICKLAND, Jessie N. of Nicholson, Ga. found dead in public road 5/10. AC 5/11/1905

STRICKLAND, Katie, Mrs., age 29, d. 33 Curran St. Atlanta, Thurs. Interred: Dunwoody, Ga. Husband: L. M. Mother: Mrs. M. A. Rosser. 6 bros., one sister. AG 5/7/1908

STRICKLAND, Maggie, colored, age 41, d. 206 Vine St. Atlanta. AG 6/19/1909

STRICKLAND, Mattie Lee, age 18 mos., dau. of Mr. and Mrs. Charles B., d. 90 Wylie St., Atlanta 12/26. Interred: Rockmart, Ga. AC 12/28/1905

STRICKLAND, Q. P., Mrs. d. 303 Simpson St., Atlanta, Mon. Interred: Westview. AG 7/23/1908

STRICKLAND, T. L., age 54, d. 101 N. Butler St. Atlanta. Wife, one dau. Interred: Waycross, Ga. AG 4/0/1908

STRICKLAND, W. B., age 23, son of Mr. and Mrs. C. J. Strickland, 11 Kennedy St., Atlanta. Remains sent Forest Park, Ga. AG 11/17/1906

STRINGER, Ben Lee, age 41, d. Mon. 282 Peeples St., Atlanta. Interred: Westview. AG 2/23/1910

STRONG, F. E., Mrs., wid. of Dr. R. B., d. 16 Bedford Place, Atlanta, Sat. Bro: Col. W. S. Thompson, Atlanta. Interred: Westview. AG 10/8/1907

STRONG, Jesse, colored, age 50, d. 7 Harrison St. Atlanta. AG 3/16/1908

STRONG, Lonnie, colored, age 38, d. rear 242 Whitehall St. Atlanta. AG 9/28/1909

STRONG, Mary F., Mrs. d. Thurs. 304 Oak St., Atlanta. Sons: Clifford I. of Portland, Ore. and Walter W. of Atlanta. Interred: Westview. AG 6/8/1906

STRONG, B. R., Mrs. d. Sat. 16 Bedford Place, Atlanta, wid. of Dr. Benjamin R. of Marietta, Ga. Ch: Danner, Memphis, Tenn.; B. R., Mobile, Ala.; Mrs. J. F. Bailey, Brunswick; Mrs. K. F. Thomason and Miss Mary Strong, Atlanta. AG 10/5/1

STROUD, Harry, colored, age 32, d. 170 Martin St. Atlanta. AG 1/17/1908

STROUD, Mary, colored, age 33, d. 10 Mildred St. Atlanta. AG 1/24/1907

STROUP, Albert, age 68, d. 81 Stonewall St., Atlanta, Mon. Interred: Oakland. AG 5/3/1910

STROUP, Julian, age 70, d. Sun. 81 Stonewall St., Atlanta. Wife. Bro: Albert, Atlanta. Interred: Oakland. AG 4/5/1909

STROUSS, Lawrence D, age 22, d. 30 East Ave. Atlanta. AG 3/23/1909

STROZIER, Blanche, inf. dau. of Mr. and Mrs. L. M., d. Wed. 305 Richardson St., Atlanta. Interred: Westview. AG 2/24/1910

STROZIER, Cosby W. d. Mon. Helena, Ga. Interred: McRae Cemetery. AG 5/11/1910

STRUNG, Henry, colored, age 30, died 288 Fulton St., Atlanta. AG 12/31/1906

STUBBLEFIELD, W. A., Dr., age 50, d. Chattanooga, Tenn. AG 5/19/1910

STUBBS, Mrs. d. near Pleasant Hill Sun. Interred: Bethel Methodist Church. AG 4/24/1907

STUBBS, Sidney G., age 23, d. 26 Currier St. Atlanta. AG 6/13/1907

STUBENGER, John C. F. d. 2/18 Macon. Wife, one son, two daus. Formerly lived Marietta. AG 2/19/1910

STUCKEY, George A. suicide 5/24 Macon. AC 5/25/1905

STUCKEY, William M., Harris Co. farmer, suicide at home near Whitesville, Ga. AG 12/19/1907

STUDSTILL, Thomas, Mrs. d. Rays Mill Thurs. Interred: Alapaha Cemetery, Milltown, Ga. Several bros. and sisters, husband, three children. AG 7/31/1909

STUMP, James, Capt. d. 5/3 res. of son, Joseph, Valdosta. he was b. Germany, age 76. Res. of Baltimore. Dau: Mrs. W. A. Green, Dakota, Ga. Interred: Valdosta, Ga. AC 5/4/1905

STURDEVANT, infant of Mr. and Mrs. T. O., d. 36 DeGress Ave. Atlanta. AG 5/21/1910

STURGES, J. C., age 69, d. Grady Hospital, Atlanta, Fri. Interred: Westview. AG 7/14/1906

STUTTS, W. F.. Brunswick, Ga. old res. died res. on East St. Fri. Leaves widow and five small children. AG 12/17/1906

STYLES, Mittie, inf. dau. of Mr. and Mrs. A. B., of E. Pt., d. Fri. Interred: Crest Hill. AG 6/10/1910

SUBER, Nellie A., Mrs., age 35, d. Edgewood, Ga. Interred: Oakland. AG 8/1/1907

SUDAN, Francis, age 22 mos., son of Mr. and Mrs. P. L., of 90 Rock St., Atlanta, d. Mon. Interred: Hollywood. AG 6/28/1910

SUDDETH, Zachery Taylor, 8 mos, died 159 Alexander St., Atlanta. Interred: Gainesville, Ga. AG 11/19/1906

SULLIVAN, Bessie, Mrs., wife of Donohue Sullivan, age 23, d. 276 E. Fair St., Atlanta, Thurs. Interred: Oakland. AG 9/28/1906

SULLIVAN, Daniel O., Capt., age 81, d. Wed. dau.'s res., Mrs. W. S. Mosely, 560 Woodward Ave., Atlanta. Son: D. W. Dau: Mattie. Confed. Vet. Interred: Westview. AG 7/7/1910

SULLIVAN, Etta, colored, age 10, d. 160 Parson St. Atlanta. AG 11/12/1910

SULLIVAN, J. B., colored, age 2, d. 17 Strong St. Atlanta. AG 12/28/1907

SULLIVAN, R. F., Hon., tax collector for Franklin Co., d. Carnesville, Ga. Tues. AG 3/26/1908

SULLIVAN, Richard C. , age 26, d. Atlanta last week. Bro: Joseph. Wife was Miss Teresa McDuffie. Three children, two brothers. AG 4/30/1906

SULLIVAN, Sarah E., colored, age 75, d. 1139 E. Fair St. Atlanta. AG 4/21/1908

SULLIVAN, Sylvanus d. Waldon (near Macon). Married 52 yrs. Wife survives. Ch: L. V. Sullivan, New Orleans; E. P. and A. C. Sullivan of Walden; E. S. Sullivan, Montezuma; Mrs. Lou Clarke, Macon; Mrs. J. M. Henson, Hazlehurst. AG 3/14/1907

SULLIVAN, Theresa, Mrs. d. 76 Lovejoy St., Atlanta, Mon. Interred: Oakland. AG 3/9/1908

SULLIVAN, Warren Lockridge, age 2, son of Mrs. Theresa McDuffie Sullivan, d. Fri. 76 Lovejoy St., Atlanta. Interred: Oakland. AG 8/27/1907

SULLIVAN, W. C., age 62, d. 5 Bush St. Sun. Interred: Canton, Ga. AG 1/27/1908

SULLIVAN, William, Mrs. d. Houston Co., Ga., age 45, yesterday. Leaves husband, 4 children. AG 12/24/1907

SUMEY, Frank ., inf. son of Mr. and Mrs. W. H., d. Tues. 32 Fitzgerald St., Atlanta. Interred: Lawrenceville, Ga. AG 1/4/1910

SUMLIN, Mattie, colored, age 22, d. 415 Chesnut St. Atlanta. AG 5/15/1907

SUMMERFIELD, Fred L., Mrs. d. 11/13. Interred: Sardis Church. AC 11/16/1905

SUMMERLIN, Green, negro murdered Douglasville, Ga. AG 3/23/1908

SUMMERLIN, John M. d. Clarkston, Ga. Tues. Interred: Sweetwater Church. AG 9/24/1908

SUMMERS, Emma, Mrs., age 63, d. 230 E. Pine St. Atlanta. AG 2/19/1907

SUMMERS, J. M., Mrs. of 644 S. Pryor St., Atlanta d. while visiting dau., Mrs. J. M. Cox, Birmingham, Ala. Dau: Mrs. G. G. Hannah, 284 S. Pryor St. Atlanta. Interred: Westview. AG 6/15/1908

SUMMERS, Moody C., age 50, d. Atlanta. Interred: Conyers, Ga. AG 5/1/1906

SUMMEY, C. L., Dr. of Stone Mountain d. 12/10. 2 wks. ago his wife died. AC 12/11/1905

SUMNER, Joe L., Hon., d. son's home, Dr. Gordon Sumner, Wed., Poulan, Ga., age 65, pioneer settler to Worth Co. AG 7/16/1908

SURLES, Vivian K., age 11 days, d. 259 Crumley St. Atlanta. AG 2/11/1909

SUTHERLAND, Bob, negro, to die in gallows, Rome, Ga. AC 3/7/1905

SUTTLES, Charley, colored, age 13, d. 48 Trenholm St. Atlanta. AG 6/13/1907

SUTTLES, E., Mrs., age 18, d. 176 Nelson St. Atlanta. AG 7/17/1907

SUTTLES, Elizabeth Margaret, inf. dau. of Mr. and Mrs. W. J., d. 774 E. Fair St., Atlanta, Mon. Interred: Hollywood. AG 7/28/1908

SUTTLES, Grace, age 2, dau. of Mr. and Mrs. E. P. of 90 Ira St., Atlanta, d. Thurs. AG 11/26/1909

SUTTLES, Lizzie, colored, age 37, d. 104 Foundry St, rear, Atlanta. AG 1/12/1907

SUTTLES, W. W., Mrs., dau. of Mr. and Mrs. R. M. Barton, d. Mon. parents res. 176 Nelson St., Atlanta. Interred: Westview. AG 7/16/1907

SUTTON, Edward M., age 41, d. Mon. Decatur, Ga. Interred: Oakland. AG 8/30/1910

SUTTON, Estella, colored, age 1, d. 62 Davis St. Atlanta. AG 11/21/1910

SUTTON, Hennie, colored, age 20, d. 20 Reed St. Atlanta. AG 7/24/1907

SUTTON, John L., Mrs., age 33, dau. of late Joseph Smith, d. 570 Whitehall St., Atlanta, Sat. Sisters: Mrs. J. A. Perry, Miss Lilly Smith. Bro: J. J. Smith. Husband, 3 children, mother, survive. Interred: Oakland. AG 2/8/1908

SUTTON, Lena, age 11, d. 82 E. Hunter St. 5/3. Interred: Sweetwater, Tenn. AG 5/4/1906

SUTTON, T. C., age 35, d. McDonough Road, Atlanta. AG 5/24/1907

SUTTON, Will, colored, age 18, d. 6 Thompsons alley. Atlanta. AG 6/21/1907

SWAIN, Annie, colored, age 45, d. 10 Golden St. Atlanta. AG 2/7/1908

SWAINIE, Sallie, Mrs., age 29, d. Sun. 218 Carter St. Atlanta. Interred: Tifton, Ga. AG 5/7/1906

SWAIT, M., Mrs., age 60, d. 34 Tumlin St. Atlanta. AG 4/10/1907

SWAN, John H., Mrs. d. 11/25 Thomasville, Ga. As Miss Maynita Arnold she moved with mother to Thomasville from Atlanta several yrs. ago, marr. John Swan, 2 yrs. ago. Relatives in Atlanta and Barnesville. AG 11/27/1910

SWANEY, Austin W., inf. son of Mr. and Mrs. J. W., d. Fri. 207 Carter St.,Atlanta. Interred: Tifton, Ga. AG 6/9/1906

SWANEY, Ogden Wade, infant, d. 207 Carter St. Atlanta. AG 6/9/1906

SWANN, E. W., age 47, of Cartersville, Ga., d. Atlanta Wed. Interred: Cartersville. AG 3/24/1910

SWANN, James W., age 35, sheriff of Rockdale Co., d. Wed, typhoid. AG 10/22/1906

SWANN, William W. of Rockdale Co. d. last Fri. Dist. magistrate 30 yrs. AG 9/4/1906

SWANSON, Henry, colored, age 23, d. San Bernardino, Ca. AG 10/29/1907

SWANSON, Mary, colored, age 72, d. 64 Chestnut St. Atlanta. AG 2/22/1907

SWANSON, Thomas J. of Covington, b. Morgan Co., Ga. 4/28/1831, d. yesterday. He m. Miss Frances Cornelia Copeland of Morgan Co. He was Civil War veteran. AG 3/7/1907

SWANTON, Josephine F., Mrs., age 64, d. Atlanta Ave., Decatur, Sat. Daus: Mrs. A. A. Ivy, Mrs. W. B. Symmers, Mrs. Estell Kerr, Mrs. L. W. Thomas. Sons: John Albert and Joe W. Swanton. Interred: Decatur Cemetery. AG 8/7/1909

SWAYGERT, Mary J., age 64, d. 140 Wells St. Atlanta. AG 4/10/1907

SWEARINGEN, R. M., Mrs., age 34, d. 131 S. Pryor St. Atlanta. AG 11/11/1909

SWEAT, Kates, Mrs., age 58, d. 36 Tumlin t., Atlanta. Interred: Caseys. AG 4/8/1907

SWEAT, Mary, age 3, dau. of Mr. and Mrs. C. S., d. 666 Chestnut St., Atlanta, Thurs. Interred: Caseys. AG 12/30/1908

SWEAT, Robert J., age 8 mos., son of D. E., d. Sat. Atlanta. Interred: Waycross, Ga. AG 12/17/1910

SWEATMAN, Clyde Russell, son of Mr. and Mrs. R. C., d. 118 E.
12th St. Atlanta, Tues. Interred: Westview. AG 6/8/1909
SWEATMAN, Martha A., age 69, d. 42 E. Eleventh St. Atlanta. AG
4/20/1910
SWEATMAN, Martha A., Mrs., age 69, d. 42 E. 11th St. Atlanta Mon.
Interred: Sandy Springs Church yard. AG 4/19/1910
SWEATMAN, Martha A., Mrs., age 69, d. 42 E. 11th St., Atlanta,
Mon. Interred: Sandy Springs Church yard. AG 4/19/1910
SWEATMAN, W. R., age 42, d. 15 Bradley St. Atlanta. AG 11/17/1910
SWEET, W. C., Mrs. of Middlesboro, Ky. Sister: Mrs. S. L. Rhorer,
N. Boulevard, Atlanta. AG 1/22/1907
SWICK, William, young man, d. Mon., Dalton, Ga. Mother, wife, two
children. AG 11/10/1909
SWIFT, Willie, negro, died during riot at dance, Jackson, Ga. AG
12/6/1909
SWIFT, H. C., 75, leaped to death 204 Harris St., Savannah 2/6.
NY Merch. Daus: Mrs. M. J. Joiner, Miss Ada Swift, Savannah; Mrs.
R. F. Julian, Bircher, FL. Sons: Dr. A. K., Woodbine, Ga.; Dr. C.
G., Nome, Tx. Bur: Stockton, Ga. AC 2/8/1905
SWINDLE, G. E., of Valdosta, wealthy farmer, age 52, d. 8/17 at
Buffalo Lithia Springs, Va. Sons: L. C., Valdosta Merchant; J.
H., Valdosta. Wife, 4 sons. AG 8/18/1909
SWINSON, Ruth, age 3, dau of Mr. and Mrs. W. S. Swinson, d. Mon.,
305 S. Boulevard, Atlanta. Interred: Westview. AG 3/12/1907
SWINSON, W. S., Mrs., age 12, d. 69 Luckie St. Atlanta. AG
3/16/1907
SWORDS, J. H., Mrs. d. 35 Foundry St., Atlanta, Sat. Interred:
Oakland. AG 2/2/1908
SYKER, Joe d. Sparta, Ga. 3/16, age 73. 6 sons, 6 daus. AC
3/17/1905
SYKES, Wyley J., Sr. d. 12/24 Barnesville, Ga. Age 82. AG
12/27/1910
SYMMERS, William, age 76, d. 196 Angier Ave., Atlanta, Mon., res.
of Atlanta over 35 yrs., was b. Aberdeen, Scotland. Ch: Miss Kate
Symmers, Atlanta; dau. in Scotland; son, W. B. Symmers, Atlanta.
Interred: Westview. AG 12/15/1908
SYMMES, John C., age 64, d. Wed. Atlanta. Interred: Hollywood. AG
9/9/1910
SYMONDS, W. A., age 68, Confed. Vet., d. Old Soldiers' Home,
Atlanta, Mon. Interred: Westview. AG 12/27/1910
SYMONS, W. F., age 68, d. Old Soldiers' Home. Atlanta. AG
12/28/1910

TABOR, Nathan T., pioneer of Gilmer Co., d. 6/14 Cartecay, Ga., age 83. Son: Judge J. H., Ordinary of Gilmer Co. AC 6/16/1905

TACKETT, W. P., Douglas Co. Tax Receiver, d. age 63. Confederate Veteran. Wife, 3 daus., survive. AG 12/9/1907

TAFF, Evaline, infant dau. of Mr. and Mrs. R. M. Taff, d. Mon. in East End. Interred: Greenwood. AG 6/10/1907

TAGGART, Ola May, colored, age 2, d. 41 Mary St. Atlanta. AG 5/4/1909

TALBOT, K. B., Mrs., many yrs res. of Atlanta d. home of dau., Mrs. William G. Boyer, Saugerities, N. Y. Daus: Mrs. A. W. Davis, Mrs. R. Frank Hawkins, Mrs. W. S. Helms, Atlanta. AG 5/8/1906

TALLENT, Edna, age 1 yr., d. 54 Glenn St. Atlanta. AG 7/22/1907

TALLEY, Amanda, age 65, d. Decatur, Ga. AG 2/19/1910

TALLEY, J. D., age 64, d. Thurs. Funeral at Abbeville, Ga. AG 8/15/1907

TALLY, John Hugh d. Chattanooga, Tenn., home of his sister, Mrs. W. O. Smith. Sisters: Mrs. W. O. Smith; Mrs. John M. Kenny of Nashville and Mrs. A. L. Alsobrook of Louisville, Ky. AG 10/25/1909

TALLY, Silas, colored, age 60, d. 281 Parks Ave. Atlanta. AG 10/1/1908

TALTON, Bennie, son of Mr. and Mrs. R. E., accidently shot while playing with rifle. Interred: Montreal, Ga. AG 1/22/1907

TANKLESLY, Eliza A., Mrs. d. Thurs. Twiggs Co., Ga. at family res. Interred: Family Burial Grounds. AG 9/18/1908

TANKS, John killed Christmas night, Spring Place, Ga. by Roscoe Russell of Eton. AG 12/27/1907

TANNER, George Henry, Judge, age 53, d. 766 Peachtree St. Atlanta. AG 10/20/1909

TANNER, J. I., age 21, killed in railroad accident. Interred: Auburn, Ga. AG 5/29/1906

TANSLE, Alice, colored, age 47, d. 33 Maple St. Atlanta. AG 3/31/1908

TAPP, Maud, Miss, d. Mon. 139 Redford St. Atlanta. Interred: Hollywood. AG 8/21/1906

TAPP, Oliver, colored, age 29, d. 101 N. Butler St. Atlanta. AG 12/3/1907

TAPPAN, Ann, Mrs. d. White Plains, Ga. res. of son, age 74. Ch: Prof. Edward Tappan, Gibson, Ga.; John Tappan, Macon; G. R. Tappan, White Plains; C. A. Tappan, Atlanta. AG 9/21/1910

TARBUTTON, Herschel, Sandersville, Ga., the young man shot in duel with Mr. Tyre in Laurens Co. last week, died yesterday. Tarbutton owned considerable property in Washington and Johnston Co.'s. AG 11/13/1906

TARETON, Louise Frances, Mrs., age 32, d. 101 N. Butler St. Atlanta. AG 3/5/1907

TARRANT, A. L., age 6 yrs., died 114 State St. Atlanta. AG 12/28/1906

TARRANT, Sarah A. E., Mrs. d. Fri. Atlanta. Interred: Oakland. AG 1/15/1910

TARRANT, Sarah E. V., Mrs., age 79, d. Stockbridge, Ga. AG 1/19/1910

TARTER, Fannie, Mrs. of Madison Co., Ala., d. 9/22, res. of bro., E. T. Martin, Madison, Ala. Age 84. AG 9/22/1910

TATE, Glennes, infant dau. of Mr. and Mrs. W. H., d. Mon. 17 Glenn St., Atlanta. Interred: Wesley chapel church yard. AG 9/10/1907

TATE, Hauron, colored, age 23, d. 11 Flynn St. Atlanta. AG 9/28/1907

TATE, Jerry, colored, age 82, d. 9 State alley. Atlanta. AG 5/15/1907

TATE, July, colored, age 40, d. rear 163 Ellis St. Atlanta. AG 8/14/1907

TATE, Louise, colored, age 26, d. 9 Treyholm St. Atlanta. AG 2/8/1909

TATE, Oliva, colored, age 70, d. 32 N. Jackson St. Atlanta. AG 1/1/1908

TATE, Willis, age 60, d. 56 Tye St. Atlanta. Son: Walter Tate, Rome, Ga. AG 7/27/1907

TATE, A., colored, age 54, died 182 Ashby Street, Atlanta. AG 12/8/1906

TATUM, Clarence, colored, age 1, d. 252 Chestnut St. Atlanta. AG 3/3/1909

TATUM, P. S., age 47, d. Atlanta Sun. Interred: Abbeville, Ga. AG 4/18/1910

TATUM, Shepherd, colored, age 40, d. 10/27 29 Trayholm St. Atlanta. AG 10/28/1910

TAURMAN, Randolph, age 40, d. Milledgeville, Ga. AG 2/27/1907

TAYLOR, Augustus, age 40, of 360 Hill St., Atlanta, d. Thurs. Interred: Conyers, Ga. AG 4/22/1909

TAYLOR, B. W., Dr., Col. in Confed. Army, d. 12/27 Columbia, S. C., age 72. Grandfather was Colonel in Rev. War. AC 12/28/1905

TAYLOR, Belle, Miss, dau. of Mr. and Mrs. T. W., d. parents res. Fri., Amsterdam, Ga., age 19. Interred: Henderson, S. C. AG 4/20/1909

TAYLOR, Bruce, colored, age 44, d. 244 E. Cain St. Atlanta. AG 12/10/1908

TAYLOR, C. C., Mrs., age 83, wid. of late Dr. G. F., d. Thurs. res. of son-in-law, W. C. Fowler, 281 Rawson St. Atlanta. Interred: Opelika, Ala. AG 7/9/1908

TAYLOR, C. C., Mrs., mother of Mrs. R. C. Fowler, d. week of 7/10. AG 7/17/1908

TAYLOR, Catherine, Miss, age 23, d. 92 Luckie St. Atlanta. AG 9/2/1909

TAYLOR, Charles H., age 74, died at Charleston, S. C. AG 11/20/1906

TAYLOR, Charley, negro, d. Thurs. Dublin, Ga., on plantation of A. H. Adams from blow on head by Joe Deal, another negro, who escaped. AG 1/5/1907

TAYLOR, E. C., Mrs., age 48, d. Dallas, Ala. 5/11. AC 5/13/1905

TAYLOR, F. C., Mrs. of Waresboro d. Mon. Leaves two children, husband. AG 9/12/1906

TAYLOR, Fannie, colored, age 50, d. 154 E. Cain St. Atlanta. AG 9/30/1908

TAYLOR, Helen, colored, age 8, d. 345 1/2 Butler St. Atlanta. AG 12/14/1908

TAYLOR, infant son of Mr. and Mrs. J. H., d. Peachtree Park, Atlanta, Mon. Interred: Chamblee, Ga. AG 8/9/1910

TAYLOR, inf. son of Mr. and Mrs. W. M., d. 169 E. Georgia Ave, Atlanta. Interred: Conyers, Ga. AG 3/23/1908

TAYLOR, James Ernest, colored, age 7 mos. d. 232 Williams St. Atlanta. AG 3/22/1909

TAYLOR, John, colored, age 50, d. 101 N. Butler St. Atlanta. AG 3/15/1907

TAYLOR, John T., age 60, Atlanta res. 43 yrs., d. Thurs., age 60. Son: Virgil. Interred: Oakland. AG 1/28/1910

TAYLOR, Lee, Mrs., age 29, d. 69 Luckie St. Atlanta. AG 2/11/1907

TAYLOR, Leila A., Mrs. d. Fri. 59 Garden St. Atlanta. Interred: Hollywood. AG 4/16/1910

TAYLOR, M. R., age 65 (or 61), Confed. Veteran, d. Tues. Atlanta. Interred: Louisville, Ky. Daus: Mrs. Gilbert C. Smith, Louisville, Ky., Mrs. Will A. Crook, Chicago, Ill. AG 9/30/1908

TAYLOR, Mary, colored, age 37, d. 30 Glennwood Ave. Atlanta. AG 4/19/1907

TAYLOR, Nancy, colored, age 54, d. 111 Bradley Ave. Atlanta. AG 11/7/1907

TAYLOR, Oscar d. Hawkinsville. AG 12/9/1907

TAYLOR, Pearl, Miss, dau. of Mr. and Mrs. G. W., d. Blackshear, Ga. Sun. from burns, exploding lamp. AG 8/30/1910

TAYLOR, Ralph S. of Toccoa, Ga. d. 2/19, at res. of stepfather, Col. A. H. McAllister. AC 2/15/1905

TAYLOR, Robert, colored, age 18, d. Briceville, Ga. AG 5/8/1907

TAYLOR, Sallie, colored, age 26, d. 24 Jones alley. Atlanta. AG 8/14/1907

TAYLOR, Sallie, Mrs. d. Fri. 401 Central Ave. Atlanta. Interred: Miss. AG 5/24/1907

TAYLOR, Sarah J. b. Jasper, Ga. d. Graham, Tx. 12 ch. 9 live: Mrs. Lem Cagle, Talking Rck; Lula Cage; Laura Allred, Jasper; Mrs. W.B. Archer, Sharptop; Mrs. Chas Taylor, Rome; Mary Keeter, Florence Allred; Ophelia Mullinax, Tx. Interred: Atlanta. AG 1/29/1910

TAYLOR, Von, age 17, son of Mr. and Mrs. W. M., of Jackson, Ga., d. Mon. Interred: City Cemetery. AG 8/1/1910

TAYLOR, W. E. d. Tues. Atlanta. Family in Griffin, Ga. AG 10/11/1910

TAYLOR, William killed by street car Sat. Atlanta. Interred: Westview. AG 2/16/1910

TAYLOR, William, age 72, d. Copenhill Ave. Atlanta. AG 2/14/1910

TEAGINS, Susie, colored, age 30, d. 101 N. Butler St. Atlanta. AG 2/7/1908

TEAGUE, Floyd, age 18, d. Baltimore, Md. Father survives. Interred: Atlanta. AG 9/8/1909

TEAGUE, Julia, Miss, age 34, d. Fri. corner 14th and E. Fair St. Atlanta. Interred: Rock Springs, Ga. AG 5/10/1907

TEAGUE, R. H., Jr., age 22, son of Mr. and Mrs. R. H. of 35 Mesha St. d. Phoenix, Arizona Fri. AG 6/29/1908

TEAL, Carl, age 3, d. 3112 Angier Ave., rear. Atlanta. AG 7/22/1907

TEDDER, Walter, age 25, d. 61 DeKalb Ave. Atlanta. Interred: Peachtree Church. AG 8/31/1908

TEEPLE, J. W., furniture dealer in Savannah, d. Bull and Broughton Streets. AG 4/30/1907

TELAFAIR, Bertie May, died Grady Hospital,burns recd at her home, 36 Reinhardt St. AG 11/17/1906

TELFAIR, Little, colored, age 50, d. 12 Madison St. Atlanta. AG 10/23/1907

TELFAIR, Berta May, age 10, died Grady Hospital, Atlanta. AG 11/19/1906

TENNELL, Mary, Mrs., age 49, d. Atlanta. AG 9/9/1908

TENNENT, M. G., age 76, d. Atlanta Mon., res. of Marietta. Ch: Lt. Gilbert Tennent, US Marine, J. M., D. J., Charles, William; Mrs. J. T. Stansell. Interred: Marietta, Ga. AG 12/9/1907

TENNINBAUM, J. M., age 59, d. 267 Capitol Ave. Atlanta. AG 4/28/1908

TERESNELL, Clarence, age 18 mos., d. Mon., 550 Crew St., Atlanta. AG 7/31/1906

TERRELL, Jertie, colored, age 20, d. 9 Smith alley. Atlanta. AG 10/12/1909

TERRELL, Julia F., Mrs., age 84, d. Sun. res. of son-in-law, Corpl. John Fay, Ft. McPherson. Daus: Mrs. Fay; Mrs. Henry O'Hine, of Revenna, Ohio. Interred: Baptist Church yard. AG 5/16/1910

TERRELL, N., colored, age 21, d. rear 54 Greensferry Ave. Atlanta. AG 12/3/1907

TERRELL, Robert, colored, age 85, d. 187 Little St. Atlanta. AG 10/25/1909

TERRELL, Sallie, colored, age 70, d. 133 E. Baker St. Atlanta. AG 7/6/1909

TERRELL, Sallie B., Mrs., age 37, d. Fri. 33 Orange St. Atlanta. Husband, N. J., and one child survive. Interred: Westview. AG 6/1/1907

TERRELL, Susie, colored, age 29, d. 71 Clifton St. Atlanta. AG 7/20/1907

TERRELL, Washington, colored, age 41, d. 15 Johnson row. Atlanta. AG 8/11/1908

TERRETT, Corrine, colored, age 5 mos., d. 27 Mechanic St. Atlanta. AG 2/19/1907

TERRIE, E. L. C., Mrs., formerly of Atlanta, d. Pendleton, S. C. recently. Husband, one child. Mother: Mrs. Laura A. Steele. Four bros. of Atlanta. AG 7/6/1909

TERRY, F. A., Mrs. d. Tues. Interred: Westview. AG 7/25/1907

TERRY, Florence A., Mrs. of 364 Decatur St., Atlanta, d. Tues. AG 7/24/1907

TERRY, Jane Russell, Miss, age 58, d. 3/16 Summerville, Ga. Interred: New Haven, Conn. AC 3/23/1905

TERRY, Marshall, colored, age 75, d. Alms House. Atlanta. AG 11/30/1910

TERRY, Mary A., Mrs., age 45, d. 147 Kirkwood Ave. Atlanta. AG 3/4/1907

TERRY, Mary, Mrs. d. Greenville, S. C. Thurs., age 82. Bro: L. B. McCrary of Talbot Co. InterredL Ephesus Presbyterian Church yard. AG 1/17/1908

TERRY, Mildred, inf. dau. of Mr. and Mrs. T. J., d. Tues. 147 Kirkwood, Atlanta. Interred: Sylvester. AG 5/31/1906

TERRY, R. W., age 60, d. 408 Simpson St. Atlanta. Interred: Westview. AG 5/1/1907

THACKER, J. E., age 51, d. Fri. Wife: Dolah. Ch: Mrs. C. A. Lowe,

Roy, Irma; Loma Thacker. AG 12/18/1910

THACKER, Glennie, Miss, age 8, dau. of Mr. and Mrs. J. E., 440 E. Fair St., d. Tues. Interred: Westview. AG 2/2/1910

THAMES, Lester A., inf. son of Mr. and Mrs. P. L., d. Tues. 188 Davis St., Atlanta. Interred: Westview. AG 7/25/1907

THARPE, Fallie, Mrs. d. Macon 2/20, wife of R. A. Ch: L. A., R. A., Jr., Lester, Mrs. W. P. Barnes. AG 2/2/1910

THARP, J. D., Hon., age 78, of Kathleen, Ga., Houston Co., d. Wife, 5 ch: Mrs. J. B. Riley, Macon; Gus Tharp, Macon; Mrs. J. C. Solomon, Atlanta; Mrs. R. S. Henry, Chattanooga; Coalson Tharp, Kathleen. Interred: Perry, Ga. AG 2/26/1908

THATCHER, Hall, age 18, d. Atlanta Tues., 416 E. Georgia Ave. Interred: Westview. Son of Mr. and Mrs L. M. Thatcher. AG 10/6/1909

THATCHER, Hall, age 18, d. Atlanta Tues., 416 E. Georgia Ave. Interred: Westview. Son of Mr. and Mrs L. M. Thatcher. AG 10/6/1909

THATCHER, Harold, age 18, d. 92 Luckie St. Atlanta. AG 10/8/1909

THAXTON, Jackson, Mrs. d. Pepperton, Ga., Sun. Husband, several children. Interred: County Line Church Cemetery (near Jackson, Ga.) AG 8/9/1910

THEBAUT, Carrie V., Mrs., d. Mon. Atlanta, dau. of C. A. Simmons. Interred: Clarkston. AG 4/16/1907

THEISE, C. H., Kentucky man, suicide, 143 Deaborn Ave., Chicago, Ill. AG 5/10/1909

THEISLER, David E., age 1 yr., d. Howell Sta., Atlanta. AG 8/26/1907

THOECKER, Osin, colored, age 55, d. 206 Robbins St. Atlanta. AG 8/26/1908

THOMAS, Alexander, colored, age 35, d. 162 Bell St. Atlanta. AG 8/7/1908

THOMAS, Annie May, colored, age 4 mos., d. 54 Elizabeth St. Atlanta. AG 10/5/1908

THOMAS, Bessie, age 14 mos., d. Atlanta. AG 12/17/1909

THOMAS, Bud, Columbus, Ga. negro, sentenced to be hanged 1/10/1908 by Judge Martin. AG 11/29/1907

THOMAS, Bud, negro deck hand on steamer Bradley, fatally cut in fight with Frank Wade. Columbus, Ga. AG 8/14/1907

THOMAS, Charles, age 4, son of Mrs. C. C., d. Mon. 573 Edmon St., Atlanta. Funeral at Union Point. AG 10/18/1910

THOMAS, Clay, desperate negro who shot Policeman Anderson 12 yrs. ago, shot and killed today by Policeman Mark Riley and Bailiff J. D. Burson while defying arrest. AG 8/6/1906

THOMAS, Cosby, age 9 mos., son of Mr. and Mrs. W. E., d. Sat. 5 Bluff St., Atlanta. Interred: Canton, Ga. AG 8/6/1910

THOMAS, Dillie, colored, age 42, d. 101 N. Butler St. Atlanta. AG 7/9/1909

THOMAS, E. C., Mrs., wife of A. W., age 49, d. Atlanta Thurs. Interred: Westview. AG 11/29/1907

THOMAS, Edward Floyd, age 16, son of Colonel and Mrs. L. P. Thomas, d. Tues. at 43 W. North Ave., Atlanta. Interred: Oakland. AG 6/20/1907

THOMAS, Ernest, age 3 mos., d. 597 Marietta St. Atlanta. AG 4/27/1907

THOMAS, **Francina**, age 9, dau. of Mr. and Mrs. Frank, fell from tree 6/9. AC 6/10/1905

THOMAS, **Frank G., Mrs.** accidental burning death 7/7 of Sparta, Ga. Husband, 9 children. W. W. Thomas, eldest son. Bro: H. R. and Sidney Lewis. AG 7/8/1908

THOMAS, **Frazier**, age 1 mo., d. Simpton St. Atlanta. AG 8/3/1908

THOMAS, **George**, colored, age 75, d. 5 Rhodes St. Atlanta. AG 9/11/1907

THOMAS, **Gertrude**, Miss of Athens, dau. of late W. W. Thomas of Savannah, buried Athens. Sis: Mrs. Richard Johnston, Macon. AC 1/17/1905

THOMAS, **Gertrude**, Mrs., age 73, d. 54 E. Alexander St. Atlanta. AG 5/15/1907

THOMAS, **Gus**, age 60, d. 62 Fain St. Atlanta. AG 10/29/1907

THOMAS, **infant** of Lottie, colored, age 1, d. 139 E. Baker St. Atlanta. AG 12/17/1910

THOMAS, **Iona**, colored, age 25, d. rear 5 Bryan St. Atlanta. AG 9/2/1909

THOMAS, **Irene**, colored, age 25, d. 46 Johnson St. Atlanta. AG 9/22/1910

THOMAS, **J. A., Mrs.** d. Macon Sat. Interred: Riverside. AG 11/22/1910

THOMAS, **J. A., Mrs.** of Dublin, Ga., d. Macon Sat. Husband: Major J. A., of Dublin. Sons: Ansel, of S. C., J. A., Jr. of Macon, HJill G., of Dublin. Dau: Mrs. Chalres P. Bannon, Macon. Interred: Rose Hill. AG 11/21/1910

THOMAS, **J. B.**, Confed. Vet., d. 12/18 Atlanta. Interred: Westview. AC 12/19/1905

THOMAS, **James** of Pine Grove, Ga., Confed. Vet., d. 4/18, age 60. Wife, 5 children. AG 4/19/1910

THOMAS, **James**, age 18 d. Edgewood, Ga. Wed. Interred: Decatur, Ga. AG 11/6/1907

THOMAS, **Jane**, colored, age 72, d. 286 Wylie St. Atlanta. AG 3/12/1908

THOMAS, **Jim**, colored, age 27, d. 101 N. Butler St. Atlanta. AG 3/3/1908

THOMAS, **John S., Mrs.** of S. Boston, Va., d. Atlanta Tues. Body removed to res. of Mrs. T. J. Thomas, 482 Woodward Ave., Atlanta. Husband, one son, three bros., two sisters. AG 4/7/1909

THOMAS, **Joseph T.**, age 10 mos., d. Inman yards. Atlanta. AG 8/27/1909

THOMAS, **Lena**, colored, age 3, d. 4 Travis St. Atlanta. AG 9/8/1908

THOMAS, **Lester**, colored, age 18, d. 13 Bell St. Atlanta. AG 3/25/1907

THOMAS, **Lester A.**, age 3 mos., d. 188 Davis St. Atlanta. AG 7/26/1907

THOMAS, **Mabel**, colored, age 5 yrs, d. 199 McDaniel St. Atlanta. AG 1/16/1907

THOMAS, **Mack**, colored, age 87, d. 53 Courtland St. Atlanta. AG 11/27/1909

THOMAS, **Mary**, colored, age 30, d. Fulton Co. almshouse. AG 9/14/1908

THOMAS, **Mattie**, colored, age 19, d. 5 Royal St. Atlanta. AG 7/10/1908

THOMAS, Mildred, age 14, d. 29 Luckie St. Atlanta. AG 9/8/1909

THOMAS, N. B., age 45, d. yesterday 4th St., South Macon, Ga. Wife, three children, mother, bro., Dr. H. J. Thomas of Lizelle, Ga. Sisters: Mrs. J. H. Bullock, Mrs. J. Herring of Macon, and Mrs. J. J. Jones of Jones Co. AG 6/28/1907

THOMAS, Nathan, colored, age 25, d. 235 W. Hunter St. Atlanta. AG 10/25/1907

THOMAS, Nellie, colored, age 19, d. 12 Lyons Ave. Atlanta. AG 3/26/1908

THOMAS, Oscar, colored, age 26, d. 233 Mangum St. Atlanta. AG 12/9/1907

THOMAS, R. O. funeral at Bellvue, near Macon 9/4, age 61. Wife, 5 children. Interred: Bass Chapel Cemetery. AG 9/4/1909

THOMAS, Robert B., age 55, d. Thurs. Atlanta. Interred: Westview. Wife, one son, Joseph W. Thomas. Daus: Misses Alva, Vera, Thelma. AG 10/2/1908

THOMAS, Robert J., age 38, d. 318 N. Boulevard, Atlanta, Thurs. Mother, wife, and two children: Misses Mildred and Virginia. Interred: Westview. AG 4/1/1910

THOMAS, Squire, colored, age 70, d. 112 Haynes St. Atlanta. AG 3/22/1909

THOMAS, W. H., Mrs. d. Sat., 390 Woodward Ave. Atlanta. Husband, three sons: Elmore, Curtis, Hugh. Sis: Mrs. John F. Connally. Interred: Oakland. AG 10/6/1906

THOMAS, Will, age 22, d. 101 Fraser St. Atlanta. AG 1/16/1907

THOMAS, Will, colored, age 22, d. 101 N. Butler St. Atlanta. AG 6/3/1909

THOMAS, Willie Grace, age 1 yr., dau. of Mr. and Mrs. C. E., d. Plaster Rd., Atlanta, Fri. Interred: Tucker, Ga. AG 1/24/1908

THOMAS, Zepta, colored, age 80, d. Fulton Co. Alms House. AG 10/26/1907

THOMASON, A. A., age 88, d. Atlanta Tues. Daus: Mrs. S. C. Webb, Mrs. N. E. St. John. Sons: A. J., J. A. AG 4/12/1910

THOMASON, Hulda, Mrs. d. Fri. 282 W. Fifth St. Atlanta. Interred: Hollywood. AG 1/19/1907

THOMASON, infant of W. D., d. 16 Pelham St., Atlanta, Mon. Interred: Norcross, Ga. AG 10/2/1907

THOMASON, James A., inf. son of W. R., d. 408 Railroad St., Atlanta, Wed. Interred: Westview. AG 5/10/1906

THOMASON, Joseph R., infant, d. 428 Railroad St. Atlanta. AG 5/8/1906

THOMASON, Maurice, age one, d. Tues., son of Mr. and Mrs. C. A. Thomason, Peachtree Rd., Atlanta. Interment: Sandy Springs Church. AG 9/19/1906

THOMASON, R. d. Vineville, Ga., 33 Riverside. AC 8/25/1905

THOMASON, Rebecca A., Mrs., age 54, d. Simpson St., Atlanta, Thurs. Husband: J. C. Interred: Elliotts Cemetery. 10 children. AG 5/13/1910

THOMASON, Willie, age 2, d. 11 Welborn St. Atlanta. AG 6/11/1910

THOMPSON, Americus buried Winder, Ga. Fri., d. from pistol wound of his 13-yr. old son. Leaves 4-5 children, oldest being 13. His wife d. 1-2 yrs. ago. AG 12/16/1907

THOMPSON, Brooks, age 22, of Madison, Ga. d. Thurs. Atlanta. Wife. Mother: Mrs. L. M. Thompson, Atlanta. Interred: Madison, Ga. AG 6/10/1910

THOMPSON, Charles W., age 64, d. niece's res., Mrs. C. H. Stiegiltz, 267 Formwalt St., Atlanta, Wed. Sons: William S., of Etowah, Tenn., J. H. of Douglasville. AG 4/21/1909

THOMPSON, Elizabeth, Mrs., age 66, died 37 Hendrix Ave. Atlanta. AG 8/27/1906

THOMPSON, Ella, Mrs., age 40, died 167 1/2 Decatur St., Atlanta. Interment: Riverside. AG 12/21/1906

THOMPSON, Emma Livingston, age 44, d. 845 Peachtree St. Atlanta. AG 7/31/1908

THOMPSON, G. O., age 55, d. Mon. Atlanta. Interred: Norcross, Ga. AG 7/6/1910

THOMPSON, George I., age 25, d. 30 Crew St. Atlanta. Wife survives. Interred: McDonough, Ga. AG 2/26/1908

THOMPSON, Harry, formerly of Atlanta, removed 2 yrs. ago to St. Louis, interred: Atlanta, Westview Cemetery. Father: George E. AC 2/24/1905

THOMPSON, Helen, colored, age 3, d. 46 Kennesaw alley. Atlanta. AG 11/15/1907

THOMPSON, Henrie E., Miss, dau. of Mr. and Mrs. W. H., Decatur, Ga., age 17, d. Grady Hospital. Atlanta. Interred: Decatur, Ga. AG 8/29/1907

THOMPSON, infant of Mr. and Mrs. B. S., d. Sat. Atlanta. Interred: Buford, Ga. AG 6/4/1910

THOMPSON, J. H., Mrs., age 44, d. College Park, Ga. Thurs. Husband, one child, one sister, three bros. Interred: Opelika, Ala. AG 1/20/1910

THOMPSON, J. N., age 27, d. 143 Kirkwood Ave. Atlanta. Wife, one child. Parents: Mr. and Mrs. C. A. Thompson. Two bros., two sisters. Interred: Westview. AG 8/28/1909

THOMPSON, James Robert, age 26, d. Atlanta Tues. Father: A. J., 299 Crew St. Interred: Covington, Ga. AG 5/3/1910

THOMPSON, Jeannette Gail, inf. dau. of Mr. and Mrs. L. M., d. 235 Ira St., Atlanta, Thurs. Interred: Odessadale, Ga. AG 3/27/1908

THOMPSON, Julia, colored, age 59, d. 240 Williams St. Atlanta. AG 3/25/1907

THOMPSON, Mary, Mrs., wid. of late George Thompson, d. res. of son, W. H. Thompson. Interred: Oakland. AG 1/28/1908

THOMPSON, Mattie, Mrs., age 52, wife of A. ., of 57 Tye St. Atlanta, d. Mon. Interred: Gloster, Ga. AG 4/29/1908

THOMPSON, Mattie L., Mrs., age 41, d. 421 E. Fair St. Atlanta. AG 2/11/1909

THOMPSON, N. D., Mrs., age 63, d. 449 N. Boulevard. Atlanta. AG 1/21/1910

THOMPSON, Rebecca, 88, d. 21 Irwin St. Atlanta. Sons: David, Atlanta; Russell, Gainesville; John, Everett, Wash. Daus: Mrs. David G. Peel, Mrs. Jane Miller, Mrs. Carrie Meyers, Mrs. Garrett Meyers. 23 grch, 12 ggrch. Bur: Oakland. AG 11/24/1910

THOMPSON, Robert C., Mrs., age 35, 495 Crew St., Atlanta, pregnant, d. of fright as negroes killed. Two sons, age 10 and 7. Interred: Westview. AG 9/25/1906

THOMPSON, W. H., Mrs. d. Cataula, Ga. 4/27. Ch: J. W., Eugene, Mrs. John A. Lewis of Columbus, Ga. AC 4/28/1905

THOMPSON, W. W., age 77, d. 92 Luckie S. Atlanta Tues. Interred: Smithville, Ga. AG 9/9/1903

THOMPSON, Wiley, age 72, d. Atlanta. Interred: Westview. AG 12/30/1907

THOMPSON, Will bitten to death by large possom, Indian Springs, Ga. AG 10/18/1906

THOMPSON, William d. 72 Jett St. Atlanta, age 30. Wie, two children survive. Interred: Chamblee, Ga. AG 4/25/1906

THOMPSON, William, former tax receiver of Dalton, Ga., d. yesterday, aged abt 76. Wife, four daus, all married. AG 3/5/1908

THOMPSON, William, negro, killed by lightning near Walton Co. line. Mother, wife, children. AC 6/25/1905

THOMPSON, Z. T., age 61, d. 117 Cherokee Ave., Atlanta. AG 3/5/1908

THOMSON, William S., Mrs., wife of Col. W. S., d. Tues. 449 N. Boulevard, Atlanta. Interred: Oakland. AG 1/20/1910

THORNE, Mabel, colored, age 19, d. 244 N. Butler St. Atlanta. AG 11/30/1910

THORNTON, Albert E., age 54, d. 593 Peachtree St. Atlanta. AG 4/4/1907

THORNTON, C. N., age 21, d. Wesley Memorial Hospital. Atlanta. AG 11/20/1907

THORNTON, Clarke d. 23 Yorke Ave. Atlanta. Interred: Westview. AG 11/19/1907

THORNTON, Josephine, Mrs., age 46, d. 10/15 12 Tilton St. 4 daus. 3 sons. Interred: Athens, Ga. AC 10/16/1905

THORNTON, Julia, colored, age 74, d. 55 Delbridge St. Atlanta. AG 10/23/1907

THORNTON, M., age 42, died Atlanta. AG 11/26/1906

THORNTON, Marshall, age 2, son of Mrs. James Stacey Thornton, d. Middletown, Ohio, Wed. Formerly of Atlanta. AG 4/30/1908

THORNTON, Parker, colored, age 28, d. 101 N. Butler St. Atlanta. AG 3/25/1907

THORNTON, T. P., age 62, d. Atlanta. Interred: Chattanooga, Tenn. Four daus., one son, survive. AG 9/29/1908

THORNTON, William, colored, age 13, d. Minor, Ga. AG 3/28/1907

THRAILKILL, infant of Mr. and Mrs. Brent, d. Hapeville, Fri. Interred: Slack Rock church yard. AG 7/16/1909

THRASH, Lawson, age 15, son of Mr. and Mrs. Lawson Thrash of 636 Highland Ave., Atla<nta, d. Sat. Interred: Griffin. AG 9/5/1908

THRASH, Mary Dunn, Mrs., age 28, d. Smyrna, Ga. Mon. AG 8/10/1909

THRASHER, D. R., age 69, d. Sun. Marietta, Ga. Interred: Forest Park, Ga. AG 4/20/1908

THRASHER, Sophie, colored, age 58, d. 146 Garden St. Atlanta. AG 1/28/1908

THRASHER, T. B., age 35, d. 46 Buena Vista Ave. Atlanta. AG 10/11/1909

THRASH, Lawson, Jr.,, age 17, d. 636 Highland Ave. Atlanta. AG 9/8/1908

THRESHER, David E., inf. son of V. E., d. Thurs. Howell's Sta. Atlanta. AG 8/23/1907

THROWER, Eugene, former Atlanta, d. Opelika, Ala. Tues. Interred: Atlanta. AG 5/20/1908

THROWER, F. M., Mrs., age 61, d. Jacksonville, Fla. AG 2/19/1910

THROWER, Nolan O., age 35, d. Mon. 43 Orleans St. Atlanta. Interment: Oakland. AG 8/22/1906

THROWER, O. A., Mrs., age 65, d. Thurs. Jacksonville, Fla. Interred: Atlanta. AG 2/17/1910

THURMAN, Callie, Mrs., age 57, d. 640 S. Pryor St. Atlanta. AG 4/3/1908

THURMAN, Cornelius, Mrs. funeral Mon. 23 Pavillion Ave. Atlanta. Interred: Oakland. Husband, one dau., survive. AG 6/4/1906

THURMAN, Elizabeth T., age 46, d. Wesley Memorial Hospital. Atlanta. AG 8/9/1907

THURMAN, J. M. fell to death in Chattahoochee River. Wife. Ch: Miss Mamie Thurman; Mrs Z. D. Sharp. Mother: Mrs. James Banks. Interred: Westview. AC 5/1/1905

THURMAN, J. O., age 60, d. Atlanta. AG 2/7/1910

THURMAN, R. G. d. Mon. Smyrna, Ga. Interred: Family Cemetery, near Marietta, Ga. Wife, three daus: Misses Lilly, Bessie and Izzie. AG 10/5/1909

THURMAN, Robert W., sheriff of Dade Co., d. Sun. Chattanooga. Interred: Trenton, Ga. AG 5/18/1910

THURMAN, Rosa L.,ge 2 yrs., d. 32 Edwards St. Atlanta. AG 6/10/1907

THURMOND, Clinton, colored, age 44, d. 101 N. Butler St. Atlanta. AG 9/8/1908

THURMOND, W. T., Mrs. d. Sat. Atlanta. Interred: Westview. AG 10/19/1907

THWEATT, Ben d. 4/11 Barnesville, Ga. Interred: Ft. Valley, Ga. AC 4/13/1905

THWEATT, Ben, Mrs. d. 4/12 Barnesville, Ga. Interred: Baptist Cemetery. AC 4/13/1905

THWEATT, William B., age 55, d. Maitland, Fla. Was Forsyth, Ga. merchant. Leaves wife and children, bro., several sisters. AG 1/1/1907

TIBBS, Mary F., Mrs., age 63, widow of W. C. Tibbs, Atlanta, d. dau.'s res., Mrs. Dr. Jabez Jones, Thurs. Sons: S. T., W. C., Atlanta; T. E., Utoy, Ala. Dau: Mrs. Jones. Interred: Westview. AG 10/1/1909

TIBBS, William H., Col., age 92 on 6/10th, Confederate vet., managed farms in Whitfield and Murray Co.'s. Funeral Sat. AG 10/23/1906

TIBBS, Walter H., age 37, died at 35 Strong Street, Atlanta. AG 11/21/1906

TICKELL, Helen Louise, age 9 days, d. Columbus, Ga. Interred: Hollywood cemetery. AG 10/25/1907

TICKNOR, F. O., Mrs. d. Albany, Ga. Sat. Husband, dau., several bros., sisters. AG 1/3/1910

TIDMARSH, T. F. d. Atlanta Mon. Interred: Warm Springs, Ga. AG 10/30/1907

TIDMARSH, T. T. of Warm Springs, Ga. d. Mon. AG 10/29/1907

TIDWELL, Arthur Paul, age two, son of Mr. and Mrs. A. W., Broad St., Macon. Interred: Riverside Cemetery. AG 3/29/1909

TIDWELL, C. F., age 27, d. 475 Whitehall St. Atlanta. AG 11/3/1909

TIDWELL, Frank W., age 41, d. Tues. Rock Springs Rd., Atlanta. Interred: Macon, Ga. AG 5/11/1910

TIDWELL, R. M., age 64, d. 404 E. Fair St. Atlanta Tues. Interred: Villa Rica, Ga. AG 5/26/1908

TIGAS, Martha, colored, age 52, died at 52 Jeptha Street, Atlanta. AG 12/11/1906

TIGERT, Bishop J.. Memory Of Bishop of Methodist Episcopal Church. AG 12/11/1906

TIGNER, Charles O., age 50, d. 171 Decatur St. Atlanta. AG 8/12/1908

TIGNER, Ben F., Mrs. of White Sulphur Springs, Meriwether Co., d. 5/29. Interred: Fam. Ground at Ogletree home, near Stinson. Dau. of late Dr. J. F. Stinson, Meriwether Co. Ch: Dr. George S. and Hope, Atlanta; Dr. Edround at Ogletree home, near Stinson. Dau. of late Dr. J. F. Stinson, Meriwether Co. Ch: Dr. George S. and Hope, Atlanta; Dr. Ed, Milledgeville; Frank, TIGNER, Ben F., Mrs.....Columbus; Mrs. Dr. N. H. Boddie of Chipley; Misses Carrie and Julia, White Sulphur Springs. Attd funeral from Atlanta: Dr. George S. Tigner and wife; Mrs. C. H. Johnson; Mrs. H. C. Black; Miss Kate Neal. AC 5/30/1905

TILANDER, Mattie, Mrs., age 23, d. 12 Ponders Ave. Atlanta AG 9/21/1908

TILFORD, Mary Adaline, age 9 mos., d. 65 Bass St. Atlanta. AG 6/26/1908

TILLANDER, Della, Mrs., age 32, d. Atlanta Thurs. Mother: Mrs. Eliza Rice. Husband: G. A. 2 small children. Bros: R. M., J. M., and Joseph Bice. Sis: Mrs. William Robinson. AG 4/21/1910

TILLER, J. W., age 50, d. Fri. 706 N. Boulevard, Atlanta, Sat. Interred: Blakely, Ga. Wife, 5 sons, 4 daus, survive. AG 10/23/1909

TILLINGHAST, J. W., Capt. of Kirkwood, Ga. d. Ocean Springs, Ms. Wife, three sons: J. W. and J. H. of Kirkwood and J. H. of Mobile, Ala. Sis: Miss Hermia Tillinghast, Mrs. F. K. Aram, of Kirkwood. Interred: Ocean Springs, Ms. AG 10/8/1909

TILLMAN, William M. T., age 61, d. res. of son, W. H. Tillman, 4 Ponders Ave., Atlanta. Daus: Miss Ora Tillman, Montgomery, Ala.; Miss Rena Tillman, Americus, Ga. Interred: Americus, Ga. AG 3/12/1907

TILLY, Ross, negro, killed by J. M. Parks 5/15. Parks exonerated. AC 5/16/1905

TILSON, W. P., Mrs. d. 294 Hunter St. Funeral: Thurs. Atlanta. Interred: Greenwood. AG 10/13/1910

TIMA, Michael, colored, age 71, d. East Point, Ga. AG 9/2/1909

TIMMERMAN, M. B., age 61, d. Old Soldiers' Home, Atlanta. AG 10/20/1909

TIMMONS, Dalton H., age 10 mos., son of Mrs. N. H. Timmons of Anniston, Ala. d. Atlanta while attending funeral of her sister, Bessie Jaillette. Interred: Fairburn. AG 7/30/1906

TINSLEY, T. W., Mrs. d. Fri. Atlanta. Interred: Cartersville, Ga. AG 6/25/1910

TIPPIN, Mary Jane, Mrs., age 72, d. 216 South Ave. Atlanta, Wed. Sons: J. E., W. E. Dau: Mrs. G. D. Huey. Interred: Woodstock, Ga. AG 8/1/1910

TOBIN, P. T., age 9 mos., d. 9 Iswald St. Atlanta. AG 6/21/1906

TODD, Freddie, Miss, age 22, d. res. of parents, Mr. and Mrs. J. P., 10 Todd St., Atlanta, Tues. Bro: Thomas. Interred: Chamblee. AG 6/16/1909

TODD, Henry E., age 20, d. Hapeville, Ga. Wed. Parents: Mr. and Mrs. Robert Todd. 3 bros., 3 sister. Interred: South Bend Church yard. AG 7/28/1910

TODD, R. L. d. Columbus, Ga. 3/24. Interred: Columbus, Ga. AG 3/25/1908

TODES, inf. dau. of B., d. LaGrange, Ga. Interred: Atlanta, Oakland Cemetery. AG 12/12/1910

TOEPEL, Helen M., dau. of Dr. and Mrs. C. O., age 11 mos., d. 186 Park Ave. Atlanta. Interred: Westview. AG 10/14/1907

TOLAND, A. P., age 87, Confederate Veteran, ex-deputy sheriff, d. College St., Hapeville, Ga. Thurs. Wife. Son: L. J. Dau: Miss Nannie Toland. AG 6/11/1909

TOLBERT, Annie, colored, age 38, d. 209 Mangum St. Atlanta. AG 5/24/1910

TOLBERT, B. J., Rome, Ga., 11/29/1906. Tolbert, age 65, died N. Rome. Survivors: Wife, several children. Interment: North Rome Cemetery. AG 11/29/1906

TOLBERT, Elba, Miss, age 24, d. 169 Mills St., Atlanta, Fri., dau. of Mr. and Mrs. J. T. Sisters: Mrs. L. H. Zurline; Mrs. L. Stutz. Bro: T. W. Tolbert. Interred: Villa Rica, Ga. AG 9/10/1909

TOLBERT, Ludie, Miss, age 18, dau. of Mr. and Mrs. H. T., d. parents res. near Sharon Church, Atlanta Mon. Interred: Sharon church yard. AG 4/20/1909

TOLBERT, M. M., Mrs., age 73, d. 87 Luckie St. Atlanta. AG 3/7/1907

TOLBERT, M. S., Mrs., age 64, d. Boulevard and Woodward Ave. Atlanta. AG 2/13/1908

TOLBERT, Mark L., young attorney, d. Sat. Atlanta. AG 1/26/1907

TOLBERT, Mark S., age 23, d. 29 Luckie St. Atlanta. AG 1/18/1907

TOLEN, Anderson, colored, age 19, d. 19 Lee St. Atlanta. AG 9/26/1910

TOLERSON, Ida, Miss, age 19, d. Wesley Chapel, Atlanta, Thurs. Parents: Mr. and Mrs. W. H. Tolerson. Interred: Family Cemetery. AG 7/10/1908

TOLHURST, Marie, age 1, d. 469 W. Hunter St. Atlanta. AG 12/30/1910

TOLLENT, Edna, inf. dau. of Mr. and Mrs. R. R., d. Sun. 54 Glenn St., Atlanta. Interred: Westview. AG 7/22/1907

TOLLISON, Vinie, Mrs., b. Cobb Co.-d. 1/19, age 92, dau.'s res., Mrs. Lizzie Willis, Douglasville. Son: Jeff D., Atlanta. Daus: Mrs. Sussie Profitt, Vinings. Sis: Mrs. Rebecca Whitley, Atlanta; Mrs. Cage, Sandy Spgs. AG 1/21/1910

TOM, Lee, Chinese, age 46, d. 59 E. Hunter St. Atlanta. Atlanta. AG 9/2/1909

TOMBS, Mamie, colored, age 20, d. 24 Jones alley. Atlanta. AG 4/4/1907

TOMLIN, Lula, Mrs., age 31, d. 348 Howell Mill Rd. Atlanta. AG 2/8/1909

TOMLINSON, Hugh, age 78, d. 194 Smith Ave. Atlanta. AG 12/17/1910

TOMLINSON, M. E., Mrs. d. Sat. Atlanta. Sis: J. E. Stallings, grocer in W. Peachtree St. She d. his res. Rallings St. Interred: Valdosta, Ga. AG 10/8/1907

TOMLINSON, M. E., Mrs., age 32, d. 30 Crew St. Atlanta. AG 10/8/1907

TOMLINSON, W. M., Mrs., age 63, d. yesterday, Macon. Daus: Mrs. J. W. Owens, Mrs. B. A. Goosby of Macon. Interred: Ft. Hill. AG 5/10/1907

TOMPKINS, Addie, colored, age 38, d. 6 Chestnut Ave. Atlanta. AG 9/14/1908

TONALL, Leroy, colored, age 49, d. 167 Beckwith St. Atlanta. AG 2/26/1908

TONEY, Ernest, age 16 mos., son of Mr. and Mrs. J. L., d. 84 W. Georgia Ave., Atlanta, Sun. Interred: Forest Park Cemetery. AG 12/5/1910

TONEY, J. M., age 70, d. Fri. Forest Park, Ga. Interred: Forest Church yard. AG 6/25/1910

TONEY, Marion, age 1, d. 5 Guyton St. Atlanta. AG 10/13/1908

TONTASS, H., age 60, d. 60 Conally St. Atlanta. AG 7/14/1910

TOOKES, James, colored, age 28, d. Atlanta. AG 5/24/1906

TOON, V. R., age 24, d. Atlanta. Father: res. of Whiteville, N. C. AG 2/14/1910

TORBERT, Edward, little son of Mr. and Mrs. Grover, buried Greensboro, Ga. 10/27. Aged abt 2 yrs. AG 10/28/1910

TORBETT, Callie Barrow, age 22, d. 269 Courtland St. Atlanta. AG 4/6/1907

TORRENCE, Arthur A., age 38, d. 31 Markham St., Atlanta, Tues. Interred: Hollywood cemetery. AG 12/18/1907

TORRENCE, Kate, Mrs., age 55, d. 26 W. Peachtree St. Atlanta. AG 6/22/1910

TORRENCE, Stephen James, d. St. Peters Hospital, Charlotte, N. C. yesterday. Bros: Walter H., Charles L. AG 7/28/1906

TORRENCE, Kate C., d. 62 W. Peachtree St. Atlanta, wid. of John E., dau. of late Wm W. Clayton. Sons: Wm C., Richmond, Va.; John E. & Paul S., Atlanta. Sis: Mrs. Sarah C. Crane. Bros: Smith & Thomas A. Clayton. Bur: Oakland. AG 6/20/1910

TORVISH, infant dau. of Mr. and Mrs. C., d. Tues. 176 Echo St., Atlanta. Interred: Westview. AG 5/13/1907

TOWERS, Chatham M., d. Washington, Ga. 6/21. AG 6/22/1908

TOWNLEY, J. J. d. Wed. dau.'s res., Mrs. J. A. Robinson, 162 Park Ave., Atlanta. Daus: Mrs. Robinson, Mrs. C. M. Boggs, Mrs. E. L. Boggs. Son: J. W. Townley. Interred: Lawrenceville, Ga. AG 9/22/1910

TOWNLEY, William F., age 9 mos., d. home of grandparents, Mr. and Mrs. B. F. Roberts, Ben Hill, Ga., Mon. Interred: Wesley Chapel grave yard. AG 5/21/1906

TOWNS, Eliza, Mrs., age 80, d. Atlanta Wed. Son: V. C. Interred: North Side Park, Ga. AG 5/31/1910

TOWNSEND, Elizabeth, Mrs., age 85, d. Tues. 44 Emmett St., Atlanta. Dau: Mrs. S. F. Tolan. Interred: Conyers, Ga. AG 10/18/1910

TOWNSEND, M. A., Mrs. of Tifton, age 84, d. Sun. AG 3/1/1910

TOWNSEND, Robert, age 6 yrs., son of Mr. and Mrs. Robert of 237 Luckie St., Atlanta, d. Sat. AG 3/13/1909

TOWNSLEY, L. S. of Perry, Ga. d. Fri. Wife, two sons: S. S. Townsley, Atlanta and S. S. Townsley, Atlanta, and L. S. Townsley, Jr., Perry, Ga. Interred: Perry. AG 7/31/1908

TOWNSLEY, William S. funeral Tues. Atlanta. Interred: Wesley Chapel grave yard. AG 5/21/1906

TOY, A. G. of Norwood, Ga. d. 2/1. Interred: Camak. AC 2/4/1905

TOY, Mary Bockover, Mrs., age 55, wife of Robert B., d. 401 Ponce de Leon Ave., Atlanta, Fri. AG 1/29/1910

TRABER, Sarah, Mrs., age 30, d. 60 King St. Atlanta. AG 7/1/1907

TRAMMEL, Marguerite, inf. dau. of Mr. and Mrs. J. D., d. Atlanta Sat. AG 5/6/1907

TRAMMELL, D. B., Mrs., age 21, died 116 E. Twelfth St. Atlanta. AG 11/19/1906

TRAMMELL, Mamie Wise, Mrs., age 22, d. 104 Venable St. Atlanta, Thurs. AG 4/17/1907

TRAMMELL, W., Hon., age 90, d. res. of son-in-law, B. R. Blakely, Griffin. Ch: Mrs. B. R. Blakely, Mrs. Charles Beeks, Mrs. J. W. McWilliams, Walter Trammell, of Okla. Interred: Atlanta, Oakland Cem. AG 2/28/1910

TRAPNELL, B. A., Mrs. of Swainesboro d. 8/14 Bulloch Co., youngest dau. of Hon. and Mrs. Jerry J. Coleman of Graymont. Sis, bros: Dr. E. T., Wallace, Fred, Lowis, Walter of Bainbridge; G. H., Swainesboro; Mrs. W. C. Burton, Adrain; Mrs. Dennis Durden; Mrs. Robert Walsh, Graymont. Interred: Lake Church near Metter, Bulloch Co. AC 8/18/1905

TRAVIS, Dora, age 37, d. rear of 109 Woodward Ave., Atlanta. AG 5/26/1906

TRAVIS, Fred E., age 31, d. 702 Glenn St. Atlanta. AG 12/14/1909

TRAVIS, John d. Macon, Ga. 12/11. Interred: St. Josephs Cemetery. AG 12/12/1910

TRAVIS, John B. of Macon d. 12/10, sister's res., Mrs. Ed Cassidy, Oak St., age 58. Born in Ireland, to America as young man. 2 sisters in Phila. One bro. in Ireland. AG 12/10/1910

TRAVIS, D. W., Mrs. of Gainesville, Fla. d. res. of sil, Frank D. Milstead, Kirkwood, Ga., Sat., dau. of Mr. & Mrs. N. B. Phillips. Sisters: Mrs. C. B. Wilmer and Mrs. L. R. Woods, Tampa, Fla. Interred: Gainesville, Ga. AG 1/13/1908

TRAWICK, M. T. d. Opelika, Ala., age 58. Widow. 3 ch: Rev. Henry, Birmingham; L. M.; Ophelia; Mrs. Sam Trawick, N. Y. AC 4/23/1905

TRAYNOR, Maud, Miss, age 26, d. 55 Johnson Ave. Interred: Fish, Ga. AG 7/12/1909

TREADWAY, James L. suicide Tues. Columbus, Ga. AG 11/5/1910

TREADWELL, Hardey. Covington, Ga., near Oxford, d. age 65. Graduated Emory College before civil war; taught school. 3 ch: Will and Forrest Treadwell, Columbus, Ga.; Miss Mae Treadwell, missionary to Brazil. AG 12/18/1906

TRENT, Oregon Saine, Mrs., age 26, d. 110 Ivy St., Atlanta, Sat. Sis: Miss Julia Saine. Interred: Westview. AG 10/23/1909

TRIBBLE, Clark A., age 2 mos., d. Lakewood Heights. Atlanta. AG 12/29/1908

TRIBBLE, John, age 6 mos., d. 2 D'Alvigny St. Atlanta. AG 5/12/1909

TRIBBLE, S. J., Mrs., age 67, d. 21 English Ave. Atlanta. AG 2/20/1909

TRIBBLE, Sarah F., Mrs., age 79, d. bro.'s res., Dr. J. M. Bosworth, 23 E. Georgia Ave., Atlanta, Sun. Interred: Oakland. Bro., only relative. AG 5/3/1909

TRIMBLE, Mary J., colored, age 1, d. 184 Cooper St. Atlanta. AG 7/14/1908

TRIPP, Kate, Miss, age 18, d. Greenwood Sta. Atlanta. AG 2/8/1909

TRIPP, W. H., livery stable man, horse trader, killed Cordele 12/23 by W. P. Kendall, policeman. AG 12/23/1909
TRIPPE, David, colored, age 11, d. 432 Crumley St. Atlanta. AG 6/18/1909
TRIPPE, R. J., age 47, d. 267 Capitol Ave. Atlanta. AG 2/11/1909
TROMBLAY, Louise, Mrs.,ge 68, d. Atlanta. AG 6/11/1910
TROPP, Fannie, age 18, d. from attack. AG 5/8/1906
TROPP, Hyman, age 6, son of A. Tropp of 46 Armstrong St., Atlanta, beaten by playmates, d. Tues. AG 5/8/1906
TROUP, Glenn, 9 mos., d. Wed., 6 Rhinehart St., Atlanta. Interred: Hollywood. AG 8/2/1906
TROUT, Elizabeth, Mrs., age 62, d. Mon. 78 Capitol Ave. Atlanta. Daus: Mrs. A. Brooks, Douglas, Ga.; Mrs. W. J. Jones; Mrs. J. E. Johnson; Mrs. W. Swinford. Sons: C. E., W. H., E. C., J. C., W. C. Interred: Westview. AG 6/13/1910
TROUTMAN, J. F., Col. d. Ft. Valley, Ga. 9/12, age 83. Wife. 3 ch: J. F., Jr., J. H. of N. Y.; Miss Dedie Troutman, Atlanta. Confed. Vet. AC 9/14/1905
TROWBRIDGE, H. F. funeral 11/19 Atlanta. Interred: Westview. AC 11/19/1905
TROWBRIDGE, John, Mrs., former res. of Atlanta, d. Watertown res. of sister, Mrs. S. P. Judson. Sister: Mrs. J. C. Peek, Atlanta. AG 11/8/1907
TRUELOW, Ira d. Alburquerque, N. M. last Wed. Bro: A. R. Truslow, formerly of Atlanta, now Jacksonville, FL. AG 6/25/1907
TRUITT, Alice M., colored, age 12, d. Fulton Co. Alms House. AG 8/11/1908
TRUITT, Bessie May, colored, age 1, d. 4 Middlebrooks row. Atlanta. AG 5/11/1908
TUBBESING, Frank, native of Germany, age 68, d. Sat. res. of Mrs. J. T. Wynn, 482 Houston St., Atlanta. Interred: Natl Cemetery, Marietta. AG 6/25/1907
TUCK, Bobbie, age 7 mos., son of Mr. and Mrs. Z. T. Tuck, died at home, 49 Kirkwood Ave., Atlanta. Interment: Lawrenceville AG 12/8/1906
TUCK, Eliza, colored, age 46, d. 47 Byman St. Atlanta. AG 10/30/1908
TUCKER, A. E., Mrs., wife of pres. of Chattanooga Paint Co., d. 4/20 Chattanooga, Tenn. AG 4/21/1909
TUCKER, A. S., Dr. of 438 Pulliam St., Atlanta, physician, d. Fri. Grady Hospital. Wife and several children survive. Interred: Conyers. AG 1/11/1907
TUCKER, Annie Farren, Mrs., age 60, d. 46 E. Mitchell St. Atlanta. AG 11/3/1909
TUCKER, Eliza, colored, age 7 yrs., d. rear 146 E. Ellis St. Atlanta. AG 5/1/1908
TUCKER, Henry. Macon, Ga., 12/1/1906. Officer of U. S. Dist Court in Macon, died as result of train crash. AG 12/1/1906
TUCKER, Lula, Mrs., age 41, d. 13 Kirkwood Ave., Atlanta, Thurs. Interred: Blackston, Ga. AG 6/8/1906
TUCKER, R. P., age 65, d. Wed. 158 Plum St. Atlanta. Wife, 7 ch. Daus: Lizzie, Clyde. Sons: Gus, Guy, Earl, Walter, Carl. Interred: Crawford, Ga. AG 9/1/1910
TUCKER, Richard killed in Macon 4/9 by Clifford Kemp, negroes. AC 4/11/1905

TUGGLE, Charles S., infant son of Mr. and Mrs. E. M., d. Tues., 31 Meldrim St., Atlanta. Interred: Buford, Ga. AG 5/28/1907

TUGGLE, Frances Adelaide, inf. dau. of Mr. and Mrs. W. B., d. Macon Sat. Interred: Atlanta, Oakland Cemetery. AG 6/29/1909

TUGGLE, Frank Logan, Jr., inf. son o f Mr. and Mrs. F. L., d. 92 Woodson St. Atlanta Tues. Interred: Stone Mtn, Ga. AG 5/26/1908

TUGGLE, Lodwic A., age 18, d. 22 Hammond St., Atlanta Wed. Parents: Mr. and Mrs. J. T. Tuggle. AG 8/19/1908

TUGGLE, Milton B., Rev., age 63, d. Atlanta. AG 1/12/1910

TUGGLE, Minnie, Miss, age 28, dau. of Mrs. L. G., d. Sat. Decatur, Ga. Interred: Clarkston. Mother, two sisters, Miss Aurie and Miss Gertrude Tuggle; three bros., Ben, John and Lucius Tuggle. AG 5/18/1907

TUKES, Charlie, alias Brown, negro tried for murder of Frank Kelley, negro, on C. C. Greer farm, Cordele, Ga., sentenced to hang 8/27. AG 7/24/1907

TUMLIN, George Wingfield, age 2, son of Mr. and Mrs. G. W., d. 179 Oglethorpe Ave., Atlanta, Mon. Interred: Westview. AG 8/4/1908

TUMLIN, J. M., Mrs. of Hogansville, Ga., d. Macon Tues. Husband, 3 daus., 2 bros. survive. Interred: Westview. AG 5/20/1910

TUMLIN, Lester, age 1, d. 189 Cherokee Ave. Atlanta. AG 5/4/1907

TUMLIN, Mary A., Mrs., age 68, d. Atlanta Sat. Interred: Sardis church yard. AG 5/30/1910

TUMLIN, Sam, colored, age 81, d. 63 Lindsay St. Atlanta. AG 10/30/1908

TUMLIN, W. H., age 3, d. 331 N. Jackson St. Atlanta. AG 12/24/1907

TUMLIN, Willie Haynes, age 3, son of Mr. and Mrs. J. C., d. 331 N. Jackson St., Atlanta. AG 12/23/1907

TUPPER, Deas Frost, Mrs., age 47, d. Philadelphia, Pa. Husband, 7 children, 3 bros., 4 sisters. Interred: Westview. AG 4/26/1907

TURK, R. M., age 79, d. Delwood Ave., Atlanta, Wed. Sis: Mrs. L. Elliott, Atlanta; Mrs. Kate Riggs, Chattanooga, Tenn. Interred: Elliotts Cemetery. AG 7/7/1909

TURK, T. W., pioneer to Milledgeville, d. Mon. Leaves wife. No children. Interred: Baptist Church Cemetery. AG 9/3/1907

TURLEY, Julia Tate d. Tues., dau. of late John A. Turley of Athens, Tenn. AG 4/7/1910

TURLINGTON, Henry E., age 26, d. 7/4th while swimming, Tampa, Fla. Res. of 45 1/2 Peachtree St. Wife, parents, 8 bros. and sisters of Atlanta. Interred: Hollywood. Atlanta. AG 11/1/1910

TURMAN, Q. E. d. Live Oak, Fla. 8/25/1907. Friends in Atlanta. AG 9/2/1907

TURNELL, J. T., age 67, d. Madison, Ga. 10/25. AG 10/27/1910

TURNELL, Mattie, Miss of Madison, Ga., d. Petersburg, FLA. 1/22. Interred: Madison, Ga. AC 1/23/1905

TURNER, A. Q. Mrs., wife of chief of police, d. Greensferry Rd., Atlanta, Sun. Interred: Westview. AG 6/25/1906

TURNER, Alice E., age 10, d. Fri. Macon. Interred: Riverside Cemetery, Macon. Bro: Harry Turner. Parents: Mr. and Mrs. J. L. Turner. AG 9/19/1908

TURNER, Allen, age 21, d. Atlanta Wed. Bro: I. J. Turner, Atlanta. Interred: Dallas, Ga. AG 6/4/1908

TURNER, Annie Margore, age 14 mos., dau. of Mr. and Mrs. A. F. of Tampa, Fla., d. 3/27 res. of J. A. Fulcher. Interred: Tampa, Fla. AG 8/28/1909

TURNER, Belle, Mrs., age 50, d. 46 Hightower St. Atlanta. AG 2/26/1908

TURNER, Belle, Mrs., age 50, d. son's res., I. F. Turner, 23 Ponders Ave., Atlanta, Sat. AG 2/20/1908

TURNER, C. W., age 41, d. W. Linden St. Atlanta. AG 12/28/1910

TURNER, Edgar, colored, age 35, d. Milledgeville, Ga. AG 4/13/1909

TURNER, Elizabeth, inf. dau. of Mr. and Mrs. J. L., d. Thurs. 385 Cherokee Ave., Atlanta. Interred: Westview. AG 5/14/1908

TURNER, Elsie, inf. dau. of Mr. and Mrs. A. W., d. 18 Exposition Ave., Atlanta. AG 5/17/1910

TURNER, Florence, age 1, dau. of Mr. and Mrs. Charles R., d. 28 Morgan St., Atlanta, Sat. Interred: Pleasant Grove Church. AG 9/5/1908

TURNER, Hose killed Commerce, Ga. Sat. night by J. J. Pace, deputy, who was acquitted of murder. AG 5/8/1907

TURNER, Ida Elizabeth, age 2, dau. of Mr. and Mrs. J. L., d. 385 Cherokee Ave. Atlanta Thurs. Interred: Westview. AG 5/15/1908

TURNER, infant of Mr. and Mrs. C. C., d. 20 Pope St., Atlanta, Fri. AG 6/10/1910

TURNER, J. A., age 83, Confederate Veteran, d. Thurs. Son: J. W. Dau: Mrs. M. O. Head. AG 10/23/1908

TURNER, J. B. d. Fri. 139 Nelson St. Atlanta. Leaves wife, two children. Interred: Westview. AG 7/6/1907

TURNER, J. B., age 36, d. 69 Luckie St. Atlanta. AG 7/6/1907

TURNER, J. D., Dr., age 70, d. Tues. 925 Peachtree St., Atlanta. Interred: Oakland. AG 7/17/1909

TURNER, J. W., Rev. d. Fitzgerald, Ga. 3/25. AG 3/25/1908

TURNER, James B. d. Atlanta 4/5. Wife. Parents: Mr. and Mrs. Thomas Turner of N. Y. Bro: Thomas, Jr. of N. Y. Sis: Mrs. Sam Carter, N. Y. C. Interred: Atlanta, Oakland Cemetery. AG 4/6/1909

TURNER, James B. d. Mon. 70 E. Baker St., Atlanta, Wed. Body temporarily placed in receiving vault at Oakland Cemetery pending shipment to N. Y. for interment. AG 4/7/1909

TURNER, James B., age 33, d. 94 Courtland St. Atlanta. AG 5/4/1909

TURNER, Jennie Louise, age 4 yrs, dau. of Mr. and Mrs. L. S. Turner, d. Sat., 56 McDonough St. Atlanta. Interred: Westview. AG 8/11/1906

TURNER, Mabel, colored, age 22, d. Milledgeville, Ga. AG 10/25/1909

TURNER, Mary Ella, colored, age 19, d. rear 526 North Piedmont St. Atlanta. AG 9/21/1909

TURNER, May, age 1 yr., d. 133 Oakland Ave. Atlanta. AG 10/18/1906

TURNER, M. L. T., age 41, d. Atlanta. AG 4/1/1908

TURNER, Naby, colored, age 17, d. 18 Fort St. Atlanta. AG 12/10/1910

TURNER, Pearl, Miss, age 14, dau. of Mr. and Mrs. J. C., d. Wed. 76 W. Peachtree Pl. Atlanta. AG 9/1/1910

TURNER, S. F., Rev. d. Americus, Ga., age 28. AC 7/14/1905

TURNER, S. M., age 49, d. 93 Stonewall St. Atlanta. AG 3/27/1908

TURNER, Sallie, colored, age 7, d. Bell St. Atlanta. AG 2/13/1908
TURNER, Virgie T., age 33, d. College Park Sat. Interred: College Park, Ga. AG 9/21/1907
TURNER, W. W., Mrs. d. Sat. Athens, dau. of late Dr. Charles W. Lane of Athens. Sis: Miss Louie Lane. 3 sons. AG 7/11/1910
TURNER, William, age 82, funeral Sat. Interred: Westview. Died Old Soldiers' Home, Atlanta. AG 3/26/1910
TURNER, William L. d. St. Louis Sat. Interred: Oakland cemetery, Atlanta. AG 3/14/1907
TURNER, Willie T., Mrs., age 40, d. 144 Wylie St., Atlanta, Wed, wife of H. M. Mother, father, one son. Interred: Mt. Zion Church yard. AG 12/2/1909
TURNIPSEED, Edna, infant dau. of Mr. and Mrs. H. F., d. Mon. 52 Columbia Ave. Atlanta. Interred: Sardis Church. AG 8/14/1906
TURPIN, C. W., Mrs., age 20, d. 101 N. Butler St. Atlanta. AG 10/2/1907
TURPIN, Mirta (Myrta), Mrs., age 18, dau. of Mr. and Mrs. C. W., (another notice says, wife of C. W.), d. Grady Hospital, Atlanta, Mon. Interred: Westview. AG 9/28/1907
TURPIN, W. H., age 66, d. 431 Leggetts Ave. Atlanta. AG 8/22/1910
TURRENTINE, Carrie, Miss d. Ensley, Ala. Sun. Interred: Forest cemetery, Atlanta. AG 10/30/1906
TUTWILER, N. P. funeral Sun. Atlanta. Interred: Oakland. Wife. Daus: Misses Lillian, Grace and Sadie. AG 6/4/1910
TWEEDY, Ordis, age 3, dau. of Mrs. Carrie Belle, d. E. Point, Thurs. Interred: College Park. AG 1/7/1910
TWEEDY, Thelma G., inf. dau. of Mr. and Mrs. R. A., d. 767 Ashby St., Atlanta. Interred: Hollywood. AG 10/19/1907
TWEEDY, W. T. N. of 60 W. Georgia Ave., Atlanta. Interred: College Park, Ga. AG 2/6/1908
TWILLEY, Mary, age 2 yrs., dau. of Mr. and Mrs. Ed Twilley, d. yesterday. AG 3/25/1907
TWILLEY, Mary, age 32, of 153 Central Ave., Atlanta, d. Tues. Husband: C. P. Parents, 4 bros., survive. Interred: Knoxville, Tenn. AG 7/27/1909
TWITTY, Curtis killed by John Tucker Dorsey, who surrendered to Sheriff Crow, Gainesville. AG 5/4/1906
TWITTY, Mary, Mrs., old age, and son, James, d. Jan. 30, laid away together, Americus, Ga. Son: Late Rev. Peter Twitty of S. Ga. Conference. AC 2/1/1905
TYE, Drury E., Sr., 70, Atlanta pioneer, d. 141 Whitehall St. Born Barboursville, Ky., Knox Co. Confed. Vet. He md. Miriam Sparks, Barboursville (d. 12 yrs. ago). Bro: Dep. Sheriff Joshua Tye. Nephew: Drury Tye, Jr. Bur: Oakland. AG 2/25/1908
TYNER, Mary, Mrs., wid. of late Martin V., d. dau's res., Mrs. Henry Hataway, S. Macon. Interred: Hillsboro. AG 8/30/1908
TYSON, Florence, Mrs., age 54, d. S. Moreland Ave. Atlanta. AG 12/9/1910
TYSON, Lain, S., Mrs., age 38, d. 69 Luckie St. Atlanta. AG 2/12/1907
TYSON, Lula, Mrs. d. Tues. Interred: Villa Rica. AG 2/12/1907
TYSON, Pressia, Mrs., age 32, d. Tues. 153 Central Ave., Atlanta. Husband: C. P. Parents, 4 bros. Bur: Knoxville, TN. AG 7/27/1909
TYUS, D. W., Sheriff, of Grady Co. d. from pistol shot wounds inflicted Mon. by negro, Charley Williams. AG 8/23/1907

UFFORD, Jane, colored, age 65, d. 184 Houston St. Atlanta. AG 12/3/1908
UHL, John of Augusta, Ga., age 78, d. 7/19. AC 7/21/1905
ULMAN, G. H., traveling man of Zanesville, Ohio, found dead in bed at Piedmont Hotel, Atlanta, Tues. Interred: Zanesville, Ohio. AG 5/31/1910
UNDERWOOD, Henry M., age 74, 246 Edgewood Ave., Atlanta. AG 11/9/1906
UNDERWOOD, Cora, Miss, age 25, d. Sun. Edgar, Ga. Parents: Mr. and Mrs. W. B. Underwood. Sis: Mrs. N. S. Johnson. Bros: Jewel, Clarence and Pinkton Underwood. Interred: College Park Cemetery. AG 5/9/1910
UNDERWOOD, Ellison, inf. son of Mr. and Mrs. T. S., interred Hollywood Cemetery. AG 1/30/1908
UNDERWOOD, J. I., age 36, d. 182 Plum St. Atlanta. Interred: Westview. AG 11/2/1907
UNDERWOOD, Louis D., age 5 mos., son of Mr. and Mrs. H. S., d. 900 Marietta St., Atlanta, Fri. AG 1/31/1908
UNDERWOOD, T. H., age 44, d. 80 Western Ave. Atlanta. AG 11/8/1909
UNDERWOOD, William A., former cowboy and circus rider, d. Fri., Atlanta. People from Wallace, Va. AG 10/25/1907
UNDERWOOD, Lillian Girard, Mrs., age 25, wife of William Wilding Underwood, d. 556 Greensferry Ave.,A tlanta, Sun. Parents: Mr. and Mrs. J. G. Ramsey. Bros: Hartwell Ramsey, Milwaukee, Wis.; Paul and Aeneas Ramsey, Atlanta.
UPCHURCH, Fred C., age 19, d. Oakland City. Atlanta. AG 9/21/1909
UPCHURCH, Richard T., age 52, d. 11 Berean Ave. Atlanta. AG 7/30/1906
UPDIKE, Katherine, Mrs. d. Ft. McPherson last Sat. Interred: Kingston, Ohio. AG 5/1/1906
UPSHAW, Marshall E., age 72, d. Fri. 98 Jefferson St., Atlanta. Wife. Two sons. AG 5/6/1910
UPSHAW, Myra H., colored, age 64, d. McDaniel Rd. Atlanta. AG 4/15/1908
UPSHAW, Peter, colored, age 95, d. 242 E. Cain St. Atlanta. AG 11/2/1907
UPSON, Henry, colored, infant, d. 104 Old Wheat St. Atlanta. AG 6/6/1906
URWITZ, May, Dr. d. Houston, Texas 10/2. Wife survives. AC 10/3/1905
USHER, John T. of Lumpkin, Ga., drowned in pond. AG 6/25/1907
UTZ, A. L., age 30, d. 140 Spring St., Atlanta Sat. Interred: Marshall, Mo. Wife, parents, 4 bros, 2 sister, survive. AG 11/23/1908
VALDES, Digna, 8 yrs. old dau. of Mr. and Mrs. S. Valdes, d. 274 Whitehall St. Atlanta. Interred: Westview. AG 6/23/1907
VALDES, Digna, age 8, dau. of Mr. and Mrs. S., d. Thurs. 174 Whitehall St. Atlanta. Interred: Westview. AG 6/21/1907
VALENTINE, M. C., Mrs., age 70, d. 28 Tumlin St. Atlanta. AG 10/29/1907
VALENTINE, Mary A., Mrs. interred Smyrna, Ga. Tues. AG 10/29/1907
VAN BIBBER, Sarah J., age 74, d. 81 Park Ave. Atlanta, at dau's res, Mrs. J. K. Thrower. Interred: Oakland. Day, and one son, survive, W. H. Van Bibber of Washington, D. C. AG 11/25/1906

VAN DEVENTER, Roberts, Mrs. d. 5/16 Savannah, Ga., formerly Miss Callie Woodward of Edenton, N. C. AC 5/17/1905

VAN EPPS, J. C., Mrs. d. Fri. Atlanta. Interred: Oakland. AG 7/11/1910

VAN EPPS, Minnie T., Mrs., age 54, d. 127 Washington St., Atlanta. AG 5/24/1906

VAN HORN, J. T. funeral Wed. Atlanta. Interred: Westview. AG 3/29/1910

VAN HORN, W. C., Mrs., age 63, d. Atlanta Mon. One dau: Miss Mamie Van Horn, Washington, D. C. AG 3/29/1910

VAN HORNE, Dorothy, inf. dau. of D. S. of Monroe, Ga., d. res. of grandfather, A. W. Jones, 113 Tuscaloosa St., Birmingham, la. Interred: Griffin, Ga. AG 4/20/1908

VANCE, John M., age 70, d. Soldiers' Home, Atlanta. AG 5/21/1907

VANCE, Norwood K., Dr., age 46, d. New Kimball Hotel. Atlanta. AG 4/3/1908

VANDERGRIFF, E. S., age 44, d. Fri., 145 Kelley St., Atlanta. Interred: Nelson, Ga. AG 8/17/1907

VANDERGRIFF, Ella, Mrs., age 42, wife of J. V., d. 228 Pulliam St., Atlanta, Tues. AG 6/23/1908

VANDERGRIFF, Laura, age 2, d. 40 Gaskill St. Atlanta. AG 4/22/1909

VANDERGRIFF, Sarah J., Mrs., age 36, d. Atlanta Sun. Interred: Tickanetley, Ga. Husband: J. W. 6 children. AG 5/3/1909

VANDEVENDER, A. M., Mrs., mother of Horatio, manager of Wes. Union Telegraph of Atlanta, d. Meridian, Miss 2/6. AG 2/7/1908

VANDIVERE, A. G. B., age 84, d. 202 Luckie St. Vet., Mexican, civil wars. Survivors: S. L. & W. J. Vandivere, Atlanta; Mrs. O. M. Montgomery, Atlanta; Mrs. John Hill, Cartersville. 15 grch. Bur: Cartersville. AG 12/29/1906

VANDIVER, Eva, age 1, d. 50 Fortress Ave., Atlanta, Wed. Interred: Cartersville. AG 8/2/1906

VANN, Annie M., Mrs., age 32, d. 10/17 1621 Fourth St., Macon, Ga. Interred: Jones Chapel Cemetery. AG 10/18/1910

VAN VALKENBURG, Wilfred R., age 43, d. 3/19 Huntsville, Ala. Wife, 4 children. AC 3/20/1905

VAN VORST, C. E., age 70, d. bro.'s res., W. O. Van Vorst, near Clarkston, Ga., Sat. Interred: Savannah. Bro., three children. AG 9/28/1908

VARDAMAN, Mary F., Mrs., mother of James K., d. 3/18 Jackson, Miss. Interred: Greenwood. Son: John F. of Cripple Creek, Colo. AC 3/20/1905

VARNELLE, Paul, age 14 yrs., son of Mr. and Mrs. Varnell, d. Newburgh, N. Y. 8/17/1907. Interred: Greenwood AG 6/13/1908

VARRIS, Barbara, Mrs., age 77, d. 55 E. Georgia Ave. Atlanta Sun. Interred: Westview. AG 1/3/1910

VAUGHAN, Caroline T., Mrs., age 62, d. 131 S. Pryor St. Atlanta. AG 9/3/1908

VAUGHAN, Effie Clyde, age 10 mos., dau. of Mr. and Mrs. H. B., d. 172 Whitehall St., Atlanta. Interred: Westview. AG 7/13/1908

VAUGHAN, Eva, inf. dau. of Mr. and Mrs. Frank V., d. 627 Whitehall St., Atlanta, Mon. Interred: LaGrange, Ga. AG 4/18/1910

VAUGHAN, J. R., Mrs., age 44 d. Mon. her res. 32 Fortress Ave. Atlanta. AG 1/1/1907

VAUGHAN, Maggie, Mrs., age 29, d. 18 Rhinehart St. Atlanta. Husband. Mother: Mrs. Mary Ware. Bur: Athens, Tenn. AG 7/8/1908
VAUGHAN, Willie, age 14 mos., dau. of Mr. and Mrs. Vaughan of 65 Formwalt St., Atlanta, d. Sun. AG 1/17/1910
VAUGHAN, Willie, age 14 yrs., d. 201 Capitol Ave. Atlanta. AG 1/19/1910
VAUGHN, Carroll D., age 13, son of Mr. and Mrs. J. E. Vaughan, Jr., d. Thurs, 139 Courtland St. Atlanta. Interred: Camden, S. C. AG 8/10/1906
VAUGHN, Charity, Miss, age 68, d. 84 Hampton St., Atlanta, Tues. Interred: Mt. Perrin. AG 4/13/1909
VAUGHN, David, Mrs., Sr. d. S. Conyers 6/19, age 75. Husband, several children, grandchildren. AG 6/20/1910
VAUGHN, J. W., Mrs. age 40, of Waynesboro, Ga., d. Thurs. Atlanta. AG 7/16/1908
VAUGHN, James, colored, age 51, d. 95 Luckie St. Atlanta. AG 5/18/1908
VAUGHN, Lee, colored, age 56, d. 101 N. Butler St. Atlanta. AG 5/20/1909
VAUGHN, M. D., age 56, d. 150 Whitehall Terrace. Atlanta. AG 11/8/1909
VAUGHN, Mattie, age 11, dau. of Mr. and Mrs. Hiram, d. Grady Hospital, Atlanta. Interred: Hollywood Cemetery. AG 12/7/1908
VAUGHN, Miss d. in the Tower (jail) Atlanta. AG 2/4/1907
VAUGHN, Willie, colored, age 48, d. 36 Collier St. Atlanta. AG 10/2/1908
VAVIS, Barbara, age 77, d. 55 E. Georgia Ave., Atlanta. AG 1/4/1910
VEAL, Columbus, age 19, d. Wed. Atlanta 60 Delta Pl. Atlanta. Interred: Sylvester Cemetery. AG 9/15/1910
VEAL, Lucy, Mrs., age 50, wife of B. H., d. Austell Tues, dau. of Capt. B. W. K. Peacock of Cartersville. Daus: Hattie, Sarah, Lucyh. Son: Coleman. AG 6/22/1910
VEAL, Sarah, age 68, d. 573 Marietta St. Atlanta. AG 1/25/1910
VEAZEY, Gray, son of late Rev. T. J. d. near Barnett, Ga. Fri. Wife, 2 small children. Interred: Norwood-his mother was buried same cemetery one wk ago today (5/4). AG 5/4/1907
VENABLE, Ethel d. Grady Hospital, Atlanta 3/26. AC 3/27/1905
VENSON, Addeline, colored, age 60, d. corner Smith and Crumley Sts. Atlanta. AG 3/16/1907
VENTURA, Albert M., inf. son of S. V., d. Thurs. 133 Kelly St. Atlanta. Interred: Westview. AG 5/24/1906
VERDIEL, Joseph, Jr., colored, age 14, d. 19 Proctor St. Atlanta. AG 9/30/1910
VERHIME, J. E., age 67, d. 12 Oliver St., Atlanta, Oct. 16. AG 10/18/1910
VERHINE, Robert C., 14 mos. son of Mr. and Mrs. J. R., d. 617 W. North Ave., Atlanta, Fri. Interred: Acworth, Ga. AG 1/17/1908
VERNON, John M., Mrs. of Cussta, Ala. d. 3/2. West Point, Ga. Interred: Cusseta Cemetery. Husband, 4 daus., 2 sons. AC 3/4/1905
VERNOY, James, age 89 d. Thurs. res. of son, W. A. Vernoy, 219 Cherokee Ave., Atlanta, Sat. Interred: Westview. AG 1/14/1908
VICKERS, Emma, Miss d. Fri. res. of mother, Mrs. Julia Vickers, near Hahira, Ga. AG 12/17/1910

VICKERY, Josh, Mrs., and her 11 mos. old baby were murdered Helena, Ga. Her father-in-law, Jack Vickery, arrested. AG 3/28/1909

VIENTON, S. W., age 65, d. Tues. 350 E. Georgia Ave. Atlanta. Interred: Westview. AG 6/13/1910

VINCENT, J. T., age 31. Atlanta. Wife. 2 children. AC 12/21/1905

VINHINE, W. F., Mrs., age 20, d. Griffin St. Atlanta. AG 12/13/1909

VINING, Ethel, age 5, dau. of D. F., d. 499 Chestnut St., Atlanta, Sun. Interred: Hollywood. AG 11/7/1910

VINING, Hester J., age 23, from Mobile, Ala. Macon, 11/12/1906. Fatally crushed coupling car, Central of Ga. yards. AG 11/12/1906

VINING, Ruby L., age 1, d. 513 Simpson St. Atlanta. AG 12/8/1910

VINSON, Effie, Miss, age 20, dau. of J. H. Vinson, merchant of E. Gadsden, Ala., d. Sat. AG 7/24/1906

VINSON, Lora, colored, age 48, d. 46 Hardin St. Atlanta. AG 4/10/1907

VINSON, Lula, Mrs., age 47, wife of Dr. George A., d. 338 Washington St., Atlanta, Tues. Bro: William Arnold. Halfsisters: Mrs. C. E. Bennett, Mrs. May Finney. Halfbro: G. W. Arnold. Interred: Westview. AG 7/27/1909

VITTUR, C. K., Mrs., age 70, wid. of late B. D. Vittur, mother of Col. Charles Vittur, died 95 Orange St., Atlanta. AG 11/17/1906

VON HADEIN, Willie C., age 28, d. 328 Formwalt St., Atlanta. Interred: Westview. Parents: Mr. and Mrs. J. F. Bros: J. H., Jacksonville, Fla.; J. F., Jr. of Lead, S. Dak. Sisters: Mrs. G. G. Waters, Miss Lullie Anna Von Hadein. AG 11/22/1909

VON REEDAN, Elsie J., Mrs., age 47, d. S. Atlanta. Two children. Interred: Westview. AG 9/30/1908

WADDELL, J. E., age 19, d. Mon. 64 Hampton St. Atlanta. Interred: Oak Grove Church yard. AG 11/22/1910

WADDELL, John Newton, age 10 mos., inf. of Mr. and Mrs. J. N., of 275 E. Hunter St. Atlanta. Interred: Oakland. AG 5/1/1906

WADDILL, Frank A., Dr. d. 5/22 Cheraw, S. C. AC 5/23/1905

WADE, Sallie, wife of H. S., d. Fri. AG 10/6/1906

WADE, William, colored, age 53, d. 347 Smith St. Atlanta. AG 10/21/1908

WADKINS, Lula May, colored, age 13, d. 45 Graves St. Atlanta. AG 3/29/1909

WADLEY, Rebecca Barnard, Mrs., wid. of William M., d. her res. Great Hill Place, Bolingbroke, Ga., age 87. Interred: Family Burial Grounds. AC 6/6/1905

WADSWORTH, Maggie Nora, Mrs., age 31, d. 28 Strong St. Atlanta. AG 10/13/1906

WAGNER, Frederick L., inf. of Mr. and Mrs. F. L., age 17 days, d. Decatur, Ga. AG 10/18/1907

WAGNER, Henry Leo, age 2, son of Mr. and Mrs. R. A., d. 787 Ashby St., Atlanta, Tues. Interred: Caseys Cemetery. AG 6/30/1909

WAGNON, Louis, age 28, d. Hendersons crossing on Sou. Railway. AG 3/22/1910

WAINSCOTT, Albert, age 2, son of Mrs. Effie, d. Fri., Atlanta. Interred: Sylvester Cemetery. AG 12/14/1907

WAIT, Malcolm G., Mrs., age 55, d. 301 N. Jackson St. Atlanta. AG 5/9/1910

WAITE, Henry C. d. at "The Rocks" on the Satilla River, 6/19 (Waycross). AG 6/20/1910

WAITS, George, age 48, d. 47 Stewart Ave. Atlanta. AG 10/1/1907

WAITS, William A., age 78, d. 84 W. Georgia Ave. Atlanta. Interred: Mt. Gilead church yard. AG 5/29/1906

WAITS, W. P. d. 8/30 Battle Hill. Interred: Mt. Gilead Cemetery. AC 10/3/1905

WAKEFIELD, Mary, Mrs. d. 4/20 res. of son, age 71. Born Bulloch Co., Ga. 3/10/1839. Interred: Laurel Grove Cem., Savannah, Ga. Son: Charles E. AG 4/21/1910

WAKEFIELD, Mary, Mrs., age 71, d. 4/20 res. of son, Cordele, Ga.. She was b. Bulloch Co., Ga. 3/10/1829. Interred: Savannah, Ga., Laurel Groce Cemetery. Son: Charles E. AG 4/21/1910

WAKEFORD, W. M., Mrs., wife of Postmaster Wakeford, of Adel, Ga., d. AG 8/31/1910

WALDEN, Floyd of Dahlonega murdered. Bud, Carl and Wash Jarrard and Cage Baker are charged with the murder last Christmas evening. AG 2/8/1907

WALDEN, N. A., Mrs., age 73, d. dau.'s res., Mrs. Lula Stamps, 161 W. Hunter St., Atlanta. Sis: Mrs. M. C. Shell; Mrs. Philo Holcomb. Bro: Willis C. King (decd). Interred: Bremen, Ga. AC 4/8/1905

WALDEN, T. E. of E. Macon d. yesterday, age 33. Mother, father, 5 bros., 3 sisters. Interred: Ft. Hill cemetery. AG 9/23/1907

WALDER, Charles d. Atlanta Sat. Interred: Westview. AG 6/1/1908

WALDREP, E. H., age 64, d. 90 S. Boulevard. Atlanta. Interred: Hardemans Church yard. AG 1/27/1910

WALDROUP, Mary L., Mrs., age 79, d. Wed. 329 Cooper St. Atlanta. Daus: Mrs. M. S. Veal, Mrs. J. A. Thomas, Mrs. Annie Binton. Sons: M. L., J. W. Interred: Woodville Church yard. AG 9/22/1910

WALKER, inf. child of Mr. and Mrs. G. W., d. 203 Means St. Atlanta, Thurs. Interred: Casey's Cemetery. AG 7/1/1910

WALKER, Allen, age 7, d. 464 Bass St. Atlanta. AG 5/13/1907

WALKER, Augusta R., Mrs., age 74, d. 49 W. Cain St. Atlanta. AG 11/9/1910

WALKER, Beulah, colored, age 34, d. 27 Adams alley. Atlanta. AG 10/21/1908

WALKER, Beulah, Mrs. d. Tues. 82 Virgil St., Atlanta, age 21. Interred: Westview. AG 5/31/1906

WALKER, C. A., age 36, d. Inman yards. Atlanta. Res: 403 Luckie St. Interred: Westview. AG 10/25/1907

WALKER, C. V., age 41, former res. of Augusta, d. Atlanta, Whiteford Ave., Wed. Wife, 4 children, bro., 3 sisters. Interred: Augusta, Ga. AG 10/17/1907

WALKER, Charles, colored, age 40, d. Fulton Co. Alms House. Atlanta. AG 12/5/1907

WALKER, Charles A. killed by freight train Thurs. Inman yards, Atlanta. Relatives in Virginia. AG 10/25/1907

WALKER, Charlie to hang Decatur, Fri., for murder of motorman, S. T. Brown. AG 7/28/1910

WALKER, David L., 76, Conf. Vet., Macon, d. sil's home, Chas. B. Rhodes, Forsyth St., Vineville. Sons: Berrien & Legare, NY. Daus: Mrs. N. G. Evans, Edgeville, S. C.; Mrs. C. B. Rhodes, Macon. Bros: B. Presley, John M., Macon. AG 10/25/1907

WALKER, Dora, Mrs., wid. of Gen. W. S., d. dau´s res., Mrs. H. C. Peeples, 719 Piedmont Ave., Atlanta, Sat., age 79. To Atlanta from S. C. 30 yrs. ago. Daus: Mrs. E. L. Anderson, Mrs. H. C. Peeples. Son: W. Walker. Bur: Oakland. AG 1/4/1907

WALKER, Ella B., Mrs., wife of H. H., d. Atlanta Fri. Interred: Westview. AG 6/22/1908

WALKER, Ella M., Mrs., age 38, d. Atlanta. AG 6/22/1908

WALKER, Emma, Mrs., age 27, d. 502 Gordon St. Atlanta. AG 10/6/1906

WALKER, Eveline, Mrs., age 73, d. 9/10 683 Woodward Ave., Atlanta. Several children. Buried in the country. AC 9/11/1905

WALKER, G. L., age 62, d. 7 Boss Ave. Atlanta. AG 1/28/1907

WALKER, George, colored, age 46, d. Peters and Haynes Sts. Atlanta. AG 11/21/1910

WALKER, Gilbert C., Mrs., age 78, widow of ex-Gov. Walker of Virginia, d. 12/16 Binghamton, N. Y., res. of sister. AG 12/17/1910

WALKER, H. H., age 87, d. Tues. res. of dau., Mrs. Mary McAfee, 222 E. Fair St., Atlanta. Sons: W. H.; Chamblee, Frank; Norcross; and Charles of Waco, Texas. AG 6/13/1910

WALKER, Harriet E., age 2, d. 59 Hilliard St. Atlanta. AG 5/15/1907

WALKER, Henry Heyward, age 87, d. 222 E. Fair St. Atlanta, Tues. Interred: Chamblee, Ga. AG 6/15/1910

WALKER, J. F., Jr., age 6 mos., d. 80 Magnolia St., Atlanta. AG 5/12/1909

WALKER, J. L., Confederate Veteran, d. Sun. Atlanta. Interred: Westview. Wife, two daus., two sons, survive. AG 1/28/1907

WALKER, J. M., College Park mayor (res. since 1891), Confed. vet, b. Greene Co. 1/1841, m. Mary L. Dorsey, Clayton Co., rel. Judge R. T. Dorsey, Atlanta. Sons: F. E., Okla., J. L., Tx, R. A., W. M., C. Park. Daus: Mrs. J. O. Blalock, Jonesboro, Mrs L. L. Loving, C. Park, Mrs J. B. Adams, Riverdale, Mrs. J. A. Joyner, Jackson, Mrs. C. Y. Smith, Tennille. Bros: Z. T., Greene Co.; Chas, Savannah; Judson, Atlanta. Sis: Mrs. J. W. Benton, C. Park. AG 4/15/1907

WALKER, Jessie, age 10, dau. of Mrs. J. G., d. Mon. 459 E. Georgia Ave., Atlanta. Interred: Westview. AG 10/11/1910

WALKER, Jessie, age 10, dau. of R. H., d. Mon. 459 E. Georgia Ave. Atlanta. Interred: Westview. AG 10/11/1910

WALKER, Joel T., age 73, d. Bonaire, Ga. Interred: Perry, Ga., Evergreen Cemetery. Confed. Vet., Co. K., 11th Ga. Regt. Wife, 2 daus., 3 sons. AG 3/24/1910

WALKER, John d. 145 W. aker St., Atlanta Tues, age 59. Wife, two sons, L. R. and G. C. Walker. Daus: Misses Alice and Nellie Walker. Interred: Westview. AG 8/26/1908

WALKER, John, colored, age 30, died Decatur & Yonge Sts., Atlanta. AG 12/11/1906

WALKER, John B., age 59, d. 145 W. Baker St., Atlanta Tues. Interred: Westview. AG 8/27/1908

WALKER, John H., age 55, d. Fri. 161 Formwalt St., Atlanta. Wife. 4 daus., 2 sons. Interred: Westview. AG 7/2/1910

WALKER, Lillian B. L., colored, age 7 mos., d. 114 Robbins St. Atlanta. AG 5/26/1908

WALKER, Lillie May, age 9 yrs., dau. of Mr. and Mrs. J. P., of
Riverside, Ga., interred: Union City, Ga. AG 9/24/1910
WALKER, Lucy, Mrs., age 50, wife of John, d. Fri. 115 Jefferson
St. Atlanta. Interred: Hollywood. AG 2/7/1908
WALKER, M., colored, age 25, d. 101 N. Butler St. Atlanta. AG
12/14/1907
WALKER, M. L., Mrs., age 74, d. 157 Crew St. Atlanta. Interred:
Oakland. AG 6/23/1907
WALKER, M. T., Mrs. d. Wed. 167 Crew St. Atlanta. Sons: Rev.
William Bohler Walker of Macon, George I. and Matt T. Walker of
Atlanta, Henry Walker of Illinois. Interred: Oakland. AG
6/20/1907
WALKER, Madge, age 2, d. 464 Bass St. Atlanta. AG 9/21/1908
WALKER, Mary A., Mrs., 76, d. 42 Auburn Av. Daus: Mrs. A. M.
Hollinshed, Mrs. V. E. Bailey. Buried: Hollywood. AG 9/20/1906
WALKER, T. Blake, age 17, son of Mrs. Lucy, d. 343 Ormond St.,
Atlanta, Sun. AG 1/28/1908
WALKER, Mary E., age 34, d. 88 S. Pryor St. Atlanta. Remains sent
to father's home, E. S. McGee, Patterson, Ga. AG 1/27/1910
WALKER, Mary J., Mrs., mother of Mrs. Ira VanDuzer. d. 6/30,
Elberton, Ga. Son-in-law: Col. VanDuzer. Interred: McDonough, Ga.
AG 7/1/1909
WALKER, Matilda, colored, age 54, d. 19 Raspberry St. Atlanta. AG
7/19/1907
WALKER, Mattie R., inf. dau. of Mr. and Mrs. E. W. of 209
Kirkwood Ave., Atlanta, d. Fri. Interred: Monroe, Ga. AG 9/5/1908
WALKER, Myrtis, age 4, dau. of Mr. and Mrs. G. W., d. 203 Means
St., Atlanta. Interred: Caseys Cemetery. AG 7/2/1910
WALKER, Nat, age 58, killed by Tom Misz, age 48, farmer,
Alpharetta. AG 1/20/1910
WALKER, Osilee drowned 6/10 at Landale, 6 mi. below West Point,
Ga., in Chattahoochee River. AG 6/12/1906
WALKER, Rachel Maggie, age 3 yrs., d. Sun. res. of parents, Mr.
and Mrs. J. P., on Poplar St., Atlanta, Mon. Interred: Union
City. AG 10/18/1909
WALKER, Stephen, colored, age 50, d. 25 Mays St. Atlanta. AG
2/25/1907
WALKER, Thaddeus, Morman elder, age 23, d. Fri. Atlanta.
Interred: Inkon, Idaho. AG 4/16/1910
WALKER, Viney, colored, age 34, d. 77 Haynes St. Atlanta. AG
10/30/1908
WALKER, Virginia, inf. dau. of Mr. and Mrs. Edward, of Bolton,
funeral at res. of her grandfather in Bolton. Interred:
Hollywood. AG 7/1/1910
WALKER, W. H., age 60, d. Thurs. Peachtree Rd., Atlanta.
Interred: Prospect Church yard. AG 9/15/1910
WALKER, W. S., Mrs., 503 Gordon St., Atlanta, d. Tues, age 27.
Had been married 6 yrs. Leaves husband, little dau. Interment:
Oakland. AG 10/3/1906
WALKER, Will, age 48, d. 101 N. Butler St. Atlanta. AG 3/8/1907
WALKER, William H. d. Dublin 3/10, age 64, res. of Dublin for 16
yrs., native of Stewart Co., Ga. m. Miss Willie Finch,
Jeffersonville, Ga. Sons: Freeman, Cicero, Finch, Benjamin,
George, Lawrence. Dau: Miss Sallie. AG 3/10/1910

WALKER, Willie T., age 1, young son of Mr. and Mrs. S. A., d. 104 Summit Ave. Atlanta. Interred: Westview. AG 6/25/1910

WALL, Arthur, Mrs. d. Iron Springs Dist., Jackson, Ga., Sun. Husband, one son, dau. Sis: Mrs. C. A. Pittman. Interred: Milledgeville, Ga. AG 8/9/1910

WALL, Ester, colored, age 71, d. 18 Jeptha St. Atlanta. AG 9/26/1907

WALL, Florence A., Mrs., age 28, d. 117 Bass St. Atlanta. AG 3/27/1909

WALL, Henrietta H., Mrs., age 69, d. 127 Oakland Ave. Atlanta. AG 4/1/1907

WALL, Lawrence, age 7, d. 103 Fowler St. Atlanta. AG 4/19/1907

WALL, Martha, Mrs., age 47, d. 30 Crew St. Atlanta. AG 3/25/1907

WALLACE, Anderson, age 70, d. 101 N. Butler St. Atlanta. AG 7/8/1909

WALLACE, Annie, Mrs., wife of F. H., d. 8/30, 10 mi. from Opelika, Ala. Husband. 5 ch: one is C. B. Wallace, Atlanta. AC 9/2/1905

WALLACE, D. J., age 70, d. Tues. E. Pt., Ga. Interred: Lawrenceville, Ga. AG 6/29/1910

WALLACE, Daly d. Sun. Dalton, Ga., age 23, son of Mr. and Mrs. Will Wallace. AG 6/7/1910

WALLACE, Della M., Mrs., age 26, d. 342 Frazer St. Atlanta. AG 4/6/1907

WALLACE, E. W., Mrs., age 26, d. Thurs. 342 Fraser St., Atlanta., dau. of Mr. and Mrs. T. P. Whitley. Husband, two children survive. Interred: Westview. AG 4/6/1907

WALLACE, Helen Wells, Mrs., wife of Prof. S. S., d. Wed. She was b. Poultney, Vt. 1874, removed Ga. 1899. She md. 6/17/1896 in N.Y. Husband, three ch: Janet Read Wallace, Samuel Stewart Wallace, Jr., Edward Victor Wallace. AG 8/14/1907

WALLACE, J. J., age 69, d. Thurs., 5 Homer St., Atlanta. Wife, 6 children. Interred: Douglasville, AG 7/12/1906

WALLACE, James, age 63, d. 267 Capitol Ave. Atlanta. Interred: Roswell, Ga. Ch: Mrs. J. Miller, J. A. Wallace. AG 10/13/1906

WALLACE, Lena, dau. of Mr. and Mrs. F. H., d. Sun. Oakland City. Interred: Wesley Chapel church yard. AG 5/28/1906

WALLACE, Lizzie, Mrs., age 65, d. Mon. 45 Cameron St. Atlanta. Interred: Lithonia, Ga. AG 5/13/1907

WALLACE, M. M., Mrs., age 77, d. 35 Chapel St. Atlanta. Interred: Marietta, Ga. AG 11/12/1907

WALLACE, Mary B., Mrs., age 42, d. 71 Howell St., Atlanta, Fri. Husband, 3 sons, 3 daus., survive. AG 10/8/1909

WALLACE, Mary Elizabeth, Mrs. of Washington, Ga., age 48, d. 3/30. Daus: Mrs. F. E. Miller, St. Louis; Misses Berta and Mamie Wallace, Washington, Ga. Interred: Pierce's Chapel, family burial grounds. AC 3/31/1905

WALLACE, Mattie, colored, age 30, d. rear of 159 N. Piedmont Ave. Atlanta. AG 1/14/1908

WALLACE, Ola, age 2, dau. of E. E., d. Thurs., 18 Bluff St. Atlanta. Interred: Westview. AG 7/6/1906

WALLACE, R. R., age 63, d. 115 Kirkwood Ave. Atlanta. Interred: Westview. AG 5/19/1910

WALLACE, Roy, age 18 mos., son of Mr. and Mrs. W. M., d. 14 Gospero St., Atlanta, Fri. Interred: Marietta, Ga. AG 1/25/1908

WALLACE, S. S., Mrs. d. Wed. Atlanta, wife of Prof. S. S. at Ga. Tech. AG 8/15/1907

WALLACE, S. T., switchman on Sou. rrr, d. from rr. accident. AG 10/27/1906

WALLACE, Sallie, colored, age 32, d. Atlanta. AG 4/17/1908

WALLACE, Sam, age 20, d. Atlanta Sat. Interred: Hollywood. AG 7/5/1909

WALLACE, Stephen T., witchman killed Sat. by engine Chester, S. C. Interred: Atlanta. AG 10/29/1906

WALLACE, W. A., age 64, d. Wesley Memorial Hospital. Atlanta. Interred: Austell, Ga. AG 8/15/1907

WALLACE, W. M. d. Atlanta Wed. Interred: Casey's Cemetery. AG 7/8/1909

WALLACE, William, age 39, d. Sat. 115 N. Pryor St. Atlanta. Interred: Westview. AG 2/25/1907

WALLER, Robert killed 11/15 West Point, Ga. in train accident. Res. of 222 Hilliard St. Atlanta. Interred: Jackson, Ga. AC 11/17/1905

WALLING, W. T., age 76, d. Wed. near Lacy Springs (Decatur), Ala. AG 7/10/1908

WALLS, Oliver, age 99, 4 mos., 7 days, d. Sun. Thomaston, Ga. Interred: Antioch Church. AG 5/18/1910

WALRAVEN, A. J., age 56, father of Councilman Don S. Walraven, d. Atlanta, 434 Luckie St. Wife. Bros: John and Bryant. Sister: Mary. Funeral: Marietta. AG 9/1/1908

WALRAVEN, George L., age 30, d. 225 Capitol Ave. Atlanta. AG 8/31/1908

WALRAVEN, John, Mrs., age 61, d. 63 Cherry St.,tlanta, Tues. Interred: Westview. AG 7/23/1908

WALRAVEN, Luther. Calhoun, Ga., 12/17,son of Jasper Walraven, drowned in Ooostanaula river near Plainville last night. AG 12/17/1906

WALSEMANN, L. F., age 52, d. Ocala, Fla. AG 9/3/1909

WALSH, James d. 65 E. Mitchell St., Atlanta, Tues., Atlanta pioneer. Ch: Emmett D. Walsh, James Walsh, Jr., Paul Walsh, Mrs. Maymie Walsh Frieze, Mrs. W. E. Taylor. Interred: Oakland. AG 1/9/1908

WALSH, James, Jr., age 39, d. Cincinnati, Ohio. Former Atlantan. Sis: Mrs. Mamie Walsh Friese; Mrs. W. Taylor. Bros: Emmett, Paul. Father: James, Sr. Mother d. over 2 yrs. ago. AG 4/14/1910

WALSH, James, Mrs. d. Tues. 67 E. Mitchell St., Atlanta, age 58, wife of James. Sis: Mrs. M. J. Young. Ch: Emmett, Paul, James, Jr., Mrs. Maymie Walsh Friese and Mrs. W. E. Taylor, all of Atlanta. AG 12/3/1907

WALTER, George A., age 80, d. Thurs. res. of son-in-law, George Corley, 282 Lawton St. Atlanta. Leaves 2 daus., 3 sons. Interred: Westview. AG 6/8/1906

WALTER, Michael, Father, priest of Marist Society, d. 10/30 Atlanta, age 30. Born Lorraine. Interred: Cincinnati, Ohio. AC 10/31/1905

WALTERS, Alonzo found dead last night at Windsor Hotel, Americus, Ga. with bullet in head, age 55. Leaves large family, grandchildren. AG 8/25/1908

WALTERS, C. W., age 64, d. 33 Orange St.,tlanta, Sun. Interred: Oglethorpe, Ga. AG 12/13/1909

WALTERS, J. L., Mrs., age 77, d. 427 Gordon St. Atlanta. AG 9/22/1908

WALTERS, W. A. d. Sun. Pittsburg, Pa. Interred: Westview. AG 2/12/1907

WALTHALL, Frank colored, age 38, d. 101 N. Butler St. Atlanta. AG 4/3/1908

WALTHALL, Frank colored, age 38, d. 101 N. Butler St. Atlanta. AG 4/3/1908

WALTON, Annie May, Miss, age 16, dau. of Mr. and Mrs. W. M., 174 Lindsay St.,tlanta, Tues. Interred: Hollywood. 6 bros, 2 sisters. AG 6/16/1909

WALTON, Dorcus, colored, age 60, d. 125 Larkin St. Atlanta. AG 6/20/1907

WALTON, Ed, colored, age 26, d. Grady Hospital, Atlanta. AG 5/23/1907

WALTON, Kitty Mae, 5-yr. old dau. of Mr. and Mrs. S. O. Walton, d. Sun., Atlanta. AG 2/12/1907

WALTON, Lizzie, Mrs., wife of Jack, d. Wed. home of parents, Mr. and Mrs. T. W. Pitt, 107 Logan St., age 23. Bros and sisters: Tom Pitt, Atlanta, John A. Pitt, St. Louis, Mrs. W. W. McAfee, Atlanta. AG 7/12/1906

WALTON, S. E., Mrs., age 62, d. Center Hill, Ga. Tues. Sons: T. E., A. R. Daus: Mrs. D. E. Lyle, Atlanta; Mrs. B. S. Cook, Culman City, Ala. Interred: Tallapoosa Cemetery. AG 7/8/1908

WALTON, S. O., Mrs., Jr. d. Sat. bur. Methodist cemetery, Lumpkin, Ga. AG 3/5/1907

WALTON, Sarah E., Mrs., age 63, d. Center Hill, Ga. AG 7/9/1908

WALTON, Annie E., Mrs., age 30, d. Moreland Ave. Atlanta, wife of E. R. Infant son. Father: J. W. Hollingsworth. Sis: Mrs. W. G. Sharkey, Mrs. Y. R. Norris, Mrs. I. E. Estes, Misses Willie and Irene Hollingsworth. Bur: Westview. AG 5/9/1910

WALTON, Robert Hall, age 35, d. Sun. 176 Luckie St. Atlanta. Interred: Decatur. AG 3/11/1907

WAMBLE, Edna, dau. of George, negro, killed by sweetheart, Oscar Stinson (also killed himself), Woodbury, Ga. AC 5/3/1905

WARD, Alex, his 2-yr. old child was burned Thurs. night, wounds may prove fatal. Mr. Ward is bro-in-law of Ordinary J. Milligan of Carrollton, Ga. AG 12/6/1908

WARD, Alman killed by Sonnie Williams. Date not given. AG 6/20/1908

WARD, B. C., age 51, d. Atlanta Thurs., 179 Spring St. Interred: Westview. AG 6/8/1910

WARD, Christine, colored, age 22, d. 101 N. Butler St. Atlanta. AG 7/13/1908

WARD, E. B., age 27, d. 12/13 Ft. McPherson, Ga. Wife. Interred: Columbus, Ga. AC 12/14/1905

WARD, Ed of Columbus, Ga. d. 12/12. Interred: Girard Cemetery. AC 12/15/1905

WARD, Fannie, colored, age 28, d. 226 Wylie St. Atlanta. AG 12/30/1910

WARD, J. S. d. 3/11 Norwood, Ga. Wife, one dau. AG 3/12/1907
WARD, J. T., Mrs. d. West Point, Ga., 12/26, other of W. A. Ward,
Atlanta, age 69. Husband. Children: W. W., Atlanta; Mrs. J. B.
Hodnett, West Point; John W. Ward, Montgomery, Ala. AG 12/28/1909
WARD, Joseph, colored, age 55, d. 101 N. Butler St. Atlanta. AG
5/26/1908
WARD, Juliette, age 2, d. 54 Wyman St. Atlanta. AG 5/15/1907
WARD, Loretta, Miss, age 17, d. Thurs. 156 Chapel St., Atlanta.
Interred: Westview. AG 5/31/1907
WARD, Mary, Miss, age 24, d. Atlanta. AG 2/16/1910
WARD, Mary, Miss, age 65, d. 291 Seaboard Ave. Atlanta. AG
3/21/1910
WARD, Ollie, colored, age 65, d. 13 Longview Ave. Atlanta. AG
7/15/1909
WARD, Roy, colored, age 27, d. 78 S. Delta St. Atlanta. AG
3/5/1907
WARD, W. T., Jr., age 2, d. 718 Woodward Ave., Atlanta Sun.
Interred: Dallas, Ga. AG 4/11/1910
WARD, William, age 61, d. Tues. 54 Weyman St., Atlanta. AG
5/7/1907
WARD, Willie, colored, age 40, d. 17 Tyler St. Atlanta. AG
11/3/1908
WARD, infant of Mrs. William d. Tues. 54 Wyman St. Atlanta. AG
5/13/1907
WARDLAW, L. E., Mrs., age 56, d. Thurs. res. of stepmother, Mrs.
E. A. Smith, near College Pk. Bur: Connally's Cem. Sons: W. O.,
J. E. Bros: J. G., J. Wyley, T. B. and Berry Smith. AG 7/17/1908
WARE, Addie, Mrs., wife of Prof. C. R., d. Atlanta Sat. Interred:
Lawrenceville, Ga. AG 10/19/1907
WARE, Annie F., infant of Mr. and Mrs. A. W., d. Tues., 1079
Marietta St. Atlanta. AG 5/7/1907
WARE, Charles E., d. 12/16 Macon. Interred: Rose Hill. Wife,
little dau., and parents, survive. AG 12/17/1909
WARE, Columbus B., colored, age 32, d. Washington, D. C. AG
7/9/1908
WARE, Duncan, second son of Mr. and Mrs. S. A., of Hyde, Ga., d.
2/5, age 26. 2 bros., 2 sisters. Interred: Fishing Creek
Cemetery. AG 2/7/1905
WARE, John S., age 72, d. Thurs. 403 E. Georgia Ave. Atlanta.
Wife. Sons: G. H., J. A., E. R. Dau: C. E. Battle. Niece: Miss
Pearl Ware. Sis: Miss Mary E. Ware. Bur: Westview. AG 9/22/1910
WARE, John Thomas, Atlanta pioneer, d. E. Point Tues, b. Atlanta
1844 (Marthasville). Sons: George H., E. Point; H., San
Francisco, Cal. Interred: Oakland. AG 6/2/1909
WARE, Ruby, age 9 mos., inf. dau. of Mr. and Mrs. E. R., d. 88
Rankin St. Atlanta. Interred: Duluth, Ga. AG 6/8/1908
WARNELL, Z. S. of Pembroke killed by negro 10/22, aged abt 40. He
was from Bulloch Co. Leaves wife, no. of children. AG 10/23/1908
WARNER, Alice, colored, age 25, d. Fulton Co. Almshouse. AG
6/6/1906
WARNER, Edward G., age 42, d. 217 Juniper St. Atlanta. AG
10/12/1909
WARNER, J. H., age 66, d. Decatur. AG 6/3/1909
WARNER, Lizzie, age 40, d. 368 Crumley St. Atlanta. AG 1/1/1908

WARNER, Nannie, Mrs., wife of Frank H., d. Columbus, Ga. 9/8. She was dau. of Mr. and Mrs. Getzen of Fortson, Ga. Leaves 3 children, two sisters. AG 9/9/1908

WARNOCK, E. D., Mrs., age 65, d. Sun. 18 Howell Pl. Atlanta. Son: Dr. E. J. Interred: Allendale, S. C. AG 5/30/1910

WARNOCK, James T., Mrs. funeral 286 W. Peachtree St., Atlanta Sat. Interred: Westview. Kin: Dr. Samuel D. Warnock, T. P. Warnock, Misses Charley and Lillian Warnock. AG 7/26/1907

WARNOCK, Mary J., Mrs., wid. of late Dr. J. T., d. Thurs. 285 W. Peachtree St., Atlanta. Interred: Westview. AG 7/27/1907

WARNOLD, William H., colored, age 95, d. 247 Chapel St. Atlanta. AG 10/30/1908

WARREN, Henry, age 14, d. Thurs. 101 N. Butler St. Atlanta. Interred: Westview. AG 5/17/1907

WARREN, J. A., Mrs., age 26, d. Atlanta. AG 9/30/1908

WARREN, J. C., Mrs., age 26, d. Atlanta Mon. Interred: Waverly Hall, Ga. Father: D. C. Hendrix. AG 9/29/1908

WARREN, Mary E., Mrs., wid. of Thomas J., d. 7/5 res. of dau., Mrs. C. E. Earle, Elberton. Ch: Mrs. Ben H. Thornton, Mrs. C. E. Earle; Jesse J. Warren, of Elberton; John H. Warren, Marietta. Interred: Elmhurst Cemetery. AG 7/6/1910

WARREN, William, Mrs., age 60, d. Fri. Husband. Sons: P. L., J. L., Tilden. Daus: Misses Mattie, Mary, Annie Lou of Swainesboro, Ga. Bros: Willis Watson of Worth Co., Ga.; John Watson, Emanuel Co. Interred: new city cemetery. AG 6/30/1908

WARTMAN, Lenia, Miss, age 32, d. 80 Julian St. Atlanta, Fri. Interred: Caseys. AG 1/11/1907

WARWICK, Louise E., Mrs., age 89, d. Sat. 84 Davis St., Atlanta. Interred: Greenwood. AG 2/22/1910

WARWICK, William P. d. Oshkosh, Wisc. Sev. Atlanta relatives: Mrs. Susannah Wafers; Mrs. Belle McLean, sisters; J. C. Warwick and G. W. Warwick, bros.; E. A. Warwick of Clarkston, Ga.; and T. F. Warwick of Claxton, Ga., bros. AG 12/10/1910

WASHINGTON, Belle, Miss d. Mon. Swainsboro, Ga. Interred: Westview (Atlanta). AG 5/17/1910

WASHINGTON, George, colored, age 37, d. Atlanta. AG 8/1/1907

WASHINGTON, Josephine, colored, age 32, d. 59 Jetha St., Atlanta. AG 5/24/1906

WASHINGTON, Willie May, colored, age 6, d. 6 Grady Ave. Atlanta. AG 11/14/1908

WATERMAN, Lena, Miss, age 32, d. 80 Julian St. Atlanta. AG 1/12/1907

WATERMAN, Walter T., age 38, former res. of Marietta, Ga., d. Wed. Atlanta. Interred: Terre Haute, Ind. AG 8/19/1909

WATERS, Clarence E., age 27, d. near Fitzgerald, Ga., his home, Sun. Interred: Westview, Atlanta. AG 8/19/1908

WATERS, J. C. d. Jackson, Miss. AG 7/22/1907

WATERS, Louise, Mrs. d. 162 Ridley St., Atlanta, Mon. Interred: Casey's Cemetery. AG 7/20/1909

WATERS, Lula Moore, colored, age 36, d. 277 Old Rawkin St. Atlanta. AG 1/7/1907

WATERS, M. A., Mrs., age 73, d. Sun. res. of dau., Mrs. H. W. Fitch, 196 Bellwood Ave., Atlanta. Daus: Mrs. J. B. Tribble, Mrs. Lula Irwin, Mrs. Aggie Jordan, Mrs. Fitch. AG 11/22/1909

WATERS, R. C. d. Sat. dau´s home, Mrs. Charles Derby, Atlanta. Daus: Mrs. Derby, Misses Lynwood and Vera. Bur: Westview. AG 5/13/1907

WATERS, W. A. of Pittsburgh, Pa., formerly of Atlanta, d. Interred: Atlanta. Wife, one child. AG 2/11/1907

WATERS, W. T., Sr., 70, former Atlanta merchant, d. Chattanooga, Tenn. Wife. Son: W. T., Jr., Atlanta. Daus: Mrs. Lois Yarbrough, 832 Piedmont Ave.; Mrs. Thomas J. Wesley, 462 W. Peachtree St. Interred: Fayetteville, fam. cem. AG 12/1/1910

WATKINS, Benjamin of Douglasville, age 74, killed by car on E. Point line Sun. Died home of son, J. P. Watkins, E. Point, Ga. Leaves wife, 6 children. Confederate Veteran. Interred: Douglasville, Ga. AG 10/17/1907

WATKINS, C. A., age 77, d. 14 Addie St. Atlanta Thurs. Interred: Alpharetta. AG 9/21/1906

WATKINS, G. J., age 75, d. Mason and Turners Ferry Rd. Atlanta, Tues. Sons: T. M., G. J., Jr., Charles. Daus: Mrs. W. B. Maynard, Miss Maggie Watkins. Bur: Fam. bur. ground near res. AG 6/15/1910

WATKINS, H. D., Mrs., dau. of Mr. and Mrs. J. M. Stevens of Whitesburg, Ga., age 20, died. Married two years. AG 3/30/1907

WATKINS, J. C., Mrs. d. Martin, Ga. 6/16. Husband, 4 children. Interred: Martin Cemetery. AG 6/17/1910

WATKINS, James D., age 5 mos., son of Mr. and Mrs. S. D., 359 W. Third St., Atlanta, d. Tues. Bur: Union Grove, Ga. AG 3/29/1910

WATKINS, Laney J., inf. dau. of Mr. and Mrs. C. G., d. Sat. 706 Ashby St., Atlanta. Interred: Hollywood. AG 6/4/1910

WATKINS, M. L., age 29, d. 14 Addis St. Atlanta. AG 7/13/1908

WATKINS, Maggie, Mrs., age 24, d. 14 Addis St., Atlanta, Thurs. Husband, three children. Interred: Alpharetta, Ga. AG 7/10/1908

WATKINS, Margaret Louise, inf. dau. of Mr. and Mrs. T. M., d. near Masons Church, Bolton Rd., Atlanta. Interred: Family Grave Yard. AG 10/16/1907

WATKINS, Mayson, colored, age 28, d. Buford, Ga. AG 8/25/1908

WATKINS, R. F., Mrs. funeral Sun. from sister´s res., 514 Boulevard, Atlanta. Intered: Oakland. AG 9/14/1907

WATKINS, Van Dyke, age 12, son of Mr. and Mrs. J. L., d. 144 Addie St., Atlanta, Wed. Parents, 3 bros., 2 sisters, survive. Interred: Alpharetta, Ga. AG 10/7/1908

WATKINS, Velma C., inf. dau. of Mr. and Mrs. Randolph, d. 173 Hampton St., Atlanta, Thurs. Bur: Alpharetta, Ga. AG 5/27/1910

WATKINS, W. C., age 41, d. 29 Luckie St. Atlanta. AG 7/8/1909

WATKINS, William E., age 35, res. of Edison, Ga., d. Atlanta Tues. AG 7/6/1909

WATSON, A. H., Jr., inf. son of Mr. and Mrs. A. H., d. Wed. 74 Doane St., Atlanta, Thurs. Interred: Oakland. AG 4/15/1909

WATSON, Blake, colored, age 1, d. 172 E. Harris St. Atlanta. AG 1/28/1908

WATSON, Charles, Mrs., age 41, d. Tues., 11 North Moore St. Atlanta. Interred: Westview. AG 2/27/1907

WATSON, Eliza, colored, age 30, d. Alms House. Atlanta. AG 7/27/1907

WATSON, Eula T., Miss, age 18, d. parents res., Mr. and Mrs. B. C. Watson, 120 Curran St., Atlanta, Thurs. AG 12/24/1909

WATSON, Fannie, colored, age 16, d. 221 Chestnut St. Atlanta. AG 11/4/1908

WATSON, Georgia M., age 16 mos., dau. of Mr. and Mrs. L. M. (or L. R.), d. Sat. 78 Ormond St. Atlanta. Bur: Oakland. AG 5/9/1908

WATSON, Hattie, colored, age 58, d. 182 Houston St. Atlanta. AG 4/10/1908

WATSON, infant of Mr. and Mrs. John W., d. 229 W. North Ave., Atlanta. Sat. Interred: South Bend Cemetery. AG 12/7/1907

WATSON, J. P., Mrs.,ge 30, d. 249 Central Ave. Atlanta. AG 5/11/1908

WATSON, J. S., age 68, d. 82 Doane St. Atlanta. AG 11/30/1910

WATSON, J. W., colored, age 20, d. 297 Magnolia St. Atlanta. AG 11/12/1910

WATSON, L. D., Capt. d. Jackson, age abt 77. Confed Vet., 6th Ga., Regt. Wife. Daus: Mrs. Clayton Matthews, Atlanta, Mrs. L. L. O'Kelley, Tifton. Sons: Joe of Michigan; Douglas of Charlotte, N. C. Interred: City Cem., Jackson. AG 11/8/1910

WATSON, Ray, age 2, d. 5 Carroll Pl. Atlanta. AG 8/31/1908

WATSON, Sidney P., age 56, died res., 137 Richardson St., Atlanta. Survivors: Wife, dau., Miss Anna C. Watson; two sons, Sidney P. Watson, Jr., Charles P. Watson. AG 11/29/1906

WATSON, W. A., Mrs., age 75, d. Bushville, Banks Co., Ga., 3/12. Interred: Hebron, Ga. AC 3/14/1905

WATSON, W., Mrs., age 40, d. 11 Moore St. Atlanta. AG 3/1/1907

WATSON, Zelmer, age 6, colored, d. 267 Mangum St., Atlanta. AG 5/26/1906

WATT, Frank, colored, age 45, d. 51 Bellwood Ave. Atlanta. AG 3/26/1908

WATT, Ruth, age 2 yrs., d. 133 McDaniel St. Atlanta. AG 9/4/1907

WATTERS, J. C., former chief of Jackson, Miss. fire dept. d. Thurs. Jackson, Miss. Interred: Oakland, Atlanta. AG 7/22/1907

WATTERS, Katherine Moore, Mrs. d. dau.'s res., Mrs. Percy E. Wood, Atlanta, Wed. Interred: Rome, Ga. AG 8/12/1910

WATTERS, T. G., Mrs., age 82, d. Wed. dau.s' res., Mrs. Percy E. Wood, 87 W. Peachtree St., Atlanta. Bro: A. T. Moore, Rome, Ga. Sons: J. H., Augusta; W. W., Rome, Ga. Bur: Rome. AG 8/10/1910

WATTS, Charles, colored, age 35, d. 32 Fairfax St. Atlanta. AG 12/16/1907

WATTS, Elizabeth, Mrs. of Macon d. Thurs., wid. of John. Bros: B. J. Knight, Ben Knight. Son: David Watts. AG 2/28/1908

WATTS, J. A. d. 201 Carter St., Atlanta, Mon. Interred: Hollywood. AG 9/14/1907

WATTS, J. L., age 62, d. 52 Cameron St. Atlanta. Interred: Westview. AG 3/5/1908

WATTS, J. Q., Rev., age 36, d. Lakewood Heights, Atlanta, Sat. Wife, 2 daus. Bur: Oak Hill Cem., Cartersville, Ga. AG 2/19/1910

WATTS, John A., age 58, d. 201 Carter St. Atlanta. AG 9/17/1907

WATTS, Joseph E., age 36, d. Macon, Ga. AG 7/15/1909

WATTS, Kendricks, colored, age 3, d. 32 Fairfax St. Atlanta. AG 1/31/1908

WATTS, May, age 17, d. 101 N. Butler St. Atlanta. AG 9/17/1907

WATTS, Robert Lee, blind, son of Mr. and Mrs. William of Valdosta, d. 1/4 Atlanta. AC 1/3/1905

WATTS, Sadie, colored, age 23, d. 130 McDaniel St. Atlanta. AG 5/13/1907

WATTS, Walter F., age 21, son of Mr. and Mrs. T. P. Watts, died at family res. on Decatur Rd. Mon. Interment: Wesley Chapel church yard. AG 12/17/1906

WATTS, William Haywood, colored, age 4 mos., d. 27 Gunby St. Atlanta. AG 3/3/1909

WAXELBAUM, E. A. funeral from res. Oak St., Macon. Interred: William Wolff Cemetery. AG 9/10/1908

WAY, Fred, former Atlantan, d. 7/23 Dallas, Tex. Interred: Westview, Atlanta. Wife, father, mother, 2 sisters. AG 7/27/1907

WAY, Martha, dau. of Mr. and Mrs. Hilliard, d. 99 Rawson St., Atlanta, Fri. Interred: Westview. AG 6/11/1909

WEAKS, Benjamin Patrick, age 1, d. 25 Hugh St. Atlanta. AG 4/13/1909

WEATHERFORD, W. C., Mrs., age 39, d. 17 W. Cain St. Atlanta. AG 7/12/1907

WEATHERS, Robert Lee, age 18 mos., d. 101 Butler St. Atlanta. AG 10/11/1909

WEATHERSBEE, W. G., Mrs. of Hephzibah died Augusta. AG 2/12/1907

WEATHERSBY, George Rix, age 26, d. 42 E. Baker St., Atlanta Thurs. Interred: Oakland. AG 12/26/1908

WEAVER, Annie, colored, age 45, d. 101 N. Butler St. Atlanta. AG 5/4/1909

WEAVER, Benjamin F., age 43, d. 267 Capitol Ave. Atlanta. AG 2/8/1909

WEAVER, C. W., age 41, d. 54 W. Luckie St., Atlanta, Mon. Interred: McClenny, Fla. AG 12/27/1910

WEAVER, Harry, Mrs. d. Sat. Montgomery, W. Va. Interred: Opelika, Ala. Sisters: Florence, Annie and Kate Fallaw, Mrs. W. Pruitt (Rhine, Ga.) Bros: J. R., T. H. and Smith Fallaw. AG 1/21/1908

WEAVER, Henry, colored, shot and killed by Richard Jackson, Donalsonville, Ga. AG 3/22/1907

WEAVER, J. H., age 75, d. Milledgeville, Ga. AG 3/7/1907

WEAVER, J. H., Rev., age 78, d. Atlanta; b. 1829 Newton Co.; 1858 m. Eliza, dau. of Rev. Joshua Callaway, Jonesboro, who lived 1-yr. after marriage. Sisters: Mrs. Jane Hendry, Mrs. Martha Hendry, Cuthbert. Bur: Sharon Church. AG 3/5/1907

WEAVER, James H., Dr., bro. of Mrs. Mary Brown, d. several mos. ago., Atlanta. AC 4/3/1905

WEAVER, Mary, Miss, age 20, d. Ellijay, Ga. AG 12/28/1910

WEAVER, Mary, Mrs., age 79, d. Fri. Lithonia, Ga. Interred: Redan Methodist Church yard. Sons: H. W., Atlanta; J. F., Lithonia. AG 7/22/1910

WEAVER, P. H. killed by lightning Sun., Decatur, Ga. Interred: Kellys Chapel. Had lost leg in Battle of Fredericksburg. His little son was killed by cyclone several yrs. ago. AG 5/25/ 9 0

WEAVER, Tom, negro, lynched by citizens after he fired at Mayor Wilson, Cordele, Ga. AG 8/22/1910

WEAVER, W. M., Judge, d. Mon. Greensboro, Ga. AG 6/16/1906

WEBB, A. M., age 25, d. Thomasville, Ga. AG 6/11/1910

WEBB, Albert M., age 21, d. Thomasville, Ga. Thurs. Interred: Decatur Cemetery. AG 6/10/1910

WEBB, Andrew, Mrs. d. Doves Creek, Ga. Sun., age 66. Husband, 5 children. AG 11/15/1910

WEBB, Austin d. res. of dau., Mrs. J. M. Scarbrough, 5 Tilden St., Howell St., Ga., Sun. Bur: Casey's Cemetery. AG 1/20/1908

WEBB, Eliza, colored, age 60, d. 101 N. Butler St. Atlanta. AG 1/1/1908

WEBB, Ella, Mrs., age 27, d. near Kirkwood, Atlanta, Mon. Interred: Decatur, Ga. Husband, 3 children, 3 sisters, 4 bros. AG 3/10/1909

WEBB, H. R., age 39, d. 23 Glesham St. Atlanta. AG 11/11/1907

WEBB, Harry, colored, age 21, d. Atlanta. AG 7/19/1909

WEBB, Laura, Mrs., age 77, d. Tues. Centerville, Ga. Interred: Masons church yard. Sons: Owen, C. A., D. W., Atlanta. Dau: Mrs. Josie Hetrick, Atlanta. AG 12/29/1909

WEBB, Lawrence, Mrs., age 22, d. 639 E. Fair St., Atlanta Thurs. Husband, mother, Mrs. Amanda Womack, and three children survive. AG 5/14/1908

WEBB, Malinda, Mrs., age 72, d. res. of dau., Mrs. J. M. Scarborough, 5 Tilden St., Thurs. Husband: Austin Webb. 5 daus. AG 3/8/1907

WEBB, Martha, age 10, of Canton, Ga., d. Atlanta. AG 9/21/1910

WEBB, Maude, Mrs., wife of Jesse, age 24, d. 85 Wells St. Atlanta. Interred: Winder, Ga. AG 7/10/1908

WEBB, Odessa, Miss, dau. of Hon. J. P., d. 11/24 Carrollton, age 15. AC 11/26/1905

WEBB, Robert funeral 11/18 mother's res., Mrs. S. C. Webb, 26 Capitol Ave., Atlanta. Interred: Hollywood. Relatives: Mr. and Mrs. J. B. Norton; Mr. and Mrs. J. W. Tuck. AC 11/18/1905

WEBER, William Lander, Dr., Pres. of Mansfield Female College, Mansfield, La., d, former faculty member of Emory College, Oxford, Ga. 3 children, wife, who is dau. of Bishop Wilson, Baltimore, Md. AG 10/4/1910

WEBSTER, Catherine, Mrs., age 26, d. Atlanta. AG 5/4/1908

WEBSTER, E. A., Mrs. d. Tues. Interred: Decatur, Ga. AG 6/10/1909

WEBSTER, George T., Mrs., age 24, of 238 Central Ave. Atlanta, d. Fri. AG 5/1/1908

WEBSTER, Mildred, age 14, dau. of Mr. and Mrs. Frank A., d. Thurs. Interred: Savannah, Ga. AG 10/16/1907

WEBSTER, Mildred Helen, age 14, dau. of Mr. and Mrs. Frank A., d. 161 E. Pine St., Atlanta, Wed. AG 10/9/1907

WEBSTER, S. Z. d. Valley Grove, Ga. 9/2. Interred: Valley Cemetery. AC 9/3/1905

WEBSTER, W. S. d. Norcross, Ga. 12/17. Wife, 5 ch: Misses Harriet and Sarah Webster, Joe, Kiser and Edward Webster. Sisters: Mrs. H. S. Barfield, Miss Georgia Webster of Columbus, and Mrs. J. A. Reynolds of Macon. AG 12/18/1909

WEBSTER, infant of Mr. and Mrs. A. E. d. last night Mt. Airy, Ga. Interred: Eastview. AG 6/28/1906

WEDENMEYER, Frances, Mrs., age 76, d. 11 Orange St. Atlanta, mother of musician, Fred. She was b. Germany 1831. Sons: Fred of Atlanta, Albert of Omaha, Nebr. Daus: Mrs. John Shelton of Highland Park, Ill.; Mrs. James Roberson (or Robinson), Atlanta. Kin: Misses Lena & Josie Wittig, Mr. & Mrs. Fred Wedemeyer, Mr. & Mrs. Albert Wedemeyer of Omaha, Nebraska. AG 3/16/1907

WEEDEN, Howard, Miss d. Huntsville, Ala. 4/11. AC 4/13/1905

WEEKES, Charles, Mrs., age 75, d. Mon. at son's res., W. H. Weekes, DeKalb Co. She was wife of late John W. Weekes. Ch: W. H., C. L., P. L., L. P., J. W., Clara, J. W., Mrs. J. R. George. Interred: Decatur. AG 5/21/1906

WEEKLEY, L. E., age 50, d. 396 Capitol Ave. Atlanta. AG 11/12/1910

WEEKS, Clara, Miss, of Decatur, d. Mon. Bro: W. H. Weeks, Decatur. Interred: Decatur Cemetery. Bros: W. H., C. L., Poleman L. and L. P. Weeks of Decatur and J. W. Weeks of Lithonia. Sis: Mrs. John R. George, Lithonia. AG 6/16/1908

WEEKS, Clarisa, Mrs. funeral Decatur, Ga. Tues. Interred: Decatur. AG 5/23/1906

WEEMS, Chester, age 18, d. res. of mother, Mrs. Sallie Weems, Riverside, Ga., Tues. Bros: Charles, Fred. Sis: Mrs. M. L. Redd. Interred: Westview. AG 5/11/1910

WEEMS, Grady S., son of Mr. and Mrs. E. C., d. 107 Kennedy St., Atlanta, Sun. Interred: Marietta, Ga. AG 2/10/1908

WEEMS, Missouri, colored, age 6, d. 256 Greensferry Ave. Atlanta. AG 10/9/1907

WEEMS, W. A., age 28, d. Atlanta Fri. Interred: Meade, Fla. AG 5/8/1910

WEEMS, Winnie, colored, age 31, d. 215 Hubbard St. Atlanta. AG 11/5/1907

WEEMS, J. A., Mrs., Union Springs, Ala., formerly Pauline Jeter, sis. of late William Lamar Jeter and of Mrs. Samuel Carter, Carters, Ga. d. yesterday. Husb., sis., 2 grown ch. survive. Sons: Randle, Jeter, Walter, Atlanta. AG 12/9/1907

WEICHER, Newton, Mrs. d. Tues. Tunnel Hill, Ga. Interred: West Hill Cemetery, Dalton, a. AG 8/4/1910

WEIMER, Conrad, age 43, d. Fri. S. Kirkwood, Ga. Interred: Oakland. AG 6/21/1907

WEINBERGER, Mary, Mrs. d. Fri. 282 Piedmont Ave., Atlanta. Husband, two daughters, son, survive. AG 5/26/1906

WEINHOLTZ, Wilhelmina, age 75, d. Thurs. 209 Bass St. Atlanta. AG 7/12/1906

WEISS, Jennie, wife of William, age 63, d. Tues. 432 Central Ave., Atlanta. Interred: Westview. AG 9/9/1909

WELBORN, C. O. d. East Point, Ga. Interred: Oakland. AG 9/14/1907

WELBORN, Emma, age 8 mos., d. Rhinehart St. Atlanta. AG 10/8/1907

WELBORN, Emma, inf. dau. of Mr. and Mrs. T. A., interred Hollywood cemetery. AG 10/8/1907

WELBORN, Etta M, Miss, age 27, d. Atlanta Tues. Granddau of George Griffin of Atlanta. AG 3/1/1910

WELBORN, Etta, Miss d. Atlanta Tues. Interred: Statham, Ga. AG 3/2/1910

WELCH, C. E., Mrs., age 676, d. 283 Marietta St. Atlanta. AG 9/9/1908

WELCH, Edward, abt 40 yrs. old, d. Sun, suicide, Sandersville, Ga. AG 6/26/1906

WELCH, Herren, infant son of Mr. and Mrs. T. W., d. 248 W. Mitchell St. Atlanta. Interred: Jackson, Ga. AG 11/2/1906

WELCH, J. T., Mrs., age 21, d. 9/27 Columbus. AG 9/28/1909

WELCH, Robert, colored, age 49, d. 12 Jennings St. Atlanta. AG 3/3/1909

WELCH, Theodore, age 3, d. 248 W. Mitchell St. Atlanta. AG 11/5/1906

WELCH, W. A., colored, age 25, d. 412 McDaniel St. Atlanta. AG 2/7/1908

WELCH, William, age 105, of Acworth, Ga., b. 3/26, was over age 60 when enl. in Co. F, 14th N. H. Vols. Draws pension. AC 1/29/1905

WELL, Ella, colored, age 32, d. Emmett St. Atlanta. AG 4/12/1909

WELLBORN, Asbury H., 18 mos. old, d. from street car accident. Atlanta. AG 9/8/1906

WELLBORN, Etta, Miss, age 27, d. 30 Crew St. Atlanta. AG 3/3/1910

WELLBORN, Ida, Mrs., wife of A. J. of Rock Spring, Chickamauga, buried today. AG 9/19/1906

WELLBORN, J. M., age 87, d. Conyers, where res. for 25 yrs. Several children. Interred: E. View Cemetery. AC 5/14/1905

WELLBORN, S. N., of Union Springs, Montgomery, Ala. d. yesterday. Interred: Eufaula, Ala. AG 8/31/1906

WELLHOUSE, Fannie, Mrs., funeral Sun., res. 245 W. Peachtree St. Atlanta. Relatives: Mr. and Mrs. Louis Wellhouse, Mr. and Mrs. Alvin Wellhouse, Mr. and Mrs. Leo Wellhouse, Mr. and Mrs. Max J. Young, Mr. and Mrs. Moerne Young. AG 10/6/1906

WELLMAKER, William, colored, age 11 mos., d. Edgewood, Ga. AG

WELLONS, Elizabeth, Mrs., age 89, from N. C., d. 4/6 res. of dau., Mrs. J. R. Miller, Perry, Ga. 2 daus., one in La. She was widow of W. S. Wellons, Soldier in War of 1812. AC 4/8/1905

WELLS, son of Edward. Murdered by his father, Edward Wells 72 Mills St. Atlanta. AC 9/16/1905

WELLS, A. P., Mrs., age 79, d. Thurs. res. of son, J. Mitt Wells, 161 Gordon St., Atlanta. Interred: Westview. AG 5/17/1907

WELLS, Andrew J., age 32, d. son´s res., E. F. Wells, Forest Park, Fri. Wife, several children. Interred: Forest Park, Ga. AG 9/11/1909

WELLS, Carl, age 5, d. 29 Tye St., Atlanta. AG 9/8/1909

WELLS, Charlie killed Wed. by falling door, 616 Marietta St., Atlanta. Pallbearers: Elma Wadkins, Clyde Roper, Joe Loveless, John Doyl, Ernest Owings. AG 9/21/1906

WELLS, Cincinnatus H. LWT probated. Fannie B. and Henry G. Wells qualified as exrs., Fulton Co. AG 9/26/1908

WELLS, Cincinnatus Henry, age 49, d. 61 E. Tenth St. Atlanta. AG 9/14/1908

WELLS, Clifford, inf. son of Mr. and Mrs. John, d. Sun. 17 Bluff St., Atlanta. Interred: Westview. AG 8/19/1907

WELLS, Curtis, age 2, d. home of parents, Mr. and Mrs. William, 11 Downie St., Atlanta. Interred: Winder, Ga. AG 6/15/1906

WELLS, E. A., Mrs., age 79, d. 161 Gordon Ave. Atlanta. AG 5/18/1907

WELLS, Frank L. d. Knoxville, Tenn. 10/21. AG 10/21/1910

WELLS, James R., Mrs., age 30, funeral 6/2. Kin: Dr. James R. Wells, Mrs. M. E. McLendon, J. F. McLendon. Interred: Oakland. Husband, dau., father, James S. McLendon. AG 6/1/1908

WELLS, Jessie, Mrs., age 25, d. 68 Johnson Ave., Atlanta, Mon., wife of E. A. One child. Interred: Stone Mountain, Ga. AG 6/28/1910

WELLS, Joel H., age 39, d. 56 West End Ave. Atlanta. AG 3/28/1907

WELLS, Joseph H., age 40, d. his res. 56 West End Ave. Atlanta. Wife, baby girl, survive. AG 3/25/1907

WELLS, Julia B., infant dau. of Mr. and Mrs. L. A. Wells, d. Sat. Oakland City, at res. of grandparents, Mr. and Mrs. H. C. Hutcheson, College Park. AG 6/17/1907

WELLS, Katie Lucie, age 2, d. 49 Lyle St. Atlanta. AG 9/6/1910

WELLS, M. M., age 66, father of P. A., d. Fri. Campbell Rd. Atlanta. Wife, 7 children. Interred: Westview. AG 8/6/1910

WELLS, M. M., Mrs., age 62, d. 566 Central Ave. Atlanta. AG 11/8/1909

WELLS, Mary E., Mrs., age 84, d. 380 W. Peachtree St. Atlanta. AG 7/20/1907

WELLS, Miramlee, Mrs., age 57, d. 466 W. Hunter St. Atlanta. AG 2/24/1908

WELLS, Miranda, Mrs.,a ge 57, wife of H. H., d. Sat. 466 W. Hunter St., Atlanta. Husband, 5 children. Interred: Hollywood. AG 2/24/1908

WELLS, Raymond, age 19, son of Dr. and Mrs. J. S., d. Atlanta 7/27. Interred: Griffin, his res. AG 7/28/1910

WELLS, Raymond B., age 20, of Griffin, Ga., d. Wed. Atlanta, son of Dr. J. B. Bros: J. H., H. P., W. O., all of Griffin. AG 7/28/1910

WELLS, Ruth, inf. dau. of Mr. and Mrs. W. M., funeral Mon. Nancy Creek. AG 6/4/1906

WELLS, S. H, age 58, d. 510 N. Jackson St. Atlanta. He removed to Atlanta from Elkton, Ky. yr. ago. Wife, 3 children: Mrs. Bromfield Ridle, Miss Annie Nold Wells, Horace Wells, Jr. Interred: Elkton, Ky. AG 4/3/1908

WELLS, S. P., Capt., bro. of late Charles of Atlanta, d. Greenville, S. C. 9/20/ AG 9/21/1909

WELLS, Sammie W., age 60, d. Long Branch, N. J. AG 4/22/1907

WELLS, Stewart, age 14, d. East Point, Ga. AG 9/6/1906

WELLSBORN, J. P. d. El Paso, Texas. Funeral 12/9 res. of parents, 284 Connally St., Atlanta. Interred: Westview. AC 12/10/1905

WELL, E. A. of Savannah d. 7/10 Atlantic City. Born Laupheim, Wurtenburg, Germany 11/17/1834. Came to America age 20, res. Statesboro, Ga. Enl. Bulloch Co. 5th Ga. Cav., Civil War. m. Miss Babette Meinhardt. Daus: Mrs. David Stern, Quincy, Ill.; Mrs. I. H. Hirsch; Mrs. James H. Hirsch; Mrs. Jack H. Hirsch, all of Atlanta; Miss Rita Well, Savannah. Son: Arthur L. AC 7/12/1905

WELMAN, J. H., Mrs., age 55, d. 17 W. Cain St. Atlanta. AG 11/6/1907

WELSH, Helen, Mrs., age 55, d. 352 Whitehall St., Atlanta, Tues. Daus: Mrs. Joseph Strauss; Mrs. Sam Neill of Clio, S. C.; Misses Henrietta and Rosa Welsh, Atlanta. Son: C. S., San Antonio, Tx. Interred: Charleston, S. C. AG 3/9/1910

WELSH, Henry, colored, 42 Green St., Atlanta, killed Atlanta race riot. AG 9/24/1906

WELSH, James P., age 33, bur: Marietta. Wife was Miss Pearl McClatchey (survives). Mother: Mrs. E. I. Welsh. Sis: Mrs. E. P. Swetman, Slidell, La.; Mrs. J. H. Groves; Misses Martha, Ava, Louise. Bros: George, Stanley. AG 10/12/1909

WENTWORTH, Blanche, Mrs., age 49, d. 101 N. Butler St. Atlanta. AG 5/18/1907

WESLEY, Delia, colored, age 5, d. 68 Johnson Ave. Atlanta. AG 3/16/1908

WESLEY, Charles, colored, age 70, d. Fulton Co. Alms House. AG 3/10/1908

WEST, Anderson, colored, age 48, d. 197 Bell St. Atlanta, Oct. 27. AG 10/29/1910

WEST, B. F., age 65 or 70, of Gainesville, Ga. found dead in woods, near Peachtree Sts. and W. Peachtree Sts. Atlanta. Interred: Gainesville. AG 3/28/1910

WEST, Delilah F., age 61, d. 107 Broyles St. Atlanta. AG 6/15/1910

WEST, Eltrude E., Mrs. d. Sun. 220 Beacon St., S. Macon, Ga. Interred: Rose Hill. AG 10/22/1907

WEST, Eugene, inf. son of Mr. and Mrs. George W., d. 65 Almore Ave. Atlanta, Tues. Interred: Hollywood. AG 5/13/1908

WEST, Fay T., age 1 mo., infant dau. of Mr. and Mrs. T. B. West, d. Mon. 243 N. Boulevard, Atlanta. Interred: Westview. AG 7/8/1907

WEST, G. E., Mrs. d. 116 Main St., Atlanta, Wed. Interred: Hollywood. AG 4/8/1908

WEST, George, Mrs., age 45, d. 284 Courtland St. Atlanta. Res. of Carrollton, Ga. Interred: Carrollton. AG 10/1/1909

WEST, Henry, age 4, d. 89 Foundry St. Atlanta. AG 7/17/1907

WEST, Henry, colored, age 55, d. 8 Beard St. Atlanta. AG 3/16/1907

WEST, J. Oxford, age 19, d. res. of father, Dr. S. F. West, Fri., Atlanta. Interred: Bethesda Church yard. AG 11/5/1910

WEST, Joe, colored, age 32, d. 101 Butler St. Atlanta. AG 10/11/1909

WEST, Madison, colored, age 61, d. 194 E. Ellis St. Atlanta. AG 10/7/1909

WEST, Rosa Helen, age 9 mos., d. 9 Berean Ave. Atlanta. AG 11/22/1909

WESTBROOK, Charles, colored, age 46, d. 197 Little St. Atlanta. AG 6/21/1909

WESTBROOK, Garnett, age 1, d. 97 Carroll St. Atlanta. AG 10/4/1910

WESTBROOKS, Alice, colored, age 25, d. Nashville, Tenn. AG 1/3/1908

WESTBROOKS, infant of J. O., d. Mayson and Turner Rds. Atlanta. AG 7/3/1910

WESTBURY, Mr. believed to be body of, a raft hand, found in Altamaha River near Dents rice plantation 4/1. AC 4/3/1905

WESTER, J. T. d. 7/17, age 35. Interred: Newnan, N. C., his old home. AC 7/18/1905

WESTFALL, Mamie A., Mrs., age 34, d. 92 Luckie St. Atlanta. Husband. One son, three bros., three sisters. AG 5/6/1909

WESTFALLS, J. W. of Atlanta d. Sun. Funeral: Dug Gap Church, Dalton, Ga. Age 54. Wife. One child. AG 5/3/1910

WESTFIELD, Philip, colored, age 25, d. Milledgeville, Ga. AG 1/28/1908

WESTLEY, L. F., age 80, d. Fulton Co. almshouse. Atlanta. AG 10/22/1906

WESTLEY, Sam, colored, age 3 mos., d. 32 Diamond St. Atlanta. AG 5/20/1908

WESTMORELAND, Hattie B., colored, age 21, d. 134 Crumley St. Atlanta. AG 10/18/1909

WESTMORELAND, Sarah, Miss, 2nd dau. of Col. and Mrs. George, d. Decatur Tues. Interment: Westview. AG 10/1/1906

WEY, Jennie B., Mrs., age 43, d. 131 Spring St. Atlanta. AG 6/1/1907

WEYMAN, Elizabeth, age 1, d. 53 E. 14th St. Atlanta. AG 6/1/1907

WHARTON, M. B., Rev. Dr. d. Atlanta Mon. Interred: Eufaula, Ala. AG 7/23/1908

WHATLEY, Jett, Mrs. d. Sun. Helena, Ga. Husband, children-2 girls, 1 boy. Interred: McRae Cemetery. AG 8/10/1909

WHATLEY, Rebecca R., Mrs., age 38, d. 315 Highland Ave. Atlanta Sun., wife of Sgt. Whatley of Atlanta police dept. Interred: Lithonia, Ga. AG 6/1/1908

WHATLEY, S. J., Mrs., mother of Sgt. Whatley of police dept., d. Sun. 321 W. Fifth St. Atlanta. 10 children. interred: Meansville, Ga. AG 10/24/1910

WHEAT, Margaret A., Mrs. d. Sat. Atlanta, age 56. Sons: Frank C. Whet, John D. Wheat, 86 Hill St., Atlanta. Bros: William Carroll, Richmond, Va.; John Carroll, Covingtin, La. Interred: Oakland. AG 12/3/1907

WHEELER, A. A. run over and killed by street car Sun. at Crumps Park, Macon. AG 7/10/1906

WHEELER, Alberta, colored, age 21, d. 210 Parson St. Atlanta, Nov. 3. AG 11/5/1910

WHEELER, Bedford, colored, age 56, d. 42 Electric St. Atlanta. AG 11/21/1910

WHEELER, Edward W., colored, age 9, d. 310 Fort St. Atlanta. AG 10/3/1908

WHEELER, Geo. W., Mrs., bur. Warrenton. Daus: Mrs. Kate Pilcher, Warrenton; Mrs. W. B. Emory, Atlanta. Sis: Mrs. J. L. Cox & W. A. Orme. Bros: W. H. Heath, Washington, DC; R. H. Heath, L. Rock, AR; Geo. Heath. Sons: C. A., Will. AG 8/7/1908

WHEELER, Joseph, Gen., native of Augusta, b. 9/10/1831 d. 4/26/1906. W. Point Cadet, Lt. in US Army, representative of Congress. At Shiloh, Murfreesboro, Chickamauga, age 26 when in battle of Murfreesboro. Lived Ala. aftere war. AG 4/26/1906

WHEELER, Kate, colored, age 2, d. 240 Foundry St. Atlanta, Nov. 4. AG 11/5/1910

WHEELER, Lura, age 16, son of W. C., d. Atlanta, Sat. Interred: Duluth. AG 8/3/1908

WHEELER, O. D., Mrs. of Piedmont Ave., Atlanta. Interred: Oakland. AG 5/4/1906

WHEELER, Pinke V.,, wid. of O. D., d. Charlotte, N. C. 5/2, formerly Pinke Walker, Atlanta, dau. of late B. F. Mother survives. Sis: Mrs. Noyes, Mrs. Frank Clement, Atlanta. Bros: Dr. W. P., H. Lee, W. B., J. M. Bur: Oakland. AG 5/3/1906

WHELCHER, Walter, age 2 yr., son of Mr. and Mrs. L. C., d. 720 E. Fair St. Atlanta. Interred: Canton, Ga. AG 7/10/1908

WHELEN, Pat, age 63, d. Atlanta Wed. Interred: Westview. AG 12/39/1910

WHIDBY, William A. d. Sat. Father: W. E. of Peachtree Rd. Interred: Sardis Cem. Wife, one child. AG 3/29/1909

WHIPPLE, Herschel, colored, age 52, d. College Park. AG 5/20/1909

WHIPPY, F. C., Mrs., age 53, d. 35 W. Peachtree St. Atlanta. AG 8/8/1906

WHIPPY, Mrs., of Cinn., visiting Atlanta for her health. d. Wed. Husband: C. F. Whippy. AG 8/3/1906

WHITAKER, Audley, age 3, son of Mr. and Mrs. J. H., d. Fri. Atlanta. Interred: Gaffney, S. C. AG 8/6/1910

WHITAKER, Henry J., age 69, d. 127 S. Forsyth St., Atlanta, Wed. Wife. Ch: Mrs. S. P. Sims, Atlanta; Cyrus, W. Springfield, Mass.; Arthur, Enfield, Conn. AG 1/5/1910

WHITAKER, M., colored, age 49, d. 170 Markham St. Atlanta. AG 9/30/1908

WHITAKER, Thomas S. d. Wed. Atlanta. Funeral res. of parents, Dr. and Mrs. S. T. Whitaker, in Oakland City. Interred: Westview. AG 9/15/1910

WHITAKER, W. B., Dr. d. Elberton, Ga. 5/26. Wife, one child. Born and reared in Enfield, N. C., moved to Elberton 12 yrs. ago. Interred: Elmhurst Cemetery. AG 5/27/1910

WHITBY, William A., age 23, d. Ponce DeLeon Springs. Atlanta. AG 3/29/1909

WHITCOMB, Dorothy, Miss, age 33, d. Tues. Clifton Springs, N. Y. Interred: Atlanta, Westview Cemetery. AG 2/19/1910

WHITCOMB, John, Capt. of Dawson, Ga. d. 3/28, age 81. Wife. Several grown children. AC 3/30/1905

WHITE, Alma, Mrs., wife of Q., Atlanta, d. 12/10, 443 Edgewood Ave., age 25. 2 children. Interred: Flowery Branch, Ga. AC 12/11/1905

WHITE, Annie, Mrs., age 63, wife of B. S., d. McDonough Rd., Atlanta, Fri. Interred: Marvin's Cemetery. 4 sons, 2 daus, 1 bro., 4 sisters. AG 10/8/1909

WHITE, Arthur, age 14 mos., son of Mr. and Mrs. Frank, d. 71 Tennille St. Atlanta. Interred: Westview. AG 12/4/1909

WHITE, Arthur C. d. on train near Atlanta Mon. Interred: Winchester, Va. AG 3/17/1910

WHITE, Berry, inf. dau. of Mr. and Mrs. W. V., of 59 Jefferson St., Atlanta, d. Wed. Interred: Westview. AG 2/24/1910

WHITE, Dennis, colored, age 48, d. 10 Old Wheat St. Atlanta. AG 2/24/1908

WHITE, D. O. killed Birmingham, Ala. Thurs. Res. of 12 Gilmer St., Atlanta. Interred: Westview. AG 12/7/1907

WHITE, E. O., railroad man of Atlanta, killed in rr yards, Birmingham, Ala., Thurs. Res. of 12 Gilmer St. Atlanta. Widowed. No ch. Interred: Westview. AG 12/6/1907

WHITE, Ed, colored, d. age 24 of dynamite explosion. Atlanta. AG 3/28/1907

WHITE, Edward A. d. Denver, Colo. Funeral in Atlanta 9/10. AC 9/11/1905

WHITE, Eliza A., age 79, d. Oakland City, Atlanta, Fri. Bro: Francis M. White. AG 8/7/1909

WHITE, Elizabeth, age 1, d. 22 Garden St. Atlanta. AG 10/29/1907

WHITE, Elizabeth Jarrett, inf. dau. of Mr. and Ms. V. A., d. res. of Dr. C. P. Ward, 226 Gordon St., Atlanta. Interred: Tugalo, Ga. AG 10/26/1907

WHITE, Gertrude, Miss, age *33, d. 286 Peachtree St. Atlanta. Dau. of late Capt. and Dora White. Sis: Mrs. James Davenport, Americus; Mrs. S. W. Beck, Griffin. Interred: Griffin, Ga. AG 9/30/1909

WHITE, Gertrude, Miss, age 33, d. 286 Peachtree St. Atlanta. Dau. of late Capt. and Dora White. Sis: Mrs. James Davenport, Americus; Mrs. S. W. Beck, Griffin. Interred: Griffin, Ga. AG 9/30/1909

WHITE, Gus, a negro, fatally stabbed, 54 Decatur St., Atlanta Mon. AG 8/26/1907

WHITE, I. K., age 68, died at 11 Castleberry Street, Atlanta. AG 12/20/1906

WHITE, J. A., age 42, d. 26 North Henry St., Atlanta, Sun. Dau: Stella. Sister: Mrs. L. P. Williams. Bros: J. T., J. M. and G. A. White. Interred: Family Burial Ground. AG 7/27/1908

WHITE, J. K., age 68, died at res., 11 Castleberry St., Atlanta. Survived by wife. Body sent Fairburn, Ga. for interment. AG 12/18/1906

WHITE, J. M., Mrs. d. Flat Shoals Rd. Atlanta Sat. Survived by husband, 3 daus., 9 sons. AG 5/25/1908

WHITE, John, colored, age 90, d. 101 N. Butler St. Atlanta. AG 3/11/1909

WHITE, Joseph, colored, age 34, d. 25 Orange St. Atlanta. AG 5/8/1908

WHITE, Katie, Mrs., age 17, d. 281 S. Humphries St. Atlanta. Interred: Flippen, Ga. AG 10/18/1907

WHITE, L. D., Mrs. d. Sun. AG 9/27/1909

WHITE, L. W., colored, age 53, d. 42 Auburn Ave. Atlanta. AG 9/14/1908

WHITE, Laura E., Mrs., age 82, widow of late John C., Atlanta pioneer, d. 206 Ivy St. Atlanta Sun. Interred: Oakland. Daus: Mrs. George M. Hope, Mrs. Walter Tomlinson. Nephew: Charles E. Currier. AG 3/29/1909

WHITE, M., colored, age 5, d. 270 Ivy St. Atlanta. AG 3/18/1909

WHITE, M. A., Mrs., age 73, d. 523 Highland Ave., Atlanta. AG 1/1/1908

WHITE, M. B., Mrs., age 72, mother of atty T. Hudson, and pioneer of E. Tenn., d. Chattanooga, Tenn. 5/3. Interred: Bristol. AG 5/4/1910

WHITE, Maggie A. S., age 35, d. 523 Highland Ave. Atlanta. AG 2/15/1910

WHITE, Mamie H., Mrs., age 29, d. 166 W. Alexander St., Atlanta, wife of S. H. Interred: Westview. AG 8/30/1910

WHITE, Mamie, Mrs., age 37, d. 212 Murphy Ave. Atlanta. AG 9/29/1909

WHITE, Martha, Mrs. d. 153 Emmett St., Atlanta, Sat. Interred: Austell, Ga. AG 5/11/1908

WHITE, Mary A., Mrs., 75, d. 523 Highland Ave., Atlanta Tues. Ch: V. A. White, Dencourt, Ga.; Mrs. J. P. Green, Brookwood, Ala.; E. A., C. L. and J. A. White; Miss Maggie White, Atlanta. Interred: Austell, Ga., Fam. Grounds. AG 12/30/1907

WHITE, Mary E., Miss, age 70, d. 97 Washington St. Atlanta. AG 5/16/1910

WHITE, Mary, Mrs. d. Sat. 169 Echo St., Atlanta. Interred: Athens, Ga. AG 5/26/1906

WHITE, Mary, Mrs., age 69, d. 303 Rawson St., Atlanta, Thurs. Interred: Hollywood. AG 3/10/1910

WHITE, Mary, Mrs., age 77, mother of Hon. W. Woods White and Menzo White of Atlanta, d. 10/30 College Park, Ga., where buried. AC 10/31/1905

WHITE, Maude, Mrs. d. Thurs. Jacksonville, Fla. Res: 168 E. Georgia Ave., Atlanta. Mother, Mrs. H. N. Moore, and sister, Mrs. N. H. Bullock. Interred: Westview. AG 6/14/1907

WHITE, Minnie, colored, age 32, d. corner Luckie and Bartow
Streets, Atlanta. AG 10/1/1907
WHITE, Odessa, Mrs. interred family cemetery, Cobb Co., Ga.
Husband: Jack. AG 9/20/1909
WHITE, Oliver T., Jones Co., bur. Milledgeville. Confed.,
Hampton's Legion. Md. sis. of Mark Johnson, niece of journalist,
Malcomb Johnson. Daus: Mrs. Stallings, Alice White, Atlanta.
Sons: Dr. Oliver T. Mt. Airy; Dr. Mark. AG 10/29/1906
WHITE, Roscoe, age 17, d. Atlanta Sun. Interred: Westview. AG
5/21/1906
WHITE, S. M., age 2, d. Atlanta. AG 12/17/1910
WHITE, Sallie, colored, age 24, d. 156 E. Harris St. Atlanta. AG
1/14/1908
WHITE, Sidney E., age 3, son of Mr. and Mrs. Cecil, d. Wed.
Birmingham, Ala. Interred: Birmingham. AG 8/8/1907
WHITE, Thelma, 22 mos., d. 311 S. McDaniel St. Atlanta. AG
8/24/1906
WHITE, Vivian, age 8, d. yesterday, dau. of Mr. and Mrs. H. M.,
574 S. Pryor St., Atlanta. AG 5/3/1906
WHITE, W. A., age 63, d. 346 Humphries St. Atlanta. AG 11/27/1907
WHITE, W. C., telegraph operator, Jonesboro, Ga. shot by Will Lee
10/11. AG 2/8/1907
WHITE, W. H., Sheriff of Heard Co., Ga. d. Mon. AG 6/18/1907
WHITE, William Floyd, infant son of Mr. and Mrs. J. A., d. 168
Echo St., Atlanta. Interred: Hollywood. AG 6/5/1907
WHITE, Willie, inf. son of Mr. and Mrs. W. S., d. Mon. 15 Short
St., Atlanta. AG 3/21/1910
WHITE, Wilson, colored, age 28, d. 192 Fraser St. Atlanta. AG
1/14/1908
WHITE, Zippie, miss, sister of Mrs. A. S. Clay, d. this morning
at res. of Senator Clay, Marietta, Ga., age 35. Survived by
mother, Mrs. M. V. White of Marietta, Mrs. Clay and one bro., L.
J. hite of Douglas Co. AG 3/1/1907
WHITEFIELD, Albert, son of Mr. and Mrs. J. T., d. 21 McDonald
St., Atlanta, Sun. Interred: Dunwoody, Ga. AG 12/30/1907
WHITEFORD, Robert, colored, age 36, d. 58 Culver St. Atlanta. AG
11/19/1909
WHITEHEAD, Emil of Carlton, 64, wid of Geo., Oglethorpe Co., d.
2/22, dau's res., Mrs. Walter Martin. Ch: Hon. W. E., Theotoric,
Mrs. Martin of Carlton; George of Comer; Mrs. T. C. Stevens,
Herbert Whitehead of Sandy Cross. AG 2/23/1910
WHITEHEAD, John C., age 70, d. 3/25 Winder, Ga. Wife, 4 children.
AG 3/26/1910
WHITEHEAD, Joseph B., age 42, died, Thaxton, Va. AG 8/29/1906
WHITEHEAD, Joseph J., age 6 mos., d. 74 Alamo St. Atlanta. AG
7/9/1906
WHITEHEAD, Thomas Y. of 159 Central Ave., Atlanta, age 49, b.
Athens, Ga. 1857. Killed in train accident. Cousin: Charles
Whitehead. Wife, former Miss Ada Armspaugh of Athens and 14-yr
old son, Frederick, survivors. AG 9/12/1906
WHITEHEAD, Joseph Brown, d. Thaxton, Va., funeral at res. 582
Peachtree St., Atlanta. Interred: Westview. AG 8/29/1906
WHITEHURST, J. C. d. Columbus, Ga. 2/21. Wife. Several ch. Bro:
F. M., Atlanta. AG 2/22/1910

WHITEN, S. A., age 21, employe of Sou. Bell, d. Grady Hospital, Atlanta. Res: 674 E. Fair St., Atlanta. Interred: Marietta. AG 7/25/1906

WHITES, W. B., Capt. of Atlanta, d. home of A. H. Kohn, Prosperity, S. C. Tues., age 69. Native of Newberry. Mbr of Co. H., 3rd S. C. Regt., Capt. D. A. Dickert. Interred: Prosperity. Son: R. L. Whites. AG 7/12/1906

WHITESIDE, Addie, Miss, age 45, d. res. of sister, Mrs. Flora Rapp on W. Hunter Rd. Atlanta. AG 4/24/1907

WHITFIELD, Allison, inf. son of Mr. and Mrs. B. P., d. 211 Fox St., Atlanta, Mon. Interred: Casey's. AG 2/16/1908

WHITFIELD, Cora, Mrs., age 27, d. Tues. 135 English Ave., Atlanta. Husband, two children. Interred: Caseys. AG 2/11/1907

WHITFIELD, Dessa Lucile, age 1, dau. of Mr. and Mrs. F. C., d. 697 Chestnut St., Atlanta, Wed. Interred: Casey's Cemetery. AG 7/2/1908

WHITFIELD, E. H., Mrs., wife of late Robert W. of Milledgeville, d. yesterday, Macon. 4 children, mother, 9 brothers, all of Macon. AG 1/5/1907

WHITFIELD, Eva, dau. of Mr. and Mrs. W. H., d. Sun. 161 Jefferson St. Atlanta. AG 4/23/1907

WHITFIELD, George, age 82, d. Decatur, Ga. AG 7/2/1908

WHITFIELD, Jones, colored, age 29, d. New York City. AG 3/26/1908

WHITFIELD, Joseph T., 18 mos., d. 697 Chestnut St., Atlanta, Thurs. Interred: Caseys. AG 8/4/1906

WHITLEY, Emma O., Miss, age 22, d. Mon. 342 Frasier St. Atlanta. Interred: Westview. AG 1/29/1907

WHITLEY, W. L., Mrs., 83, Rome, dau: Mrs. J. C. Crawford. 4 ch. AG 12/28/1906

WHITLOW, W. C., age 57, d. 178 Luckie St. Atlanta. AG 2/27/1907

WHITMAN, Earl d. Atlanta Tues. Bro: James R., 184 Forrest Ave., Atlanta. Interred: Westview. AG 2/25/1909

WHITMAN, J. R., Jr. killed Wed. night by street car. Res. 184 Forrest Ave., Atlanta. Interred: Westview. AG 4/2/1909

WHITMAN, William, age 14, d. Atlanta. AG 3/28/1910

WHITMEYER, Evans, age 13, son of Mr. and Mrs. J. M., drowned Tues, res. of 616 S. Pryor St. Thurs. Interred: Westview. AG 5/21/1908

WHITMIRE, Helen Marguerite, age 1 yr., dau. of Mr. and Mrs. H. F., d. Thurs., 343 Ormond St., Atlanta. Interred: Westview. AG 10/13/1906

WHITMIRE, James d. 42 Bass St., Atlanta Tues. Interred: Westview. AG 9/1/1909

WHITMORE, Mary P., Mrs. d. this morning at her home near Rome, wife of late Col. W. P. who served with distinction in Fla. wars. Age 65. Sis: R. N. Berrien, Atlanta. AG 3/4/1907

WHITNER, Charles H. d. Sanford, Fla. 1/5. Wife: Sadie Wallace Whitner, Atlanta. Sons: Charles H., Jr., Atlanta; Donald, Jacksonville, Fla. Interred: Sanford, FLa. AG 1/7/1910

WHITNER, E. M. S., Mrs., age 77, d. 34 Pulliam St. Atlanta. AG 11/1/1910

WHITNER, Elmira, colored, age 58, d. 11 Rawson St. Atlanta. AG 5/28/1906

WHITNER, Sarah Martha, Mrs., LWT filed for probate, Fulton Co., Ga. Exrs: sons, J. A., T. C. and C. F. Whitner. AG 11/14/1906

410

WHITSIT, Ruby, Mrs., dau. of J. G. Evans of E. Pt., Ga., d. Messina, N. Y., Sat. Interred: College Park Cemetery. Husband: Lyle. 4 bros. AG 11/15/1910

WHITT, Carrie, colored, age 30, d. rear of 201 Little St. Atlanta. AG 10/30/1909

WHITTEN, Effie, age 18, d. Terminal St. Atlanta. AG 3/10/1910

WHITTIER, Georgiana, Mrs., age 52, d. 209 Luckie St. Atlanta. AG 11/6/1907

WHITTLESEY, George C. funeral Mon. 177 E. Georgia Ave. Atlanta. Interred: Westview. AG 6/13/1906

WHITWORTH, Bessie, Miss d. res. of mother, Mrs. F. S. Whitworth, 124 Echo St., Atlanta, Sun. Her father was killed in Exposition Cotton Mills two mos. ago. Interred: Caseys. AG 4/1/1907

WHITWORTH, Floyd, inf. son of Mr. and Mrs. W. C., d. 117 Echo St., Atlanta. AG 2/11/1908

WICHARD, J. R., Mrs., age 42, d. 91 Summit Ave. Atlanta. AG 7/31/1908

WICKER, F. A., age 40, suicide, at 2 Haygood Ave., Atlanta. AG 11/20/1906

WICKER, J. A., age 54, d. Capitol View. Atlanta. AG 2/7/1910

WICKLIFE, William H., age 32, d. Sun. Atlanta. Interred: Branch, N. J. AG 5/4/1908

WIEBMAN, Edna, colored, age 1, d. 9 Robinson's alley. Atlanta. AG 3/27/1909

WIGGINS, Eugene, age 7 mos., d. 207 Grant St. Atlanta. AG 6/1/1907

WIGGINS, Jesse, Mrs., age 44, d. 118 Mangum St., Atlanta, Tues. Survived by husband, Jesse, and two daus. Interred: Dallas, Ga. AG 3/26/1907

WIGGINS, L. W. of Marietta suicide. AC 6/4/1905

WIGGINS, Lela G., Miss, age 17, d. Thurs. at Vannoy station. Interred: Morgan Church, Ga. AG 7/6/1907

WIGGINS, Lucie, Mrs., age 44, d. 118 Mangum St. Atlanta. AG 3/28/1907

WIGGINS, Matilda, Mrs., age 60, d. 112 Curran St., Atlanta, Wed. Interred: Lithia Springs, Ga. AG 6/16/1910

WIGGINS, Sanford, colored, age 37, d. 309 Fraser St. Atlanta. AG 10/3/1907

WIGHMAN, Annie L., Mrs. d. 6/4 res. of mother, Mrs. C. E. Young. Husband: George W. Wighman of Columbia, S. C. One child. AC 6/6/1905

WIGHTMAN, A. C., Dr. d. Richmond, Va. 11/12. AC 11/13/1905

WIGHTMAN, Mary, Mrs., age 72, d. Wed. 508 S. Boulevard, Atlanta. Interred: Westview. Dau: Mrs. Walter Hughes. AG 10/28/1909

WIGLEY, W. G., age 72, d. 345 E. Georgia Ave. Atlanta. Daus: Mrs. J. E. Scott of 345 E. Georgia Ave.; Mrs. W. H. Rice, 210 Grant St. Interred: Norcross, Ga. AG 8/29/1907

WILBANKS, Effie, colored, age 6, d. rear 137 Oakland Ave. Atlanta. AG 8/7/1908

WILBANKS, Minnie, Miss, age 22, d. 92 Powell St. Atlanta Wed. Father: W. C. Wilbanks, policeman. Interred: Hollywood. AG 10/2/1909

WILBERN, E. A. d. Grady Hospital. Atlanta. Age 45. AG 8/5/1907

WILBURN, John, colored, age 4 mos., d. 15 Phoenix alley. tlanta. AG 5/20/1908

WILBURN, Joseph G., age 56, d. Mon. Decatur, Ga. Interred: Decatur Cemetery. Wife, three daus: Miss Leila, Alice and Llewellyn Wilburn. Sons: Joseph G., Walter. One sister, two bros. AG 3/1/1910

WILCOX, B. E., age 44, of Fitzgerald, Ga., d. Atlanta. AG 8/6/1910

WILCOX, J. W., age 55, d. Atlanta. Son: Fred of Chicago, Ill. Interred: Westview. AG 12/6/1908

WILD, Antone, Savannah, Ga. ironworker, hanged himself during wife's funeral Millstadt, Ill. AC 12/15/1905

WILDER, Charles A., Mrs. d. Royston, Ga. Tues., age abt 60. Husband, C. A. Stepdau: Mrs. R. A. Willbanks of Lavonia, Ga. AG 7/22/1910

WILDER, Elizabeth, Mrs., age 67, d. Sat. 220 S. Boulevard, Atlanta. Interred: Sylvester, Ga. AG 3/16/1907

WILDER, J. W., age 26, d. 23 Ponders Ave. Atlanta. Interred: East Point, Ga. AG 2/24/1908

WILDER, J. W., age 26, d. 46 Hightower St., Atlanta, Sat. Leaves bride of several mos. AG 2/20/1908

WILDER, Judson J., age 51, d. city hospital, Macon, Thurs. No relatives in Macon. Interred: Gainesville, Ga. AG 3/29/1907

WILDER, S. A., Mrs., age 64, d. 506 Woodward Ave., Atlanta, Sun. Interred: McDaniel, Ga. AG 11/29/1909

WILDER, W. E., age 31 d. yesterday 2111 Second St., Macon. Mother, brother, Oscar, sisters: Mrs. H. A. Bankston, Mrs. W. N. Strayer, Mrs. M. E. Hobbs, Mrs. C. A. Smith. Interred: Cedar Ridge cemetery. AG 8/29/1907

WILDER, F. L. of Albany d. 12/17. He was survived by wife, many near relatives. AG 12/17/1906

WILDER, J. T. of Covington, age 60 d. Soldiers Home. Bur: Westview. AG 8/27/1906

WILEY, C. M., Mrs., wife of Col. Charles M., d. Fri. Marietta. Dau: Mrs. Lawson Brown, Macon. Interred: Macon, Ga. AG 8/10/1907

WILEY, Henry, colored, age 35, d. McDaniel St., Atlanta, Thurs. AG 12/3/1907

WILEY, L. V., Mrs., age 57, d. Buford, Ga. AG 3/10/1909

WILEY, Mamie M., Mrs., wife of R. Frank, of Gulfport, Miss., d. res. of bro., Matt Murphy, Columbus, 11/9. Husband, 6 yr. old dau. Interred: Linwood Cemetery, Columbus, Ga. AG 11/8/1910

WILEY, Susan P., age 72, d. 109 W. Peachtree St. Atlanta. AG 3/29/1910

WILEY, Susan P., Mrs. funeral Wed. 109 W. Peachtree St., Atlanta. Interred: Oakland. AG 3/29/1910

WILEY, W. H., age 26, d. 50 S. Jackson St. Atlanta. AG 3/22/1907

WILHOIT, Wirt H., age 20, son of Mr. and Mrs. Will F., of Newnan, Ga., d. Thurs. Interred: Macon. AG 12/30/1908

WILKERSON, Annie, age 22, d. Hapeville, Ga. AG 12/29/1910

WILKERSON, Carrie, Mrs. d. Sat. Atlanta. Interred: Redan, Ga. AG 12/1/1907

WILKERSON, Hassie, colored, age 40, d. 18 Grace St. Atlanta. AG 3/1/1907

WILKERSON, James C., colored, age 4 mos, died 79 Tattnall St. AG 12/10/1906

WILKERSON, M. E., colored, age 5, d. 79 Tattnall St. Atlanta. AG 2/26/1908

WILKERSON, Mark, age 2 mos., son of Mr. and Mrs. W., d. Fri. Atlanta. Interred: Westview. AG 6/25/1910

WILKERSON, Mary, colored, age 1, d. 44 Collier St. Atlanta. AG 10/19/1907

WILKERSON, Merk, inf. of M. C., d. 701 Seaboard Ave. Atlanta. AG 6/25/1910

WILKES, Charley shot by Dan Lott, Adel, Ga. 12/24. AG 12/27/1909

WILKES, Ella B., colored, age 3 mos., d. 37 Reed St. Atlanta. AG 9/2/1909

WILKES, Luna, Mrs., wife of W. A. H., d. Sun. Atlanta, 310 Marietta St. Interred: Mableton, Ga. AG 5/2/2910

WILKES, J. E., Mrs. d. 9/16 Thomson, Ga. AC 9/18/1905

WILKINS, Ann Maria, Mrs., age 96, d. Old Soldiers' Home. Atlanta. AG 12/2/1910

WILKINS, Ethel Constance, Miss, age 18, d. Thurs. res. of parents, Mr. and Mrs. George W. Wilkins, 88 E. 9th St., Atlanta. Interred: Westview. AG 11/26/1909

WILKINS, John, age 4, son of Mr. and Mrs. William, d. near Pine Log 9/25. AG 9/26/1908

WILKINS, W. A., Major, his LWT entered for probate, Waynesboro, Ga. Wife and son: W. A., Jr. AG 3/4/1907

WILKINS, Walter, police officer, shot and killed by E. M. Fuller, Augusta, Ga. 2/25, mistaken for burglar. AG 2/26/1907

WILL, Louis, age 59, d. Tues. Atlanta. Interred: Hollywood. AG 1/8/1907

WILL, Sam, age 54, d. at Home for Incurables. Atlanta. AG 1/9/1907

WILL, Wilhelmina, age two, dau. of J. L. of Flat Shoals Rd. AG 9/20/1906

WILLCOX, D. F., Mrs., AGE 75, d. res. of grandson, F. G. Lumpkin 3/18. Ch: Archibald Willcox, Mrs. Robert Ransom. Sis: Mrs. W. N. Hawkes, Atlanta. AG 3/18/1908

WILLCOX, Mrs. d. Sat. Jacksonville, Ga. Leaves husband, several small children, father, mother. AG 11/12/1907

WILLEFORD, Etta, Mrs., age 30, d. Atlanta Sat., wife of O. A. Interred: Chestlehurst, Ga. AG 2/8/1908

WILLHOLT, Samuel H., age 35, d. 50 Larkin St. Atlanta. AG 3/8/1909

WILLIAMS, infant dau. of Mr. and Mrs. A. L., d. Depot St., Dalton, Ga., Mon. AG 8/10/1910

WILLIAMS, Alex, colored, age 26, d. 25 Oakland Ave. Atlanta. AG 9/11/1908

WILLIAMS, Alice, colored, age 28, d. 5 Airline St. Atlanta. AG 7/29/1908

WILLIAMS, Alton, age 17, d. E. Point, Ga. Sun. Interred: East Point Cemetery. Mother: Mrs. Anna Williams. 4 sisters, two brothers. AG 10/19/1908

WILLIAMS, Annie L., age 5 mos., d. 140 Gilmer St. Atlanta. AG 12/9/1909

WILLIAMS, Annie, Mrs., age 31, d. 200 Decatur St. Atlanta Mon. Husband: D. W. Interred: Westview. AG 6/8/1909

WILLIAMS, Asa L., age 14, d. 11 Rush St., Atlanta, Thurs. Interred: Hollywood. AG 10/30/1908

WILLIAMS, Askew, colored, age 12, d. 70 Markham St. Atlanta. AG 12/27/1910

WILLIAMS, Ben, colored, age 31, d. 200 Maple St. Atlanta. AG 7/20/1907

WILLIAMS, Ben, colored, age 98, d. 19 Taliaferro St. Atlanta. AG 3/16/1908

WILLIAMS, Benjamin B. d. Rev. Mr. Coile Res. near Winterville, Ga., while returning from Lexington. Age 60. Wife, 4 children: Joe, Dutch, Maud Williams and Mrs. E. H. Youngkin (Athens, Ga.). Interred: Family Burial Grounds. AG 4/21/1910

WILLIAMS, Berry, colored, age 50, d. Edgewood. Atlanta. AG 9/21/1909

WILLIAMS, Bertha, colored, age 25, d. 406 Davis St. Atlanta. AG 9/3/1909

WILLIAMS, C., colored, age 3, d. 282-A Williams Street. Atlanta. AG 5/1/1907

WILLIAMS, C. T., Mrs. d. E. Huntsville, Ala., recently removed there from Russellville, Ga. Husband, 4 sons. AG 2/24/1910

WILLIAMS, C. W., age 76, d. 79 Lee St. Atlanta. AG 9/21/1909

WILLIAMS, Chester, age 1 mo., d. 10 Fitzgerald St. Atlanta. AG 3/18/1909

WILLIAMS, Columbus, colored, age 70, d. 24 Lyons Ave. Atlanta. AG 3/10/1908

WILLIAMS, Dora, age 1, d. 170 Grant St. Atlanta. AG 4/22/1907

WILLIAMS, Dorothy, age 4 mos., d. 530 Pulliam St. Atlanta. AG 4/12/1909

WILLIAMS, E. B., Mrs., age 32, d. Sun. 164 South Ave., Atlanta. Interred: Palmetto, Ga. AG 8/19/1907

WILLIAMS, E. G. killed. Donald M. Bain charged in Fulton Co. AG 8/6/1909

WILLIAMS, E. P., Mrs. d. Sat. Atlanta. Interred: Rome, Ga. AG 9/2/1907

WILLIAMS, Effie, colored, age 58, died at 161 N. Boulevard. AG 12/8/1906

WILLIAMS, Elizabeth, colored, age 60, d. 1000 S. Pryor St. Atlanta. AG 12/3/1908

WILLIAMS, Ella, Mrs., age 26, d. Home for Incurables, Atlanta. AG 9/3/1907

WILLIAMS, Elton, negro, age 29, shot and killed at 25 Beard St., Atlanta. Beckie Randolph, negro woman, held as slayer. Also held: Vine Smith, William Baker, Lizzie Pryer, negroes. AG 3/25/1907

WILLIAMS, Emma, colored, age 26, d. 79 Newton St. Atlanta. AG 3/1/1907

WILLIAMS, Ethel, Mrs., age 32, d. 17 W. Cain St., Atlanta Fri. Mother: Mrs. Callie Thurman. Bro: Guy Thurman. Interred: Sylvester Church. AG 3/27/1908

WILLIAMS, Eunice, age 1, d. Edgewood, Ga. AG 12/11/1908

WILLIAMS, F. T., of W. Pt. d. 4/2 dau's res. Mrs. H. W. Miller. Daus: Mrs. E. C. Little, Waycross; Mrs. W. W. Little, W. Pt; Mrs. J. C. Blanton, Blanton, Al; Mrs. J. J. Truitt, Whitesville. Son: L. O., Gabetville. Bur: New Hope, AG 4/3/1909

WILLIAMS, Fannie, age 6 mos., d. 101 N. Butler St. Atlanta. AG 6/12/1907

WILLIAMS, Fannie, infant dau. of F. Williams, d. Mon. Atlanta. Interred: Westview. AG 6/10/1907

WILLIAMS, Fannie L., colored, age 1 yr., d. 38 Hilliard St. Atlanta. AG 6/1/1907

414

WILLIAMS, Fannie, Mrs., age 29, d. Sun. 33 Inman Ave. Atlanta.
Relatives in Miss. Interred: Westview. AG 4/22/1907
WILLIAMS, Fannie, Mrs., wife of I. V., d. 33 Inman Ave. Sun.
Interred: Westview. AG 4/25/1907
WILLIAMS, Fred A. d. Barrow S., Athens. Wife, one child. AG
9/12/1906
WILLIAMS, G. H., Mrs., age 22, d. 101 Butler St. Atlanta. AG
11/20/1909
WILLIAMS, G. M., Mrs. d. Sat. Atlanta. AG 2/11/1908
WILLIAMS, G. O., age 60, d. 70 Walton St. Atlanta. AG 7/15/1910
WILLIAMS, Garfield, colored, age 30, d. 101 N. Butler St.
Atlanta. AG 7/10/1908
WILLIAMS, George, colored, age 39, d. 223 E. Pine St. Atlanta. AG
11/17/1907
WILLIAMS, George, suicide. Wife, three children. AG 11/3/1906
WILLIAMS, H. R., Dr., age 43, d. Opelika, Ala. AG 11/12/1910
WILLIAMS, Harriett, colored, age 64, d. rear of 102 Martin St.
Atlanta. AG 3/29/1909
WILLIAMS, Henry, age 26, d. 734 Elliott St. Atlanta. Parents: Mr.
and Mrs. W. H. Williams. Interred: Utoy church ard. AG 7/9/1908
WILLIAMS, Henry, colored, age 27, Grady Hospital, Atlanta. AG
11/19/1906
WILLIAMS, Henry murdered by Will Smith, colored, found guilty of
voluntary manslaughter in Superior Court, sentenced 7 years in
penitentiary. AG 12/15/1906
WILLIAMS, Homer L., age 30, d. near Centerville, Ga. 12/23.
Interred: Snellville. AG 12/28/1909
WILLIAMS, infant of Mr. and Mrs. J. C., d. Bonnie Brae Mon.
Interred: Westview. AG 10/22/1907
WILLIAMS, infant of Mr. and Mrs. L. A., d. Egan, Ga. Sun.
Interred: Hollywood Cemetery. AG 7/26/1909
WILLIAMS, infant killed by Dallis Taylor, Louise Taylor, Annie
Jones and Gertrude Williams, Dublin, Ga. (in jail.) Gertrude
Williams is infant's mother. AG 12/3/1909
WILLIAMS, Ira D., Mrs., age 33, of Senoia, d. Sun. Atlanta.
Interred: Senoia, Ga. Husband: J. T. Williams of Senoia. AG
11/29/1909
WILLIAMS, J. L. shot by V. T. Stowers, died 4/4, Hazlehurst, Ga.,
age abt 30. Wife, child abt 5 mos. old. Bro: Eugene Williams. AG
4/5/1909
WILLIAMS, J. L., age 19, d. 69 Luckie St. Atlanta. AG 2/25/1907
WILLIAMS, James, colored, age 16, d. 14 Bradsberry Ave. Atlanta.
AG 12/22/1908
WILLIAMS, James W., age 43, d. Atlanta. Interred: Lawrenceville,
Ga. AG 3/17/1910
WILLIAMS, Jim, colored, age 42, d. 101 N. Butler St. Atlanta. AG
12/14/1907
WILLIAMS, John, colored, age 80, d. 101 N. Butler St. Atlanta. AG
12/3/1908
WILLIAMS, Joseph d. 512 Washington St., Atlanta, Oct. 19. AG
10/20/1910
WILLIAMS, Julia E., inf. dau. of Mr. and Mrs. J. C., of 38 Rock
St., d. Atlanta Sat. Interred: Rean, Ga. AG 5/11/1908
WILLIAMS, Lem, colored, age 100, d. 212 Smith St. Atlanta. AG
3/27/1909

WILLIAMS, Lena, colored, age 31, d. Alms House. Atlanta. AG
8/21/1907
WILLIAMS, Leroy, colored, age 4, d. Brotherton St. Atlanta. AG
12/2/1910
WILLIAMS, Lewis, colored, age 30, d. Fulton Co. Alms House. AG
3/10/1908
WILLIAMS, Loyd, age 1 mo., son of Mr. and Mrs. G. H., 101 Butler
St. d. Atlanta Mon. Interred: Lawrenceville, Ga. AG 12/13/1909
WILLIAMS, Lucy, Mrs., age 32, d. 164 South Ave. Atlanta. AG
8/20/1907
WILLIAMS, L. Volney, Mrs. d. Sun. Waycross. Husband: L. V.
Williams. Father: C. W. Wiggins. Sis: Mrs. R. B. Groover of
Pelham, Ga. Bros: Tom Wiggins of N. Y.; Eugene Wiggins of Fla.;
Charlie Wiggins of Waycross. AG 12/7/1908
WILLIAMS, M., age 2, d. Flora Ave. Atlanta. AG 1/1/1908
WILLIAMS, M. M., Mrs., age 78, d. S. Kirkwood (Atlanta) Fri.
Interred: Greenwood., AG 2/27/1910
WILLIAMS, Mamie M., Miss, age 23, d. 28 Flat Shoals Rd., Atlanta,
Sat. Parents: Mr. and Mrs. J. M. Williams. 4 bros., one sister.
Interred: Greenwood Cemetery. AG 11/14/1908
WILLIAMS, Mamie S., Miss, age 39, d. Concord, Ga. AG 8/8/1910
WILLIAMS, Margaret, inf. dau. of Mr. and Mrs. W. L., d. 15 Pope
St., Atlanta. Interred: Chamblee, Ga. AG 5/11/1908
WILLIAMS, Marian, age 3, dau. of Mr. and Mrs. R. A., d. 187 N.
Jackson St., Atlanta, Tues. Interred: Westview. AG 1/28/1908
WILLIAMS, Marie, age 2, dau. of Mr. and Mrs. W. S., d. Flora
Ave., near Edgewood, Ga., Mon. Interred: Buford, Ga. AG
12/30/1907
WILLIAMS, Mary C., colored, age 28, d. 55 Elizabeth St. Atlanta.
AG 8/14/1908
WILLIAMS, Mary Elizabeth, age 5, d. Atlanta. AG 9/8/1909
WILLIAMS, Minnie, Miss of Concord, d. Sat. Atlanta, age 19?.
Nice: Mrs. C. O. Maynard. Sis: Mrs. W. H. Coppedge, Mrs. T. A.
Johnson. Interred: Zetella, Ga. AG 8/6/1910
WILLIAMS, Morris of Barnesville, Ga. d. 2/2, res. of mother: Mrs.
Jennie Williams, age 28. AC 2/4/1905
WILLIAMS, Mose, colored, age 37, d. 140 Houston St. Atlanta. AG
10/11/1909
WILLIAMS, Moses, colored, age 25, d. 212 Smith St. Atlanta. AG
4/20/1908
WILLIAMS, Nevelle, age 8, dau. of Mr. and Mrs. N. H., d. 55 W.
Alexander St., Atlanta, Tues. Interred: Westview. AG 4/12/1910
WILLIAMS, Nora, Mrs., age 26, d. 42 Hood St. Atlanta. AG
12/12/1910
WILLIAMS, Ola Grace, age 9, dau. of Mr. and Mrs. M. W., d. 121
Curran St., Atlanta, Sun. Interred: Powder Springs, Ga. AG
11/23/1907
WILLIAMS, Pleas, colored, age 51, d. 52 Berkle St. Atlanta. AG
10/21/1908
WILLIAMS, Polly, Mrs., relict of late J. D., age 84, d. 6/8
dau.'s res., Mrs. A. B. King, Harris Co., Ga. AC 6/9/1905
WILLIAMS, Ralph, colored, age 1, d. 178 State St. Atlanta. AG
10/20/1908
WILLIAMS, Riley, negro, hermit, found dead in room at 124 Glenn
St., Atlanta. Interred; Southview Cemetery. AG 5/14/1906

WILLIAMS, Riley, negro, former servant to Gen. Robert Toombs, d. Tues. Kirkwood. AG 4/17/1907

WILLIAMS, Robert, colored, age 16, d. 103-A Randolph St. Atlanta. AG 10/13/1909

WILLIAMS, Robert, colored, age 70, d. Fulton Co. Alms House. Atlanta. AG 12/30/1908

WILLIAMS, Ruby P., age 2, infant dau of Mr. and Mrs. D. E., d. Wed. 74 E. Georgia Ave. Atlanta. Interred: Westview. AG 5/9/1907

WILLIAMS, Ruth, inf. dau. of Mr. and Mrs. F. M., d. Willow St., Atlanta, Wed. Interred: Maccabee Cemetery. AG 7/22/1909

WILLIAMS, Samaria, Mrs., age 32, d. 15 Pope St. Atlanta Fri. Interred: Chamblee. Husband: J. A. Williams. One child. AG 6/5/1909

WILLIAMS, Serena, Mrs., age 78, d. 119 Grant St. Atlanta. AG 2/19/1907

WILLIAMS, Silas W., age 77, Atlanta pioneer, d. Sat. 375 Piedmont Ave. where res. since 1875. He was b. Lebanon, Ohio 1832. Wife: Mary E. Dau: Jeanette. Son: Harry. Bur: Westview. AG 4/16/1910

WILLIAMS, Sonnie hanged for killing Alman Ward 6/19, Colquitt, Ga. AG 6/20/1908

WILLIAMS, Susie, colored, age 25, d. 318 Taylor St. Atlanta, Oct. 16. AG 10/18/1910

WILLIAMS, Susie, colored, age 52, d. 2 Johnston St. Atlanta. AG 11/20/1907

WILLIAMS, T. C., Mrs., age 35, d. Sat. Atlanta. Interred: Sardis Church yard. AG 8/30/1910

WILLIAMS, T. F., Mrs. d. Montgomery, Ala. Mon. Interred: Edgemont Cemetery, Anniston, Ala. She was formerly Miss Jessie Hannon, dau. of Rev. W. Y. of Anniston, Ala. AG 2/2/1910

WILLIAMS, T. H., age 75, d. 185 Forrest Ave. Atlanta. AG 6/11/1910

WILLIAMS, V., colored, age 23, d. 101 N. Butler St. Atlanta. AG 12/6/1907

WILLIAMS, Virginia Noble, Mrs. funeral Thurs. Atlanta. Interred: Oakland. AG 6/6/1906

WILLIAMS, W. E., employee of Central r.r., struck down by train, d. Thurs. Wife, one small child, father, mother, three sisters, four bros., all of Fla., survive. AG 3/28/1907

WILLIAMS, W. R. d. Atlanta Fri, res. 230 S. Boulevard. Interred: Newnan, Ga. AG 7/13/1909

WILLIAMS, W. S. funeral 4/30 173 Oak St. Atlanta. Interred: Westview. AG 5/1/1906

WILLIAMS, Will, colored, age 28, d. corner Bartow and Luckie Sts. Atlanta. AG 3/7/1907

WILLIAMS, Will, negro killed by Deputy Sheriff, Fuller Fields, Swainsboro, Ga. 11/27. AC 11/29/1905

WILLIAMS, Will, negro, living on plantation of Elias Graham, 4 miles East of Ocilla, Ga., found dead. AC 1/10/1905

WILLIAMS, Willie, colored, age 33, d. 238 Windsor St. Atlanta. AG 1/31/1908

WILLIAMSON, B. C., Mrs., 34, d. 42 W. Baker St. Atlanta. Sons: Cooper, John T. Dau: Mary. Sis: Mrs. R. M. Allen; Mrs. T. E. Hamilton, Thomson, Ga. Bros: J. D., Jr., (Macon) & W. M. Minor, Savannah. Parents: Mr. & Mrs. J. D. Minor. Interred: Riverside Cemetery, Macon, Ga. AG 9/28/1909

WILLIAMSON, Burt H., age 47, d. Atlanta Sun. AG 8/2/1909

WILLIAMSON, E. G., age 27, d. 101 N. Butler St. Atlanta. AG 5/10/1907

WILLIAMSON, Frank J., Jr., age 21 mos., inf. son of Mr. and Mrs. Frank J., d. 536 Washington St., Atlanta. Interred: Oakland. AG 8/14/1907

WILLIAMSON, George, colored, age 34, d. 1 Florence St. Atlanta. AG 12/4/1908

WILLIAMSON, Ida May, Miss d. Sun. at Mt. DeSales Academy, Macon, dau. of Mr. and Mrs. Henry E. of Macon. Bros: James A., Frank J., Henry, Jr. and Claud. Interred: Oakland Cemetery, Atlanta. AG 5/28/1906

WILLIAMSON, Nathan, age 4 mos., young son of Mr. and Mrs. R. B. of 226 Highland Ave., Atlanta. Interred: Westview. AG 5/9/1908

WILLIAMSON, Zelda Lyda, age 3, dau. of Mr. and Mrs. R. R., funeral Mon. 4 Angier Pl. Atlanta. Interred: Westview. AG 10/24/1910

WILLIAN, F. A., Mrs. funeral Wed. Kin: F. A. Quillian, Col. R. J. Redding, S. A. Redding, R. A. Redding, W. C. King, S. B. Sawtell. AG 7/8/1908

WILLINGHAM, Calder B. d. Mon. Macon. Interred: Rose Hill Cemetery. 8 bros: Rev. R. J., Richmond, Va.; Thomas L., Rome, Ga.; Edward J., Pringle, Pauld D., Broadus E., Osgood P., Ben B., Macon. AG 10/23/1908

WILLINGHAM, E. V., age 53, d. 192 Courtland St. Atlanta. AG 3/7/1910

WILLINGHAM, Henry Wallace, age 16, d. Atlanta. Interred: Westview. Son of Mr. and Mrs. B. L. Willingham of Forest Park. Older bro: Judson. Sisters: Carolyn, Emmie. AG 7/27/1909

WILLINGHAM, Mack, age 2, d. 205 Gordon St. Atlanta. AG 3/25/1907

WILLINGHAM, Mary, Miss, age 60, d. Atlanta Thurs. Interred: Westview. AG 11/20/1903

WILLINGHAM, N. A., Mrs., wife of Capt. W. A., d. 3/19 Toccoa, Ga. AC 3/20/1905

WILLINGHAM, Thomas A. d. Thurs. near Helena, Ga. on train. Interred: Sandy Springs church yard. AG 12/18/1910

WILLINGHAM, William, son of Alexander of Lincolnton, Ga., d. 2/21. AC 2/23/1905

WILLIS, Annie, colored, age 42, d. 322 Smith St. Atlanta. AG 2/26/1908

WILLIS, Annie, Mrs., age 27, funeral Wed. Atlanta. Interred: Family Burial Ground. AG 3/25/1908

WILLIS, C. C., age 40, of Creystal River, Fla., d. Atlanta Wed. He was sea captain. AG 3/3/1909

WILLIS, Emma, Mrs., wid. of late Judge J. T., d. 2/2 Columbus. AC 2/4/1905

WILLIS, Ester Tate, age 36, d. Wed. Atlanta, res. of 26 Delta Pl. Interred: Cleveland, Tenn. AG 8/31/1910

WILLIS, Fletcher colored, age 35, d. Perry, Ga. AG 12/30/1908

WILLIS, James L., age 44, d. Inman St., Atlanta, Sun. Son: John.
Sis: Mrs. John McKeller, Mrs. M. Sanders, of Wrightsville, Ga.,
and Mrs. H. Bell. Bros: Harry, Pike Co., J. D., Texas, and
Thomas, Baldwin Co. Interred: Westview. AG 5/16/1910

WILLIS, Jessie, colored, age 50, d. 123 Sims St. Atlanta. AG
3/28/1907

WILLIS, Jim, age 18, shot and killed by J. B. Rowan of Massie,
Ga., age 45. AG 5/7/1910

WILLIS, John, colored, age 86, d. Grady Hospital. Atlanta. AG
8/6/1907

WILLIS, Joseph, colored, age 1, d. 342 Fulton St. Atlanta. AG
12/3/1907

WILLIS, Joseph D., age 64, d. Fri. East Point, Ga. Leaves wife, 6
children. Confederate veteran. AG 3/8/1907

WILLIS, N., colored, age 21, d. 216 Clark St. Atlanta. AG
4/22/1907

WILLIS, Pency, Miss d. Thurs near Walden, Ga. One bro., one
sister. AG 5/8/1908

WILLOUGHBY, Tom, age 40, carpenter, killed Junction City by work
train. Interred: Hampton. AG 9/11/1906

WILLSON, J. S., Dr., d. Mon. Atlanta. Interred: Oakland. AG
2/12/1907

WILMER, Mattie, colored, age 39, d. 29 Ami St. Atlanta. AG
7/13/1908

WILMOUTH, Benjamin of Hampton St., Atlanta, killed by Walter
Hightower of 144 Gaskell St. 3/1906. AG 12/24/1906

WILSON, A. E., Jr., inf. of Mr. and Mrs. A. E. interred Westview
Cemetery, Atlanta. AG 2/12/1908

WILSON, Annie B., colored, age 30, d. 40 Henry St. Atlanta. AG
9/2/1910

WILSON, Annie, Mrs., age 47, d. 29 Luckie St. Atlanta. AG
9/5/1906

WILSON, Benjamin F., age 65, d. Wed. 31 Green Ave. Atlanta. Wife,
several children. Interred: Sylvester, Ga. AG 7/28/1910

WILSON, Clifford, inf. son of Mr. and Mrs. C. F., funeral Mon.
Atlanta. Interred: Westview. AG 7/11/1910

WILSON, Clifton, age 5 weeks., d. 710 Seaboard St. Atlanta. AG
7/11/1910

WILSON, Cora L., age 28, d. Atlanta Wed, wife of W. E. 3
children, 3 sisters, 2 bros. Interred: Temple, Ga. AG 5/12/1910

WILSON, Dora, age 3 mos., dau. of Mr. and Mrs. H. H., d. Atlanta
Sun. Interred: Oakland. AG 12/6/1909

WILSON, E. G., age 92 yrs., d. near federal prison. Atlanta. AG
8/9/1907

WILSON, Edith, ge 1 mo., d. Atlanta. AG 12/17/1910

WILSON, Elizabeth, age 17 mos., dau. of Mr. and Mrs. D. W. of
Duluth, d. 6/13. Interred: Buford, Ga. AG 6/14/1909

WILSON, Ernest, negro, killed by Will King, negro. Atlanta. G
10/14/1907

WILSON, Eva, age 11 mos., d. Wyman St. Atlanta. AG 4/12/1909

WILSON, Fannie, age 12, negro girl, shot and almost instantly
killed on plantation of B. T. Hatcher, 8 miles below Columbus,
Ga., Wed. Henry Howard, age 10, claimed he did it accidentally.
AG 6/2/1906

WILSON, G. W., patrolman, Atlanta, d. Auburn, Ga. Interred: Auburn. AG 8/30/1906

WILSON, George, colored, age 40, d. 270 Irwin St. Atlanta. AG 2/28/1908

WILSON, George, Jr., inf. son of Mr. and Mrs. George, d. Fri. Atlanta. Interred: Westview. AG 5/18/1907

WILSON, Georgia, Mrs. d. Thurs. Atlanta. Interred: Hollywood. AG 1/4/1910

WILSON, Green, colored, age 50, d. 82 Old Wheat St. Atlanta. AG 3/3/1909

WILSON, Harry, age 2 mos., son of Mr. and Mrs. S. R., d. Atlanta Mon. Interred: Westview. AG 6/30/1908

WILSON, Henry, Dr. d. M. R. Emmons' res., 795 Peachtree St., Atlanta, Thurs. Leaves two daus. Interred: New York. AG 2/15/1908

WILSON, J. E. d. Thurs. Waycross, Ga. Bro: H. W. AG 9/9/1910

WILSON, J. W., 4 mos. infant of, d. 17 Corleys St. Atlanta. AG 8/27/1906

WILSON, Jack M., Mrs. d. Wed. Atlanta. Interred: Westview. Funeral at her late res.., 83 Spring St. AG 9/3/1907

WILSON, Jerry, colored, age 9 mos., d. 470 Smith St. Atlanta. AG 3/30/1908

WILSON, John, merchant, age 55, of Comers Rock, Va., d. Bristol, Tenn. Wife, one dau. AG 10/6/1909

WILSON, John W., age 40, d. Fri. Atlanta. Interred: Greenberg AG 12/6/1907

WILSON, Julia Jinks, age 2-1/2, 23 Hayden St., Atlanta, Sun., funeral Mo. AG 11/12/1906

WILSON, L. B., Mrs., mother of Capt. John J. Seay of Rome, Ga., Mrs. G. A. Park of Louisville, Ky. and Mrs. L. B. Langford and Mrs. E. E. Caldwell of Atlanta, d. Louisville, Ky. Mon. Interred: Atlanta. AG 9/14/1908

WILSON, Lee Royal, negro child of 68 Fitzgerald St. Atlanta buried Sun. Southview Cemetery. AG 5/14/1906

WILSON, Leila, age 27, d. Water Works Rd. Atlanta. AG 5/12/1910

WILSON, Lizzie, colored, age 40, d. 7 Glennwood Ave. Atlanta. AG 9/30/1909

WILSON, Mam, colored, age 1, died 21 Bryan St., Atlanta. AG 12/26/1906

WILSON, Margaret A., Miss, age 78, d. Thurs. 163 N. Jackson St., Atlanta. Sisters: Mrs. Mary E. Roberts, Miss Mattie L. Wilson, Mrs. Jane G. McElroy. Bro: R. C. Wilson, Doraville, Ga. Interred: Doraville, Ga. AG 11/12/1909

WILSON, Mary Elizabeth, 2 mos dau. of R. L., d. E. Rome. Interment: Buford. AG 9/20/1906

WILSON, Mattie, colored, age 38, d. rear 18 W. Peachtree St. Atlanta. AG 4/13/1909

WILSON, R. A. d. 3/19 Fitzgerald, Ga. AC 3/20/1905

WILSON, R. E., age 10, d. 69 Luckie St. Atlanta. AG 4/28/1908

WILSON, Robert H., Mrs. d. 124 E. North Av. Ch-Mrs. Haywood Hansel, Wharton O., Harvie & R. H., Jr. Sis-Mrs. Mary Buckner, Mrs. Harvie Phillips, Miss Ellen Wharton, Atlanta, Mrs. Laura Plummer, Memphis, Tenn. Bur: Oakland. AG 5/6/1907

WILSON, Roy Edward, age 6 yrs., son of Mr. and Mrs. C. R., 455 W. Simpson St., Atlanta, d. Sat. Interred: Casey's Cemetery. AG 4/25/1908

WILSON, S. A. d. Sun. Atlanta. Interred: Sardis church yard. AG 11/29/1909

WILSON, S. A., Dr., physician of Battle Hill, d. Sun. Wife, son: S. A. Wilson, Jr. Interred: Westview. AG 8/7/1906

WILSON, Sarah, Mrs., age 59, d. 55 Weyman Ave., Atlanta, Mon. Interred: Sylvester cemetery. AG 12/30/1907

WILSON, Sophronia, Mrs. of Henry Co., relative of Uriah Askew of Stockbridge, d. Tues. Interred: Noah's Ark Methodist Church cemtery. AG 3/3/1910

WILSON, Thomas stabbed in Macon by James H. Landers 2/11, age 64, Carroll St. AC 2/12/1905

WILSON, Thomas Bennett, age 67, Confederate veteran, d. Mon. 155 Mangum St., Atlanta, age 67. Served Co. F, 56th Ga. Regt. Interred: Hollywood. AG 2/16/1908

WILSON, Tom, colored, age 28, d. 57 Collier St. Atlanta. AG 5/8/1909

WILSON, Virgil T. d. sister's res., Mrs. Mattie Thompson, E. Point, Ga. Interred: College Park. AG 9/23/1907

WILSON, W. H. d. Griffin 3/18. AG 3/21/1910

WILSON, W. K., age 44, d. 5 Brown Pl. Atlanta. AG 3/25/1907

WILSON, W. Leake, Mrs. d. Adamsville, Ga. Sat. Interred: Family Burial Grounds. AG 12/23/1907

WILSON, W. R., age 57, formerly of Atlanta, d. Elberton, Ga. Interred: Westview. Bro: E. H. AG 2/25/1909

WILSON, W. W., age 40, d. 31 E. Fair St. Atlanta. AG 8/31/1908

WILSON, William L., infant, d. 1250 Marietta St. Atlanta. AG 8/31/1906

WILSON, William M., colored, age 7 mos., d. 436 Smith St. Atlanta. AG 8/30/1910

WILSON, William T., age 55, carpenter, d. 558 Decatur St., Atlanta, Thurs. Wife, three children. AG 7/31/1908

WILSON,, Z. R., Jr., age 2 mos., d. 246 Park Ave. Atlanta. AG 10/22/1909

WILSON-HOUSER, E. E., Mrs., age 63, d. Atlanta Mon. Interred: Westview. AG 4/13/1909

WIMBERG, Ester, age 8 mos., d. 93 Gilmer St. Atlanta. AG 6/21/1906

WIMBERLY, Emory Speer, age 6, youngest son of Mrs. O. J., d. Oglethorpe St., Macon, 12/28, son of late Olin J. Wimberly of Macon. AG 12/29/1910

WIMBERLY, Olin J. d. Tatnall Square, Macon, Ga. Funeral 1/17. Interred: Rose Hill Cemetery. AG 1/18/1910

WIMBERLY, W. H., age 51, d. Orme, Tenn. AG 2/11/1907

WIMBERLY, William H. of Macon d. Interred: Rose Hill. AG 2/12/1907

WIMBISH, Grace, age 5, dau. of Mr. and Mrs. J. T. of 117 Kirkwood Ave., Atlanta, d. Sun. Interred: Casey's Cemetery. AG 4/13/1908

WIMBLEY, Hattie, colored, age 13, d. 199 Houston St. Atlanta. AG 2/25/1907

WIMFEE, Arthur E. d. Erlanger Hospital, Chattanooga, Tenn. Mother, father, wife, two bros., three sisters. Funeral at Chickamauga Baptist Church. AG 2/23/1910

WIMPEY, John A., age 70, d. 221 Courtland St. Atlanta. Interred: Oxford, Ga. AG 6/12/1907

WIMPY, J. M., Mrs., age 64, died 125 E. Georgia Ave., Atlanta. AG 12/10/1906

WINANT, Laura, Mrs., age 54, d. 57 Hardee St. Atlanta. AG 10/3/1906

WINBORN, George W., age 73, d. Wed. Funeral at brothers: D. W. Winborn, 394 Auburn Ave., Atlanta. AG 9/27/1906

WINBURN, Charles E., Mrs., age 39, wife of Charles E., d. 83 Angier Ave., Atlanta, Fri. Interred: Westview. AG 10/19/1907

WINBURN, J. B. M. Mrs. wife of Judge, mother of W. A., V. Pres. of Central RR., mother of Congressman Thomas M. Bell, d. Washington St., Gainesville, Ga. 4/15. AG 4/16/1910

WINDHAM, infant of Mr. and Mrs. E. G., d. 154 Hill St., Atlanta, Thurs. Interred: Reynolds, Ga. AG 10/4/1907

WINFREY, Scott, colored, age 45, d. 224 Elliott St. Atlanta. AG 10/30/1909

WING, Henry Cary, age 4, son of Mr. and Mrs. C. C., d. Wed. Interred: Oakland. AG 4/25/1907

WING, Orrin Arthur d. parents home in Lowell, Mass. He left Atlanta in June, and was m. 6/14 to Miss Sophie White. AG 7/14/1908

WINGERBERG, Mary, Mrs. funeral Sun. Interred: Westview. AG 5/28/1906

WINGFIELD, Bessie, colored, age 14, d. 225 Randolph St. Atlanta. AG 8/17/1908

WINGFIELD, Elizabeth, Miss, age 52, d. Wed. res. of Dr. T. J. Wills, Washington, Ga. Interred: City Cemetery, Washington, Ga. She was one of 6 daus. of late Judge and Mrs. Charles E. Wingfield. AG 7/16/1909

WINGFIELD, Thomas B. of Eatonton d. Jan. 30, age 54, son of late Col. Junius A. Unmd. Bros. and sisters. AC 2/1/1905

WINMAN, Charles, age 56, d. Bolton, Ga. AG 9/4/1908

WINN, Gertrude, age 1, dau. of Mr. and Mrs. W. F., d. 6 Berrian Ave., Atlanta, Sun. Interred: Hollywood. AG 3/10/1908

WINN, Harriet B., Mrs., age 62, d. Washington St. Atlanta. AG 11/27/1910

WINN, Minnie, Miss d. Wed. Bolingbroke, Ga. Interred: Family Burying Ground, Bolingbroke. AG 10/20/1910

WINN, Nancy E., age 57, d. Milledgeville, Ga. AG 1/31/1907

WINN, P. P., Mrs., wife of Rev. P. P., d. Thurs. Decatur, Ga., age 60. Interred: Decatur. AG 4/19/1907

WINN, W. H., Mrs. of 61 Cherry St., Atlanta, d. Tues. Husband survives. Sons: W. Thomas Winn, Joseph H. Winn. AG 1/29/1907

WINN, W. J., Colonel. Savannah, Ga. 11/27/1906. City engineer, Savannah since 1881 died yesterday of would recd at battle of Peachtree Cr., Atlanta, 6/20/1864. Survivors: two sons, daughter, of Savannah. AG 11/27/1906

WINNINGHAM, Mike, age 34, formerly of Atlanta fire dept., d. Stone Mtn, Ga. Thurs. Wife, two children, parents, Mr. and Mrs. O. Winningham, and several bros. and sisters. AG 6/5/1908

WINNINGHAM, Mike, age 34, formerly of Atlanta fire dept., d. Stone Mtn, Ga. Thurs. Wife, two children, parents, Mr. and Mrs. O. Winningham, and several bros. and sisters. AG 6/5/1908

WINSTON, John C. d. home in Marshall Co., Ala. few days ago, age 60. AG 7/20/1906

WINSTROM, Mary, colored, age 26, d. 522 W. Mitchell St. Atlanta. AG 9/1/1908

WINTER, Charles W., age 74, Atlanta pioneer, b. West Point, Ga. d. 220 S. Blvd., Atlanta. Leaves wife, dau., Mrs. J. W. Horsey of Atlanta. Sons: J. A. Winter of Durant, Ind.; T. and Charles W. Winter, Jr. of Thomasville, Ga. Interred: Oakland. AG 2/6/1907

WINTER, James L., Col. d. 8/10 Atlanta. Interred: Oakland. AC 8/12/1905

WINTER, James L., Mrs. d. Knoxville. Bur: Oakland. Ch: Mrs. C. E. Kauffman, 56 Currier, Atlanta; Mrs. L. W. Smith, Macon; Mrs. L. M. Morrow, Knoxville; Mrs. A. S. Nash and Annie Winter, Knoxville; Mrs. C. M. Taylor, Covington. AG 3/8/1907

WINTER, Joe, former res. of Atlanta, d. Dallas, Texas. Interred: Richmond, Va. AG 8/9/1910

WINTERBOTTOM, Lula Jane, Mrs., age 40, d. 908 Marietta St., Atlanta, Sun. Husband, 3 children, and parents, Mr. and Mrs. A. W. Elrod, survive. Interred: Casey's Cemetery. AG 5/25/1908

WINTERMUTE, G. A., age 27, d. Atlanta. AG 8/22/1910

WISE, Addie, Mrs., age 63, d. 101 N. Butler St. Atlanta. Interred: Bogart, Ga. AG 10/26/1907

WISE, Joseph, Dr., age 77, died at 44 Highland Ave., Atlanta, AG 11/20/1906

WISE, Marvin A., age 5, son of Mr. and Mrs. M. T., d. Fri. 641 Woodward Ave. Atlanta. Bur: Jenkinsburg, Ga. AG 10/5/1907

WISHART, William M. funeral Tues. Atlanta. Interred: New York City. AG 9/21/1910

WITHERS, Richard Carlyle, age 1, infant son of Mr. and Mrs. W. T. Withers of Oakland City, d. Tues. AG 6/27/1907

WITHERS, W. E., age 73, d. Oakland City. AG 8/1/1907

WITHERS, W. S., Atlanta pioneer, d. Wed. Oakland City. Funeral: J. B. Withers, Oakland Ave., Oakland City. Wife, three sons, two daus., survive: Mrs. Mary Cherry, Mrs. Julia Sanders, W. G. Withers, J. B. Withers, W. T. Withers. AG 8/1/1907

WITHROW, John, Fannin Co. murderer, to die on gallows on 11/18. AG 10/20/1910

WITHROW, Pearl, Miss, age 19, d. Atlanta. AG 5/4/1909

WITT, Adolph, age 34, d. Atlanta. AG 5/6/1908

WITT, M. P., age 50, of S. Macon d. 4/20. Wife, 6 children. Interred: Culloden, Ga. AC 4/21/1905

WITT, W. C., age 65, of Old Soldiers' Home, Atlanta, d. Sat. He was b. Walker Co., Ga. 1/1842. Interred: Westview. AG 2/29/1908

WITTLES, J., Mrs., age 45, d. 101 N. Butler St. Atlanta. AG 3/22/1909

WOESTMAN, O. D., formerly of Atlanta, d. Fri. his res. San Antonio, Texas. AG 12/13/1909

WOFFORD, C. C., age 30, d. Birmingham, Ala. Aunt: Mrs. Sarah Johnson, 547 Woodward Ave., Atlanta. Bur: Westview. AG 7/19/1907

WOLF, Clarence B., age 11 mos., d. 268 Waldo St. Atlanta. AG 8/31/1908

WOLFE, John R., Judge, pioneer to Dublin, d. last night, age 68. AG 1/26/1907

WOLFORD, Jacobs, age 70, d. 26 Alaska Ave. Atlanta. AG 6/2/1910

WOLFSHEIMER, Marion R., age 8, d. 387 Washington St. Atlanta. AG 3/14/1910

WOLPERT, William J., age 39, funeral Sun. 3/17 late res. 65 Fraser St. Atlanta. Kin: William J. Wolpert, William Wolpert, W. S. Wolpert, J. J. Wolpert, Mr. & Mrs. J. B. Morgan, Mrs. S. C. Saye, Mr. & Mrs. Edward D. Saye. AG 3/16/1907

WOMACK, Bert A., Mrs., age 36, d. 138 Hill St. Atlanta. AG 4/10/1907

WOMACK, Emmet, Col., former res. of Covington, Ga., graduate of Emory College in 1870, d. Washington, D. C. Sat. AG 1/15/1908

WOMACK, Will, negro, age 30, was lynched by mob 4 miles n. of Eastman 5/13. AG 5/14/1906

WOMBLE, C. T., Mrs., age 48, wife of H. W., d. Atlanta, Fri. Interred: Thomaston, Ga. AG 10/12/1908

WOMMACK, Mary V., inf. dau. of Mr. and Mrs. R. W., d. Sun. 73 Sylvan St. Atlanta. Interred: Elvan church yard. AG 7/22/1907

WOOD, A. A., Confederate veteran, d. Thurs. at Soldiers' Home, Atlanta. Interred: Scarboro. One sister, one bro. AG 5/3/1907

WOOD, Abbie, colored, age 36, d. Jeptha St. Atlanta. AG 1/28/1908

WOOD, B. C., age 51, d. Atlanta. AG 6/9/1910

WOOD, Bertha, Mrs., age 22, d. 151 Williams St. Atlanta. Husband: J. W. Sis: Mrs. C. F. Johnson, Mrs. R. I. Dickey, Misses Mamie and Ella Conway. Bro: Jesse Conway, Quanah, Texas. Interred: Greenwood. AG 9/2/1910

WOOD, E. D., Jr., age 4, d. 31 Dalney St. Atlanta. AG 2/8/1909

WOOD, Flournoy, age 45, d. 129 Payne St. Atlanta. AG 11/15/1909

WOOD, G. W., Mrs. d. Sat. at Log Cabin, Macon, Ga. Sat. Res. Macon all her life. AG 11/16/1909

WOOD, George LeForest, age 64, d. 132 Lucile Ave., Atlanta, Sat. Wife, one dau. Interred: Gloversville, N. Y. AG 7/6/1908

WOOD, Henry Clinton, Major, citizen of Briston, Tenn., Confederate Soldier of 43 engagements, wounded Chancellorsville, d. 12/8, age 72. 2 terms State Sen. of Va. AG 12/9/1909

WOOD, infant of Mr. and Mrs. J. R., d. 305 Means St., Atlanta, Tues. Interred: Lawrenceville, Ga. AG 10/9/1907

WOOD, infant of Mr. and Mrs. J. W., d. Thurs. Interred: Lawrenceville, Ga. AG 10/16/1907

WOOD, J. C., res. of Auburn, Ga., d. Atlanta Mon., age 31. Interred: Auburn, Ga. AG 11/8/1910

WOOD, J. S., age 24, d. Atlanta. AG 4/7/1908

WOOD, Jane, Mrs., age 41, d. 19 Paynes Ave. Atlanta. AG 9/6/1907

WOOD, Joseph W., age 75, d. Simsville, on River Rd., Mon. 4 daus., 3 sons, 3 bros, 1 sister. Bur: Dallas, Ga. AG 1/17/1910

WOOD, Julia E., age 15 mos., dau. of Mr. and Mrs. W. D., d. 10 Guyton St., Atlanta Tues. Interred: Hollywood. AG 5/10/1909

WOOD, L. J., Dr., 45, Union Co., d. Md. Bessie Parham, Bennettsville. 5 daus, 4 sons. Bros, Sis: T. W. Wood, Atlanta; S. M. & Smith Wood, Mrs. J. T. Bailey, Spartanburg; A. D. Wood, Williamston; Mrs. L. J. Gaunt, Kelton. AG 12/29/1909

WOOD, Laura, Mrs. bur. West Hill Cem., Dalton, Ga. 2/18. She d. Chattanooga res. of dau., age 64. 2 daus., 1 son. AG 2/19/1910

WOOD, Lee of LaGrange. Troup Superior Ct. trial 11/12 of T. J. Denney for killing Lee Wood, Hogansville, last Apr. AG 11/13/1906

WOOD, Mary Elizabeth, age 14 mos., dau. of Prof. and Mrs. H. P., d. 395 S. Boulevard, Atlanta, Thurs. AG 6/18/1908

WOOD, Mary Elizabeth, inf. dau. of Mr. and Mrs. M. A., d. 149 Pearl St., Atlanta, 5/27/1907. AG 6/5/1907

WOOD, Maude, inf. dau. of Mr. and Mrs. Williams Wood, d. Sat. 78 Jefferson St., Atlanta. Interred: Highland cemetery. AG 8/5/1907

WOOD, R. J., age 43, d. 26 Beecher St. Atlanta. AG 5/18/1907

WOOD, R. M. d. 12/7 Milledgeville, Ga. Interred: Westview. AC 12/10/1905

WOOD, Susan Jeanette, Mrs, age 78, died at res. of granddau., Mrs. J. C. Childs, 89 Capitol Ave., Atlanta, Fri. Son: J. W. Wood, of New York. AG 1/29/1906

WOOD, T. W. d. 11/12, age 66, Richmond, Va. AC 11/13/1905

WOOD, W. B., age 38, d. Hampton St., Atlanta. AG 11/6/1907

WOOD, W. G., formerly res. of Atlanta, d. San Antonio, Texas. Interred: Westview. AG 9/19/1907

WOOD, W. H., age 75, d. 339 Seabord Ave. Atlanta. AG 5/11/1908

WOOD, W. J., age 70, d. Columbus, Ga. Mon., res. of 30 yrs. from S. C. Wife, 4 children. AG 3/2/1910

WOOD, W. Luke, age 44, d. 29 Luckie St. Atlanta. AG 9/8/1909

WOOD, William H., infant son of Mr. and Mrs. M. A., d. Tues. 149 Pearl St., Atlanta. Interred: Sylvester. His sister, Mary Elizabeth, d. 10 days ago. AG 6/5/1907

WOODALL, Junius P. d. 10/26 Charlotte, N. C. Wife. AG 10/27/1910

WOODALL, Rhoda A., Mrs., age 56, d. 698 S. Pryor St. Atlanta. AG 8/8/1906

WOODALL, Will, age 12, died from dogbite, Flatwood's District, Rome, Ga. 11/30. AG 11/30/1908

WOODEN, Cherokee, colored, age 35, d. rear of 334 Courtland St. Atlanta. AG 3/26/1908

WOODFIN, N. H., age 28, d. Fri. Atlanta. Wife lives Greenville, S. C. AG 8/28/1909

WOODLIFF, Maude, Miss, age 21, dau. of A. H., Forsyth Co., d. 2/22, buried Flowery Branch 2/23. 3 bros., 5 sis: T. J., M. B., R. B.; Mrs. Addie Harrison; Mrs. May Wallace; Mrs. Janie Roark; Misses Emmie and Pearl Woodliff. AG 3/10/1910

WOODRUFF, Helen, Mrs. d. Macon at res. of Mrs. W. A. Goodyear, Orange St., age 74, wid. of late Henry L. Woodruff who d. last Oct. Interred: New Haven, Conn. AG 12/30/1907

WOODRUFF, Henry L. d. 10/1906. AG 12/30/1907

WOODS, Carl L., 19 mos. d. 180 Echo St., Atlanta. Buried: Westview. AG 8/29/1906

WOODS, inf. dau. of Mr. and Mrs. G. N., d. Thurs. 58 Rock St., Atlanta. Interred: Adairsville, Ga. AG 9/2/1910

WOODS, O. A., Mrs., age 35, d. 16 Fair St. Atlanta. AG 2/4/1908

WOODS, Oliver, Mrs., age 35, d. Atlanta Sat. Sis: Mrs. T. J. Grey, NYC. Interred: New York. AG 2/2/1908

WOODS, W. Houston, age 80, of Sutherland, Iowa, d. nephew's res., W. Woods White, 201 Capitol Ave., Atlanta, Thurs. AG 3/26/1909

WOODSON, Edward Shreue, age 5, son of Mr. and Mrs. G. H. Woodson, died at residence, 215 Highland Ave. Atlanta. Interment: Westview. AG 12/16/1906

WOODSON, W. D., age 49, d. Biddeford, Maine. AG 2/8/1910

WOODWARD, Daniel, age 70, d. 63 McAfee St. Atlanta. AG 5/18/1907

WOODWARD, I. T., Mrs. d. Thurs. Mountville, Ga. AG 2/15/1907

WOODWARD, Mary, negro, age 42, d. Atlanta. AG 9/8/1908

WOODWARD, Mittie, Miss, age 23, dau. of Mr. and Mrs. W. N., d. Jacksonville, Fla. Bro: Samuel Woodward, Atlanta. 5 sisters. Interred: Westview, Atlanta. AG 2/24/1908

WOODWARD, Samuel B., age 40, d. 131 Payne St. Atlanta. AG 4/18/1910

WOODWARD, Walter N., age 60, d. 144 Spring St. Atlanta. Wife, 6 daus: Mrs. Richard Drake, Mrs. William Hemphill, Mrs. D. E. Guerrant, Mrs. Albert Carr, Miss Susie Woodward and Miss Bessie Woodward. Son: Sam. D. Woodward. AG 12/4/1908

WOOLF, Annie Kate, age 5, d. 268 Waldo St. Atlanta. AG 6/22/1909

WOOLFOLK, Ann, Mrs., wid. of late I. W. Woolfolk, d. at home, 2 miles N. of Perry, Ga. Survivors: 12 sons, 2 daus. AG 11/26/1906

WOOLFOLK, W. W., Mrs., d. 5 mi N Perry. Survivors: Husb., child. AG 12/27/1906

WOOLFORD, Edward, colored, age 7 mos., d. 48 Elm St. Atlanta. AG 2/28/1908

WOOLINGTON, William, age 22, actor, d. Atlanta several days ago. Interred: Westview. Wife, one child and mother of Winchester, Va., survive. AG 12/28/1908

WOOLLARD, Della, Mrs., age 43, of Savannah, d. Sun. res. of W. C. Bishop, 461 Pulliam St., Atlanta while visiting. Wife of Frank of Savannah. Interred: Savannah. AG 9/25/1906

WOOLLEY, Mildred, age 7, dau. of Mr. and Mrs. W. H., d. 697 E. Fair St. Atlanta, Thurs. Interred: Conyers, Ga. AG 2/28/1908

WOOSTER, Carl (Karl), age 24, of Atlanta killed in Jackson, Miss., son of Mr. and Mrs. C. A. Wooster. Bro: Kirk. AG 9/24/1909

WOOTEN, E., Mrs., age 55, d. Fri. Sis: Mrs. M. C. Tolleson, 148 Central Ave., Atlanta. Interred: Westview. AG 8/29/1907

WOOTEN, J. E., Judge d. 12/27 Eastman, Ga. Interred: Covington. AC 12/29/1905

WOOTEN, W. C., age 43, of Washington, Ga., d. Interred: Family grave yard, Ophelia, Ga. AC 1/18/1905

WOOTTEN, M. E., Mrs., age 71, d. son's res., W. F. Wootten, 34 Oak St., Atlanta, Fri. Interred: Canton, Ga. AG 2/8/1908

WORD, Cora, Miss, age 17, d. 35 Lawshe St. Atlanta. AG 8/27/1909

WORD, Howard, age 3 mos., son of Mr. and Mrs. Word of 493 Washington St., Atlanta. Interred: Hollywood. AG 9/1/1908

WORD, J. K., inf. son of Mr. and Mrs. Harry, d. Tues. Tomlin St. Atlanta. AG 10/18/1910

WORD, Matilda J., wife of J. L., age 54, d. 17 Wellborn St. Atlanta. Interred: Westview. AG 11/20/1907

WORDLAW, Anna Elizabeth,, age 38, wife of Paul, dau of Capt. & Mrs. J. M. Liddell, d. Rocks Springs Ave., Atlanta. Bros: Dr. F. A., Cameron, Tx, D. W., J. G., A. P. & Roy Liddell, Atlanta. Sis: Mrs. J. D. Johnson. Bur: Rock Spgs Presb. Church. AG 9/30/1908

WORDS, Georgia, colored, age 26, d. 51 Lowe St. Atlanta. AG 5/21/1907

WORLD, Sam, age 14, died Fulton Co. Jail. Atlanta. AG 12/26/1906

WORRELL, E. E., negro, age 32, d. Fulton Co. Jail. AG 10/15/1909

WORSHAM, Elizabeth, Mrs., wife of Dr. H. D., age 71, d. 5/22 Macon. Son: Eugene. Interred: Riverside. AC 5/24/1905

WORSHAM, J. H. D., Dr. funeral Sun. at late res., 321 Coleman Ave., Macon. Interred: Rose Hill. AG 5/27/1907

WORTH, M. C., Mrs., age 75, d. 57 Morrison Ave. Atlanta. AG 1/29/1908

WORTHINGTON, John, age 3, son of Mrs. Annie, d. Mon. 5 Lucile Ave., Atlanta. Interred: New Jersey. AG 3/9/1910

WORTHY, Bartow, negro, age 26, d. Atlanta. AG 12/14/1907

WRAY, Martha Katherine, age 6 mos., dau. of Mr. and Mrs. J. W. of 100 Park Ave., Atlanta, d. Sat. Interred: Westview. AG 8/12/1909

WRAY, Mary May, Miss, age 31, d. 377 Glennwood Ave., Atlanta Wed. Bros: J. W., G. C., Edward, W. P. Sis: Misses Mildred, Viola, Susie. Interred: Westview. AG 4/1/1910

WREN, Mike, policeman, killed by Ernest Wells, Knoxville, Ga. AG 3/18/1906

WRIGHT, Alfred, colored, age 6 mos., d. 77 Gardner St. Atlanta. AG 12/22/1908

WRIGHT, Allie E., Mrs., wife of D. S. of Atlanta. Interred: Luxominio, Ga. AG 5/1/1906

WRIGHT, Annie B., Miss, age 16, dau. of Mr. and Mrs. M. J., d. Thurs. Atlanta. Interred: Westview. AG 9/9/1910

WRIGHT, Ben, colored, aged 54   5/10/1906

WRIGHT, C. S., Mrs., age 60, d. 17 W. Cain St. Atlanta. Came to Atlanta from Griffin for treatment. Husband and niece, Miss Mary McGrath of Lexington, Ky., survive. AG 3/22/1907

WRIGHT, Connie, colored, age 18, d. Atlanta. AG 8/7/1908

WRIGHT, Ethel, colored, age 25, d. 113 Bell St. Atlanta. AG 12//9/1908

WRIGHT, Franklin, Mrs., wife of F. W., age 77, of Covington, d. 2/20 dau´s res., Mrs. J. B. Chestnut, Savannah. Ch: Hon. Boykin Wright, Augusta; Mrs. Frank Weldon, Atlanta; R. F. Wright, Atlanta; Mrs. Chestnut. Bur: Covington. AC 2/21/1905

WRIGHT, H., age 1 year, died Atlanta. AG 11/26/1906

WRIGHT, H., d. Mon. Survivors: Wife, 8 children. Interred: church church yard. AG 11/26/1906

WRIGHT, H. C., Capt. d. Sat. Macon. Interred: Riverside Cemetery. Age 80, Confed. Vet. Sons: Thomas F., New York; Harry, Macon; Albert, Havana, Cuba. Dau: Mrs. B. B. Bullock, Ocala, Fla. AG 7/25/1910

WRIGHT, Harriet, Mrs., age 86, d. 132 Main St., Atlanta, Tues. Interred: Hollywood. AG 12/15/1909

WRIGHT, Helen Frances, 18 mos. dau. of Mr. and Mrs. Charles Wright, 17 Connally St., d. Fri. AG 1/11/1907

WRIGHT, J. E., age 28, d. Atlanta. AG 3/7/1910

WRIGHT, J. I., Col., former citizen of Rome, Ga. d. last night Ft. Worth, Texas, age 83. at son´s home. Leaves 3 ch. AG 2/28/1907

WRIGHT, J. S., Mrs., age 59, d. 294 Courtland St. Atlanta. AG 10/13/1906

WRIGHT, James K., age 33, suicide Atlanta. Leaves wife. AG 8/ 9/1907

WRIGHT, John mortally wounded by another negro in saloon fight on Edgewood Ave., Atlanta. AG 4/1/1910

WRIGHT, John H., age 65, d. sister´s res., Mrs. Martin J. Argard, 582 Highland Ave., Atlanta, Sat. Interred: Savannah. AG 10/17/1910

WRIGHT, John S., age 51 funeral Sun. Lovejoy Methodist Church. Bros: L. O. Wright, Atlanta, former Newton Co. sheriff; J. O. Wright. Wife, ten children, survivie. AG 8/5/1907

WRIGHT, John W., Jr., age 18 mos., son of Capt. and Mrs. John W., d. Ft. McPherson, Tues. AG 6/28/1910

WRIGHT, Leigh, colored, age 35, d. Oakland City, Ga. AG 2/1/1908

WRIGHT, Lilly Mae, infant dau. of Mr. and Mrs. W. A., d. Fri. 179 Wylie St. Atlanta. Interred: Caseys. AG 6/14/1907

WRIGHT, Maggie, colored, age 4 mos., d. 148 E. Baker St. Atlanta. AG 1/29/1908

WRIGHT, Mary E., Mrs., age 55, d. New York. AG 2/8/1909

WRIGHT, Patsy, colored, age 48, d. 11 Rose St. Atlanta. AG 5/8/1906

WRIGHT, R. C., age 44, d. Sun. Atlanta. Wife, 7 children. AG 7/11/1910

WRIGHT, Ralph E. d. Atlanta, native of Columbus, Ga. Bros, sisters: Arminius, Homer (Whitman, Ga.), Mrs. C. W. Smith (Atlanta, Mrs. Joel Davis (Griffin), Mrs. T. A. Mell (Athens), Mrs. W. B. Bonnell (Macon). Bur: Columbus, Ga. AG 10/19/1907

WRIGHT, Ruth E., Mrs., age 29, of Sylvester, Ga. d. Wesley Memorial Hospital. Atlanta. Interred: Helena, Ga. AG 4/10/1907

WRIGHT, W. S., Mrs. d. 208 Hunnicutt St., Atlanta. Interred: Westview. AG 9/14/1907

WRIGHT, W. T., age 37, d. Battle Hill. AG 12/2/1910

WRIGHT, W. T.. Macon, Ga., 12/8/1906. Died at City hospital due to wreck at Elko yesterday. AG 12/8/1906

WRIGHT, Walter A., age 30, d. Chattanooga, Tenn. Funeral res. of uncle, 15 Echo St., Atlanta. Interred: Hollywood cemetery. AG 7/24/1907

WRIGHT, Will, colored, age 20, d. N. Butler St. Atlanta. AG 1/28/1908

WRIGHT, William, colored, age 40, d. 27 Reed St. Atlanta. AG 11/2/1907

WRIGLEY, Mike d. 9/4 in Acambre, Mexico, engineer for C., N O. & T. P. Railroad. AG 10/25/1909

WYATT, George, colored, age 42, d. 10 Bunker St. Atlanta. AG 3/27/1909

WYATT, J. W., colored, age 2 mos., d. rear 200 E. Ellis St. Atlanta. AG 10/25/1907

WYATT, L. W. d. Mon. Funeral Bethel Church, Dalton, Ga. He lived Dalton 2 yrs, having removed from Tenn. Age 64. Confed. Vet. AG 3/9/1910

WYATT, S. I., Mrs., age 78, d. dau.´s res., Miss S. D. Miot, 42 Crew St., Atlanta, Mon. Dau., one son: Walter Miot, Columbus, Ga. AG 6/16/1908

WYATT, W. B., aged German killed in railroad accident. Funeral: New Hope Church. AG 12/21/1906

WYCHE, E. M., Mrs., d. Anniston, Ala. yesterday. interred: Hillside cemetery. AG 9/17/1907

WYCHE, Gus, colored, age 28, d. Grady Hospital. Atlanta. AG 8/27/1907

WYCK, Nina Van, mrs., age 35, d. Talbotton, Ga. AG 6/1/1907

WYLIE, Stewart, colored, age 67, d. 136 Howell St. Atlanta. AG 7/13/1908

WYLIE, David G., age 70, d. 530 Spring St. Atlanta. AG 12/28/1910

WYNN, Glen B. d. Aberdeen, Ga. Wed., son of Mrs. O. Sis: Misses Annie, Louise, Ruby. AG 8/8/1910

WYNN, Lucy, Mrs. interred Oakland Cemetery, Atlanta. AG 6/4/1906

WYNN, Mary, colored, age 54, d. 206 Bell St. Atlanta. AG 9/21/1910

WYNN, Thomas S. J., age 23, d. 33 Cone St. Atlanta. AG 2/8/1909

WYNN, W. C. of Whitesburg lived at Hutcheson Mills, d. Wed., age 50. Leaves wife, several children. AG 7/5/1907

WYNNE, Hugh Douglas, age 3, d. 180 Cleburne Ave. Atlanta. AG 11/3/1909

WYNNE, Martha A., Mrs., age 81, d. 29 Whitehall Terrace. Atlanta. Interred: Westview. AG 6/13/1910

YANCEY, E. H., Mrs., wife of late Dr. E. H. of Covington, d. Atlanta Sat. Interred: Covington, Ga. 1/2. Dau: Mrs. Olena Pritchard. Four sons. AG 1/3/1910

YANCEY, Marshall, age 78, d. 210 Railroad St. Atlanta. AG 6/8/1907

YANCEY, O. H., Mrs., age 21, d. Smyrna, Ga. AG 1/3/1910

YANCEY, W. R., Mrs., age 74, d. Forest Park, Ga. Fri. Interred: Forest Park Cemetery. AG 6/20/1908

YARBOROUGH, Hazel M., infant, d. 61 DeKalb Ave. Atlanta. AG 1/20/1910

YARBROUGH, C. S., Mrs. d. Sat. Beulah, Ala. AG 5/3/1910

YARBROUGH, Florence, Miss,ge 24, dau. of Mr. and Mrs. J. D., d. 269 Glenn St., Atlanta, Sat. Interred: Westview. AG 1/20/1908

YARBROUGH, Larry, colored, age 22, d. 13 Smith's alley. Atlanta. AG 10/7/1909

YARBROUGH, Mary Elizabeth, age 8 mos., d. 5/11 Macon, res. of parents, Mr. and Mrs. W. J. AG 5/12/1909

YARBROUGH, M., age 27, d. Fri. Vinings Station, Interred: Hollywood cemetery. He was son-in-law of Sgt. W. H. Turner of Atlanta police force. AG 12/8/1906

YATES, W. V. of Macon, engineer, d. train wreck Macon. AG 2/15/1911

YATES, William, Capt., from Ga., age 36, Troop A, 14th cavalry, thrown from horse Boise, Idaho while drilling. May not live. AG 7/18/1906

YEAGER, Frank, age 40, d. 203 Telfair St., Macon., son of Mrs. F. P. Yeager and late F. P. Yeager, once Lt. in Macon Police Force. Leaves 2 bros., 2 sisters. Funeral yesterday at Macon. Interred: Riverside. AG 1/16/1907

YEATES, William S., Professor, age 52, d. 180 Pine St. Atlanta. AG 2/20/1908

YERGAN, Harold, age 14, son of Mr. and Mrs. H. T., d. Tues. Atlanta. Interred: Anderson, S. C. AG 6/8/1910

YONGE, May, colored, age 15, d. Demorest, Ga. AG 10/9/1907

YOPP, O. S., son of Mr. and Mrs. L. P. of 298 Central Ave., Atlanta, d. Lovett, Ga. Mon. Interred: Westview. Atlanta. AG 6/23/1908

YORK, Clifford B., age 5, d. 20 Franklin St. Atlanta. AG 10/29/1907

YORK, H. L., aged citizen of Varnell Station (near Dalton), d. res. of son, Will York, Fri. Confed. Vet. Funeral at Dawnville. AG 4/25/1910

YORK, Lula, Mrs. funeral Tues. Interred: Riverview Cemetery, Atlanta. AG 3/24/1908

YOUNG, Addie, Mrs., widow of John, sister of William B. Emmert, formerly of Va., but now Washington, D. C., d. 3/13 Briston, Tenn, age 38. One son. AG 3/10/1910

YOUNG, C. T., age 37, d. Fri. Interred: Westview. Wife survives. AG 9/29/1906

YOUNG, Carolee, Mrs., age 53, d. Sat. Baker St., Atlanta. Ch: P. W., Charles; Mrs. E. H. White; Mrs. J. E. Dennis; Mrs. H. H. Walter. Interred: Columbus, Ga. AG 4/25/1910

YOUNG, Elsie, colored, age 33, d. 52 S. Humphries St. Atlanta. AG 3/18/1908

YOUNG, George funeral Mon., son of G. T. Young of McDonough Rd., Atlanta. Interred: Marvin church yard. AG 6/13/1906

YOUNG, Inez, inf. dau. of Mr. and Mrs. J. R., d. 102 Poplar St., Atlanta, Sun. Interred: Hollywood. AG 7/5/1909

YOUNG, Isaac, colored, age 30, d. 85 Hunnicutt St. Atlanta. AG 4/9/1908

YOUNG, James, negro from Macon, brakeman of Central Railroad, d. rail accident. AG 7/23/1906

YOUNG, M. E., Mrs., age 67, d. Ash St., Macon., Mon. her res. of 25-yrs. Dau: Mrs. E. H. Leonard of Macon. Sons: E. F. of Macon, D. T. of Chattanooga; J. T. of Indiana. Bur: Ft. Valley. AG 3/6/1907

YOUNG, Marion, age 6 mos., dau. of F. L., d. Gainesville, 144 Lee St. Sun. Interred: Westview. AG 7/7/1906

YOUNG, Mary B., Miss, age 15, d. Demorest, Ga. Tues. AG 9/27/1907

YOUNG, Mary W., age 1, dau. of Mr. and Mrs. A. B., d. 224 State St., Atlanta, Tues. Interred: Westview. AG 2/4/1908

YOUNG, Mary W., colored, age 1, d. 224 State St. Atlanta. AG 2/7/1908

YOUNG, Mattie C., Mrs., age 26, d. Mon. 242 Powell St., Atlanta, wife of E. L. Two small children. Interred: Hollywood. AG 7/11/1910

YOUNG, Mittie E., Mrs., age 21, d. Perryton Rd., Atlanta, Thurs., wife of Clinton Young. Parents: Mr. and Mrs. L. C. Waits. Interred: Sharon Church yard. AG 7/10/1908

YOUNG, Montain, age 6 mos., d. 120 Bryan St. Atlanta. AG 7/14/1910

YOUNG, Nathan B., age 16, son of Mr. and Mrs. C. B., d. Sun. 161 Crew St., Atlanta. Interred: Westview. AG 9/10/1910

YOUNG, S. C., age 53, d. Edgewood (Atlanta). AG 4/27/1910

YOUNG, T. T., colored, age 50, d. 20 Lyons Ave. Atlanta. AG 2/24/1908

YOUNG, William Elliott, age 63, d. 259 Hill St., Atlanta, Mon. Interred: Westview. Wife. Dau: Miss Anna Young. Bro: Capt. John Young, Paducah, Ky. AG 9/21/1909

YOUNG, William S., ex-convict, committed suicide Fri. Atlanta. Interred: Westview. AG 5/30/1910

YOUNGHEAD, S., colored, age 42, d. Grady Hospital. Atlanta. AG 3/22/1907

YOUREE, Henry H. d. 5/12 Shreveport, La. Interred: Scottsville, Texas. AG 5/13/1910

YU CHEOW, Chinese, age 57, d. 68 McDaniel St. Atlanta. AG 12/2/1910

YUEN, Loo, Chinaman, d. Tues. 16 Madison Ave., Atlanta. Interred: Westview. AG 10/25/1909

ZABAN, M., age 47, d. Atlanta. AG 2/15/1909

ZACHEM, Joseph, 2, son of George d. 70 Butler St. Bur: Westview. AG 8/27/1906

ZACHERY, Amanda, colored, age 80, d. 2 Allens alley. Atlanta. AG 1/1/1908

ZACHRY, John M., Capt., age 75, Confed. Vet., d. 210 Spring St., Atlanta, Wed. Interred: Westview. AG 12/29/1910

ZACHRY, Mary J., Mrs., age 81, d. 76 Dixie Ave. Atlanta. Interred: Oakland. AG 4/28/1908

ZACHRY, Mamie, Mrs., wife of W. I. d. Apalachee, Ga., Thurs. The Zachrys moved to Madison, Ga. 3 mos. ago. Daus: Mrs. Lucien harris, Mrs. J. J. Martin. Son: L. H. Zachry. Interred: Atlanta, Ga. AG 6/19/1908

ZELLARS, Margaret K., Mrs., wife of ex-repr., W. S., d. 3/
of late Benjamin A. Camp of Atlanta. Sis: M
formerly of Douglasville, Ga., now of Texas; Mrs. Willis of Ark. AC 3/4/1905

ZIMMER, Mary J., Mrs., age 71, d. New Kimball House. Atlanta. AG 1/20/1910

ZIMMERMAN, William H., age 72, d. Sun. near Griffin, Ga. Interred: Brazil, Ind. Son: A. H. AG 11/23/1908

ZORN, Willa, Miss, dau. of Mr. and Mrs. D. W., d. Fri. Glennville, Ga., age 17. Interred: Philadelphia Cemetery, Glennville, Ga. AG 6/1/1908

ZUBER, Margaret, Mrs. funeral 154 N. Jackson St., Atlanta, Mon. Interred: Oakland. AG 5/21/1906